What Great Paintings Say

Volume 2

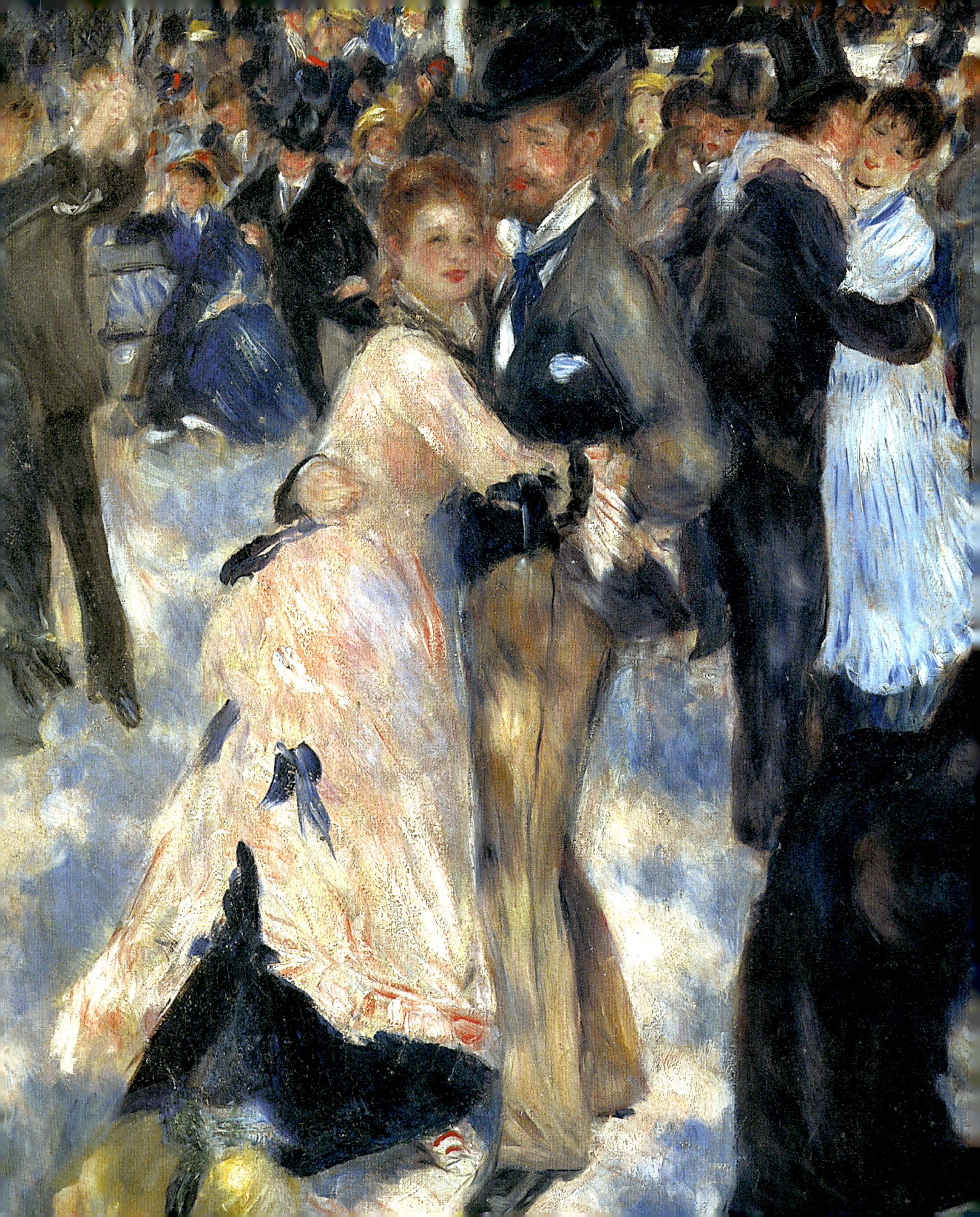

What Great Paintings Say

Volume 2

Rose-Marie and Rainer Hagen

TASCHEN

KÖLN LONDON LOS ANGELES MADRID PARIS TOKYO

Cover:
School of Fontainebleau
Gabrielle d'Estrées and one of her sisters (detail), c. 1600
96 x 125 cm
Paris, Musée du Louvre
Photo: Réunion des Musées Nationaux, Paris, Photo © G. Blot

Back Cover:
Jan van Eyck
The Arnolfini Marriage, 1434
82 x 60 cm
London, National Gallery
Photo: © National Gallery Picture Library, London

Illustration Page 2:
Auguste Renoir
Au Moulin de la Galette (detail), 1876
131 x 175 cm
Paris, Musée d'Orsay

The texts of this book are based on articles which were written for the magazine *art*, Hamburg.

Hohenzollernring 53, D–50672 Köln
www.taschen.com

Coordination: Annick Volk, Cologne
Production: Tina Ciborowius, Cologne
Cover: Claudia Frey, Angelika Taschen, Cologne
Translation: Karen Williams, High Raw Green; Michael Hulse, Coventry

Printed in Germany
ISBN 3–8228–1372-9

Contents

Foreword

Pictures are windows. They open up a view that extends beyond the familiar horizons of everyday life. They bring us face to face with figures we do not know, with buildings from times gone by, and with landscapes that no longer look the same or indeed never existed at all.

Pictures offer adventure. At least to those who are willing to step out of the four walls around them and – using their physical senses, their powers of intellect and their own life experience – discover all that the work of art holds in store.

This book aims to assist in this process of discovery. It answers questions that lead us further on our quest, and it magnifies details that are important for the whole. The book does not offer an overview of the epochs and schools of art history; on the contrary, each painting is introduced separately, almost as if no others existed – each picture, so the authors believe, a unique window, each picture a new adventure. Those who return from a successful journey into a picture are enriched by the experience.

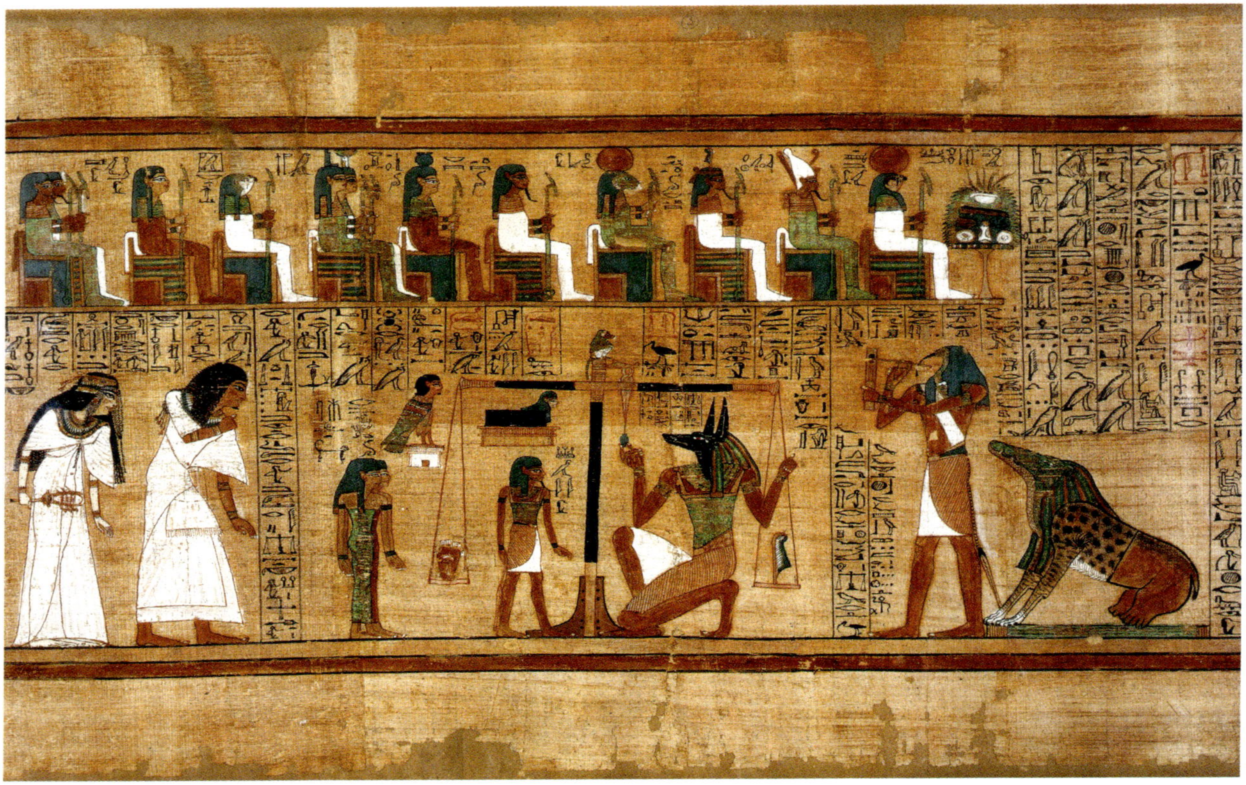

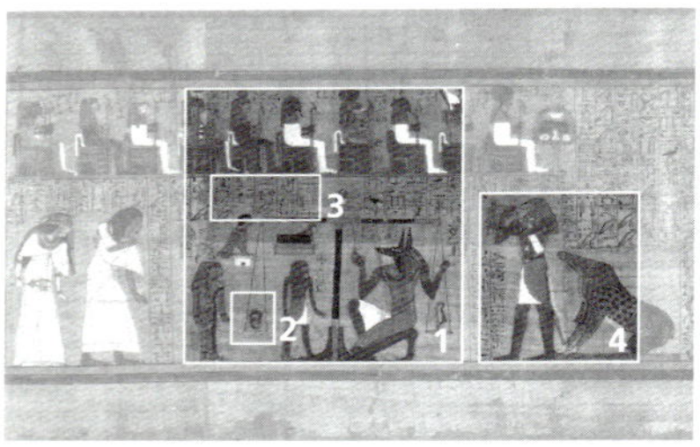

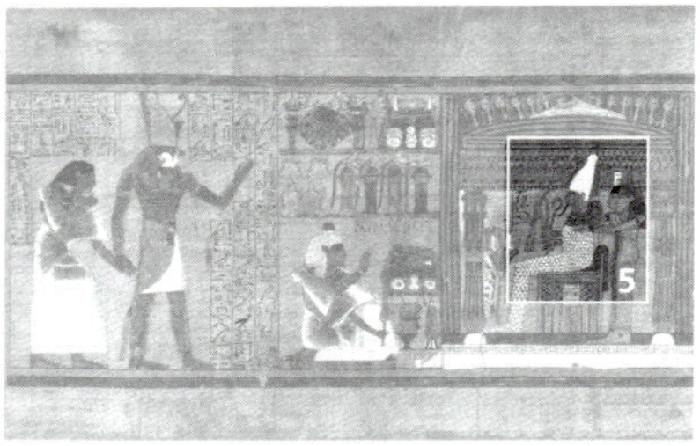

Anonymous: From the Papyrus of Ani, c. 1300 BC

Counsel for the afterlife

Scrolls of papyrus have been found resting between the legs of many Egyptian mummies, wrapped up along with them in the linen shrouds in which these dead were laid to rest. The scrolls contain both text and images and constitute a kind of guide to the kingdom of the dead. They were intended to familiarize the deceased with the underworld, and assist him in the trials he would face there and with his passage back from the dark depths into the light of the sun. For this reason the Egyptians called a book of this kind a guide to emerging into the day.

It was 19th century grave robbers who dubbed the mysterious scrolls "books of the dead". Presumably it was from one such grave robber that the English Egyptologist Sir E.A. Wallis Budge purchased what is known as the Papyrus of Ani (part of the Theban Book of the Dead), in Luxor in 1880. The scroll measures 23.79 metres in length by 38 centimetres in breadth, and has been on view in the British Museum ever since, albeit cut up into 37 separate leaves. According to Budge's own account, the colours of the papyrus – more than 3,000 years old – were

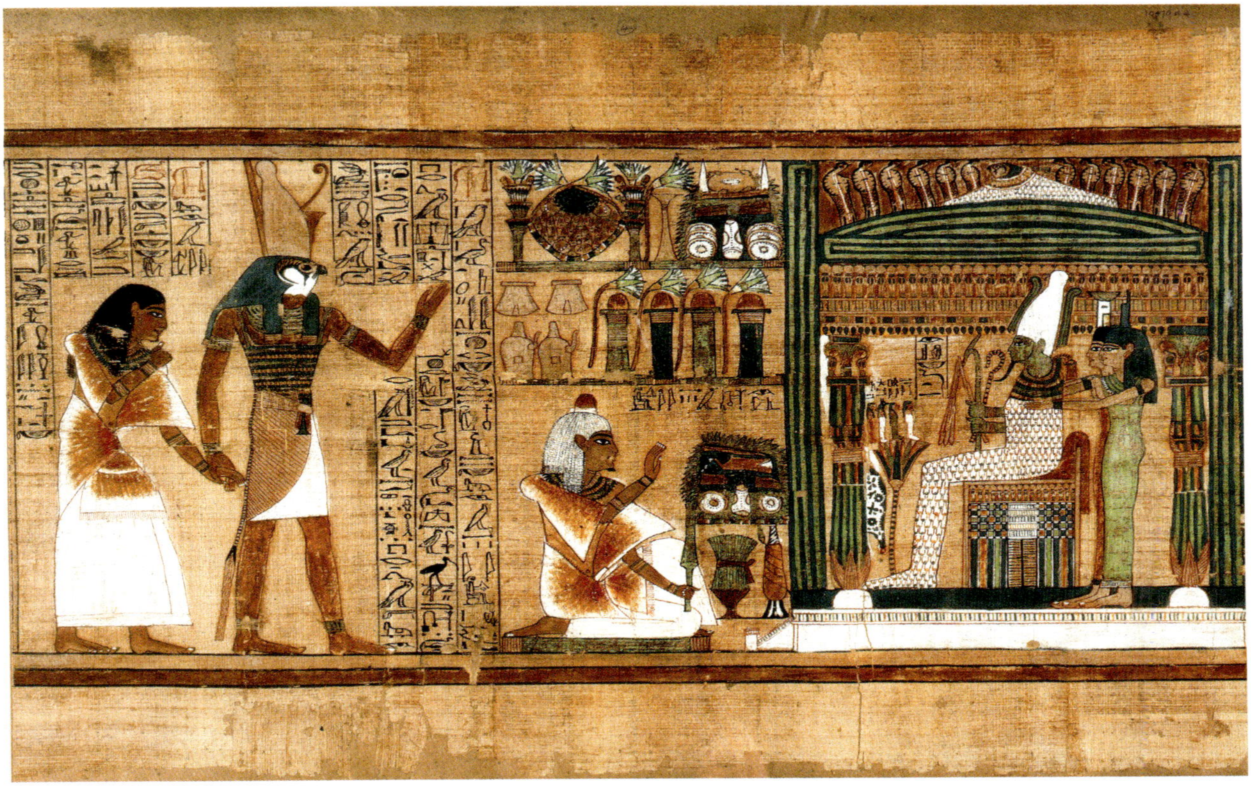

still light when it was first unrolled, but quickly darkened on contact with the air.

Leaves 3 and 4 of the papyrus are reproduced here. Both of them depict the royal scribe Ani, for whom this book of the dead was prepared, entering into the kingdom of the dead. Judges await him and weigh his heart on a balance; a monster awaits him too, threatening to devour him; and finally, in the right-hand picture, there is the god Osiris, lord of the underworld.

Ani's demeanour is somewhat bowed, and deferential. The position of his arm, folded across his breast, is indicative of submissiveness toward superiors. Behind him, in the left-hand picture, is his wife Tutu, who probably predeceased her husband. She accompanies him for a part of the way. When alive, she was a priestess at the temple of Amon and sang in the choir: she is still holding the sistrum, the ancient Egyptian rattle that was used to accompany temple singing. The couple are wearing ceremonial vestments and artfully curled and plaited wigs, and their eyes are made up black.

Ani apparently lived around 1300 BC in Thebes, the capital of the Egyptian empire, not many years after the famed Pharaoh Tutankhamun (1332–23 BC). Clearly the "true royal scribe" occupied high rank in the Egyptian temple hierarchy. One title recorded on the papyrus describes him as the overseer over all the votive offerings brought to the gods at Thebes and Abydos. In addition it was probably he who fixed the not inconsiderable dues that wealthy Egyptians regularly paid to the temple in the form of grain and livestock, and also administered the immense property belonging to the temple. In a word, he was a hard-working man who enjoyed his monarch's favour.

Ani was one of the caste of affluent officials who could afford a book of the dead. For some 1500 years, from 1550 BC till Roman times, the custom was to place these scrolls in the tomb with the deceased. They were either prepared especially or were bought ready-made with only the name of the owner to be entered. The price was about that of a slave, or half the annual income of a worker, which meant that these books were unaffordable for the lower classes.

Indeed, in earlier times a guide to the underworld had been the royal prerogative alone. The texts were not inscribed on papyrus, however, but were painted onto the walls of the secret burial chambers in the pyramids. A certain degree of democratization, at least with regard to the afterlife, later enabled well-to-do servants of the state to equip themselves with a book of the dead as well.

Henceforth, having one's own book of the dead was an essential part of the elaborate preparations for death that every pious and well-to-do Egyptian made in his lifetime. He would have an inaccessible burial chamber filled with all the requisites he would want in the afterlife: stores, furniture, effigies of his servants and wives. A stone sarcophagus was made, and a plaster or card death-mask. The burial rites were also decided in advance. Only when these preparations had been made could a contemporary of Tutankhamun rest easy in the contemplation of the day when he would "cross to the other shore".

The jackal-headed god Anubis is seen kneeling under the right part of a scales crossbar. "He of the scales" had the task of making the first examination that Ani the scribe would undergo in the afterlife: his heart would be weighed against a feather.

Anubis was also known as the Lord of the Westerners. To the west of every Egyptian city, separated but within seeing distance of the living, was a necropolis or city of the dead, and Anubis was the presiding deity. The wild dogs and jackals that strayed in these places threatened the repose of the dead, digging up graves and dragging off the remains found in them. By making a jackal-headed god the protector of their dead, the Egyptians were hoping to contain this nuisance.

Anubis also oversaw the complex embalming rites. These lasted seventy days; during this period the corpse was dried in sodium and conserved using resins, oils and spices. The exact composition of these mixtures has remained the secret of the priests of Anubis.

The centrepiece of the scene is the large scales, a balance such as was used to weigh gold or silver. Less valuable metals such as copper were counted by the bar, while grain was measured out in bushels. The balance was used only for the most precious materials. In our picture, a baboon is ensuring that the balance is working properly; this is Thoth, god of letters and scribe of the gods. He is sitting on the upright post from which the crossbar is suspended. The pointed triangular indicator is firmly attached to it. Only if it points vertically down are the pans of the scales perfectly balanced. Anubis is doing the balancing, using a heart-shaped weight hanging from a hook.

Below the left part of the crossbar are deities of lesser rank: Shai, the god of destiny, and behind him the two goddesses Meshkent and Renenet. These have long known Ani. It was Meshkent, at the time of his birth, who determined the span of his life and the hour of his death. The head of this deity can be seen a second time in our picture, above Shai, on the birth brick. Egyptian women delivered their children crouched on a birth brick. Renenet, the nurse-goddess, gave suck to Ani and watched over his childhood development. Both of these deities preside over the fate of mankind, and might testify on Ani's behalf at the last judgement. Beside them, represented as a bird with a human head, Ani's spirit is watching the weighing from the roof of his tomb. The spirit can fly, but it always has to return to the body. Its fate too depends on the outcome.

The Lords of Justice are enthroned high above the scales. Gods of heaven, earth and light, they are the judges who will pronounce upon Ani, according to the result of the weighing. Judgement is passed in the Hall of Pure Justice, where this world and the next meet. Mayet, the goddess of justice and truth, is present only in symbolic form, in the emblem of divine order: the feather lying on one of the pans. Ani's heart must prove as light as the feather if it is to pass the test. The conduct of a man on earth is being weighed here against the ideal of divine justice.

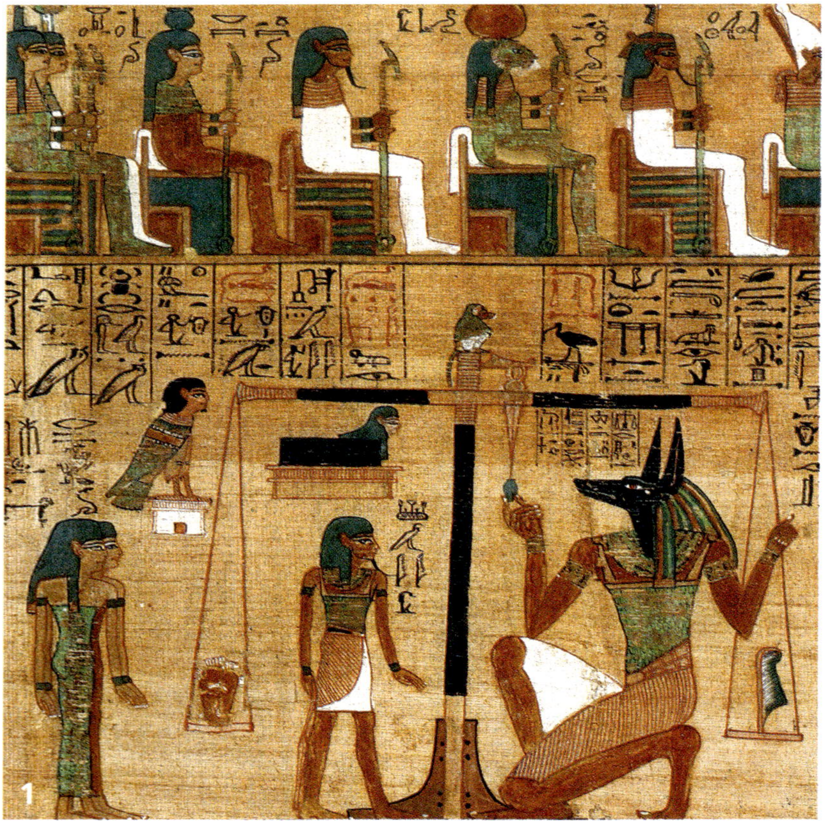

1

The god Anubis weighs the dead man's heart

Very few could hope to be equal to such a test. Everyone feared it. The one source of hope was the help afforded by the book of the dead, which not only identified the dangers of the underworld, but also offered the means of mitigating them. In other words, it contained magic spells.

Almost two hundred spells were given to the deceased on his journey. If he said them at the right moment, it was possible to achieve a favourable result. Spell number 125 was the one to recite before the judges. It contained the "negative confession", and was very long, beginning "I have done no injustice towards mankind" and continuing "I have not mistreated animals" and concluding "I have not shamed the god of my city".

Nor was an assurance forgotten that was all-important for lands made fertile by the waters of the Nile: "I did not hold back the flood waters in their season." From the "negative confession" we gather what the worst crimes were in ancient Egypt: untruthfulness and lies, embezzlement and fraud. This recitation did not include a truthful account of the deceased's conduct on earth; indeed, it was designed to prevent the truth coming to light. It was a conjuration.

The Egyptians also believed that visual representation of the book of the dead possessed magical power. They thought that the likeness of an object or creature partook of its virtues: thus, the servants whose *ushabti* effigies were placed in the tomb would continue to clothe and feed their master in the afterlife, and depicting the celestial scales on the papyrus as perfectly balanced would magically ensure that the heart and feather weighed the same. This hope countered some of the terror inspired by the ceremony.

Ani is found innocent. The judges pronounce him to be in harmony with the divine order: he is a just man, and "the Devourer" shall have no power over him.

Naturally a book of the dead did not depict this menacing "Devourer" eating the guilty. Kept at bay by the spells, its reptilian mouth remained shut. The monster was a hybrid of various beasts: crocodile, hippopotamus and lion. If a "guilty" deceased really were devoured by this creature, it would be the worst punishment conceivable to the Egyptians: complete and utter annihilation, the second and definitive death, with no hope of future reincarnation.

The heart is the seat of personality

In the left pan of the scales is a heart, red with white veins to the top and sides. It is not the whole human being who is weighed against the ostrich feather, symbol of the cosmic order, but only that part of him which the Egyptians considered the true centre of the personality, the seat of reason, will and conscience. Unlike the other inner organs and entrails, the heart was not removed when the body was embalmed and kept in jars. It was the most important organ and remained in the mummy.

The heart constituted a potential source of danger at the moment of judgement. What if it should testify against its owner? It might expose the "confession" as lies, nullify the spell, and tip the balance of the scales. The book of the dead anticipated this problem and had another spell to counteract it, number 30. It is headed: "Spell to ensure that the heart (of the dead) does not oppose him in the realm of the dead."

In our picture, the text is in hieroglyphics to the left over the crossbar of the scales. It begins at the top right and runs in vertical columns. Twice a crouching man can be seen behind a heart hieroglyph that closely resembles the heart on the scales. In the second column from the right we

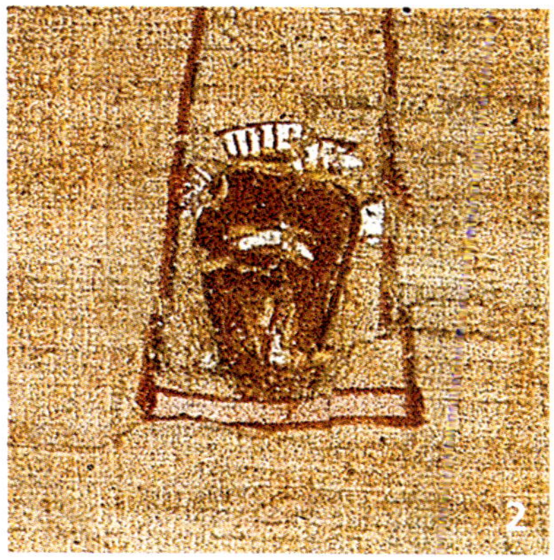

find the name of the scribe, Ani, in black script, and above it the insignia of the guild of scribes (a stylized palette with writing implements) and, below, a bird, a stylized water-lily, two reeds, and a crouching man.

In this spell, Ani twice calls upon his heart to be silent. First, he addresses "the heart of my mother", meaning the heart he was given when he came into the world; then he addresses his own heart, the heart that has evolved through his lifetime "in ever-changing form". This spell, which has also been found frequently on heart-shaped amulets, was seemingly in use more than two thousand years before Christ – which would make it one of the oldest prayers of humankind.

The Egyptians believed that the book of the dead was the work of Thoth, god of

My heart of my mother, my heart of my mother
My heart of my ever-changing form
Do not rise up to bear witness against me
Do not oppose me in the hall of judgement
Do not turn against me before the master of the scales
(prayer of the scribe Ani)

letters and scribe of the gods, seen here recording the outcome of the weighing. In a civilization that believed in the magical power of written or drawn signs, anyone who was able to make them enjoyed the highest reputation. Thus Thoth was credited with the invention of the arts and sciences. He was the lord of magic and the mysterious god of the moon. He was also a lord of justice and truth, and ensured that the divine order of the cosmos was observed. He appears in our picture as the baboon atop the scales post, and again as an ibis-headed official. The marsh-dwelling ibis seemed a mysterious bird to the Egyptians, on account of its secluded manner of living. The birds seemed forever looking for something, so skill in finding was ascribed to them, and thus special experience and cleverness.

In his left hand the god has a palette with depressions for the black and red ink used in headings. He is standing to write, with a sharpened rush (more of which he has in the palette), on the wall of the hall. It was usual to sit to write, without a desk, on a scroll held on the knees. Writing was normally done on papyrus processed from the steeped and pressed pith of the plant, which grew in the marshlands of the Nile delta.

"Thoth has examined Ani in writing," the inscription reads, which means that the deity has registered the name of the dead man among those of the just. Not until this registration has been made is judgement concluded, for a result or sentence was only legally binding when recorded in writing. The Egyptians were meticulous in this point: they wanted to record everything for eternity, if at all possible. They had a veritable mania for collecting and recording.

Every event of importance, in town and country alike, was set down by official scribes, from the sale of a slave to the yield of the grape harvest. The scribes noted how many baskets of grapes were delivered, and on every wine pitcher they noted the year, the vineyard, and the vintner's name, before transferring all the data to a special ledger. This information served both to monitor labour and to fix the level of taxes. Apparently there was one scribe to every ten workers.

The caste of scribes, along with the castes of priests and soldiers, played a key role in the centralized and rigidly hierarchical ancient Egyptian state. Their education was lengthy and demanding: their training lasted some twelve years, in schools attached to the temples, and consisted in copying old texts. Subsequently they would be employed as book-keepers, technicians, scholars or artists, and above all as officials in the administration. Like Ani, they oversaw the property of the gods or the king. They fixed and collected taxes, and dispensed justice. They were state officials for life, and the positions could generally be inherited. Thus they were the immediate representatives of the highest caste, and "the eye of the king", and were themselves a proud caste: "Come to me, Thoth, holy ibis", one Egyptian scribe prayed, "guide me, make me diligent in my profession, for your profession is the finest of them all. They say that he who excels in it will be elevated to the aristocracy."

In this select company, Ani was designated a "true scribe", which means that his title was not merely conferred as an honorific. Ani had learnt the skills of the god Thoth from scratch, and quite probably he composed at least parts of his own book of the dead himself.

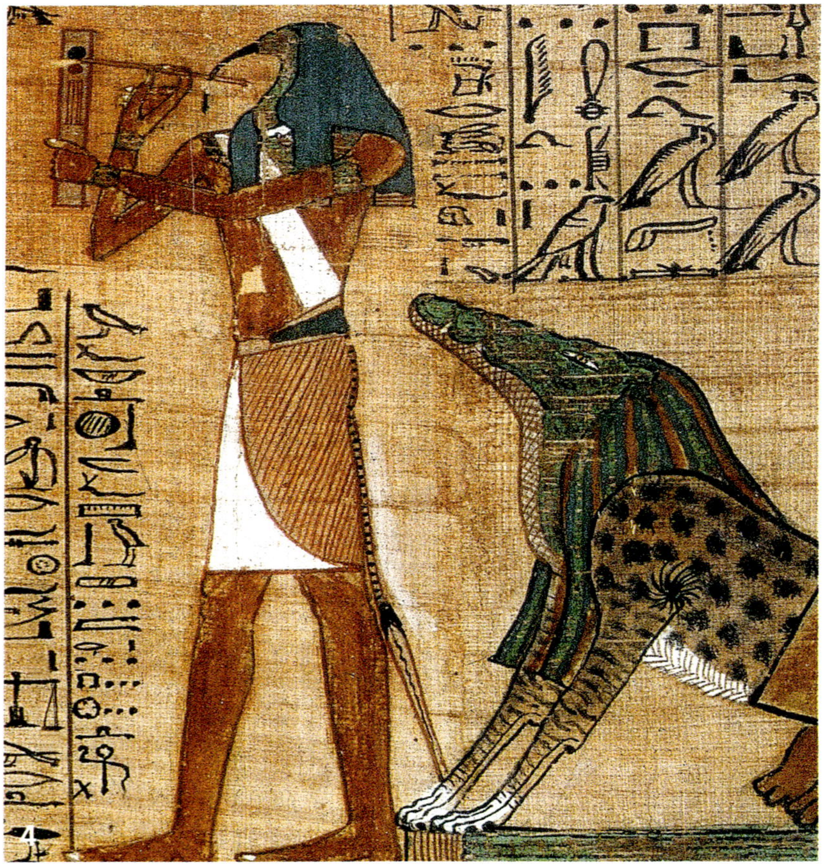

Those who write endure

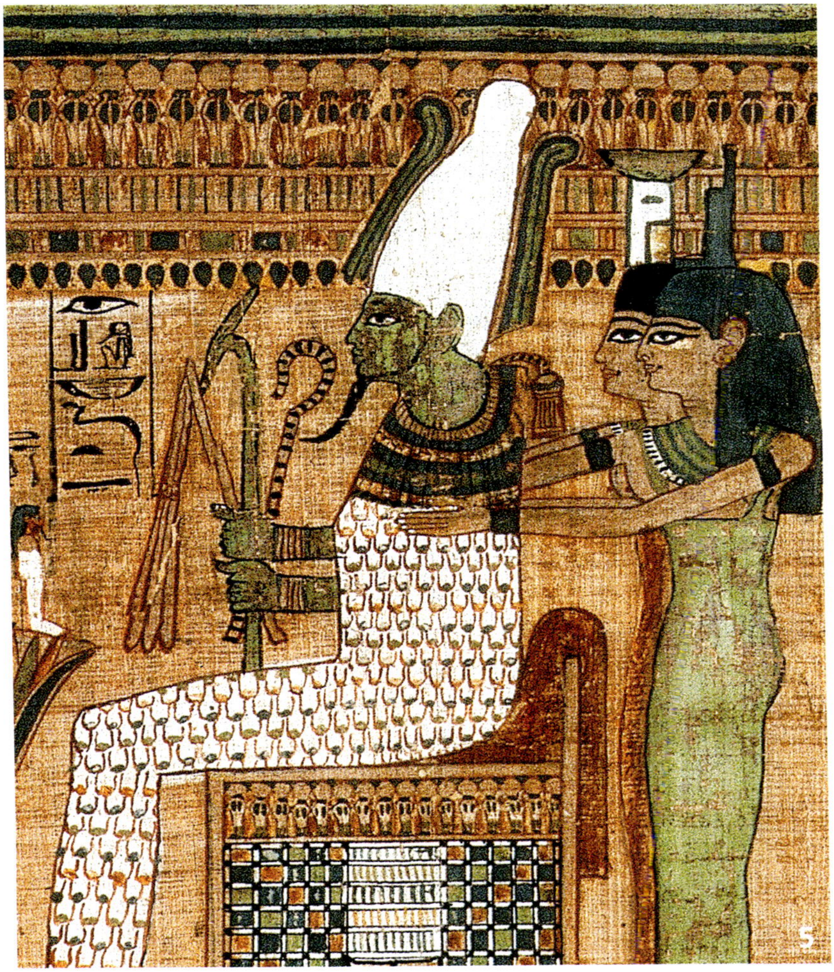

Osiris, god of the dead, confers a second life

The falcon-headed god Horus conducts the acquitted Ani to a sacrificial table on which are confections, meat and fruit. In the background are vessels containing wine or beer. Ani the scribe kneels; all of these earthly things are his offering to the god Osiris, king of the dead.

The lord of eternity is enthroned on a *naos*, a magnificent wooden shrine such as were used to carry the images of gods in processions on feast days. The canopy rests on lotus stems, recalling the fact that Osiris was apparently originally a fertility god. The green colouring of the deity's face recalls this too. Green was the colour of the primeval mud from which the Egyptians believed all life came, the colour of the Nile when it flooded the land every year and made it fertile.

Osiris is holding the insignia of power: the crooked staff, sceptre and whip. On his head he is wearing the *atef* crown, composed of a white mitre-like crown and two ostrich feathers. These are the emblems of the highest station in all Egypt, that of the all-powerful Pharaoh. But the figure of Osiris is rigid and unmoving, a mummy shrouded and artfully painted. In other words, although he is a mighty king, Osiris is still subject to the fate of humankind. Like his subjects, he too had to die. It was on the fact that this destiny was shared that the great hope of Ani the scribe and his contemporaries was based.

According to Egyptian legend, the good king Osiris had an enemy, his brother Set. Set lay in wait for Osiris, seized him and killed him. He cut up the body and threw the parts into the Nile. But Isis, the wife of Osiris (in our picture she is standing guard behind the throne with her sister Nephthys), went in search of him. "Woefully she roved the land, never resting until she had found him."

Jackal-headed Anubis re-assembled the fourteen parts of the corpse, bound them in shrouds, and thus created the first mummy. Isis metamorphosed into a kite and "created the air with her wings". At this the dead god began to revive. And, while he could no longer resume his first life on earth, he was able to embark on a second. Thus he became the king of the underworld: "Now grief is at an end, and laughter returns."

This comforting myth of the conquest of death and the possibility of a second, fresh beginning meets a deep-seated need in mortal humanity. So the meeting of the deceased with Osiris constitutes one of the most significant moments in the book of the dead. The Egyptians believed that, in the divine order of things, everything was repeated, and that anyone must therefore be able to repeat what happened to Osiris. Every mortal hoped that magic would assist him to become one with Osiris, that he might be resurrected into a new and different existence. From the start, the book of the dead refers to the scribe as "Osiris Ani", meaning that this mortal has become Osiris, and trusts that this will place the deceased under the protection of the god of resurrection.

But even Osiris could not protect Ani from all the dangers that threatened him. In the afterlife there were abysses, demons and terrors, reflecting the primeval fears rooted in the human spirit, phenomena that even a deity would go in fear of. A considerable number of them are still in Ani's way as he journeys on. The remaining thirty-five leaves of the book of the dead try to familiarize him with these dangers. They provide him with expertise, prayers and spells that will conduct him safely to the paradisal "fields of the rushes", that place "where every wish is fulfilled". There, Ani will be able to "drink his jug of beer every evening" in perpetuity, or accompany the gods by day as the barque of the sun crosses the heavens. The gates of the great beyond are open to him. Ani can go on, out into the day.

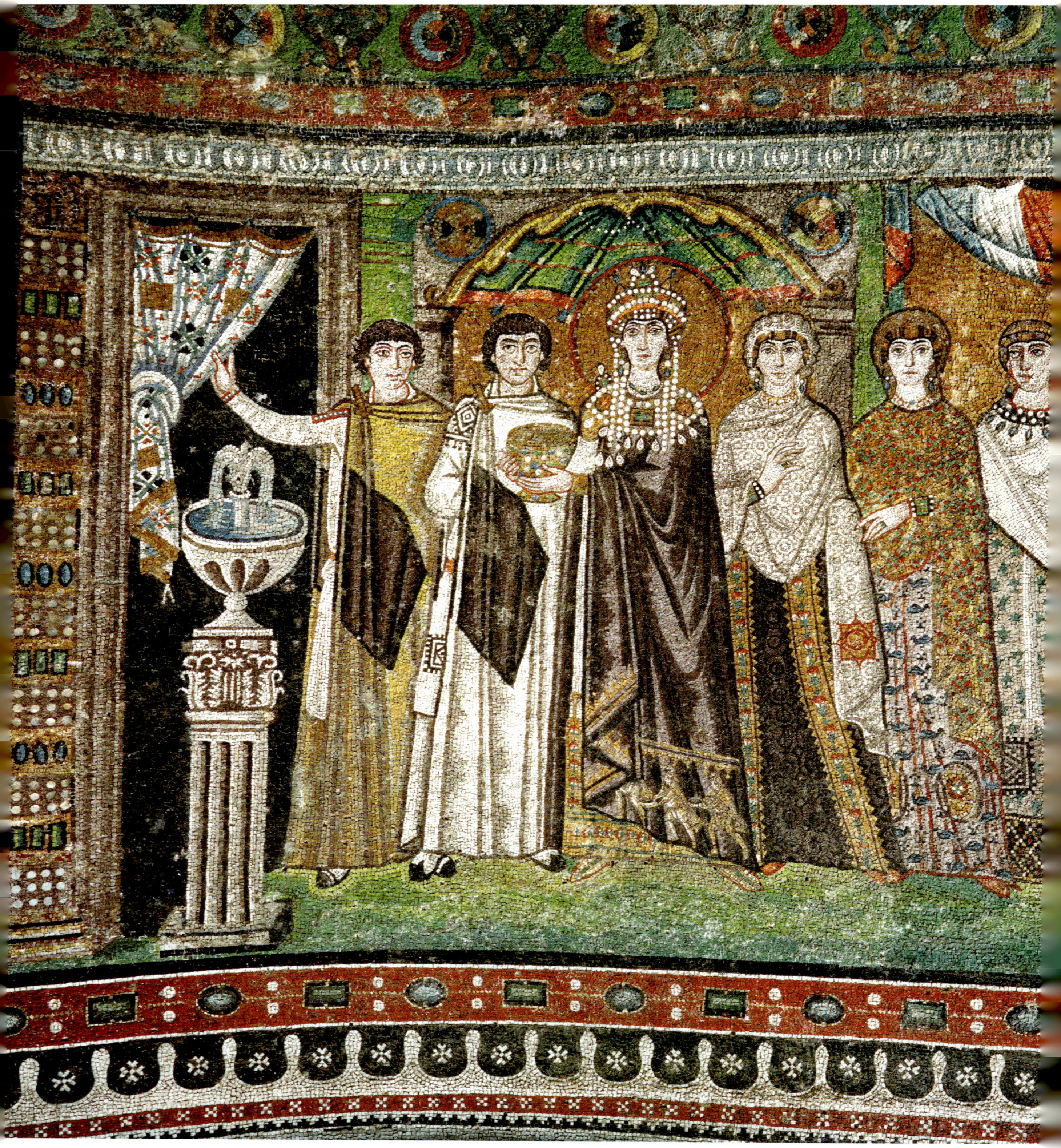

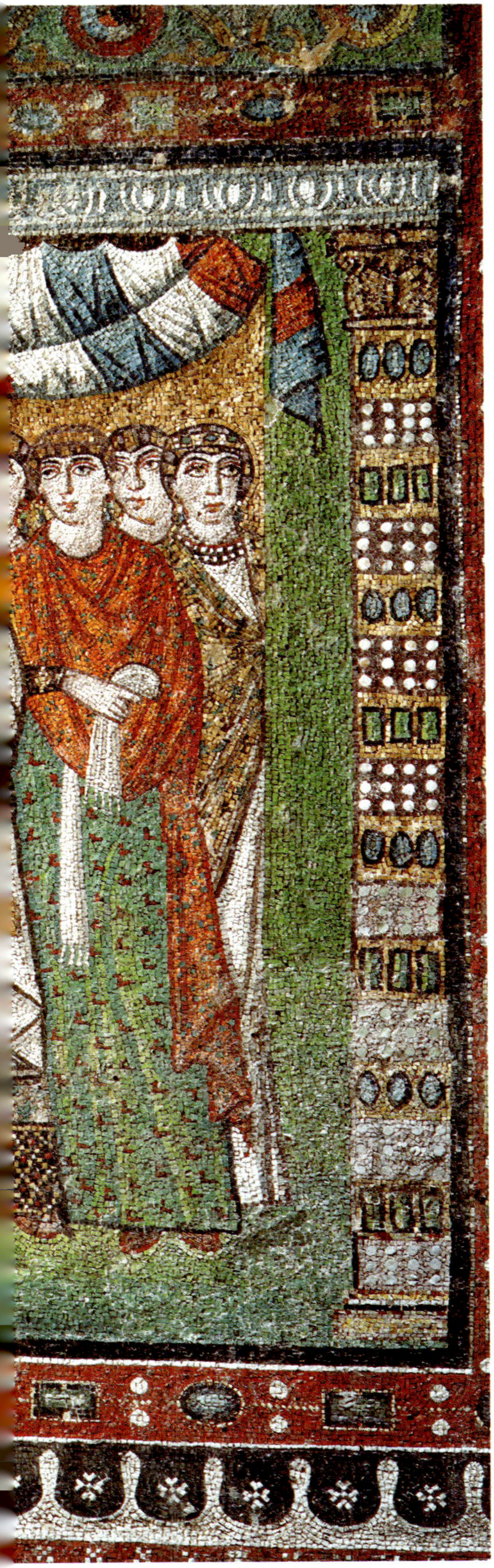

Anonymous: The Empress Theodora with her Retinue, c. 547

Group portrait with empress

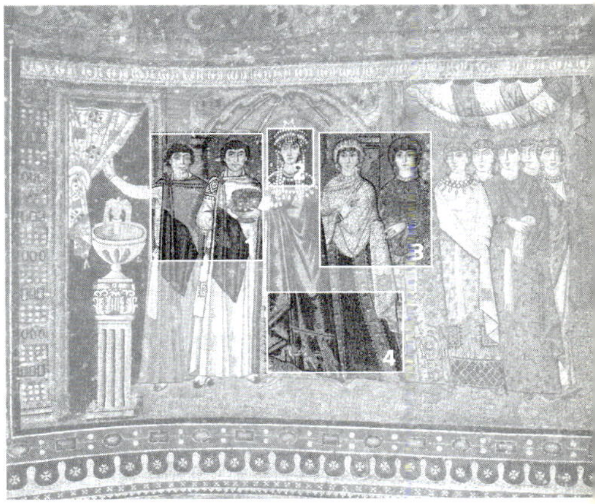

Whether we want to or not, we have to look up to Theodora. For her portrait is in a mosaic high over the heads of beholders. It is in the church of San Vitale in Ravenna. From the opposite wall her husband, Justinian, emperor of the East Roman Empire, looks out across us. Theodora too bears the insignia of power, clearly visible: the bejewelled triple diadem with the long chains of pearls, over a jewel-encrusted cap, and over her shoulders a cloak of imperial purple.

The empress is not aligned with her retinue; hers is the only figure over which no other overlaps. She is going ahead of those who accompany her, leading a procession and bearing a communion chalice to the church. An official is pulling back the drape from a portal, and the dark opening contrasts with the golden brightness of the outdoor scene. The procession is moving across an area of greenery; a fountain is splashing; and over the ladies is a colourful awning. The empress is standing exactly underneath a baldachin borne on stone columns. Although accounts describe her as short and petite, Theodora dominates her court, thanks to her foreground position and her high head-dress. Protocol dictated as much to the artists who worked on this mosaic in the mid-6th century.

The images of the imperial couple in Ravenna served a political purpose. They underlined the presence of the rulers in a city they had only recently reconquered for their empire. They were in a church because the emperor of the East Roman Empire was a religious leader and Christ's vicar upon earth. Hence the golden nimbus behind Theodora's head, a reflection of the light divine. This places her on a par with saints and apostles, quite a career for the daughter of a bear-tamer at the Constantinople hippodrome.

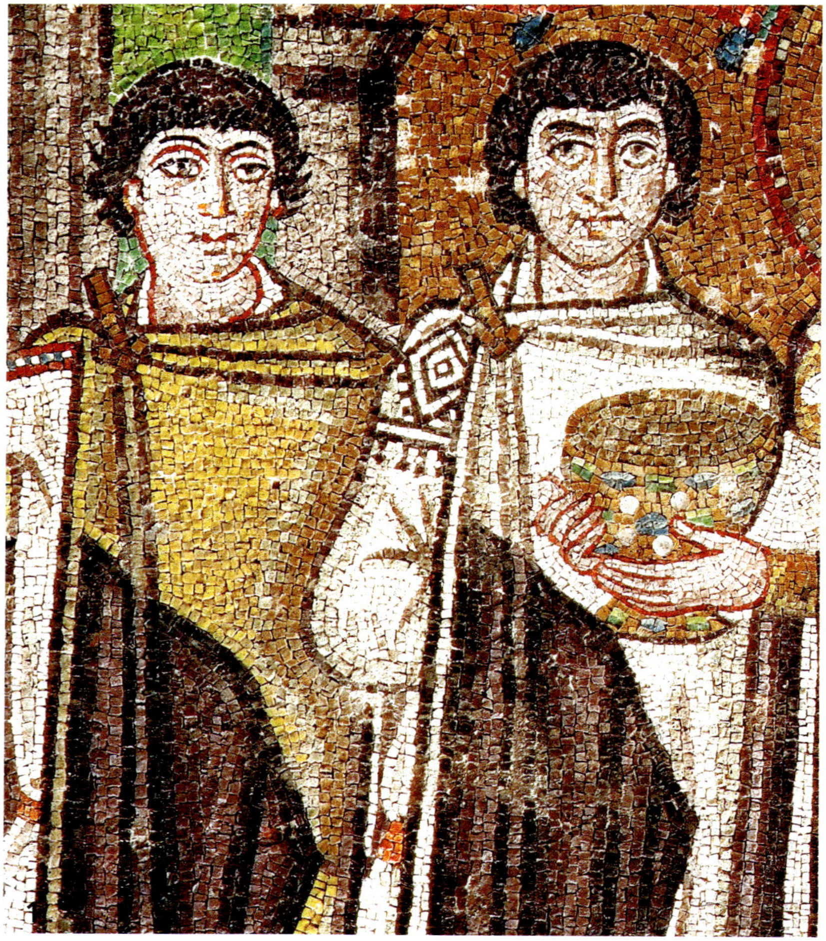

Eunuchs helped with the affairs of government

Meteoric careers were by no means unusual in mobile Byzantine society. The empress's closest confidant, Narses, probably shown here at her side, was born into slavery in Armenia in 480. Uneducated, and "a slight, to all appearances weakly man", he made his way by his appetite for hard work and his expertise, both of which he exhibited in political and military positions. Rulers could rely on him. Narses is seen in the modest attitude prescribed by etiquette, both arms concealed beneath his cloak; for it was forbidden to approach the divine rulers with "impure hands".

Both of the men portrayed in the mosaic are dressed as Byzantine officials, in the uniform of the civil administration, which was organized along military lines. The officials' belt over the white tunic is almost concealed by the long cloak fastened at the right shoulder. The rank of the wearer was proclaimed by the colour of the cloak and the large rectangular piece of material sewn onto it. This was called a *tablion*; the emperor's was gold, that of Narses is the precious purple reserved to the most senior of the seven ranks of official.

Even the black and white footwear was part of the uniform. It was part of an official's salary and was presented to him by the emperor, together with his certificate of appointment. Many officials studied law and passed difficult examinations; others, such as Narses, had a background in hands-on work. Parents who wanted their sons to rise more easily to high office had them castrated at an early age. Narses too was a eunuch. Only eunuchs and priests could not become emperor in Byzantium – and so posed no threat to the ruler.

The East Roman emperors lived dangerously, in spite or maybe because of their seemingly infinite power. They went in fear of potential rivals in high office, for they were constantly beset with court intrigues, military conspiracies and popular uprisings. In theory the ruler was elected directly by the "people"; in practice, however, it was a small military clique that voted him in.

Thus in the late 5th century Justinian was a rural lad living in a village in Thrace, till his uncle, a dependable professional soldier, was unexpectedly proclaimed emperor by the soldiery. Shortly afterwards, Justinian moved to the capital, Constantinople, where he received an excellent education and presently became the right-hand man of the ruler. This provided him with the means to assure himself of the throne. In 527, on the death of his uncle, Justinian became the official successor of Caesar and Augustus, the absolute overlord of an empire still known as "Roman" although for the past two centuries it had no longer been ruled from the banks of the Tiber but from the Bosporus. Rome's first Christian emperor, Constantine, had moved his capital there in dangerous times when tribes were on the move. Before the city was named after him, it was called Byzantium.

Justinian inherited a vast empire centred on the eastern Mediterranean, united only by the Christian religion and the person of the emperor. The western territories of the old Roman empire had fallen to barbarians. When Justinian came to the throne, the Ostrogoths ruled in Rome and Ravenna. The new emperor took as his great task in life the restoration of the old borders of the Roman empire, and he succeeded; but the areas of North Africa and Italy that were conquered by his generals were lost once more after his death. The East Roman or Byzantine Empire, however, survived until 1453.

The only certain likeness that we have of the empress Theodora is this one in Ravenna: large dark eyes, gazing from a narrow face. At this point she was no longer young, about fifty (we do not know when she was born). She died in 548, at about the same time as the church containing her image was consecrated. The portrait was copied from an original done in Constantinople, for in fact Theodora never set foot in Ravenna.

Theodora's features bear signs of illness (historians suspect cancer) or of the arduous toil of government affairs in an especially difficult time. About 540, plague spread through the East Roman Empire, taking a heavy toll on the population and ruining the economy. When Justinian too was stricken with the plague, the responsibility of government fell squarely upon Theodora. She proved well able to manage, pre-empting potential conspiracies and dealing with the administrative affairs of the empire as well as with military ventures – albeit not to the delight of the generals. This marked the peak of her power. For months, the empress was the absolute ruler in a patriarchal state that normally preferred her sex to be confined to the ladies' apartments. She was experienced in matters of government, since Justinian had involved her in them from the outset. This was envisaged neither by tradition nor by the constitution; but Justinian wished to share everything with the wife he worshipped his whole life long. He called her his "sweetest delight" or, from the literal meaning of her name in Greek, "the gift of God".

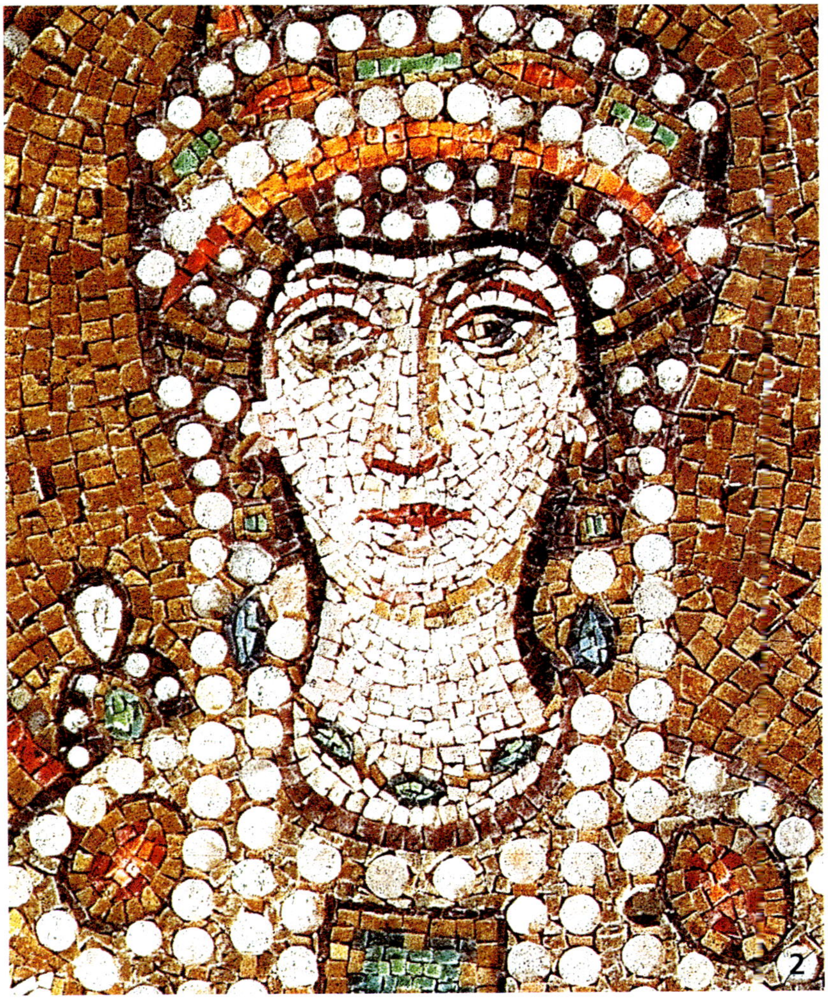
2

A woman well able to manage

When he fell head over heels in love with Theodora, then a mere girl and twenty years younger than he, Justinian was already a counsellor to the emperor and in line for the throne. Theodora, by contrast, was from the lower classes. Since her early youth she had been performing on revue stages. "Fair of countenance, and graceful of form", she could neither dance nor sing, but nonetheless scored immense success with her comic striptease number. In a Leda burlesque she performed with a goose that was trained to pick out grains of corn from between her thighs whilst she writhed in transports of delight. In his *Secret History*, from which we know these things, Procopius (the contemporary who also wrote the official histories) described Theodora as "the sort of girl who if somebody walloped her or boxed her ears would make a jest of it and roar with laughter". The bishop of Ephesus was even blunter: "Theodora was from a brothel."

No one, not even the church, raised any objection when the emperor's confidant fell so madly in love with this girl that he resolved to make her his lawful wife. Theodora was crowned empress at Justinian's side, and from that moment on even her arch-enemies (among them Procopius) could find not the slightest misdemeanour to accuse her of. She acquitted herself with dignity in her new role. She did not forget her earlier experiences, as is shown by an edict she promulgated against prostitution. Doubtless she owed her realism and tough will to the hard youth she spent in the hippodrome, the sleazy pleasure district of the capital: in 432, when whole quarters of the city were burnt to the ground in a popular uprising, and a mob besieged the palace, the emperor and his advisers were already debating flight, going into exile overseas, but Theodora, the one woman in a counsel of men, urged a fight and refused to flee. "I shall never take off the purple", she declared, "nor shall I ever see the day when those around me do not address me as the empress. The purple will make a good shroud." At her urging, Justinian's generals put down the insurrection. Some forty thousand were left dead. Sixteen years later, Theodora went to the grave in the imperial purple.

The two ladies immediately beside Theodora cannot be identified with certainty, but while the five companions in the background are all to a similar schematic design, these two have individualized features: the elder, with the high cheekbones, may be Antonina, the chatelaine of the palace and wife of the famous general Belisarius; the younger, who bears a resemblance to her, would then be Johannina, her daughter.

Like the empress, Antonina had had quite a career on the stage; both were strong-willed women who exerted a powerful influence on their partners, an influence that their contemporaries were at a loss to explain except by supposing them to use magic potions. Belisarius did indeed seem very much under his wife's thumb. Even on campaign he was inseparable from her; and time and again he turned a blind eye to her many blatant affairs.

If Theodora took her friend under her wing despite her scandalous life-style, it was not only out of loyal friendship. Through Antonina she had the popular general Belisarius, who might have been a dangerous rival for Justinian, where she wanted him. And in dealing with countless intrigues, the dependable Antonina proved her worth. In the "silken apartments of the holy palace", ably informed by a secret service organized by Narses, the two women deliberated strategies to put the empress's policies into effect and wipe out anyone who got in her way. For one powerful minister of finance, for instance, who had dared to bear tales about Theodora to Justinian, Antonina set a cunning trap: she led the unwary unfortunate to admit, with reliable witnesses listening in concealment, that he had his eyes on the throne. His fate was sealed.

It was also Antonina who carried out Theodora's plans in Italy in 537. She accompanied her husband there, persuading the reluctant Belisarius to depose the newly and lawfully elected Pope Silverius in Rome, on the orders of the empress. The Pope was replaced by force with a favourite of the empress's. Indeed, Silverius is said to have been first banished and then murdered, by a servant of Antonina's, at the empress's command.

But charges such as these were made by Procopius, the secretary of Belisarius, who hated Theodora, or by authors who disliked her policy on religion. Her whole life long, the empress supported the Christian sect of the Monophysites, even hiding a persecuted bishop in her own apartments for years. The Monophysites were found chiefly in Egypt and Syria, and held that Christ had but one divine nature, and not an additional second, human nature, as the Orthodox Church taught. The Monophysites were persecuted as heretics, and that included the man concealed by the empress. Theodora's aim, which Justinian tolerated, was to place a Pope at the head of the Church who sympathized with her protégés. That end justified any means; and when the pontiff whom Belisarius had placed on St. Peter's chair failed to satisfy her expectations too, she had him abducted from Rome and brought to Constantinople, where she could put pressure on him. Shortly before her death she seemed to be within sight of her goal: the Pope was yielding, and the Monophysites were rehabilitated. They praised the empress as "sent by God, to protect his persecuted people in the dangers of the tempest". But in fact the Orthodox Church was victorious in the long term. It was the church that wrote the history books; and Theodora was not portrayed favourably in them.

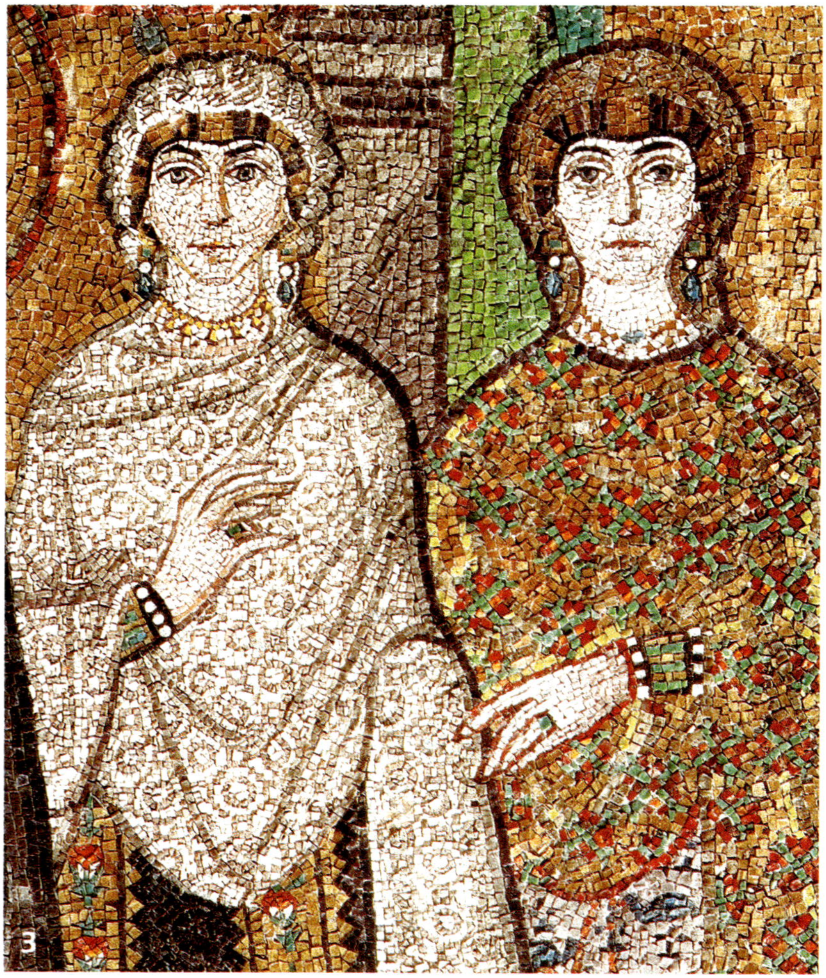

Intrigues in the holy palace

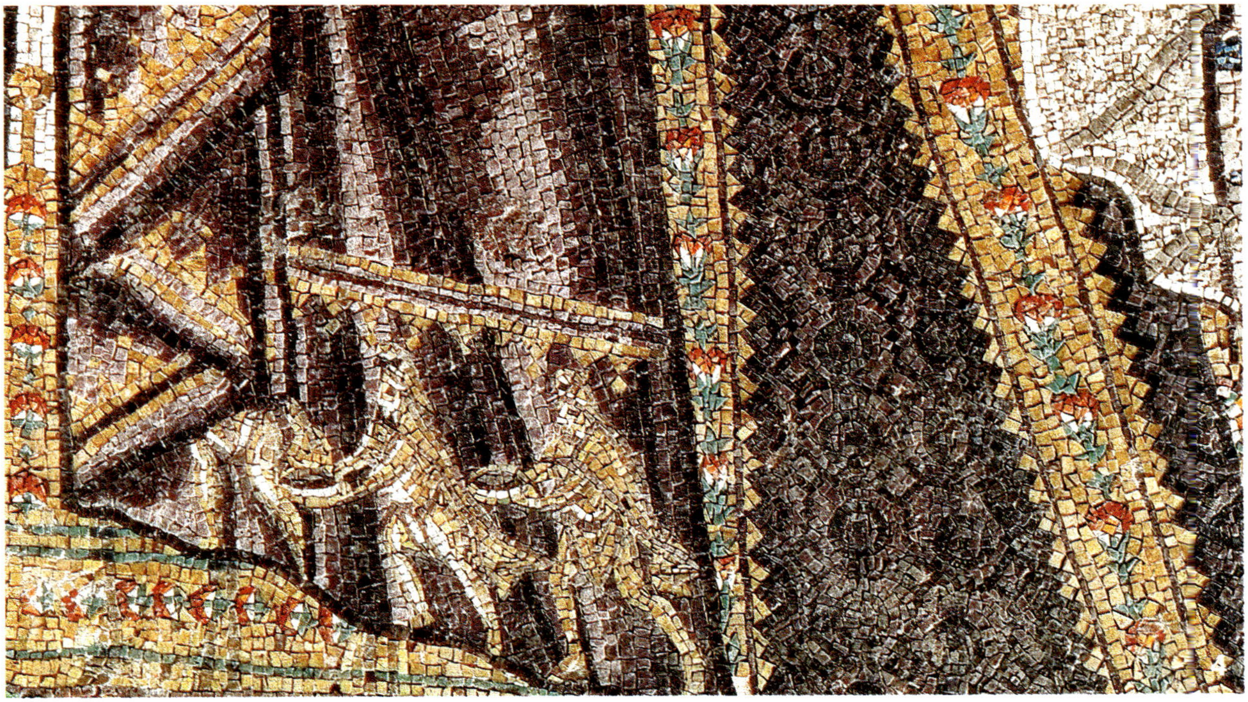

The hem of Theodora's long cloak, worn over the bejewelled white robe, is adorned with figures embroidered in gold: the Three Kings bearing their gifts. The detail is minutely done, in coloured-glass mosaic stones of various shapes. The number of pieces used for the two imperial mosaics in San Vitale is put at 322,560, many of them gold. A thousand years on, they still shine. Bedded upon an uneven ground of mortar, they still reflect the light in manifold ways.

We know neither who designed nor who made these works, for the masters who made mosaics did not sign their achievements. They may have been from Italy, where the Roman tradition was still alive, or equally from Constantinople. There were many outstanding Byzantine craftsmen, and throughout the Middle Ages Constantinople supplied Europe with luxury items: implements crafted of ivory, jewellery, and above all costly fabrics. Textiles were the most important sector of the Byzantine economy, assuming almost industrial proportions. But that splendorous workshop that was Byzantium produced not only for the export market (carefully monitored by customs), above all, their wares were produced for the imperial court. The exhibition of wealth was a deliberate act of policy.

"Through the beauty of its ceremonies", one Byzantine official noted, "imperial power appears a yet more splendid and magnificent thing. It makes as profound an impression on foreigners as it does on subjects of the empire." The emperor was good at the kind of show one might expect of God's vicar on earth. One contemporary poet described barbarians admitted to an audience supposing themselves already in heaven when they had barely crossed the threshold of the palace, so great was the splendour.

The protocol that set the emperor apart from mere mortals (and afforded him protection from them) extended to his clothing. Certain colour shades were reserved for the imperial family, and the death penalty could be inflicted on anyone who dared wear those shades. Tyrian purple in particular, the prized genuine purple from Tyre made from snails, was the colour of imperial garb. The shades it came in ranged from scarlet to the costliest brownish-purple amethyst hue, which has been used to dye the silk we see Theodora wearing. The fact that her neighbour is wearing a similar shade indicates her privileged status. Antonina and the other ladies of the court are furthermore wearing white patterned stoles of the latest oriental fashion. All of them, on certain feast days, received their rich clothing from the hands of the empress; for silk fabrics were a state monopoly.

Silk as a status symbol

Silk came from remote China, on the caravan route that crossed Persia, where the trade might be interrupted at any time. Not until years after Theodora's death did wily Byzantine monks contrive to smuggle silkworms out of China in hollowed-out walking staffs. Byzantium likewise guarded the secret of silk well, and the material remained a status symbol.

The motif of the Three Kings embroidered onto the silk is found again in the mosaics of Ravenna, in Sant' Apollinare Nuovo. There we can see clearly what we can only guess at here: the biblical magi are not entitled to the imperial purple, nor are they assigned the aura of a halo – unlike the Empress Theodora.

Limburg Brothers: Miniature for the month of January from the Très Riches Heures of the Duke of Berry, c. 1415

Palaces crumble but books remain

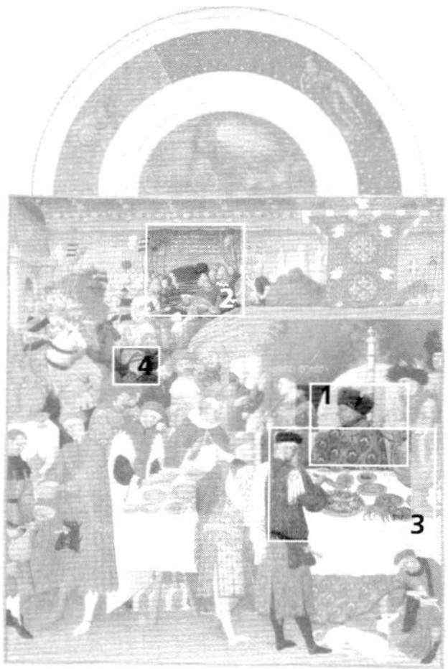

The scene, a New Year gathering hosted by John, Duke of Berry, probably on 1 January 1413 at his Paris city palace, the Hôtel de Nesle. The seventy-three-year-old duke is seated beneath a baldachin, as befits his high rank; he is the uncle of the king of France. On the fabric of the canopy are the royal *fleur de lis* and the duke's two heraldic animals, the bear and the swan.

Behind the Duke of Berry, a fire is blazing, screened off by a reed fireguard. It must be cold outside, to judge by the arriving guests warming their hands at the fire whilst a court officer invites them to approach: "aproche, aproche" is written over his head, like a speech bubble. In the background hangs a tapestry, both as a protection against the cold and damp, and for decorative purposes. It is meant to show the Trojan war, though the figures in it are dressed and armed like the duke's contemporaries. Before the old man, who is wearing a fur cap even inside the palace (which is doubtless draughty), the table is sumptuously laid. The floor is covered with straw matting, as was customary in winter.

All of this is depicted on a sheet measuring 29 by 21 centimetres, painted by the Limbourg brothers in the early 15th century for the *Très Riches Heures* of the Duke of Berry. The manuscript, which runs to 206 sheets of finest vellum, owes its name to the keeper of the duke's treasures, Robinet d'Estampes. His task it was to keep an inventory of the treasures in his master's possession, and in 1416, following the death of the duke, he noted: "Item, in a cassette, numerous leaves of a very rich book of hours, which Paul and his brothers decorated and illuminated very richly."

He additionally noted a "fine book of hours", a "large" one and a "small" one. The Duke of Berry possessed fifteen books of hours in all, as well as fourteen Bibles, sixteen psalters, six missals and seventeen breviaries, every one of them listed and described by the diligent Robinet, in part during the lifetime of the duke, who ennobled him in recognition of his services. For the duke was a collector, buying illustrated books of prayer or receiving them as gifts or commissioning them. It was in accordance with his wish for a magnificently illuminated book of hours that the *Très Riches Heures* was made.

A book of hours was a prayer book for personal use in everyday devotions. It contained the words of prayers that were said at various hours during the day. The initial letters were illuminated – that is, decorated in colour, and especially with red lead, *minium*. This evolved into small-format illustrations, or miniatures: hence the word. The sumptuous beauty of these illustrations gradually outshone the prayers themselves, and the everyday utility object became something that afforded aesthetic pleasure, and in due course a sought-after collector's item.

At the beginning of a book of hours there was almost invariably a calendar. It contained the twelve months of the year, each with an illustration, in the manner prescribed by medieval tradition. Usually these pictures showed rural people going about the work that the land required of them at the season: in April cutting the vines, in July making hay. In the pictures illustrating February, the countryman would be warming himself by the hearth. But in January, the month of leisure and festivity, an elderly aristocrat would be seated banqueting at table. Thus the tradition. In the *Très Riches Heures*, for the first time, it was not just any old man. The Limbourg brothers portrayed the man who had commissioned the book from them, the Duke of Berry, amidst all that was dear to him: loyal friends, servants and dogs, fine raiment, costly gold plate, and, not least, good food. The duke was a gourmet. He is credited with having made truffles a part of French cuisine.

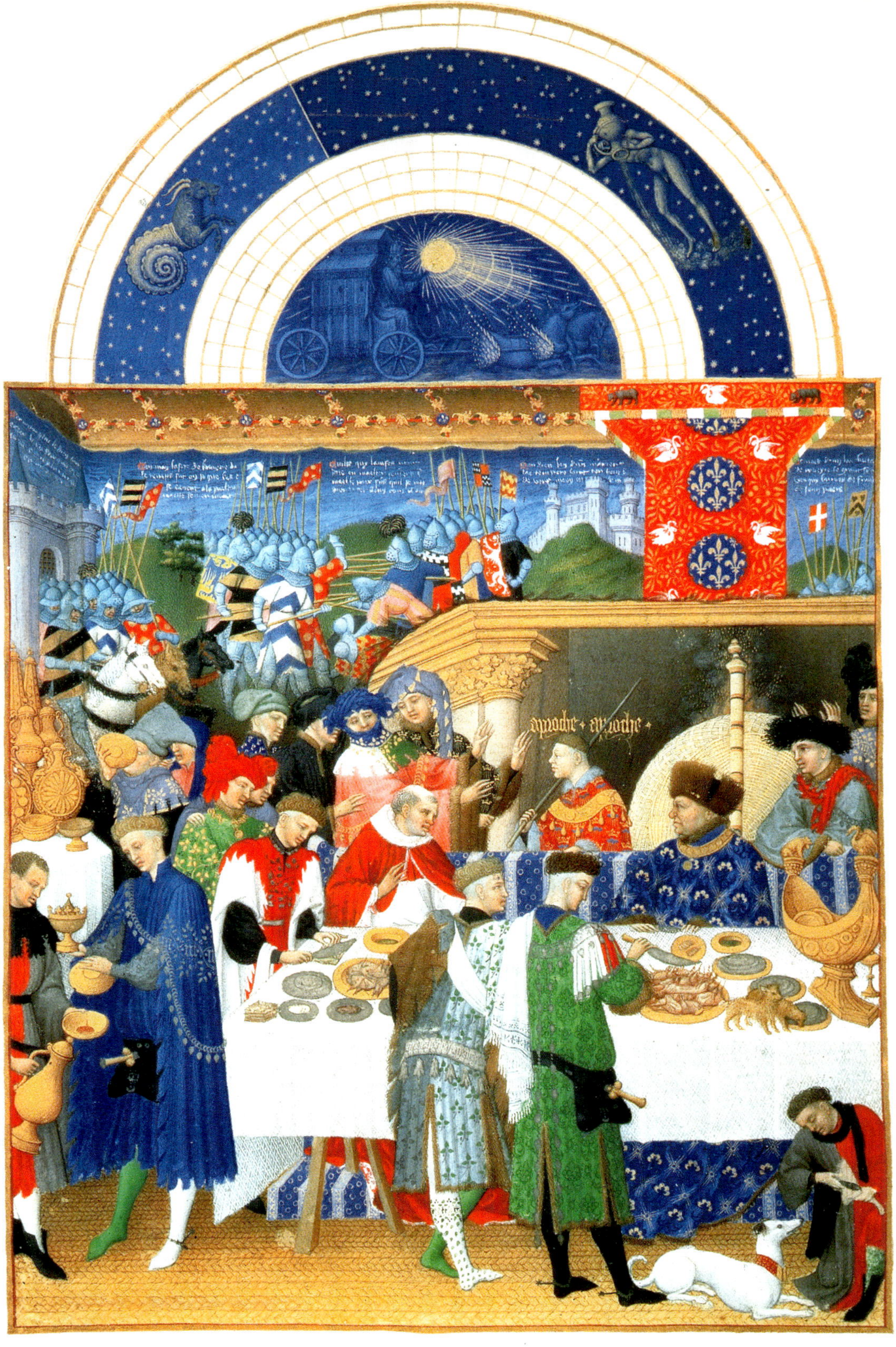

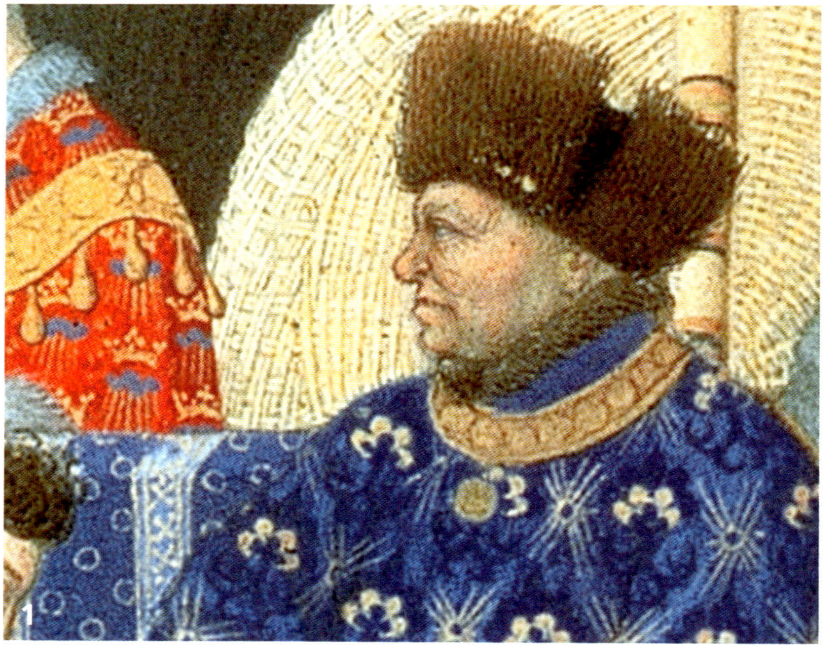
1

The most covetous man in the world

Festivities, giving and receiving gifts – nothing was closer to the duke's heart. Here he was in his element. The first day of January was *his* day; it is an old French custom to give presents to mark the start of the year, at every level of society. Kings and princes of the blood royal exchanged precious jewels and gave their officials and household servants substantial sums of money in recognition of their loyal service. Courtiers tried to acquit themselves well in this ceremony by making their master a present that would give him particular pleasure.

Thus in 1408 the Duke of Berry was given a rare manuscript of Terence by Martin Gouge, his treasurer and later Bishop of Chartres. In the picture, Gouge is probably the one man of the church we see at table. A general made a gift of a curiosity from Italy: a magic stone which changed colour on contact with poison. This would be useful in uncertain times. In this way, much of the ducal collection was assembled. Robinet d'Estampes recorded that the Duke of Berry received 350 items as new year gifts in the course of the years, including 80 manuscripts and 177 gems. He in turn made 281 presents, not including gifts of money. They cannot have been paltry gifts, for the duke was a generous man; one contemporary quoted in Froissart's chronicles remarked that he had given so much to his servants that every one of them was rich.

Generosity was a political tool: a duke needed people he could rely on, devoted followers, his own party on which he could depend when struggling for power or simply for survival. Not for nothing did Berry's brother, the Duke of Burgundy, always take a few barrels of Beaune wine on his travels, to augment his popularity.

The Duke of Berry was even openhanded with money that did not belong to him. He was forever spending more than he had, his financial difficulties were chronic, and yet he never hesitated to incur huge debts (at interest rates as high as 78%!) in order to stage lavish entertainments. In 1385, with money entrusted to him by the king for the waging of war, he held magnificent tournaments in southern France ... Generosity as a political strategy coincided in the Duke of Berry with an innate spendthrift vein. (It is true, of course, that in the Middle Ages no high nobleman dreamt of being discreet when it came to displays of luxury.) Even at the age of seventy-three, Berry participated in every festivity, thinking it important to be thought the most stylish of French noblemen. His expense ledgers show that in the winter of 1413 the duke bought no fewer than three new state robes: one for Christmas, "lined with 447 fine black marten furs"; a second, gold-embroidered, for New Year's Day, presumably the robe seen in the Limbourg brothers' picture; and one of blue velvet for the Feast of the Epiphany.

It is striking, and perhaps a sign of his age, that there are hardly any ladies near the duke in this miniature. After all, he once remarked, as Froissart tells us, that "a lord's castle is nought without a lady and a man is nothing without a woman". A mere five months after the death of his first wife he resolved to re-marry. Then already forty-eight, he chose a twelve-year-old girl for his new bride, to the astonishment of all around him and of his royal nephew – who (thus Froissart) demanded of him, "What will you do with so young a wife?" To which Berry replied, "If the girl is young, I shall spare her for three or four years." And the king: "But will she spare you?" Unlike his first, this second marriage of the duke's does not appear to have been particularly happy. The duchess led most of her life apart from her husband, in the provinces, and Robinet's inventory makes hardly any mention of gifts from her.

The Duke of Berry's principal passion, however, cost him sums far larger than any garments, festivities or presents. He invested in something he felt would be permanent and would assure him everlasting fame after his death: he built palaces, in the capital, Paris, and in the provinces of Berry, Auvergne and Poitou, which the king gave him as his appanage. One palace after another. Ever larger, ever more magnificent, more luxurious. He had a full seventeen palaces in the town and in the country, and almost all are pictured in the *Très Riches Heures*. This rage to build cost Berry dear. The revenues from his provinces were not sufficient. He raised the taxes and ruthlessly exploited every other territory too where he represented the king – so much so that the cities of southern France, already ruined by war, rose up in arms against him. Froissart notes that "the duke was the most covetous man in the world and did not care where he took his money". And one Parisian decried Berry in his diary as "a man as cruel towards the common people as ever any Saracen tyrant".

One hundred years of war and chaos

In the Middle Ages, a prince of the blood royal had no need to be concerned about the people. Jean of France, Duke of Berry, was the third son of the French King John the Good. For his nephew Charles VI, who succeeded to the throne when still a minor and went mad in 1392, Berry conducted the affairs of government, working together with – or against – other princes of the royal family. When the citizens of Paris tried to air their political views, his message to them was: "It is no business of yours … the king, and we who are of his blood, will wage war when we please, and if we please we shall make peace."

This applied to policy both foreign and domestic. And it was this high-handed stance of the powerful, their greed for money, and their personal ambition, that plunged France into chaos in the early 15th century. Plagues, and the Hundred Years' War, laid waste the land. The war had begun in 1337 when a king of England laid claim to the French crown. Ever since the war had dragged on, punctuated by cease-fires of various duration. France, the chief theatre of war, was in a sorry state, racked economically and financially by the burdens of war and by the woeful and self-serving administration of the princes. In a period when there was a royal power vacuum, the Duke of Berry's thoughts turned to enriching himself. The Dukes of Burgundy, however, had loftier ambitions. They took advantage of the weakness of France to extend their territory and transform Burgundy into a major power. When the Duke of Orléans crossed them, their rival was murdered in cold blood; and this, in 1407, led to the outbreak of an additional civil war between the parties of Burgundy and Orléans.

Berry was no warrior. He was a diplomat; and time and again, as far as he was able, he tried to mediate between the two enemies, while at the same time upholding the rights of the king. He made concessions in every direction, and too many of them. The duke was not the equal of the determined power politicians who steered the course of Burgundy. In 1412, Berry was besieged in his provincial capital, Bourges, by the troops of Burgundy and (paradoxically) the king, and was forced to capitulate. The English forces he had called to his assistance arrived too late. To get rid of them again, and to pay his own soldiers, Berry needed money; so he had the gold treasures which he had given as an endowment to the cathedral of Bourges melted down and minted into coin.

The working capital of a nobleman

On a sideboard to the left, artfully arranged, we see the Duke of Berry's gold plate: finely chased pitchers, goblets, bowls, plates. Most of these were probably gifts. The custom was for a city to present golden goblets to its lord on the occasion of his first visit.

Gold plate was practical; it could easily be transported from palace to palace, and used everyday. It was also decorative: it asserted the wealth of its owner with every glint and gleam. Still more, though, it was the working capital of a medieval nobleman, to cover any and every eventuality. It could readily be pawned or sold if the need arose. On his death, Berry's brother, the powerful Duke of Burgundy, did not even leave enough money to pay for mourning clothes for his sons. His widow paid the pall-bearers with golden plates.

Gold plate could be melted down, too, as the chalices of Bourges cathedral were. Gold works of art, often crafted in long years of patient labour, thus tended to have a short life. The story goes that one goldsmith was so distressed to learn that yet another of his masterpieces had been melted down that he entered a monastery and abandoned his craft for good.

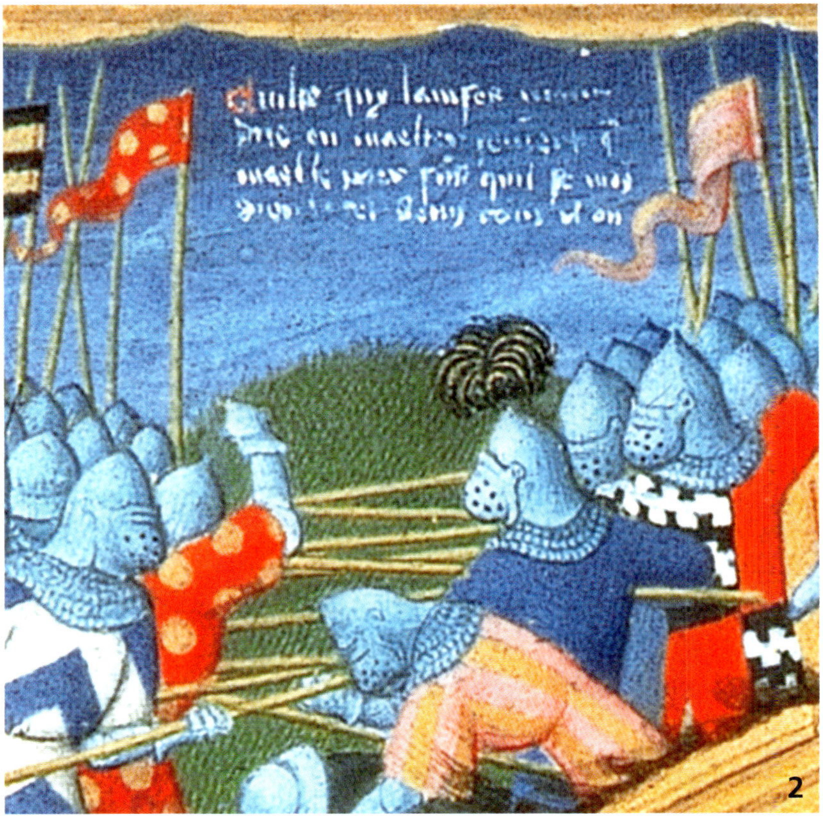
2

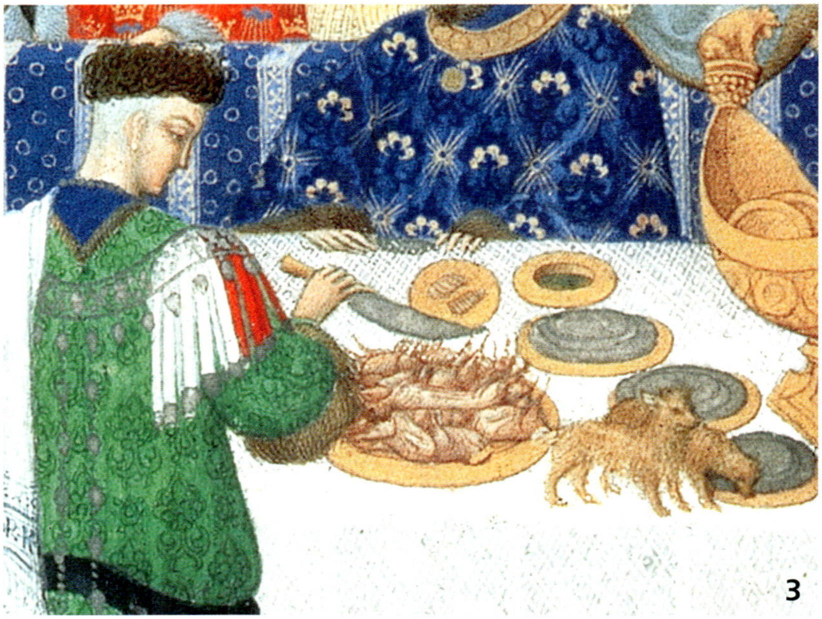

3

Forever on the move with the court and the bear

A ducal household was a bottomless pit. In 1413, the Duke of Berry's household numbered almost three hundred, and he was concerned that they should constitute a suitable setting for his own person. Like other great noblemen, on New Year's Day he made gifts of splendid clothing to every one of them, from the first chamberlain to Hannequin the court jester, from his two personal physicians to the barber.

Amongst the most important positions at court, normally reserved for aristocrats, were those of waiters, carvers and cup-bearers at the duke's table. A complex and sophisticated ceremonial ritual governed their actions. To the left in the foreground we see a cup-bearer fetching a drink (or perhaps only water for a finger-bowl – food was eaten with the three first fingers of the right hand). This is clearly intended for the duke because the goblet and bowl have lids, which was the prerogative of rulers. The carver is at work on the fowl (probably pigeons, partridges or quail), observing elaborate and fixed rules. The choicer parts are reserved for the duke, while the remainder is for guests of lower rank. Each carver has a collection of knives, which he looks after with great care and keeps in majestic sheaths at his belt. The slices of poultry are placed on thick slices of bread; these are not eaten, but are later, soaked in sauce and fat, given to the dogs and the poor. The poultry is followed by countless other courses; according to the Duke of Berry's expense ledgers, every Sunday and feast day three oxen, thirty sheep, 160 partridges and the same number of hares were consumed. After the banquet, or between courses, the duke's entertainers would perform music, dances, and crude capers. A concluding sweet course would consist of spices such as aniseed, coriander, fennel and ginger, almonds and other nuts, and exotic candied fruits. Hot and spicy mulled wine was served with this course.

In 1413, the Duke of Berry had ceased to travel much and resided mostly in his Parisian palace. His advanced age, considerable for the era, had finally compelled him to abandon the nomadic life-style that was characteristic of the highest noblemen at the time, kings included. Until not long before he had moved about constantly, from province to province, from palace to palace, seeing to his affairs and collecting revenue. On these travels he was always accompanied by his entire court and the larger part of his treasures. Nor should we forget the duke's favourite bear, his heraldic animal, which also went with him everywhere in a specially constructed wagon, under the watchful eye of a warder.

A greater love of dogs than of mankind

In addition to his bear, the duke was accompanied by dogs. An enthusiastic huntsman, the Duke of Berry purportedly possessed fifteen hundred dogs in the year 1388. They were so famous that he received the hand of his second wife only when he agreed to present her guardian "six hunting hounds, of the finest and keenest". The duke's "great greyhound" had servants of its own (dog and attendant can both be seen at bottom right), and a noblewoman, the Abbess de Villiers, was exclusively charged with the care of Berry's favourites, his small white Pomeranian spitzes. These were from Germany; their sire was a gift of the emperor, named Prinz. Another spitz named Löwe (lion) is seen in numerous miniatures accompanying the duke when he went out riding or was at prayer. These dogs were indulged in everything; in the January miniature they are even seen wandering amongst the dishes of food on the table.

From the ducal expenses ledgers we know that one servant was handsomely rewarded when he rescued Prinz from a cess-pit into which the dog had fallen. If any dog was under suspicion of rabies, it was sent to the seaside to recover its health. There was no doubt about it: animals were dear to the Duke of Berry's heart. So dear, indeed, that in 1393 he awarded a life-long pension to a loyal dog that refused to budge from its departed master's grave. The duke's contemporaries were not so far from the truth when they asserted that he had a greater love of dogs than of mankind.

The Duke of Berry's miniaturists

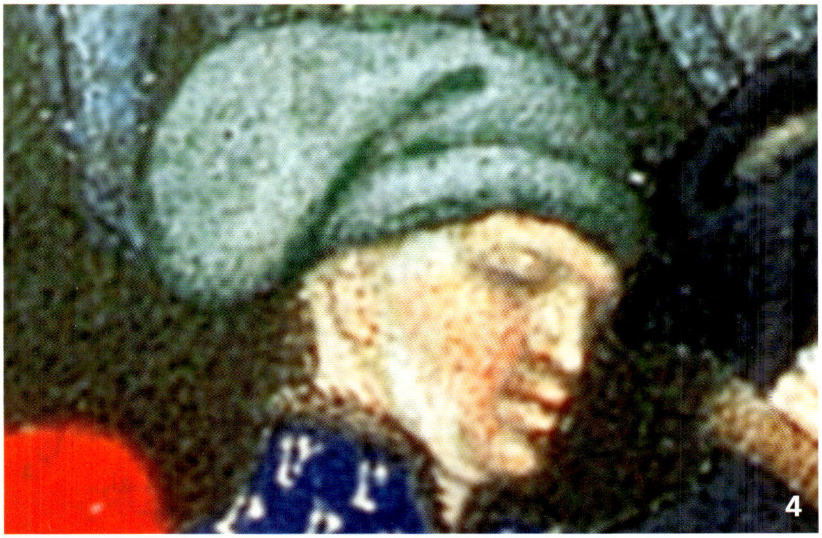

The duke's love of art also exceeded his love of mankind. For his magnificent building projects he hired the best architects and sculptors, and the palaces they created had an elegance altogether new, with slender towers, pointed roofs and artful ornamental stonework, a far cry from the ponderous castles built by the nobles of old.

By 1400, when all seventeen of the Duke of Berry's palaces were as good as finished, he had the leisure and means to take an interest in another art form: miniatures. His parents and brothers had already collected manuscript books, but the duke was bent on collecting finer, richer works than ever. For this purpose he established a miniaturists' workshop in his province of Berry and presently hired the three Limbourg (or Limburg) brothers, Paul, Jean and Hermann, Flemish artists originally from Nijmegen, in today's Netherlands but then in the Rhenish duchy of Geldern. Two of them are known to have qualified as goldsmiths in Paris, but left the French capital when it was threatened by plague in 1399. From 1400–03 they worked for the Duke of Burgundy, but after that they do not reappear until 1408, in accounts, the only reliable source we have (for miniatures were rarely signed). We do not know which miniature was done by which brother, though in all likelihood they all worked on them together, one perhaps doing the background and another the figures. Paul was the boss of the workshop.

The Duke of Berry's accounts show that from 1410 regular payments were made: "to Paul of Limbourg, 6 thalers"; "to the aforementioned Limbourg, 10 thalers"; and "50 thalers to Paul of Limbourg, chamberlain to His Excellency ... in recognition of the good and pleasing services he has performed for him, continues daily to perform, and, it is to be hoped, will perform in the times to come, for his raiment, and that he may be the most highly regarded in his service".

The title of chamberlain to a duke is a high honour, but Berry did more to bind the esteemed artist to him; he made him a gift of a house in Bourges, and furthermore, in 1408, had a girl just eight years old kidnapped, which brought his excellency considerable trouble with parliament in Paris. The child's name was Guillotte Mercier and she was of bourgeois family. The duke had her kidnapped "in order to marry her, against her mother's will, to a Dutch painter who was working for him in the Hôtel de Bicêtre in Paris". This can only have meant Paul of Limbourg. Christine de Pisan, a contemporary Parisian poet and feminist, lamented the notorious waywardness, intemperateness and immorality of artists.

It is assumed that Paul of Limbourg introduced several self-portraits into the *Très Riches Heures*. Here, he would presumably be the man in the plain woollen cap, who is in contrast to the richly-garbed guests. The man drinking, likewise wearing a grey cap, might be one of his brothers, and the half-concealed woman in the plain blue head-scarf might be Paul's wife Guillotte.

There is no doubt that the duke's artists were present at his New Year festivities; in his inventory, Robinet d'Estampes describes an item "which Paul Limbourg and his two brothers ... made a gift of at the New Year celebration". Bound in white velvet and with gilded silver clasps, this was "a deceptive imitation book made from a single piece of wood, containing no pages and nothing written in it". A dummy, in other words. The painters permitted themselves a little joke in the gift they made to their master.

A mere three months after the New Year festivities of 1413, disaster struck the gathering depicted in this miniature. The duke fell seriously ill. This meant that political governance was effectively suspended; and the civil war erupted anew. In April 1413 the people of Paris revolted, and the city fell prey to a bloodthirsty reign of terror. At about the same time, the English landed once more on the coast of France, summoned to assist now the one and now the other party in the civil war. In October 1415 the French army was totally annihilated by the triumphant English at Agincourt. The larger part of France now came under foreign rule; the dauphin fled to the provinces and set about re-conquering his realm from a new base, a long and arduous task. The Maid of Orléans, who was to afford such invaluable assistance in the process, was born at about the same time that the Limbourgs painted their book of hours: Joan of Arc.

But neither the artists nor the Duke of Berry was to live to see that day. When the latter died in 1416, his painters had already gone to the grave before him. Their book of hours was unfinished. But it has survived, just as the ducal account books have. Unlike the duke's gold treasures – all melted down. And unlike the palaces intended for posterity – destroyed. Only the surviving books now tell us how the Duke of Berry celebrated New Year, and how much the mourning shoes cost that the "attendant upon the little dogs" wore to his master's funeral.

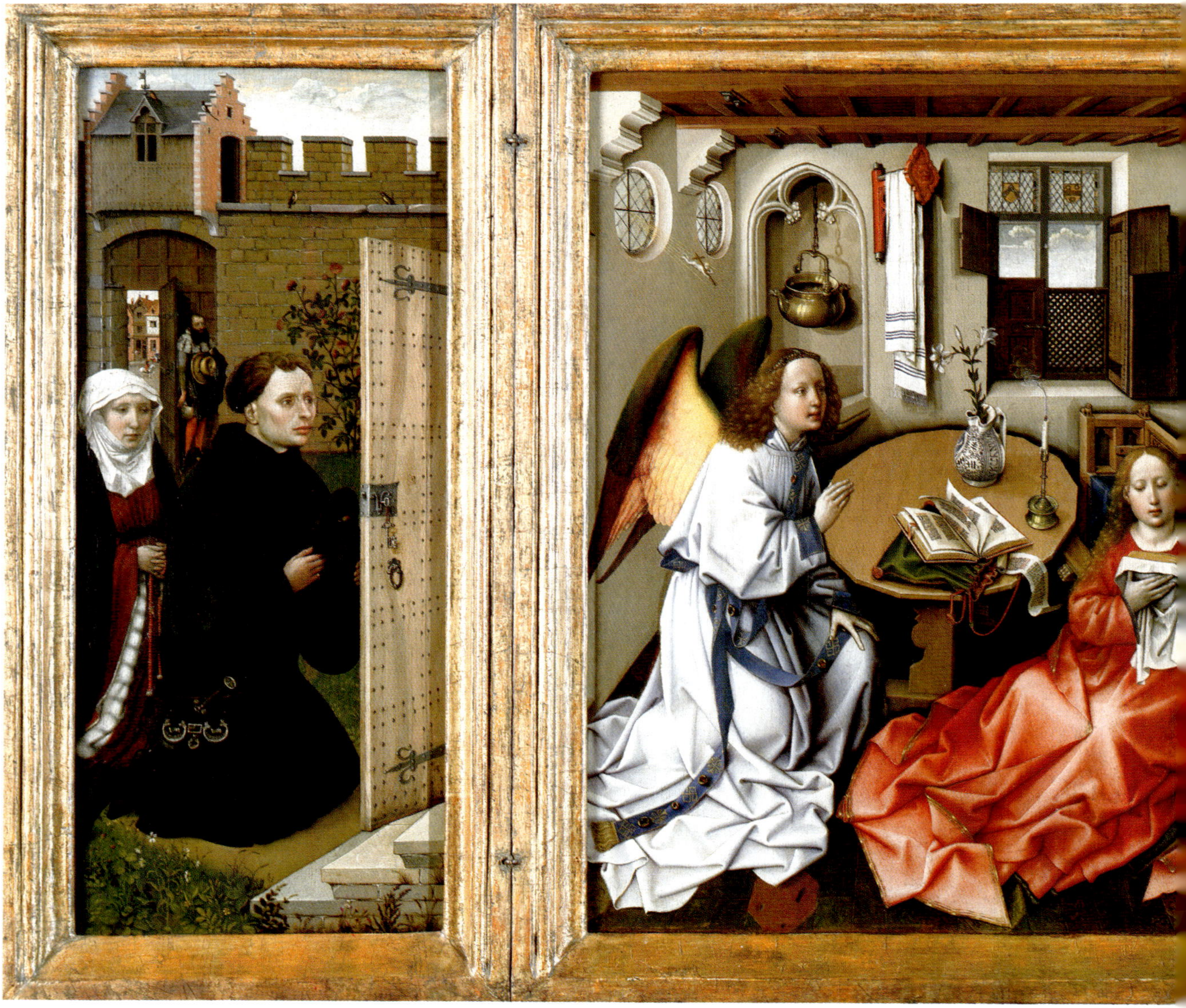

Robert Campin:
The Mérode Triptych, c. 1422/1430

An angel in the living room

A living room, a workshop, a walled garden: interiors and nature, with glimpses of a city, its streets and squares. Seeing a reproduction, we might suppose this three-panelled painting to be large, but in fact it is relatively small, just 120 centimetres in total breadth and 64 centimetres high. It was intended not for a church but for a room rather like that in the centre portion, the annunciation scene. The triptych served as a house altar, standing against or hanging on a wall, and the couple who endowed it would pray their daily *Ave Maria* before it. These words, meaning "Hail, Mary", were the Archangel Gabriel's words

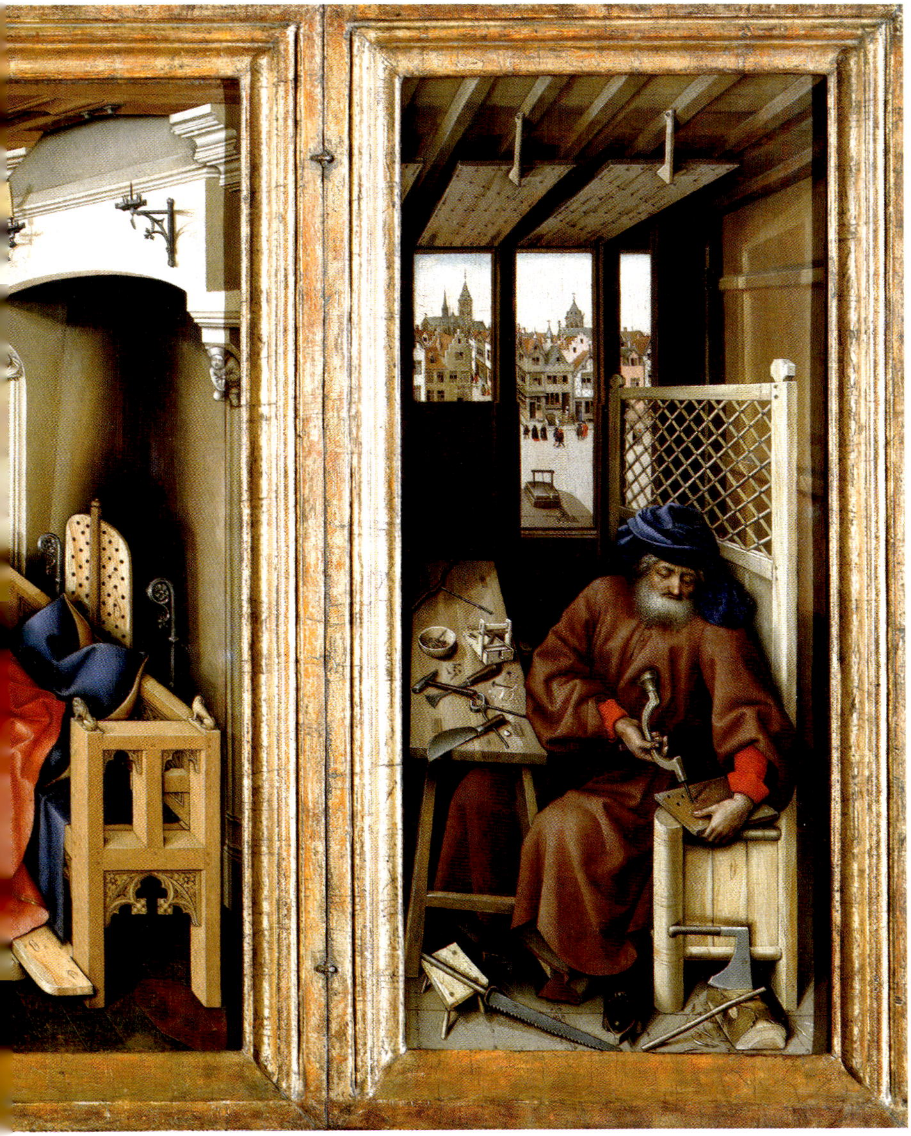

of greeting to the Virgin Mary when he came to tell her she would bear a son.

The annunciation marks the beginning of the Christian story of salvation, and in order to underline the significance of the event, artists liked to re-locate it to a church or palace. Until well into the Middle Ages they presented it, as they presented all biblical events, against a golden background. But in this version from the Netherlands, the annunciation happens in an urban, middle-class setting.

The two figures in the centre panel are no ordinary burghers, but we perceive this (disregarding the angel's wings) only by comparing with the others in the two sides: the faces of Mary and the angel are less realistic and individual, and their garments far more splendid. The folds in the fabric alone constitute an entire chapter of art history.

Examination of the wood on which the triptych was painted has shown that the wood for the centre panel was felled around 1373 and that of the wing panels somewhat later. Art historians date the painter's work (though more than one may have worked on the picture) to between 1422 and 1430. And at that date an annunciation set amongst the ordinary people was quite new.

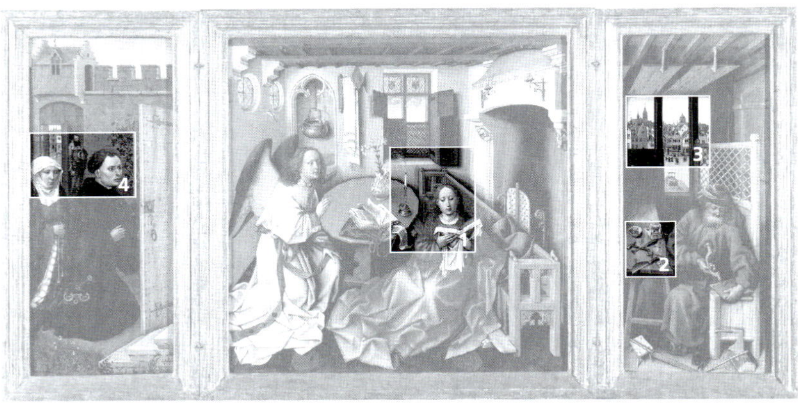

The Holy Ghost snuffs the candle

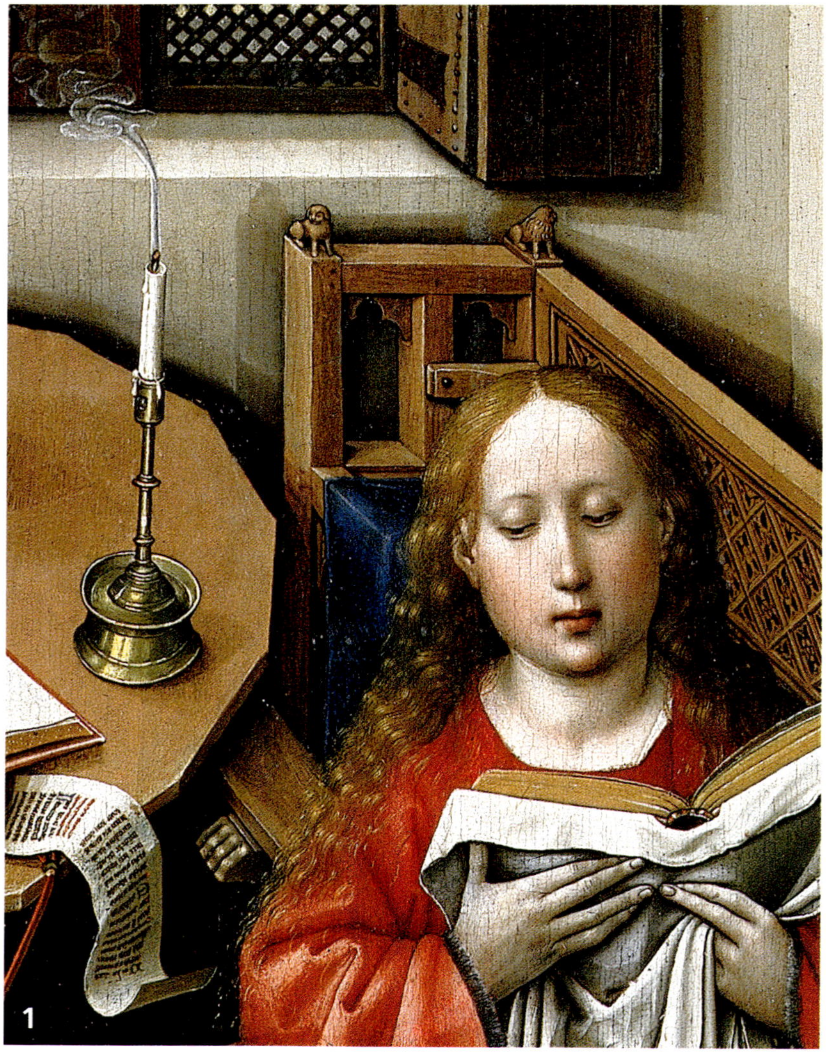

1

Neither Mary nor the Archangel Gabriel, sent by God, has a halo. Apart from the wings of the angel, there is only one other indication that what is happening here is of a mystical, indeed divine nature: the tiny naked figure seen approaching Mary on seven golden rays from the round window nearer to us. This is Jesus, and the cross over his shoulder is a reminder that it is his suffering that will redeem humanity. Theologically, the annunciation was equivalent to an act of conception, and God's seed was imagined as a miniature but fully-formed body of Christ.

There are no haloes, no dove representing the Holy Ghost, no ecclesiastical or palace architecture, but instead a medium-sized room with a table, a long seat, windows and a fireplace. The perspective is admittedly not quite faultless, but the individual objects, like the manner in which the ceiling and bench are constructed, have been faithfully recorded. At the far end of the bench we can even see a wooden pin, one of the pivots on which the back-rest of the bench could be swung over to the other side. In winter, this meant one could sit cosily in front of the hearth.

The centre panel is one of the earliest pictorial representations of a room in an ordinary home. Even now we can still sense something of the relish with which the things of everyday life were taken note of and declared worthy of record in a painting.

One reason why the things of this world entered into Christian panel painting was the order that followed the rules formulated in 1223 by St. Francis of Assisi. This saint retains his popularity to this day; he preached to the birds, giving his attention to creatures in need, whether human or animal, rather than engaging in the dogmatic scholastic debates of the age. His mendicant followers were itinerant friars, and as they travelled they interpreted the Bible in terms of the reality their listeners lived in. Thus the Dutch preacher Geert Groote, for example, suggested in the late 14th century: "Let us imagine ourselves living in the same house as Christ and Mary." And that is exactly what our artist has done.

That said, many of the seemingly realistic details do in fact possess a theological significance. The white lilies in the majolica jug, the white towel, and the vessel of water, all illustrate Mary's immaculate purity; the half-closed windows and the absence of doors highlight the secluded retirement in which she lives. She is sitting not on the bench but in front of it, which betokens her humility. She is not touching the book she is reading with her hands but is holding it in a towel, demonstrating her respect for the sacred text. The lions on the bench arm-rest recall the throne of Solomon, and thus the wisdom of the Old Testament king. These are all symbols that can also be found in many an earlier painting of the Virgin.

The snuffed candle, however, is an unwonted touch. It has only just been extinguished, as we can see from the smoke curling up from it. The painter was presumably aiming to show something that is not visible, a sudden draught of air: along with the angel and the divine seed, the Holy Ghost or the divine breath are also in the room. This is a moment beyond the human senses, registered in everyday terms.

The value of work

On pictures of Christ's nativity, Joseph is always present, for as the future father who would raise Jesus he has an important role to play in the Holy Family. But he played no part in the conception, and was therefore normally absent from annunciation scenes. The triptych breaks with this tradition – and, once again, it was probably through the Franciscan influence. The friars had elevated Joseph, often relegated to a supporting role and indeed a butt of ridicule in crude mystery plays, into a saint close to the people: in their version, Joseph had neither performed miracles nor suffered martyrdom, but he embodied the virtues of the believing and dutiful citizen. His was the example that might be followed in everyday life.

He is portrayed on the right wing panel as an artisan. The various precisely-rendered tools, and Joseph's concentration as he positions his drill, suggest how important his occupation and station seemed to the artist, and to the man who commissioned the painting.

This was not something that could be taken for granted. As long as only the church and the nobility commissioned paintings, little attention was paid to artisans. In the 14th and 15th centuries, however, as the cities grew, the power and self-confidence of the ordinary citizens increased as well. If they ordered a picture, they wanted to see their own world in it. Paintings were now commissioned by merchants making profits out of fine textiles traded afar, for example; or by master craftsmen whose large workshops had brought them prosperity.

A higher valuation has been placed upon Joseph, though at the same time the higher standing of Mary remains clear. His workshop is wooden, whereas Mary's room is stone-built. No door connects the two places. Joseph is excluded from the holy event. He does not know what is happening, and his concentration on his work could also be interpreted as a lack of awareness or imagination.

Along with his tools and nails there is a wooden box-like contraption on Joseph's table. This has been identified as a mouse-trap, and a reconstruction has demonstrated that it works. Why the mouse-trap is in the picture, though, is a moot point; indeed, its meaning has been debated so long that the triptych has sometimes been referred to as the "mouse-trap annunciation". Supposedly there are even two mouse-traps in the panel, the second being on the counter-flap opened to the outside; this is said to be an older type of trap, but no one knows how it works. A theological explanation for the mouse-trap(s) has been proposed from St. Augustine, who described Christ as the *muscipula diaboli*, the devil's mouse-trap. By this he meant that Christ had saved the world and thus entrapped the devil.

But were the artist and the donor really familiar with this 4th century analogy? It is possible, but not certain; and, looking at the painting, we may well wonder if those who seek for symbols everywhere do not sometimes find more than the painter ever concealed in the first place. Would allusions to St. Augustine really be in a picture meant for the everyday devotions of a family in business? Must high art really exclude all reference to banal everyday realities – such as the presence of mice in a house?

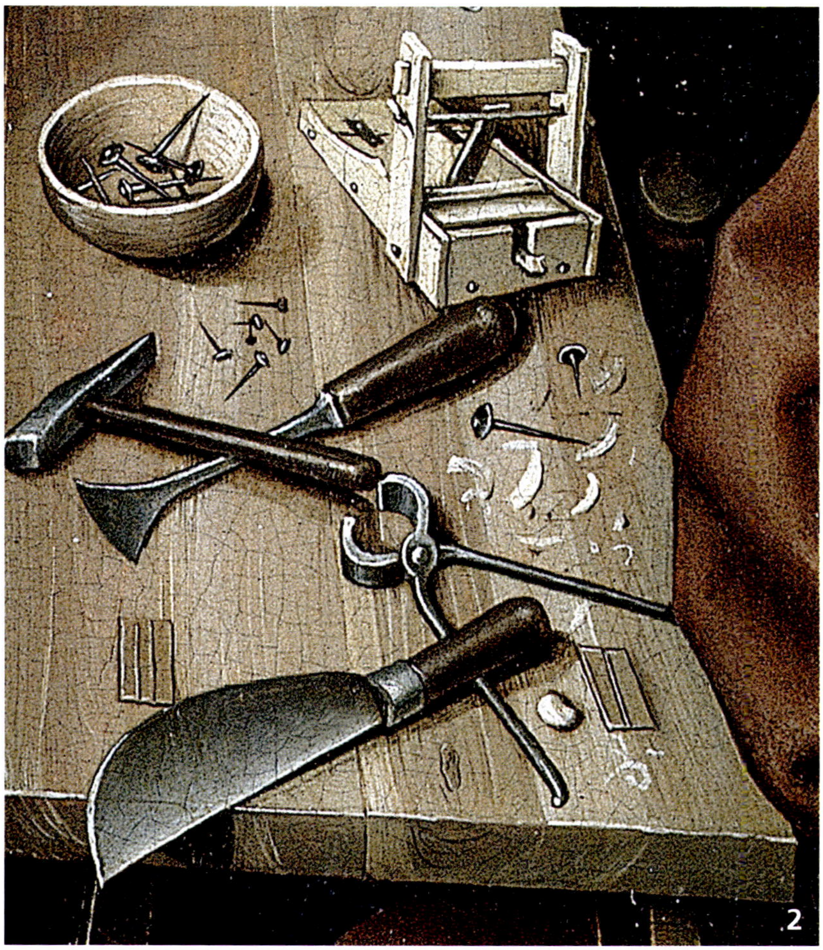

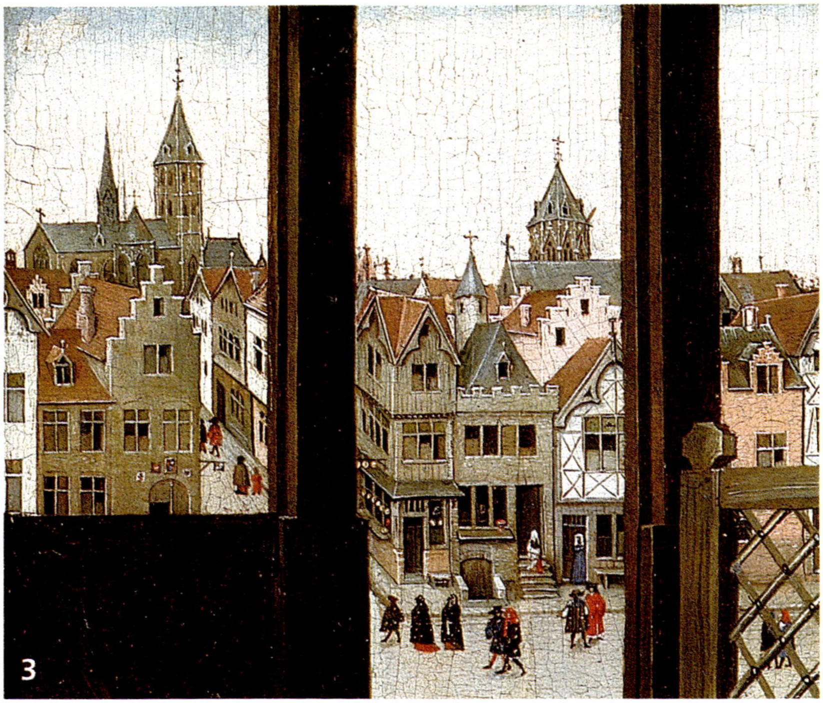

3

A city apparently peaceful, in troubled times

Through the half-opened windows in the annunciation room we see a little sky, but in the background in the wing panels we see a city. In the religious part of the triptych, our gaze is directed upwards; to the right and left, we see the earthly home in which this great event is to be accommodated.

The different seasons are distinctly earthly and yet can only be interpreted through religion. On the left panel, roses and wild flowers are in bloom; on the right, there is a hint of snowfall. The church calendar affords an explanation: the couple who endowed the painting are celebrating the Feast of the Annunciation on 25th March, and the painter is denoting springtime with flowers, whilst Joseph only enters into his paternal role with the birth of Christ, at Christmas.

Many attempts have been made to identify the city in the painting, but none has been definitive. Ghent and Liège have been proposed, but it might equally be Tournai, where the artist lived, or Mechelen, which may have been where the man who commissioned the triptych lived. The buildings we can see were characteristic of northern France and Burgundy in the early 15th century. Some are half-timber; some have stepped gables. Church towers are visible too. To the right may be a barber shop, with three gleaming barber's basins in the window. All the figures in the right panel are warmly dressed, the women in black hooded cloaks over red skirts; the men have fashionably high head-gear.

The impression is peaceful, but the times were troubled. The English had occupied large areas of France, and it was not until 1429 that Joan of Arc, the Maid of Orléans, led the French king to victory. The Duke of Burgundy, an uncle of the king, took advantage of his weakness in order to extend his own territory.

In addition to these wars there were civil wars. Europe was racked by a succession of urban revolts, in Florence (1378), in Paris (1418), in Bruges (1438), in Ghent (1451). In 1423, artisans and labourers seized power in Tournai and kept it till 1428. This was the city where Robert Campin was at work on his annunciation.

Campin (c. 1375–1444) had a large workshop in Tournai, several houses, and the respected office of city painter. He took the part of the insurgents, served as a member of one of their committees, and was sentenced, after the old oligarchy returned to power, to make a pilgrimage to Saint-Gilles in Provence. Probably, however, he paid a fine instead.

Three years later he was in court again, this time on a charge of adultery, though this may have been a pretext. His sentence of a year's banishment was suspended, but he left the city nonetheless, staying away for several years. Possibly he gave up his workshop before he left. Documents show that he discharged three men who had worked for him for many years, first ensuring that they were designated masters in their craft. One of them was Rogier van der Weyden, the co-founder with Campin and the van Eyck brothers of Netherlandish painting.

Van der Weyden may have done some work on the left wing of the triptych. X-rays have shown that both the woman and the man in the background were added later. This bearded man holding a straw hat has been identified as the Mechelen town herald.

The woman was probably the wife of the man who commissioned the painting, and she was presumably added later because the triptych was painted before the marriage. The man who ordered the picture may have wanted it as a votive image, expressing a pious wish for a family. But this is speculation. The woman's hair and throat are chastely covered, as was customary then amongst married women. She is kneeling behind the man, holding a red coral rosary in her folded hands.

Research has focussed on the coats of arms in the windows on the centre panel in the attempt to identify the person who commissioned the triptych. The left one is uninformative, but the right points to a family named Ymbrecht or Inghelbrecht or Engelbrecht (names did not yet have the fixed written forms they would have today). This name could be read as "angel brings", and it is conceivable that an annunciation scene was ordered by way of allusion to the family name, as well as to the wish for a family. And perhaps what Gabriel has brought in this triptych is not only glad tidings but also Holy Scripture; the bag on the table may point to this. Still – an archangel descending from the throne of God to deliver a bag?

In terms of their dates, two men might have commissioned the triptych. Both lived in Mechelen, which is north of Brussels and about a hundred kilometres from Tournai. The Metropolitan Museum of Art in New York, which now owns the work, considers that the donor was "probably" one Jan Engelbrecht, a well-to-do carrier or trader. German art historian Felix Thürlemann is adamant that it was one Peter Inghelbrecht or Engelbrecht, who came from Cologne and had a cloth business in Mechelen; but the evidence advanced by Thürlemann is similarly no more than probability.

The part played by the bearded herald is also open to debate. He occupies a prominent position, between the couple's heads, and his face, unlike that of the archangel, is so individual that it must be a portrait. Perhaps this man brought some important, good news.

The work is unsigned and takes its name, the *Mérode Triptych*, from its last private owners. The artist was long anonymous, and known as the Master of Flémalle from work he did in the Flemish monastery of Flémalle. Not until the early 20th century did Robert Campin emerge from the obscurity of this sobriquet. To what extent the triptych is indeed by his hand, however, and how much might have been by others in his workshop, is disputed.

Much as the triptych, with its plenitude of simple everyday things, is of this world, it nevertheless remains enigmatic. One puzzle is the wall separating Mary's room from the garden. On Mary's side there is no door in this wall, but on the side where the couple are kneeling there is. This inconsistency can be resolved on the symbolic level: the enclosed space in which we see the Virgin is intended to show that she leads a secluded, immaculate life, apart from the world. The donor is imagining that she has entered into his house. From without, he has opened the door; with his own eyes he beholds the Mother of God and petitions her for a family.

A pious wish for a family

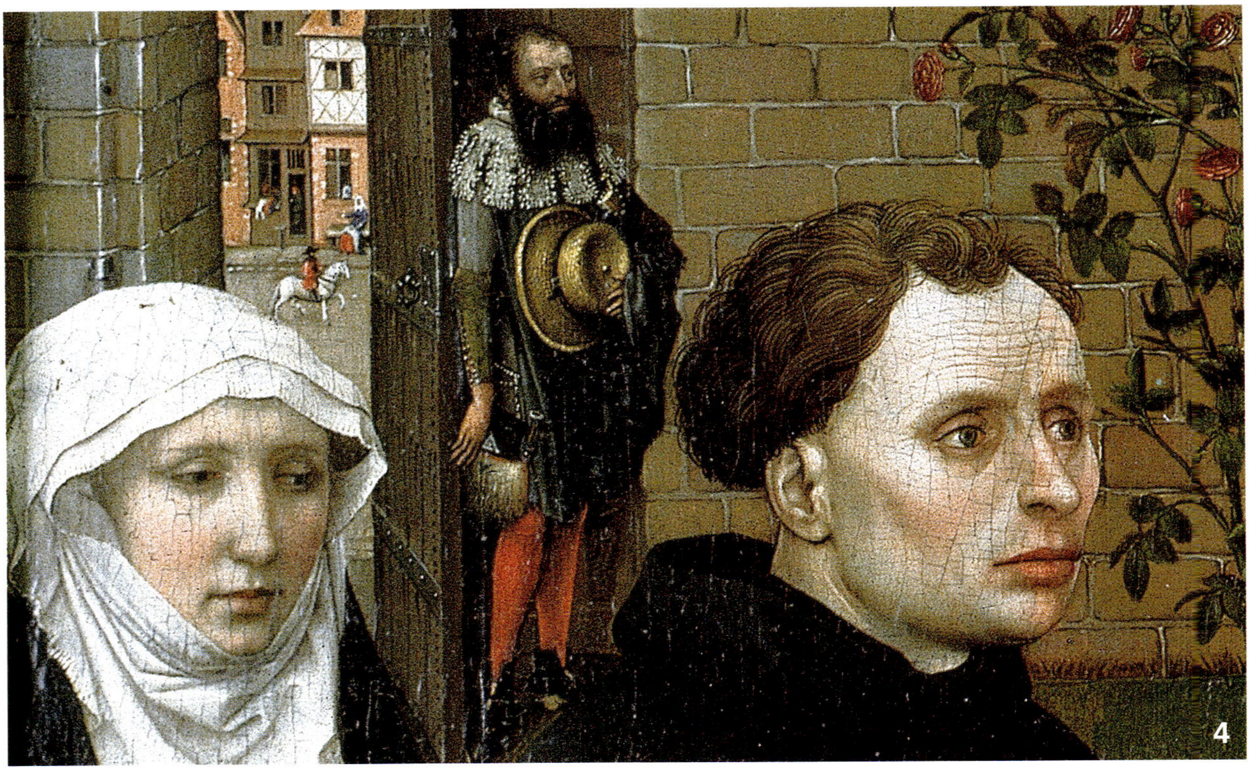

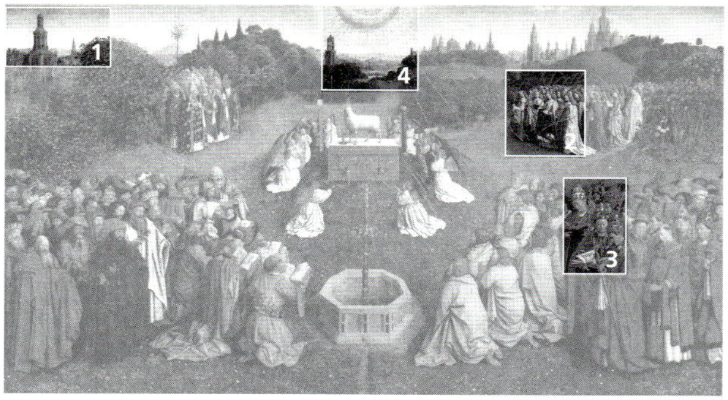
1
4
3

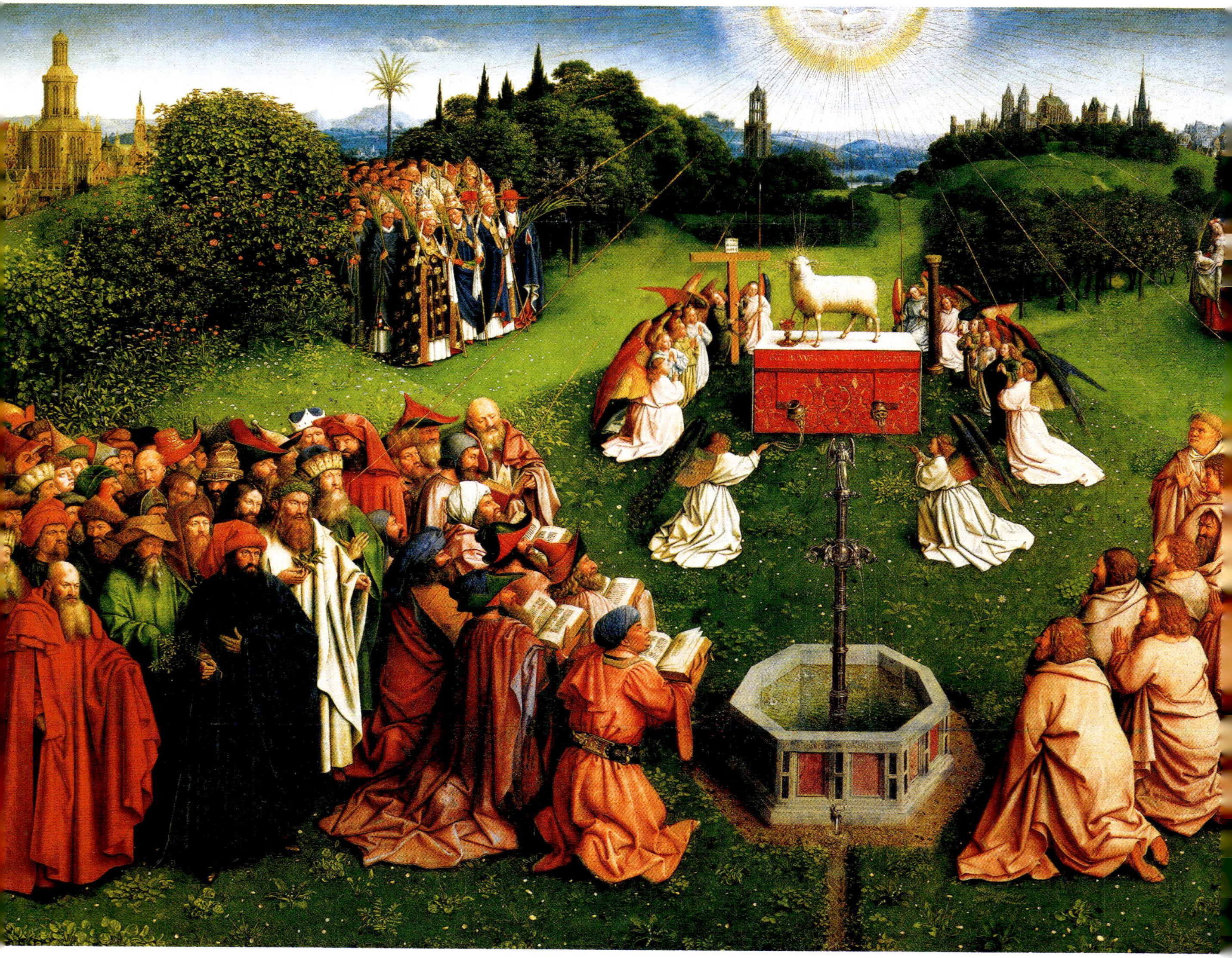

Hubert & Jan van Eyck: The Adoration of the Lamb, 1432

Jerusalem on the horizon

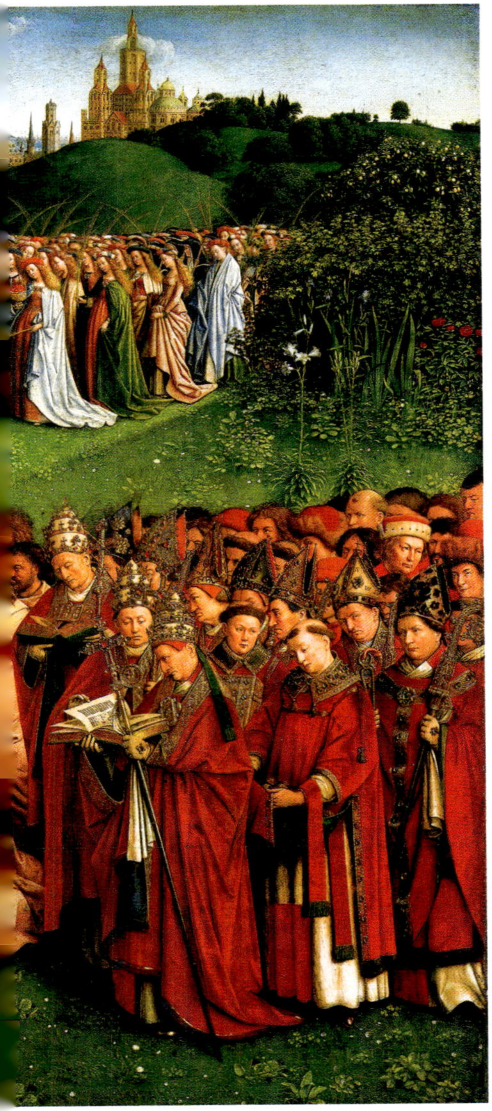

At first glance this picture seems well outside our familiar world. Many of the details are unfamiliar to the contemporary eye, and, even if they can be identified, viewing them together is a taxing undertaking. This broad field, for instance, with its flowers, trees and bushes, a city silhouetted against the sky, and a blue prospect of distance, goes very well with our idea of a panorama. This is how we have learnt to see landscape. The bleeding lamb on the altar, however, does not go with the setting, to our way of thinking.

We may recall that the lamb has its place in Christian symbolism: the Lamb of God represents Jesus Christ, who gave his life's blood to redeem humanity. Today, however, symbols are more likely to be rendered in abstract or stylized fashion, whereas this lamb is painted with such precision that it would not be out of place in a zoological textbook.

The grouping of the figures may also strike an unprepared viewer as curious. Rather than going their own ways in this appealing natural setting, they are seen walking, kneeling or standing in a closely bunched-up manner, as if under orders to seek physical contact. They look like cutouts. Why this contradiction between the fresh and lively landscape and the stiffness of the figural grouping?

The painting was completed in 1432, and at that date was not seen in isolation but as one of twenty panels which together constituted the Ghent Altar. *The Adoration of the Lamb* is the centre panel. Above it and next to each other are pictures of God the Father, the Virgin Mary, and John the Baptist, and to their sides angels making music, and the first man and woman in Creation. The wings beside the centre panel also feature groups of figures; all of them are making their way towards the centre, towards the bleeding lamb. On the rear of the altar, visible only when it is folded shut, the donors are seen kneeling, and in an annunciation the Virgin is told that she will bear a son. The altar is still – or rather, once again – in the place where it was positioned in 1432: St. Bavo's Church in the city of Ghent in Flanders, in today's Belgium.

The centre panel measures 134 by 237 centimetres and is the largest. It contains the most motifs, and also poses the most difficulties. These begin with the subject itself, which has meanwhile effectively disappeared from art and which is rarely visualized even in sermons any more: the second paradise. The first paradise, in which God created Adam and Eve, is still a part of the familiar repertoire of motifs. But the second paradise, where God's chosen people dwell after death, or after resurrection, is now the stuff of cartoons – people reposing on clouds somewhere up high in heaven.

Five hundred years ago, the second paradise did not have to be thought of as high up; it could readily be imagined on earth, as a beautiful landscape with vegetation from every region known to man, a climate invariably pleasant, and the dove as symbol of the Holy Spirit, its rays touching all the ranks of the blessed.

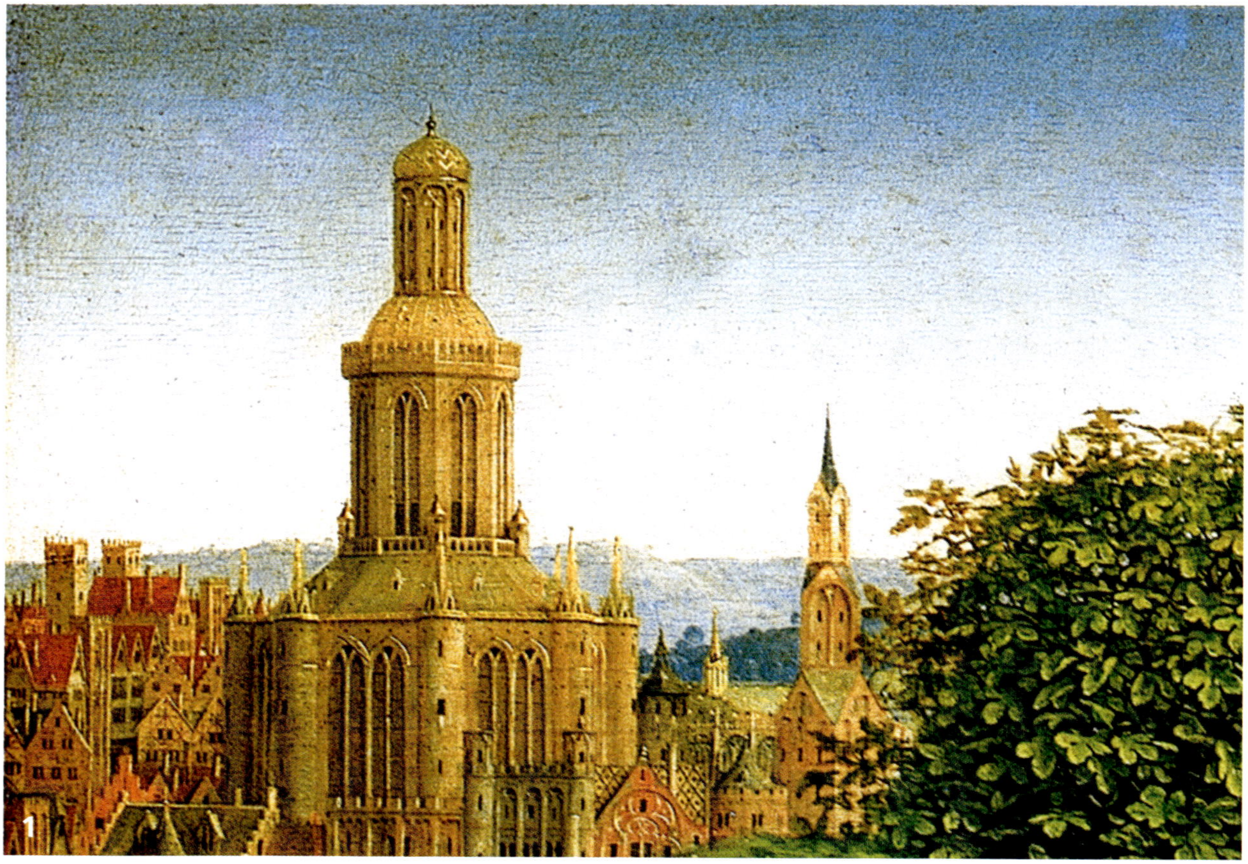

1

Life in the city is better

This new paradise is not only a pleasant landscape. The panoramic prospect is delimited by tall buildings; beyond the fields there is a city. Today, if we can credit the fields of the blessed at all, we may envisage a paradisal natural setting, but to locate paradise in a city goes against the grain of our times.

In the Bible, the city bears the name of Jerusalem. In Revelation 21, John the Divine says, "And I John saw the holy city, new Jerusalem, coming down from God ... And the city had no need of the sun, neither of the moon, to shine in it: for the glory of God did lighten it, and the Lamb is the light thereof."

In St. John's vision, at the end of time the holy city came down to earth. The end of time and the redemption of the world occupied medieval man acutely, as is apparent in numerous visions. Even on the northerly periphery of Christendom, in a village in Holstein, a poor peasant "beheld the city". His name was Gottschalk, and his visions were recorded by the clergy. He described accompanying the dead through the torments of hell unto the holy city. In his account too, the suffering and the movement all happened in groups. "Now Gottschalk turned to the south and beheld something like a city on a broad plain; it was unendingly long and wide, so that he could not make out where its end might be." On approaching, he realized that the city was laid out on a strict, orderly plan, with "dwelling after dwelling in a straight line".

Gottschalk had his vision in the year 1189. There is much evidence like it to suggest that at that time the city was a desirable goal to be aimed at. It held promise of a better life: straight and paved streets, markets, opportunities to earn a living, help for the poor. City dwellers were better able to take refuge behind their walls when marauding armies arrived. City dwellers were not so much at the mercy of capricious feudal overlords as those who lived in the country were.

The notion that the city was an auspicious place where God's chosen people might lead a blessed, contemplative life was not so remote from reality at that time in Europe as it is today.

The churches, towers and other buildings in the altar painting resemble the Flemish buildings of the age, but cannot be clearly identified. Following northern Italy, the late Middle Ages saw Flanders and the Netherlands rise to become the region with the most cities in Europe. It was progressive in industry, it was favourably located as trade routes increasingly turned to the Atlantic coast rather than the Mediterranean, and it enjoyed the patronage of dukes who well realized that cities were good tax-payers.

The enigmatic artist brothers

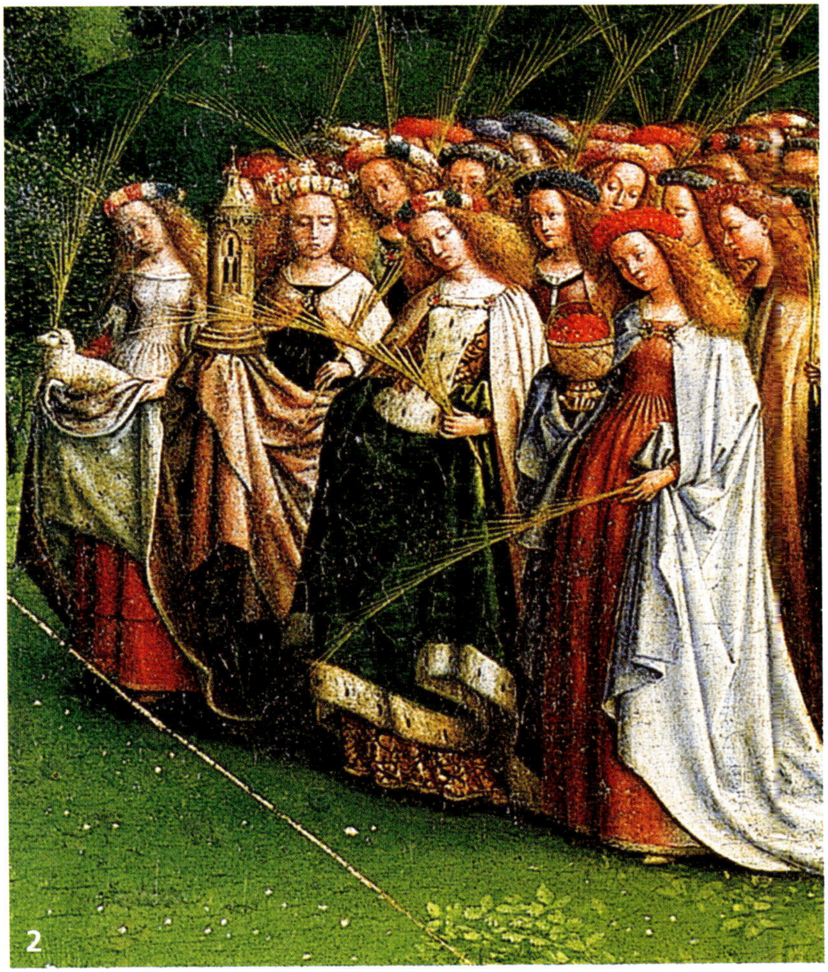
2

In the eyes of the rural community it was one thing for the city to attain the status of an ideal; from the viewpoint of city dwellers, despite the benefits, things looked rather different. To take the example of Ghent: this city, where the altarpiece was painted and installed in 1432, had achieved wealth through its cloth. A large number of craftsmen lived there, which resulted in specialization, which in turn meant especially high quality. Flemish cloth was famed throughout Europe. The notably colourful garb of the martyrs might almost be a catalogue of local products.

Prosperity had made the people of Ghent self-assured; like the other cities of Flanders, Ghent had its own administration, though it had to observe the imperatives of the lord of the land, the Duke of Burgundy. To negotiate this accommodation was the task of the council, which mediated between the Duke and the citizenry. Membership of the council was not only honourable, it was also dangerous. In 1432 a number of Ghent's councillors were murdered because they had allegedly been "bought" by the Duke; the following year, the council had a revolt against ducal officers suppressed and the ringleaders beheaded. Among the councillors who took action on this occasion was the deputy mayor, Josse or Jodocus Vijd. It was he, together with his wife, who endowed the altar.

The unrest was sparked by the Duke's financial demands. At times the municipal tax revenue was not enough for him, and he attempted to improve the state of his coffers by reforming the currency. When this happened, all the gold and silver coinage then in circulation had to be exchanged for new coins, and the Duke retained a third or a quarter of the precious metals. Doubtless this loss had a more severe impact on artisans and tradesmen than on the patrician classes, who were property owners. The Vijds were of the patrician class and evidently enjoyed good relations with Duke Philip of Burgundy, for he honoured them with his presence when the altar was consecrated.

According to an inscription, the work on the altar was performed by Hubert and Jan van Eyck. What precisely was done by each of the two brothers is not ascertainable. Of Hubert, art history knows next to nothing, except that he died in 1426. Of Jan we know that in 1425 in Lille he entered the service of Duke Philip, with the not particularly high rank of chamberlain. In his master's service he undertook a number of diplomatic journeys. In Portugal he painted Princess Isabella, subsequently the Duke's wife. In 1430 Jan van Eyck settled in Ghent, then the most affluent and appealing city in the vast duchy of Burgundy, a city in which he could expect to receive commissions for work from wealthy burghers.

In the 15th century, ordinary burghers were increasingly commissioning artworks. It was their influence that led painters to pay more attention to their real environs, such as a field, the bushes and flowers that grew there, and the buildings in the background. The task of artists working for the Church was to make visible the invisible: the afterlife and the nature of redemption. Ordinary citizens, on the other hand, wanted to see their own surroundings, the locale where they had made their way and achieved wealth and influence, that wealth that permitted them the luxury of endowing a painting or an altar or indeed an entire chapel.

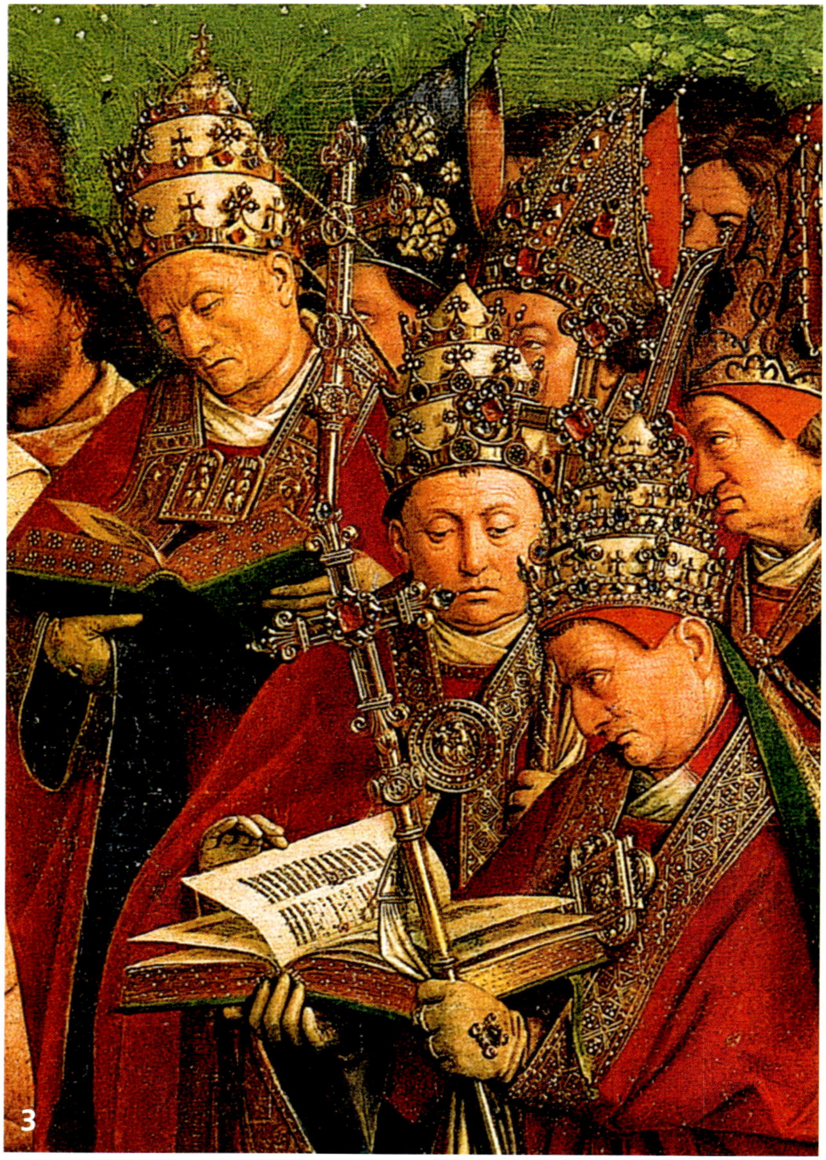

3

The competing Popes

Although the landscape in the painting is faithful to this world rather than the next, it nevertheless articulates the afterlife, and does so in a strictly hierarchical manner. On the central axis we see the dove, symbol of the Holy Spirit, above; beneath it, the Lamb of God; and below, the fountain of everlasting life. The artist has the groups of figures arriving from four different directions, and distinguishes them carefully. The groups at the top are saints and martyrs, clearly segregated according to sex. At the lower left are the prophets and the peoples who lived before the birth of Christ, while at the right are men of the Church. The programme of the painting was probably designed by theologians, as was customary at the time. The fact that only one of the four groups consists of women is a reminder of the low esteem in which women were held by the Church.

At the head of the churchmen we see the apostles, kneeling, wearing simple garments. Behind them are three Popes in fine regalia. The Church, with the Pope at its head, was seen as an earthly image of the divine order. Structures of hierarchy and subordination were considered not only practical but also God-given. In the Middle Ages they governed conceptions of both this world and the next, and for this reason people were profoundly disconcerted when the Church underwent a great schism. This was in 1378, a good half century before this altar was installed. Suddenly there were two Popes, one ruling in Rome, the other in Avignon.

The schism lasted four decades, and in this period West European Christendom was split. Three Popes in particular helped end the schism, and the three pontiffs in the painting resemble them strongly. In the middle is Alexander V. He was elected at the Council of Pisa in 1409, after the assembly had deposed the two Popes currently ruling. But Alexander died in the following year, and the two other Popes considered themselves still the incumbents. During the Council of Constance which followed, the Roman Pope, Gregory XII, resigned the papal chair voluntarily; he is seen standing rearmost. The new Pope of the reunified Church was Martin V, who is to the fore in the group of three.

It was not only the schism in the Church that had left the faithful full of uncertainty, but also the attempt to restructure the hierarchy. In order to depose a Pope, a Council had to declare itself the supreme authority. Many at the Councils wanted this to be established not merely as a crisis measure but on a permanent basis, so that the Council, representing the whole community of the faithful, would be higher than the Pope. This view did not prevail, but in 1431 a Council convened at Basle, where another Pope was deposed and a new one elected. Since the incumbent refused to be ousted, a new schism resulted; this was the last in the history of the Church, and lasted only a few years. In that year of 1431, Jan van Eyck's work on the altar was nearing its end. For the faithful, the happenings in Pisa, Constance or Basle were not merely the remote bickering of theologians. From the topmost to the lowest levels of society, they were disconcerted. Van Eyck's painting was conceived in a spirit counter to these realities in the Church. Indeed, this may even account for the stiffness in the painting.

Naturally the precision and symmetry were first and foremost dictated by tradition. What was new was the broad field, the attempt to make a third dimension visible. If we recall the symbolic, statue-like figures painted against a gold ground, customary in past ecclesiastical art, we can clearly see that this centre panel of the Ghent altar must have seemed revolutionary.

The use of oil paints was also new. At times the brothers van Eyck are described as the inventors of oil paint, which they assuredly were not. But they were the first to make consistent use of oils and to draw on the advantages they afford: the overlaying of layers of paint without running, leaving the lower layers visible and giving lustre and depth to the painting.

The Vijds not only endowed the altar and had themselves portrayed on the outer flaps, they also paid to have the side chapel where the altar is housed extended, and agreed by contract to have mass celebrated their daily. In doing this, the Vijds were purchasing a privilege which until then had been the prerogative of the nobility: their name and their merit were saved from oblivion.

Just as the altar reflects something of the period in which it was created, so too its fate tells us something of the history of the ensuing centuries. Spain's King Philip II, in whose realm the Netherlands then lay, laid claim to the altarpiece. The cathedral chapter had a copy made for him (1557–59). In 1566 the Netherlands saw a growing movement against the decadent clergy, the all too worldly life of the monks and prelates, the luxury of the churches and monasteries. The incensed masses "purged" the churches. That the Ghent altar might not fall victim to this iconoclastic fury, it was hidden in the church tower and subsequently in the town hall.

It was twenty years before it returned to its chapel. Two hundred years now passed without notable event. In 1781, Emperor Joseph II of Austria had the panels with Adam and Eve removed. The ancestors of all humanity were naked, and Joseph, son of Maria Theresia, was a prudish man. In 1794 the southern Netherlands, which then belonged to Austria, were occupied by the French revolutionary armies, and the soldiery looted the panel showing the Lamb of God, together with some others, and sent them to Paris. Prussia's Marshal Blücher returned them to Paris following the final defeat of Napoleon.

In 1821 parts of the altar were sold off, some to Berlin; after the First World War they were returned. By 1920 the altar was once again complete, including Adam and Eve. In 1940 the Germans invaded Belgium and, like the French before them, once again looted the altar. The altar survived the fighting that ended the Second World War in a salt mine at Alt Aussee, and in 1945 was returned to Ghent, where it now stands as it did five hundred years ago.

The tribulations of a famous altar

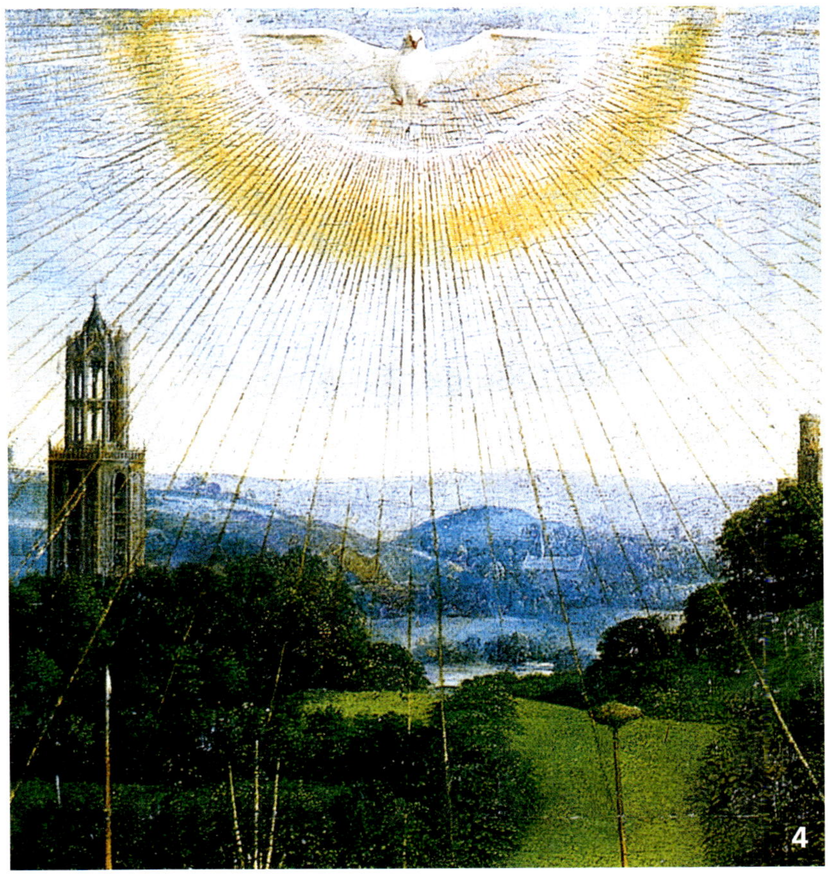
4

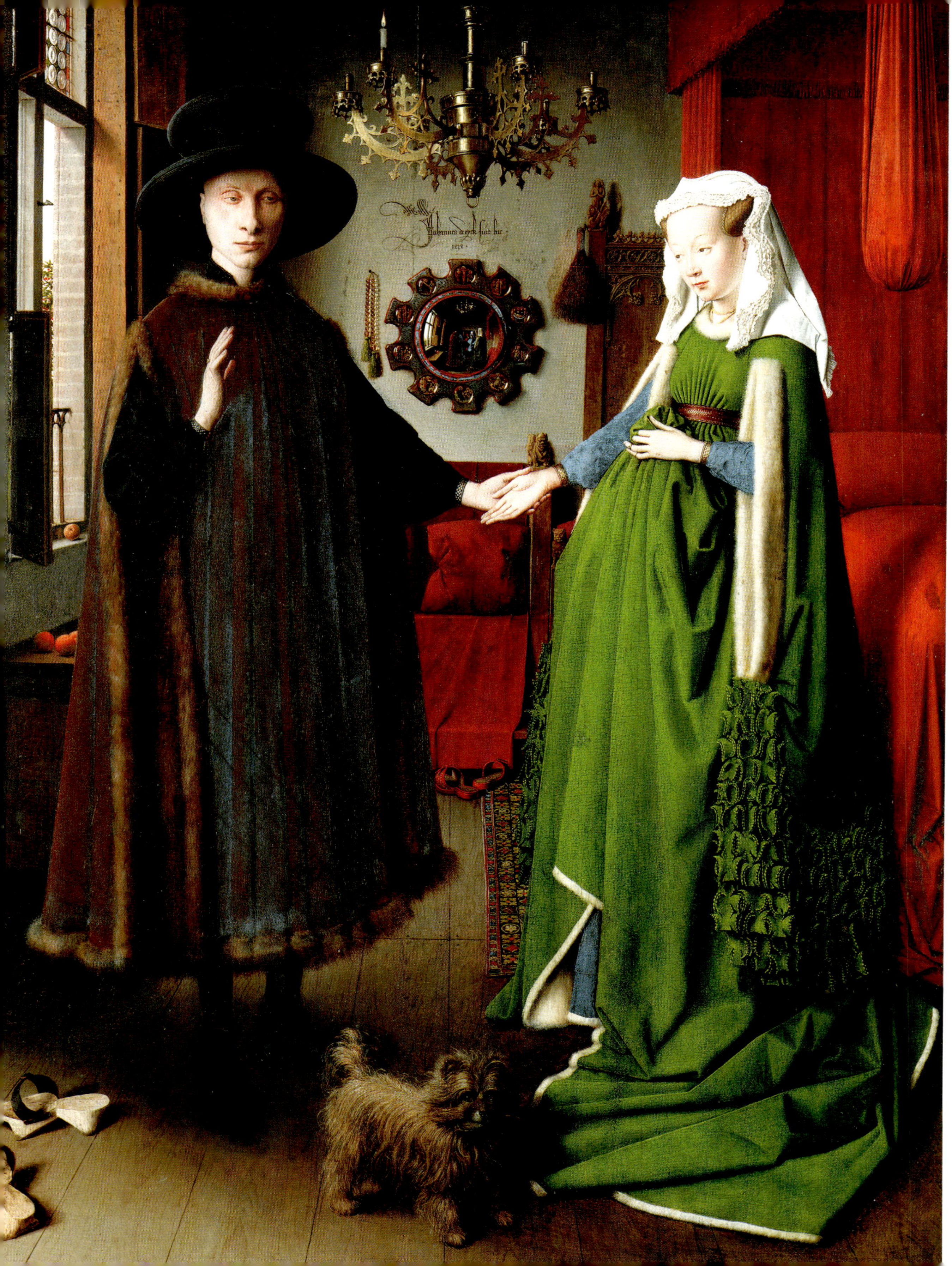

Jan van Eyck: The Arnolfini Marriage, 1434

An Italian in Bruges

An aristocratically dressed couple in middle-class surroundings: slippers and clogs lie on the floor, and the woman's artfully pleated train tumbles not onto the gleaming marble tiles of some grand palace but onto plain floorboards. There is much that appears contradictory and mysterious in this panel.

It was executed in 1434 in Bruges, the leading centre of trade in northern Europe. Wood and furs arrived here from Russia and Scandinavia, silks, carpets and spices from merchants in Genoa and Venice, and lemons, figs and oranges from Spain and Portugal. Bruges was a wealthy place, "the most famous city in the world on account of the goods that are traded there and the merchants who live there", according to Philip the Good, Duke of Burgundy from 1419 to 1467. It was the chief port of his own duchy.

Burgundy stretched from the shores of the North Sea right down to the Swiss border, and for several decades was the most powerful political unit in Europe. Its dukes owned many palaces, including one in Bruges, and were lovers of luxury. Recognizing that Burgundy's might rested on the industriousness of its workforce, and in particular on the trading activities and textile industries of the Flemish towns, Philip the Good let his citizens improve their own standard of living and grow wealthy under Burgundian rule.

The couple in van Eyck's painting are undoubtedly rich. This is most evident in their clothing: the woman's outer garment, with its voluminous swathes of material, is trimmed with ermine. The folds at the bottom could only have been arranged so skilfully with the help of a maid, and the train, too, would have needed a second person to carry it when moving about. To walk at all in such a dress presupposed a degree of practice normally only acquired in aristocratic circles.

The man is wearing a sumptuous velvet cloak trimmed or even lined with mink or sable. But the cloak is only calf-length and is slit down the sides, allowing movement and activity. The fact that this man does not belong to the aristocracy is indicated by the wooden clogs in front of him, which were slipped on to avoid having to wade through the dirt in the streets. The high and mighty didn't need clogs – they travelled on horseback or were carried in litters.

Van Eyck gives no indication of the identity of his sitters either on the panel or in any other document, and it was only some 100 years after the work was executed that it was described in an inventory as: "A large panel painting, Hernoult le Fin with his wife in a room." Hernoult le Fin was the French version of the Italian surname Arnolfini. The Arnolfinis belonged to a family of merchants and bankers, originally from Lucca, who had opened an office in Bruges.

This foreign businessman was thus living in Bruges in aristocratic luxury. He owned oriental carpets, chandeliers and mirrors; he had glazing in at least the top half of his windows; he could even afford expensive oranges. The room's cramped dimensions, however, are those of a middle-class home. As in all private chambers, the bed is dominant. During the day, the curtains were tied up into a ball; people sat on the edge of the bed and even received visitors lying on top of the covers. At night, the curtains were drawn around the bed to create a new living space, a room within a room. In the Italian city-republics, the middle classes were permitted to live in their own palaces if they could afford it; in the Burgundy of van Eyck's day, however, that was uncommon. Only one man is said to have done it in Bruges – a Florentine compatriot of the Arnolfinis, the manager of the powerful Medici bank.

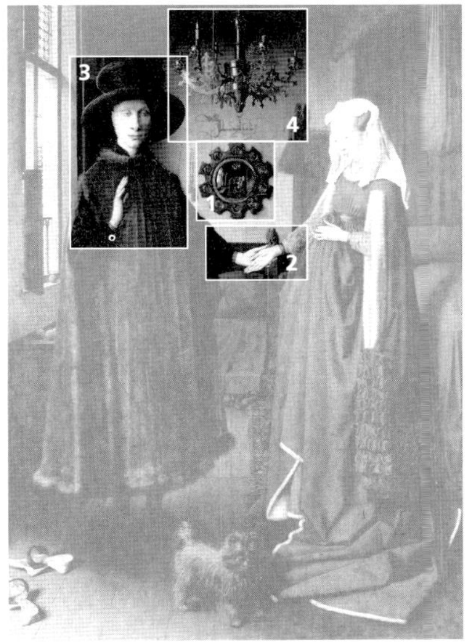

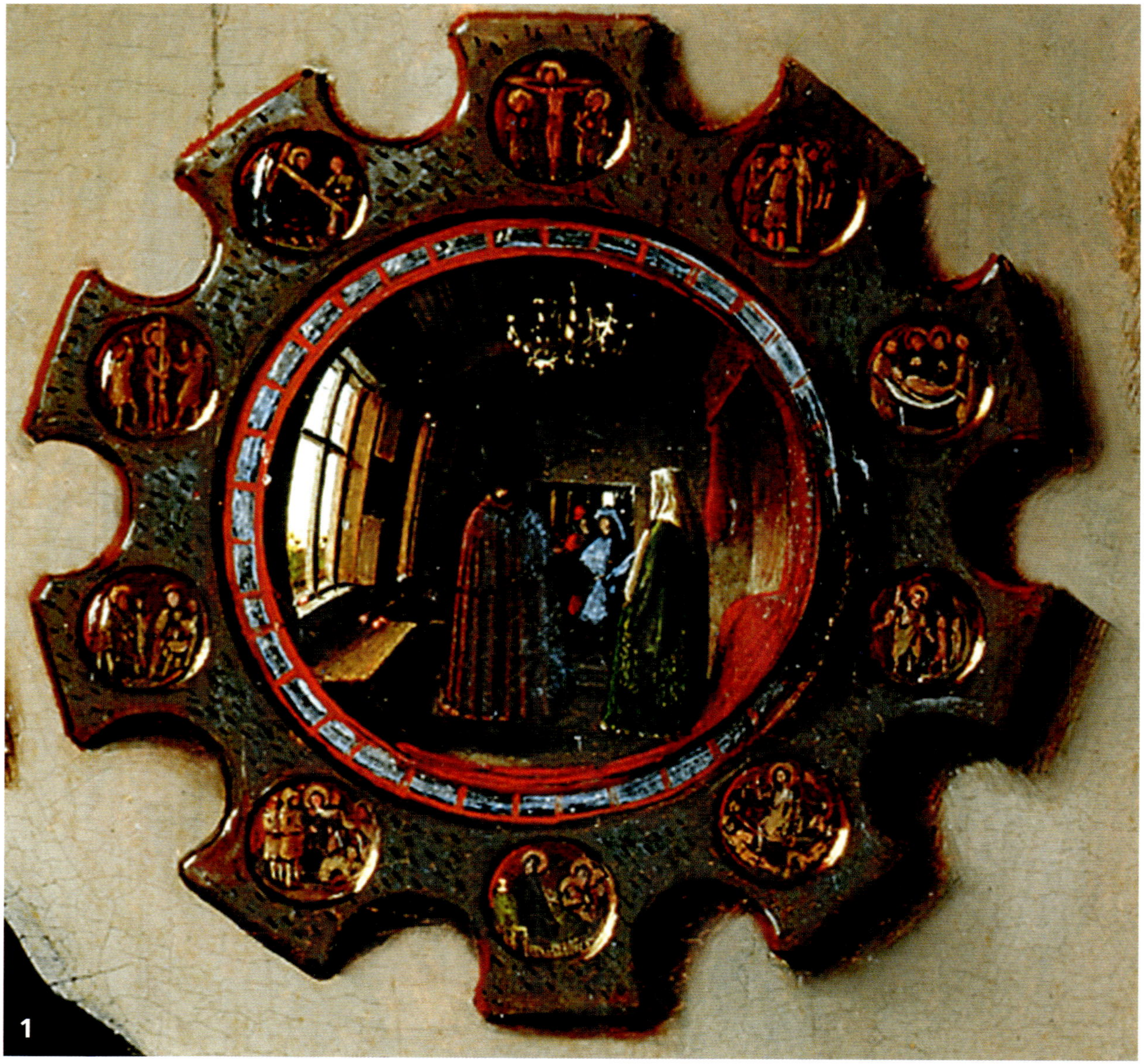

1

A mirror with magic properties

In the central axis of the composition, on the far wall of the room, hangs a mirror. Its frame is adorned with ten painted medallions containing scenes from the Passion of Christ. Glass mirrors in a middle-class home were unusual in van Eyck's day; people normally made do as best they could with polished metal. Only princely households could afford flat mirrors, which were considered a valuable rarity because they were so difficult to manufacture – the crystal base usually shattered when the hot liquid metal was poured over it. It would still be some time before a mixture of mercury and tin was invented which could be applied cold. Augsburg glass-blowers, however, had arrived at an interim solution whereby they poured a metal mixture – evidently heated to not quite such a high temperature – into a glass sphere, and thereby obtained a convex mirror.

These curved mirrors were more affordable than flat ones. In French they were called *sorcières*, or "witches", because they magically expanded the viewer's field of vision. In this picture, we can see in the mirror the beams of the ceiling and a second window. Behind us, so to speak, we can see another room, and where we ourselves are standing the mirror shows us two figures who are just entering the room.

This effect was repeated 200 years later by the Spanish painter, Velázquez, in the flat mirror which appears in his large canvas *The Maid of Honour*. It is probable that van Eyck's *Arnolfini Marriage* was at that time part of the Spanish Royal Collection, of which Velázquez was the curator.

The woman lays her right hand carefully in the man's left. There is a solemnity to this joining of hands, which the artist places in almost the very centre of the composition and which is thereby lent particular significance. The two figures themselves adopt very formal poses within their everyday surroundings. The woman's train has been carefully arranged, and the man raises his right hand to take the oath. For van Eyck's contemporaries, the joining of hands and the gesture of oath-taking were sure indications that two people were pledging each other their troth.

In the 15th century, you needed neither a priest nor witnesses to enter into a Christian and legal marriage. A wedding could be performed anywhere, including – as here – in a private bedchamber. The sacrament of marriage was conducted not by priests but by husband and wife themselves. To officially announce their marriage, the newly-weds would attend Communion together the following morning, although even this was not compulsory.

Only at the Council of Trent a good century later did the Church succeed in making the attendance of a priest and two witnesses a necessary element of the marriage ceremony. It did so not for religious reasons, but in order to clamp down on the abuse and deception possible under the old system. Even after this, however, the ceremony still did not have to take place before the altar, but at most in front of a church door.

Although witnesses are not required at the Arnolfini wedding, two are nevertheless clearly visible in the mirror. They are needed for a different reason, namely to legalize a written contract of marriage. Such contracts were common where – as here – large amounts of money were involved; they regulated financial matters between the marriage partners and had to be signed by two witnesses.

It may well be that the financial agreement in the present case was particularly important, since this is clearly a "left-handed" marriage. The man takes the woman's hand in his left hand, not his right as was otherwise the convention. Such marriages were concluded between partners of unequal rank, and are still occasionally practised in ruling houses in our own times. More precisely, it was always the woman who came from the lower class. She had to relinquish all rights of inheritance for herself and her children and thus could not continue the family lineage, but was guaranteed sufficient financial means to support herself in the event of widowhood. These means, or title-deeds relating to them, were originally presented on the morning after the marriage. It is from the Low Latin *morganatica*, meaning a gift from a bridegroom to a bride, that we derive the term more politely given to this sort of union, namely a "morganatic" marriage.

The bride in this painting is not getting married in white – that would only become the convention in the second half of the 19th century – but in her most sumptuous Sunday best. Her bulging figure is not intended to indicate that she is pregnant, but like her small, high-laced bosom illustrates the ideal of beauty held in the Late Gothic era. The copious folds of cloth which she carries with her also reflect the fashion and lavish style of the Burgundian empire – and elsewhere besides. Women dressed in such ample robes and often wearing large bonnets were compared by contemporary writers to ships under full sail, and an unkind French tongue commented that it was hard to distinguish the "empty" vessels from the pregnant ones.

The bride in van Eyck's picture must have been very young. The carved monster above her hand forms part of a seat standing against the back wall. It recalls the gargoyles which served as waterspouts on cathedral roofs. These, like the pose of the bride, were typical of the era which we call the Gothic.

A very private ceremony

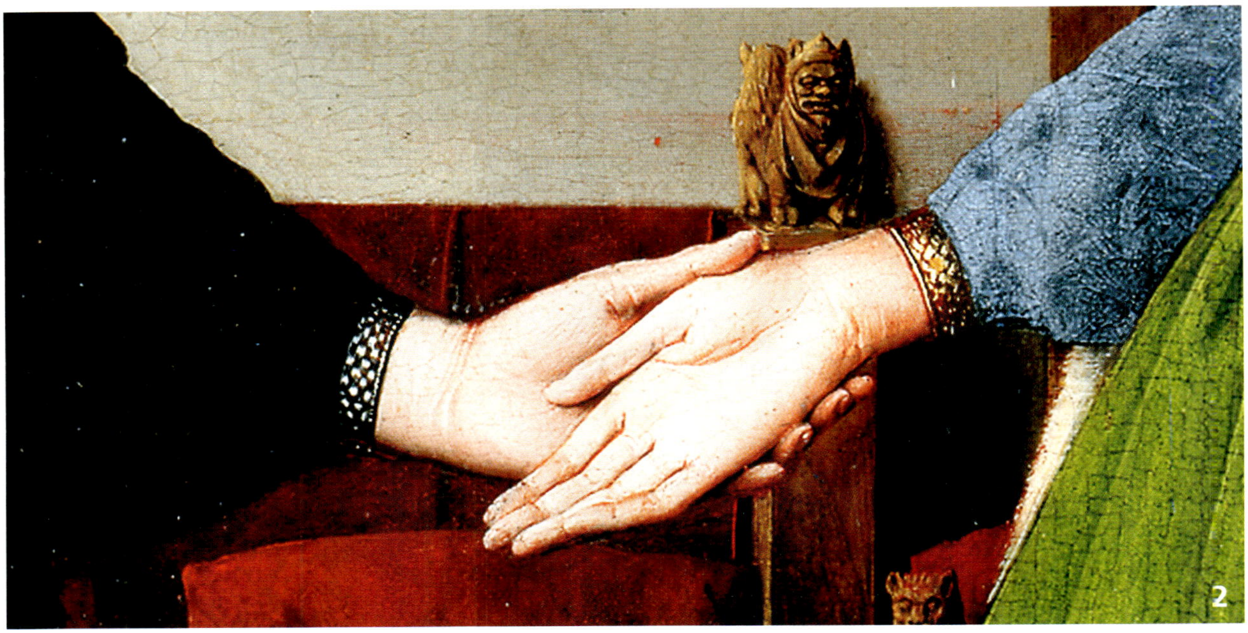

At the Burgundian court and amongst the social circles surrounding it, it was not just women's fashions that were extravagant – so, too, were the men's. They wore elaborately wound turbans or top hats of monstrous proportions. Philip the Good introduced dark colours for official occasions, as worn by Arnolfini here. These would later evolve into the black of Spanish court dress.

The bridegroom's hands are as white and well manicured as those of his bride. His narrow, sloping shoulders also indicate that he does not need physical strength to assert his position in society. Some see hints of a cool, calculating sophistication in his face. It is possible that the French version of his name, Hernoult le fin, is also intended to characterize him – as Hernoult the Refined, the Shrewd.

His forename is sadly missing from the inventory. Around 1434, however, at least two male members of the Arnolfini family were living in Bruges. The more prominent of them, Giovanni di Arrigo Arnolfini, was financial adviser to the Burgundian dukes and the French king, and wed an Italian banker's daughter, Giovanna Cenami, who inherited his estate after his death. This seems to rule out a morganatic marriage. It is possible, however, that his brother Michele made such a marriage, for we only know the first name of his wife. Perhaps he went against convention and married not a wealthy young woman from his home town, but a local Flemish girl. No document bothers to record her surname – evidently it was not worth mentioning.

The two Arnolfinis in Bruges dealt not just in goods, but also in money. In those days, Italians had virtually the monopoly on banking across the whole of Europe. Italy was the leading economic power and developed the techniques of banking, bills of exchange, letters of credit and even double-entry bookkeeping. Italian banks opened branches in all the major centres of trade. In Bruges, their representatives met daily with the city's merchants in the house of a Mr van der Burse. He would give his name to capitalism's most important institution: the bourse, or as we more familiarly know it, the stock exchange.

The customers of the Italian banks included not just businessmen, but also monarchs. The relationship between the bankers from Lucca, the city from which the Arnolfini brothers came, and the dukes of Burgundy was particularly close. One of the former had put up the enormous ransom needed to buy the freedom of a Burgundian heir imprisoned in the Orient. Lending money to rulers implied great honour, but also increased risk – they didn't always pay it back. Enforcement was out of the question. Every political defeat meant losses for the banks. Thus the death in battle in 1477 of the last Duke of Burgundy, Charles the Bold, also meant fatal losses for the Bruges branch of the Medici bank – the bank that had allowed itself to own a palace there. In the long term, the bank's ruin in Flanders probably also contributed to the fall of the Medici in Florence.

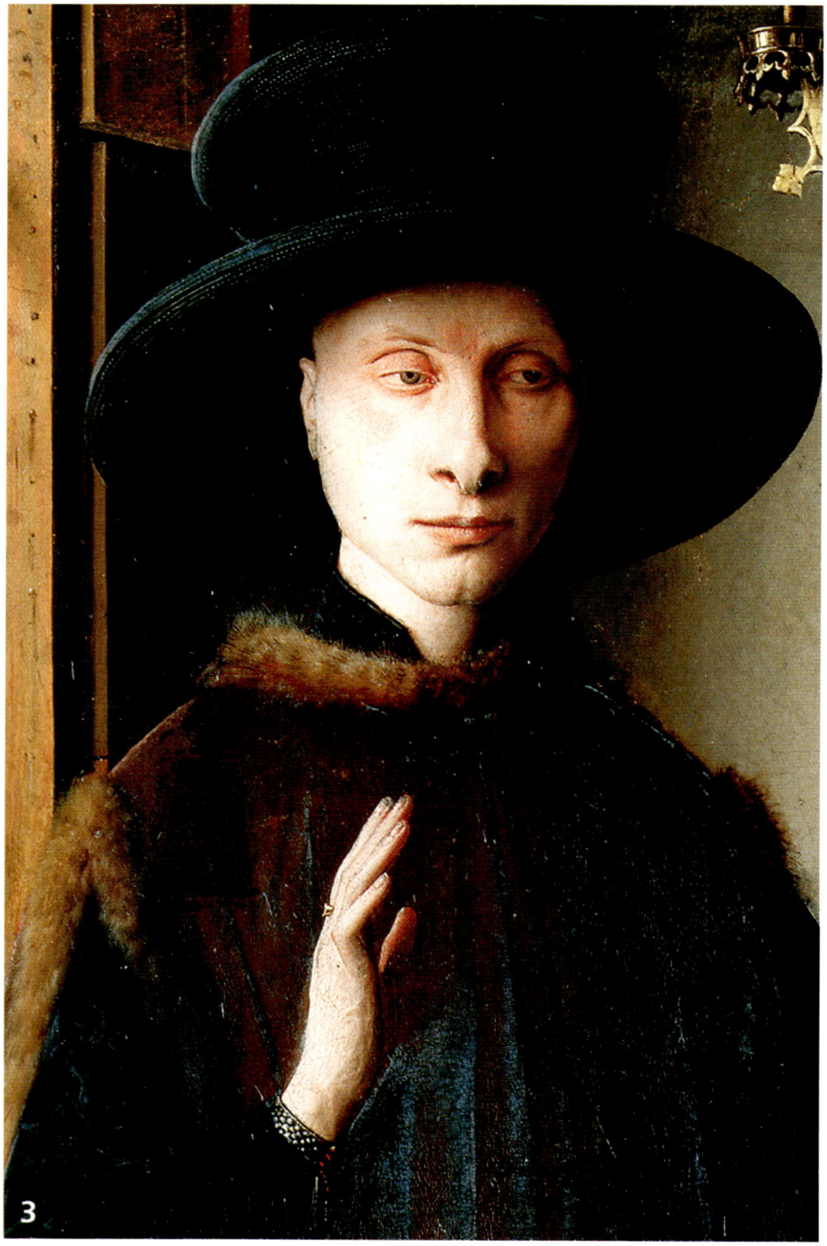

3

An industrious banker

The secret language of everyday objects

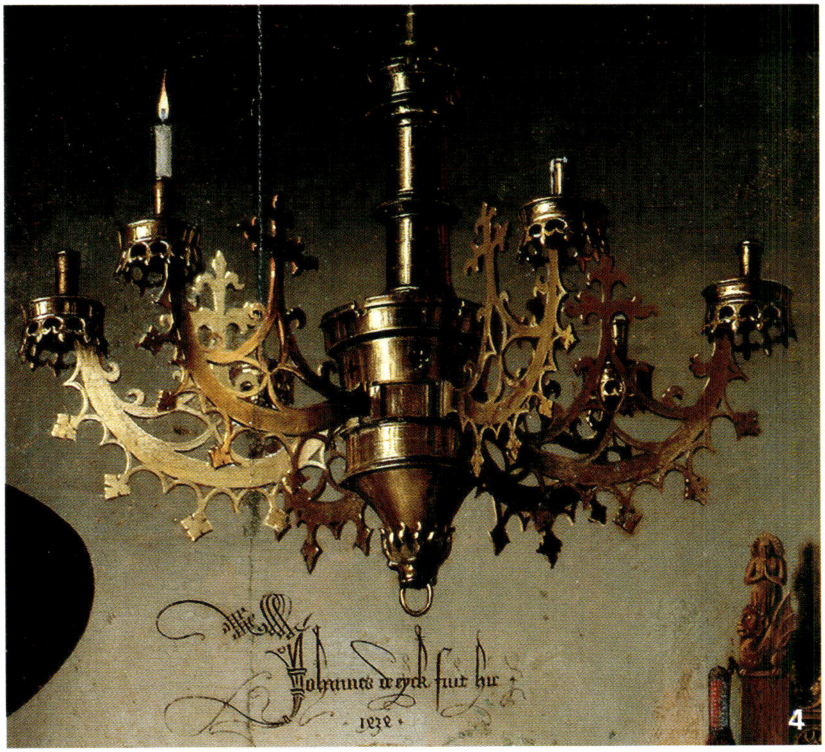

4

Hanging above the couple's heads is an ornate chandelier of a kind manufactured in Flanders by art metalsmiths of the day. We know from records from the Bruges branch of the Medici bank that a similar chandelier was shipped in pieces to Italy.

A solitary candle burns in the chandelier. There is no obvious practical reason why just one flame should be lit; symbolically, however, it ties in with a popular medieval tradition, whereby a large burning candle was carried at the head of wedding processions or handed ceremonially by the bridegroom to the bride. The flame signified the all-seeing Christ, who is witness to the marriage vows. Earthly witnesses to the ceremony were thus not really required.

Visible beneath the right arm of the chandelier is a wooden figure forming part of the tall back of a chair. It represents St Margaret, the patroness of pregnant women, subduing the dragon. The chair stands directly beside the marriage bed. Like the candle and the carved chair decoration, most of the other objects in this room also have a hidden meaning. At the same time as giving us one of the earliest realistic portrayals of a middle-class interior, van Eyck also gives us symbols. For him, as for his contemporaries, objects carried a message. They spoke. Sadly, it is no longer always possible for us to decipher this secret language of objects.

A little dog, like the one between the bride and groom for example, was a symbol of prosperity, but also of faithfulness. On tombstones of the day, a lion is frequently found at the feet of the husband, symbolizing strength and courage, and a dog at the feet of the wife. Fidelity in marriage was clearly only expected from the woman.

Several of the seemingly random objects in the room speak of the purity of the bride – the spotless mirror, for example, and the translucent beads of the rosary hanging beside it. These symbols are familiar from paintings of the Virgin and altarpieces. Indeed, it was in the churches of the Middle Ages that this type of imagery arose: a congregation which couldn't read needed "talking" images which it could contemplate and learn from.

Van Eyck himself painted a number of famous altarpieces, but he lived in a century in which devotional subjects began to be overtaken by secular images. *The Arnolfini Marriage* testifies to this process of transition: it uses the pictorial language of religious art to portray a domestic interior and a scene which, although it incorporates the presence of Christ, records not saints or martyrs but a banker and his wife.

Also to be understood symbolically are the slippers and clogs. Taken literally, they might indicate unseemly haste or an untidiness inappropriate for such a solemn ceremony. For van Eyck's contemporaries, however, they contained a reference to the Old Testament: "Do not come any closer. Take off your sandals, for you are standing on holy ground." Thus God spoke to Moses (Ex. 3:5). When a bride and groom administered the sacrament to each other, then even a simple wooden floor became "holy ground".

Van Eyck's painting illustrates the transition not just from sacred to secular art, but also from aristocratic to bourgeois subject-matter. Portraits of the nobility had existed for a number of decades, some of them executed by van Eyck himself in his capacity as court painter. Philip the Good of Burgundy made him a chamberlain and occasionally also his envoy in confidential affairs. But Philip also allowed him to work for the middle classes, because he knew that his own power rested on their industriousness, their contribution to the economy and also their willingness to take financial risks.

Of particular significance in this painting is the signature of the artist. It is placed not modestly in the bottom right-hand corner, as was otherwise the convention, but prominently on the rear wall between the mirror and the chandelier. Even its formulation is unusual: instead of "Johannes de Eyck fecit" (Jan van Eyck did this), it says "fuit hic" (was here). This inscription transforms the panel into a document. The artist signs not as the painter of the picture, but as a witness to the marriage. Perhaps the man who can be seen in the convex mirror, entering the room wearing a turban and a light blue gown, is in fact the artist himself.

Paolo Uccello: The Battle of San Romano, c. 1435

Monument to a military leader

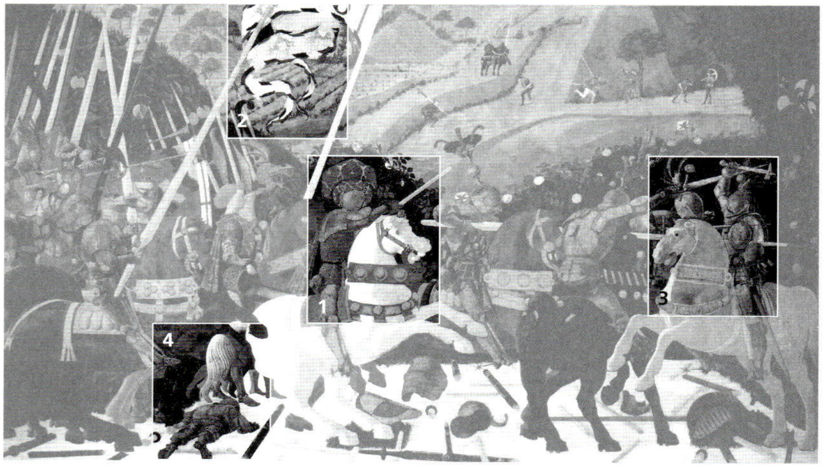

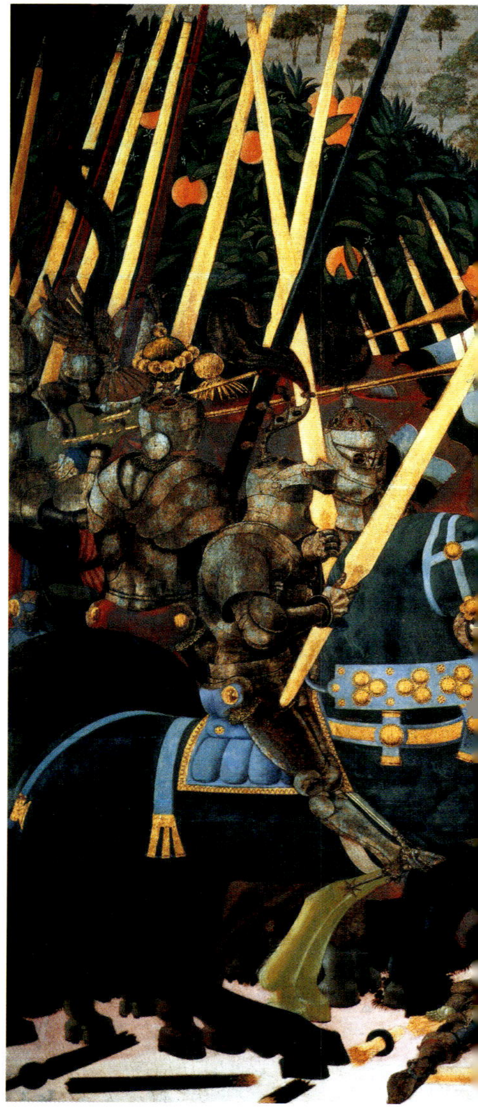

The battle of San Romano was portrayed by Paolo Uccello in a cycle of three panels. Five centuries ago, all three hung together in the Medici Palace in Florence, in the large ground-floor room known as the Sala di Lorenzo. This we know from an inventory of 1492. Today, the panel discussed here hangs in the National Gallery in London, with the second in the Uffizi in Florence and the third in the Louvre in Paris.

We do not know the exact year in which Uccello executed his cycle of paintings, but we do know the date of the battle: 1 June 1432. San Romano is located halfway between Florence and Pisa. The battle itself represented a minor defeat by the Florentines of the Sienese and, were it not for Uccello, would have long been forgotten; it was one of the countless skirmishes which characterized the political situation in 15th-century Italy.

Italy differed from most of the rest of Europe at that time in lacking a central ruling power. Its nominal head, the Emperor, came only on brief visits from Germany; the Pope had no political authority, and no more or less power than any of Italy's other princes and cities. With no one above them to settle their disputes, these latter were constantly at war with one other, frequently switching their allegiances but usually with Milan on one side and Florence on the other.

It was during this period of permanent warfare that Renaissance culture experienced its greatest flowering – a culture which also infuses Uccello's panels. The fact that art and warfare flourished side by side shows that normal life in the cities and courts was largely unaffected by the many conflicts of the day. Nor did the citizens, courtiers or priests do any of the fighting themselves. They let others do that for them. As Niccolò Macchiavelli (1469-1527) would later write: "Italy thus found itself almost entirely in the hands of the Church and a few republics, but since neither priests nor civilians were accustomed to taking up arms, they began to hire armies."

The word for such a hire agreement was *condotta*, and the military commanders with whom they were signed were *condottieri*. These contracts set out what the employer had to pay weekly or monthly, how any spoils were to be divided, and the numbers of cavalry and infantry which the condottiere promised to supply. The condottiere guaranteed to fight on his employer's behalf as long as the money kept coming. Should the employer run out of funds, the contract immediately became void and the condottiere could hire himself and his troops out to another power. The condottiere was a professional soldier who feared only one thing: peace. A condottiere is once said to have tossed a coin to a beggar, who thereupon thanked him with the words "Peace be with you". Incensed, so the story goes, the condottiere

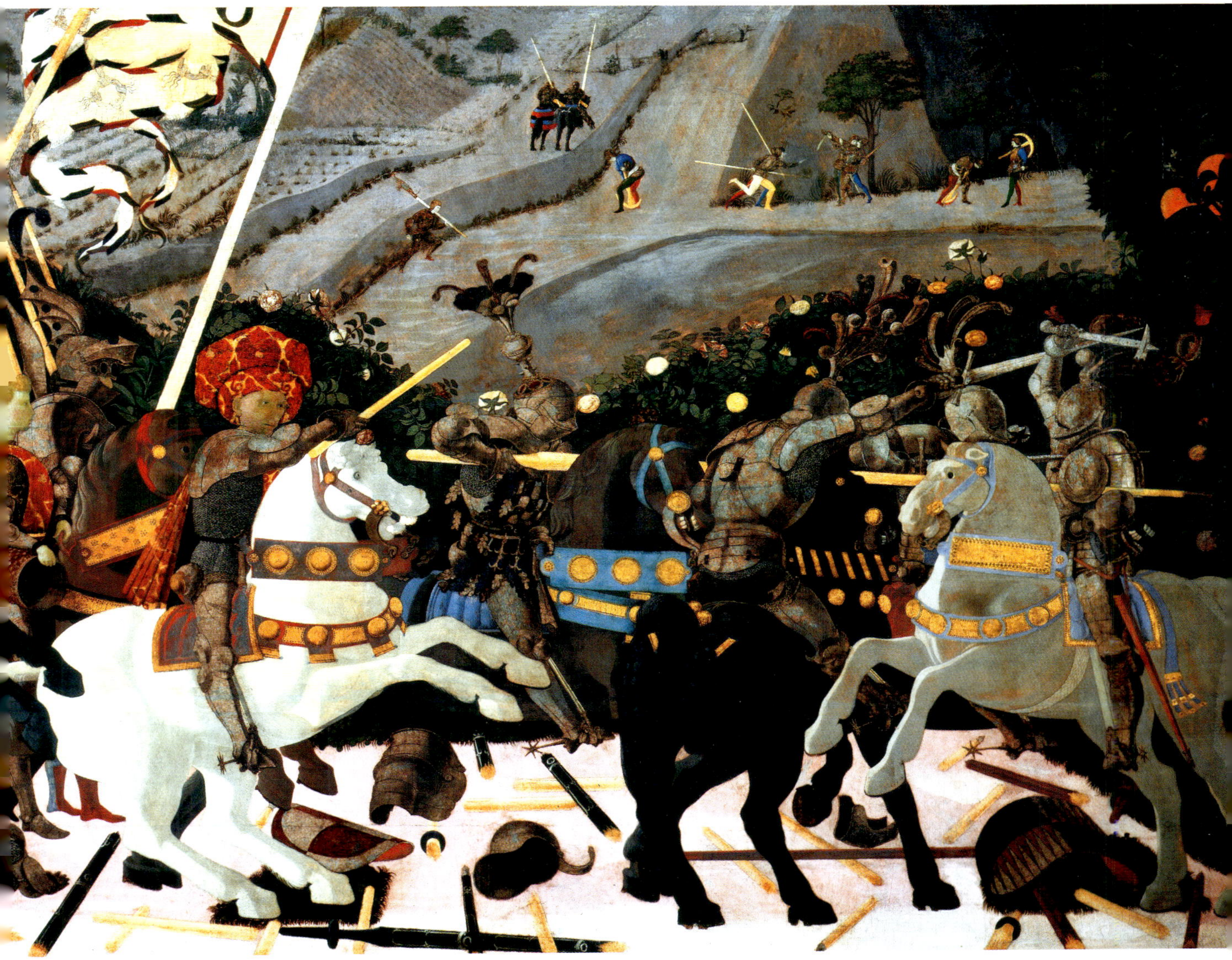

turned around, shouted at the beggar and snatched back the money.

Uccello paints his condottieri with their troops. There were two reasons why the use of hired armies had become so widespread in Italy. Firstly, the absence of a central ruling dynasty also meant that Italian society lacked the class which was granted land by its lords and which raised armies for them in return. Secondly, the growth of the mining industry in the 15th century had boosted the money supply across Europe, and much of this money found its way into the commercial centres of Italy. The city states were rich and could afford to pay for private armies.

The relationship between the warring republics and their condottieri was characterized by money and mistrust. For military power lay in the hands of the condottieri, not with the cities themselves. A city never allowed the army it was paying to pass through its own gates – only its commander. Wherever possible, the city fathers tried to keep back the wife or children of the condottiere as a sort of deposit. Or they employed several condottieri within the same army, in the hope that, in the event of attack, at least one of them would consider it to his advantage to defend the city. This naturally gave rise to issues of hierarchy amongst the various commanders.

Condottieri came from all classes of society. We know that the father of the condottiere in the Louvre panel was a peasant. All his sons became mercenaries; some of them rose up in the world, and the most famous of them produced a son who, as a condottiere in his own right, became Duke of Milan: Francesco Sforza. He was not the only one to rise up to become a ruling prince. In the words of one contemporary: "In our change-loving Italy, where nothing is set in stone and there is no long-established ruling house, stable-lads can easily become kings."

The chances of advancement were great, but so were the risks. The condottiere

Carmagnola, for example, won an important battle for Venice, but subsequently upset his employers with his – to their minds – dwindling military zeal. The Venetians suspected that he was more eager to make pacts with the enemy than to fight for Venice's interests. So they instructed him to report to the Doge. Instead of being granted an audience, however, Carmagnola was imprisoned in the Doge's palace and then beheaded. This took place on 5 May 1432, just a few weeks before the battle of San Romano. Macchiavelli is matter-of-fact about Carmagnola's fate: "As soon as they realized his commitment was waning, in other words that they were unlikely to profit further from him, but that they could not dismiss him, or they would lose what they had gained, they felt compelled to kill him for their own safety."

Lack of enthusiasm was an accusation levelled at many condottieri, but it arose directly out of the nature of their business: soldiers, horses and arms were their capital, and they naturally wanted to keep their assets more or less intact. And since they all felt the same way, they developed a certain professional etiquette: enemy horses were spared, and prisoners not killed but returned on payment of a ransom. Although Uccello portrays a terrifying war machine on two of his three panels, it seems that the battle of San Romano, like most others, was bloodless. There are no reports, at least, of any dead or injured. Macchiavelli again: "The wars in Italy were begun without fear, fought without danger and finished without losses." They sooner resembled military ceremonies than real battles.

Niccolò Mauruzi da Tolentino is the name of the condottiere with the general's staff. Uccello portrays him wearing a magnificent hat of red and gold velvet brocade. Tolentino might have worn such hats at official receptions or military parades, but certainly not on the battlefield. The page riding behind him is carrying his master's helmet, but this is itself too ostentatious for a real battle. Realism, however, was simply not on the agenda. All three paintings were intended to serve as visual propaganda and in particular to celebrate the feats of Niccolò Mauruzi da Tolentino.

The condottiere's praises had already been publicly sung a year after the battle of San Romano, when Florence's official speaker, Leonardo Bruni, declared that Tolentino possessed all the virtues of a great military leader: "courage in the midst of danger, perseverance, an overview of all operations and the gift of foresight".

Many Florentines held a quite different view, however. Giovanni Cavalcanti, for example, considered Tolentino a reckless fighter and a poor tactician. He describes how, at San Romano, Tolentino advanced too deep with a small unit of men and involuntarily embroiled them all in a fight. "When the battle went badly, Tolentino despaired and could hardly hold back his tears. He saw no escape until Micheletto [the condottiere in the Louvre panel] appeared and rescued us from the serious danger into which Niccolò had led us."

Matteo Palmieri (1406-1475) disagreed: Tolentino advanced so deep not out of

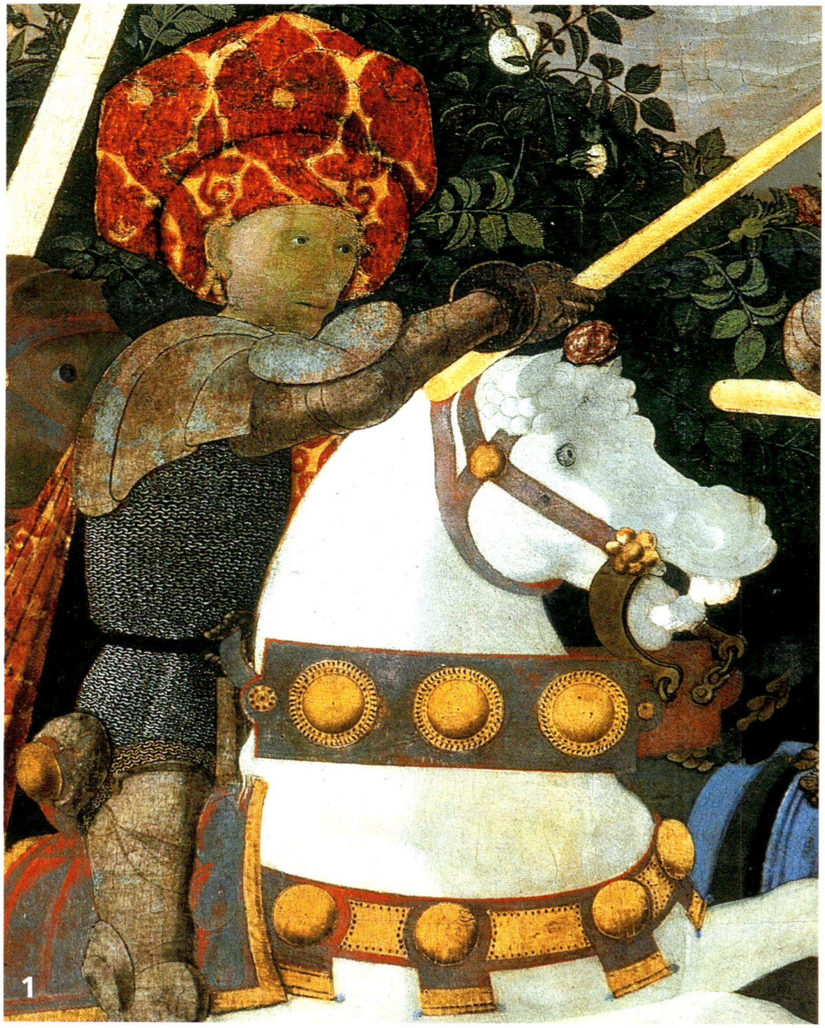
1

recklessness, but in order to lure the enemy into a trap. The arrival of Micheletto had been a precisely planned outflanking manoeuvre, not a piece of good luck. What really happened, who won the battle of San Romano, we do not know; we have only conflicting reports, partisan commentaries.

Such partisanship arose out of the political situation in Florence. Cosimo de' Medici ruled the city via middlemen, but in 1433 was ousted and imprisoned by Rinaldo degli Albizzi. Cosimo had engaged Tolentino's services and lent him financial support, and his opponents now claimed that Cosimo was seeking to set himself up as absolute ruler with Tolentino's help. Rightly or wrongly, Tolentino was branded a member of the Medici camp. When the condottiere heard that Cosimo had been taken prisoner, he rode up to the city with his troops and only withdrew when he was told that Cosimo would be killed immediately if Tolentino attempted to force his way in.

Cosimo was spared execution but was exiled to Venice, while Rinaldo's men sent Tolentino north, as far from Florence as possible. On 28 August 1434 he was captured by the Milanese near Bologna. As his employer, Cosimo would normally have bought his release; in this case, however, Rinaldo didn't. With no prospect of fetching a ransom, Tolentino was of no value to the Milanese – he fell off his horse and died. To what extent he was pushed is unknown, but whatever the case, it was an inglorious end.

According to one anecdote from the period, the city fathers were discussing how best to get rid of a condottiere who had rendered good service but who had now grown dangerous. The solution: have him killed and then proclaim him one of the city's patron saints. Something similar happened to Niccolò Mauruzi da Tolentino. His inglorious end was followed by his apotheosis. After the Medici party had seized back the reins of power and Cosimo had returned from Venice, he had the condottiere's body brought back to Florence and buried in the cathedral. An uncommon honour for someone who was not a native Florentine. The service, which was held on 20 March 1435, was even attended by Pope Eugenius, freshly expelled from Rome.

Tolentino became a martyr for the Medici cause, but it is unlikely that this was the sole reason why Cosimo honoured his memory so publicly. Through the celebrations surrounding Tolentino, Cosimo celebrated himself. He showed himself a man who remained loyal to those who fought on his side, and reminded the world that the (supposedly) magnificent victory at San Romano was won for Florence under his rule. More propaganda, in other words. The fact that he commissioned no less than three paintings of the battle can probably be explained in the same way. Paintings, like commemorations of the dead, served to glorify the house of Medici. In 1456 Cosimo commissioned Andrea del Castagno to paint a fresco of Tolentino mounted on his horse in Florence cathedral. To be immortalized on horseback in a public place was evidently the wish of many condottieri, and in his eulogy Leonardo Bruni made discreet reference to the fact that the ancient Romans also honoured their heroes with equestrian statues. This tradition had been forgotten in the Middle Ages but was revived around 1450, when Donatello executed the first equestrian statue of the Renaissance. It was, moreover, dedicated to a condottiere, Erasmo da Narni, known as Gattamelata, and stands in Padua. Venice also erected an equestrian statue of its condottiere Colleoni, although not – as the latter had wished – on St Mark's Square. The Florentines, economically-minded as ever, held back; their condottieri were commemorated not in bronze, but in paint.

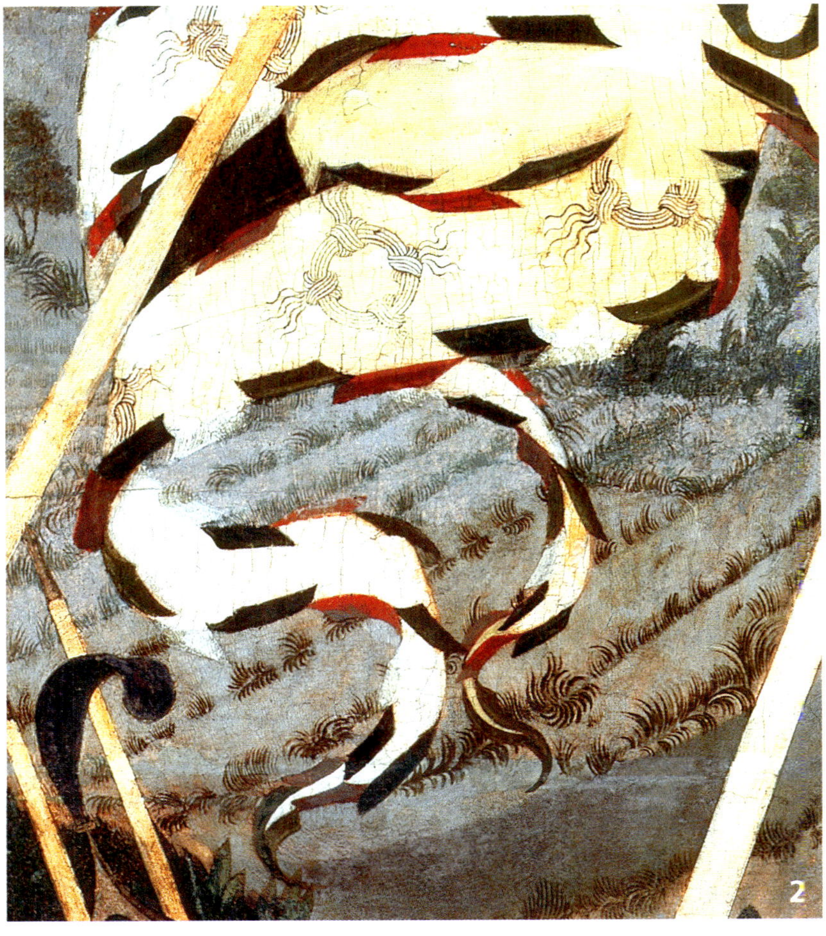

2

Flags as a means of orientation

Like most flags in the Middle Ages, Tolentino's pennant is not rectangular, but ends in two long tongues. The emblem of the mercenary leader is a ring of rope with knots. He may have chosen this himself, or it may have been awarded to him. Coats of arms in those days could be made up of anything and were constantly changing.

The condottiere Muzi Attendolo Sforza, for example, chose a quince as his emblem. He was then granted permission to adopt the lion from the arms of the prince employing him. He combined the two by placing his quince on the paw of a lion, and later added a dragon.

The practice of adopting a visual emblem had established itself during the Crusades, when knights from different countries and speaking different languages had to fight in the same army. Flags, like coats of arms, became particularly important following the introduction of visors. Since knights could no longer be recognized by their faces, they needed other forms of identification. Condottieri often omitted coats of arms from their shields, however, so as not to attract their enemies' attention unnecessarily. But flags showed friend and foe alike where everyone was. They acted, as one contemporary described it, "like a torch in a room that lights everything up. If, by some misfortune, they should go out, everyone is left floundering in the dark and will be defeated."

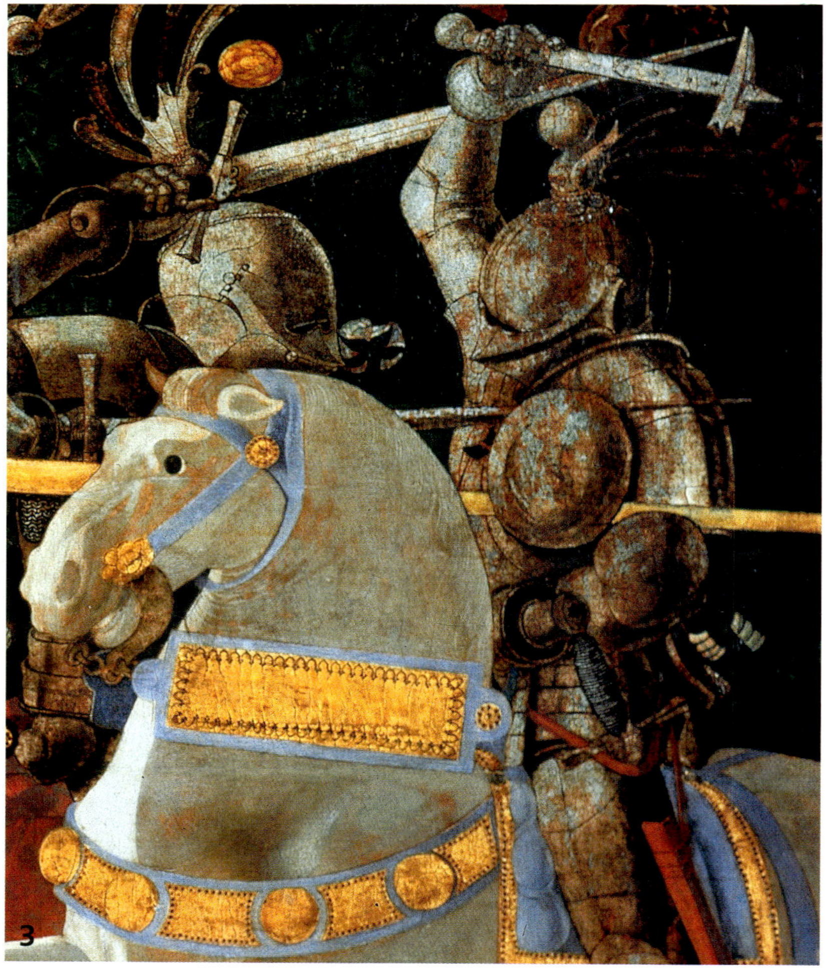

The cavalry decide the battle

Tolentino is said to have had 2000 cavalry and 1500 infantry under his command, but only the cavalry really counted. In attacks, the foot soldiers – armed with pikes and crossbows – advanced first. They cleared any obstacles for the horses, shot their arrows from as close to as possible, and then let themselves be overtaken by the cavalry. After this they withdrew, usually to the side, to harrass the enemy from there. A few individuals stayed with the riders in order to help them if they were unseated. They were purely auxiliaries.

The condottieri skirmishes of the 15th century were always decided by the cavalry. With their heavy horses, they trotted towards each other at moderate speed. The blow of a lance was not normally fatal, but could lift a rider out of his saddle. Weighted down by some 20-30 kg of armour, he was unable to get back onto his feet unaided and was thus temporarily out of the fight.

After their lances, riders used maces or swords. A sword could only wound or kill, however, if it found a chink in the opponent's armour. As Uccello illustrates, swords were forged with sharp tips so as to better penetrate such chinks. A particularly vulnerable part of the body was the armpit, and the rider with the mace in Uccello's panel protects it with a so-called "floating disk".

The unhorsed riders and numerous pieces of broken lance are precisely positioned along lines which converge in the head of Tolentino's white mount at the centre of the panel. But although the effect is almost academic, as if taken straight out of a textbook, Uccello was in fact here deploying something entirely new. He was namely one of the first artists to attempt the mathematical representation of space in painting. "Oh, what a lovely thing this perspective is!" he is said to have declared.

The perspective composition extends only as far as the hedge, however. The landscape behind fails to take up the receding lines of the foreground composition and remains spatially ill-defined. It is impossible to tell just how far apart the fields, the trees and the soldiers drawing their crossbows are supposed to be. The composition thus falls into two parts. Perhaps Uccello was not yet capable of continuing into the background the perspective system which he achieves in the foreground. Perhaps, however, he simply wasn't as interested in what was happening on the far side of the hedge. There are reasons why this might be so – and they arise out of 15th-century military tactics. Battles were decided by the cavalry, and the riders needed level terrain on which to attack. They couldn't fight uphill, nor could they jump obstacles. They needed firm ground to mount their charge. In front, therefore, we have the carefully chosen – and mathematically idealized – battleground, and behind it the surrounding, militarily less important landscape.

The calculation of distances was important not just in art, but also in the burgeoning science of artillery. Gunners had to be able to use a plumb and square and, like painters, have a firm grasp of the basics of geometry. In 1453 Mohammed II destroyed the walls of Constantinople with his cannon; his biggest gun fired cannon-balls almost a metre in diameter a distance of 1500 metres. The advent of artillery signalled the end of the arms wielded by Uccello's condottieri – it arrived in the same century as perspective in painting.

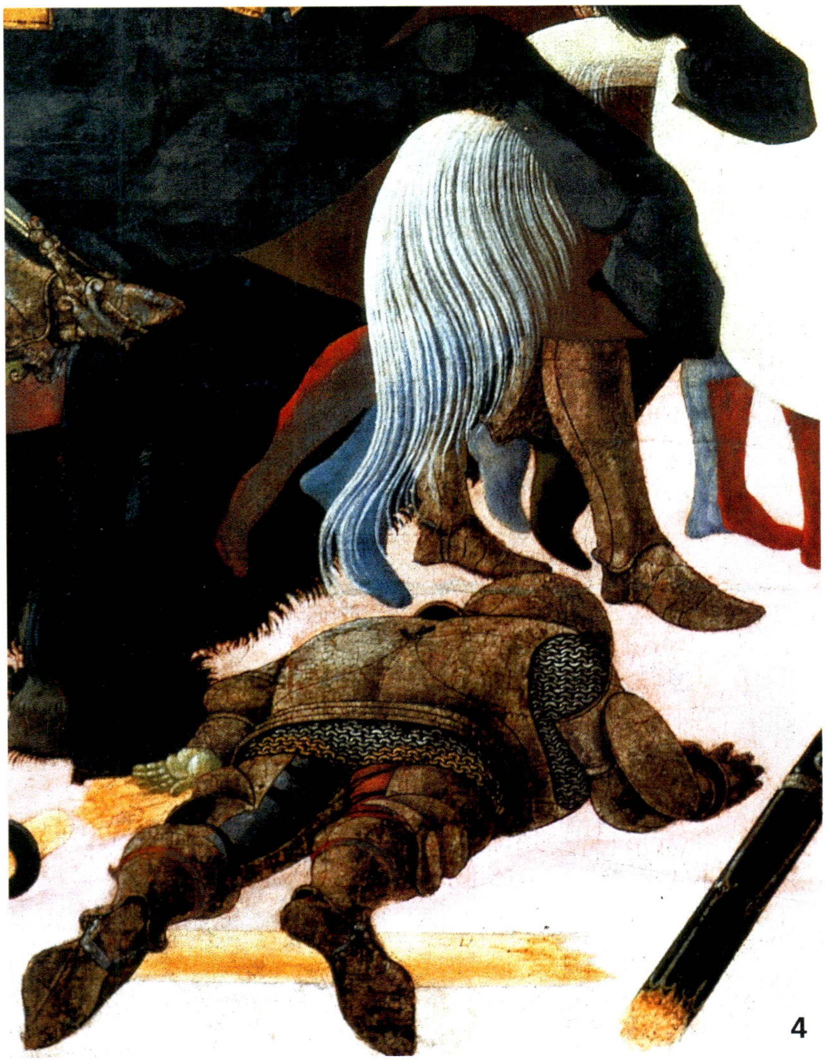

4 **The discovery of perspective**

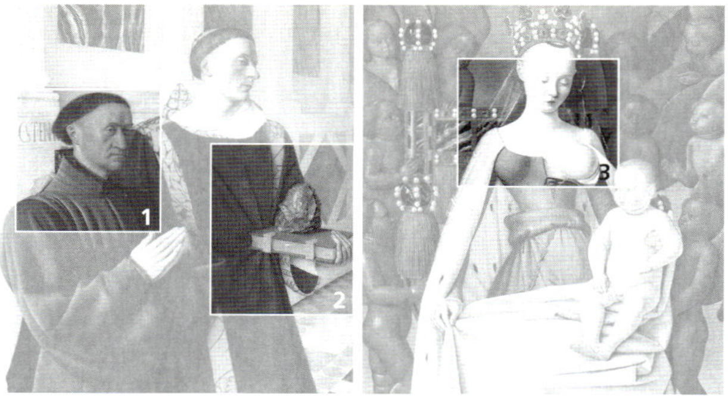
1
2
3

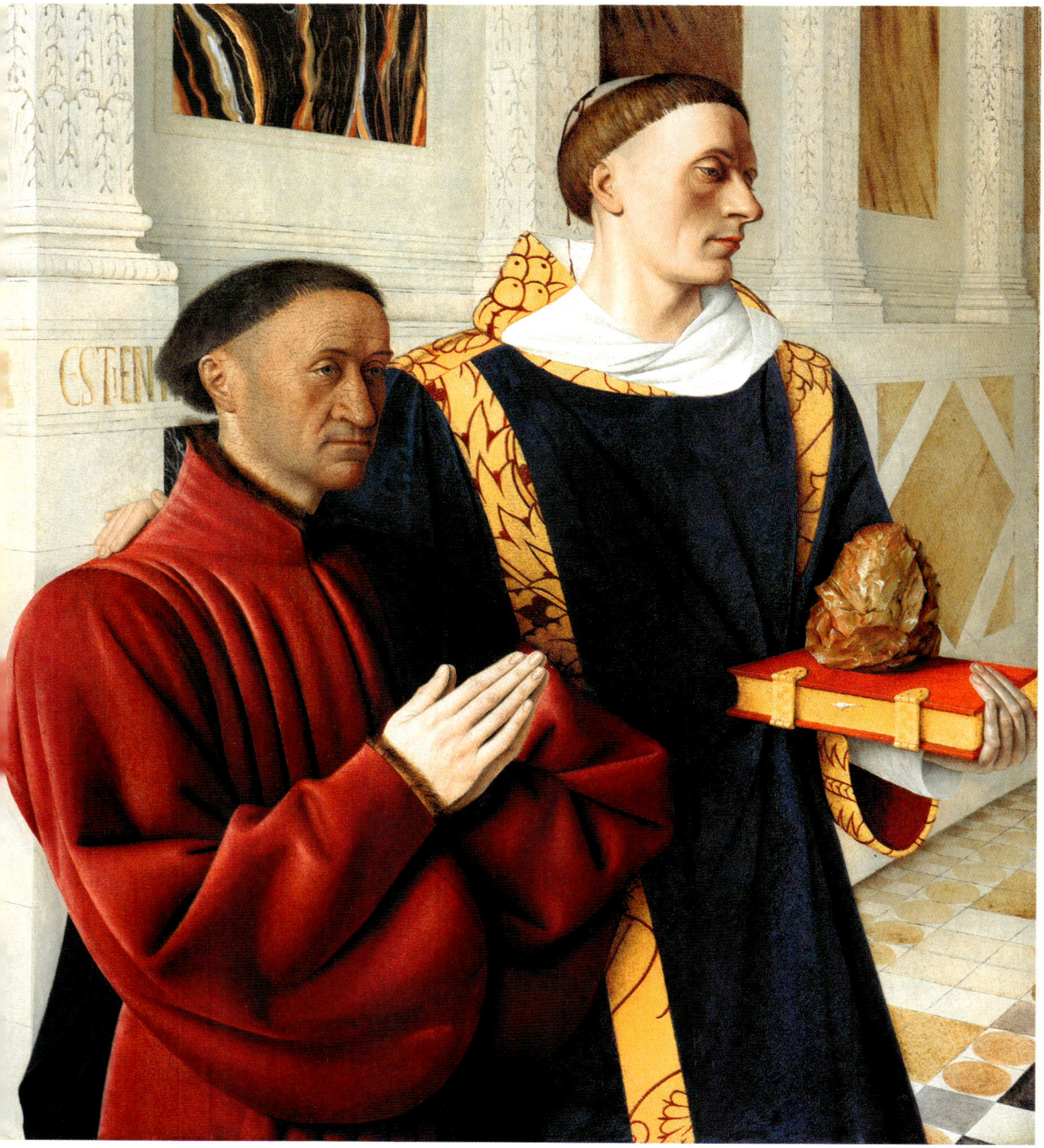

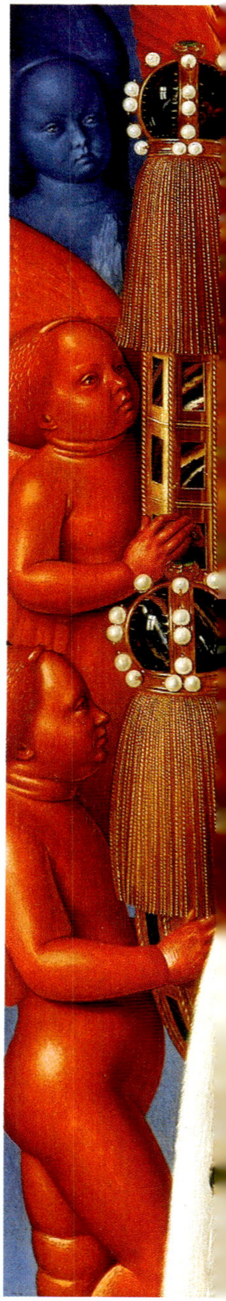

Jean Fouquet: The Melun Diptych, c. 1456

The King's mistress posing as the Virgin

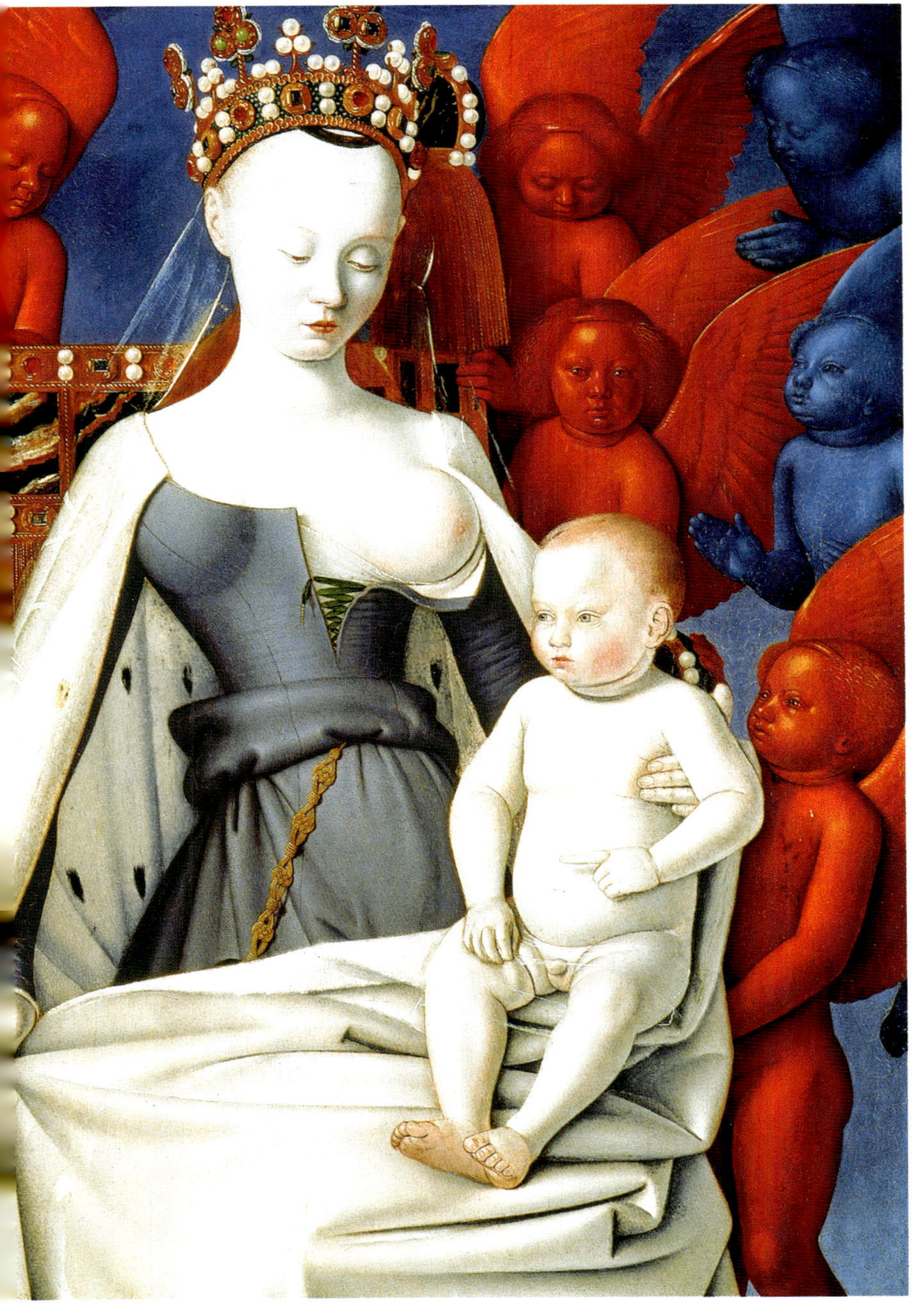

The work is in two parts, but today they appear together only in reproductions. In reality the two parts are in two different cities, the left panel in Berlin, the right in Antwerp.

Art historians had long suspected that they belonged together, but it was left to modern scientific examination of the wood on which they were painted to supply the evidence. Two boards of the Berlin panel and one in the Antwerp panel came from one and the same oak tree. It was felled, according to dendro-chronological analysis, about 1446. Following the usual seasoning period of ten to fifteen years, the boards fetched up in the workshop of the French painter Jean Fouquet (1415/22–c. 1481), who painted a two-panel devotional picture, or diptych, on them, in about the year 1456.

The donor was Etienne Chevalier, the royal treasurer, and he is portrayed on the left panel, kneeling at prayer. Beside him stands St Stephen (Etienne in French), identifiable by his attributes: the Gospels, and one of the stones with which he was martyred. St Stephen's role is to intercede for Chevalier with the Virgin Mary, seen on the right panel, in the non-terrestrial sphere, on a throne borne up by angels. One of the Virgin's breasts is exposed, and in her lap sits the infant Jesus, pointing a forefinger in the direction of the treasurer by way of indication that his prayer is heard and he may hope for divine clemency.

For centuries the diptych hung above Etienne Chevalier's tomb in the church of Notre Dame in the town of his birth, Melun, south of Paris. There it was intended to preserve the donor's memory "in perpetuity", together with the masses said every morning at six for the repose of his immortal soul.

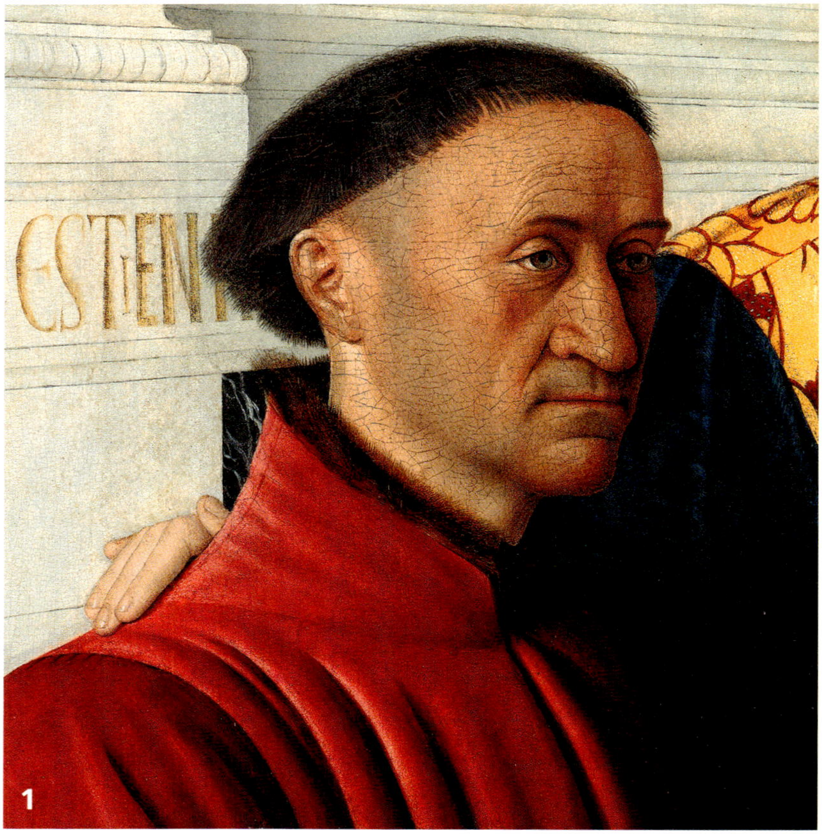

1

A trustworthy treasurer

The donor's name, "Estienne" (in the old spelling), is inscribed in the marble pillar behind him in gold letters. The treasurer is seen wearing a solemn maroon fur-lined robe – with the padded shoulders then in fashion and stiff pleats – and kneeling in a palatial hallway. Rooms of this kind, with marble walls and floors in the style of the Italian Renaissance, were uncommon in 15th century Paris, but Chevalier's house in rue de la Verrerie was reputedly magnificent, with as many glass windows as there were days in the year. King Louis XI dined there in 1465, a high honour for an official, and a recognition of his services to France and the monarchy.

Chevalier's services were chiefly to Louis' father, Charles VII (1403–61). At his court, Chevalier (born around 1400) served as the royal secretary, notary and auditor in succession. Around mid-century he was the treasurer, responsible for the finances of the realm, with a seat in the royal council – that is to say, not merely in the larger, ceremonial council, but in the smaller privy council through which Charles VII conducted the daily affairs of government. The king liked to have non-aristocrats such as Chevalier about him, commoners who owed everything to him. They were the only ones on whom he could rely in the struggle against the nobility, a hotbed of ambition, intrigue and revolt.

Towards the end of his reign, Charles had indeed managed to subdue the nobles. By concluding peace with his powerful cousin and enemy, the Duke of Burgundy, he had put an end to the civil war. And more: Charles VII has gone down to posterity as a weak king (dramatists from Schiller to Shaw portrayed him as an unfortunate or even ridiculous figure alongside Joan of Arc), yet it was he who brought to a victorious conclusion not only the civil war but the Hundred Years' War. Little by little his forces drove out the English, who had occupied the larger part of France for almost fifty years. The invaders were obliged to yield province after province, until in 1453 they were finally driven to escape back across the sea. Charles VII (in another portrait by Fouquet) was justly celebrated as "the most victorious king".

The king owed his success to a group of hard-working officials in his service. One of these was Etienne Chevalier. It was he who procured the immense sums necessary to finance protracted military campaigns – and thus victory. Tax revenue came in very slowly indeed (not until 1444 had an assembly of the estates granted the king the right to levy taxes directly) and the royal coffers were forever lacking in ready cash to pay for the war. On one occasion, Chevalier himself made the king a personal loan of 1100 livres. He had to wait years till the sum was repaid.

Of course a portion of the incoming revenue went to pay the servants of the state, and the treasurer was among those who amassed a fortune; but he appears to have been more cautious than others, for at court, where according to the contemporary chronicler Georges Chastellain "nobody tells the truth", the man with the stern features enjoyed the reputation of being incorruptible and trustworthy. It was no accident that the king's personal physician, the king's mistress, and even King Charles VII himself, appointed Chevalier the executor of their wills.

A patron in heaven as powerful as St Stephen, depicted here in a blue dalmatic with gold braid standing supportively at the treasurer's side, could be of good use to a man in a prominent and vulnerable office at the intrigue-ridden court of Charles VII. The king was fickle in his favours, as two others in his service had discovered.

An enterprising merchant of Bourges, a commoner by the name of Jacques Coeur, had risen to become Master of the Privy Purse. But he became too wealthy. In 1451 Charles had him arrested without warning. Coeur was banished and his fortune confiscated and transferred to the coffers out of which the king paid for his war.

St Joan, too, was left in the lurch by Charles. She had lent assistance to the young heir to the throne when his fortunes were at their nadir, and had wrenched him out of his depressive, passive state. The English invaders, having inflicted a crushing defeat on the French at the battle of Agincourt in 1415, had occupied France and had nothing but scorn for Charles, who now held little more of France than the city of Bourges itself. Charles withdrew to that city, where he remained inactive and resigned to his fate until the warlike maid appeared in 1429. Joan declared that she had been sent by God. She took back the city of Orléans for France, and conducted Charles to Rheims, where he was crowned the rightful king. Joan it was who restored courage to this despairing man and thus sparked the reconquest of his realm. But subsequently, when Joan fell into the hands of her enemies and was sentenced and burnt as a witch in 1431, the king never lifted a finger to help her.

More than twenty years were to pass before "the most victorious" Charles hesitantly started the process of appeal against that sentence – doubtless to counter the notion that he owed his successes at war to witchcraft. Not until 1456, the year in which Etienne Chevalier's diptych was painted by Fouquet, did a court rehabilitate Joan. She was nevertheless granted no place in official portraiture. A maid who had claimed to hear the voice of God was of necessity suspect in the eyes of the church. It was not until 1920 that she was canonized.

St Stephen, on the other hand, was a recognized martyr, indeed the first. He was a patron from whom the treasurer might hope for efficacious help. And it was more than the name alone that linked them: the volume bound in red leather which the saint is holding, with its gold blocking and bookmark, was quite possibly from the treasurer's own library. For Chevalier was a collector of illuminated manuscript books, as were the king himself and his uncle, the Duke of Berry.

Chevalier had already ordered an illuminated book of hours from Jean Fouquet in 1448. This was a prayer book for the laity such as the great used at their private devotions, and in all probability it was not finished until about the same time as the diptych, since the work, both for the scribe who wrote the text and for the artist who illuminated the book, was long and arduous. All forty-seven of the miniatures which Jean Fouquet painted for Eitienne Chevalier's magnificent book of hours have survived.

In certain scenes, whether biblical or depicting the lives of the saints, the treasurer can be seen – clad in black at the entombment of Christ, or in portrait style, as in the diptych, praying to the Virgin. In the book of hours too, his name or his *imprese* appears – a golden doubled 'e', the two letters tied by decorative love-knots. These symbols, which evolved from traps for game, were taken (in contrast to wedding rings) to stand for an extra-marital liaison.

Love-knots of this kind apparently adorned the lost frame of the diptych

St Stephen's stone

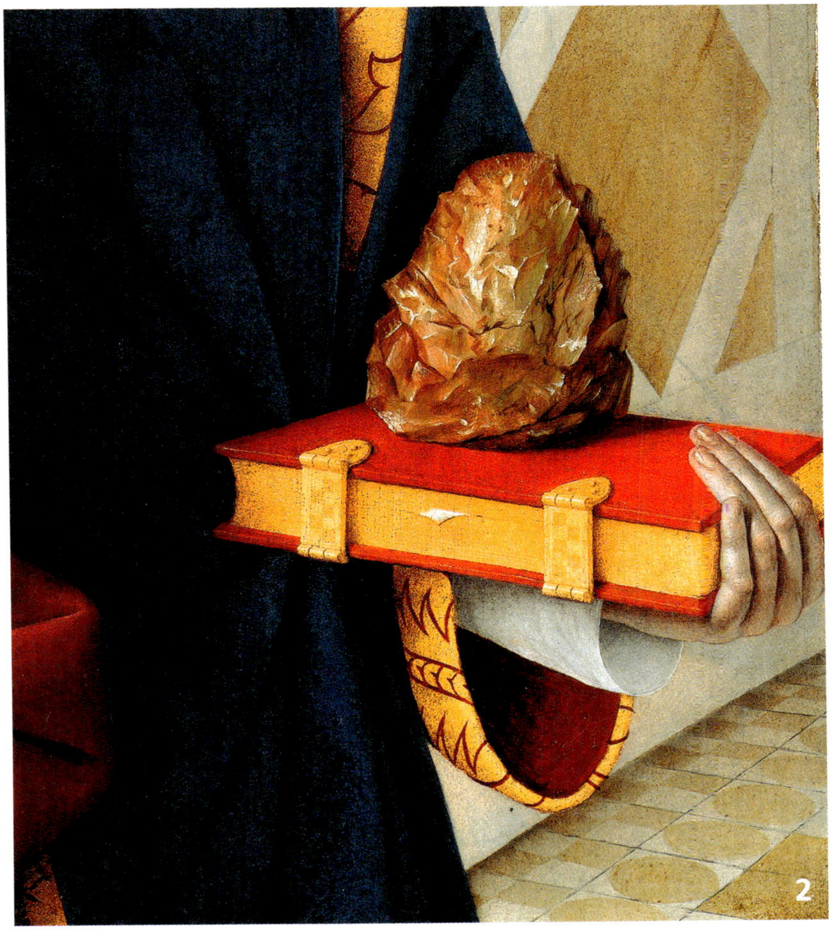

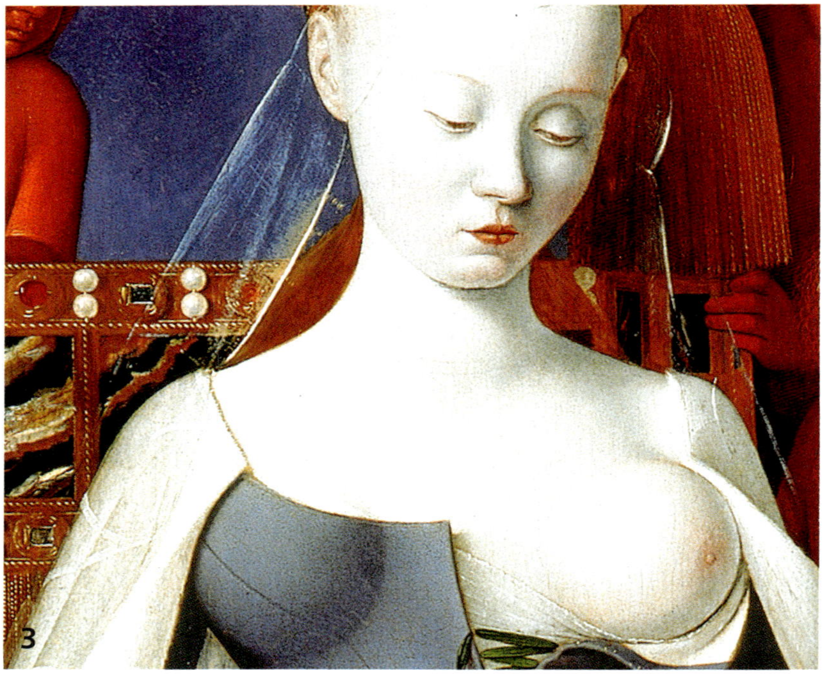

3

The most beautiful woman in the world

The attractive Virgin poses conundrums. The great Dutch art historian and chronicler of the Middle Ages Johan Huizinga detected "a whiff of decadent godlessness" about her. Fouquet has not depicted her giving suck to the infant Jesus; indeed, her pert bosom is not one that prompts thoughts of breast-feeding. Yet there is a theological justification for exposing the breast: just as Christ displays the wounds in his side to God the Father, so too Mary displays her breast, underlining her role as intercessor for human kind, on earth and in purgatory.

It is possible that this madonna bears the features of Katherine, the goodly wife of the donor, who died in 1452 and was buried beside him in Melun. More likely, however, is that this is a portrait of Agnès Sorel, a lady who had advanced Chevalier's career significantly and indeed may have meant even more to him, according to one persistent tradition. This rumour is even supported by an inscription on the reverse of the panel, dated 1775 and attested by notary: "The Holy Virgin, with the features of Agnès Sorel, mistress to King Charles VII of France, deceased 1450." To contemporaries, Agnès Sorel was quite simply "the most beautiful woman in the world". Barely had she appeared at the French court in 1443, aged about twenty, but the king, twice her age, was utterly captivated. We have this from Chastellain, the court chronicler of the Duke of Burgundy, and also from Enea Silvio Piccolomini, later Pope Pius II, who noted in his memoirs: "Whether at table, in bed, or in the council chamber, she must needs be always at his side."

Charles' wife, Queen Marie, was fully occupied with raising her fourteen children. She was a devout woman, and, according to Chastellain, "had a face that would have struck fear even into the English".

The king's mistress, by contrast, was the only woman to appear before the court mounted on a stallion at a tournament, in gleaming silver armour studded with jewels. In church, we are told, she was good at exhibiting "a pretty anguish at her sins"; but while she was about it she held her head high and wore "the most monstrous" lace head-dresses and trains, fully a third longer than any other princess had ever worn. She lowered her décolleté so far that a bishop made a complaint to the king about "cleavages that exposed the women's bosoms and nipples to view".

The influence of Agnès Sorel was felt not only in fashion but in politics. Like Joan of Arc fourteen years previously, she had the gift of arousing the king from the lethargy he recurrently subsided into. She inspired him with courage and the will to action, and motivated him to resume the fight against the English enemy after a lengthy period of inactivity.

The services rendered to France by this beautiful woman, who died young in childbirth, were later hymned by no less a personage than King Francis I (1494–1547), in lines of poetry that translate roughly as: "Her love deserves more praise, / since it brought about the revival of France, / than anything a nun may do in a convent / or a hermit in the wilderness."

To memorialize such a woman in a painting, as treasurer Chevalier did, seemed legitimate. At any rate, few would then have considered it blasphemous to portray and transfigure a presumed sinner, after her death, as the Virgin Mary. The monarch, anointed by God himself, was considered holy, and he conferred holiness on all he touched.

So it was only right and proper that the left panel of the diptych should be entirely in red, white and blue, since these were the heraldic colours of the king.

The artist, Jean Fouquet, was also in service with King Charles VII. He had painted his portrait – not very flatteringly, giving him a bulbous nose and pop eyes. Born in Tours between 1415 and 1422, Fouquet worked chiefly for the king, who resided mainly in the Loire valley, and his courtiers. When Charles died in 1461, a rider bore his death-mask from Bourges to Paris, where Fouquet was at the time, so that the artist might overpaint it for the obsequies, in which a royal likeness as true to life as possible played an important part.

Fouquet, like Chevalier the treasurer, was one of the few to remain in service under Charles' successor. In 1475, indeed, Fouquet was appointed court painter. But Louis XI was a power politician, with little time for art, and seems to have ordered mainly book illustrations from his painter.

We know nothing about the youth or training of the artist. Features of Dutch panel painting are apparent in his work: a psychological sensitivity in rendering the ascetic features of Chevalier, and a love of nature and of detail. It is possible that Fouquet had been apprenticed to a miniaturist.

What is certain is that from 1446 to 1448 he was in Italy, probably in the retinue of a legation of French churchmen. Be that as it may, he excited considerable attention with a portrait of Pope Eugenius IV. This painting is lost, but the Florentine Francesco Florio was still declaring in 1477 that the Frenchman "outdid the painters of every other century with his art".

We can assume that in Florence Fouquet enjoyed contact with Fra Angelico, Paolo Uccello and Masolino – and took the opportunity to learn perspective, spatiality, and a sense of the monumental, from these second generation Renaissance artists. As well as the features of Italian architecture, the three-dimensionality of the protagonists in the Chevalier diptych betrays their influence.

We have another pointer to Fouquet's familiarity with the work of the Italians. Like Lorenzo Ghiberti (1378-1455), who had introduced a relief self-portrait into his bronze doors for the Florence baptistery, Fouquet too immortalized himself in his own work. In the Louvre in Paris there is an enamel medal inscribed "Johes Fouquet", bearing a portrait which was evidently that of the artist, which was clearly forcibly broken out of the frame of the diptych.

Fouquet was famous in his day, and seen as the founder of a modern French school of painting, but now only few of his panels have survived: the diptych, the portrait of the king (Paris), Gonella the court jester (Vienna), Chancellor Jouvenel des Ursins (Paris), and the pietà in the church at Nouans. Paradoxically, his fragile miniatures have stood the test of time better, being tucked away in folio volumes in the safe keeping of libraries.

The painter himself was forgotten. In 1775, when the cathedral chapter of Notre Dame in Melun needed to raise money for restoration purposes, the diptych was separated into two portions and sold, despite the express stipulations of the donor. After the French Revolution, the two halves appeared on the market separately. The right panel was bought in Paris by a lord mayor of Antwerp, and since 1840 it has been in the museum in that city.

The left panel was discovered at a dealer's in Basle, Switzerland, by the German poet Clemens Brentano (1778-1842). Like many another Romantic, he was concerned to seek out and save the "countless doomed works of the most sublime art". The panel painting reminded him of the book of hours of Etienne Chevalier, which was in the possession of his brother, Georg Brentano, a Frankfurt banker. Only a short time previously the miniatures had been ascribed to Fouquet, of whom only the name was known. But the poet saw the similarity of the diptych figures to those in the book of hours, and this led in due course to the identification of the treasurer and his painter. Subsequently, in 1896, the painting joined the Berlin collection.

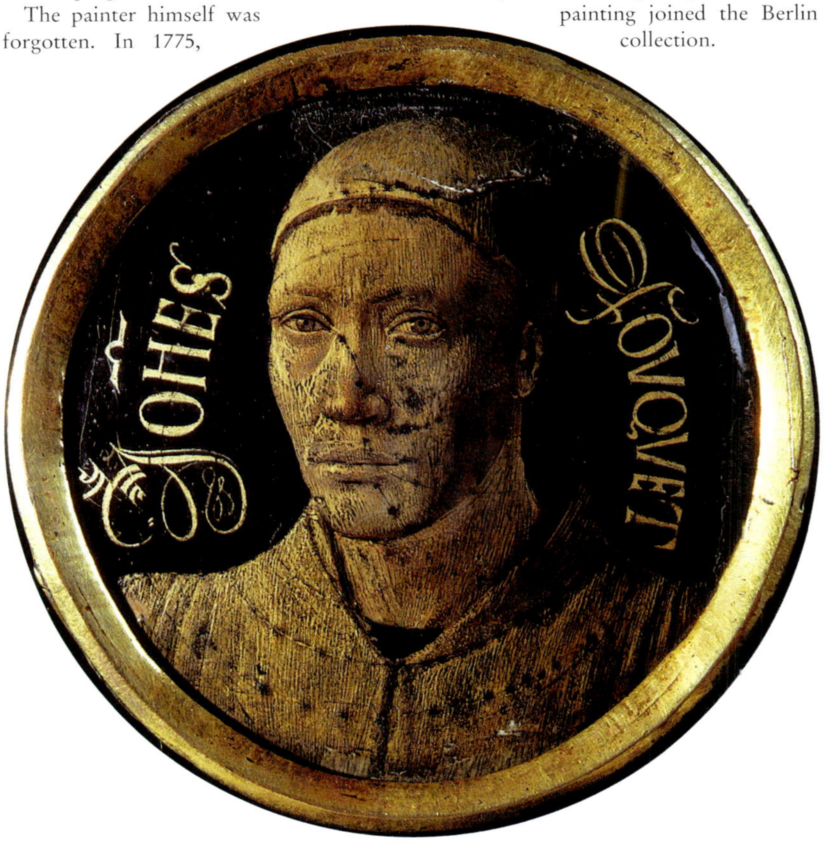

A German Romantic identifies the donor

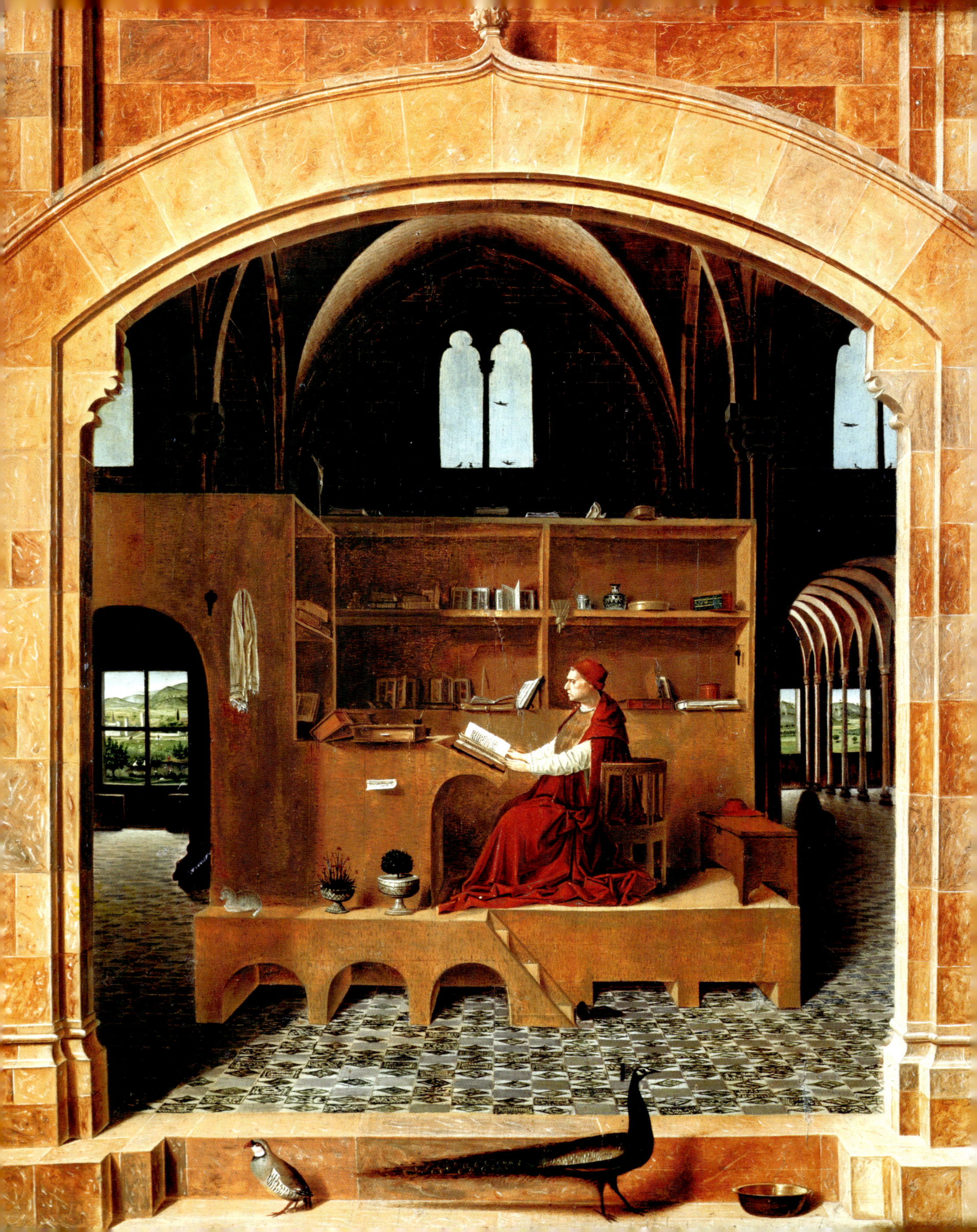

Antonello da Messina: St Jerome, between 1460 and 1475

A Small Saint in a Vasty Building

Antonello painted his St Jerome in Messina. The year in which he did so is disputed but was between 1460 and 1475. At that time the Sicilian town had a population of 25,000 and depended for its livelihood on its port. Its position on the Mediterranean was favourable, and shipping bound in every direction stopped there to take provisions on board or to trade goods. On the shelves behind Jerome are ceramic vessels from the Netherlands.

But Messina was also a provincial town, on the periphery of Europe, far from the cultural centres. None of the significant authors of humanism lived there; there was no school of painting deserving of the name. In 1550 Giorgio Vasari, the first chronicler of art, wrote of Antonello: "Messina could offer no life that was to his taste." Nevertheless, apart from some journeys it was there that he spent his life, from his birth around 1430 till his death in 1479.

This was the early period of the Renaissance, and Florence was its hub. There the Medicis were in power, men open to the world, who developed banking and made shrewd profits out of the growing need for capital, but who also brought to their own city men of learning exiled from Constantinople, founded libraries, and supported writers, architects and artists. In Florence, unlike Messina, a new era was dawning.

The artists and the men of learning, often in the service of the Church, broke through religious barriers and discovered the physical world afresh, with the help of ancient philosophers.

One achievement of the painters was the conquest of physical space. Beyond a thin strip of earth, Gothic artists had tended to see the heavens, as a symbol of eternity and the kingdom of God. The painters of the early Renaissance showed space as it appears to the eye. With the help of perspective they evolved the ability to relate objects near and far. The innovative artist Paolo Uccello, painting around 1450, transformed the battle of San Romano into a geometrical construct such as had never been seen before.

Antonello was also fascinated by distance, as we see in this painting. It measures 46 by 37 centimetres, and is now in the National Gallery in London. We are looking into an ecclesiastical building, and the growing distance from the viewer is perfectly clear. In the foreground, a wall serves him as a kind of frame, and beyond it is a spacious hall containing the cell in which Jerome is at work. To the right and the left, either side of the cell, our gaze is drawn through vaults to the rearward windows. Antonello deploys light and shadow to emphasize the size and spaciousness of this church-like interior. And further on, outside, a far-off landscape opens up to the view.

One means frequently employed in the Renaissance to indicate perspective distance was tiles or stone slabs on a floor, the lines running toward their notional meeting at the vanishing point. Antonello shows these lines in the foreground portion and continues them at the sides, albeit not so distinctly. He robs the central lines of their impact, however, by placing the saint's cell in the middle of the composition, which obscures the impact of the perspective and weakens the optical triumph.

Exactly where the centre lines of the tiles ought to have been running toward their meeting point, Antonello locates Jerome's book and hands. This is an important point in the composition; the window diagonals cross here too. The effect is to place the act of reading, of study, in the centre. Yet the saint is astoundingly small, his head smaller than the blocks of stone in the walls. The painter neither endowed him with substantial size, nor positioned

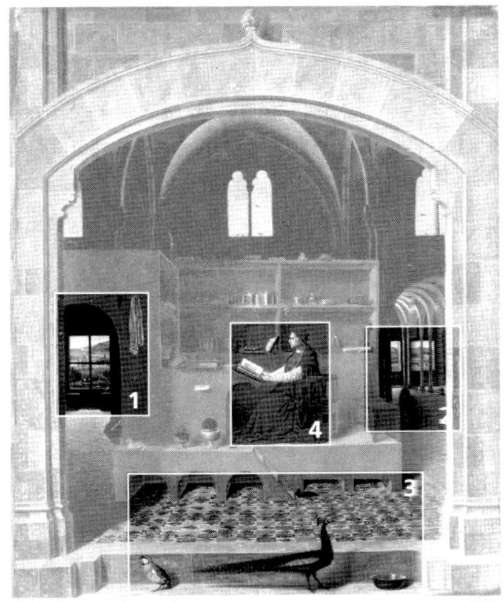

him in the foreground. Instead, he adopted an approach familiar from jewellery boxes in the Renaissance, when precious stones were presented on outside velvet cushions. In Antonello's painting, this translates as exterior walls, then spatial depth, the study, and in the heart of it all the great church father at work.

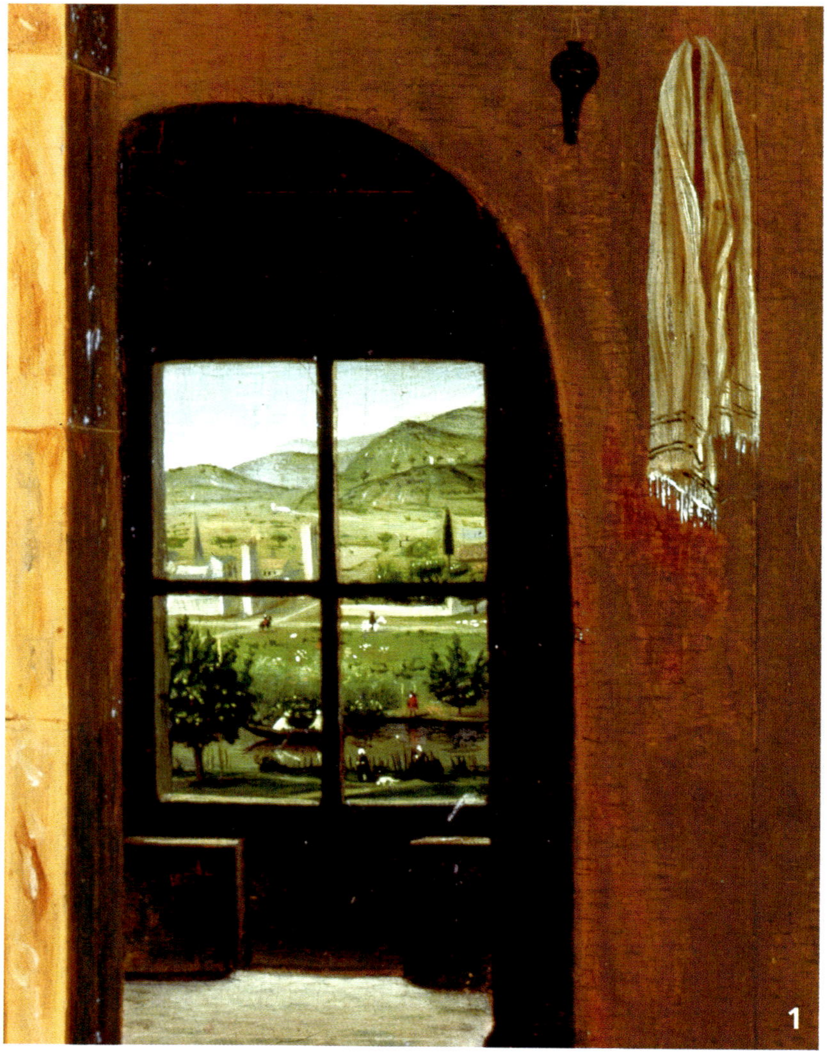

1

A window and a towel

Mountains, rivers, towers and white perimeter walls are characteristic of Messina, and the view through the window on the left recalls the place where Antonello spent his life. His father was a bricklayer and stonemason, and options for his son were limited; he probably moved to Naples, the nearest city which valued art. At Naples there was a court and all the stately functions that go with a court; for a long time, Sicily was ruled by the Neapolitan kings. The kingdom of Naples belonged to the Dukes of Anjou, and later to those of Aragon. These houses were enemies, but the rulers were agreed on one point: their predilection for contemporary Flemish art, for artists such as Jan van Eyck, Hugo van der Goes, Rogier van der Weyden or Petrus Christus.

In Italy this taste was shared by others, and the art produced in Ghent and Bruges was highly esteemed by many collectors. A new and bracing art was being created in the north too, as painters discovered the uniqueness of every human face, the many sides of the natural world, and the thousand things that everyday life presents to the view. On several occasions, the representatives of the Medici bank sent paintings home from Bruges; but not all of them arrived at their destination. In 1473 pirates seized a sailing ship that was transporting an altar by Hans Memling, ultimately intended for Florence, and it ended up in Danzig. In 1445 a ship bound for Naples had been plundered, and the inventory of stolen treasures included tapestries, fabrics, furs, vases, candelabra, and mirrors in costly frames. The Flemish cities were considered important centres of the arts, of fine crafts, and of good taste. Italian princes tried to tempt weavers south, and sent their own court painters to visit the north.

Naples was probably the city with the greatest number of Flemish works and the most artists pursuing a Flemish style. The reasons for this were to be found in the strange political circumstances of the period: Flanders was then a possession of the mighty Burgundy. The French prince, poet and art lover René of Anjou came to value Flemish art whilst in captivity as the Duke of Burgundy's prisoner. From 1438 to 1442 it was he who ruled southern Italy, including Sicily, and in this way the art of the north found its way to Naples. René was succeeded by a Spanish king, Alfonso V, who had made the acquaintance of Jan van Eyck when the artist painted the king's sister Leonora. The portrait had been commissioned by another Duke of Burgundy, who hoped to marry Leonora. This made two coincidences; and the coincidences were to have consequences.

Alfonso reigned from 1442 to 1458, bringing works by van Eyck and Rogier van der Weyden to Naples and urging local painters to imitate them. One Niccolò Colantonio was especially assiduous in following this pointer, and his *St Jerome* can be admired to this day in the Museo di Capodimonte in Naples: it shows a book-crammed study, exaggerating the northern innovations to the point of caricature.

It is believed that Antonello was Colantonio's pupil. Even if he was not, it is manifest that the study of his Jerome is under the Flemish influence: the plants, the ceramic ware, the boxes, the books arranged in different positions, the towel, the well-observed position of the saint's fingers in the pages of his book. This plenitude of detail originated in the northern school. The deserted interior prospects at either side of the painting, on the other hand, conform to the ideals of the Italian Renaissance. Antonello has married two different styles, and it is the tension between them that makes for the extraordinary appeal of this picture.

Faith that tamed a lion

Antonello's reputation was founded not only upon his artistic abilities; he also used a new medium. Unlike the painters of the Middle Ages, or indeed the Florentine artists of the early Renaissance period, he used a variety of oils rather than egg to bind his colour pigments. The advantage of this was that the paint could be applied more thinly and several layers of paint could be overlaid and better nuanced; a luminous quality of lustre unknown to traditional methods became available to the artist.

This new technique came from Flanders too, where Jan van Eyck was one of the first masters to employ it. Antonello probably learnt it in Naples. It is no accident that works from his hand were erroneously ascribed time and again over the succeeding decades and centuries to Flemish painters, usually to van Eyck himself. An altarpiece by van Eyck, now lost, was in Naples and showed St Jerome. Antonello was doubtless familiar with it.

Jerome was invariably identified in paintings by the accompanying lion. Legend had it that a lion came limping into the monastery, and all the other monks fled. Jerome, however, so the story goes, "approached him as if he were welcoming a guest". He called back the other monks, and together they sought the lion's injury, found a thorn, and pulled it out. In art, the saint was portrayed performing this treatment himself. Generally he is seen at his lectern, looking as if interrupted in profound thought, while the lion, like an obedient child, is uplifting a forepaw. Antonello, however, has placed the lion at some distance, limping through the hallway to the right, one forepaw drawn up.

The story of the lion is recorded in the *Golden Legend*, a collection of saints' lives and legends compiled around the year 1270. They were intended to entertain and instruct: the function of the king of the beasts in this tale, for instance, was to show that even wild Nature could be tamed by Christianity. But the *Golden Legend* also tells that one night the monks placed a woman's dress by Jerome's bed, whereupon he put it on in the dark and appeared at the dawn mass wearing it. This practical joke was played on him, says the pious narrator, by those whom Jerome had punished for "sexual offences". Historians, though, have noted grounds for suspecting the saint himself. In Rome he had given ascetic instruction to a patrician lady and her daughter with striking frequency, and at length he moved with both from Rome to Bethlehem, where the lady's fortune funded the building of several monastic institutions.

Jerome wrote letters most emphatic in tone to the daughter, calling upon her to preserve her virginity, lead a pure life, and read only Christian books. He confessed that he himself had not always resisted the tempter, and had suffered appalling torments in consequence. For later centuries, these letters were a source of instruction and edification, but today they are more likely to be read as desperate attempts to lay his own sins to rest.

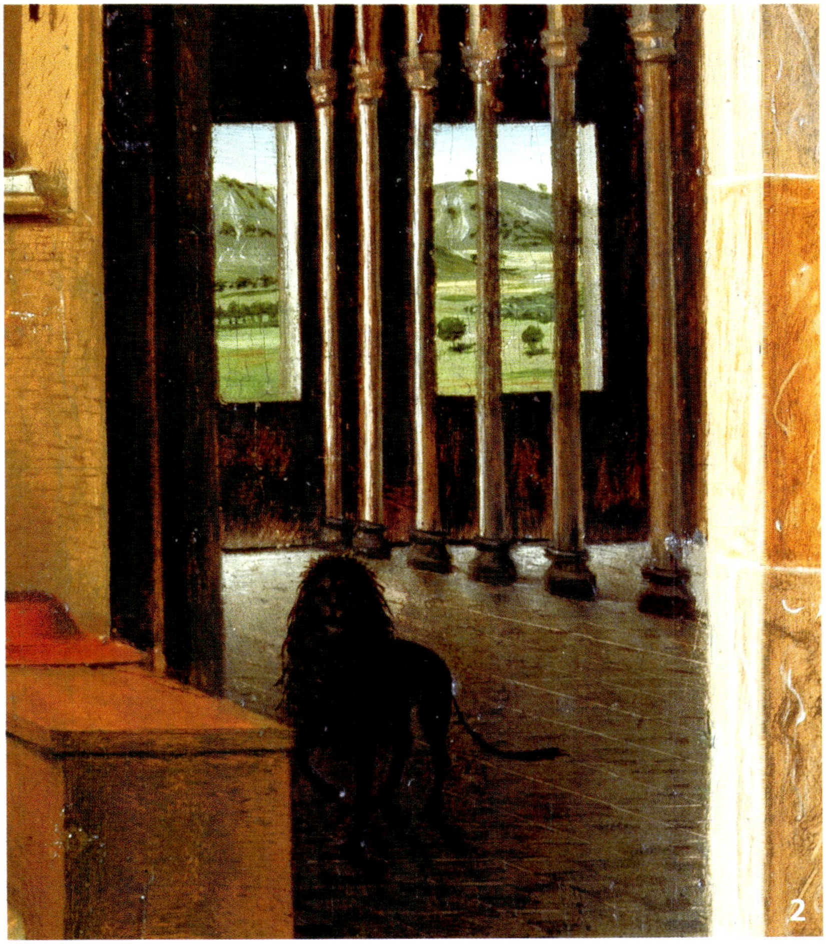
2

Jerome, who was born in 347 and died in 420, was and remains a controversial saint. His critics describe him as vain, unjust and dissipated. The Church, however, forgave him his weaknesses because his merit as monk and scholar was so extraordinary. Having spent some years as a hermit on the eastern margins of Syria, he later passed more than three decades as the prior of several monastic institutions in and near Bethlehem, and drew upon his own experience to set down guidelines for the ascetic life of a monk. Above all, he translated from the Greek and Hebrew, establishing portions of the Vulgate, the Latin Bible used by the Church from the Middle Ages on and the text to which Christian theologians refer to this day. In tribute to his significant status, painters often portrayed him in the red robes of a cardinal, a rank which in fact he never achieved.

In Antonello's day, the beholders of paintings would instantly wonder whether a depicted animal represented more than itself, and what message it might be intended to convey. Most of the symbols that originated in Greece and the Orient and were absorbed into Christianity had multiple connotations. The context would indicate what was meant.

Leaving aside birds and a horse seen through the windows, Antonello has assigned four creatures to his saint: a lion, a cat, a partridge, and a peacock. The lion, as we have seen, derives from the legend. The cat may simply be there to catch mice: since mice nibbled away manuscripts, they were the avowed enemies of scholars. A mouse nibbling paper is to be seen in Colantonio's painting of Jerome.

That leaves the partridge and the peacock, conspicuous in the foreground and painted with greater precision than the other creatures in the picture, so presumably more than merely decorative in function. Both are thoroughly familiar in the Christian visual repertoire. The story went that the partridge stole the eggs of other birds, and it was used as a symbol of the devil trapping the young. On the other hand, partridges were also said to steal each other's eggs, and yet the young were said to return invariably to their real mothers, just as the faithful return to Christ. The peacock was said to have been in paradise, and thus stood for eternal life. It was depicted on the walls of Roman catacombs, on medieval tombstones and on sarcophagi. It was not until the early Renaissance that it acquired an additional function, symbolizing vanity. The vessel by the peacock is also more than a mere dish of water set out for the birds. Antonello's contemporaries would think of a baptismal font, the water that washes us free of sin, the water of paradise that confers life eternal.

The question is what all of this has to do with Jerome. In 1976 an American student came up with a plausible explanation. She gave her attention not only to the possible meanings of the symbols but also to the views through the windows: to the left, a town and people rowing, riding or walking, and to the right, trees and hills with not a building or human being to be seen. Antonello is contrasting town and country, the world of social pleasures with that of solitude.

That polarity is to be found throughout St Jerome's writings. He saw the city as a place of the devil, the "smoke-filled dungeon" where he had suffered from "the burden of the flesh". The wilderness, by contrast, he described as "the loveliest city of them all, a true paradise". Advocating the ascetic monastic life, Jerome declared: "The Holy Spirit does not care to dwell amongst crowds, confusions and conflicts. The dwelling place of the Holy Spirit is solitude." His demand was: "Hold human kind cheap, seek the angels, flee the cities to find Christ in the wilderness!"

Through the window to the left Antonello shows us the place of temptation as described by Jerome, through that to the right the dwelling place of the Holy Spirit. Positioned accordingly to the left are the thieving partridge, and above it a cat, perhaps not only as a catcher of mice but also as a symbol of sexual desire. Above the cat hangs a towel, an attribute often assigned to the Virgin as a symbol of purity, but in Jerome's case clearly stained. On the opposite side, below a window which reveals the wilderness to be gentle countryside, are the positive symbols: the king of the beasts in submission to Christianity, the bowl of baptismal water, and the peacock without the displayed span of tail-feathers which would have rendered him a symbol of vanity.

Thus if we consider the animals, the objects, and the views through the windows in a symbolic light, Antonello is in fact showing us far more than a scholar at study in his quiet cell – he is portraying a man in danger, a cardinal caught between the fronts, between good and evil, between God and the devil.

A cardinal poised between God and the devil

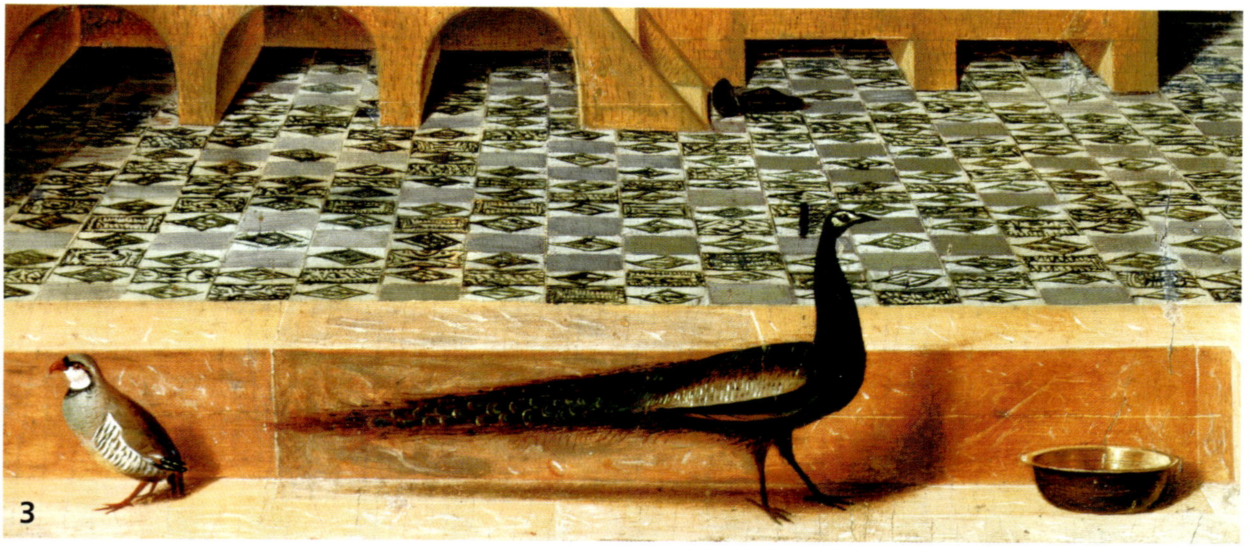

3

The patron saint of humanists

In the visual arts, the life of St Jerome is ordinarily reduced to three episodes: he is either a hermit in the wilderness, or a monk extracting the thorn, or a churchman at his studies with the lion at his feet. He is also often shown as bearded, to suggest venerable age.

In Antonello's version, there is no indication that Jerome is old. He is sitting upright and unsupported, and seems to be concentrating fully on the book. Antonello was famed for his male portraits, and this cardinal is so individualized that we inevitably wonder whom he may have portrayed. It was not considered sacrilegious to give Jerome the facial features of the living. Around the year 1525, Lucas Cranach the Elder painted Cardinal Albrecht of Brandenburg as Jerome. The profile Antonello painted bears a striking resemblance to that of Nicholas of Cusa, also called Cusanus.

Nicholas, indeed a cardinal, was a contemporary of the artist's. He was born in 1401 in a village on the river Moselle, was prince bishop of the diocese of Brixen and adviser to Pope Pius II, and died in 1464. Nicholas went down in church history as a thinker and as a diplomat, as the man who attempted to establish consensus and restore harmony between the Pope and the Council, between the Church and secular rulers. Pope Pius owed him much, and it is possible that in gratitude he commissioned a portrait of the cardinal as St Jerome from Antonello.

Antonello might have visited Rome and seen the cardinal there, or he might have worked from a medallion. But whether the cardinal is Nicholas of Cusa or some other altogether, why did the painter, or the source of his commission, choose Jerome of all the saints and church fathers? Probably because the saint was renowned for his work in a discipline which then enjoyed high esteem, that of translation. One might think of him as the patron saint of humanists: he had given the text of the Bible its Latin form, and humanists were engaged in locating, translating and penning commentaries on the writings of the Greeks and Romans. To locate and purchase an ancient manuscript or a medieval copy of one was counted a deed worthy of high fame, and the wealthy competed in building up libraries. Nicholas of Cusa too was an impassioned collector. He had numerous texts translated, and to this day portions of his library are preserved at the hospital of St Nicholas in the town of his birth, Bernkastel-Kues.

In 1475 Antonello travelled to Venice, where among other things he painted an altar and doubtless enjoyed a quite different order of recognition, in a city of artists and connoisseurs, from what would be his due back home in Sicily. The Duke of Milan wooed him as court painter, but in vain: in 1476 Antonello returned to Messina. He was now a man of some means; in his will he left his workshop to his son, made bequests to all the members of his family (including an illegitimate daughter), and gave an Ethiopian slave her liberty. He died in February 1479 and was buried in the habit of a monk, in accordance with his wishes.

Antonello was the only great artist to have spent his life in Messina. His coffin was lost in 1863 during flooding.

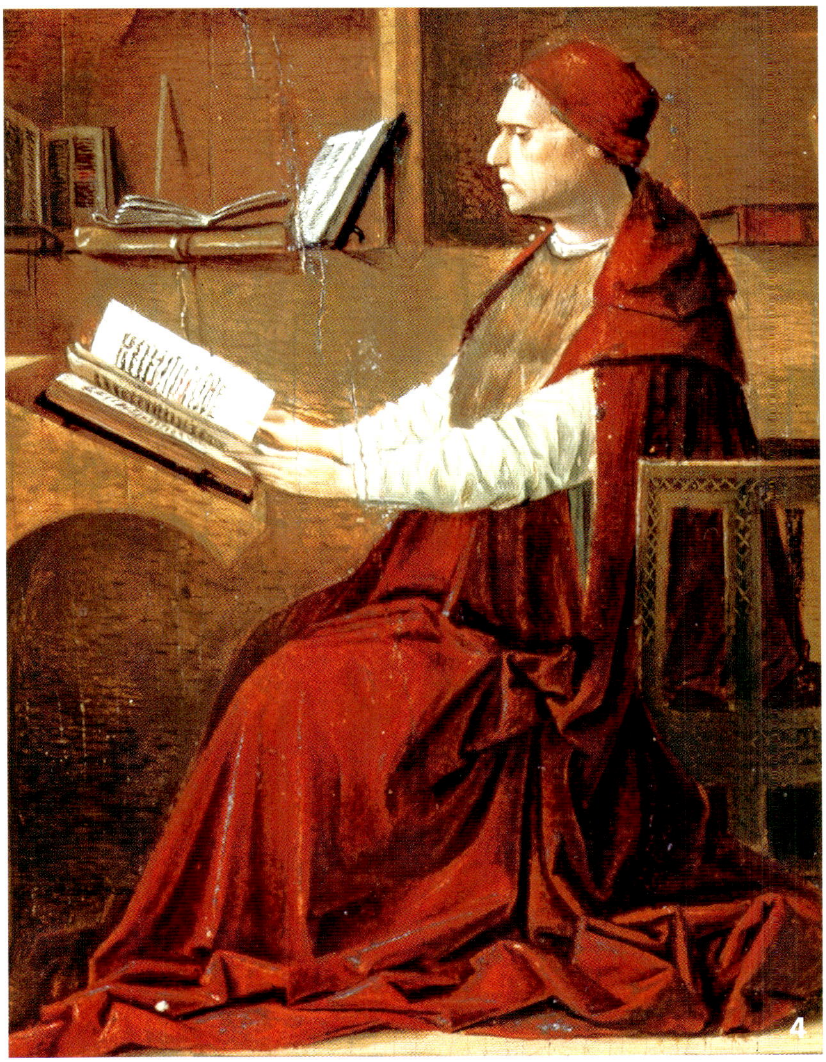

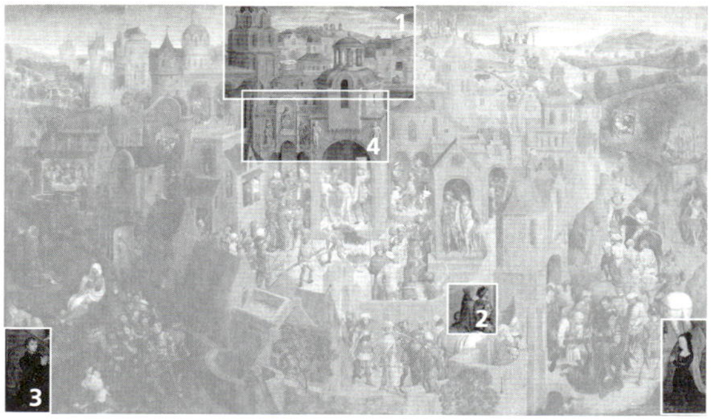
1
4
2
3

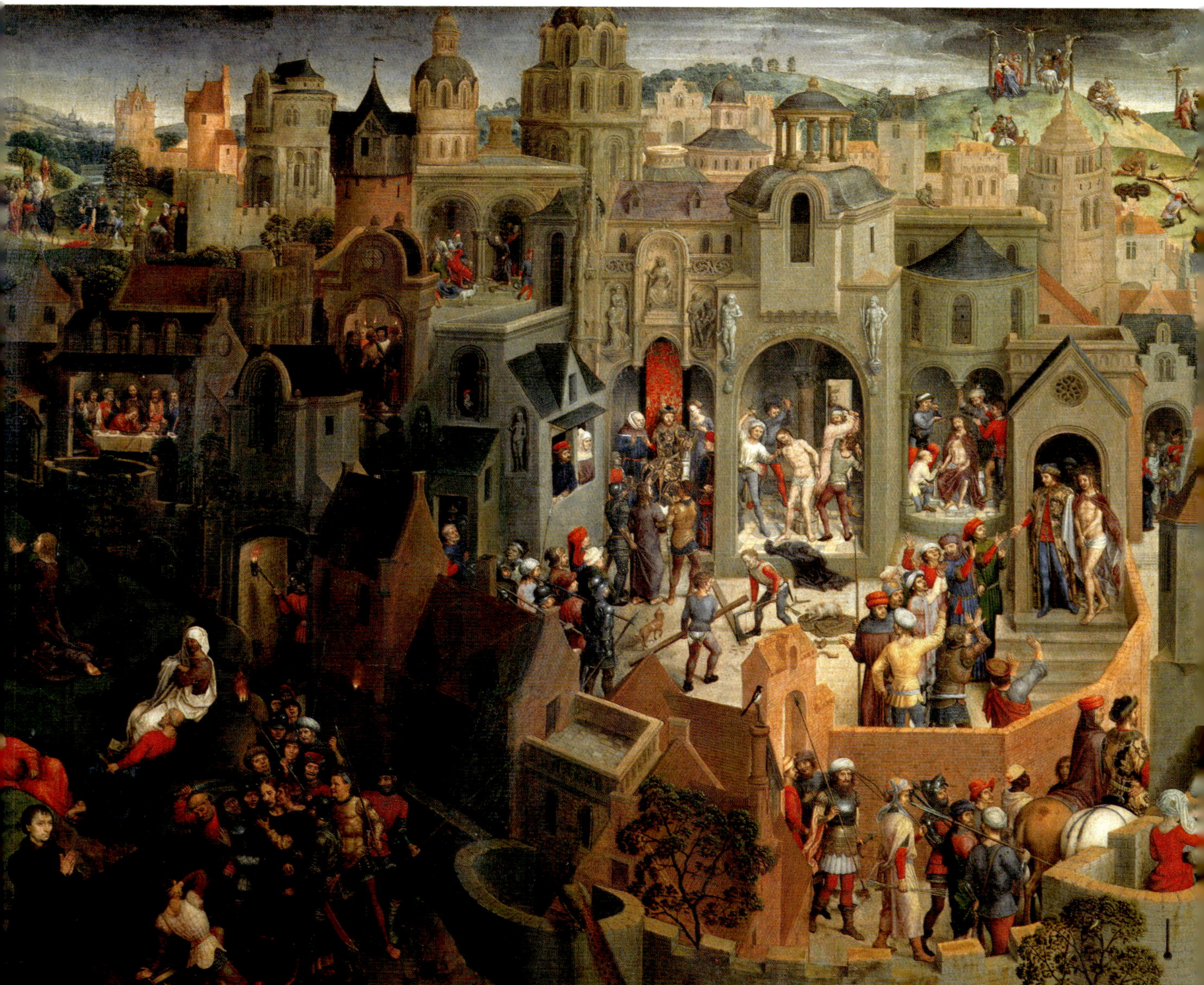

Hans Memling: The Passion, c. 1470/71

Looking back to the Middle Ages

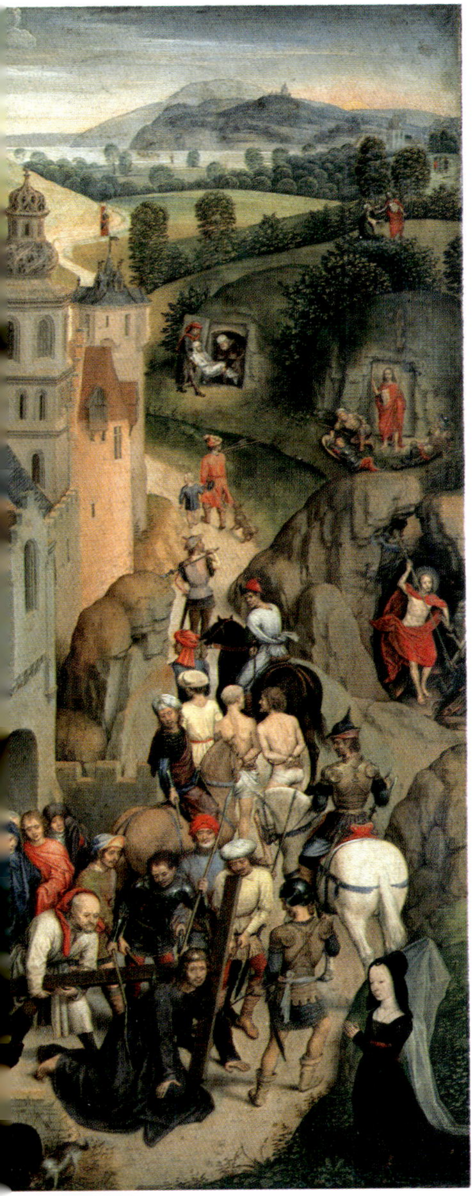

Memling painted *The Passion* around 1470/71, on the cusp of the Middle Ages and the modern era. The work does not look forward into the future, but rather recapitulates the medieval understanding of pictorial images: it exhibits neither a mathematically precise perspective nor any reservations about presenting simultaneously to the view events that did not happen simultaneously. The reality of space and time is not important. All that matters is to show the passion of Christ, station by station.

The panel measures 55 by 90 centimetres. Memling begins his account at the top left, where Jesus, hailed as the Messiah, enters Jerusalem and casts the traders and money-changers out of the temple. In the night portion of the painting he is seen taking the last supper with his disciples, and Judas is also seen betraying him to the high priests. After the supper Jesus prays in the garden of Gethsemane, the multitude come and Judas identifies Jesus by kissing him. Peter attempts to defend his master with his sword. Later, when the soldiers recognize Peter, he denies having been one of the disciples, and the cock above him recalls Jesus' prophecy: "this night, before the cock crow, thou shalt deny me thrice".

Memling shows the main square of Jerusalem brightly lit: Jesus is accused by the high priests before Pontius Pilate, the Roman governor; Pilate proposes to release him, but the people protest. On the way to the place of execution, Jesus falls at the city gate and turns his face to us.

At the upper and right margins of the painting we see the crucifixion, deposition, burial, descent into hell, and resurrection. At the top right, very small, Memling includes several appearances of the resurrected Christ. In all, the picture presents more than twenty episodes, which in Memling's times were familiar to all, including those who could not read or write.

For medieval mankind, the earth was a flat disc surrounded by water. Below it was hell, and above, beyond the visible sky, was the realm of God. At the centre of the disc was Jerusalem, the place where the son of God had died and had ascended to his father. A number of world maps have survived on which the seas and continents then known were grouped around Jerusalem in the middle; they document a Christian understanding of geography.

Memling was active in the Flemish city of Bruges, and people both there and throughout the rest of Europe knew full well which roads and shipping routes led to the real Jerusalem. After all, it was almost 400 years since French, German and Italian knights had embarked on the first of the crusades, with the aim of liberating the centre of their world from infidel rule. The crusades had failed; since 1244, Jerusalem had been firmly in the hands of Islam, though Moslem rulers did permit pilgrims who came in peace to visit the city.

In the 15th century, according to cautious estimates, some thousand pilgrims a year ventured on the journey to the Holy Land, taking ship in Marseilles or Venice, usually in the hope that this expensive undertaking, with its many privations, would purge them of sin. Jerusalem and Santiago de Compostela were considered the most important of all places of pilgrimage, and guaranteed visiting believers the most comprehensive indulgence to erase their sins.

Anyone in Europe who wanted could obtain information about present-day Jerusalem. There were accounts that included advice on the routes to take, and there were woodcuts showing famous buildings. Memling evidently took no interest in this. His Jerusalem is a collection of imaginary buildings, the roofs and towers looking more European than Middle Eastern. An interest in realistic views of cities was just developing at the time, and they began to appear in the backgrounds of paintings, simplified to the prominent churches and towers.

Memling's buildings are so close together, the roofs seem so full of movement, the city is so clearly delimited by its walls, that it is like an organism. At that time it was widely held that a city was not merely a grouping of buildings enclosed within walls, but a living creature, comparable to a protective woman.

All of the buildings, albeit not large or splendid, are solidly stone-built. There are no cottages built up against the walls, no half-timber houses posing a fire risk, no derelict or half-finished buildings, nor any of the dirt usually found in streets. What Memling is painting is an ideal city.

It may be that his intention was to locate the last days of Jesus' life in a pure, transfigured and appropriate setting. But it is also possible that, in painting this city, Memling was thinking of another Jerusalem, the new Jerusalem of Revelation 21, which according to John the Divine will come down from God at the end of time: "And the building of the wall of it was of jasper: and the city was pure gold ... and the street of the city was pure gold, as it were transparent glass."

It is true that the city Memling painted is not golden, nor did he otherwise follow John's detailed description in Revelation, but his Jerusalem nonetheless matches conceptions of a city placed like a great jewel, by the hand of a higher power, in its landscape setting.

Jerusalem, the ideal city

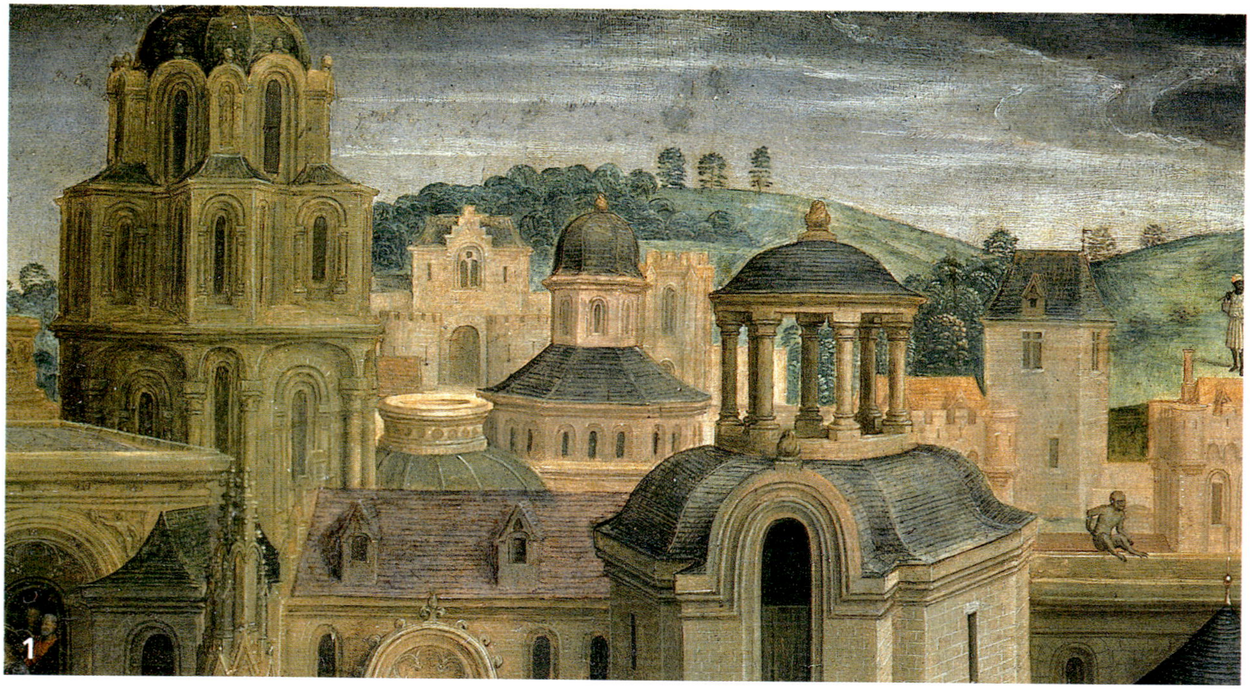

The cities of Europe were studded around the continent's affluent regions, and in the 15th century that meant the most cities were in northern Italy and in Flanders. The foremost city in Flanders was Bruges, where Hans Memling worked. It was linked to the port of Sluys by canal, and was favourably situated on the trade routes of the age, from Spain to Novgorod. From the north came grain, wood and furs, from the south lemons, figs and oranges, and via the Mediterranean silk, carpets and spices. Bruges was "the most famous city in the world, for the goods traded there and the merchants who live there," wrote Philip the Good (1396–1467), Duke of Burgundy and lord of the realm to which Flanders, and Bruges, belonged.

The people of Bruges earned their prosperity not only by trade but also by making textiles of high quality. A third of the population made a living in this sector, spinning, dyeing, weaving and tailoring. Guilds controlled the numbers of masters and journeymen and ensured that the same purchase conditions for raw materials applied to every textile venture. Protective measures of this kind safeguarded individual workshops in relation to each other, and the contracts agreed with the Duke prohibited competition in the near vicinity: weaving and spinning were forbidden within a precisely defined radius of the city, and the municipal militia destroyed the looms of offenders.

The cloak of the rider on the right suggests the widespread taste for fine fabrics at the time. This is Pontius Pilate, the Roman governor, whom Memling depicts in a number of scenes. He alone, of the Biblical personae, has fur trims on his cap and collar, which under the rules that governed apparel in the 15th century was reserved for men of especially high rank.

The man beside him in the cape-like garment and the round red cap may be a Pharisee. At all events, men clad similarly are among those shouting "Crucify him!" when Pilate proposes to release Jesus. They are gesticulating wildly, arms upraised; under the unbending courtly code of the house of Burgundy, which set the standard for the upper classes in Flanders too, gestures such as these were a sign of uncouthness and undignified behaviour.

Bruges owed its wealth not only to its well-organized artisan sector and its advantageous location near the coast. It was also the city in which the Dukes of Burgundy resided. Their realm extended from the North Sea to Switzerland, and they were the wealthiest rulers in Europe. The city of Bruges benefited from this. In 1468, two years before Memling painted his *Passion*, the new Duke Charles the Bold made his ceremonial entry into Bruges, confirmed the privileges of the city, and held tournaments and festivities. Three months later there was a further occasion for revels when his bride entered the city; it was indeed a year of rejoicing and celebration.

But the festivities had to be paid for, and the price tag carried by the new Duke's soldiers was even higher for the cities and taxpayers of Burgundy. The Duke was not one to be squeamish when it came to filling the coffers. He went to war in an attempt to regulate the boundaries of his patchwork realm, and in 1477 fell in battle at Nancy. The Burgundian empire fell apart.

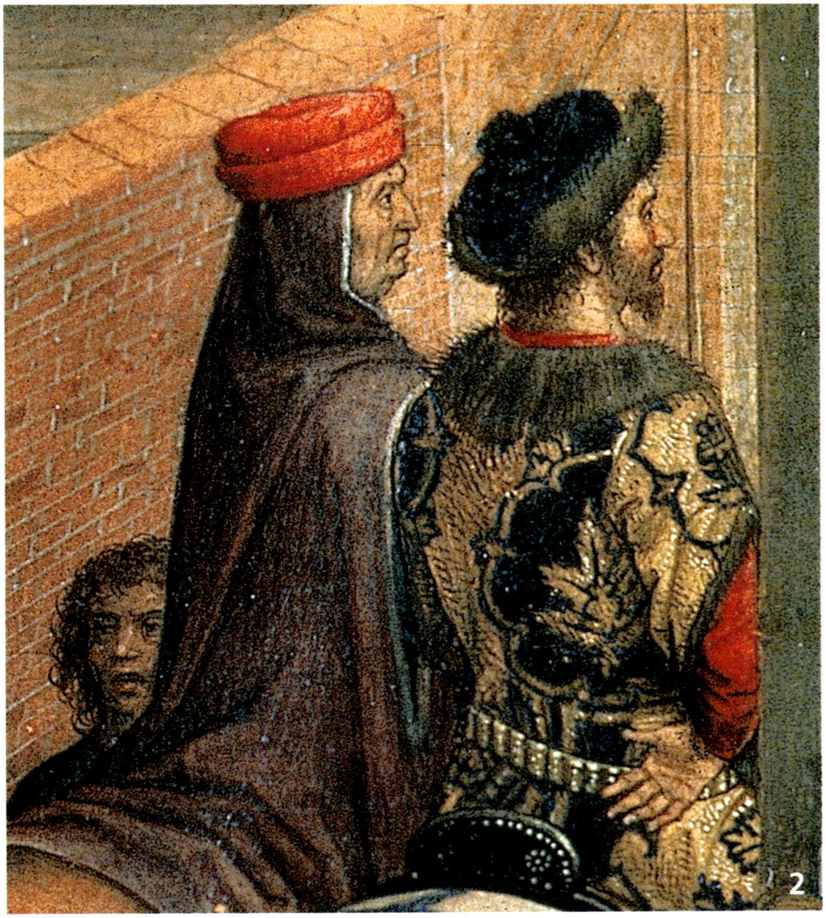
2

The fine cloth of Bruges

The death of Charles also marked the end of the greatest period in the history of Bruges, not because the splendours of the ducal residence were a thing of the past, but more seriously because the guilds had ossified and were cripplingly procrastinatory when it came to introducing new capitalist forms of production. Moreover, the port and canal silted up. Before long the merchants had deserted the city. The artists followed. The new metropolitan centre of trade and the arts was to be Antwerp.

Tommaso Portinari's art and debts

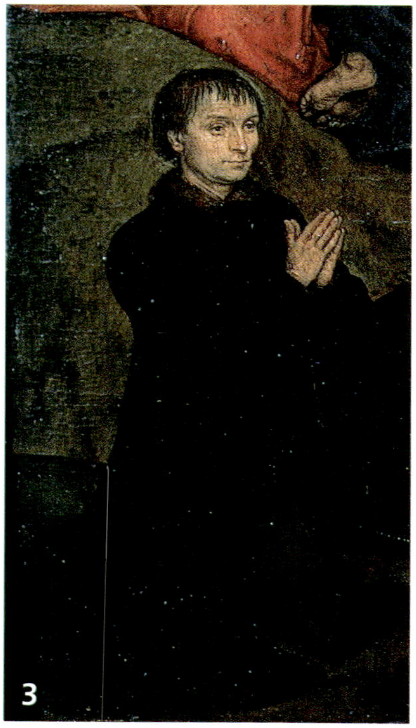

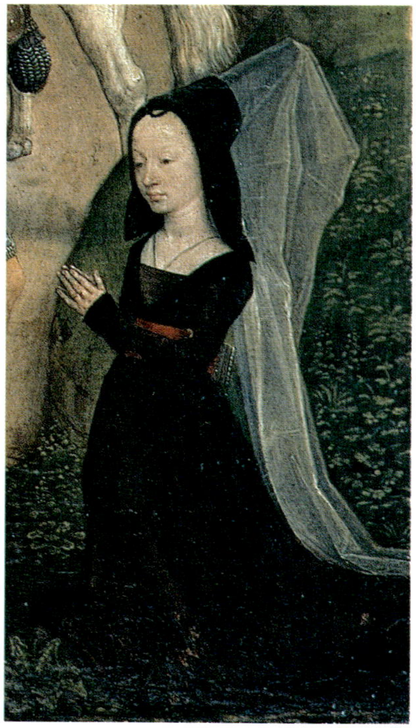

Bruges was also of unusual importance as a city of finance. Italy had developed the techniques of banking, such as bills of exchange, notes of credit, or double-entry book-keeping, and Italian banking houses had branches in every major trading city. In Bruges, the banks' representatives met with the city's merchants at the home of one van der Burse, and it was his name that came to stand for the most important of capitalist institutions, the *bourse* or stock-exchange.

The resident representative of the powerful Medici bank was Tommaso Portinari, and he had himself and his wife, as the donors, portrayed in the lower left and right corners of the painting. They married in 1470, when Tommaso was forty-two and his wife fourteen or fifteen, and their marriage was probably the occasion for commissioning this painting. Both were of respected Florentine family. Memling painted the banker with a fur trim on his collar and the young Florentine woman dressed in Burgundian fashion, wearing a tall pointed hat with a long veil, and with her hairline shaved back because a high forehead was counted a sign of particular beauty.

The records of the Medici bank have survived, so we can trace Portinari's career quite closely. He entered the service of the bank at the age of seventeen. His father was the managing director at head office, and two brothers were the managers of the Milan branch in succession. In 1465 he became manager of the Bruges branch, and, buying a fourteen percent share of the business capital, was entitled to a quarter of the profits.

Following the death of Piero de' Medici in 1469, Lorenzo (later known as "the Magnificent"), then aged just twenty-one, took over the bank. Lorenzo was more interested in politics and in ostentatious splendour than in the ramified Medici business empire; he gave Portinari in Bruges a free hand, and no longer placed limits on the credit granted the Duke of Burgundy, as his father Piero had done.

This proved Portinari's undoing. Evidently he was an ambitious man, and, like his new boss, prone to ostentation. He aspired to be respected at the court of Burgundy, and acted as adviser to Duke Charles, loaning him substantial sums. For purposes of show and status, he bought a house in Bruges of a magnificence that outdid all the rest.

But the losses incurred by the Medici bank when Charles the Bold died in 1477 were enormous. Portinari's other speculative ventures misfired too: a Portuguese voyage of exploration to Guinea failed, and long-term supply contracts for wool yielded losses. Lorenzo severed his connection with Portinari, obliging him to run the Bruges bank single-handed, with few assets but immense liabilities. The unfortunate financier spent the following decades, now in Bruges and now in Florence, collecting debts and evading his creditors. When he died in 1501, his son refused the inheritance, consisting as it did chiefly of debts.

The Portinaris have gone down in honourable memory through a number of paintings which they commissioned, presumably all between 1470, the year they married, and 1477, the year they were ruined. Two portraits of the couple painted by Memling are now in the Metropolitan Museum of Art in New York; the Portinari altar by Hugo van der Goes is in the Uffizi in Florence.

Memling's *Passion* was likewise removed to Florence and given to the hospital of Santa Maria Nuova. The hospital had been founded by a forefather of Tommaso Portinari the banker, and every generation of the family made further gifts of money and art to it. The van der Goes altar, too, was originally there. From the hospital, or the church of San Egidio which was attached to it, the Memling passed into the keeping of Duke Cosimo I de Medici, who gave it to Pope Pius V, who in turn gave it to a Dominican monastery he had founded at Bosco near Alessandria.

When Napoleon's forces were in Italy in 1796, dissolving and looting monasteries, a monk concealed the painting, and in 1814, when French rule was at an end, retrieved it. The monastery gave the work to King Victor Emmanuel I of Sardinia, who gave it to the Galleria Sabauda in Turin, which has been a public art collection since 1832. There this Flemish *Passion* has hung ever since, and recently it was superbly restored.

How little Memling was concerned to show a realistic Jerusalem is indicated by his painted sculptures too. At the time of Christ and in Memling's day, both under Jewish and under Moslem hegemony, the portrayal of the human image was prohibited in Jerusalem. In Bruges, open as it was to all the world, these religious bans would surely have been familiar.

In Flanders, on the other hand, it was customary to place sculptures, generally madonnas, on churches and public buildings, as one can see to this day in the marketplace in Bruges. Memling's painting depicts what was customary in his own part of the world: the buildings on the square, the administrative precincts, bear sculptures, and these are discreetly related to the events.

Where Jesus is accused before Pilate, Memling represents the judgement of Solomon. Two women were disputing over a child, and Solomon ordered the child to be divided in half, whereupon one of the women resigned her claim, showing herself to be the true mother. Both Pilate and Solomon were seekers after the truth.

Above the doorway where Peter denies Christ are Adam and Eve covering themselves, after they have eaten the apple, lost their innocence, and, in the Christian world view, brought down original sin upon humankind. This is a comment upon the weak disciple, Peter, who has now incurred his own guilt. The bearded naked men above the scourging scene are probably Cain and Lamech. Cain is carrying the bone pick with which he slew Abel; Lamech, according to a non-Biblical tradition, killed Cain with an arrow shot from his bow. At the time, Lamech was already old and blind but nonetheless liked to go hunting. One of his sons indicated where he thought their prey was. In earthly terms, the killing was an accident, but on a higher plane the message the painter is endorsing here is clear: those who do violence unto others shall die a violent death.

It is striking that Memling depicts Cain and Lamech naked and indeed with physical grace: both are resting their body weight on the left leg while the right is idly angled. Here the painter is depicting two well-formed male bodies as understood by classical Greek sculpture, which had just been rediscovered in Florence, the centre of the early Renaissance. They are out of place in a medieval painting; might the donor, being from Florence, have expressed a wish? Or was the artist delicately indicating that he was familiar with the new aesthetic movement, even if he did not follow it?

Whatever the answer, these nude bearded men are absorbed into the harmonious fabric of the painting. The forms and colours contribute to a sense that in Memling's Jerusalem all things are taking their foreordained course, and indeed in the rest of the world too.

It is this trust in God and the world that distinguishes Memling from many of his contemporaries. There is no new-fangled mathematical grasp of space, no arresting clarity in the rendering of natural detail, no fear of lurking demons as in the work of Hieronymus Bosch, some ten years younger. Memling must have held a profound conviction that all things were in the hand of God, and that conviction is here expressed, in powerful colours, as the higher security afforded by this vision of Jerusalem.

Renaissance sculptures in Christ's Jerusalem

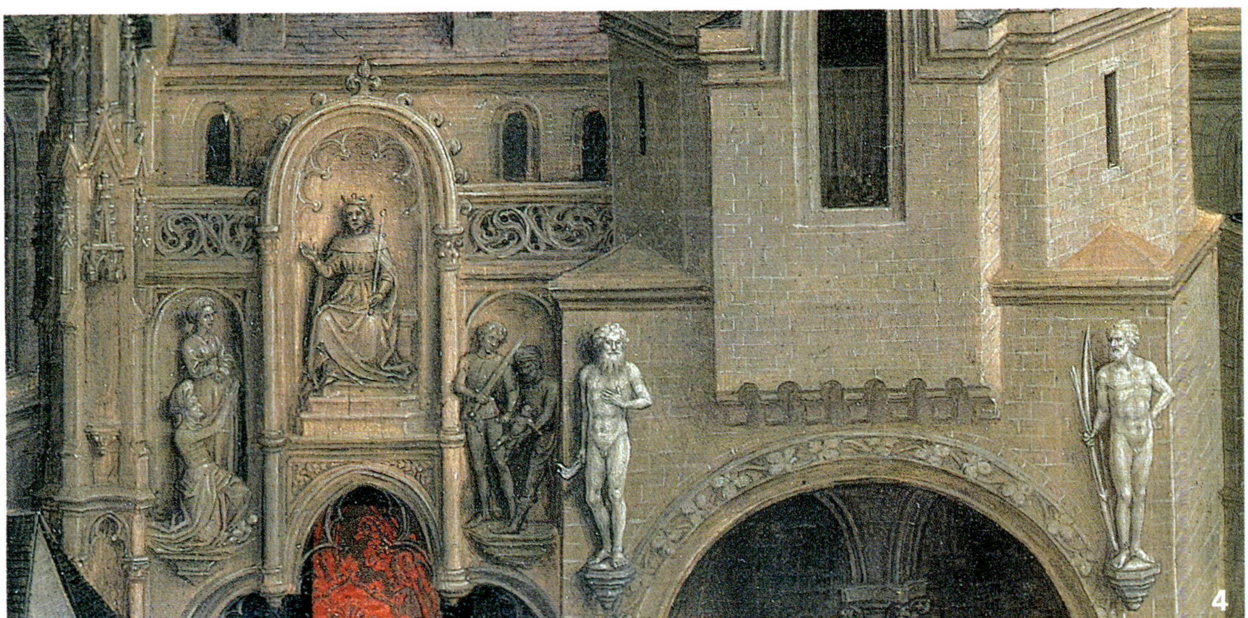

4

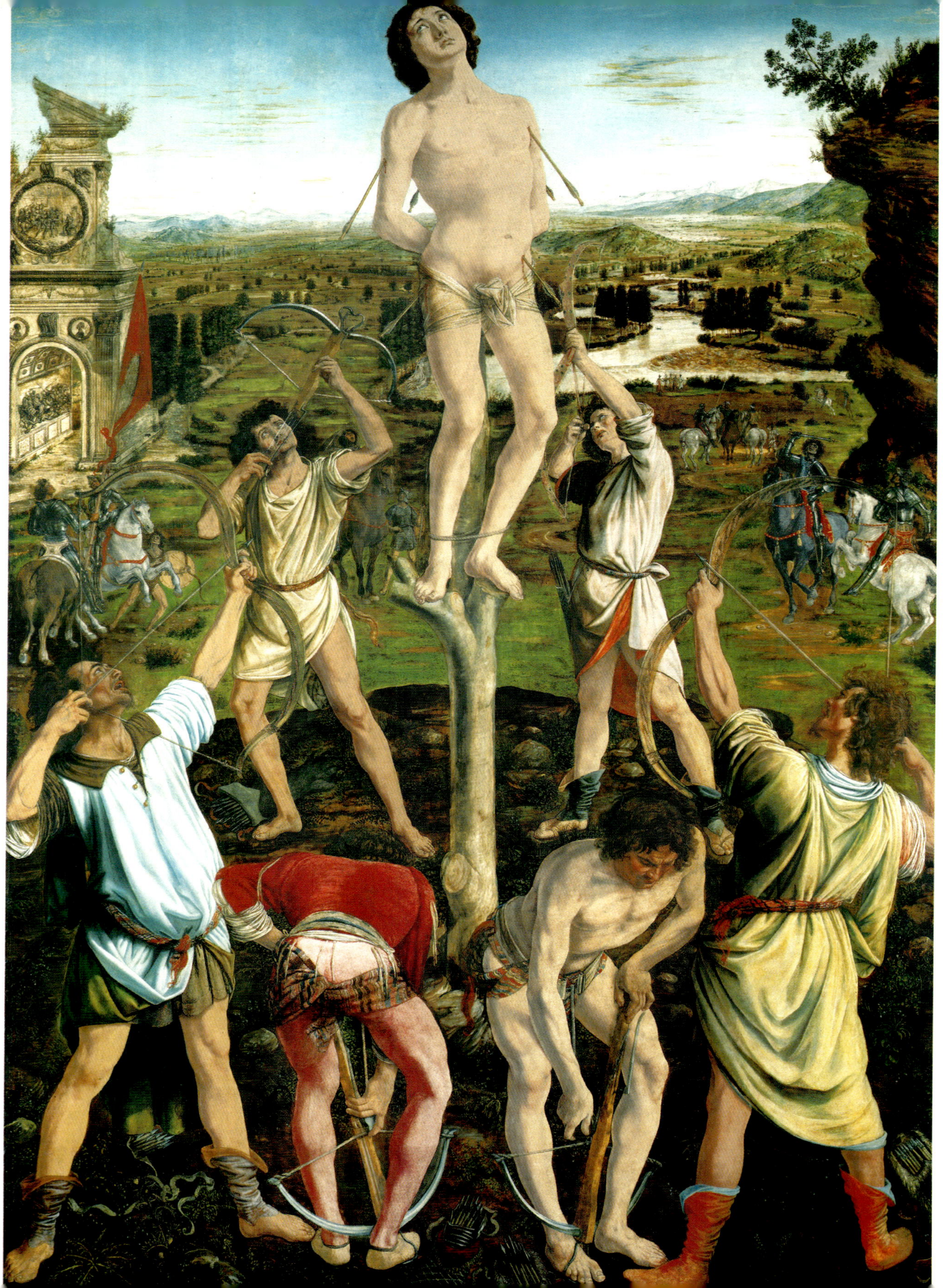

Antonio and Piero del Pollaiuolo: The Martyrdom of St Sebastian, 1475

A grim male ballet

A young man, almost naked, tied to a dead tree. He is standing right at the top of the painting, his head up in the hazy blue of the sky and touching the upper edge of the picture. He makes a passive impression, transported into some other realm, exalted above the things happening beneath him. Below, all is activity, a kind of male ballet in which the painter displays strong, muscular men. Four of them are holding longbows or crossbows, aiming at the young man's body and perhaps awaiting an order to fire from the armour-clad horseman in the background. The archers furthest to the fore are touching the lower edge of the picture. Their feet mark the base of a compositional pyramid, the tip of which is the young martyr's head. The whole of the composition, top to bottom, is governed by this pyramid structure of moving bodies. It is an unusual and somewhat disconcerting composition.

The story goes that this defenceless victim, St Sebastian, lived in the 3rd century AD. He was an officer in the army of the Roman emperors Diocletian and Maximian. Sebastian enjoyed their high esteem and was entrusted with the first cohort, according to the 13th-century hagiologist Jacobus de Voragine in his *Golden Legend*. But Sebastian was a Christian, lending assistance to his persecuted fellow believers and destroying more than two hundred images of pagan deities. Thereupon "Diocletian commanded that he be bound to a stake in the middle of a field, and soldiers shoot arrows at him". It was done as the emperor ordered, till Sebastian "resembled a hedgehog". Despite his wounds, however, he remained in good cheer, seeing in martyrdom a certain road to eternal salvation. Our painter reflects the twofold view of the world held by Sebastian: life on earth "enjoins sin, commands misdeeds, and urges injustice". Martyrs go straight to heaven, where they prepare for all the faithful "a dwelling place amongst the stars".

It was with this certainty of faith that Sebastian braved the piercing arrows, till the soldiery left the field, believing him dead. "But within a few days", the legend runs, "there he stood, hail and hearty, on the steps of the emperor's palace!" Sebastian had survived the first part of his martyrdom. The circumstance that it had not resulted in his death tended to be forgotten in succeeding centuries, along with the sequel of the story, since what happened to Sebastian next was much less spectacular and exalted: "The emperor had him clubbed till he gave up the ghost", Jacobus de Voragine tells us. "And he had his body cast into the sewers, that the Christians might not venerate him as a martyr."

Needless to say, the remains of Sebastian were nonetheless retrieved after this ignoble end, given fit burial, and venerated. In the year 680, according to a chronicle written at the court of Charlemagne, the remains were transferred to the Church of San Pietro in Vincoli in Rome, reputedly on direct orders from heaven. The saint's altar can still be seen there. This transfer was not without consequences: an outbreak of the plague came to an end, and for centuries Sebastian was the saint whose intercession was prayed for in times of plague.

When it came to depicting Sebastian, artists almost invariably chose to paint him pierced with arrows. In the latter half of the 15th century, the scene was one of the most popular subjects in Italian art. Around 1470, Andrea Mantegna painted the young officer as an athlete of antiquity, powerful and masculine; more often he was depicted as a soft, almost feminine ephebe, as Sandro Botticelli painted him in 1474 and as the brothers Pollaiuolo painted him the following year. Invariably, though, the saint seems unharmed despite

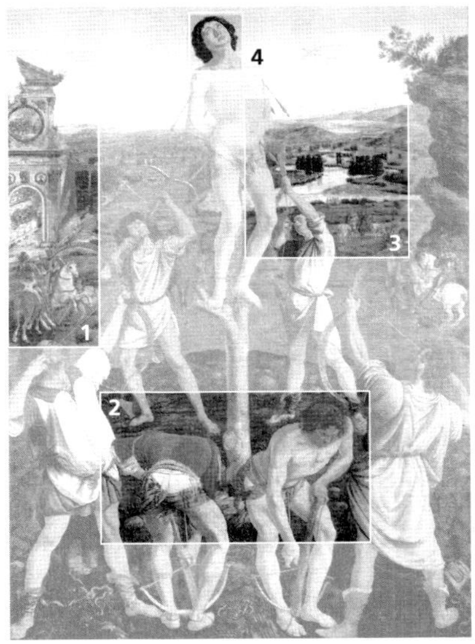

the arrows, possessed of a noble beauty: he is a hero, bound for the stars. Sebastian was the perfect saint for an optimistic era that was embarking on a new age and took particular pleasure in beautiful bodies – the early period of the Italian Renaissance.

Pollaiuolo's Sebastian was done to a commission, according to the painter and artists' biographer Giorgio Vasari (1511–74). Antonio Pucci, a Florentine banker, ordered it for the family chapel (consecrated to the saint) in the Servite Church of Santissima Annunziata. It was "an excellent, choice work", wrote Vasari. "Antonio Pucci recognised as much and gave him 300 scudi, avowing that the sum barely paid for the paint." The satisfied client was at that time one of the most influential citizens of Florence.

The rise of the Pucci family had accompanied that of the Medici, and they had supported the great dynasty's policies. It was no coincidence that placed Pucci's striking bald head right beside that of Lorenzo Il Magnifico in a fresco by Domenico Ghirlandaio. Like the Medici, he became a patron of the arts, and (for example) commissioned a number of panel paintings from Botticelli. For the rulers, art was a tool of propaganda, among other things: the Medici built palaces, churches, and libraries, collected Greek manuscripts, welcomed in the humanists who poured in to Italy after Constantinople fell to the Turks in 1453, and were thus a driving motor of the Renaissance.

This dynamic development had its roots in the economic rise of the city, its flourishing textiles industry, and its pan-European banking ventures in the first half of the 15th century. The guilds of Florence were commissioning work intended to beautify the city, and the artists were taking their bearings from antiquity, now rediscovered. When Antonio Pollaiuolo was born, in 1432, the dome of Florence cathedral, the symbol of the new architecture, was nearing completion. The goldsmith and sculptor Lorenzo Ghiberti (1378–1455) was at work on the famous bronze doors of the Baptistery. The young Antonio Pollaiuolo (whose sobriquet derived from his father's farming chickens, *pollo* in Italian) is said to have been apprenticed to Ghiberti.

In homage to antiquity, our painter has placed at the left of his picture a ruined Roman triumphal archway with a shattered pediment. Four reliefs can be made out on it: two medallions bearing Roman busts, a battle scene, and a court scene in which prisoners are being led before their judge. Beyond the triumphal arch, Pollaiuolo shows us the countryside from which he himself came, the valley of the Arno, with the river winding amongst hills and cypresses, presumably towards Florence somewhere in the background. Antonio Pollaiuolo led a happy life, Vasari tells us, "for the artist found favour in his home city, which was then at the peak of its fortunes".

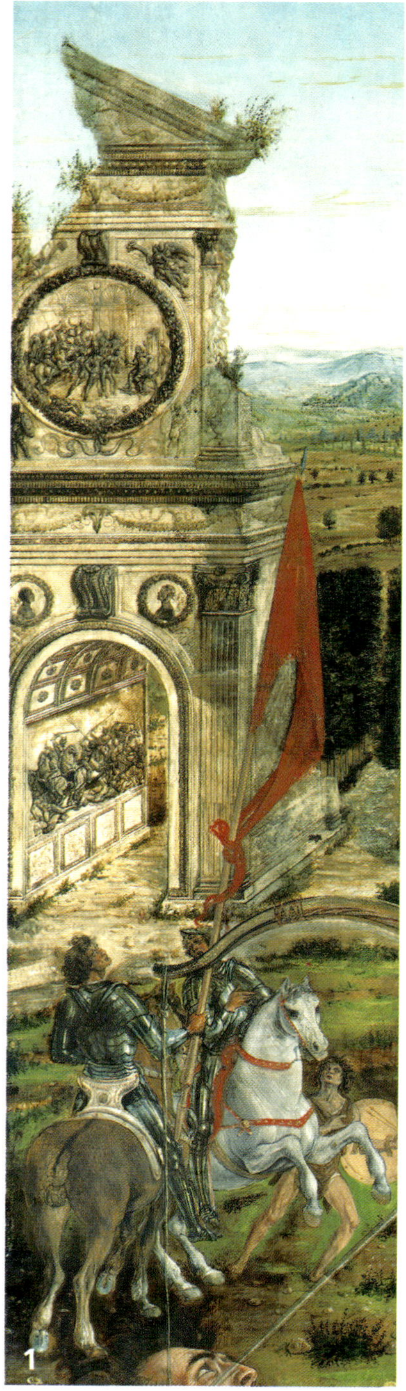
1

Homage to antiquity

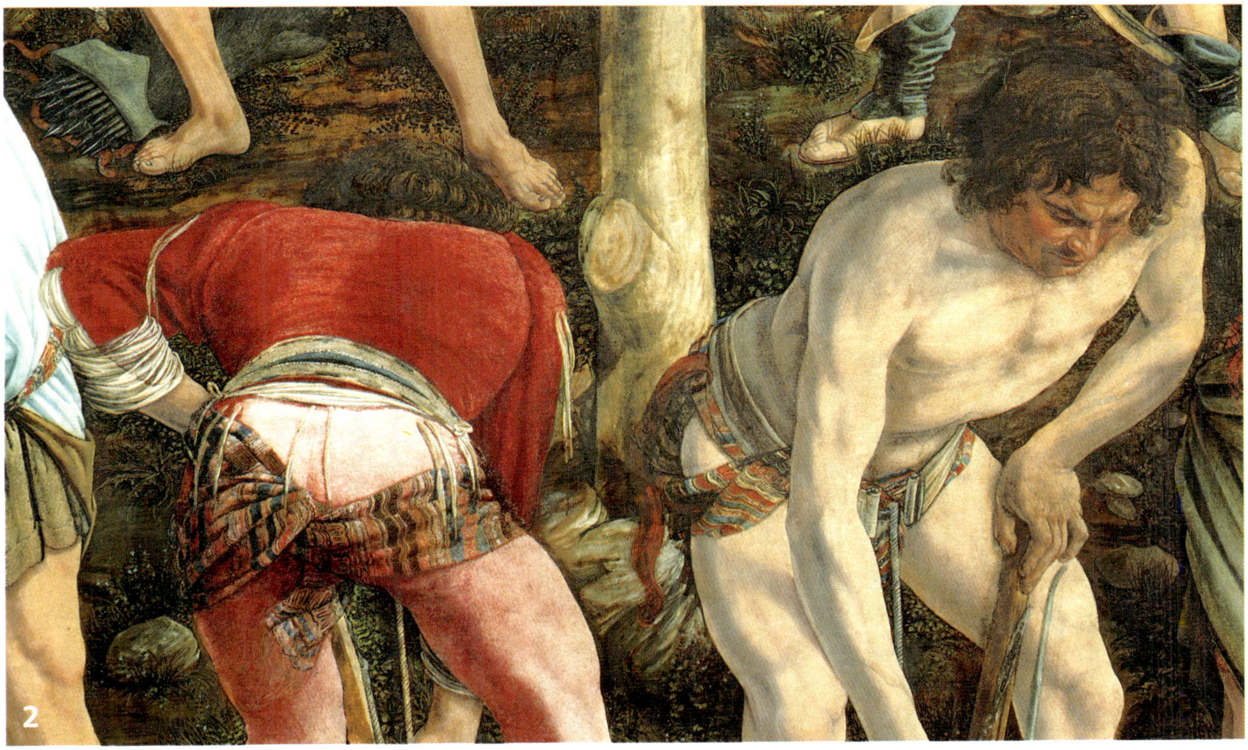

Of the archer at the lower right, Vasari wrote: "One sees his veins swelling, his muscles tensing, and the man himself holding his breath to enhance his strength." The painter "imitated nature as faithfully as he possibly could". Vasari declared that this painting of the martyrdom of St Sebastian was "the most celebrated of all the works Antonio ever accomplished".

We can account for this high praise in terms of two important goals that Renaissance artists set themselves. They aimed to rediscover the human body, which had been the dominant subject of art in antiquity; and they aimed to make visible the spatial nature of the places in which the body was moving. They began by liberating their figures from clothing notable for its many folds and for its sense of shame; artists such as Antonio Pollaiuolo used living models to study human anatomy, the play of the muscles and sinews, or the rush of blood to the head after physical exertion. Once the human form had been precisely studied and grasped, the object was to extrapolate an ideal of physical beauty. Pollaiuolo illustrates his skills as a realist in the two near-naked men at the feet of the saint, while in the figure of Sebastian himself, who even has one foot angled in the manner of antiquity, he exemplifies his ideal of the male body.

The Florentine sculptor Donatello had preceded Pollaiuolo in this quest for physical perfection. His sculptures served purposes less of a devotional than of an aesthetic nature. The famous bronze David, dating from around 1442, was not conceived for the usual niche in a church wall; it was placed in all its nakedness and independence in the garden of the Medici palace, where one might walk around it and admire the sculpture from every angle. Donatello's figure already possessed what the painters had yet to achieve: a sense of three-dimensionality. Pollaiuolo, who liked to experiment, had also worked as a sculptor, making a number of statues of Hercules, and was one of the first to tackle the problem.

Vasari referred to his "new manner". One particular feature of this manner involved showing the same person from various angles, thus establishing a new spatial and bodily sense. In the present painting, Pollaiuolo puts a number of models through their paces. The man with the crossbow in the foreground is seen twice, once from the front and once (revolved by 180 degrees) from the rear, once nearly naked and once clothed. The archers aiming at the saint are positioned around the vertical axis of the bare tree, each turned at an angle of 90 degrees to the next. Artists of the High Renaissance, such as Michelangelo and Raphael, reaped the fruits of such artistic exploration.

A new manner of portraying bodies spatially

Antonio Pollaiuolo, like many of his fellow artists, had learned the goldsmith's craft. Around 1460, with his younger brother Piero, he founded a workshop for the design and manufacture of candelabra, crucifixes, and armour. Piero experimented in the use of oil paint, following the Dutch example; in the present painting, the landscape behind St Sebastian with its gradations of colour tonalities and its transparency of atmosphere, could not have been painted in the traditional tempera. But Sebastian himself was the product of Antonio's mind. It was he who was the head of the workshop.

The six bowmen and the saint are arranged in the shape of a pyramid, and the arrows and outstretched arms guide our gaze upward, but also to the background. "What a charming thing perspective is!" another great experimenter, Paolo Uccello (c. 1397–1475), is said to have exclaimed. In order to convey spatial depth in rooms or on squares, Renaissance artists would draw in perspective lines meeting at a notional vanishing point in the distance. In the present painting, that vanishing point would be on the horizon behind St Sebastian's body. But the arrows, of course, are aimed not into the distance but at the body in the foreground, a bewildering ambiguity and a token of highly inventive artistry.

Sebastian was the patron saint of bowmen, and yet, notwithstanding the fact that their actions and weapons occupy two-thirds of the picture, it was not painted for any archers' clubhouse. The members of such clubs were of a humble walk of life, and if they commissioned works, they were simple and affordable ones. The popularity of Sebastian as a subject did not soar until the Church and private patrons began consecrating altars and chapels to the saint. This occurred when the plague swept Europe in the 14th century, bringing death to a third of the continent's population. Florence was not spared; as the writer Boccaccio observed around 1350 in his book of tales, the *Decameron*, "brother was taken from brother, sister from brother, and often man from wife".

Generally death resulted within three days of contracting the plague. The causes of the disease were unknown, and there were no effective medicines. All the more reason to place hope in divine intercession. People prayed to the saints, and especially to Sebastian. Just as he had survived the arrows, so too he would ward off the deadly darts of the plague. Classical mythology influenced this notion: in Homer's *Iliad*, a god had inflicted disease on the Greeks by means of poisoned arrows. In paintings of Sebastian, the arrows are usually shown piercing those parts of the body where plague spots first became visible in the infected – the loins and armpits. If these spots were cut open, the resulting wound was apparently much like that left by an arrow.

Pollaiuolo and the other Italian Renaissance artists who tackled the subject in the 15th century give us little real sense of this. Very little blood flows; there are no spots or black marks to sully the immaculate body of the saint as he undergoes his martyrdom against a serene landscape backdrop.

Pollaiuolo located the scene in his own native parts, on a hill near Florence, overlooking the valley of the bright River Arno. The setting might be the country estate of the Pucci family, or it might be the location to which affluent society flee from the plague in the first tale of the *Decameron*. "The house was on a low hill, situated on every side at some fair distance from our country roads, and with a variety of green trees and plants around it." So Boccaccio describes the refuge where his characters, young men and women, rejoice at still being alive. They mean to enjoy stories, music, and dancing together, and forget disease and death. And even the narrator declares his intention, "where there is so much suffering", to pass over in silence "what may properly be passed over". The visual artists of the 15th century took the same approach.

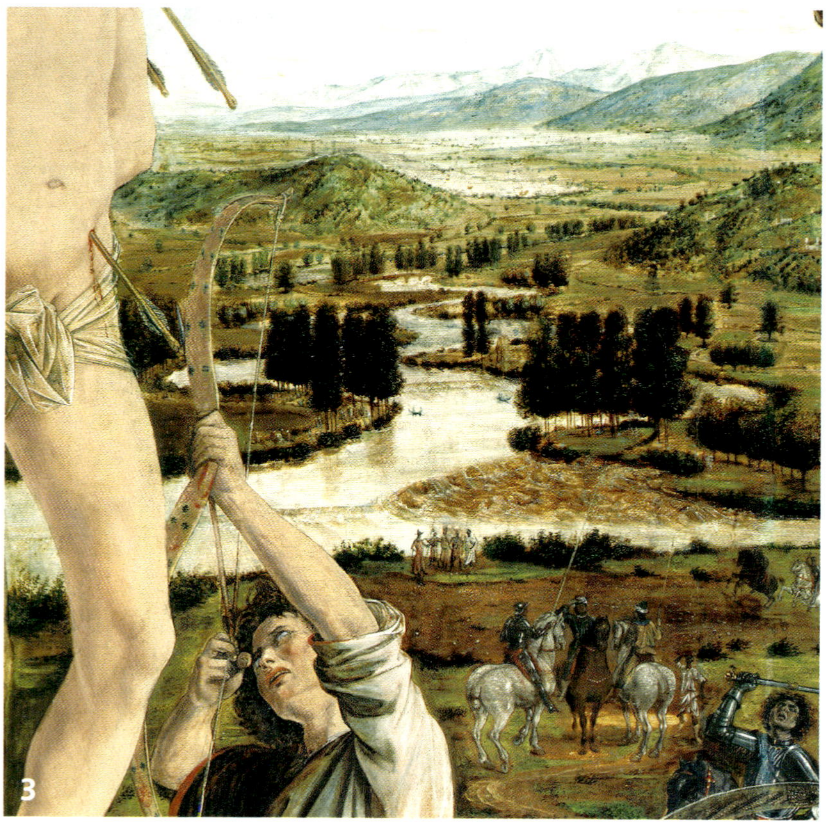

Idyllic countryside near Florence

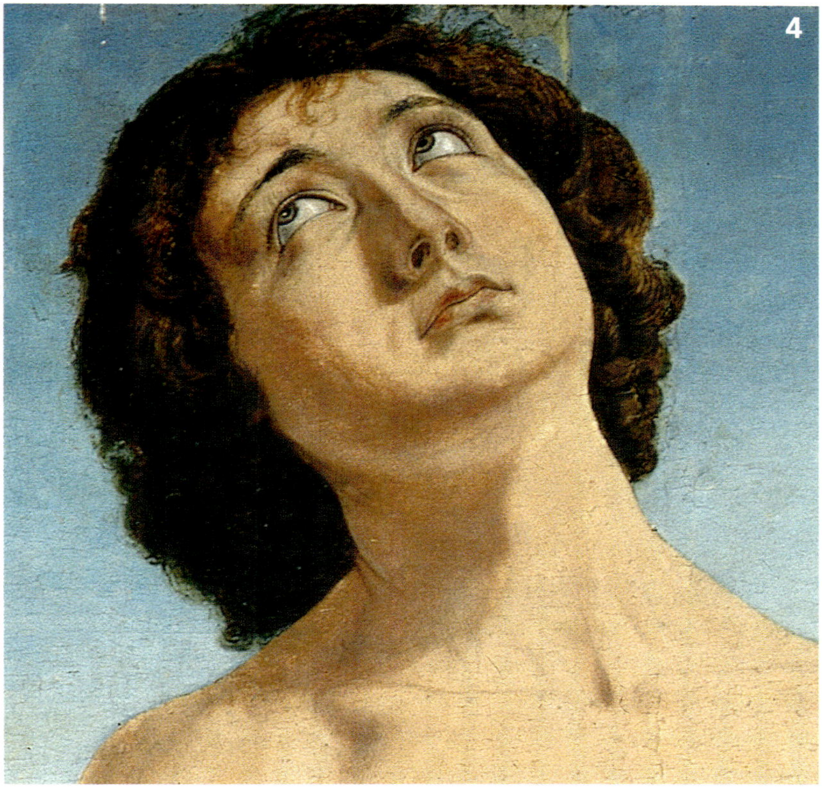

The Christian Apollo

In the 15th century, outbreaks of plague became less frequent, and the services of the patron saint, Sebastian, were no longer required so often. Nevertheless, the number of church and chapel commissions for paintings of Sebastian, symbolizing as he did an optimistic view of the future, steadily climbed. Doubtless in response to requests by the clients, the artists reduced the number of arrows, so that the saint no longer "resembled a hedgehog" but was simply an attractive, nearly naked young man.

Pollaiuolo gave Sebastian a transparent loincloth, and emphasized the soft femininity of his body by contrasting it with the older and more muscular bodies of the bowmen. These changes paradoxically left the Christian martyr looking rather like that very pagan idol he had once fought, according to legend. He became a kind of Christian Apollo, suggestive of Adonis, the darling of the gods, or even of Cupid with his love arrows. To behold so much triumphant corporality adorning the altars of churches shocked only a few monks. They admonished that the beauty of St Sebastian might distract those at prayer – of both sexes.

One watchword that went unchallenged in Florence in those days was, "If it's pleasure you want, do it a lot with boys!" Roughly every second male in the city sooner or later had trouble with an authority established in 1432, the records of which have been preserved in part. Its brief was not so much to extirpate as to monitor homosexuality. The "passive" partners, boys between puberty and their first shave, were not targeted by this body, and the "active" adults were generally risking no more than a fine. Sexual relations with boys were accepted as a passing phase in life, with marriage lying ahead of men but young women meanwhile out of reach. Elder citizens introduced youths to sexual practices, in a sort of initiation ritual and within the bonds of neighbourly ties or friendships.

Those mentioned in the records of the monitoring authority range from dyers and wool carders to members of the upper classes. The young Gino Capponi, whom Vasari names as a model of Pollaiuolo's, came from one of the city's principal families. Humanists, writers, and artists were denounced with particular frequency. In 1473 a man who worked for Botticelli was arrested and punished; three years later, Leonardo da Vinci was charged, but acquitted. In 1502, Botticelli himself was anonymously accused of having had homoerotic relations with a young apprentice, but evidently charges were not pressed – and this in an age that was no longer so tolerant. In 1494, the fundamentalist monk Savonarola had proclaimed Florence the Republic of God. He decreed the death penalty for homosexuality, and "lascivious" paintings were publicly burnt. Even after his fall, the city did not return to its former tolerant ways, and during the Counter-Reformation naked images were banned from the churches. This mood took its toll on St Sebastian. As a protector against the plague, he was supplanted by St Rock, who was depicted in art as an old, bearded man, above all fully clothed, in accordance with the strict requirements of the Council of Trent.

Antonio Pollaiuolo did not abide in Florence to see Savonarola's regime. "The foremost master of our city", as Lorenzo de' Medici called him, had been summoned to Rome in 1484, and there he created the tombs of two Popes, which further augmented his fame. He died there in 1498, held in high esteem, a happy artist to the last. Today, however, his name is almost forgotten. He lacks the harmony and elegance of a Botticelli, whose stock now stands so much higher. What once fired Pollaiuolo's contemporaries with enthusiasm now tends to prompt indifference: his eagerness to experiment, his technical virtuosity. But the fact is that he helped to formulate the laws of the Renaissance.

Sandro Botticelli: The Adoration of the Magi, c. 1475

A magnificent picture for a dubious moneychanger

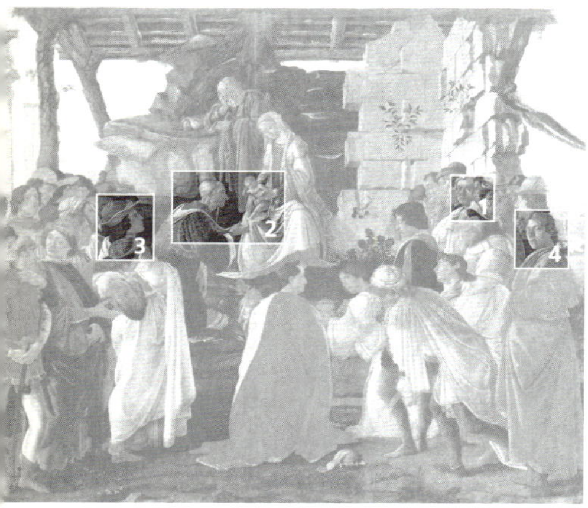

The stone wall is crumbling, and the only shelter for the Virgin Mary and the Infant Jesus is a flimsy wooden structure. This is not the manger sought out by the Holy Family when there was no room for them at the inn, not the manger familiar from traditional illustrations of the Christian nativity. This is a ruin. The old heathen world has collapsed; of a Roman temple in the background, too, only fragments remain. Mary, Joseph and the child are enthroned upon a massive rock at the centre of the painting. On this rock, the new church of Christendom will be built.

This scene by the Renaissance painter Sandro Botticelli, now in the Museo degli Uffizi in Florence, is not in fact a nativity. The manger, ox and ass are not present here; and the shepherds who hastened to the place have moved on once more (they can be seen in the distance, at the foot of the temple columns). This is an occasion that is said to have taken place in Bethlehem on the thirteenth day after Christ's birth, an occasion which the church celebrates as the Feast of the Epiphany. On this day, Jesus Christ is revealed (this is the meaning of the word "epiphany") to the three "wise men from the east", who are seen with their retinue at the infant's feet.

These wise men or magi appear to have been astronomers, who took a star in the heavens as a sign that a king of the Jews had been born: "the star, which they saw in the east, went before them", St Matthew tells us (2, 9), "till it came and stood over where the young child was." In the painting, the golden rays of the star are shining through the roof-beams onto where the baby Jesus lies in Mary's lap. "And when they were come into the house", the evangelist continues (2, 11), "they saw the young child with Mary his mother, and fell down, and worshipped him: and when they had opened their treasures, they presented unto him gifts; gold, and frankincense, and myrrh."

The Feast of the Epiphany was celebrated by Christians everywhere, but the festivities in 15th century Florence were especially lavish. The relics of the three kings, it is true, lay elsewhere, in faraway Cologne; but on account of the journey they had made, they were considered the patron saints of pilgrims and travellers, and by extension of travelling merchants. Small wonder, then, that Florence, a city that owed its wealth and importance to trade, was particularly diligent in venerating them.

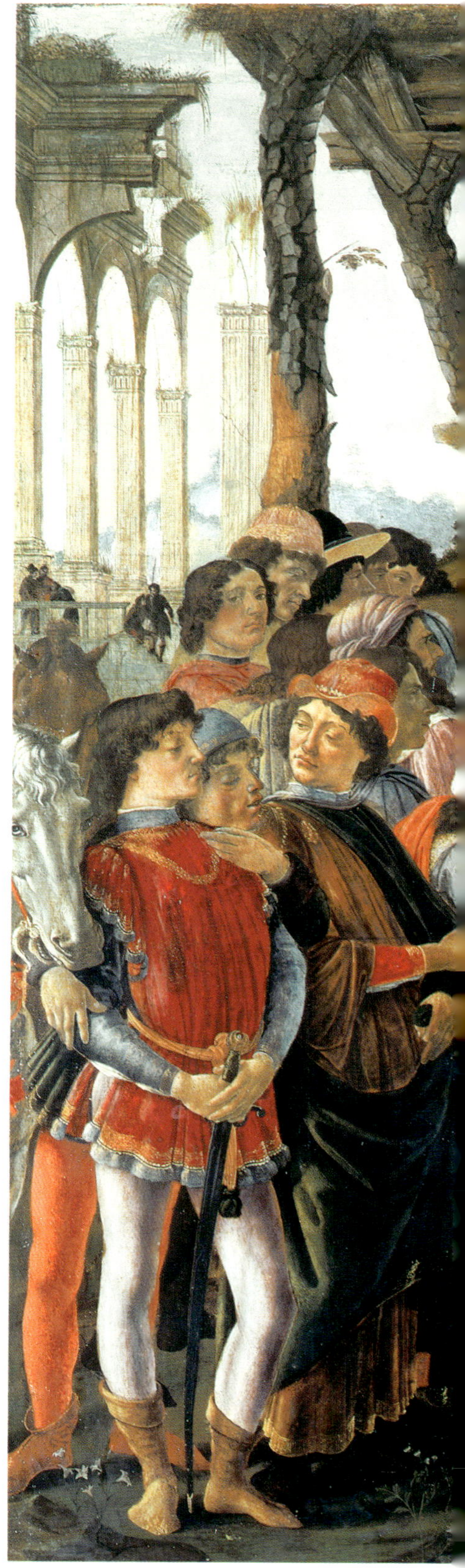

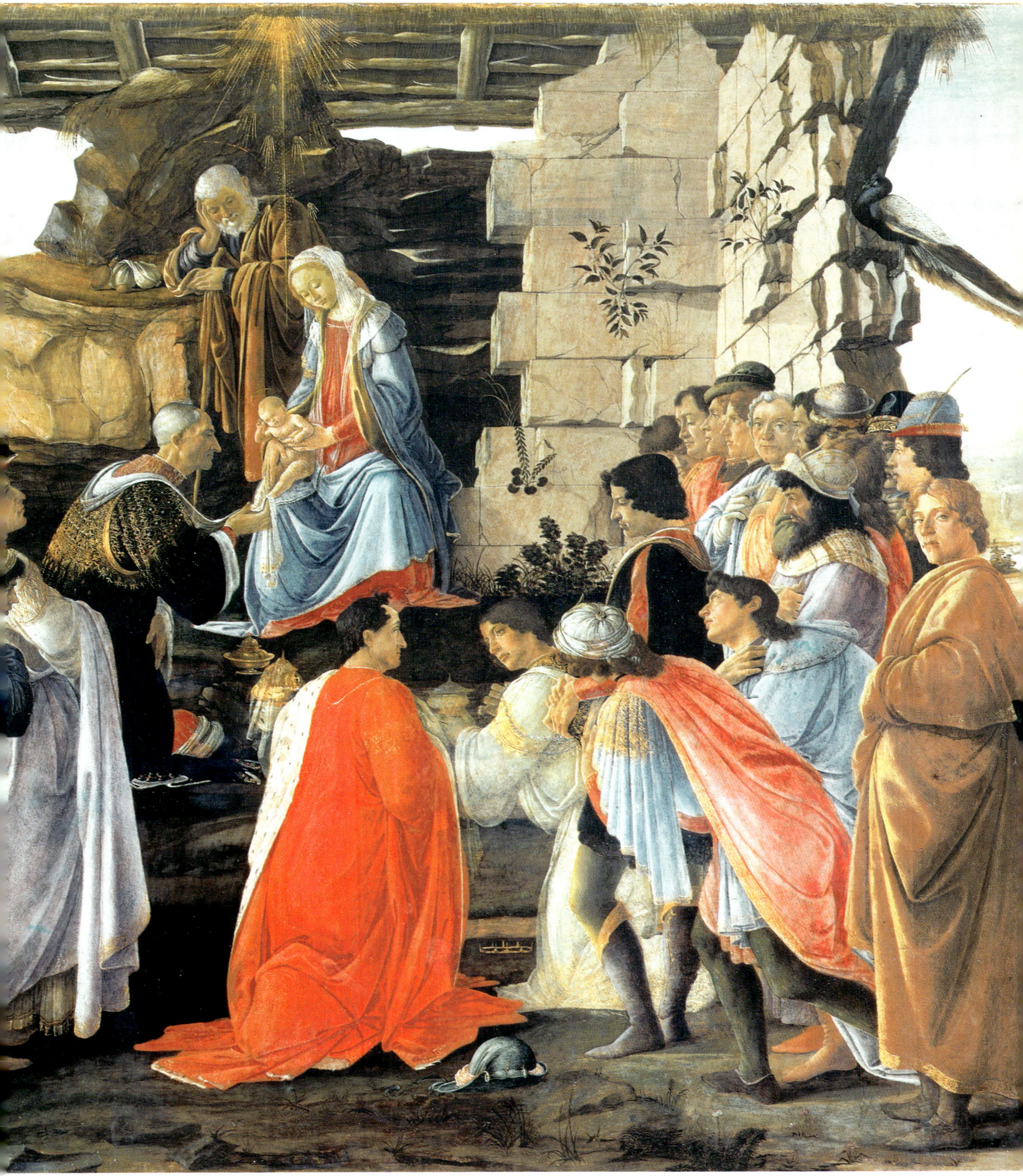

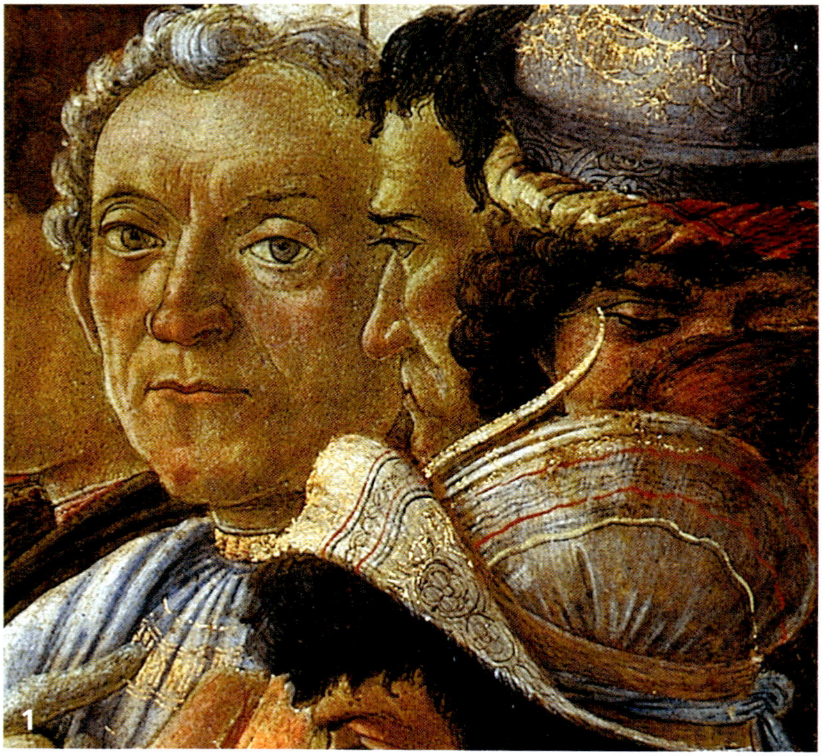

Whining to the tax office

Guasparre del Lama, who commissioned this altar-piece from Botticelli, was himself a Florentine businessman. The grey-haired man in the midst of the group of followers on the right has an air of self-assurance as he gazes out of the picture, his forefinger to his breast appearing to proclaim: I am he who endowed this painting.

What we know of this man, born the son of a barber in 1411, derives (tellingly) chiefly from his tax returns. The people of Florence had to declare their property annually to the city's "catasto", or tax office, and only if they made a proper tax return were they able to hold office. Like many of his fellow citizens, del Lama tried to soften the hard tax collectors' hearts: "Have pity on me," he groaned in 1446, for instance. "I married a wife who brought me no dowry, which is a real woe! These two years I have had nothing, neither money nor house."

Other documents show that his wife Cosa did in fact bring 200 florins with her when she married, and del Lama inherited a plot of land from his father – but in 1451 he was still whining that as an apothecary's assistant he earned a paltry thirty florins a year. "I am a sick man and have nothing to live on!" Three years later, though, he was buying a house in Via della Scala; and fifteen years later he made 556 florins from the sale of two houses and some land. He even owned a Turkish slave woman, for whom he had paid fifty florins. Evidently his circumstances had notably improved.

By 1469 he seems finally to have established himself as a man of means, for he was now listed as a *sensale de' cambi* or a currency exchanger. No doubt, he was to be seen seated in the new marketplace at his *tavola*, his table covered in green baize, with his money chest and ledgers before him. In 1473 his name appeared in a notary's contract for a major transaction which involved exchanging Neapolitan currency for Florentine.

The Arte del Cambio, the influential bankers' guild, monitored these money-changers very closely, since they were suspected of usury and other dubious practices, and their number was continuously growing. And no wonder: the profession was exceedingly lucrative.

Guasparre del Lama will have been among those who amassed a tidy fortune. Because his marriage remained childless, he decided as he approached his sixtieth year to invest in a tomb suitable to his station. He was prepared to spend a substantial sum to preserve his name from oblivion; and so, in his own lifetime, he had a burial chapel built in Santa Maria Novella, one of the city's largest and most distinguished churches, located very nearly opposite his own home in Via della Scala. It was on the inner wall beside the main door and, though modest in size, the tomb and altar were elaborately ornamented in marble.

An exclusive tomb for a simple money-changer – it may be that del Lama owed it to the good relations he enjoyed with the Dominicans at Santa Maria Novella. In his will, made on 29 May 1469, he left them the income from his property, some sixteen florins a year, with instructions to say mass for him once a week and additionally on the Feast of the Epiphany. He also left modest sums to "seven poor girls", for their dowries.

Del Lama had his chapel, evidently under construction at the time, consecrated to the three kings; the eldest of them, Caspar, was his own namesake. And he commissioned the altar-piece from the young painter Sandro Botticelli.

Devout and tender, the eldest of the three kings is bending to kiss the saviour's foot. A century after the painting was done, the artist and biographer Giorgio Vasari discerned in this figure the features of the elder Cosimo de' Medici, ruler of Florence. The Roman profile of the man, positioned centrally in the composition, is indeed very similar to that of Cosimo as seen on a medal struck after his death in 1464 to honour the "Pater Patriae", the father of the fatherland.

Cosimo the Elder was the richest man in Florence. Under him, the Medici bank became the biggest banking house in Europe, with branches in Bruges, London and Rome. In order to secure his wealth he sought political power as well, achieved it with the help of the party of the common man, and exercised it with the greatest discretion. That fiction dear to the people of Florence – that they were living in a republic – was respected: the people never lacked for opportunities to vote. But the Medicis' men ensured that the right candidates were elected.

The uncrowned ruler of Florence, born in 1389, is seen in Botticelli's painting bowing before the infant Jesus. In point of fact, Cosimo in the last years of his life was so stiff that he was not even able to kneel to kiss the Pope's feet. He suffered from gout, as did his two sons Piero and Giovanni. It was probably their features that Botticelli gave to the other two kings, proffering their gifts to the saviour a step lower than Cosimo. Together with their father, they represent the three ages of man, a traditional gesture in pictures of the three kings.

The Medici had a special relationship with the magi: in 1440, when Cosimo had consolidated his power and was building his palace, he chose the three kings as the family's patron saints. At least four pictures of these popular figures were in his possession; in 1459 he had Benozzo Gozzoli paint a fresco showing the procession of the kings through the Florentine hills on the walls of his private chapel; and of course the Medici were always there when the people of Florence marked the Feast of the Epiphany with their version of a royal procession, parading through the streets – indeed, the family were members and patrons of the Compagnia de' Magi, a lay fraternity which organized the festivities.

The humble appearances of the powerful

Generally the citizens of Florence were urged to observe a "republican" simplicity – but the procession at Epiphany gave them a chance to put on their full finery in honour of their saints. Splendour of this order was permitted only on high feast days or at state occasions, when it was important to display the city's wealth and power to the outside world.

The rulers themselves were obliged to put on humble appearances, for they too were expected to be of republican convictions. Any ostentation would have been taken amiss and held against them by the Florentines; Cosimo's cloak is embroidered in gold, it is true, but like his son Piero he is shown in the picture wearing his fur discreetly, as an inner lining. None of the three Medici is shown wearing a crown; Florence hated this symbol of rule.

When Botticelli painted his picture, all three Medicis in it were in fact already dead: Giovanni died in 1463, Cosimo in the following year, and Piero in 1469.

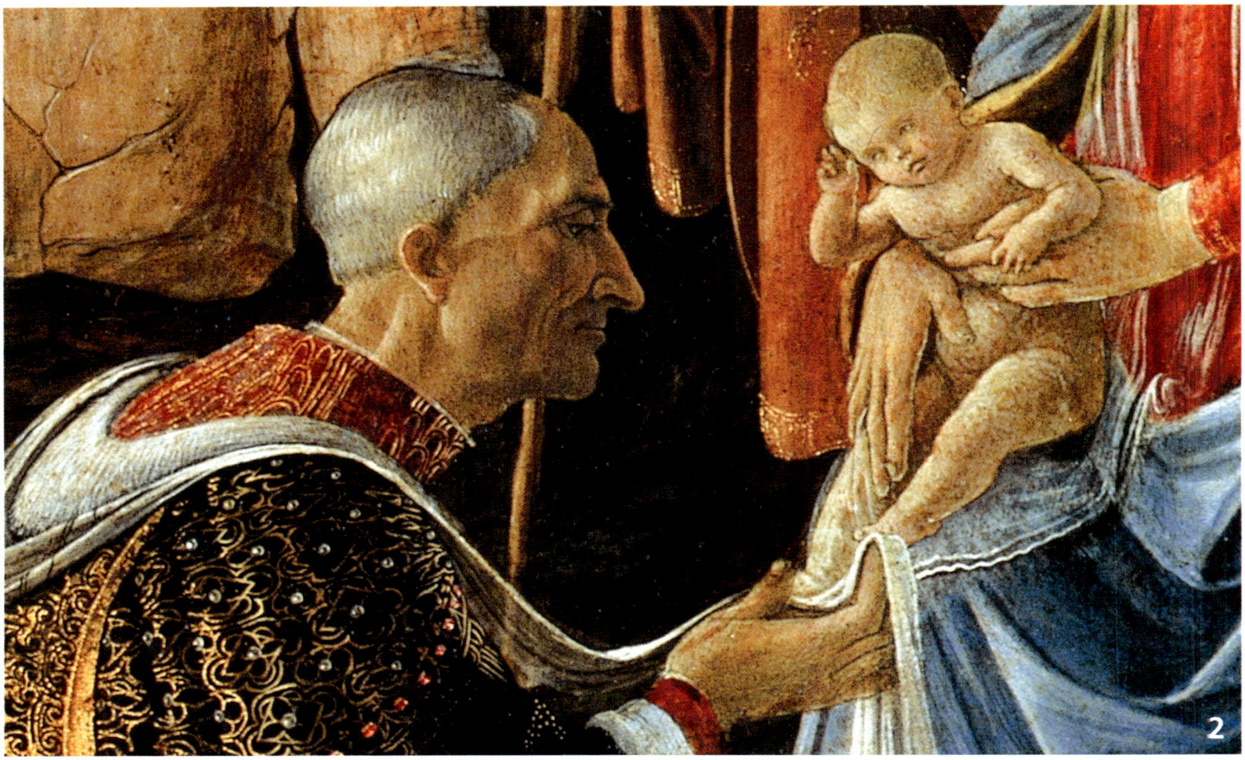

2

The ugliness of Il Magnifico

When the picture was painted, Florence was ruled by Lorenzo de' Medici, known subsequently as Il Magnifico, or the Magnificent. In 1469, following the death of his father Piero, he entered upon the succession aged just twenty. Probably Guasparre del Lama had the Medici family placed so prominently in the painting to secure the protection of the new ruler for himself, or to thank him for some favour.

Il Magnifico is standing right behind his grandfather Cosimo, conspicuous in his white cloak. He is not a king but a member of the retinue. Botticelli has idealized his features; with his squash nose and protuberant eyes, Lorenzo was reportedly an ugly man, unlike his younger brother Giovanni, known as the Handsome, who is to the right in the painting, wearing a black jerkin.

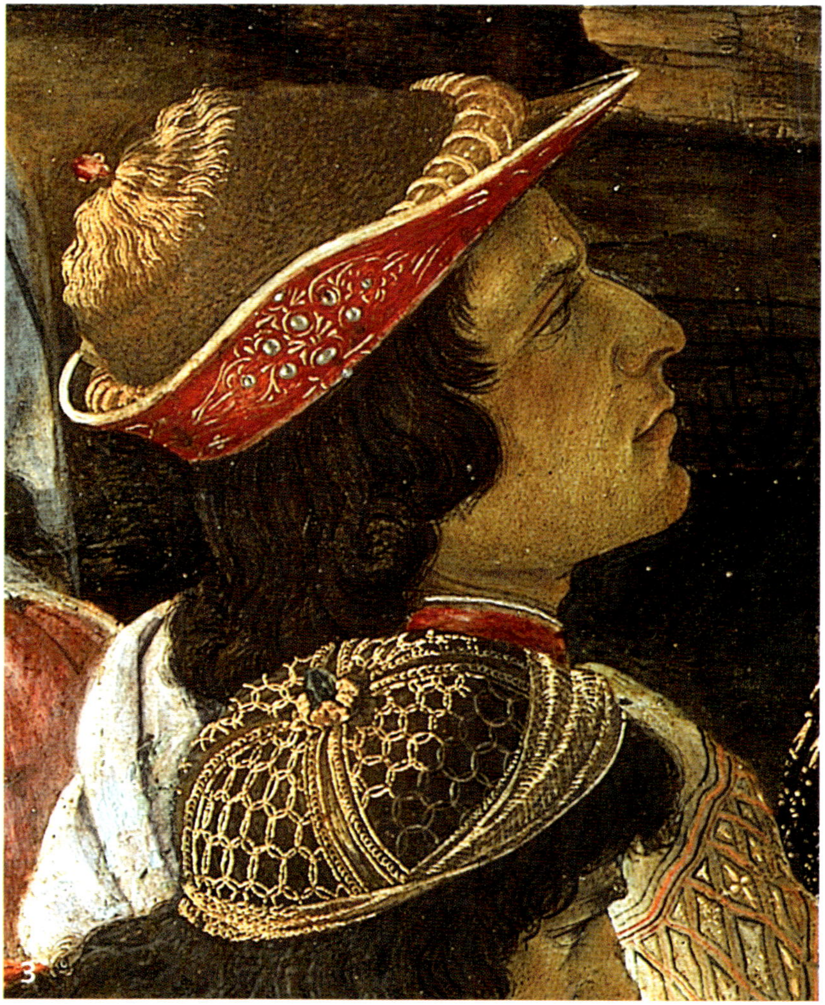

Lorenzo took more interest in politics than in business, and so the family bank made losses under him and had to close branches abroad. Nevertheless, he retained control of the bankers' guild: del Lama's career would scarcely have been possible without Lorenzo's approval. There were ample opportunities for contact between the moneychanger and the ruler, who liked to be close to the people – for instance, at the weekly meetings of the Compagnia de' Magi. The fraternity met every Tuesday for devotions and to prepare the Feast of the Epiphany, and also to cultivate the relations and dependencies that assured the city's rulers their power.

But no amount of protection could ward off the disaster that hit del Lama in 1476. The Mercanzia, the Florentine court of trade and fiscal affairs, found him guilty of an irregularity; it lay in the past, but somehow it had emerged that seventeen years previously del Lama had forged the figures in a letter of credit in his main ledger (the sum involved was eleven florins). Because he also tried to deny the offence, he was ordered to pay a fine of ninety florins, ten times the minimum fine prescribed by law. But above all, he was debarred from the guild.

Del Lama's business career was over. Before long he was lamenting his woes in his tax returns again. But once more his life took a turn: in 1480 his wife Cosa died, and within a week the sixty-nine-year-old remarried, making an advantageous match. Madonna Angelica de' Malefici brought him a dowry of three hundred florins and was also pregnant before long.

This unhoped-for good fortune prompted del Lama to revise all his existing plans. It was not his splendid tomb, he now felt, that would ensure the survival of his name, but his descendant, who would inherit his fortune. In 1481, in a new will, del Lama attempted to rescind his legacy to the Dominicans. He also forgot about the "poor girls".

When the moneychanger died shortly afterwards, the monks of Santa Maria Novella allowed his remains to be interred in the church, but only once his widow had agreed to observe the stipulations of the first will. Madonna Angelica did so; but when the funeral was over, she proved inordinately tough, and the Dominicans had to sit out a forty-year legal action before they saw a penny of del Lama's money.

Botticelli will have painted the work commissioned by the moneychanger between 1469 and 1476 – that is, between the date of the first will, with its generous provision for the monastery, and del Lama's career disaster. Evidently the painter saw his money rather more speedily than the monks were later to do; but then, it was probably a fairly small sum. The altar-piece measures just 111 by 134 centimetres, and moreover, the painter (born in 1445) was not yet well known.

In his self-portrait at the far right, though, Botticelli has as self-assured an air as the younger Medici and the man who commissioned the painting. His gaze is cool and sceptical, and his upper lip has an arrogant twist to it. Vasari described Botticelli as "a man of inquiring mind" given to living in "haphazard fashion" and to playing practical jokes. But in Renaissance Florence the protection of the all-powerful (and art-loving) Medici was as indispensable for an ambitious artist as it was for a moneychanger; so it may have been Botticelli's idea to introduce portraits of the rulers into his *Adoration of the Magi*.

The artist fared better with the painting than the moneychanger did. Vasari described it as "a marvellous painting which today amazes every artist by its colouring, its design, and its composition." And he continued: "His *Adoration of the Magi* made Botticelli so famous, both in Florence and elsewhere, that Pope Sixtus IV, having finished the building of the chapel for his palace at Rome and wanting to have it painted, decided that he should be put in charge of the work."

Botticelli's painting triumphantly satisfies very different requirements. Naive viewers would be happy to see a pious scene featuring familiar faces. The more sophisticated would discern a subtle allegory of the decline of the old religions and the blossoming of the new church of Christ. And art connoisseurs would be surprised by the fresh perspective the innovative artist chose for this scene: rather than showing the magi and their retinue in procession, from the side, as had conventionally been done by Benozzo Gozzoli and others, he opted for a frontal view, the figures ceremonially grouped about the Holy Family. The disposition and the harmony of this multi-layered work are a harbinger of the artistic style of the High Renaissance.

In the years ahead, Botticelli received the commissions he hoped for, not only from the Pope but also from the rulers of Florence. As early as 1475, shortly before Guasparre del Lama's altar-piece was completed, Giuliano de' Medici ordered a painted banner from him. Lorenzo had his country residences decorated by Botticelli. His masterpieces too, such as *Primavera* (c. 1482) and *The Birth of Venus* (c. 1485), were painted for a branch of the Medici family.

With his *Adoration of the Magi*, the youthful Botticelli attracted the attention of those who knew about art, as he had hoped. So this masterpiece is not only a document of Christian piety; it also bespeaks the canny career strategies of both an artist and a businessman. It reflects the destinies and dependent relations of people in a Renaissance city where the ruling bankers were pleased to don the attire of the three kings.

An artist's strategic career planning

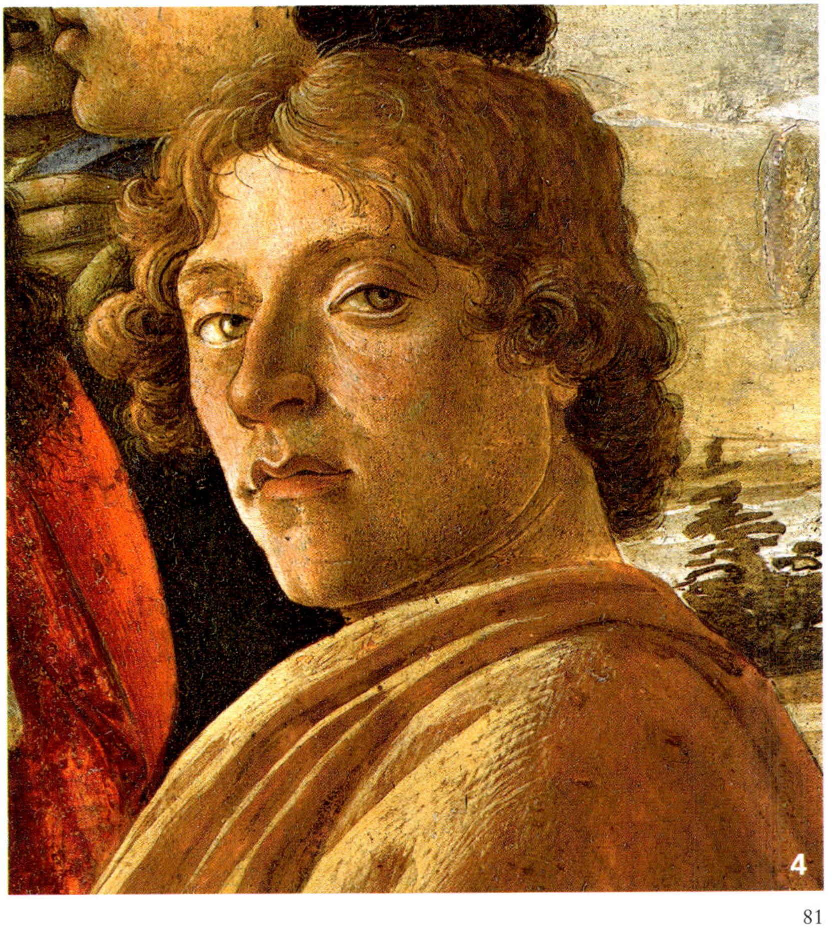
4

**Ercole de' Roberti/Lorenzo Costa:
The Ship of the Argonauts, c. 1480/1490**

Jason sails for unknown shores

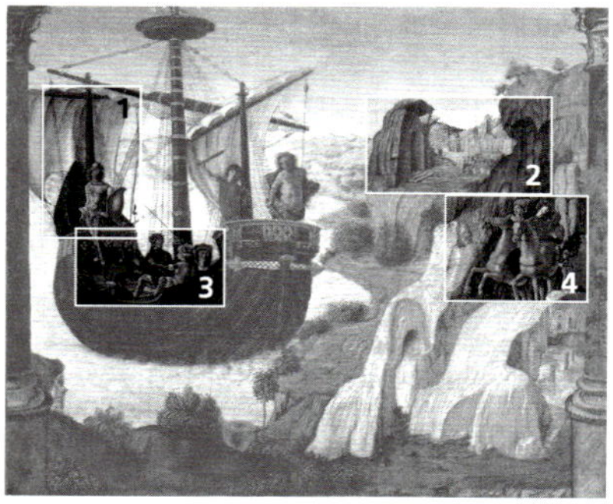

The sails are billowing in the breeze, the ship casts off, and the crew gaze back. On shore, bizarre rock formations tower up. The dark mass of the vessel seems to be hovering over the milky-white waters of the sea. It is almost a surreal landscape, a strange mixture of the fantastic and the real.

This type of ship was common in the 15th century, and was used for cargo transport. But the golden embellishments on the forecastle and stern suggest that this vessel is not putting to sea for a trading voyage. This is an adventurous expedition, and her crew are important people. The athletically built man at the stern, stripped to the waist with a lion's fell over his shoulder and a club in his fist, has the attributes of Heracles, the hero of Greek myth who had superhuman powers. Beside him, wielding a club, is Hylas, his arms-bearer and darling, and in the fore of the ship stands Jason, the captain.

What we see in the ship are some of the fifty heroes assembled, according to myth, by the son of King Aeson to undertake the first ever long-distance sea voyage and fetch the Golden Fleece, a ram's fleece guarded by a dragon at Colchis on the Black Sea. For this enterprise, Jason built the largest ship ever seen, the *Argo*. From the ship, the members of the expedition took their name, Argonauts.

They set sail from the Greek port of Iolcus, were embroiled in adventures, demonstrated their mettle, and enjoyed themselves. In Thrace they rid a blind seer of the fearful harpies plaguing him; on Lemnos they bestowed their favours on the women, whose husbands were dead. At length in Colchis Jason succeeded in seizing the fleece with the help of Medea, daughter of King Aeëtes and an adept in magical charms. She had fallen in love with Jason; he married her and took her back to Greece, but their union ended in tragedy when Medea, abandoned, took fearful revenge and murdered their children.

The first part of the story is one of the oldest adventure yarns in world literature and was retold by many writers, among them Valerius Flaccus, a Roman author of the first century AD. In 1474 his *Argonautica* was printed in Bologna and thus made available to a wide public, so the subject had currency when this painting was made in nearby Ferrara between 1480 and 1490. It now hangs in Padua, is neither signed nor dated, and poses numerous problems for art historians.

Measuring 46 x 53 cm and painted on oak rather than the usual poplar, the painting will once have adorned the front of a chest, together with other panels. Five more pictures showing episodes from the myth of the Argonauts, are in museums and private collections in Paris, Madrid, London and Florence. They were probably attached to two matching chests, each bearing three panel paintings. Subsequently they were in the possession of the Roman collector Vincenzo Giustiniani. His 1638 inventory notes: "They are believed to be from the hand of Ercole da Ferrara."

Ercole de' Roberti was active in Bologna at the time the panels were painted, as was Lorenzo Costa, who probably helped him with the work. Both painters were from Ferrara.

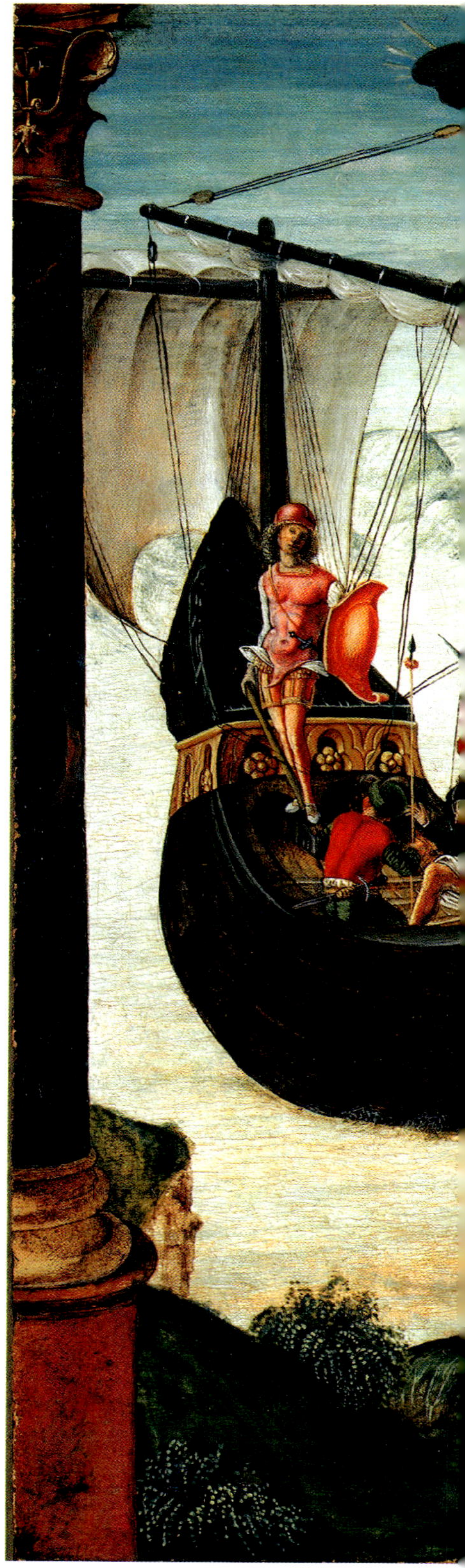

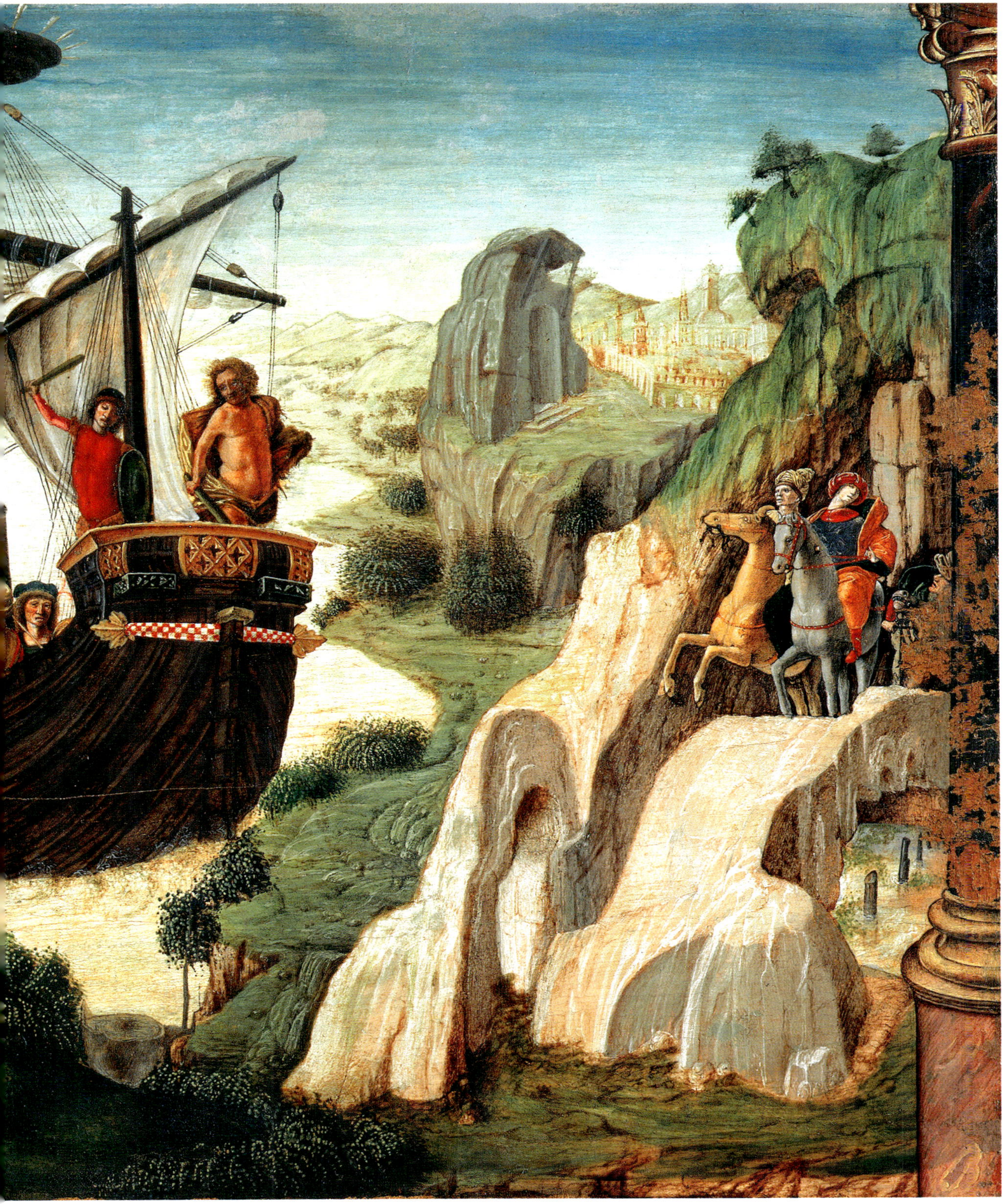

It is unclear, however, which artist did which panels – the weaker ones were possibly done by an assistant. Nor do we know for which bride the chests were made.

Bridal chests were a must in Italy when a young woman married: one or more, depending on her property. In these chests, the bride's dowry was ceremonially carried from the house of her parents to that of the bridegroom, where they were assigned a place in the bedroom, beside the bed. Originally plain wooden chests, in the 15th century they were adorned with family coats-of-arms and colourful pictures, ever more splendidly; during the Renaissance, the decorative motifs chosen would often come from Greek or Roman mythology. Artists who were normally occupied mainly with painting saints and rulers could indulge their imaginations with a little unaccustomed licence in painting these heathen tales of love.

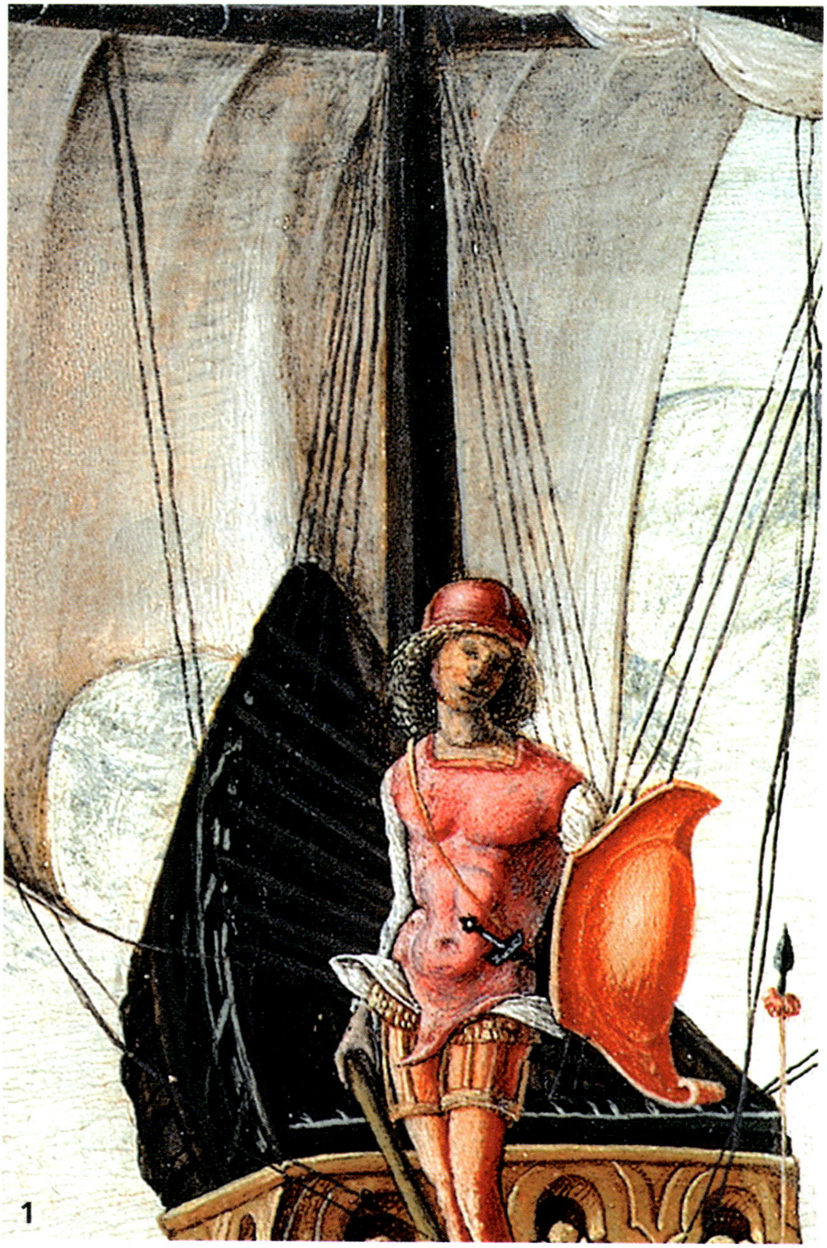

1

As well as mythical love affairs, the subjects depicted on these chests were frequently steadfast women such as the Romans Lucretia and Portia, whom brides were recommended to take as examples. Other popular themes were the rape of the Sabine women or Jason and the Argonauts returning with Medea. If the unhappy fate of Medea might be read as an ill omen for a marriage, that consideration evidently played no part in the choice of motif.

Doubtless the chests adorned with Argonaut scenes were made for a bride from the highest social circles. On that the experts are agreed; but the identity of the family who commissioned them is disputed. On two of the less skilfully painted panels, the remains of a coat-of-arms can be made out, with a lily and two stars. These might signify the Guidotti family of Bologna, which had two lilies and six stars in its device. In 1486 a son of the family married an illegitimate daughter of the Bentivoglio family, the Signori or masters of Bologna. Their wedding may have been the occasion for which the chests were ordered.

However, the dominant position of the ship on the two loveliest Argonaut panels, in the Padua and Madrid collections, may turn our thoughts to another and more famous family, the dynasty of the Estes. The dukes of Ferrara likewise had a lily in their coat-of-arms, and also married off their two daughters, Isabella and Beatrice, in the years 1490 and 1491. Ships were the *impresa* of the family; an *impresa* was not an official heraldic device but a symbolic image which great families in Italy liked to use for decorative purposes and also to express a key quality. The Estes' *impresa* featured ships sailing before a strong wind. It appeared time and again on their frescoes, paintings, and even coins: the gold ducats of Leonello d'Este, who reigned from 1441 to 1450, have the head of the ruler on the obverse, and on the reverse two men in a ship, the sails of which have filled with the wind. And when Leonello d'Este's men went into battle, their war-cry was "Vela", meaning "sail".

"Vela" was the war-cry of the Estes

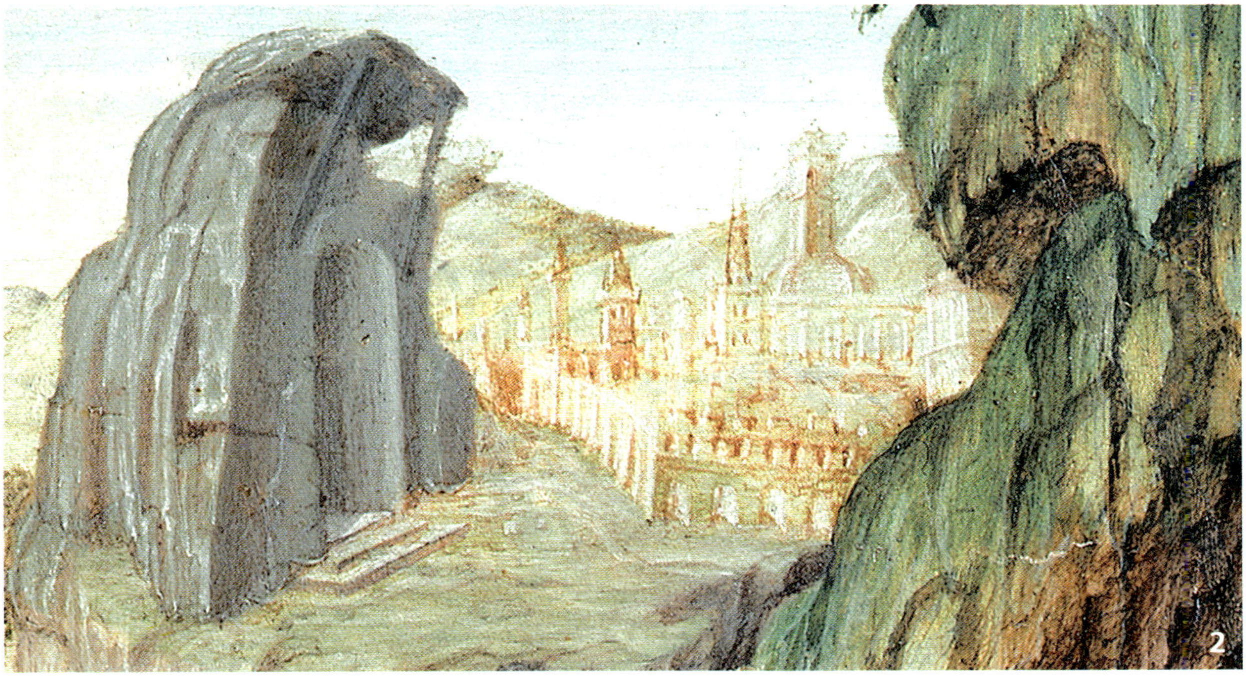

2

For the Este family, Heracles was an important symbolic figure. There were statues of Heracles in their palaces, and frescoes on their walls told of his heroic deeds. The Estes traced their own descent from the ancient superman, claiming ancestry in ancient mythological times – though the fact of the matter was that the Estes had held the ducal title only since 1471, as a fief granted by the Pope. The Estes were absolute rulers, or despots, and if they acquitted themselves with distinction over several generations it was not through any elected kinship with club-wielding heroes.

They made shrewd use of the city's strategic position in the Po river delta, developing its port and thus controlling the major waterway into the plains of Lombardy. Customs duties levied on trade goods were a principal source of revenue for the dynasty, and if the sails on their ducats were billowing in the wind we may take it as one more reminder of just how important the maritime sector was for Ferrara.

The people of the city enjoyed a modest degree of prosperity. Their rulers had flood barriers built to protect Ferrara from the waters of the Po. The Estes also kept war at bay, playing off the larger powers of Milan, Venice, Florence and Rome against each other and pursuing a risky policy of routinely changing sides, now leading the armies of the one party as *condottieri*, now of the other.

The dynasty and state were served by an efficient civil service. Indeed, Ferrara was the envy of all of turbulent Italy for its order and stability. In 1442, following a visit to the city, the Renaissance architect Leon Battista Alberti wrote: "It was there that I grasped what good fortune it is to live in a state where nothing troubles one's peace of mind, beneath the rule of the best of fathers, who respects law and custom."

The Estes were adept at using their prosperity to good ends. As early as 1391, Alberto I founded a university. His work was continued by Niccolò III, and by the latter's three sons, Leonello, Borso and Ercole, who reigned in succession. They brought humanists to the city and prosecuted so many building projects that "the din of the masons' hammers could be heard far and wide". Thus by their efforts a small and marshy place "where only frogs and mosquitoes dwell" was transformed in the course of the 15th century into a centre of courtly culture and style that irradiated all Italy.

Duke Ercole I, who reigned from 1471 to 1505, gave the name that was at once his own and that of the Greek hero to his favourite project. He designated as the "addizione ercolea" a residential extension which tripled the area of the prosperous city. The duke's project was an early and successful example of well-thought-out urban planning: within just ten years, wide straight streets and some twenty palaces and a dozen churches had come into being, to designs by architect Biagio Rossetti.

An early example of urban planning

These new buildings and streets, known also as the *terra nuova* or new land, were the result of an immense effort. It may be that the city we can make out in the distance in the Argonauts panel is an allusion to this development. The picture was painted at a time when the planning of the *terra nuova* and its funding from taxes and levies were in everyone's thoughts, one way or another.

On the 11th of February 1490, Ercole's eldest daughter Isabella (1474–1539) married Francesco Gonzaga, the earl of nearby Mantua. The nuptial ceremonies were arranged by that very Ercole de' Roberti to whom the Giustiniani inventory ascribed the Argonauts chests.

From letters we know that, in the year before the wedding, the painter Ercole de' Roberti was sent to Venice to procure the finest, costliest pigments, such as ultramarine and gold. Eleven thousand gold platelets are reputed to have been used in adorning Isabella's dowry. This included the marital bed, a golden boat, a triumphal carriage, and thirteen bridal chests – everything made to the designs and under the supervision of Ercole de' Roberti. He had begun back in 1483, as soon as the betrothal of Isabella (then aged nine) was announced, possibly with the help of Lorenzo Costa in Bologna; both Ferrara-born artists were decorating churches and palaces in that city.

As painter to the court of Este, and master of the nuptials, de' Roberti escorted Isabella to Mantua, but made a premature return, weak and exhausted. A year after the wedding, he petitioned the duke in all humble submission for the payment due to him. In fact it was to be another four years before he received it.

For painters the situation in Ferrara was particularly delicate, because there was hardly anyone but the duke who might commission work, in contrast to Venice, Florence or Rome, where many families were forever competing to hire the best artists. Ferrara's painters were often obliged to earn their living elsewhere – in Bologna, for instance. The teachers of de' Roberti and Costa had done this; they were Cosimo Tura (c. 1430–95) and Francesco del Cossa (c. 1435–c. 1477), the founders of the Ferrarese school.

Ferrara's painters did Renaissance subjects in a Gothic style

These artists had developed an elite style for their courtly clientele which differed from the Renaissance style of their fellow Italian artists in the major centres. Art history refers to it as "humanist Gothic". The great breakthroughs of the modern era – such as the discovery of mathematically exact perspective, the realistic representation of the human body – were of limited interest to the artists of Ferrara.

The Ship of the Argonauts is a case in point. The artist gives us little indication of precisely how the crewmen are sitting in the vessel; the elegantly elongated figures of Jason and Hylas are decoratively placed, rather than standing squarely on the boards of a tossing ship. Of more importance to them than capturing reality was the element of the fantastic, as seen in the weightless, hovering appearance of the vessel, or a landscape in which cliff and city gate, nature and man-made architecture, seem to meld.

Thus the painters at the court of Este interpreted in this "Gothic" style the new subject matter that Renaissance humanists borrowed from antiquity; the style and the theme were in fascinating and highly idiosyncratic contrast. If the art of Ferrara is not well known today, it is because of the fate of the Estes.

The main line became extinct, and in 1598 the Estes had to quit Ferrara. The fief returned to Rome, and Pope Clement VIII systematically destroyed everything that recalled the erstwhile rulers. He had churches and palaces demolished, or let them fall down, and with them the great numbers of large-scale frescoes that had been a chief part of Ferrara's art disappeared for ever. The Estes are said to have possessed more frescoes, in terms of area covered, than any other rulers. All that remains to attest the splendour of the Estes are a few partially-ruined astrological scenes of the months, painted in the Palazzo di Schifanoia by Tura and Cossa.

The Este art collection was also carted away and sold off. Today, pictures from the Ferrarese school are scattered around 125 cities and some 300 collections around the entire world. In Ferrara, though, scarcely any remain.

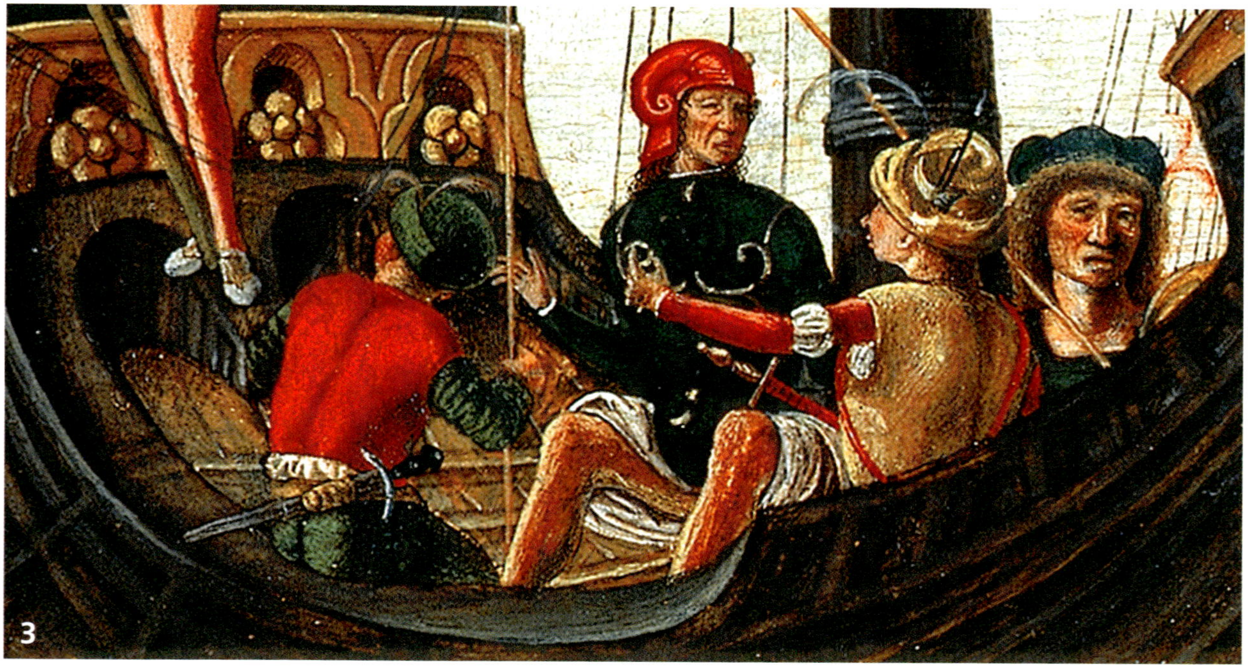
3

The life and style of the Estes can be glimpsed in two famous works of literature. From 1472 to 1494 an Italian count at their court, Matteo Boiardo, wrote the lively *ottava rima* narrative poem *Orlando Innamorato*; and in the early 16th century, the poet and diplomat Ludovico Ariosto wrote his great continuation of it, *Orlando Furioso*. Writing in Italian rather than Latin, these poets told of damsels and knights, feats of arms, love, valour and adventure, taking their personae from the legends that had accrued around Charlemagne and King Arthur. Their heroes, knights errant, were purportedly crusading against the heathen Saracens, but in reality they were chiefly interested in acquitting themselves courageously in duels and saving beautiful damsels from dragons or evil sorcerers before making a conquest of them in an idyllic setting.

That at least was what the nostalgic taste of the aristocratic audience demanded, those who listened to the poets "with delight and good cheer" at the court of Ferrara, as Boiardo tells us. At a time when firearms were beginning to decide the outcome of battles, the Estes still saw themselves as knights. In their youth, all of the dukes learnt the arts of war, which were considered essential in a feudal lord, and they were greatly in demand as highly-paid *condottieri* leading the armies of Naples, or Florence, or Milan.

In times of peace they jousted at tournaments or went hunting or embarked on long journeys on the pretext of making pilgrimages. In a letter to Isabella d'Este, Baldassare Castiglione wrote of "that accursed vagabond streak that some ancestor of the house of Este bequeathed to all his descendants". Isabella's grandfather Niccolò III and a number of companions had made it as far as Jerusalem in 1413.

That vagabond streak, a taste for risk and for venturing upon the unknown, is apparent (in the symbolic idiom of the age) in another figure associated with the Argonauts. Light of foot like Jason and Hylas, she is seen in other panels standing below billowing sails. She is Dame Fortune, blown hither and thither at the whim of the winds. She is a sister to Ventura – what may come but is not to be foreseen – and of Adventura.

For a *gioco di ventura*. a game of chance, Duke Ercole once neglected the affairs of government for weeks on end, we are told. He was on the river Po, on a pleasure boat, playing cards with a wealthy Jew by the name of Abraham, who allowed him to win large sums. Perhaps that pleasure boat of the Estes had the red-and-white chessboard pattern on it which has so puzzled scholars of heraldic devices when confronted with the ship of the Argonauts. Red and white was the strip of the Este jockeys at horse races, where large sums were staked; the colours may have been associated with all of their riskier ventures.

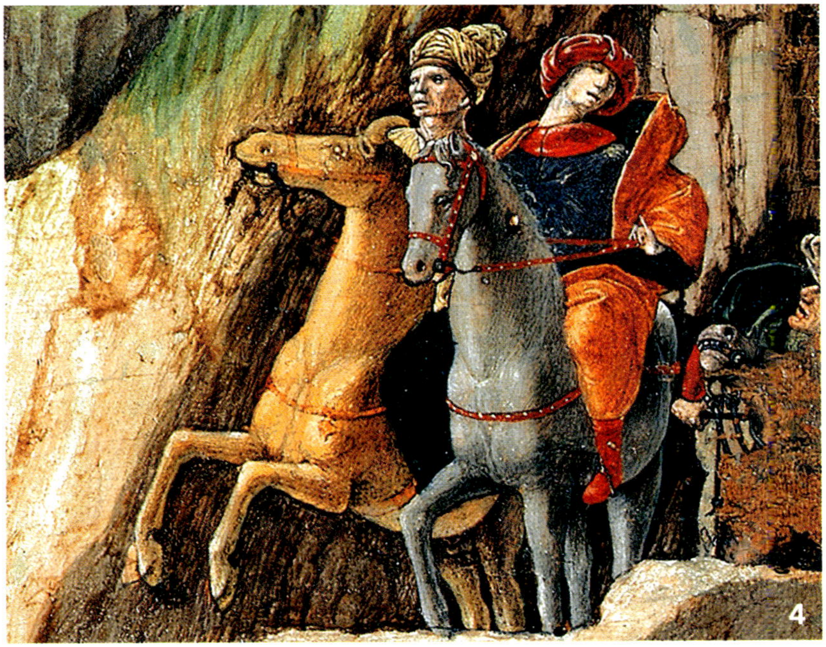
4

A taste for games of chance and adventure

Ercole's daughter Isabella chose as her *impresa* another symbol of Ventura, a bundle of lottery tickets, for she too was a dedicated gambler. The motif of the Argonauts on a bridal chest, standing for pluck and venturesomeness, would have been apt to this strong woman.

Much later, around the year 1512, she ordered a painting from Lorenzo Costa, to adorn her private apartments. Costa was now the successor of the great Andrea Mantegna as court painter in Mantua. He was given a programme to observe, according to which the subject was to be the coronation of Isabella by divine love. In the background of this work, which is now in the Louvre, the ship of the Argonauts appears once again. But this time she is in port, and her sails are furled.

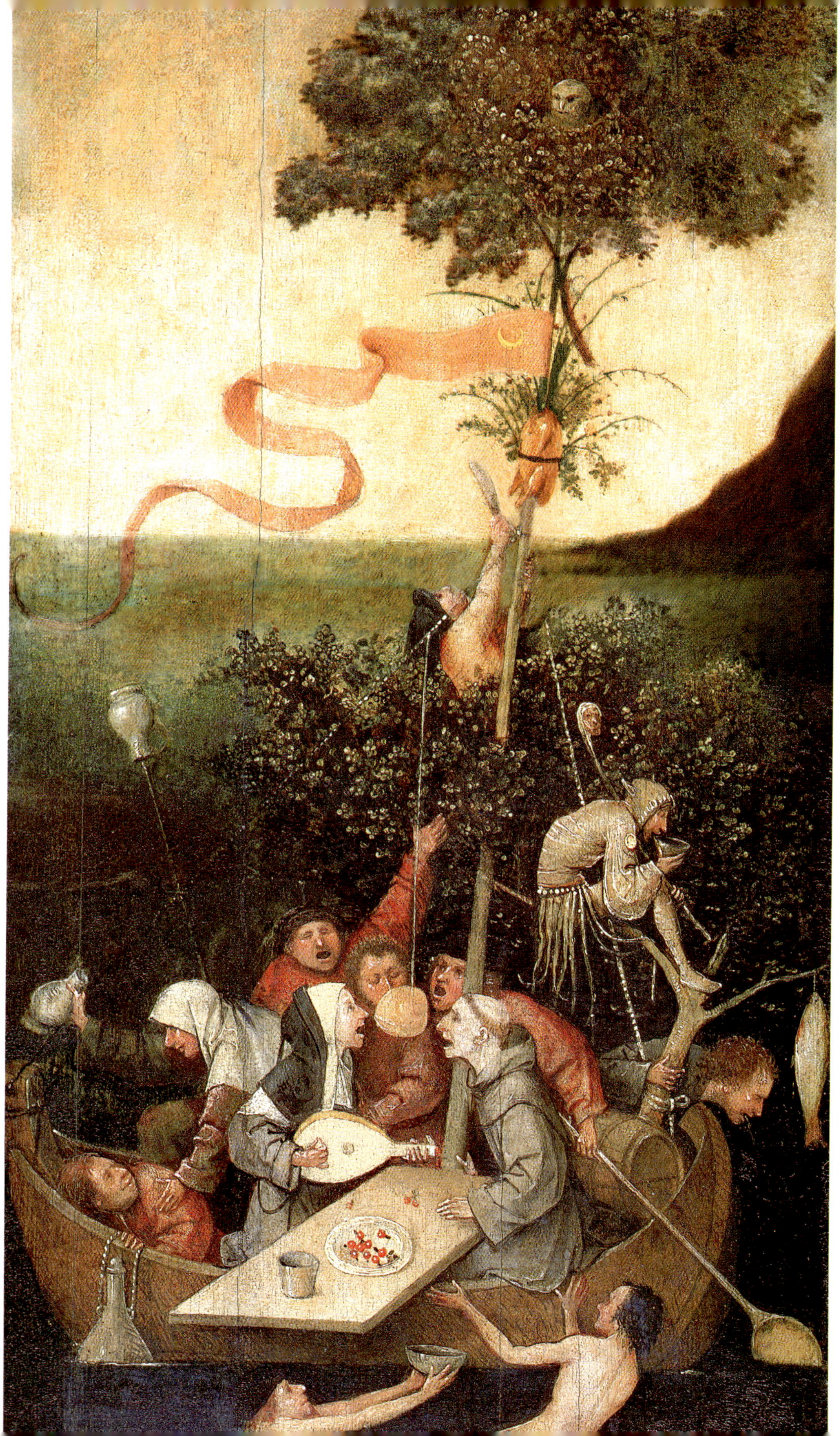

Hieronymus Bosch: The Ship of Fools, between 1480 and 1516

The Sinner and the Eccentric

In 1399 the City of Frankfurt ordered a madman who had run naked through the streets to be removed from the city and deposited further down the river Main. In 1406 some fishermen were instructed to carry a lunatic from Frankfurt to Mainz in the night. In 1418 the citizens of Frankfurt had a madwoman transported by ship to Aschaffenburg. In 1427 a blacksmith's lad who had lost his wits was taken down the Main and then along the Rhine to the Kreuznach area.[1]

Such deportations are known to have occurred in other European cities, as well. Sometimes the unfortunates were taken away by boat, although the majority were sent off overland, attached to goods transports. Those expelled were not just the unsound in mind, but also beggars, journeymen, discharged soldiers, cripples, and the sick. At the close of the Middle Ages, the number of people thus moving from one place to the next with no permanent home was large – in some areas it represented up to 30% of the population. The walls and gates which surrounded medieval cities protected them not just from their enemies, but also against these bands of vagabonds. Should individuals nevertheless manage to find their way in, after a few days they were sent on their way or indeed ejected by force. Only in the case of people who were clearly insane was a boatman or ferryman instructed to remove them. He would take them back to their hometown, or simply abandon them somewhere. The main thing was, they didn't come back.

A clear distinction was made between a town's own lunatics and those from elsewhere. Those from local families were not driven out. They would be at most imprisoned if they assaulted another citizen. They would then be put in the "fool's chest" or the "madhouse", usually small huts rather than solid buildings, where they were cared for by a lowly employee of the town. They were confined there, but not treated. No cure was expected, barring a miracle. The same was true of other serious diseases – patients and their relatives pinned their hopes more on God and the saints than on medicine.

There were two reasons for this: the lowly state of the doctor's art and the dominant role of religion. The kingdom of heaven was ever present in the Middle Ages. People's lives were defined by God. True life only began in His presence; this earthly vale of sorrows was seen as a place of transition, only important insofar as people could qualify here for admission to heaven.

This intensely felt, ever-present power of God also determined people's relationships with each other. They were all on the same path, all pilgrims on the road to salvation. In the face of this common goal, the differences between them as individuals assumed less importance. Even the differences between the insane and the not insane. They lived side by side. Families kept their sick members at home. The insane were integrated in society. Only when they had no family or when their relatives could no longer control them were they sent to the madhouse.

The insane were not simply suffered, however; they also served a religious function, by offering a means for the healthy to do good. Alms, endowments and other acts of charity were all good deeds that would increase one's chances of going to heaven.

In Bosch's day, this attitude was changing. He lived at the end of the Middle Ages and the start of the Renaissance, during which the Christian world picture would slowly lose its coherence and power. Bosch painted *The Ship of Fools* sometime between 1480 and 1516 – the precise date is unknown. In 1517 Luther nailed his theses to the door of the church in Wittenberg. He, like other protagonists of the Reformation, doubted the value of good deeds as a ticket to heaven. The insane, together with the cripples and beggars to whom one could also demonstrate one's brotherly love, thus lost their religious worth. From being necessary, they now became undesirable. They began to be cast out.

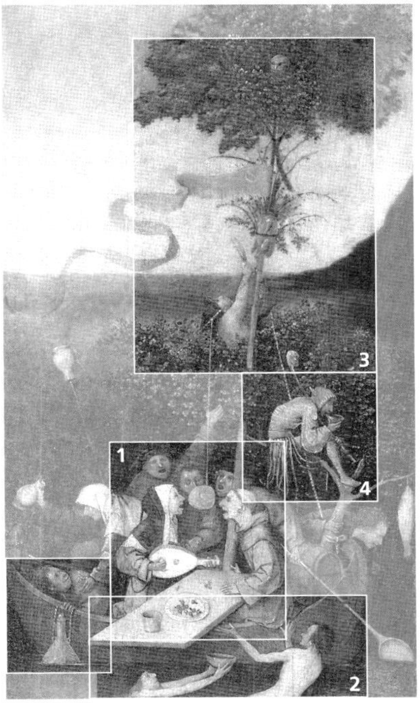

Fornication on board

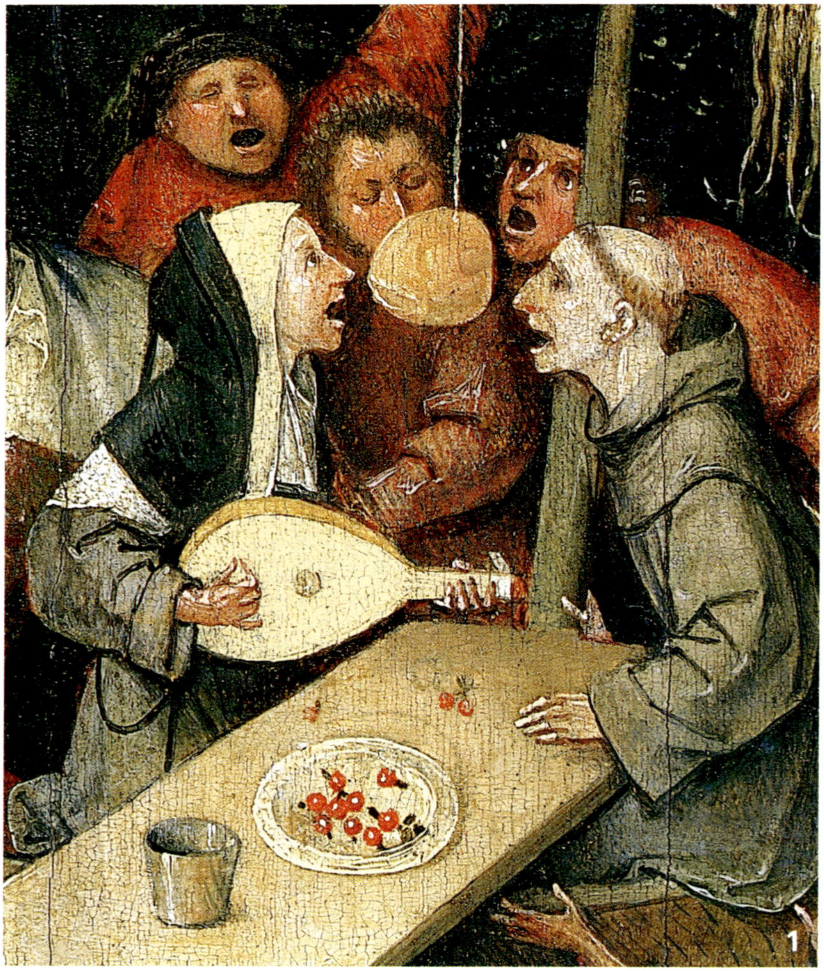
1

The number of prisons grew, and workhouses were introduced, where the mentally ill were shut up alongside thieves, beggars and those unwilling to work.

Although there is no proof that the insane were indeed packed off in boatloads, it would be easy to interpret Bosch's *Ship of Fools* as symbolizing the widespread process of segregation that started in his day. But that would be to view the picture solely through modern eyes. It is unlikely that Bosch's contemporaries would have interpreted the painting in such a way; they would have seen it in quite a different light.

In the middle of the boat sit a Franciscan monk and a nun. The nun is playing the lute, and both are singing or trying to catch with their mouths the pancake hanging from a string and being swung by the man with the outstretched hand. On the table between the monk and the nun lie some small fruits, which look like cherries. More of these fruits can be seen on a plate, beside which stands a cup, perhaps containing dice.

Bosch's contemporaries were used to looking for a meaning in such arrangements of people and objects. In this case their thoughts might have run thus: monks and nuns are supposed to live separately – if they are seated together, they are acting improperly. The lute, the white instrument with the round hole, recalls a vagina, and hence playing the lute means fornication. (In the symbolism of the time, the bagpipes represented the male pendant to the lute.) The childish game with the pancake signifies gluttony, the large number of jugs and barrels drunkenness, and the cup possibly the disreputable game of dice. The people on the boat do not know what is right and proper. They are fools. Not for nothing is one of them even dressed in a fool's costume.

The image of a ship laden with fools would have been thoroughly familiar to Bosch's contemporaries; they would have encountered it, for example, in carnival processions in which boats filled with fools were pulled on wheels through the streets. In several Netherlandish towns and cities there were festival associations by the name of "Blauwe Scuut". People who wanted to drink and be merry would gather together in these "blue ships". Viewers of the present painting may also have read a book entitled *Das Narrenschiff* (The Ship of Fools), a bestseller published in Basle in 1494 and translated into several languages. Written by Sebastian Brant, it describes more than 100 different types of fool and foolish behaviour. Thus "A fool is someone who counts on getting someone else's inheritance...", or "A fool is someone who scorns God and rails against Him day and night...".[2] All these characters get into a boat headed for the Land of Fools.

But a fool in those days was somewhat different from a fool today. In the Middle Ages, the term meant more than it does in today's language. It was applied not just to someone who flaunted God's commandments and the rules of social coexistence, but also to the mentally ill. We must bear this in mind if we are to understand how Bosch's painting would have been received in its own day. Of course it was appreciated even in the Middle Ages that there were differences between the two categories of fool. But these differences were not taken very seriously. At the end of the day, it boiled down to the same thing: both were unable to recognize the straight and narrow path to God. All fools were sinners. It was simply that the insane among them were given a better chance of forgiveness.

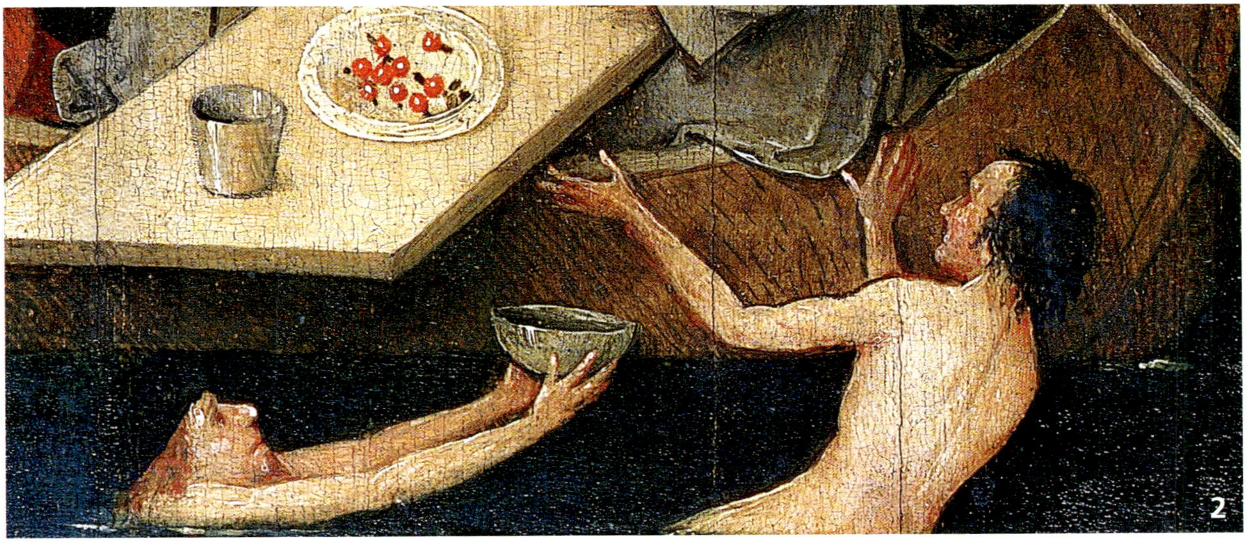

2

Meanings of water

The artists of the Middle Ages employed a language of symbols which they drew upon in the composition of their paintings and which the viewer subsequently used to "decipher" them. A number of reference books were even compiled, explaining the significance of the individual symbols, and these books continue to serve as vital sources of information for us today. They demonstrate, among other things, how many different meanings one image could carry. A ship might symbolize the City, the Church, faith or life itself. Bosch's ship full of fools could thus be interpreted as an allegory of life or the Church. Criticism of representatives of the Church was widespread in the late Middle Ages. The two interpretations are not mutually exclusive, however.

Like the ship, water could signify a number of different things. On the one hand, it was associated with purification, renewal and baptism. On the other hand, it could mean danger, a threat or sin. Naked figures in the water are almost always sinners in the metaphorical imagery of medieval times.

Water was also frequently associated with madness. Perhaps because water, like madness, was something which couldn't be grasped. In the Netherlandish town of Meulebeck the mentally ill were led across the bridge of a river: passing over the water was supposed to bring healing.

On the pennant fluttering from the mast, Bosch has depicted a crescent moon. This was the symbol of the Turks, who were threatening Europe. In painting, however, the crescent moon was also used to identify the mentally ill: the fools as lunatics under the flag of the enemy of Christendom.

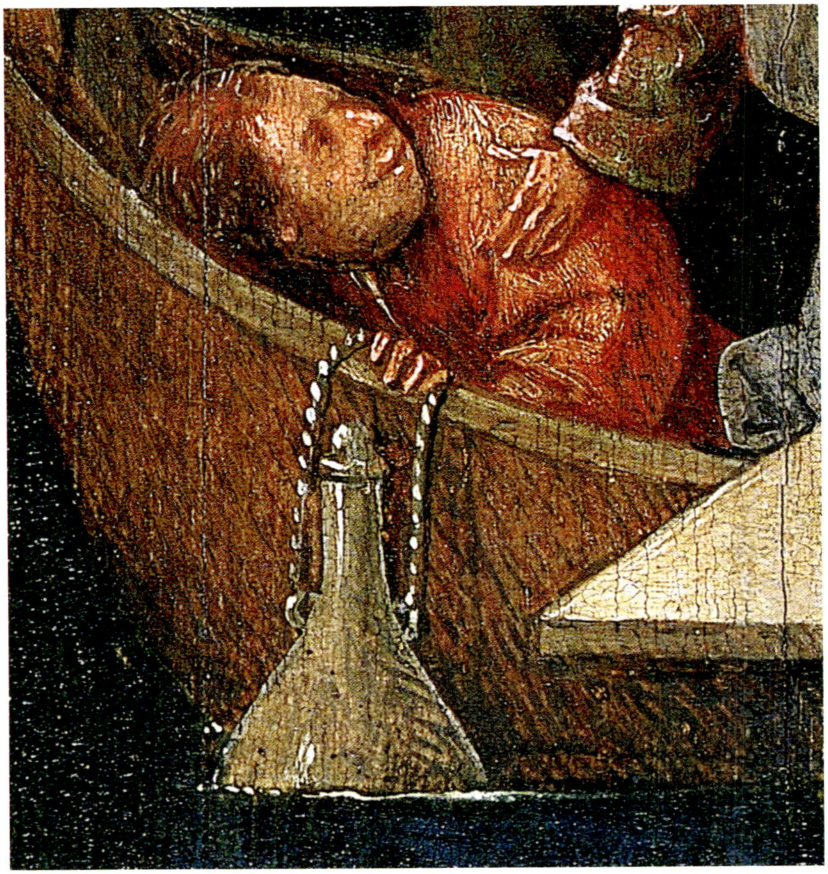

A mast without a sail

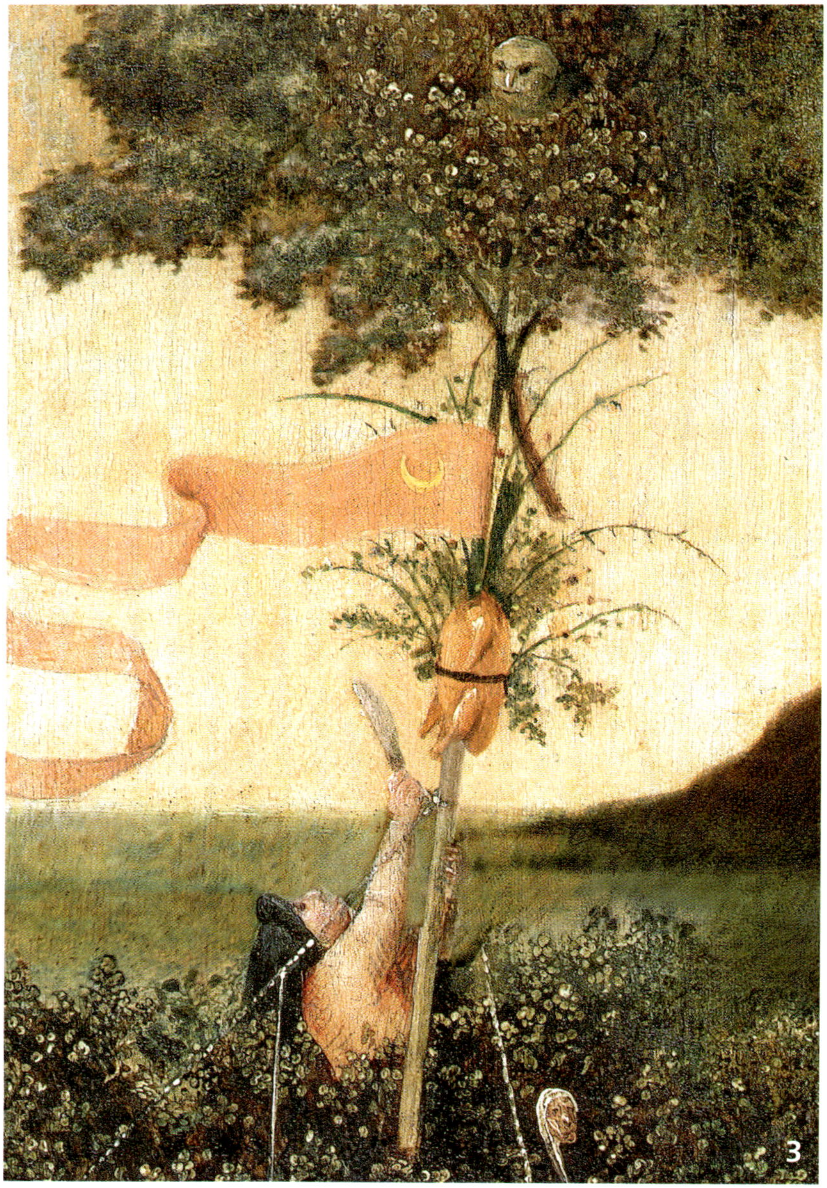
3

Trees appear in two guises in Bosch's picture, and they occupy a large area of the panel. One serves as a rudder, the other as a mast. The rudder-tree is lashed to the stern. A fish hangs from a dead branch on the right, while on the left – on a branch bursting into a leafy bush – sits the fool. It is a very unbalanced helm, difficult to move; it lacks the most fundamental qualities that a good rudder needs.

In the bush stands a man, who is reaching upwards to cut down a roast goose from the mast. His action recalls games associated with maypoles, which were commonly erected in the Netherlands in Bosch's day. Items would be tied to the maypole, which young people would then compete to cut down. The leafy crown of the mast does not grow out of the main trunk, but consists of branches that have been tied on. Only the inner section with the gleaming highlights was executed by Bosch; the rest was added later by a different hand.

The mast is unsuitable for setting sail, the rudder unsuitable for steering. Both features are useless, and the giant cooking spoons will be of little help, either, in propelling the boat forwards. Yet the passengers are intoxicated and in high spirits, and fail to see that they cannot steer their ship. They will never reach the Land of Fools.

In the pictorial symbolism of the Middle Ages, and in the imagery of other cultures, too, the tree (like water, ships and rocks) is of great significance. For the Germanic peoples, the tree was the great ash Yggdrasil, which held heaven and earth together. The Buddhists have a tree of enlightenment, the fig tree. In the Judaeo-Christian Paradise stands the Tree of Knowledge.

The Christian Tree of Knowledge forms the background against which the mast of this ship of fools assumes its particular meaning. It bears no apples, but only a goose tied to its trunk. The man who is cutting the goose down is not thereby transformed; he does not, like Adam, suddenly acquire a thirst for knowledge, but will get no more than a full stomach.

Bosch portrays a reversal of the mysterious process allegorized in the Bible as the Fall and Expulsion from Paradise – a very realistic, materialistic reversal: the displacement of spirit by gluttony.

The fact that the crown of the tree does not grow out of the trunk, but rather is added on, fits both the image of the maypole and the symbolism of the composition as a whole. The tree of fools is dead; it bears not a single leaf or fruit. Although the bush beneath it has foliage, its only fruit is a dead fish. It is also deformed.

Above, in the rapidly wilting crown topping the mast, sits or hangs something which the present condition of the painting no longer allows us to identify with certainty: it may be a skull, or it may be an owl. The owl represents the bird of wisdom and of death. While wisdom on this boat is surely no more than a distant memory, death, on the other hand, is near. This ship of fools will founder and sink.

In Sebastian Brant's *Narrenschiff*, all the characters are constantly moving. They are ceaselessly engaged in some senseless activity or another, as if standing still were dangerous. Bosch's passengers, too, all appear emotionally or drunkenly animated – with one exception: the figure in the fool's costume. He sits apart from the rest, turns his back on them, sips quietly from a bowl. One might think he was meditating. Fool's costumes were very popular in Bosch's day, and were worn by professional jesters at court and in carnivals and processions. There were even carnivals devoted solely to fools. The fool's costume included bells, which were supposed to jingle constantly - something they would only do so if the wearer kept moving. In his hand the fool held either a mirror – symbol of narcissistic vanity – or, as in Bosch's panel, a fool's sceptre. This sceptre usually bore a carved jester's face and was understood as a phallic symbol. The fool himself sometimes wore a coxcomb on his cap; the comb and the sceptre represent uncontrolled sensuality. The asses' ears indicate stupidity. Even the fact that the cap fits tightly on the fool's head, almost like a second skin, has a symbolic significance: the fool's costume can't simply be slipped off like other garments, but sticks fast to the wearer. With its symbols of stupidity and lust, the costume is an aspect of human nature: man is not just spirit, but also animal.

This concept of the fool held an extraordinary fascination for the people of the late Middle Ages and early Renaissance era. They thought in metaphors. The fool symbolized the human condition: such is man, a hemaphrodite belonging partly to the world of spirit and partly to the sphere of instinctual urges.

By their very nature, however, symbols are never clearly defined. They permit different interpretations, and as they pass down through the generations, so they are assigned new meanings. Fundamentally, every person was a fool. At a not quite so fundamental level, fools were those who acted wrongly – like the passengers in Sebastian Brant's *Narrenschiff*. Such fools stray from the straight and narrow path and fail to get to heaven. At the start of the Renaissance era this vision of divine redemption, this goal of all human endeavour, lost its cogency. The Christian world picture faded. People began to rely more on their own experience than on Biblical authorities. The earthly vale of sorrows metamorphosed into an attractive landscape. The people within it discovered their individuality. They sought a new metaphor for their new outlook on life, and alighted once again upon the fool. He was reinterpreted: no longer a sinner, but an eccentric, someone who is different from the rest, who flaunts his individuality. Around 1500 – a point in time which saw the publication of a great many books about fools – there appeared in German literature a character who epitomizes this new type of fool: Till Eulenspiegel. He lives not wrongly, but differently. Instead of being slower-witted, he is cleverer than the townsfolk, farmers and thieves. He hoodwinks them, teaches them lessons the hard way, and then makes his getaway. He belongs to the vagrants, the homeless who drift across Europe. Amongst the ruling classes, the Renaissance prince became an idol of individualism, obeying only his own will. Lower down the social scale, in certain regions this role of idol was taken over by Till Eulenspiegel: the fool as hero.

The person in the fool's costume in Bosch's painting falls into the Eulenspiegel category. He doesn't join in with the rest, he thinks for himself, an eccentric. All the other passengers represent the old type of fool: they are behaving badly, they are sinning, instead of steering their ship of life towards the kingdom of heaven. Bosch thus brings together in one panel two different interpretations of the fool, one belonging to the Middle Ages and the other to the early Renaissance. His *Ship of Fools* thereby documents the transition from the old era to the new.

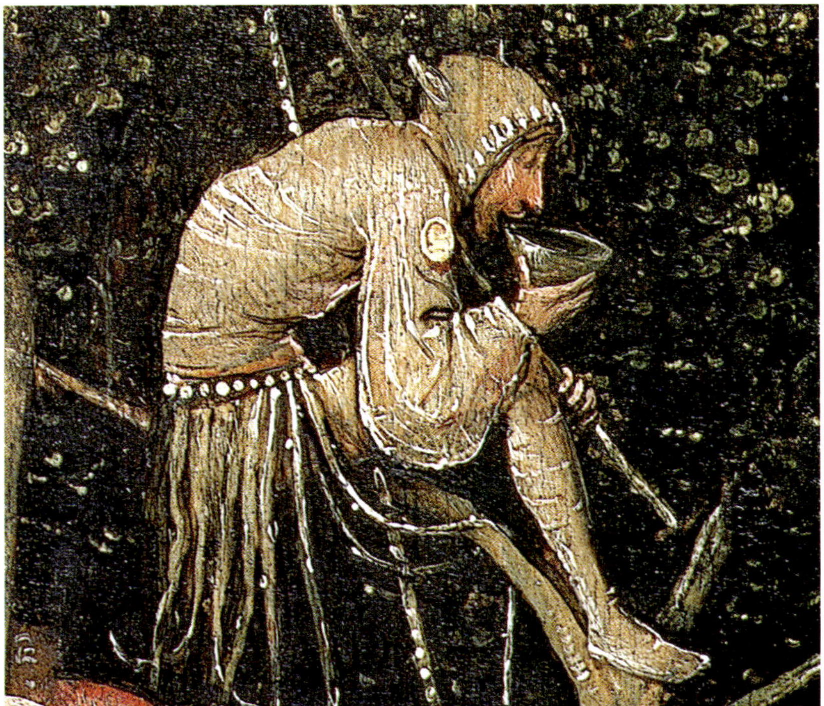

4

The birth of the eccentric

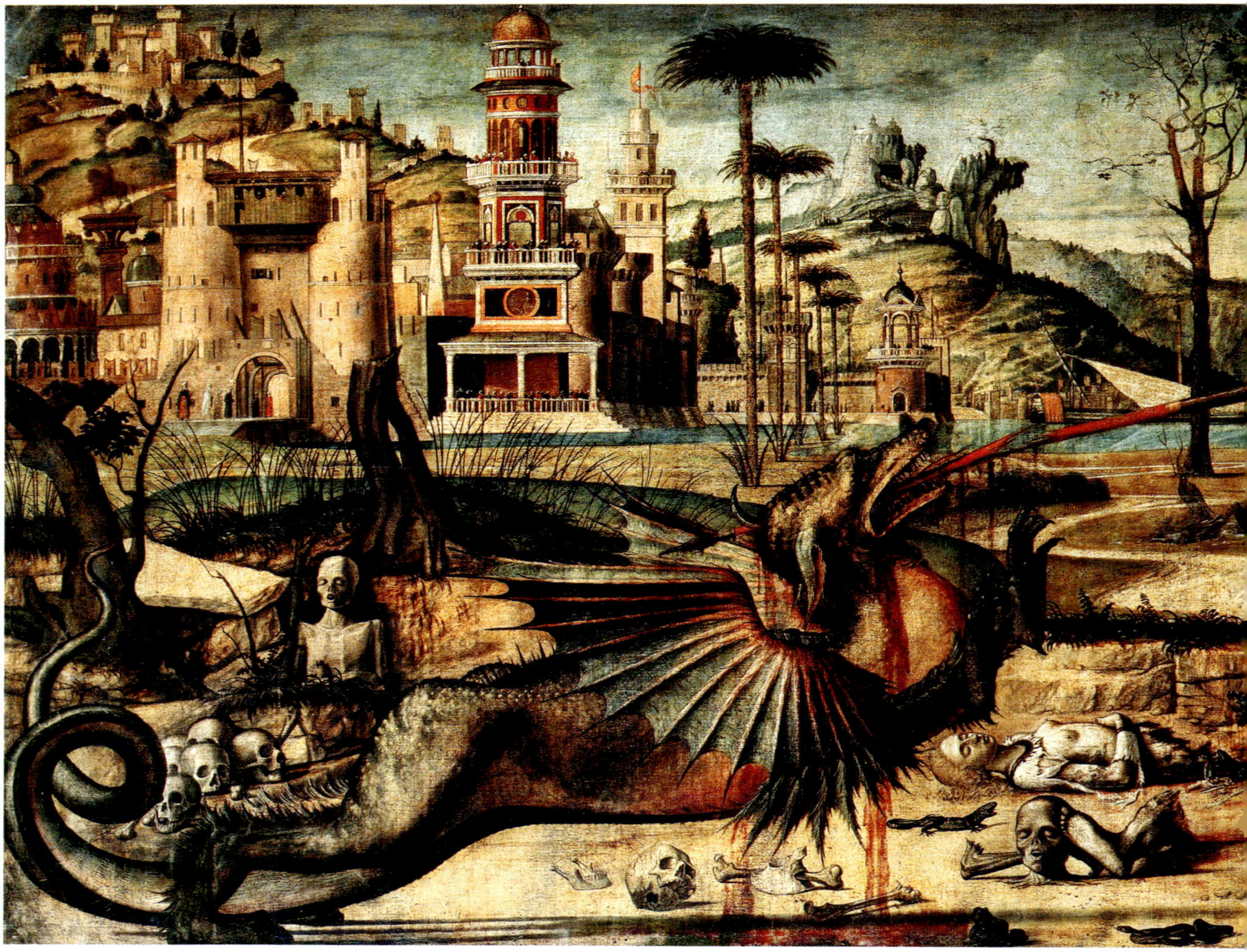

Vittore Carpaccio: St George and the Dragon, 1502/1507

A fearless charge for the myth of Venice

The knight in armour thrusts his great red lance straight down the monster's throat. It splinters, but the dragon is brought down. The city's inhabitants, watching the battle from the distance, can safely come down from their towers to welcome St George as their saviour.

St George then goes on to kill the captured dragon in one of the city's squares, whereupon the heathen members of the population convert in their masses to Christianity, the religion of the man who saved them from the beast. The Venetian artist Vittore Carpaccio portrayed these episodes on two further canvases. Together with *St George and the Dragon*, in the unusual format of 141 by 360 centimetres, they form part of an ensemble of scenes from the lives of the saints executed between 1502 and 1507 in oil and tempera on canvas. They adorn a chapel in a modest building situated on a side canal in the centre of Venice, namely the Scuola di San Giorgio degli Schiavoni.

The Venetian *scuole* ("schools") were religious confraternities of lay individuals devoted to pious practices and works of charity. According to the founding charter of one such association: "It is a good and joyful thing to live together and be humble for the love of God." They were financed by legacies and by contributions from members, and provided services that we today leave largely to the state. They ran hospitals and supported members who had fallen on hard times. In the 15th century Venice was home to six wealthy and influential *scuole grandi* and over 200 "small" ones, in which social classes or associations of immigrants joined forces.

The small Scuola degli Schiavoni was founded by immigrants from Dalmatia. In

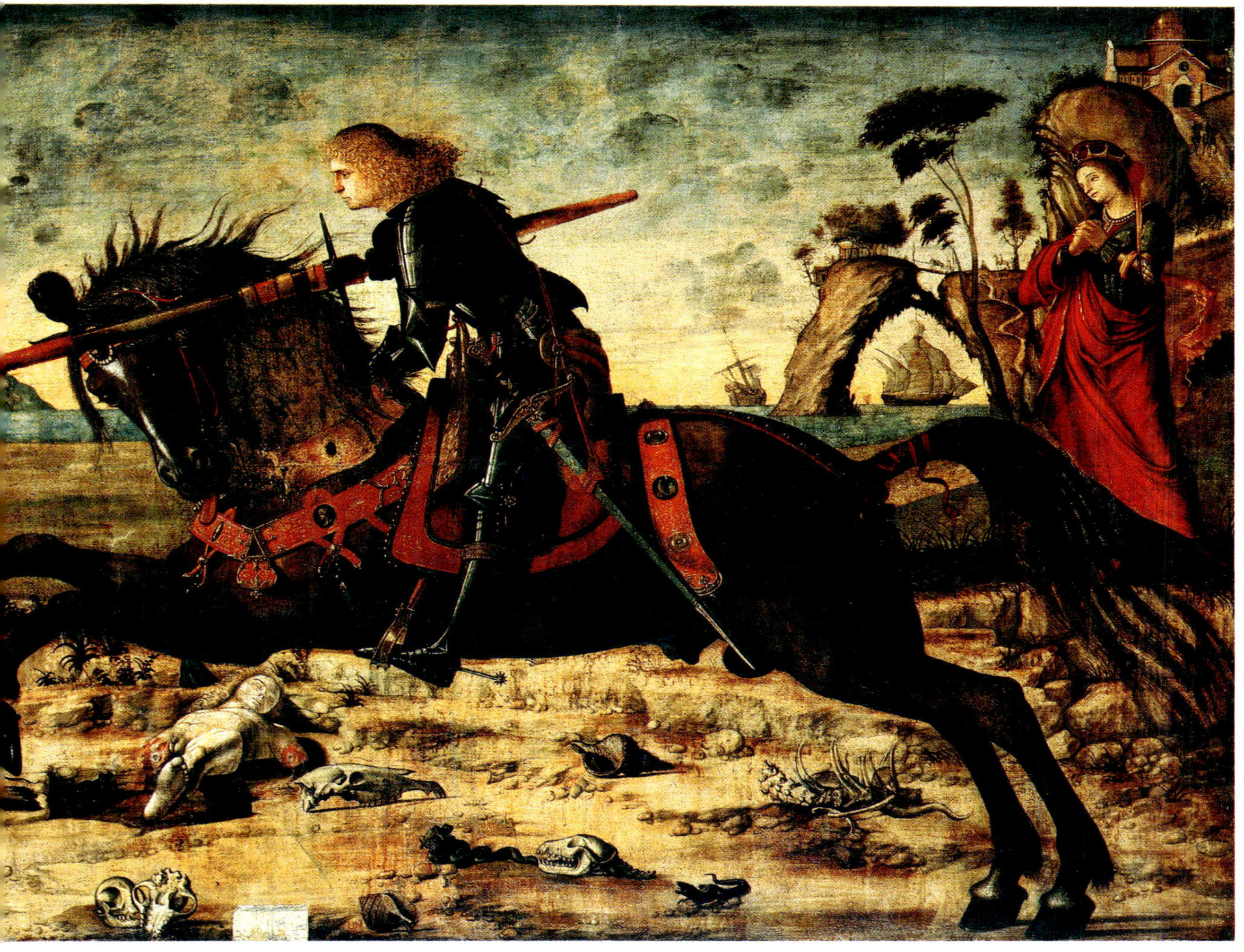

their application for recognition by the Council of Ten in 1451, the founders refer expressly to the precarious situation of the many Dalmatian sailors fighting the Turks on Venetian galleys, far from their homeland. Since the welfare of this immigrant group was in the interests of the Serenissima, the "Most Serene" maritime Venetian Republic, the application was approved and the Scuola founded under the protection of the patron saints of Dalmatia, St George and Tryphon (and later Jerome). Their lives and miraculous deeds are the chief subjects of the paintings that decorate the Scuola's chapel and assembly hall.

Sponsoring works of art was considered just as much a pious deed as funding hospital beds or candles for the chapel. Who commissioned and paid for the paintings in the Dalmatian Scuola is not stated in the records, but the St George cycle probably arose in conjunction with a donation to the confraternity by the Venetian captain Paolo Valaresso. He had served as the commander of fortresses in Dalmatia and the Peloponnese, and upon his return to Venice in 1499 brought back a precious relic of St George, formerly in the possession of the deceased patriarch of Jerusalem. In 1502 Valaresso carried it to the Scuola degli Schiavoni in a ceremonial procession "with many priests, drums, and pipes and with great devoutness".

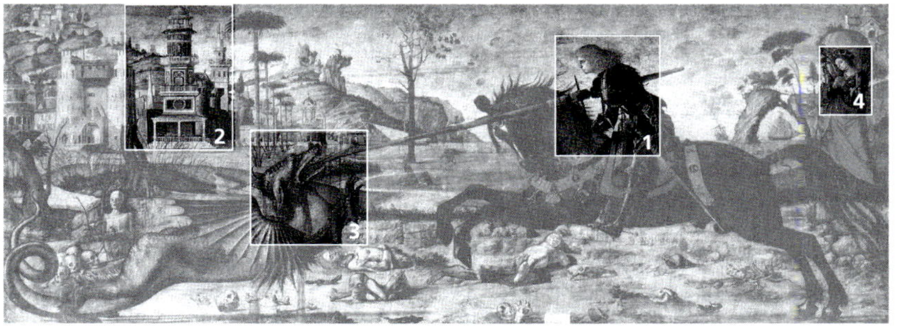

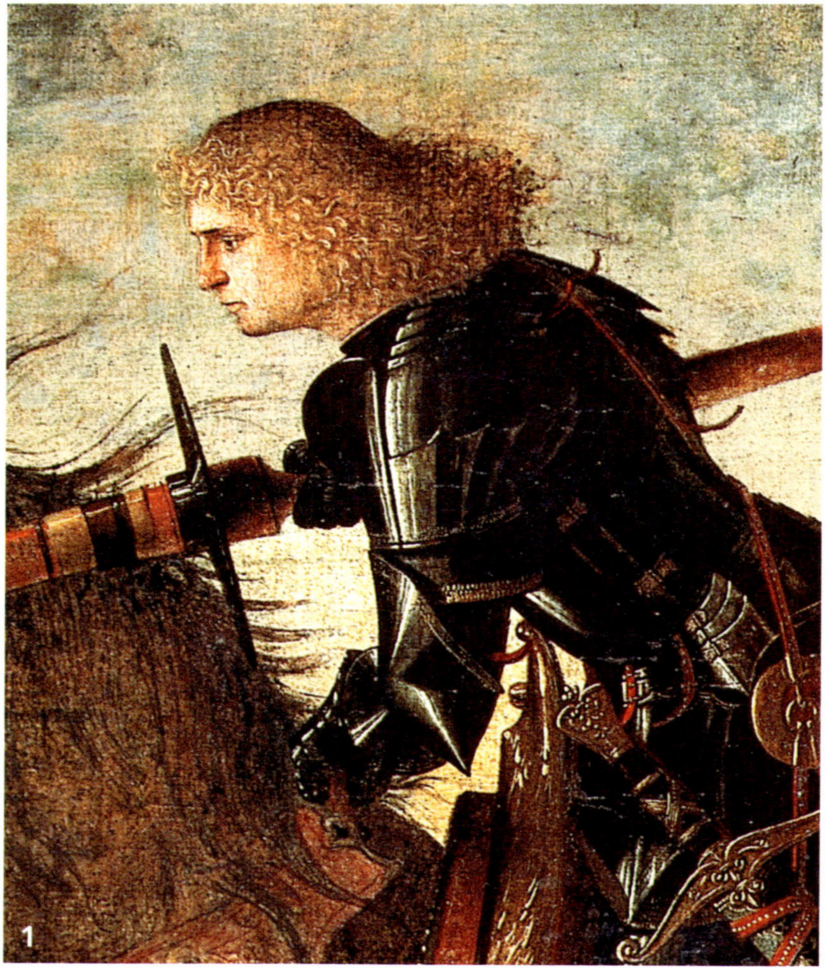

1

A soldier of Christ

Relics of St George had been housed on the Venetian monastery island of San Giorgio Maggiore since 1296. Together with St Mark, George was the patron saint of the city in the lagoon. He originated from the East. The historical George is thought to have come from Cappadocia, present-day central Turkey, and to have served as a cavalryman in the Roman army in the 3rd century. Because he declared himself a Christian, he suffered a martyr's death. The legend of his battle with the dragon, however, only appears from the 12th century onwards.

"George ... once travelled to the city of Silena in the province of Lybia", wrote Jacobus de Voragine (c. 1228–98), archbishop of Genoa, in his *Golden Legend*. Near this town was "a lake where a plague-bearing dragon lurked"; this dragon "used to come up to the city walls and poison everyone who came within reach of his breath. To appease the fury of this monster, the townspeople fed him two sheep every day ... But in time they were running out of sheep ... so ... they paid him tribute of one sheep and one man or woman." One day the lot fell upon the king's only daughter, and she was left beside the lake for the dragon. "At this moment blessed George happened to be passing by ... and arming himself with the sign of the cross, set bravely upon the approaching dragon, and commending himself to God, brandished his lance, dealt the beast a grievous wound, and forced him to the ground."

The "soldier of Christ", who here conquers Satan in the guise of the dragon with the sign of the cross, is part of a long pagan tradition. The sun god Apollo and the heroes Hercules and Perseus are just some of the figures from antiquity who fought the Manichaean battle of good versus evil in the shape of a monster, the battle of light against darkness. There are no fewer than fifty-five dragon-slayers in Christian tradition. George, the most popular of them all, is usually identified in paintings by his white horse.

Carpaccio seats his George on a brown stallion, a heavy tournament horse in blood-red harness captured in mid-gallop. The knight thundering across the canvas is dressed in gleaming black armour. In the pose of an experienced jouster, such as could be admired on St Mark's Square in the artist's own day, he charges at his opponent with lance tilted.

George here appears not as a luminous figure on a white horse, but as a mighty fighter – the sort of patron saint upon whom the Venetians could call in times of danger. Such was George's popularity that even the statue of St Theodore, looking down from a column between St Mark's square and the lagoon, was referred to in common parlance as George.

The Orient lay close to Venice

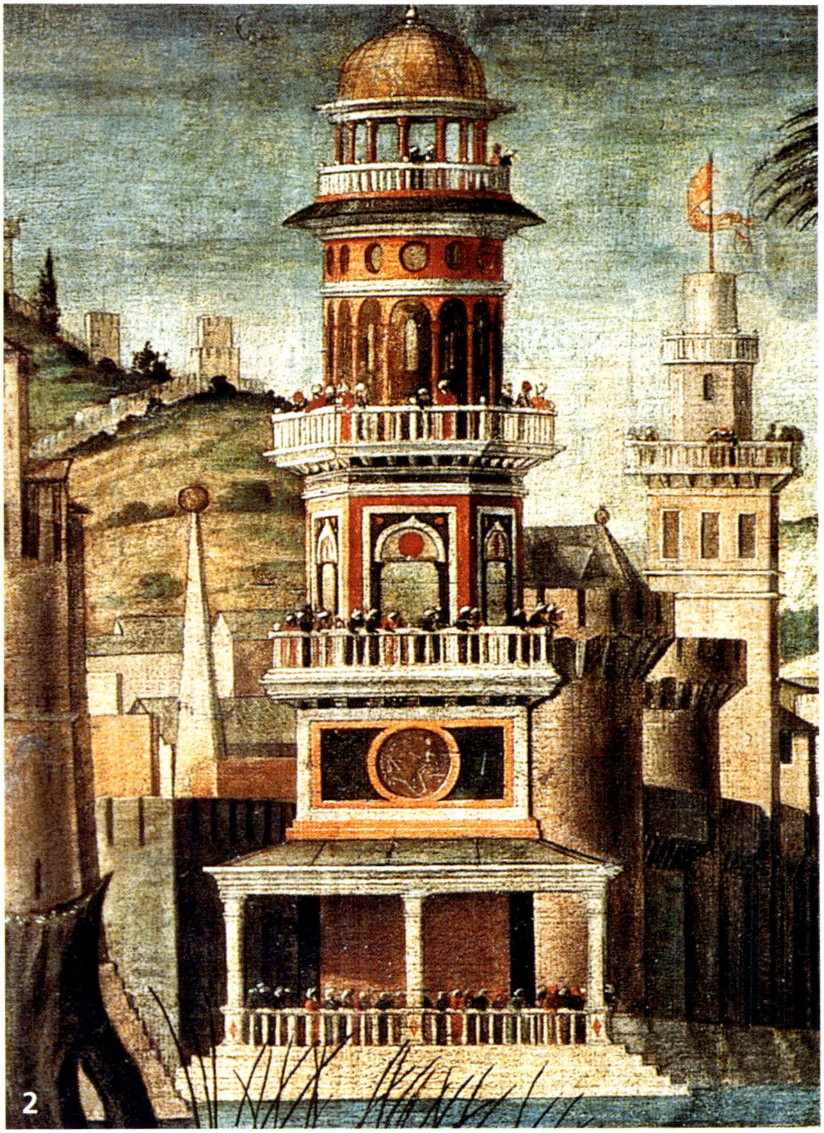

2

Vittore Carpaccio, who was born in c. 1460, is said to have accompanied his teacher Gentile Bellini to Constantinople, acting as his young assistant. But Carpaccio probably never saw the Orient at first hand, relying instead for his inspiration on the illustrations which accompanied the travel writings of other contemporaries.

Tall date palms, an obelisk, elegant pavilions by the water and a series of towers lend the Lybian city of Silena, mentioned in the *Golden Legend*, an air of exoticism. Its inhabitants are watching the battle with the dragon from the airy terraces of a tall building of multicoloured marble. Only a handful have ventured as far as the bridge in front of the city walls, via a massive fortified edifice in which we can recognize the Bab el Futuh, one of the city gates of Cairo. Carpaccio could have found it in a woodcut by Erhard Reuwich in *Pilgrimage to the Holy Land* by Bernhard von Breydenbach, published in Mainz in 1486.

There were naturally plenty of Venetians who had sailed the seas as mariners, merchants and diplomats in the service of the Serenissima, and who could describe the architecture of the East to the artist in great detail. The Venetian Republic, which had originally formed part of the Byzantine Empire, had maintained close links with the Levant ever since its foundation. The wealth of its patricians rested on the maritime trade in spices, silk and other oriental luxuries. To ensure safe shipping routes for its galleys, the Republic had established coastal bases along the Adriatic and Aegean and expanded its power in the East.

By the beginning of the 16th century, when Carpaccio painted his *St George*, Venice was starting to lose its control of the seas. Since the conquest of Constantinople in 1453, the Ottoman Empire had grown in strength. It went onto the offensive, engaged the Republican fleet in constant skirmishes and thereby captured one Venetian port of call after another. In 1479, for example, Paolo Valaresso, the donor of the St George relic, had to abandon the Peloponnes ports of Modon and Coron under his command, leaving the sea routes increasingly more dangerous for Venetian traffic. The Orient, previously so close, slipped out of reach and withdrew to an uncertain distance. It is probably no coincidence that, during precisely this period, the fascination with the Orient increased: never before had Venice's artists painted so many exotic buildings, landscapes, caftans and turbans.

"Everyone was in fear and trembling", wrote the Venetian Domenico Malipiero in his diary in 1470, following the fall of Negroponte on the island of Euboea (Évvoia). "People were afraid the whole empire would be destroyed." Banks collapsed and in 1499 the Republic even found itself obliged to levy a special tax to meet the costs of war and to cut the salaries of all its civil servants. All of Venice's efforts to organize a European league to defend Christianity from the Ottoman threat came to naught. Instead, the German emperor, France and the Pope allied themselves against the weakened Venice. It was forced to fight against half of Europe on land and against the Turks at sea. The assistance of St George must surely have been invoked by many a Venetian of the day.

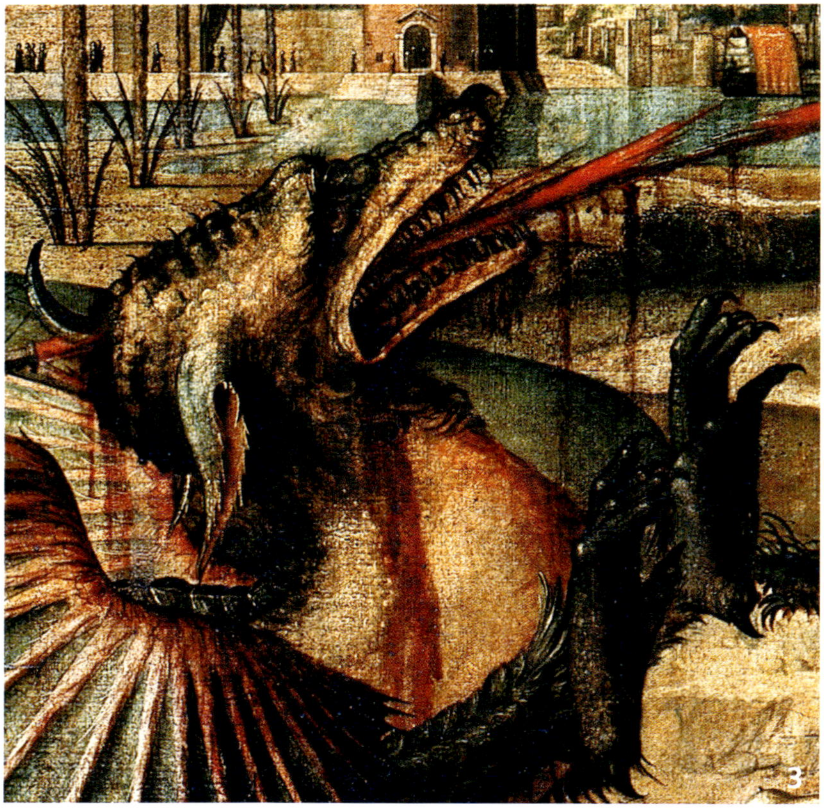

Dangers lurk in the water

"When it rises, the mighty are afraid, gripped by terror." Thus the monster Leviathan is described in the Book of Job. Carpaccio's fearsome dragon rears up on its muscular hind legs, ready for the fight, a worthy antagonist for the saint in armour.

The legends surrounding St George do not specify the type of dragon he fought; the final composition of the fabulous beast is left to the artist's imagination. Carpaccio gives him the tail of a snake, the body of a lion, the claws of a bird, the wings of a bat and the head of a wolf. The gruesome remains of a previous victim testify to the monster's cruelty. This scene of horror provides the backdrop against which the battle with the dragon is staged.

Nearby lies a body of water. Leviathan, records the Book of Job, "makes the waters boil with its commotion. It churns the depths. The water glistens in its wake. One would think that the sea had turned white." For psychologists, the dragon also embodies the threatening chaos within. It lives in water or dark caves, both symbols of the subconscious. The cathartic example of the legendary dragon-slayer serves to prove that it is possible for man to overcome his instinctual drives.

For Carpaccio's contemporaries, there were very real dangers lurking in water. 150 citizens of Venice drowned in a severe storm in 1504. The city regularly flooded at certain times of year, and it is said that only the intervention of SS Mark and George saved the city from being swallowed up by the sea shortly after its foundation.

In addition to storms and Turkish soldiers, the Venetians were in danger from yet another threat – the plague. In both 1498 and 1503 the "Sensa", an important trade fair, had to be cancelled due to major outbreaks of the plague, brought to the lagoon by rats on ships from the Levant. The source of the epidemic was suspected by doctors of the day to lie in "venomous vapours", related to the plague-bearing dragon in *The Golden Legend*, who poisoned "everyone who came within reach of his breath". The people sought their salvation in flight or by invoking the protection of St George.

The Venetian government, however, did not simply leave it at that. For almost twenty years, since 1484, a special body – unique in Europe – had been in charge of city hygiene. It monitored deaths, isolated the sick on a hospital island and imposed a strict quarantine on all incoming ships. The measures were effective; by 1513, everything seemed to be under control. The efficient Serenissima had defeated the plague dragon.

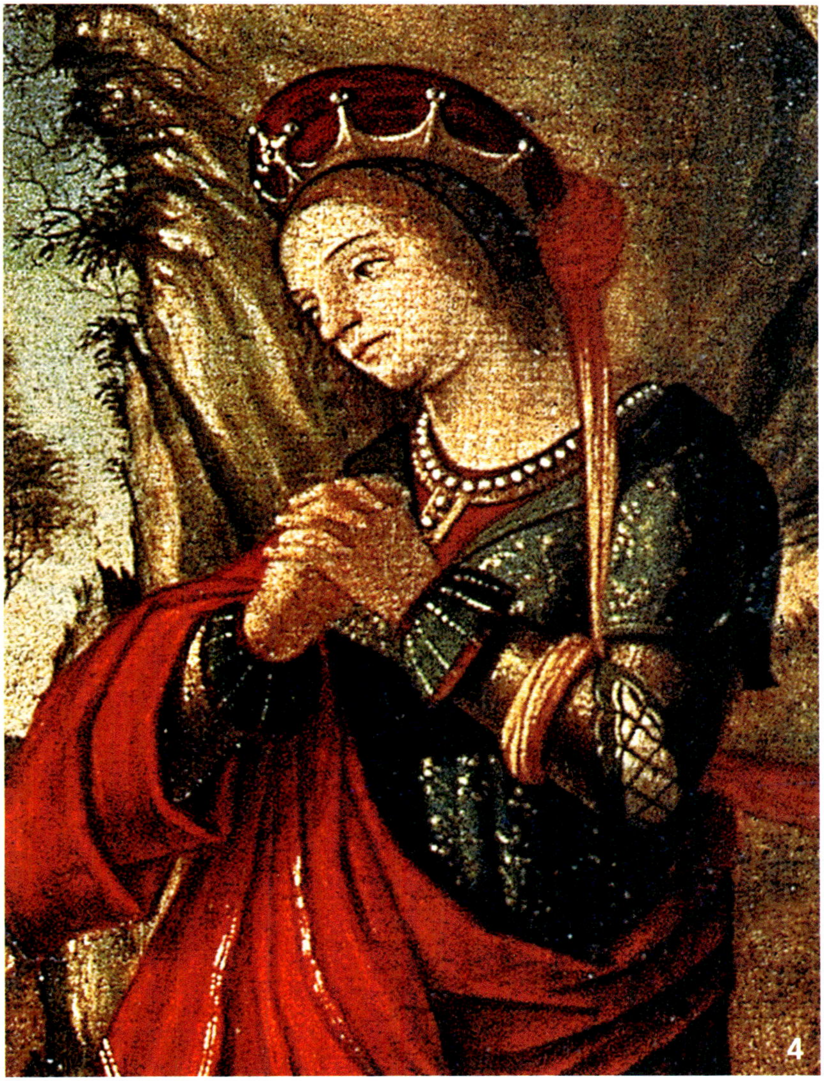

4

Barbers and tailors donated paintings

Carpaccio does not paint the princess who is to be sacrificed as a naked, alluring victim, as later Venetian artists saw her. She watches the battle with her hands clasped, her hair modestly covered, and wrapped in her mantle. The artist might have portrayed the Virgin Mary in a similar fashion, or the equally virginal "Queen of the Sea", Venice herself.

"Have no fear, child! Throw your girdle around the dragon's neck!", St George commands the princess in *The Golden Legend*. "When she had done this, the dragon rose and followed her like a little dog on a leash." Pitifully, like a little dog, the dragon goes off to the slaughter – in the next painting in the cycle. Carpaccio assigns generous space to the triumph of the saint and the subsequent festivities: he shows joyful celebrations attended by richly dressed people in front of magnificent buildings. Such images of order and social harmony reinforced the myth that Venice had woven around its system of government for centuries. It was the myth – celebrated in countless stately processions and ceremonies, as well as in official paintings – of an invincible, just, ideal Republic.

The dutiful citizens of Venice were expected to exert themselves selflessly for the good of the state and the general public. The Dalmatian immigrants who had banded together to form the Scuola degli Schiavoni consisted, according to their official register, of barbers, tailors and fruiterers, in other words lower-class citizens with absolutely no political rights, even if they were born in Venice.

The ruling patrician class defused the social tensions that arose in times of war insofar as they allowed the "people" to take charge of certain areas of social work, for example, through the *scuole*. Within these "schools", the lower classes could also hold office and advance to high rank. As a group, they were allowed to take part in processions and their senior representatives were granted an appropriate place in official ceremonies. As collective sponsors of works of art, they were even allowed to produce their own state propaganda.

Between 1470 and 1520 – a period during which Venice was under particular threat from within and without – there thus arose on the walls of the small *scuole* at least ten *istorie* (histories), monumental cycles devoted to the lives of the saints. They were to convey, even to those who could not read, a "true", i.e. pious and patriotic, message. George's triumph is at the same time the triumph of the myth of Venice.

Because its senior officer defiantly opposed the disbanding and secularization of the Scuola degli Schiavoni under the French occupation of 1806 – the only such chief officer to do so – the worshipful confraternity still meets there today. Its works of art have survived intact. Thus the walls of the Scuola, with their reassuring message that in times of danger a saviour is always near at hand, continue to reflect both the former glory of the Serenissima and the threat that hung over it.

Gentile Bellini: St Mark Preaching at Alexandria, 1504–1507

How Bellini imagined a city

Gentile Bellini painted his vision of Alexandria between 1504 and 1507 in Venice. He was not familiar with the city at first hand, but he was the only Western artist of high standing who had ever travelled to the Islamic world of the East. He worked in Constantinople and may have gone as far as Jerusalem, but never to Egypt.

The painting is dominated by the enormous façade of a church with curving buttresses incorporating a number of arched openings. No such façade is to be found either in the West or in Constantinople or indeed anywhere else in the Mediterranean – it is a product of the artist's imagination. Although perhaps not entirely: if we forget the buttresses and concentrate upon the three cupolas and the upper arches, we are reminded of the top section of St Mark's cathedral.

The picture was commissioned by a Venetian religious confraternity that named itself after St Mark, and formed part of a cycle of altogether seven paintings depicting the life and works of the Evangelist. For the viewer studying the almost eight-metre-wide canvas from the distance it needs, however, it is difficult to locate Bellini's St Mark. Artists around 1500 were no longer allowed – as they had

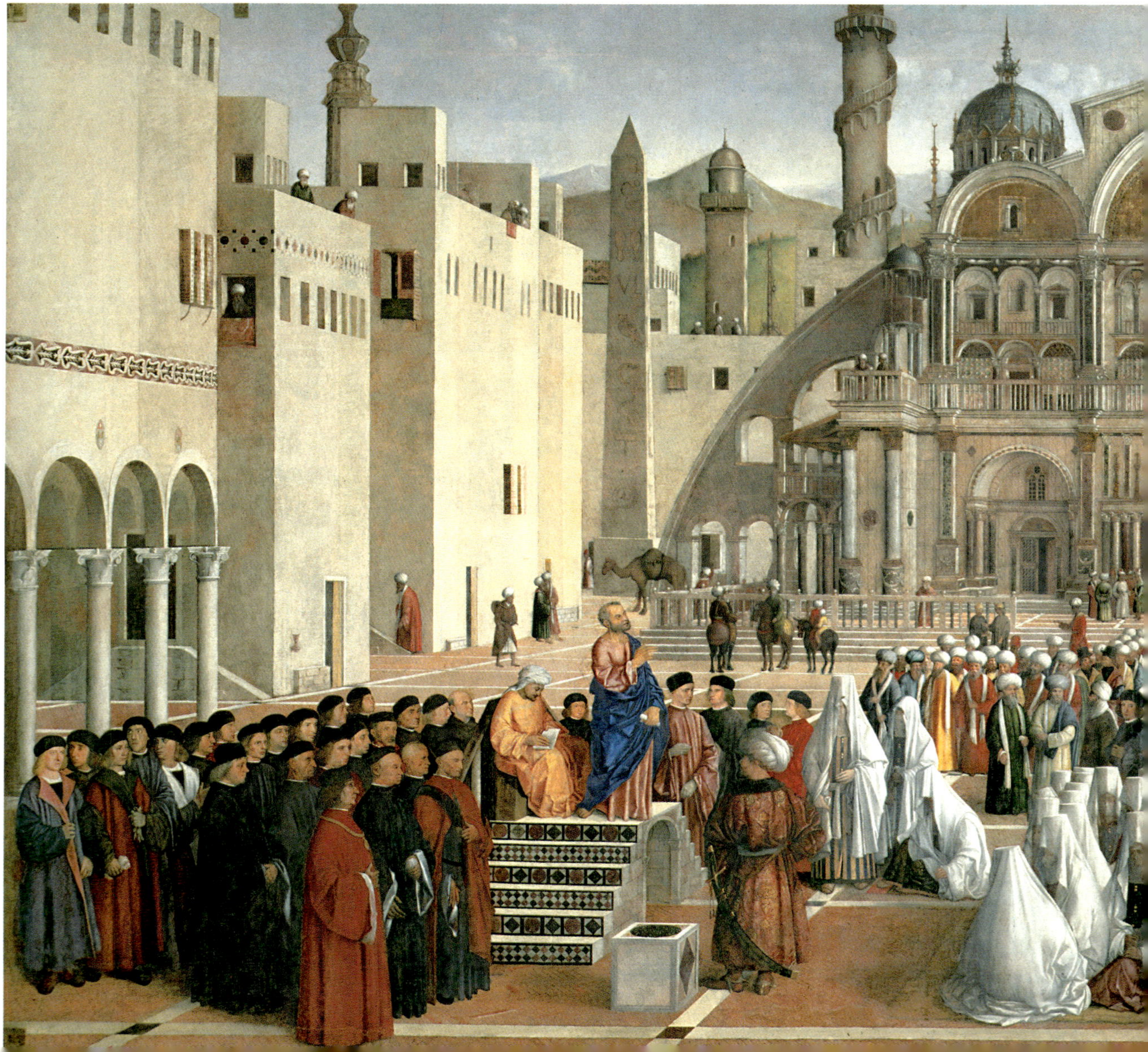

been in the Middle Ages – to make figures who were particularly important much larger than the rest. Bellini, it would seem, used the church façade instead: St Mark was considered the founder of the Christian community in Alexandria, a community whose missionary activities had extended far beyond the bounds of the city, and in the church façade the artist creates a broad-reaching structure that appears to hold both halves of the picture, heathens and Christians, in a maternal embrace.

For Bellini's contemporaries, however, the saint was probably not quite as inconspicuous amongst the crowd as he appears to us today. Bellini honours him with a sprecial colour, which in those days would have caught the eye of viewers from afar.

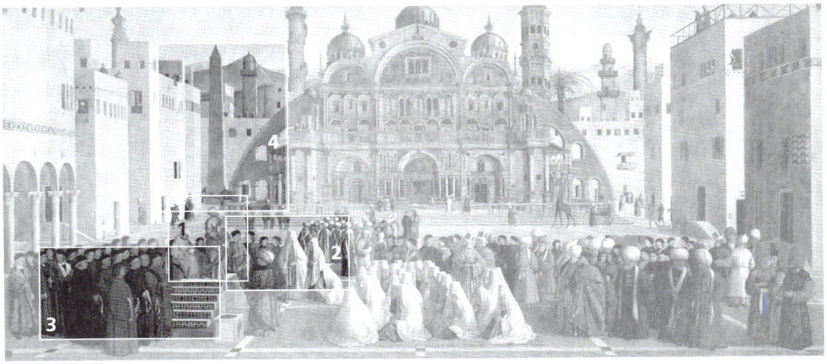

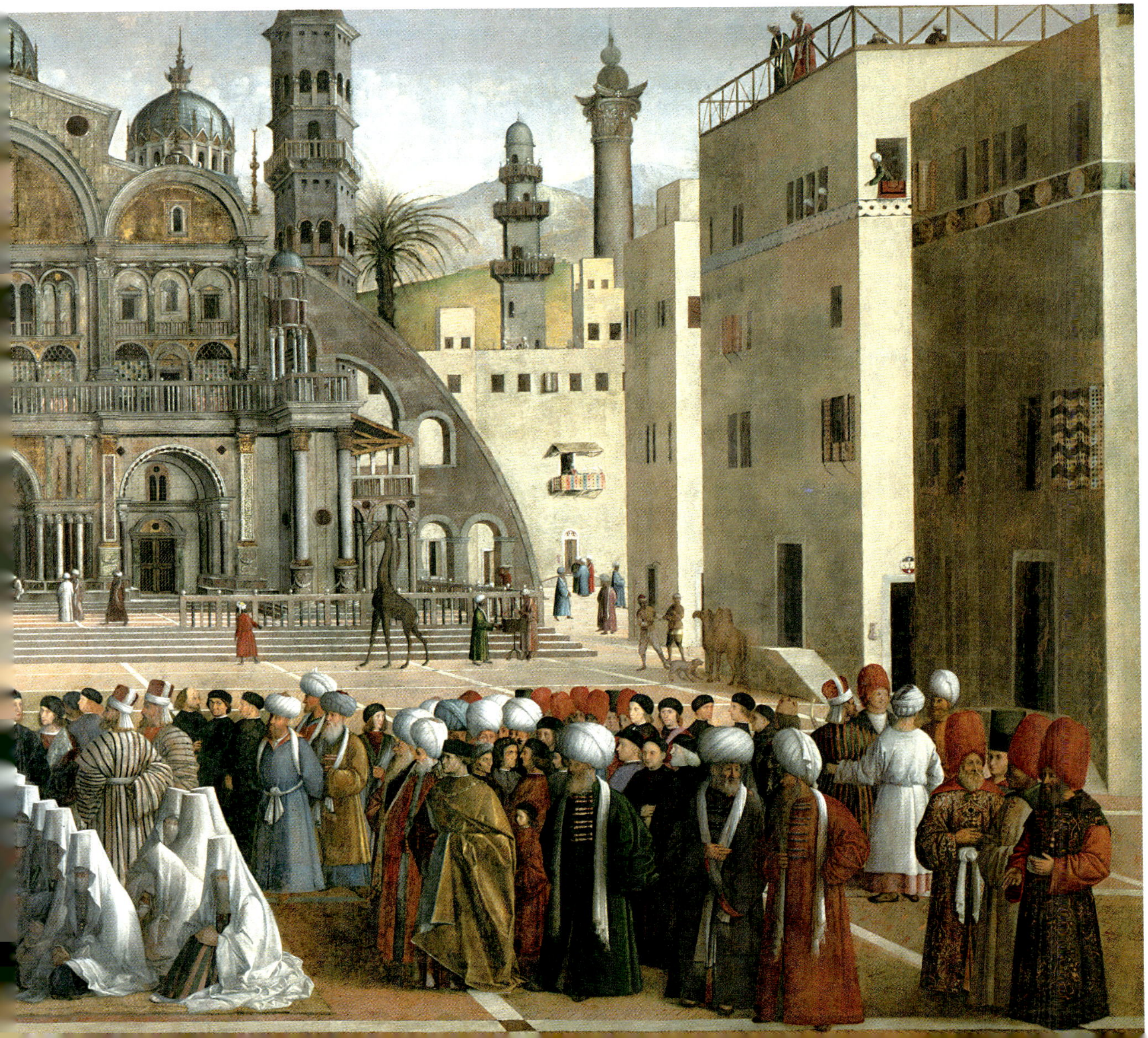

The rise of the colour blue

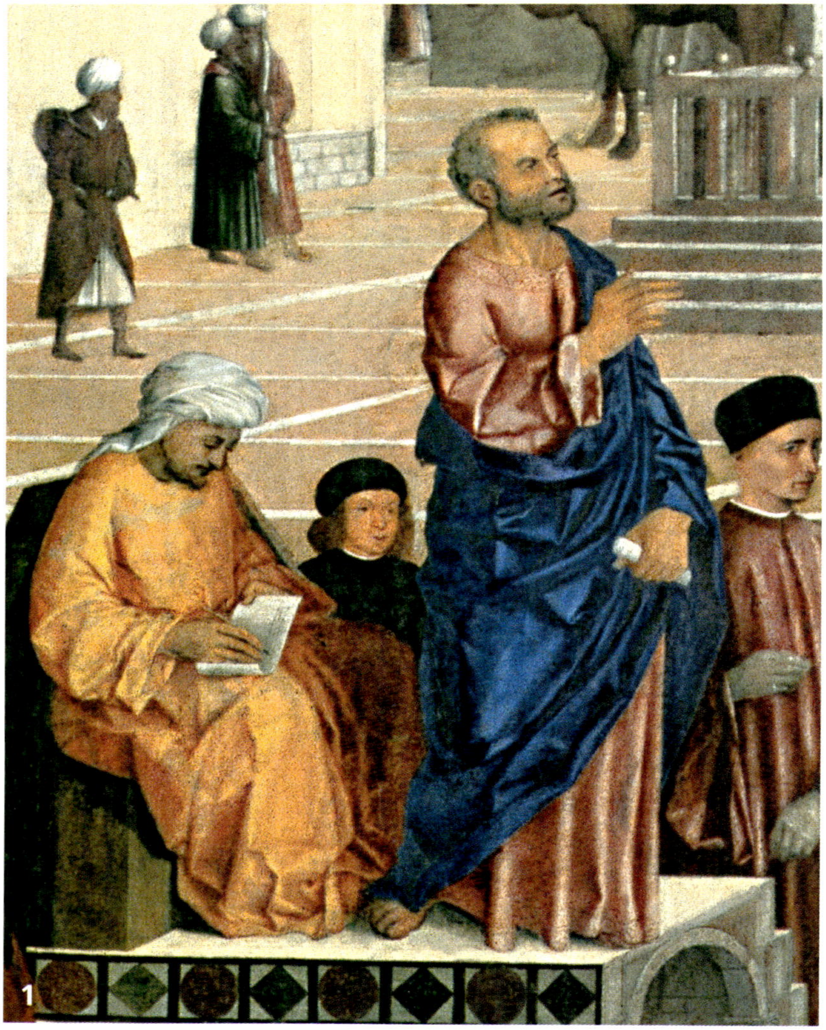
1

Colours, too, have their own story. In the first century, during Mark's lifetime, no preacher would have chosen a blue stole; in the hierarchy of colours, blue ranked very low down. At the top stood white, black, and red; these were the colours in which Greeks and Romans clad themselves. In wall-paintings, such as those in Pompeii, blue generally appears only in the background. For the Greeks, there was no blue in the rainbow. Blue was positively despised by the Romans, for whom it held numerous bad associations: the eyes of the barbarians in the North were blue, for example. Caesar and Tacitus recorded that the Celts and Teutons dyed their bodies blue in order to frighten their enemies.

Blue, so little valued for so long, began its rise in 1200, as can be traced in earthenware and fabrics, church windows and most clearly of all in the Virgin's draperies. Around 1500, in Bellini's day, artists almost always dressed the Queen of Heaven in robes of blue, and several of Europe's kings now also took to wearing blue cloaks on ceremonial occasions. In order to make a person's high rank visible in paintings and miniatures, artists used a particularly brilliant blue, mixed from an extremely expensive pigment obtained from the precious stone lapis lazuli. Bellini – it is to be suspected – did the same thing in the case of the saint's stole. No other blue in this painting shines with such luminosity as that of St Mark.

In his left hand, St Mark is holding a roll of paper, papyrus or parchment. The man behind him, probably an assistant scribe, is also writing in or leafing through a sort of book. St Mark is always associated in pictures with writing of some kind, for it was as an author that he achieved his elevated status; it is to him that we owe the earliest of the four Gospels and thus one of the documents on which the Church was founded.

But who this Mark was remains shrouded in darkness. Whether he was with Peter in Rome, whether he was a bishop in Alexandria and there died a martyr's death – either is possible, but cannot be proved. He remains anonymous, without a face, without a character, without a biography. And yet in Bellini's Venice he was one of the most popular figures, enveloped in a wealth of legends. The story of his martyrdom, of which nothing is known, was nevertheless related in great detail: how he was seized at the altar by heathens while celebrating mass on Easter Sunday, how Christ appeared to him in prison, how the following day he was dragged to his death through the streets of Alexandria, how the pagans wanted to burn his body, but how a mighty storm arose and sent them fleeing, and how Christians were then able to give him a worthy burial.

Mark's remains are supposed to have been transported to Venice in 828. Once again, a storm broke out over Alexandria, driving the pagans into their houses, so that the Venetians could carry the body unchallenged onto their ship. In order to keep the abduction secret from Alexandria's Christians, another corpse was placed in the grave, and to dissuade the Muslim customs officials from inspecting them more closely, the Venetians concealed St Mark's remains beneath slabs of ham and pork. So the story was told in the city lagoon – a story of cunning and courage to the glory of Venice.

Amongst Gentile Bellini's contemporaries was Marino Sanudo, Secretary to the Senate, famous for his book on the lives of the doges, written in the 1490s. There is a sentence in the book that, although unconnected with St Mark, reveals how a historical survey judged something to be accurate. Sanudo writes: "If this had not been so, our good Venetians would not have had it painted." A picture that shows St Mark preaching in an imaginary Alexandria amongst Venetians and Egyptians confirms, in other words, that the saint was active there.

From the 10th century onwards St Mark became established ever more firmly as the patron saint of Venice, and countless legends sprang up linking the saint with the city. Thus he was said to have visited Venice during his time in Rome, where Peter had told him of the life of Jesus. He had a prophetic dream that revealed that he would be laid to eternal rest in Venice, and indeed on the very spot where the first St Mark's church was subsequently erected. When the original church was destroyed by fire and a new one was built, and nobody knew exactly where the body was buried, it helpfully revealed itself by cracking open a column. It was not just the Venetians who venerated St Mark; the saint also declared his allegiance to Venice.

A psycho-social process: the city selects its own saint, creates an entirely imaginary figure and lends it a religious reality which bears no relation to the facts or lack of them. This process succeeded particularly well in Venice because faith in the Republic and Christian faith had grown into one. The cult of St Mark became a state religion. Anyone who mocked St Mark was insulting Venice, while anyone who paid him homage was also paying homage to his city.

The Venetians had previously venerated as their patron saint one St Theodore, whose religious standing was far below that of the Evangelist. The more highly regarded St Mark corresponded to the city's growing might. Venice reached the pinnacle of its political power in the 13th and 14th centuries. Its fleet held sway over the Adriatic and its ships pushed ever further eastwards, establishing ports along the coast of Greece and the Levant. Here, under the suspicious eye of the local populace, the Venetian merchants built themselves large residences that doubled as warehouses. They would have done the same in Alexandria. Their ships carried spices, silk, carpets, and precious woods back to Venice, where they were sold on the Rialto to the merchants of western Europe, making the city in the lagoon the most important point of trans-shipment of luxury goods from the Orient.

When Bellini painted his picture, this era of power and profit was over. Vasco da Gama had discovered the sea route past Africa to India, and exotic goods could now be shipped direct to the ports along the west coast of Europe. Mediterranean trade shrank, and Venice lost its central significance. The Turks posed an immediate threat. For several decades they had been conquering the Venetian settlements in the eastern Mediterranean and decimating the Venetians' once famous fleet of ships. A city in crisis. An age in which all hopes were pinned on St Mark and on the pictures in which he was portrayed.

Faith turns pictures into documents

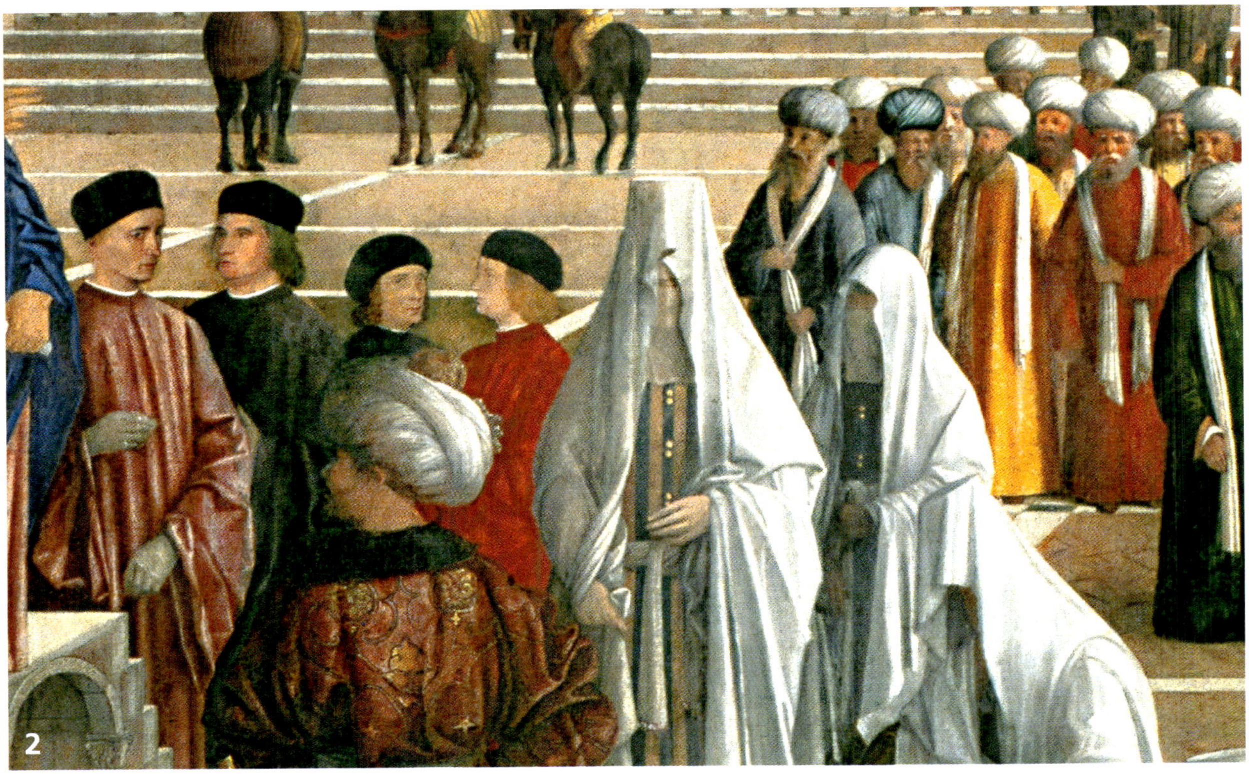
2

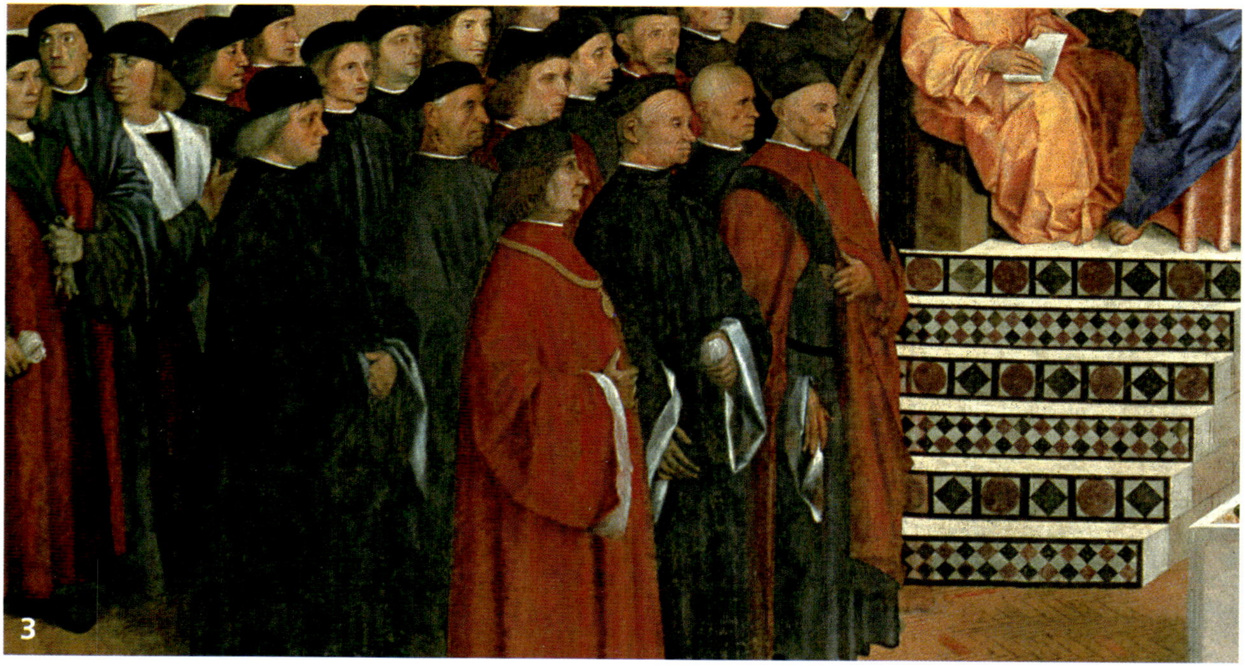

3

In St Mark's day, that is to say the first century AD, Alexandria was a flourishing city and a spiritual metropolis. Priests guarded the knowledge handed down from the age of the pharaohs, Greek and Roman scholars came to study it, and a growing Christian community enlivened the debate over God and the gods, the meaning of life, and what happens after death. In his own vision of Alexandria, Bellini invented an architecture whose magnificence corresponded to the fame of the setting.

He had never been to Alexandria, and even if he had seen sketches by other travellers, they wouldn't have helped him. When Bellini came to paint it, the city was a run-down provincial outpost. Only a fraction of the area encompassed by the city wall was still occupied. The Genoese merchants who had been Venice's great rivals had already secretly left the city. A chronicler in 1515: "At that time there were no more large merchants in Alexandria, neither Muslims nor Christians. As a consequence of the tyranny of the governor and the tax collectors, the city had fallen utterly into decline ... It is even said that if you try to buy bread there, you won't find any."

Gentile Bellini portrays himself in a red toga with a chain of honour around his neck. This latter had been presented to him by Sultan Muhammad II in Constantinople. No one knows if Bellini went to the Ottoman capital of his own free will. He was probably obeying the urgent wish of the Senate. Having once again suffered heavy losses in battle against the Turks, in the spring of 1479 Venice had concluded peace and in August had received an envoy from the Sultan, who requested that artists should be sent over to Constantinople. The painter was joined on the journey by a bronze founder and several assistants.

Born in 1429 and thus at that point fifty years old, Gentile Bellini was a famous man. His father Jacopo is considered the founder of an independent Venetian school of painting, and both Gentile and his younger brother Giovanni trained in the family workshop. In 1479 he was working in the Doge's Palace, painting for no fee because the Senate had promised him the position of broker at the Fondaco Tedesco. Since this honorary post at the German warehouse guaranteed him a permanent income, he was free to work for the Senate as a sort of state artist. That the Venetians should interrupt this favoured artist during his work on their own chambers of government and dispatch him to the Sublime Porte was an act of almost servile politeness.

Bellini is sent to Constantinople

What Bellini's artistic vocabulary gained from his experience in the East is evidenced in the present canvas in the clothing, rendered with great precision. The men in the tall red hats on the far right of the picture can be identified as Circassian members of the military aristocracy, while the man with the scimitar in front of St Mark is a high Ottoman dignitary. It must have been in Constantinople, too, that Bellini originally encountered the squatting figures of the women in tall headdresses covered by a white veil; although Turkish men paid occasional visits to Venice, it is most unlikely that such women would ever have been seen in the artist's native city. It must similarly have been in Constantinople that Bellini discovered the decorated wall-tiles on the steps of St Mark's podium. He paints them with striking precision, for they belong to the Islamic culture and he wants to identify his Alexandria as an Islamic city.

Bellini's painting was commissioned by the Scuola Grande di San Marco, a religious confraternity devoted to good works. How much money its members raised can still be estimated today by standing on the Campo SS Giovanni e Paolo in front of the magnificent façade of the Scuola, or by visiting its spacious interior. Gentile Bellini's canvas, together with six other paintings devoted to St Mark, hung in the "library" on the first floor. As well as offering mutual aid and assisting the general welfare, the Scuole also offered their members an opportunity to cut a more public figure, for example in processions and in paintings. Several Scuola members may be portrayed amongst the group of Venetians.

Venetians from around 1500 have thus been taken back in time to the first century and removed from their own city to a foreign one. Turbans, dromedaries, and a giraffe serve to characterize the scene. Bellini uses the obelisk to indicate that this is a city in Egypt, and the tower with the round cupola to show that it is Alexandria. This tower represents the lighthouse of Alexandria, world-famous in the days of the Ptolemies and Romans. By Bellini's time it had long since collapsed, and no one knew what it used to look like. But it could be seen in a mosaic in the cathedral of San Marco. The mosaic tower was also a work of imagination, but the Venetians considered it to be authentic. For would their forefathers have let it be portrayed in any other way?

A few years earlier, for another Scuola, Bellini had painted a procession on St Mark's Square. Both paintings are laid out in the same fashion: a crowd of people assembled in a square with a church façade in the background. In those days, squares of this kind were new. In 1504, the year in which Bellini started work on *St Mark Preaching at Alexandria*, the Senate had just resolved to clear St Mark's Square of huts, trees, and vines, because it was like a "filthy latrine" fouled by all and sundry.

Bellini transferred his compatriots' desire for civic spaces laid out on a geometric plan to far-off, run-down Alexandria. He thereby employed the new Renaissance methods of evoking spatial depth through the use of centralized perspective. The converging lines of pale stone patterning the square, and the buildings on either side similarly converging towards the rear, convey the impression that we are indeed looking into a large space.

Bellini's picture thus illustrates something of current trends in both art and civic design around 1500. It shows, too, how the artist and his contemporaries had little feeling for what was foreign and for what lay in the past. And while it is true that historical knowledge was still very limited, it seems the artist simply had no desire to portray an event that took place in the first century AD as something long past, nor the wish to depict a setting in far-off Egypt as somewhere foreign. The distant city, like the distant past, was absorbed into the present: Alexandria – just another sort of Venice.

Gentile Bellini died in 1507, leaving the picture unfinished. It was completed by his brother, Giovanni. Three hundred years later, under the Napoleonic occupation, all the Scuole were dissolved. The painting today hangs in Milan.

4

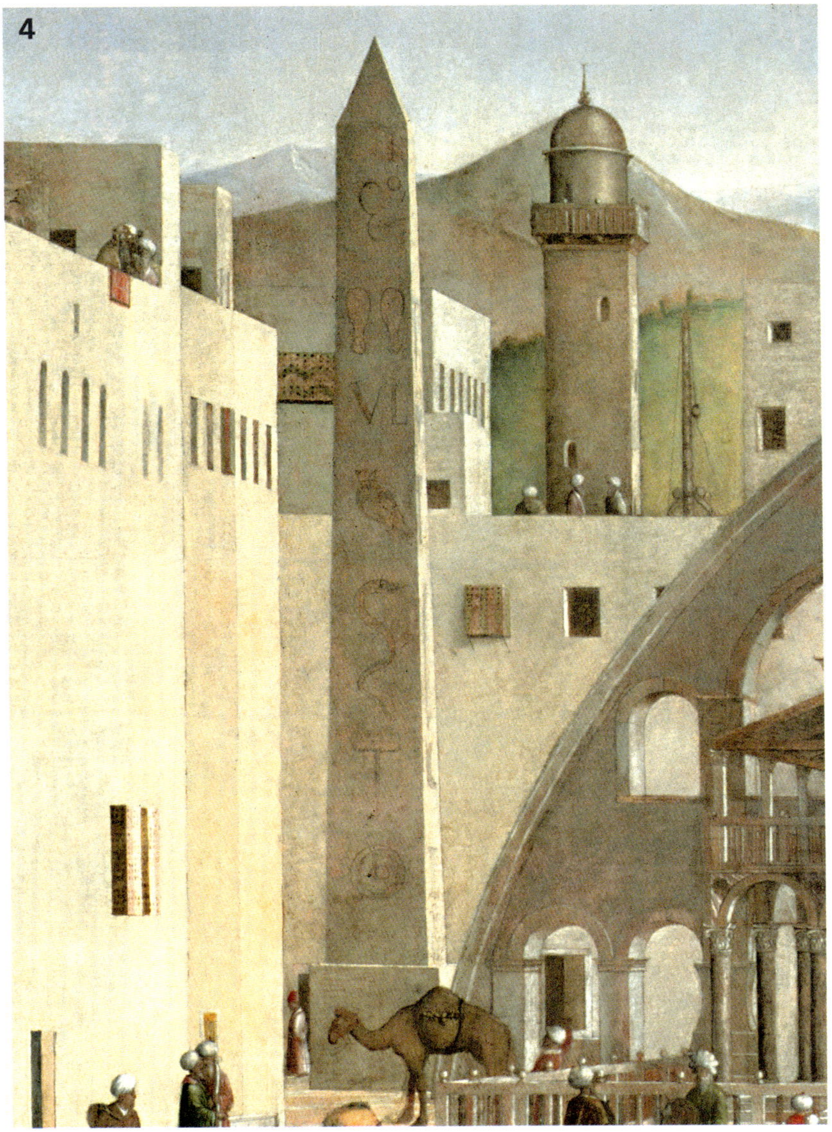

Public squares on a geometric plan

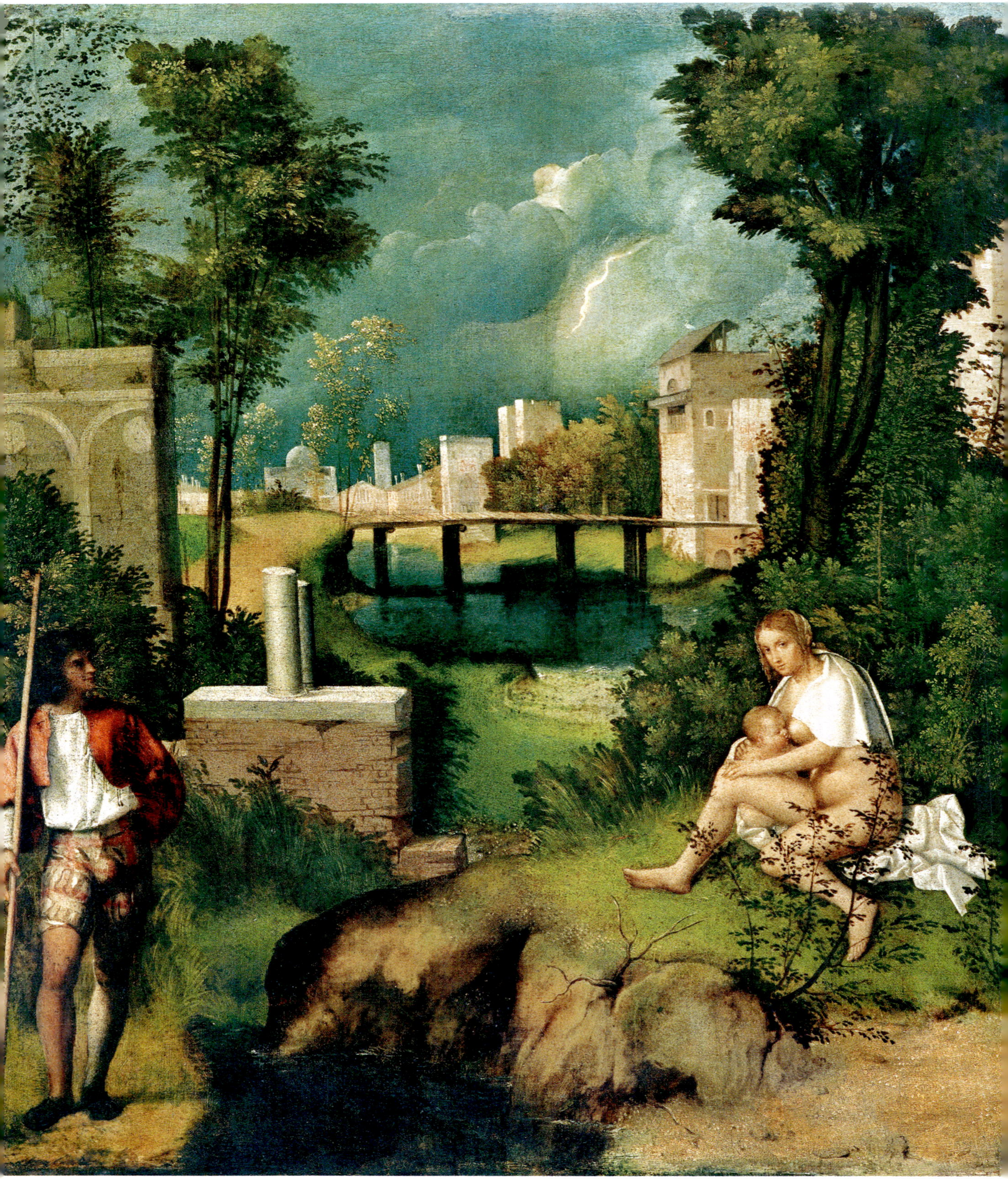

Giorgione: The Tempest, c. 1507

The man, the naked woman and the bolt of lightning

The painting, which was executed in Venice around 1507, is first documented in 1530 as "the small landscape with the tempest, the gypsy woman and the soldier". The blonde with the pale skin – a gypsy?

With a population of over 120,000, Venice at that time ranked amongst the largest and wealthiest cities in Europe. Trade with the Orient had been channelled through the city's canals for over three hundred years and the Venetians had profited richly. By the time Giorgione came to paint his picture, however, those times were past: Columbus had discovered America in 1492 and Vasco da Gama the sea passage round Africa soon afterwards. The trade routes no longer passed through the Mediterranean.

The majority of patrician and middle-class families remained prosperous enough, nevertheless, to own a second home in the country. The Venetians, living on top of each other on their cramped islands, sought nature and a freer life on the mainland. They started by buying farmhouses with dovecotes and chicken yards; later they built country houses, then villas, including architectural masterpieces such as those by Andrea Palladio, born in 1508.

This yearning for the countryside was reinforced by contemporary literature. Like the Greeks and Romans before them, Renaissance authors now composed pastoral idylls celebrating the life of the rustic shepherd. 1506 saw the first performance, in Urbino, of a bucolic play; two years earlier, Jacobo Sannazaro (1457–1530) had published his novel *Arcadia*, the tale of a young man who seeks to forget his beloved in solitude, with only animals for company. This love of nature and the pastoral idyll is also echoed in a letter written by the Venetian humanist, historian and cardinal Pietro Bembo (1470–1547): "I have come to my little villa, which has joyfully welcomed me", he wrote. "The only noise I can hear is that of nightingales trying to out-sing each other ... I ride, I go for walks in a small wood, pick a basket of strawberries with my own hands ... In the evenings, I take a small boat out on a lovely stream."

Giorgione's picture, with its two people in the heart of nature on the outskirts of a city, might have pleased Bembo. The man with the staff, described in 1530 as a soldier, is referred to as a shepherd in an inventory of 1569. He looks calmly across at the naked woman with the child. The woman herself looks questioningly out of the picture, towards the viewer.

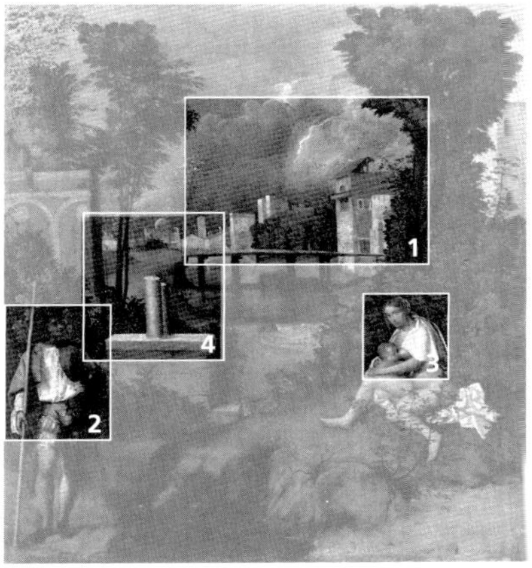

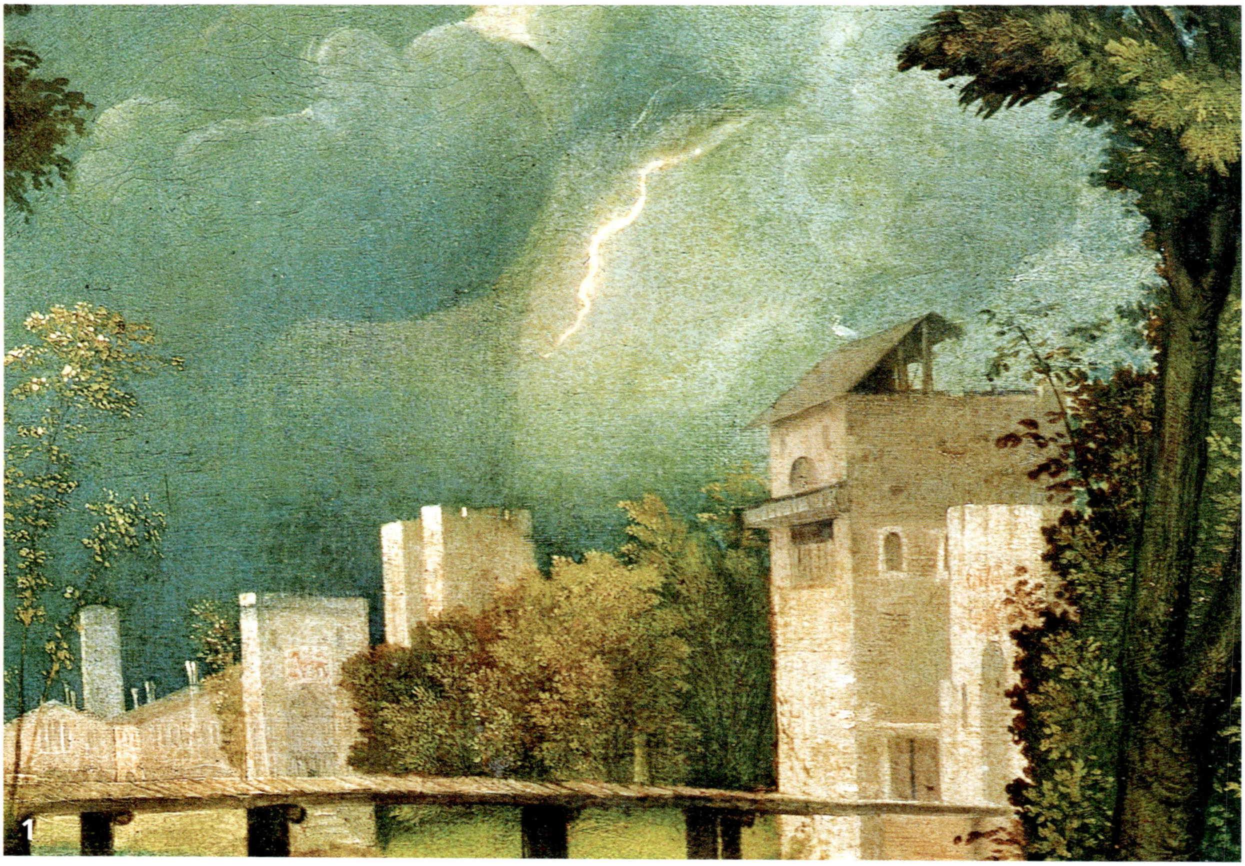

1

Eternity and the moment

After the writers, so too the painters began to celebrate nature. In the Middle Ages, this earthly vale of sorrows was considered barely worthy of portrayal; art stood solely in the service of the Church. Worshippers were to be offered visions not of the world around them, but of the saints, figures from the Bible, Heaven – everything inaccessible to the eye. If a painting featured a flash of lightning, it signalled the wrath of God.

With the end of the medieval era, the earth began to appear in art. Saints were no longer set against an indeterminate background of gold, but appeared in front of hills and trees. These seemed as eternal and unchanging as God's Heaven itself, however. The seasonal changes in nature were only recorded for the first time in books of hours, written and illuminated not for a broad public but for wealthy patrons. In addition to prayers, such manuscripts often included a calendar with miniatures accompanying each of the months and showing landscapes first covered in snow, then in their spring green, next with their fields ready for harvesting, and later in their brown autumnal foliage.

The Venetian Giovanni Bellini (c. 1430–1516) went beyond such seasonal changes and distinguished even between times of the day, making the difference between dawn and dusk visible in his art. He was Giorgione's teacher. Giorgione took this process yet another step further. In *The Tempest*, he shortens the "exposure", going beyond season and time of day to capture a natural phenomenon that is over, literally, in a flash. Dark thunderclouds conceal the sun, the light grows wan, shadows disappear. A dangerous bolt of lightning sears across the sky. The artist captures an instant in time.

This focus on the immediate moment was not the artist's declared aim, but rather a side product of the investigations into nature being conducted in many disciplines during the Renaissance. Philosophers wanted to know whether the earth or the sun was the centre of the cosmos; doctors and theologians argued over whether or not dead bodies could be dissected for the purposes of research; cartographers were combining maps into atlases; botanists were classifying the species of plants. For their part, painters were learning how to create the illusion of spatial depth on a flat canvas, looking at how colours changed in the distance and studying nature in close-up detail. In 1503 Albrecht Dürer executed a watercolour of a patch of grass, something which no one before his day had considered worthy of attention. Dürer, who came from Nuremberg, was in Venice in 1507; it was his second visit. Like Giorgione, he was amongst those artists who were discovering nature as a subject for painting.

A man from a well-to-do home

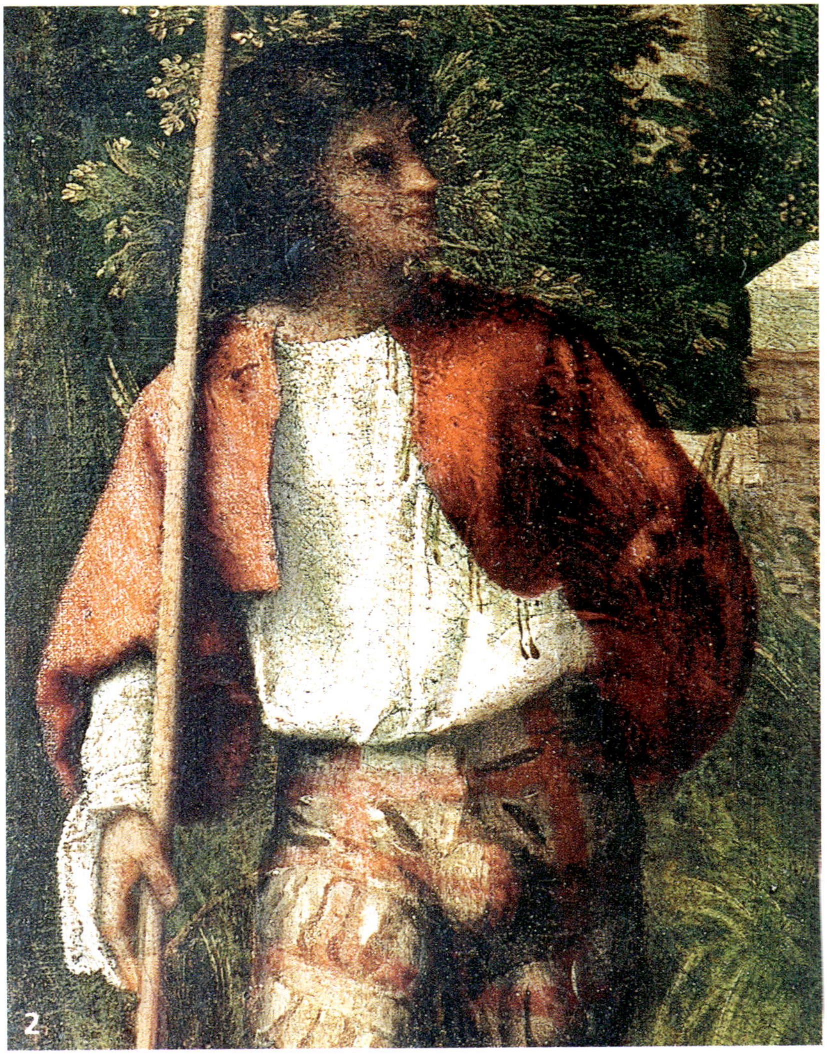
2

The trousers with the slits in their fabric were typical of mercenary dress. The staff, however, is without a metal tip and is therefore not a lance, suggesting that its bearer is a shepherd rather than a soldier. The short jacket with wide sleeves seems to have been fashionable amongst young men from well-to-do families. When the painting surfaced in the Palazzo Manfrin in Venice in the 19th century, it was called "Giorgione's Family". This erroneous title was so firmly rooted that in 1878 a statue of the artist himself was based on the male figure draped so elegantly against his staff.

The statue was commissioned by the town of Castelfranco Veneto, which lay some 30 kilometres from the Venetian lagoon. It was here that the artist was born, probably in 1477. The name Giorgione means "great Giorgio" – so-called "because of his physical appearance and his moral and intellectual stature", according to Giorgio Vasari, author of the famous *Lives of the Artists*, first published in 1550. Giorgione's surname has not come down to us, but he is thought to have come from modest circumstances. In 1510 he died of the plague, and his surviving oeuvre comprises fewer than 30 paintings. In comparison with other great painters of his day, such as Bellini and Titian in Venice, Michelangelo, Raphael and Leonardo, it is striking that he carried out virtually no public commissions. No works by him for the Doge's palace or the churches and *scuole* ("schools", or religious confraternities) of Venice. His only altarpiece was painted for a family chapel. He evidently worked for a circle of patricians who hung his pictures in their private apartments. The formats he adopted were correspondingly small. *The Tempest* measures 82 by 73 centimetres and is today housed in the Galleria dell' Accademia in Venice.

It is thought to have been commissioned by Gabriele Vendramin. It was certainly in his ownership in 1530 and, together with other items from his palazzo, is listed in an inventory of that same year. Gabriele came from a family that had recently yielded a doge. At the time the painting was executed, he was 23 years old and thus a few years younger than the artist. Even if it is not a portrait, both artist and patron could identify themselves with the young man in the landscape.

Gabriele Vendramin's house was famed as a "meeting place for the city virtuosi". Giorgione himself played the lute and sang "so beautifully ... that his services were often used at music recitals and social gatherings". The artist thus moved in circles in which class differences, at least temporarily, seemed suspended. All were bound by a common love of music, art, nature and also the past. Amongst the books and paintings in Vendramin's apartments were antique bronzes, marble sculptures and medals. He was considered an "antiquary", a connoisseur of classical antiquity, the era to which the Renaissance looked back in reverence and in which it saw its artistic ideal.

That Vendramin's love of art was not some passing whim emerges from his last will and testament. In it, he speaks of his concerns for Venice – his heirs are to learn how to sail and wage war on water like their forefathers, to the credit of their family and country. But he also speaks movingly about his pictures, which "are so dear and precious to me ... because it is they who have given me a little peace and solace amongst the stresses and strains of managing the family affairs."

Considerably less elegant than the man standing on the left is the woman sitting awkwardly on the white sheet on the right. Her legs extend in different directions as she leans her upper body slightly forward – a natural, but not very comfortable position in which to nurse an infant. Modern viewers are struck by the fact that the child is sitting beside her, rather than lying across her lap. It must already be somewhat older. In those days children were breastfed for several years – not by their mothers, if they could afford it, but by wet nurses. A mother's milk was the safest form of nutrition.

Why, however, the naked woman is sitting beside the water with broken columns nearby while a storm approaches is a question that has troubled generations of viewers. Especially since the 19th century, when the painting was put on display in the Palazzo Manfrin in Venice and in 1866 was reproduced as a lithograph. Few other works of European art have posed such an enigma as Giorgione's *Tempest*.

The majority of its would-be interpreters, both professional and amateur, started from the assumption that *The Tempest* was based on a literary source. The child might be Dionysus, the son of Zeus, in the care of a nymph who is hiding him from Hera, Zeus's angry wife. Or it might be Moses, who was rescued from his basket on the Nile by the Pharaoh's daughter and was straight away handed over to a wet nurse. Or Cain, conceived by Adam and Eve after their expulsion from Paradise and the first murderer in world history.

This biblical interpretation for a long time enjoyed the most support. The city in the background, empty of people, was thought to symbolize Paradise, the tempest the wrath of God. Problems are posed by the supposed figure of Adam, however, who is not portrayed in the conventional manner as working the soil "by the sweat of his brow" while covering himself with a fig leaf or animal skin. This man does not look like someone just expelled from Paradise, but surveys the world, woman and child with a calm and sovereign expression.

Such a positive picture of the first man had been recently painted by the Italian philosopher Pico della Mirandola (1463–94). In Mirandola's eyes, Adam – at least before the Fall – offered a shining example for humankind, because in contrast to the animals, Adam had free will and could choose between good and evil, could "lower himself to the level of the beasts ... or raise himself to the greatest heights". Pico set out these thoughts in his famous *Oratio de hominis dignitate* (*Oration on the dignity of man*), which was reprinted in Venice in 1498, some ten years before Giorgione painted *The Tempest*. An oration, characteristic of the self-assurance of the men of the Renaissance, which would undoubtedly have been read and discussed by the young Venetians for whom Giorgione worked.

More persuasive than the biblical interpretation, however, is the suggestion that we are looking at the figure of Paris, son of the king of Troy. His mother dreamt that he would bring destruction on his native city, and so he was exposed in the wilderness and left to die. A shepherd and his wife found him and brought him up. It is not this scene we are shown here, however, but a later one. Like his foster father, Paris becomes a shepherd. He falls in love with a river nymph and together they have a child. One day Hermes, the messenger of the gods, brings Hera, Athene and Aphrodite to see Paris, who has to decide which of them is the fairest. He chooses Aphrodite, who promises him Helen in return. Paris abandons the nymph, and it may be this scene that Giorgione had in mind.

This interpretation, at least, is supported by a number of details: the river representing the home of the nymph, thunder and lightning heralding the destruction of Troy. Paris will defend Troy, and so is characterized not just as a shepherd, but also as a soldier. He is wounded in battle; the nymph he abandoned has the power to heal him, but refuses. Paris dies and the nymph, inconsolable, kills herself.

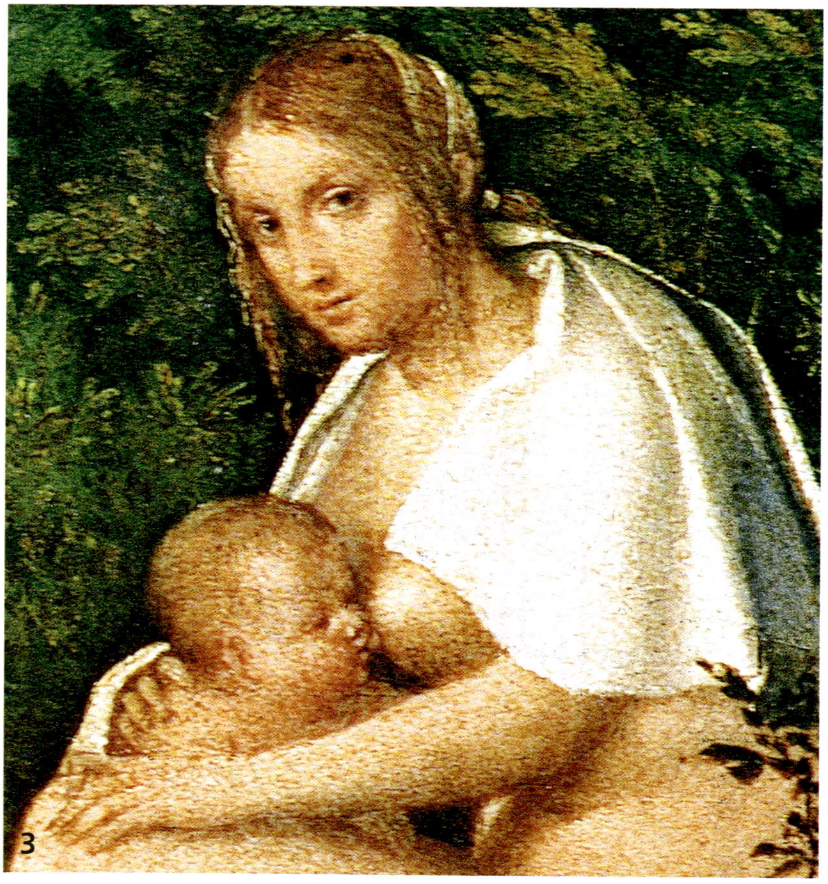
3

Who is the woman nursing at her bosom?

A brainteaser for those in the know

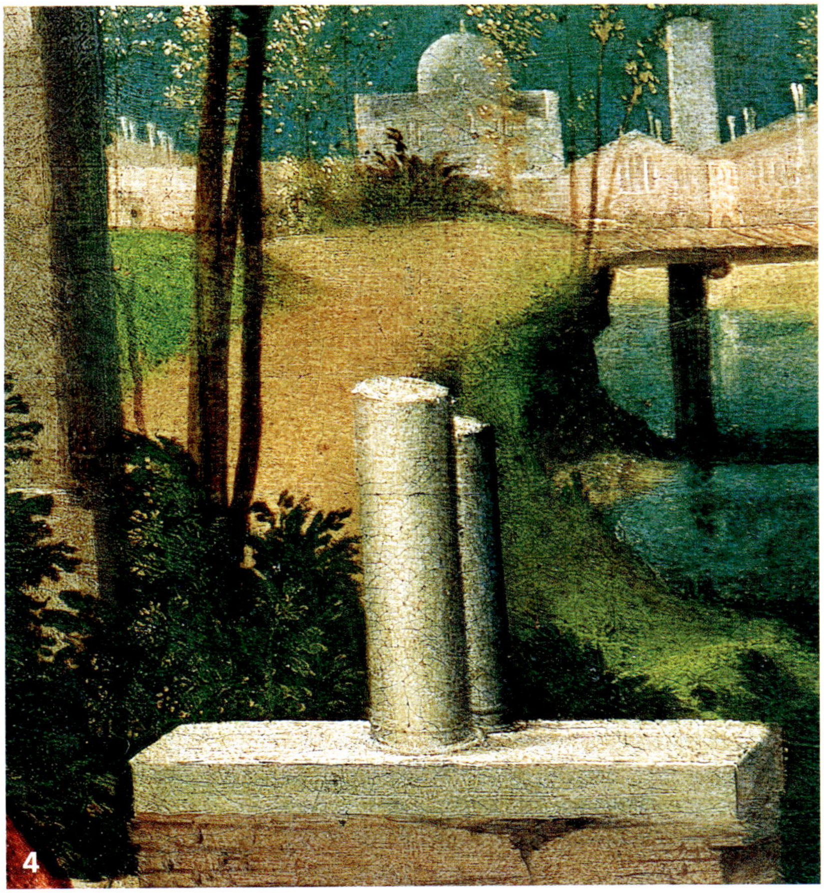

Venetian and Florentine art lovers took particular delight in disguising the subjects of their paintings. Only they knew what was being portrayed, and they revelled in the fact that others could only guess. "Many express their opinion, and no one agrees with anyone else; all that is even finer than the painted picture." Thus Giovanni Aurelio Augurelli, a humanist who was a frequent visitor to Venice around 1500. Perhaps it was some sort of upper-class fancy, a game whose pleasure lay in withholding knowledge from other people. Art that was commissioned for a public place had to be comprehensible to all. At the other end of the spectrum lay art for the initiated, for viewers in possession of the special code.

Perhaps, too, there was a taste for pictures without symbolism or meaning. A work, relieved of content, which was designed solely to please the eye and which lent free rein to the viewer's imagination. One such painting may be the *Concert Champêtre* in the Louvre, painted either – we still do not know for certain – by Giorgione or Titian. It portrays two naked women and two clothed men with a flute and a guitar in front of a spacious landscape – a composition with no identifiable source in literature, created, so it would seem, simply for the pleasure of a beautiful scene.

These are works designed to allow free association. Thus the column fragments are reminiscent of antiquity, of Greco-Roman pastoral poetry. Yet the men in the *Concert Champêtre*, like the man in *The Tempest*, are wearing contemporary dress. If they clearly belong to the artist's own day, then so must the naked women. This posed a problem for the 16th-century viewer: a female nude could only represent Eve or Venus or a nymph, never a real Venetian or Florentine woman. At least not in works destined for a wider public. That was forbidden by the conventions of the day, which banned sex and nudity and which largely reflected religious strictures. In private circles, however, it may have been different. Perhaps it was precisely in their breach of social convention that their special thrill lay. And perhaps also in the fact that the artist refused to be specific. This ambiguity may have given rise to the curious identification of the naked woman as a "gypsy", a female figure who, although not taken from classical mythology, nevertheless belongs to a people with their origins in the mysterious Orient.

Giorgione seems to have taken a while even to decide upon the final layout of *The Tempest*. An X-ray taken in 1939 reveals, in place of the man, a seated female nude with her legs in the water. The nursing woman was added later.

The way Giorgione saw people and nature was admired even in his own day. In the paintings of Giovanni Bellini, in whose workshop Giorgione learnt much, the figures are clearly outlined and thereby isolated in space. In many cases they give the impression of having been cut out and glued on. In Giorgione's work, by contrast, figures and objects arise not out of outline sketches but out of colour, which the artist juxtaposes and overlays. One thing grows out of another – body and surroundings, water, path, bush and dome form a visual unity, as previously seen perhaps only in backgrounds by Raphael, but nowhere else.

Since his figures are not defined by outlines, they often seem to be very slightly moving. The naked woman might be just about to change position. Into a tradition of painting which prized the eternal, the abiding, and ideals of beauty, Giorgione introduces the fleeting, the ever-changing. Not the morally charged motif of ephemerality, but the snapshot in time, the very second in which the lightning flashes, and thus something of that which the Impressionists would later, and in a very different way, seek to capture.

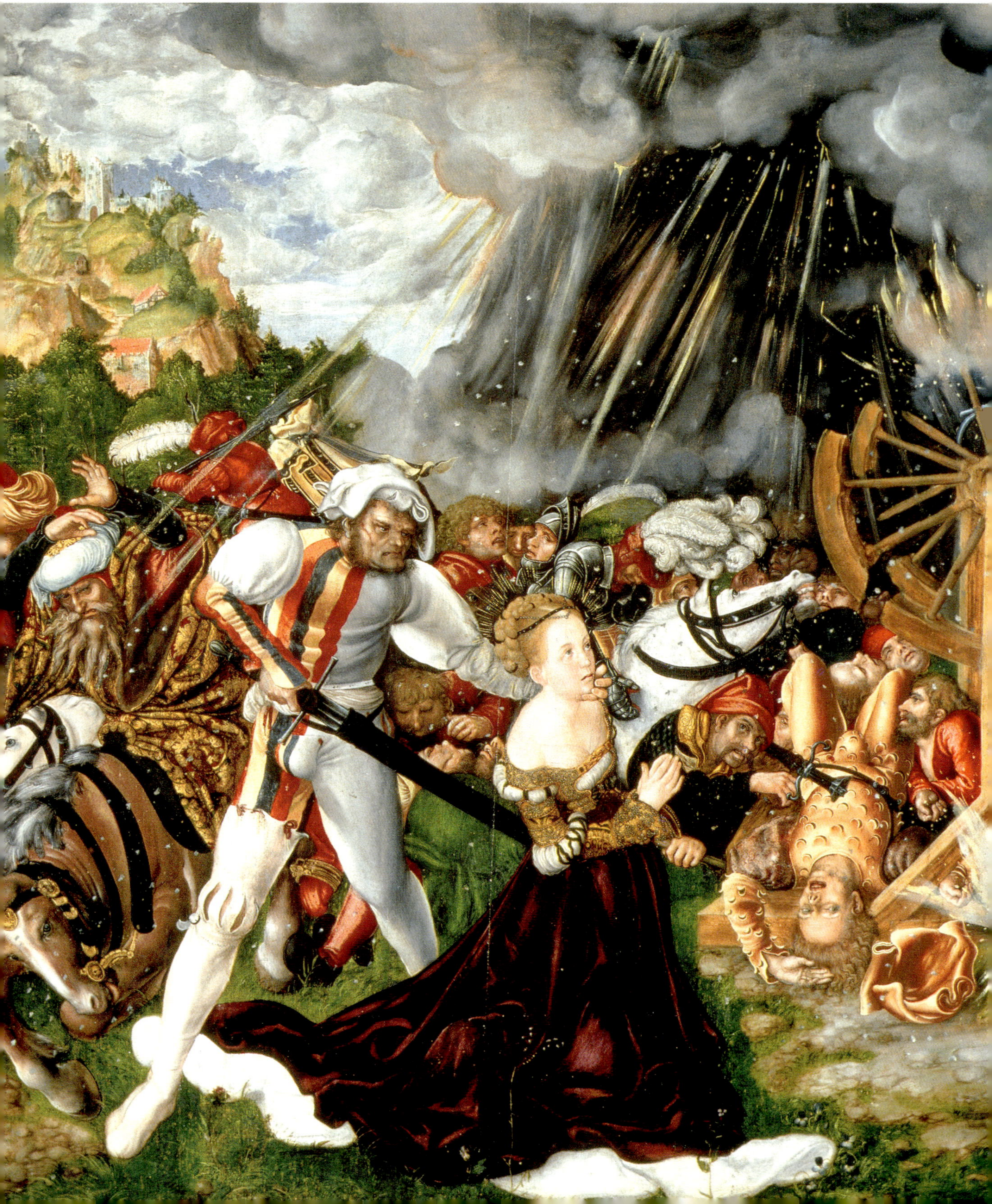

Lucas Cranach the Elder: The Martyrdom of St Catherine, c. 1508

Heaven's gates are already opened to receive the bride

Princess Catherine was born on Cyprus; she was beheaded in Alexandria, supposedly in the time of Emperor Maxentius, who drowned in AD 312. His successor was Constantine I, who became the first ruler to tolerate Christians in the Roman Empire. But if Constantine was willing to allow a small proportion of the population to worship a foreign god, Maxentius, his predecessor, continued to insist upon the state religion. According to Christian legend, he ruled from Egypt, which at that time formed part of the Roman Empire.

The city of Alexandria, with its famous libraries, was considered the cultural centre of the Western world and was home to a particularly active, but more or less underground community of Christians. Maxentius wanted Catherine, so the story goes, as a wife for his son. Catherine didn't want him. She demanded a spouse who was as noble, handsome, wise and rich as she; handsome and wise, however, the emperor's son was not.

Maxentius was powerful, and the princess's exacting demands got her mother into trouble (her father, the king of Cyprus, was dead). The two women went to a hermit for advice. The hermit recommended Jesus Christ as a spiritual husband, for Jesus possessed all the desired qualities in excess. Catherine embraced the new faith and was baptized. One night, she dreamt that the Virgin Mary was showing her the infant Christ, who held out a ring to her and said: "O my beloved Catherine, in your faith I will make you my bride."

Thus it is recorded in the *Passional*, the oldest collection of lives of the saints to be published in book form in the German language. The *Passional* first appeared in Augsburg in 1471 and 1472 and was reprinted over fifty times within the space of just a few years. Like all Christian legends, the story of St Catherine is one of Christian virtues and prejudices. It demonstrates that divine love is greater than physical love; that God helps when he wants to; that pagans are savagely cruel and infinitely inferior in debate.

This inferiority becomes apparent when Catherine challenges the emperor to a debate. He is unable to compete with her learning and so summons all the wise men of the land to refute her arguments. Instead, the virgin princess converts the many clever orators to Christianity.

Enraged, the emperor commands the wise men to be burned and throws Catherine into prison, where she is to be left to starve. When hunger again fails to persuade her to renounce her Christian beliefs (she is fed in prison by God in the shape of a white dove), Maxentius orders the building of great wheels studded with sharp knives, which are to tear her body to pieces. Catherine prays to God for assistance; he shatters the sadistic instrument of death with thunder and lightning and thereby kills 4000 pagans. The fact that God was here also acting cruelly would not have disturbed Christian readers, for pagans were considered enemies.

The emperor next orders Catherine to be beheaded. She prays, and hears a voice from Heaven saying: "Come, my beloved daughter and my spouse, Heaven's gates are opened to you." After her death "the angels took up her body and carried it to Mount Sinai, where God gave Moses the Ten Commandments. For there was no one worthy to bury the saint, only the angels."

St Catherine's convent, founded in the 6th century at the foot of Mount Sinai, is still one of the most impressive monuments of Christian history. The wheel became the symbolic attribute through which the saint is identified in art, although in Cranach's version it is not furnished with the usual sharp knives.

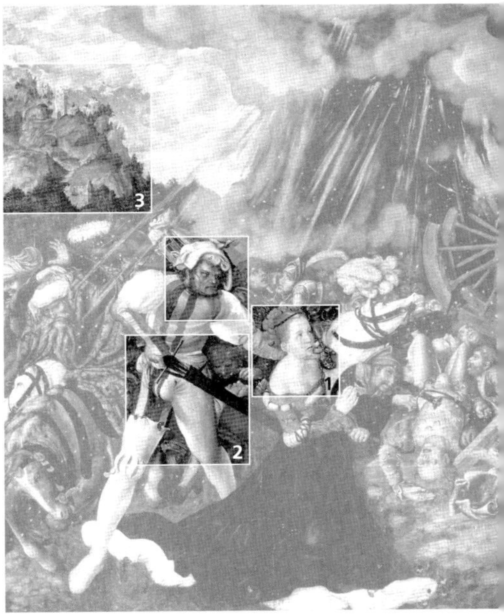

In his painting Cranach combines two different events which occur in chronological order. In the middle ground, we are shown the destruction of the gruesome wheel and the punishment of its builders. Horse and rider are hurled to the ground by fiery bolts of lightning raining down from God. In the foreground, we see Catherine, her eyes turned piously heavenward, on the point of execution. Taken together, the two scenes contain – for Christians – a visual message that goes beyond the legend of St Catherine itself: only faith in God can deliver you from the evil and misery of this corrupt world.

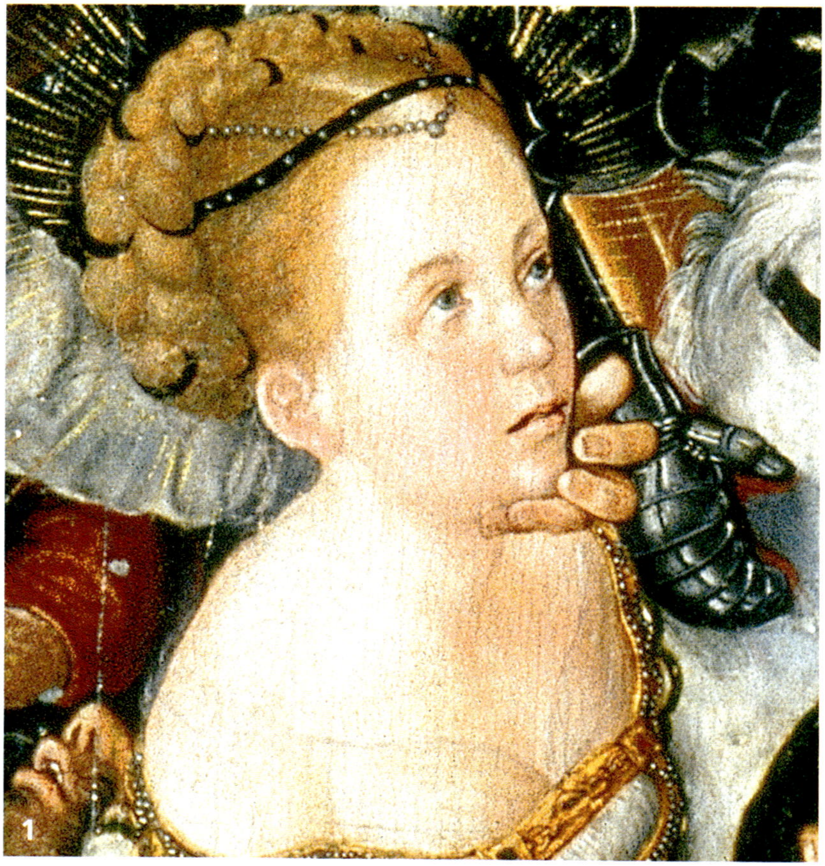

A beautiful martyr, sumptuously dressed

Catherine does not tremble, shows no trace of fear, kneels with her eyes raised in prayer. She is wearing a sumptuous dark red dress, its bodice and sleeves embroidered with pearls. Her dress and underskirts have been carefully arranged around her, as was the convention at royal weddings. Striking, too, are her bare shoulders and plunging neckline, her bosom covered only by transparent fabric. The painter has given her a sensual charm, and one would like to ask him why.

For the flesh of humankind, in Catholic thinking, was wicked, depraved, corrupt – a burden for the soul ever since the Fall. Throughout the entire Middle Ages, contempt for the body was one of the major themes of religion. The flesh was seen as a prison in which the soul is incarcerated and within which its view of God is obstructed. And when the church fathers were not describing the body as a prison, they were proclaiming that the flesh dulled the senses, that carnal pleasures were false distractions from true joy. The pious distinguished themselves by practising self-mortification and by quashing the desires of the flesh, be it for food, sex or even a conversation about earthly affairs. From this point of view, St Catherine ought to be awaiting her death shabbily dressed, without jewellery or ornament, and with sunken cheeks and bony shoulders.

Cranach follows another tradition, in which victory over carnal desires was idealized in the figure of the Virgin. According to Christian thinking, Mary, the mother of Jesus, was untouched by man and was taken bodily up to Heaven after her death. Catherine, who had refused to marry the emperor's son and had thereby rejected children, wealth and worldly honours, was emulating her model. In the language of the Church, she was "pure". Her soul purified her body making it a "temple of the Lord". In this context, the beauty and adornments with which Cranach endows her are not to be understood materially, but as symbols of her spiritual victory over the world and its temptations.

Cranach characterizes danger and temptation to dramatic effect through the large pubic pouches worn by the executioner and the knight in the golden armour lying on his back. Stylish pouches for the genitalia were a fashionable feature of young men's dress. "The flies must be as big as a calf's head", ran the words of a contemporary song. The fact that the artist includes them twice, in front of and behind Catherine, lends them a programmatic significance: they highlight the constant threat facing a "temple of the Lord" – or at least the difference between the Christian saint and the heathens around her.

There are thus theological grounds for Catherine's beauty and lavish dress. In portraying her as a handsome figure of a woman, however, it is also possible that Cranach was simply obeying his patron's wishes. The painting (112 x 95 cm; Budapest, Ráday Collection of the Reformed Church) was executed around 1508, and thus during the Renaissance. The body was being rediscovered, and everywhere in Europe the traditional portrayals of saints and martyrs were being used to satisfy the demand for figures of physical beauty. In an altarpiece that Cranach painted for the palace chapel of Frederick the Wise of Saxony in 1506, Catherine is showing less flesh. Frederick may have commissioned the present, more liberal *St Catherine* for his private apartments. He was certainly a great venerator of St Catherine; his collection of relics included twenty-six "particles" of her hair, bones and dress, and of Mount Sinai.

Although the executioner plays no prominent role in the legend, Cranach brings him right into the foreground. Through his size and colourful clothing, the artist grants him the same significance in visual terms as his victim.

If we are to believe the stories of the lives of the saints, the majority of martyrs seem to have died by the sword. Barely one of them met his or her death in the manner most commonly practised in the Middle Ages and the 15th century, namely on the gallows. Death by hanging was considered ignoble, shameful; only common people were hanged, and the saints were not to be associated with them. When the specific manner of their martyrdom – through stoning, for example, or by roasting on a gridiron, disembowelment or being shot with arrows – was unknown, narrators had their saints killed by the sword, like members of the upper classes.

In executions of this kind, the victim had his collar removed and shoulders laid bare; in the case of Cranach's Catherine, that is not necessary. With his left hand, the executioner makes sure the saint's head is upright. For 16th century viewers, this was an action with a dual significance. On the one hand, they saw a low-born man touching a person who was so far superior to him that, according to the laws of the day, he was forbidden to touch her at all. On the other hand, the gesture is a reminder of the teamwork required between victim and perpetrator: only if the victim remains kneeling in an upright position right up to her last breath, only if – in line with classical and aristocratic ideals of upbringing – she can maintain her composure even *in extremis*, can the executioner bring his sword down cleanly between her head and shoulders and fulfil his duty with a single stroke.

Like Catherine, the executioner is also dressed in his best, although this probably owes more to an artistic pleasure in festive clothing than to a desire to lend splendour to the preparations for the mystical marriage. His tall white boots, made of leather, are laced to his trousers and slit at the knee. Slits at the knee and the elbow were the height of fashion, as was sporting them on just one side. The stripes, too, fall on just one side only, the right, by coincidence in the German federal colours.

To Cranach's contemporaries, striped clothing signalled that the wearer was a social outsider. Such outsiders included executioners, lepers, prostitutes, travelling jugglers and clowns. The 13th-century Saxon Code also named serfs, bastards and convicts as wearers of striped clothing. When Cranach wanted to identify individuals within his paintings as particularly inferior – tax collectors and Pharisees, or the soldiers casting the dice over Christ's clothes at the foot of the Cross – he often gave them striped stockings.

Striped clothing was unknown in medieval Europe; where it came from, and why it was condemned, has yet to be fully explained. Crusaders in Palestine probably encountered opponents wearing striped cloaks. Christian theologians viewed striped dress as worldly adornment and therefore damnable. In the 16th century it was worn with pride only by mercenaries – but they, too, were social outsiders. Stripes as a way of marking people out from mainstream society have survived – in prison dress – right up to the present.

Stripes identify the outsider

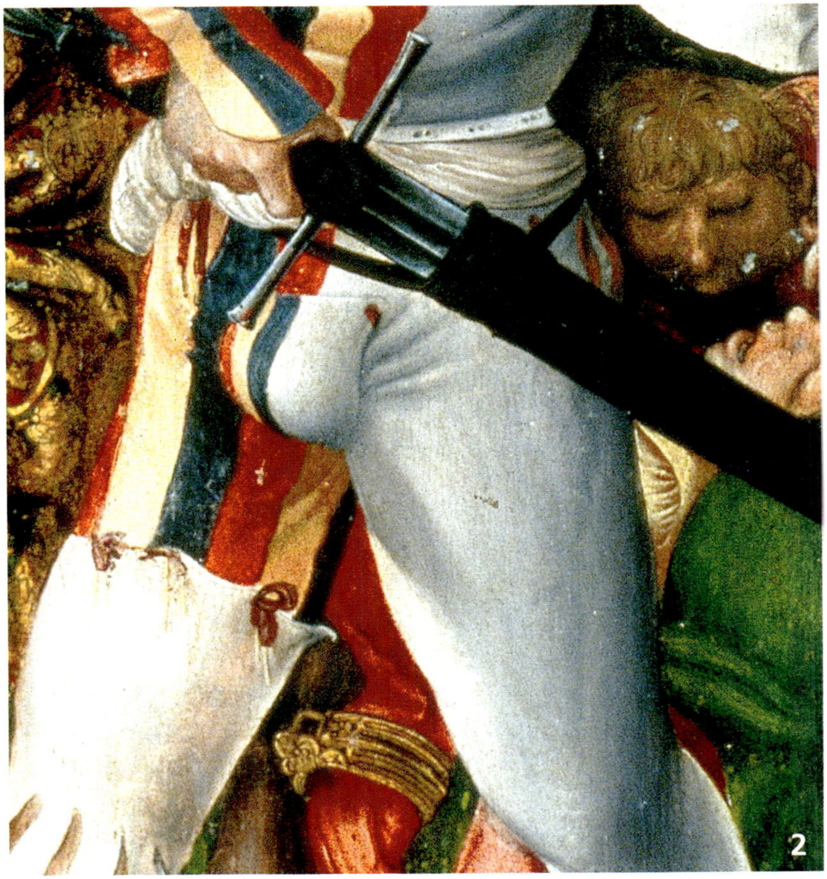
2

Castles on mountainsides, often perched on top of unnaturally jagged rocks, were by no means exclusive to Cranach, but formed part of a widespread pictorial repertoire. They played a role similar to that of little dogs in interiors. Just as dogs were a means of injecting life into empty areas of the foreground, so castles reaching up to the skies added decorative interest to the background.

But while they served as aesthetic pieces of scenery, they also reflected the social order. Castles symbolized power. Every feudal lord had a least one, in which he could shelter from his enemies and from which he could exercise his might. So it was in the Middle Ages, at least. But in Cranach's day, their importance began to wane. The newly developed cannon tore through their thick walls, and the growing wealth and power of the cities weakened the hold of the old ruling families. Cranach's towers already seem threatened with ruin.

In place of the medieval fortresses there now appeared palaces, magnificent complexes with large windows and broad flights of steps. One such palace was created in Wittenberg, the city in which the present picture was painted. Elector Frederick III of Saxony, called Frederick the Wise, opened up and extended the old castle to bring it in line – as far as his finances allowed – with contemporary ideas of what a palace should be, namely an appropriately splendid reflection of its owner's status. Building work was completed in 1509; Cranach's *St Catherine* was executed around 1508.

Frederick the Wise of Saxony has gone down in history as the protector of Martin Luther, but in every other respect he was one of the many regional princes typical of Germany at that time. While centrally-controlled states were taking shape in England, France and Spain, Italy and Germany were ruled by cities, bishops and princes. The princes sought to expand their spheres of influence through marriage; after their deaths, the same lands were divided up again amongst their heirs. In 1485 Saxony, too, had been split, and Frederick III had made Wittenberg his seat of residence.

Around 1508 Wittenberg boasted some 2000 inhabitants and a university. Of its some twenty-two professors, half were Augustinian monks, for they cost the ruling prince nothing. In 1508 the Augustinians sent one of their very advanced students, the monk Martin Luther, from the University of Erfurt to Wittenberg. He was 25 years old and was to teach Moral Theology for beginners while continuing his own studies.

It was not until 1517, almost ten years later, that he nailed his famous ninety-five theses to the door of Wittenberg palace chapel. In them, he argued against the idea, widespread within the Church, that it was possible to shorten the length of time spent by the deceased in purgatory by means of indulgences.

Such indulgences had to be bought; the money paid for them found its way into the pockets of ecclesiastical and secular rulers. No one took the indulgence industry further than Albrecht of Brandenburg, who purchased three bishoprics from the Pope. He borrowed the necessary money from the Fugger bankers and paid them back with the revenue generated – with the Pope's approval – by massive sales of indulgences. Frederick the Wise also permitted the sale of indulgences. He used the income thus raised to fund his university and probably also his collection of relics.

In 1508, the year in which Luther arrived in Wittenberg and Cranach probably executed his *St Catherine*, the sale of indulgences was not yet a controversial subject. While there were complaints about the financial and worldly interests of the church leaders, particularly in Rome, and about the licentiousness of many monasteries and nunneries and the inadequate education of the clergy, there was not yet any talk of a split in the Church or of the abolition of its many saints. That would come with the Reformation.

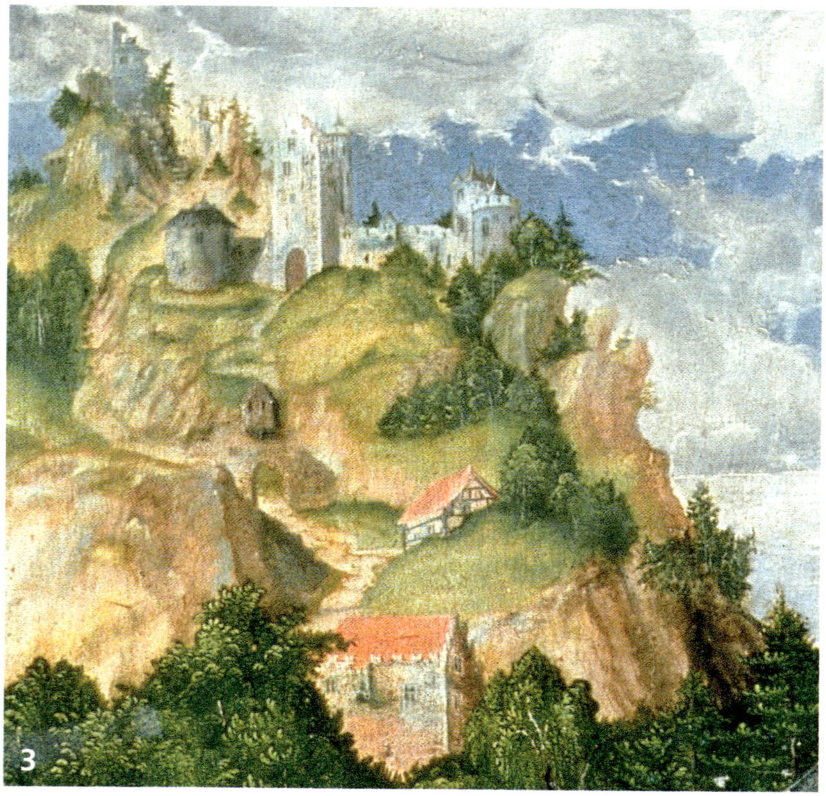

The end of the castle

The face of the executioner is like the psychological study of a thug. With the exception of the red scar, it bears a certain resemblance to the face of the artist and is thus far removed from the schematically simplified heads frequently found in Cranach's paintings. In other ways, too, the *Martyrdom of St Catherine* is full of carefully executed details – from which we may conclude that the entire painting was executed by the master himself.

Cranach was born in Kronach in 1472. In 1505 he came to Wittenberg as court painter to Frederick the Wise. In 1507 he is recorded as having an assistant, in 1509 two apprentices, and later ten journeymen. His workshop was soon one of the largest of its day. Cranach was not only an artist but also a businessman: he purchased several pieces of land in succession, bought an apothecary's shop, invested in a printing business and became alderman, mayor and the second richest man in Wittenberg.

After his death in 1553, he remained famous in particular as a painter of the Reformation. It is thanks to him and the countless portraits which issued from his workshop that we know what Luther looked like. Cranach illustrated many of Luther's writings and furnished many leaflets with polemical anti-papal woodcuts. The artist and the reformer were friends; Luther was god-father to one of Cranach's children, and the artist a witness at Luther's marriage to Catherine of Bora. The reformer thereby wedded a former nun, a woman brought up to view Jesus Christ as her bridegroom, just like St Catherine before her.

Cranach, Luther's friend and an advocate of the Reformation, also worked for Luther's opponents. For Albrecht of Brandenburg, for example, whose sales of indulgences had so incensed Luther that he called for a public debate. Cranach worked for this opponent of the Reformation long after Luther had nailed up his ninety-five theses in 1517. In the 1520s his workshop contributed almost 180 paintings to the decoration of Albrecht's collegiate church and palace in Halle, and in the 1540s Cranach's nephews supplied the Brandenburg Elector Joachim II with almost as many pictures for his ecclesiastical foundation in Berlin. Cranach himself was involved only in the designs, but a considerable proportion continued to portray the saints, the figures from Catholic tradition so emphatically rejected by Luther.

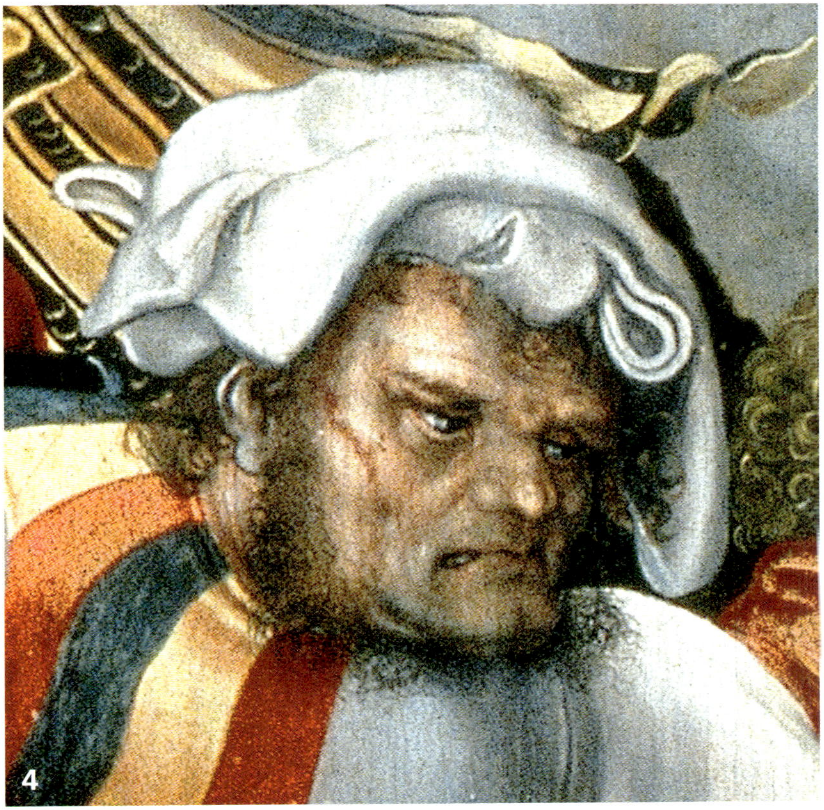

4

The executioner resembles the artist

There is no evidence to suggest that Luther took offence at his friend's work for the opposition. The powerful Cardinal Albrecht of Brandenburg, for his part, was equally aware of Cranach's support for the Reformation. These were unclear times; long after 1517, the indulgence issue continued to be seen as an internal Catholic dispute and Martin Luther dismissed as a rebellious, runaway monk, even by men such as the cardinal. That his protest might give rise to a split in the Church was, at least in the mid-1520s, not yet apparent, nor even something Luther wanted.

And as far as Cranach was concerned, his workshop was a large business that had to finance itself, quite independently of his personal allegiances. Those who see the painter as first and foremost a propagandist of the Reformation overlook his many Catholic works. *The Martyrdom of St Catherine* is one of the finest of them.

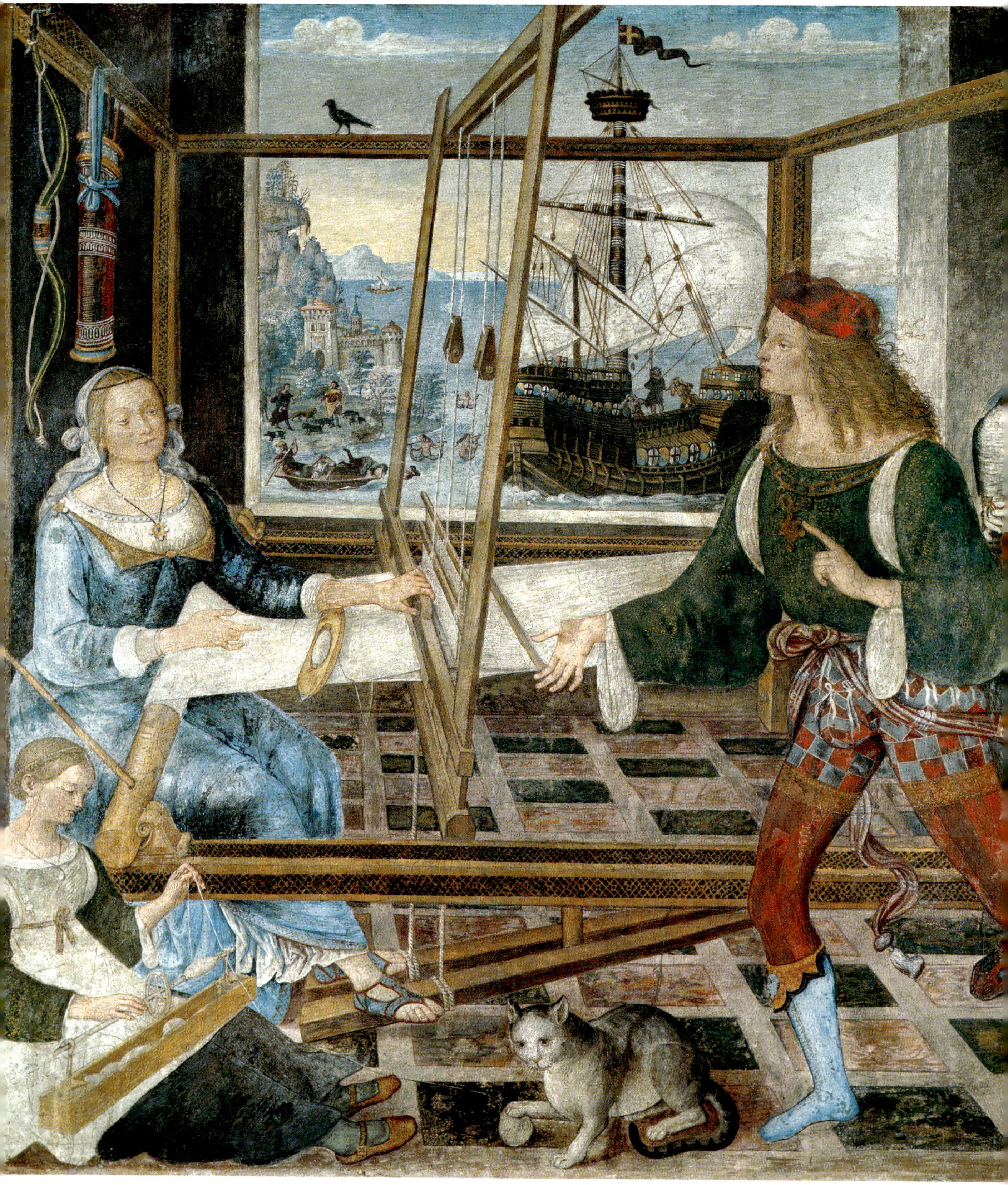

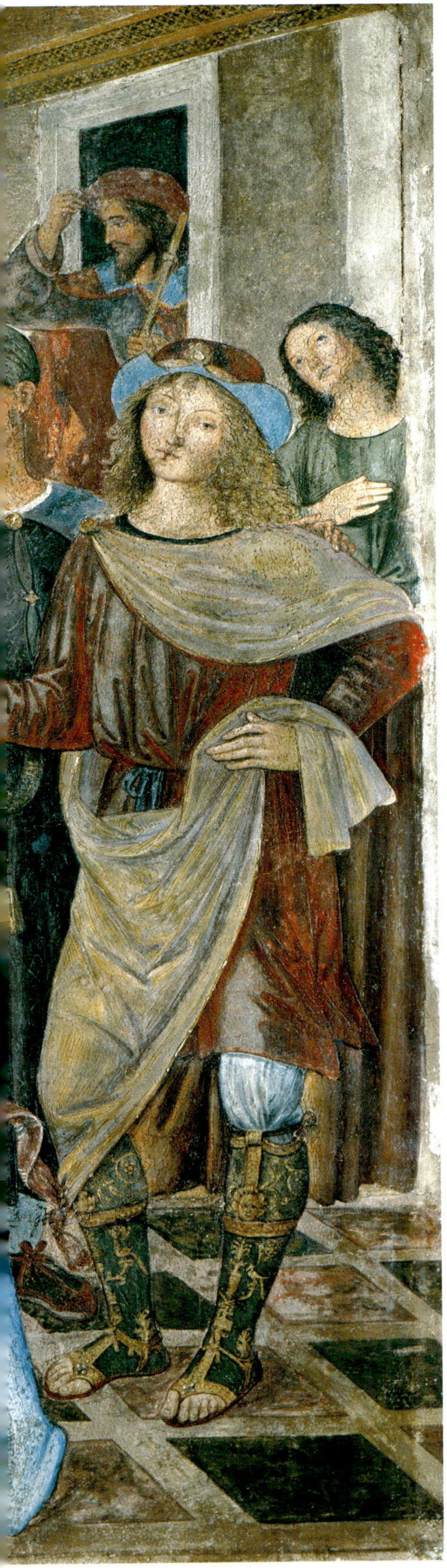

Pinturicchio: Penelope and the Suitors, 1509

In praise of lies and deceit

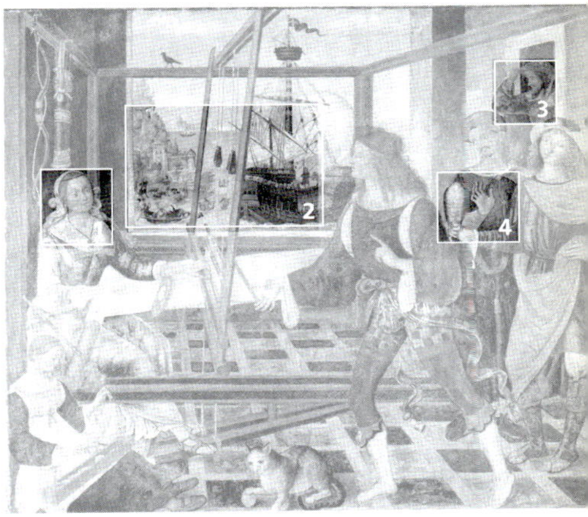

The Palio horse race is held in Siena twice a year. Representatives of the different districts of the city come together in Siena's scallop-shaped market square to compete against each other; their historical costumes recall the traditional battles for control of the Tuscan city. At the start of the 16th century, the reins of power were held by Pandolfo Petrucci. He was considered a "tyrant", a term which in those days was not solely negative, and liked to be known as il Magnifico, the Magnificent, like Lorenzo de' Medici in nearby Florence before him. Petrucci commissioned the present painting in 1509.

It measures 125 by 152 centimetres and was painted on the wall of the stateroom in the Petrucci palace, in conjunction with seven further frescos by other artists. Three of the original frescos have since disappeared, two are housed in the Siena Museum of Art, and three – Pinturicchio's *Penelope and the Suitors* amongst them – in the National Gallery in London. It was removed from its original wall in Siena in 1843, at the request of a Parisian art collector; from Paris it passed into a private collection in England and from there, in 1874, into the National Gallery. The work was badly damaged; unlike other works by Pinturicchio in Italy, it has never quite been restored to its original glory.

Despite its evident age, the work continues to tell the story of Penelope in the liveliest fashion. Penelope, the wife of Odysseus, waited twenty years for her husband, the king of Ithaca, to return from the Trojan Wars. All the while she had to ward off the suitors who harried her. Whether the men whom Pinturicchio portrays are truly suitors, however, is by no means as certain as the title of the painting would suggest.

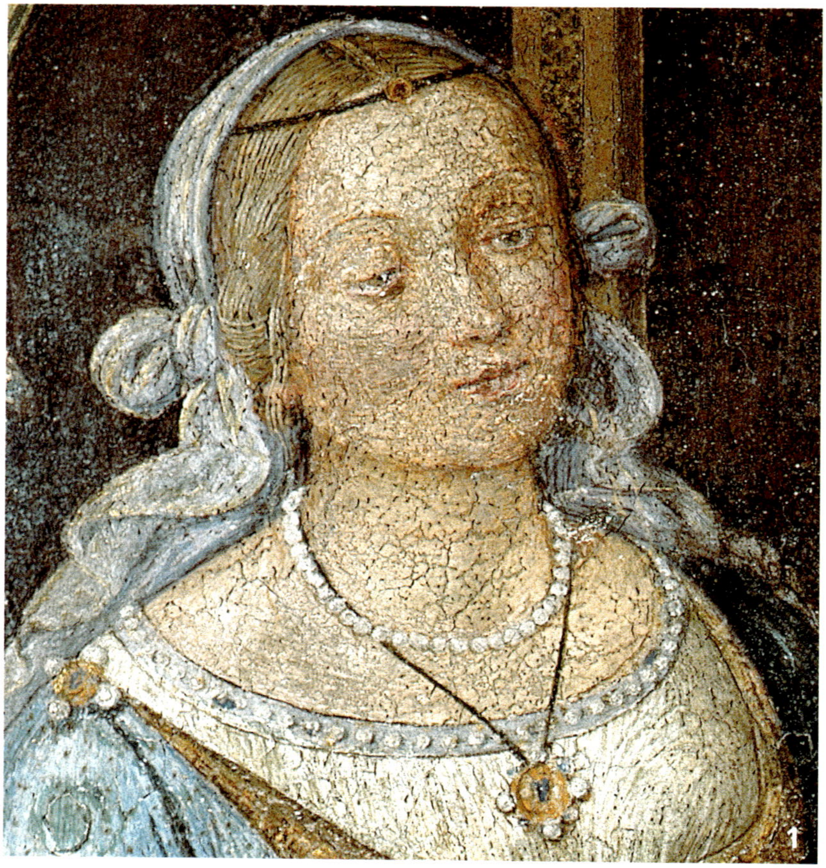

1

The details were not so important

Penelope was the model of a virtuous wife. She had no idea if her husband was still alive, or if he would ever return from the siege of Troy, but she remained faithful to him. Meanwhile, she was constantly harassed by suitors who wanted to marry her. These suitors moved into her house, drank her wine and ate her meat, and even planned to murder her 20-year-old son, Telemachos. For if they could get rid of him and win Penelope, they would also inherit Odysseus' lordly possessions.

Penelope, wooed and threatened, devised a cunning ruse to keep the men at bay: when she had finished weaving a shroud for her husband's elderly father, she announced, she would make up her mind. Each night, however, she secretly undid everything she had woven during the day.

In the background of the picture, Pinturicchio shows us two of her husband's adventures. On the ship with the billowing sails, Odysseus has had himself tied up so that he cannot succumb to the enchanted singing of the Sirens, who swim round the ship in the shape of mermaids. On the left rises the island of Circe, a sorceress who changes all men into beasts. The god Hermes, however, gives Odysseus a herb which protects him against Circe's magic.

Odysseus is watched over most zealously of all, however, by Athene, the goddess of wisdom. She also lends her advice to his son Telemachus, back in Ithaca: "she herself, taking the shape of a swallow", runs Homer's verse, "darted aloft to perch on the smoky main beam of the hall."

Although Pinturicchio places a bird on the rear strut of the loom, it is not a swallow; and while he shows Odysseus tied up on his ship, he is not bound to the mast as Homer describes him in *The Odyssey*.

Neither the artist nor his humanist advisors would have read Homer's text. Written some 800 years before the birth of Christ, it was largely forgotten during the Middle Ages since it offered little of relevance to Christian teachings. Right up to the Renaissance, it existed only in fragments and was known only from references in other works. Although it may have been available in Latin in 1509, when Pinturicchio painted his fresco, it had probably not yet been translated into Italian. Even if it had, printing was still in its infancy and hand-written copies were rare. Thus the artist had to base his work on oral tradition, on hearsay. But it was not the details that mattered – all that was really important was that the walls of Petrucci's palace should cite antique motifs, for thinking around 1500 was dominated by the rediscovery of pre-Christian culture.

The search for classical painting – figural representations were known primarily from vases – fuelled a wave of excavations. In Rome, for example, digging had been going on since 1490 at the Esquiline Hill, beneath which lay the famous palace of Emperor Nero. A report written in verse describes touring such excavations as a subterranean adventure. Supplied with ham, bread and wine, and guided by a local expert, visitors crawled on all fours into a world of frogs, owls and bats. The rooms themselves were blocked up with earth, but curious visitors could look into them by torchlight through holes knocked in the walls. It was difficult to make things out clearly, but apparently all physical discomforts were outweighed by this glimpse into a bygone world, lying almost 1500 years in the past.

A frequent feature of antique frescos was an uninterrupted view into the distance. It was a speciality described by such Roman authors as Vitruvius and Pliny. Pinturicchio was one of the first to take up this classical motif: he gives the room in which the loom is located a window as large as the rear wall and thereby provides his composition with a second plane of action.

To establish a coherent perspective which led the eye smoothly from foreground to background was one of the new challenges of the Renaissance. Tiled floors whose lines converged upon a vanishing point in the background were a popular means of solving this problem.

Pinturicchio also uses the loom, whose wooden frame fills almost the entire foreground room, to establish perspective depth. The floor and the frame indicate that we are viewing the picture from a position slightly to the left of centre, beneath the feet of Penelope and her maid, where one of the rows of tiles descends almost vertically to the bottom of the painting. In the right-hand side of the composition, it becomes apparent that the artist had some difficulty with the perspective construction of the frame: the gesticulating men have to walk through the loom.

In contrast to his space, Pinturicchio's people seem flat. As in Gothic art, they lack the shading through which painters can model the human figure. The man nearest the foreground is imprecisely located in space; he seems to float rather than walk. Bemoaned by critics in the past, these lingering traces of the Gothic style in a Renaissance spatial construction are today precisely what lend Pinturicchio's work its distinctive charm.

The artist was born around 1454 in Perugia. His real name was Bernadino di Betto, but he was known as *il Pinturicchio* (the little painter) on account of his slight stature and modest manner. For art lovers of later generations, he was entirely overshadowed by his contemporaries Leonardo da Vinci and Michelangelo, but in his own lifetime his work was much in demand. In 1492/95 he decorated the Vatican apartments of the Borgia Pope Alexander VI, and from 1501 to 1508 worked in Siena on one of the largest pictorial cycles of the Renaissance, a ten-part fresco of scenes from the life of Pope Pius II, better known as the humanist Enea Silvio Piccolomini.

The commission from Petrucci must have especially pleased the artist, because he set aside his usual modesty and included himself in an altarpiece receiving the letter of invitation from Siena. On the envelope we can clearly read the words "Eximio Viro Pictori digniss. Magistro Bernardino Perrusino alias il Pinturicchio nobis car ...", which might be translated thus: "To the extraordinary man and painter, the most noble Master Bernardino of Perugia, called il Pinturicchio, our dearest ..."

The expansion of space

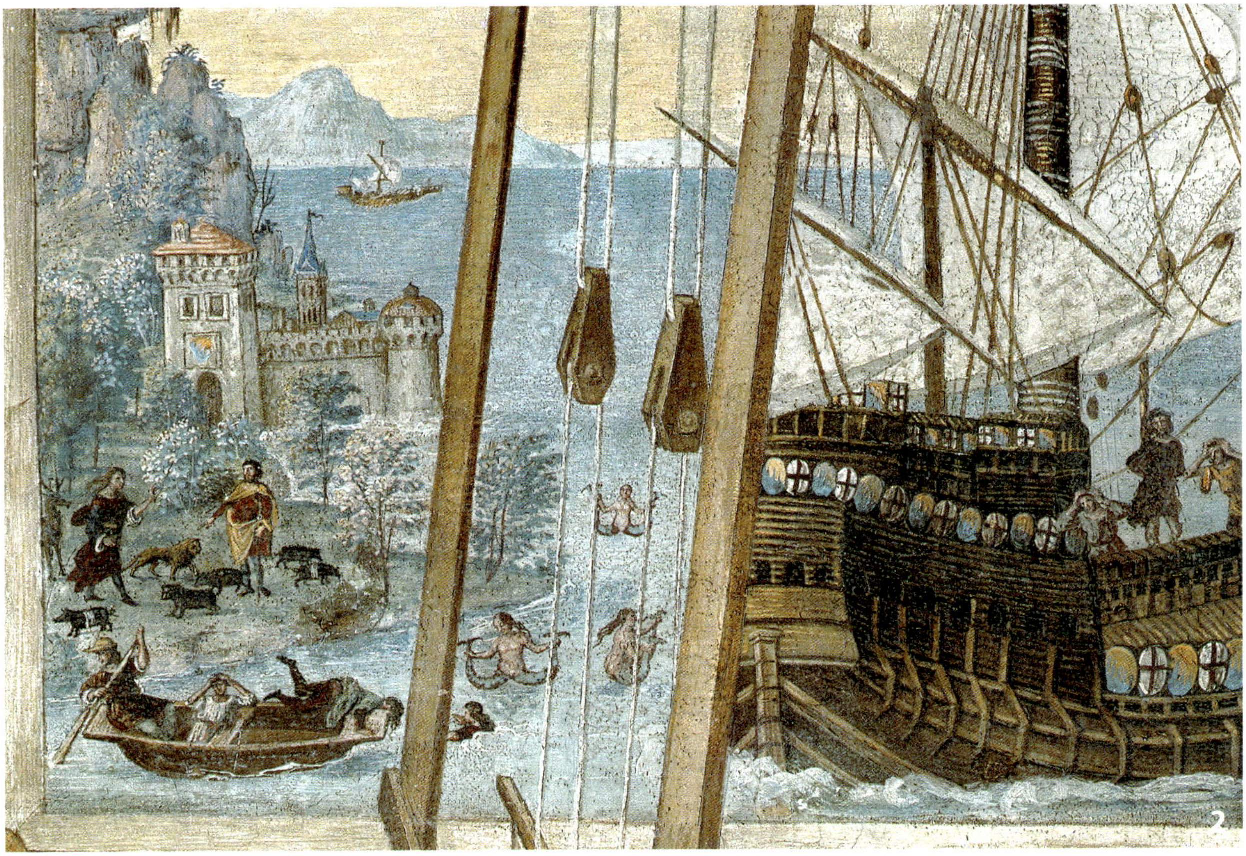

2

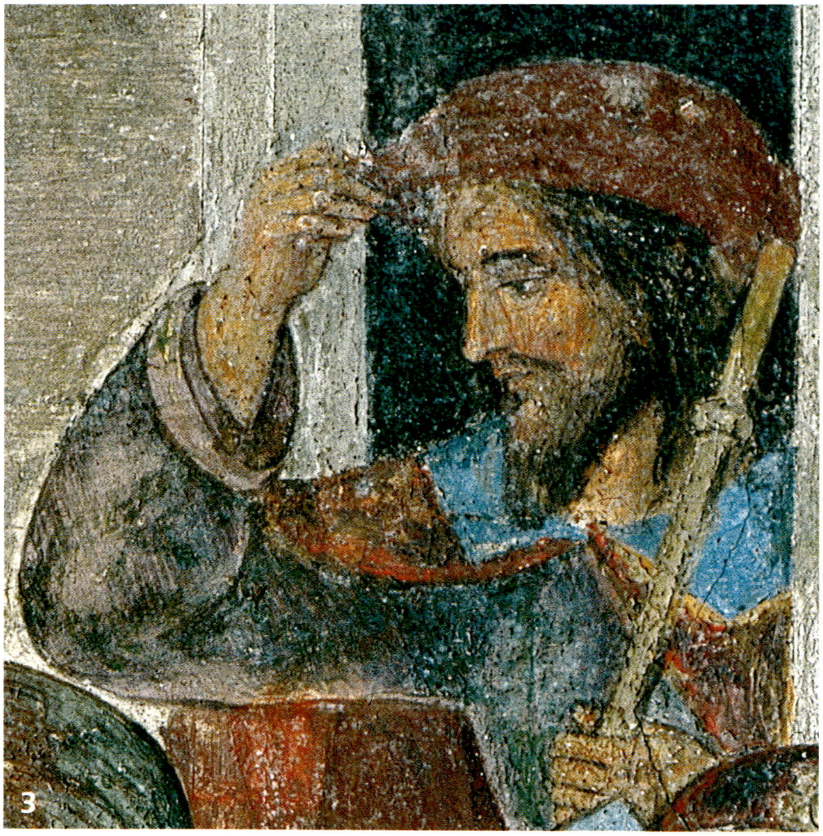

Strong, clever and calculating

Odysseus did not return to Ithaca in triumph, but disguised himself as a beggar and sounded out the situation in secret. He was ridiculed by the suitors and reviled by one of his own servants. He learned that Penelope, whose trick of undoing the cloth she had woven had been discovered by the suitors, was now hoping to stave them off with a test: the one who could shoot an arrow through an iron ring with Odysseus' bow would be allowed to marry her. In Pinturicchio's fresco, Odysseus, the only man who is unshaven, is looking through the doorway on the right, clad in a simple cap and with a staff in his hand. His bow and quiver are hanging on the opposite wall. Not one of the suitors is even able to string the bow; only Odysseus is strong enough, and uses it to fell one suitor after another.

Odysseus creates a bloodbath in his own home, killing unfaithful servants and exacting revenge without mercy. That was considered fairly normal behaviour not just in ancient Greece, but also in the era during which this fresco arose. Italy consisted of a large number of small territories whose political climate was characterized by constant intrigues and struggles for power. These lesser states were continuously changing their allegiances, asking now the Spanish, now the French to help protect them against aggressive neighbours. Siena was no exception.

In 1487 Pandolfo Petrucci, the man who would commission the *Penelope* fresco, had played Siena's warring factions off one against the other, cold-bloodedly murdered his rivals and even his own father-in-law, and seized some of the assets of Siena's rich. In 1499 the city came under threat from the French to the north and, to the south, from the troops of Cesare Borgia, son of Pope Alexander VI, who wanted to acquire Siena for the Papal States. Petrucci signed treaties with both sides, although this did not stop him from secretly supporting a plot against Cesare Borgia. Cesare invited the main conspirators to a friendly meeting and killed them. Petrucci was also invited, but smelled a rat and didn't go. When Cesare subsequently occupied Siena, Petrucci had to flee, but was restored to power by the French. He died in 1512; Pinturicchio died a year later.

When the Pope asked one of Petrucci's advisors, the scholar Antonio da Venafro, how his master had managed to govern the unruly Sienese, he replied: "With lies and deceit, Holy Father!" And with cruelty, too: one of Petrucci's summer pastimes was rolling boulders down a nearby hill without caring who or what they hit. If pursuits of this kind were tolerated in a powerful leader, the ability to deceive others and keep hold of power through trickery was positively celebrated. In 1513 Petrucci was cited by Niccolò Machiavelli, in his book *The Prince*, as a model example of a wise and clever tyrant.

It is easy to see why a man such as Petrucci should feel drawn to a figure such as Odysseus. A mythical leader in uncertain times, the hero of antiquity was strong, clever and frequently described as "calculating". Just as Odysseus would not allow himself to be seduced by the Sirens or robbed of his human form by Circe, so Petrucci refused the friendly invitation from Cesare Borgia and thereby escaped death. And just as Odysseus killed all the suitors, so Petrucci removed his opponents one by one. Calculation, lies, deceit and murder were necessary means of self-preservation for city rulers in Renaissance Italy. The more skilfully they were employed, the greater one's chances of survival. Machiavelli justified them as necessary techniques for holding on to power. Even Penelope, the virtuous wife, kept the suitors at bay by deceitful means, namely, by secretly undoing the length of shroud she had woven during the day.

Hands do the speaking, not mouths

The National Gallery in London calls Pinturicchio's fresco *Penelope and the Suitors*, and there is much to support this title: the young man seems to burst forcefully in on the unprotected woman, and his gestures imply animated words. The hand raised as if in defence near the falcon, on the other hand, suggests reserve. This was the artistic convention in Pinturicchio's day: messages were conveyed with the hands, while mouths remained permanently closed. Unfortunately for the modern-day viewer, however, such hand gestures can rarely be deciphered with certainty.

Rather than reproaching Penelope or demanding that she finally choose one of the suitors, the young man nearest to us may be saying something quite different. The artist has clearly distinguished him from the others and assigned him a prominent role. With his handsome ringlets, chequered hose and fluttering sash, he does not necessarily appear a negative figure. It is possible that he represents Telemachus, Penelope's beloved son, who has come to tell his mother that his father has returned.

This deviates from the original version of events as told in *The Odyssey*, in which Homer has the news brought to Penelope by an old servant woman. Penelope refuses to believe her, and even when she meets Odysseus face to face, she does not fall immediately into his arms. Afraid that this is a stranger masquerading as her missing husband, she first asks him a question that only Odysseus can answer. Their reunion is one of the most moving scenes in the epic. Pinturicchio portrays in his own way, it might be argued, the moment before it takes place.

But what about the falcon? Those who see the men bursting in on Penelope as suitors might view the hunting bird as a reference to their extravagant pursuits. Those who see them as the friends and followers of Odysseus, on the other hand, might point to another scene in Homer's epic, in which a hawk kills a dove. The incident occurs while Telemachus is making his way back to Ithaca from Lacedaemon, just prior to the return of Odysseus himself. One of Telemachus' companions, a seer, interprets this divine omen to signify: "In all Ithaca there is no more royal house than yours. Yours is the power for all time!" Power, in this case, over Ithaca.

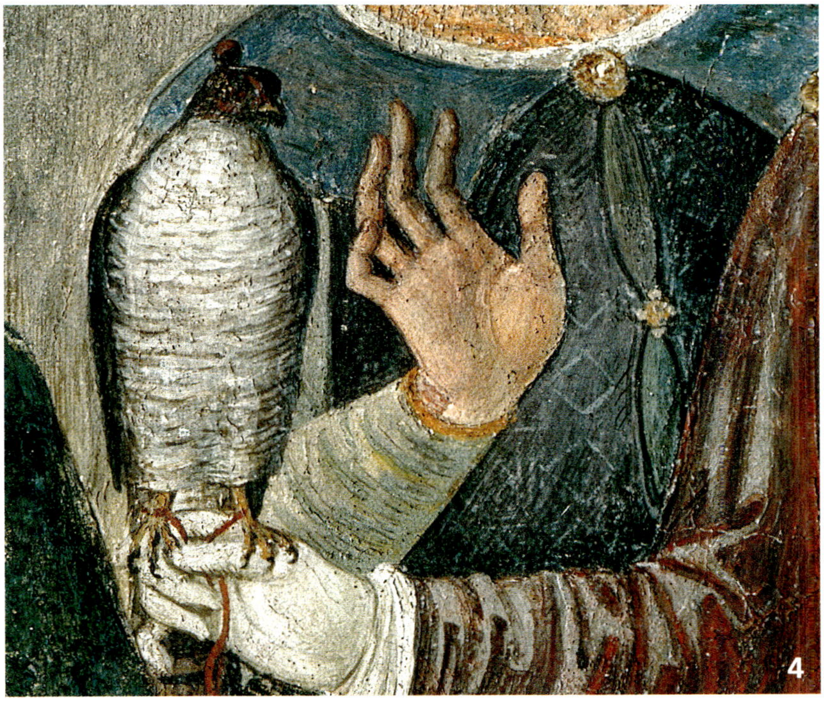
4

What the fresco might also mean, however, is power over Siena – in the hands of Petrucci's own son. In 1509, the year in which the painting arose, his son got married and in 1512 indeed took over from his father as city tyrant. In one of the other frescos in Petrucci's stateroom, a son is again given striking prominence. There are good reasons to suppose that the present paraphrase of *The Odyssey* was conceived as a marriage painting: Pinturicchio praises unswerving marital fidelity and prophesies success for the future ruler.

This proved of little use; Petrucci's son was deposed after just a few years. It is doubtful that the love between the young couple was as unswerving as that of their Greek forebears: the two came from rival Sienese families and were married solely for political reasons. The mother of the bride is said to have died of grief over the arrangement.

Nor did the painter of the faithful Penelope, if we are to believe the Sienese gossip, have a happy marriage. He chose a dominating wife who regularly cuckolded her diminutive, often absent husband and who even married their daughter to one of her own lovers.

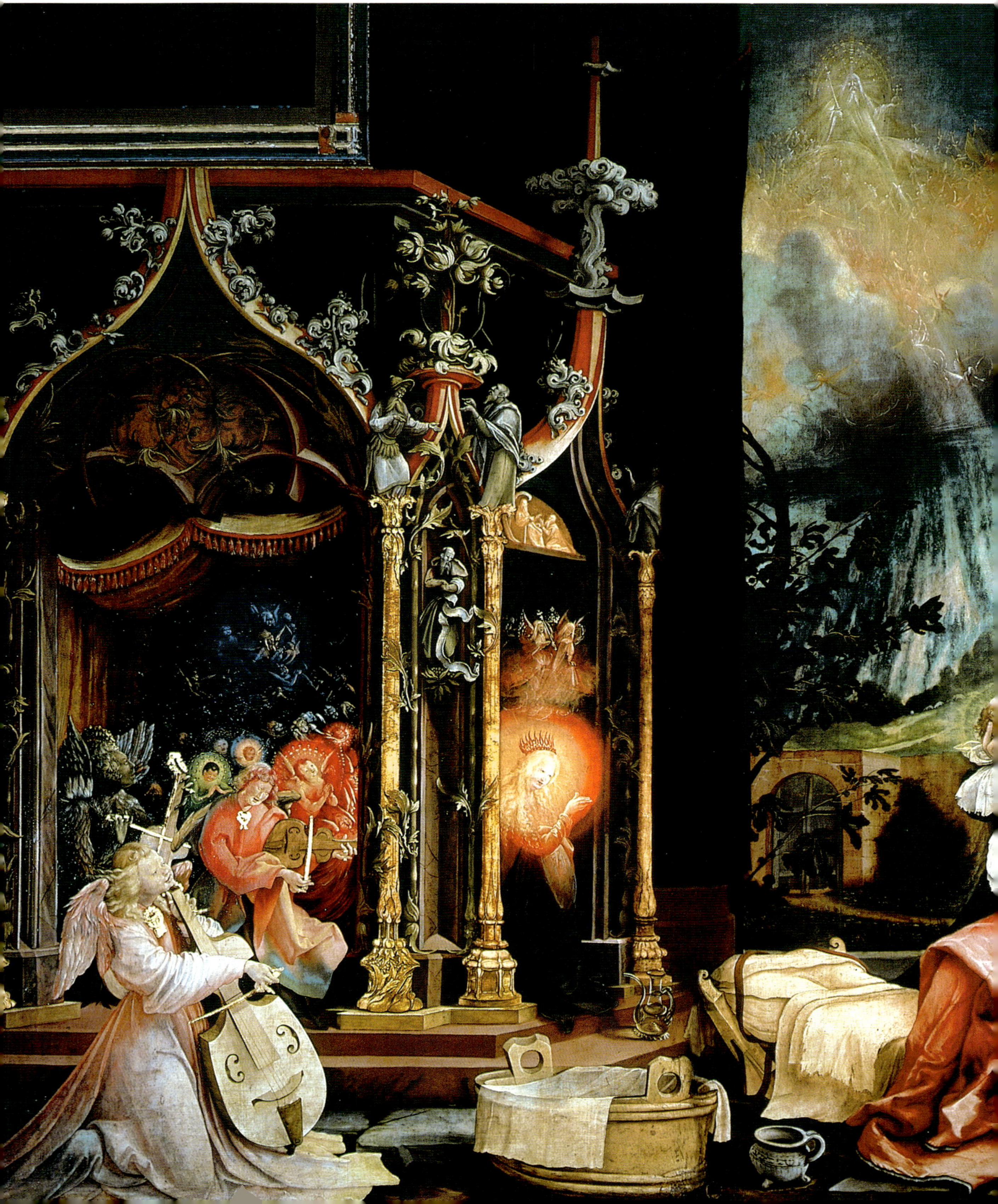

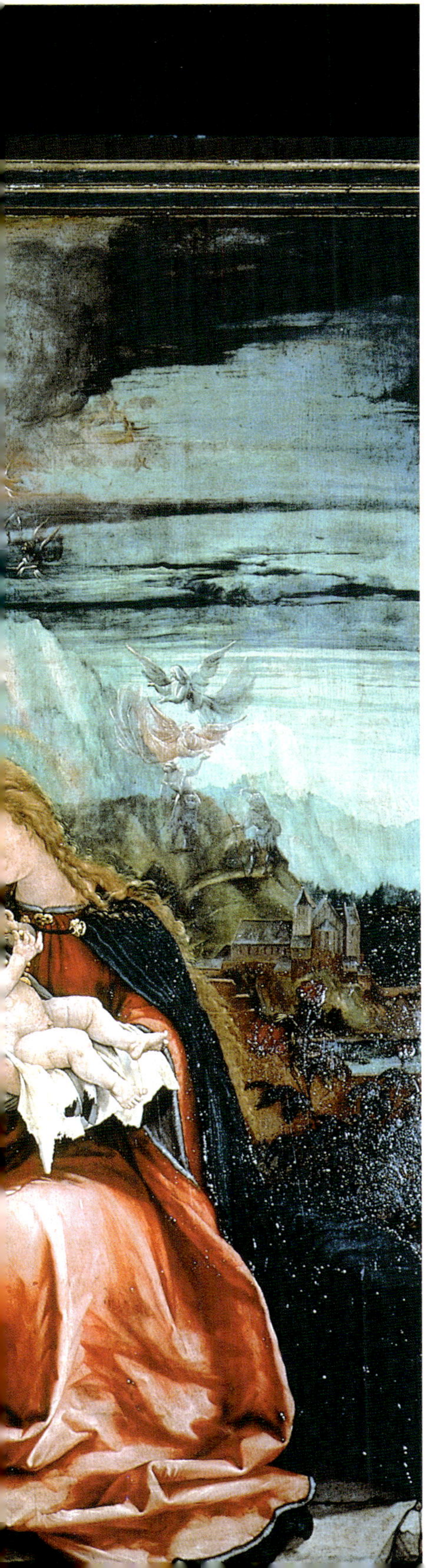

Matthias Grünewald: The Nativity panels from the Isenheim Altar, 1512/1516

The music of the spheres on earthly instruments

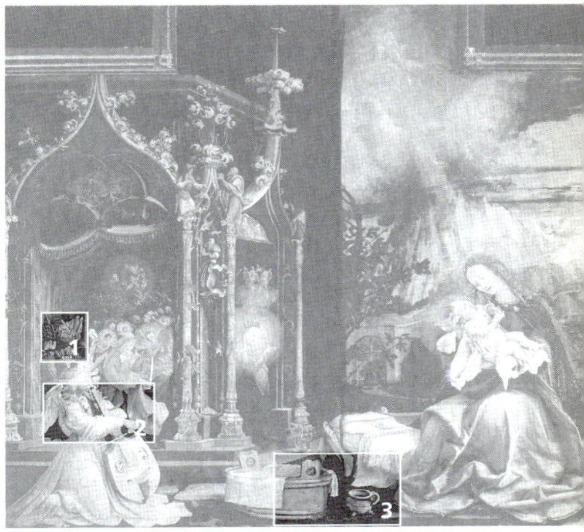

Grünewald's Nativity panels form part of the Isenheim Altar, executed between 1512 and 1516. The ten panels making up the altarpiece depict, alongside a number of saints, scenes from the life of Christ on earth, from the Annunciation to the Resurrection. Even today, the subject of each scene can be identified almost at first sight. Only the Nativity panels seem confusing. Rising in a flourish of rampant growth on the left is a fantastical work of architecture, its pillars decorated with figurines of debating men. Opening up on the right is a view of a distant landscape, in front of which sits a Virgin who is so big that she would be unable to stand upright in the chapel on the left. Instead, she appears over there a second time – smaller, but already as Queen of Heaven with nimbus and crown.

In the distant landscape, we can make out two shepherds to whom angels are proclaiming the birth of Christ in Bethlehem. But Mary and her son are seated not in a stable but in the open countryside, with neither Joseph nor an ox or donkey in sight. And as items of domestic use, the washtub, chamber pot and bed belong to a very different kind of reality than the angels and God the Father in the heavens above.

To the modern viewer, the painting exudes an atmosphere similar to works of Surrealism, which typically bring together objects and creatures from different realms and times as in a dream. But while the Surrealists sought to create a world outside the sphere of logic, Grünewald's altarpiece was constructed with a logic that extends right down to the last detail.

Fear not the angels

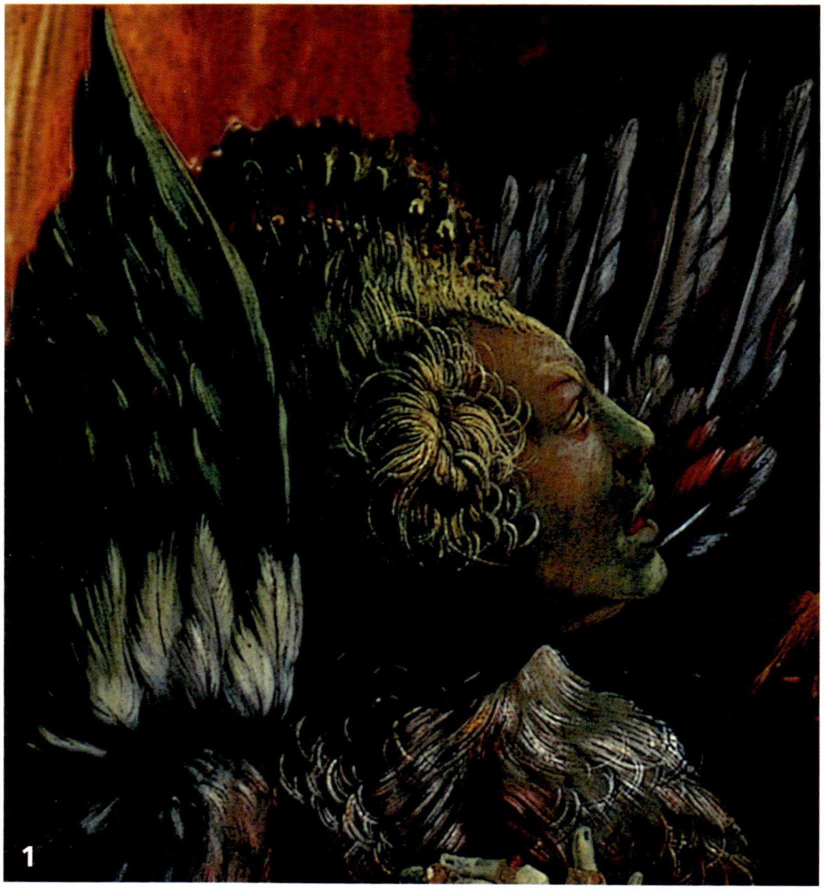

1

The Christmas angels of our own day are the sorry remains of once mighty beings. They have come down to us as sweet-smiling spirits, but they were once seen as thoroughly unsettling figures of superhuman size. They seemed dangerous. "Fear not!", the angels had to cry in order to stop the shepherds from running away. At their appearance, people turned their faces away in fear – like Grünewald's Mary in the *Annunciation* panel which is hinged immediately to the left of the *Concert of Angels* seen here, and in which she is confronted by a frighteningly large angel.

Sumerians, Assyrians and Babylonians also believed in angels; the majestic representatives of God's will mostly appeared as hybrids of man and beast. Angels in Greece originally took the form of sirens, heavenly male singers. They later became female and attempted to lure seafarers such as Odysseus to their deaths. They were portrayed as birds with human heads, similar to Grünewald's gamba player. His green head is as far removed from popular images of angels today as that of the bearded angel floating above the Virgin's shoulders.

God's heavenly hosts were originally all male, like him. The God enthroned in glory at the top of Grünewald's picture wears a long, two-pointed beard, a symbol of his sex. But Grünewald portrays his angels sometimes as male, and sometimes – as in the case of the angel kneeling in the foreground – with more feminine traits. In the artist's day, both sexes were acceptable. Thus Michelangelo's angels are male, while in Dürer and Titian they mostly resemble young girls. The theologians of the Middle Ages, however, were preoccupied with a quite different problem, that of substance. Did angels possess a body and gender at all, they wondered, or were they composed of pure spirit? The church fathers believed they also existed in material form, while for the Scholastics of the 12th century, seeking to reinforce the Christian faith through philosophical argument, they were beings of spirit.

Artists usually indicated otherworldliness by means of an aureole, understood as a spiritual radiance. Grünewald surrounds several of his angelic figures with these bright circles of light, as well as his figure of Mary as Queen of Heaven. Art historians are not agreed, however, as to who the angels here granted aureoles are meant to be.

Every colour held its own meaning: green was the colour of Paradise and thus of eternal life. Green shows that angels are immortal. On the right-hand side float a red and a blue angel: red denoted the order of angels called the seraphim, blue the cherubim. Red symbolized the morning sky, blue the midday sky. There was no evening sky, for to the faithful God and his angels are eternal.

The angels were divided into two groups: into messengers, who announced and implemented God's will on earth, and into those who stood around the throne of God lauding and magnifying him. The music of the spheres produced by these beings, who consist only of sound, is no invention of the Bible. The Egyptian God Thot had already said: "I have harmonized the singing voices of the heaven's revolutions." According to Plato's *Republic*, too, on each of the eight revolving heavenly spheres stands a siren singing a specific note. And Caesarius of Heisterbach, a 13th-century theologian, wrote that only those who departed this earth could hear the music of Heaven: "The melody which a dying person hears is so sweet that no choir, be it of voices or instruments, can be compared with it."

Since the harmony of the world could not be perceived by the living, they had to content themselves with a substitute – music. Angel musicians are similarly a substitute. Divine beings producing the sounds of the spheres or existing purely of sound were difficult to capture in paint, and thus in Grünewald's panel they sing with their mouths slightly open as they draw their bows across the strings. Why the angel in the foreground is bowing from the left remains a mystery. Perhaps it is meant to suggest that angels make music differently to humankind.

Who had written the music sung and played in Grünewald's day was mostly unknown. Composers ranked as artisans; it was generally believed they simply assembled existing material into new arrangements. God alone was creative. Giovanni da Palestrina, Samuel Scheidt and Orlando di Lasso were not yet born.

Music played no great role in everyday church life. It consisted of monodic liturgical chants that were sung by the priests, occasionally augmented by a small (male-voice) choir, at times accompanied by a portable organ. The words were all in Latin; the congregation remained passive. Instrumental music and (polyphonic) motets were only performed on feast days or during royal visits. Even then, it was not normal to use strings, as depicted by Grünewald, but rather wind instruments, and above all trumpets. Each instrument was assigned to its own social sphere. Thus the trumpet was associated with rulers and their wars. Its blast promised strength and power. In a religious context, too, the Last Judgement is announced with trumpets.

Stringed instruments, on the other hand, belonged inside the home, or in the hands of wandering fiddlers who provided the music at village dances. Members of the aristocracy and wealthy middle classes often learned to play an instrument themselves. In the *Book of the Courtier* published in 1528, the author Baldesar Castiglione declares that "music is not only an ornament but a necessity for the Courtier", although he must only play in private company "when there are ladies present" and "not in the presence of common people". Castiglione argues the case for "music of great skill and suavity" such as produced by viols. When Grünewald painted his angels, he must also have been thinking of this type of intimate chamber music, of music for a family celebration, in which mother and child were to be bathed in sweet sounds, not disturbed by triumphal trumpets.

No stringed instruments in church

Contrary to what Grünewald's concert of angels seems to suggest, by no means all theologians of the 16th century wanted to hear music in church. Many considered its sensual harmonies a temptation of the devil. The reformers John Calvin and Ulrich Zwingli banned all instrumental music from church services, and in 1527 fanatics even destroyed the organ in Zurich cathedral. In 1562 the Council of Trent, at which the Catholic Counter-Reformation was conceived, also considered doing away with all instruments in church. The reformer Martin Luther, on the other hand, praised music as a "gift of God".

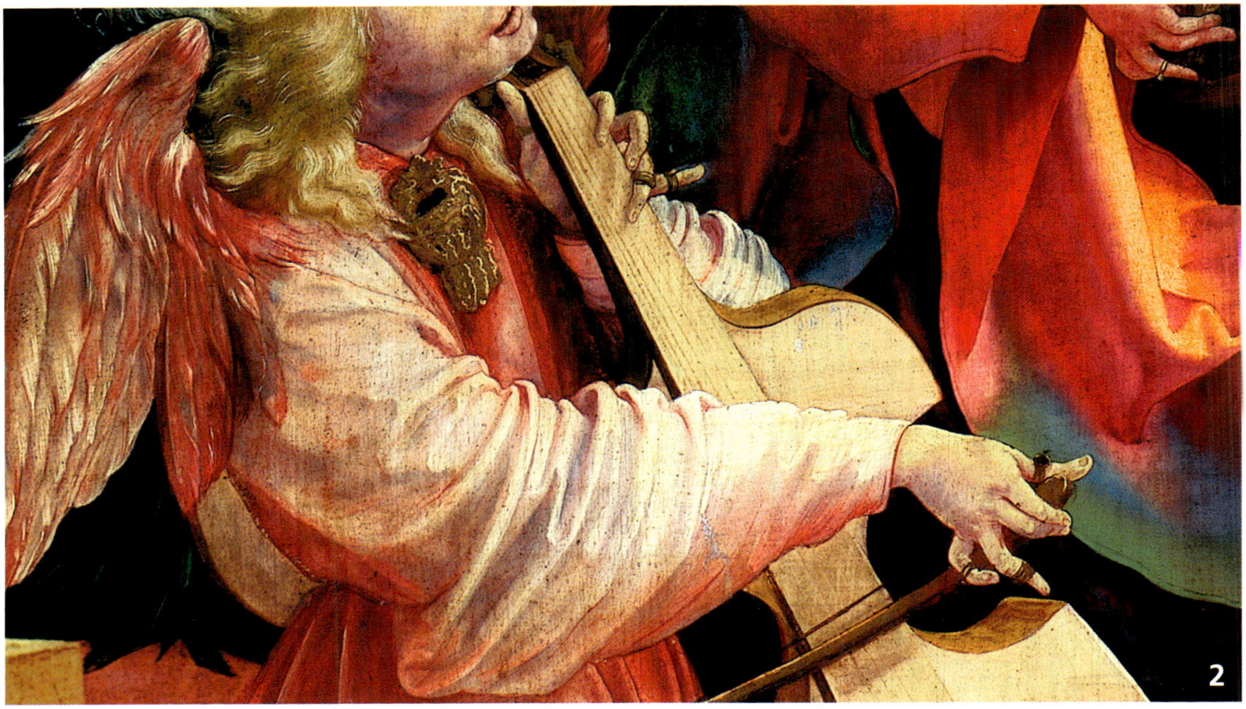

2

In the central foreground stand a wooden washtub, an earthenware vessel and a bed. Some interpreters (the Swiss art historian Jacob Burckhardt in the 19th century, for example, and the Catholic theologian Joseph Bernhard in 1921) have taken the vessel to be a chamber pot and thereby a sign that God had indeed given his son all the attributes of a mortal. But the spherical patterned vessel is probably just there for ladling water. The fact that it has feet shows that it cannot have been intended to take a person's weight.

Other interpreters of Grünewald's painting see a symbolism in the wooden bathtub and the jug – cleansing in water as a reference to Christ's baptism. The picture is steeped in symbolism, not just in the colours of the angels. Mary, for example, is compared with a rose without thorns, while the enclosed garden in which she sits is a symbol of her virginity.

But if rose and garden were well-known pictorial symbols, the wooden washtub was not. Grünewald paints it with such realism and places it in such a prominent position that he, or the client who commissioned the altarpiece, may not have intended it symbolically at all. It might refer simply to the washing of the body, for example. The altarpiece was painted for a convent of Antonites, an order of hospitallers whose members were dedicated not just to the spiritual welfare of those in their care, but also to their physical healing. They provided accommodation for pilgrims on their way to Rome and Santiago de Compostela. In the Middle Ages, they mainly looked after people suffering from poisoning by ergot-infected grain, a disease that became known as St Anthony's fire after the patron saint of the order. For the Antonites, tub and jug belonged to their daily routine, to the tools of their charitable work. Reason enough to include them in a sacred painting.

There may be a political context to these objects, too. In Crucifixion paintings of the Middle Ages, the emphasis was laid upon the divine nature of Christ. He had overcome suffering, and with his widespread arms he seemed to embrace humankind in forgiveness. Grünewald, by contrast, portrays – on another panel of the Isenheim Altar – the dead Christ as a tortured body. He shows his human nature, the agonies he has endured. Grünewald thereby aligned himself with those who deplored the current state of ecclesiastical affairs – the secularization of the Curia, the financial greed and material ostentation of the heads of the Church. Priests and artists protested by focusing on the poverty and suffering of Christ, on his earthly existence. In 1516 the Isenheim Altar was completed; in 1517 Luther nailed up his theses in Wittenberg and initiated the Reformation.

The jug and the washtub with the cloth draped over it are reminders that infants are usually washed immediately after birth and thereby emphasize the physical presence of God's son on earth – even if the vessel is a jug and not a chamber pot.

Just how important these domestic items were to the artist is also reflected in the fact that many of the elements that normally belong in a Nativity are omitted. There is no Joseph, there are no animals, there is no star, no crib and no hint of a stable.

Chamber pot or jug?

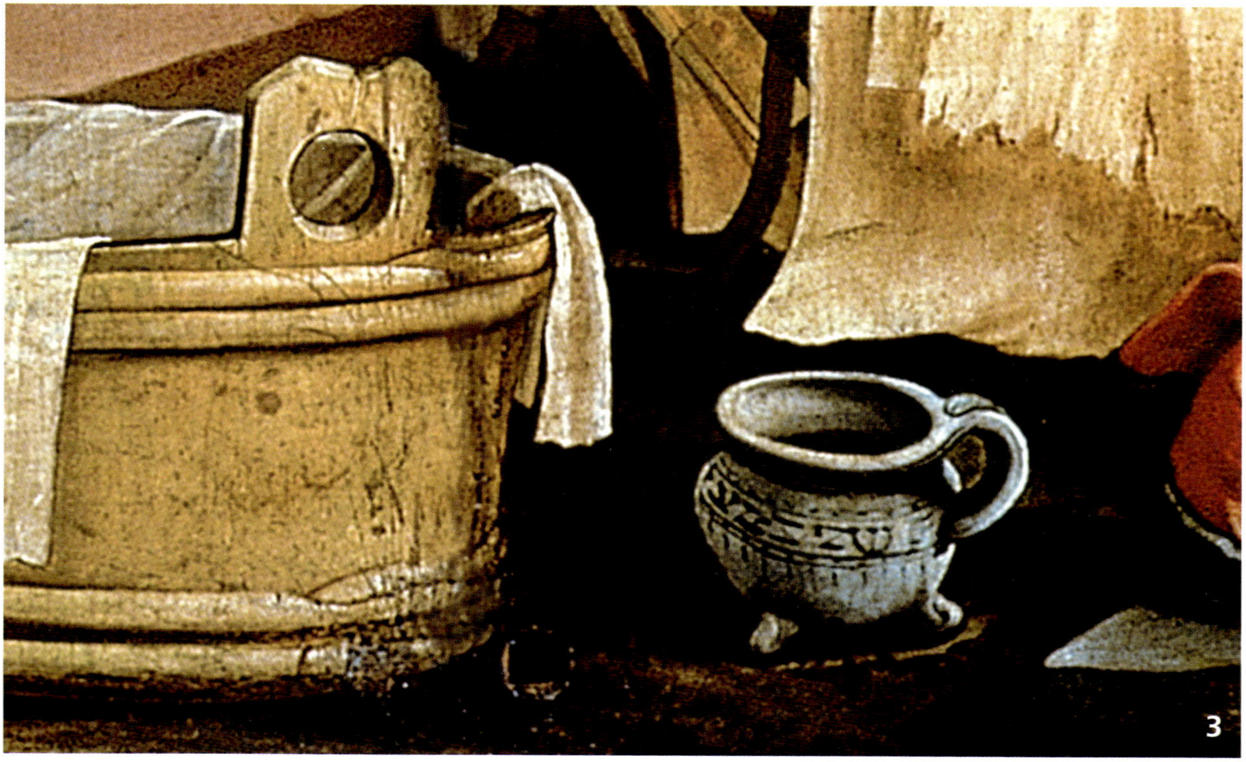

A many-sided altarpiece

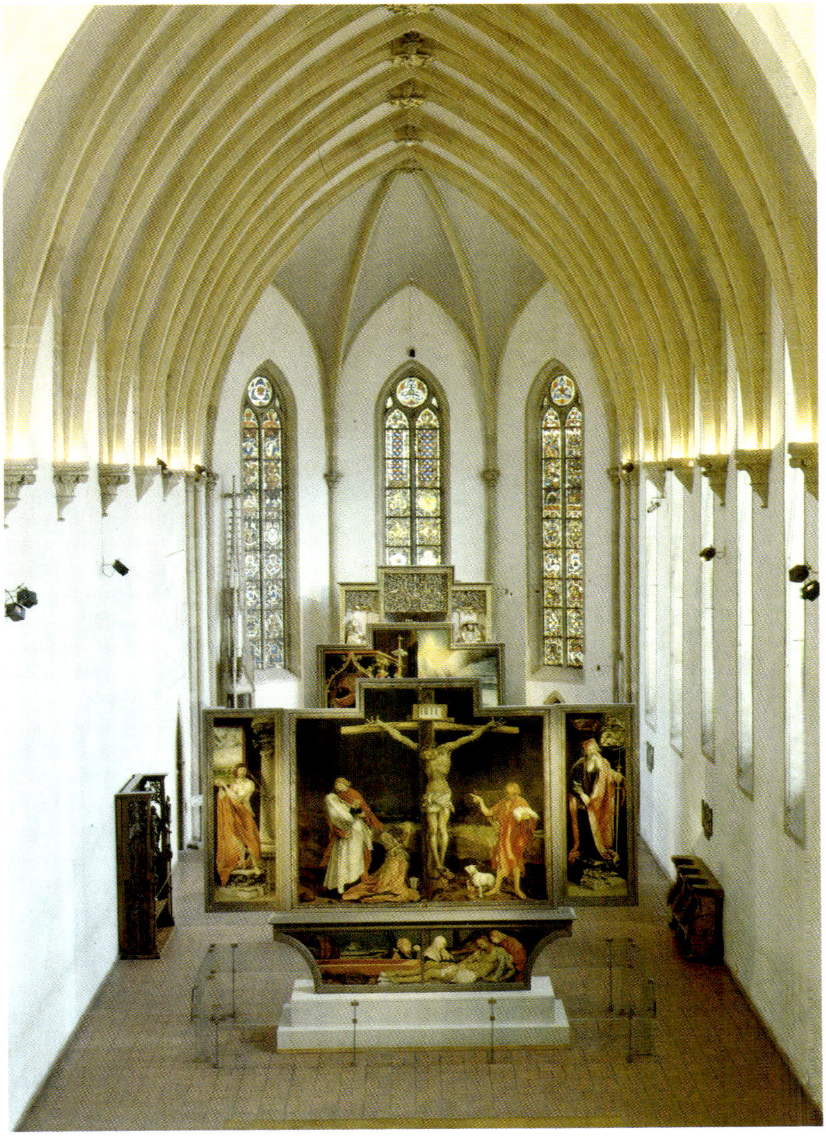

The Nativity panels featuring the *Concert of Angels* and the *Virgin and Child* total 304 centimetres in width and 265 centimetres in height. The two panels could be opened out to reveal behind them woodcarvings of saints, with St Anthony, patron saint of the Antonite Order, in the middle. The Nativity panels could themselves be concealed behind a set of outer wings, which in their closed state showed Christ tortured to death on the Cross. These three main compositions have since been separated and are on display one behind the other in the Musée d'Unterlinden in Colmar.

The sculptures are probably the work of Nikolaus Hagenauer, as was also a huge carving of branches, leaves, turrets and figures which rose above the altar wings and gave the altar a height of some eight metres. When the panels left the church in Isenheim in 1793, the carved surround remained behind. By 1860 it had disappeared: "Two carts with painted and gilded sculptures", notes a museum catalogue of 1860, "were removed long ago to be sold in a neighbouring province."

The panels of the altarpiece owe their own survival in such good condition first and foremost to two commissioners of the still young French Republic. Following the upheavals of the Revolution, the two were dispatched in 1793 to draw up an inventory of works of art in the Upper Rhine region. They probably thought the village of Isenheim – the Antonite Order no longer existed – was not safe enough for Grünewald's altarpiece, and so they had it moved to the district capital of Colmar.

The altarpiece has only left Colmar twice since that time, in each case during wartime. In 1917 – when Alsace belonged to Germany – it was taken to Munich, and in 1939 – when Alsace belonged to France – it was removed to safety in the Périgord region.

Almost nothing is known about its artist. He was born between 1460 and 1480 in Würzburg and died either in 1528 in Halle an der Saale or in 1532 in the Odenwald area. In the intervening years he can be found in Aschaffenburg, Frankfurt and Isenheim. Like the dates of his birth and death, uncertainty also surrounds the question of whether this Matthias Grünewald was assisted (at least occasionally) by one Mathias Nithart, in other words, whether perhaps two masters were involved on the present altarpiece.

That the artist should conceal the story of his personal life so completely behind his work is no coincidence: the master of the Isenheim Altar was steeped in the world view of the late Middle Ages. In the face of God and his angels, man appeared small and laden with sin; he had no originality, no powers of invention of his own.

Not so Grünewald's contemporary, Albrecht Dürer, born in 1471. He lived with the new ideas of the Renaissance, considered his contribution as an artist important, and even painted himself in the likeness of Christ, in other words as a creature of God. While we are excellently informed about Dürer's life, the master of the Isenheim Altar remains enigmatic – just like many a detail in the theological programme underlying his painting.

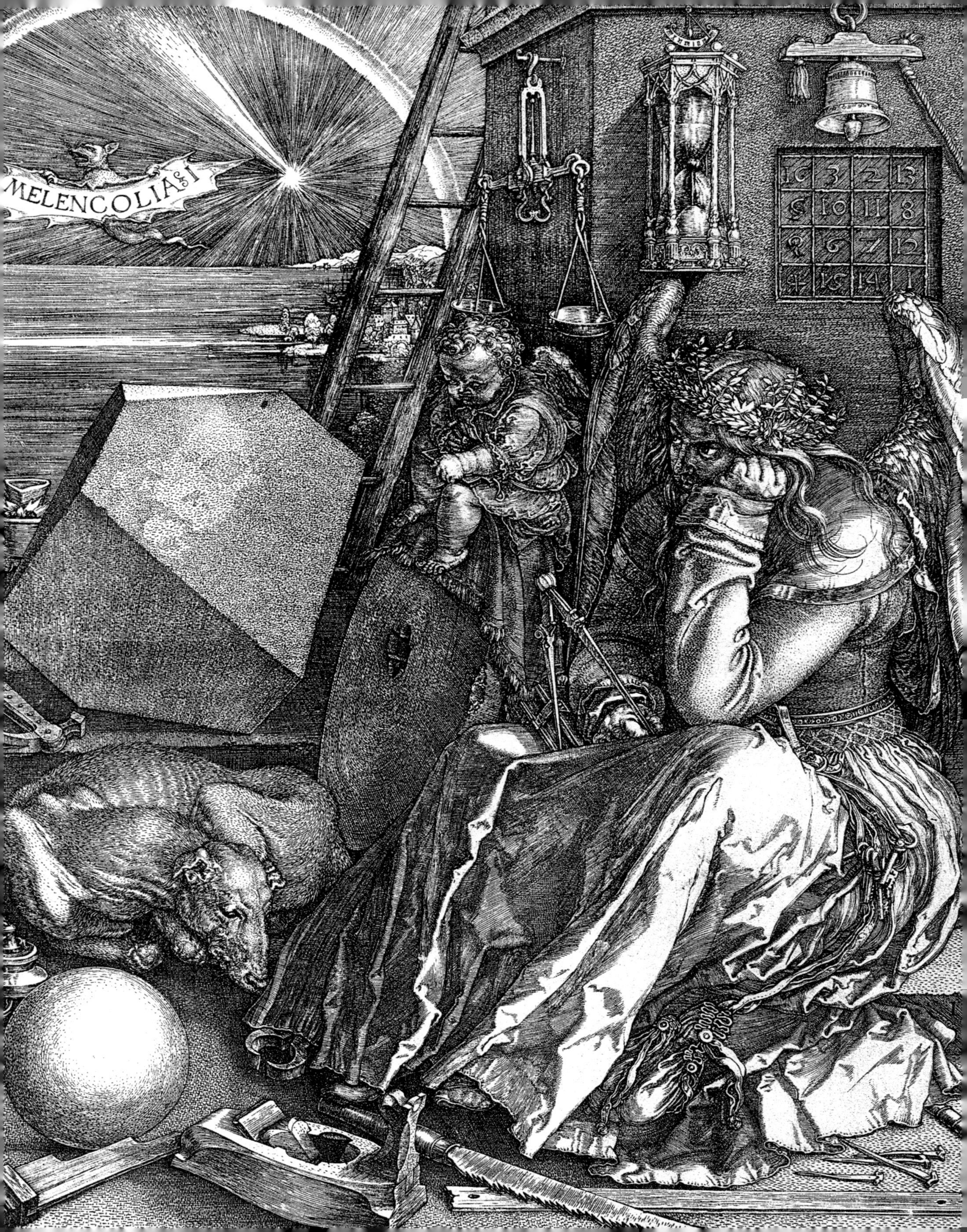
MELENCOLIA I
16 3 2 13
5 10 11 8
9 6 7 12
4 15 14 1

Albrecht Dürer: Melencholia I, 1514

When wings no longer soar

During his lifetime Albrecht Dürer executed some 450 copperplate engravings and woodcuts, but only eighty paintings. He was sooner a draughtsman than a painter, both in terms of his output and with regard to the wealth and potency of his inventions. As one of a number of superlative single plates, *Melencholia* ranks among his finest works.

The copperplate engraver works with a burin, a tool with which Dürer was familiar from his childhood on, since his father was a goldsmith. Only after Albrecht had trained under his father was he apprenticed to a painter; and only after the son had learned to use a burin was he taught to handle a brush.

Engraving was at that time still a new technique, one that had evolved out of the methods employed in goldsmiths' workshops. Goldsmiths had always worked from printed sheets of ornaments, plant motifs and lettering; these patterns were engraved with a burin on metal plates and reproduced. It was only a small step from these pattern books to the engraving of entire scenes, as pioneered by the artist Martin Schongauer in around 1430. Schongauer, active in the Alsace region, elevated the new technique to an art form. Dürer was eager to visit the celebrated master on his first extended trip away from home. He set off in 1490, but by the time he reached Colmar, Schongauer was already dead.

Dürer was away for four years, and like all travelling journeymen he had to earn his own living. The earliest testaments to his income and success come from Basle, where he worked for printers and publishers, cutting woodcuts, engraving copper plates and contributing to book illustrations, such as those for *Das Narrenschiff* (*The Ship of Fools*) by Sebastian Brant. He thus earned his first wages as a graphic artist, and later too he would work for long periods solely with a burin and pen, and not with a brush.

Like copperplate engraving, book printing too had only been invented just a few decades before Dürer's birth in 1471. Both techniques proved ideal for a man with such enormous powers of invention. After Schongauer, Dürer became the second great master of engraving and set new standards for book illustration. In his *Apocalypse*, the accompanying woodcuts for the first time enjoy equality of status with the text. After Dürer had settled back in his native city of Nuremberg, he quickly acquired his own printing press. His wife and mother sold his engravings at fairs and markets, and agents carried them as far south as Rome.

The people who bought them were almost all from the urban middle classes. Members of the feudal aristocracy could usually afford to commission expensive paintings, but the middle classes didn't normally have that sort of money to spend. It was only with the advent of printing technology that works of art became affordable for bourgeois citizens. And since, at the end of the Middle Ages, the middle classes were increasing in number and power, the demand for art was also growing. A Dürer engraving in those days cost about half the day's wages of a city stonemason.

Dürer's love of the graphic arts is only partly explained by the fact that engraving and printing were new techniques still offering a wealth of possibilities, and that he had learnt early on how to use a burin. Such external factors were joined by more personal considerations. As his writings and self-portraits show, Dürer was a self-confident man. He wanted to work with the greatest possible freedom. Paintings destined for churches, however, had to adhere to strict conventions, and portraits had to reflect the wishes of those who

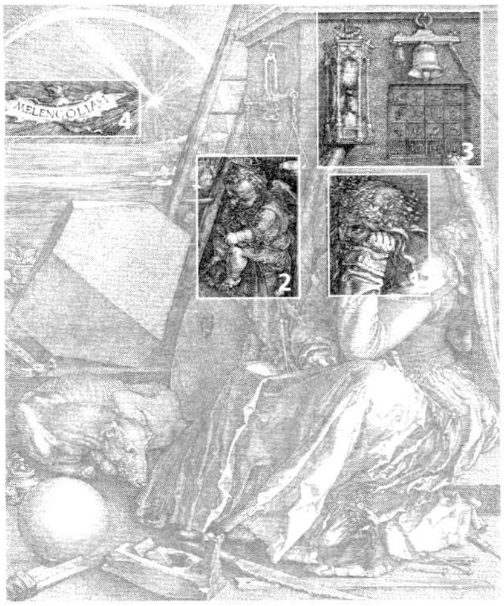

commissioned them. Graphic works, on the other hand, or at least the majority of them, could be produced on Dürer's own artistic terms and at his own risk. Here he was no longer the servant of the rich and powerful, but a free artist and self-employed salesman.

There was another reason, too. A good painter, wrote Dürer, was "full of figures inside". That was also true of himself: he was full of ideas for pictures, had more in his head than he could ever put down on paper. This is evident from the wealth of his drawings, of which he left more than 1000 at his death. Many of these are by no means preliminary stages in the evolution of later works, but are distinct compositions that never got any further. Bearing in mind that an altarpiece would take him several years, it becomes clear why he liked engravings and woodcuts – they were quicker. He could render visible more "figures" than was possible in paint, and he could earn more than with a drawing. His prints made him famous across Europe.

In his writings, Dürer warns against allowing apprentice artists to practise too much, because otherwise "melancholy" might "get out of hand". As a remedy for melancholy of this kind, he recommends playing a stringed instrument for a short while in order to "enliven the blood".

Dürer is probably referring here to a passing mood. To find out today what people understood by melancholy in the old days, we cannot rely on the written word alone. The majority of people could not read, which is why the language of pictures was so important. The pictorial motif of the head resting on the hand appeared frequently. Inscriptions reveal that it was associated not only with melancholy, but also with acedia, or accidie, a term deriving from medieval monastic life and denoting spiritual torpor, the inability "to raise one's soul to God". It was considered a temptation and for a long time also ranked as one of the deadly sins. Acedia characterizes the most severe form of melancholy: not just a depressed mood, but a much more profound inability to want or do anything. Today we would call it a deep depression.

The word "melancholy" and the pictorial motif of the "head in the hands" were also employed in another context, namely to designate one of the four humours. The physiological theory of the humours originated in antiquity and had recently been aired afresh by the humanists. According to this system, body and disposition (humour) are determined by four distinct fluids. In the ideal person, these fluids are in balance; in humankind, however, they are out of balance. Someone with too much red blood, or *sanguis*, is of a sanguine disposition. Those with too much phlegm are phlegmatics. An excess of yellow bile, or choler, makes someone a choleric, and too much black bile a melancholic.

The theory of the four bodily fluids failed to stand up to scientific investigation, but the division of humankind into four humours remained popular. According to old descriptions, the sanguine humour is the happiest, the melancholic the worst: antisocial, gloomy, tightfisted, apathetic, in other words lazy. The physical characteristics of a melancholic included a dark face, something emphasized in Dürer's figure via the contrast with the whites of her eyes. Relationships were established not just between bodily fluids and humours, but also between the four times of day, seasons of the year, ages of man and elements. Dürer includes at least two of these "foursomes" in his engraving. The element assigned to melancholy was earth, implying dryness. One way of warding off its ill effects, it was believed, was through the application of wetland plants, such as the watercress and crowfoot that Melancholia here wears on her head. The time of day assigned to melancholy was the evening – in Dürer's engraving, it is dusk, as illustrated by the comet and the bat-like creature bearing the inscription.

Even in Dürer's day, few people would have been educated enough to understand all these references. What is striking is their profusion, the large number of meaningful details that at first sight make the print appear overloaded, disordered, almost chaotic. Perhaps that was what Dürer wanted. His plate creates an initial impression that is not dissimilar to the melancholic's view of the world: the order that might enable him to act has disintegrated, and the world appears full of oppressive mysteries.

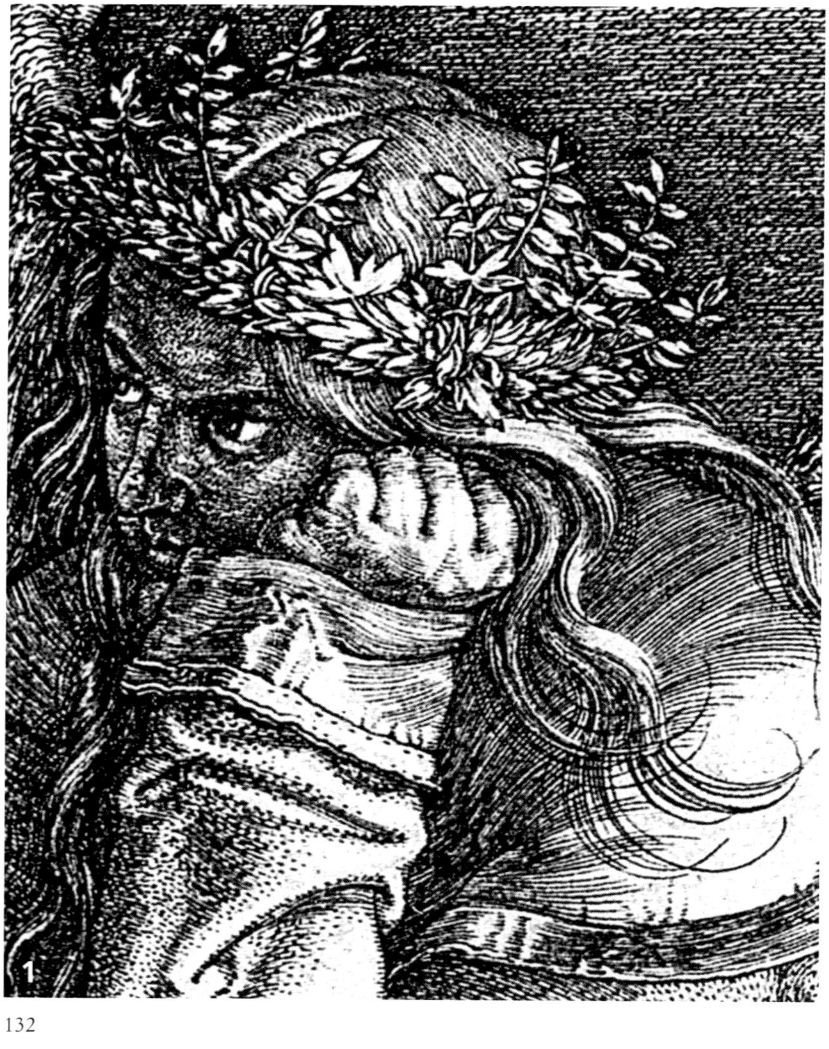

Melancholy is more than just a mood

The other face of melancholy

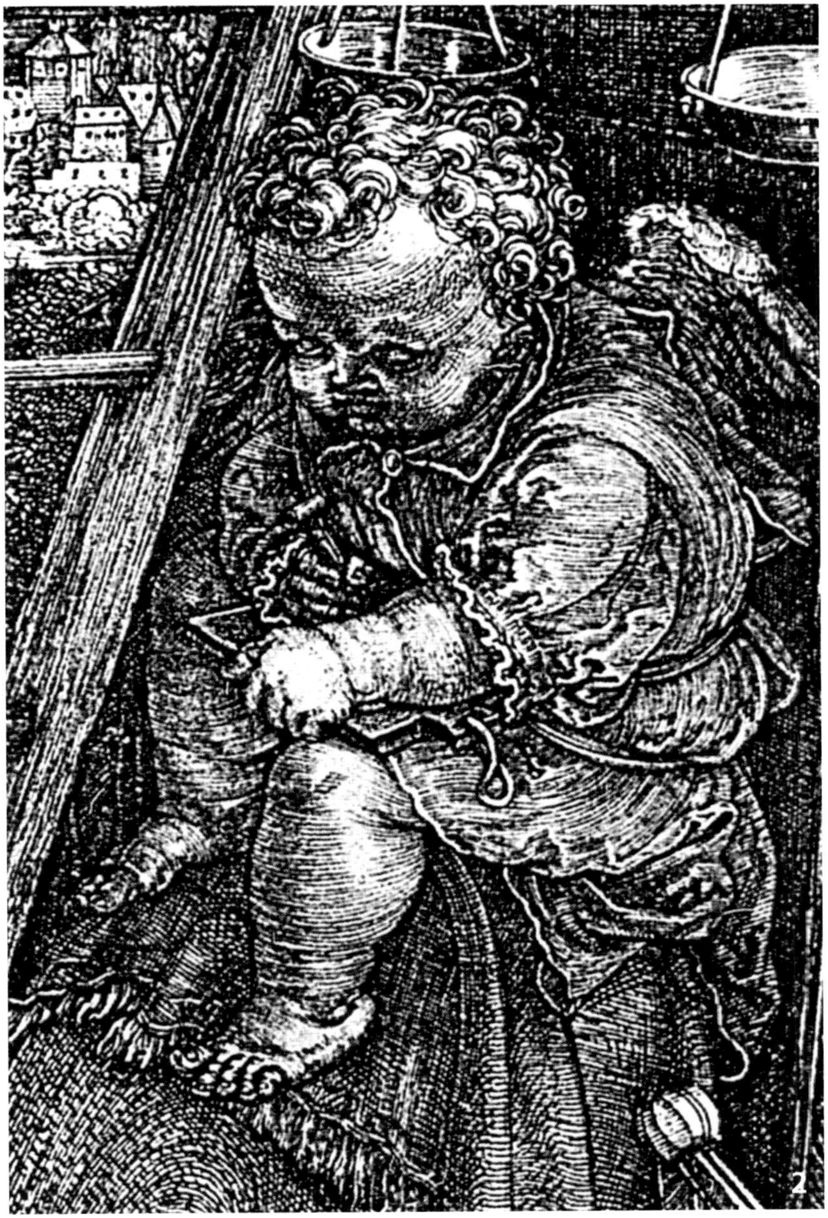

2

Amongst Dürer's many watercolours, the majority of them calmly cheerful in mood, there is one in which torrents of dark water are streaming from the sky. Dürer noted in connection with the painting that he had dreamt of rain that had fallen like a deluge. Such nightmares, in which man finds himself trapped in a hopeless situation with no way out, are one of the characteristics of melancholy.

There were reasons enough for such phases of depression in Dürer's life. Some experts view his *Melencholia* engraving in conjunction with the death of his mother, who lived with him and who died in May 1514. But no one knows whether the loss of his mother actually affected him deeply. What is undisputed, however, is that he was living in a joyless, childless marriage. In 1514 he was 43 years old – perhaps he was experiencing what we today refer to as a midlife crisis. He was a venerated figure in Nuremberg and in 1509 had been appointed to the Grand Council, the highest distinction possible for a non-patrician. But he knew how much more highly artists were regarded in Italy, and what an influential role art and artists played south of the Alps. He had written from Venice a few years earlier: "Here I am a gentleman, at home a parasite."

Dürer had brought back from Italy an interest in artistic theory. He published three books and repeatedly put forward the argument, new in Germany, that the artist should not rely solely on his own hand, but that he needed to know a great deal if he wanted to produce something good. He was chiefly interested in the proportions of the human body and wanted to define the ideal human shape, an ambition he relinquished, however, in recognition of the fact that bodies could assume many different beautiful forms. A reference to these theoretical deliberations and the difficulties they posed is perhaps – and this can only be speculation – included in *Melencholia*: the sketching putto, representing the naïve, "uneducated" painter, is contrasted with the adult figure with the compasses in her hand, representing the artist who, in his striving for knowledge, has come to his wit's end.

The putto child can also be interpreted quite differently, namely as the positive side of Melancholia. Aristotle was the first to describe the melancholic disposition; he saw melancholics as living under great tension which expressed itself in low spirits, but could also inspire great achievements. "All truly outstanding men, whether they have distinguished themselves in statecraft, literature or the fine arts, are melancholics." This positive aspect of melancholy was similarly rediscovered in the 16th century. From a humour associated with purely negative characteristics, genius suddenly shone out. Naturally Dürer was also considered a melancholic in this regard. Thus Philip Melanchthon, a humanist and a colleague of Luther, described Dürer as a "most noble melancholic".

Nuremberg could not compete with Venice or Florence as a centre of art, but as a centre of technology and precision engineering it was famed far beyond the borders of Germany. Tools and instruments from Nuremberg possessed an extraordinary reputation, and during Dürer's lifetime the city produced no less than two ground-breaking inventions. In 1492 Martin Behaim constructed the first globe, and in 1510 Peter Henlein built the first pocket watch with a spring mechanism. The watch became known as the "Nuremberg egg" owing to its oval shape.

Watch and globe – both items use counting, measuring and dividing as a means of apprehending and portraying the world more accurately, and they are characteristic of the scientific awakening which accompanied the start of the Renaissance.

The magic of numbers

The world was no longer seen as God's garden or as a human vale of sorrows, but as something which could be measured by man. Dürer's studies of the proportions of the physical body were all part of this new interest in science, and we know that he was attacked as a consquence, probably by Christians, who argued that God's children should not be measured in terms of centimetres. The *Melencholia* engraving also reflects this interest; Dürer includes within it a whole series of measuring instruments – an hourglass, a sundial, a bell for ringing the hour, scales and a level.

The panel of numbers belongs entirely, however, to the old era, the Middle Ages. Here the numbers serve not the mastering of reality but as a form of intellectual exercise, symbolism, magic. Such arrangements were called a "magic square" or "*tabula iovis*", Jupiter table, and are distinguished by the fact that the verticals and horizontals, as well as the two diagonals, all add up to the same sum, in this case 34. Dürer has built in other plays on numbers: 34 reversed is 43 – his age in the year 1514. The year itself appears in the bottom row of the table. It is also the year in which his mother died, in the month of May, referred to in the number 5 appearing upside down in the second row. In the language of symbols, a torch pointing downwards or the tree of life with its roots pointing upwards were understood to represent death.

The square is connected in another, quite different way to the subject of the engraving. Each of the four humours was associated with a star and hence a god, and melancholy thereby came under the sinister influence of Saturn. According to Greco-Roman mythology, the god Saturn was defeated by the god Jupiter; in the shape of the Jupiter table, therefore, Dürer invokes the protective presence of Jupiter.

More difficult to answer is the question of why Dürer should include not one, but two timepieces. Perhaps he was thinking of the fact that time passes differently during a period of depression. It seems to evaporate; like the melancholic's surroundings, it becomes unreal. The melancholic lives outside time and space. Dürer's figure, too, seems to gaze vacantly before her, seeing neither the landscape nor either of the timepieces.

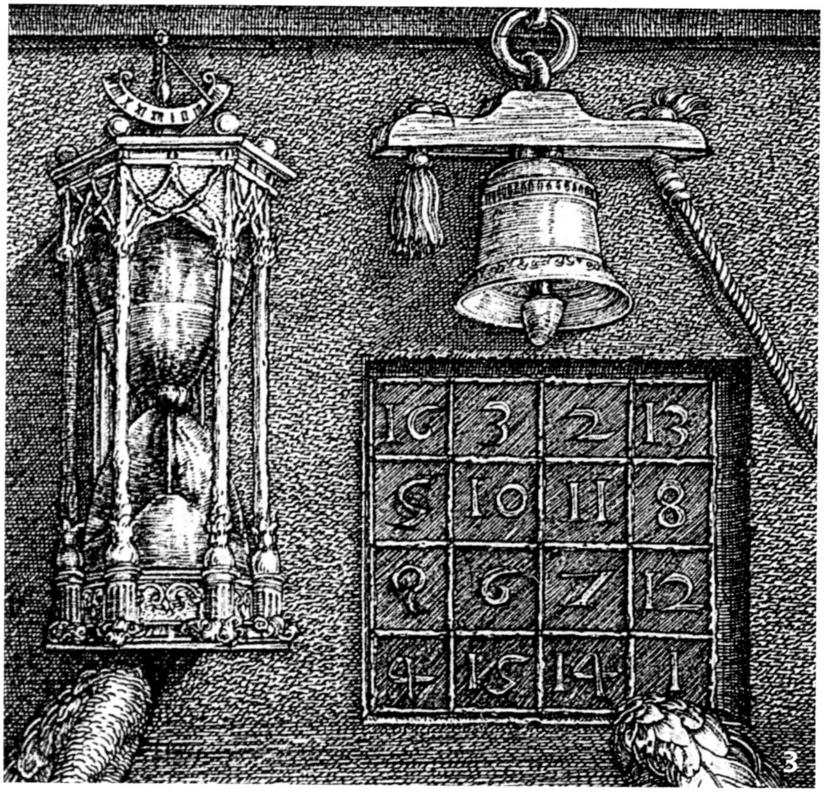

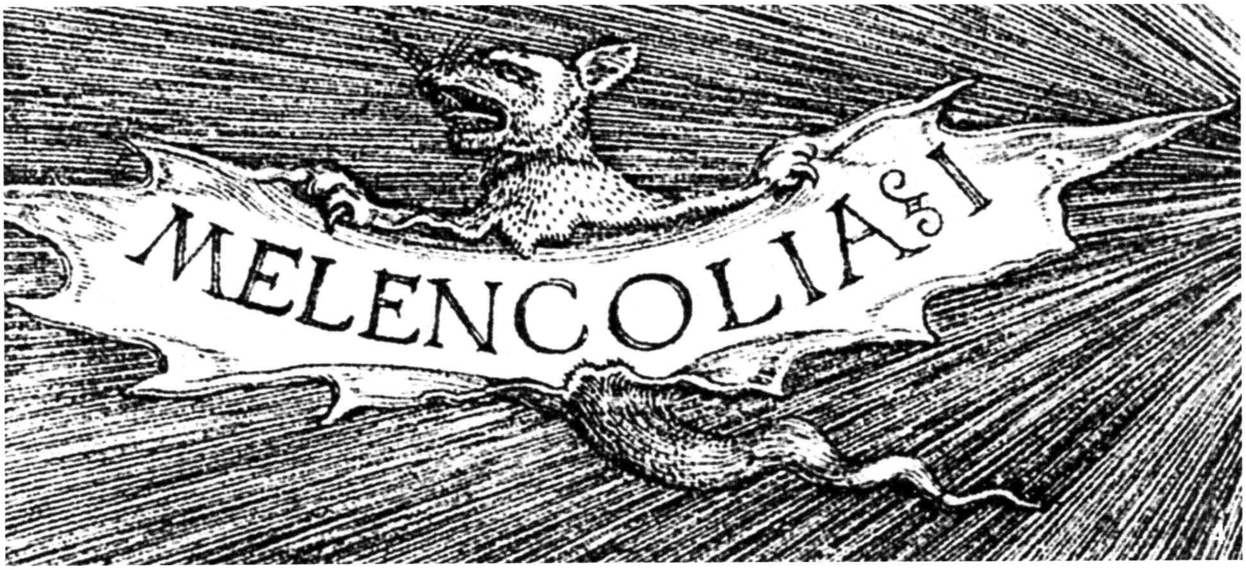

Not just at the start of the Renaissance …

Why Dürer placed a "I" behind the Latin word *Melencolia* in the inscription has not been satisfactorily explained. Perhaps he was planning to portray the other three humours, or perhaps he wanted to indicate that melancholy had a number of different forms and effects. Perhaps the "I" is not intended as a number at all, but rather as the letter "i". In this case, the title of the engraving would mean "Melancholy, go away!"

In certain epochs Melancholia appeared particularly frequently, albeit not always under her own name. The Germans in the 18th century spoke of the "illness of Werther" (in reference to the novel *The Sorrows of Young Werther* by Goethe), the French in the 19th century of the "mal du siècle". Common to most "melancholic" periods in history is a social situation clouded by confusion, in which it is difficult to see what's what and to act appropriately. This may be compounded by a sense of weariness and boredom, as well as one of threat. A prime example of a melancholic is Hamlet, who returns to the corrupt Danish court, who broods and dithers, who is appalled by the reality of the social situation, who withdraws into a feigned madness, before finally being forced to act by external circumstances.

Shakespeare wrote *Hamlet* in 1601, at the end of an era at whose beginning Dürer conceived his *Melencholia*. It was an era of dramatic change. Alongside the Christian world view, there evolved a scientific one. The institution which during the Middle Ages had presided over intellectual and spiritual activity, namely the Catholic Church, lost it omnipotence. The consequences of these changes were felt even in daily life. For centuries, for example, the Catholic Church had taught that Christians could earn themselves a place in the kingdom of Heaven though good deeds. Luther, however, rejected this thesis out of hand. If people could no longer expect a heavenly reward for the bread they daily gave to the poor, however, why should they be so generous any more?

Another example: two major groups within the population disappeared, the monks and the knights. Monasteries in Protestant regions were abolished, while the knights had already seen their financial basis undermined by the growing power of the cities and princes. Two groups that, through their existence and their ideals, had decisively shaped society had now disappeared. If the monastic and chivalric way of life was no longer valid, to what were people supposed to look for orientation?

We are accustomed to seeing the dawn of the Renaissance as a forceful new beginning, but it was accompanied beneath the surface by a strong wave of melancholy. Amongst the more sensitive minds of the epoch, in particular, there were many who were plagued by dark visions and anguished faces. It is not impossible that we have entered another melancholic phase in our own times. There is much to suggest this, even if the word is unfashionable. We speak instead of fear and depression. Our cinemas are full of films about cataclysmic destruction, and our authors testify year after year to introspection, to the withdrawal into the self that follows when it is so difficult to act meaningfully in the outside world, in the face of the many catastrophes that seem to be looming, be they real or imaginary. Seen in this light, Dürer's engraving remains highly contemporary, despite all its 16th-century symbolism and details.

Niklaus Manuel Deutsch: The Judgement of Paris, between 1516 and 1528

The goddess with the mercenary's hat

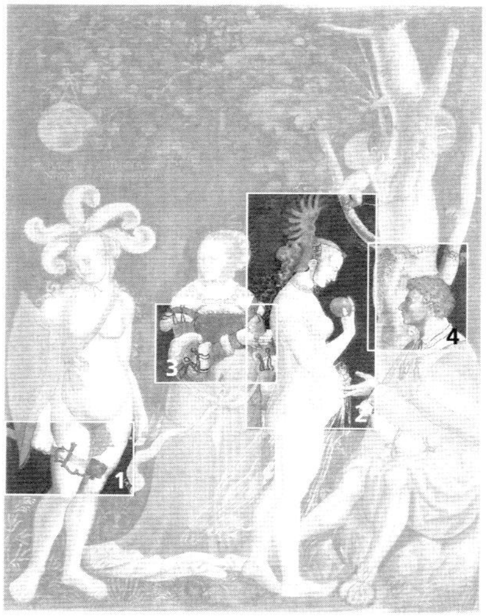

Against a dark background suggestive of night, a curious company has assembled beneath the leafy boughs of a tree. A young man is staring deep into the eyes of a beautiful, transparently clad woman, while two other ladies, one naked, the other sumptuously dressed, stand beside them like extras with their eyes averted.

The figures are identified by inscriptions within the painting. The words PARIS VON TROY DER TORECHT (Paris of Troy, the foolish) are written in gold and silver lettering over the head of the man. The lady equipped with shield and sword is identified as IUNO EIN GÖTTIN DER ÜBERWINDUNG INN STRITS (Juno, the goddess of victory in battle). The woman in the transparent dress is named as Venus – the words FENUS FENUS can be read in gold on her crested bonnet. Around the circumference of the ball in her hand it is also possible to make out the words EN DIESER OP, probably the beginning and end of the German phrase DIESER OPFEL DER SCHÖNSTEN, meaning "This apple for the fairest".

It is clearly a reference to the golden apple marked "For the Fairest" which, in the world of Greek mythology, the goddess of Discord threw onto the table during an Olympian banquet. When three of the goddesses argued over who should have it, the king of the gods announced that the final decision should be made by the fairest of all men. That was Paris, son of the king of Troy, whom the goddesses found tending his father's flocks. Each goddess attempted to win the young man's favour: one offered him fame, the second power and riches, while the goddess of love promised that the fairest woman in the world should be his. It was to Venus that Paris awarded the apple, and with her help he won Helen, wife of the king of Sparta. Paris abducted her, so the legend goes, and thereby unleashed the war between the Greeks and the Trojans that would form the subject of Homer's *Iliad*.

While the artist demonstrates his familiarity with mythology, he has muddled up his inscriptions. The goddess he describes as Juno, wife of Jupiter, is in fact the warlike Minerva, clearly identified by her weapons. Juno herself is the one standing in the middle, richly dressed. The artist naturally calls the goddesses by their Latin names rather than their Greek ones, for at the time this undated painting was executed, probably between 1516 and 1528, Greek antiquity was still in the process of being rediscovered by humanist scholars. Niklaus Manuel was not a Greek expert, and even his two trips to Italy were not made for the purposes of study.

The artist probably derived his knowledge of the Greek myth from a medieval novel, in which the legend had taken on a moralizing slant. Paris was reproached for choosing not the positive virtues of fame and power, but the pleasures of physical love, which in the Christian Middle Ages was considered sinful. Manuel, too, describes Paris as "foolish" in his inscription, and the painting can thus be considered a warning. This provided the painting with an excuse for its portrayal of naked women and also made it acceptable to the stern city councillors for whom it was probably executed.

The two coats of arms hanging in the tree, a bluish swan and a square white well belonged to the family of a certain Bendicht Brunner, a member of the small ruling class which at that time held sway in Berne. It was here that Manuel was born in c. 1484, in the narrow confines of a medieval city of some 5000 inhabitants, which lay off the main trade routes. Together with twelve other towns, the "noble Republic of Berne" formed the smallest of the Swiss confederations.

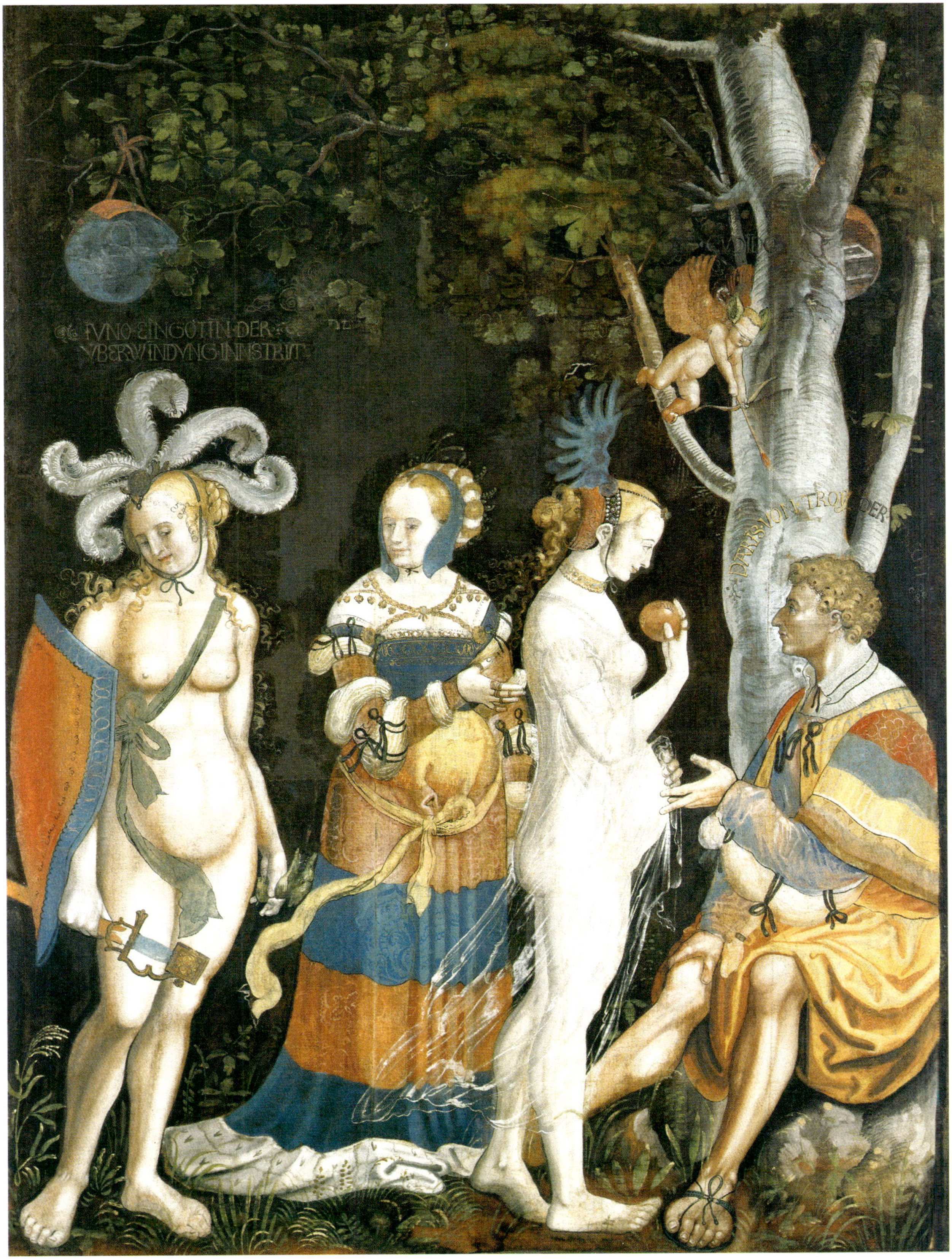
IVNO EIN GOTIN DER
VBERWINDVNG IN STRIT

In the early 16th century, war was the confederates' chief occupation. According to the German humanist Jakob Wimpheling, they were "obstreperous, sullen and arrogant wild men" ... "taught from their youth onwards to take up arms and go to war." For the majority of Swiss, there was little else for them to do – their limited land provided neither jobs nor sufficient food, so mercenaries became the Alpine region's biggest export.

Niklaus Manuel also twice left his wife and children to travel to Italy, around 1516 and in 1522, as a mercenary soldier in the French army. He was skilled in the use of the long, narrow sword for "one and a half hands" which Minerva here holds so casually by its blade. Made in Milan, this magnificent weapon with its richly worked gold handle was one which Swiss mercenaries liked to take home with them. More common in Berne was the so-called "Swiss sword": Niklaus Manuel liked to sign his works with the symbol of this simple dagger, which for a long time formed a sort of Swiss national symbol, on a par with the Confederation Cross. That a nation should make a weapon its emblem says much about its self-image.

The Swiss earned their military reputation at the end of the 15th century, when the "cowherds" unexpectedly succeeded in crushing the knights of Burgundy. The services of the "invincible giants" were subsequently sought by the main European powers. In Manuel's day, Italy was the battlefield of Europe. It was here, for fifty years, that the French kings, the emperors and the popes fought each other in constantly changing alliances. Thanks to their geographical position, the Confederates could descend upon Italy, France or Germany with 30,000 men within two weeks; as long as the king of France had them as allies, he could manage without his own army in Italy.

The Confederate cantons hired out their troops for a healthy fee. Individual mercenaries often set off on their own initiative too, to sell their services. You could count on the Swiss as long as you paid them regularly; if the money didn't materialize, they would simply pack up and go home or seek compensation some other way. Manuel came away with a hand injury from the plundering of Novara: when the money they had been promised for conquering the city failed to appear, the angry Confederates burned it down and killed anyone who stood in their way. Manuel was also present at Bicocca when the Swiss, contrary to orders, attacked an enemy in a superior position. They had embraced the ideals of the Burgundian knights and considered waiting or playing tactical games to be dishonourable. "We want at them!" they bellowed – and suffered a crushing defeat. Shortly afterwards Manuel composed a satirical song in which he mocked the victors for being so cowardly as to dig themselves entrenchments.

The Confederates also refused to wear helmets or armour; they attached importance to agility and elegance on the battlefield. Thus the goddess of war in the present painting also does not wear traditional armour, but instead the extravagant plumed toque sported by the boldest Confederate mercenaries.

Taking up arms for king, emperor and pope

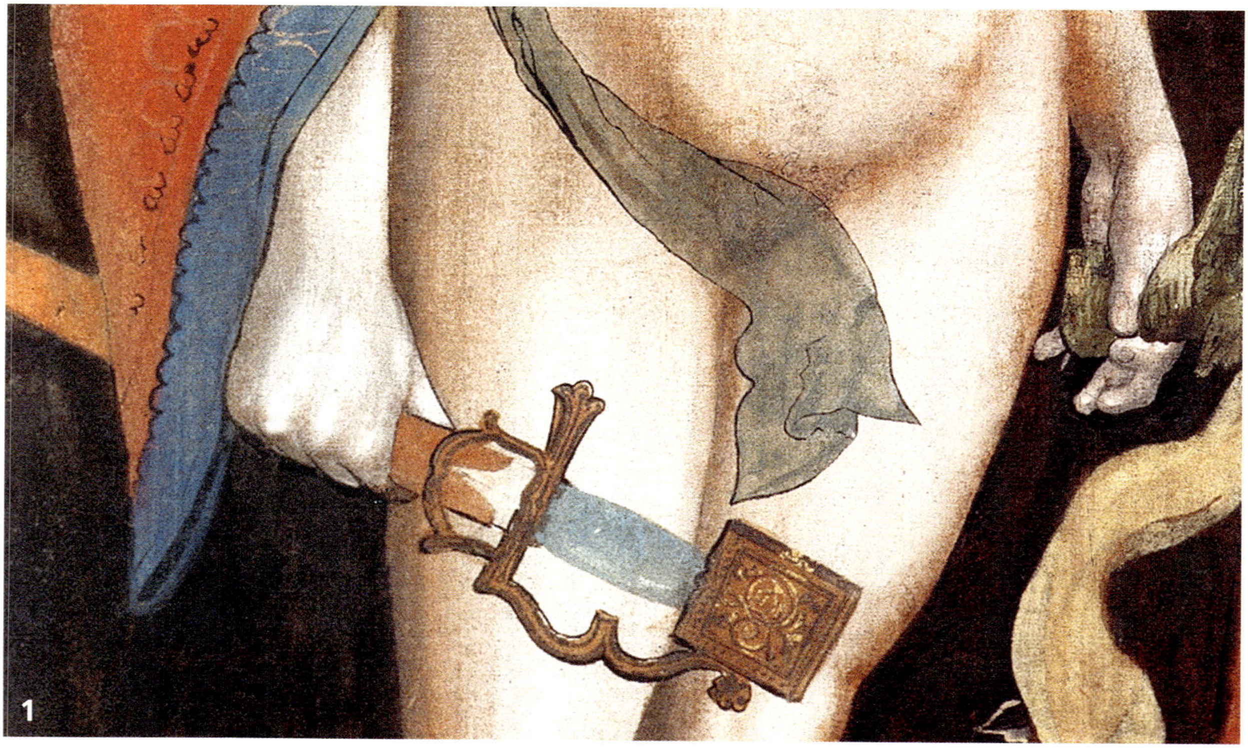

1

While the goddess of war exposes her tanned naked body unclad, Venus heightens the shapeliness of her body with a transparent shift. With her small, firm breasts above a rounded belly, whose curves promise fertility (but by no means necessarily imply pregnancy), she thereby falls fully in line with Gothic ideals of beauty in the Middle Ages. The pale, frosty white colour of Venus' skin testifies to her gentility and idleness, but may also be interpreted as a reference to her devilish, wicked nature. Venus the medieval woman knows how to ensnare men, how to cast a spell over them like Parsifal or make a "fool" of them like Paris. The beginning of the 16th century saw a particular spate of warnings regarding the sinful, sensual charms of women. In countless satires and pamphlets, the goddess of Love and the ruinous "power of women" which she represented were attacked with such vehemence that one can only assume that Manuel's contemporaries were particularly susceptible to her arts of seduction.

Venus dominates the picture and the scene; Paris is fascinated by her. The artist probably felt the same way. The attractive naked female body remained one of his favourite subjects. In a number of drawings he furnishes his ladies with "lassos" which with to capture their lovers. In one of these lassos the artist symbolically places his own monogram and dagger: he too is a captive. Women in his paintings almost always appear armed, somehow connected with war, danger and death.

Swiss mercenaries setting off for Lombardy were spurred on not only by the promise of rich rewards and military action, but also by the hope of an amorous affair with a camp follower or an Italian beauty. That service under Lady Venus was not without its own dangers emerged when the first mercenaries returned from Italy in 1495. The Bernese authorities found themselves obliged to open a "pox house" in which to isolate the many soldiers suffering from syphilis – victims of the perilous power of women.

Lady Venus and the power of women

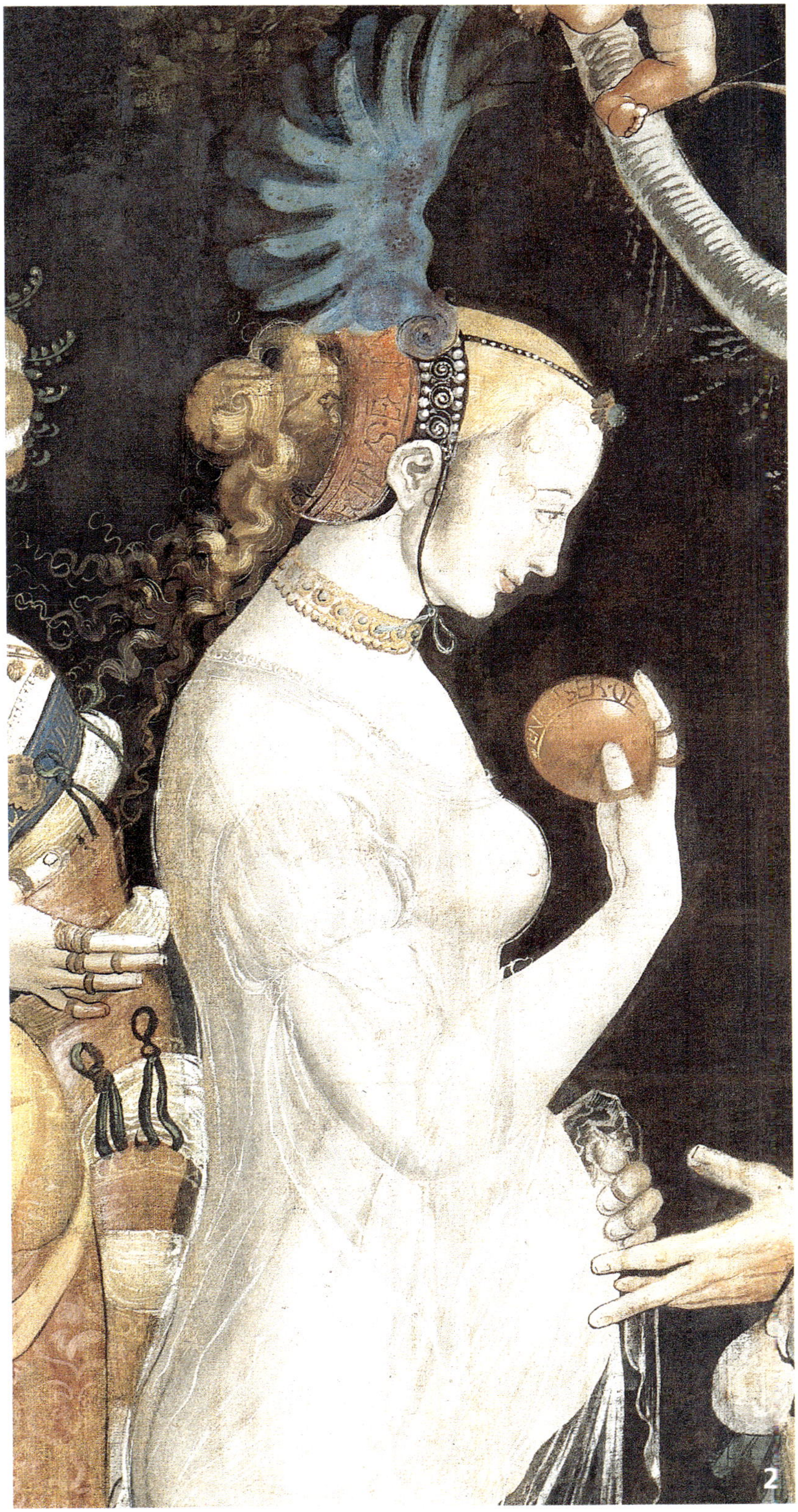

Wealth is what Juno offered Paris the shepherd, and wealth is stamped all over her appearance. This both corresponds to her status as Jupiter's wife – the bonnet concealing her hair indicates that she is married – and at the same time reflects fashion trends in Niklaus Manuel's day. Her dress, in several shades of sumptuous velvet, ends in an ermine train. The sleeves, a particularly important element of her costume, are slit in four places to reveal a pleated white lining, bunched up to create the popular puffed effect. The sleeve sections are connected at the shoulder and elbow only by decorative black ribbons laced through eyelets. This made it possible to mix and match the various sleeve sections in the latest colours and thereby give the appearance of owning a larger wardrobe than was perhaps the case. The broad sleeves of Paris's shirt are also slit, puffed and laced; at the start of the 16th century, men's fashions were if possible even richer and more splendid than women's. This trend seems to have been set by a piece of male, soldierly inspiration. After their victory over the Burgundians in 1476, a rich booty of velvet and silk fell into the hands of the Confederates. They cut up their plunder, so the story goes, into pieces and embroidered them onto their shabby clothes. Instead of armour, they wore thick quilting to protect themselves against injury and the cold. To give themselves mobility, they slit this quilting at the knee, elbow and shoulder, lined the "holes" with the expensive fabrics and thereby invented their colourful "slashed" style of dress. The German mercenaries liked it so much that they adopted it too. "One must let them have one pleasure in their wretched and miserable lives", felt Emperor Maximilian I, and gave permission for his foot soldiers to wear such costumes, even though they contravened the official dress code.

Mercenaries set the trend

Thanks to their high military standing, the Swiss cowherds from the back woods were soon dictating the style of dress worn by men and women of every class in large parts of Europe. Their extravagantly provocative mercenary fashions caused preachers everywhere to fulminate against the devilish impropriety of their slits and puffs. Within the Confederation itself, there were those who bemoaned the loss of "the old Helvetic modesty and simplicity". The Bernese chronicler Anshelm condemned the ostentatious dress worn by certain ladies, including the wife of military commander Albrecht von Stein, who wore an "underskirt of silver and shoes of gold" and more jewellery "than has ever been seen in Berne before". Perhaps Manuel was thinking of her when he painted Juno with her gold necklaces, brooches and numerous rings.

Albrecht von Stein, under whose banner the artist fought twice in Italy, drew a fat pension from the French king even between campaigns; he was a so-called "crown-eater". Many others in Berne were similarly in the secret pay of foreign powers: influential members of the military, councillors, mercenary agents and recruiting officers. Even the authorities accepted money without a scruple: around 1623, French subsidies accounted for a third of Berne's entire income.

Ordinary soldiers had the chance of making more money in short campaigns than in years of working in the fields or in a workshop. Vast quantities of money suddenly came into circulation in a society that had previously been predominantly agricultural. Prices and standards of living rose; everyone was tempted to spend more than they earned, especially on clothes. Envy, dissatisfaction, venality and corruption were the consequences. "This people", observed an advisor to Charles V, "has got so used to the income that buys it idleness, inebriation and luxury, that it can no longer do without foreign money."

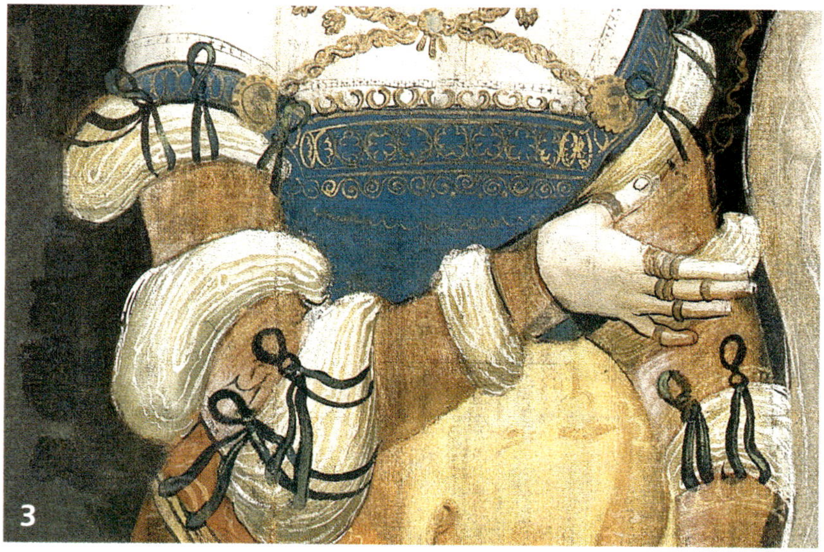
3

A social climber goes into politics

Manuel took full advantage of the restructuring taking place in Bernese society, brought about by the mercenaries and their new-found wealth. He rose from being the son of a "foreigner" – his father appears to have been a spice seller in Piedmont – to being a member of the small ruling class, previously strictly closed to outsiders.

Nothing reliable is known about Manuel's early years or his artistic training. It is possible that he studied under a Bernese glass painter. By 1509, however, he had done well enough to marry into a respectable middle-class family, and shortly afterwards he bought a house in the street today called Gerechtigkeitsgasse. His workshop executed altarpieces for churches and monasteries. One of Manuel's most important works, a monumental *Dance of Death* on the wall of a Franciscan monastery, has long since been destroyed, and is known to us only through a later copy. The head of Paris, with its bold profile and golden curls, reappears in the copy as a portrait of the artist, who paints himself at work at the end of the macabre roundelay. Death awaits him just as it does the other citizens of Berne in the painting, but in his case the skeleton is kneeling humbly at the feet of the clearly very self-confident artist. Like Paris, he is dressed as a magnificent mercenary.

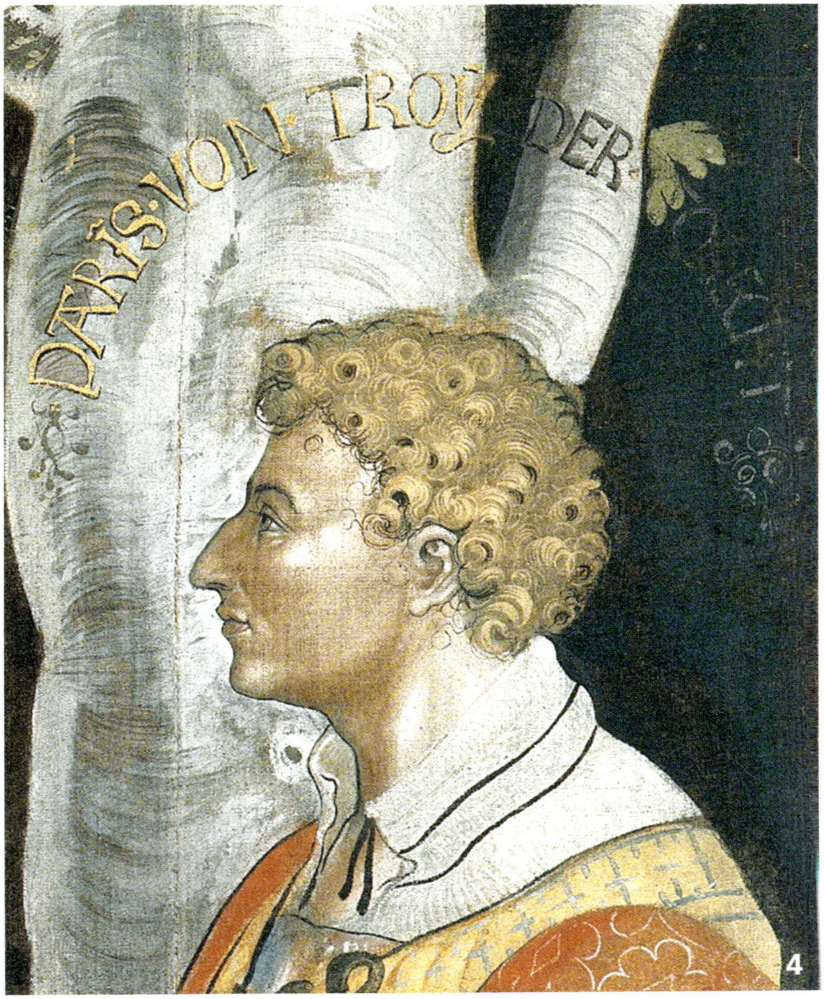

4

A letter that Manuel wrote from Italy in 1522, applying for a job in the Bernese administration, indicates that he must have been dissatisfied with his position both as a painter and a mercenary. "I am a young journeyman and have many small children ... whom I would like to educate properly but which as an artist I cannot afford to do ..." Soon afterwards Manuel was appointed bailiff of Erlach and spent over five years managing estates not far from the city of Berne, in a position which not only absolved him of material cares, but also prepared him for more senior positions in government. He probably stopped painting at this point, although he continued to draw. His only known journeyman, Elysius Walter, also changed horses and became a sexton.

As well as being eager to rise up through the social ranks, Manuel had another reason for wanting to give up his job as an artist. In 1517 Luther had nailed his theses to the door of the palace chapel in Wittenberg. With the advent of the Reformation, artists in northern Europe lost their main employer, the Church. Many Swiss, their confidence shaken by their military defeat at Pavia, also embraced the new Protestant teachings. Too many of them had also experienced at first hand the Catholic priesthood and its lust for earthly possessions: Albrecht von Stein had swopped his own grey stallion for a general indulgence for himself and 500 of his men.

"The Indulgence Seller" was the title of a pamphlet with which Manuel threw himself into the religious debate that would soon divide Berne. The politically very active bailiff of Erlach penned several polemical sketches and essays and thereby played a major role in ensuring that the Reformation triumphed in Berne in 1528. As a member of the executive, from now on – until his death in 1530 – he was directly responsible for a series of strict decrees that put an immediate end to a chaotic, dissolute era.

The churches were cleansed of their "idolatrous images" (some of them painted by Manuel himself). The secularization of Church assets restored the city to financial health and enabled it to "do without foreign money". Serving as a mercenary was forbidden, as was the costume that went with it. The slits in clothes had to be sewn up; gambling, drinking, dancing and whoring were all banned. The power of Lady Venus was crushed. With the active assistance of the artist who had celebrated her beauty in his paintings, the goddess was driven out of Berne.

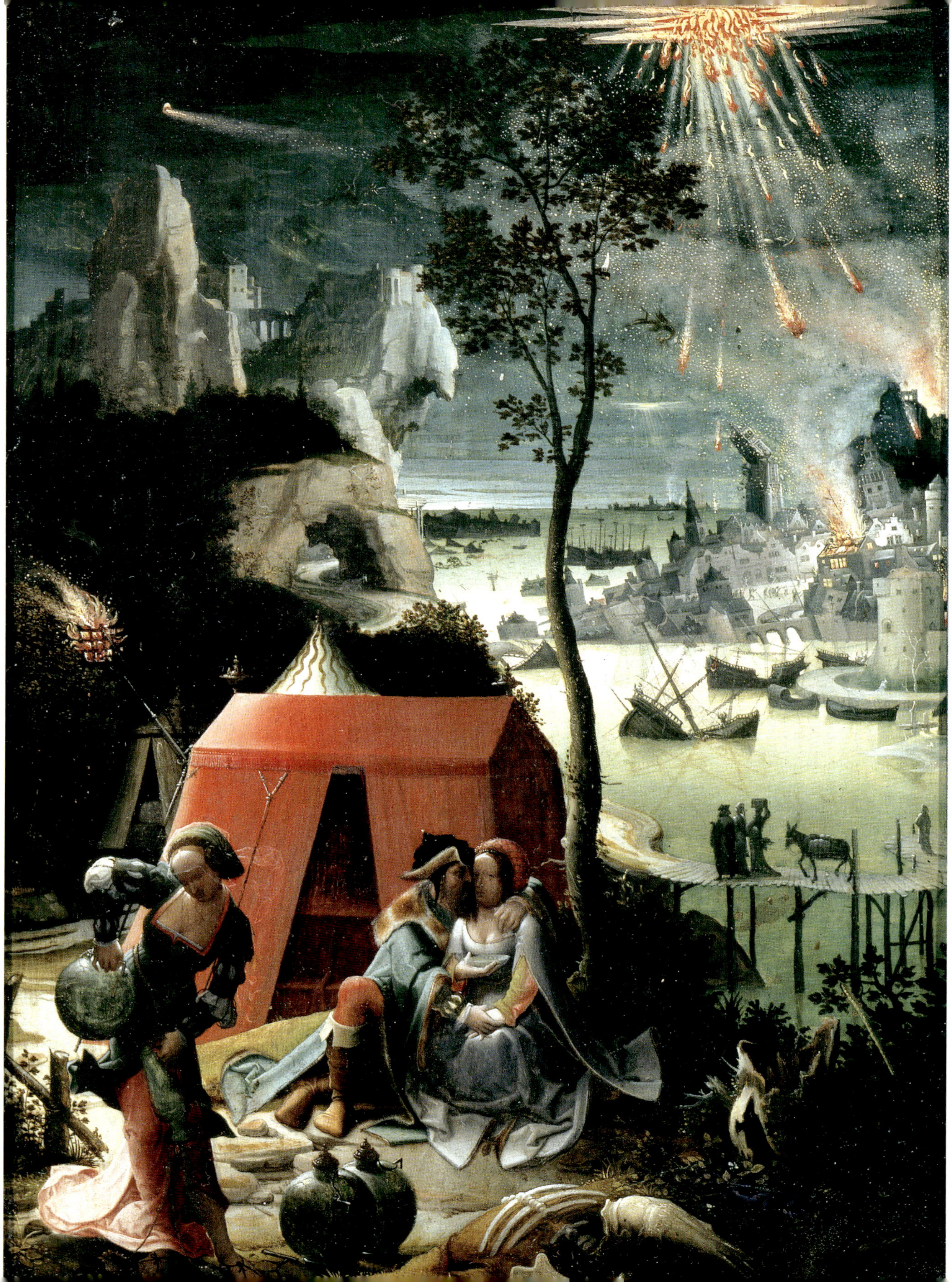

Netherlandish Master: Lot and his Daughters, c. 1530

Sodom burns, while those who have escaped celebrate

In the foreground women and wine, in the background the end of the world – two scenes composed within triangular fields of the same size which meet at the diagonal running from top left to bottom right and which are held together by the pallid half-light. A clearly constructed painting which tells a dark, chaotic tale.

The story of Lot is related in chapters 18 and 19 of Genesis, the first book of the Old Testament, which tells of the creation of the world and the subsequent direction of God's wrath towards humankind. Having expelled Adam and Eve from Paradise after they disobey him, the depravity of their descendants leads God to destroy all but two of them in the Flood. When the people of Babylonia challenge him by building the Tower of Babel, his punishment is to confuse them by giving them many languages and scattering them across the earth. When he hears of the sinful lives of the inhabitants of Sodom and Gomorrah, he decides to destroy the two cities.

God told Abraham of his plan. Abraham's nephew, Lot, had settled in Sodom and so the Patriarch started negotiating with God: "Suppose you find fifty innocent people there within the city – will you still destroy it, and not spare it for their sakes?" God replied: "If I find fifty innocent people in Sodom, I will spare the entire city for their sake." Abraham spoke again: "Suppose there are only forty-five? ... only forty?" Abraham eventually managed to get the number down to ten innocent people. God sent two angels, dressed as ordinary men, to Sodom, to assess the situation. These are the events leading up to the present scene.

The angels met Lot, who invited them to have dinner and spend the night at his home. All the men of the city of Sodom, godless and immoral, banded together and surrounded Lot's house, demanding that he yield up his two guests. "Bring them out so we can have sex with them." They wanted to homosexually abuse the supposedly defenceless strangers. Lot, the pious, virtuous patriarch, offered the Sodomites his two virgin daughters in place of the strangers: "Do with them as you wish, but leave these men alone, for they are under my protection."

The Sodomites were not interested in the young women; they wanted the strangers. They attacked Lot and tried to break down the door into the house. The two angels pulled Lot inside and revealed their power by blinding the men of Sodom. They then told Lot of God's intention to destroy the city and urged him to leave with his family immediately. "At dawn the next morning, the angels became insistent ... When Lot still hesitated, the angels seized his hand and the hands of his wife and two daughters and rushed them to safety outside the city." There they warned him: "Run for your lives! Do not stop anywhere in the valley. And don't look back!" As Lot hurried to safety, God "rained down fire and burning sulphur from the heavens on Sodom and Gomorrah. He utterly destroyed them ... But Lot's wife looked back as she was following along behind him, and she became a pillar of salt."

The artist shows Lot and his daughters, safely removed from Sodom, in front of some luxurious tents. The Bible describes them differently, namely as refugees living in a cave in the mountain. Nor are the faces of the three etched with worry and despair, as might be expected after losing one's wife and mother, home, city and possessions. Lot's daughters believed that the whole of the rest of humanity had been destroyed. So the older daughter said to her sister: "There isn't a man anywhere ... for us to marry. And our father will soon be too old to have children. Come, let's get him drunk with wine, and then we will

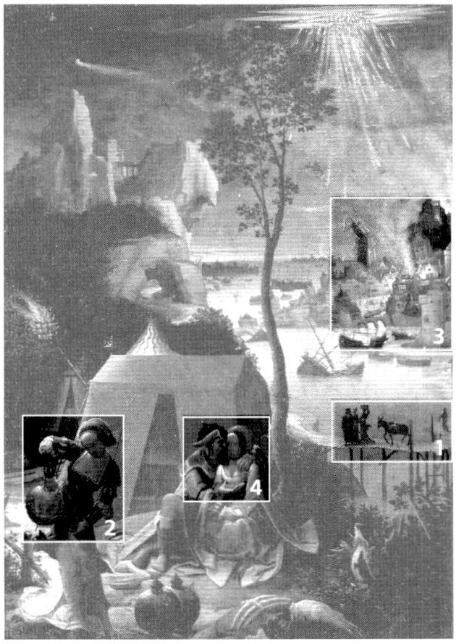

sleep with him. That way we will preserve our line through our father." So that is what they did, the eldest daughter the first night, and the youngest the second, and on both occasions Lot "was unaware of her lying down or getting up again".

Nothing of this incestuous story can be seen in the present painting. The destruction of Sodom, on the other hand, is portrayed in dramatic detail – the fire falling from the sky and the city going down in flames. The fact that the father was prepared to prostitute his daughters, and that his daughters are now trying to dupe the pious old man – these were things the viewer was expected to know. The artist transforms the misery of the refugees into a conventional love idyll. Conventional, too, insofar as it is the man who is taking the initiative, and not one of the daughters.

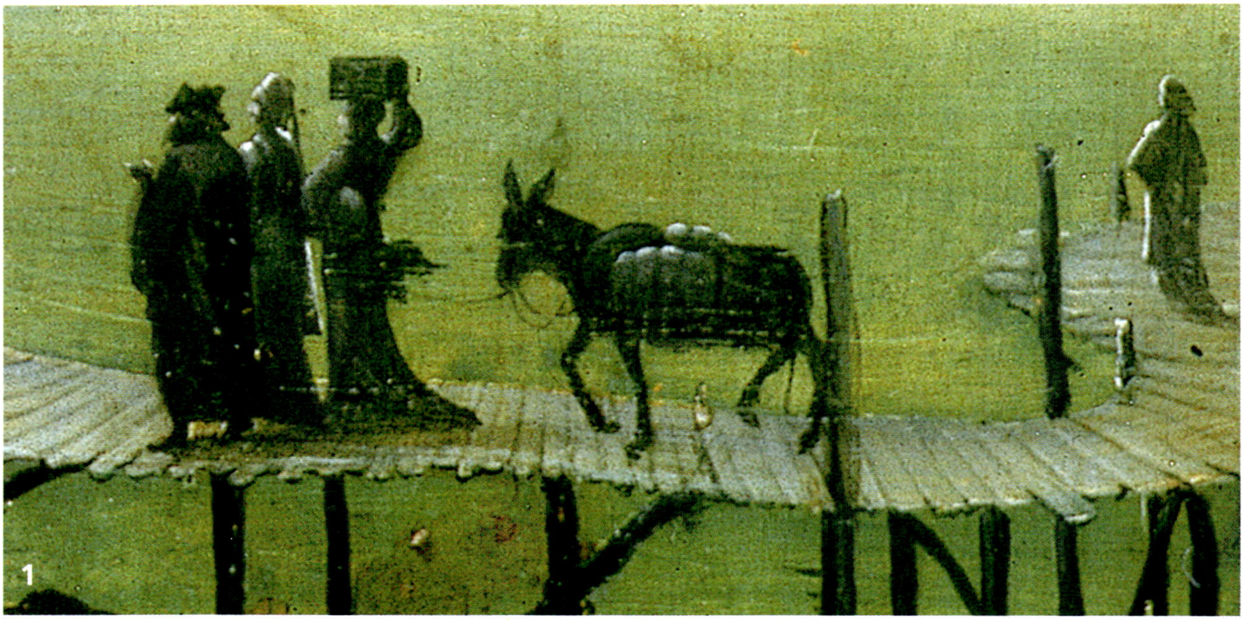

Sodom was also called Rome

The artist portrays Lot and his daughters twice within his composition, large in the foreground, and small and shadowy in the background, where they can be seen crossing a narrow raised walkway. One of the daughters carries a piece of luggage of her head, and a laden donkey follows behind. They do not appear to be afraid of falling off (otherwise they would be walking in single file), nor do they seem to fear catching sight of the disaster by mistake. The mother, who was turned into a pillar of salt for casting a forbidden look back, is standing on the winding walkway at the right-hand edge of the picture. The three survivors seem to be strolling along at an unhurried pace, as if on their way to a picnic, which they then consume in the foreground.

Every epoch has taken from the monstrous story of Lot and his family what seemed relevant to its own time. For the peoples of the Old Testament, for example, it was the law of hospitality. As nomads, they lived in a semi-desert; there were no inns, and travellers were dependant upon the help of local inhabitants. These viewed strangers with scepticism, but the law commanded that they gave them food and shelter. Lot, who was even willing to offer his daughters to the Sodomites to be raped so that the strangers in his house should escape injury, thereby upholds this vitally important law.

Prostituting one's own daughters was scandalous, however, as was committing incest, and these two elements posed a challenge for everyone who subsequently tried to interpret the story. One of the earliest, the Jewish philosopher Philo of Alexandria, who died in c. AD 50, solved the problem by simply denying that the story was an actual historical event.

Martin Luther took a very different view. Luther exerted a decisive influence upon Northern European thinking in the 16th century – the century in which this painting arose. For the father of the Reformation, the story of Lot's family was a real one, and he made many allowances for the behaviour of its members. Why had Lot's wife looked back? "She succumbed to human weakness and temptation, because she could hear such a terrible noise and thunderstorm behind her." Was it possible for a father to sleep with his daughters and know nothing about it? Lot would know about it, granted Luther the psychologist, but he would forget, because "a heart that has been so terribly shocked and overtaken by such a dreadful fate loses all sense of itself." As he explained: "We see the same thing on a much more minor scale in melancholic, depressed people and lovers, who say and do many things that they quickly forget." With his sympathetic commentaries, Luther wanted to distance himself from the sorts of monk who had no idea what real life was like. He was also, of course, pointing a warning finger at Rome. Just as God had destroyed Sodom and four other cities, Luther argued, he would also destroy the church of the papists if they did not change their ways. For while the Pope "sits on high, he thinks he has the power to do whatever he pleases, and will endure no criticism or punishment, just as the Sodomites did here. Where neither advice nor assistance is accepted, it must of necessity follow that one will ultimately go to wrack and ruin."

Experts date the painting to around 1530 or earlier. The artist, a contemporary of Luther, is unknown. He probably lived in Leiden in the Netherlands, i.e. in an area which during the Reformation liberated itself from Spanish hegemony, and where Luther's writings were widely read.

The present master is unlikely to have known them. Although Luther had nailed his ninety-five theses to the door of Wittenberg palace chapel in 1517, at the time this picture was painted, his commentaries on the Bible were not yet written or distributed. It is certain, however, that during the Netherlands' 80-year war against Spain and Catholicism, people looking at the collapse of Sodom would have associated it with the "depraved" city of Rome.

The big round wine jars are heavy, and it is astonishing how the artist succeeds in showing the strenuous act of decanting them as a graceful movement. Three such jars can be seen. Who carried them and the tents all the way up here? It cannot have been Lot's servants, for they and his herds of cattle were all destroyed along with the Sodomites. After all, Lot's daughters justified their seduction of their father with the argument that he was the only man left on earth.

Both the painting and the Old Testament account leave questions unanswered. One thing that is clear is the role played by alcohol – and long would be the list of Christian preachers who would cite the story of Lot in their campaign against excessive drinking. One such was John Calvin, a contemporary of Luther and the present unknown master. As a reformer in Geneva, he used the threat of severe punishments to coerce his fellow citizens into leading a godly life. He even presumed to declare that God had made Lot's story known so that we should "abhor drunkenness". For it was "true that God demonstrates every day through grave punishments how much this vice displeases him".

Just as Luther barbed his commentaries with criticism of Rome, the monasteries and monks, so Calvin used his own writings to crusade against drinkers. Those who drank too much, he warned, would invoke "the wrath of God". While there is a sense of Lutheran tolerance about the camp in the foreground, the fiery background is Calvinistically harsh.

The story of Lot remained popular over the centuries not because of its drunkenness, however, but because of its incest. Amorous relationships between family members are found as far back as Greek mythology, and today it is not only psychoanalysts who suspect that such ancient legends give expression to forbidden and repressed desires. The story of Oedipus, who unwittingly murdered his father and married his mother, is the best known of all.

Another story handed down both orally and in writing since antiquity is that of the King of Tyre. He loved his daughter, forced her into his bed, and kept suitors at bay with a riddle that they had to solve. If they failed, they were beheaded. If they succeeded, they were also killed, because the solution betrayed his forbidden relationship with his daughter. The ancient legends explore various incestuous combinations; thus father loves daughter, son loves mother, brother and sister love each other. But it is rare to find a daughter seeking sexual union with her father.

Psychoanalysts are familiar with daughters who are so jealously attached to their fathers that they wish their mother dead or far away, so that they can take her place. But in neither the psychiatric nor the forensic literature does there seem to be a known case of a daughter actually turning her incestuous desires into reality.

Except in the shape of the defence put forward by an accused father. For feminist writers argue that the story of Lot – like the entire Bible – is written from a male perspective. It is deliberately designed to defend a pious man and preserve his reputation untarnished. In fact, however, Lot – so the accusation goes – was the active party. One might see the rigid, passive position of the daughter being embraced by Lot in the present picture as supporting this thesis. The graceful way in which the other daughter is decanting the wine shows that the frozen attitude of her sister cannot be blamed on any lack of artistic skill on the part of the painter.

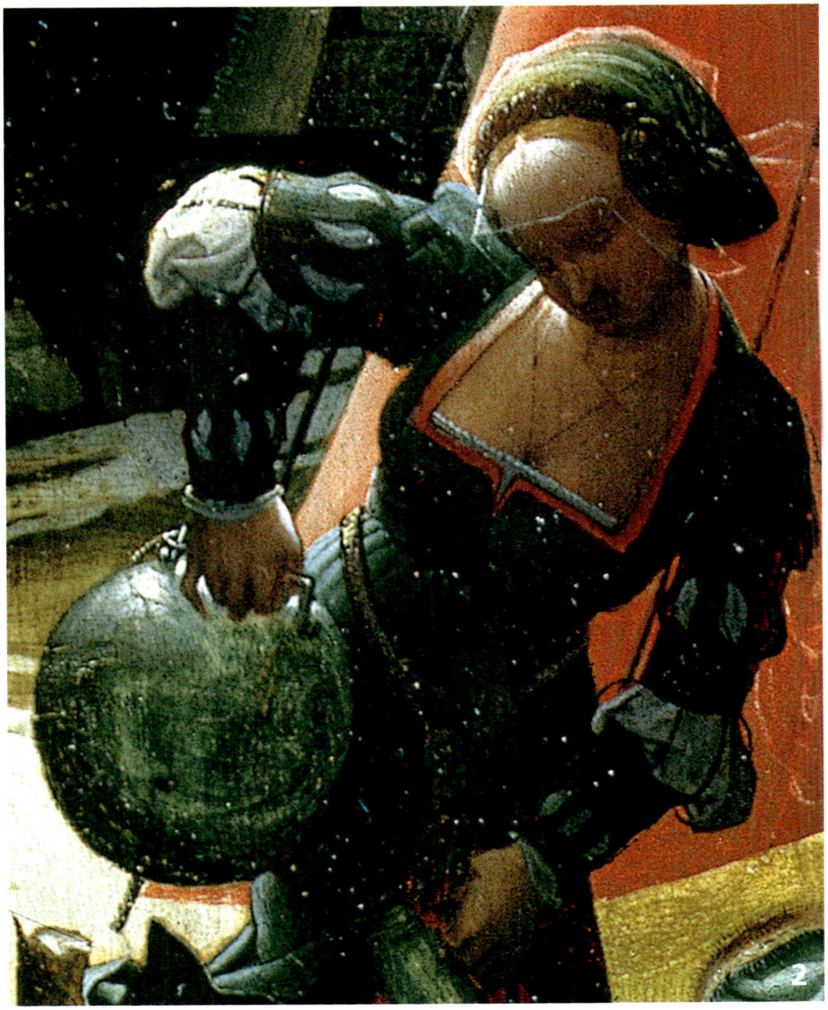

Drinkers invoke the wrath of God

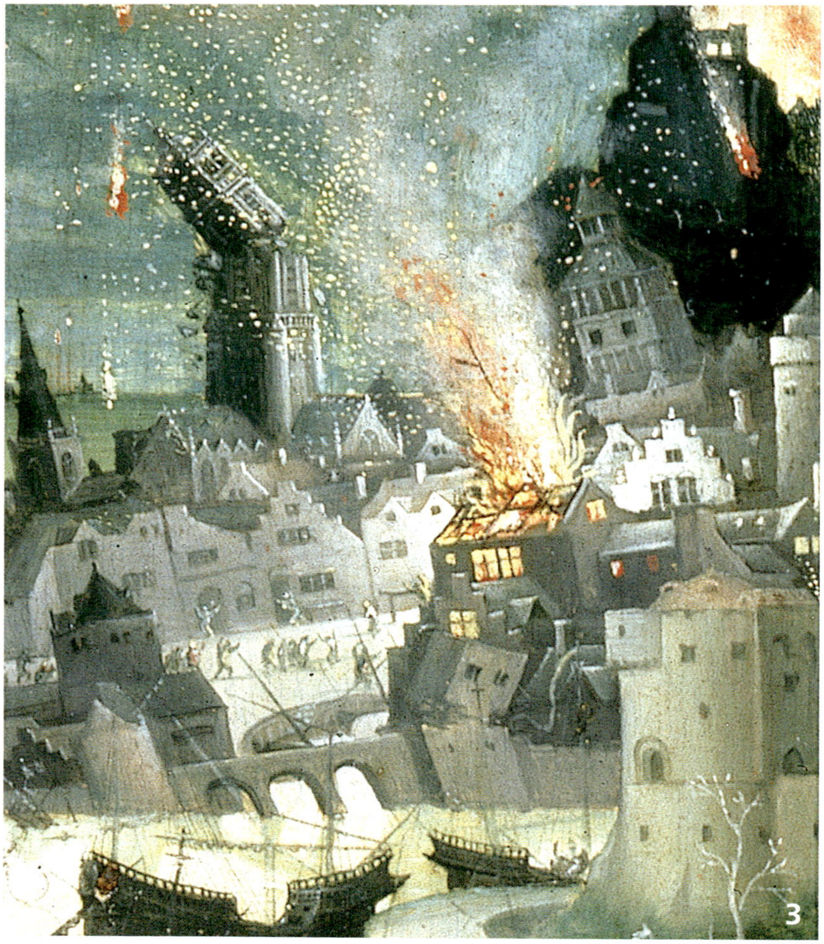

Houses collapse, boats sink – the world is sliding towards destruction

Geologists believe they can date the destruction of Sodom and its neighbouring cities to the year 4350 BP. At that time, a severe earthquake shook the region around the Dead Sea. Hydrocarbons forced upwards out of the depths ignited and sulphur dioxides produced acid rain. The people, animals and plants had no chance. Thick black clouds made the deadly catastrophe visible for miles around.

For the Bible, the fire came not out of the earth but from the skies; the artist visualizes it as a volley of blazing darts streaking downwards. No less unnerving than the bombardment from above is the tilt of the buildings and the main square: like a slowly capsizing platform, the city is sinking leftwards as if it is about to slide into the sea. The church tower is already collapsing, perhaps as the spire of St Peter's in Leiden had done during a fire in 1512.

Ships, too, are breaking up and sinking. Fire is raining down on the city lying on the distant horizon, while another in front of the cliff on the left remains unscathed, as does the tower on the right-hand edge of the picture. The surface of the water, meanwhile, remains smooth and untroubled. This abrupt juxtaposition of catastrophe and calm – a juxtaposition demonstrated not just by the two main scenes, but also within the vision of destruction itself – heightens the viewer's sense of the uncanny and unfathomable nature of these events.

The Bible makes no mention of a sea or any other expanse of water; it has been added here by the painter. Since artists in those days had no hesitation in relocating distant events to the present, and since ports were emerging as the leading economic centres in the Netherlands, such embellishment of the Biblical narrative seems quite natural. In 1497, however, Dürer too turned Sodom into a port. Because he had just been to Venice? Whatever the case, artistic considerations would also have played a role: the search for effects, for powerful visual contrasts – such as those offered by fire and water.

Fire and water are joined in this painting by the contrast between the flat plain and the mountainous landscape. Also disconcerting is the single tree growing the full height of the picture. The water, the towering rocks, the tree as a structural device, and beyond them all a sweeping view into the distance – these were all components of what might be termed "universal landscapes", artificial constructs which combine a range of different elements which in real life do not belong together. This genre of painting was developed by the Netherlandish artist Joachim Patenier (c. 1480–1524); similar landscapes provide the backdrop to the visions of Patenier's contemporary, Hieronymus Bosch (c. 1450–1516).

Patenier kept to the surface, to what could be seen in the landscape. In the work of Hieronymus Bosch, and later Pieter Bruegel the Elder (after 1525–69), the ground opens up, hellfire blazes upwards and a yawning mouth provides a gateway to the underworld. Just as Sodom is in danger from above, in the pictorial fantasies of Bosch, Bruegel and their followers, the world is threatened from below.

For the majority of people at the start of the 16th century, the earth was not just solid ground on which to build houses and in which to sow corn, but was permanently at risk from the powers of Hell or divine Judgement. The eschatological gloom that had hung over the end of 1400s lingered into the new century. "Since the world is on the decline", wrote Luther, "our own day, as the blasphemers, the papists never stop fuming, will be followed by the end, that is, by the Last Judgement."

The painting, which measures 58 by 34 centimetres, was acquired by the Louvre in Paris in 1900. Over the years, many art historians have turned detective in their desire to uncover the identity of its artist. The majority come down in favour of Lucas van Leyden (c. 1494 –1533), who is famed primarily for his engravings. If not Lucas himself, then an artist in his circle, others have suggested. Others again consider the landscape to be by Patenier, the figures to be by Lucas. Yet others attribute the preliminary drawing to Lucas, the final execution to a pupil. According to the latest research, the artist is unknown, but probably worked in Leiden and perhaps also in Antwerp.

A question mark also hangs over the painting's date. The earliest it has been dated to is 1504. Next comes 1512, the year in which the tower of St Peter's church in Leiden collapsed – but is that reason enough? The latest date proposed is 1530. It thus probably arose in the 1510s or 1520s – at the beginning of a period in which the fate of Lot and the destruction of Sodom became extraordinarily popular in art. Between 1500 and 1600, an American art historian has calculated, the Old Testament story of Lot was painted at least 210 times. Before and after this century, on the other hand, the motif appears much more infrequently.

Why was this subject so popular from 1500 onwards? Several developments coincided. Firstly, people were generally more familiar with the Bible. In around 1450 Johannes Gutenberg had invented printing with movable type, and in the wake of the Reformation the Bible was translated into the vernacular languages of northern Europe. For the first time, its text could be read by the laity. Many people lived their entire lives afraid that the world was about to end, and were particularly drawn to descriptions of God's wrath. Others again were attracted by the shockingly risqué element of this chapter from the Holy Book.

Accompanying this increased familiarity of the Bible was the fusion of the story of Lot with two thoroughly secular pictorial motifs highly popular during this era. First, the motif of the "unequal couple", also known as the "wiles of women". Pictures of this type show an older man and beside him a young woman who is making up to him or allowing him to fondle her. The man has money or a purse in his hand. The message: women sell their sexuality, and old men obtain sexual gratification only with the help of money.

The motif of the unequal couple was joined somewhat later by that of the *conversation galante*. Such pictures showed persons of both sexes engaged in flirtatious conversation, more or less advanced along the path to intimacy. If we screen out the catastrophe taking place in the background of the present painting, what remains is a picnic in the hills; servants have put up the tents and poured out the wine and have even lit a fire in an iron brazier in anticipation of falling evening temperatures. In Lot paintings from the second half of the 16th century onwards, the catastrophe recedes increasingly into the distance; what remain are the delights of love, sex and tenderness.

Particularly large numbers of Sodom and Lot compositions issued from the Netherlands. Perhaps because so many artists lived and worked there, and because popular demand for works of art was greater there than anywhere else. Perhaps, too, because nowhere else in Europe were people and their needs viewed with so little prejudice. It is possible that even incest fantasies were admitted with less embarrassment.

It is for other reasons, however, that this painting continues to fascinate us today. It recalls the imagery of our dreams; figures, objects, events seem to emerge out of the darkness of the subconscious. Rocks, fire, the solitary tree, the smooth surface of the water assemble themselves in a way that is only seen in dreams. The viewer senses something threatening at the same time as sensing tender intimacy, and he suspects that both may be connected – but how remains a mystery.

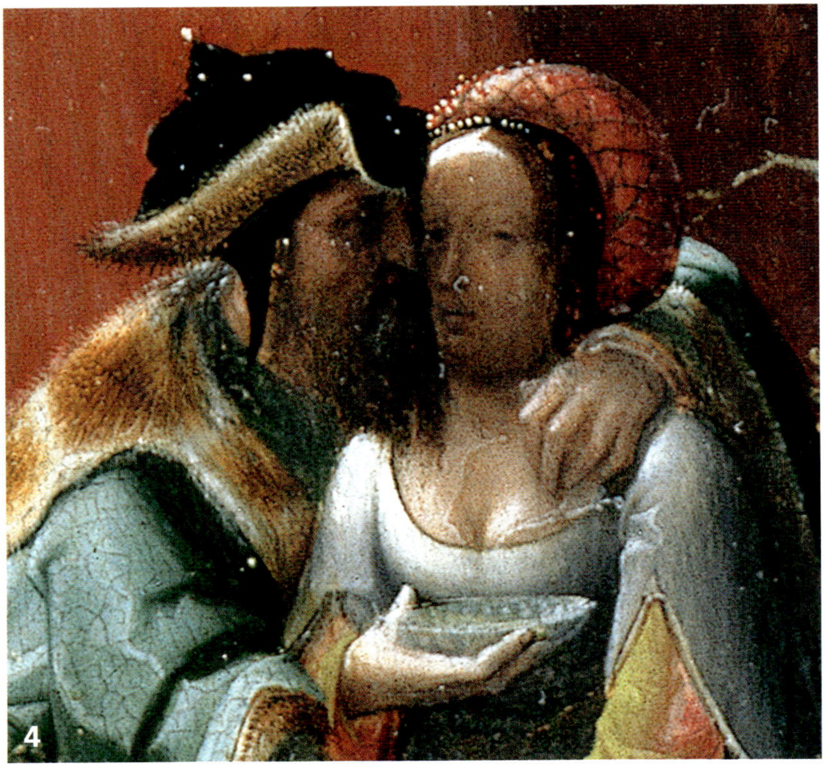

4

The catastrophe recedes into the background

Hans Holbein the Younger: Portrait of the Merchant Georg Gisze, 1532

A foreign merchant in his office

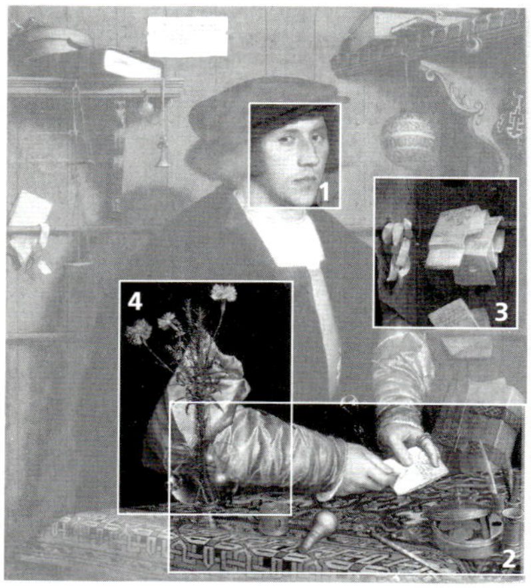

Holbein portrays a Danzig merchant in London. The merchant is standing in his office, the *skrivekamere*, and is opening a letter. The address on the folded sheet of paper reads: "Dem erszamen Jerge Gisze tu Lunden in Engeland Mynem broder to handen" ("For the hand of my brother, the honourable George Gisze in London in England").

For his portrait sitting, Gisze wears a white shirt, a silk doublet of light red and a black jacket with slits above the elbow, through which he has passed his arms. Holbein emphasizes the two arms and uses them, in conjunction with the ample jacket and the dark shadow cast on the wall behind, to lend the figure breadth and volume. And yet, even as he does so, he obliges the merchant to squeeze into one corner of the office. There is almost no room behind the table, and Gisze's left elbow seems to knock against the panelling of the back wall.

It may be a coincidence, but the contrast between his splendid clothing and cramped office characterizes the situation in which Gisze was living. He represented a trading company based in Danzig. The city was a member of the Hanseatic League, the association of towns that formed to protect its merchants against pirates, competition, and princely despotism. For centuries the Hanseatic League was a powerful force in the North Sea and Baltic sphere, and merchants derived status from belonging to it.

And yet, despite money, power, and status, life abroad was very restricted. The Hanseatic merchants in London all lived in the Steelyard, a building complex on the banks of the Thames with just one entrance, and even that was closed at night. They were not allowed to be married nor could they bring women into the complex. They all ate together. Contact with locals was monitored, since the English government feared espionage and the spread of subversive ideas. The merchants feared thieves. Their goods were warehoused where they lived, and storerooms were secured with several locks; a bunch of keys is hanging from Gisze's belt and from beneath the shelf on the right. The inhabitants of the Steelyard were also worried that individual members would forge business links outside the Hanseatic League, or get involved in pub brawls that might set the local populace against the foreigners. Merchants like Gisze who were stationed abroad lived no lives of luxury, but rather a sort of barracks existence.

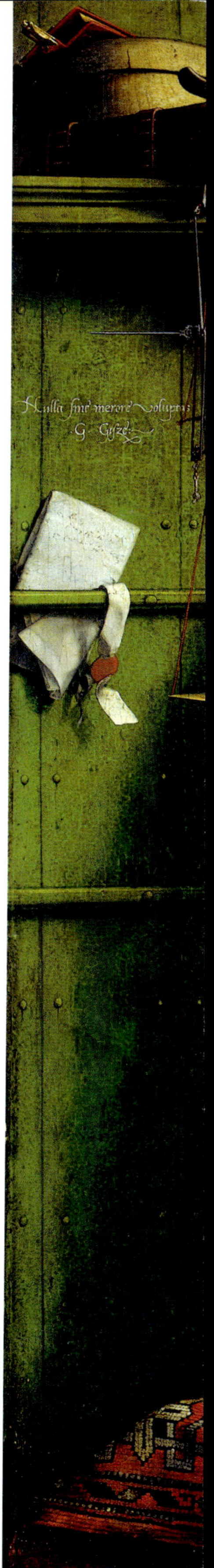

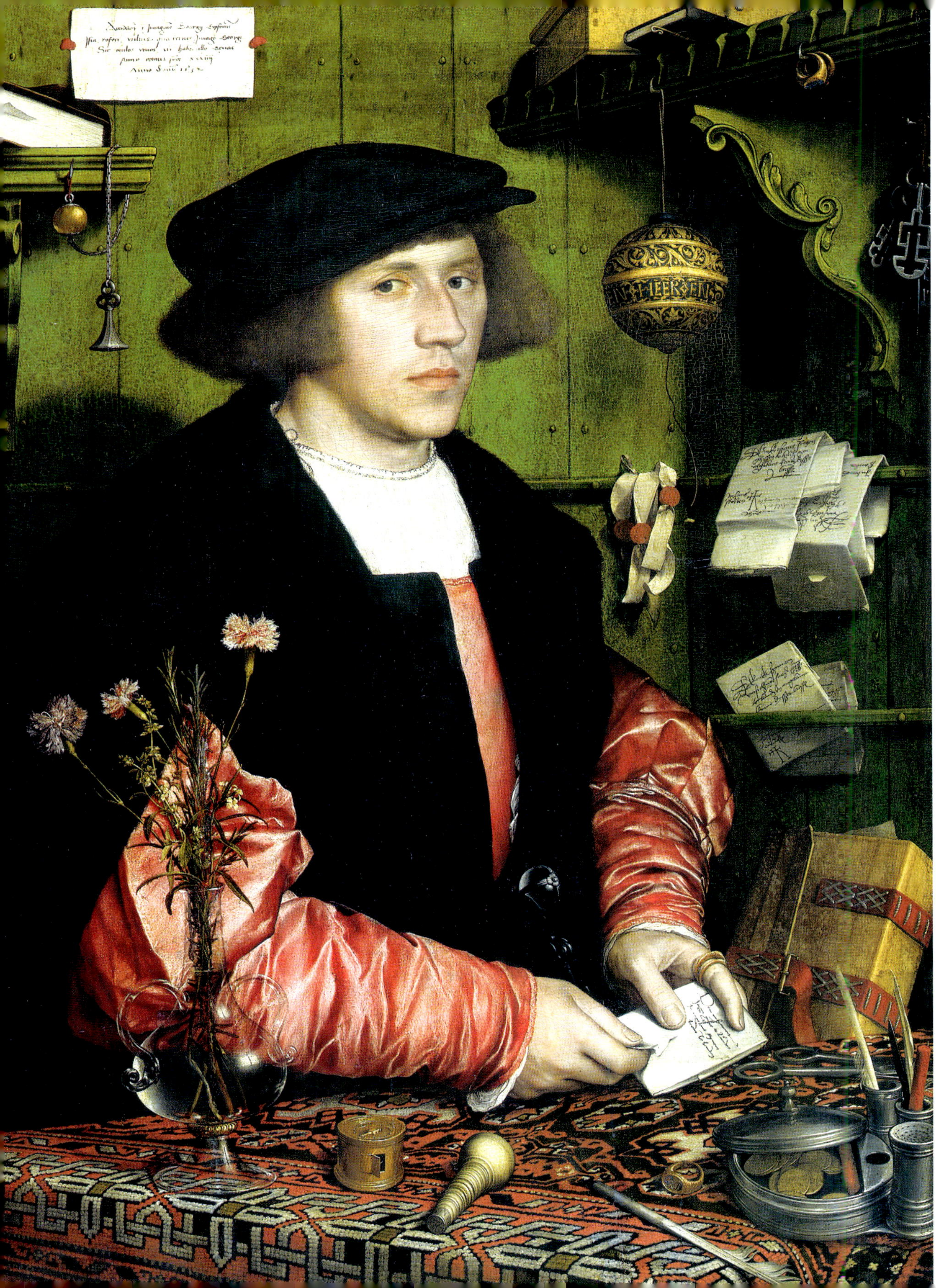

The white sheet of paper pinned to the back wall tells us that Gisze was in his 34th year: *Anno aetatis suae XXXIIII*. He was born in Danzig, was baptized Georg, was known as Jerge. Danzig (modern-day Gdansk) was an important centre of commerce thanks to its advantageous location near the River Vistula and the Baltic coast. Having expanded under the Teutonic Order, it now stood under the protection of the Polish kings and was governed by members of its local patriciate, to which the Gisze family also belonged. One brother became a bishop, Georg was made a councillor.

The artist, born in Augsburg in 1497 or 1498, was about the same age as the Danzig merchant. The two men probably received a very similar education in the early part of their lives: reading, writing, arithmetic, and religion with a tutor, perhaps followed by a few years at a grammar school studying a little philosophy and history, and improving their style and oratory by reading classical authors. Next an apprenticeship, probably first with their fathers in the business or the workshop. We know that Hans Holbein moved to Basle, and then – because work was not forthcoming – to London, and from there back to Basle, and then in 1532 back to London again. Basle at that time had a population of some 12,000, Danzig 25,000, and London 80,000. Someone arriving in London from either of these German-Swiss or German-Polish cities thus had to adjust to living amongst an unfamiliarly large number of people. He would also find himself caught up in a power struggle between the Church and the Crown. Gisze was a member of a large organization that guaranteed him protection and an income. Not so Holbein. He arrived as a freelance artist with a few connections. On his second visit, however, these were of little value, since his most important contact was Sir Thomas More, who had just resigned as Lord Chancellor. More was a devout Catholic and refused to recognize Henry VIII as head of a separate, Anglican Church. In 1535 King Henry had him beheaded.

In these uncertain circumstances, Holbein initially attached himself to his German compatriots at the Steelyard. Perhaps these latter considered that they were getting a good product at a cheap price. In 1532 and over the following years Holbein painted the portraits of about a dozen German merchants in London; Gisze's was probably the first of them. None of the others is represented in such a large format and surrounded by the paraphernalia and papers of their profession, and it is conceivable that Holbein offered Gisze this elaborate treatment in order to demonstrate his art in detail. The other Hanseatic merchants appear against a monochrome background. While this may have been a matter of price, it is also possible that the sitters wished to be seen differently: a figure appears more regal, more powerful when seen against a neutral background than when having to vie for attention with too many other objects. But this is speculation. X-rays of the painting have revealed that Holbein originally intended to portray the head frontally, but subsequently turned it to one side; only the pupils remained directed towards the front. For this alteration, too, we have no explanation.

1

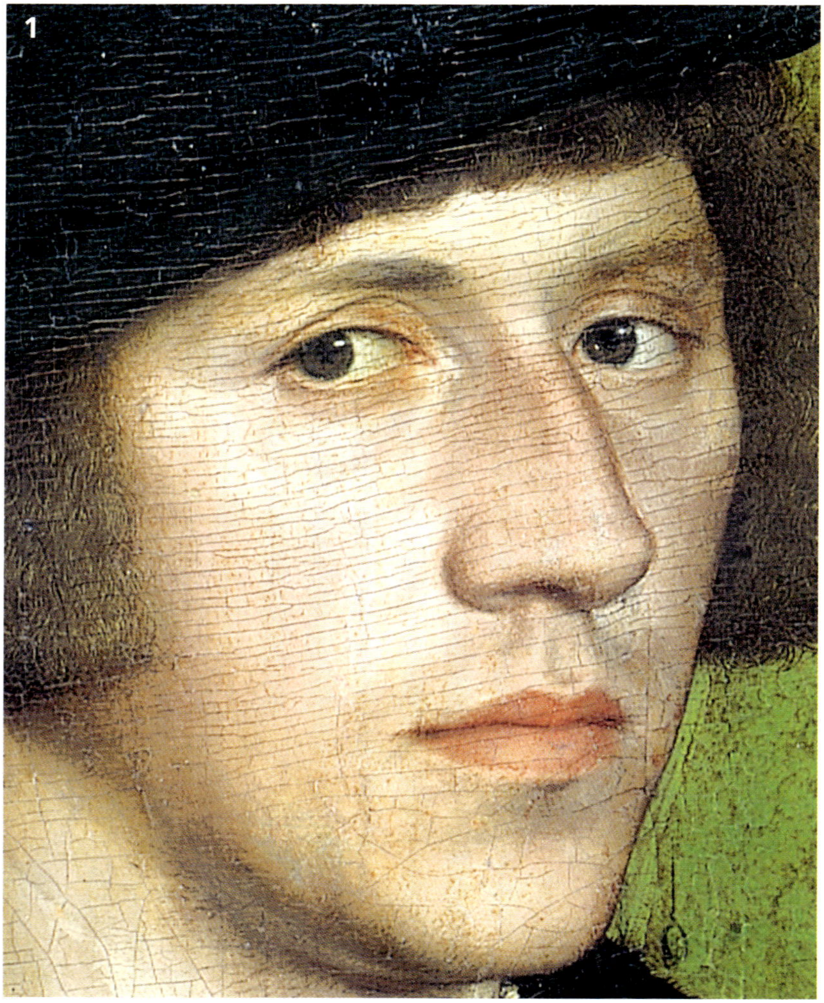

Eye-to-eye contact

The oriental carpet on Gisze's table probably reached Europe via Venice. While it was surely unsuitable as a surface for writing on, it demonstrated that money was available to add a decorative touch to the *skrivekamere*. Perhaps it was also intended to make the room look more homely, since as well as the office it was also the bedroom. Further decorative features include the vase of flowers and the exquisite decoration around the spherical string-dispenser. Nor is the presence on the table of a small timepiece – a type with just one hand on the dial at the top – mere coincidence. The majority of the populace continued to rely on the striking of the clocks on church towers and town halls, whose mechanisms were operated by weights. The newer, small pocket watches and table clocks, on the other hand, were mechanically driven by steel springs. They might not be very accurate, but they held an entertainment value and at the same time let it be known that their owner was open to all things new and could afford such small miracles of engineering.

Next to the clock lies a signet: a die used to make seals of wax or lacquer. A second signet, more decorative in its design and attached to a ball of amber, hangs from the shelf on the left. Also on the table are a number of quills, a box of coins or wax discs and sticks of lacquer, and beside it another container with small holes, used for sprinkling fine sand onto freshly penned letters in order to make the ink dry faster. Lying further back is a pair of scissors; these assumed a role in a certain type of contract, whose text was written out twice, once at the top and once at the bottom of the same piece of paper. Each party then received one half. In the event of a dispute, the two halves were compared to see if they fitted together.

All these objects can be found in paintings by other masters, including the signet ring lying on the tablecloth in the foreground. But only Holbein painted three or four such rings within one and the same canvas. Another can be seen on Gisze's index finger, while two more are hanging from a hook on the shelf above. Four signet rings in one office? The fact that Holbein draws no particular attention to them within his composition, but includes them almost in passing, suggests that he is simply making a dutiful record of his subject. Today, however, the rings provide us with a clue to the nature of Gisze's job.

The way people worked had changed radically since the formation of the Hanseatic League three hundred years previously. At the beginning, merchants travelled in person across the country or overseas to do business. They bought and sold their goods themselves, usually trading by barter. In Holbein's day, however, they stayed behind in their offices, relying on sea captains and travelling sales staff, and on business partners in other centres of trade, sometimes members of their own family. The handshake that had formerly concluded a deal was replaced by the written agreement, a contract or a letter from distant parts bearing a seal. There are two possible explanations as to why Gisze should have half a dozen signets and seals in his office all at one time, both of which may be correct. Perhaps he gave them to members of his sales team to take with them on trips, or perhaps he himself represented a number of different companies whose seals he used when working on their behalf.

Tools of a merchant's trade

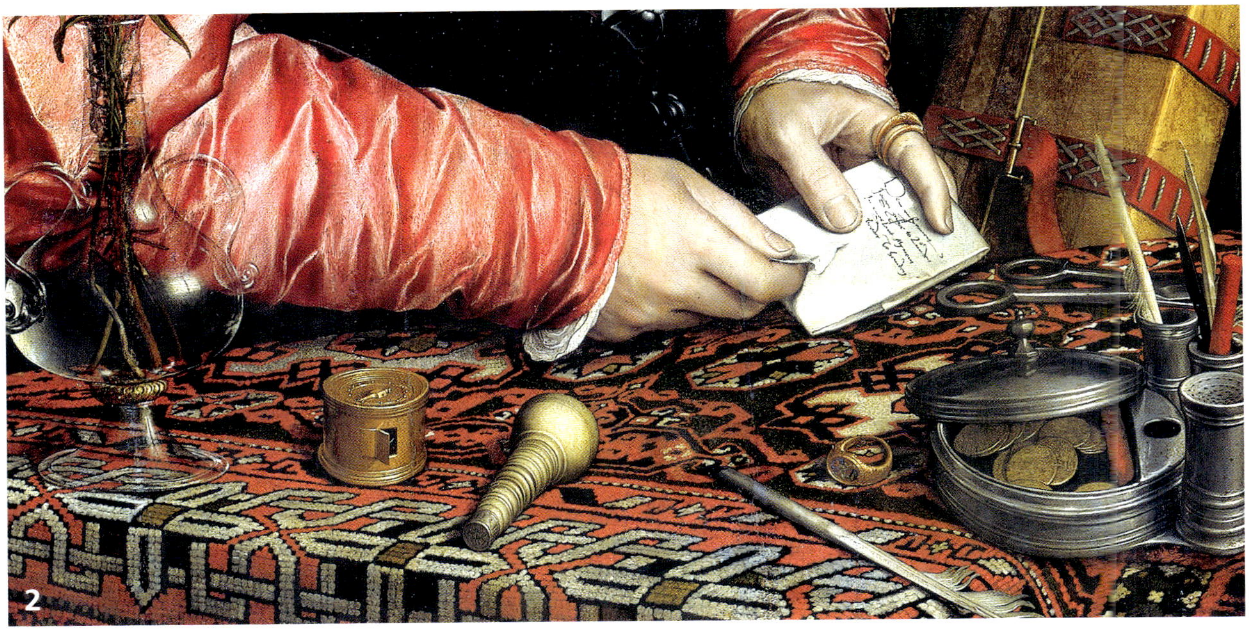

2

Many letters and no postal services

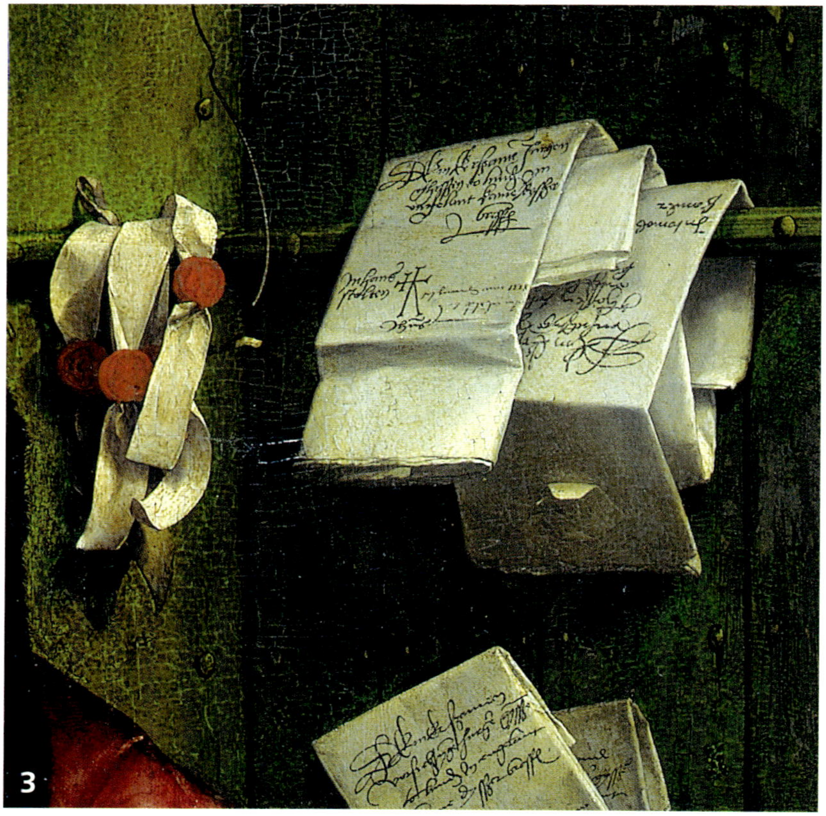

3

The Hanseatic League owed its success in England to the special privileges it enjoyed. In order to secure the island a particularly attractive position within the wide-reaching network of trade between the countries of northern Europe, the English kings exempted the foreign merchants from taxes and duties. England's most important exports were wool and cloth, of which, in the 15th century, a third was shipped by the Hanse alone. London imported stockfish from Norway, iron from Sweden, wine and salt from Germany, and honey, wax, and wood from Russia. Wood was needed in particular for shipbuilding; the discovery of America and the sea route around Africa to India meant that every seafaring nation was expanding its fleet. Wood also arrived from Danzig, although the prime export from here was Polish grain. Famines in Germany, the Netherlands and France were also alleviated by grain surpluses in the east. For several centuries, the Hanseatic League provided the network through which supply and demand were regulated in the north of Europe.

General correspondence was filed in boxes and folders, while letters that the recipient wanted to keep handy were tucked over strips of wood on the wall, as can be seen in Holbein's picture. The wall was made of panelling, and like most London buildings the Steelyard was probably constructed largely of wood. Envelopes were not yet the norm. Letters were folded, the address and occasionally the company's stamp placed on the back, and sealed. Regular postal services did not yet exist, and merchants gave their letters to messengers, sea captains and travelling colleagues. The Hanseatic businessmen conversed with their English customers and the Russian merchants in the Hanseatic base of Novgorod, for example, in their own respective languages, while amongst themselves they spoke Middle Low German, which was understood all the way from Tallin to Bruges.

In Gisze's day, however, the language was changing in the wake of Luther's Reformation. Luther wrote a German as it was spoken in Saxon pulpits; today called New High German, its use was spread by his sermons and his books. In northern Germany, too, the written and spoken language began to alter in the individual towns and cities where Luther's influence made itself felt.

Whether employing the old Low German or the new High German, one thing common to writing everywhere was a relatively arbitrary orthography. The adjective *erszam* (honourable) appears sometimes with a capital letter, sometimes without. Nor was there a fixed way to spell surnames in Gisze and Holbein's day, either. As his letters reveal, the former is variously addressed as Giesze, Gysse, and Ghyssen. Thus Holbein's painting not only documents the type of duties performed by a foreign merchant, but also testifies to an age in which people were successfully able to make themselves understood even though they spelled things in different ways, and in which a person's identity was not bound up with an officially approved sequence of letters. Orthography would be uniformly regulated only in the 19th century, when the cities and states joined together to form the German Empire.

The language employed for legal disputes, theology, science, and submissions to the authorities was Latin, whose universally valid rules surmounted all national barriers. Gisze and Holbein, it may be assumed, both understood it. Where – independently of the letters – the sitter wishes to make statements about himself, it is to Latin, the language reserved for "higher" things, that he turns, for example on the white card at the top of the picture, or up on the wall on the left near the scales. There, in slender capitals and signed with his own name, appears a personal motto: *Nulla sine merore voluptas* – "no joy without sorrow".

On the piece of card pinned to the top of the wall, the client has the artist confirm in Latin that this is indeed a portrait of Georg Gisze in the 34th year of his life. It was not unusual for the name and age of the sitter to be included, but Gisze goes a step further: he lets it be known that his cheeks and eyes look exactly as painted. This additional piece of information indicates some of his surprise, indeed his astonishment, that such a likeness is possible, and perhaps even his pride that he, the *gemeene kopman* (general merchant) from Danzig, is himself to be seen in this marvel of painting.

The vase and flowers are the only objects in the portrait that are not directly related to Gisze's profession, and their perilous position between his elbow and the edge of the table strengthen the suspicion that they are not intended as literally as the other items of practical use. They seem a little like a picture within a picture, added afterwards. Out of the glass vase, the flowers, and the fabrics behind them, Holbein conjures a stunning feast for the eyes, as if wanting to demonstrate what else he can do when released from his duties as a chronicler. His exquisite bouquet also carries a heightened significance: carnations were symbols of the Passion of Christ, as well as of love, chastity, and fidelity. They were considered engagement flowers. Through them, other dimensions, otherworldly and private, penetrate the sober room. In 1535 Gisze got married in Danzig; it is possible that he was already engaged and wanted to send his future bride this portrait.

What made and continues to make Holbein famous, however, was not his use of symbols, nor was it the large-scale allegorical compositions that he executed in Basle and for the assembly hall at the Steelyard. Rather, it was the accuracy with which he rendered objects and faces, and his ability to portray people just as they are without offending them. That he should hone precisely these skills can be explained not least by the economic situation. England and many of the German states were breaking away from Rome, and with the Catholic Church artists lost their most important patron. They had to find new fields of employment, one of which was portraiture. Having entered art at the end of the Middle Ages as the donor portrait, this subsequently became a genre in its own right. At first reserved solely for churchmen, princes, and scholars, it spread from southern Europe to the North. After the Hanseatic merchants, Holbein painted a lengthy series of members of the English nobility. As painter to King Henry VIII, he was dispatched on several occasions to paint the portraits of potential brides so that the king could gain an idea of what they looked like – a delicate diplomatic task. In 1543 Holbein died in London. Georg Gisze survived him by almost twenty years, dying in 1562.

By now the Hanseatic League was long since past the height of its influence. It faced tough competition from Dutch and English rivals in all the centres of trade, and when the aggressive "Merchant Adventurers" were expelled from Germany, Queen Elizabeth I responded in 1598 by closing the Steelyard. In 1666 its premises fell victim to the Great Fire of London. Holbein's painting provides us with the only surviving picture of what its offices once looked like.

Money isn't everything

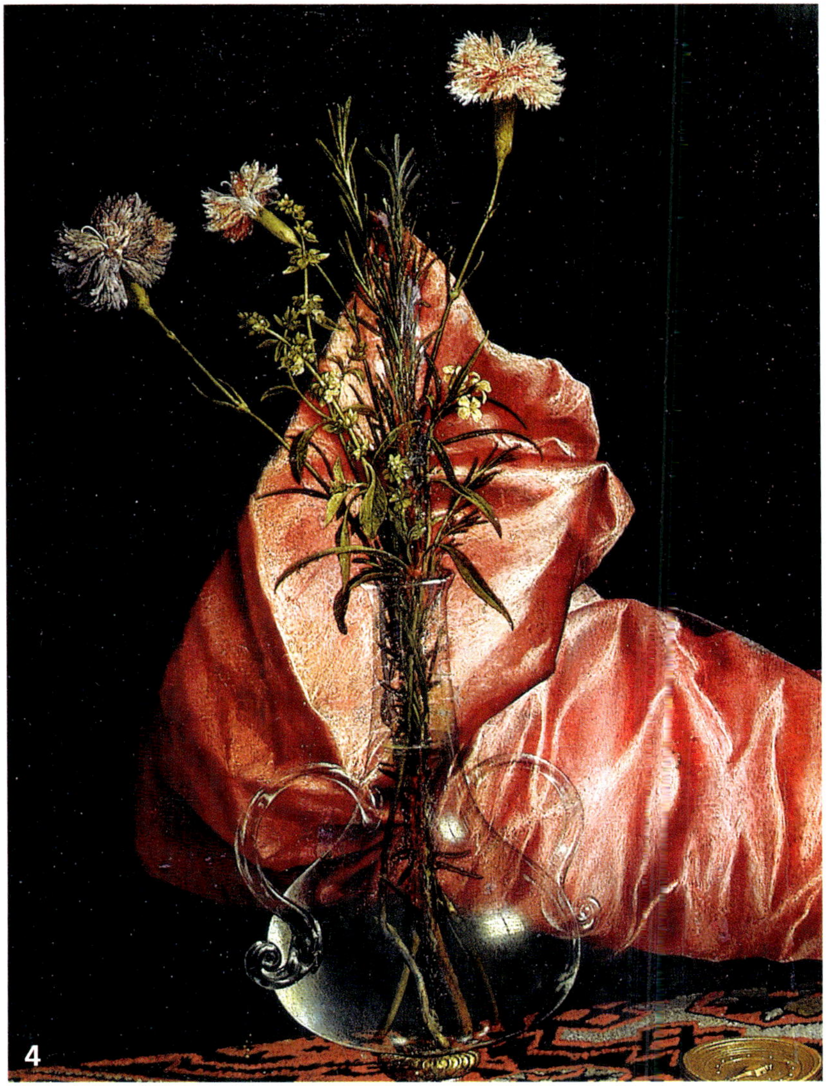
4

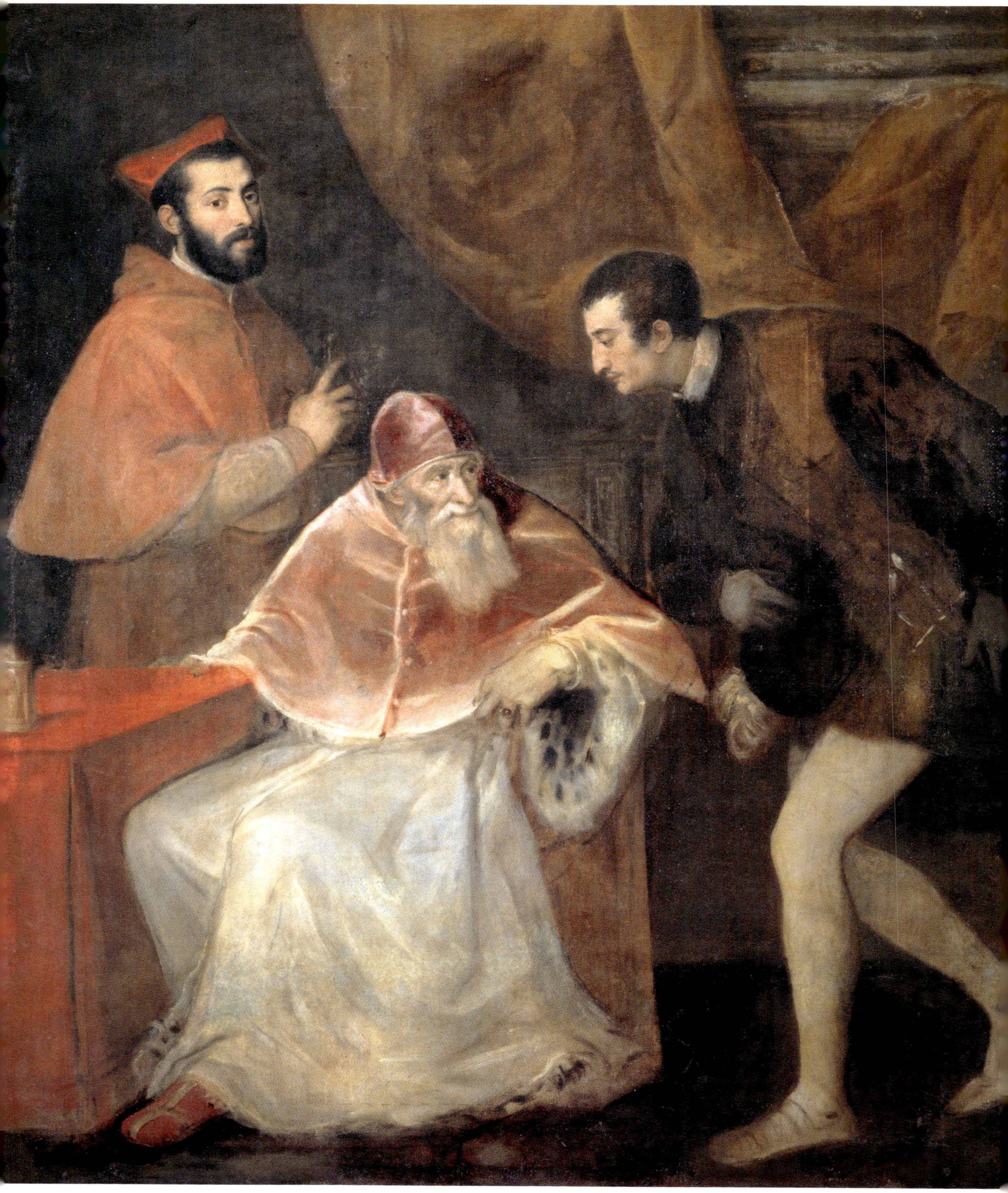

Titian: Pope Paul III and his Grandsons, 1545

In the end the artist, too, was cheated

When Titian left Venice in the autumn of 1544 to travel to Rome, he was around 55 years old. It was only with reluctance that he said goodbye to his home, his workshop and Venice itself, whose lagoon setting made it well protected against attack.

Tiziano Vecellio (born between 1488 and 1490, died 1576) was at that time regarded not only as the most famous painter in Venice, but also as the most outstanding portraitist in southern Europe. Princes in particular valued his ability to ennoble individual characteristics with ceremonial dignity. Charles V, Holy Roman Emperor, preferred Titian above all other artists when it came to having his portrait painted. He even made the artist a count and a member of the imperial court, and promised him an annual pension – even if it usually wasn't paid.

The long-standing dispute over who held the highest rank in Europe, the Holy Roman Emperor or the Pope, also extended at times to the issue of who had the best artist in his employ. Charles had already been painted by Titian when Paul III, a member of the Farnese family, ascended the papal throne in 1534.

The Farnese naturally wanted to engage the artist's services for themselves. They knew Titian didn't like travelling; on the other hand, it was beneath their rank to visit him in his Venice studio. So they established preliminary contact with him via a child: they sent the Pope's grandson, twelve-year-old Ranuccio Farnese, who was studying in nearby Padua. His portrait today hangs in the National Gallery of Art in Washington.

That was in 1542. The contact had been engineered by Cardinal Alessandro Farnese, who appears standing behind the papal throne in *Pope Paul III and his Grandsons*. He now asked Titian if he would like to move to Rome and enter the full-time service of the Pope. The artist declined. In 1543 the cardinal invited him to Bologna, where Paul III was meeting Emperor Charles V. It was here that Titian executed his first portrait of the Pope. This was followed by an invitation to come to Rome at least for a few months. The Venetian agreed.

Two factors prompted Titian to accept. Firstly, although already an old man by the standards of his day, he had never been to Rome or the far south and had thus never seen Italy's classical architecture, ruins, mosaics and sculptures with his own eyes. He was a Renaissance artist who had not had the obligatory exposure to antiquity. He had been offered several invitations to work in Rome, but had never accepted – perhaps because he was afraid that the works of the great masters would throw his own ideas on art into disarray. Now, however, he felt secure enough in himself. He is said to have spent his first few weeks doing nothing but gazing in wonder at the remains of Rome's classical culture.

The second factor prompting Titian's trip to Rome was his paternal desire to help his own family. His son Pomponio had embarked on a career in the Church and was hoping to be offered a living at a monastery or church. Titian thought of the prosperous abbey of San Pietro in Colle, which bordered on some land he owned. Cardinal Farnese gave him reason to be hopeful; in Bologna, he implied that the matter had already been decided in Titian's favour.

A year later, in March 1544, Titian made enquiries on the subject but received no answer. Cardinal Alessandro Farnese was clearly aware how much the artist wanted St Peter's in Colle for his son – and used this as a sort of covert blackmail. In September 1544 the Venetian nuncio informed the cardinal in Rome that because of the benefice the artist was now prepared

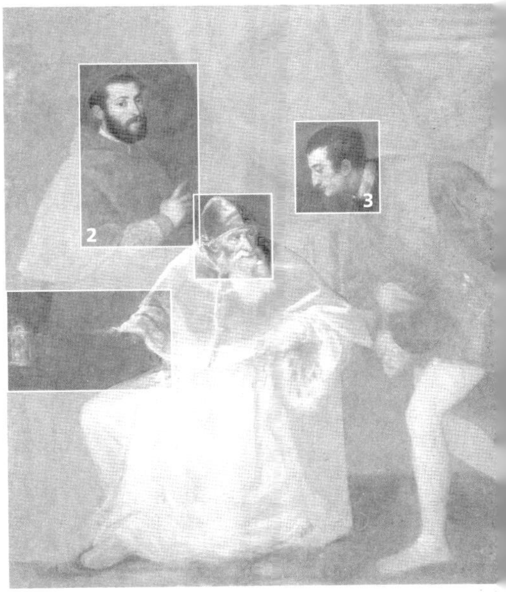

"to paint Your Honour's highly illustrious household in its entirety, right down to the cats."

The country which Titian crossed in autumn 1544 was fragmented and unstable, and consisted of cities and duchies which, although for the most part formally independent, in practice could only exist in alliance with a foreign power – in other words, with France or the emperor, resident in Spain. Armies of mercenaries were constantly marching through Italy; the Duke of Urbino, whom Titian visited along the way, even decided to supply the artist with a bodyguard for the last stage of his journey.

In Rome, Cardinal Farnese received the artist with great ceremony and had an apartment made ready for him in the Vatican palace.

Frail and full of energy

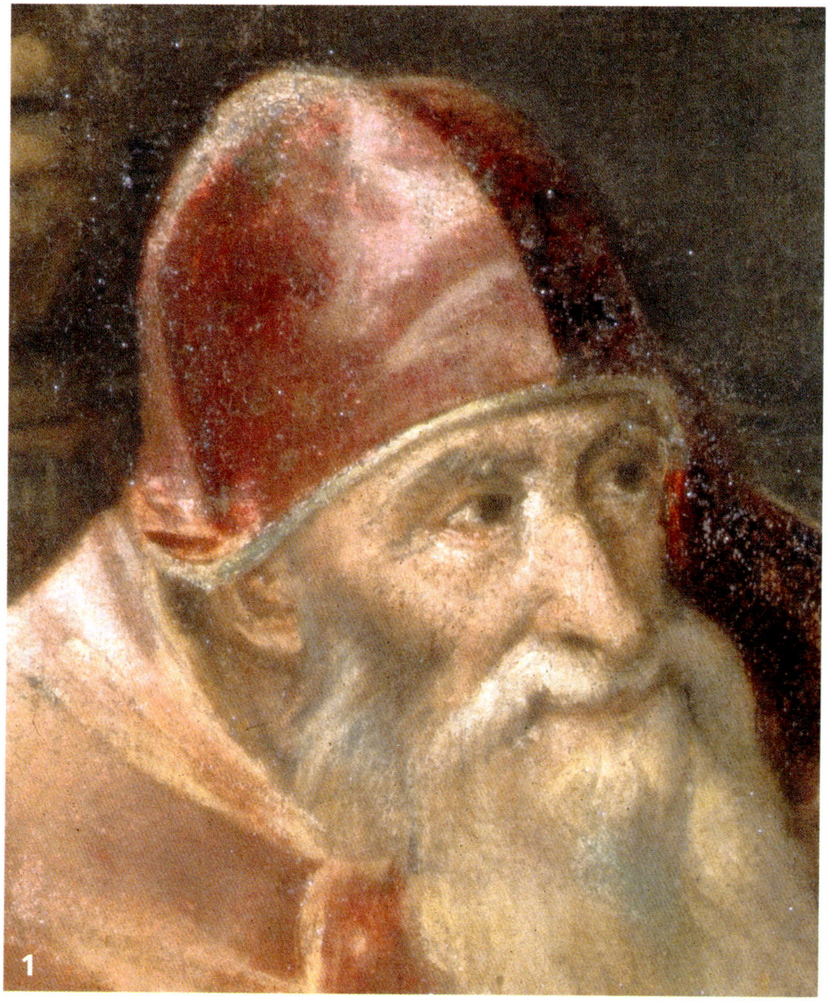

In order to hold his own against Spain and France and their Italian allies, the spiritual head of the Catholic Church needed soldiers, money and good connections. Without them, the Pope risked being steamrollered, even on religious issues, by his powerful international neighbours. Pious monks were thus considered unsuitable for such high office – the leader of the Papal States needed to be a man with experience of diplomacy and war and someone happy to use their cunning and power.

Paul III had no scruples on that score, as his own career reveals. He came from the lower aristocracy, from a family with no useful contacts within the Curia, but he had a very attractive sister. He sent her off "to have an affair with the Pope", as Martin Luther described it, "and was made a cardinal in return".

As a cardinal, Paul III also kept a concubine, with whom he fathered three sons and a daughter. This prompted Luther, in far-off Wittenberg, to accuse him of being an "epicurean swine". In Rome, however, such behaviour was considered justified because it ensured the preservation of the family line. The latter's perpetuation – or even simply the plan to found a dynasty of rulers – provided a legitimate excuse for breaking the rule of chastity. Since his elder brother had only produced a sickly son who died young, the later Pope was obliged to make provision for the future. There is no evidence that he did so unwillingly.

There is also little evidence that he applied any of the Church's precepts to himself. For men such as him, a religious career meant first and foremost the opportunity to profit from the income of the Church. The Vatican possessed countless pastorates, abbeys, land holdings, woodlands, villages, towns, bishoprics and offices. They all brought in money and were awarded as sinecures to senior members of the clergy. As a cardinal, the later Paul III owned several bishoprics, even though he had not taken the higher orders necessary to be a bishop. So he appointed someone to represent him, paid this deputy a percentage of the takings and thereby put him in a position of dependency. Dependants strengthened one's influence and power.

When the Farnese Pope had himself painted by Titian with two of his grandsons, he was 77 years old and in a tricky situation. North of the Alps, Protestantism was growing and Germany's Lutheran princes had combined their military forces into the Schmalkaldic League. Charles V needed to fight the League and imperiously demanded financial support from Paul. At the same time, however, Charles called for the convocation of an ecclesiastical council which would agree reforms and not least remedy the deplorable state of affairs which Paul had unscrupulously exploited for his own benefit.

Quite what sort of man we are looking at in the present portrait Titian makes it difficult for us to tell. On the one hand, he shows us a shrunken old man whose shoulders are barely able to support his head upright, whose flesh is melting from his face and whose beard is unkempt. Yet on the other hand, the Pope seems full of dynamism: the fact that his body and head are pointing in different directions creates a sense of tension and movement. While his bent back and head jutting forward imply frailty, they also call to mind someone who is getting ready to pounce. The pontiff's eyes are also wide open and full of energy, unlike those of most elderly people. This ambiguity, this blending of two aspects of the same person, lends Titian's pope an unsettling air.

Paul's son Pier Luigi produced four sons, the two eldest of whom – Alessandro and Ottavio – are included in the present portrait. They were called "nepots", an expression which meant both nephew and grandson, and which thus elegantly veiled the fact that the Pope was getting his picture painted with blood descendants he was not supposed to have.

Alessandro was appointed a cardinal at the age of 14. That was in 1534, directly after his grandfather's election as Pope. For the majority of Curia members, there was nothing improper about this: at the end of the day, a Pope needed as many votes as he could get in the college of cardinals. Paul also wanted to be able to pass on the benefices that he had assembled over the previous years to a member of his own family. Protection of one's family, expansion of one's power and possessions – these were absolute priorities, not just amongst the Farnese, and not just in Italy. The Pope put his grandson Alessandro in the way of some thirty bishoprics.

Alessandro Farnese felt himself no more obliged to model his behaviour on the teachings of the Church than his grandfather. On several occasions he came close to giving back his cardinal's hat. He kept a mistress (and possibly several), fathered a daughter and, in his early years as papal ambassador to the French court, danced so elegantly that Queen Catherine de' Medici could still remember it thirty years later. He used the money that flowed so copiously his way to extend the Palazzo Farnese in Rome and fill it with antique treasures and contemporary works of art.

An X-ray of the canvas has revealed that Alessandro was originally positioned further left. It was probably he himself who persuaded Titian to move him closer to the Pope and portray him grasping the knob on the back of Paul's chair with his right hand – as a sign that he was laying claim to the papal succession. His claim failed: he attended seven conclaves but was not elected. The Counter-Reformation demanded a different sort of person to the type represented by Alessandro, his grandfather and the earlier Renaissance popes from the houses of Borgia and Medici.

Alessandro is the only one of the three figures in the painting who is looking out at the artist – and like the figure of the Pope, the look he casts is difficult to judge. Is he staring intently at the man behind the easel, or gazing more generally out into space? Does Titian portray him as impassive, as the English art historian Harold E. Wethey believes? Or is the young cardinal looking to see whether the elderly man at the easel will swallow a Farnese's vague promises? It was Alessandro, after all, who lured Titian to Rome with the prospect of a living for his son, and the artist establishes with him, so it seems, fleeting, meaningful yet expressionless eye contact.

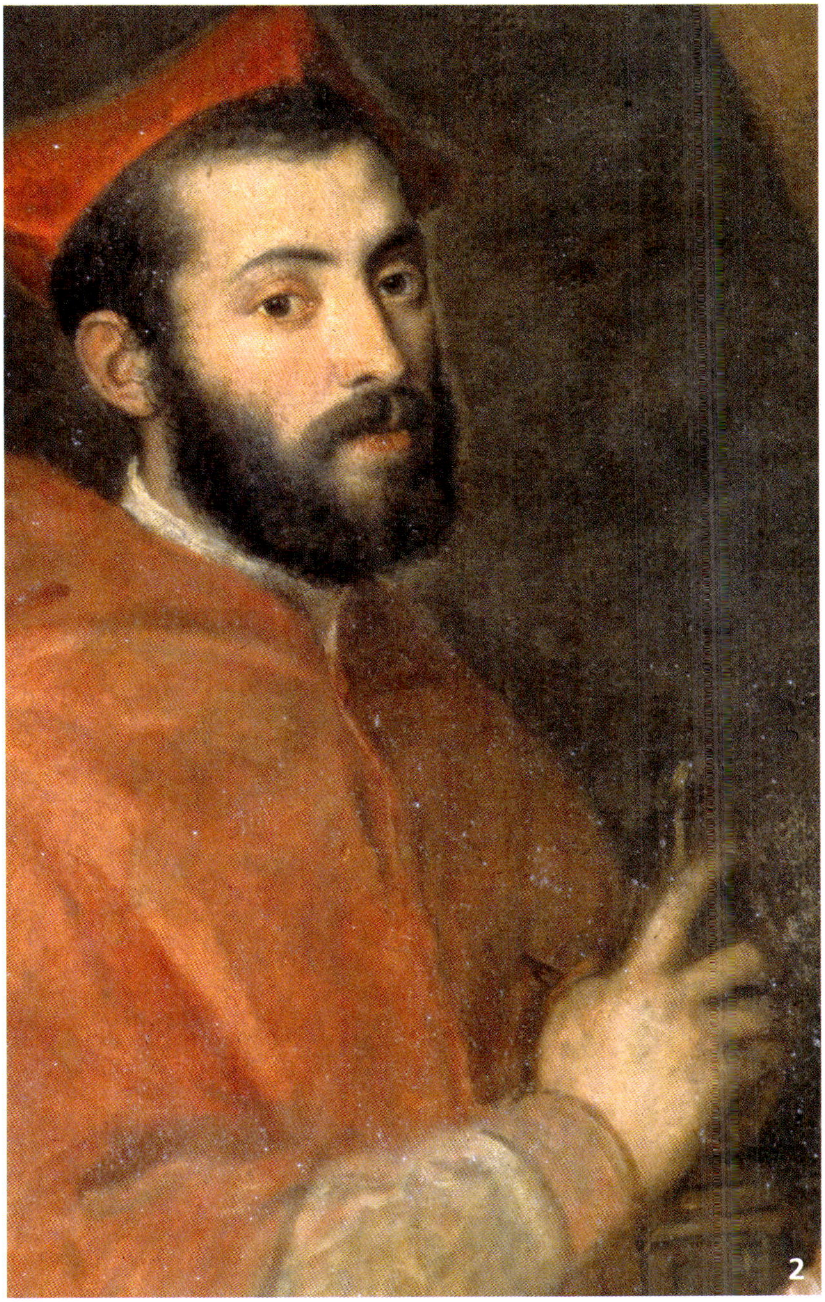

2

How to stake a visible claim

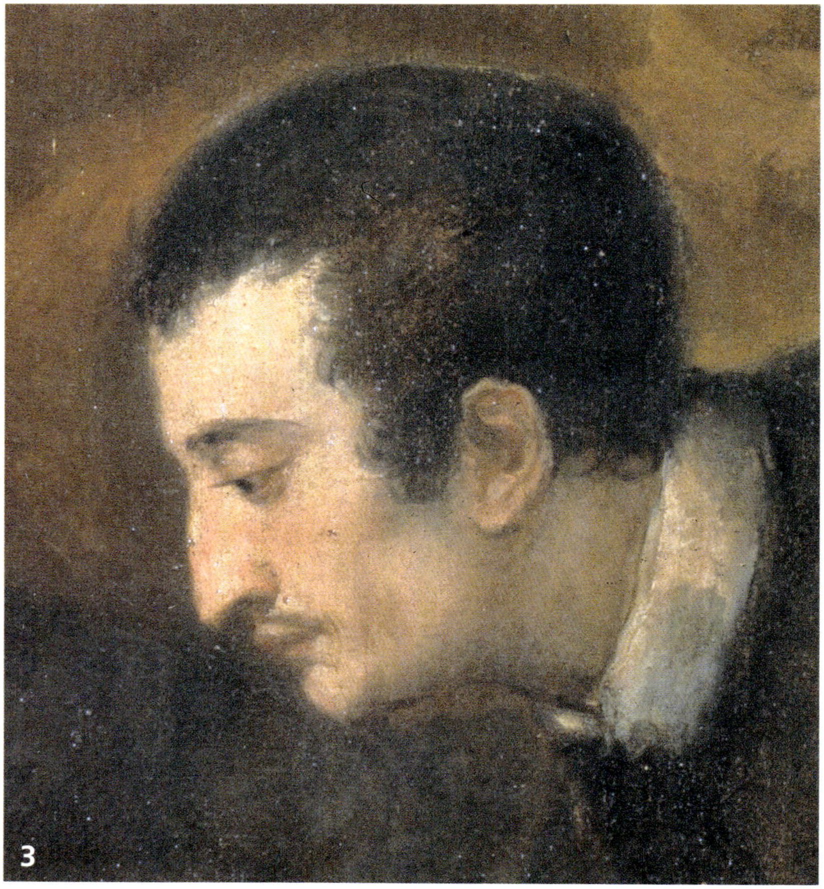
3

No upright grandson

Titian portrays Ottavio Farnese, the 21-year-old grandson, paying reverence to the Pope in the prescribed fashion. Persons approaching the Pope had to bow three times and then kiss the papal foot. Paul's red shoe can be seen at the bottom edge of the painting and signals how low the young man in his secular dress will have to stoop.

Ottavio had a lump on his nose, and the X-ray of the painting shows that Titian had not overlooked this feature. In the finished work, the bridge of Ottavio's nose is impressively straight, almost as sharp as a knife – an improvement common in portraits, but which lends the face a smoothness which, together with the lowered eyelids, rounded back and bent knees, seems somehow suspicious. Titian was a master of body language, and in Ottavio's smoothness and the snaking pose of his body the artist portrays – without disparaging caricature – a person who is not "upright".

Nor did the young man have much incentive to behave in a straight and upright fashion. Paul III deployed his grandsons like pawns in a political game; he used Ottavio to create a family alliance with Spain, marrying him at the age of 14 to a daughter of Charles V. In 1545 the emperor needed money from the Pope for his campaign against the Protestants. The Pope gave, but demanded in return the rights to the imperial cities of Parma and Piacenza, with which he wanted to establish a duchy for his family. He sweetened the deal by promising that Charles's son-in-law Ottavio would become duke and his own daughter duchess.

Thus far the interests of Paul III were identical to those of his grandson. The situation was complicated, however, by two members of the family who do not appear in the painting. One was Ottavio's father, Pier Luigi. He demanded the new duchy for himself. The Pope said yes, the emperor no: he let it be known that he would tolerate his son-in-law as duke, but on no account the latter's father. Ottavio's prospects of a dukedom were thus directly threatened by his own father. He plotted secretly with the emperor against his father and grandfather.

The second member of the family to question Ottavio's right to the new duchy was a younger brother. The Pope had been planning for several years to marry him to a French princess, for he wanted a family alliance not just with the emperor, but also with France, the second major power in Europe.

In order to make the marriage proposal more attractive, the Pope decided to promise the new duchy not to Ottavio, but to the future son-in-law of the French king. The split newly emerging between Paul III and the emperor made a change of allegiance necessary. Ottavio thus saw himself cheated of his future both by his father and his brother, and beyond them by the Pope. If Titian paints him as someone whose devotion masks only anger and hatred, he is simply portraying the situation as it really was. Two years later, Ottavio finally succeeded in becoming duke – after his father was murdered by one of the emperor's henchmen.

The wrangling over the duchy took place in the first half of 1545. Titian stayed in the Vatican palace until the end of May and must therefore have been well informed about what was going on. He must have been aware, too, that the cardinal was jealous of his younger brothers: as the first born, the new dukedom should have been awarded to him. Only with difficulty was Paul able to restrain him from taking action himself; he mollified his grandson by assuring him that, once Pope, he would have far more power than some duke of Parma and Piacenza.

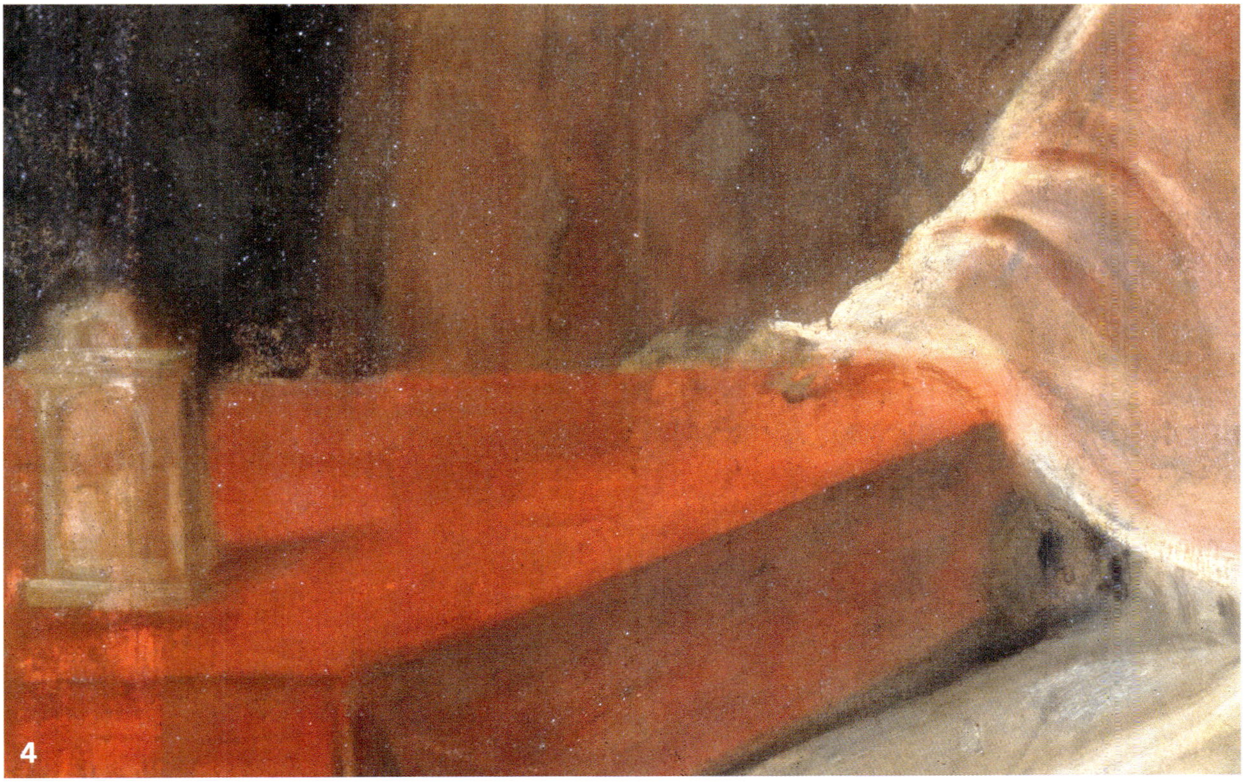

4

Strictly speaking, the Pope's hand should be visible on the far edge of the table, but Titian has not painted it. Nor did he sketch it in prior to painting; he seems to have worked for the most part directly with the brush. Michelangelo (1475–1564), who dominated the art scene in Rome, criticized the lack of *disegno*, or design based on drawing, in the Venetian's work, but praised his colouring. In *Pope Paul III and his Grandsons* this is centred – as so often in Titian – on red, which the artist explores in all its variety and in dramatic nuances.

The Pope's right hand is not the only thing missing; other parts of the canvas, too, have been primed but then taken no further. The painting is unfinished, and why work on it should have been abandoned has been the subject of much speculation. There is no evidence of any quarrel between the artist and one of his subjects. A letter that Titian later wrote to the cardinal rules out any suggestion of an open disagreement.

It would be quite understandable if Titian felt let down, distrustful and full of resentment towards the Farnese, for the anticipated benefice for his son never materialized. Although, in Rome, he received his board, lodging and an honorary citizenship, as far as we know he was not paid a fee. Nor was he paid for the other paintings he executed for the Farnese during the same period. It all went towards the bill for the abbey, so to speak, for which he would have to wait a while longer.

The Italian historian Roberto Zapperi has looked closely at all the conceivable reasons why Titian should have stopped work on the portrait, and concludes that the likeliest explanation is the shift in political allegiances which took place even as the painting was in progress. When the canvas was begun in December 1544, Spain was the Pope's preferred ally; when it was abandoned in May 1545, the ally was now France. Since large-format portraits (the present work measures 200 x 173 cm) also served as something of official statements, Titian's work was politically no longer opportune. And so the picture vanished unframed into the Farnese cellars in Rome. Over a hundred years would pass before it was honoured with a place on the wall.

The Pope's hand is missing

Today it hangs in the Museo Nazionale di Capodimonte in Naples and is revered as a masterpiece of portraiture which both venerates and questions its dignitaries, as a masterpiece of colour, psychology, eye and body language. Deceit and hypocrisy were considered important qualities and were highly prized by Paul III. Titian possessed the ability to make them transparent: in the tranquil assembly of *Pope Paul III and his Grandsons* he conceals hints of the secret war of emotions and interests. He also points to the transience of hopes and dreams – the ink bottle that stood on the table has been replaced by an hourglass.

Vain, too, were Titian's own hopes. He never got the living he had expected to earn with this painting. Instead, his son was fobbed off with a small parish – a humiliating reward for Titian's hard work in Rome and a sign of autocratic arrogance. Another quality captured for posterity by Titian's brush.

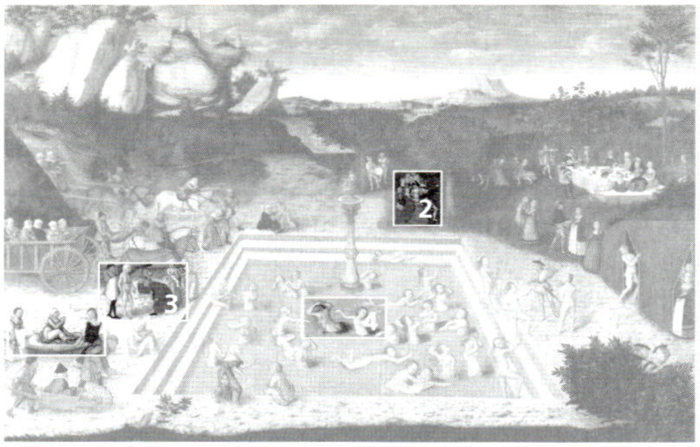
2
3

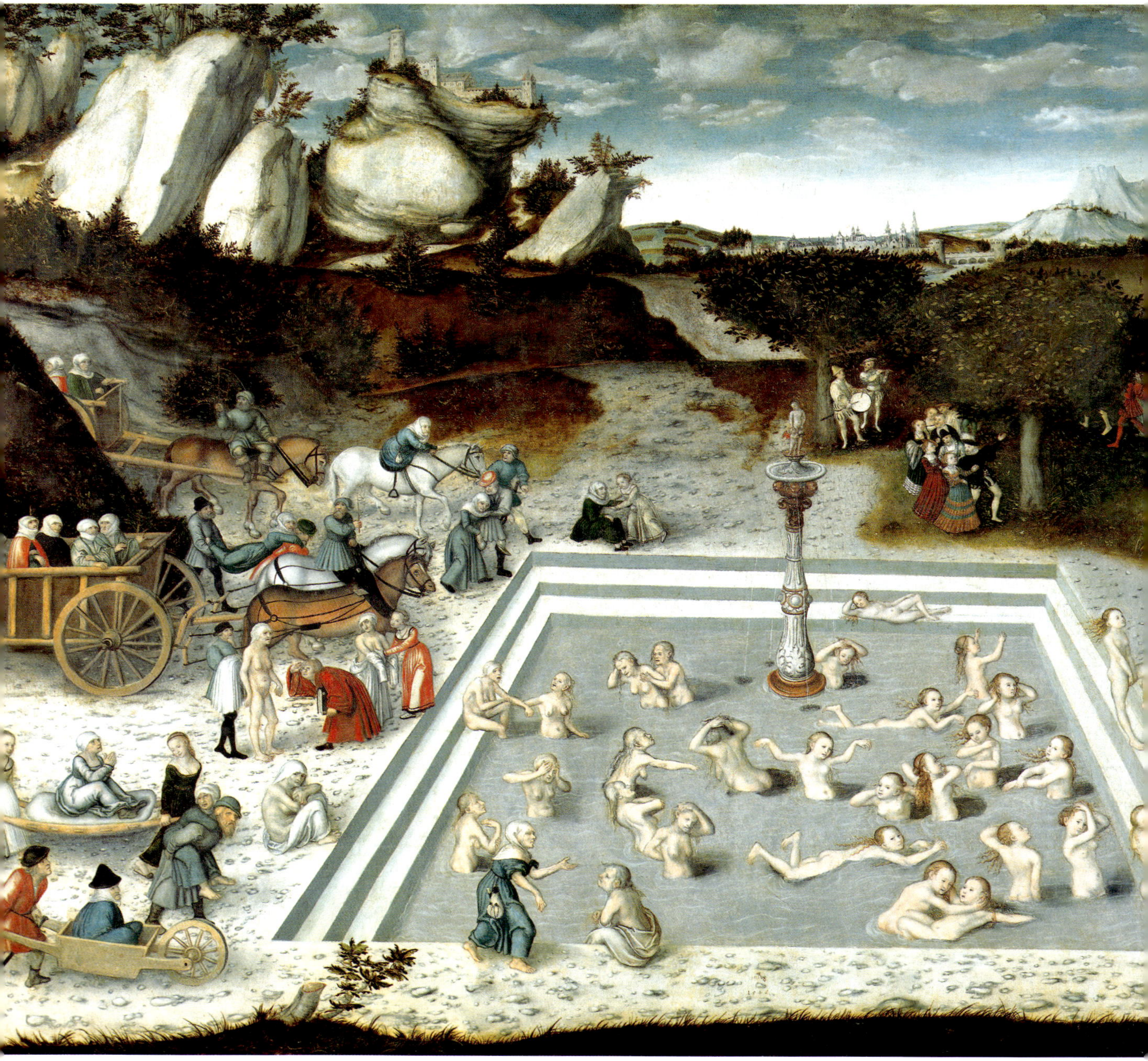

Lucas Cranach the Elder: The Fountain of Youth, 1546

The miracle in the water

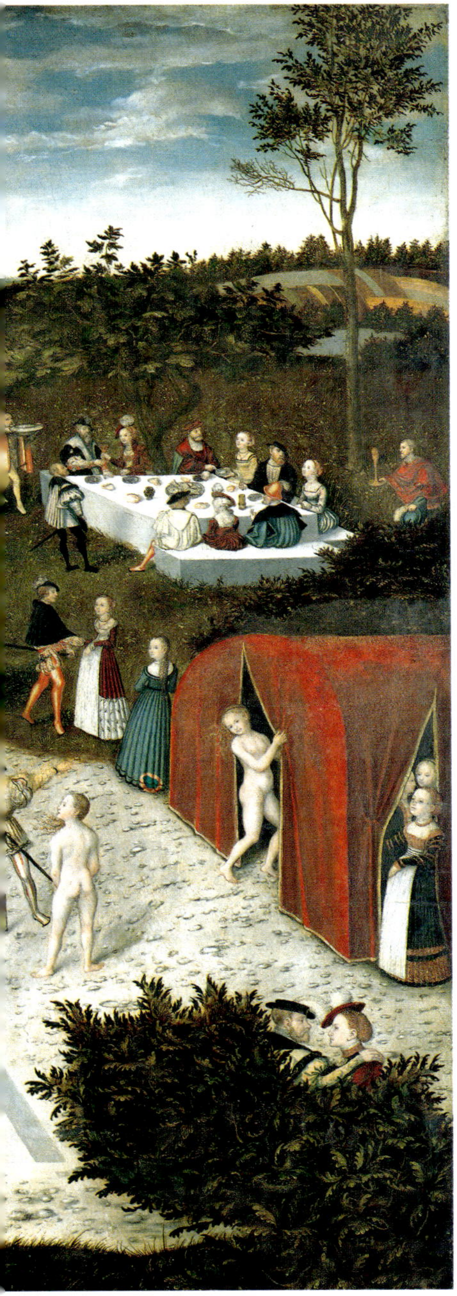

In 1578, a professor of medicine describing the Swiss town of Baden and its curative waters noted: "The open-air pool, also known as the *Bürgerbad* [public pool], lies beneath the clear skies." The pool "is 30 feet long and 24 feet wide, so that over a hundred people can bathe in it at once." It was lined with stone slabs "and contains a number of seats".

Not everything in Cranach's painting of the legendary fountain of youth is thus invented. Such pools existed and were open to the general public. The professor continued: "In this pool everyone, both locals and visitors, can bathe for free ... On Saturdays, in particular, the people come from the town and the countryside in their masses, and women and men seek to enjoy themselves and improve their looks."

It was forbidden to carry weapons in the vicinity of baths. When Cranach portrays the men in the right-hand half of the picture with swords, he is departing from contemporary convention. The fact that only women are shown bathing in the pool is another departure from 16th-century reality; normally, both men and women sat in the pool, occasionally separated by a wooden partition. Ladies did not bathe entirely naked, but wore shifts that were bound beneath the bosom and covered at least the lower half of their bodies.

Therapeutic spas seem to have been popular throughout the Middle Ages; civic and church records occasionally mention the fact that such and such a number of days were granted for a trip to a spa. Poor citizens were awarded travel allowances from the public purse. As for the rich: in 1534 Count Palatine Philip travelled to Gastein with sixty horses, stayed seven weeks and returned home cured; in 1584 Elector August of Saxony set off with 225 horses in order to bathe in the waters of Schwalbach, which he had carried to a nearby palace for him.

Such journeys were not always made on health grounds alone. In Lucerne in 1566, a number of canons "asked the Council for permission to go to Baden with their wives to take the waters, something which was refused on account of the scandal". The fact that they asked, however, suggests that such pleasurable excursions with ladies were nothing out of the ordinary.

Wealthier visitors to Baden did not use the open-air pool but went to guesthouses with indoor baths. "Some of them visit three or four such baths daily, and spend the large part of the day there singing, drinking and – after their bath – dancing." The indoor pools were surrounded by galleries from which people could look down on the water below. "Nothing can be more delightful to the eye or the ear than when budding maidens or those fully blossomed into young women open their mouths to sing, with the most beautiful open faces, like goddesses in their figures and conduct, their garments floating on the water and each a different Venus."

This enthusiastic description comes from a papal secretary who visited Baden in 1417 while attending the nearby Council of Constance. His references to dance and music were confirmed in 1573 by the doctor to Pope Sixtus V, who added that these were normal practice in all German baths. In the case of the dancers and musicians in the right-hand half of the present composition, Cranach is thus adhering to the reality of his day.

News sheets that have survived from the 16th century frequently relate to sightings of unexplained phenomena, such as calves with five legs, fishes with human faces, a hand coming out of the clouds, and fire in the heavens with streaks as long as a lance, first white, then blood red – "a sign from God sent to warn us and make us lead better lives".

Just as much in Cranach's mythical scene is actually taken from real life, this belief in miracles was also – however paradoxical it may seem – normal for the time. People took for granted the fact that extraterrestrial forces might directly intervene in earthly affairs at any time, be they sent from God or the devil. Luther really "saw" Beelzebub when he threw his inkpot. The distinction between the natural sciences and religion with which we are familiar today was not yet clear. Science was still in its infancy. This is particularly clear in the sphere of medicine. Anatomical studies of corpses were still rare, and medical treatment continued to be based on the classical theory of the four humours. If you fell ill, it was because these humours were out of harmony, and so you were bled. It is understandable that patients should trust God rather than medicine, and that they should hope for a miracle from heaven sooner than a cure by their doctors – the elderly woman unable to walk is praying as she is carried to the water.

The mineral spas were amongst those who benefited from the primitive state of medicine. In 1568 one Martin Rulandus wrote: "Since no medicine has been discovered or invented up till now to preserve the health", there remained "only water and baths". He pronounced drinking mineral water and bathing in spas as a cure-all, albeit with a shrewd proviso: "if you do it correctly". The beneficial effects, if they made themselves felt, were naturally ascribed to God. This emerges from many documents, including the testimonial which three men took with them to the Luthernbad baths near Willisau in 1583. This confirms that they have by no means left their wives and children to come and have a good time, but solely to be able to "enjoy this divine gift".

In the 16th century, a spa in the county of Spiegelberg (present-day Bad Pyrmont) acquired an almost sensational reputation for its miraculous properties. In its waters, "Almighty God generously displayed his charity and goodness to the people every day". Around 10,000 people are supposed to have descended upon the spa in the space of four weeks; all the neighbouring villages were full to overflowing with invalids and the sick. The next year, however, almost no one came. The spa had lost its alleged power, as it had done 300 years earlier. In both cases it was God who had personally withdrawn his blessing from the waters, in order to punish certain people. The first time it was the Count, because he had charged money for the use of the spring. The second time it was the visitors, because they had fornicated openly in its waters.

Praying and bathing

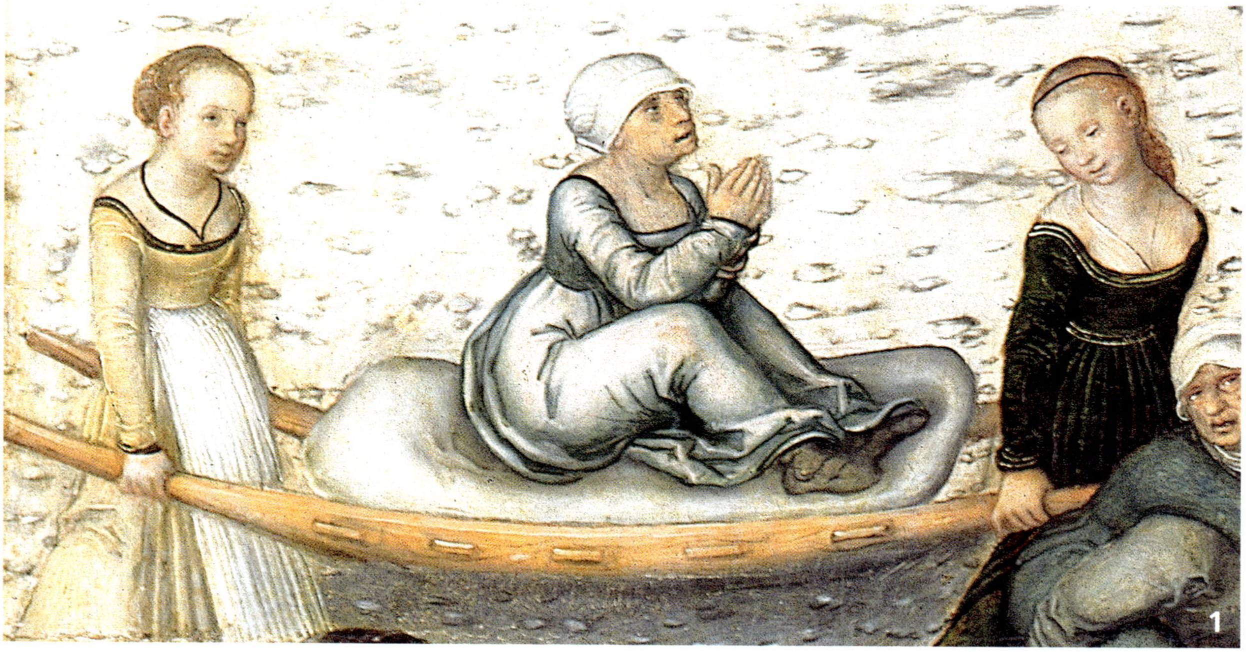

Those who are healthy feel young

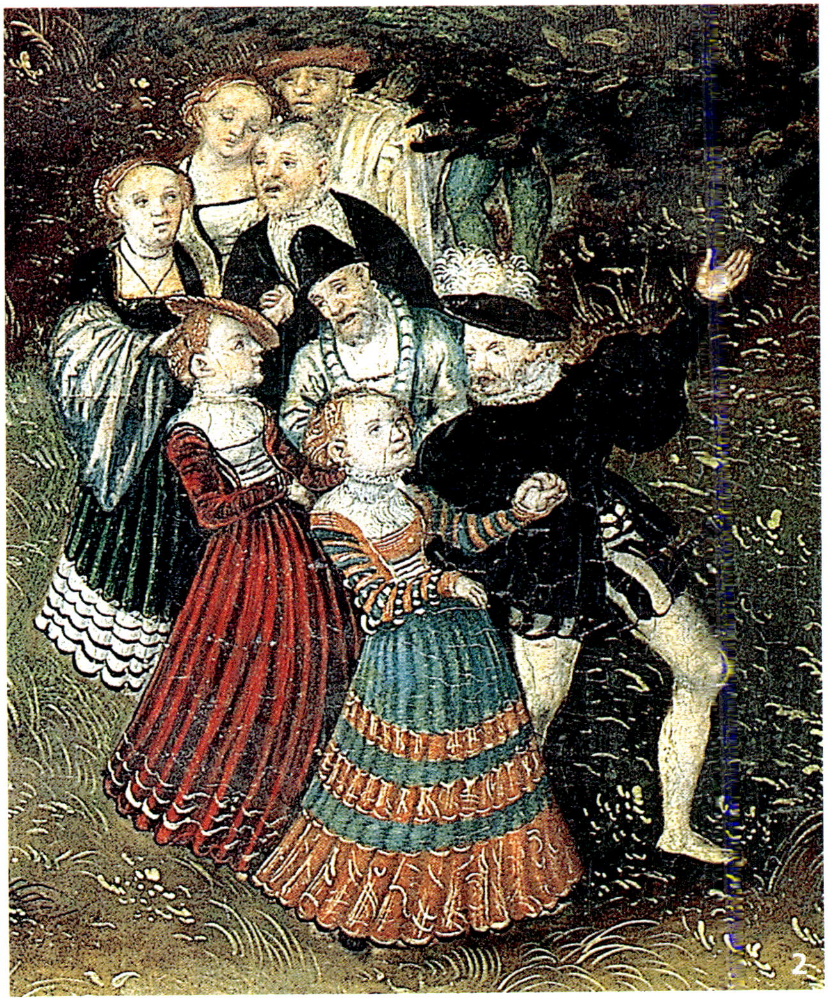

The waters of Spiegelberg-Pyrmont were supposed to heal stab wounds, gaping cuts and shot wounds, eye and ear complaints, all types of rash, and sprained or stiff arms and legs. Anyone who regains the use of their limbs and sense organs and comes away with a clear skin is going to feel not just healthy but usually rejuvenated, too. Every health spa is at the same time a little bit of a fountain of youth.

The existence of a spring that could really restore aged bathers to their youth, which could really turn fragile elderly people into vigorously dancing and flirting young men and women, was probably something that few people even in the 16th century thought likely, for all their belief in miracles. Even in those days, the fountain of youth belonged to the world of myth and legend: Jupiter is supposed to have turned the nymph Juventa into a spring that rejuvenated all those who bathed in it. In Norse mythology, one of the springs near the great ash tree Yggdrasil had the power to restore people to youth and beauty. In the medieval Wolfdietrich epic, the coarse Else is transformed by water into a lovely young woman. The motif appears again and again, indicating just how widespread was the desire to renew oneself through baptism in water, to undo things that had happened or to start life over again as a young person with the experience of old age.

It was a dream also dreamed by the German poet Hans Sachs, a contemporary of Cranach, who naturally turned it into verse. As he slept, it seemed to him that he came to a large pool "of brightly polished marble". There were many people around him, coming "from every country far and near, in litters, sleighs and carts". They were "wrinkled, toothless and bald, trembling and itching all over". But after an hour "they leapt out of the round pool, beautiful, shapely, fresh, young and healthy, light-hearted and cheerful, as if they were twenty years old."

Hans Sachs was 62 when he composed the poem about his fountain of youth dream; Lucas Cranach was 74 when he painted his fountain of youth picture. If it was indeed he who painted it, and not his son, Lucas the Younger. It is a question that has yet to be resolved. Nor is it important. Most of Cranach's paintings are workshop productions on which his sons and assistants were also involved to a greater or lesser degree. Copies of his most popular compositions were regularly turned out to meet demand. Cranach saw himself as an artisan, as the head of a manufacturing team. Only at the start of his career did he initial his own works; later he used the workshop emblem of a winged snake.

The Fountain of Youth also bears the snake emblem, but as far as we know was only painted once. The decorative Venus and Cupid motif on the splashing fountain, however, left the workshop some thirty times in only slight variations. Lucretia holds her dagger to her attractive bosom no less than thirty-five times in Cranach's oeuvre. Cranach's workshop supplied the pictures that people wanted. Alongside impressively splendid paintings for churches and palaces, it produced pictures for private apartments: devotional scenes for the ladies, transparently clad young women representing Lucretia, Venus, nymphs or graces for the gentlemen. *The Fountain of Youth*, with its large numbers of young women lolling naked in the water, must also have been produced for a male client. In its style, the painting corresponds to the gently satirical poem by Hans Sachs. The only question that remains open is at whom its satire is directed: the women with their desire for youth, or the men with their desire for young women?

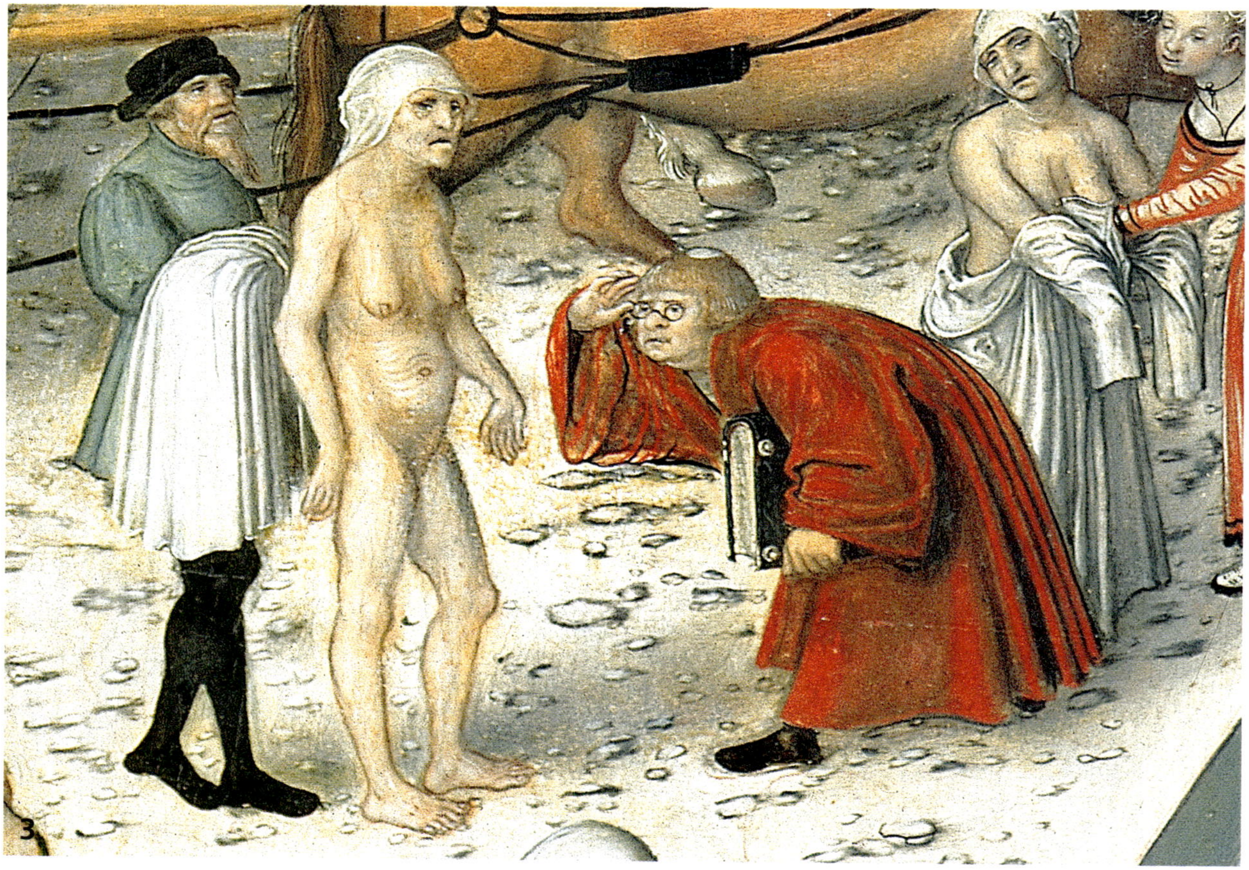

3

The small scene with the man in the red coat contains more than just gentle satire. He is bending down in front of an old woman with not a stitch on her body and ogling her sagging flesh. Whether he is intended to be a doctor or a clerk compiling an official register of miracles, what he is doing seems shameless, at least to us today.

In the 16th century, however, people had different ideas about what was embarrassing and what not. They lived closer together and knew each other more intimately. But even in those days, the aged body did not number amongst the usual subjects of painting. Although the Renaissance is celebrated as the era in which the human body was rediscovered, it was only the young body in its physical prime. The elderly remained covered up.

Young bodies were not simply discovered, however, they were also strongly idealized at the same time. The pattern this followed is clearly illustrated in Cranach's picture. The feminine ideal of beauty included a swollen belly and gently curving lines throughout. Bones were unsightly and were left out. Backbone, collarbone, hipbones, knees – like the rest of the body, they were all enveloped in a soft mass of flesh hiding any sharp edges. Some of Cranach's young women give the impression of being as boneless as mermaids. Accompanying these soft curves are long flowing locks, which Cranach portrayed as golden in all of his rejuvenated young women, in line with the ideal of his day.

Just as edges and corners were avoided, so too were all sexual characteristics. It is true that the painters of the Renaissance vied with each other when it came to portraying a beautiful bosom; indeed, they virtually established a standardized bust – not too small, not too full, and always high. But the nipples and their areolae were only hinted at, and pubic hair was usually omitted. Nipples and pubic hair together provide the most important colour accents in the adult female body, however. They signal that it does not want

Young is beautiful and old is ugly

to be appreciated solely as an aesthetic object. Leave them out, and the body is desexualized and at the same time translated into a prepubescent state; it appears childlike, innocent, an impression which the gay splashing about in Cranach's painting only serves to reinforce.

The bodies of the elderly women do not fit into the Renaissance ideal of beauty. Other painters confirm this insofar as they show naked old women, if at all, only as witches or – as in the case of Dürer – as the personification of miserliness. The situation remains little changed today. It is true that, in the last hundred years, a few artists have portrayed the bodies of elderly people in a slightly kinder light than was the case almost 500 years ago. But the taste of the public in general – as evidenced above all by advertising – continues to uphold the cult of youth dating back to the Renaissance and antiquity.

Cranach's fountain of youth differs from those of other artists of his day insofar as only women are bathing in it. The men on the right clearly don't need to: they are all in their prime, smartly dressed and waiting simply for the next naked young woman to climb out of the water, get dressed and allow herself to be wooed. Wishful male superiority? A product of age-old male fantasy?

Not entirely. In the 16th century, this fairytale was not just about lust and its satisfaction, but about solving a practical problem. Young women were necessary to ensure progeny. An heir was vital, be it to run the farm, take over the workshop or beg for alms. In an era in which there was no state pension for the elderly, women of childbearing age had to provide the only form of security available – offspring.

This cost far more of them their lives than is the case today. They died in childbirth or, weakened by repeated pregnancies, were carried off by one of the many epidemics. In the population aged between 40 and 60, there were only two women for every three men. One man in three thus remained a widower or unmarried, unless he married a young woman in his advancing years. Seen in this light, the idea of rejuvenating some of the remaining elderly women and thereby boosting the numbers of the next generation of young women made logical sense.

The high mortality rate among women and the economical situation very often led to marriages between partners of very different ages. A widower with children couldn't carry on without a new wife; a farmer's widow could not manage her farm without a strong man. An apprentice would marry his master's widow and thereby inherit both his wife and his position. These marriages between young and old were a frequent target of satire. Hans Sachs wrote a poem about them in *Altweiber-Roßmarkt* (Old Women's Horse Fair) and Lucas Cranach painted the motif of the "unequal couple" some twenty times.

There is no trace of such mockery in *The Fountain of Youth*, however. The young women are met not by toothless old men, but by dignified gentlemen who to some extent suit them in age – a miracle probably attributable less to the God of the Bible than to the pagan deities Venus and Cupid, who stand and watch on top of the fountain near the centre of the painting.

The myth and the reality

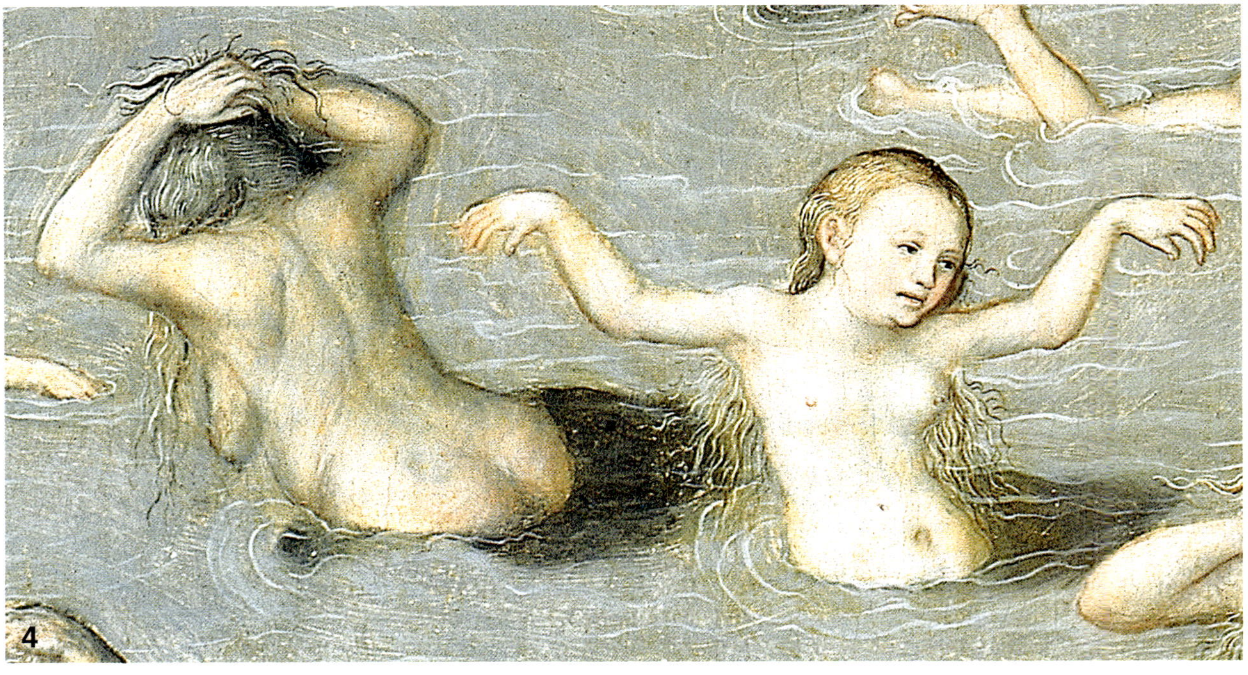
4

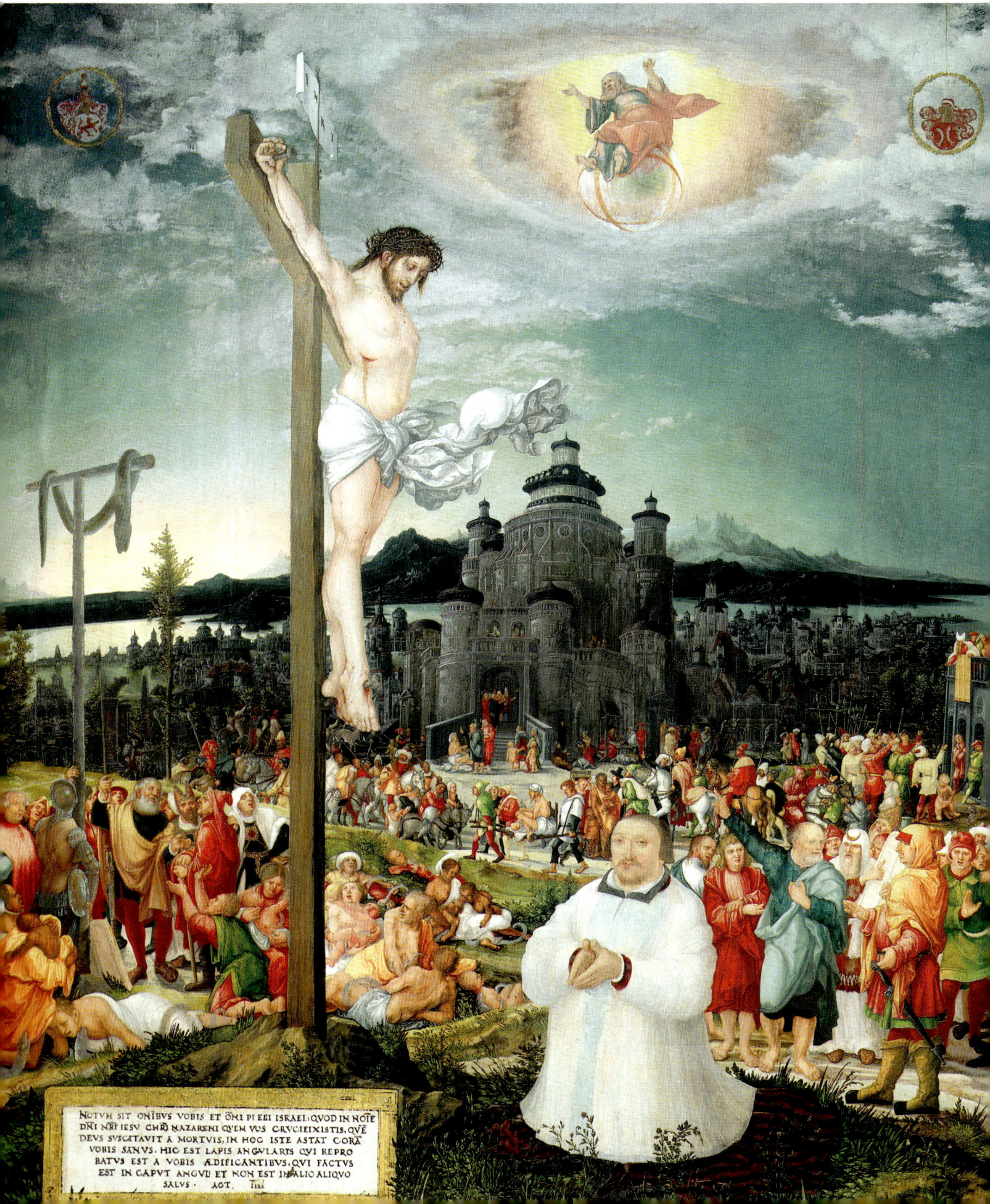
NOTVM SIT OMNIBVS VOBIS ET OMNI PLEBI ISRAEL: QVOD IN NOIE
DNI NRI IESV CHRI NAZARENI QVEM VOS CRVCIFIXISTIS, QVE
DEVS SVSCITAVIT A MORTVIS, IN HOC ISTE ASTAT CORA
VOBIS SANVS. HIC EST LAPIS ANGVLARIS QVI REPRO
BATVS EST A VOBIS ÆDIFICANTIBVS, QVI FACTVS
EST IN CAPVT ANGVLI ET NON EST IN ALIO ALIQVO
SALVS. ACT. IIII

Wolf Huber: Crucifixion Allegory, c. 1550

A Catholic makes an approach to the Protestants

The painting is dominated by Christ on the cross. Wolf Huber portrays him with muscular arms, a chest arching powerfully forwards and straightened knees. The dead man is not hanging from the nails that have been driven through his palms, but is standing, holding himself upright. His body is almost uninjured; his face bears no sign of the pain he has suffered and betrays nothing of his fear, expressed in the Bible, that God has forsaken him. He seems to have his eyes peacefully closed and the viewer sees his father awaiting him in Heaven with open arms.

The history of art is familiar with a very different kind of Crucifixion, one in which Christ appears with dislocated shoulders, a face streaming with blood, fingers straining desperately upwards, his body emaciated and his knees sagging.

Theologians speak of the dual nature of Christ, who was both "true God" and "true man" (Martin Luther). Crucifixion paintings in Western art allow us to see which one of these two aspects of Christ was uppermost in the mind of the person executing or commissioning the work.

In the Gothic era, Christ was mostly portrayed as a suffering man. During the Renaissance, the emphasis shifted in Italy to the divine nature of Christ, expressed in terms of the physical ideals of classical antiquity. North of the Alps, on the other hand, the start of the 16th century brought a spate of brutally realistic images of the dead Christ (as produced, for example, by Hans Holbein the Younger, Lucas Cranach the Elder and Matthias Grünewald).

Wolf Huber painted his *Crucifixion* in around 1550 in Passau, during a period of great religious and political uncertainty. The Muslim Turks had conquered south-eastern Europe and laid siege to Vienna, no more than 200 kilometres from Passau, and it was unclear whether they would continue to push westwards. A combined defence initiative collapsed as a result of the usual rivalries between kings, princes and cities, but also because of the religious disputes setting Christian against Christian. The papacy was in deep crisis. Reformers such as Ulrich Zwingli, John Calvin and Martin Luther were developing new forms of Christianity. In 1545, a year before his death, Luther again expressly condemned "the papacy in Rome" as "instituted by the devil".

The desertion of so many believers forced the Catholic Church to take a long, hard look at itself. The way ahead became the focus of the Council of Trent, which was convened in 1545 and which ended, after many delays and interruptions, in 1563. One of the resolutions passed at the Council related to religious art. Like religious life as a whole, it was to come under much stricter supervision and control. Saints were to be portrayed as they truly were, elevated above earthly things, and not shown with dusty feet, for example. The figure of Christ was always to be given particular prominence and never be allowed to disappear into a crowd. Crucifixions were to focus on the divine nature of Christ; he was to "triumph".

In the face of the Islamic threat hanging over Europe and the danger posed to the papacy by the Protestants, the Catholic Church wanted to portray itself as powerful. This was to extend into art, too: its paintings were to exude confidence. Christ's moment of despair on the cross, or his physical humiliation, were not opportune. One of the means of indicating the Saviour's divine status was the loincloth billowing out before him in defiance of all the laws of nature.

Passau at that time formed part of the lands owned by the Catholic Habsburgs, and Huber's painting reflects the artistic criteria of the Council of Trent. But even Martin Luther would probably have

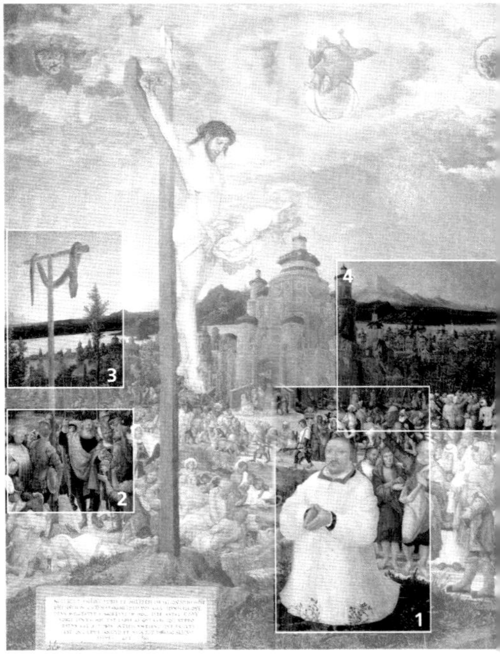

found it acceptable. Although the physical martyrdom of Christ lay at the heart of Luther's theology – humankind, he preached, could only be redeemed by Christ's suffering and God's grace, and not by credits run up on earth or purchased from the Church – the reformer would surely have appreciated the way in which Wolf Huber demonstrates so convincingly that Christ belongs both to earth and to Heaven, in other words unites both spheres in one body. The painting, which measures 154 by 131 centimetres, today hangs in the Kunsthistorische Museum in Vienna.

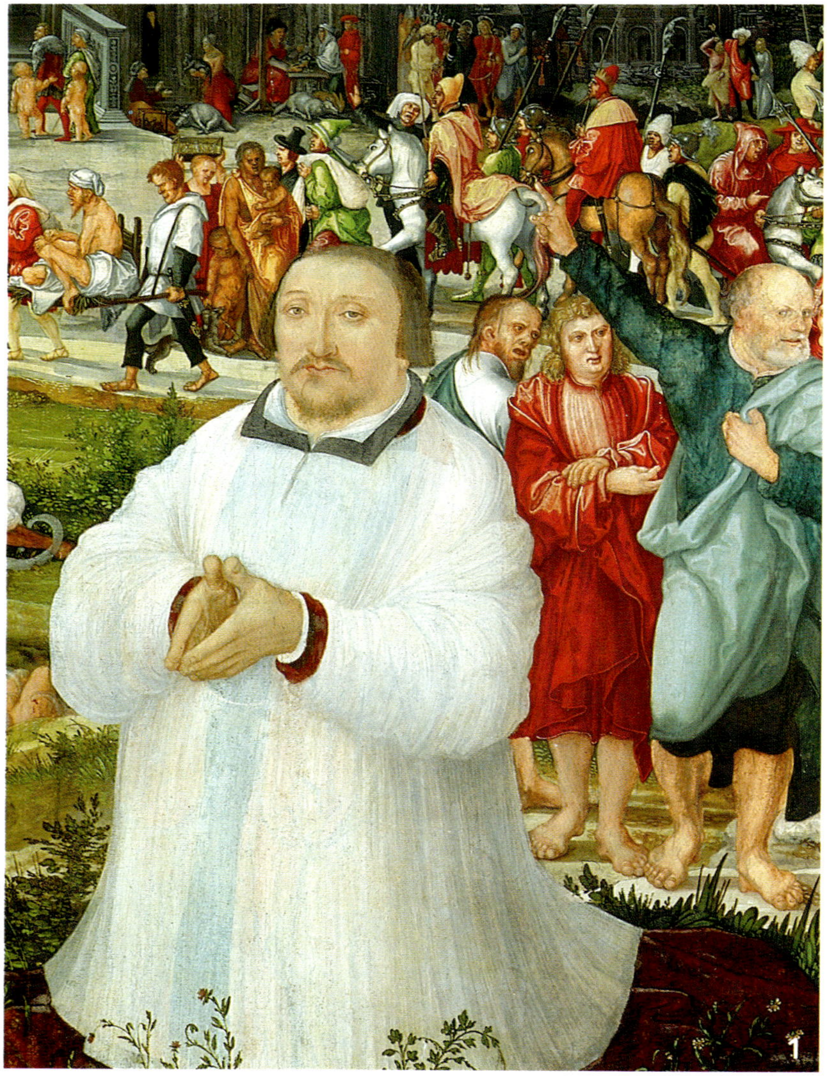

The viewers are meant to join the donor in prayer

The kneeling, somewhat plump figure of the donor was long painted over; whether this was done for aesthetic or political reasons, we do not know. In his place was a meadow. Although his figure was only uncovered in 1954, the donor's identity was never in doubt; it can be deduced from the two coats of arms in the top corners of the picture – on the left the emblem of the bishopric of Passau, and on the right (with the two fish back to back) the arms of the counts of Salm. Wolfgang, Count of Salm, headed the diocese of Passau as prince bishop from 1542 until his death in 1555.

He would have been happy to live the quiet life of a scholar, but the political situation didn't allow it. His brother Niklas II was "councillor and chief chamberlain" to the emperor; his father, a general in the Habsburg army, had fallen in 1529 while defending Vienna against the Turkish armies. His own Passau diocese extended all the way to the border with Austria and was thus directly threatened by the Muslim Turks. In view of this and on account of his father's fame, King Ferdinand sent him to the Imperial Diet in Speyer in 1544 and to the Imperial Assembly in Regensburg in 1546. On both occasions he was tasked with motivating the German princes to put aside their differences and unite in the fight against Islam.

The donor is portrayed here in a simple surplice, which falls in line with the modesty for which he was widely known. He was also a gentle, tolerant man who abhorred violence. Although a Catholic, he did not want to pursue the Protestants with "fire and the sword" as the previous holders of his office had done. Count Salm had studied in Italy; he spoke Latin, Greek, Italian and French, and strove to gather as many scholars as he could at his Passau court. Whether he persuaded Father Nicholas Bobadilla to join him or whether the latter was sent by Rome remains unclear. The Italian Bobadilla was a member of the strict Jesuit order founded in 1534, whose members were directly subordinate to the Pope and which sought to further the Counter-Reformation. Father Bobadilla undoubtedly supported the prince bishop in his efforts to bring the unsettled faithful back into the Catholic fold; he may also have contributed to the complex programme underlying Huber's *Crucifixion Allegory*.

The painting shows the bishop praying to the Crucified Christ and narrates in detail two episodes from the Bible, one in the Old Testament and one in the New. In the pictorial language of Huber's day, if a donor is shown praying directly to Christ, it means that he is praying for the salvation of his own soul. If the donor is looking out at the viewer, however, it means he is urging the viewer to do the same as he, in other words to kneel down and pray.

The message the bishop particularly wants to give the viewer is written on the panel next to him. The text is taken from the story of the healing of the lame man by Peter and John (Acts 3 and 4). The disbelieving priests ask the disciples by what power, or in whose name, they have performed such a miracle. Peter replies "that he was healed in the name and power of Jesus Christ from Nazareth, the man you crucified, but whom God raised from the dead" (Acts 4:10). Huber naturally includes the text in Latin; in contrast to Luther, the Catholic hierarchy was against any translation of the Bible into the vernacular.

Huber assigns the episode from the Old Testament to the left-hand side of the composition. Amidst a crowd of wailing Israelites, Moses – portrayed with a bushy beard, in line with convention – is pointing to the cross with the brazen serpent. Just one figure on the far left, standing quite still, seems uninvolved in the scene: the elderly man with short white hair. Comparisons with a self-portrait have revealed that this is Huber himself. He was between 60 and 70 years old when he painted this picture, and looks out at the viewer just as his patron does.

We know little about him. His name is first documented in a contract of 1515: in his home town of Feldkirch (in Vorarlberg), a "Master Wolfgang Hueber … now resident in Passau" was to paint an altarpiece. It can be concluded from the contract (and early drawings) that Huber or Hueber was born between 1480 and 1485 and that, after his years as an apprentice and journeyman, he settled in Passau.

A second document relates to a dispute. The guild of "painters, woodcarvers and glass-makers" are complaining to the bishop that Wolf Huber has not joined the guild, something which as a citizen of Passau he is technically supposed to do. He is refusing to supply the annual contribution of four pounds of wax and to fund a meal for the "girls and women".

There is probably more at stake here than simply guild membership dues. Citizens in virtually every city were fighting for greater rights within the system of government, be it operated by secular or religious rulers. They wanted more own jurisdiction, greater administrative powers and a higher proportion of the city's revenues.

Rights and obligations on both sides had been recently renegotiated in Passau under Wolfgang, Count of Salm's predecessors. Perhaps Huber had infringed the rules by accepting commissions from the middle classes while he was court painter. Whatever the case, in 1542, at the start of his rule, prince bishop Salm took Huber clearly under his wing and instructed his painter, woodcarver and glass-maker colleagues not to trouble his court painter again.

Huber had already worked for Salm's predecessors and in particular, too, for his elder brother Niklas, "councillor and chief chamberlain" to the emperor. Niklas may have commissioned Huber to produce some designs for his father's sarcophagus, following the latter's death in battle against the Turks. Huber was probably also amongst the delegation that travelled to Vienna to attend the ceremonial burial of the "saviour of Christendom".

Niklas also entrusted the artist with architectural projects, as was common in those days. He rewarded him handsomely: as well as an annual allowance, he gave him the small palace of Neufels on the Inn river "to live in for the rest of his life after all his service".

While Huber cannot be assumed to have lived here in princely splendour, he would certainly have been more comfortable than guild members in the city. Like the circle of scholars with which Wolfgang, Count of Salm surrounded himself, Huber's little palace brings to mind Italy, and the particularly high esteem in which artists south of the Alps were held.

Fires in Passau have destroyed many historical documents, but one that survives allows us to draw some conclusions about the relationship between prince bishop Salm and his painter. In 1553, after Huber's death, the bishop personally appointed two guardians for the artist's children. That he attended to this in person was not necessarily normal practice.

On his tombstone Huber is described as "fürstlich hoffmaller" (court painter to the prince) and vaunted as a "khunstreich man" (man of artistic skill). Missing, however, is the title of "Meister" (master), as awarded by a guild. Huber had undoubtedly earned it, but evidently the person composing the text – perhaps the artist himself – wanted to avoid all mention of guilds, any connection with the artisan classes. He was court painter to a prince bishop.

Court painter to a prince bishop

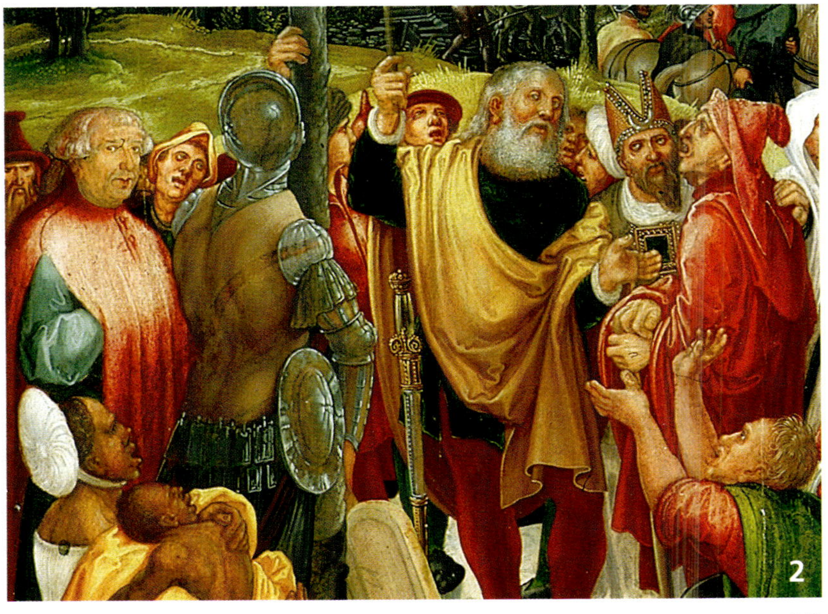

2

While the story of Adam, Eve and the serpent that tempts them remains highly popular even today, the tale of the brazen serpent is virtually unknown. The brass or bronze serpent appears in Numbers 21. Moses is leading the Israelites out of Egypt, and they have passed through the sea and across deserts. But "the people grew impatient along the way, and they began to murmur against God and Moses. 'Why have you brought us out of Egypt to die here in the wilderness?'" Jehova was angered by their complaints, and to punish them he "sent poisonous snakes among them, and many were bitten and died". The Israelites implored Moses to pray to the Lord to take away the snakes. Moses did so, and the Lord commanded him: "Make a replica of a poisonous snake and attach it to the top of a pole. Those who are bitten will live if they simply look at it!"

The very animal which had brought disaster was thus to be cast in bronze. But from the viewpoint of the narrator, the snakes were sent by Jehova and were thus his messengers. To revere the snake was to respect the omnipotence of God and acknowledge that all salvation comes from Jehova.

This visually powerful story has been forgotten, probably because it no longer fits into our conception of snakes. For us, snakes are negative, both as symbols and in real life.

It was a snake that tempted the first humans in Paradise and became – as the serpent – the embodiment of evil. It is experienced in nature, if at all, only as something dangerous. In earlier cultures along the Mediterranean, however, its significance was ambivalent. The Egyptians, Mycenaeans and Minoans worshipped snakes or snake goddesses. They apparently represented the fertility of the earth; the snake's shedding of its skin was related to the constant renewal of nature. The snake's association with healing powers has survived into the present only in the twin serpents entwined around the caduceus.

In Huber's day, things were different. The motif of the brazen serpent was widely known, not least because an antique bronze snake was venerated as the original brazen serpent in the Milan church of San Ambrogio. The motif also appears in picture Bibles published during this same era.

The particular choice of the brazen serpent is connected with the desire to find pointers in the Old Testament to the coming of Christ. Theologians were looking not just for prophecies but for events prefiguring those in the life of Christ. Thus the story of Jonah being swallowed by a whale and then spat out again after three days was interpreted as paralleling Christ's death and Resurrection. Abraham's willingness to sacrifice his son Isaac was equated with God's plan to sacrifice his own son.

Nowhere in Numbers does it say that the brazen serpent was hung on a cross or a T-bar. Artists and the clergy advising them chose this motif to make their point clear: just as the Israelites worshipped Jehova in the shape of a snake, Christians worship God in the person of the Crucified Christ. That is the only path to salvation. Huber makes this same parallel visible in another way: Peter (standing near the bishop) is pointing upwards in exactly the same pose as Moses and with an almost identical gesture. One is pointing to Christ, the other to the metal snake.

The brazen serpent stopped the complaining

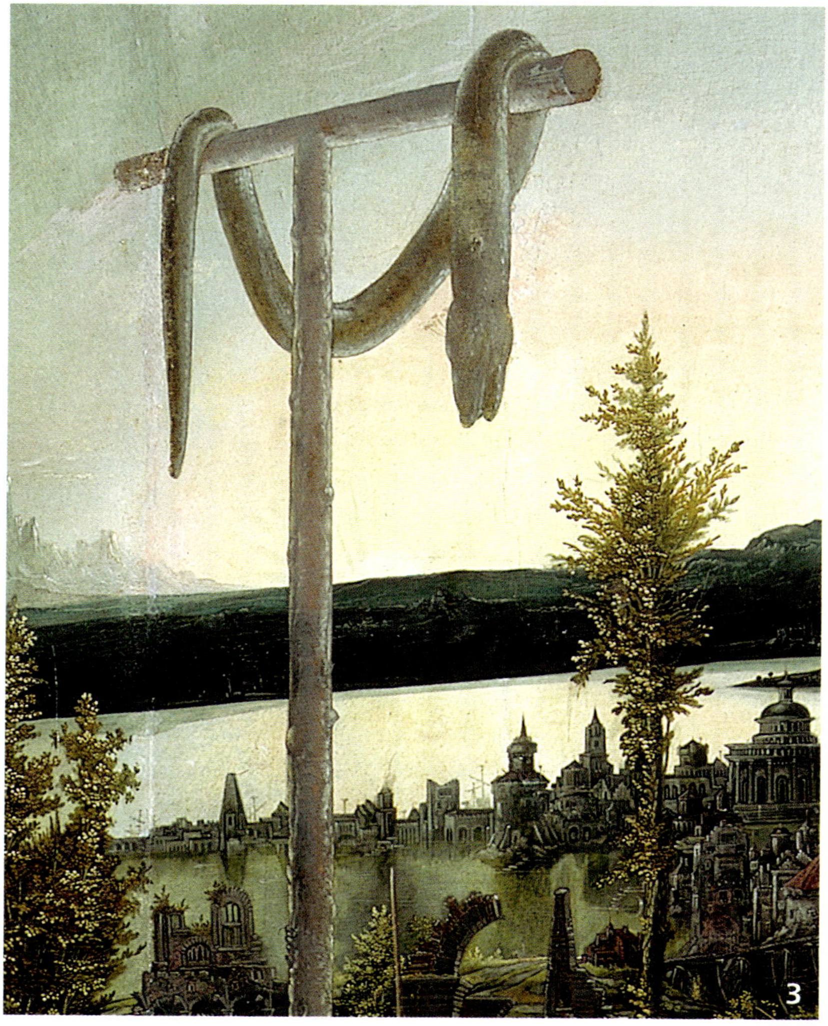

3

A picture for both Catholics and Protestants

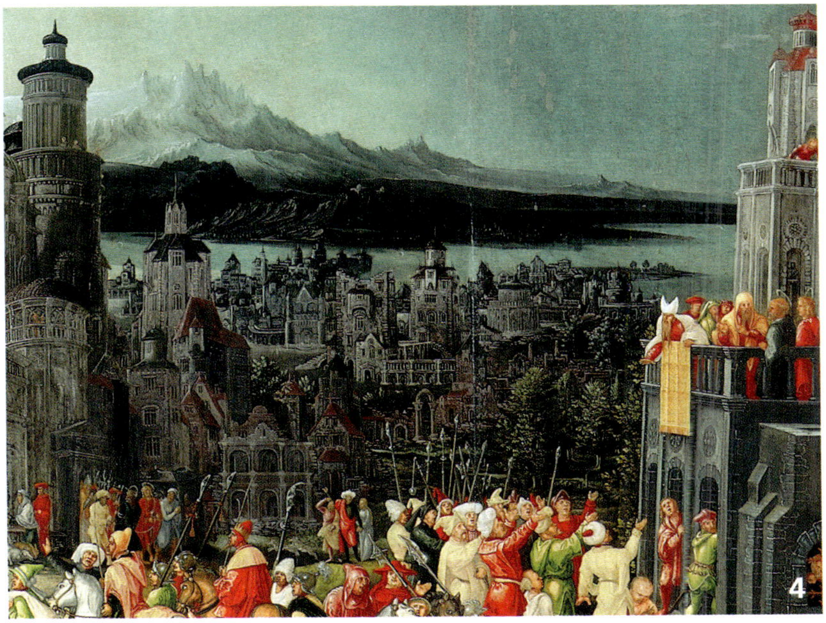

Wolf Huber belonged to the Danube school, a current within German and Austrian painting in the opening decades of the 16th century. Other members included Albrecht Altdorfer and Lucas Cranach the Elder. Among their common characteristics were an often artificial lighting and a garish palette. As in Huber's *Crucifixion Allegory*, they displayed a typical preference for expansive landscapes incorporating forests, sea, mountains, animated skies and a ground full of small figures. Altdorfer's *Battle of Issus* is another example of this type of painting (cf. *What Great Paintings Say*, Volume II).

It was untypical of the Danube school, however, to tell a story in several scenes, as Huber does with the healing of the lame man. The sequence begins to the bishop's left with the cripple being carried to the temple on a stretcher. He is then healed by Peter and John at the entrance to the temple. Peter and John are subsequently led away to prison out of the right-hand temple door; from the balcony over the prison entrance, the priests address the people. The next morning the two apostles are released but are told never to preach in the name of Jesus again. They refuse. Huber shows them in discussion with the high priests to the right of the bishop's head. With the story beginning and finishing on either side of the bishop, the painter assigns his patron a prominent position not just within the overall composition, but also within this story of the miraculous power of Jesus.

While it was common for several scenes from one story to be combined within a painting in the Middle Ages, this was not the case in the 16th century. Huber is here employing an old-fashioned device. On the other hand, he portrays a gently curving horizon, particularly evident in the prison building, which leans to the right. Huber thereby indicates the curvature of the earth. The academics gathered at the Passau court would undoubtedly have discussed the latest scientific and cosmological theories, and perhaps too the claims by Copernicus that the earth revolved around the sun, rather than the sun around the earth – a proposition which threw theologians and the entire Christian world into disarray. Huber's painting thus retains vestiges of the Middle Ages while embracing the scientific thinking of the Renaissance: it stands between two eras.

It is similarly ambivalent in its religious stance. It served as propaganda for the Counter-Reformation, and nothing in it infringes the rules laid down by the Council of Trent. But in contrast to works issuing from Italy and Spain, from regions of Europe in which Catholicism was still uncontested, Huber avoids all motifs which might offend Protestants. It contains nothing of the Virgin Mary, nothing of the cult of saints to which Luther was so opposed. Peter and John are not given haloes; the painting emphasizes only the figure of Jesus Christ, just as argued in Luther's theology.

Nor does the donor appear in his bishop's robes. Rather than demonstrating the magnificence and power of the Church of Rome, he kneels in a simple surplice. This is his own choice, albeit one which does not contravene the Council of Trent's directions. In this respect, the *Crucifixion Allegory* is also a very personal painting. Count Salm was a loyal son of the Church, but not one who gave Protestants up for lost. One might imagine he wanted not just to admonish Catholics, but also to encourage all his errant fellow believers to repent and return to the faith.

A hero takes a dip

Daedalus, according to Greek myth, was a skilled and highly inventive Athenian craftsman. He had an apprentice called Talos, however, who by the age of twelve was already proving more talented than his master. Talos is said to have designed the first saw after studying the backbone of a fish; he also invented the dividers and the potter's wheel, for which he became very famous. This angered his master. He took Talos up to the Acropolis and onto the roof of the Temple of Athena, and threw him off. The crime was discovered. Daedalus lied and said his apprentice had tripped. No one believed him. Daedalus was exiled.

He fled to the island of Crete, where King Minos was delighted to welcome such a skilled craftsman. The king's wife, however, was in love with a white bull. Daedalus built a wooden cow, in which the queen hid and was impregnated by the bull. She gave birth to the Minotaur, a monster with the head of a bull and the body of a man. King Minos, horrified, instructed Daedalus to build a labyrinth from which the monster could never escape. Daedalus did so, but was then sent into the labyrinth himself, together with his son Icarus, when Minos found out that it was he who had built the wooden cow. Minos also had every ship watched so that Daedalus would be unable to leave the island even if he found a way out of the labyrinth.

Daedalus was determined to get out, however. "He may check my escape by water and land, but the air and the sky are free. There I will go. Minos may rule over everything, but not over the skies." So he built Icarus and himself each a pair of wings. The large feathers were sewn together with thread, the smaller ones stuck together with wax, and the wings themselves gently curved like those of birds. Before they embarked upon their flight, Daedalus warned his son to keep a middle course over the sea, and not to fly too close to the water, in case the wings got wet, or too close to the sun, in case the wax melted.

Daedalus flew in front, Icarus behind. Ovid, the Roman poet, wrote: "Many a fisherman pulling in his catch with a bending rod, shepherd leaning on his crook and farmer at his plough, gazed at them with astonishment and thought that anyone who knew how to soar through the ether must be an immortal." Icarus, grown overconfident, flew ever higher, until the sun melted the wax of his wings. He plunged into the sea and was drowned.

Bruegel portrays Icarus on the point of drowning. He omits Daedalus altogether. More important in his composition are the three figures whom Ovid also mentions, albeit only in passing: the farmer at his plough, the shepherd resting on his crook and the fisherman with his rod.

Ovid (43 BC – c. AD 18) was one of the most popular classical authors in Bruegel's day. That the artist was familiar with his writings is demonstrated not only by the three figures, but also by a fourth detail. Ovid tells the story of Daedalus and Icarus in his *Metamorphoses*, a book in which he describes transformations in the world of the gods and heroes. A metamorphosis takes place in the tale of Daedalus, too. Talos the apprentice is caught in mid-fall by Athena, who turns him into a previously unknown type of bird. This new bird flies close to the ground and lays its eggs in hedges, "for it fears the heights, remembering its former fall".

This bird is present at Icarus's death and gives out "a joyful crowing ... as an eternal rebuke to you, Daedalus!" It is a partridge. Bruegel sits the partridge on a bare bough near the fisherman.

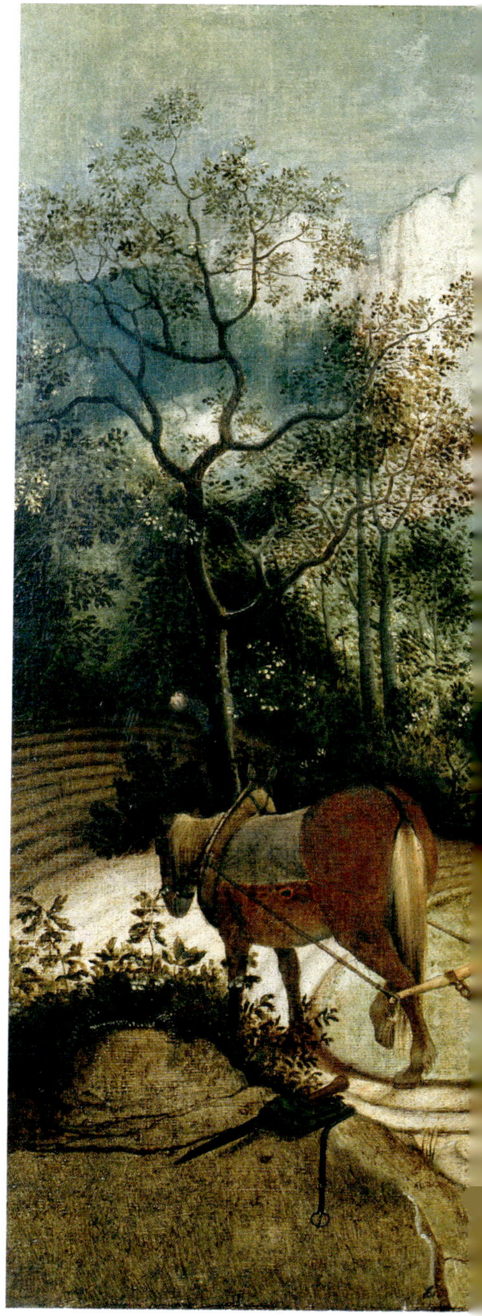

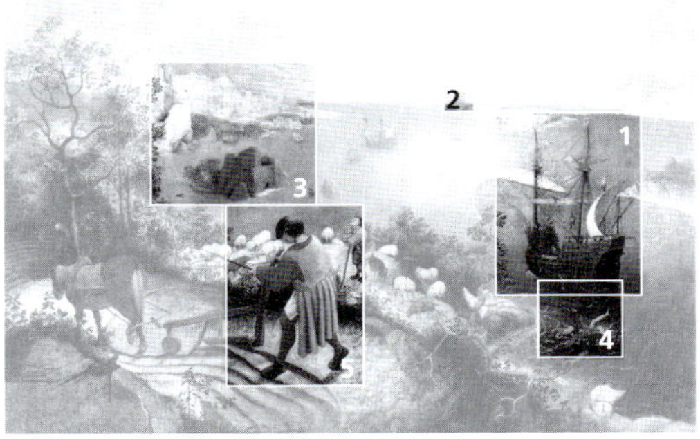
2
1
3
4

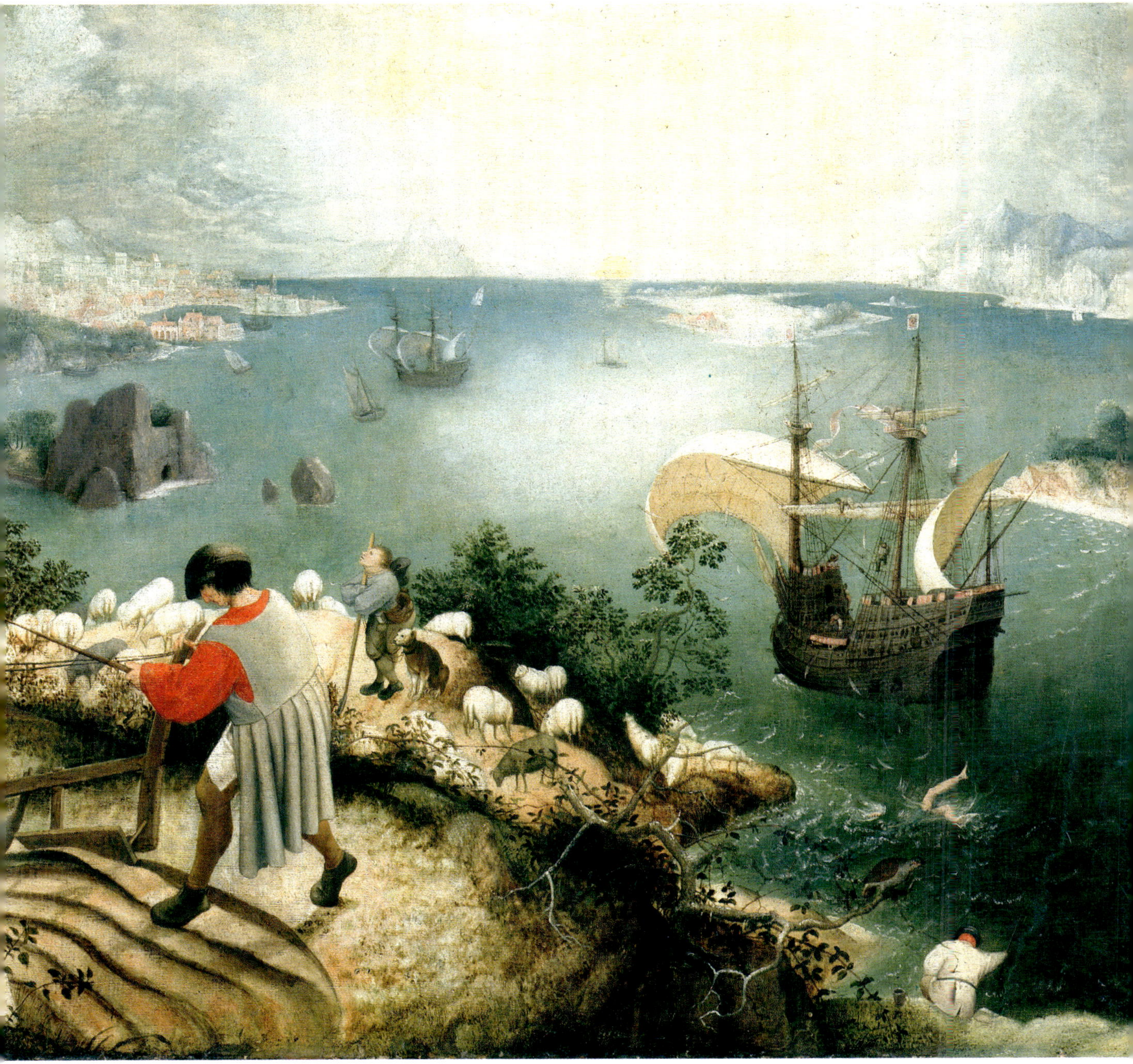

A ship such as the one behind Icarus measured some 40 metres long by 15 metres wide and was one the largest boats of its day. It had four decks and four masts. The two masts at the stern were equipped with triangular lateens, and the two mainsails could be supplemented with additional sails. The billowing foresail allows us to see how the canvas is fastened along the yard.

Cargo-laden sailing ships also carried arms. Five cannon can be seen ranged along the poop deck and seven along the side facing the viewer; there must be seven more that we cannot see on the other side. But their appearance was more threatening than their performance: the cannonballs only travelled about 100 metres and were inaccurate in their aim. They could cause damage to the masts and rigging, but couldn't sink ships. Nor, in most cases, was that their intention. Enemy ships in the 16th century were if at all possible not sunk, but captured. Everyone could use a ship. New ones were expensive.

The oval, almost spherical construction of the sailing ship was intended to make the ship difficult to board: the narrower the area of contact, the fewer attackers could climb aboard at once. The bulwarks at the bow and the stern were built deliberately high, so they could hold soldiers and provide a platform to fight invaders below. Those fighting from an elevated position had the advantage. The Spanish, who tended to take things to extremes, built up to seven decks one on top of the other; this, however, made their ships clumsy and difficult to manoeuvre. The Netherlanders were more restrained.

Bruegel painted many ships in the course of his career – large, fast, studded with cannon, driven by the wind. A particularly large number were conceived for engravings. Engravings were sold by publishers who only commissioned the subjects their customers wanted. Pictures of ships were popular. No wonder: Bruegel spent the 1550s – the decade during which *Icarus* was painted – in Antwerp, and Antwerp lived from seafaring.

This had not long been the case. Neighbouring cities such as Bruges and Amsterdam had kept Antwerp small. Up to around 1500, the town remained a minor centre of trade. Its rise was sparked by the discovery of the sea route to India around the southern tip of Africa and by the Spanish conquests in America. Spices, exotic woods and silks from the Far East had previously been transported by caravan to the Mediterranean and from there to central Europe via the Italian ports. Now goods from India could be shipped directly to Lisbon, bypassing the costs of intermediate customs duty and camel hire. With the new gold from America landing in Seville, the Atlantic coast took over from the Mediterranean as the destination for European imports. The route from the Atlantic ports on the Iberian Peninsula to the North led via Bruges, Amsterdam and above all Antwerp.

The first spice ship from Portugal landed in Antwerp in 1501; that same year, the city was granted the imperial licence for the grain trade. Ships from the cities of the Hanseatic League brought corn from Stettin and Danzig, which was then shipped on from Antwerp to Spain. The English also sold their wool to Europe via the Dutch ports, and the Fuggers and Welsers transported metals from Germany and Hungary which were sent on by ship from Antwerp. The city found itself at the hub of Europe's new trade routes. Its forward-thinking councillors offered better transshipment facilities than neighbouring

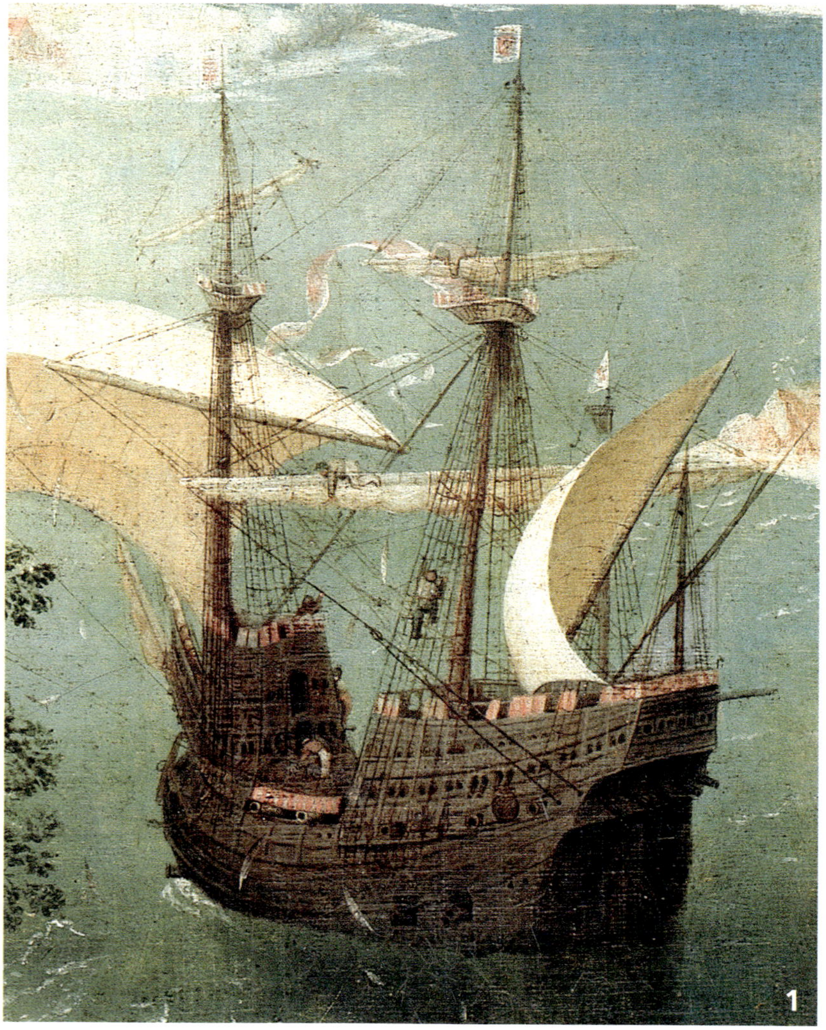
1

Seafaring was a profitable business

ports. Within fifty years, the small town had become western Europe's leading centre of maritime trade.

It was the big sailing ships which brought in the goods and thus the money, and which became a symbol for the citizens of Antwerp of the rise of their city. It grew rapidly. One contemporary believed it would soon rank amongst the "fullest places in Europe". Although many new houses were built, "they are very expensive, owing to the large influx of all sorts of people". It was thus not just merchants who profited from the boom, but also craftsmen, dockers, estate agents and of course manufacturers of luxury goods, such as goldsmiths and artists. It is no coincidence that Bruegel should have based himself in this city for so many years.

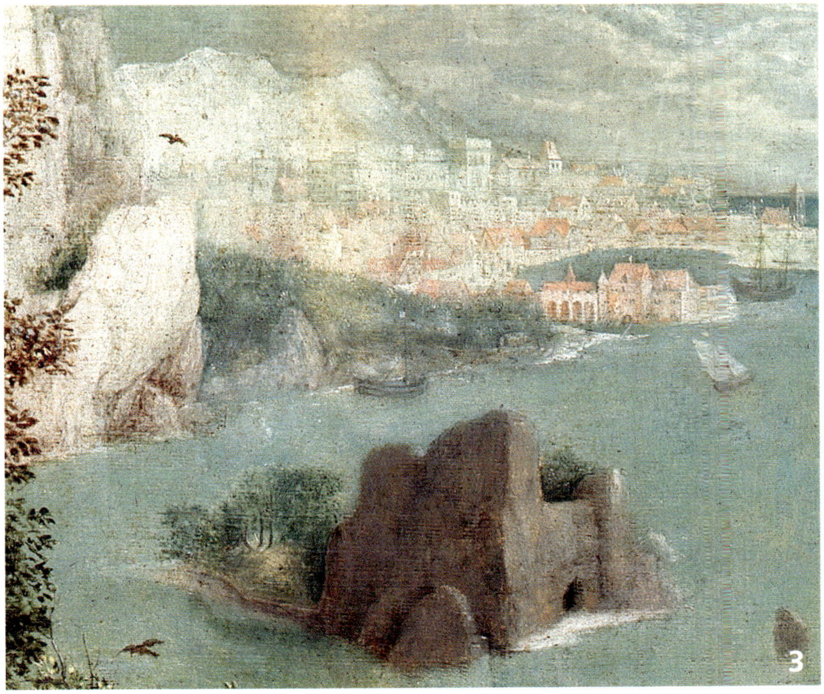

3

Things that can't be painted

Antwerp owed its rapid development to the discovery of new sea routes and distant continents. The geographical horizon was expanding: in 1520 Magellan circumnavigated the globe and thereby proved that the earth was round not just in the minds of a few scientists. In 1543 Copernicus published his astronomical treatise, in which he proved that the earth was not the centre of the universe. The discovery of the earth, new continents and space is one of the great themes of the 16th century. These new discoveries created new requirements. Geography had made almost no progress since Ptolemy (c. 85-c. 160) almost 1500 years earlier; the Middle Ages had been more interested in the world to come than the surface of the earth. Suddenly, however, people needed atlases, cartographers and cosmographers – and their centre became Antwerp.

Here, alongside many others, worked Abraham Oertel, who latinized his surname to Ortelius as was the convention among scholars. He published the first atlas of the world, entitled the *Theatrum Orbis Terrarum*, which might be loosely translated as "A portrayal of all the lands of this world". Up to that point, maps had been sold individually and employed different formats. Ortelius took the maps compiled by various cartographers and redrew them using a uniform scale, bound them together in book form and sold them in a convenient volume.

2

Ortelius is important both for his contribution to the history of geography, and for the information he provides us about Bruegel. Both men were members of the Guild of St Luke and were friends. Since no writings that might shed light on Bruegel's thinking have survived from his own hand, we must turn to Ortelius. In his *Book of Friends* he writes: "Our Bruegel paints many things that can't be painted." And: "There is often more thinking than painting in his works."

The whole world in a picture

The new interest in the earth can be seen in painting, too. In the Middle Ages, artists portrayed their figures against gold backgrounds. The gold symbolized eternity, in the face of which nature paled into insignificance. Landscape was merely a prop, a decorative accessory. A good 100 years before Bruegel, however, nature began to grow and spread across paintings. First in Italy and then north of the Alps, the landscape painting was born.

With the spread of this new type of picture, so the meaning of the word "landscape" changed. In German, it had previously been used to describe a region and the customs of its inhabitants: "The landscape itself eats no bread, but rice and fish." It now came to describe a picture, an artificial product, while the inhabitants and their customs were slowly forgotten. Dürer was one of the first in the North to use the word in this new sense; in a diary entry of 1521 he mentions a "good landscape painter", namely Joachim Patenier.

Patenier had specialized in the portrayal of landscapes and thereby discovered how to use colour to create spatial depth. He typically employed a brown foreground, a green middle ground and a light blue

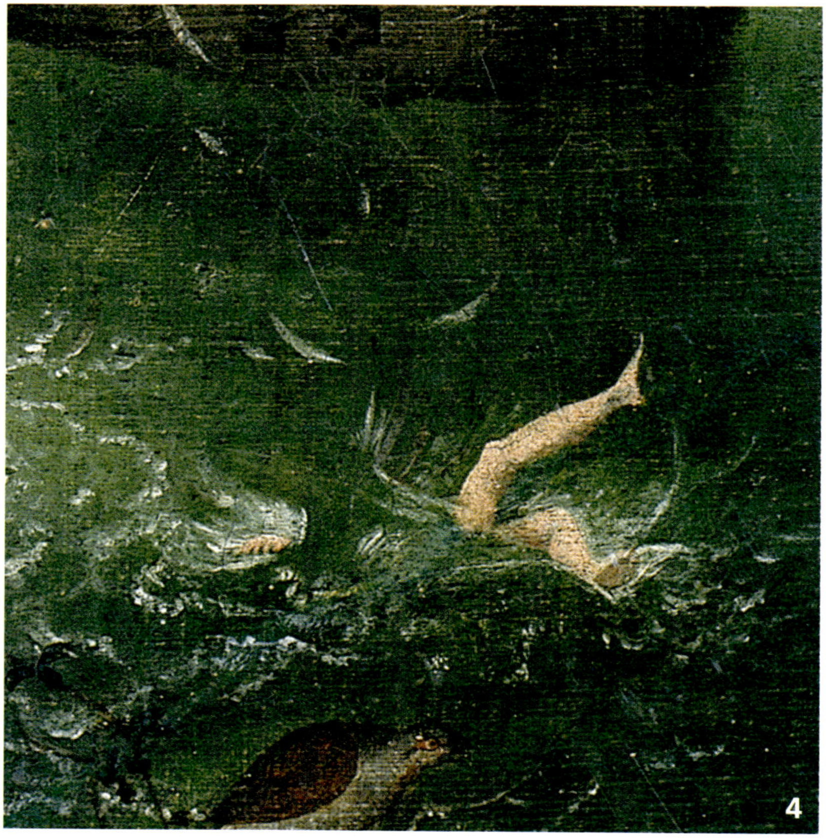

4

background, in a palette thus moving from dark to light. Bruegel, too, usually sticks to Patenier's rules.

But tonal values alone are not enough. To portray a sweeping, expansive landscape, you need an elevated vantage point. The painters of Bruegel and Dürer's day climbed to the tops of church steeples and mountains to learn what landscape looked like when seen from above. Bruegel presents his *Icarus* from a similarly elevated spot: we look diagonally down on the farmer ploughing, see the shepherd more from the side and the ship above him fully side on. Whether the perspective be accurate or not, this angled view creates the sense that we are looking across a great distance.

The impression of a space almost vast enough to contain the whole world is also suggested by the inclusion, within this one composition, of a host of motifs – far more than one might expect to see in one place in real life: fields and tall trees and a range of mountains and the sea and islands and the horizon and a port to boot. These all appear to be arranged within a flat circle that extends beyond the horizon and thereby incorporates what lies out of sight.

A very long fall

This inclusion of so many motifs was no more Bruegel's invention than the high vantage point or the use of tonal values to create spatial depth. There is something in this picture which *is* new, however, reflecting the same artistic desire to reach far into the distance and portray the height and breadth of space. This innovation, this idea reveals itself not to the eye, but to the mind. For Bruegel paints many things "that simply can't be painted", and there is "often more thinking than painting in his works".

Bruegel's invention is to show Icarus sinking beneath the waves at the same time as the sun. In usual versions of *Icarus*, the sun appears high in the heavens with Icarus beneath it, tumbling towards the sea. Bruegel himself employed this traditional layout in an engraving, in which the sun seems to be a couple of hundred metres above the water, and in which Icarus' fall can only have lasted a few seconds. While engravings were produced for a broad public, Bruegel's paintings were destined, for people he trusted to use their minds.

The person contemplating Bruegel's *Icarus* had to consider that the legendary youth must have commenced his fall somewhere above the place where he is drowning, outside the painting; that at that point the sun must still have been nearby; and that Icarus must have been falling for the same length of time as the sun has taken to drop to the horizon. Let's say that has taken six hours. This means Icarus has been falling through space for six hours. A massive distance. An extraordinary relationship between time and space. Bruegel's pictorial invention can be compared – within its own field – to the discoveries of Columbus and Magellan. However, it did not change the world.

In Ortelius' atlas, the regional maps are prefaced by a map of the world. From a practical point of view, this map serves purely as a means of orientation and provides the publisher with the opportunity to air some of his opinions. This he does in the form of quotations from Cicero and Seneca. For example: "Is this the dot that so many peoples divide up amongst themselves with sword and fire? How ridiculous are the borders drawn by mortals." Or: "What shall one who is familiar with all eternity and the size of the globe find great in human affairs?" Selected by the publisher for people who are fascinated with the size of the world, these quotations also remind them how small and imperfect they are. An atlas with a moral.

The atlas did not appear until after Bruegel's death, thus the artist never saw Ortelius' compilation of maps and texts. We may assume, however, that he was familiar with Ortelius' editorial position. Nor was it unusual for its day. It was popular in the 16th century to link the ancient Stoics with Bible concepts: the world is shaped by a sole divine power; everything that happens has a higher meaning; humankind must fit into the scheme of things.

That Bruegel thought along similar lines can be inferred from his *Icarus*. Although, unlike Ortelius, he does not cite from the classical authors, he presupposes a familiarity with the legend of Icarus, for example, perhaps in the version by Ovid. Only someone who has read Ovid will notice that Bruegel has turned subsidiary figures into main players, and that the values he attaches to the characters in the story are different to those of Ovid. For Bruegel, as for Stoic Christians, Icarus was not the courageous explorer who attempted to go beyond the bounds of what was previously known and conquered. On the contrary, for them, Icarus symbolized someone who refused to fall in line, to content himself with his lot. For that he had to die. Icarus was not a hero, but a fool. If Bruegel had wanted to portray him as a hero, he could have painted him plunging dramatically out of the sky. Instead he makes him almost ridiculous by reducing him to a pair of kicking legs.

Several poems have been written on Bruegel's *Icarus* over the past 100 years (cf. the book *Gedichte auf Bilder*, "Poems on Pictures", published by the Deutscher Taschenbuchverlag). Almost all of them see Icarus as a tragic hero. The other figures are described as indifferent; they feel no pity for Icarus and fail to sense anything extraordinary about his fall. For Bruegel – we must assume – their response is the right one.

Daedalus is no more a hero in Bruegel's eyes than Icarus; the father flying at a sensible height doesn't fit into his overall concept and is simply omitted. The artist's positive heroes are the farmer and the shepherd. Both occupy a meaningful position within the composition. As the largest figure in the composition, the farmer dominates the foreground, while the small head of the shepherd is located in virtually the exact centre of the picture. For Bruegel, these are positive figures because they are doing something useful within the bounds of their possibilities; the farmer guiding his plough, the shepherd watching his flock. They are also peace-loving, something automatically assumed of a "good shepherd" but also demonstrated in the case of the farmer, too, by the fact that he has taken off his belt and sword and laid them on the rock. The farmer is looking down at the soil he is tilling, confining himself to the earthly sphere assigned to him by God. The shepherd directs his gaze heavenwards, a traditional pictorial means of symbolizing his connection with the divine, his turning to God.

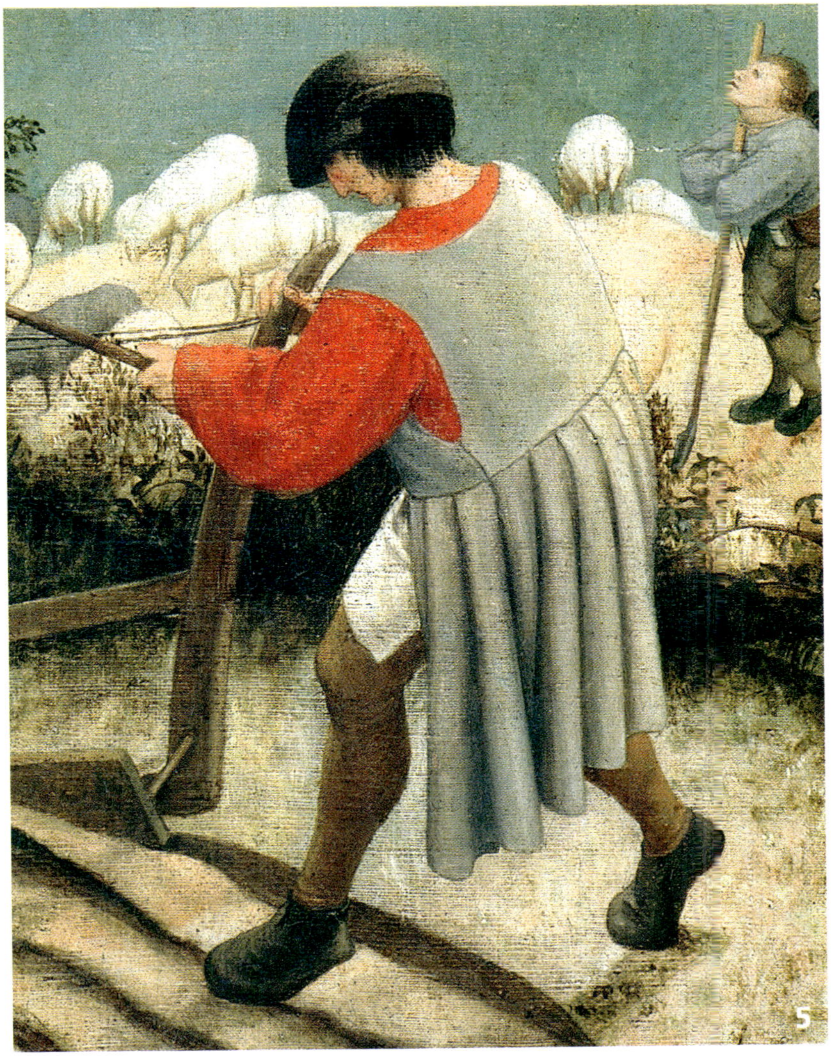

5

These figures from daily life represent *vita activa*, a conscientious, hard-working life. In 1576 the German poet Johann Fischart described it thus:

Auch keine Flügel man haben muß
Die die Sonne schmilzt wie Icarus
Nein, Standmut nur und feste Hand
Die machen fliegen durch das Land
Arbeit und Fleiß, das sind die Flügel
Die führen über Strom und Hügel.

(Nor do you have to have wings / for the sun to melt like Icarus / No, simply courage and a firm hand / will make you fly through the land / Diligence and work, these are the wings / that will carry you over rivers and hills.)

To understand these attitudes, we need to appreciate the background against which they evolved. This was an era of upheaval and insecurity. As early capitalism was changing the social structure, the Reformation was undermining the ordering power formerly wielded by the Catholic Church. Seafarers were opening up new horizons; Copernicus was proclaiming that the sun, not the earth was the centre of the universe. Practical activity took on a particular value. It became a means of keeping one's head and helping others survive. Bruegel portrays both the expansion of space and how man should conduct himself within it.

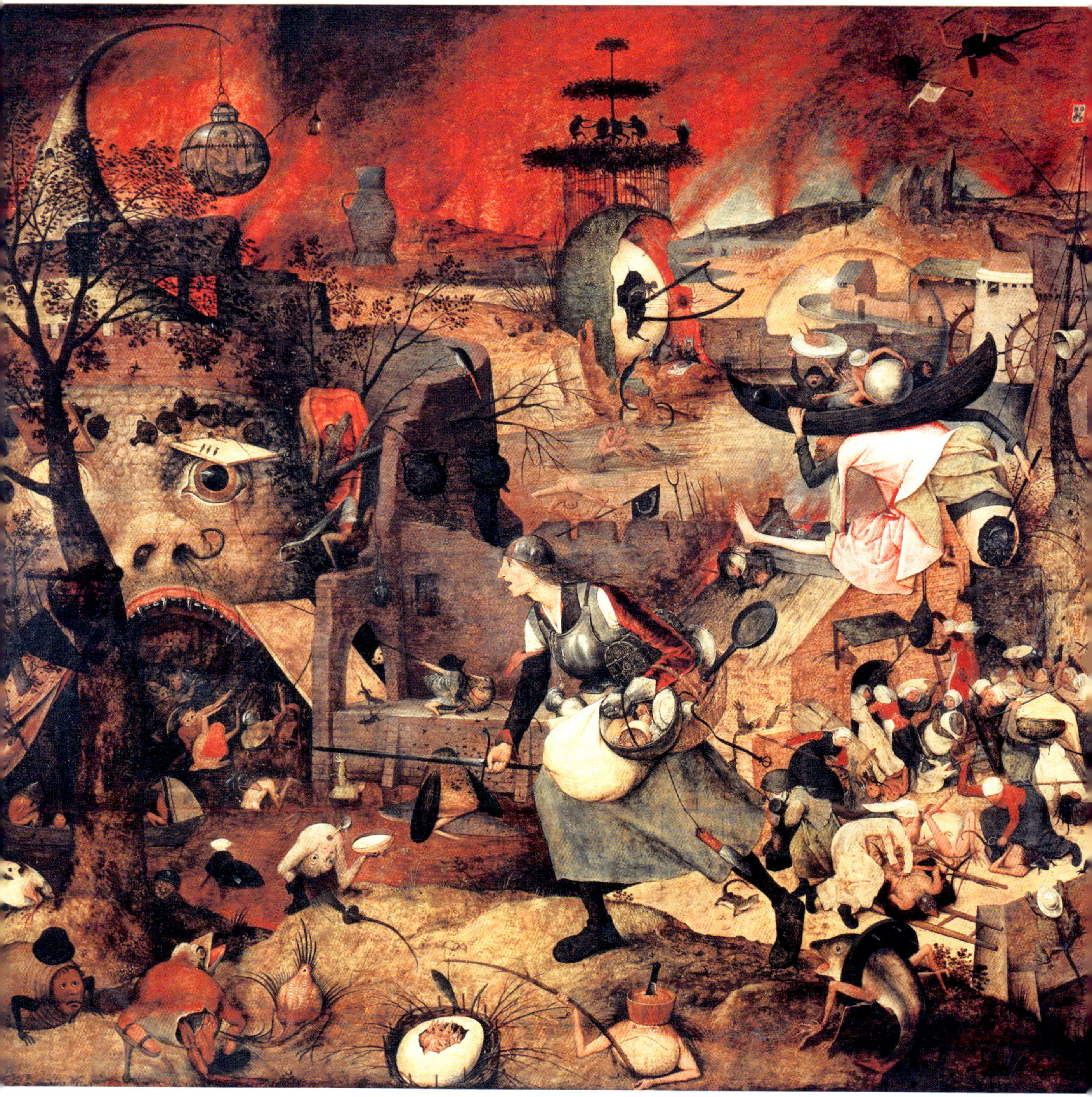

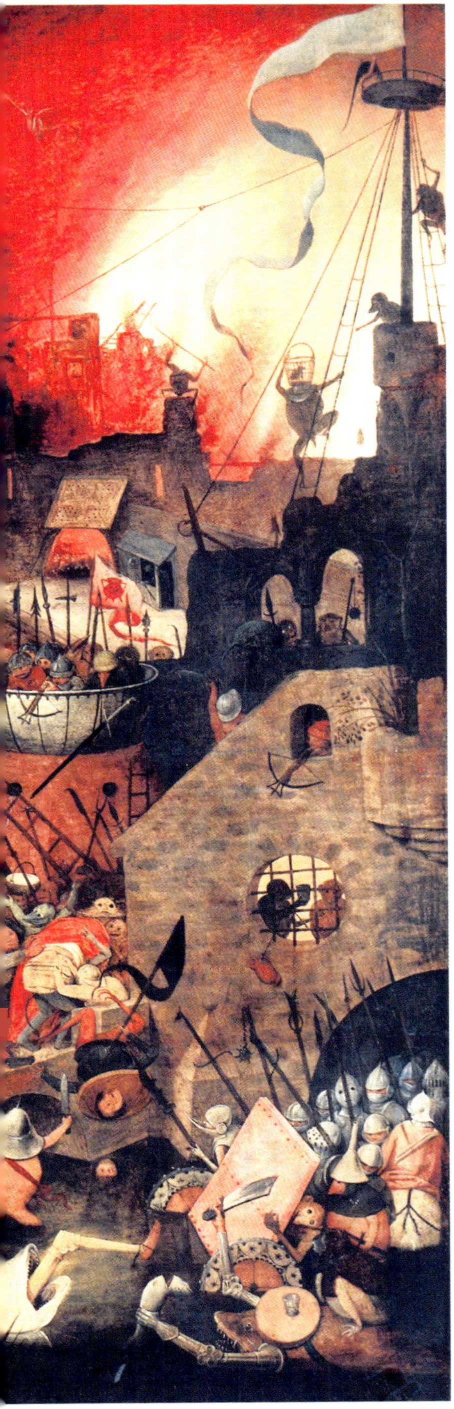

Pieter Bruegel the Elder: Dulle Griet, 1562

God's order is not in force here

The artists of the 16th century made the women in their paintings beautiful. In almost every case, women were celebrated – as nymphs, Venuses or richly bejewelled patricians, as Madonnas or martyrs. The painters thereby strove to match their models to an ideal of beauty.

Unembellished or deliberately repulsive women were the exception. Such images originated mainly north of the Alps. A picture by Dürer portrays a grinning, bare-breasted old woman with straggly hair and clutching a bag of money. Hans Baldung Grien executed a number of works on the theme of the *Stages of Life*, at least one of which shows women's bodies growing pronouncedly uglier as they grow older (cf. *What Great Paintings Say*, Volume II). But a truly very large painting, a panel measuring 115 by 161 centimetres, portraying the figure of Dulle Griet, "Mad Meg" – that was something unique even in the North. We have certainly yet to find anything similar, other than the second version of the same composition, also painted by Bruegel and today housed in Düsseldorf.

Everything about Dulle Griet flies in the face of aesthetic convention: no hair plays around her forehead, her skin looks grey, her toothless mouth is open, her clothes are shabby. There is no fullness or splendour to her bosom, which is hidden behind a breastplate hanging down over her stomach. And instead of turning graciously towards the viewer, she is running past with heavy steps.

Dulle Griet and the women behind her are nevertheless clearly human beings. The same cannot be said of the men. They ap-

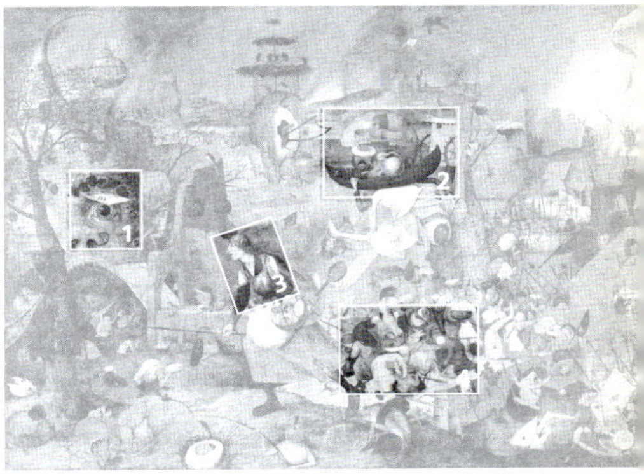

pear, at least in the foreground, as devils, demons, half-animals, and soldiers whose identity is completely concealed beneath their armour. Why this should be, and whether the chaotic landscape is part of Hell itself, the artist does not tell us. We have only a title, *Dulle Griet*, handed down via his first biographer. Uncertainty surrounds the date of the panel too. Art historians have settled upon 1562.

Jugs with a double meaning

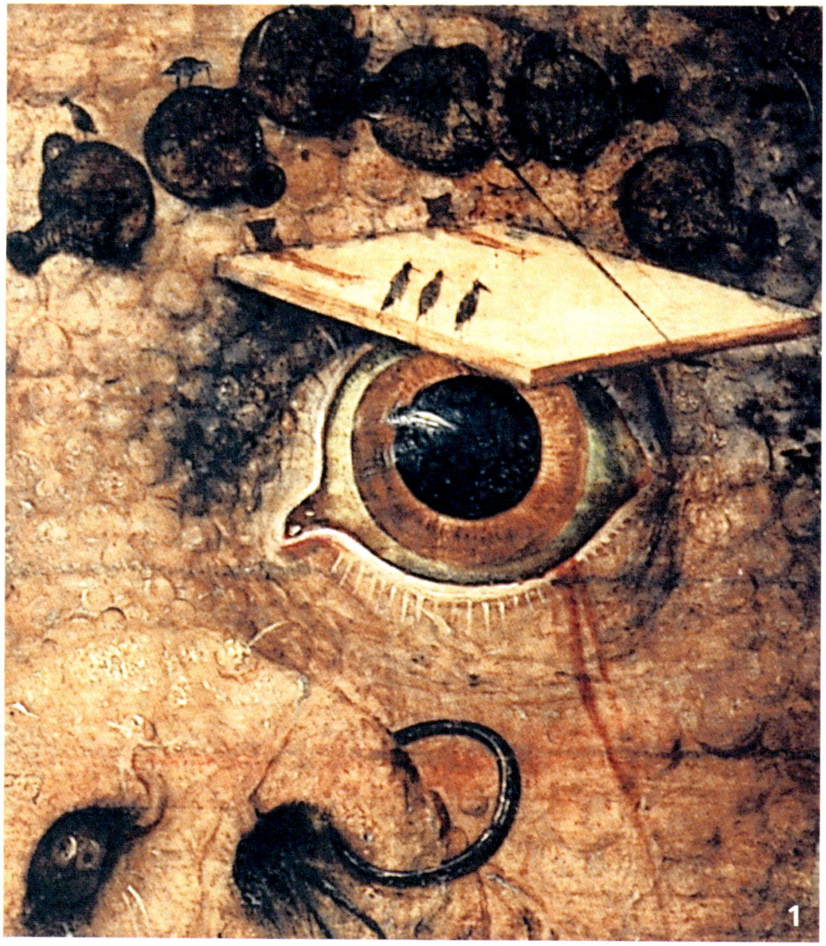
1

A board as an eyelid, a skin made out of stones, a tree growing out of the ear – the artist mixes organic and inorganic, allows animal and vegetable forms to grow together. This contradicts all experience. The order regulating our world seems to have been suspended. Contradicting the rules of nature, too, is the fact that the building representing the jaws of Hell appears as part of a creature and at the same time as a place. It is a head and the ruins of a castle. The crown on the forehead of this infernal prince is simultaneously a crenellated wall.

The eyebrows are made up of jugs. Just as they are suspended here against the masonry, so jugs in those days hung on the façades of many houses. They served as nesting boxes. Birds and bird's eggs added a touch of variety to an otherwise monotonous diet. Jugs are everywhere to be found in this picture. In the left-hand background, an enormous one stands in the landscape, not unlike the cooling tower of a modern-day nuclear power station. On the right, soldiers are sitting in a pot, and the jug appears again as their ensign on their flag. Dulle Griet, too, has gathered together several jug-like containers, one of them filled with coins.

Such a vast number of jugs in one composition is unlikely to be mere coincidence. In those days, in an age without glass bottles, tin cans or plastic bags, jugs were a handy container for foodstuffs. Obtaining and storing food took a great deal of effort and thought. Jugs thus played a central role in daily life.

But this isn't a scene from daily life, a genre picture; the jug is not just an object, but also a symbol. According to the pictorial convention of the day, it had two meanings. The first stems from the Bible. "There will always be plenty of ... oil left in your containers" promises the prophet Elijah in a period of great drought (I Kings 18:14), and at the wedding at Cana, Christ turns several jars of water into wine (John 2). Thus the jug made God's power visible.

Its second meaning arose out of its practical function. Since jugs were used for storage, full jars came to symbolize not only prosperity but also avarice. In old engravings, personifications of greed are usually accompanied – alongside sacks and chests – by jugs. Thus the jug would have reminded Bruegel's contemporaries not only of the omnipotence of God, but also of the demons of contemptible materialism. Which meaning was intended here can be easily deduced from the composition: Dulle Griet has gathered up all her household utensils, money and jewellery while, to the right of her, women are crowding around coins she has dropped.

It is a picture about avarice, about cupidity and greed. In the symbol of the jug, however, the religious connection is also established and the departure from God implied by the sin of greed made all the more clear. There are several further instances in this painting of objects that carry two meanings. The egg, for example, was considered a symbol of the Resurrection of Christ on Easter morning, and in other cultures too serves as a symbol of nature awakening in spring, of fertility and vitality. In Bruegel's bleak landscape, however, all the eggs are cracked. An ape-like demon creeps out of the double-walled egg in the background, while the egg at the bottom of the picture contains several chicks at once, in defiance of nature. The large figure on top of the house is shovelling money, money, money out of his egg-shaped behind – a perversion of the fertility symbolism. As in the mixture of organic and inorganic, God's order is not in force here.

The person shovelling money out of his own backside is carrying a ship containing a globe on his back. Hieronymus Bosch, whose work strongly influenced Bruegel's own, painted a similar motif, a St Christopher carrying on his shoulder a glass ball as a symbol of the world. Inside the ball sits the Infant Christ. Once again, a motif is turned on its head. In Bosch, the saint carries the Saviour; in Bruegel, the unsaintly figure is burdened by a globe containing only half-human creatures who are obviously consumed with gluttony and greed.

The ship, like the jug, also carried two meanings. As a positive symbol, it represented the Church, steering towards its heavenly goal through the currents of the day. Alternatively, it could represent the Ship of Fools, full of people with no idea where they are going, and unwilling to see that they are worshipping false idols such as Mammon. At some point they will meet with disaster. Neither ship nor globe is seated very securely on this back, either.

The concept of the Ship of Fools was at that time widely familiar. In Flanders such ships were towed through the streets during carnival parades, filled with people dressed in fools' costumes. 1494 saw the publication in Basle of *The Ship of Fools* by Sebastian Brant. In his book, which became a European bestseller, Brant describes over 100 different sorts of folly, many of them related to material greed. For example: "Money fools are everywhere, so many that they cannot be counted." Or: "A fool is someone who counts on getting someone else's inheritance."

Dulle Griet contains a second glass ball, which hangs like a Chinese lantern from the cap of the infernal head and contains naked human figures. Bosch, too, painted a number of transparent spheres containing humans or landscapes. Perhaps the globe motif developed out of the nimbus, or perhaps the imperial orb. It is also possible, however, that these balls came from the Far East. There they appear in much earlier art: a drawing dating from 1081, for example, shows a demon who has been trapped by the Buddha in a round glass vase. Another painting from 1160 shows a Buddhist saint in meditation; a transparent sphere surrounds his head and breast to indicate that he has removed himself from the outer world.

The possibility that western artists were familiar with such Asiatic motifs is a real one. Trade with the Far East, via the Mediterranean and the caravan routes, had been established for centuries, and the Crusaders who occupied Constantinople and fought for Jerusalem would undoubtedly have brought back works of art from other cultures as well as Islam.

There are two other details in Bruegel's panel which point to influences from outside Europe. Both are found on the infernal head: the ring through the side of the nose and the pointed cap, which is closely related to the Phrygian cap (Phrygia lay in western Asia Minor). Since all the peoples outside the Christian Occident were considered to be enslaved to the devil, Bruegel's deliberate embroidering of the face of Hell with non-European details is not implausible. It would also have had a contemporary relevance: in Bruegel's day, the Turks had occupied the Balkans and were threatening all of Christian Europe.

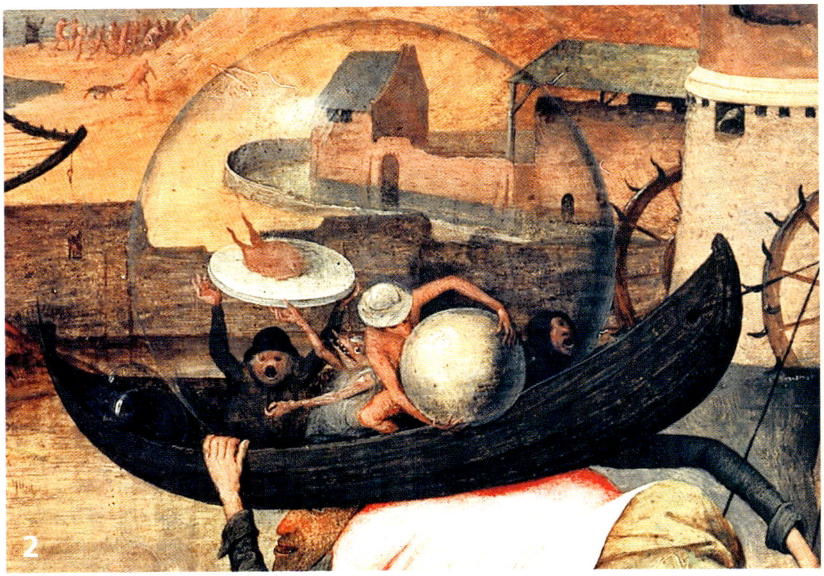

2

The world in the ship of fools

The central figure who gave her name to the painting was a character from Flemish folklore and frequently appeared in slapstick comedies and stories. As "Gret Sauermaul" (Meg Sour-mouth) she rowed with her husband, as "Schwarze Gret" (Black Meg) she pretended to be queen in her mistress's place. Outside Flanders, too, women who were particularly strong, aggressive or spiteful were given some form of the name Margaret. France had a "Margot-la-Folle" (Margaret the Mad), and "Mad Meg" and "Roaring Meg" were the nicknames in Scotland and Ireland for large guns.

The ghosts of two dangerous Margarets haunt the legends of northern Germany. One was the Countess Rantzau: "When Mad Margaret died, iron bands were placed around her coffin, and seven locks on the lid, to prevent her return ..." "Black Margaret" was the warring queen of Denmark, Norway and Sweden (1353–1412), whose military successes were put down to a pact with the devil.

It cannot be a coincidence that the name Margaret is so frequently connected with certain types of women, and it is likely that this is another instance in which an image from Christian tradition has been turned into its opposite. According to legend, St Margaret was a redoubtable woman who lived in Antioch in the 3rd century AD. The Roman governor tried to seduce her, but she resisted and proclaimed herself a Christian, giving the governor an excuse to arrest her. The devil appeared to her in prison in the shape of a dragon, which she put to flight with her cross. This model of courageous Christian behaviour was subsequently inverted into the terrifying image of a cantankerous, egotistical woman.

Bruegel's picture makes reference to everyday Flemish life not only through the figure of Dulle Griet herself, but also through a number of figures of speech that can be identified within the composition. The breastplate, for example, illustrates the Flemish expression "to get into armour", meaning to fly into a rage. Someone who sets about something with "iron gloves" is violent. To "mount a raid in front of Hell" means to defy the devil or to make a gain while ignoring danger. And a woman who ties the devil to a cushion – as is happening behind Dulle Griet – is brave, domineering or both.

At the same time as depicting a figure from folklore and "citing" colloquial idioms, however, Bruegel has also done something quite different: he has portrayed a madwoman. Psychiatrists have deduced from Dulle Griet's face and behaviour that she is suffering from a form of schizophrenia, which expresses itself in egocentricity and unsociability. Striding rapidly by, Dulle Griet seems unconnected either to the devils and demons or to the women behind her. She is alone. Schizophrenia is frequently characterized by a vacant, staring gaze, a neglect of one's hair and clothes, a fear of losing one's possessions and an inability to keep a grip on reality. For schizophrenics, their surroundings become a chaos full of threatening delusions. And this is precisely what Bruegel has painted.

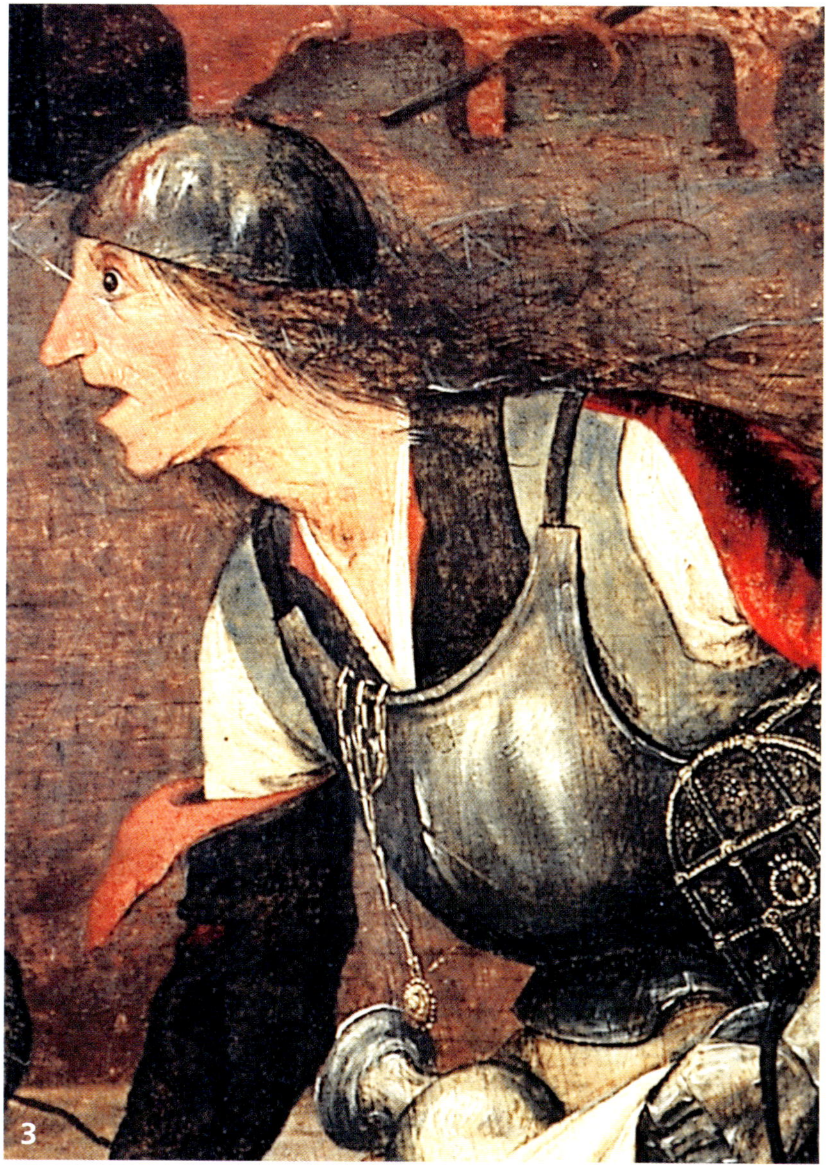
3

The mad and black Margaret

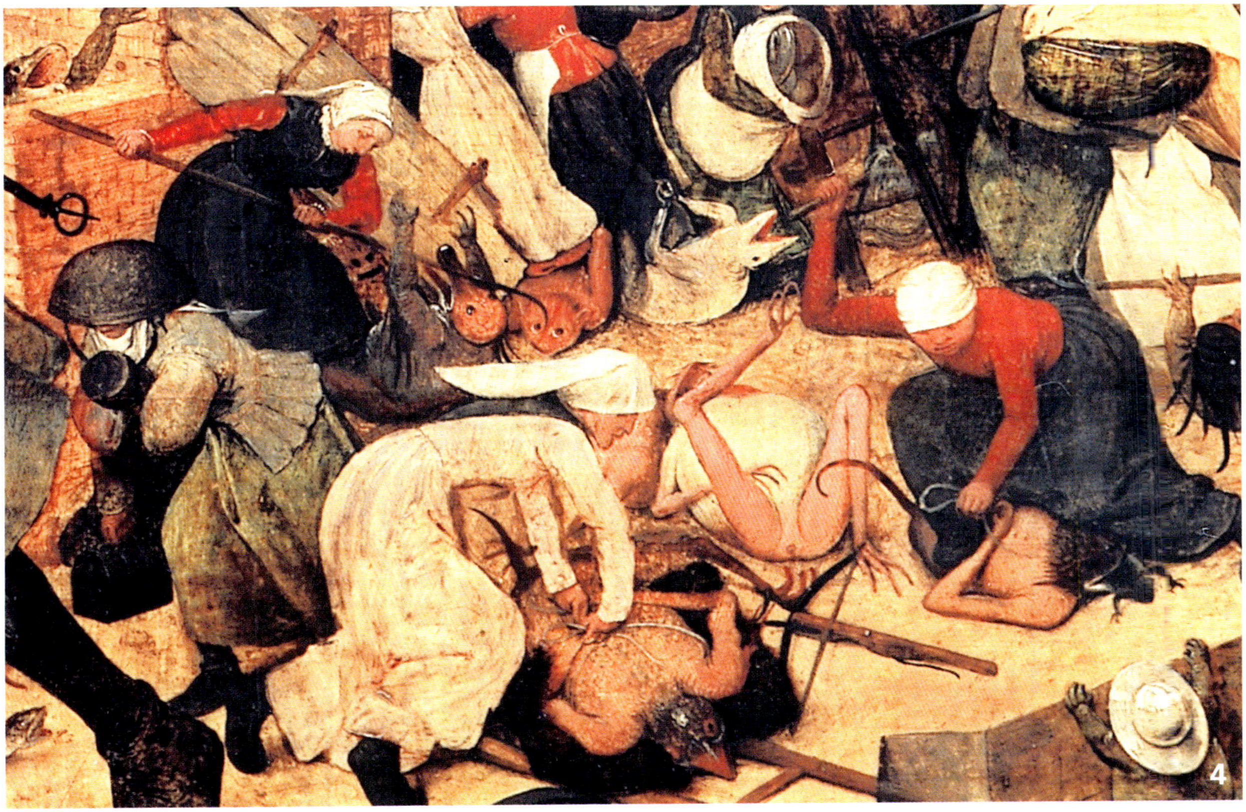

Wise women were persecuted

Bruegel left behind no commentary on this painting, and his first biographer established only its connection with Dulle Griet. We know, on the other hand, that it was common in the 16th century for pictures to contain hidden meanings, which had to be deciphered by the viewer. It was also said of Bruegel that he painted things that simply couldn't be painted. It seems fully permissible, therefore, to speculate about possible concealed messages in *Dulle Griet*.

The picture is dominated by women. In real life, however, it was men who ruled the roost. Women had few legal rights; they and their property were largely at the disposal of their fathers or husbands. In the late Middle Ages, it became increasingly difficult for many women to practise a trade; craftswomen were ousted by guilds. In the field of medicine, a similar shift occurred. The healing arts were now taught as a science at the universities, and the university doctors supplanted the folk medicine practised primarily by women.

It was the midwives and "wise women" who would become the prime victims of the witch-hunts instigated during the medieval Inquisition. They not only administered herbs and tinctures, but also uttered magic formulae that were incompatible with Christian teachings. They were also versed in methods of birth control. It was because of this, one recent theory argues, that they were persecuted by the Church – for the princes needed subjects. In the infamous *Hammer of the Witches*, a handbook compiled in 1487, it is clearly stated: "No one causes more harm to the Catholic faith than the midwives."

In the second half of the 16th century, witch-hunting reached a peak. This elimination campaign may have been precipitated by political concerns, but it was rooted in a much deeper bias against women. For in an important part of traditional Christian thinking, Eve was blamed for introducing temptation into the world. St Thomas Acquinas: "The relationship between woman and man is that of the imperfect and defective … to the perfect."

It is possible that Bruegel wanted to say something, in *Dulle Griet*, on the dangerous subject of witch-hunting or, more generally, about the defamation of women. For the men here are by no means more "perfect" than the women. On the contrary, men appear as devils and demons. The women have to protect themselves from these half-animals.

Bruegel has not presented the women in his picture as positive heroine figures, however. They overcome, but they do not triumph, nor do they win the sympathy of the viewer. The artist delivers no clear plea for a re-evaluation of women. As in many of his details, here, too, he is ambiguous. On the one hand, he shows women as superior. On the other, he seems to be saying that those who question male dominion and thereby the Christian world order are abnormal and even mad.

Pieter Bruegel the Elder: The Census at Bethlehem, 1566

A village in winter

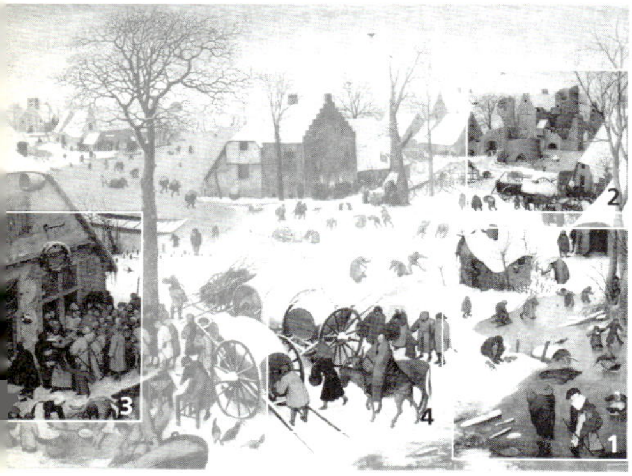

The sun is going down, the shadows are lengthening. In an hour it will be dark. The Flemish villages of 400 years ago had no street lighting, nor indeed did most of the cities. When night fell, the villagers withdrew into their houses. The rich could afford wax candles; the rest lit tallow candles, oil lamps and open fires – no more than emergency lighting by our own standards. There was little alternative but to go to bed.

Not that many people actually had a bed to climb into. Most slept on the ground in front of the fire, or on a bench or a sack of straw which was put away during the day. Even beds had only a sack of straw as a mattress. People slept and sat on hard furniture; upholstery was not yet invented. They slept in groups, usually with all the occupants of a house in one room, several in the same bed.

The farmhouses of this era were divided into three: one room for the animals, one room for the people, and the attic for straw, hay and supplies. Some also had cupboards and wardrobe beds. The heart of the house was the fireplace. It was used for cooking and roasting, and it was here that people ate, worked and slept. It was not yet customary to assign different functions – dining room, bedroom, living room – to different rooms, even in the larger homes of the wealthy. Nor was the right to privacy, to personal space, a feature of life in those days. That would not emerge until the 18th century.

Bruegel's villagers lived cheek by jowl. Their need for mutual protection – especially at night – and for mutual warmth was probably much greater than their need for solitude. Of that they had more than enough: their villages lay far apart, Europe was "empty", the roads unsafe. The population of the entire West only totalled some 80 million. That is approximately as many as in Germany today.

The few windows let in little light. The houses were dark inside even during the day. The poor light and cramped space drove people outside. As continues to be the case in southern countries, in the 16th century people further north, too, lived more on the streets, more out in the village square than inside their own homes. It was here that they did business, talked and played; it was here that a large part of social and professional life was based.

People also drank in the village square, despite the winter's cold. Someone is running a bar from the hollow trunk of a tree, with the tavern sign of a swan hanging above. The customers can warm themselves at the brushwood fire close by. On the very top of the tree sits a crow. In the contemporary language of symbols, hollow trees and crows signified something bad. Taverns were places of ill repute. Local respectable people didn't go there. They were for people passing through, travelling salesmen, itinerant students, people who earned their money in unknown ways, people who were invariably treated with suspicion by a close-knit village community. Standing around near "The Swan" are a number of soldiers with lances, perhaps the guard accompanying the census officials.

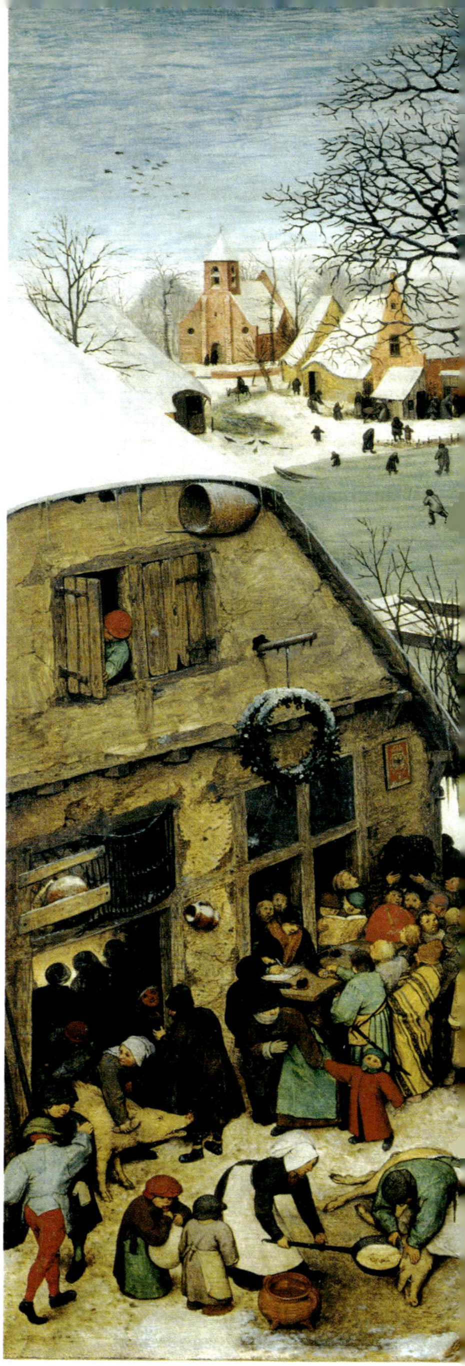

Most of the houses stand wall to wall; only the hut in the right-hand half of the picture lies well away from the rest. On its roof, an old basket without a bottom has been turned upside down to make a chimney. Attached to its gable is a cross. Its distance from the other buildings suggests that it houses a leper; the cross indicates that its inhabitant lives on alms.

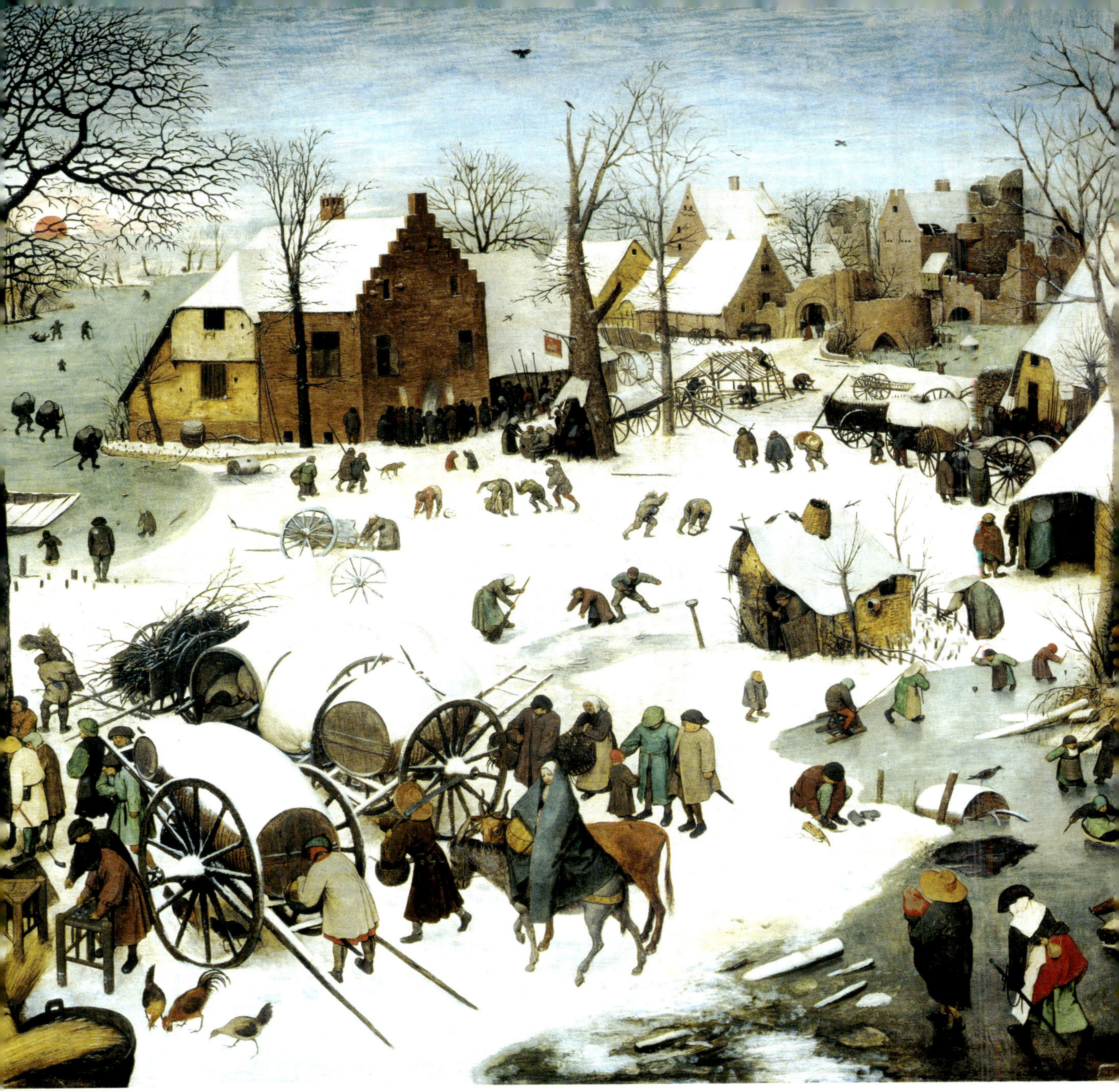

The wreath hanging from the building in the left-hand foreground indicates that this, too, is a tavern. The dilapidated condition of the building may be understood symbolically rather than literally: it reflects the bad reputation of drinking houses in general, and of this one in particular, as the temporary census office and the biblical inn, whose keeper shows Mary and Joseph to the stables. Whereby we may question whether a birth in a stable was really seen as something lowly either in Christ's own day or even in Bruegel's; for the large part of the population still lived in close proximity to their animals.

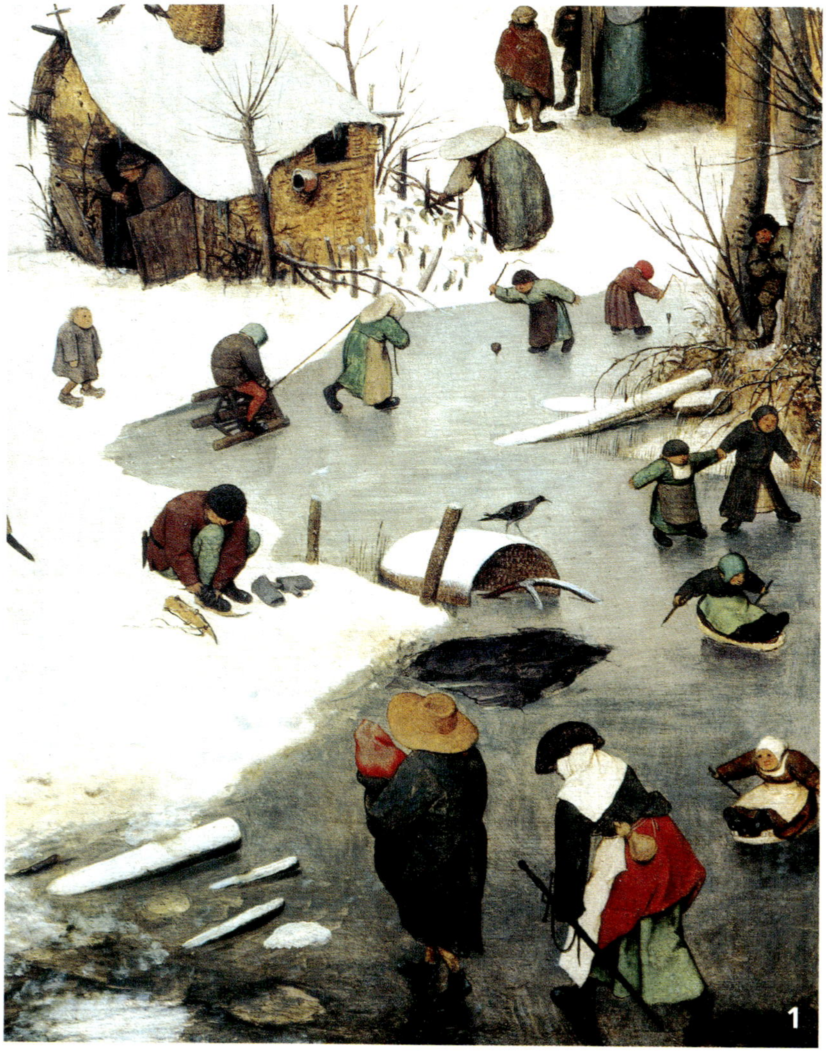

1

eaves of the tavern in the left-hand foreground hangs an old straw hive, and beside the door further below a jug – both intended as nesting boxes, and put up by people hoping to collect a few eggs or even eat the birds themselves. Meagre attempts to introduce some variety into a monotonous diet.

Childhood had not yet been discovered

Two little girls are pushing themselves on little sledges across the ice, while two more are spinning tops. The fact that they have toys to play with, however, was not typical in Bruegel's day. The grown-ups rarely made things solely for children. When children played, then with objects from the adult world. Typical of the things children used in games is the three-legged stool on which a boy is being pulled across the ice.

This lack of toys specially made for children had nothing to do with poverty, but with the general attitude towards the early years of life. Children did not get the affection given in small families today – there were too many of them for that, and too many who died. Childhood was not seen as a stage in its own right, with its own particular needs, but merely as a step along the road to adulthood. Bruegel, too, makes no great distinction in his pictures between the faces of children and those of grown-ups. Either he and his contemporaries had not yet noticed such differences, or they did not consider them important. Even the clothes the children wear are those of adults: the girl pulling the stool, and the two on the sledges, for example, are all wearing headscarves, dresses and aprons just like the women in the painting. Only the very youngest children wore special baby clothes; from the age of five at the latest, boys and girls wore the same as the grown-ups.

Nor were they treated very differently from adults: children naturally helped in the home or in the fields, as far as they were physically able. They went along to watch public executions, and were shielded neither from death nor reproduction in the crowded conditions in which they lived. The zone of protection erected around children and young people today

Meat is a luxury

In the Jewish town of Bethlehem, the consumption of pork is forbidden. This doesn't interest Bruegel; he paints a Netherlandish village in December, and the start of winter is traditionally a time when animals are slaughtered. Pigs in those days are estimated to have weighed a third less than today and were closer to wild pigs than to modern breeds. At the start of the summer they were driven out of the village into the woods, where they lived on what they could forage, mainly acorns. When the ground began to freeze, they were butchered.

Meat was expensive in the 16th century. There were many reasons for this. Passing armies, for example, fed themselves on whatever was to hand. Cattle were harder to hide than an emergency store of grain, and it took years to build up new herds. Drying, smoking and salting were the only known methods of preserving meat, whereby salt was expensive and salting only suitable for a few types of meat. Meat only became affordable to broad sections of the public all year round with the invention of the can. In Bruegel's day, the poor only had as much meat as they could eat at slaughtering time.

These poor, who made up the majority of the population, lived chiefly on cereals, pulses, milk, eggs and honey. Under the did not exist for them. Not even in front of the judge. A 12-year-old could be punished in exactly the same way as a 22-year-old.

Schooling was a relatively new thing in the 16th century. In the Middle Ages, "instruction" was given to only a very few children, mostly those destined for the clergy. With the Renaissance and the Reformation, the need for education grew: thanks to Luther, Zwingli and Calvin, lay people could read the Bible themselves – they just had to learn to read first. The expanding economy and the rise in international trade also demanded an ability to be able to write and add up – parties separated by substantial geographical distances could only agree terms by letter and in figures. After lengthy stagnation in the Middle Ages, the Renaissance brought with it a boom in education. It developed very unevenly, faster in the towns than in the country, and sooner in the economically advanced parts of Europe than in the backwaters. The Netherlands ranked amongst the prosperous regions of Europe. An Italian visiting in the 16th century reported that everyone in Flanders could already read and write – almost certainly an exaggeration.

But let as assume that lessons were also held in the Flemish village painted here by Bruegel. They would have taken place either in the village square or in some room or stable; even the towns rarely had a purpose-built school. Pupils wrote on slates. The teacher had no formal training and knew only a little more than his students. He was paid in kind. Elementary schooling lasted about two years and only took place when the children weren't needed to work at home or in the fields. After these two years, by which time the children were seven or eight, for most of them their education was over. Only a very few boys, supported by their families or the Church, went on to attend the municipal grammar schools.

The dilapidated towers and walls beyond the moat belong to a castle. In the Middle Ages, it offered the villages protection. Those times were past. The small parties of knights who used to fight each other, lay siege to each other's castles and steal each other's cattle had given way to armies of mercenaries with muskets and canon, against whom the old castle walls were no match.

The castles had fallen into ruin for other reasons, too. In the Middle Ages, the lord of the manor was usually the "owner" of the village and its inhabitants. He could demand unpaid labour with or without a team of animals and could refuse someone permission to marry or to leave the community. Over the course of time, however, feudalism began to lose its hold and in the 16th century was entirely abolished in the progressive Netherlands. In 1531 all landowning lords were reminded that they were expressly forbidden to demand gifts or compulsory service. The people in this picture are no longer serfs.

Just as the abolition of serfdom reduced the power formerly wielded by the local lords, so too did the new role of money. Money had always been in circulation, but on a small scale. With the upswing in international trade and the advance of industrialization, it now grew in volume and significance. In the Middle Ages, the measure of a person's wealth was the extent of his land holdings, the number of villages and communities he "owned". There now emerged a new measure: money and goods. The people handling these and getting rich on them were members not of the nobility but of a new, middle class. Businessmen and bankers amassed fortunes and lent them out to customers who included nobles, more and more of whom were having to sell off their castles and estates. It is quite possible that one of the farmers in this picture leases his land not from the lord of the run-down castle but from a citizen in a neighbouring town. Perhaps he has even bought his fields himself.

Feudal castles collapse

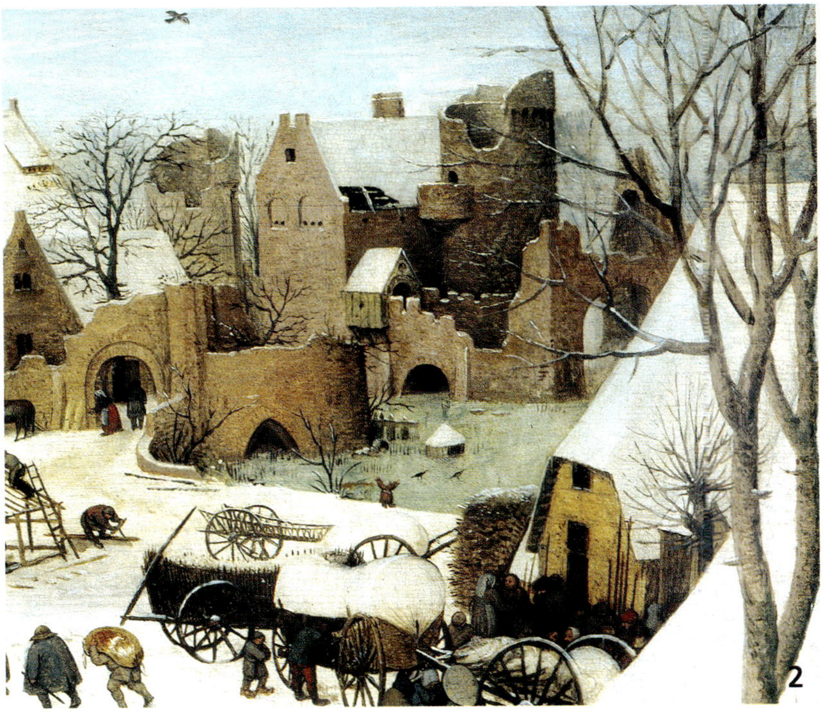

2

The double-headed eagle in Bethlehem

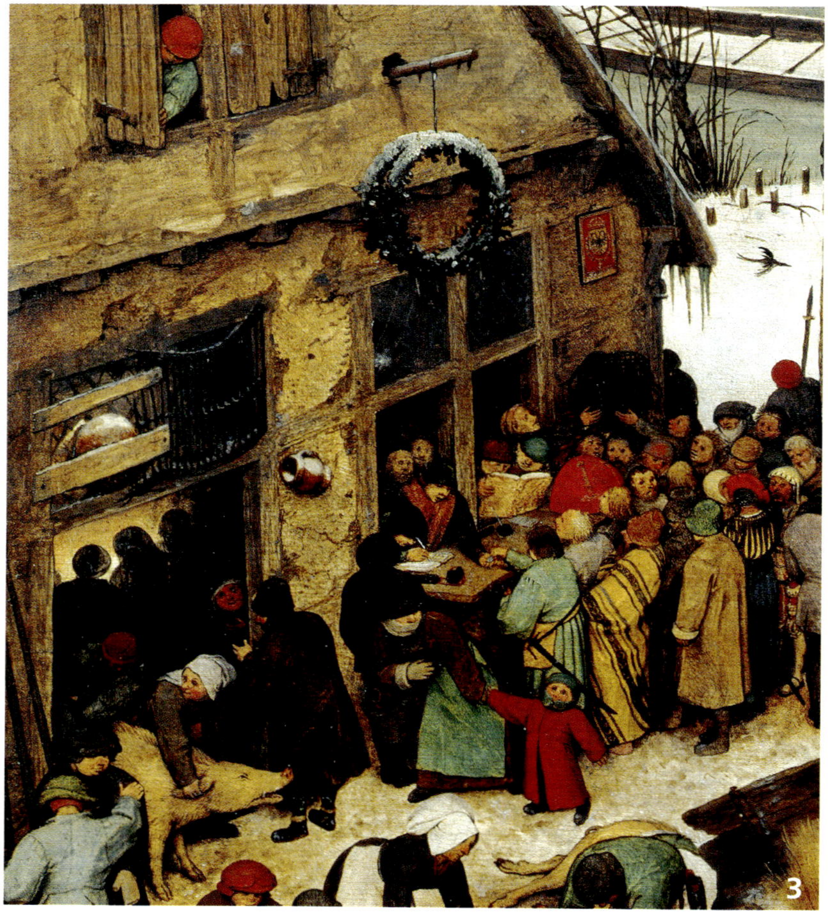

3

The ruling nobility thus saw its power diminished by the loss of its serfs, by the new role of money and by the accompanying growth of the middle classes in the cities. If it was curtailed from "below", it was also curtailed from "above" by the tendency of the kings to centralize power in their lands, to rule directly rather than via princes, dukes, counts and barons. In the 17th century, this trend towards absolutism would reach its climax under Louis XIV of France. In Bruegel's picture, the plaque bearing the double-headed eagle, hung on the front of the inn near the census officials, testifies to a similar desire by a sovereign to be personally present throughout the realm.

Bruegel's sovereign was the Habsburg Philip II in Madrid, whose empire comprised possessions in Austria and Italy, Burgundy, the Spanish heartlands of Castille and Aragon, and the Netherlandish provinces. It was an empire assembled through marriage and inheritance, scattered across half of Europe and expanded by conquests in South America; an empire in which "the sun never sets" but which is barely governable. Philip's representative in the Netherlands was not one of the local lords, but a relative, Margaret of Parma.

It was Philip's father, Charles V, who had secured the supremacy of the king and emperor by depriving the nobility of its political power, at least within Spain itself. In the Netherlands, however, neither he nor Philip succeeded in this to the same degree. Philip's crest hangs on the front façade, nevertheless. Together, the double-headed eagle and the ruined castle signal something of contemporary political reality in this wintery village, seemingly so far from the world of politics.

Also part of contemporary political reality is the money on the counter. The men using the tavern as their office are taking payments and writing things down in a big book. Bruegel has probably painted not one of the rare population censuses, but the annual collection of tax. Since the clergy and the nobility did not have to pay anything, the burden of taxation fell upon merchants, artisans and peasants. And it was a heavy burden. Charles V had already identified the Netherlands as a rich source of income; according to the Venetian ambassador Navagero, the Netherlands paid half the tax revenues of the entire Habsburg empire and four times as much as the Spanish themselves. When the Duke of Alba then came and tried to impose an additional tax – 10% on all goods sold – the Netherlanders finally rose up in rebellion.

Population censuses counted not people but hearths, households. Much to the sorrow of later statisticians. The smallest social unit was not the family but the household, which included maids, apprentices, journeymen and stable lads as well as two or three generations of one family – everyone, in other words, who lived in the house. With the high rate of infant mortality and an average life expectancy of just 32 years, a population census would anyway have become rapidly out of date. Nor were the rulers of the day interested in their subjects as individuals. They only wanted to know the number of production units, which were the households. For "hearth counting" became the basis on which taxation was calculated.

No information regarding population figures can be found in church records, either. Priests were not yet obliged to register births and deaths. Since nothing was written down, we may assume that many of Bruegel's contemporaries didn't even know in what year they were born. And why should they, indeed? No official ever asked to know it. The year of a person's birth only became an important, indeed decisive figure when it became the basis on which their whole lives were calculated – from their entry into school to their eligibility for military service, the right to vote and ultimately retirement. Whether Bruegel knew how old he was is thus also uncertain. He makes no mention of his age anywhere.

Bruegel portrays Mary and Joseph no larger than the other figures, nor does he place them in the centre of the composition or emphasize them by means of colour, dress or haloes. They are people amongst the crowd; it is almost as if Bruegel has hidden them.

He painted the picture in 1566, a difficult time for the Catholic Church in the Netherlands. One year previously, Calvinist masses had torn down and destroyed all the works of art in the Catholic churches – in protest at their pomp, and in protest, too, at the power of a Church which would tolerate no others. In August 1566 the Calvinists vented their fury not just on objects, but also on monks. The anti-Catholic uprising spread. Governor Margaret of Palma sought to defuse the situation by allowing the Protestant groups to build their own churches and by no longer hounding their preachers. She made concessions. In distant Madrid, Philip refused to tolerate such leniency. It contradicted his absolutist philosophy, and it also contradicted the task he had inherited, namely to spread the Catholic faith with all the forces at his disposal, with the cross and the sword. He would rather sacrifice 100,000 people than tolerate heresy in the Netherlands, Philip said. He dispatched the Duke of Alba with an army. In 1567 Margaret stood down, Alba took over, and the Netherlanders rose up. The ensuing war of liberation from Spanish-Habsburg hegemony would last over eighty years.

With his "secularization" of Mary and Joseph, Bruegel was responding not to the current situation in 1566, but rather to the epoch in which he lived and worked and which made that situation possible – the dawn of the Renaissance. In the Middle Ages, paintings were dominated by their biblical subjects; all worldly detail was either omitted altogether or was relegated to a position of minor importance, minor interest. In the 15th and 16th century, this perception changed. The world of the Bible and the Christian authorities gave way to a new reality, that of the natural scientists – critical observers of animals, plants and people, of the stars and the times of day, and even of such banal processes as the collection of taxes and the slaughtering of pigs.

Mary and Joseph in the crowd

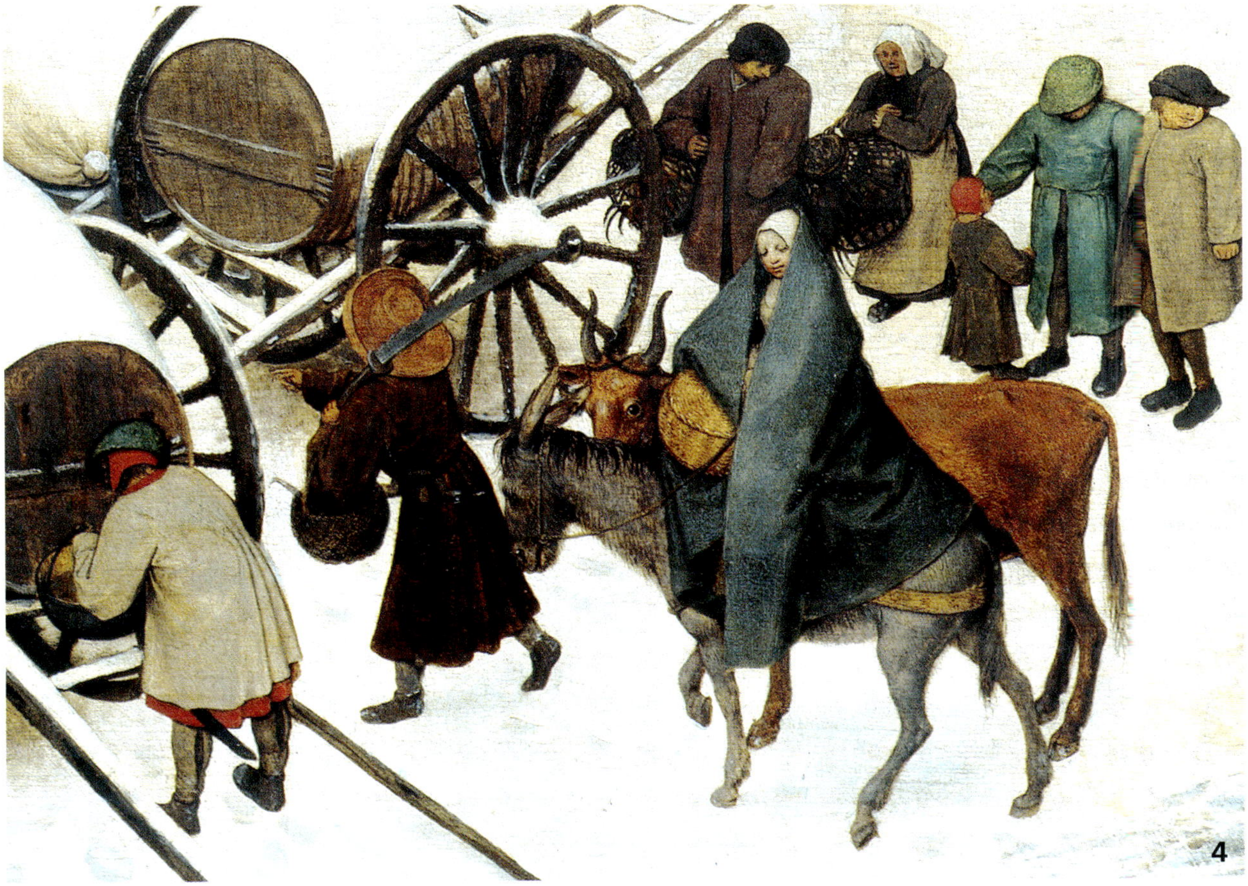

4

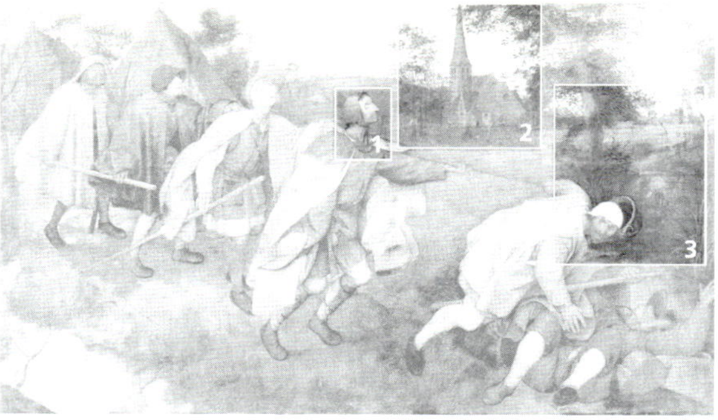
1
2
3

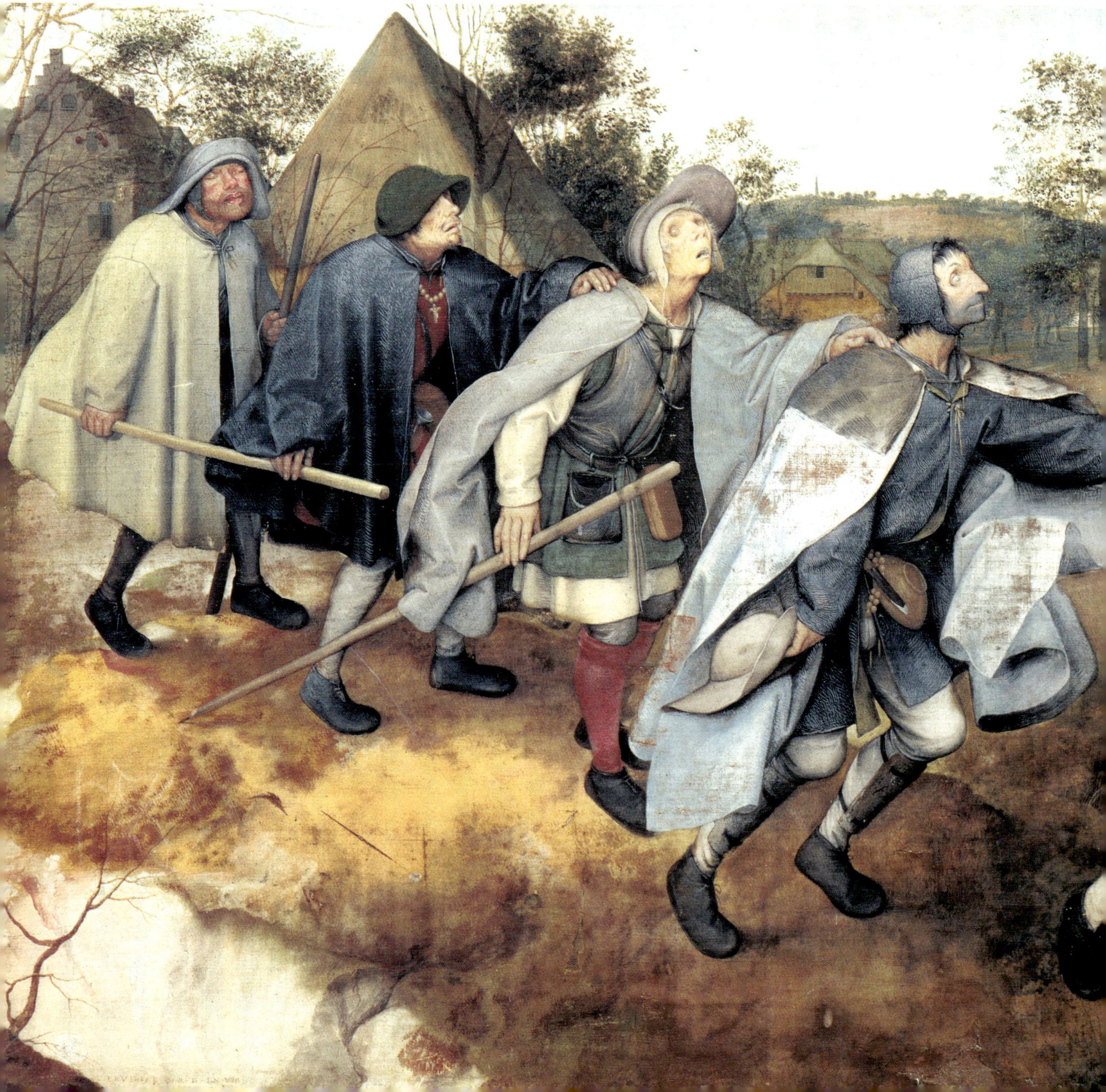

Pieter Bruegel the Elder: The Blind Leading the Blind, 1568

A downward path

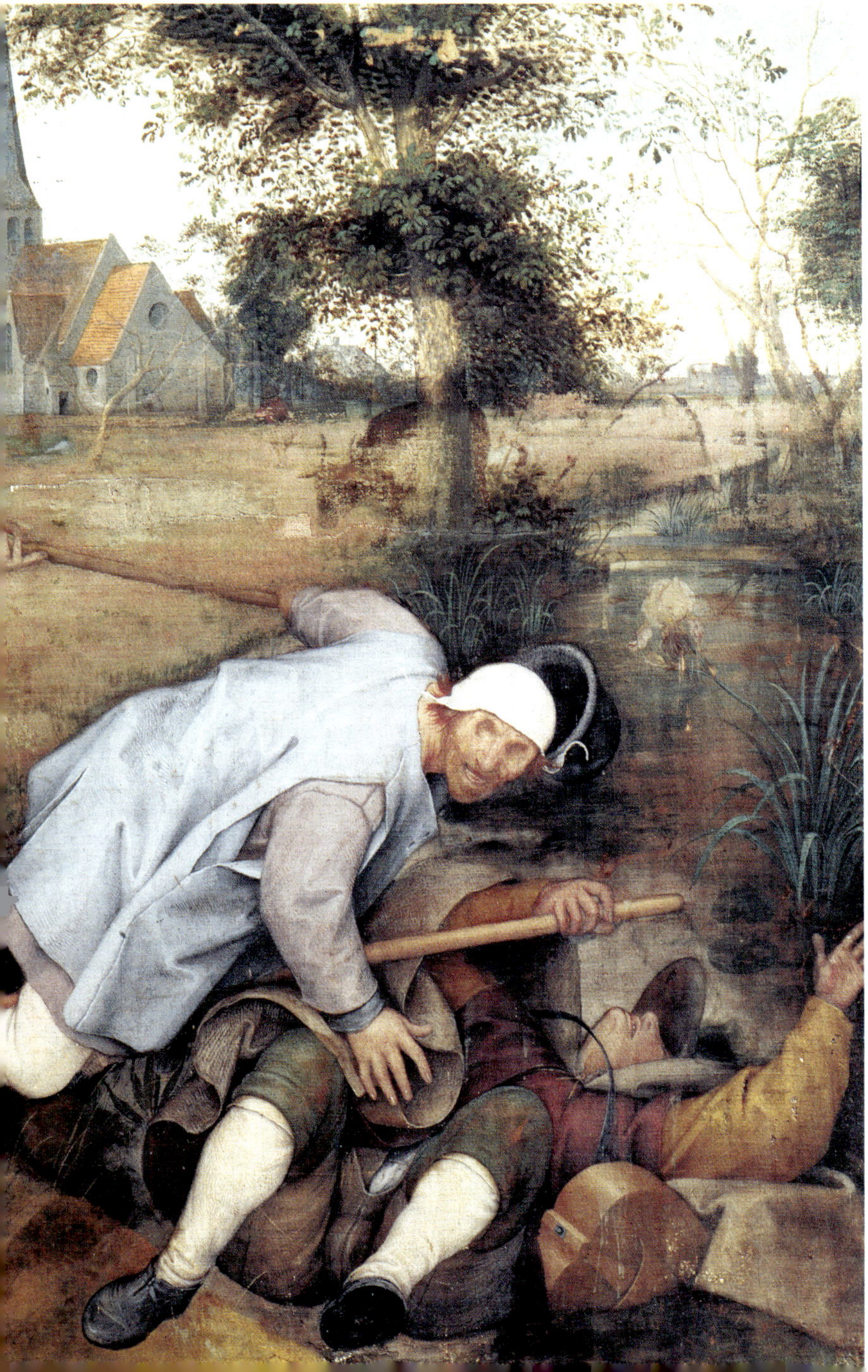

Pieter Bruegel the Elder executed this painting in 1568, the year before his death. His precise date of birth is unknown, but he was probably not much older than 40 when he died.

In 1563, following his marriage, Bruegel moved to Brussels. Brussels was the administrative capital and seat of government of the Spanish rulers, to whose empire the Netherlands belonged. A year before Bruegel painted *The Blind Leading the Blind*, the Duke of Alba had arrived with his troops; on behalf of the Spanish king, he was to wipe out every heretic in the Netherlands – Calvinists, Lutherans and Anabaptists – along with anyone who dared oppose Spanish hegemony.

In 1568, the year in which the present painting arose, Brussels was in the grip of a reign of Spanish terror. In January, eighty-four of its citizens were publicly executed, and two months later more than 1500 Netherlanders were arrested. On Whit Sunday two leading aristocrats, Count Egmond and Count Horne, were beheaded on the orders of Alba's "blood council".

The painting, which measures 86 by 154 centimetres, takes its subject from the Gospel of St Matthew. In Chapter 15, Jesus says of the Pharisees: "They are blind guides leading the blind, and if one blind person guides another, they will both fall into a ditch."

Which leader truly had vision, which was the right party – these were acutely relevant questions in the Netherlands of Bruegel's day, and many citizens, the artist undoubtedly amongst them, were afraid of heading down the wrong path and bringing disaster upon themselves.

Before his death, Bruegel asked his wife to burn a number of preliminary drawings on which he had made notes, so that they should not be made public. Although he adopts no political stance in the painting itself, or at least not one that is obvious, he may well have been influenced by the political situation, by now hurtling towards catastrophe.

Bruegel presents the six blind men as disfigured and destitute beggars. In classical antiquity, the blind were portrayed in a completely different light: in Greek myth, for example, men such as Teiresias assumed even greater stature as a consequence of their blindness. Zeus gave him the gift of prophecy, and Teiresias and blind singers were considered particularly accomplished.

In the Christian world view of the Middle Ages, there was no room for the gifts of the Greek gods. But the blind were still needed in order to demonstrate miraculous cures. Popular amongst artists thereby was the story of blind Bartimaeus, who implored Jesus to restore his sight. "And Jesus said to him, 'Go your way. Your faith has healed you.'" (Mark 10: 52) As in the case of Jesus' description of the Pharisees as "blind guides leading the blind", these words were interpreted to mean that only those with the correct faith could truly see.

The leaders of the Reformation in the 16th century had little regard for miracles and saints. As a consequence, *The Blind Leading the Blind* became a subject rarely painted in Protestant regions, and it disappeared from art even in Catholic parts. But the false guides were frequently cited in the religious and polemical writings of such as Martin Luther: "and let the Pope remain a blind leader of the blind".

Although the subject is treated in two engravings by an earlier Netherlandish artist, Bruegel's is the oldest known painting of *The Blind Leading the Blind*. Instead of portraying people who have been enriched by the gifts of Zeus or Christ, he paints beggars who stumble and fall, who feel their way helplessly through the countryside and who pull each other over.

No artist before or since has painted blind people so realistically and so powerfully as Pieter Bruegel in Brussels in 1568.

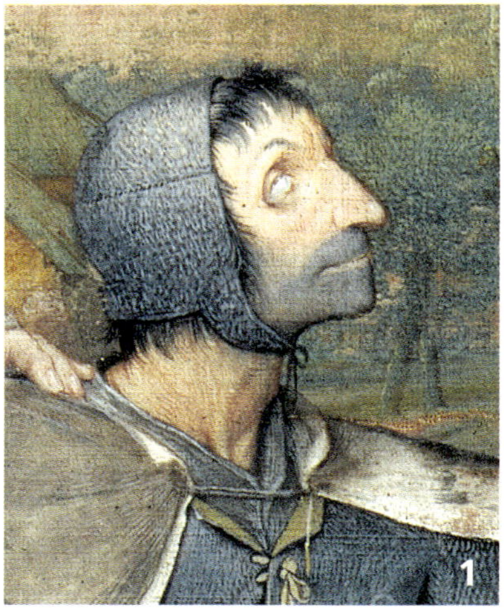

Bruegel looks the blind in the eye

In the era before Bruegel, the blind were typically characterized in art by closed eyelids. Only the fact that they couldn't see was of interest, not the medical reason why. Bruegel took a closer look.

His curiosity fell in line with the growing contemporary interest in the real world. After the theological orientation of the Middle Ages, with the advent of the Renaissance nature and the globe had once again become objects of scientific enquiry. Bruegel has portrayed the eyes of his blind with such accuracy that experts can today diagnose their conditions. The man with the blue cap, for example, is suffering from black cataracts, the one behind him has corneal leukaemia, and the one in front of him has had his eyes gouged out, either in a fight or as a punishment.

A medical textbook of 1585 lists 113 diseases of the eye. Research and cataloguing were primarily the concern of universities, however, and between them and hands-on medicine there yawned a wide gap. University-trained doctors considered surgical intervention, in particular, a menial job that should be left to others. The majority of these others were barber-surgeons and charlatans who travelled from country fair to country fair, offering their services, selling herb mixtures and proffering advice. They recommended, for example, drinking the urine of red-haired men, since this was the best "for fistulas, rashes and clouding of the eye, in order to remove the cataract and stop the weeping".

Blind people were a much more familiar sight in the 16th century than they are today. People spent more of their lives outdoors, and the proportion of blind people within the population was greater.

The situation may be compared with that in some of the developing African nations today: lack of hygiene was one of the chief causes of blindness in Bruegel's day, too. Since little was to be expected of doctors and fairground healers, people pinned their hopes for a cure on God and his saints, as sanctioned by the Catholic Church.

People suffering from eye complaints prayed especially fervently to St Lucy. A powerful heathen had wanted to marry her for her beautiful eyes and demanded that she renounce Christianity. Instead, Lucy tore out her eyes and sent them to the heathen, telling him that he now had what he wanted, but that she would stay true to her faith. This act, so the story goes, converted the heathen to Christianity, and Lucy's eyes grew back again.

In those days there were patron saints and legends associated with every infirmity, and they preoccupied the minds of sufferers at least as much as the cause of their illness and the means of its cure. The grounds on which saints became the patrons of specific medical conditions were sometimes strange: in Germany, for example, those afflicted by blindness prayed to St Augustine because his name begins with "Aug" – meaning "eye" in German.

In the absence of other statistical data, the numbers of such patron saints allow us to draw certain conclusions about the distribution of illness in the 16th century. There were no less than 123 saints associated with fevers, i.e. with inflammations and infections of all kinds, while the assistance of fifty-three different saints could be invoked against the plague. Forty-nine were associated with illnesses of the head and forty-seven with eyes conditions.

Eye complaints thus fell into the top group of 16th-century illnesses. There were thirty-seven saints for epilepsy, twenty-three for gout, twenty for gallstones, and so on. None of these patrons appears in Bruegel's work. The few saints he paints are taken from the Bible, not Catholic tradition.

The church in this picture is one of the most fought over in art history. It has been interpreted in at least three different ways.

According to the first of these, the church proves that the painting was intended to serve the viewer with a moralistic Christian warning. By deliberately placing the church above a gap in the human chain, so the argument goes, Bruegel is saying that, while the first two blind men are lost without hope of redemption, those behind them might still be saved by the Church.

The second interpretation sees the painting arguing not for but against the Church. For the 16th-century equivalent of the Pharisees – the "blind guides leading the blind" in St Mark's Gospel – were the priests and monks of the Catholic Church. The withered tree in front of the church signals that the Church is useless, dead, rotten.

According to the third voice in the debate, the church should not be considered a symbol at all, but quite simply part of the village architecture. Almost every one of Bruegel's paintings and engravings portraying a village also includes a church – precisely as was the case in the Netherlands of the artist's day.

It is a fact that religion and the Church decisively influenced the course of the 16th century. The corruption of the papacy sparked the Reformation, spearheaded by Martin Luther, Ulrich Zwingli and John Calvin, and this was followed in turn by the Counter-Reformation, in which Catholic rulers sought to crush their Protestant counterparts.

Raging around Bruegel, in particular, was the war being waged by the Spanish kings against the political and religious revolt by the Netherlands. Depending on the city or province in which a church stood, it might be used by either Protestants or Catholics. In this respect it was truly fought over.

The new teachings of the Reformation affected the blind in a very direct way. Since they were unable to work, the blind were dependent upon alms. In the past, giving money to those in need had been one of the "good works" through which, according to Catholic thinking, people could cleanse themselves of sin and earn themselves a place in Paradise. The leaders of the Reformation argued, however, that God alone decided who would go to Heaven. There was no longer any personal benefit to be gained from good deeds. One of the major incentives behind acts of charity was thus taken away, and life for the many beggars in front of the churches and monasteries became correspondingly harder.

It became harder, too, because Protestants dissolved the Catholic monasteries and nunneries and seized the assets and estates of the Catholic churches. City-based charitable organizations took over from religious associations and endeavoured to look after the beggars wandering the countryside. Their numbers were large, especially in the forward-looking Netherlands, where serfdom had been abolished and with it the responsibility of landowners for their subjects. While townspeople were willing to given alms to their own poor, non-locals were expelled after just a few days. People didn't trust them, nor could they be sure if they were really as poor or sick as they said they were. People with a roof over their head would have reacted with suspicion rather than sympathy at the sight of a party such as the six blind men here.

Justification for their reaction was provided, furthermore, by Calvin's theory of predestination. Calvin argued that the life of each individual was foreordained by God. Those who were rich need not be ashamed of their wealth (provided they gave a tenth of their profits to the Church), for God had accorded them money and possessions.

The miserable plight of those who were sick, crippled or blind, on the other hand, was also willed by God. According to Calvin's harsh teachings, such men and women simply had to accept the fate that God had inexplicably assigned to them.

The Church and the poor

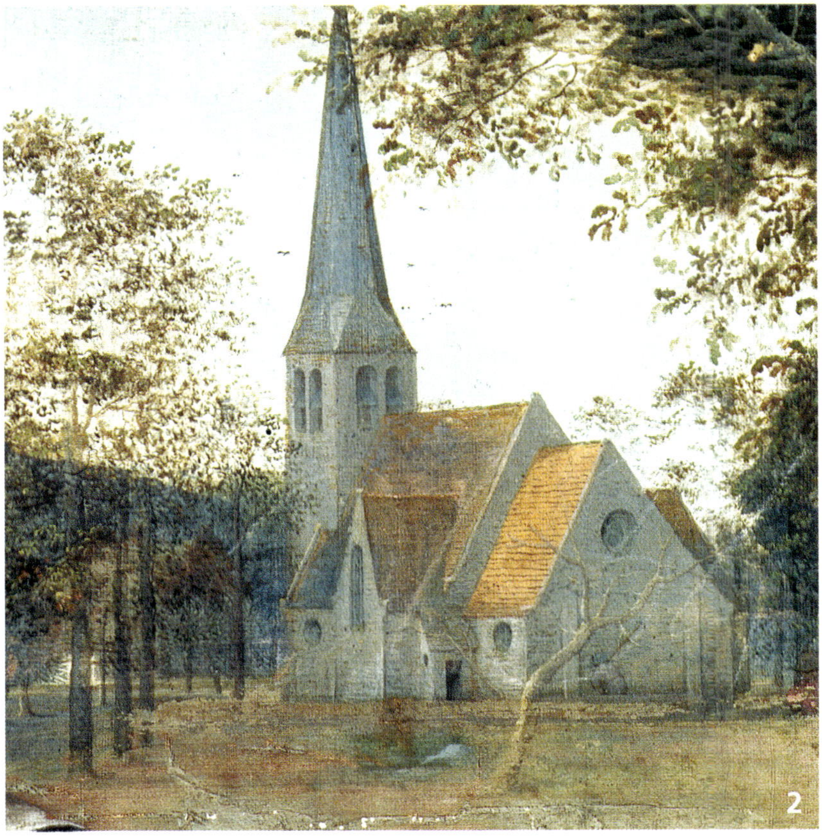

Whether Bruegel was a Calvinist or whether he remained a true son of the Catholic Church throughout his life, we do not know for sure. To judge by his pictures and his friends, however, if he was Catholic, he was a critical one to say the least. For none of his surviving paintings fits into the educational or morally instructive programme of the Church, and even when he paints biblical subjects, he usually conceals them within the composition in such a way that they appear incidental.

A number of men in his circle, such as the cartographer Abraham Ortelius and the poet and philosopher Dirck Volckertszoon Coornhert, reveal themselves as Stoics in their writings, and it is probable that Bruegel, too, embraced some of the ideas of the ancient philosophers. The Stoics believed, for example, that the universe is governed by an ordering power that assigns a place and destiny to every living creature. The virtue of man lies in calmly submitting to his fate. To relate this to our picture: loss of sight is willed from on high and a blind person is therefore not to be helped. This notion of destiny is similar to Calvin's theory of predestination; both encourage a distanced, entirely unsentimental attitude towards beggars and the disabled.

This attitude is apparent, too, in Bruegel's portrayal of the blind men. The artist could have portrayed the stumbling men in such a way as to evoke sympathy and compassion in the viewer. The opposite is true. He shows them – more or less – as rogues, as people thoroughly capable of violence and deceit. Empty eye sockets, in particular, would have been immediately associated with punishment or fighting and would have been seen as something a person had brought upon himself. This attitude, so heartless by our own standards, is also found in literature. Around 1553, the *Tale of the Life of Lazarillo of Tormes* was published in Antwerp by an unknown author. In this story, Lazarillo is a youth who is brought up as a guide to a blind man. He sees the tricks and pretences the blind man uses to make his living and comes to the conclusion: "Since the Creation of the World, God has created no one more full of cunning, more sly or more wicked than he was."

The book went through several editions and in 1554 also appeared in Spain, where as in the Netherlands – and despite being banned by the Grand Inquisitor – it quickly joined the ranks of the popular bestsellers, comparable with *Till Eulenspiegel* ("Till the Prankster") in Germany, for example. Till's practical jokes were not invented but recorded in Braunschweig around 1510. Amongst those who Till hoodwinked were a group of blind people. He promised them money, and since each one thought Till had already given the money to another of their party, they ate a lavish meal only to find themselves unable to pay and thus looking like swindlers. A story of a similar prank also circulated in France. To make a joke at the expense of a blind person was allowed; it was considered funny.

Bruegel's paintings also seem to have brought a smile to people's faces. His first biographer tells us that he was called "Pieter the Droll" by many, a nickname derived from the fact, he explains, that there are only a few paintings by Bruegel "which the viewer can look at soberly without laughing".

Laughing at *The Blind Leading the Blind*? For the modern viewer, that is hard to imagine. But those were the days when dwarves and idiots were kept at court as forms of entertainment. The tendency was the same: the sophisticated laughed at the less sophisticated, at those who were supposedly uncouth, clumsy, ignorant. Even today, children are not the only ones who snigger when someone trips and falls in a puddle.

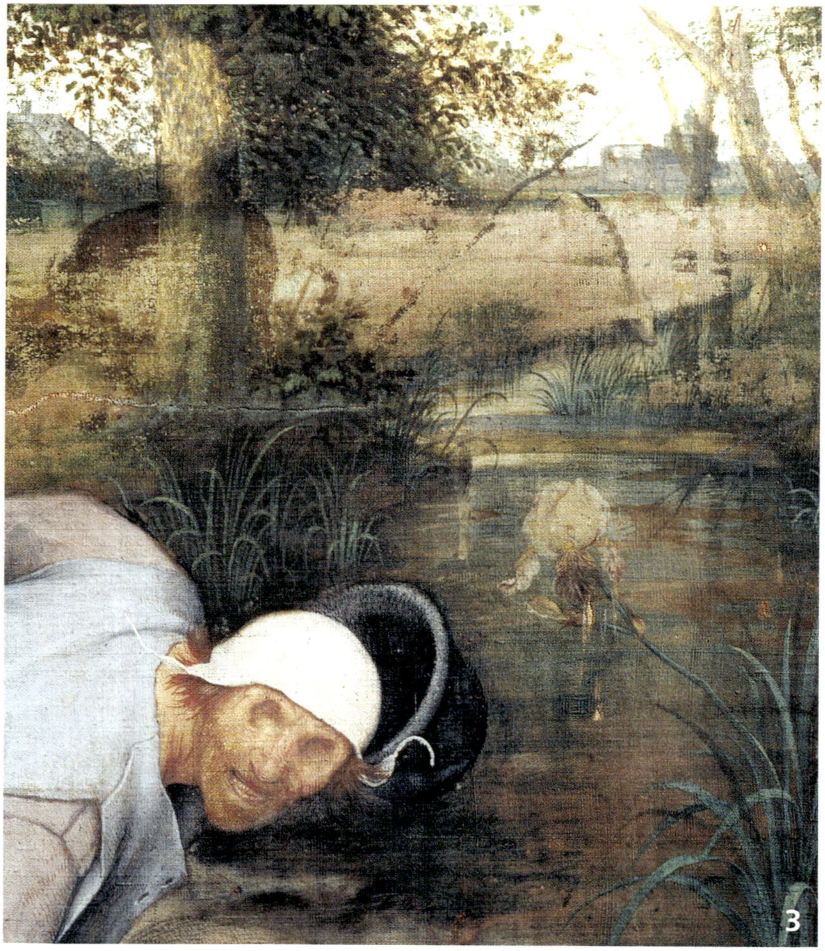

No room for sympathy

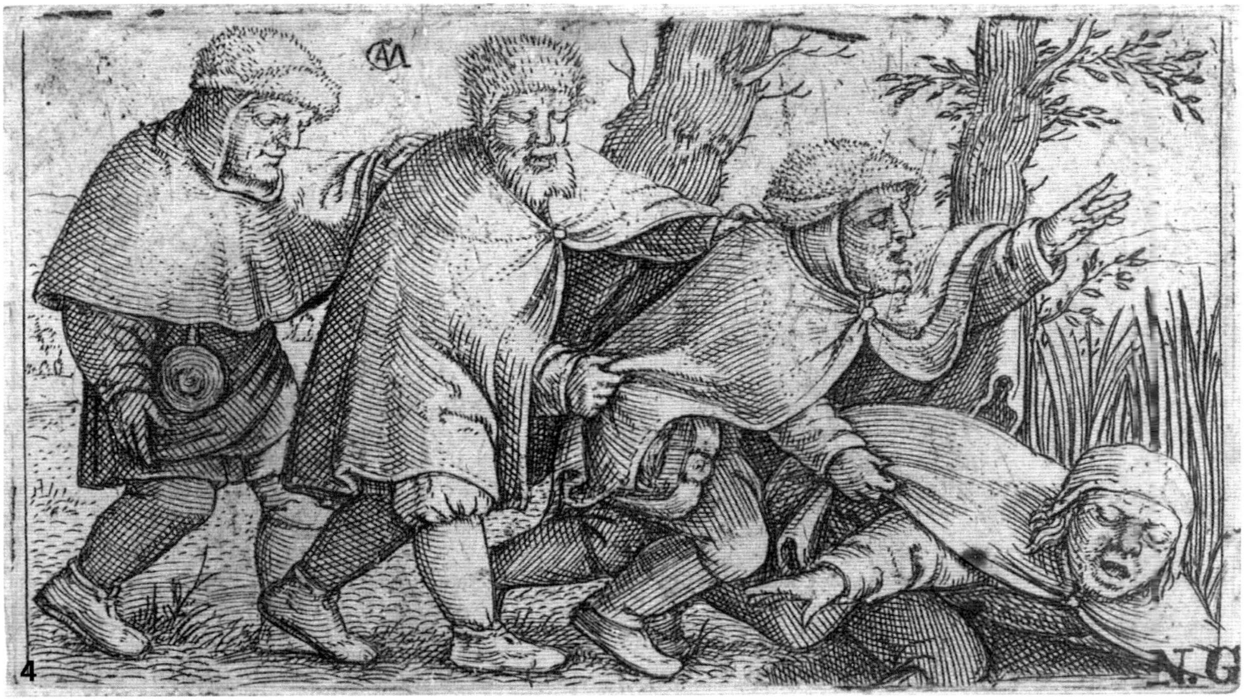
4

The subject of *The Blind Leading the Blind* had already appeared occasionally in art before Bruegel. In the 1550s, for example, it formed the subject of an engraving by Cornelius Massys. Here, the blind men are given no individual characteristics but are portrayed in the traditional manner with their eyes closed. The comparison makes the qualities of Bruegel's work clear. Bruegel paints not clichés but people, each with his own face and his own medical condition.

Bruegel individualizes. By showing not two, as in the Bible, nor four like Massys, but no less than six blind men one behind the other, Bruegel conveys the impression that his work relates to people in general. His contemporaries would have been reminded of representations of the Dance of Death, in which individual figures hold onto each other in a long procession or roundelay.

The most important difference between Bruegel and Massys, however, is that Massys's blind men are walking along flat ground, while Bruegel's are following a diagonal. This descending diagonal lends new significance to their stumble and fall.

In Massys's engraving, the blind men seem to have tripped over by pure misfortune. In Bruegel's diagonal, on the other hand, their fall seems inevitable, as if they are moving towards something final. This sense of an imminent end is reinforced by the palette, in which grey plays a dominant role. There are no lively contrasts, and red appears only in the clothing of the figures at the rear. At the front of the procession, however, the trousers, cloak and jacket worn by the leader, and the musical instrument he is carrying, are almost identical in colour to the ground and the water into which he has fallen. It is as if, the artist seems to suggest, he is returning to the soil. The heads of the blind men form a curve of life, and the man on the ground marks its termination. It is not just a picture about blindness, be it physical, moral or religious, but also about the inexorable advance towards death.

In the marshy pool above the fallen man grows a lily, whose flower is almost as big as the faces. Seen beside the heads of the blind men, painted with naturalistic brutality, the unnaturally large white bloom is like a sign from another world. White lilies were a symbol of purity and redemption – but whether the men are guaranteed salvation, whether one of them can seize the lily, are questions the artist leaves open.

The fact that Bruegel painted *The Blind Leading the Blind* a year before his death and during a time of murderous repression perpetrated by the authorities suggests that he intended to say something about the end of life.

The path of life leads downwards

But it is also possible that the subject attracted him for a quite different reason. It is possible that it presented him with a technical challenge – the portrayal of people falling. In another painting of 1568, the *Nest Robber*, he places in the middle ground a monumental figure who seems to be falling forwards towards the viewer. In *The Blind Leading the Blind* he chooses to show the men from side on, falling almost in slow motion. Nothing of the sort had previously been seen in painting. Bruegel's interest in solving a technical problem, coupled with the nature of the society within which he worked together made this extraordinary painting possible.

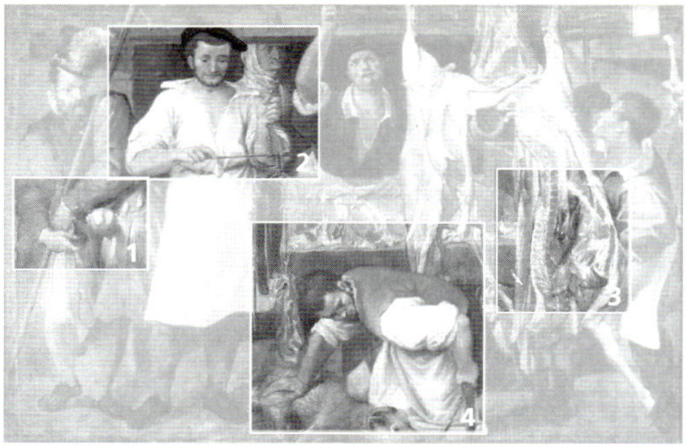
1
2
3
4

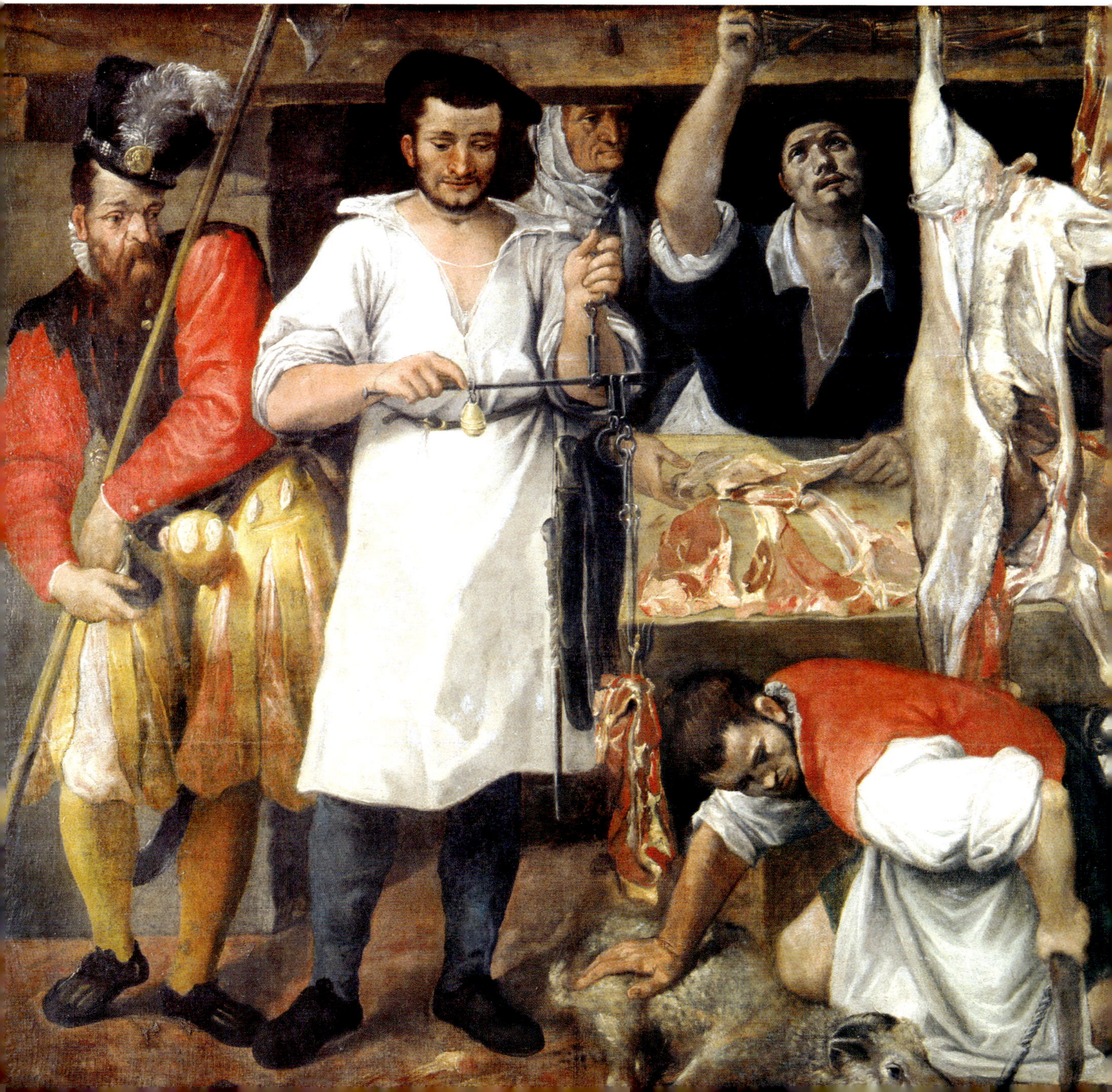

Annibale Carracci: The Butcher's Shop, c. 1583

A painter discovers life in the raw

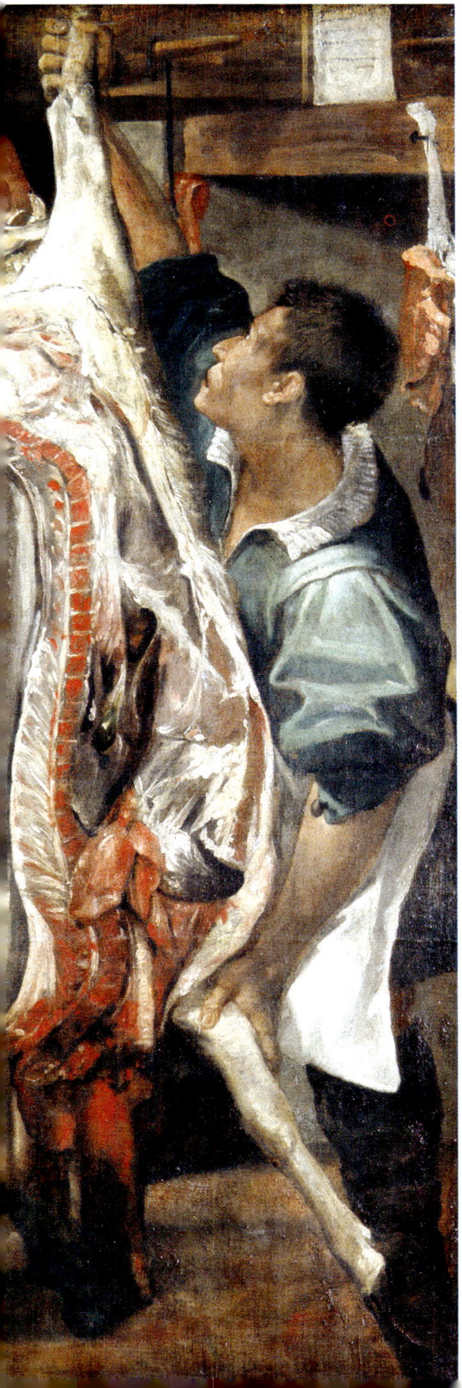

In 1993 the British artist Damien Hirst exhibited a calf, cut lengthways in half, in a glass cabinet filled with formaldehyde. A good 400 years before him, in around 1583, Annibale Carracci in Bologna painted sides of beef in a butcher's shop. In both instances, raw meat as art: in the case of the Italian, realistically portrayed, in the case of the Englishman, the real thing itself.

The shock in 1993 was great; it would have been the same in 1583. The Bolognese were used to paintings which showed antique gods or Christian saints, executed in delicate, light colours. Carracci brought his contemporaries back into the crude present with his forceful palette and reminded them of one of the foundations of human existence, killing. In his painting, the living animal is turned into the commodity meat.

The artist shows us a side of beef hanging up, a skinned lamb and various cuts of meat, along with four butchers at work, an old woman with her hand on a piece of meat and a member of the Swiss guard. Beneath the butcher's block, a dog is waiting for scraps. At the bottom of the picture, in the centre, a ram with its back legs tied together is about to have its throat slit.

The Butcher's Shop was purchased by King Charles I of England after 1627, and in 1765 the painting passed to Christ Church College in Oxford. The English wondered why the Italian had chosen such a vulgar subject. They speculated that it might be a family portrait, showing Carracci's brother and cousin dressed up at the butcher's block and the artist himself holding the scales. But even this failed to earn the large canvas a place in the college's noble halls. Instead it was hung in the kitchen. In 1956 it was rediscovered, brought out and cleaned of a thick layer of fat and soot for the large Carracci exhibition in Bologna. Today it forms the showpiece of the college's art gallery.

Bologna is known in Italy as *la Grassa*, the fat. The city had always been famed for its good food, and in Carracci's day a prolonged period of peace had enabled the economy to recover sufficiently for people to be able to afford to eat well. Since 1512 the city had formed part of the Papal States, and was governed by a papal legate. Robbed of all genuine power, the patricians compensated by surrounding themselves with at least the superficial trappings of authority, which included Swiss guards. One such guard is standing on the left near the butchers. He is buying the meat, and is already rummaging in his purse for some money.

The artist tells us what he thinks of this guardsman in the way he portrays his fulsomely padded genital pouch, his ostentatious slit trousers and his awkward attempt to retrieve coins from the purse without losing his halberd in the process. The guard appears old and gloomy next to the young butcher clad in gleaming white.

The Swiss guardsman symbolizes the constraints of a class society against which the young artist rebelled. Annibale Carracci, born in 1560, came from the artisan class. His forefathers were tailors. His father, however, having achieved modest prosperity, paid for his elder brother Agostino (1557–1602) to complete an apprenticeship as a goldsmith and then train as a copper engraver and painter. Annibale started out by working in the tailor's workshop but then followed the path taken by his brother, who had meanwhile proved that there was money to be made as an artist.

His cousin Ludovico (1555–1619) also became an artist. The three joined forces and after their apprenticeship formed – in defiance of all guild rules – their own school of art, the Accademia degli Incamminati, the "academy of those who have set off on their way". This proud title signalled their desire to follow a different path to that of the established masters.

Annibale was the most talented and the boldest of the three. The idea of making a butcher's block the subject of art was not conceived by him, however, but originated in the Netherlands. The Netherlandish artists of the 16th century became the first to paint the world of craftsmen, peasants and housewives, people who in Italy were not considered worthy of art. When some of these works reached the South, Annibale's teacher, Bartolomeo Passarotti, took up the motif of the butcher's shop and painted two butchers, one with a squint and the other toothless. It was a satirical portrait, painted from the perspective of wealthy patrons. Annibale Carracci does not treat his figures as socially inferior. He painted two versions of *The Butcher's Shop*, the first in a smaller format and then in life size and with more figures in the highly regarded manner of history paintings.

The ridiculous authorities

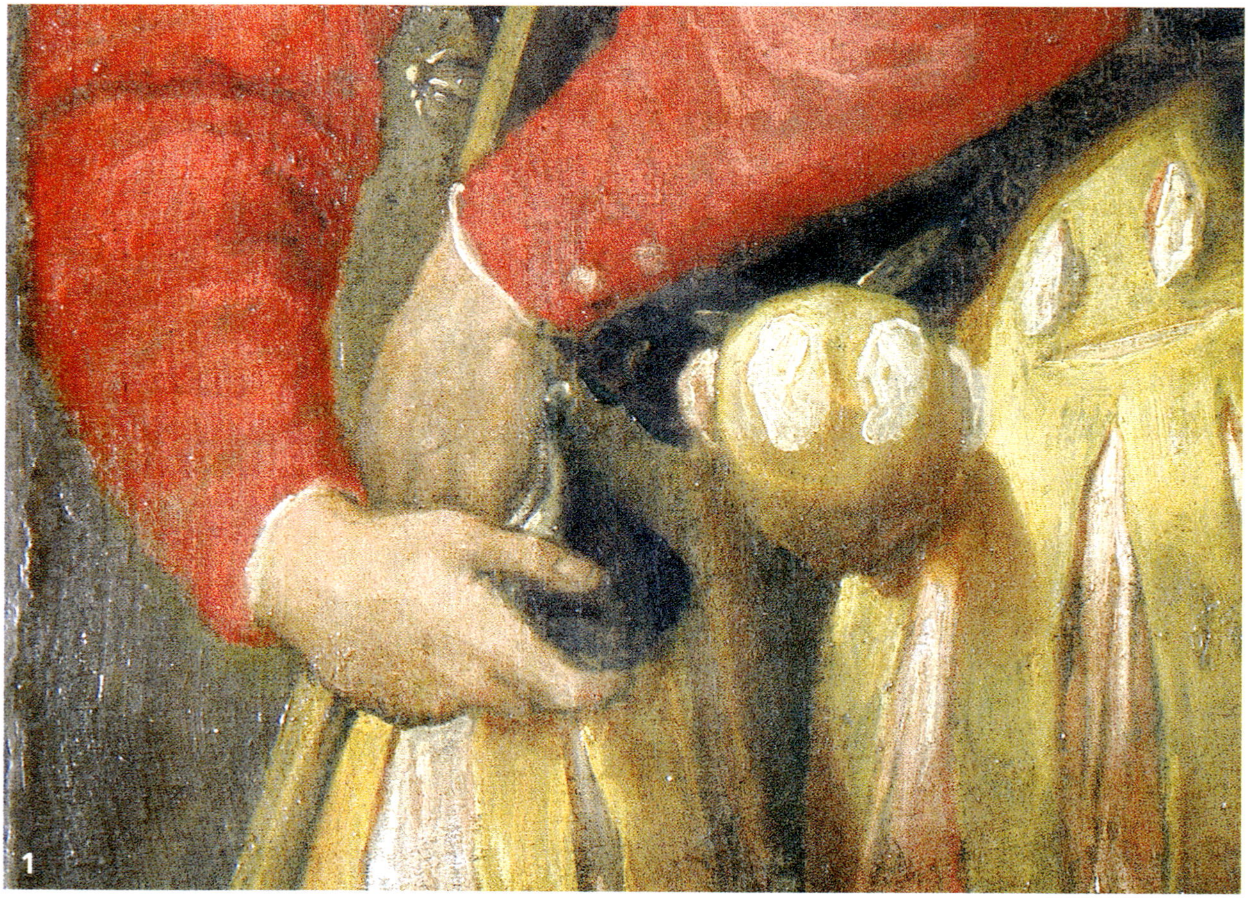
1

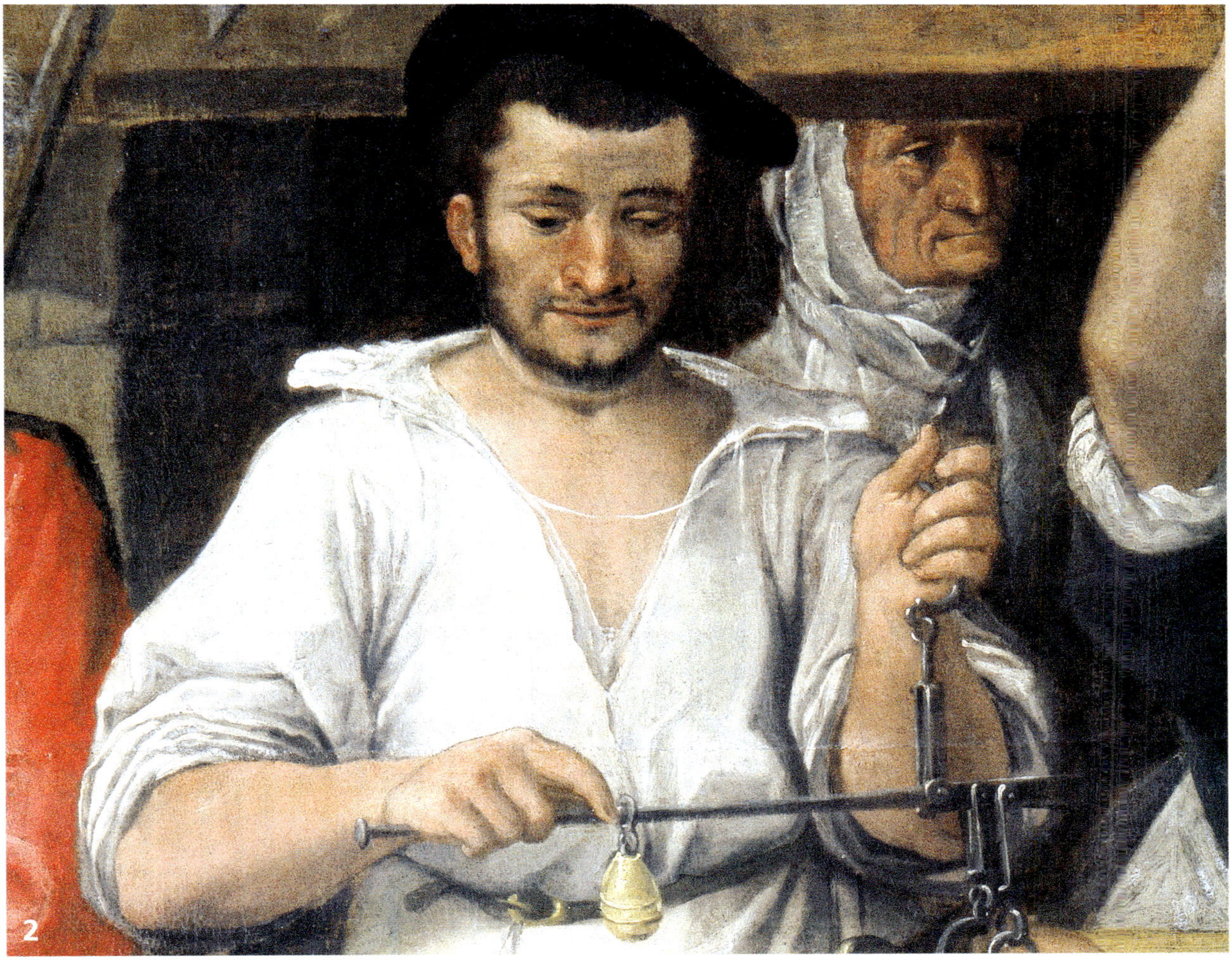

2

Only the master may weigh the meat

The man with the hand-held scales must be the owner of the butcher's shop, for weighing the meat, calculating the price and taking the money were all tasks carrying a particular responsibility. The price list laid down by the authorities is displayed against the wall in the top right-hand corner of the canvas. Inspectors made regular checks, since butchers were fond of overcharging.

Most Italian artists of the 16th century slavishly followed the works of the Renaissance masters, adopting and varying gestures, poses and stylizations from their famous predecessors. The young Carraccis refused to go along with this trend. In a note, Annibale wrote angrily to an older colleague: "Stupid Vasari doesn't notice that the good old masters fashioned things from life." A painter should first and foremost study "living things".

It was not difficult for Annibale to get a close look at the workings of a butcher's shop. His uncle, Vincenzo Carracci, owned one in Bologna's Saligado di San Francesco, now Piazza Malpighi, and his cousin and fellow artist Ludovico had also learnt the butcher's trade there. Annibale is little interested in the shop itself: he shows beams, indicates walls, but no more. He concentrates entirely upon the people and the meat, portraying both in such detail and with so many subtle nuances that he must have studied his subject again and again. The work shirt with the lace to tie the collar, the different shades of red characterizing the various sorts of meat, the longitudinal section through the side of beef, the gleam of the blade sharpener – these things couldn't be learnt from the Old Masters.

The theory that Annibale has here painted either his uncle's family or his own seems plausible but cannot be proved. A self-portrait by the artist bears little resemblance to the man with the scales. Three of the faces are seen from angles more awkward than would normally be employed in portraits. Perhaps the work was commissioned by a member of the Canobi family, who rented slaughtering blocks in one of the largest butcher's in the city. But that is speculation. Artisans who had become wealthy enough to have their portraits painted did not wish to be portrayed practising their trade, but preferred to pose dressed in black as members of the upper middle classes.

During the same period as *The Butcher's Shop*, Annibale also painted a farm labourer shovelling cooked haricot beans, the food of the poor, into his mouth. He leans over the bowl with unkempt hair. Rather than some handsome "shepherd" in line with the taste of Bolognese patricians, Annibale shows a man assuaging his hunger.

The poor fed themselves on soups and vegetable stews; eating meat was the privilege of the wealthy. Banquets were simultaneously a demonstration of power. In Bologna in the 15th century, it is reported that the platters of food "were paraded around the square in front of the palace ... so that the people could see their magnificence".

Those who supplied meat often earned good money, but were also tainted by a somewhat shady reputation. For part of their job was to kill, often before their customers' very eyes. Only in later centuries would live animals be sent off to be slaughtered in abattoirs. Carracci's contemporaries had thicker skins: they were very familiar with killing, as with dying.

Nevertheless, even in those days the act of slaughtering an animal must have disturbed those watching. This is indirectly illustrated by Annibale's picture. The artist who observes everything so closely has left one thing out: the blood that courses out of a body when it is killed. It is true that the sides of beef were only slung on the hooks once the blood had drained out of them. But even on the aprons and shirts of the butchers, there is not a drop of blood to be seen. They hang white and innocent over their wearers. The ram on the ground, too, has yet to shed a single drop of its blood: the butcher's knife is still in its sheath and the bowl to catch the blood is missing.

All the more succulent is the meat laid out in front of the viewer, complete with sinews, fat and offal. Meat that is still recognizable as beast exudes a peculiar, contradictory fascination that both attracts and repels. Perhaps it stirs primitive memories of hunting for food; perhaps it holds links with sensual excesses or arouses a fear of death and transience. Meat also has a ritualistic past: animal and human sacrifices served to pacify the gods. With the heart of his dead enemy, the victor believed he could appropriate his powers.

This response to the sight of meat has nothing to do with art. Yet Carracci's *Butcher's Shop* cannot be understood without it. And the fascination of butchered animal carcasses, captured so powerfully by Carracci for the first time, would inspire artists after him to their own variations on the same theme – from Delacroix and Francisco de Goya, via Eugène Delacroix, to Marc Chagall and Chaim Soutine. The Austrian Hermann Nitsch has been celebrating a cult of slaughter and blood in performances since the 1960s, and Damien Hirst speculates on an "unartistic" shock with his half calf, standing as if alive.

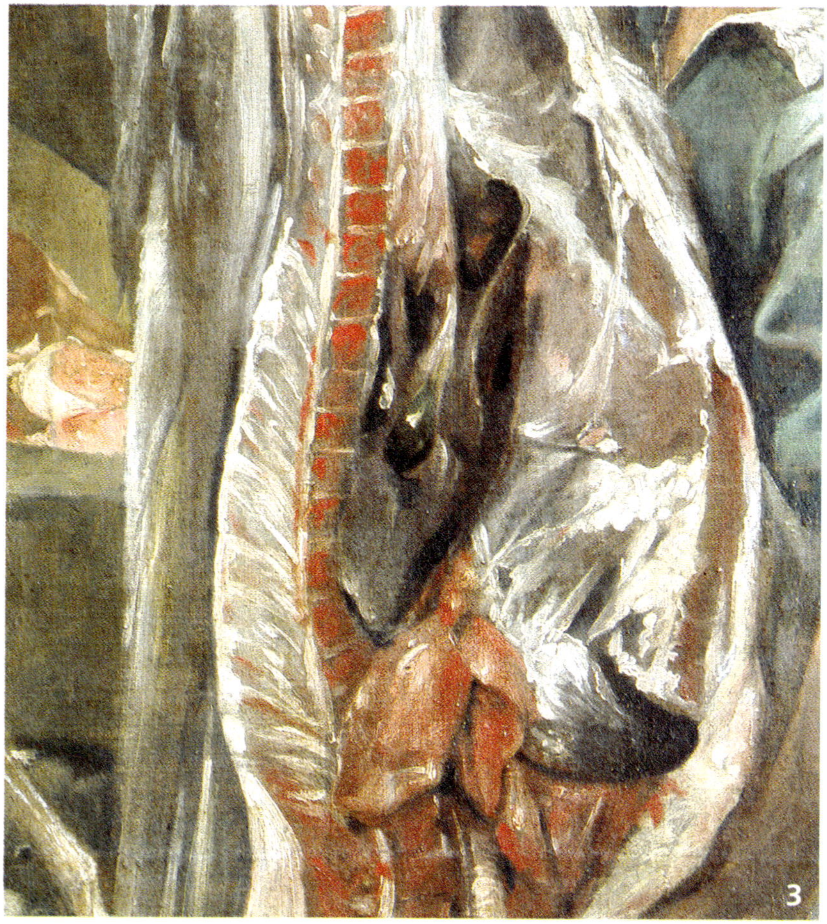

Not a drop of blood spatters the canvas

A biblical figure becomes a butcher's boy

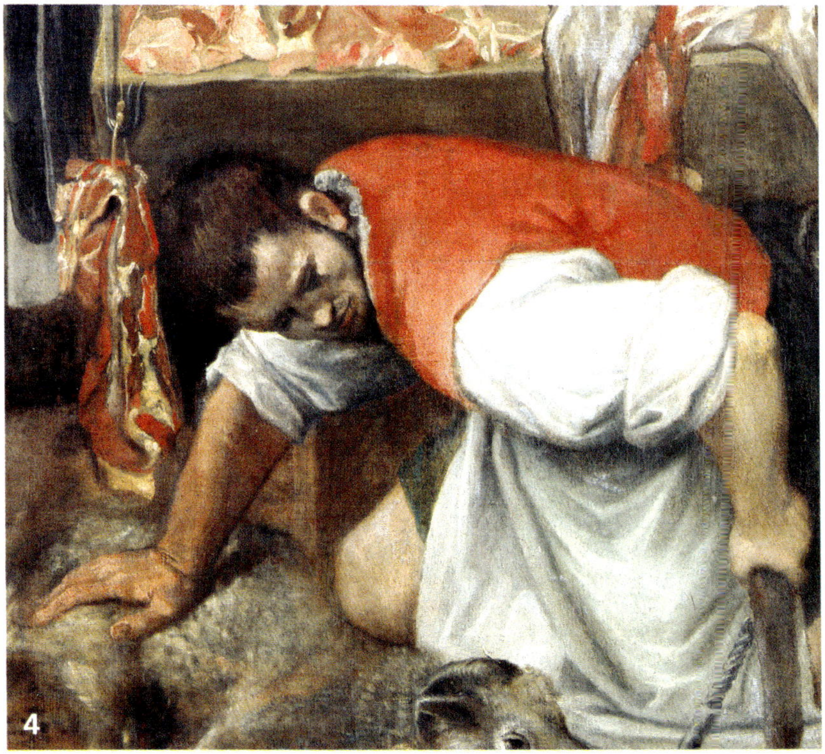
4

In the Carracci academy, everyone worked in front of the object and on location. According to one contemporary, the brothers and their pupils repeatedly drew and painted "living people, partly or entirely nude, weapons, animals and fruits, indeed everything ever created". Their motto was "Viva la carne!" – "Long live flesh!" And perhaps Annibale, with his two *Butcher's Shop* paintings, was making a play upon his artistic programme.

But for all his rebellious attention to reality, he was also firmly rooted in the traditions and preferences of the epoch in art that we call Mannerism. One of the characteristics of Mannerism are twisted and bent bodies; in Annibale, these appear in the figure of the Swiss guard delving into his purse and the butcher grasping the side of beef. Both differ from typical Mannerist figures in two ways, however: the detail with which they are observed and the plausible reason for their poses and facial expressions within the compositional narrative.

Nor did Annibale totally refuse to borrow from the figurative repertoire of earlier masters. The butcher kneeling on the floor corresponds to a figure in *The Sacrifice of Noah* executed by Raphael (1483–1520) in the Vatican Loggia. *The Sacrifice of Noah* portrays the episode in which Noah, having safely survived the Flood, makes a sacrifice of thanksgiving to God. In front of the altar lies a ram, and beside it kneels one of Noah's sons, clasping the knife in his hand. It is the same pose, the same head turned to the side, as in *The Butcher's Shop*. Raphael's naked, idealized youth has simply become a sturdy lad in working clothes. There is no doubt that Carracci would have recreated the scene in his studio in order to study the folds in the clothing and the tension in the muscles.

The artist was some 23 years old when he painted the two butcher's shops and the man eating the haricot beans. But although he continued to study and sketch the world of tradesmen and peasants, he never devoted another large-format canvas to them. *The Butcher's Shop* thus represented a brief, exciting deviation from what Italian art lovers wanted to see. It was followed by conventional subjects – pictures of saints, Crucifixions, scenes from Greco-Roman mythology. In Bologna, Annibale decorated a palazzo with the legend of Europa and the bull, another with the founding of Rome. In 1595 he moved to Rome, where on the walls and ceilings of the Palazzo Farnese he celebrated the power of love and the exploits of Hercules and Odysseus. Obeying the wishes of his patrons, he transported cardinals and art lovers far from the present and into a more beautiful world.

Here, too, however, he portrayed the idealized figures with a naturalism that made them seem real. He breathed so much life into them that he became – together with his contemporary Caravaggio – one of the major influences upon subsequent generations of artists. As a person, he fitted neither into Bologna nor Rome: despite all his successes, he remained true to his artisan origins. His peasants and butchers accompanied him unseen all his life. He died in 1609.

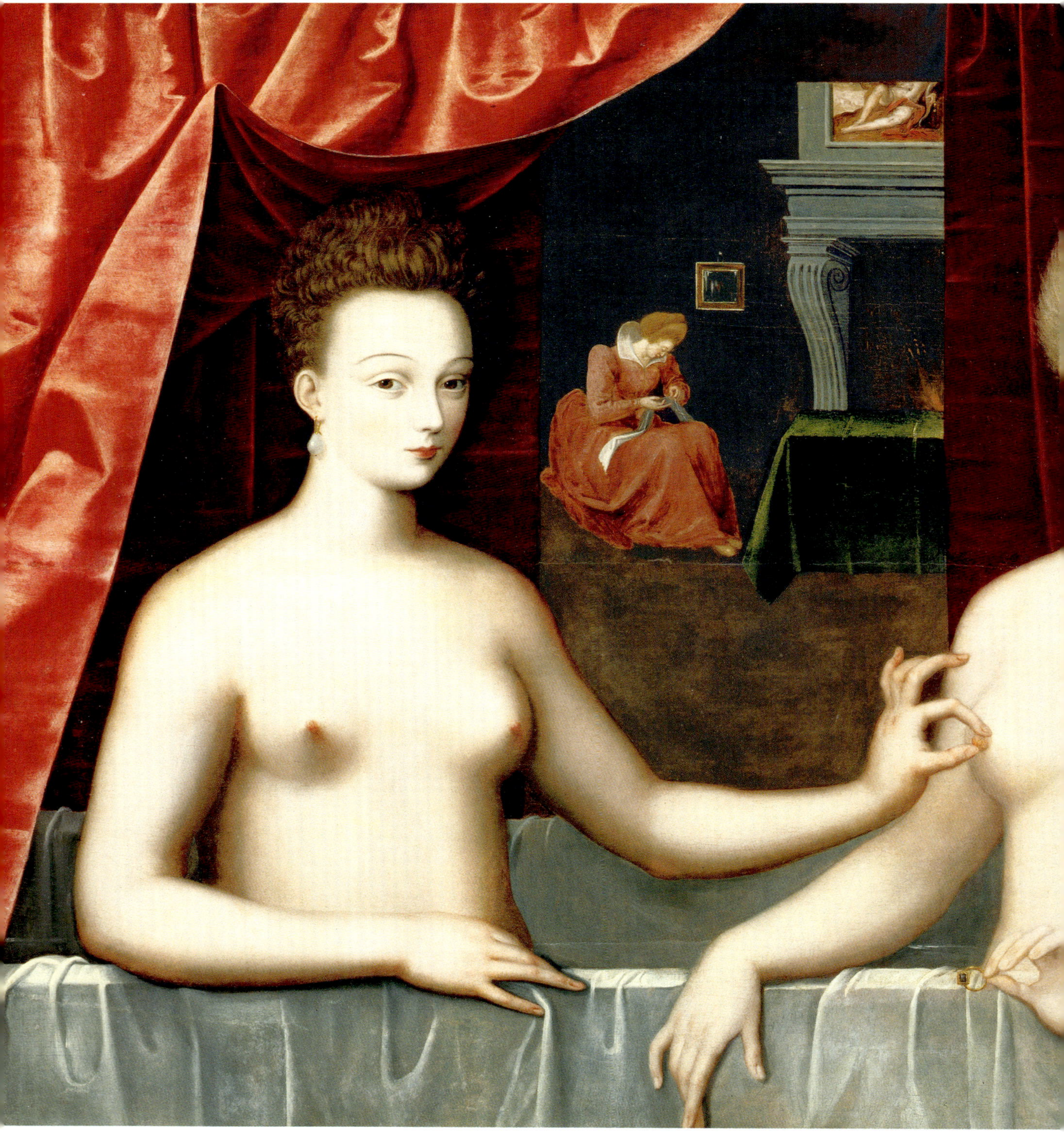

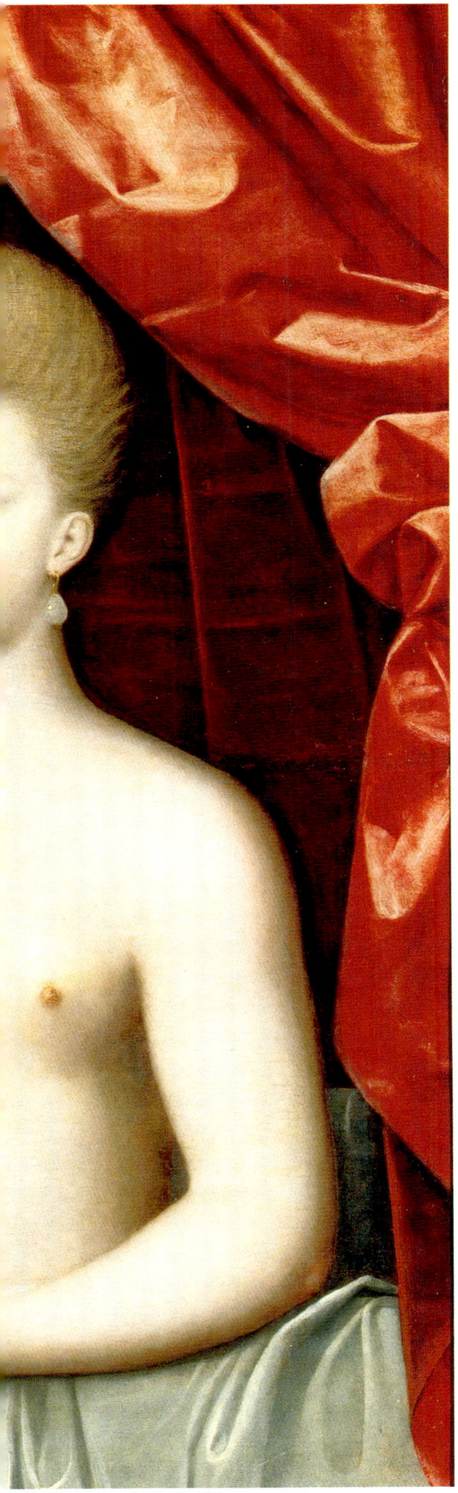

School of Fontainebleau: Gabrielle d'Estrées and one of her sisters, c. 1600

Two cool beauties in the tub

Two naked ladies disporting themselves in a bathtub. They are protected from the cold of the marble by a light, shiny cloth draped over the edge of the tub. Heavy red silk drapes hang down from an invisible baldachin, gathered up at the front and half drawn closed at the back, to screen off draughts.

At the time when this picture was painted, very few people in France took a bath. In the 16th and 17th centuries the general condition of every class of people was one of incredible filthiness. The baths and steam-houses that were so numerous in the Middle Ages had long been shut down, at the urging of the moral watchdogs of the Reformation and Counter-Reformation, who condemned places where men and women not only bathed but met socially and for amusement. Syphilis, in all probability brought from America in 1493, had transformed bath-houses into dangerous places of contagion. Before long the doctors too were approving the trend away from bathing, and even warning against it: one's hands might be washed, wrote medical scientist Jean de Renou, but the feet should only rarely be in contact with water and the head, if possible, never.

Evidently the last thing the two ladies in our picture would dream of is to bring their heads, and their beautifully styled hair, into contact with this dangerous element. They are made up and wearing pearls, and are most assuredly not taking a bath as a means of cleansing themselves but for beauty purposes. Quite likely the tub is filled not with water but with wine or milk, which since antiquity had been considered a means of perpetuating youth. In 1610 a Hungarian lady, Countess Bathory, went even further for her beauty's sake and bathed in the blood of slaughtered virgins.

Magical powers were often ascribed not only to blood but to other fluids too.

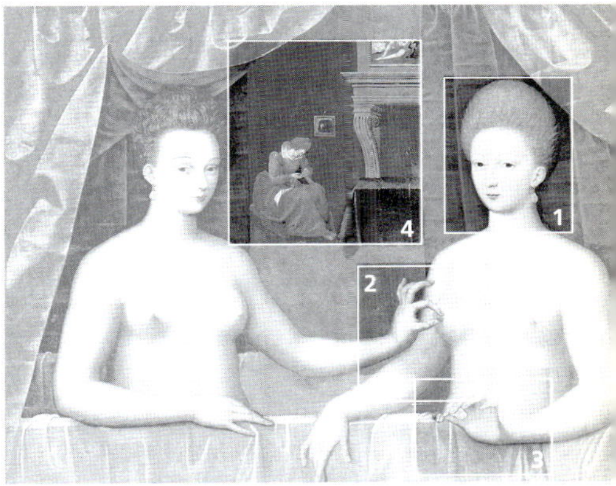

Bathing, indeed, was generally seen in superstitious terms. Astrologers advised that baths should be taken only when the moon was waning and the stars were "hot". At St John's Eve, water was said to wash away threatening evils. St Walburga's Eve (the "Walpurgisnacht" of witching fame) was thought especially auspicious for all kinds of bathing magic. Witches prepared for their sabbath by taking a bath; they heated the tub with rotting firewood and burnt herbs that had a deadening effect – according to the records of witch trials, at least. Since the clergy condemned not only witchcraft but also bathing, the two transgressions were often linked. The devil was said to copulate with witches in the bathtub, and he would show them the faces of their future husbands reflected in the water.

But at the time when this picture was painted, people associated not only magic, the fear of contagious disease, and ecclesiastical damnation with bathing. From Italy, the rest of Europe derived the ideas and visual code of the Renaissance, and with them the numerous unclothed goddesses of antiquity. In France they came into fashion, and court beauties had themselves painted rising from the waves of bathing in

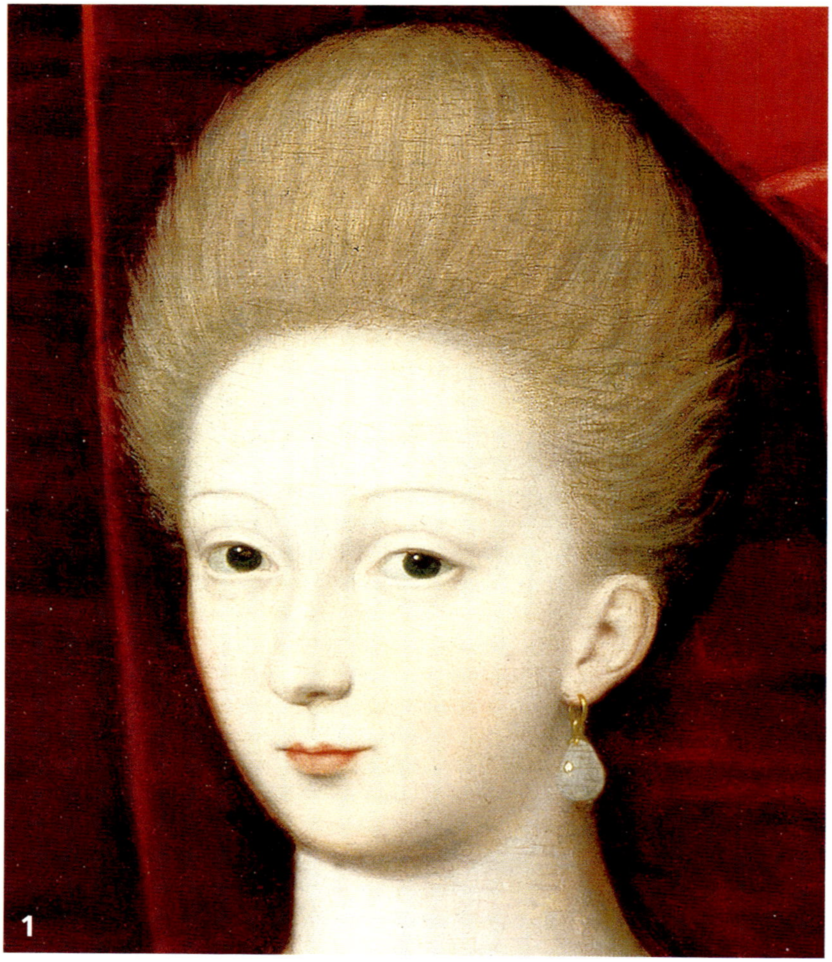

springs, feeling close to the heathen deities in the process and profiting from their prestige. Painters from Florence and Bologna decorated the rooms in the palace of Fontainebleau ("beautiful fountain") with goddesses and nymphs. The architects devised a suite of *appartements des bains* which included resting rooms, changing rooms and marble baths. It was here that King François I (1494–1547) hung the finest paintings in his possession, such as Leonardo da Vinci's *Mona Lisa*. Here too there doubtless hung a large number of pictures such as this one of two beauties in the tub. Only a few have survived. Many were overpainted with "decorous veils", and most the Queen Mother Anne of Austria had burnt in 1676, as indecent and "the work of the devil".

We do not know who painted our picture; it is unsigned. And we can only guess when it was painted. The hair styles of the two ladies in the tub were fashionable between 1594 and 1598. The inscription on a later copy of the work alleges that the blonde woman on the right was Gabrielle d'Estrées, one of the most beautiful and most hated women of her century, the favourite of a king. Indeed, she very nearly became queen herself.

Born in 1573, Gabrielle was fifteen when she arrived at the court of the last Valois king, Henri III. The court was a hotbed of scandal, and before long she was reported to have had various affairs, one with the handsome M. de Bellegarde. Henri III was assassinated in the course of the religious wars that divided France into two armed camps for decades, and his legitimate heir and successor, Henri IV, first had to conquer his own realm – for he was a Protestant, and his Catholic subjects did not recognize him. M. de Bellegarde was the master of the royal stables and fought alongside the monarch. During a pause in the fighting, he was so incautious as to tell Henri of his beautiful lover, Gabrielle d'Estrées. And on the 7th of November 1590 Bellegarde introduced the two.

Gabrielle d'Estrées must have approximated pretty exactly to the feminine ideal of her age: long-limbed, blonde and pale of complexion. Her face "was as smooth and translucent as a pearl, with all its delicacy and lustre". This was not written by some flattering courtier but by a woman who had reason to be critical of Gabrielle: Mademoiselle de Guise, a rival for the king's favour. She continued: "Though she wore a dress of white silk, it seemed black compared with the snow of her skin."

Of course this pallor was assisted artificially. Thick white make-up was applied not only to the face but also to the shoulders and bosom. The mouth and nipples were rouged. At the court of the cultivated Valois kings, the immediate predecessors of Henri IV, the arts of make-up had evolved to the utmost degree of sophistication, for both sexes. The ladies at least continued to practise these arts under the new and distinctly ill-groomed "masculine" king. They continued to pluck their eye-brows and draw in a fine line in their stead; if they did not wear wigs, they coloured their hair with white lead and powders. To achieve the popular blonde, they bleached their hair with acrid tinctures and then exposed it to the sun for several days, taking care all the while that the sunlight did not fall upon their white skin. Parts of the body that were not covered by clothing were protected with gloves or facial masks of silk or velvet when out riding or even walking. Ladies exposed their skin only within thick walls or behind silken drapes.

Gabrielle's diminutive blonde head seems relatively small on an over-long neck and a sturdily built body, and her

Eloquent hands

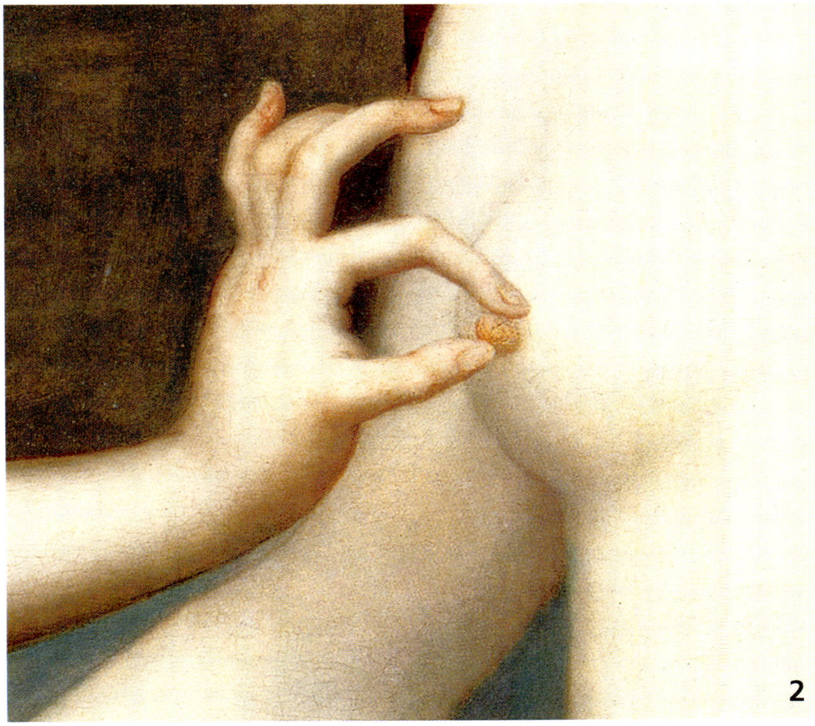

2

finely waved hair, taken up in a severe coiffure, reinforces this impression. It is a head designed to surmount a broad starched ruff or a high stiff lace collar. There was no room for long hair or tumbling curls in this idea of the head. At that time, the costume of the Spanish court was worn in France too – stiff and unnatural clothing, a product of the Counter-Reformation's hostility to the body. Women's bodies were forced into straight, tube-like iron corsets and a stiff, padded, wide skirt. It was as if the bosom, waist and hips did not exist. Even on Gabrielle's naked body we can detect the evidence of this fashion, for it is a body without curves, and even liberated from its corset it remains straight and smooth. In addition to their clothing, the ladies generally wore so much and so heavy jewellery that they had to proceed at a measured pace, "as if they were reliquaries". Only when out hunting did the provocative Gabrielle, who preferred to ride in a man's saddle, occasionally display a leg – encased in a green silk stocking.

On her mother's side, Gabrielle d'Estrées was of a family which the chronicler Tallemant des Réaux described with palpable relish as "the richest in spirited ladies that France has ever seen. There are at least twenty-five or twenty-six of them, nuns and married ladies alike, all of whom delight in sexual congress." Among the married ladies was Gabrielle's mother, who ran away with a lover when the children were small. One of the nuns was Gabrielle's sister, the abbess of Maubuisson, who was eventually obliged to leave her convent after bearing twelve children, by different fathers.

Another sister is probably seen here with Gabrielle in the bathtub: Julienne d'Estrées, Duchess of Villars. She did not balk at sitting bare-breasted below the pulpit when a Capuchin monk she fancied was preaching. The God-fearing man was forced to flee the confessional and indeed the city, so persistent were her passionate advances. No wonder Julienne, the abbess, Gabrielle, three further daughters, and the one son of M. d'Estrées were widely known collectively as "the seven deadly sins".

Sitting in the bathtub, the Duchess of Villars is tweaking one of her sister's rouged nipples with her fingertips. It is a gesture guaranteed to monopolize our attention.

The face and hands alone were not concealed by court costume, which meant that around 1600 they were of especial importance. Convention dictated that the subjects' faces be innocent of all expression, and as long as their impassive gaze is fixed on nothingness, as in our picture, it is only the hand movements that tell us these wax dummies are in fact creatures of flesh and blood. Only from their gestures can we infer what feelings, what hopes and fears, lie within them.

Juliette de Villars' gesture, a tender and highly intimate one, might imply that the sisters had a lesbian relationship. Not for nothing had they come of age at the court of the decadent Henri III, who liked to be seen wearing women's clothing. For a certainty, nothing human was unfamiliar to "the seven deadly sins". But the gesture not only suggests a lesbian tie, a notion that lends the painting a thrilling aura of the taboo: to contemporaries it could also suggest something else entirely – that Gabrielle d'Estrées was pregnant.

Today we would look to the belly for the first sign of pregnancy, but a rounded belly was in any case an essential feature of feminine beauty in the medieval and Renaissance view of things. Even virgins delighted to have rounded bellies. For this reason, numerous paintings showing the biblical Mary and Elizabeth in pregnancy have them extending their hands to each other's bodies, perhaps to feel the heartbeat or movements of the child within. The gesture was the painters' code to signal pregnancy; the artist who painted the present picture rang a charming change on it.

Gabrielle d'Estrées expected a child by Henri IV on four occasions; in 1594 she bore him a son, César, and subsequently another son and then a daughter. In 1599 she was pregnant once again, and precisely this fertility endeared her to the king. His queen, Margaret of Valois, from whom he had long been living in separation, had borne him no children, so that he and his realm still lacked an heir. He had fathered bastards, and had recognized them as his children, but with none of the pomp and ceremony that now accompanied the birth of Gabrielle's children. For the first time in his life, the king found everything he prized in women united in one, Gabrielle:

in addition to her fertility, her "beauty of form, modest demeanour, gentleness of nature and spirit".

At first, Gabrielle was apparently not especially attracted to the king, and preferred the master of the stables. But she was bartered for substantial material advantages for the Estrées, and sent to the king's bed. Report had it that at times Bellegarde would still be departing hastily by the window of Gabrielle's bedchamber when the king came in at the door. Fearing the two might still wed, the king married Gabrielle off to an impotent and obedient courtier.

In time, Gabrielle began to enjoy her life as the king's recognized concubine. She savoured the king's triumphal progress, which was the more successful after his conversion to Catholicism. When Paris was finally conquered, she entered the city at the king's side. She accumulated titles and gold; others could not approach her without kissing the hem of her robe; more and more she enjoyed the status of a rightful queen. But she did not reside in the Louvre with Henri. She lay there in the bed of queens for only a single night, could not sleep, and next morning fled the ghosts of the dead Valois, moving to a nearby city residence. Gabrielle did not care for Paris, and even followed the king into the field, for, as a courtier named de l'Estoile reports, "she was tormented more by her conscience than anyone, and did not feel safe in Paris whenever the king left the city".

The ring that Gabrielle d'Estrées is holding over the rim of the tub was placed on her finger by the king on the 2nd of March 1599. It was the investiture ring, with which France was ceremonially entrusted to Henri IV at his coronation. He gave it to Gabrielle when she was pregnant as an engagement ring: Henri meant her to be his lawful wife and queen. It was an outrageous notion. Moreover, he wanted to marry her within a few weeks, on the first Sunday after Easter. Gabrielle publicly declared her confidence that now only God or the death of the king could come between her and her happiness.

In 1599, Henri had achieved his aims. He was at the peak of his power. For eighteen years he had led the Protestant forces in the civil war, and then in a further five years of fighting, as designated king of France, he had conquered his realm by the sword. At long last he sat securely on his throne. The country had been pacified, and was at peace at home and abroad. Now Henri wanted to found a dynasty, with the woman who had already borne his heir and who had stood by him in the years when he was mocked as "a general without funds and a king without a throne". He had long since informed his horrified ministers of his intention; Gabrielle's marriage was annulled, and the dissolution of his own was being pursued in Rome.

"The redoubtable sovereign was on the point of committing the grossest stupidity that anyone can, and nonetheless he was resolved," writes Tallemant des Réaux, and most contemporaries fully shared this conviction.

Everyone was opposed to the marriage, which the Pope described as "a stain on the honour of France". The French nobles were outraged at the prospect of one day having to accept as king the bastard César, the fruit of a twofold adultery (both Henri and Gabrielle being married to other partners at the time of his birth). The French people hated and despised the king's mistress, the "queen of filth", for her extravagant gowns, her expensive jewellery (with which she even "outshone the torches"), her parties, and her lavish life-style, which contrasted so starkly with the king's own simplicity and the wretchedness of the country. Almost fifty years of civil war, sieges and epidemics had left their mark. "The king is a decent man", one poor Seine fisherman told Henri, not recognizing him in his hunting outfit, "but he keeps a dreadful whore who is ruining us all."

At this the king merely laughed; the objections of the Pope, his ministers, and the nobles, he brushed aside. He ordered preparations to be made for the wedding. The bridal gown had already been sewn. On April 5th, Henri sent Gabrielle, now extremely pregnant, back to Paris alone to spend Easter there. His beloved accepted the hospitality of a wealthy Italian banker named Zamet, who was famed for the cuisine at his table and who helped cook personally for distinguished guests. Gabrielle was taken with pains; on April 8th she gave orders to be removed to her aunt's house, and there, the following day, gave birth to a stillborn child. Her condition deteriorated and she began a fearful struggle with death; neither doctor nor priest attended upon her, and everyone deserted the dying favourite. On April 9th, the king was informed that she had died, to prevent him from hastening to her. In fact Gabrielle d'Estrées died on April 10th, "a revolting and terrible death, her eyes rolling, her neck contorted and bent back upon itself". When doctors finally went to her, they declared "this was the hand of God" – not daring to say "the hand of the devil" aloud.

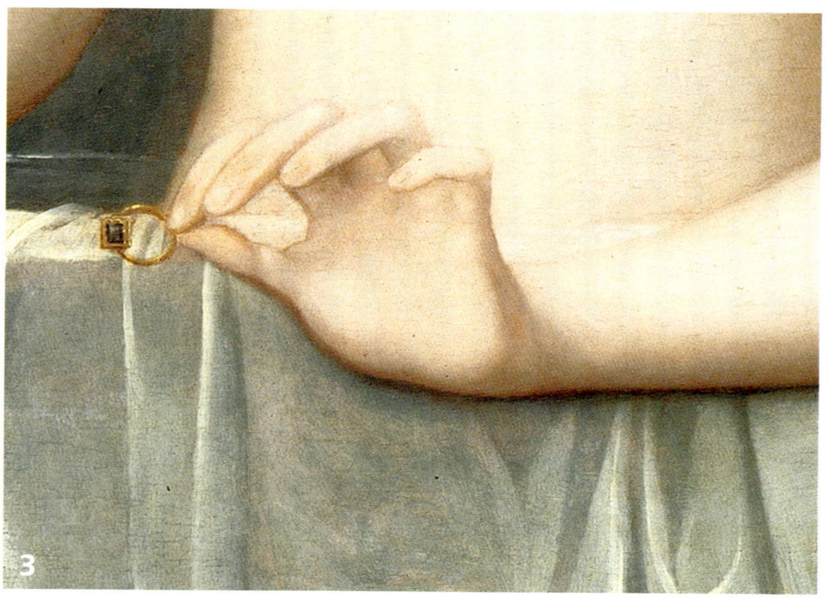

A stain on the honour of France

There are more things between heaven and earth

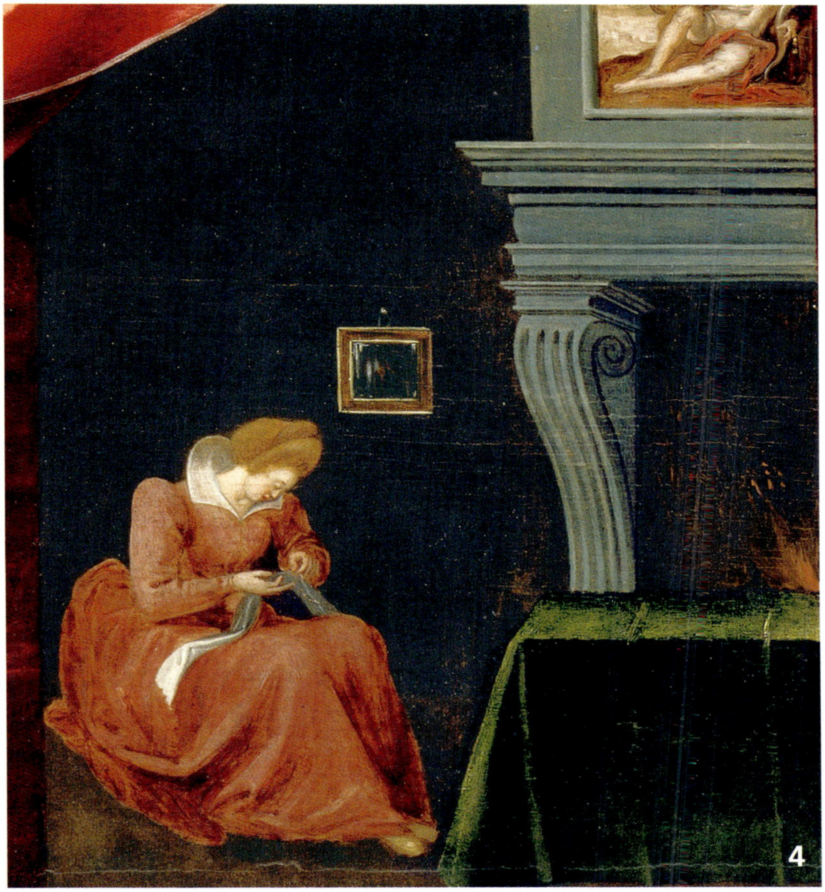

The official version given out by the French court was that Gabrielle d'Estrées died of complications in her pregnancy. But no one believed the story at the time. Tallemant des Réaux, for example, assumed Zamet had poisoned her, and thus "had done Henri a great service". The king might have ended the religious wars that had so long cleft France into two warring parties, but there were still countless religious fanatics in the country. To them, killing an enemy of the "true" religion (which invariably means one's own) was not only legitimate but also pleasing to God. There was no end to the attempts on the king's life, and his mistress, his counsellor "in the hours of the day and of the night", was detested by Catholics and Protestants alike. Rather too many people had an interest in getting Gabrielle d'Estrées out of the way.

Others inclined to a different explanation of her death. They saw in it the direct intervention of higher powers. As they generally did in times of war, catastrophe and woe, people tended to blame whatever went wrong on the evil one and his helpers. Never since the darkest Middle Ages had belief in witches and sorcerers been so widespread. Like Shakespeare's Hamlet (the play was first performed in 1600), Gabrielle's contemporaries were convinced that there were more things between heaven and earth than were dreamt of in their philosophy. More powerfully even than religious zeal, superstition governed their thinking, and led them to suspect the worst even where we would see only a prosaic everyday scene – as in the background of our picture.

Between the curtains we see a woman, possibly a wet-nurse, sewing at a table by the fireplace. To the superstitious eye, though, the scene looks very different. The heavy silk, the red of royal purple or shed blood, hangs over the bathtub and reveals the dark room to the rear. The fire of life is a mere flicker in the hearth, and a Fate or witch is unpicking the thread of Gabrielle's life. Beside her is a coffin, covered with green velvet, Gabrielle's favourite colour. All we can see of the picture on the wall is the bare nether parts of a man, an allusion to the immoral conduct of Gabrielle with the king. The mirror is dark; it reflects no life. This is a symbol of death, a prop associated with witches and devils.

"All witchcraft is borne of the lust of the flesh, which is insatiable in women," declares a 1489 treatise on witches, the *Hexenhammer*, a handbook used by persecutors everywhere. Among the seventeen tell-tale signs by which a witch may be recognized, were "distorted features" and "rolling eyes and a revolting manner". Rumours were rife following report of Gabrielle's appearance on her death-bed. The devil, people said, had probably taken her. Everyone knew that the evil one liked to enter into beautiful women, or seal a contract with them. People remembered poor Louise de Budos, to whom the devil had evidently promised that he would make her the lady of some great man, for she was unexpectedly taken to wife by the Constable de Montmorency. But one evening when she was holding court, a guest in mourning was announced who did not wish to join the others. Louise burst into tears and bade farewell to the ladies present. Shortly after she was found dead in the ante-room. There was no trace of the man in black.

Henri IV was surely one of the very few men of his time who was free of all religious zeal and superstition. In his lifetime, political circumstances had obliged him to convert more than once; in any case he was a sceptic by nature. In that same month of April 1599, because he realized the part superstitious fears had played in Gabrielle's death – no one had dared go near this woman "possessed" – the king ordered an immediate stop to the persecution of witches. But the word was that there were more than one hundred thousand warlocks and witches in France at the time; one of their number had only recently confessed as much under torture. Even a sceptical king could not save them all. In the years that followed, the pyres kept on being ignited, and in 1609 in Bordeaux a single judge condemned eighty witches to the flames in a single session.

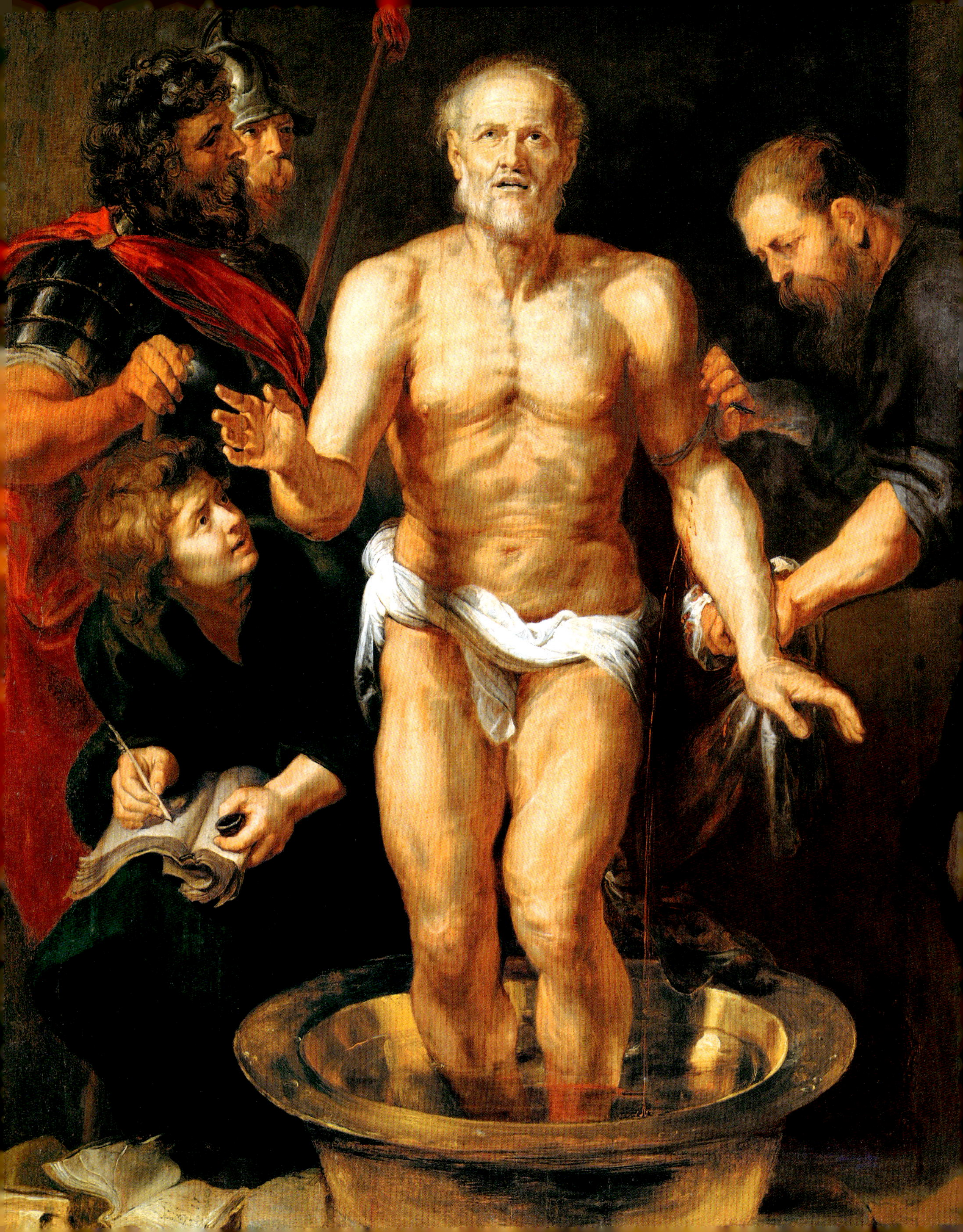

Peter Paul Rubens: The Dying Seneca, 1611/1615

A hero dies upright

An old man standing in a bathtub. He is naked and is looking up. A crouching youth is noting down what he says. A bearded man has opened a vein in the old man's arm, and a jet of blood is pouring into the water in the tub. A soldier and an officer are looking on. Thus the baroque painter Peter Paul Rubens (1577–1640) depicts the death of the Roman philosopher Seneca.

The painting (185 by 155 centimetres) is undated but was probably painted between 1611 and 1615, and is now in the Alte Pinakothek in Munich. Rubens was then in his mid-thirties, lived in Antwerp, and was much in demand as an artist. He had enjoyed a humanist education, had a command of several languages, and was familiar with the works of the ancient authors who were discussed in his day. One of these was Seneca, who was felt to be relevant because the Dutch humanist Justus Lipsius (1547–1606) had newly edited his works.

Seneca's impact derived as much from the example he set in his life as from his writings. He was a philosopher at the very centre of power. Originally from today's Córdoba, then one of the westernmost provinces of the Roman empire, he was born in about the year BC 1. His father sent him to Rome because it was only there that a young man could qualify for higher office.

When Seneca was about twenty he was taken ill, suffering feverish fits in which it seemed he would asphyxiate, and went to Egypt to regain his health. He did so, as he later wrote, thanks not only to the hot dry climate and good nursing but also to stoical philosophy. It showed him how a man could live in harmony with himself and the world about him. He had to control his passions, forego pleasures and possessions, and endure inevitable misfortunes without lamenting. If it was in his power, he should judge and act justly. Till his death, Seneca observed the ethical code of the Stoics.

Some six or seven years later he returned to Rome. His extraordinary rhetorical gifts placed him in the senate under Caligula. But the emperor was envious, and wanted Seneca dead. Only the circumstance that Seneca was suffering from consumption saved his life.

Caligula was himself assassinated, and was succeeded by Claudius. He in turn suspected Seneca of conspiring with his opponents and banished him to Corsica, then an inhospitable and almost uninhabited island.

Seneca saw his punishment as a test, and wrote to his mother: "I am not unhappy. And that you may be the more certain of this, I add: I cannot be unhappy." For the true Stoic accepts what he cannot change. He was on Corsica for eight years; then Claudius had his wife Messalina murdered, and through the influence of her successor Agrippina, the emperor's new wife, Seneca was recalled to Rome. He was to be the tutor to her son, later the emperor Nero.

The attempt to instil the ideals of stoicism in Seneca's pupil failed. Nero turned out a psychopath, bent only on the gratification of his own passions. He revelled in the sufferings of torture victims, delighted when Rome burned, sought after fame as an actor – anything rather than rule. For some years it was Seneca, with others, who conducted the affairs of the empire – till he fell out of favour with the youthful emperor. Seneca withdrew to one of his country homes.

In the year 65 a group of Roman politicians and army officers planned a coup. The conspiracy was betrayed, and Seneca was denounced as one of the plotters. Nero despatched an officer bearing orders to Seneca to commit suicide. The philosopher sat dining with his wife and friends, and with the help of one friend he

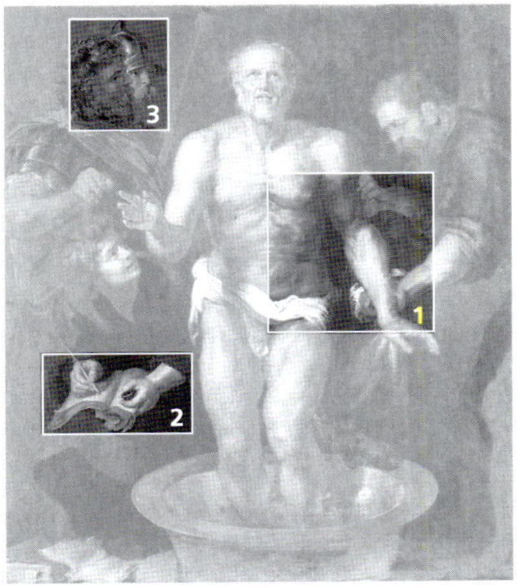

opened his veins, first in an arm, then in his legs. The blood flowed too slowly, so he drank a cup of hemlock, the selfsame poison with which Socrates, his great philosophical exemplar, had killed himself. This too did not work. In the end the soldiers dragged the dying man off to the steam bath, where he asphyxiated.

Copying the wrong original

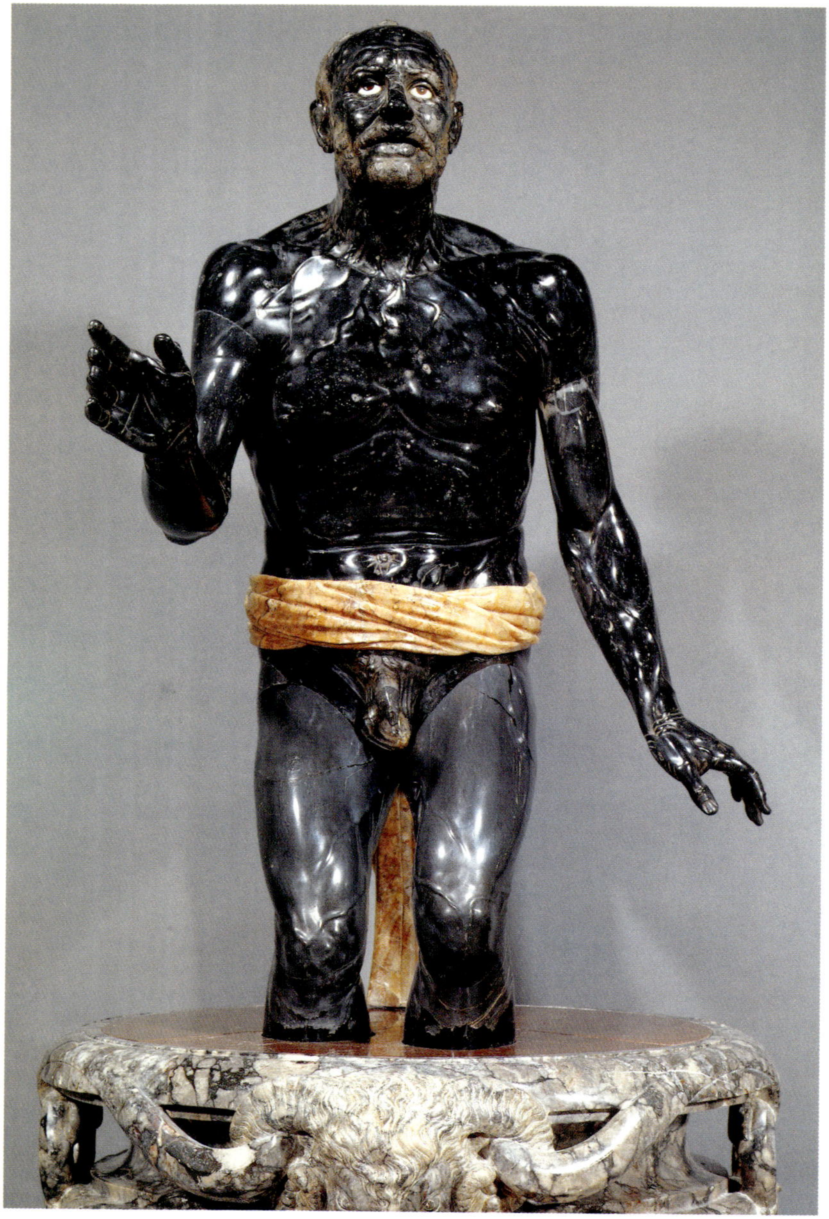

The veins are best opened when reclining in hot water, if the aim is suicide. That way the person cannot fall, and the water also prevents the bleeding wounds from closing too quickly. This had been the practice since antiquity. Lipsius observed that Seneca, as a Stoic, had always bathed in cold water, and therefore this would presumably have been both his first and his last hot bath.

The Roman historian Tacitus, who left a detailed account of Seneca's final hours, makes no mention of his having died standing; indeed, the philosopher presumably followed the customary practice. But this did not interest Rubens. He had a quite different image in his mind's eye, that of an ancient statue he had seen in Rome which was said to depict the dying Seneca.

The piece in question is the figure of an old man, 118 centimetres tall. The body is of black marble and the hip wrap of alabaster. The statue, apparently rediscovered in the late 16th century, had repairs made to the arms, hips and nose; the legs, broken below the knees, remained fragments. The statue was positioned on a coloured stone shaped like a bowl and with every appearance of being filled to the brim with liquid. Napoleon's art commissars shipped the statue from Rome to Paris and gave it a new base, and today it is in the Louvre.

Rubens saw it in Rome, probably in the collection of a patron, Cardinal Scipione Borghese. The artist lived for much of the period from 1600 to about 1608 in Italy, painting portraits of minor rulers and pompous altar-pieces and failing to win the recognition he felt was his invariable due.

Of more significance for his work as an artist was his activity as collector at this period. Rubens copied and sketched paintings and statues, establishing a store of heads and gestures, single figures and groups, which he could draw upon in later years. The statues of antiquity were then seen as matchless exemplars for the representation of man. Rubens made at least six drawings of this black statue.

Back in Antwerp, he transformed the shiny surface of the marble figure into life-like skin, making of the statue a human being of flesh and blood. He retained the stance and gesture but made the stocky body slimmer, extended the legs downwards, and converted the stone bowl into a bronze tub half-filled with water. He also endowed the facial features with his own notion of spiritual beauty. If the face of the statue was on the ugly side, the fact was explained away by the philosopher's being from Spain, which was close to Africa and thus to a possible touch of the tar-brush.

Nowadays the statue is thought to represent an African fisherman. He may have been holding a bucket in his left hand and in his right a fishing rod.

Disguising the fact of suicide

Rubens lived in a time when conflict was rife between the Catholics and Protestants. Antwerp, the city where he lived and worked, was in the southern Netherlands; unlike the northern provinces of the Netherlands, the south did not achieve independence from Catholic Spain. The Jesuits and other orders, as instruments of the Counter-Reformation, monitored any sign of Protestant or heathen departure from the orthodox line in the arts.

Seneca was a heathen, but his ethical code was close to the moral code preached by the Church. He wrote one treatise on charity, another on the brevity of life, another on the peace of the soul. He condemned the lust for fame, gluttony, and the abuse of power; he stressed that all men were brothers; and he urged followers of the stoical way to live each day in the knowledge that death is always present – we are forever approaching closer to death, he wrote, and die with every day that passes.

In the early Middle Ages, the Church affected that the philosopher was one of her own, making believe that he had corresponded with the apostle Paul, who was beheaded at about the same time that Seneca was ordered to commit suicide. The Stoic was often quoted in Christian moral writings; St Jerome (c. 340–420) considered him "almost a Christian"; and Lipsius even credited him with *sanctitas*, which means innocence, moral purity, and of course sanctity.

Rubens was a Catholic and was familiar with Lipsius' view of Seneca, so he painted the philosopher in the attitude of a Christian martyr. He did not give him a halo, but his whole body is glowing, as if it were made of some different matter from that of the other men by him. Rubens has given Seneca a more refined appearance, less stocky, with a finer head and nose. The head of the statue was tilted back into the nape of the neck, no favourable angle for the painter to adopt if he wanted the face to possess dignity. Rubens lowered the angle of the head a little, but also emphasized the heavenward gaze and gave the thinker a larger forehead, a forehead that gleams as if with enlightenment in the last minutes of his life.

The artist also adapted the figure to his time's code of decency. The statue has an alabaster wrap about the hips, but it does not cover the genitals. Given the Church's hostility to sexuality, this would have been seen as a provocation; so Rubens lengthened the wrap into a loin-cloth that covered the relevant parts.

The suicide of Seneca was difficult for his Christian admirers to accept. Rubens solved this problem by giving the philosopher no active part in his own death; instead, a physician friend is assisting him, just as Tacitus reported. He is supporting the forearm with a cloth while with his right hand he is loosening the tourniquet with which he has compressed the vein. In this way Rubens implies that it was possibly not Seneca himself who opened the veins.

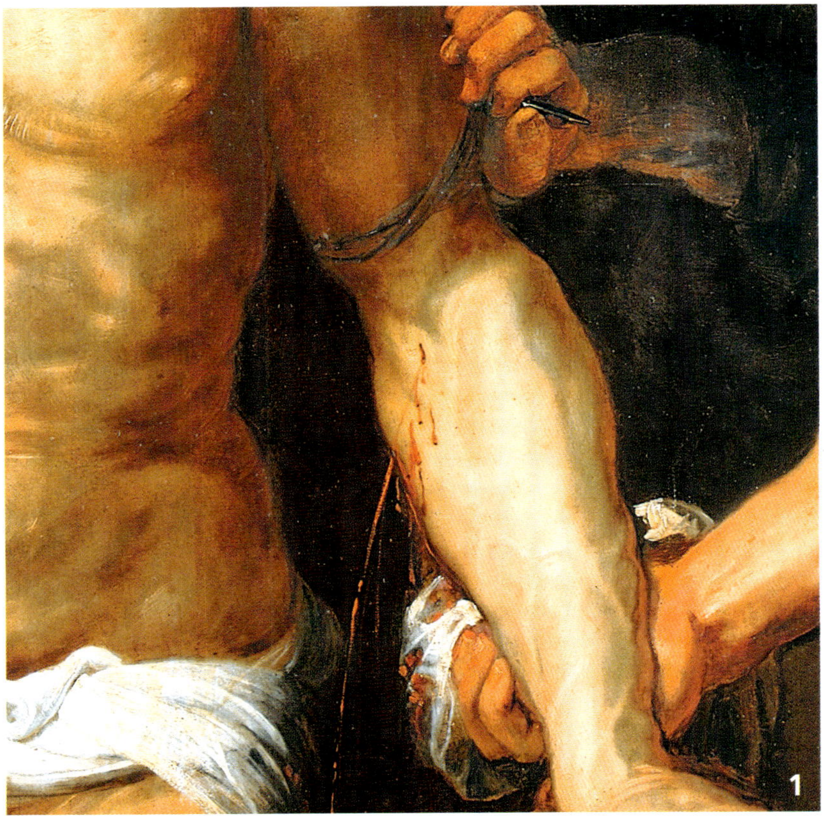

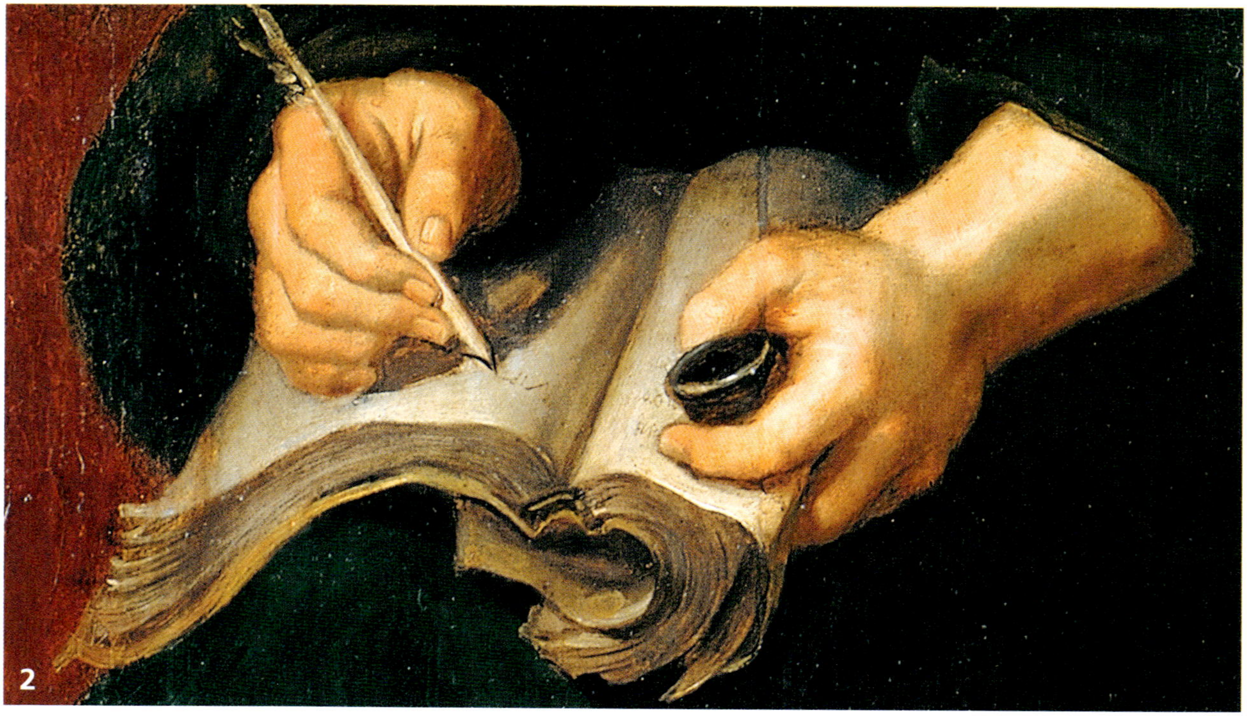

2

A scribe notes the philosopher's last words

Suicide had been a popular subject in the visual arts for centuries, but only for female figures. Lucretia, the Roman lady dishonoured by rape, stabbed herself; Cleopatra put an asp to her bosom. The reason for this preference is clear: the dagger or snake afforded an opportunity to display a young female body to view even as a tragic fate or the transience of all earthly beauty was mourned – erotic pleasure compounded with pity and morality.

This dual impact was unavailable to pictures showing Judas hanged or King Saul falling upon his sword – or Seneca. As a result, male suicide is rare in the history of art, as is also a naked old man's body. Painters and clients alike wanted youth and beauty. The bodies of old women were admissible only in pictures showing the different ages of life, or as witches, or (as in Albrecht Dürer) with a bag of money as the personification of miserliness.

Naked old men were seen as personifications of Death, but usually without any sense of reality. Prophets, church fathers and philosophers, on the other hand, were almost invariably shown clothed. The dying Seneca in Rubens' painting constitutes an exception, not only in the work of the artist but in western art: paintings dominated by the body of an old man, and intended to arouse only positive thoughts and feelings, are rare indeed.

Other painters showed the dying Seneca reclining in the bath, or supported by slaves; after all, we normally imagine dying in a horizontal position. This derives from experience but also possibly from primeval images of sleep and death that are dormant in our subconscious. Standing upright, by contrast, represents alertness, life and self-control.

The horizontal versus the vertical. People lie down to die; but Seneca stands. It is perfectly possible that it was this seeming contradiction that intrigued Rubens in the ancient statue. According to Seneca himself, true heroes die unvanquished and upright. The words referred to Leonidas and the Spartans, and were doubtless meant figuratively. In many languages the word "upright" refers both to a physical and to a moral stance, and if a painter shows a dying man in an upright position, the suggestion is that he has remained in control of himself, unto death and beyond.

Rubens, however, not only shows Seneca upright but moving. Seneca is taking a pace forward: his left leg is raised, his right arm extended. Rubens is presenting the philosopher, standing in the bathtub and dying, as if he were coming towards us.

And his opened mouth seems to want to tell us something. His words are being recorded for posterity by the young scribe. With an ink-well in his left hand and a quill in his right, he is writing down the philosopher's last words. He has just written "vir", which might be the beginning of the word "virtus" (virtue), which the Stoic is urging upon us. The scribe is mentioned in Tacitus, and so is historically authentic. Rubens is using him to imply that Seneca lives on in his writings. It was this that he aimed to show by presenting the philosopher as he has done, and that is why he has reconciled irreconcilables: dying with standing, taking a pace forward with the stasis enforced by the situation.

After the death of his first wife in 1626, Rubens wrote that he did not aspire "ever to achieve a stoical equanimity", nor did he feel "that all earthly things are equally insignificant".

Rubens was never a true Stoic. Seneca the man, and his fate, interested him far more than his teachings. He may even have seen the philosopher as a warning against depending on the powerful.

Rubens himself had been court painter to the Duke of Mantua whilst in Italy, and, while he had been allowed every freedom, the position nonetheless presently palled. Back in Antwerp, he was so beset by the stadtholder of the Spanish throne in Brussels that he was unable to decline the position of court painter. But he dug in his heels: he negotiated a contract that permitted him to remain resident in Antwerp and not at court, and the only obligation he agreed to was a monthly salary.

An occasion to look at his sketches of the Roman statue may have been afforded Rubens in 1611 by the death of his elder brother Philip. Rubens had loved his brother; they had lived together in Rome. Philip had been a pupil of Lipsius the humanist, and had been entrusted with the duty of presenting his teacher's edition of Seneca to the Pope.

It must have been Philip who acquainted his younger brother with Seneca. After his brother's death, Rubens painted a picture in which Lipsius, Philip, the artist himself, and the scholar Jan Woverius are seated together beneath a bust of Seneca. It is a painting of friendship and of recollection. The picture of the dying Seneca, though painted in tribute to the philosopher, will have been inspired by grief for Rubens' brother.

Tacitus tells us that Seneca's wife wanted to join him in death. The philosopher agreed in order that she should be safe from Nero's capricious cruelty. But riders bore word of this arrangement to the emperor, who forbade her death. Her wounds were dressed, and she survived. Since Seneca's country house was beyond the gates of Rome, and the messengers thus had to cover a considerable distance, the death of the philosopher must have taken a matter of hours. It was a hard and painful death, and at the end will undoubtedly have had little of that beautiful dignity that Seneca envisaged.

The whole thing has a rather theatrical air: the death of a Stoic, with the author in the main role, freely adapted from the death of Socrates. But the final act of the play did not quite go as planned, and the opening too was disrupted. Seneca had intended to read his will, but the officer forbade him to do so. In that case, Seneca responded, he could leave to his wife and friends only one thing, the finest and most precious thing in his possession: his *imago vitae*, the image of his life. Dying, he had always written, is a part of life. "I work upon myself and shape myself and endeavour to rise to a monstrous goal."

Perhaps the artist was familiar with these words, and was alluding to them in showing Seneca rising from the tub. Although in modelling his figure on the statue Rubens had followed the wrong original, and moreover had imposed a false Christian dimension on it, his picture remains to this day one of the most interesting commentaries on Seneca's *imago vitae*, the image of an exemplary life.

The philosopher dies, his works live on

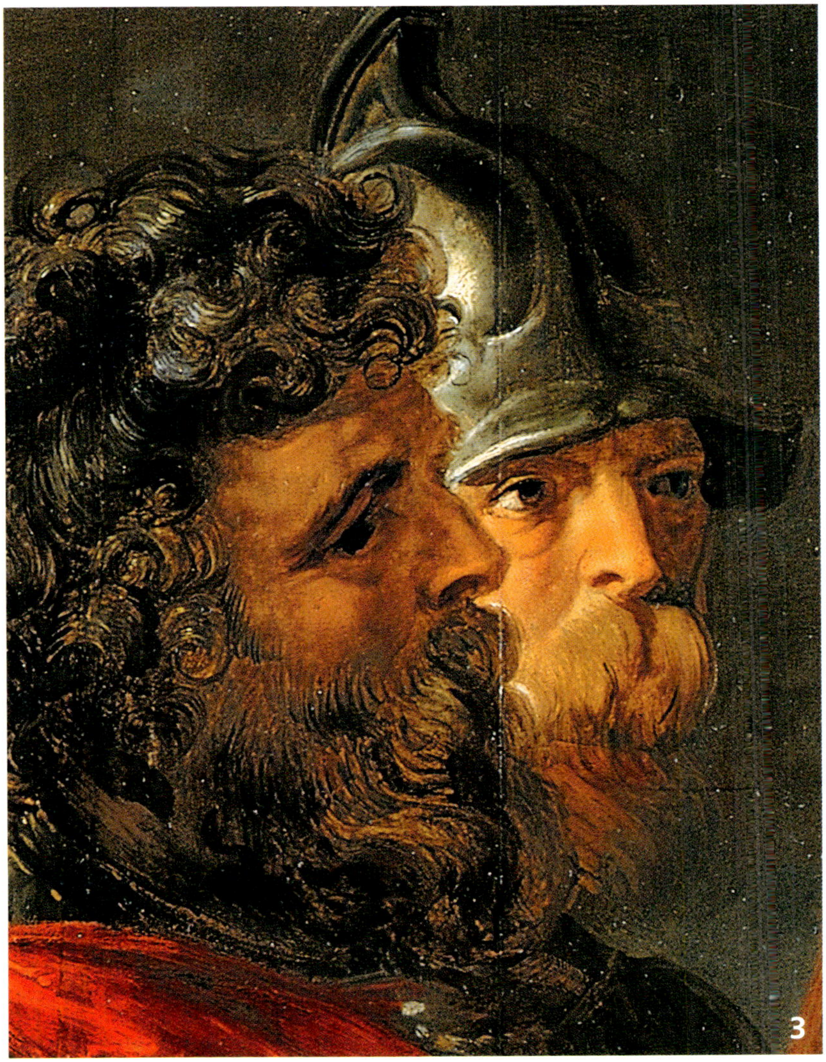
3

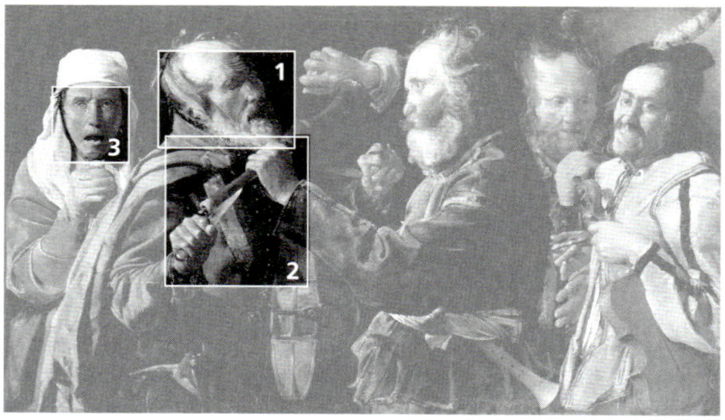
1
3
2

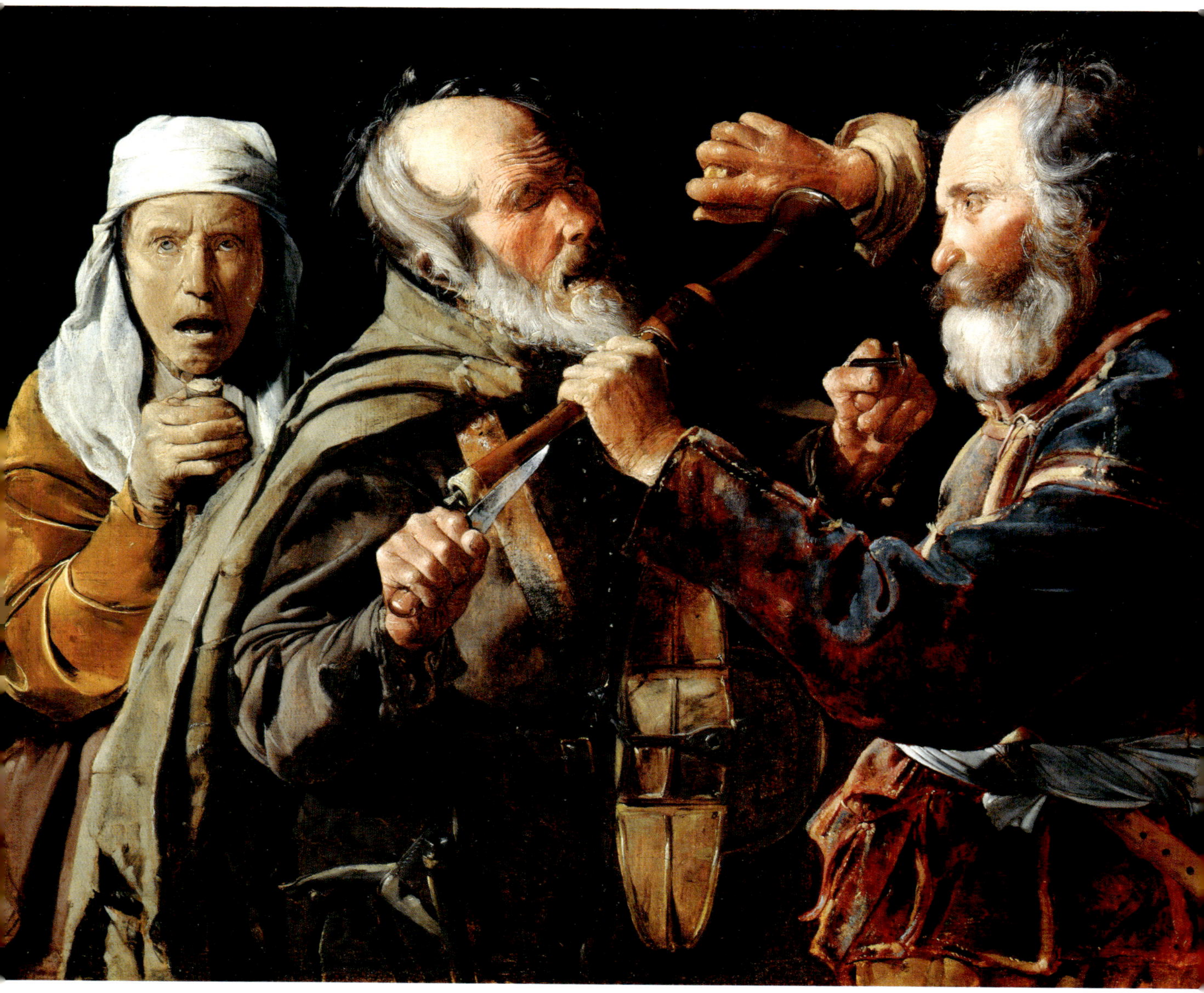

Georges de La Tour: The Musicians' Quarrel, 1620/1630

Courtly delight in the vagrant life

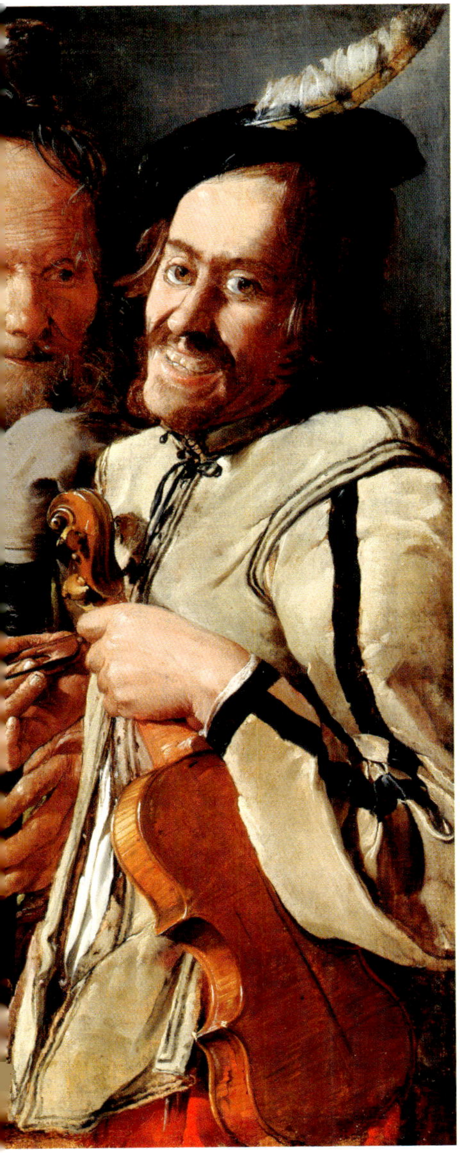

Two old men are quarrelling. One of them has a knife in his grip, the other is forcing him back with a musical instrument which he is holding horizontally like a stick. The instrument is a shawm. Another wind instrument is at his belt. The old man with the knife has a hurdy-gurdy at his belt. These are itinerant musicians.

Two other musicians, a piper and a fiddler, are at the right of the picture. They are keeping out of it, and are not trying to separate the quarrelsome two. Evidently they find the fight funny. One of them is grinning at us. The old woman at the left, on the other hand, is gripping her stick and crying out in despair.

The Lorraine artist Georges de La Tour (1693–1652) derived this scene from real life on the streets at night and his impressive portrait gallery from the lowest classes. He painted the picture some time between 1620 and 1630. This was the time of the Thirty Years' War, and the small duchy of Lorraine was being trampled through and devastated by the major powers.

In his own day, La Tour was a famous artist, but after his death he was quickly forgotten. Not till the 20th century did art historians rediscover him. His works were tracked down in museums and private collections, where they hung anonymously or under the wrong name. Mostly they were nocturnes showing saints by gentle candlelight.

The Musicians' Quarrel (94 by 141 centimetres) turned up in the late Fifties in Wales, in the possession of Lord Trevor of Brynkynallt, Chirk, in Denbighshire, where it was falsely attributed to the Italian artist Caravaggio. The first experts to examine the painting were hesitant to ascribe it to La Tour, the painter of saints. Not until the 1972 Paris exhibition of the artist's work afforded an opportunity for direct comparison was this picture declared an authentic La Tour.

Some months later, *The Musicians' Quarrel* was sold at auction by Christie's in London for 380,000 guineas, to the Getty Museum in Los Angeles.

The right eye of the man with the hurdy-gurdy is closed, the left open just a little. The man is blind; or perhaps he is pretending to be blind. This seems to be what the other man is bent on determining. He has something in his hand that might be a lemon – doubtless to squirt the juice into the blind man's eye, to test whether it is sensitive to the acid.

We can only speculate whether La Tour was out to show one musician exposing another as a fraud. But this brutal test squares with the poor reputation itinerant musicians had, especially those who traded on the pity aroused by disabilities. "Before giving to the blind, ascertain whether they are indeed blind," was the advice of the 16th century *Liber Vagatorum*, a book about vagrants that was popular in Germany. The old woman beside the supposedly blind man is presumably his guide. One reason why she is crying out is that she will be out of work, and out of a modest income too, if he is exposed.

A sedentary society based on property ownership and civil rights was suspicious of any outsider. This suspicion was not unfounded, for those who had no fixed abode were poor and thus obliged to live off those who had – by begging, cheating or stealing. "There are blind men", warned the *Liber Vagatorum*, "who sit outside churches singing songs from foreign countries they have never set foot in, and then telling lying tales about how they lost their eyesight."

The cities tried to keep the poor away as well as they could. In Nancy, the capital of Lorraine, so-called *chasse-coquins* (crook catchers) demanded to know the name, origin and destination of every penniless new arrival – and saw to it that these uninvited visitors were on their way again next morning at the latest. Only the local poor had the right to remain and to receive alms.

Eye diseases were widespread in the 17th century. A doctor has diagnosed everyone in La Tour's painting except the fiddler as having an eye illness or injury. Other than begging or making music, the blind had no means of making a living. If they quarrelled about a good place to stand – which may be what is happening here – it was a fight for survival.

In the city of Bourges, south of Paris, the church helped the blind to help themselves: players with the gift of sight taught the blind to play, or build, violins. Perhaps a similar charitable venture existed in Lunéville, the town in Lorraine where La Tour lived and painted from 1620.

A handbook's warning against the blind

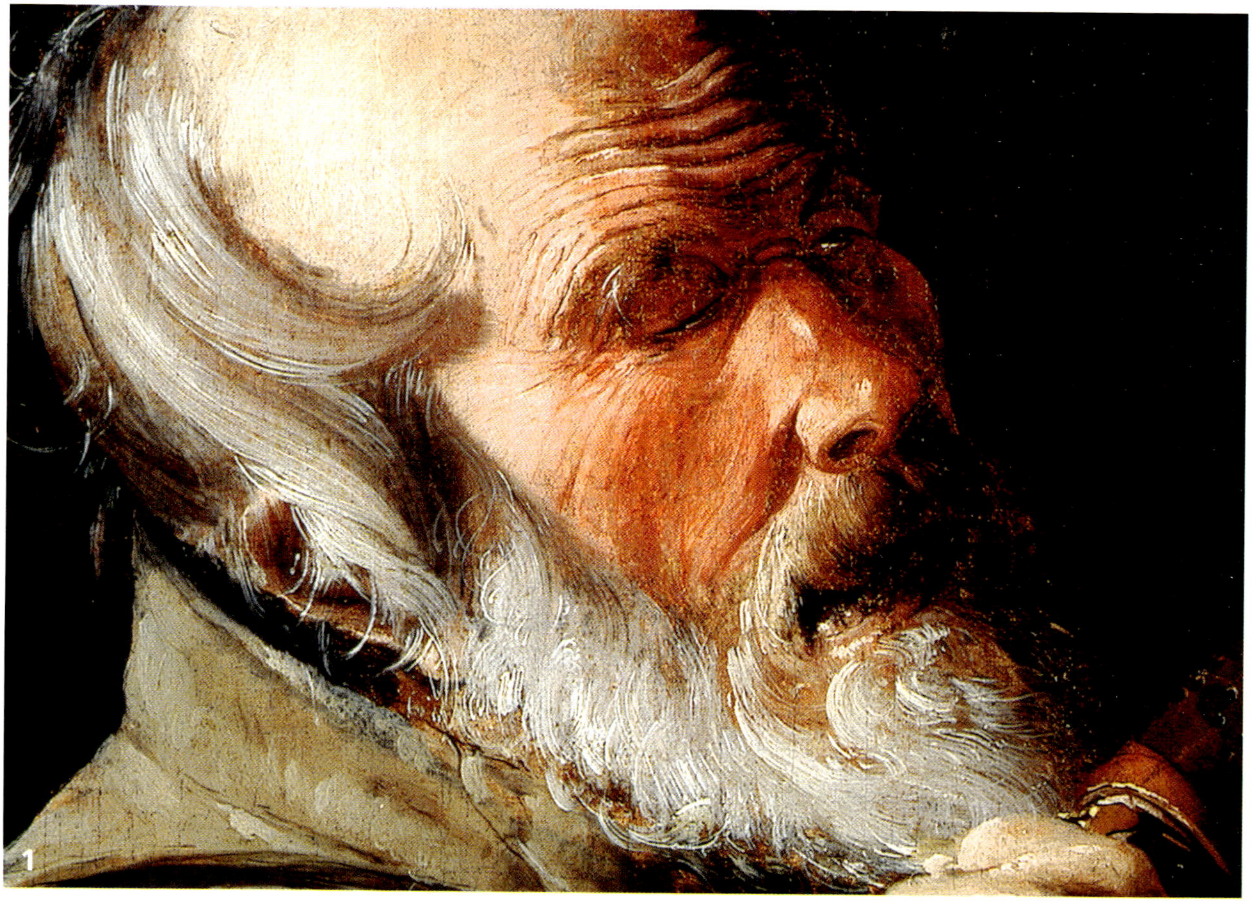
1

The blind man with the knife is a hurdy-gurdy player; the instrument is suspended before him, hanging from a broad belt. La Tour painted the selfsame ugly old man with the long hair around his bald pate at least five times, virtually life-size. In a painting (162 by 105 centimetres) now in Nantes he makes a less ragged impression than here. There he is playing a richly ornate instrument, wearing old rose breeches and white stockings and, over his cape, a fine neckerchief. On the floor lies a red hat with a feather. Musicians tried to attract attention by wearing colourful clothing.

In the solo portrait we can see the instrument rather better than in the group scene. The wheel fixed inside the hurdy-gurdy touches the strings, producing the sound. The player turns a crank at the head; the old man has it in an awkward grip. The strings all sound simultaneously; the player can use mechanical keys to adjust the pitch of some of them. The result is a varied rasping, scraping sound, tricked out with a simple melody. The blind man with the stylish hat is singing to his tune.

In the Middle Ages, the hurdy-gurdy was a popular instrument which singers at court might use as an accompaniment; there are indeed altar-pieces which depict angels performing on the instrument. But in the 17th century, when La Tour painted his picture, its prestige was a thing of the past. Because it was so easy to play, the hurdy-gurdy had become an instrument of the street, usually played by the blind or the mentally retarded. The outcast status of those who played it was extended to the instrument, and by La Tour's day it merely served to prompt compassion or at best to start a dance.

The other instruments in the picture of the quarrel were similarly held in low esteem. The bagpipes of the second from the right, and the shawm, were instruments associated with herdsmen; the fiddle held by the jolly man at the far right is the same shape as its modern descendant, but the instrument has a long crack, and was probably quite a simple affair anyway. At this period, fine violins were already being built in Italy, at workshops such as that of the Amati family in Cremona. Before long the simple fiddle would rise to become the violin, and from being a dance instrument it would evolve into a valuable and highly regarded concert instrument.

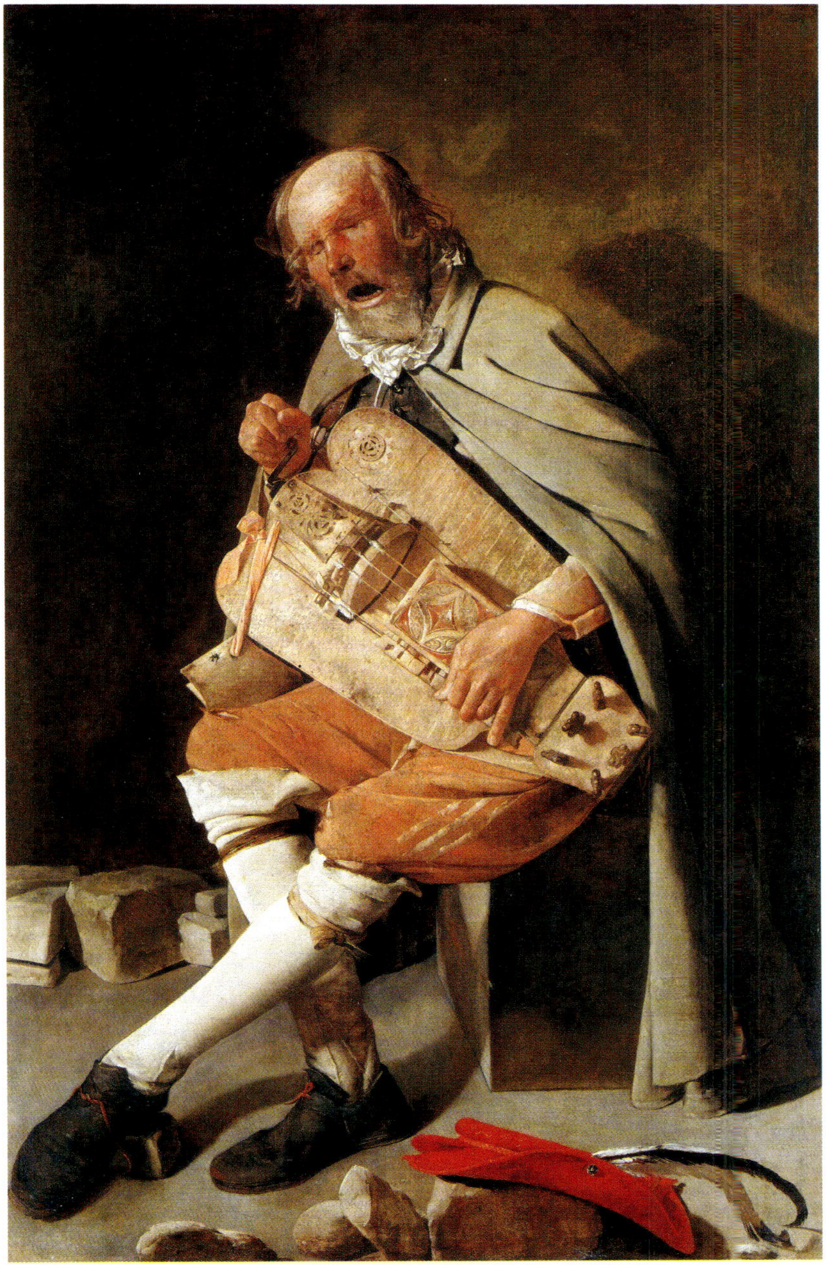

But at this time the fiddle was still considered vulgar. The to-and-fro stroking movement of the bow had long been taken as a sexual innuendo; the bagpipes too were seen as a sexual symbol. Indeed, to the pious mind, secular music in general was the work of the devil. Musicians were riff-raff, wastrels, a work-shy and quarrelsome lot. In the popular perception they deserved a good thrashing.

The hurdy-gurdy was the instrument of the street

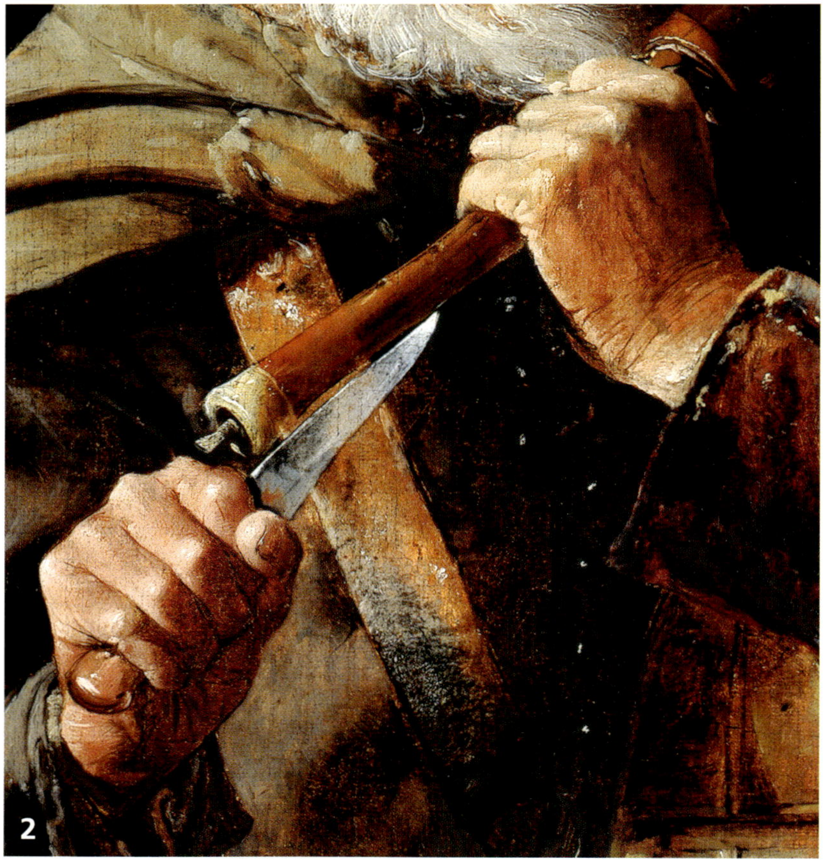

A painter with a reputation for violence

Documentary evidence that has survived in Bourges records that in 1620 a blind man brought charges against two guides who had beaten him up. His assailants were found guilty and ordered to pay the medical and legal costs. In general, French legal documents show that acts of violence, such as robbery or fighting, were more common in the first half of the 17th century than offences against property. By the end of the century that had changed, but in La Tour's day a speedy bout of fisticuffs was considered an acceptable way of resolving conflict, not only amongst beggars. The *vicarius rixosus* or quarrelsome vicar was proverbial; aristocrats were prepared from childhood for war and combat, and might reach for their weapons on the smallest of pretexts. While their coachmen jumped down from their boxes and started to fight over who had right of way, their masters climbed out of their carriages and drew their swords. The rage for duelling was at a peak among aristocrats in France when La Tour painted *The Musicians' Quarrel.*

Georges de La Tour was not an aristocrat; it was his son who was later ennobled. The father was a social climber, and evidently an arrogant type. In 1646 townsfolk in Lunéville submitted a petition complaining about the artist, "who has made himself unpopular with the people because of the number of his dogs ... which he keeps as if he were the lord and master of the place, hunting hares in the cornfields, damaging and trampling them".

La Tour came of the well-to-do bourgeoisie. The records show that he bought houses, signed apprenticeship contracts, adopted children, but also had a violent streak. "He kicked me hard", one tax collector complained in 1642, "slammed his door, and raged that he would put a bullet through the first man who came any closer." In 1648 La Tour had to pay ten francs in compensation for beating someone "with a cudgel", and in 1650 he injured a man of Lunéville so badly that the victim required surgical treatment. It was not the painter but his son who put matters straight, settling the medical and legal bill and paying the plaintiff compensation of 140 francs, a substantial sum at the time.

All the records of violence by the artist date from the last decade of his life, when he was no longer painting fights or mendicant musicians but mainly saints in the warm glow of candlelight. Perhaps his aggressive conduct was a sign of old age; or perhaps the records documenting similar conduct in earlier decades have been lost.

Or perhaps the artist's behaviour was his way of responding to the disasters that had befallen his country. For thirty long years, Europe's rulers fought over religion and power – and the small but affluent duchy of Lorraine lay squarely in the path of every army. When troops passed through they made heavy demands, and brought with them inflation, starvation and epidemics. When Duke Charles IV of Lorraine sided with the Holy Roman Emperor in 1633, Lorraine itself became a theatre of war. It was looted, and burnt to the ground; half the population reportedly died.

The war does not appear in La Tour's work. His contemporary and countryman Jacques Callot (1592–1635), on the other hand, impressively recorded all of its horrors in his 1633 series of engravings, *The Miseries of War.*

In autumn 1638, the French burnt down Lunéville, the town where the artist lived; they were followed by imperial troops, looting; then the French returned. In the end there were just thirty families still remaining in the town. La Tour and his family had probably got away in good time to the safety of Paris or Nancy. But many of his early paintings perished in the flames.

The undated *The Musicians' Quarrel* is an early work, in the view of the experts. La Tour's early paintings show everyday folk: *The Tax Collector* (now in Lemberg), *Old Man* and *Old Woman* (San Francisco), *The Pea Eaters* (Berlin). He probably found his models in the streets – among them the musicians or the old woman with her black teeth, reddened eyes and the lower lids rolled inward, a product of senility.

La Tour was not the only one to paint vagrants, beggars and strolling musicians in large formats. In the picture galleries of the aristocracy, the poor were in vogue. There may have been religious reasons for this: with the Counter-Reformation there arose in France a movement that saw poverty, sickness and suffering as not necessarily the victim's own fault, a movement that aimed to ensure that the hordes of itinerant beggars were not always simply driven out of the cities.

The initiator of this movement was the subsequently canonized St Vincent de Paul (1581-1660). His followers cared for abandoned children, galley slaves, cripples; the men who organized life for the blind in Bourges were probably among them. In Lorraine, traditionally a Catholic region, they established numerous monasteries. The Capuchins founded one in Lunéville; La Tour must have been close to them, for he left them a plot of land.

The unknown purchaser of *The Musicians' Quarrel* may well have been at the court of Lorraine or of France, like many of La Tour's secular clients. He will scarcely have been wanting to see a religious dimension in the work; more likely he wanted something quite different in his residence, to counterbalance the otherworldly pictures of saints, the idealized mythological figures, or the portraits of family members posed to heroic advantage. What he wanted was people expressing their gut feelings, their mouths gaping wide in fright, or grinning as they clutch their fiddle.

Gut feeling was irreconcilable with courtly etiquette; but King Philip IV of Spain wanted to see it. Like his courtiers, he himself was always portrayed with his features rigid and unyielding – but in his private apartments he had a painting that showed beggars, workmen and soldiers. Painted by Diego Velázquez in 1628, it was titled *Bacchus* and one of the tipsy men in it is even leering at the beholder. In the royal palace at Commercy too, which formerly belonged to the dukes of Lorraine, a hurdy-gurdy man by Georges de La Tour hung in 1764.

One of the pleasures that paintings featuring beggars afforded the aristocracy was doubtless that of looking down on those depicted. Their squalid wretchedness underwrote the superiority of the nobles. An official justification was that these pictures frequently contained a moral or a warning. "Poverty leads to deceit," is written on a painting of a blind hurdy-gurdy man done about the same time as La Tour's; under a print showing a fight is inscribed, "Mendicus mendico invidet" – the beggar envies the beggar. In other words, even the have-nots quarrel over the little they do possess.

And yet it does seem unlikely that someone would hang so superb a painting as *The Musicians' Quarrel* on his wall simply to learn a moral message or have one confirmed. Presumably purchasers were first and foremost after pleasure: they derived satisfaction from perfect craftsmanship and artistic achievement. La Tour's aristocratic contemporaries had a taste for the thrill that derives from the contradiction between true-to-life verisimilitude and extreme artifice, between realistically depicted faces and garments and instruments and a succession of faces as in a portrait gallery.

What counted was clearly to lend harmony and beauty to wretched figures of squalor by means of colour and light.

Pictures of beggars in the palace

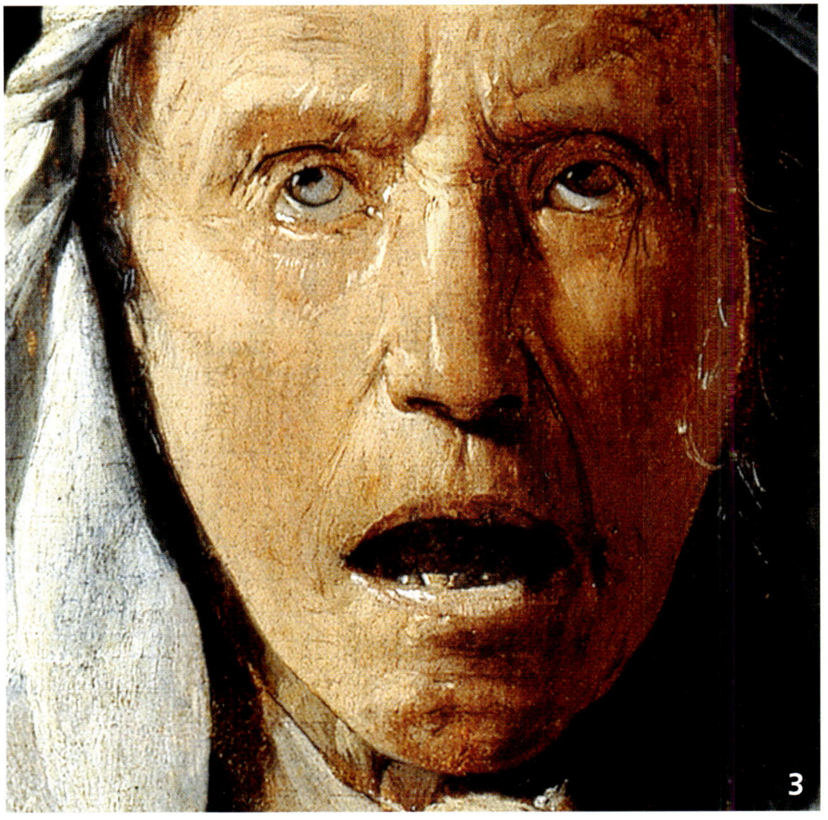
3

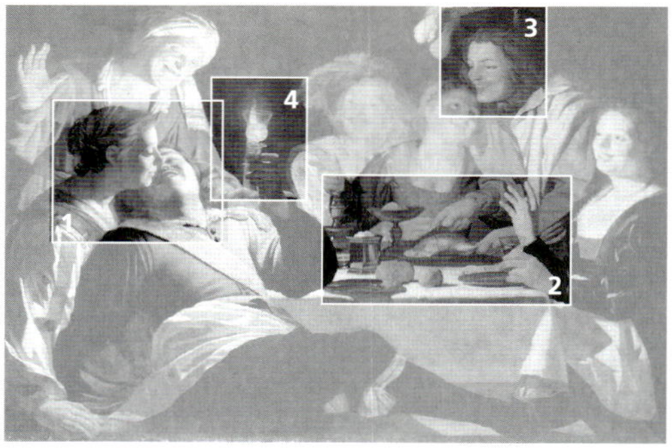
1
2
3
4

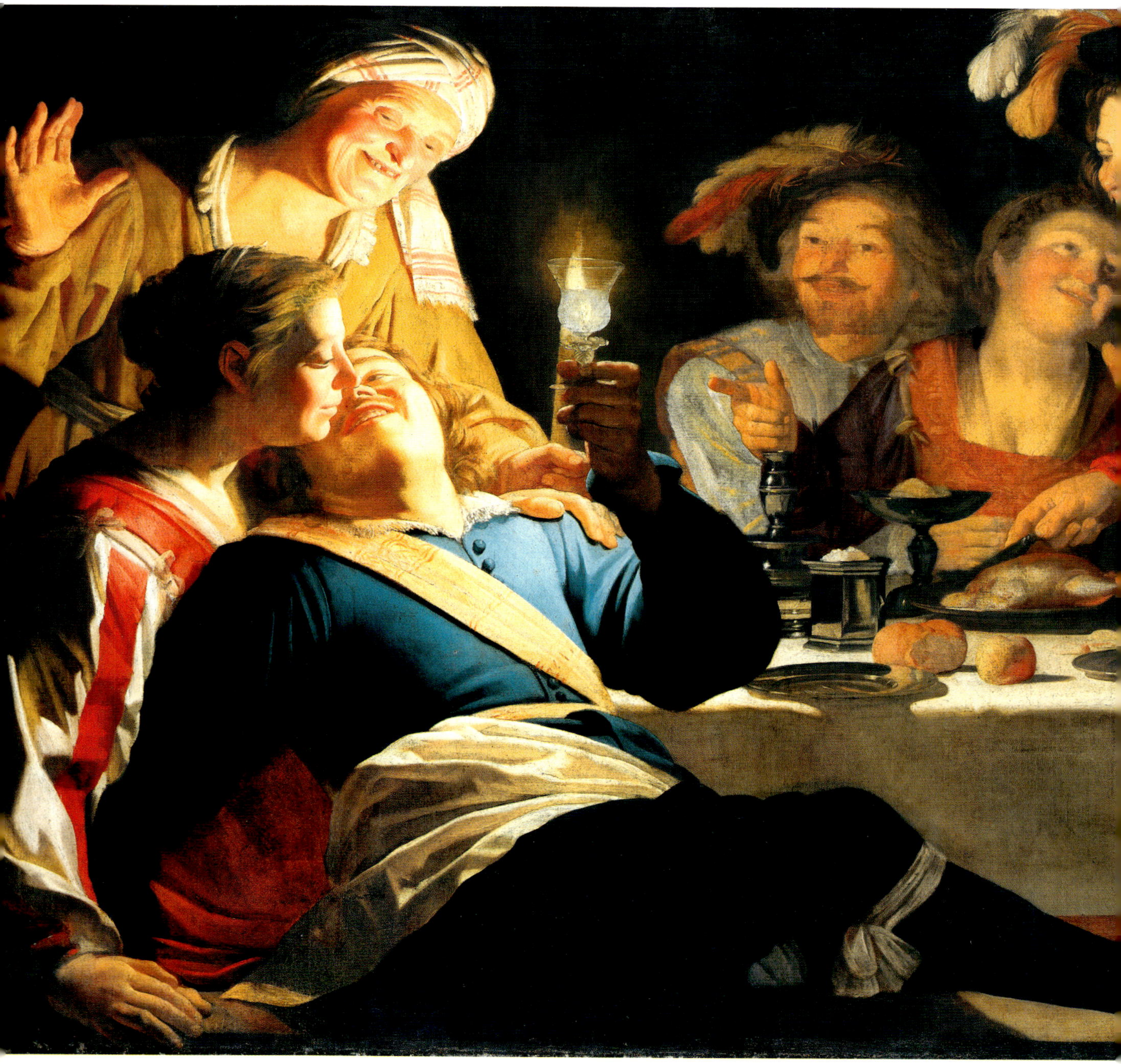

Gerard van Honthorst: Jovial Company, 1622

Not the Prodigal Son

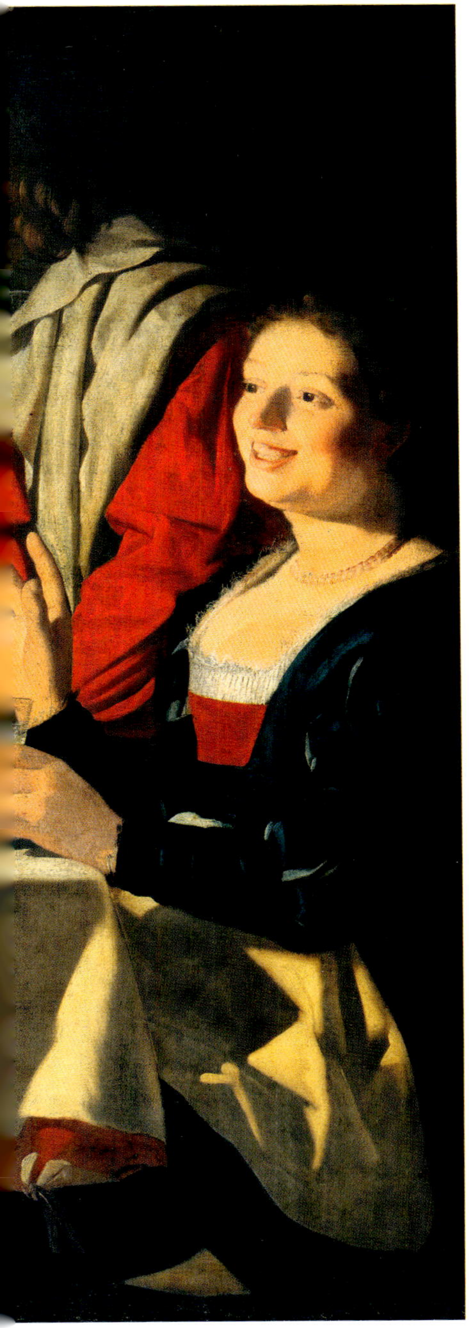

On the 26th of July, 1620, they were celebrating in Het Poortgen, a tavern in Utrecht in the Netherlands. The carousers were merchants, painters, art dealers, copper engravers – and Gerard van Honthorst, who had just returned from Rome "to the great delight of his friends".

We know of the occasion from the diary of one man who was present, Aernout van Buchell. He was a lawyer with a penchant for art, but also the local director of the West India Company. This made him an important figure in the Asian trade, which was then so profitable for the Netherlands. Buchell made a note of some of the topics of conversation. The returnee's skills as a painter were praised in the highest terms. His Flemish fellow artist Peter Paul Rubens (1577–1640), then at the height of his fame, was declared by contrast to possess little genius and to owe his success "rather to luck than to endeavour". The carousers at Het Poortgen were furthermore agreed that copper engravings after Rubens' paintings were too expensive.

Buchell did not record whether women were present, too, but it is likely that they were, because not long after, in October 1620, Honthorst married the daughter of the proprietress of the inn. Nor did the diarist think it worth mentioning what they ate, but it will have been quite an amount, as was usual on such occasions. Probably they drank wine rather than the local beer: the landlady's husband was a prosperous wine merchant.

Honthorst was twenty-seven when he made his return journey from Rome to Utrecht. He had made a name for himself in Italy with altar paintings, portraits of Roman noblemen, and candlelit scenes of the birth of Christ. He had painted one of his convivial dining scenes for Cardinal Barberini, subsequently Pope Urban VIII, and another for the Grand Duke of Tuscany. The present scene was painted in 1622, two years after his return. It measures 130 by 196 centimetres and is in the possession of the Alte Pinakothek in Munich. Previously, though, it belonged to Elector Wilhelm of the Palatinate, who called it *The Prodigal Son*.

The full title as entered in the Elector's inventory of 1716 was in fact *The Prodigal Son, Seduced in a Brothel with Drink and Caresses.* The story of the young man who squanders his inheritance is in the Gospel of St Luke. In the traditional iconography associated with the parable, the old woman would be a procuress, the young women prostitutes, and the other young men accomplices helping to strip the young man in the yellow sash of his fortune. The playing cards and other indications of cheating or theft that were normally part of the pictorial presentation of this subject are absent, however.

Whoever drew up the Elector's inventory surely made a mistake. Honthorst's painting is lacking in any Biblical background. The artist was not out to warn the beholder of the dangers of vice, of alcohol and women. He painted a profane tavern scene, in the manner of the *fête galante*.

Evidently he had made a number of sketches in Rome which he then put to use over and over: the girls with their inviting smiles, round cheeks, and low décolletées, the young men with feathers on their hats and longish hair.

At that time a number of Dutch painters were living in Rome. Others from Utrecht included Hendrick Terbrugghen (1588–1629) and Dirck van Baburen (c. 1595–1624). There was a Dutch artists' colony between Porta del Popolo and the church of Trinità dei Monti; an apprenticeship in Rome was very much a part of the northern European tradition, and it was considered important to see the ancient monuments with one's own eyes. Furthermore, in one academy at the time of Honthorst's stay, nude painting was done in life classes from living models – Rome afforded not only the classical legacy but also progressive teaching methods.

What was more, there was money to be made. The Counter-Reformation, and a taste for stately display, had led to a building boom. All Christendom was to be confirmed in its faith, and prompted to make donations, by the new or renovated churches, chapels, monasteries and palaces; and it was the painters and sculptors who adorned the altars and walls with religious motifs.

But along with this hectic boom went disorder and violence. Gangs of thugs in private pay terrorized whole quarters and fought pitched battles with the papal police. "The Papal States are in chaos", read *Avvisi*, a handwritten broadsheet. On the Ponte San Angelo, severed heads were stuck on poles by way of deterrent – more, it was reported, than there were melons at the market.

Among the artists, too, there were those with a violent streak, such as Michelangelo Merisi, called Caravaggio. He was obliged to flee the city after he had killed a gambling partner.

Honthorst and his fellow Dutch artists had heard of Caravaggio even in faraway Utrecht. He may even have strengthened their resolve to make the journey to Italy: "Then there is Michael Agnolo of Caravaggio, who has done wondrous things in Rome", the Dutchman Karel van Mander wrote in his *Schilderboeck*, published in Haarlem in 1604.

Gerard van Honthorst (1592–1656) was not of a violent bent. In 1620 the Italian doctor and art lover Giulio Mancini described him as "withdrawn and melancholy". Honthorst, he added, was "cultivated and courteous". Furthermore, "if he has promised something for a certain date, he keeps his word".

From about 1616 the painter was under the patronage of the Marchese Vincenzo Giustiniani, and lived in the nobleman's palace. Giustiniani was a banker, the brother of a cardinal, and a well-travelled man. We know of his palace that it "had a great many large halls, galleries, magnificent rooms", all of them "filled with the most famous paintings and antiques by the finest of the masters old and new". It was the perfect place for Honthorst, both aesthetically and in terms of security and useful connections.

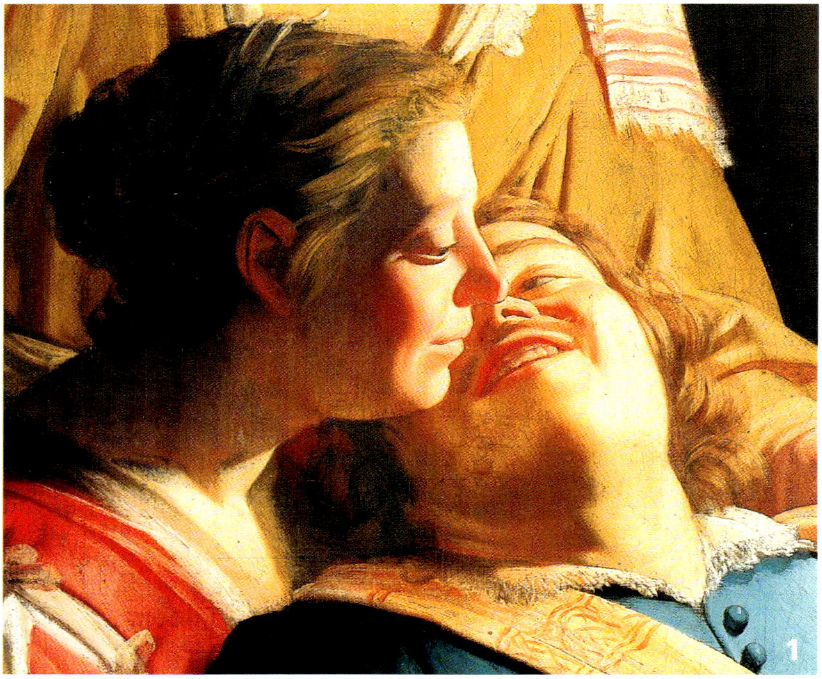

The first sketches were done in Rome

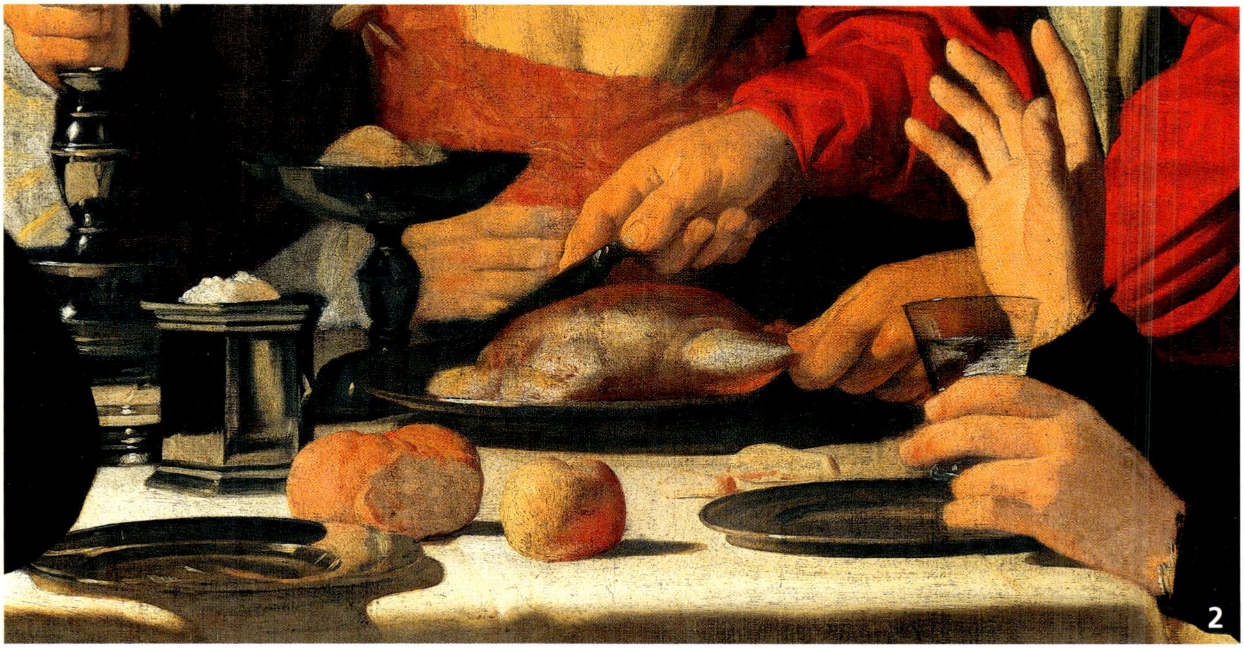
2

Honthorst did not lead a bad life in Rome, but returned nonetheless to Utrecht. The other Dutch painters did likewise, and married wives not from Italy but from the Netherlands.

Four months after his return, in October 1620, Gerard van Honthorst married Sophia Coopmans, a distant relative who had prospects of a substantial inheritance. They set up home together in Snippevlucht, a lane in Utrecht that numbered just five humble houses.

Why did this man return from the great world to the more cramped confines of Utrecht? In Rome, Honthorst had dwelt in a palace, albeit probably in a small room. Artists ate with the servants, and, even if their works were bought by aristocrats, the gulf that remained between their persons was unbridgeable.

Dutch society was more open. There were few aristocrats, and society effectively meant the burgher classes, the merchants and artisans. Artists were included in their number. And they could cross the road without fearing robbery or assault.

In the 1620s, however, it was not peacetime that Honthorst returned to in Utrecht. The provinces of the Netherlands were fighting Spain, struggling to cast off the yoke of Habsburg rule from Madrid. The struggle had begun with an uprising in 1568 and was not to end until 1648, when the Treaty of Westphalia left the southern provinces (today's Belgium) in the possession of Spain but recognized the sovereign independence of the northern provinces (in which Utrecht was situated).

The conflict was not over political power only, but over ecclesiastical power as well. The Spanish were fighting for Roman Catholicism, the Dutch for Calvinism. Honthorst was a Catholic. This meant that he was debarred from government service in Utrecht, and indeed was on several occasions obliged to bail out his brother, a priest, from gaol.

The suppression of the Catholics in the northern provinces, and the antipathy of the Calvinists to the making of images, meant that artists received no more commissions from the church. Neither – in Utrecht – could they paint any more of the large-format pictures of militia guilds. Throughout the Netherlands, armed citizens had associated in these guilds, and group portraits of the members were a Dutch speciality. Not in Utrecht, though. There the militia companies were prohibited. The Calvinist council went in fear of the city's Catholic majority, which might have become organized and taken up arms.

At the same time, however, the provinces of the Netherlands, and especially the cities, were seeing a period of economic revival. The war was no longer pursued with much seriousness, and the number of prosperous citizens was on the increase. These were now commissioning works of art in the church's stead. Being Calvinists, they observed certain rules in life: their clothing must not be ostentatious, they eschewed all luxury or self-indulgence, and the houses of the wealthy remained plain on the exterior. Only inside was decoration permitted, such as pictures on the walls and fine things for everyday use.

An expensively set table for Utrecht burghers

Such fine things would include good, ironed table linen such as we see on the table in this painting. In burgher households, the plates and serving dishes would be pewter. The poor ate off wood, but the rich ate off silver, and, from the late 16th century, off porcelain imported from China. The people at Honthorst's festive table are evidently well-to-do burghers, as we can tell from the cut glass and the hexagonal salt cellar. The sheer size of this last indicates that the necessities of life are present in abundance.

In the Palazzo Giustiniani, where Honthorst lived in Rome, hung fifteen works by Caravaggio. Of all Italian artists, he was the most influential at that time. Honthorst never met him. The young Dutchman went to Rome some time between 1610 and 1615, whereas the impulsively violent Italian had had to quit the city in 1606.

Caravaggio had revolutionized art. Instead of taking his bearings from the idealized figures who peopled the works of artists before him, he looked at living people, taking his men from the marketplace, his women from the brothel, and transforming them into martyrs and saints. If their feet were dirty, so be it. If the nose of a man carving a hot roast fowl was gleaming with perspiration, he painted it that way.

In our painting, the man with the friendly smile and a large napkin over his shoulder is supposedly Honthorst himself. He had "made good use of his good fortune", Joachim von Sandrart wrote. He painted "very rapidly, in his own manner" and before long his house "was famous, and full of the offspring of respected persons, bound in apprenticeship to him". Sandrart was among those who learnt from Honthorst; in his day the painter had some twenty-five apprentices, each of them paying 100 guilders a year to him.

In 1627 Honthorst left his humble home on Snippevlucht and bought a large house on Domkerkhof. There he was visited by Peter Paul Rubens, a good fifteen years older than Honthorst, court painter to the Habsburg stadtholders in Brussels, an artist and a diplomat, and – though the carousers on this or that festive occasion might belittle him – a man highly regarded throughout Europe. Honthorst threw a banquet for him, and Rubens, our chronicler Sandrart reports, praised his younger fellow artist's "perfect style of painting, especially in night pieces".

Like Rubens, Honthorst had the gift of moving with ease in aristocratic circles. He was educated, he corresponded in four languages, and from Rome he had letters of recommendation that opened doors to him. In the year following his return, the English envoy was already writing from The Hague to London: Here abouts there is a young man at present who is making a name for himself. At the envoy's home, Honthorst subsequently met the sister of King Charles I of England; and in 1628 Charles summoned the artist to England.

Within six months he had completed an immense painting of Apollo and Diana in the royal Banqueting House in Whitehall. He gave the two gods the features of the king and queen, and their favourite, the Duke of Buckingham, was included as Mercury. Honthorst's new masters were flattered and delighted, and rewarded him royally with a twelve-piece silver service, a costly horse, English citizenship, 3,000 guilders in cash, and an annual pension of £100. On the 15th of December, 1628, he returned from England to Utrecht, "where he was received with great respect".

But the rules that govern allegorical ceiling paintings are different from those that apply to realistic dining scenes, and an artist paints differently for monarchs than for his fellow citizens. Perhaps it was because he now expected to paint for the aristocracy, or perhaps his creative powers simply failed – either way, after 1640 Honthorst's personae came to lack their fullness, they became stiff and slick, and doubtless they were increasingly done by assistants and apprentices. By the time Honthorst died, in 1656, his fame was a thing of the past.

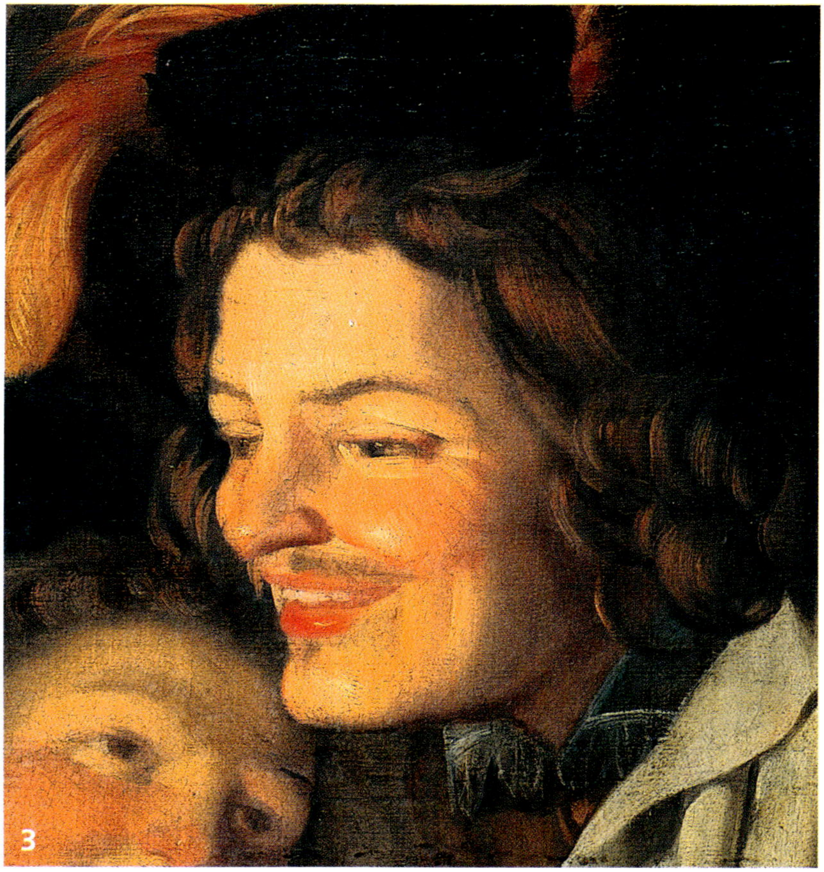

The painter enjoys his good fortune

A candle as the sole source of light

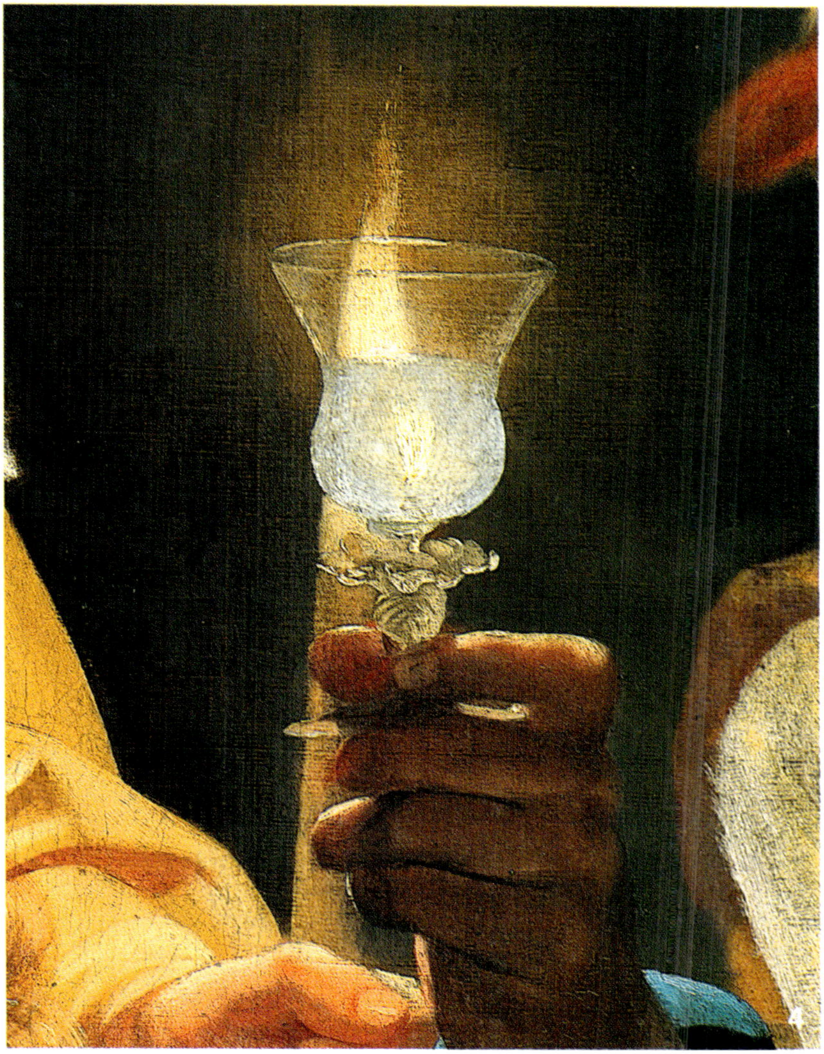

In the 17th century there was a strong tendency to assign symbolic meaning to plants, animals or objects. Candles, "blaeckerende vlammen der Minnen", stood for love, but also the vanity of earthly things, the burning down symbolizing the transience of beauty. It is no coincidence that the artist has placed an old and a young woman side by side.

It is difficult now to visualize the importance of candles in the past. Nights were very dark in the 17th century. There was no universal street lighting, and no way of seeing further than a candle, torch, or fire might illuminate. The outer darkness in Honthorst's painting was no more than the reality of every evening.

The candle is one more indication that this is no poor household. The poor used oil lamps, which shed little light. Tallow candles gave a better light, but the best, aside from the torches customary in palaces, was given by wax candles such as that in Honthorst's painting. The artist uses the candle for narrative purposes: the old woman has removed the candle from its holder (below the hand with the extended index finger) and has surprised the couple kissing in secret under cover of the half-light, much to the delight of the others at table.

The candle in the old woman's hand is the sole source of light in this painting; the wine glass before it partly covers but does not obscure it. Compositions that were unevenly lit, in which a single light source or maybe two emphasized what was of interest and left the remainder in the dark, was one of Honthorst's specialities. In Italy he was known as "Gherardo delle Notti", Gerard of the night scenes. He used this approach not only to paint dining parties but also for religious works; in his Roman period, for example, for a bound Christ who, in Sandrart's words, "clad in a white tunic, stands before Pilate, who is examining him, the light from the candles and tapers illuminating all things with such natural verisimilitude that this art has never been exceeded".

It was Caravaggio who developed this uneven distribution of light and made it famous. Honthorst had learnt from the Italian's work how to place and mask the light, how to handle darkness, and how to position the figures. But just as the two painters differed in character, so their use of chiaroscuro differed in impact, too: in the paintings of the Italian, prone to violence, living in streets that were unsafe, the contrast expressed lurking danger and the drama of events, while the peaceable-spirited Dutchman, at home in the safety of Utrecht, used the effect of the light to reveal the friendship between affectionate people and the fellow-feeling amongst burghers. Candlelight lends to his night pieces a distinctive, seductive glow.

Honthorst can be credited with making Caravaggio's chiaroscuro technique popular in the Netherlands. In so doing, he showed artists who did not make the trip to Rome new approaches to composition, which they could develop further. The most famous of them was to be Rembrandt Harmensz van Rijn, born in 1606, fourteen years after Honthorst. In his hands, light became a sign of enlightenment, of the divine presence in a dark world. Rembrandt achieved effects that went beyond Caravaggio or Honthorst. But the man from Utrecht, who had the mastery to paint such details as a cut glass held before a burning flame, showed him the way.

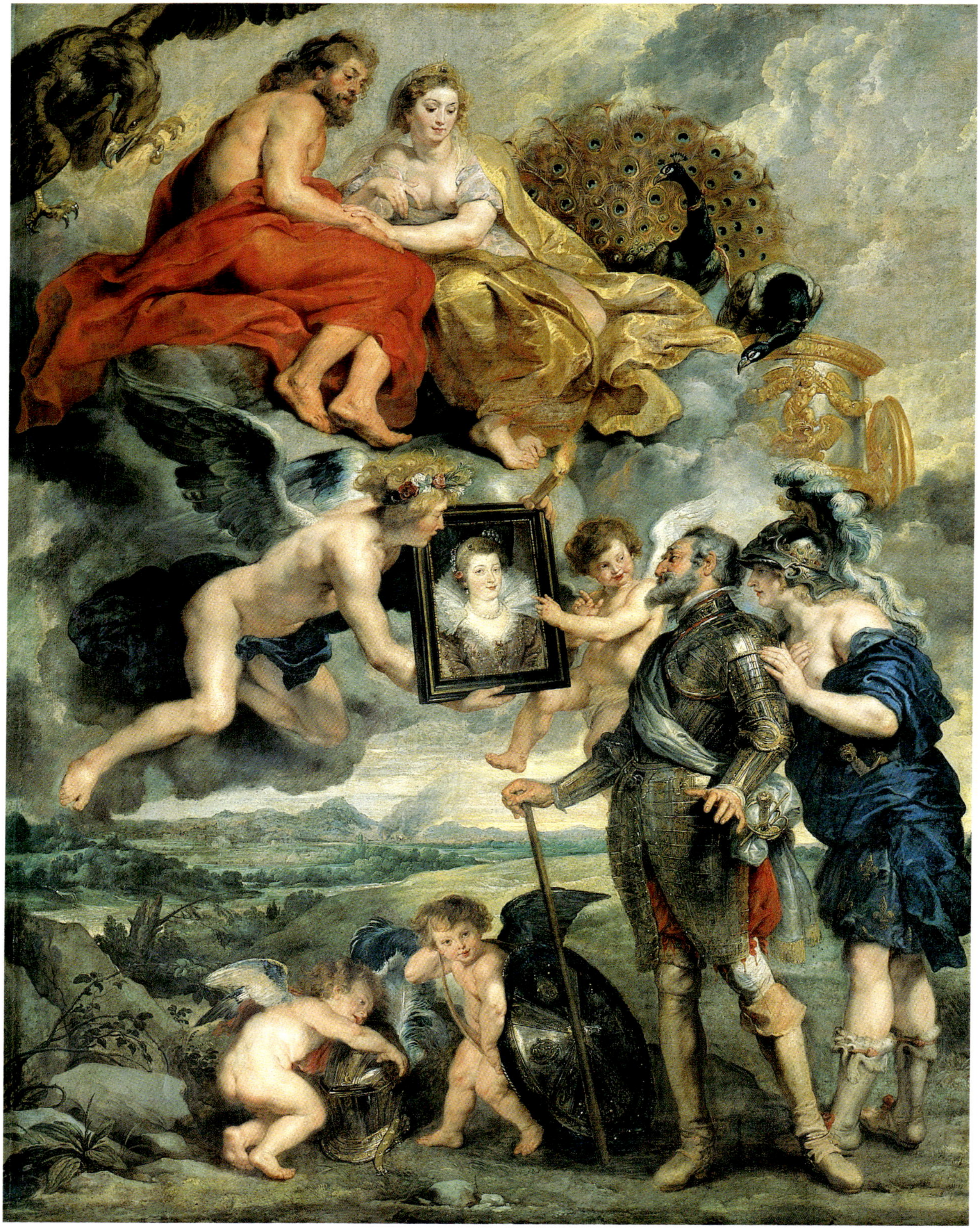

Peter Paul Rubens: Henri IV receives the portrait of Maria de' Medici, 1622/1625

A royal match

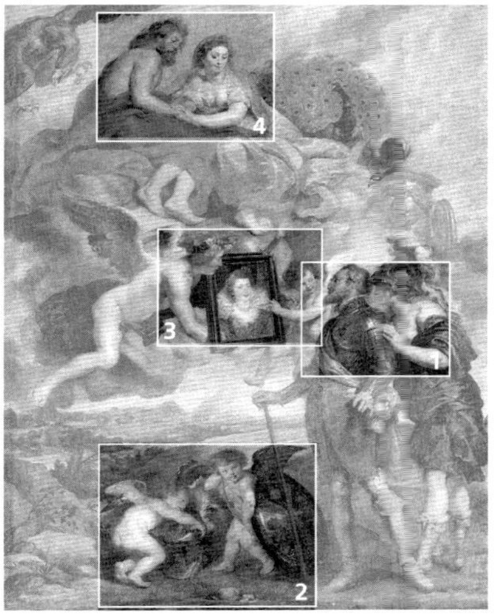

The gods of marriage and of love, Hymen and Eros, have descended to the earth in order to present to the king of France a portrait of his bride. She is smiling seductively at him from out of the wooden frame. Her name is Maria de' Medici and she is from Florence. She was betrothed to Henri IV in 1600 after they had become known to each other through go-betweens and portraits. They were not to meet until two months after the wedding.

At the time she became engaged, Maria was twenty-seven, an old maid at a time when fifteen was considered a suitable age for a girl to marry. Her family tree did not amount to much. The king could trace his ancestry to St Louis, whereas the Medici were parvenus; while they were descended from the once mighty banking family, the uncrowned rulers of Florence, the fact was they had never worn a crown. Still, Maria's uncle, the Grand Duke of Tuscany, was a wealthy man, and played a decisive part in bankrolling the monarchs of Europe. This uncle loved his niece, and the dowry he proposed to give with her made her (despite her unprepossessing family tree) the most desirable match in Europe. So the uncle wanted to see her on a throne. She wanted the same. It was an aim that was worth waiting to achieve.

Beside that lofty ambition, her life in the Pitti palace was fairly grim. All around her were sickness, intrigues, and murder. Her parents died in mysterious circumstances. Her uncle, who after all meant well, remarked that she "was excelled in beauty and intelligence by her sisters"; and indeed, her education was adapted to her modest talents. Henri IV's first wife knew Latin and Greek; Maria did not even speak French. But she was very religious, and knew court etiquette, though she would forget the rules of protocol when she was seized by one of her fits of rage. The Duke of Saint-Simon described her thus: "An altogether limited mind, always under the thumb of the scum of the court, bereft of any knowledge and without the slightest insight, hard, haughty, domineering". But certain of her external features pleased the taste of the time: her blonde hair, rosy complexion, and an element of the voluptuous – in the 16th and 17th centuries, a double chin was an essential mark of female beauty. Maria was majestic when she walked; fawning poets likened her to the goddess Juno, while sharp-tongued French ladies-in-waiting saw her as "the cow that bore the calf".

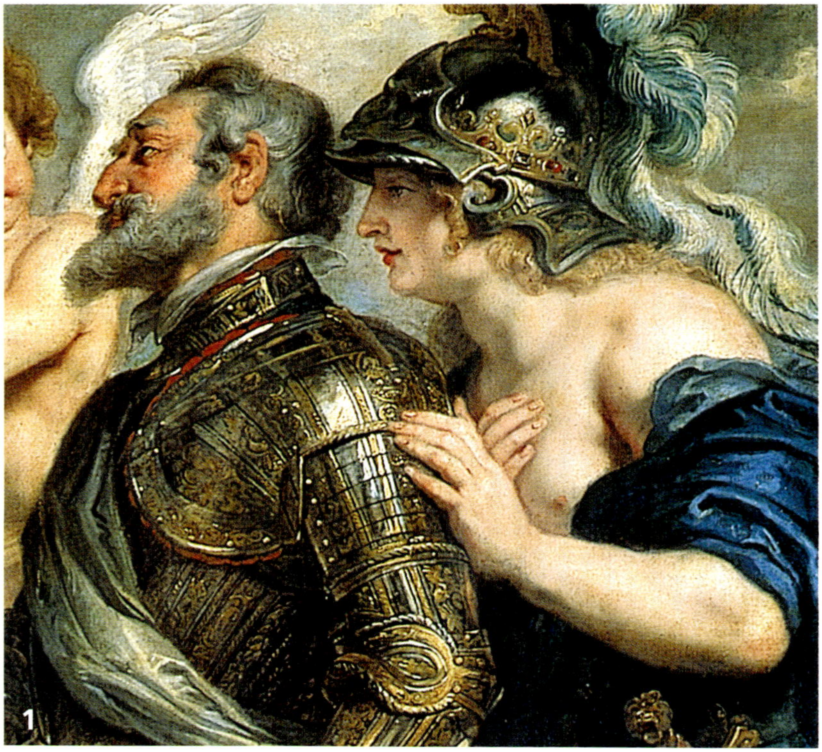

1

Gazing in admiration at the portrait of his bride, Henri IV is shown standing in shining dress armour, a white sash about his breast. White was the colour of the dynastic house. Rubens has painted him in a noble stance, all majesty, every inch a king. His country, personified as the helmeted amazon Francia in a blue dress with lilies, is looking over his shoulder with manifest interest. She is leaning trustingly on her king, who rightfully declared in a letter: "France is deeply obliged to me, for I have worked well on her behalf."

Henri IV was the most popular of all the French kings, and the hero of countless anecdotes. Generally they began with the king talking incognito to the ordinary people, who told him the truths that were in their hearts. It was not Henri's majesty but his simplicity, joviality, and closeness to his people that made him the stuff of legend. "Henri did *not* look majestic", Tallemant des Réaux noted.

When he became betrothed to Maria de' Medici, Henri was forty-seven. He was twenty years older than his bride, and his age was an advanced one in a time when average life expectancy was thirty-three. His beard was already white, his teeth were falling out, he was troubled by the first twinges of gout. He was shorter than he appears in the painting, and needed steps to mount his horse.

He rarely stood in the quiet contemplation depicted in the painting, for even in advanced years he was so active a man that contemporaries were astounded and his staff were left out of breath. He would deal with the affairs of state whilst walking at a brisk pace, and it was said of him that "he went through more boots than shoes, and spent less time in bed than others at table". He divided up his time between war, hunting, sports, gaming, and women, "and was ceaselessly on the move or at his exercises". He was not normally dressed in such finery as he is in the painting; quite the contrary, a good horse meant more to him than fine clothes, and one courtier noted that "he is often to be met wearing a torn jerkin, his face ... moist with sweat, his beard and hair thick with dust". Beneath his jerkin he wore ragged shirts, and "he was not fond of tidying or styling his hair, or indeed of combing it, and hated all who took pains with their hair". If the king seldom washed, that was a trait he shared with most of his contemporaries, but the stench Henri emitted apparently surpassed what was usual, for it was often referred to: "he had odorous feet and armpits," one source reports, while one mistress told him to his face that he stank "like a rotting carcase". Henri had grown accustomed to neglecting his clothing and physical hygiene in twenty years of leading the life of a soldier, almost always in the field. His friend and fellow soldier, the poet Agrippa d'Aubigné, commented: "on his skin, his many toilsome endeavours have left the dirt of poverty".

An unusual king

Henri grew up in the time of religious and civil wars that racked France in the second half of the 16th century. From his mother he inherited the small kingdom of Navarre on the Spanish border, and the Protestant faith; this inheritance predestined him to be the leader of the Huguenots. His marriage to a sister of Charles IX, conceived as a symbol of reconciliation between the Protestants and the Catholics, led instead to the horrors of the St Bartholomew's Day massacre in 1572. Thousands of Protestants were slaughtered. Henri escaped, and from that moment on was in the field, first as the leader of the Huguenots and soon as the spokesman of all who aimed to end the civil war by compromise.

By 1589, quite unexpectedly, every heir with a closer claim to the French throne than Henri was dead; but the majority of the French were not prepared to recognize a Huguenot as their king. Now Henri was fighting for his own kingdom; but Paris defeated him. Only when he renounced his Protestant faith in 1593, declaring "Paris is worth a mass", did he secure the throne for himself. Even now Henri still had to fight for his kingdom, arduously taking it city by city (or buying it with bribes, which cost a fortune). By the end of the century he had at last attained his goal. He was the acknowledged, crowned king of France, lord of the entire land, and the sole king of France, who owed his crown not to the grace of God but to the power of his own sword. This gave him prestige and authority. His achievement as general and politician was unique, and now he stood victorious. His country, however, was in ruins, and he himself fearfully in debt and exhausted. "France and I", he remarked, "need to get our breath back at last."

Now, with peace abroad in the land, two winged putti at the bottom of the picture are removing his warlike attributes, his shield and his white-plumed helmet. Since Ivry in 1590, when Henri had led his troops into battle against the Catholic army, that white plume had been his emblem. Before the battle, d'Aubigné (who was there) tells us, Henri told his forces: "My friends, God is on our side. Over there are His enemies and ours. Here stands your king. Attack! If you should lose your standard, rally behind my white plume – you will find it on the way to victory and honour!" Rosny, the king's companion in arms (and later, as the Duke de Sully, his minister of war and finance), was wounded and had to withdraw under a tree. He thought the battle was lost. But suddenly he saw the king, "two lengths ahead of the rest, charging like a madman into the forest of enemy cavalry lances. His people hesitated for a moment, then hastened after him, encircled him, and with him launched a fearful attack, led on by the white standard borne aloft by Pot de Rhodes. And when he was hit by a shot between the eyes and could no longer guide his wild horse, it was only the king's white plume that led on his noblemen."

This incredible attack confounded the enemy. Panic spread, and Henri won the day. "With his own hand he killed seven of the enemy and captured a standard." From then on, the white plume stood for the king and his unusual valour. It is worth adding that the evidence suggests that at Ivry he wore the plume not on a helmet but on a plain hat, which according to the records of the Navarre treasury he had bought back in 1588 for a hundred ducats. This plain hat was perhaps not so plain, though, being bejewelled with pearls and amethysts.

Now that the arms could be laid aside, Henri had the opportunity to display his statecraft, which proved as remarkable as his valour. When Henri took up the reins of government at the close of the century, the foreign enemy (Spain, summoned by the Catholics) had been pushed back over the border, but France, after almost forty years of civil war, was in a chaotic state of marauding and robbery, disorder and disintegration. The peasantry, pillaged time and again, refused to pay their taxes. The state finances were bankrupt, the administrative and judicial sectors in a state of collapse.

With the support of able ministers (Henri chose well), the king set about the work of reconstruction. His aim was to restore royal authority, order, and prosperity in the country. Might every Frenchman have a chicken in the pot on Sundays! A revival of agriculture, trade, and industry was the goal. To attain his ends, Henri chiefly needed two things: money and time. Money could be obtained by a wealthy marriage. Time was at a premium, though, not least because of the king's advanced years. He was under constant threat, the intended victim in a series of assassination attempts. The religious war might be over without either side having won a victory, but the passionate feelings of hatred and fanaticism that it had prompted still ruled the land.

Henri was living dangerously and he knew it. But what he really wanted was to savour life at last, "enjoy a good day", as he put it, "as recompense for all the bitterness, trouble, unpleasantness, toil, horror, and danger I have been through, from my childhood to my fiftieth year".

The white plume

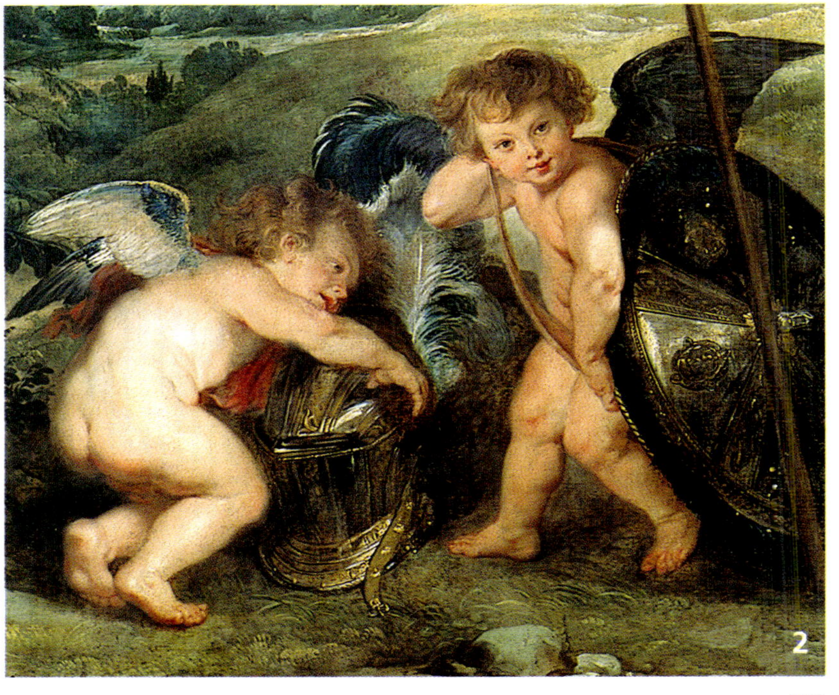

2

In Rubens it is the gods of love and marriage, Eros and Hymen, who present to the king the portrait of his bride, Maria de' Medici; in reality it was people such as his minister of finance, Sully, who alerted him to the potential match. For the king needed not only money, he needed a legitimate heir. Henri's first marriage to the brilliant, beautiful, and highly educated Margaret of Valois, whom he was obliged to marry in youth for reasons of religious politics, remained childless. For many years he had been living in separation from Margaret. Her own brother felt compelled to lock her in a fortress because of her scandalous lifestyle. Henri wanted a divorce and offered substantial amounts if she would consent. Steps to obtain a divorce had also been taken at the papal court. Meanwhile, Henri led a bachelor life in every respect: "His majesty's usual pursuits are hunting and love", we are told. He took his lovers from every level of society. "Often", d'Aubigné writes, "his conquests had an odour of dishwater about them." Not till the closing years of the century did Henri begin to reduce the number of his adventures. At last he had found a woman who could captivate him for good. She was Gabrielle d'Estrées, known as "la belle Gabrielle". But just a few days before they were to be married, she died.

The king was in deep despair. His condition worried his friends. They counselled him to marry according to his station, "for his own peace, that of his country, and his own satisfaction". The more reckless among them suggested that he should first take another lover, and proposed a variety of ladies to him. Incautiously, the king opted to pursue both courses simultaneously, which was to cause him considerable trouble. The number of potential brides was far smaller than the number of possible mistresses. The Infanta of Spain was old and ugly, and Henri did not care for German princesses: "I do not like the women of those parts", he declared; "if I were to marry one of them, I should forever be thinking I had a barrel of wine lying beside me". Presently Henri was convinced that the niece of the Duke of Florence, "though from a house not at all old", was the right match. In the autumn of 1599 the king told a courtier "that there was a virtuous princess in Florence by whom he hoped shortly to have children, that he already owed her uncle more than 500,000 thalers and would be able to settle the debt in this way, and that in addition he would receive a handsome sum of money that he would be able to use for his affairs and to relieve his realm of its heavy burden of debt."

Wooing the bride consisted mainly in negotiating the size of the dowry. Initially the French court demanded a million, since Henri's debts stood at 1,174,147 gold thalers. In late December the parties agreed on a dowry of 600,000 gold thalers, of which 350,000 were to be paid out and the remaining 250,000 offset against the French crown's debts. The marriage contract was signed in Florence in April 1600.

More speedily, though with no smaller degree of haggling, the king embarked on a new affair. Just three weeks after the death of la belle Gabrielle, Henriette d'Entragues was presented to him: "She was dark-haired, saucy, agile, lively, mischievous, jolly, forever finding witty replies and bonmots that made one laugh, perverse, a wasp made to sting back to life a heart that supposed itself dead." She was also a calculating intriguer, and took immediate aim at the crown, putting pressure on the king by denying him her favours. Once he was quite beside himself with lust, she seduced him into making a formal promise of marriage. Sully, incensed and forgetting the deference he owed his king, tore up the document; but it was drawn up afresh. In it, Henri promised "to marry Henriette if she becomes pregnant within six months and is delivered of a son". It was only then, in mid-October, that she slept with him.

Six months later, when the Medici marriage contract was signed in Florence, the king, who had meanwhile bestowed his favours on at least three other ladies, asked Henriette to give him back his pledge, as if this were the most natural demand in the world. She refused. Henriette was pregnant. The king was in an embarrassing predicament, but chance came to his rescue: Henriette, frightened by lightning, had a miscarriage, leaving the relieved Henri to go to meet his bride Maria. In July he wrote to her: "I urge you to look after your health, so that when you arrive we may make a fine child who sparks laughter in our friends and makes our enemies weep." But even on the journey to Lyons, where Henri was to meet Maria, Henriette accompanied the king. Mockingly she enquired when his "fat bag of money" was due to arrive. To which the king retorted: "As soon as I have chased all the whores out of my court." But in fact he did no such thing.

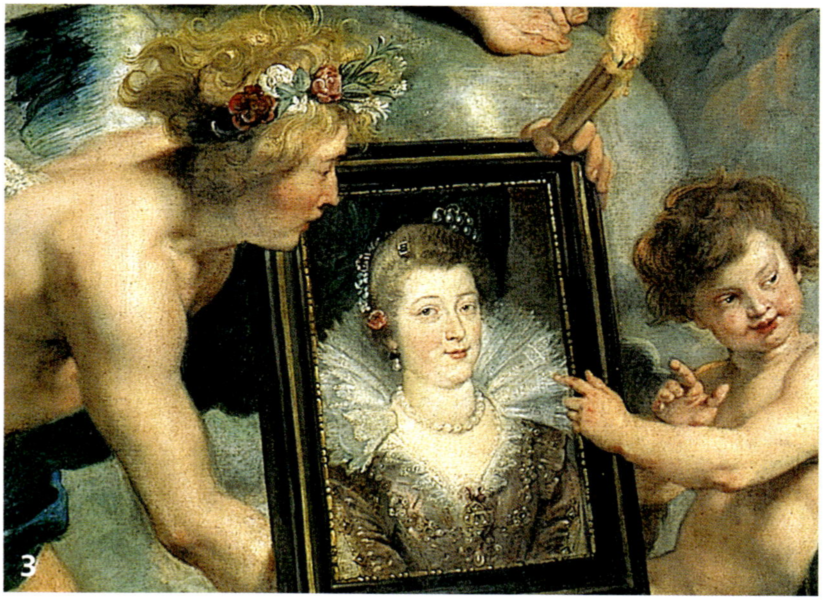

A marriage made by Eros?

A hall of fame for an infamous life

Enthroned upon clouds, the supreme god, Jupiter, and his spouse Juno, are gazing graciously down at the bridal couple. Behind Jupiter is his emblem, the eagle, while Juno's peacock carriage waits beside her. Mythology contains many a tale of the marital strife and jealous scenes that raged between these two deities. A similar lack of harmony awaited Henri and Maria in their ten years of marriage. Sully reports that he "never saw them together for a week on end without a quarrel". The differences between the lethargic and limited Maria and the active, highly intelligent king were too great. But the principal cause of their rows was Henri's continuing affairs. His father had been denounced by Calvin as "in thrall to Venus", and Henri was a chip off the old block: in the last years of his life he went through women at an almost pathological rate. As well as his countless affairs (the last being a thirteen-year-old maid of honour), he thought nothing of keeping Henriette at court, despite the fact that she was involved in several conspiracies against him and was forever threatening to have his marriage to Maria declared null and void. Henri had children by both Maria and Henriette at the same time, and had his bastards from every conceivable bed brought up together. The Tuscan ambassador exclaimed: "Truly, has anything ever been seen that was more like a brothel than this court?" Maria, needless to say, was jealous. But jealousy, in the view of the Venetian ambassador, was "really very bourgeois". Queens did not display such feelings.

Still, Maria did fulfil two expectations. She brought with her the money Henri craved, which enabled him to rebuild his country and equip his fleet for a campaign against Spain, which he hoped would finally crush Habsburg aims to major power status. And she dutifully bore him six children in eight years. The heir to the throne was just nine years old when Henri was assassinated in 1610.

While her son was not yet of age, Maria ruled France. Her political inability and her stupidity made her easy prey to Florentine intriguers whose only thought was of enriching themselves. Without a fight she conceded the dominant role in European power politics to the Habsburgs; aimlessly she squandered the state's resources; she was weak when confronting rebellious nobles. Henri's achievement crumbled in her hands. In 1617 Maria was removed from power by her son, Louis XIII; her confidants were eliminated and she herself imprisoned. She escaped in the most adventurous of manners, down a rope ladder, and without hesitating joined the rebel nobles in their fight against the king.

Presently, however, Maria's protégé, the young Cardinal Richelieu, managed to mediate between mother and son. To celebrate their reconciliation, Maria was permitted to commission a series of twenty-four monumental paintings from the Flemish painter Rubens, immortalizing the various episodes in her life – a hall of fame for herself. This was a task of some delicacy, and called for extreme wariness and consideration in the artist. But this was nothing new to Rubens, a man of the world with diplomatic experience. His style and his angle of perception coincided perfectly with the requirements of the court.

And so he transformed this life of failure, intrigue, and pettiness into something exalted and exemplary. He placed the protagonists in the company of the gods, casting a noble light upon their squalid reality with the help of allegory and myth. The completion of this mammoth cycle, in 1625, was the last climax in Maria's life. Witless as ever, she fell out with the king's counsellor, Richelieu, who had her imprisoned anew. A second time the old woman escaped, this time fleeing abroad. Unwelcome wherever she went, she travelled on, embittered and forever scheming against France, till in 1642 she died in Cologne, alone and far from Rubens' pictures, from those works that have magnified her name down through the ages.

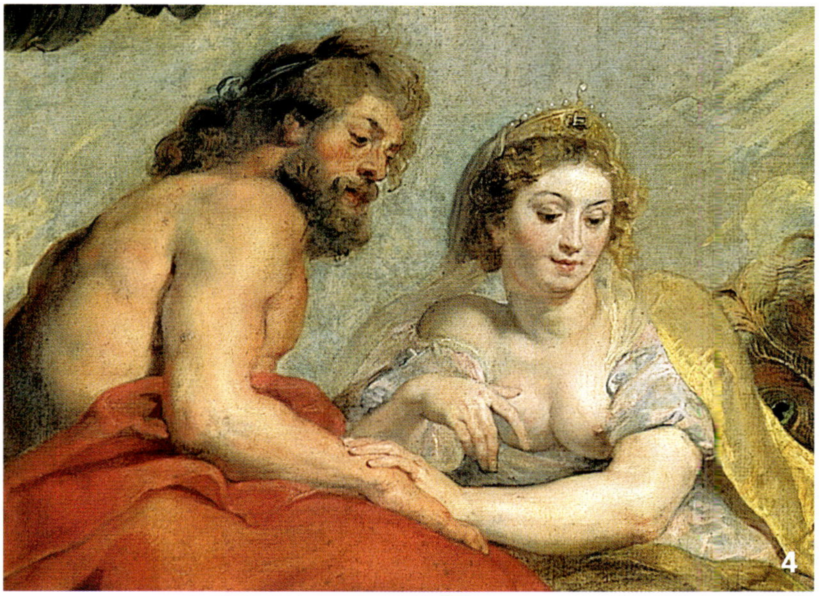

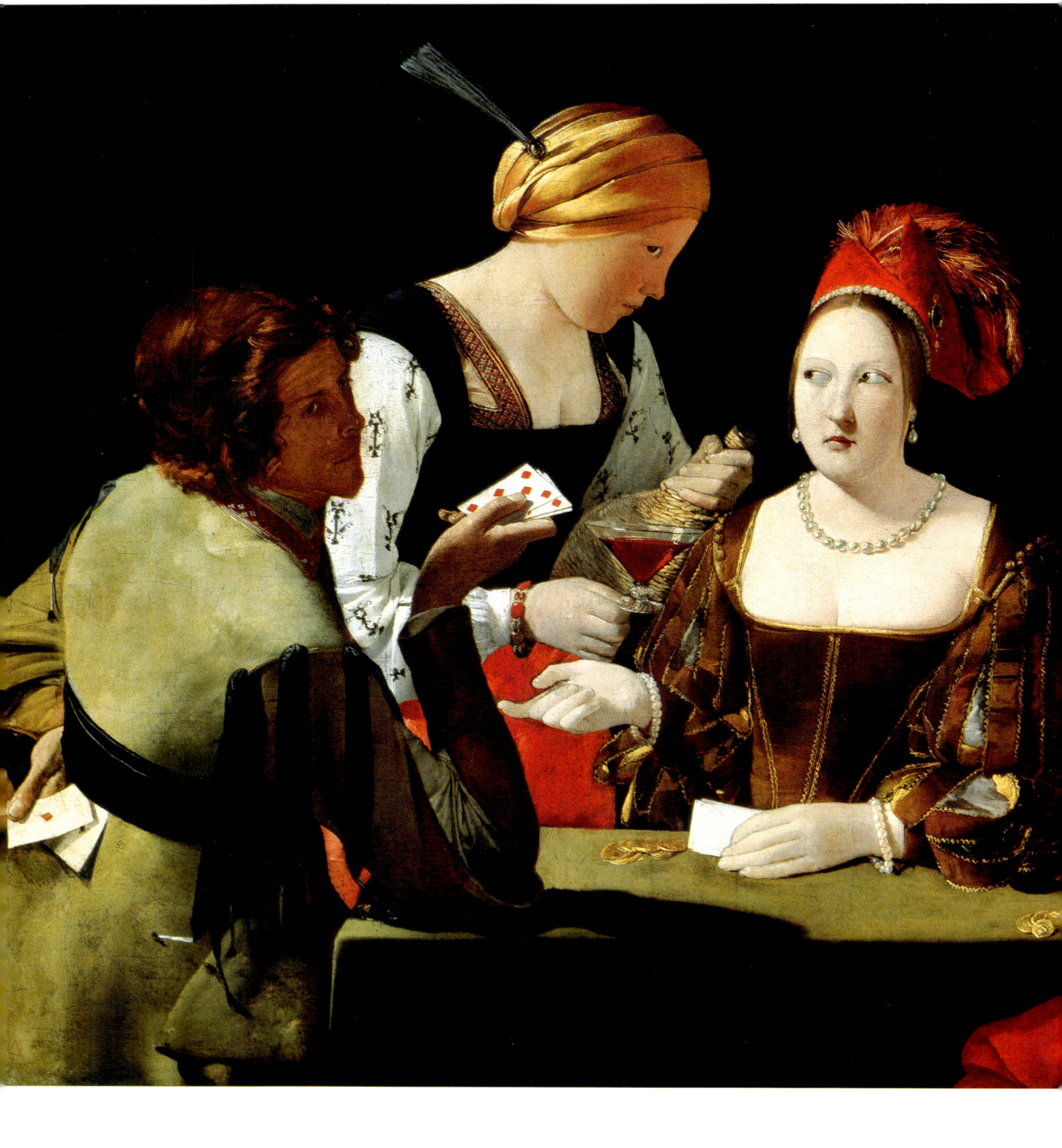

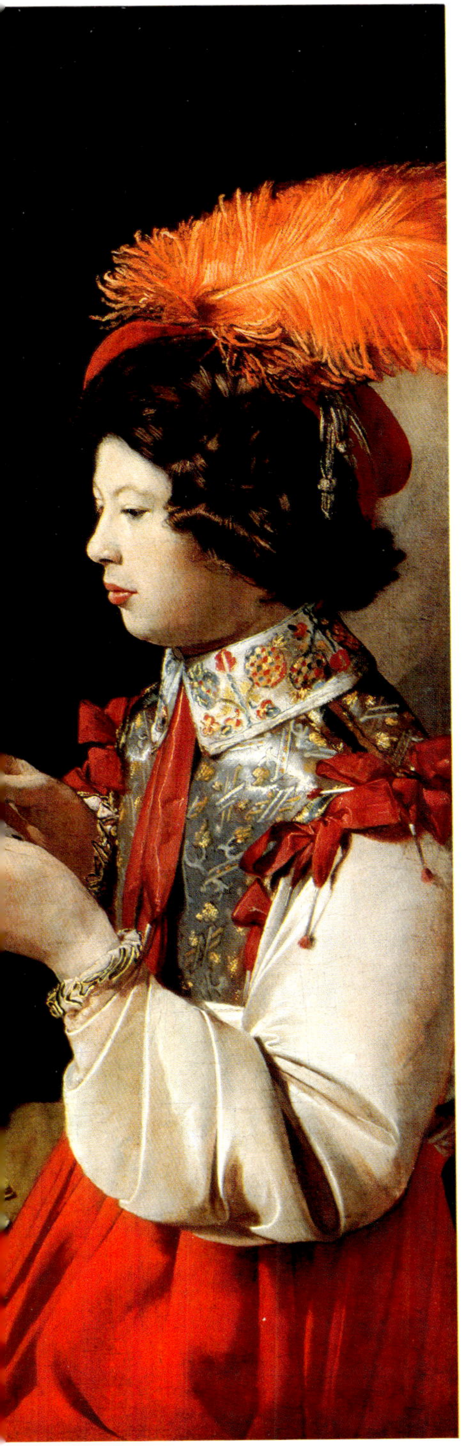

Georges de La Tour: The Sharper, c. 1630

Bad company

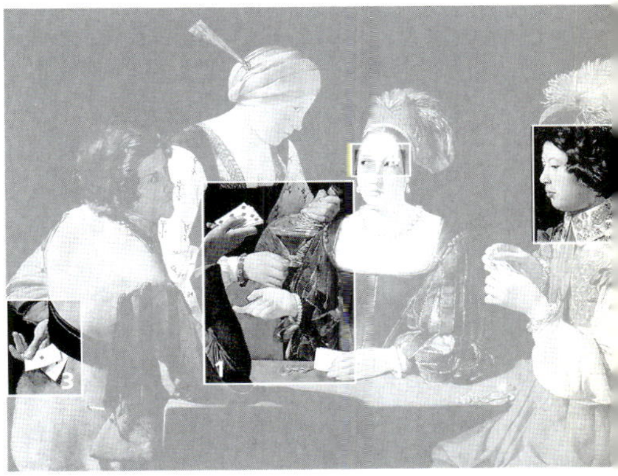

The people at the table are communicating only with looks and economical gestures. They are playing for high stakes, as we can see from the gold coins on the table. One heap lies before the ornately dressed young gentleman, while the man opposite him is carefully leaning his elbow on his cash reserves and is secretly producing a card he has hidden away behind his back, the ace of diamonds.

Georges de La Tour painted another version of this scene, with some changes of colour tone and of detail. The most striking is that, instead of the ace of diamonds, the card-sharper is producing an ace of clubs from his belt. Both works are undated, but were probably painted between 1620 and 1640.

The dark background tells us nothing about the place where the game is being played – it might equally be a salon, an inn, or a brothel. Even so, the meaning of the scene was clear to the artist's contemporaries, and we come across it in the novels and comic dramas of the time as well. It must have been an everyday occurrence: a young greenhorn is invited to a festive dinner by a young courtesan, and after the repast she suggests a hand of cards, together with "an acquaintance who happens to be here". Together, these two rogues cheat the greenhorn of all he has. Instead of a roll in the hay, all he has to look forward to is the loss of his money, and derision.

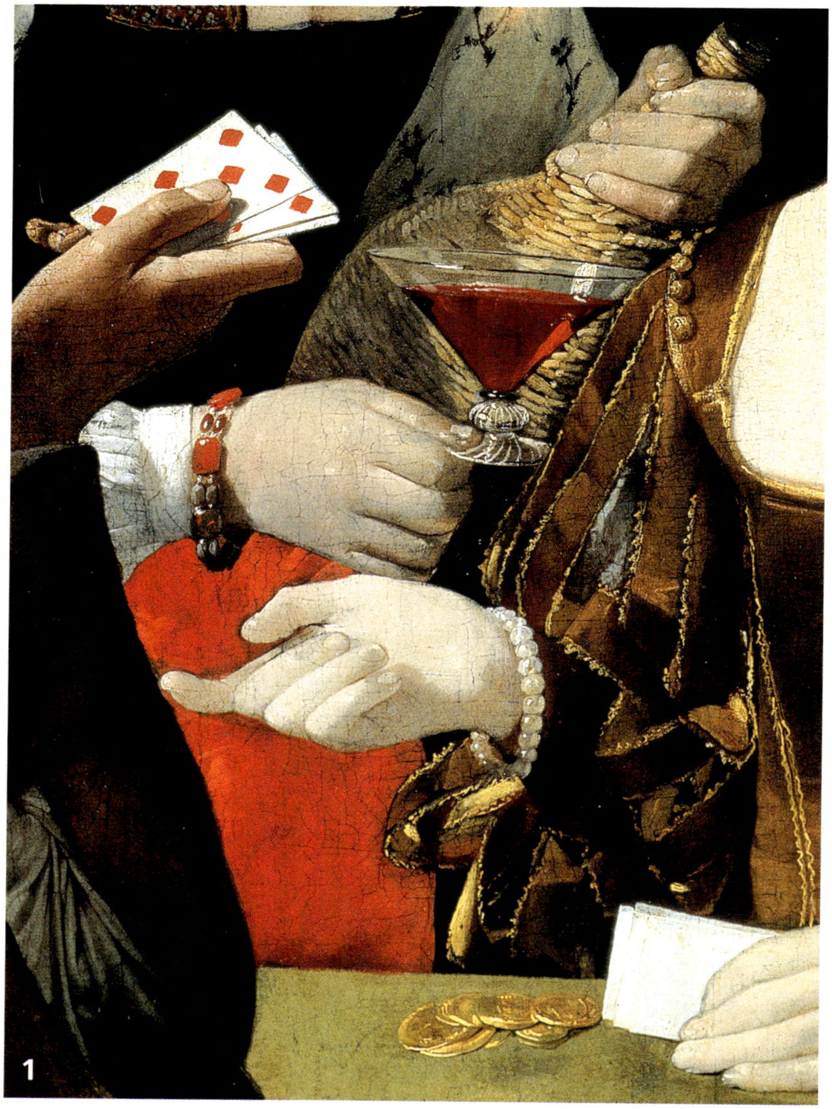

1

A rigged game

Four busy hands are working hard to ruin the fancily dressed youth. The signal to play the diamond ace is being given by the white, manicured hand of the woman. With her pearls and her feminine allures, it is she who has bewitched the victim and tempted him to the card table. The coarser hands of the maid bear signs of hard work, and the flashy stones in her bracelet are too big to be genuine. From a straw-bound bottle she is pouring red wine into precious Venetian crystal glasses for the players. The alcohol will muddy the greenhorn's wits and prevent him from spotting the tricks the sharper's tanned hand is up to.

Drunkenness, lust, and games of chance – the dangers to inexperienced youth were the universally prized amusements of life for men in the 17th century. In France and neighbouring Lorraine, where La Tour lived, wine was thought of as liquid bread and was used as a supplement to meagre victuals. One or two litres a day were considered normal. Babies were given wine by wet nurses to keep them quiet. Wine was prescribed as a medicine for many ailments. One doctor, Joseph Dubois, even recommended his patients to get drunk at least once a month.

For La Tour's contemporaries, playing games was almost as important as drinking wine. Not just children, but adults of every social class spent a good deal of time at games. Games of any kind helped them forget the troubles of everyday life – wars, civil wars, epidemics, and famines raged throughout the 17th century – and every soldier carried dice or cards about him.

Games were also a welcome break from the monotony of an existence that, in the country at any rate, was always conducted amid the self-same circle of persons. In Paris, too, there were forty-three officially registered gaming houses in the early 17th century, silently tolerated despite the fact that the king repeatedly decreed a ban. Indeed, Henri IV used to gamble himself, all night long, for high stakes, and his son, later Louis XIII, was introduced to playing cards at the age of five. At seven, so the court physician Hérouard tells us, "he took part in games of chance and won large sums". Henri IV's queen, Maria de' Medici, in her old age "did nothing else but play games and pray to God".

Piety and gambling were not mutually exclusive, then. Even the rigorous Marshall de Caillière gave it as his view, in a handbook of advice for young aristocrats, that "a man of the world" ought to play games of chance, on the grounds that this opened the doors "of the best circles".

The woman in La Tour's painting, so plainly in league with the card-sharper to dupe the greenhorn, presumably did not belong to the best circles. But it is only the situation in which we see her that permits us to draw conclusions concerning her dubious morals. In fact the woman and the maid are quite decorously dressed by the standards of the time (a plunging décolleté was perfectly usual). Even the cloth on the card table is neat and orderly; here, vice wears a proper, decent face. There is no hint of loosened undergarments, tumbled hair, remains of food, or knocked-over glasses – as in other paintings of the period that showed the same popular theme of the prodigal son squandering his inheritance on gaming and high living, a sobering example of the transience of all earthly pleasures.

It is well worth duping this young man. As well as his gold coins, he can be stripped of his costly garments. "I have seen more than one leave the gaming room with neither short nor breeches," one Venetian legate wrote home from Paris, "even when it was raining or snowing outside."

The youngster has dressed to the nines for his date with the underworld: his jerkin is of sheeny pearl-grey satin, richly embroidered in gold and silver, and he is wearing a cravatte and shoulder bands of red silk. The cuffs of his white shirtsleeves are delicately pleated and trimmed in black gold. It is all expensive, signalling that the young man is probably an aristocrat. In the 17th century, elaborate garb of this kind was still a privilege of the nobility, and was worn even if families whose wealth was chiefly tied up in property had to sell off an entire village to afford court dress appropriate to their station. The visible boundaries between ranks were beginning to blur, however, and in La Tour's time burghers who had made their own wealth were also taking to clothing themselves and their families ostentatiously. So the young man might also be the son of a well-to-do merchant or official.

The features beneath the curls are not yet defined. This is a chubby-cheeked youth with an immature mouth and protuberant lips. He may be no more than fourteen or fifteen – still a child, to our way of thinking. For his contemporaries, he was an adult. Childhood was short in those days: when he was just seven, the future Louis XIII quit the care of the ladies, threw off his children's clothing and put on a jerkin, knee-length breeches, cloak, and sword, exchanged his boyhood toys for playing cards and arms, and went hunting with the men. A child was generally treated as grown-up from the age of seven, and left home to enter upon adult life.

Boys might become apprentices, or if their station and means permitted they would attend a college; in Lorraine, for instance, there was the Jesuit college of Pont-à-Mousson, founded in 1572. Those who were not intended for the church left school at fourteen or fifteen and often went to war as officers right away; or, in times of peace, young aristocrats would be "finished" by a lengthy sojourn abroad. This lavish tour of Italy and Germany, which was not always without risk, was replaced in the 17th century by a new institution, the academy. In 1594 a Monsieur de Pluvinel, master of the king's stables, founded the best-known of these establishments in Paris. In these academies, a callow youth would be transformed into "a man of the world". He learnt to dance, to play the lute, and to conduct himself by court etiquette; but the emphasis of this education was on riding and fencing.

To practise the use of arms was essential, since it was necessary almost every day. "There is hardly a Frenchman of honour who has not killed a man", one English legate reported. The skills of self-defence and attack were required even if neither war nor civil war happened to be raging, since the highly undependable state forces of law and order could not be relied on for much. Society was ruled by violence. Young scholars, both aristocratic and bourgeois, went to their classes armed, with daggers in their jerkins and swords at their sides. They fought mock duels, brawls, and student revolts, aping the French nobility, which rebelled against the king time and again and was forever engaged in internecine duelling and feuding. Even the threat of the death penalty could not deter them from taking arms against each other on the slightest pretext.

If our young man realizes what his partners at the card table are up to, the rules of society will oblige him to draw his sword. So he may end the evening by losing more than his cash. He may lose his life.

A young gentleman of wealthy house

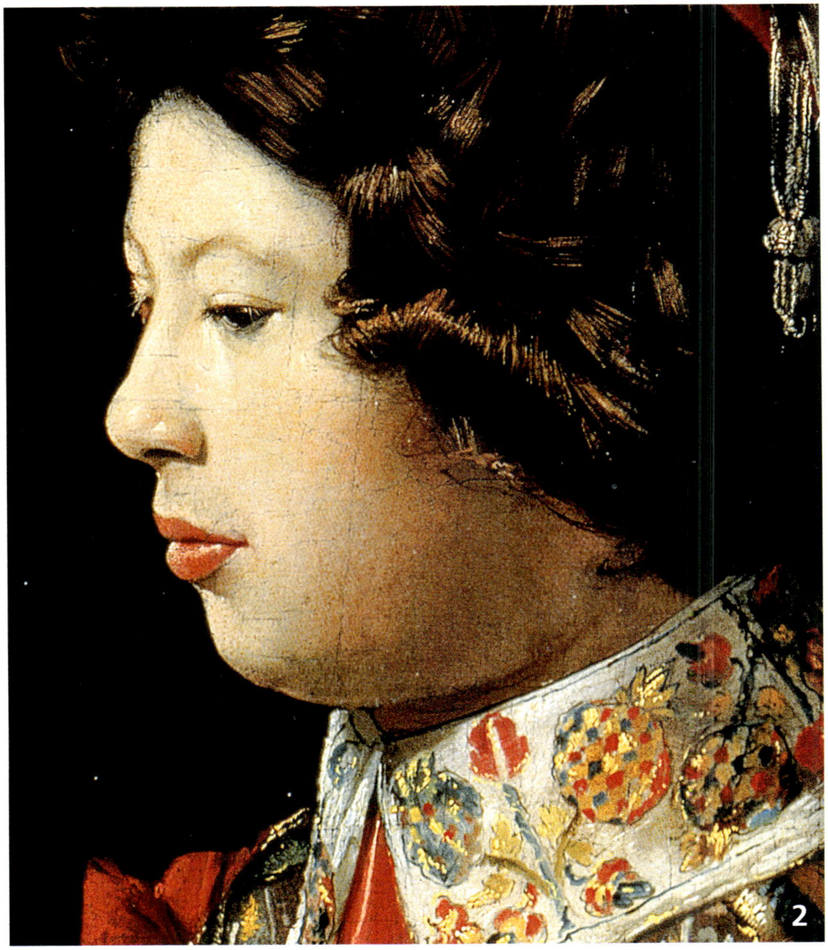

The devil's prayer-book

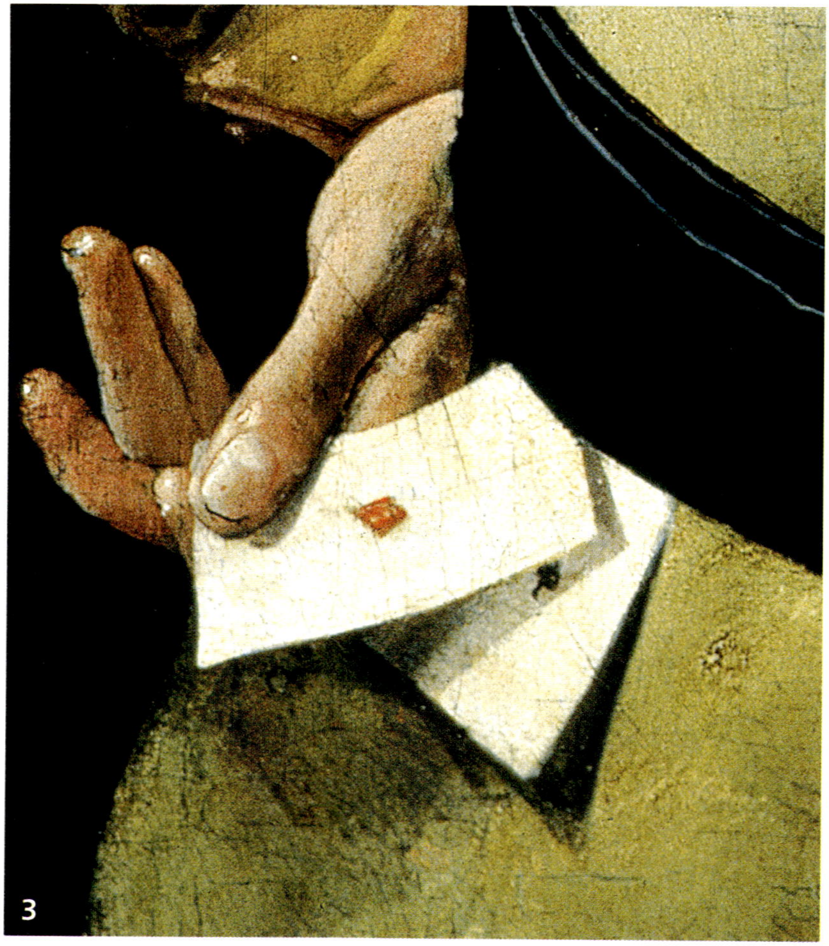

3

Diamonds and spades (and hearts and clubs) were known as the "French suits" and became established amongst card players throughout Europe in the 17th century, ousting other suit motifs that had been traditional in other countries until then. We have documentary records of playing cards dating back to Florence in 1376 (a ban), but in earlier times they were hand-painted and extremely expensive. It was not until copper engravings and woodcuts were developed about a century later that cards could be produced in large quantities. They now became affordable and popular among the aristocracy and the middle classes, while soldiers, peasants and servants continued to make do with dice.

Some of the card games then played are still known today, such as vingt-et-un (known by various other names such as blackjack or pontoon). The ace is a particularly important card because it can be counted as one pip or ten, as desired, in order to reach the target of twenty-one. The card-sharper in La Tour's picture is evidently trying to substitute the ace for one of the low-denomination cards in his hand, so perhaps the game being played is vingt-et-un. (Poker, in which the ace also has a special importance, originated in America much later.)

In 1540, an Italian named Francesco Marcolini introduced the custom of cutting the deck before play begins, since cheating whilst shuffling had become a recognized common practice. But of course there were still plenty of tricks to ensure the card deal went as one preferred. Generally they were also marked to be on the safe side, easy enough at a time when cards did not yet have printed backs. As we see from those in the woman's hand, they were plain white on the back, and on those white backs there would soon be sweat-marks and dirty patches, which a professional gambler would swiftly commit to memory, so that before long he knew exactly which cards were in his opponent's hand. As well as being a good observer, he needed nimble fingers and had to be a sound judge of character. It was important to let the opponent win at first and lull him into a false sense of security, till he became inattentive and could be pounced on.

While he is performing his substitution, the card-sharper is leaning on the table with a relaxed, nonchalant air. Good nerves were a prerequisite for those who tried to *corriger la fortune*, to adjust the imbalance in worldly justice, which gave to idiots the gold coins that a man of skill could put to far better use. "I know of some men", wrote the Marshall de Caillière, "whose sole source of income are their cards and three dice, and who are better off on the strength of that than some of the provincial landed gentry." So alongside discharged soldiers and lackeys on the make, impoverished aristocrats and the younger sons of good families might be found trying their luck at the lucrative business of card-sharping. And this they did in the teeth of the high risk – for, if they were caught, they might lose a thumb or a whole hand, or be branded, or even executed. One way of averting this danger was of course to cut in the miserably paid guardians of the law on the proceeds.

It was not only the law but also religion and superstition that were against card playing. A pack of cards was popularly known as "the devil's prayer-book". The evil one himself, with his taste for gambling for souls, was said to have invented games of chance, and anyone who used playing cards was yielding himself into Lucifer's clutches. When they went into battle, soldiers would throw away their playing cards. They were said to draw cannon fire, death, and eternal damnation.

The sideways glance the courtesan is casting her accomplice, according to one critic, betrays "the crooked ways of the world", which are leading the greenhorn to his ruin. It is a cold and calculating look, whilst in the eye of the maid we detect both curiosity and an interest in the victim. The sharper is the only one looking straight out of the canvas, involving the beholder, too, as an accomplice. From his posture we may guess that La Tour was painting a self-portrait from his mirror image.

We have no proven likeness of the painter, nor have any letters, diaries, or sketches survived from La Tour's hand. All we have are about thirty pictures, and these were not rediscovered until the early 20th century. Long they languished in provincial museums and private collections, often attributed to other artists, until the detective instincts of some art historians linked these paintings to a totally forgotten artist from Lorraine named Georges de La Tour, recorded in archives.

At first the rediscoveries were all pious, nocturnal scenes showing saints by candlelight, so the artist was declared to be a mystic and ascetic. But then, in 1926, *The Sharper* was found, in 1932 the counterpart painting with the ace of clubs, and in the 1950s a picture of a fortune-teller with similar subject matter: the accomplices of an old gypsy woman are robbing a youth who is listening to her with rapt attention. These were anything but otherworldly, mystical works, and prompted the experts to revise the opinions they had formed about La Tour.

We know where and when La Tour was active – in the Lorraine of the Thirty Years' War, when the small border state between France and Germany was torn apart by the looting and burning armies of the warring sides as they alternately marched through. The town of Lunéville was long a centre of military operations, and a regular prey not only to occupying forces but also to fire, plague, and famine. We know from entries in church ledgers and from notarial contracts that the painter spent his life there. He was born in 1593, the son of a baker, and married into an aristocratic family. He fathered a large number of children, was paid respectable sums for his works, hired apprentices, and apparently made quite a fortune supplying wood to the armies and speculating in grain during times of famine.

Apart from these bare facts, one single document gives us an indication of how his contemporaries saw him. In 1646 townsfolk in Lunéville complained about the artist to the duke, declaring he had "made himself unpopular with the people because of the number of his dogs ... which he keeps as if he were the lord and master of the place, hunting hares in the cornfields, damaging and trampling them".

At a later date we learn in passing that the artist gave a watchman a thrashing and, shortly before his death in 1652, mistreated a farmer "who had caused damage in his fields". He seems to have had a violent streak, in times that were also violent, and, as one who had himself climbed socially, he was on the side of the winners. Much in that spirit he signed his work "Georgius de La Tour fecit". He had made his own way on the crooked ways of the world, artistically, financially, and socially. He laid the groundwork for his son to be elevated to the aristocracy, which in due course occurred in 1670. The son then did his best to ensure that posterity quite forgot that there had ever been a painter of his name who was a commoner. And in that aim he succeeded for a good two hundred and fifty years.

The crooked ways of the world

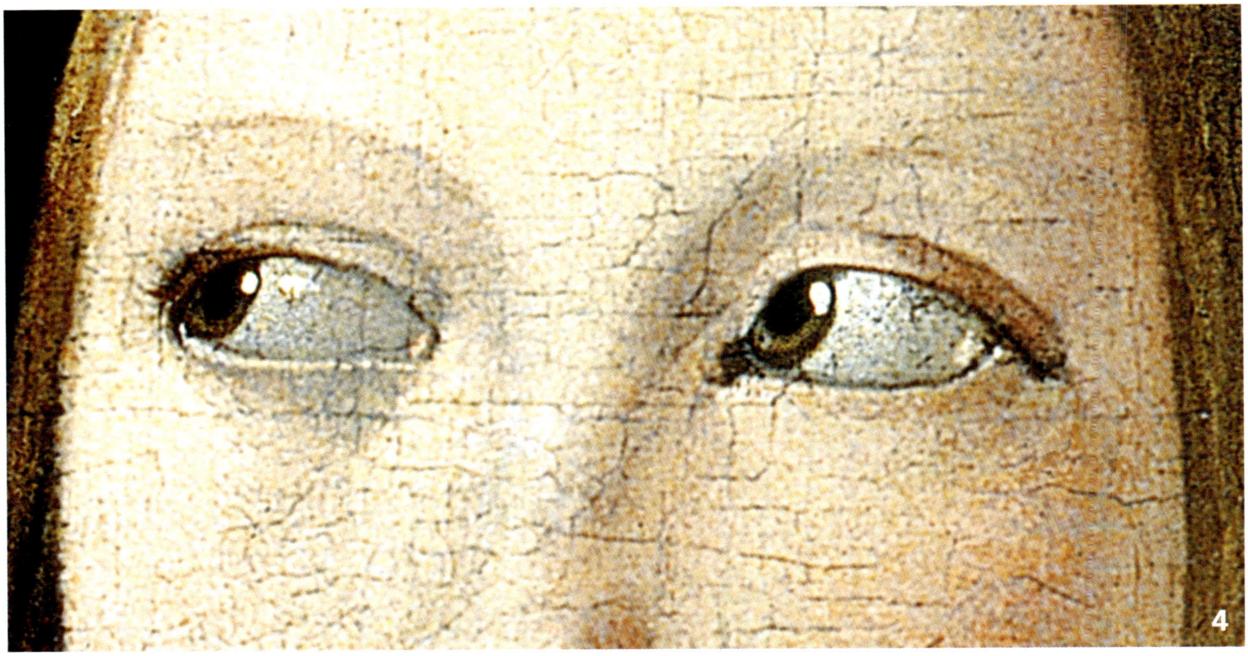
4

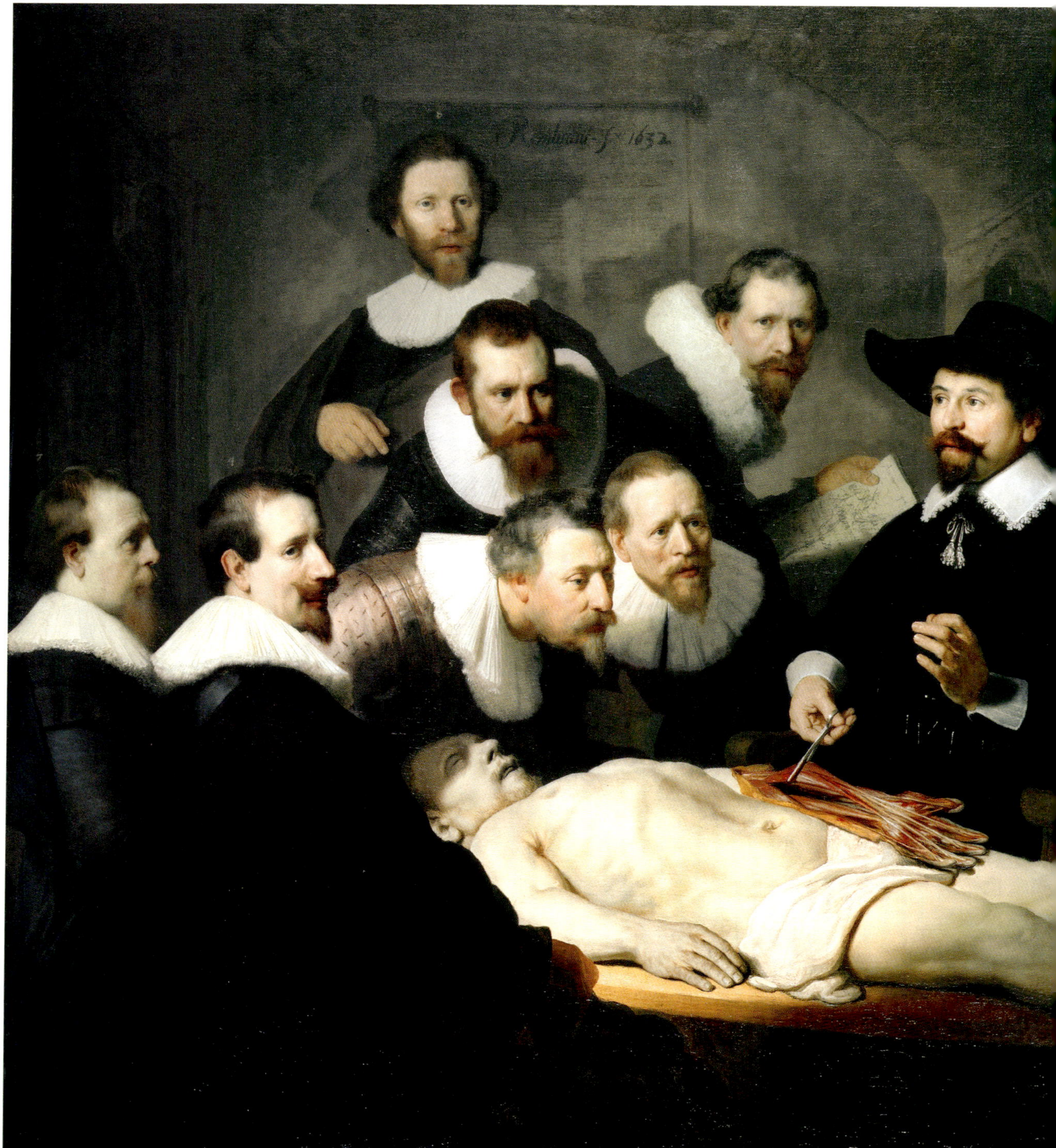

Rembrandt: The Anatomy Lesson of Dr Tulp, 1632

Surgeons lay the human being bare

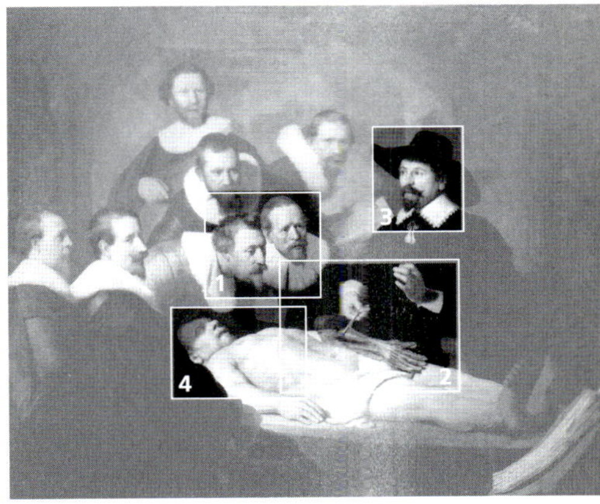

Dr Nicolaas Tulp opens up the corpse of Adriaan Adriaanszoon. The dead man had inflicted serious injuries on a prison warder in Utrecht and had robbed and beaten a man in Amsterdam; on 31 January 1632 he was hanged, and his body was made over to surgeons of Amsterdam for public autopsy.

Anatomy "lessons" of this kind, open to the public, were held not only in the Netherlands. A poster has survived from Berne in Switzerland on which a doctor declares that he will show to all who wish to know "what nature has concealed within us" and where "the soul has its dwelling place as long as you live".

The idea of the God-given soul was always present on these autopsy occasions, which took on a ceremonial and well-nigh religious character. They lasted several days, taking place only once a year, invariably in the cold months. The public who attended consisted of medical colleagues, students, dignitaries, and ordinary citizens – anatomy lectures were looked upon as social events. Laughter was expressly forbidden, and so, too, was the removal of organs.

These lectures were held in what were known as anatomy theatres, circular or semi-circular wooden constructions with rising tiers of seats or standing places from every one of which the table could be seen on which the body lay in the centre below. Little is known of Amsterdam's Teatrum Anatomicum of that period; Rembrandt himself gives only a vague indication of the space. The crowded tiers of public seating may be imagined where we as viewers of the painting are positioned.

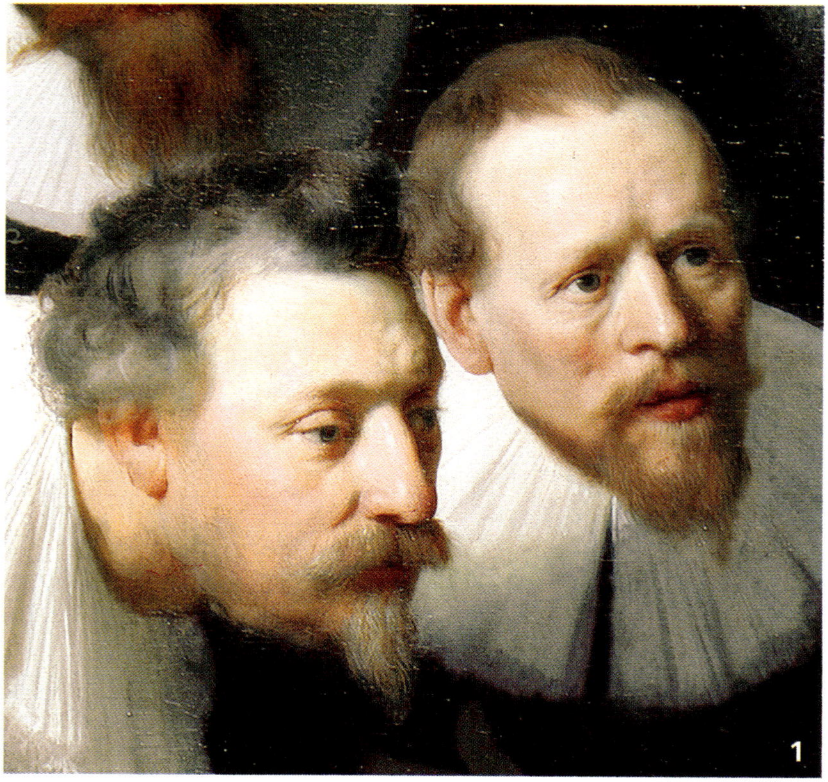

1

Working on the body

Earlier painters of these public lectures had generally shown a great deal: a large number of onlookers, a large space. By contrast, Rembrandt's *Anatomy Lesson of Dr Tulp* – the painting measures 163 by 217 centimetres and is in the Mauritshuis, The Hague – features only the corpse and eight men. There may originally have been even fewer: the man to the far left and the man at the top appear to have been added later. The list of names one man is holding was also painted in subsequently; now, it is an aid to identification.

The two who are craning forward, seated closest to the demonstration, were probably Jacob de Witt and, behind him, Mathys Kalkoen. Like the others, they are bearded and are wearing large white ruffs such as were customary on festive or official occasions. All of them were members of the guild of surgeons, and de Witt was currently an *overluyden*, or member of the board.

Convention had it that surgeons were also barbers. They treated injuries and fractures, opened veins, and also cut and trimmed hair and beards – in other words, they worked on the body. In Rembrandt's day, however, these well-groomed men seen gathered around the dead body will have left the barbering to their assistants. They were striving to give the surgeon's trade a higher standing. This was one of their reasons for inviting the public to these lectures.

None of them had been to university, though. Nicolaas Tulp is the only academic in this painting. Probably he and the surgeons depicted paid for the picture jointly; group portraits bruited the fame of those portrayed, adorned the assembly rooms of guilds, and were highly valued in the Netherlands.

Rembrandt (1606–69) adopted a new approach to the group portrait. Previously, the subject of the anatomy lecture had been painted much like a portrait gallery, one head beside the next, and most of the people shown were not looking at the corpse but into the public. Rembrandt chose instead to portray his surgeons in profile or semi-profile, seen frontally. He grouped them in a pyramid but did not place the most important person in the highest position. He also nuanced the degree of interest evinced: de Witt and Kalkoen are leaning far forward, their demeanour and gaze eloquently suggesting that they want to see everything up close and very clearly.

In actuality it is unlikely that the two surgeons would have displayed their curiosity in so unrestrained a manner at a ceremony of this nature. Nor is it probable that they would have sat quite as close as Rembrandt indicates. The artist has concentrated on the core event, eliminating the background and preferring to place the dead man in a setting of tensed life.

Capturing the quality of their gaze mattered especially to him. His whole life long, Rembrandt was fascinated by the eyes. His contemporary Franciscus Junius described them as the messengers of the heart and the windows of the soul. The eyes of the two surgeons attest to their burning, penetrating interest in the human body.

Rembrandt conceived the group of surgeons in his studio and painted their portraits individually; the exposed arm of the dead man, on the other hand, he sketched during the autopsy. The picture is thus a composite. Experts praise the precision with which he shows the tendons of the arm and hand. Possibly he consulted an anatomical atlas, such as the book at the bottom right of the painting.

It is surprising that he shows the autopsy as beginning with the arm. Surgeons invariably opened the abdomen first and removed the organs. Twenty-four years later, Rembrandt painted a second autopsy scene, *The Anatomy Lesson of Dr John Deyman* (1656; the painting was badly damaged by fire in 1723). In that work, the abdominal cavity is open; here, the artist obeyed the rules.

If Dr Tulp did not, it may have been for two reasons. Firstly, he may have been paying homage to Andreas Vesalius (1514–64), a great pioneer of modern anatomy, who was especially celebrated for his dissection of the hand. Secondly, the artist was better able to use the arm and hand to communicate religious messages than the abdominal organs. As the tendons govern the fingers, so God governs man. Scientific research was forever under the obligation of confirming God's omnipotence; only in this spirit was anatomical research permitted or indeed conceivable in the 17th century.

For a long time, the church had been generally opposed to opening up the human body. Since it was God's creation, none should violate it out of common inquisitiveness. Well into the Middle Ages, autopsies were prohibited except in the case of rulers or Popes whose cause of death needed to be ascertained. During the Renaissance this prohibition was relaxed; Leonardo da Vinci (1452–1519) is said to have been present at more than thirty autopsies.

Not until Rembrandt's century were autopsies publicly conducted, but even now they still required permission from a church or secular authority. They were organized by faculties of medicine; or in places where there was no university, such as Amsterdam (where one was currently being founded), by the surgeons' guilds.

An entrance fee of several guilders was charged. This covered payment to the hangman who had supplied the body, a fee for the doctor performing the autopsy, and payment for a chef who would serve up a substantial dinner afterwards. Often the banquet was followed by a torch-lit procession.

Research as confirmation of God's omnipotence

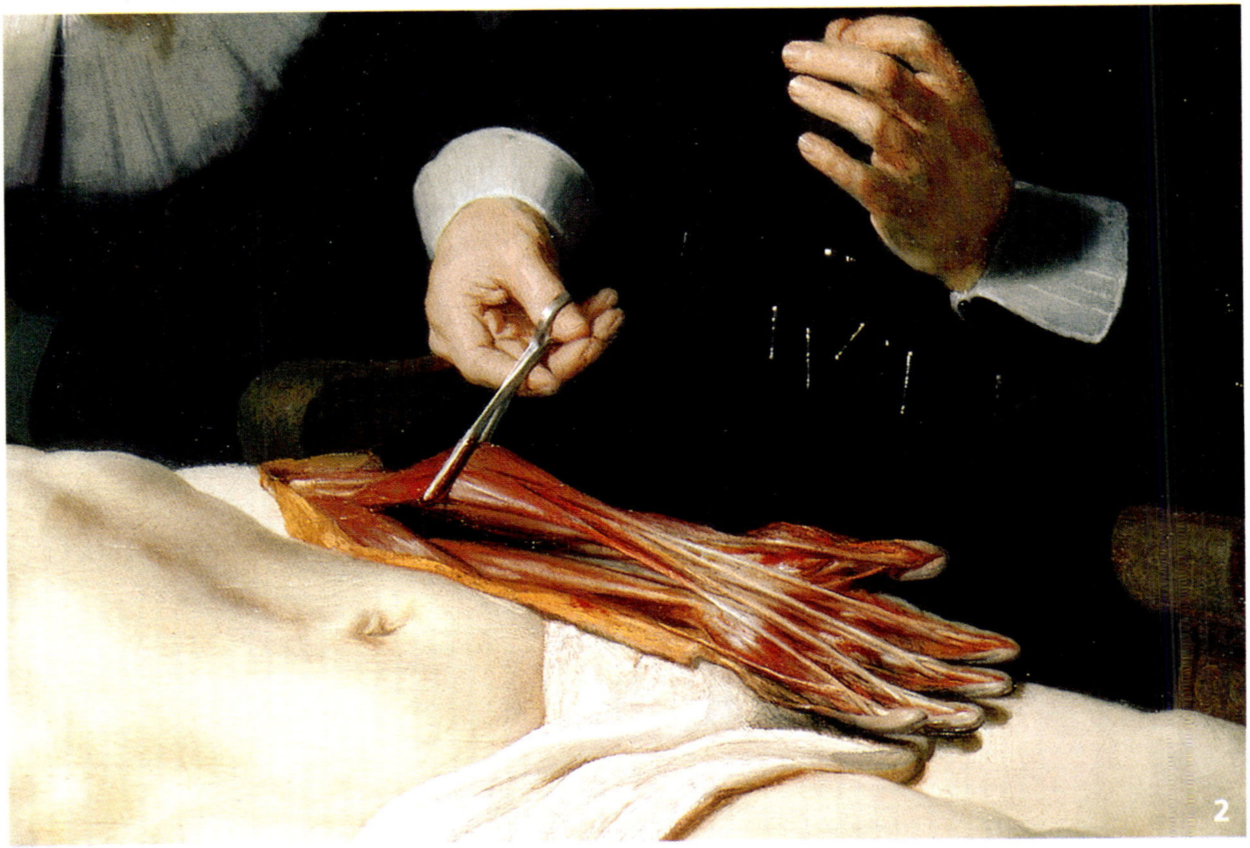

2

Theory, bones, tendons, and flesh

Nicolaas Tulp, actually Claes Pieterszoon, was born in 1593 and died in 1674. The name of Tulp was presumably derived from his parental home, which had formerly been a flower auction house. It was not uncommon to take one's name from the house or town of one's birth; the doctor's name additionally reminds us of the great Dutch vogue for tulip breeding at that time. Nicolaas Tulp was a member of Amsterdam's ruling class; he served several terms as lord mayor of the city. In 1632, when Rembrandt painted him, he was on the municipal council and was Praelector of the guild of surgeons.

The Praelector (or reader) was responsible for teaching and examinations. Tulp had his doctorate in medicine from the University of Leiden. In Amsterdam he was in general practice; anatomy was one of his special fields. He is said to have been the first to give a description of certain human organs.

Rembrandt emphasizes the special status of this man by placing him apart from the throng of surgeons. Moreover, Tulp is the only one shown wearing a hat – to keep one's hat on indoors was the privilege of persons of higher standing.

Whether it was Tulp himself who laid bare the tendons is uncertain. Working on the body was the task of practising surgeons, whereas Tulp was a scientist. Back in the Middle Ages, the gulf between these two areas had been even greater: on one level there was popular medicine as practised by the vendors of herbs, miracle healers, gem-cutters, and teeth-pullers, and on another there were the scholars who passed on the body of theory amassed by the ancients without testing it against the reality of the human body. As late as the 16th century, the difference in station was plainly visible: pictures showing autopsies have the man of learning at a lectern, far from the corpse, while the task of dissection is being performed by a surgeon. At times a third person would mediate between the two, using a cane to indicate on the body what the lecturer was describing.

If scientists did not perform the physical work themselves, did not actually dissect and touch bodies, it was altogether in accordance with an ancient line of thought. It was illustrated in the New Testament story of doubting Thomas, the disciple who beheld the risen Christ but was the only one of the twelve to doubt that he was really the same man who had died on the cross. Only when he had placed his hand in Christ's wounds was he convinced. The conclusion drawn from this was that only the young or simple-minded required physical contact in order to recognize the truth.

The man of learning, by contrast, sticks to his books. The large folio volume open at the feet of the corpse in Rembrandt's painting is not there for aesthetic reasons alone, not only to provide a counterweight and closure in that corner of the composition. It is also a reminder of the traditional book learning that dominated university thought and teaching.

To what extent Tulp himself worked with the scalpel we do not know. A panegyric written by the Dutch scholar Caspar Barlaeus in 1639 praised his skilful hands, but especially his verbal eloquence. It may be that Rembrandt omitted an assistant whose task was to perform the cutting, in order to tauten the composition. Be that as it may, the painting documents a new era in the history of medical science, an era in which academics were increasingly willing to test their teachings against the facts of reality.

The Dutch played a leading role in this evolution. Liberation from Spanish rule, and thus also from Catholic dominance, had awoken and strengthened a new sense of reality. The body remained the temple of the holy spirit, but now it could be opened. Medical science still had a lot to learn. Confidence in the profession was low, and the reputation of medical men was often poor. In the theatre, from the *commedia dell'arte* to the comedies of Molière, doctors were the butt of ridicule.

Earlier painters of autopsy scenes concealed the face of the deceased, either by a cloth or by interposing a person. The wish was that the beholder would no longer think of this body being dissected as that of a human being, an individual. Rembrandt opted for a compromise, showing the face but leaving it half obscured by shadow.

He was later to make contrasts of light and dark a hallmark of his mature style; here he was trying the method out. The painting was a work of Rembrandt's youth, done when he was twenty-five. That same year he had moved from Leiden, the town of his birth, to Amsterdam. The new metropolis of the independent Dutch provinces was a rising commercial and intellectual centre with a swiftly growing population – a good place for artists, especially those able to attract attention with a new angle on an old subject.

And precisely that was what the newcomer from Leiden supplied. His corpse is not placed parallel to the lower edge of the painting but almost diagonally, while he crowds the members of the surgeons' guild into the left half of the picture. He preserves a compositional balance with the figure of Tulp, but particularly through the gazes and movements directed toward the right. Instead of physical mass, he chose dynamism, anchoring the whole with the heavy folio volume in the bottom right corner. Compared with the catalogue-style attendance registers painted by some of his predecessors, this picture verged on the revolutionary.

The pride of place may go to Dr Tulp, but the corpse of Adriaan Adriaanszoon occupies a larger area of the canvas. The most light falls upon him. His nakedness and stiff posture mark him out from the rest. It looks very much as if Rembrandt had chosen to position the surgeons so close to him, and introduce so dynamic a quality into the picture, in order to highlight the motionlessness of the dead man, bring home the sheer nature of death.

Subsequently, death was to become one of Rembrandt's principal subjects. Not that he painted an especially large number of dying and dead people; but what lies ahead, in the end, for the people in his works becomes ever more apparent. The fading that the future will bring is glimpsed in young women, and in faces he shows what the years have etched in the skin. Rembrandt's view of life is of the approach of death.

To make this visible he uses shadow. The contrastive technique of chiaroscuro was one that Rembrandt borrowed from Caravaggio and his followers. But the interpretation he placed upon it was new. The older he grew, the more frequently he implied in the dark or semi-dark the *ombra mortis*, the shadow of death.

In this painting honouring Dr Nicolaas Tulp, that shadow lies only on the face of the hanged man. For Rembrandt at the age of twenty-five, life and death are still opposites that cannot meet.

The shadow of death

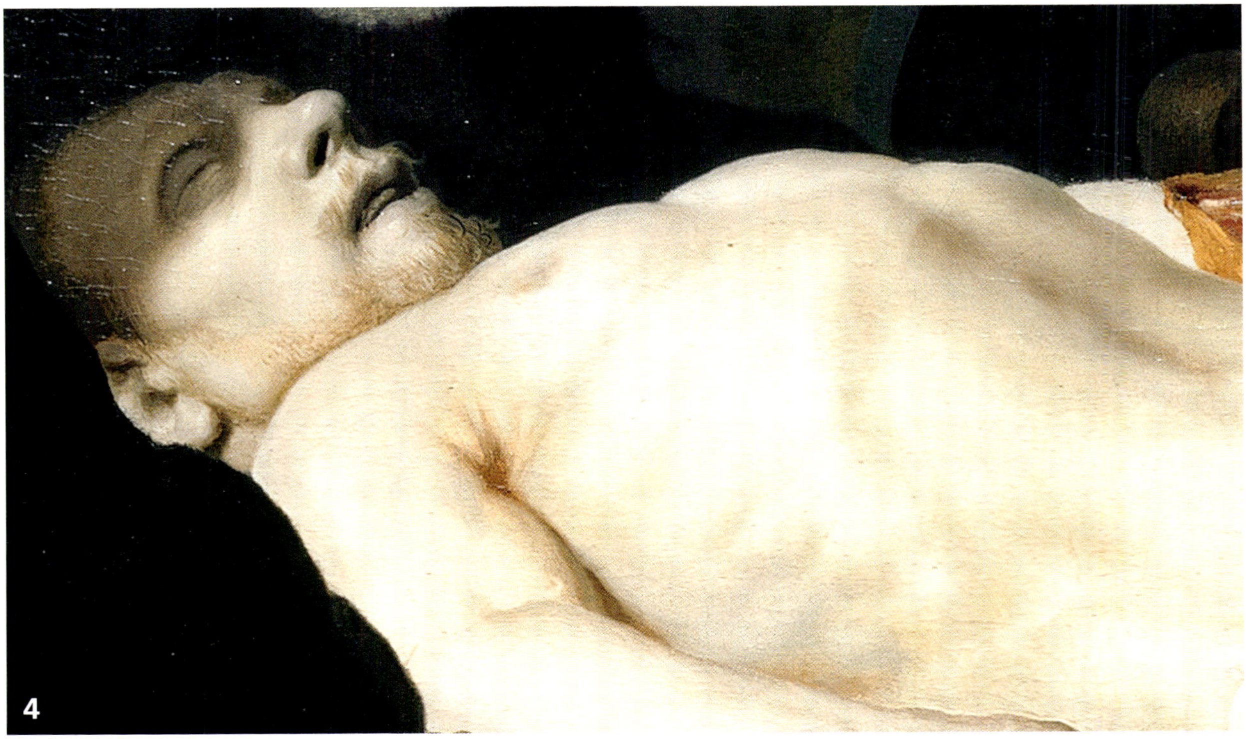

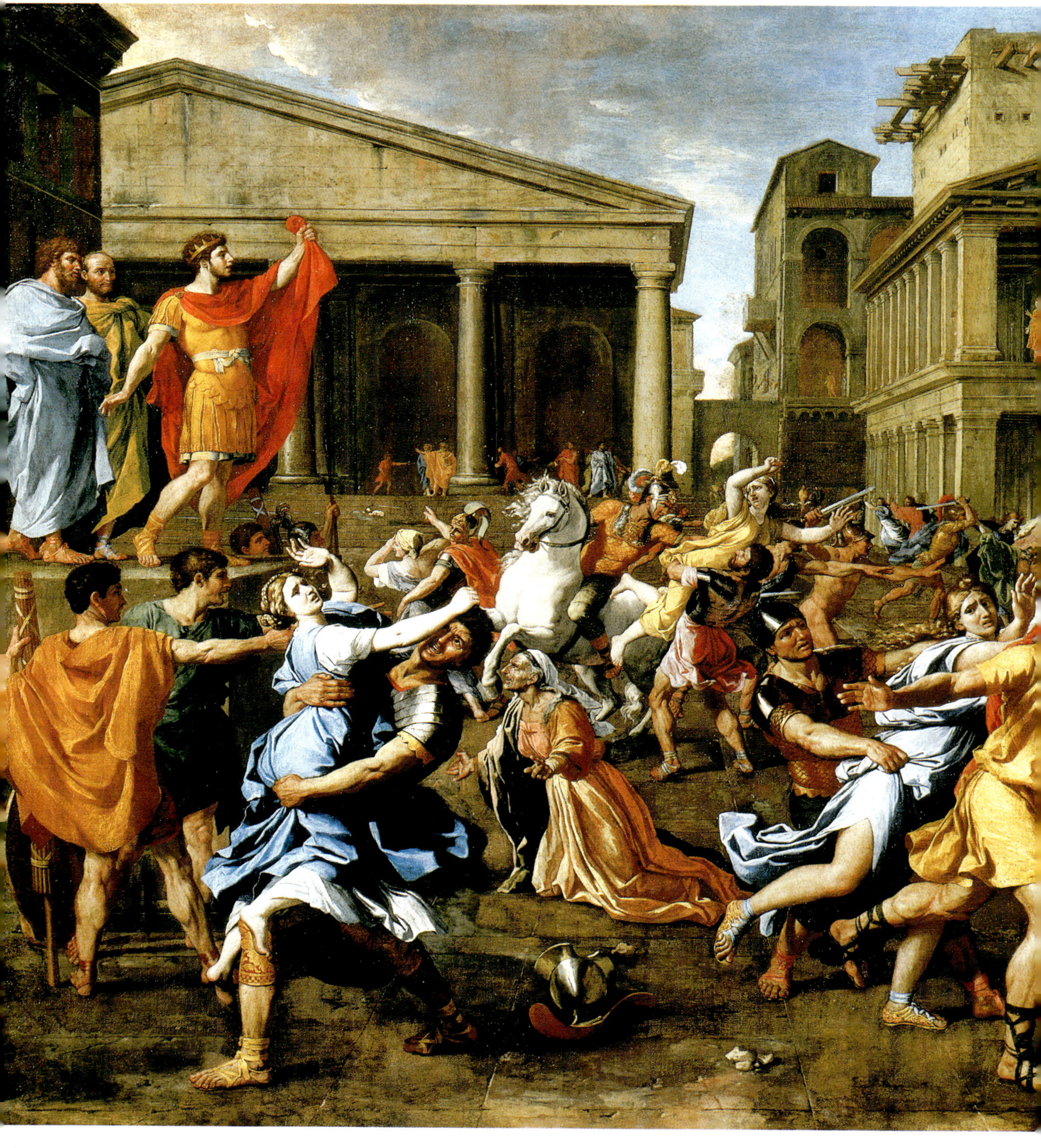

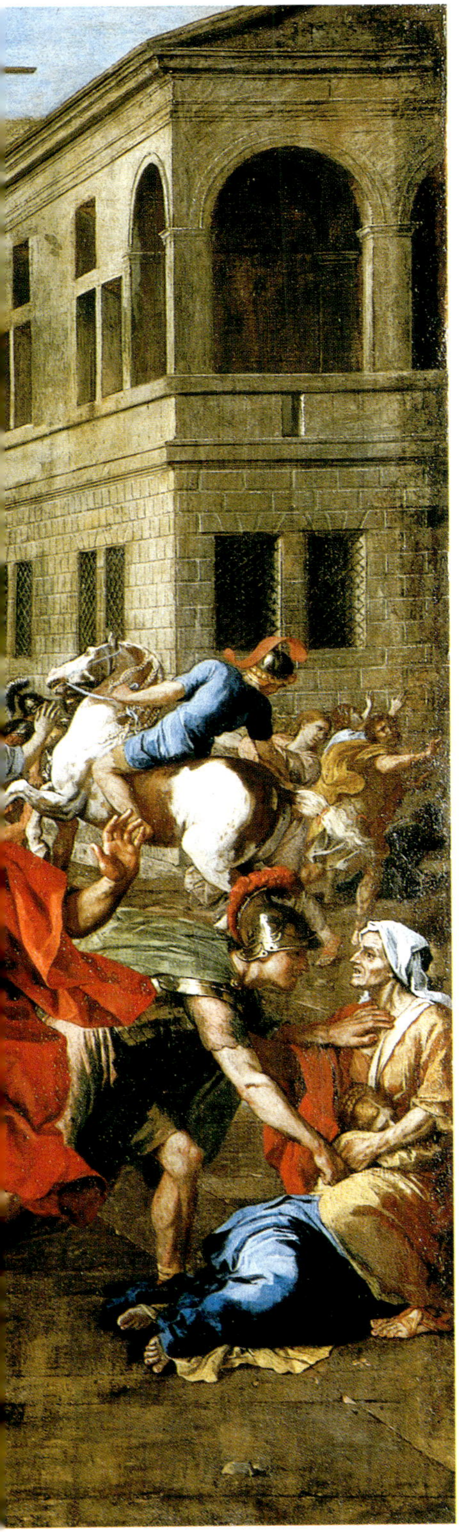

Nicolas Poussin: The Rape of the Sabine Women, 1637/1639

A Frenchman in Rome

Tumult on a square in Rome. A turbulent and chaotic crowd, with austere buildings all about. Thus the French painter Nicolas Poussin (1594–1665) saw the rape of the Sabine women.

The story of the rape is part of the foundation myth of Rome. The fledgeling settlement apparently attracted homeless and often criminal men in search of a refuge. This new rough and ready society lacked women. Romulus, the leader, proposed to obtain some; according to the Greek writer Plutarch, he spread the rumour that he had found the altar of a deity buried in the ground, and took the occasion to throw a magnificent sacrificial feast. Among the guests who came were the Sabines, a people who lived nearby. At a sign from Romulus, the Romans drew their swords and, emitting loud cries, made for the Sabine daughters and carried them off, leaving the rest of the tribe to disperse unmolested. In other words, no blood was shed; nor is any to be seen in Poussin's picture.

Plutarch considered that this breach of the rules of hospitality was justified by the need to provide a population if Rome was to have a future. Brutal though the act was, it served a higher purpose. Something similar appears to have been in the artist's mind: the chaos on his canvas in fact masks a meticulously conceived order.

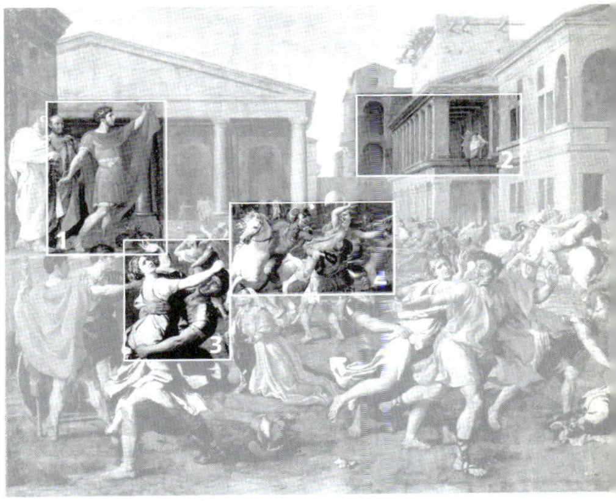

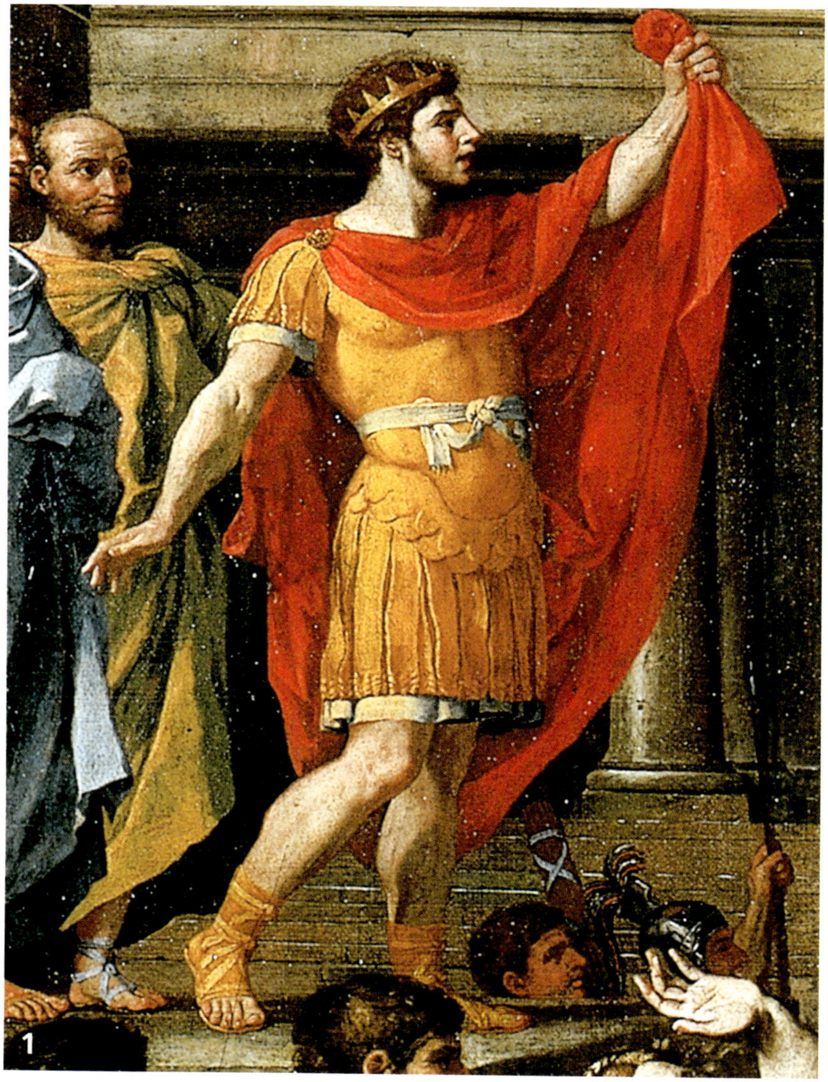

1

The ideal ancient hero

It was not easy for Poussin to get there. He was from Normandy, a poor rural region, and had to save up for a long time before he could venture the journey to Rome. His first attempt was abandoned for lack of money. In 1624 he finally made it.

In Rome, visitors had to have letters of recommendation. Poussin had one addressed to Francesco Barberini, the nephew of the Pope. Although Barberini left the city shortly after the artist's arrival, he passed him on to the Marchese Vincenzo Giustiniani, a wealthy banker from Genoa. Giustiniani gave Poussin permission to study his own collection of ancient artworks, a privilege of real importance for a young painter, for the better of the movable ancient artworks were almost all in private hands. Giustiniani also collected paintings. From Poussin he bought a *Massacre of the Innocents* and an *Assumption of the Virgin*.

Of still greater importance for Poussin was Cassiano dal Pozzo, a senior official at the papal court and a friend of the astronomer Galileo Galilei. Dal Pozzo was a well-informed collector of archaeological remains and old manuscripts. Poussin, who had probably attended a Jesuit school and unlike many other painters knew Latin, was able to extend his own education in the humanities through dal Pozzo. The collector became widely celebrated for his "paper museum": he had had drawings made of some 1500 ancient ruins, busts, and medals, and had had the leaves bound into books – an iconographic collection of outstanding quality.

For Poussin, the paper museum possessed a twofold significance: by drawing copies, the young man was able to make a living, and at the same time he was helped in his all-important quest for ideal forms. Behind his Romulus we can detect the *Apollo Belvedere* or equally an Augustus Caesar. In the decades that lay ahead, dal Pozzo was to be one of Poussin's most important clients; he bought some fifty paintings from him, a quarter of the artist's total output.

Romulus, in crown and armour, is standing at a raised vantage above the confusion. The sign agreed for the abduction, according to Plutarch, was that Romulus would stand up, unfold his purple robe, and then wrap it about him once more. Poussin thus painted the gesture that started the enterprise, with the attack of the Romans and the first frightened responses of the Sabines.

This city founder must have been an uncivilized, violent man. According to the legend, he was raised by wolves, and killed his twin brother, Remus, in the struggle for power. He obtained his women by wiles or brute force. But Poussin has depicted him as the noble and beautiful are customarily portrayed. Romulus does not have both feet firmly planted on the ground, as a man giving orders normally does, but is resting his weight on one leg, in the ancient manner, while the other is gracefully relaxed and his hip is back-turned. His arms, too, are in a harmonious balance, the one outstretched before him, the other behind. Poussin has given him a grace that recalls a dancer.

The artist was not after psychological plausibility. He wanted to reveal an inner truth, an ideal: the beauty of man. Beauty always included nobility of character. Poussin was one of many artists who saw this ideal as being embodied in the artworks of antiquity. They were best studied in Rome.

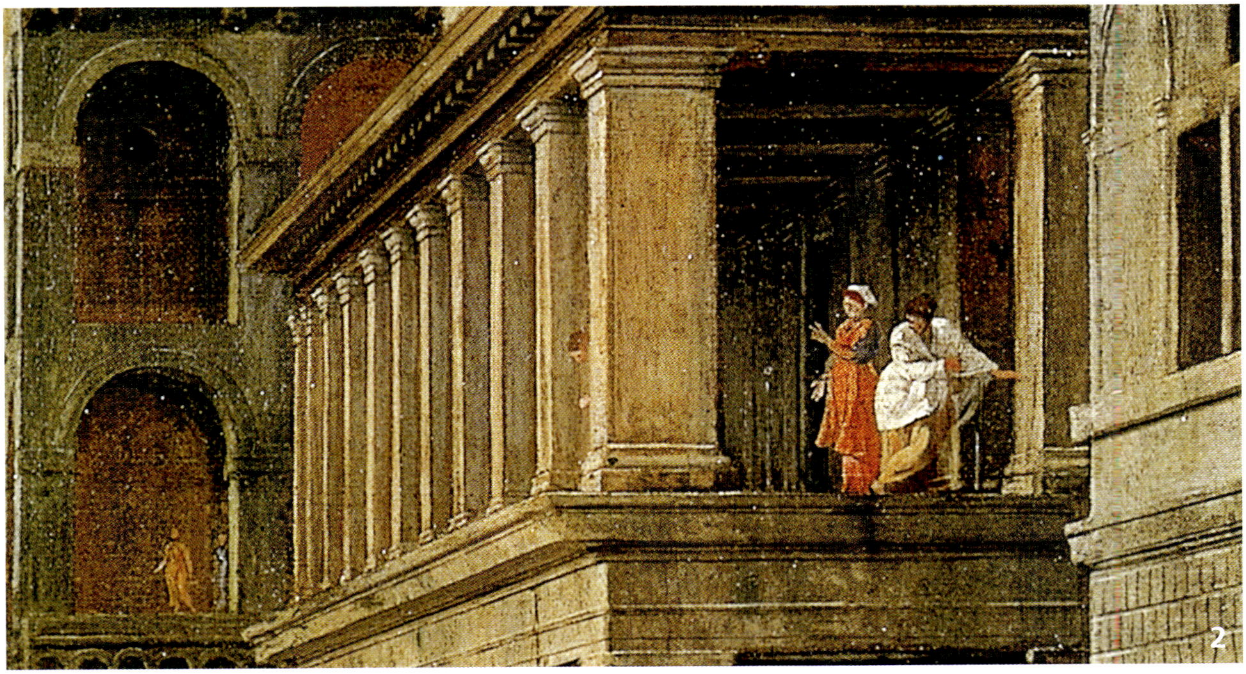

Rome, the marketplace of the world

In Poussin's day, Rome was effectively the centre of Europe. With a population of 100,000 it was one of the few large cities, and as the seat of the papacy it was the spiritual and intellectual centre of the Catholic world. Hardly any other city can have had so many diplomats in it, or attracted so many visitors – artists, pilgrims, travellers. Rome was "the marketplace of the world", wrote Pietro Contarini, the Venetian ambassador, in 1623. For its "ancient remains and also its modern sights", the city was "as much home to those from elsewhere as to its own citizens".

The financial means came from elsewhere, too. Church revenues poured in to the Vatican from many another state; and Pope Urban VIII, with his family and his protégés, spent it uninhibitedly. They endowed churches and chapels, built palaces, collected art, and had their apartments decorated with frescoes. Poussin's *Rape of the Sabine Women*, painted between 1637 and 1639, was purchased by Aloisio Onodei, subsequently appointed cardinal by the Pope and also commander-in-chief of the papal army. After a military campaign ended in defeat, however, he was obliged to sell the picture, and in 1685 it passed to Louis XIV in Paris, where it now remains, in the Louvre. A second version is in the Metropolitan Museum in New York.

The remnants of scaffolding on the tower at the upper edge of the picture are not so much a reference to the building that was proceeding apace in baroque Rome as to the founding of the city by Romulus. The architecture of Poussin's own age held little interest for him. His eye was on the ancient edifices, which he reconstructed in his paintings. At the left he has an ancient Roman temple in the background, and at the right the frontages of residences or palaces that recall Roman buildings, though they also have an air of stage sets. Since the 16th century, theatre set designers had been fond of using a perspective view along building façades to suggest spatial depth. Poussin does the same – he draws in our gaze, past pillared arcades and walls to trees and some area beyond the city precincts.

The "modern sights" Contarini referred to were Rome's baroque buildings. They were not conceived in terms of straight lines and right-angled structures; quite the opposite. Architects such as Gianlorenzo Bernini (1598–1680), Pope Urban's favourite in the field, made walls look as if they were made of sweeping folds of fabric; their windows and gables were rounded. Instead of contained order they aimed for dynamic movement; they sought to liberate masonry from the limitations imposed by statics. Many of the buildings in Poussin's paintings have the effect of a protest against baroque excesses.

Other artists adored the new style and flocked to Rome to admire it. Their prospects of work were good: all the newly built churches and palaces had to be decorated with altarpieces, frescoes, ceiling paintings and statues, and all the ancient remains had to be drawn or painted. Demand for art being so great, the artists had no need to work for one master only. They now had greater freedom. There were no guilds either, which (as in Paris) would have regulated the work of painters and imposed limits.

Poussin must have had an especially strong need for his own freedom and independence. He never stayed for long with any of the French masters from whom he learnt his craft, and in Rome, too, he preferred not to take up residence in the palace of his patron. Rather, he made his own way, as an artist without means, living with fellow artists in a part of the city that was full of the artistic, around the Piazza del Popolo.

With people of various nations living together, conflict was unavoidable. Fights and the need to escape were very much part of Poussin's experience. "Nicolas came with two of his compatriots", reports biographer Giovanni Battista Passeri, "and encountered a number of soldiers who drew their swords. He defended himself with his portfolio of drawings. ... One slash of a sword very nearly cost him the middle and index finger of his right hand." Poussin fled, and in future chose clothing that did not instantly identify him as a Frenchman.

In the painting, the turbulent crowd consists of individual groupings. In the left foreground, a Roman is picking up a Sabine woman and losing his helmet in the process. The woman is tearing at her abductor's hair with one hand. She might use the other to scratch his face or gouge his eye, but instead she is raising her arm and hand in an imploring gesture. Poussin was not so much interested in the realistic options as in art: these two figures are borrowed from a relief done by Giambologna in 1583.

A hand raised over the head, if possible with the palm upward, was part of the classical repertoire of gestures and signified an appeal or lament, despair, a cry for help. It is always a gesture made by the weaker at the mercy of the stronger. In this painting, it is assigned almost stereotypically to all the Sabine women. Indeed, gestures and attitudes play a dominant part in the composition: the graceful pose of Romulus, the backward-flung arm of the man fleeing in the right foreground, the hands of the kneeling old woman raised in supplication, the muscular grips in which the strong arms of the Romans seize their prey.

Physical gestures are the painter's way of telling us what is happening, and we are supposed to grasp the action right away. On the other hand, Poussin took little interest in faces, individualized features, and expressions. Only three heads of the young Sabine women are done with closer attention; they are turned towards us and were painted after one and the same model, a blonde woman with her hair parted in the centre and dark brows that met in the middle. The profile of Romulus is lacking in all expression. The facial expression of the Sabine woman looking back, in the right foreground, was taken from a theatre mask. Poussin took his bearings from ancient statuary, in which the individual was made to conform to an ideal. And he was opposed to Caravaggio (1571–1610), whose figures, painted with brutal realism, were widely imitated.

Poussin took his subjects from the Bible, from history, and from ancient mythology. They are large themes, but the pictures are in fairly modest formats, at least by baroque standards. *The Rape of the Sabine Women* measures 159 by 206 centimetres, a humble size compared with the frescoes then covering walls and ceilings, and considering the number of figures that crowd the canvas. Restricting himself to medium and small formats was part of Poussin's programme. He wanted to place every brush stroke personally, and, even when a successful artist, he did not employ a whole workshop of assistants and apprentices, as fellow painters did in order to cope with large-format commissions. His view was that a painter's work could contribute to the education of mankind. His ethical ambition demanded that he be as near perfect as possible.

A description of his meticulous manner of painting has come down to us from the German artist Joachim von Sandrart (1606–88). On a board, Poussin would position "a tableau of bare wax figures made for the purpose of illustrating the action". These bare figurines "he would clothe in wet papyrus or subtle taffeta, as he wished them". In this way the artist built a stage on which he could rehearse his foreshortenings, the overlap of one figure over another, the effects of light, and above all the harmony of the overall impression.

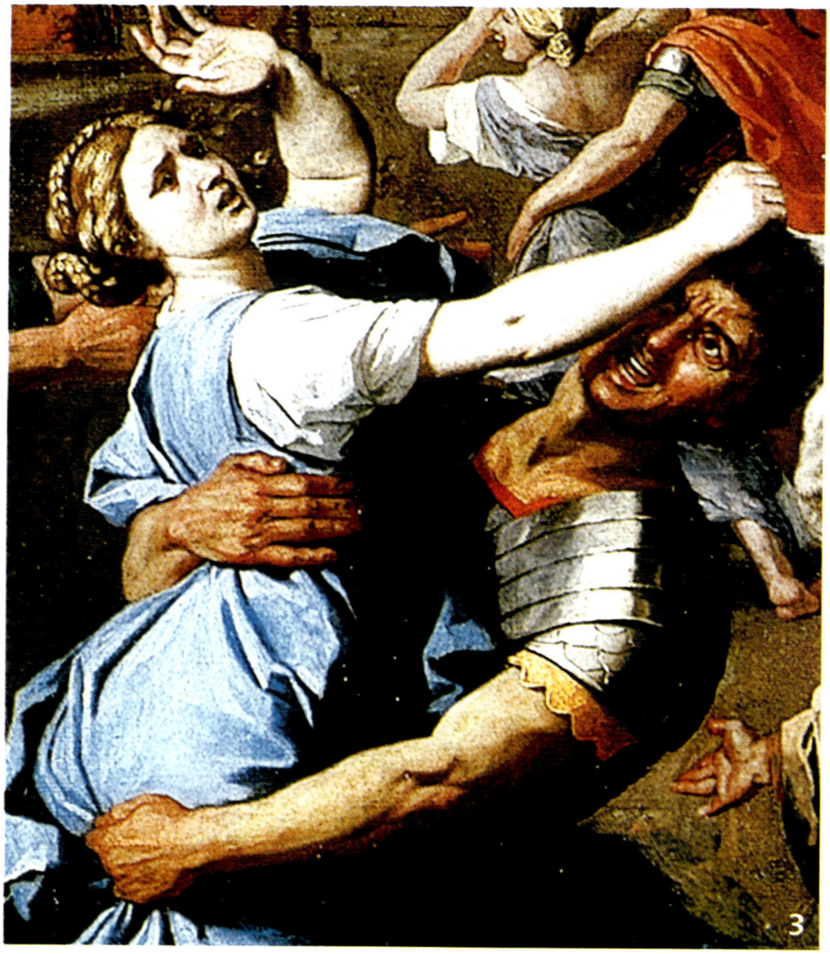

Grand gestures, ambitious ideas

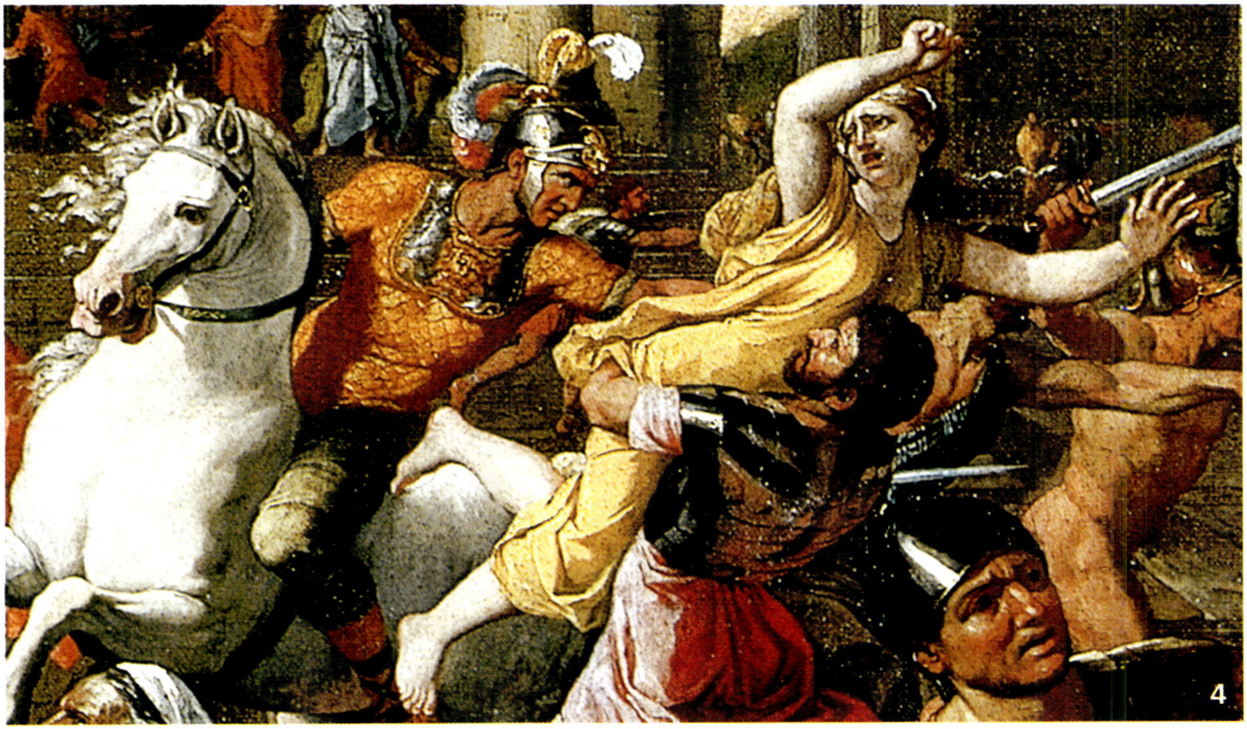
4

X-ray examination of the painting has revealed lines drawn on in the planning of the composition. The meeting-point, from which they radiate like a star-burst, is the head of the mounted Roman in the plumed helmet. This point is right beside the vertical centre axis. In the upper half of the painting, that axis is unmistakable since it coincides with the wall to the right of the temple, running down between the plumes and a woman's raised arm. The horizontal centre axis is marked by the dais Romulus is standing on. Both axes are visible at only one point in the painting; elsewhere they are out of sight, obscured by figures and so forth, since otherwise the composition could appear sterile in its too rigorous proportions. Still, Poussin is after balance. Thus to either side of the Sabine woman with upraised arm in the centre, there is another, one on the left, one on the right. There is a white horse on the left, and another on the right. To balance the group of three on the left that includes Romulus there is a twosome on the right, up on the gallery – much smaller, but then the placid temple façade on the left is offset on the right by a dynamic perspective.

All of this accords with ideas of symmetry and balance handed down from antiquity. If these were not obeyed, so the received wisdom insisted, a work of art could not be considered beautiful.

In 1640, Nicolas Poussin made a return journey to Paris. Louis XIII had badgered him to do so, leaving the artist no alternative. Poussin was needed. After long years of civil war, stability had returned to France; the economy was reviving; the country was bidding fair to become the major power on the European continent. But an art apt to this new status was lacking. Poussin was to supply it. Honours were heaped upon him, and he was appointed painter in ordinary to the king, with instructions to superintend the decoration of the great gallery in the Louvre, to design majestic fireplaces and decorative stairwells, and to supervise the labours of countless assistants. In short, his task involved all those things he had spent his life avoiding. Poussin stuck it for two years, then fled back to Rome.

There he resumed work on his own, living modestly in the Via Paolina. The small house was full of classical busts. Poussin had no servants; his wife, the daughter of a French chef, looked after him. Social climbing did not feature among his ambitions. In this he was unlike many of his

The higher order within chaos

contemporaries: Rembrandt in Amsterdam sought a secure foothold among the upper middle classes, Diego Velázquez in Madrid aspired through his art to a more exalted position in the court hierarchy, Peter Paul Rubens in Antwerp led the life of a veritable prince of art. But Poussin was true to the ideals of antiquity in the conduct of his life, too, leading it in a modest, ascetic manner, in the service of a higher task. In a self-portrait, he presents himself to us with a cloak wrapped about his shoulder like a toga.

Until his death he remained in Rome – and nonetheless he rose to be seen as the foremost painter of France. There, the impassioned excess of the baroque was not in demand. The rational vein of an artist able to bring harmony and order to chaos was more to French taste. Today, Poussin is regarded as a founding father of French classicism, albeit also as a precursor of academic painting, that manner that was to elevate the dry imitation of ancient art into a lofty goal – and drive countless artists all over Europe to distraction.

Rembrandt: The Night Watch, 1642

Parading for Amsterdam

The Night Watch, like the *Mona Lisa*, is one of the most popular works in all of Western culture. Such works are like stars that leave everything in their vicinity looking pale. And yet what is special about them is fully evident only when we understand the context and the age in which they were created, and, rather than being awe-struck by them as works of genius, bear in mind the time and society in which the artist worked. In the case of *The Night Watch*, this means asking what else was being painted, or not being painted, in Amsterdam around 1642.

Pictures for churches were not being painted, for example. The Calvinists had stripped houses of worship of all images in 1566, believing that the way to God should not be obstructed in this way. Thus the most important source of commissions for artworks since the Middle Ages had dried up, and religious subjects were no longer much in demand.

Nor were pictures of rulers being painted. There were the Princes of Orange, true, who had commanded the forces of the northern Netherlands against the Spanish, and aspired to establish a hereditary monarchy. But they led the lives of burghers rather than of kings. In Madrid at this period, the portrait of King Philip IV was painted time and again by his court painter, Velázquez, and in Paris the royal widow Maria de' Medici was glorified by Rubens in a sequence of immense paintings. But Rubens came from Brussels, in the southern part of the Netherlands, which had remained loyal to Spain and to Catholicism. In the northern part, in Holland and especially in the city of Amsterdam, this cult of monarchs was frowned upon. It ran counter to the world-view of the burghers.

The absence of a wealthy and powerful royal house was felt not only in art but in the very appearance of Amsterdam itself: there were no great palaces, no equestrian statues, and sculptors received but few commissions for tombstones. The streets and canals of the city were lined with burghers' houses topped by storage lofts and pulleys. It was these narrow houses, built wall-to-wall against each other, rather than the few large and free-standing buildings, that constituted the architectural charm of the city, and still do to this day.

In addition to ecclesiastical art and pictures of rulers, battle scenes were also almost entirely absent from the painters' repertoire, despite the fact that the Netherlands were at war. The occasion for this war had been the iconoclastic looting and burning of the churches and monasteries by anti-Catholic mobs. From Madrid, the Spanish rulers of the Netherlands responded by despatching the Duke of Alba; and it was against his reign of terror that the Dutch rose, in part, in 1568. In 1579 the northern provinces united; and in 1648, under the Treaty of Westphalia, they were recognized as an independent state.

In other words, when Rembrandt painted these finely garbed militiamen his country was still fighting for its independence. Indeed, the struggle to throw off the Spanish yoke lasted a full eighty years. Nevertheless, there are scarcely any scenes of siege, defence, or victory, no counterpart to the *Surrender of Breda,* which Velázquez painted for the Spanish king. Evidently the subject held little interest for painters. And presumably the burghers of the cities, who had the money to commission art, had no interest either.

Paintings of naval battles were all the more popular, though; and, even if they were not generally painted by artists of the first rank, the demand was great. The land forces were mainly hired mercenaries, on both sides, and the conflict was a protracted war of attrition rather than one of decisive battles; the Dutch navy, on the other hand, was as large as the French and English combined, according to contemporary sources. The Dutch were successful in their naval campaigns against the Spanish, and established colonies in the West Indies and South America. This was a sector of daring, expansion, and triumph; while the Netherlands were still struggling for their independence on land, they were simultaneously rising to become the foremost economic power in Europe. More Dutchmen are said to have died at sea, or in the course of conquests driven by economic motives, than in battles on land.

In addition to naval battles there were three other kinds of picture that enjoyed popularity: genre paintings that paid small-format homage to everyday life and domestic labour; individual or family portraits, a continuance of the ruling classes' customs by the middle class of burghers; and group portraits, usually showing the boards of merchant guilds or members of militia companies.

Like the genre painting, the group portrait is a Dutch speciality. Nowhere else were so many group portraits painted. Fifty paintings showing companies of militiamen alone are in Amsterdam to this day. Some are a full twelve square metres in size. They reflect the self-confidence of the middle classes and the pride of the new republic, and exemplify the Dutch alternative to the monarchic forms of rule in the countries all around the Netherlands. In *The Night Watch*, Rembrandt too painted members of one of these militias. According to a contemporary memo, Rembrandt has portrayed the moment when the captain gives his adjutant the order to start the company marching.

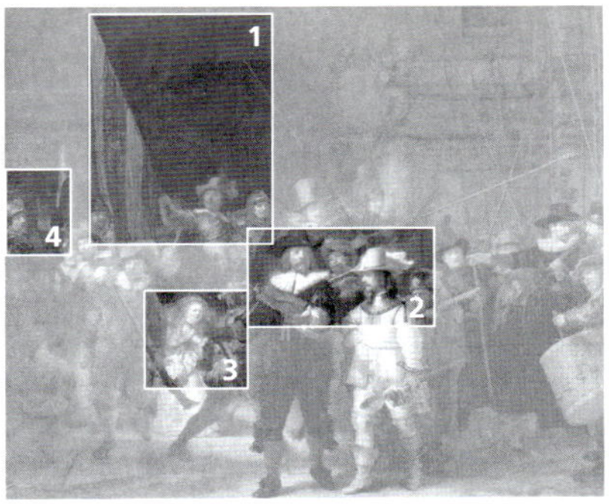
1
4
2
3

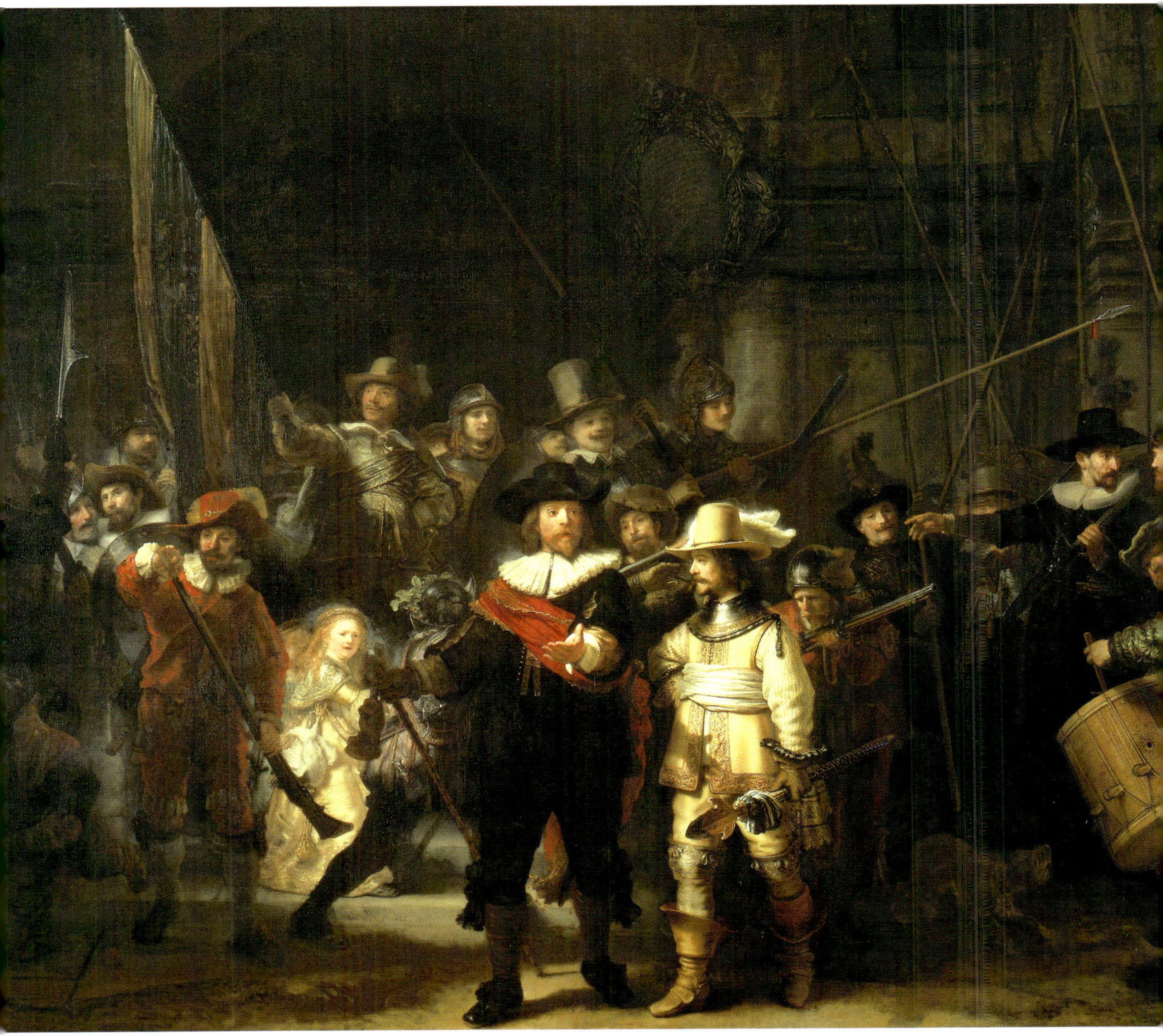

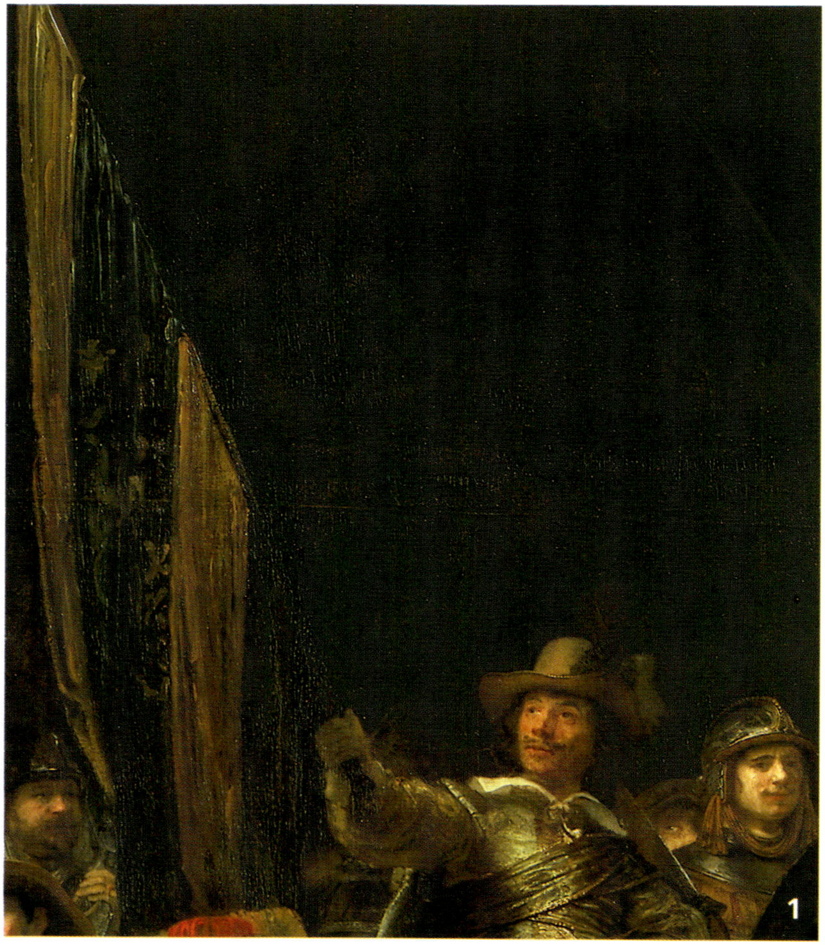

1

The rise of a city

Many an expert has tried to identify the precise place in Amsterdam where these militiamen assembled to begin their march. But in vain. The tall buildings with the archway, and the wall to the left on which the man in the golden helmet is sitting, did not exist, or at least not next to each other; Rembrandt put together the backdrop for his scene to suit himself.

The city is represented by the three crosses on the flag, which are on the Amsterdam coat of arms. The flag bearing this emblem is not held aloft with any symbolic insistence, but it is plainly visible. Amsterdam at that date was one of the largest cities in the world, and its population was growing rapidly. In 1585 it had numbered 35,000; in 1631, when Rembrandt moved to the city, it must have been 115,000; and in 1642, when he painted *The Night Watch*, the city was nearing the 150,000 mark. In just a few decades the population had increased fivefold, and the city walls had to be moved further out more than once. These were boom times for Amsterdam, such as we associate in more recent times with the cities of America's western expansion.

Amsterdam's sensational rise in Rembrandt's lifetime had a number of causes. The most important was that it was very favourably situated for trade. The mariners of Amsterdam sailed not only to far-flung destinations overseas but to northern parts as well, bringing timber and grain from Poland and Scandinavia. Antwerp, the close rival, had the same advantages of location but was part of the Spanish-ruled, Catholic southern part of the Netherlands, and ruined by the financial demands of the Spanish king and the dictatorship of the Duke of Alba. Antwerp's undoing was the making of Amsterdam: merchants transferred their businesses from the one city to the other, bringing their trading connections with them, and often their money. It was not only economic reasons that prompted them and many others to make the move. In the Spanish sphere of influence, only the Catholic church was approved. The reform movement that had been spreading right across northern and central Europe was suppressed there; Calvinists, Lutherans, and Anabaptists were obliged to flee elsewhere if they wished to practise their faiths openly. The same applied to Spanish Jews: those who declined to convert had first emigrated to Portugal and then, when that country became Spanish by marriage, many of them sailed north to the Netherlands. In Amsterdam they constituted an important and wealthy community. It was Spain's religious and power politics that inadvertently helped Amsterdam become the foremost trading metropolis in Europe.

Another key factor in that rise was the oft-praised and equally often doubted tolerance of the Dutch. Calvinism was effectively the state religion, but other churches were tolerated. Apart from the iconoclastic phase, religious fanaticism won little ground. The persecution of witches shows this clearly: the last execution took place in 1595, whereas in other countries it did not end for another 100 or 150 years. On the other hand, while various forms of Christian faith were allowed, atheism was not. When the great Jewish philosopher Baruch Spinoza doubted the god of the Jews and Christians, he was expelled from Amsterdam. The situation in terms of political leadership was similar: oligarchy, not democracy. The lord mayor of Amsterdam was admittedly elected, but those entitled to vote were a small number of wealthy burghers. Still, compared with the ever-increasing absolutism of rule and mounting religious dictatorship in other neighbouring states, the provinces of the Netherlands constituted an island of relative liberty and tolerance. Business people, and artists and artisans, too, were attracted there. Rembrandt, who was born in the small town of Leiden and the son of a miller, transferred his workshop to Amsterdam at the age of twenty-five.

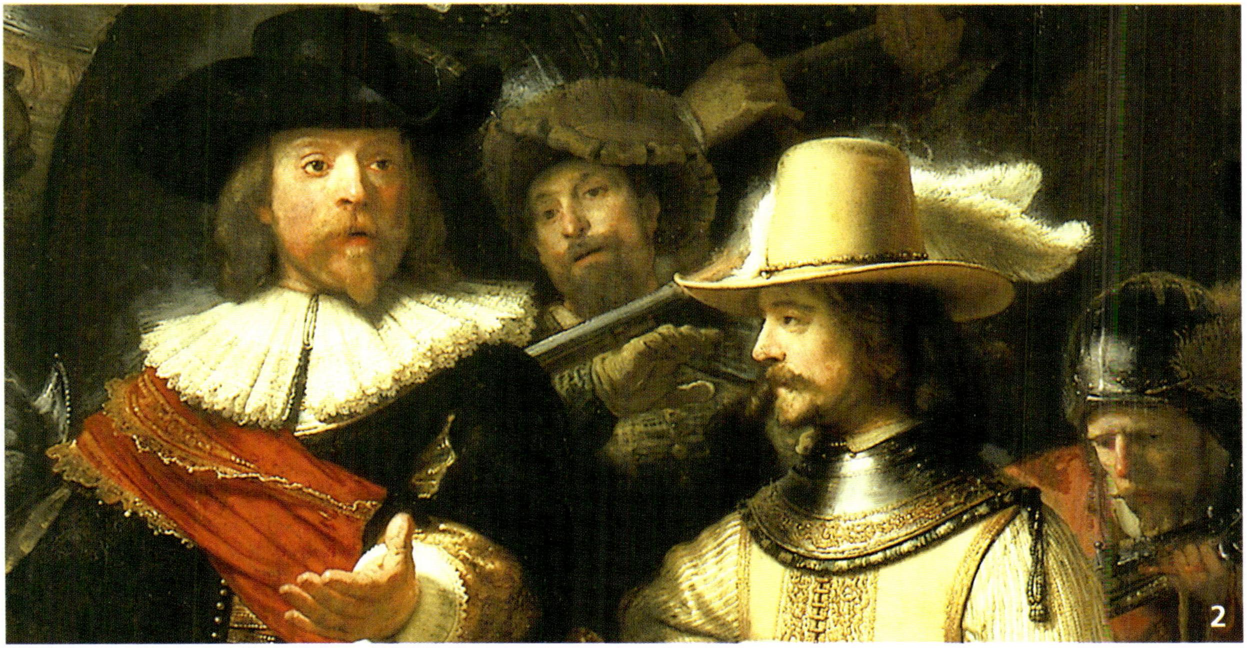
2

How to make a career

The captain of this militia company was named Frans Banning Cocq. Arm outstretched, he is pointing the way for the company. He is wearing the broad lace ruff then common in Holland, a red sash, and at his left side a sword. Like the standard-bearer and drummer, he is not in fact holding a weapon. In his right hand he has a long staff, a symbol of his military rank, and a glove, a sign of his social standing.

Of course the captain is not actually leading his men into action. Amsterdam was not attacked during this time, and the men in this painting never in fact had to defend their city. Nor is he leading them out to do the rounds of a watch; for that, they are too finely dressed. In Rembrandt's presentation, they look more than anything as if they are going to some festivities or to provide a guard of honour such as escorted the French Queen Mother Maria de' Medici when she entered the city in 1638. According to one contemporary report, "some of the guard had dressed up as they felt appropriate and were clad in armour head to foot". But helmets, shields, and armour were no longer usual with forces that did battle: firearms were by now highly developed, and armour no longer afforded sufficient protection. All that remains of medieval armour here is the plate collar, which was occasionally worn as a symbol of an officer's standing.

The captain was the son of immigrant parents. His father was said to be from Bremen, who, as the story had it, went begging from door to door in Amsterdam. He found employment in an apothecary's, subsequently established his own, married a Miss Banning, and – perhaps because the name enjoyed a certain reputation in Amsterdam – their son, Frans, later adopted that name as a middle name. Frans Banning Cocq, born in 1605 (the year before Rembrandt), studied law, took a doctorate, and married above his own station, wedding the daughter of the mayor. At the age of twenty-five (the same age as Rembrandt was when he moved to Amsterdam) Cocq inherited the fortune of his affluent father-in-law, and thenceforth every position in the community was his for the asking. Towards the end of his life (he lived to be fifty) he himself served more than one term as one of the city's mayors. His career well illustrates the opportunities open to outsiders in a city growing so rapidly, provided they were able and hardworking, married advantageously, and possessed a fortune.

Anyone familiar with Rembrandt's predilection for strong contrasts and extreme effects of light and dark might well suspect that the artist costumed the two central figures so differently for aesthetic reasons. But this cannot be the case. These were both men of high standing, and amongst those who commissioned the painting. Their clothing expresses an attitude, at least in the captain's case. Black was the colour of the conservatives of firm burgher conviction, of councillors and great merchants, and in Amsterdam black was furthermore associated with a republican, Calvinist position. It is surely no coincidence that it is the newcomer bent on a career in the city's hierarchy who is wearing the black garb of the conservative.

The fashion in light colours arose early in the 17th century at the French court. The Princes of Orange, who did not abandon their monarchic aspirations in the Netherlands, adopted this French fashion to distinguish themselves from the Spanish and possibly also from the dark-clad citizens of "their own" provinces. Thus if a burgher dressed in light-coloured clothes, he was seen as of the Prince's party, or simply opposed to the clique of burghers who ruled the cities and provinces. He might of course merely be expressing *joie de vivre* in his choice of colours; for the Netherlands, this was the Golden Age, and the people of Amsterdam fared particularly well.

Judging by her size, the female figure is a girl; judging by her face, a woman. This figure bathed in light, and the second female figure adumbrated behind her, have attracted a good deal of speculation. Some say Rembrandt intended her as a goddess of victory. Others maintain this was his wife Saskia, who in reality then lay dying. But there is a realistic reason to introduce a girl into the picture, as we see if we consider pictures of militia exercises. There are always children present, boys tricked out in finery like their fathers, girls with baskets on their arms, apparently playing the sutler. Rembrandt's girl is in fact carrying a chicken at her belt, as a sutler woman might, and the painting also features a boy with a powder horn in the left foreground.

The claws of the chicken are particularly carefully rendered. These were an old emblem of civic guards. Three militia guilds emerged in Amsterdam in the late Middle Ages: the oldest was that of the archers, then came the crossbow marksmen, and the most recent, established after the introduction of firearms, were the Kloveniers. The word came from "kloven", the butt of a gun, and that word was cognate with "klauw" or claw; the emblem of the guild consisted of a gun and a claw.

In other words, these men of the civic guard in *The Night Watch* were members of the Kloveniers guild. But by 1642 the heyday of the militia guilds was long over. In the 16th century they had had political and military power, and for that reason had been prohibited by the Spanish in 1572. When the northern provinces united against the Spanish, it was the members of these outlawed militias who occupied the Amsterdam town hall in 1578 and deposed the vacillating councillors.

After this, the civic guards were re-constituted with all due ceremony, but in a different form. The burgher associations of old were no longer enough. The threat from without called for a greater defence capability. In every one of the Amsterdam districts (by 1640 there were twenty) a company of guards was established. Every company numbered some 120 men. These district companies, while each was grouped under one of the traditional guilds, were no longer the exclusive preserve of the wealthy, but instead socially mixed and municipally organized units with officers assigned by the city council. At least, that was the official version. Within the companies, groupings of the rich emerged once again. And this can be seen on the group portraits of militia companies. Thus there were some 120 men in Frans Banning Cocq's company, but only nineteen of them are shown in the painting. The rest, half seen or merely adumbrated, Rembrandt deploys as part of the scenery, as it were. Of the nineteen, one – the drummer – was not in fact a member of the company; he was a city employee and assuredly made no payment for his inclusion. The others, depending on where they were positioned, paid up to 100 guilders each to be included, and the captain and lieutenant no doubt paid more than that. Their names were all recorded on the oval panel in the entry.

The painting was commissioned for the extended festivities hall of the Kloveniers guild. Seven pictures were commissioned for the hall, and Rembrandt got only one of these jobs. Some of those depicted are reported by his pupil Samuel van Hoogstraten to have been dissatisfied because he "was more interested in the overall conception than in the individual portraits he had been asked to paint". The response can be understood if the other guild paintings are taken as the standard. They present the men standing or sitting close together as in any group photograph, their heads given equally precise attention. What Rembrandt painted was a moment of action, of setting out on a march; he placed his highlights "capriciously"; and he included persons who had not paid, such as the girl with the chicken.

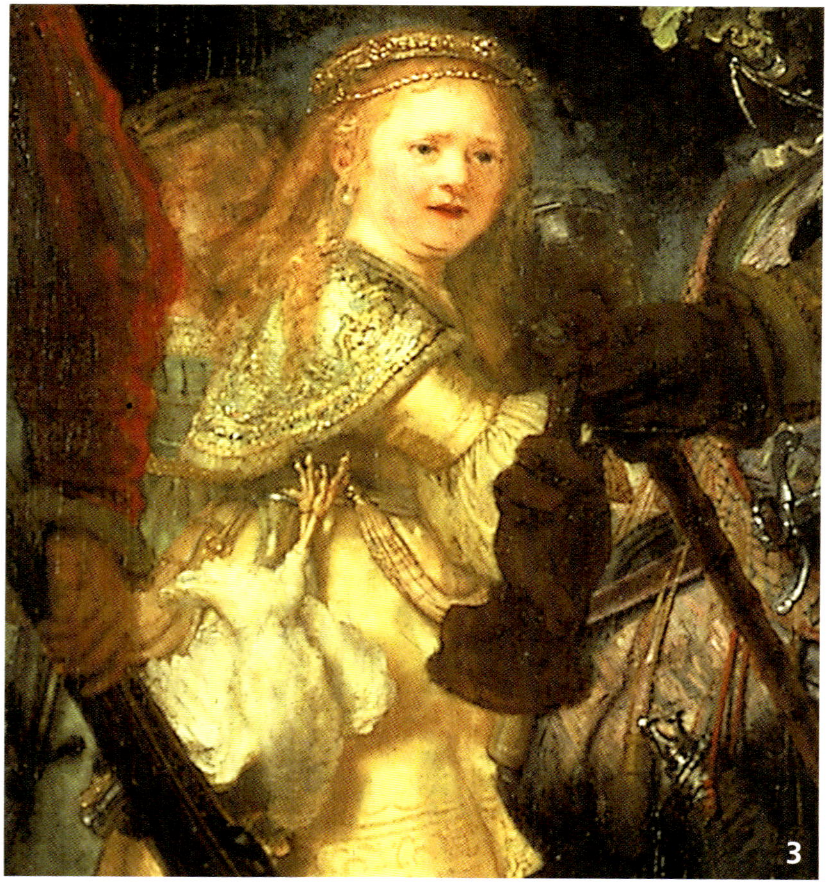

3

The girl with the chicken

From group portrait to national treasure

For the first two hundred years after it was painted, *The Night Watch* was not rated especially highly. Partly this was because the militias declined after the Treaty of Westphalia in 1648; Holland's independence as a sovereign state was recognized internationally, the guilds formed for defence were no longer active, and these group portraits were not required any more. It was not many years after *The Night Watch* till the very last pictures of this kind were commissioned.

But lack of interest was not the only reason. Aesthetic tastes were changing, too. Those who loved the light colours and delicate, fluid shapes of rococo art, or the strict symmetry and clear outlines of classicism, had little time for a painter like Rembrandt. In 1715 his picture was rehung in a hall of a military court and cut down because the wall space was too small. A broad strip was trimmed off at the top, and another, not so wide, at the bottom; together, about thirty centimetres were taken off. Previously the captain was stepping forward within the composition; now his foot was already touching the edge of the picture. At the right, the drummer was cropped, and at the left two militiamen (who had paid) behind the broad shoulders of the man in the golden helmet were removed. From contemporary copies we can see exactly what was removed. The man in the golden helmet, holding a pikestaff, was thus moved to the very edge of the painting, where he is a strong marker at the left margin, while the captain is now precisely on the centre axis: to a classical sense of composition, the trimming of the picture was a definite improvement.

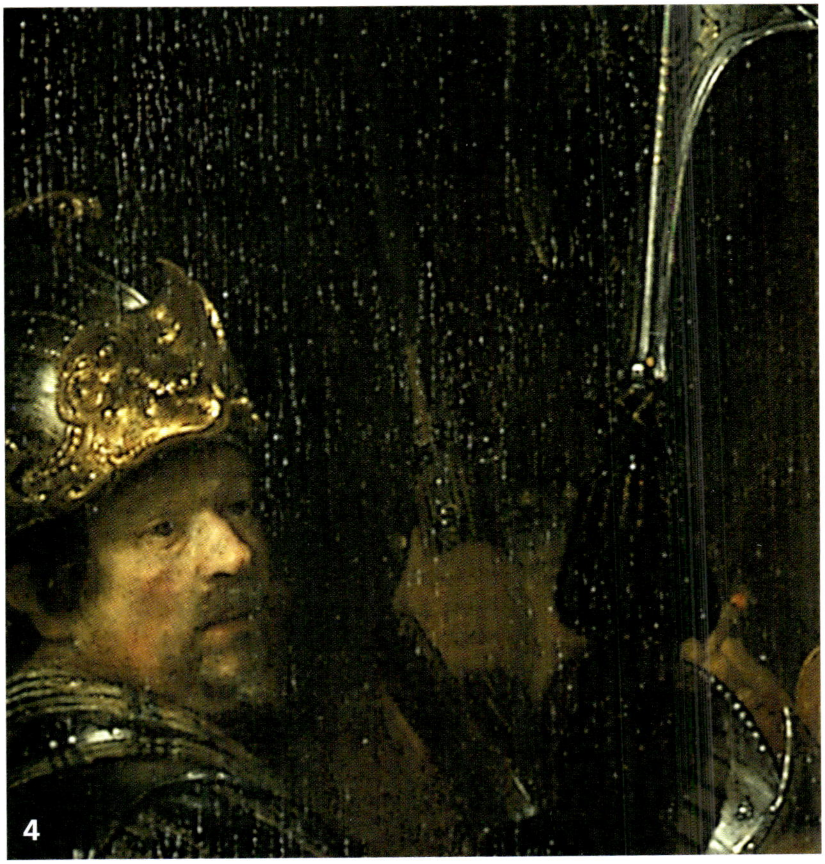
4

It was not only the format and composition that changed; the colours underwent change, too. In 1785, presumably with reference to the girl and the lieutenant, one viewer observed that "the picture is steeped in bright sunshine". Some decades later the title *Night Watch* was first used. The gradual darkening was caused by ageing of the varnish, though restoration may have assisted the process. In the 19th century, picture restorers felt that the Old Masters should be dark, and when working on old paintings they often applied a yellowish-brown varnish to give them the tonal finish desired by galleries. *The Night Watch* was not alone in being affected by this preference.

The painting became popular in its dark incarnation, in the first half of the 19th century. Again, as in the process by which it was forgotten, this was due to a conjunction of aesthetic and political reasons. The Romantics rediscovered the work for art, being fond of night and of all that was darkly intuitive, and indifferent to the bright and balanced world of classicism. Their idea of the artist included a struggle against society, wherever possible one that ended in failure. This seemed to be the fact of Rembrandt's own life: he enjoyed little recognition, went bankrupt, and spent a lonely old age.

In political terms, after the northern and southern provinces had been re-united under Napoleon, a revolution in Brussels in 1830 led to their final partition as Holland and Belgium. This partition reinforced the need for national identity. The Dutch sought it by harking back to their Golden Age, those decades that saw the political birth of their nation and were also so very fertile an era in the arts. *The Night Watch* attested to both artistic mastery and a political stance that emphasized burgher values, and moreover, not unimportantly, it was of an impressive size.

So it was that in 1885 the painting was moved to a room in the new Rijksmuseum building, where it came into its own as the principal work in the collection and indeed of Dutch art, and was revered as a national treasure. Clearly the extraordinary respect in which the Dutch hold this painting has spread to art lovers throughout the world.

To establish a cult around a painting can also provoke aggression, though, as was shown in 1975 when an unemployed teacher deliberately damaged the picture. The subsequent restoration was performed excellently, so that the painting is probably closer now to its original state than it was a hundred or two hundred years ago.

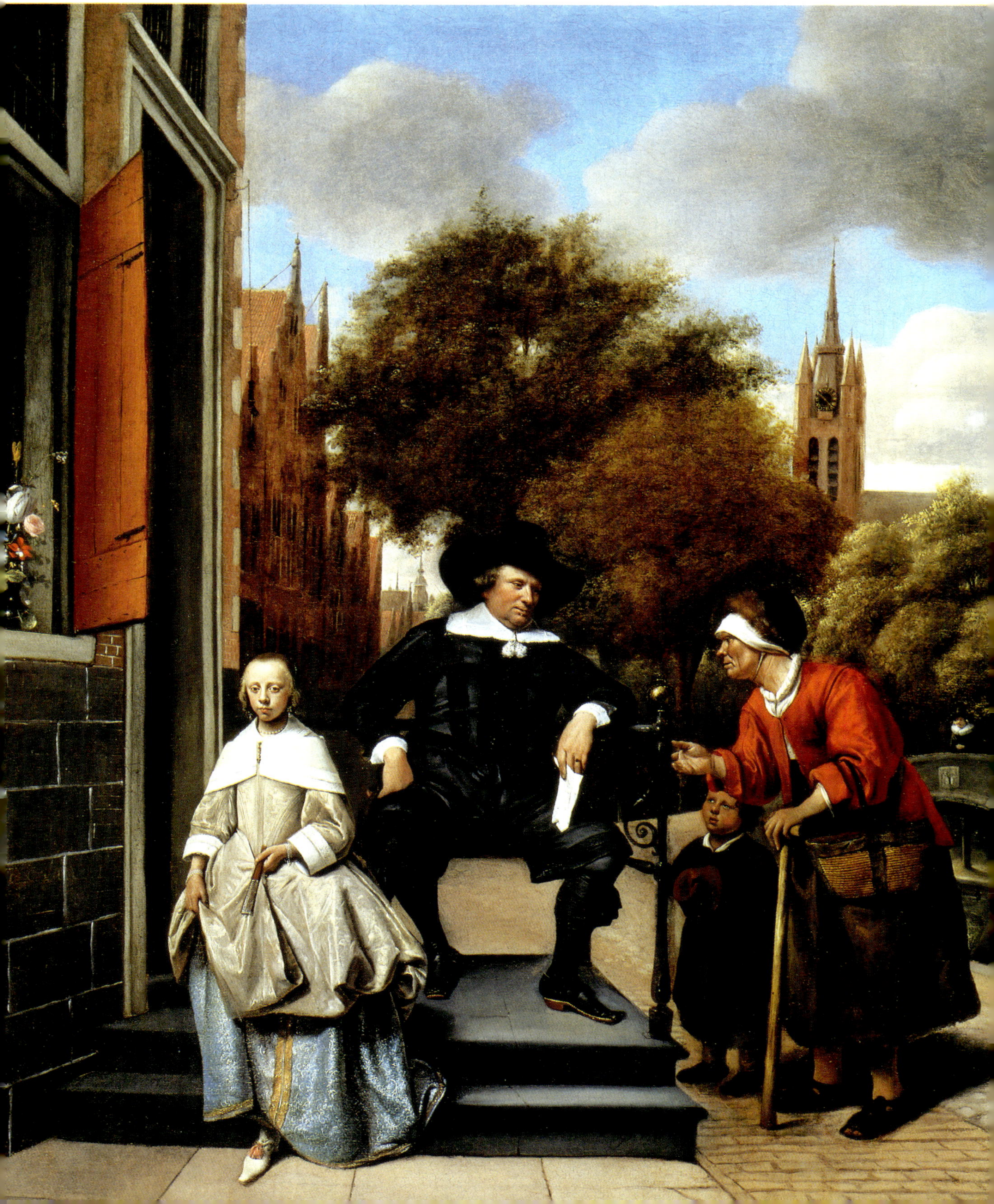

Jan Steen: The Burgher of Delft and his Daughter, 1655

A rich man sitting in the street

A man is sitting in the street. Or rather, he is sitting on the stepped threshold of his house, and thus at a place at once public and private. Not only this raised entry before his front door but also the paved area in front of the house is on his own land. Beside the paved strip is the brick public footway, on which an old woman and a boy are standing. Further to the right is the cobbled street intended for horses, carriages, wagons, and so forth.

This raised threshold, with a railing and a seat, known as a *stoep*, was often found in the Netherlands, and probably served as a place to hold conversations. Of course one might talk to passers-by from the window, where the flowers are, but it was easier without an intervening wall and on the same level. Furthermore, the seat conferred a certain dignity and placed the owner of the property on show. For someone who held public office, conversations held here could be of importance. For a long time, historians identified the man in this painting as the lord mayor of Delft, but for this there is no evidence. All we know of him is what we see. One of the things we know is that the location where he had himself portrayed is the west bank of the canal known as Oude Delft. In the background is the Oude Kerk, and to the left the twin gables of the Delflands Huis. Maps of the town show that residences on the canal-side were very narrow, and built close against each other, and extended a long way back from the street. Behind the houses were equally narrow gardens, running as far as the next canal.

Jan Steen (1626–79) painted this unknown man in 1655. At that time the town of Delft had a population of about 25,000 and was in the provinces of the Netherlands, which had thrown off Spanish rule after a protracted struggle. The Treaty of Westphalia (1648) had recognized Dutch independence. What remained contentious, however, was the form of the government. During the wars of liberation, the Dutch had made the Princes of Orange their stadtholder, but in times of peace they were too powerful for the people's liking, and in 1651 the office of stadtholder was rescinded. Henceforth, it was the patrician burghers who ruled. The man we see sitting with such self-assurance had thus been living for seven years in a newly sovereign state. And for four years it had not been ruled by the house of Orange any more but by men of his own class. The artist has portrayed him on an afternoon in late summer; by the church clock it is ten to five.

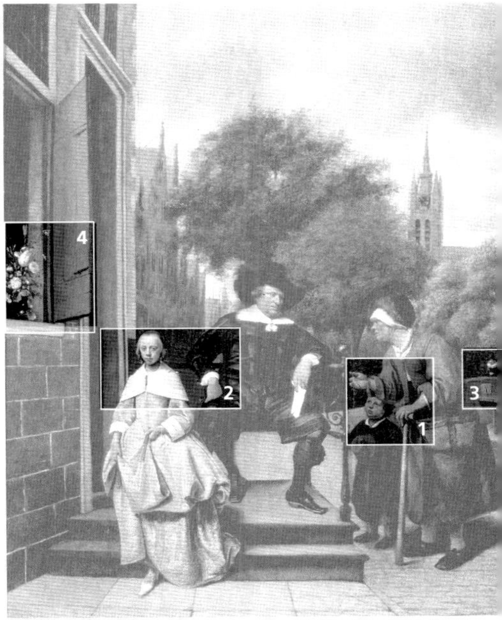

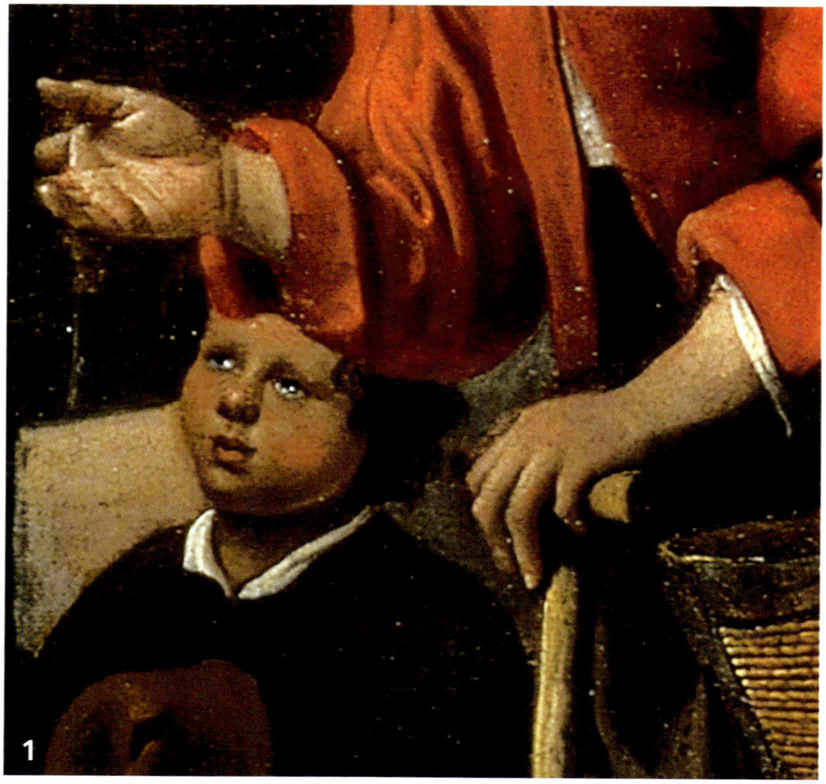

1

The registration of the poor

Steen's painting, now in a private collection, was made in the heyday of bourgeois culture in the Netherlands. One of the pillars of that culture was its strong civic sense. The government in The Hague was responsible for foreign policy and defence only; all other matters were for the provinces or cities to decide. The indigent lay in the jurisdiction of the cities, as did the administration of justice. There was no written penal code, and every town decided these matters at its own discretion, though invariably with rigour. Guilty parties were beheaded or hanged, drowned, or burnt alive; a hand was amputated; if the offence was less serious, the guilty party's shoulder was branded with a red hot iron. Executions were always held in public, as an entertainment but also a deterrent. Begging was subject to penalties.

A clear distinction was made between the poor of a municipality and beggars from without. The municipal poor were registered and had a licence permitting them to beg for alms. Their numbers included the sick, orphans, and old people unable to work, such as the woman in the painting, supporting herself on her stick and holding out a beseeching hand. The scrap of paper the affluent burgher is holding may be her licence. Steen does not portray this man as one who would spontaneously open his purse, or call back his daughter to fetch bread from the house and put it in the old woman's basket. This man is thinking it over, holding the licence in his hand as he ponders what is to be done. Such deliberation was considered a civic virtue and duty, since unreflecting charity might benefit frauds, especially those from elsewhere.

Every town was on its guard against itinerant tramps. They were strangers in the tightly woven fabric of a town and thus were invariably met with suspicion; they had no fixed abode to which a magistrate might have sent them back. They might be discharged mercenaries, landless peasants, workers from industries that had gone out of business, gypsies, or criminals fleeing justice. Since they could not always be turned away at the city gates, they would be given a permit to stay for a limited time, perhaps three days, perhaps a month, and if at the end of this period they had not found work they had to leave the city, or the municipal officers would set their dogs on them.

The magistrates and burghers took an entirely different attitude to the poor of their own municipality. They provided them with food and shelter (in former Catholic monasteries, for instance). Thus where the Sint Agatha Klooster had been (the tower can be seen over the shoulder of the seated burgher), the Oude Vrouwen Charitaathuis was built, an almshouse for old women. It may be that this old woman lived there, or that the seated burgher held honorary office there.

Despite the much-vaunted Dutch civic sense, provision for the needy was repeatedly the subject of municipal dispute. Before independence from Spain, charity had been the province of the Catholic church. In 1572, the Delft council expropriated the church there, and took over all its charitable duties. The strongest religious institution in the sequel was the Reformed (Calvinist) Church. It attempted to define social responsibilities as its own domain, while at the same time lending support to the house of Orange, which had just been ousted from power by the government representing the burghers.

So if a man chose to be painted in 1655, in a place outside the church, pondering an act of charity, this might be interpreted as a statement: against the house of Orange, against a church that arrogated social responsibilities to itself, and for the rule of the burgher.

The burgher is sitting at his ease. His left arm is resting on the railing, his right is on his thigh. Both are supporting him and thus easing his upright posture; but they also tell us something about the man. He has not the palm but the back of his hand on his thigh, which has the effect of bringing the elbow forward and so making the sitter appear broader, of more substance. The left, relaxed arm sends a message of potential goodwill and concern; the right signals that this is not a man to be trifled with.

Jan Steen was among those Netherlandish painters who discovered everyday life, and, with it, everyday gestures. He became a master of body language. In his paintings, even legs and feet talk. With his knees apart, this man again seems more substantial, while the position of his feet seems to be asserting his ownership of this plot. The right foot, below the angled elbow, is somewhat withdrawn, which may be either playful or suggestive of readiness to leap to attack or defence. It is not the posture of a scholar who spends his time at a writing desk; it is far more that of a mounted military commander.

The impression made by his daughter is quite different. She is holding the hand with the fan in front of her, and with her other hand she is raising her overskirts in the manner she has presumably been taught by her dancing instructor that is appropriate when descending steps. At the time, good (i.e. courtly) deportment required that the feet be kept close together and the arms flush along the sides, without any ostentatious or extravagant posturing.

Requirements such as these were laid down in etiquette books. Erasmus of Rotterdam, in his treatise on education published in 1532, explicitly disapproves of placing the hands square against the sides whilst sitting or standing; such a position might be permissible in a man of arms, but in others would be undignified. In *Il Galateo* (1558), Giovanni della Casa likens those who strut about with their hands against their sides to peacocks. And in 1644 John Bulwer declared the posture expressive of pride and boastfulness, and unbecoming in a gentleman.

This burgher of Delft was evidently no more troubled by such considerations than many of his contemporaries were. If pictures are to be believed, this attitude of self-confidence was highly popular. It can be seen in the groom in wedding scenes, and on many group portraits, such as Rembrandt's *The Night Watch* of 1642, in which both the showily clad lieutenant and the standard-bearer have an arm against their sides, lending to a peaceable scene of departure an air of swagger and aggression.

What the writers of etiquette books spurned was acceptable to Dutchmen; indeed, they may have adopted behaviour unacceptable in court circles as a form of provocation. Or they may have intended to demonstrate their own strength: the burghers' new self-esteem established its own repertoire of gestures. But as the century wore on, it was abandoned again, and the well-to-do took their bearings from aristocratic circles once more: the prim and proper daughter is showing her splay-legged father how those of her generation propose to conduct themselves.

A daughter dressed in the court style

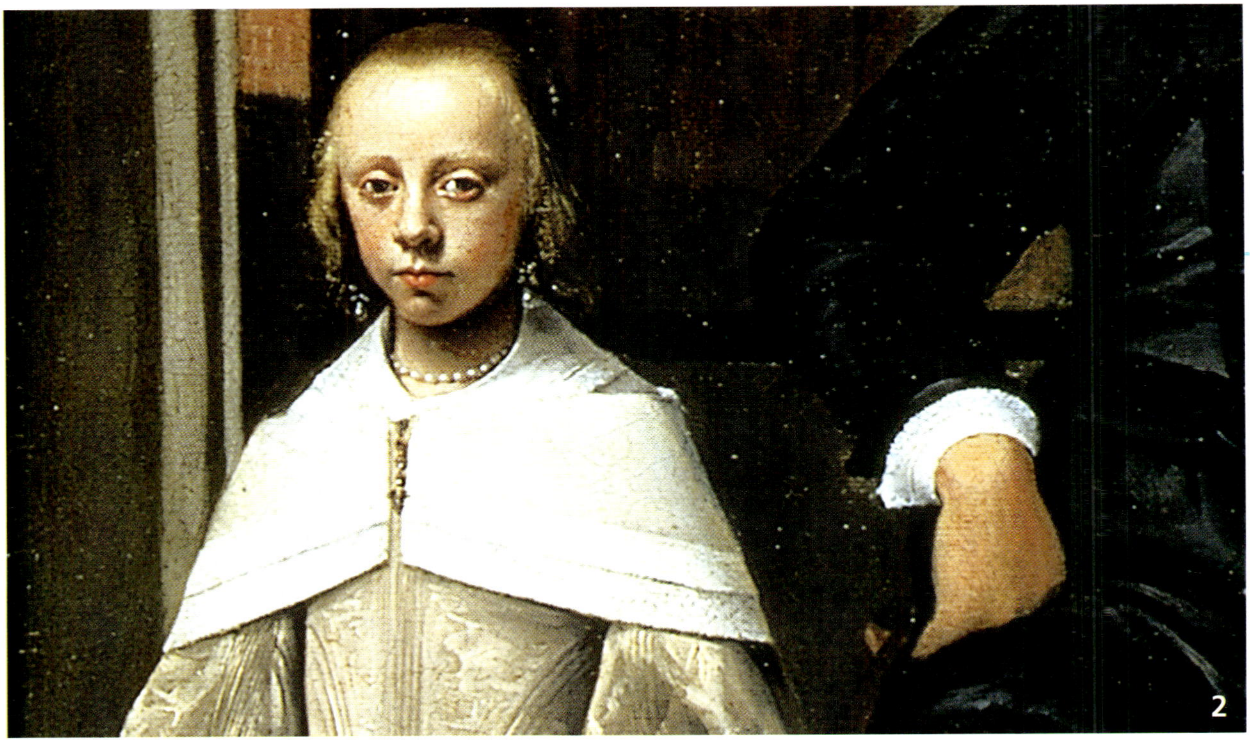

2

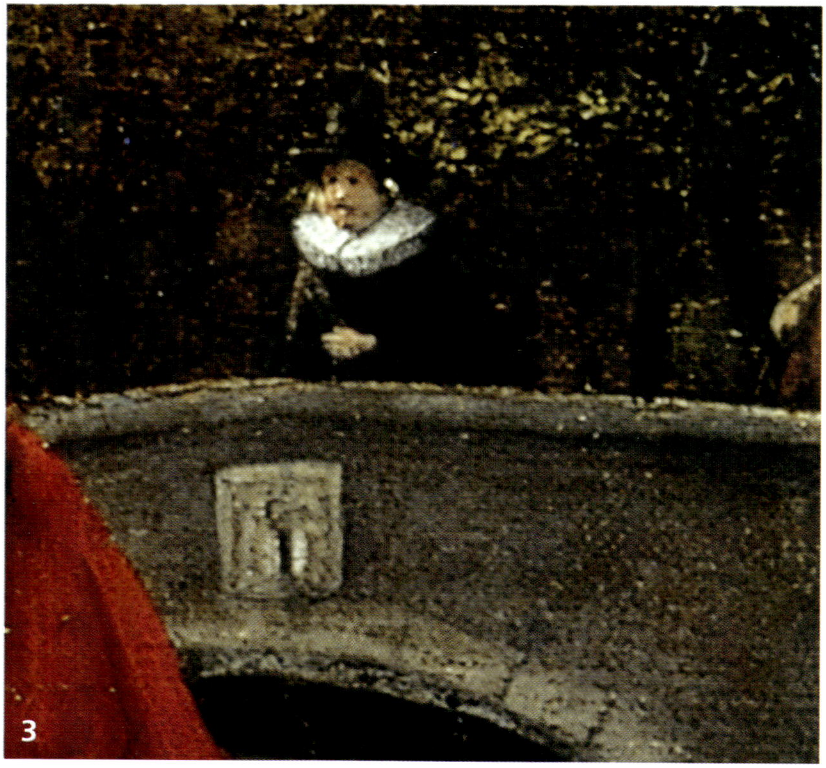

3

Looking back to the past

Jan Steen liked to tell stories in his paintings: of brawls in taverns, of twelfth-night festivities, of weddings and family outings. There is always something happening between his personae, and the father and daughter in this double portrait are no exception. The story emerges from the presence of the impoverished woman and the boy. The father is pondering what he will do; his daughter seems indifferent, self-absorbed, in a world that is all costly garments and descending steps with style.

On the bridge in the background Steen has placed two men. One, whom we can barely see, is probably a farmer, carrying a sack to the nearby market. The other is a burgher dressed in the fashion of yesteryear: his hat is taller than was usual in 1655, he is wearing a stiff ruff rather than the soft collar of the principal character in the foreground, and the cut of his beard is no longer much seen. This elderly gentleman is watching the scene in the foreground. With his black and white attire, he looks like some remote double of the foreground burgher; the quality of the gaze suggests some relationship. The artist offers no explanation, but with the gentleman on the bridge he has introduced the past into his painting, a brief look back in a picture that takes pride in the present.

Some years earlier, the bridge over the Oude Delft had been a flat, wooden construction. The arched stone bridge betokens progress and prosperity. The arms are those of the city of Delft. The Delflands Huis, the twin-gabled building seen to the left, was the seat of the office of public works, transport, and waterways. This was one of the most important of public authorities, for flat Holland was criss-crossed by a network of rivers and canals, and they constituted a major pillar of its prosperity. Neither France nor England had anything approaching so good a system of waterways, and Germany, Spain, and Italy lagged far behind. Canal transport was slower than road transport, but a horse could move fifty times the load by water. Travellers preferred gliding down the waters in the comfort of their cabins to bumpy coach rides on unsurfaced roads. All the towns of the Netherlands were linked to the seaports by the waterways, and goods arriving at the coast could thus easily be moved inland.

The Netherlands not only had the best canal system, they also had the largest of all European fleets. Their most powerful rival was England. A naval war between the two countries, from 1652 to 1654, ended in disaster for Delft: in 1654 the powder depot exploded, destroying a large portion of the city. This was the year before Jan Steen painted his burgher.

Steen himself experienced hardship during the war. Hostilities crippled trade, much reducing the chances that ships bound for America, Asia, or the Baltic would make the return voyage safely. There could be no more thought of processing English wool. The demand for faience ware, a speciality of the Delft porcelain manufactories, fell. And so, too, of course, did the demand for art. Steen had moved to Delft because his father had taken a lease on a brewery for him there. The artist could not support a family on paintings, and he had learnt the brewer's trade in his youth. Like the burgher's house, the brewery was on Oude Delft, though on the opposite bank. Steen was unable to make a success of beer in Delft.

From there he moved with his family to Leiden, later to Warmond, thence to Haarlem, and then back again to the city of his birth, Leiden, where he opened an inn. What he observed there, the revelling over-consumption of beer and tobacco, the brawls, the card-playing, is all to be seen in his paintings. To what extent he himself participated is a moot point. The fact that Steen's paintings are to be found in museums all around Europe demonstrates that he was a prolific artist; and yet he left his widow only an inn up to the hilt in debt. He died in 1679 at the age of fifty-three.

Flowers in memory of the dead

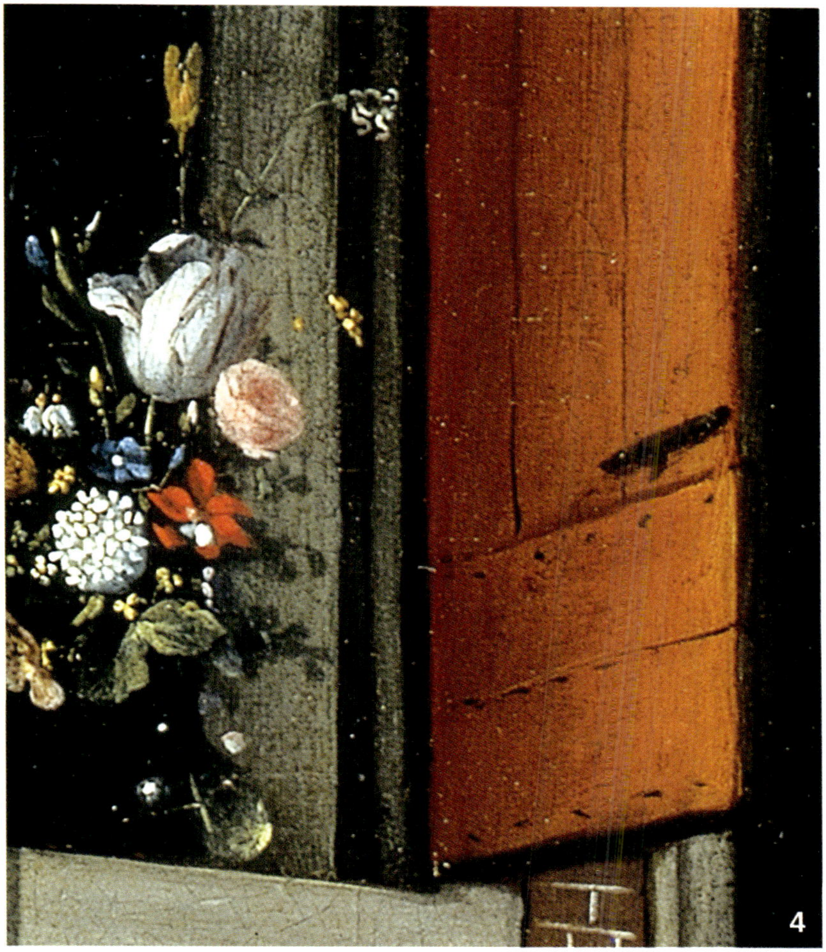

4

Painters generally positioned what was of importance in the centre of a picture. Details on the edges were not expected to excite undue attention. Steen, however, broke this age-old rule with his flowers. They are more colourful than any other part of the composition, and they are so detailed and so carefully nuanced that we might be standing right before them and not (as the structure of the work implies) a few metres away.

The flowers are isolated. They are like a picture within the picture. Like a still life. This type of painting enjoyed great popularity in 17th-century Holland, and indeed the very term came into being at this period: *still-leven*. The motionless subjects of such paintings tended to be food and kitchen utensils on a table-top, dead game birds and animals or a skull beside books, or, frequently, flowers in a vase. These pictures were notable for their relish of limited scope, and the closeness with which they scrutinized the things of the everyday world.

Steen places his vase on the window ledge and, in doing so, draws our thoughts toward the interior of the house. Well-to-do burghers felt that a presentable and indeed impressive interior, with carved chairs and tables, ornate mantelpieces, and floral decoration, was of great importance.

But perhaps the flowers are intended to point us not only to the interior but also to the person who must once have been there, the burgher's wife, now presumably deceased. The floral still life invariably prompted thoughts not just of beauty but also of transience. This miniature masterpiece on the edge of the painting may be a kind of memento mori, in remembrance of the dead. It is visible only to us as we look at the painting. It is discreetly screened by the window shutter from the family members in the painting, who live entirely in the present.

The dominant flower in the bouquet is one that enjoyed extraordinary popularity in the Netherlands at that time. In the 16th century an Austrian legate was the first to bring tulip bulbs back from Constantinople to Vienna, and in the 17th century tulips spread throughout Europe. In the Netherlands a veritable tulip mania ensued, aggravated by profiteering and botanical experimentation. The potential for creating hybrid strains seemed unlimited, and new varieties of tulip were dealt on the stock exchange (using painted images of the tulips) and resulted in wild speculation. In 1637 the Dutch tulip market crashed, and with it the financial well-being of many a small investor. Thus the tulip already had a famous, or notorious, history by the time Steen included it in his Delft bouquet.

If we take a careful look at the burgher of Delft's home, we realize that his house, with its window of flowers, does not fit in with the perspective alignment of this receding line of buildings. It is more to the fore, and seen more from the side. This is an error by the artist. But only by committing it could Steen satisfy the requirements that either he or the burgher from whom he had his commission had set: to place the head of the sitter in the middle of the composition, to leave the sitter squarely on his *stoep*, and still to present a panoramic view of the town.

We see clearly the special qualities of Steen's painting if we compare it with works by, say, his contemporary Rembrandt (1609–69). Rembrandt liked to shroud his sitters in a dark, mystical aura. Instead of that aura, Steen prefers a profusion of concrete details. Through them he gives us a character portrait of the burgher and also of his city, showing the individual as a member of the society in which he lives and works.

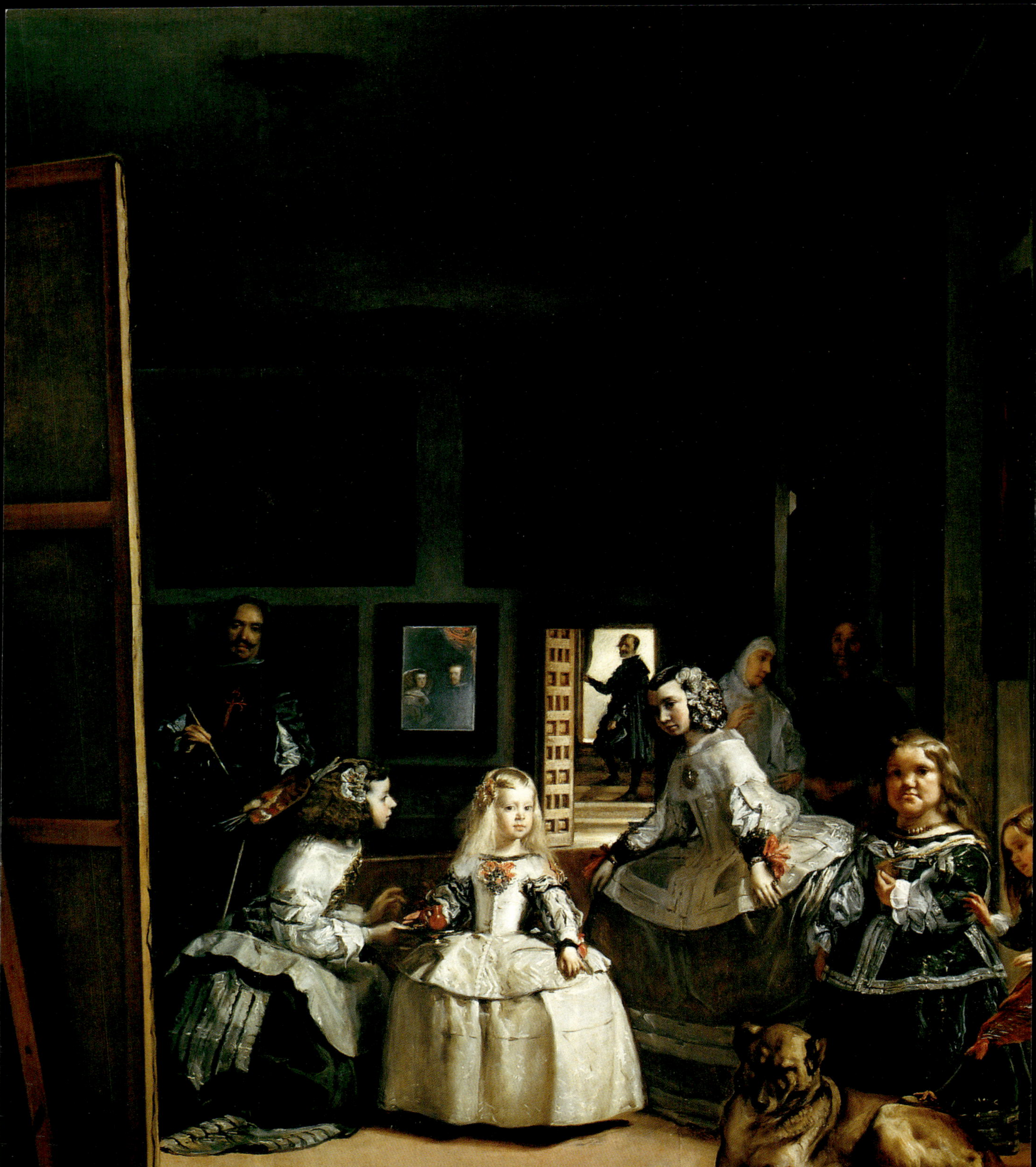

Diego Velázquez: Las Meninas, 1656

The end of the Habsburgs in Madrid

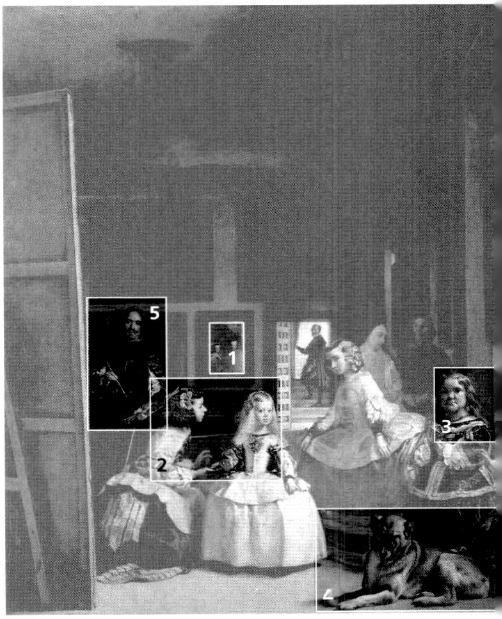

The scene: Velázquez's studio in the royal palace at Madrid. The artist is painting Philip IV and his queen, Mariana; the royal couple can be seen indirectly, reflected in the mirror at the rear. At the centre of the picture stands the five-year-old Infanta, Princess Margarita, who appears to have just come in with her maids of honour (*las meninas*) and other attendants. The light, and doubtless the gaze of her parents, are on the girl. Velázquez conveys an impression of family happiness, of wealth, and of a hopeful future, personified in the little princess.

The picture was painted in 1656. At that date the king was fifty-one, and in poor health; he had ruined Spain politically and economically; in reality the court's coffers were empty, in winter there was no firewood to warm the palace, and the fish served up on golden platters came stinking to the royal table.

The Habsburgs had been on the throne of Spain for five generations, and time and again they intermarried, within the family. The degeneration that resulted was most apparent in Philip IV, in his almost morbid weakness of will. Politically he was at the mercy of his first ministers, and in private life at that of his sensual desires. He is said to have fathered thirty-two illegitimate children, and had more mistresses than Louis XIV of France. Being a pious man, he felt that adultery was a sin. He wrote prolix, emphatic letters to a nun, confessing his sins and swearing to mend his ways; broke his word; swore his oath anew, and broke it again; and besought the nun to do penance on his behalf, with all the other nuns in her convent.

Philip IV had inherited an empire "on which the sun never set". But during his reign, Flanders was lost; Portugal and Catalonia cut their ties with Madrid; French armies ravished the country; and the routes to the colonies that produced silver were threatened by the growth of England's power at sea. Under Charles I (of Spain, simultaneously Holy Roman Emperor Charles V) and Philip II, his great-grandfather and grandfather respectively, the vast Spanish empire had already become impossible to defend militarily, but it had come through, thanks to a combination of political skill, personal dedication, and the aura of Spanish power. Now all of that was gone. The reign of Philip IV proved one long chain of disasters.

Together with the empire, Philip had inherited the Spanish commitment to fight for a Catholic Europe – under Habsburg leadership. The Habsburg emperor in Vienna had abandoned that goal following the Thirty Years' War, recognizing that a Catholic monopoly on power was untenable. Philip IV never fully grasped this insight. He bled his country for the sake of a superannuated idea, disregarding the new realities. The older he grew, the more often he withdrew to El Escorial, the palatial mausoleum where the tombs of his great ancestors were. For hours he would pray, taking refuge in religious mysticism. To bear so great a burden of personal failure as Philip IV must exhaust or defeat the powers of any man.

There is no other Velázquez painting in which the king and queen appear together. This is the only one; and here, though united, they are unclear, mere apparitions. The fact was that they had little in common. Princess Mariana was thirteen when she was sent from Vienna to Madrid to marry Philip. Then, she was a ruddy-cheeked, naïve girl who loved a good laugh, according to descriptions. One anecdote tells that, in one of the towns her procession passed through, local artisans wished to make her a gift of a hundred pairs of stockings. The Spanish lord chamberlain spurned the offer in outrage, declaring: "A Spanish queen does not have legs!" Whereupon Mariana is said to have asked whether her legs were to be cut off in Madrid.

She did not lose her legs, but she lost very nearly everything else that makes the life of a young girl worth living. Corsetted into the strict ceremonials of life at court, she had nothing to do but make a majestic impression and, more important, bear an heir. Boredom, loneliness, home-sickness, and illness in consequence of her never-ending pregnancies, transformed the lively girl into "that wilful, mulish German".

Philip gave her his attention for only a brief period. He was thirty years her senior, and her uncle. He had married the daughter of the emperor in Austria in order to consolidate the alliance between Madrid and Vienna – in vain. By 1656, the date of the painting, when the royal marriage was seven years old, hopes for an heir to the throne had still not been satisfied. Apart from the Infanta, Princess Margarita, Mariana bore an annual succession of still-born babies. Subsequently she did give birth to two sons, who died in early infancy, and to a semi-retarded boy who in due course succeeded Philip IV on the throne of Spain, and put a miserable end to Habsburg rule in that country.

An unhappy couple

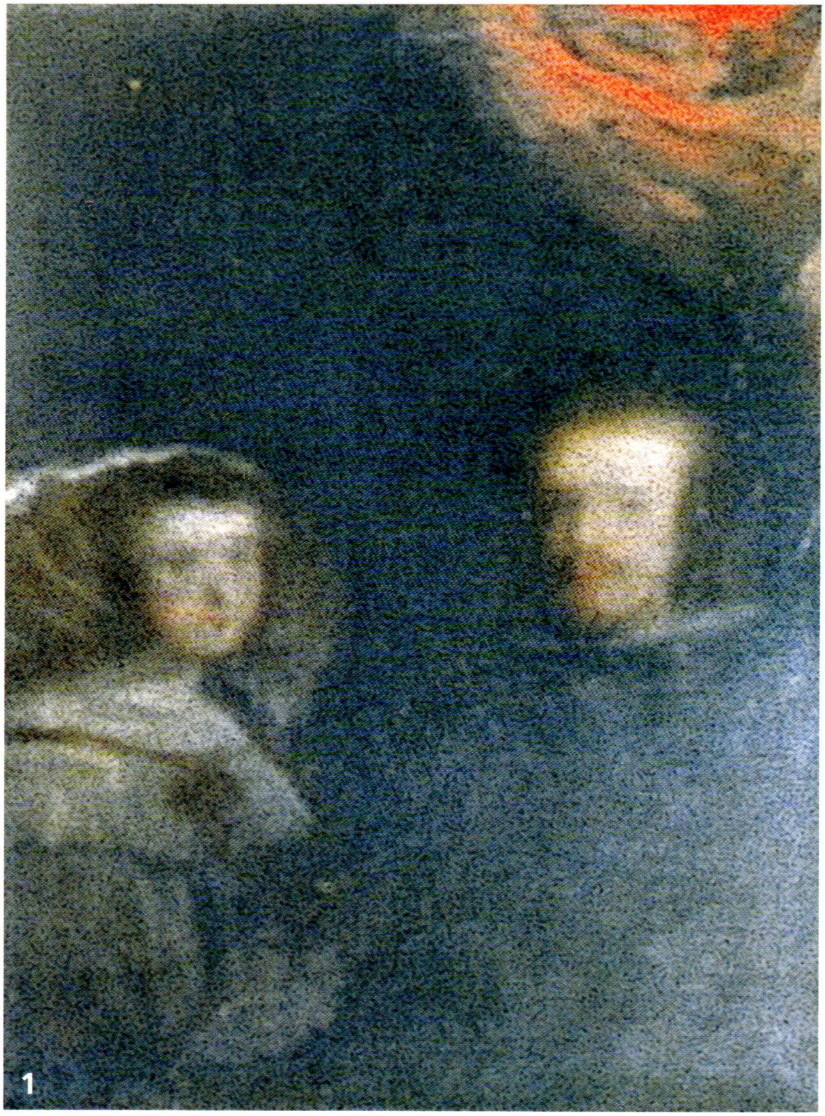
1

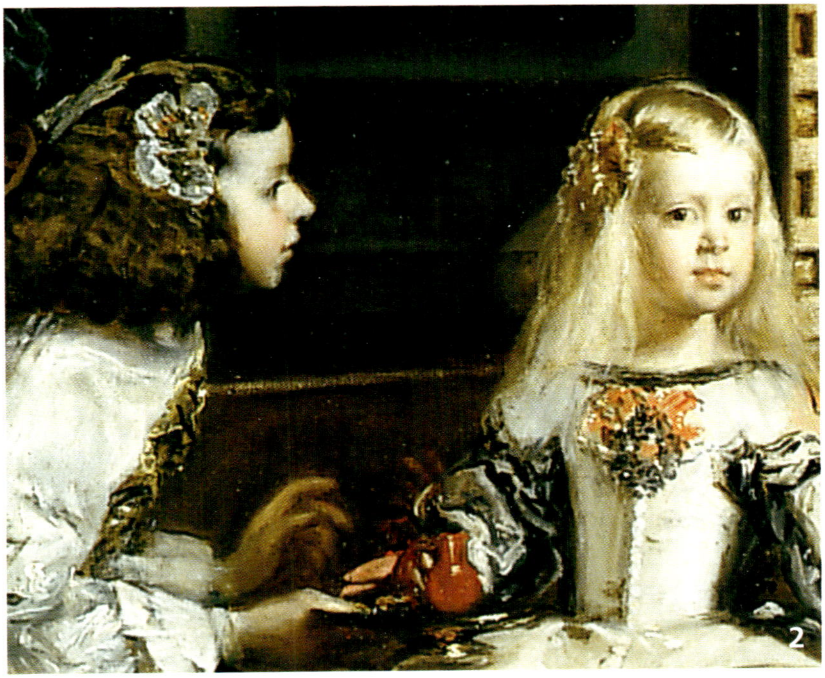

A well-bred Infanta

When this picture was painted, then, Margarita was the royal couple's only child. The fact that she was there at all, and enjoyed good health, encouraged hopes of a male heir to the throne. The periodic ebb and flow of that hope should be borne in mind if we are to understand the light upon the girl properly. Unusually in one of her age, the five-year-old is taking a jug so much as looking at the maid of honour. In this we can see the first fruits of a royal upbringing that emphasized self-control and awareness of one's station. Like most of the others in the picture, the Infanta is looking at the king and queen, whom we must imagine seated in front of the painting, as it were. Margarita is showing them how well she can already stand motionless, with a majestic manner. No doubt she already knows that a Spanish king or queen never laughs in public. This was something her mother had to be told, on the journey to Madrid. Her father was supposedly only ever seen to smile in public twice in his entire life.

The maids of honour (to either side of the Infanta) were chosen from the first families of the nobility. The one on the left is kneeling not in affection but because protocol requires her to. One had to kneel when proffering anything to a member of the royal family, and only very few were permitted to do so at all. Possibly it was the duty of the maid of honour on the right, who is dropping the hint of a curtsey, to fetch the jug: everything involved more than one person. When the queen ate, her food was reached down a succession of ladies-in-waiting of rising rank, the last kneeling as she proffered it to the queen. No other European court of the period was so riddled with protocol and ceremonials. The protocol even increased as the realm declined: when everything is going under, you cling to etiquette.

Living by rules could be literally lethal, as a story told of Philip's father, Philip III, shows. He was sitting in his study, near a coal-burning stove. The coal was giving off too much heat, too much "vapour". But the noble equerry whose office it was to tend the stove was nowhere to be found. No one else dared attend to the problem. That night, the king fell ill, and died within a few days.

The dog and the "monster"

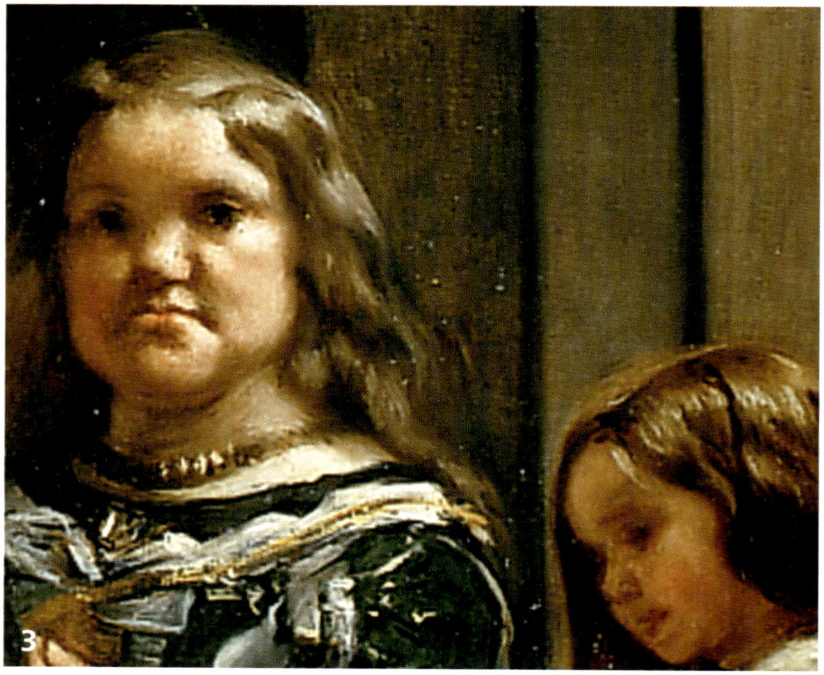

3

So that the rigid protocol and everlasting tedium of the palace might be a little more bearable, court jesters and dwarfs were part of the household. No other court in Europe had as many as the Spanish. Maria-Bárbola, the female dwarf, was from Germany; the young male dwarf at the far right, Nicolas de Pertusato, was from Italy. Both were members of the royal household. They had fool's licence, leading lives outside the court hierarchy, kept much as animals were. It is no coincidence that they are shown standing by the dog. Nor is it coincidence that Velázquez has allowed only one character in the picture a spontaneous gesture – the young dwarf is teasing the dog with his foot. Dwarfs were numbered among the "monsters" kept at a court, along with those suffering from water on the brain, physical deformities, or mental deficiencies. Maria-Bárbola, with her old woman's head on a childish body, was by no means the worst specimen. These people were dubbed "the vermin of the palace". Others, of normal stature, felt superior and attractive in the presence of the dwarfs; the "vermin" raised their self-esteem. The Infanta and her maids of honour are all the more appealing in the presence of Maria-Bárbola.

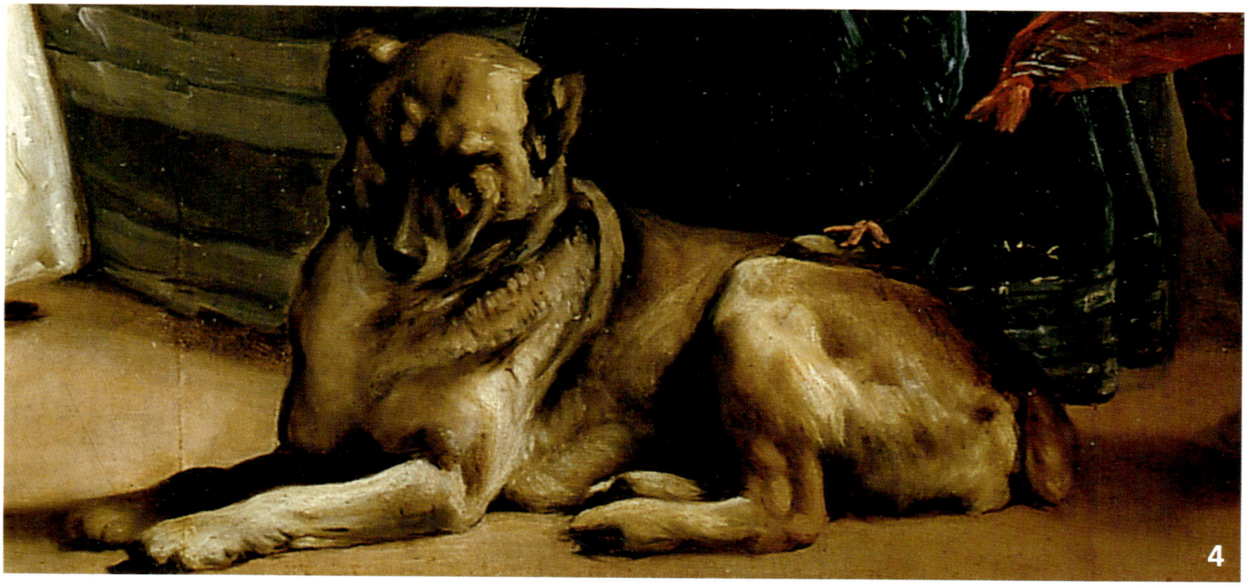

4

The end of a painter

Velázquez is wearing on his chest the Cross of the Order of Santiago; but in 1656 he was not yet a member of the order. He was not inducted into it until three years later. First, a lengthy process had to establish the "purity" of his blood (no Jews or Moors were admitted); an exception had to be made because the details of his aristocratic ancestry were incomplete, an involved business; and more than a hundred witnesses had to confirm that he had never painted for money, but only for the delight of the king. Some other hand added the Santiago Cross at a later date.

It seems that membership of this exalted order, and thus climbing the human pyramid at the top of which stood the king, mattered at least as much to Velázquez as art. There are various pointers to this suspicion. The most telling is this: four years before painting *Las Meninas*, after having spent years performing largely honorific duties at court, which allowed him time to paint, he applied for the position of marshal of the royal household. He was an experienced courtier and knew what this would entail. The position would be high in the hierarchy, but he would be bearing an oppressive burden of paltry tasks. Velázquez had to see to the king's bed linen, the straw palliasses of the guards, and the reed matting that covered the floors in winter; he had to procure firewood and coal; he had to superintend cleaning staff; at public banquets he had to hold the king's seat. A note in the 1657 archives reads: "Diego Velázquez, marshal of the royal household, reports that he is owed his salary for one year, a sum of 60,000 reals. The palace sweepers and other servants dependent upon his office have ceased to work, and, what is worse, there is not a single real to pay for firewood for His Majesty's chambers."

Even more exhausting than his duties in the palace were the tasks Velázquez had to perform when the court undertook its many journeys, to summer palaces, to theatres of war, or (in 1660) to the French border, where Philip gave his daughter from his first marriage to Louis XIV, to be his bride. In July 1660 Velázquez wrote: "I have returned to Madrid, worn out by journeying all night and working all day." A month later he was dead. In the last years of his life he scarcely painted anything at all.

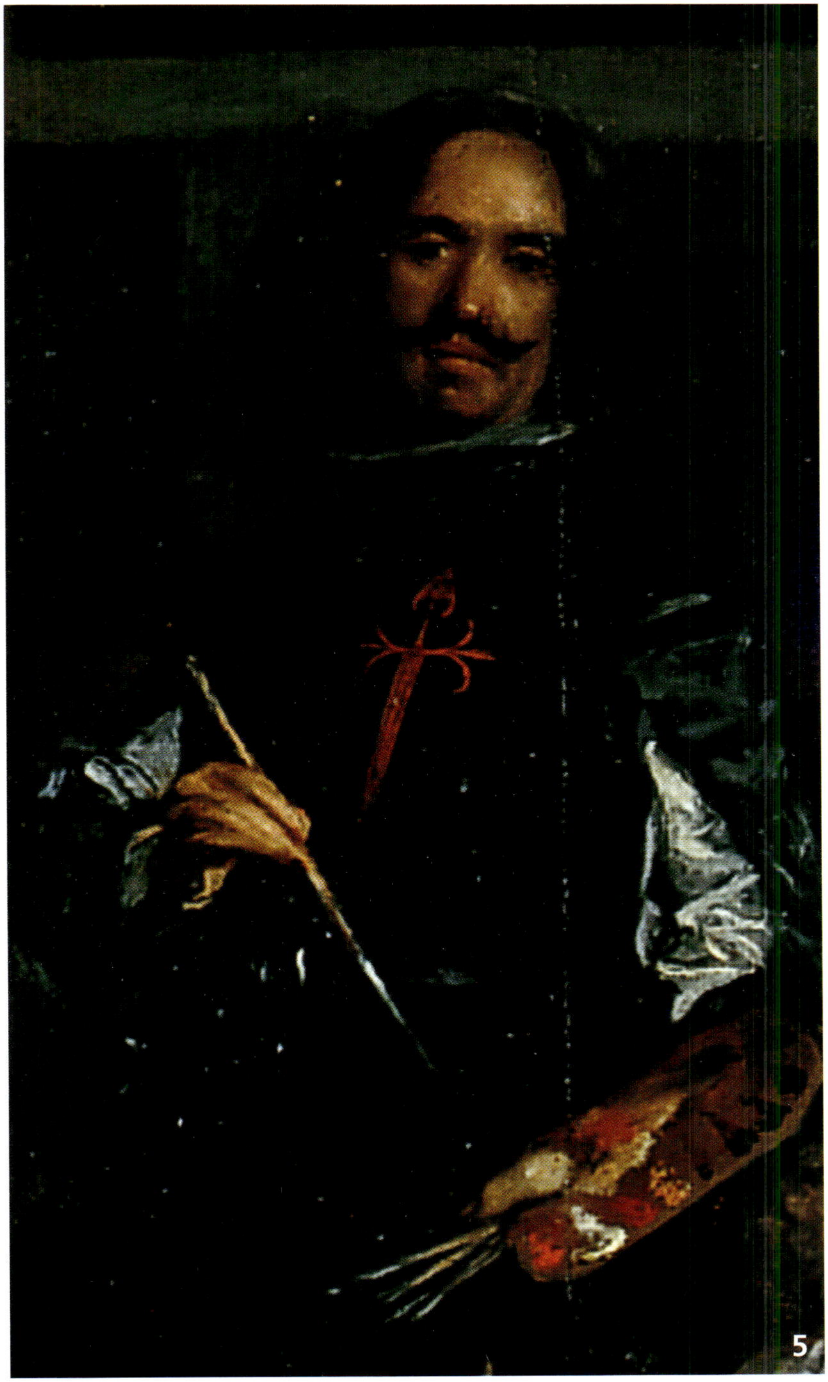

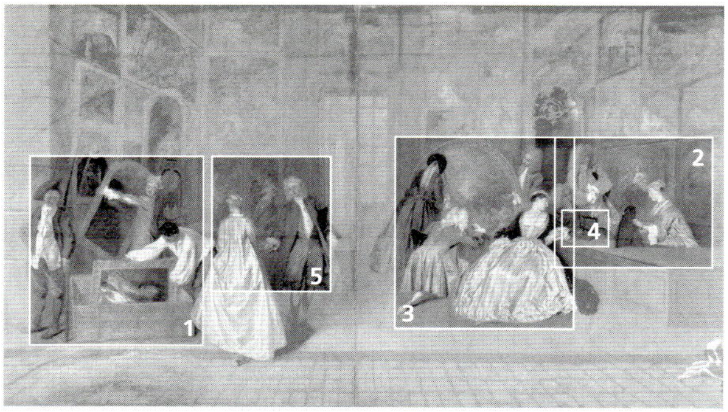
1
2
3
4
5

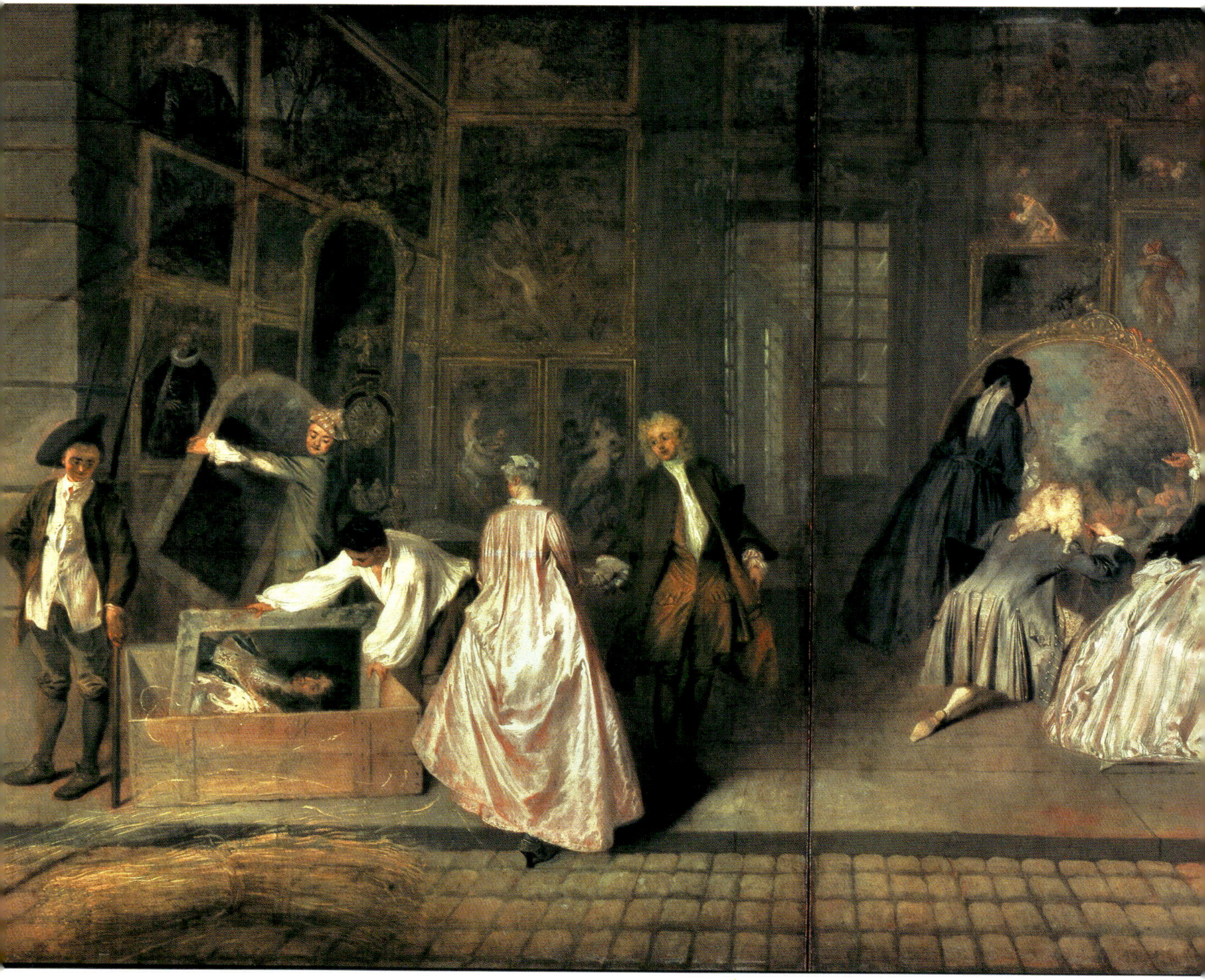

Antoine Watteau: Shop-sign for the Art Dealer Gersaint, 1720

A morning at the art dealer's

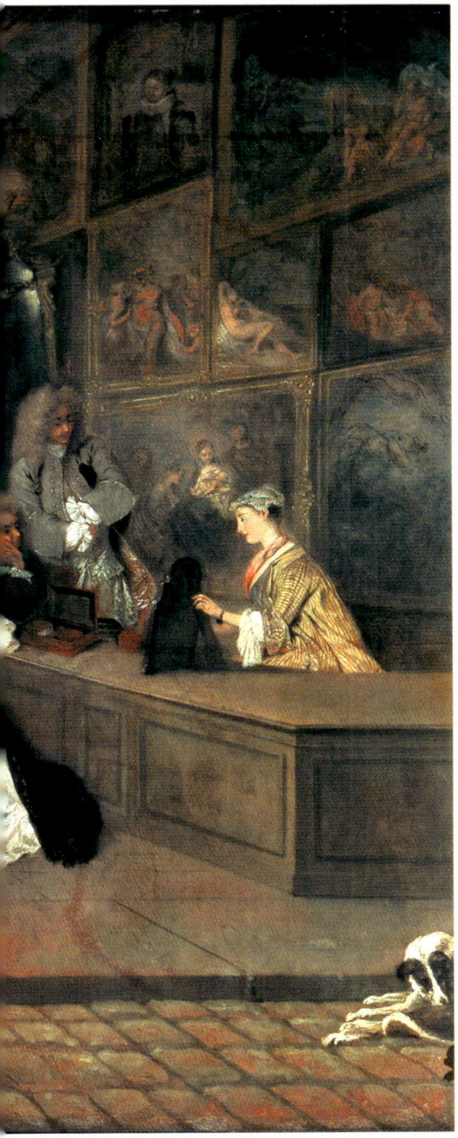

It is Paris, autumn 1720, about eleven o'clock in the morning, and we are looking into the shop owned by the art dealer Gersaint. The men and women gathered inside are familiar to us from many of Watteau's other paintings. There they are strolling through parks, chatting on terraces, basking in the carefree atmosphere of a permanent holiday. In Gersaint's shop, however, they are brought much closer to real life. Watteau's picture is about buying, selling, and money. Two assistants are packing up a painting and a mirror. To the left of the crate stands a porter with a carrier frame on his back.

It is a picture about money, but also about art, about luxury objects. It was a good address: 35, Pont Notre Dame. Gersaint's shop lay on one of the thirty bridges that crossed the river Seine. Shops had lined most of these bridges since the Middle Ages; in Watteau's day, the goods they sold were largely home furnishings and fashion items – in other words wigs, bonnets, clothes, jewellery, mirrors, and paintings.

1720 was the year in which Marseilles was swept by the plague: in August, more than 1000 people were dying a day. Large swathes of the city of Rennes were destroyed by fire. In Paris, too, fires were a frequent occurrence: two years earlier, Gersaint's first shop had burned to the ground. In March, a young aristocrat by the name of Count Horn was broken on the wheel for robbery and murder. Crime in Paris was on the rise. The major subject of conversation in 1720 was not the plague, murder, or the great fires, however, but a man called Law. The art trade was just one of the economic spheres he influenced. The people in this picture knew him well.

John Law was a Scotsman who, on 5 January 1720 (i.e. the year in which this picture was painted) was appointed French Minister of Finance, because he had rescued the country from a state of financial crisis. He had done so with the aid of two new financial instruments: paper money and shares. He guaranteed a fixed rate of exchange between paper money (which he printed in large quantities) and conventional coins. The shares he sold were in a company to which the State granted various monopolies and in the large area along the Mississippi that had recently been colonized by French settlers. The first share certificates were issued in 1718 and cost 500 livres. Demand was high, share prices rose, investors bought and sold. In January 1720 the share price peaked at 10,000 livres – an increase in value of 2000 per cent. Never would French citizens be able to make so much money so quickly. An unparalleled speculation boom set in, fuelled by new shares released by Law.

The profits being reaped had far-reaching consequences. The money was re-invested not only in new shares, but also in industry, agriculture, and in particular houses. There was a rush of new building. More cautious investors saw sinking their money into land as their safest bet. Those who didn't build at least refurbished their existing homes. New houses needed furniture, mirrors and pictures. Artists and art dealers owed Law a great deal.

In the spring of 1720 his monetary system began to waver. Share prices fell. To halt their decline, Law bought back shares at the top price, printing more and more money in order to do so and thereby causing inflation. In July the Law Bank stopped payments. Despite their guarantee, banknotes were devalued. In December Law secretly left France; he wandered across Europe and ended up in Venice, that gathering-place of speculators of all kinds, where he died in 1729.

Following the collapse of the Law system, the streets of Paris grew quieter. Those who, in the preceding years, had moved to the capital in order better to profit from the rapid circulation of money, returned to the provinces. The population is alleged to have shrunk by 25 per cent. People also left to escape the rising levels of crime. The streets were becoming unsafe; corpses drifted beneath the bridges of the Seine.

A portrait is being put into the crate. It is a picture of Louis XIV, in his bulky wig and royal ermine. The Sun King had reigned for seventy-two years. During the last decades of his rule, he had bankrupted the country with his pursuit of pointless wars. When the news of his death – in 1715 – was announced, many French are said to have burst into songs of rejoicing, and his body had to be transported secretly to church through the streets of a jubilant Paris.

The Sun King is packed away

The king was resented not just because he had burdened his subjects with high taxes and a national debt, but because he had paralyzed the country as a whole. France under Louis XIV engaged in little other than war. There were no economic innovations or social improvements, but instead the bigoted puritanism imposed by the king's secret second wife, the prudish Madame de Maintenon. When the Sun King died, the heir to the throne, the later Louis XV, was just five years old. His great-uncle Philippe, Duke of Orléans, became regent, running the country from 1715 to 1723. This short period in French history is known as the Regency. Voltaire: "Life was full of gaiety and fun during the regency of the Duke of Orléans… After the severe gloom of the latter years under Louis XIV, the regent revived the nation's spirits."

A new mood of optimism emerged. Law's financial experiment boosted the economy and the middle classes began to flourish. The regent moved from the splendid but formal palace of Versailles to the Palais-Royal in the centre of Paris. The new mood was reflected, too, in the colours people wore. During the reign of the Sun King, everything had been dark and heavy. Now clothes and fabrics became lighter, more delicate. The colours bequeathed to us in Watteau's paintings represent the new fashion.

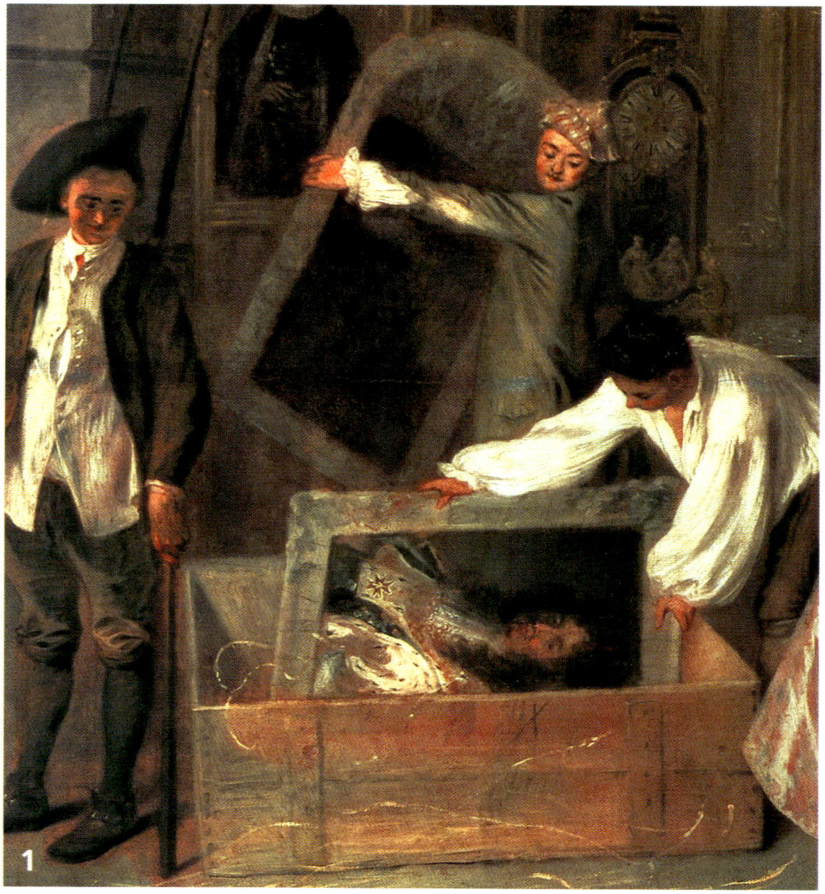
1

A bourgeois becomes a peer

Watteau liked to use his friends and acquaintances as models, and probably did so for this painting, too. The lady displaying the mirror may be Madame Gersaint, the wife of the art dealer. She was twenty-two years old, had got married two years earlier and had since given birth to two children. She would die at the age of twenty-five. Hers was typical of the short lives of women in the days before obstetric hygiene. The art dealer immediately remarried.

The model for the gentleman standing up may have been Claude Gluck. He owned a dye business and worked for the royal Gobelins tapestry workshops. Seated beside him is his nephew, Jean de Julienne, who in 1721 or 1722 took over the running of the dye works and went on to make so much money that in 1736 he was elevated to the peerage. Later, in an obituary, it was said that he rose every day at five o'clock, when it would have sufficed to have surfaced at midday to become rich.

Both men are representatives of the upwardly mobile middle classes. Louis XIV had paved the way for their rise by appointing members of the bourgeoisie to posts in his administration, a strategy designed to prevent the nobility from gaining excessive power. Commerce and industry were anyhow in bourgeois hands; as their profits grew, so too did the personal fortunes of their proprietors. The Regency then brought the great boom of the early 1720s. Despite the ever-increasing economic, administrative, and intellectual significance of the middle classes, however, they continued to lack political power. Their attempt to claim it led in 1789 to revolution.

Gluck and Julienne numbered amongst

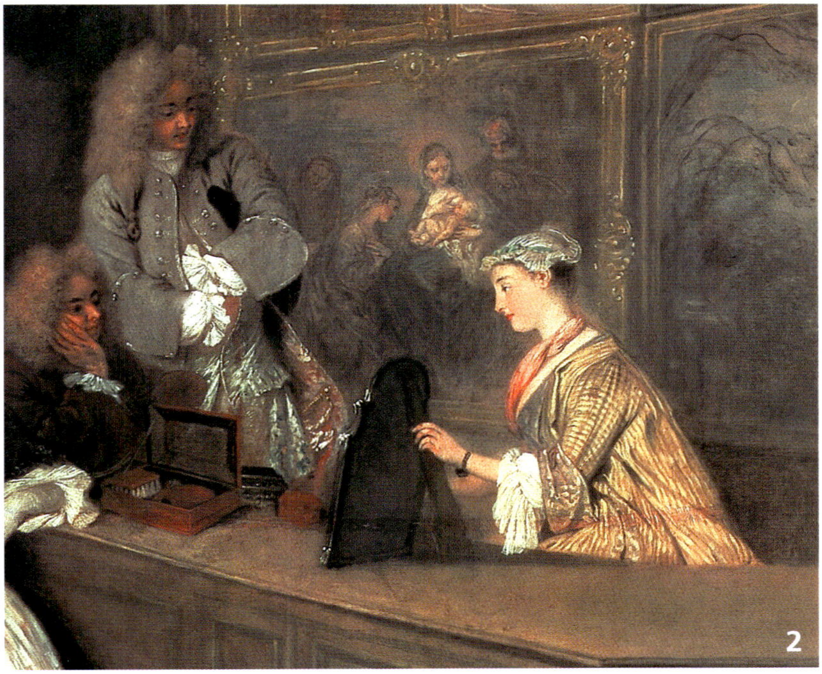

2

the newly rich members of the bourgeoisie who took an interest in art and who bought and sold pictures – even if only because it was the fashion. Julienne would even go on to be made an honorary member of the Royal Academy of Painting and Sculpture. After Watteau's death, he had his works engraved in copper and published in four volumes. Some said he was creating a memorial to the artist, others that he was cashing in on his friendship with Watteau.

Trading in luxuries

The man showing off the large oval painting must be the art dealer himself, Edme François Gersaint. He was twenty-four years old when Watteau painted his shop. It was his second shop; the first, which had burnt down, had stood on a different bridge. He was a successful young man, successful because he just happened to sell precisely the goods most sought-after in the Regency, especially during the years of the Law system – art and luxury items. It was a glittering era, made splendid "by velvet suits in every colour, lined with fabrics of gold and silver ... by magnificent braid and embroidery", as one contemporary wrote. "As for the precious stones, their brilliance dazzled the people out for a promenade and at the theatre... The frenzied eagerness to spend money and to show off, but also to horde and invest safely, emptied the shops."

Gersaint's shop is stocked full to the ceiling. While this may be an invention of the artist, it could also well have been the case in the autumn of 1720, in the months following the collapse of the Law system. As ruined buyers tried to return their pictures, painters suddenly found they had produced more than they could sell. In contrast to earlier centuries, artists were no longer engaged directly by the Church or nobility to execute specific commissions. Instead, they painted subjects of their own choice, which they then offered to the public. This shift had occurred as the circle of art buyers expanded to include the wealthier middle classes. Supply grew in line with demand. For the individual buyer overwhelmed by the size of the market, however, an intermediary was needed, and the profession of art dealer arose.

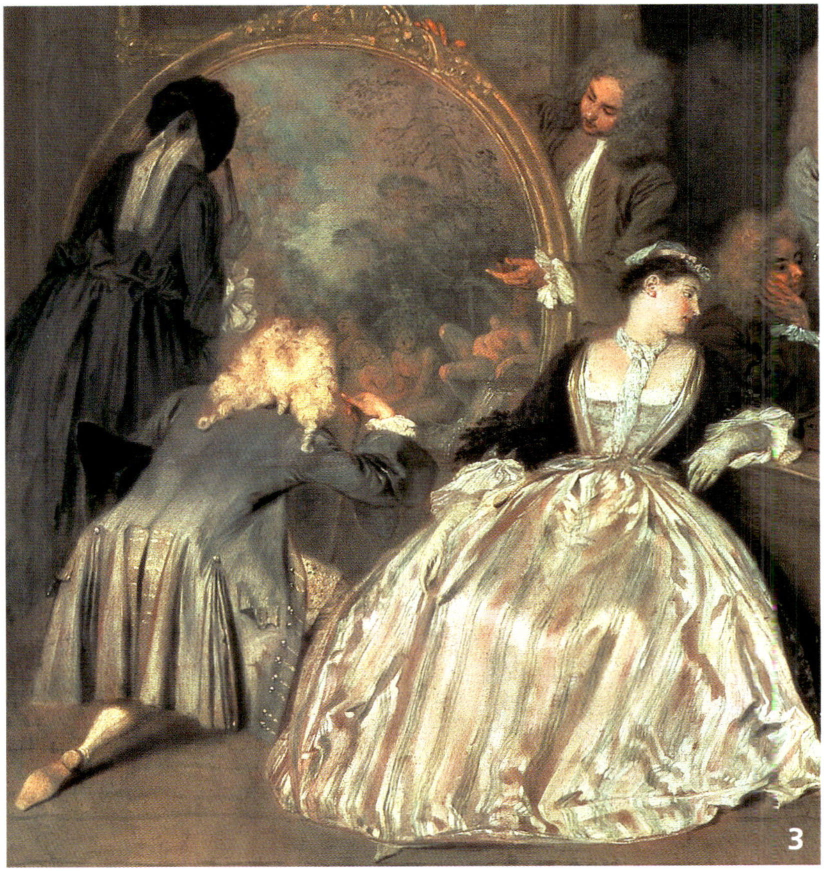

3

Dealers in art had already existed in small numbers a century earlier, but their ranks now swelled. Like Gersaint, the majority sold more than just paintings. Gersaint distinguished himself from the others with his catalogues of careful attributions. He also compiled the first *catalogue raisonné* of Rembrandt's engravings, which was published only after his death. When it came to conducting an auction, the editors wrote, there was no one better than Gersaint, "since he was always correct in what he said".

The large demand for painting during this era is undoubtedly also connected to the regent and his personal tastes, which were copied by the nobility and bourgeoisie alike. The Duke of Orléans collected pictures, commissioned Watteau to decorate his small château of La Muette, and was himself an amateur artist. His teacher was firmly of the opinion that, had the Duke not been "a great ruler", he could have been the best painter in the profession. His mother, Liselotte of the Palatinate, was more critical in her judgement. When he went to paint, she wrote, he was "primarily interested in his model, a pretty sixteen-year-old comedienne". He preferred the company of "common people, of artists and musicians", she complained, than of his well-bred peers.

His mother's remark about the young actress highlights the generally accepted relaxation of public moral standards that had taken place since the death of the strict Louis XIV. "Life was full of gaiety and fun", wrote Voltaire. It is similarly surely no coincidence that Gersaint's gallery should contain so many pictures of naked women, with famous canvases by older masters hanging beneath them – probably more of an ideal gallery as visualized by the artist than a real selection of works for sale.

In addition to pictures, the art dealer Gersaint also sold watches, mirrors, and Oriental wares such as the lacquer box on the counter. China was currently in vogue, and Gersaint was quick to respond. Whereas his first shop had been called "Au grand Monarque", in reference to the "great monarch" Louis XIV, he called his new shop "A la Pagode".

The fashion for chinoiserie, the demand for delicacy and sophistication, arose in conjunction with a new lifestyle. Opulence and pomp were giving way to intimacy and comfort. Rooms were becoming smaller and their ceilings lower; walls were being lined with wood panelling to keep out the damp. Fireplaces, too, were no longer as huge and therefore heated better. In Louis XIV's magnificent palace of Versailles, it was not unknown for wine to freeze in the glass.

So that these smaller rooms would not seem too cramped, they were furnished with mirrors. New methods of mirror-glass production led to lower prices and larger formats. In its own day, the dazzling Gallery of Mirrors in Versailles had been a display of supreme wealth. Its walls of mirrors had been made using sheets of coated glass less than one metre high. Similar sheets were now available in formats of up to 1.5 metres high and at a lower cost. Watteau paints no fewer than three large mirrors in Gersaint's shop. Glazing for windows had also become cheaper. Fewer and fewer holes in windows were being blocked up with oil-paper or simply wooden shutters. Rooms were becoming brighter, warmer, cosier.

In French, the key word for this new lifestyle was *commodité*, meaning comfort, convenience. The piece of furniture that we today know as the commode emerged during the Regency period: it was more convenient to look for something in a cabinet drawer than in a clothes trunk. The word *nécessaire* also acquired an additional meaning during this era. It came to describe a small box designed to house necessary items. Thus the regent, for example, gave the duchess a *nécessaire* containing everything needed to make and enjoy a fashionable cup of tea, coffee, and hot chocolate, including the pots, cups, and saucers. The lacquer box on Gersaint's counter is a *nécessaire de toilette*, a toilet-case containing a hairbrush and a tin of make-up or powder. This new usage of the words *commode* and *nécessaire* thus reflects, even at the linguistic level, something of the new demand in France for convenient and attractive items for everyday use.

The *nécessaire de toilette* also points to another development in French society – the growing importance of hygiene, at least amongst the upper and wealthier classes. The regent abhorred body odour. People remembered that, apart from strong perfume, there was another means of combating unpleasant smells, namely cleanliness. The doctors were still against too much washing. It was also inconvenient – if you wanted a bath, you first had to buy the water by the bucket from a street-seller, heat it up in the kitchen and then pour it into a wooden tub. Amongst those classes, at least, who were able to afford *nécessaires*, people nevertheless started washing and bathing again.

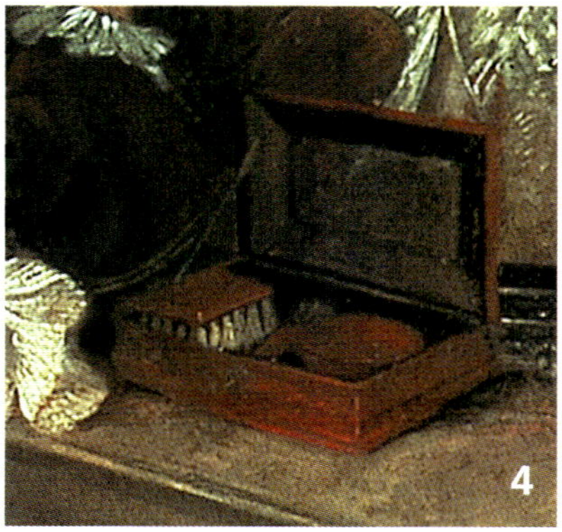

4

Chinese nécessaires

The elegant man in brown in the middle of the scene, his head inclined at a characteristic angle, bears a resemblance to Watteau himself. In 1720 the artist was thirty-six years old and was already ill. He may have been suffering the effects of paint poisoning, or may have had malaria or tuberculosis – we do not know for sure. On 18 July 1721 he died.

Little is known of his private life. Watteau, the artist who time and time again painted people enjoying themselves in the company of others, dancing in the open air, making music or out for a stroll, was a loner who did not join in himself. The pleasurable social life that he extols in his pictures was not for him. Gersaint describes him as being of "restless and changing character; he was very strong-willed; libertine in his thinking ... impatient, shy, cool and offhand in manner, silent and reserved towards strangers, a good but difficult friend, misanthropic, a harsh and even cruel critic, always dissatisfied with himself and others."

Gersaint also offers an account of how the present picture arose. Upon Watteau's return from a trip to England, he asked the art dealer to put him up, and during his stay offered to paint him a shop sign "to loosen up his fingers". A painted sign bearing a portrait of Louis XIV had hung outside Gersaint's previous shop. The sign for the new gallery, however, was to hang not out over the street, but inside the arched top of the shop entrance. Hence the upper edge of the sign was originally curved; only later was it built up to form a rectangle, by whom we do not know.

According to Gersaint, the painting was executed "in eight days, whereby he painted only in the mornings; his delicate health, or better said, his weakness, did not allow him to work for any longer". That Watteau could have completed a painting measuring 3.06 m wide and 1.66 m high in just eight mornings seems highly unlikely. Either another artist did the preparatory work or Gersaint is mistaken. He makes no mention of the fact that the sign is made up of two sections. Perhaps it was cut in half at a later date. Or perhaps it had to be executed in two parts simply in order to fit it into Watteau's studio.

This depiction of Gersaint's shop should not be taken as altogether true to life. The open front onto the street was – like the painting – a good three metres across, but appears much wider and loftier in Watteau's composition. The view through the glazed door into the rear of the house is undoubtedly also embellished. Since the houses lining the bridge stood wall to wall, they would have allowed little light to fall in from the side. The rear part of the house, the so-called *arrière-boutique*, served chiefly as a stockroom. Open shop fronts were commonly boarded up at night, being much narrower, as mentioned above, than they are made to appear in the present painting.

According to Gersaint, Watteau's painting hung for two weeks in the spot for which it was intended, over the archway entrance to the art dealer's shop. It was an enormous success; even the best artists kept walking past in order to admire it. Was such a freshly painted picture really left so exposed to the elements? Whatever the case, Gersaint very soon had a copy made. He hung the copy up and sold the original. It was bought by the man standing behind the counter on the right, thought to be Claude Gluck, who sold or gave it to his nephew Jean de Julienne, seated beside him. In 1744 it was spotted by Count Friedrich Rudolf Rothenburg, who was in Paris scouting for paintings to decorate the new palaces being built by Frederick the Great. Over the next two years, no less than six works by Watteau left Julienne's collection for Berlin, amongst them the *Shop-sign for the Art Dealer Gersaint*.

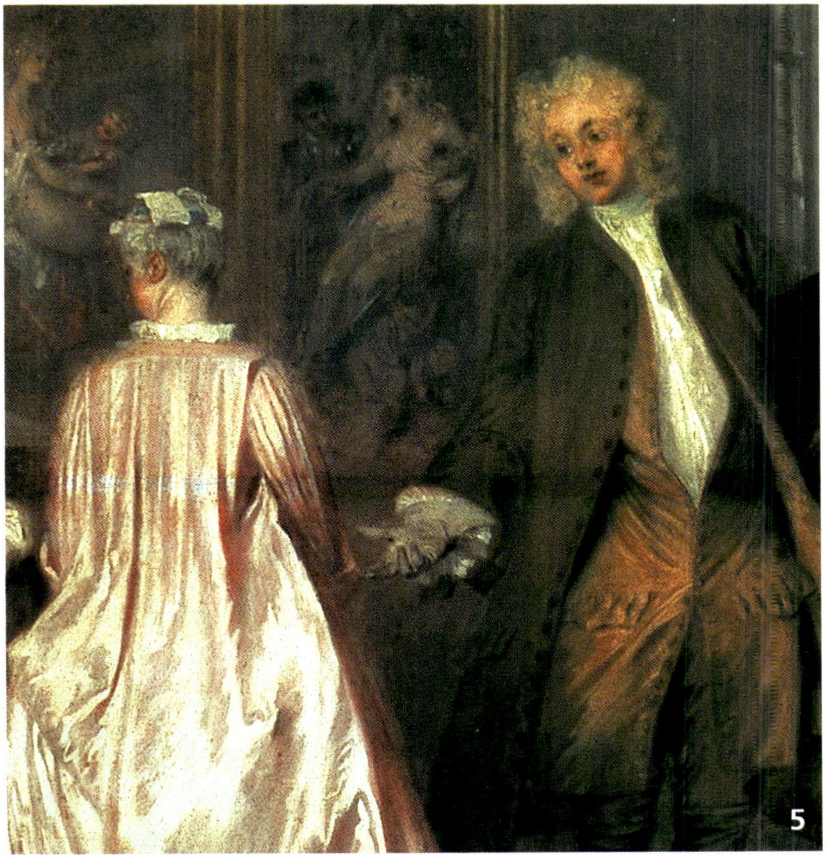

5

Paris – Berlin

In the correspondence between Frederick the Great and Count Rothenburg, the two men discuss the idea of the pendant. In those days, it was fashionable to hang two matching pictures on opposite walls, for example, or on either side of a fireplace. In 1747 Gersaint's shop-sign hung in two sections in Frederick's music room in the newly completed Knobelsdorff wing of Schloss Charlottenburg.

Thirteen years later, in 1760, after the battle of Kunersdorf, enemy soldiers plundered the palace. They stole many of its works of art, but not this one, perhaps because it was too heavy. A letter was dispatched to the king: "In Your Majesty's Music Room, one of the two large paintings by Watteau has been slashed with a sword, but can be repaired." Under Friedrich Wilhelm IV the *Shop-sign* hung in the royal palace in nearby Berlin, but later returned to Charlottenburg. During the last war it was removed to safety and thus escaped destruction when the palace burned down in 1943. Today it is once more on display in the restored rooms of Charlottenburg palace.

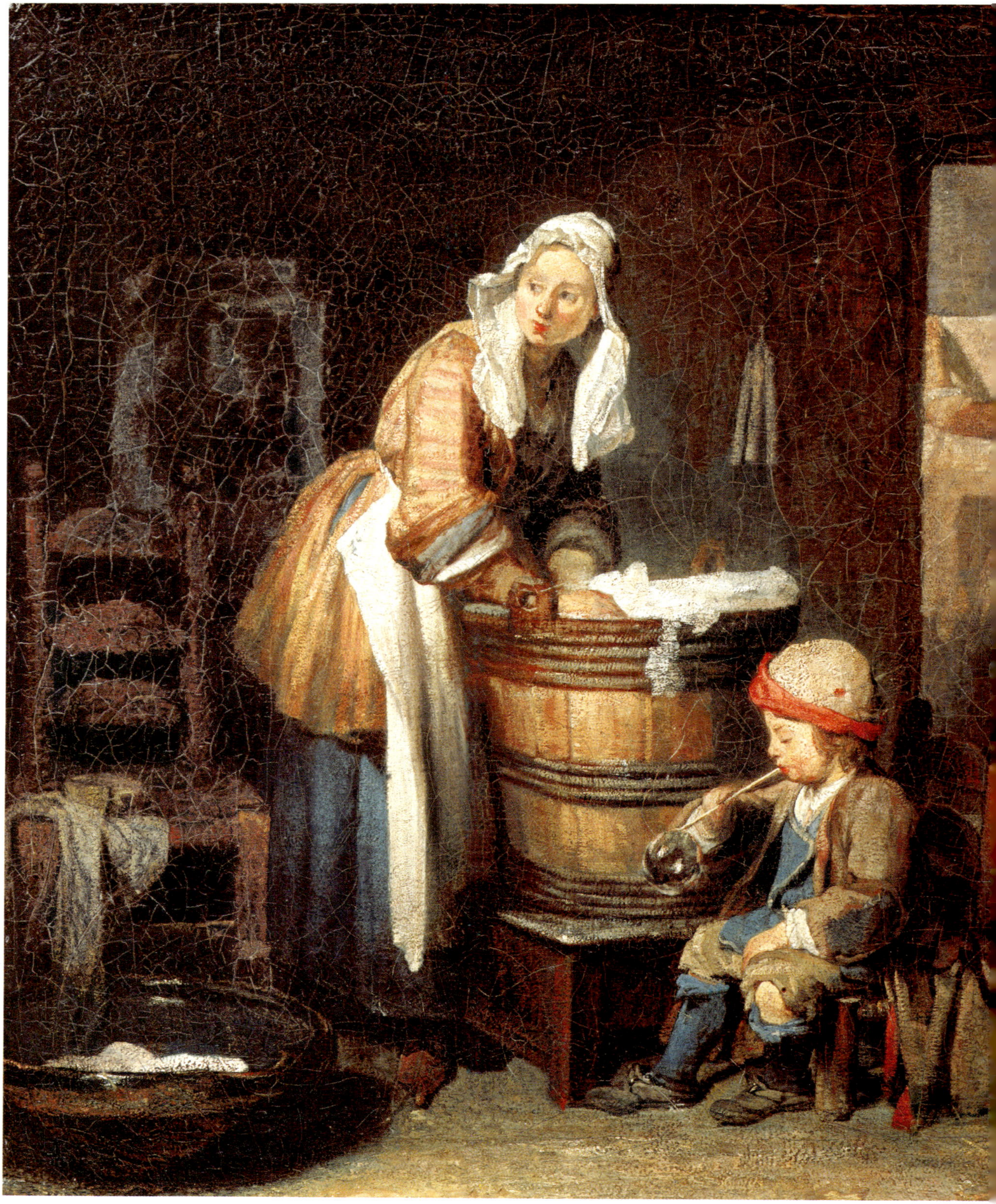

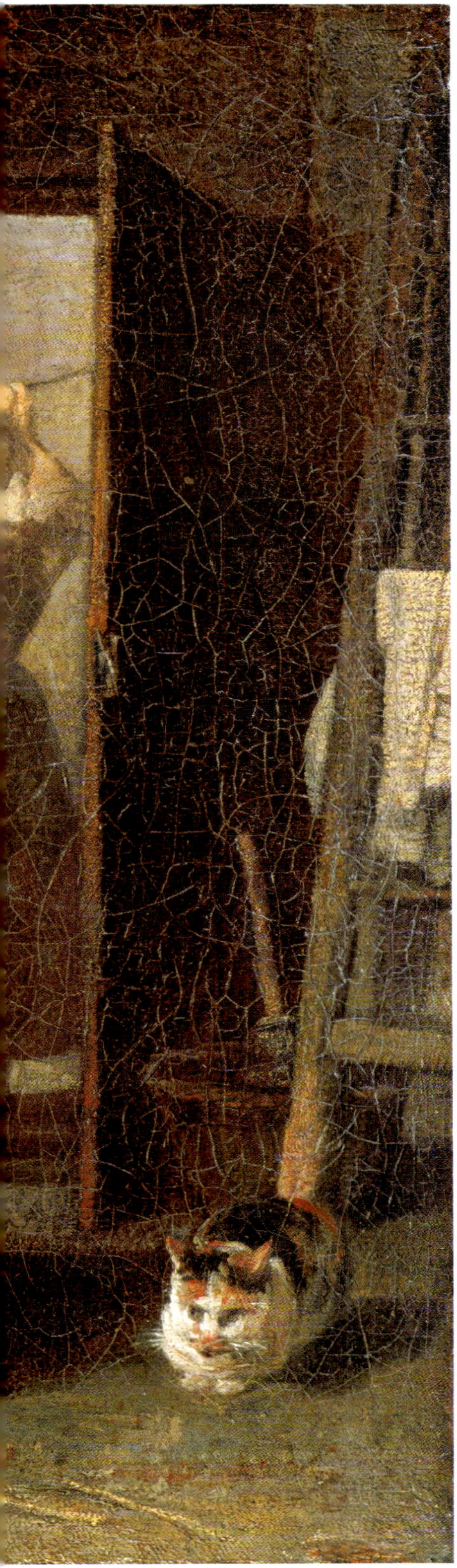

Jean Siméon Chardin: The Laundress, 1733

In praise of the freshly laundered shirt

When the picture of the young laundress was painted in Paris, France was enjoying a peace and a prosperity it hadn't seen for a long time. The expensive wars fought by Louis XIV lay well in the past; good money was to be made from trade with the colonies and other overseas territories; disposable income was being invested in manufacturing works employing newly developed production processes, for example for fabric and glass. Craftsmen became industrialists, and a new middle class took shape. The French aristocracy, meanwhile, continued to enjoy *les douceurs de la vie*, the comforts of life. The French Revolution still lay another fifty years away.

In the history of art, this era belongs to the rococo of Antoine Watteau with his *fêtes galantes*, François Boucher and Jean-Honoré Fragonard, who delighted their public with elegant portraits and subtly erotic scenes. The French painters portrayed the world and pleasures of the upper classes. They celebrate in their canvases a glittering life of ease, which unfolds against the backdrop of château terraces and smart salons. Laundries had no place in their repertoire.

Chardin was the exception. He paints the world of domestic work. His laundress is wearing neither a corset nor a hoop skirt of silk or damask, but a simple dress that she protects with an apron. On her feet are not dainty high-heeled slippers decorated with silver buckles, but shoes that are flat and perhaps made of wood. The boy blowing bubbles is clad in a patched jacket; his stockings are slipping down his legs. The scene is set in one of the ground-floor utility rooms of a bourgeois home. The door leads out to the courtyard. The kitchen, pantry, and broom cupboard lie next door.

Jean Siméon Chardin (1699–1779) was living with his parents in Paris when he painted *The Laundress* (37 x 43 cm). His father was a respected master joiner, who

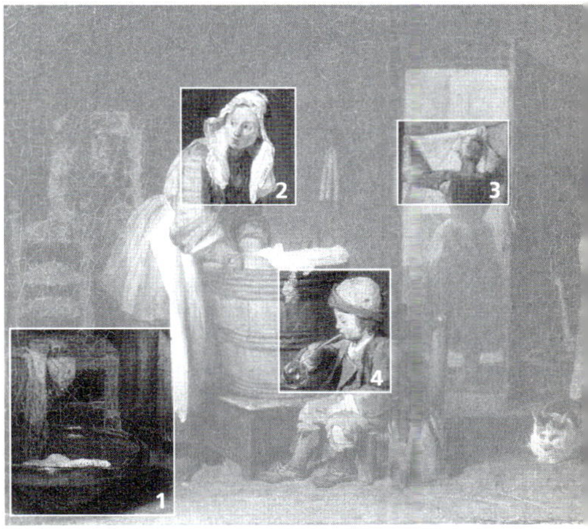

made luxury items such as billiard tables for the king. Their house lay in the rue du Four on the corner of rue Princesse, in the present-day quarter of St Germain-des-Prés. Typically of the homes of artisans and small-scale merchants, it was tall and narrow. The shop was located at street level. Behind it lay the workshop and utility rooms, followed by a small courtyard and a second building. Houses of this kind had just one largish room and a closet on each storey, and usually accommodated all the generations of one family. Some twenty-five people shared the house belonging to Chardin's parents: three sons and their families, together with a number of journeyman joiners and several maids.

Jean Siméon, the painter, lived there with his wife and two children and paid his mother 210 livres a year in rent. He was engaged for a whole eight years; his prospective parents-in-law were evidently against the idea of marrying their daughter to an artist with no regular income. His wife died in 1735. It would be nine years before Chardin got married again, this time to a wealthy widow, allowing him to move into his own home. An eight-year engagement, nine years before remarrying – these were unusually long times to wait, suggesting that Chardin was guided more by his feelings than by the usual practical considerations. In this respect, he may have been typical of a change in mentality that took place in the 18th century: affection and love began to play a more important role when it came to choosing a partner.

Looking for truth in details

The pot on the floor is made of glazed earthenware, the chair behind it has a woven rush seat, and the washtub is bound together by strips of willow. Chardin has taken a thorough look at these domestic items. Even the ones standing on the edge of the composition and in the semi-darkness are given his full attention. He has hidden his signature on the stool supporting the washtub.

These simple, inexpensive objects would have been the kind used in the Chardin family home, too. The young married couple were poor; both Chardin's parents and parents-in-law had lost their savings in a banking scandal, and the young artist had to earn a few extra crusts helping erect the scaffolding for firework displays.

He studied painting under a number of artists whose names today mean little to us. He was keen to dedicate himself to history painting, the genre in those days considered the noblest of them all and whose works commanded the highest prices. Full of drama and pathos, history paintings assumed large formats and deployed a host of people in fantastical costumes in imagined illustration of biblical, Greek, and Roman subjects. "M. Chardin was at that time of the conviction that a painter should take everything from his own head and that you needed only nature if you were lacking in imagination". He thereby echoed the opinion of the artistic Establishment.

The sight of a dead hare is supposed to have changed Chardin's thinking at a stroke. His pictures were no longer to be peopled with figures in invented poses and fancy costumes in exotic settings. Instead, he narrowed his field of vision down to a small extract from real life containing objects that did not move. Instead of making a name for himself in the uppermost echelons of the world of art, he turned his attention to the least-regarded genre of painting, the still life. In mostly modest formats, he painted mussels and fish, a copper water butt, three eggs next to a frying pan, a smoked ham on a hook. Baroque still lifes painted one hundred years earlier had carried a moralizing message: alongside magnificent arrangements of flowers lay hourglasses and skulls, reminding the viewer of the transience of life. Chardin had no message. Unless it be to say that even the most ordinary, commonplace objects can be beautiful.

He himself wanted to "rendre le vrai", to paint what was real. "I must forget everything I have seen", he told himself, "even the way in which these objects have been treated by others". But Chardin's idea of "le vrai" should not be confused with what was later called "realism". It was in the artist's head that the still life arose, that accents of light and colour were placed, that tonal values were harmonized. It would be difficult to justify the almost dazzlingly bright face of the laundress on grounds of realism, and yet within the composition it is "real", just like the arrangement of the chair and the pot in the semi-darkness.

Around 1730 Chardin's art took another new turn. He was working on a still life of a plate bearing a saveloy sausage, so the story goes, when an artist colleague observed derisively that you could make more money painting portraits. His remark seems to have reinforced slumbering

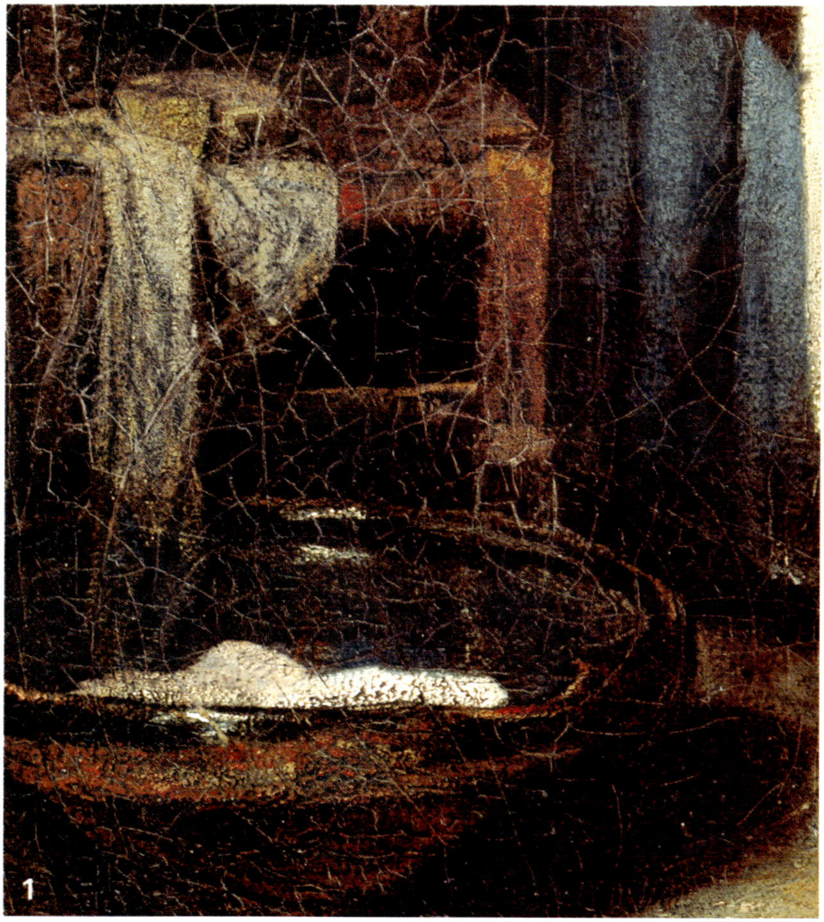
1

doubts in Chardin's mind. Although he didn't have the confidence to attempt portraits, he now turned to scenes from everyday life, such as maids doing the laundry or pouring water out of a jug.

In 1734 he showed figural paintings for the first time at an open-air exhibition in the Place Dauphine in Paris. In 1735 *The Laundress*, and a pendant, *Woman Drawing Water from a Cistern*, were officially exhibited in the Royal Academy of Painting and Sculpture. In June that same year, a glowing review appeared in the *Mercure de France*. It was written by the Chevalier de la Roque, a former officer who had become editor of the *Mercure* and who was himself an art collector. He purchased *The Laundress* and three other smaller works by Chardin.

White stood for cleanliness and order

The dominant colour in the gloomy laundry is white. The washing in the tub, the young woman's apron, her bonnet, even her forehead – all are white accents within the composition, catching our eye and thus drawing our attention.

In the fashions of the day, too, white possessed a particular significance. You could tell what class a person belonged to from what they wore. Clothes – which were much more expensive then than they are today – were an important indicator of rank and wealth. White shirts and cuffs were worn both by the aristocracy and by the bourgeoisie, and their cleanliness was a statement of the orderly circumstances in which their wearer lived – or wished to give the impression he did. A spotless shirt, or at least a pair of freshly laundered cuffs, which were visible at all times, were among the last things that an impoverished member of the bourgeoisie or nobility wanted to give up. White was a positive symbol.

In line with the social importance attached to clean laundry, washing clothes was taken very seriously. It was hard work. In households that didn't have their water delivered by porters, maids had to go and fetch it themselves from the well or the Seine. The dirty laundry was soaked in water mixed with ash, the best being the ash from beech wood, either swept out of the fireplace or purchased from an ash-seller. First the laundry was sprinkled with ash, then hot water was poured over it. Soap was expensive.

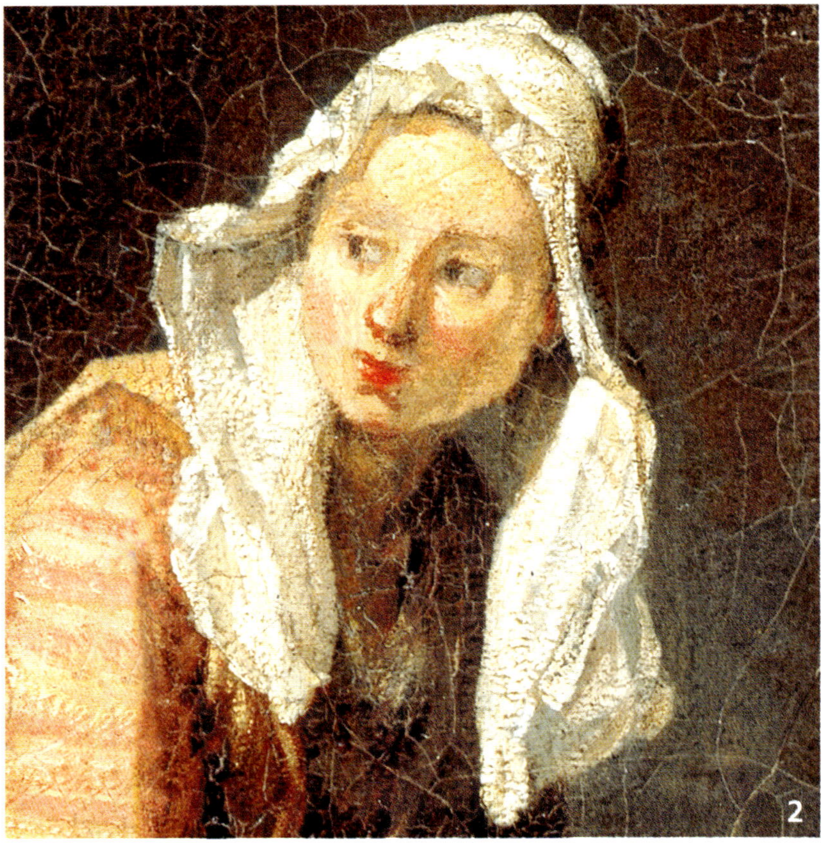

2

It was the tradition in the countryside to wash all the laundry twice a year. In the city, this grand wash was not usually carried out at home, but – if only for lack of drying space – was farmed out to laundresses on the Seine. Some 2000 washerwomen are thought to have worked in Paris in the first half of the 18th century. They gave constant rise to complaints and concerns. Items of washing were stolen and ripped, it was claimed, and the washerwomen came into contact with too much dirt to be decent people themselves. Furthermore, the Seine water left washing with a yellowish-grey tinge.

Those who could afford it, and those for whom the achievement of a truly gleaming white collar and sleeves made it worth the trouble, sent their laundry to the Netherlands. Haarlem was famed for the whitest white, attributable not just to the efforts of its laundresses and the quality of its water, but also to bleaching in the sun. Those who demanded an even higher standard of white shipped their laundry baskets off to the sunny French slave islands of Guadeloupe and Martinique.

Laundry washing was profoundly changed, indeed almost revolutionized, by the increasingly widespread use of hard soap. The oldest was the Savon de Marseilles, still sold today. Soap was less hard on the hands than a lye of wood ash and reduced soaking times. In the 18th century, the occasional big wash was replaced by smaller weekly or fortnightly washes, of the kind Chardin has evidently portrayed here. The little boy blowing soap bubbles serves to demonstrate that the laundress is using soap, at that time still very expensive. Chardin included boys of various ages blowing bubbles in three different paintings. It was a modern form of amusement, and not everyone had the opportunity to try it.

Small washes included in particular all those items of clothing that were visible to the eye, in other words shirts, collars, and cuffs, and for women tuckers, bonnets, and stockings. From an inventory compiled in 1730, i.e. shortly before this painting was executed, it emerges that a middle-class lady from the provinces owned fourteen bonnets, all made of muslin and embroidered with lace. Bonnets were practical, becoming, and extremely varied in their shapes and sizes. They could be used to conceal the hair, adorn the head, or set off the face to advantage. Since they were not expensive to make, they were a way in which even poor servant girls could add a smart splash of white to their wardrobe.

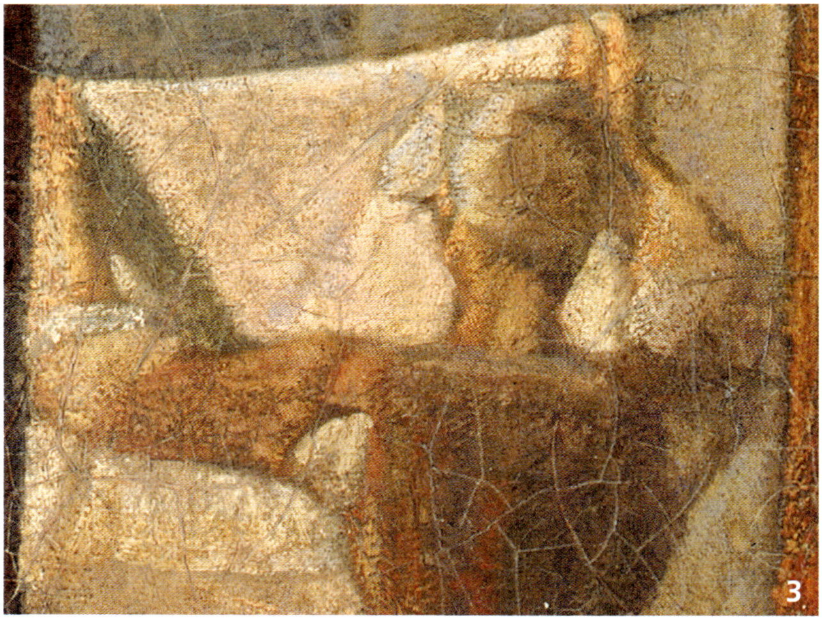

3

The hard lot of a servant girl

English tourists were struck by the fact that, although the French dressed in extremely clean clothes, they lived in relatively dirty apartments. Nor did they wash themselves very often. In the homes of the English upper classes of the day, bathrooms containing bathtubs were already being installed. In France, however, as in the rest of Europe, it was still considered dangerous for the skin to come into contact with water. Doctors were of the opinion that water could pass through the porous skin and carry germs into the body. The French therefore washed only those parts of the body that could be seen: the hands and the face.

In the 18th century, however, the desire for greater personal hygiene grew even in France. This was satisfied not with water, but with more frequent changes of underclothes. A clean shirt, it was believed, "cleansed the skin"; it absorbed sweat and perspiration and reduced bodily odours.

As a consequence, underclothes assumed a greater importance. Inventories compiled on the occasion of marriages and deaths take us inside the linen cupboards of the past. In the 17th century, the pride of every housewife was still a tall stack of bed and table linen; the average labourer, by contrast, owned an average of just two shirts, which, as we know from other sources, were washed once a month at most. In the 18th century, however, the number of shirts rose almost continuously. The lady from the provinces who in 1730 boasted fourteen bonnets also owned eighteen shirts. In the middle of the century, Jean-Jacques Rousseau, an artisan's son like Chardin, bemoaned the theft of forty-two shirts. Rousseau was young, vain, secretary to an envoy, and not yet the philosopher and propagandist of a simple life.

Like inventories, household accounts also shed light on the subject of laundry. From the records kept by an unmarried nobleman dating from the year 1759, we know that he sent five shirts, a pair of cuffs, three handkerchiefs, one pair of socks and one pair of stockings to his laundress every week. He thus wore a fresh shirt almost every day. His underpants, on the other hand, were washed just once a month; after all, they couldn't be seen. Only after his marriage did he put on a clean pair every week.

Women wore no underpants at all; they were "at the mercy of a gust of wind". Their undergarments consisted of shirts, blouses, and petticoats. Chardin's laundress is wearing a long-sleeved, salmon-pink overblouse, or "caraco"; the woman hanging up the washing is wearing, over her shirt, a close-fitting bodice, which is slit beneath the arms so as to allow her the freedom of movement she needs.

19th-century writers speculated that the laundress in the present painting represented the artist's wife, but this is unlikely. The young Madame Chardin was sickly. In 1731 she gave birth to a son, in 1733 to a daughter, and in 1735 she died. Even modest households such as that of the young Chardins kept at least one maid. Housework was hard and almost impossible to manage single-handedly – and young servant girls didn't cost much. They came from farm labourers' families who were delighted to have one less mouth to feed. The most important part of their wages was the fact that they did not have to go hungry. They often slept in the kitchen or beneath the stairs. They were given hand-me-down clothes and a bonus on special occasions.

The lot of a servant girl was hard, often cruel. Chardin does not idealize the work of laundering itself, but by showing the figures in a warm – and in the case of the woman hanging up the washing, softly diffuse – light, he undoubtedly portrays their existence as more agreeable than it actually was. Antoine de la Roque (1672–1744), who purchased this painting, wrote that it portrayed "petites femmes" going about their household duties. By "petites femmes" he meant far more than "little women", as the phrase literally translates. "Petites femmes" were not just lower down the social ladder, but were invariably young and usually attractive. The designation belongs to a male vocabulary and is charged with an erotic interest in the women it describes – who then frequently served to satisfy the same.

When Chardin painted children, it was never running about or playing boisterous games. In one of his paintings a boy is looking at a top, in another, building a house of cards. All the children seem to be lost in thought or absorbed in what they are doing. They are not far from being still lifes.

The boy blowing bubbles on the child's chair is dressed extremely plainly in a patched jacket and tattered trousers. A boy's first shirts were often made out of his father's old ones, not just for reasons of economy: it was believed the father's strength and health would thereby be passed on to his son. The boys in Chardin's paintings would later wear three-cornered hats and lace cravats, and would sit not beside a washtub, but in a drawing room. The adults, too, would no longer be maids, but governesses and smartly dressed mothers. The objects accompanying the dead animals in Chardin's still lifes would also change: pots and frying pans would be replaced by Chinese porcelain.

These changes in clothing and décor reflected Chardin's own rise in society. In 1744 he married a wealthy widow with her own house. His paintings were by now enjoying greater recognition and commanding correspondingly higher prices. He was also appointed to the post of treasurer at the Academy. In 1752 King Louis XV granted him a pension, and in 1757 he was provided with an apartment and studio in the Louvre. In order to satisfy demand, Chardin made copies of his particularly popular works; he painted *The Laundress* three times, for example. The version reproduced here hangs in Stockholm, while a second can be seen in the Hermitage in St Petersburg; the third copy was lost during the last war. He secured himself another source of income from engravings made from his paintings, for which he demanded a sort of copyright fee.

Chardin was a slow worker. Some two hundred paintings survive from his hand; spread out over a career of sixty years, that makes no more than three or four pictures a year. "I take my time because I have made a habit of not laying aside my works until, in my eyes, they leave nothing else to be desired." Other artists said the same thing, but in the case of Chardin, such a remark assumes a particular significance because it refers to small canvases, filled not with grandiose historical events but with a few modest objects and individuals. In 1751 he abandoned genre scenes for good and from then on painted only still lifes.

While engravings of Chardin's compositions were popular among the bourgeoisie, the paintings themselves were purchased by wealthy collectors, aristocrats, and kings. The philosopher and art connoisseur Denis Diderot (1713–1784) was a great admirer: "Oh Chardin!", he proclaimed, "what you mix on your palette is not white, red, or black paint: it is the very substance of objects, it is air and light that you take on the tip of your brush and apply to the canvas …". Diderot addressed the artist as a "great magician", admiring his "mute compositions" and the way in which "the air circulates around the objects".

Following the death of its first owner, Chevalier de la Roque, in 1745, *The Laundress* was put up for sale. It was acquired by Louise Ulrike, wife of Adolf Frederick, heir to the Swedish throne. She was a younger sister of Frederick the Great and, like him, was particularly fond of French rococo painting. Whereas Frederick purchased important works by Watteau, portraying festive fantasies of a life of gaiety and ease, his sister bought seven – possibly more – works by Chardin.

To what extent these still, silent, modest pictures of simple domestic life corresponded to her personal disposition or her secret desires is a question difficult to answer.

Air and light at the tip of the brush

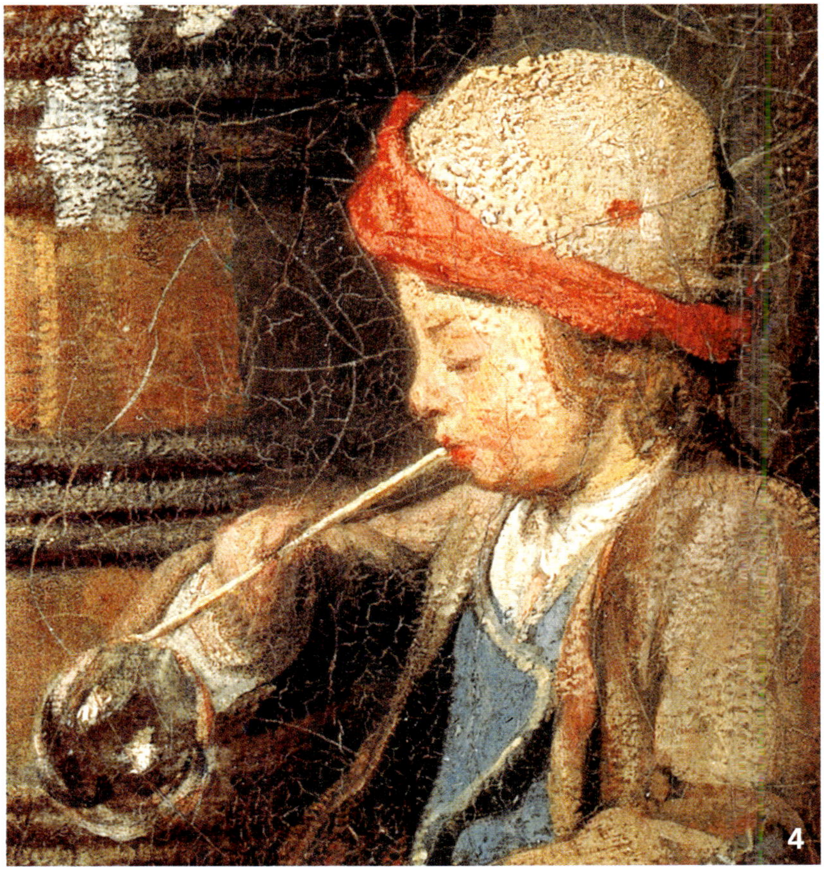

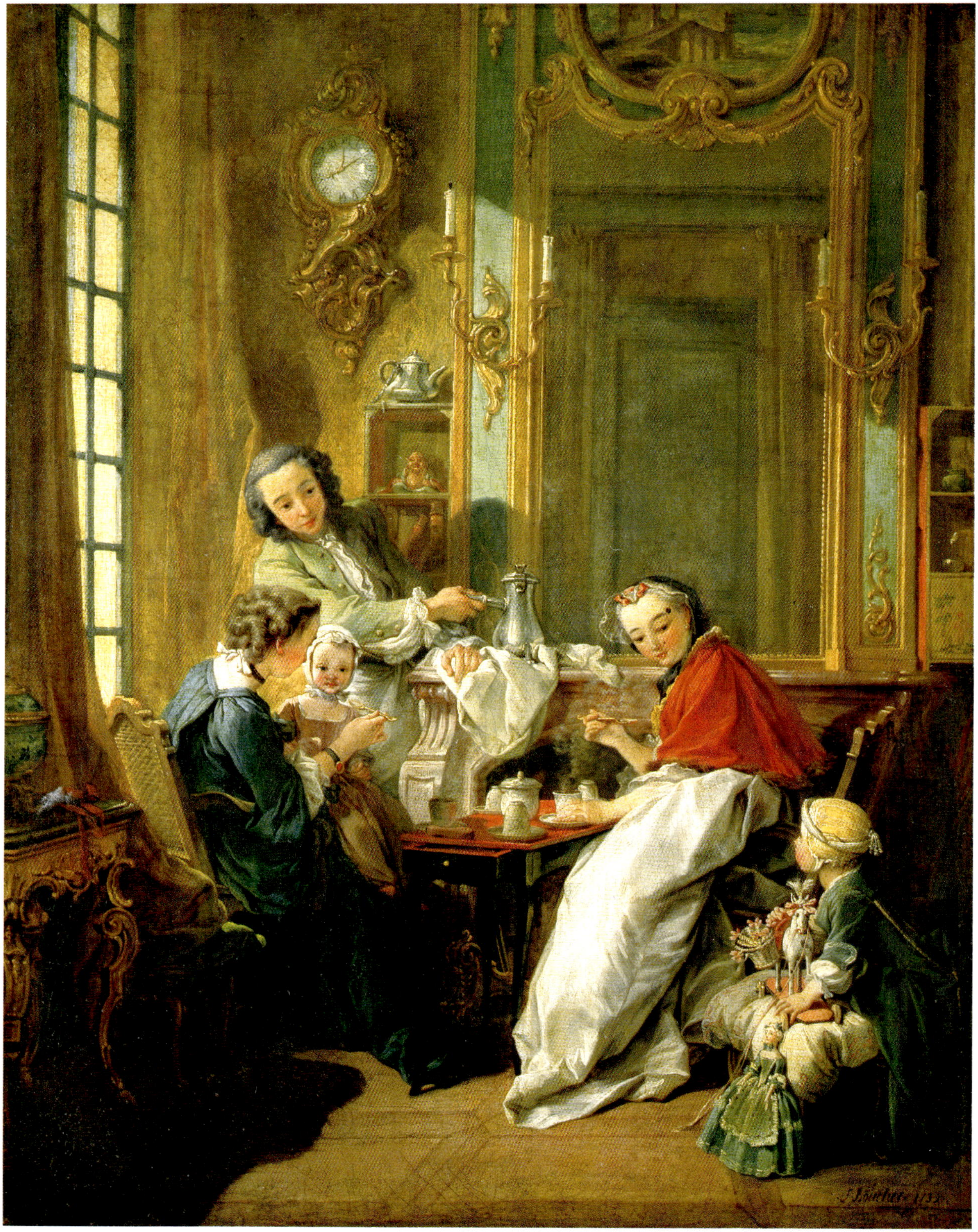

François Boucher: The Breakfast, 1739

The birth of the nuclear family

To today's viewer, this breakfasting scene has the air of a family idyll, harmless and a little conventional. To the artist's contemporaries, however, what Boucher was showing – chinaware, a large window, a small fireplace, rocaille decoration, breakfast, hot drinks, adults attending to children – was highly modern. For viewers in the 18th century, the painting reflected a new style of everyday living and also a new attitude towards life.

It was executed in Paris in 1739; the date can be read in the bottom right-hand corner, next to the signature. It was a period of prosperity in France. Louis XV (1710–1774) had so far waged no wars; good harvests had at last followed decades of catastrophic weather; commerce and industry were expanding. The lower classes had enough to eat, and in the higher echelons of society, amongst the aristocracy and industrious bourgeoisie, fortunes were being made. The family seen breakfasting here are members of one such wealthy bourgeois household.

They might even be members of Boucher's own family. In 1739 his wife, Marie-Jeanne, was in her mid-twenties. She was famed for her beauty and often served as Boucher's model. Their two children, Elisabeth-Victoire and Juste-Nathan, were four and three years old, more or less the same age as the children in the picture. The room is one that Boucher painted several times and that may well have formed part of his own apartment. The artist himself was thirty-six years old and was already earning an excellent income.

Boucher, the son of a craftsman, learned the rudiments of painting under second-rate artists, but honed his skills by studying the works of Rubens and his compatriot Antoine Watteau. He executed copper engravings of Watteau's works for a wealthy bourgeois by the name of Julienne. Painting in the gracefully ornate style of his day, he produced designs for tapestries, furnishings, theatrical decorations, and porcelain services. For his wealthy clients, he also decorated areas above fireplaces and mirrors. The lower half of such a wall painting can be seen at the top of *The Breakfast*.

The landscape above the mirror and the mirror itself are linked by a motif that recurs throughout the rococo era and the Louis XV style: the scallop shell. Just as Venus can be seen stepping out of such a shell in many of Boucher's paintings, so his contemporaries, too, rose from chairs decorated with scallop motifs. The same scallops decorated their mirrors, and the gold and silver ornaments on the walls of their apartments were similarly reminiscent of shells and waves.

Apartments were changing during this era. In 1728, an architect by the name of Patte wrote: "The art of living comfortably and by oneself was previously unknown".

"Comfortably and by oneself" – these were new ideas. Up till then, the nobility and upper middle classes had lived in large households with an emphasis upon public display. There now emerged a new desire for privacy, for a certain intimacy. Rooms became smaller, ceilings lower. So that the new rooms would not feel too cramped, large mirrors were installed, and since glass was becoming cheaper, windows were made bigger. Rooms became lighter. They also became warmer. Newly designed small fireplaces heated more efficiently than the huge fireplaces of old. In the past, it had been necessary in winter to don an extra layer of clothing when you came indoors; now you could take something off. Dressing-gowns and house-coats were no longer lined with fur as frequently as before; cold splendour was being replaced by cosiness. Even Louis XV abandoned the vast halls of Versailles

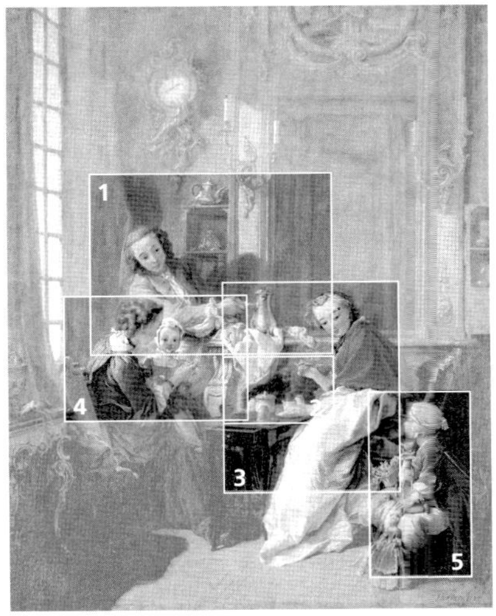

palace and withdrew, as far as court etiquette permitted, into the "petits appartements" of the entresol, with their smaller rooms and lower ceilings.

Rooms not only became smaller, but were laid out differently. Previously, each room had opened directly onto the next; to reach the one at the end, therefore, you had to pass through all the others. Now houses were given corridors. No more through traffic. An opportunity to shut yourself away, to be "by yourself".

The introduction of the corridor was accompanied by the emergence of new types of room. In the past, all rooms served multiple functions. Depending on the size of the apartment and the prosperity of its occupant, the same room might serve as kitchen and dining room, bedroom and drawing room. The aristocracy and wealthy bourgeoisie now began to indulge in a separate kitchen and a designated dining room. Visitors were no longer welcomed beside the bed. The salon arose, and between the salon and the bedroom, the boudoir. The name comes from *bouder* (to pout or sulk); it was the place where you could go and sulk.

In later eras the boudoir acquired a dubious reputation. In literature and the fine arts, it has come down to us above all as the setting for amorous encounters. Vast numbers of politely termed *galant* engravings – "through-the-keyhole" pictures of varying degrees of artistic subtlety – served to reinforce its erotic associations. The demand for such pictures almost completely obscured the other, equally if not more important aspect of the boudoir, namely as somewhere to be together with one's family, undisturbed; the boudoir as the setting for the new, growing sense of family, as a place where parents could pay loving attention to their children, too.

The boudoir arose simultaneously with the discovery of privacy, with the growing appreciation of domestic intimacy. These developments were probably in turn a reflection of the greater importance starting to be attached to the emotions in the 18th century. This was the era in which the nuclear family was born. The family was now seen as a "valuable emotional unit". Boucher's *The Breakfast* is one of the first artistic records of this development.

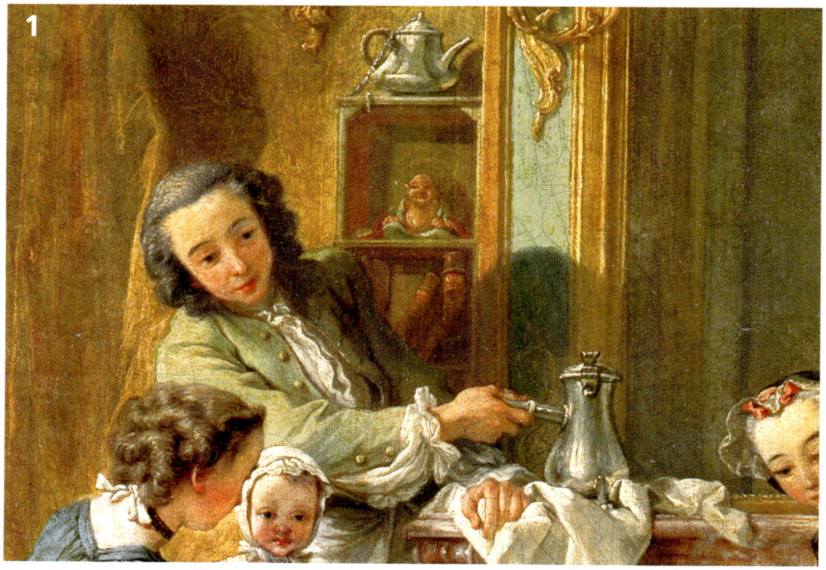

Breakfast is a French invention

The young man in the green frock coat was long thought to be the artist, François Boucher himself, serving breakfast to his family in person. Even King Louis XV is known to have warmed and poured out his own coffee when living in his "petits appartements". It was all part of the new lifestyle. But the man in green seems much younger than a thirty-six-year-old; moreover, he is wearing a white apron. (This apron is even more evident in a preliminary study for the painting.) He is thus more likely to be a servant. He has just brought the pot, wrapped in the white cloth now lying on the mantelpiece, from the kitchen, or – more probable still – from across the road. For in the first half of the 18th century, the fashionable drinks of tea, coffee, and chocolate were for the most part brewed and served in public houses. The young man with the apron is probably a *garçon limonadier* (a "lemonade boy"). He would have worked for the guild of lemonade and liqueur sellers, who towards the end of the 17th century also began serving hot chocolate and coffee in silver pots.

The idea of supplying the Parisians with hot drinks in their own homes was nothing out of the ordinary. All day long, traders selling herbal teas plied the streets; a shout would bring them hurrying to your front door. Cold and hot water was similarly carried up to people's apartments. In the early morning, the streets of the city filled with the cries of baker's boys from the suburbs selling their rye rolls, country girls touting fresh eggs, and milkmaids announcing their arrival. Boucher made their familiar cries the subject of a series of engravings. From nine o'clock in the morning the streets were thronged with bustling waiters delivering breakfasts to people in their own apartments.

Breakfast is a French invention of the 18th century. Louis XV was the first king to have bread or a roll in the morning with a hot drink. His royal predecessors had started the day with dinner at around ten o'clock. Over the course of the decades, this large, hot meal moved closer and closer to midday and eventually became lunch. Louis XIV ate his dinner at one o'clock, but did not have breakfast. This was something only introduced by his descendants.

It was because of the new hot drinks that breakfasting became so popular. Not everyone liked them, however. Liselotte of the Palatinate, married to the Duke of Orléans, wrote from Paris: "I rarely take breakfast ... Tea to me tastes of hay and manure, coffee of soot and lupins, and chocolate is too sweet for me. What I would really like to eat would be ... a good beer soup. That wouldn't give me a stomach ache."

Coffee, tea, or chocolate?

Some critics claim that the drink being consumed in this painting is coffee, but this is not true. It is hot chocolate, thick and sweet. A beverage for children, ladies and the aristocracy.

The drink can be identified from the pot that the young man has unwrapped from the cloth. It is not a pear-shaped coffee-pot, nor is it a tea-pot like the round-bellied one standing on the top shelf above the Chinese figurine. The silver or pewter pot on the mantelpiece has the traditional slender shape of a chocolate-pot with a straight handle. The spout is short and wide, so that the thick chocolate can be poured out with greater ease. It was usually whisked to a froth before serving.

In the 18th century, chocolate was made from cocoa, sugar, cinnamon, and vanilla. It was sold in tablets and enjoyed as a drink, dissolved in hot water or hot milk. It was very different to the drink we call cocoa today. Since the 19th century, cocoa beans have had the large part of their oil extracted, making them less nutritious but easier to digest.

Yet it was precisely its high nutritional value that originally made chocolate so popular. It was first imported from South America into Spain in the 16th century. During the lengthy and in those days very strict periods of religious fasting, the Church permitted the consumption of fluids. With the help of the sweet, nutritious drink, these fasts were easier to endure. When a Spanish princess, Anna of Austria, became Queen of France in 1615, she introduced chocolate to the French court. Its success was enormous: within a short space of time, chocolate had become the favourite drink of the French and subsequently the European aristocracy, and thereby a public status symbol.

It was usually enjoyed in bed or, as in Boucher's painting, in the boudoir, as a sweet upbeat, so to speak, to a day of leisure. Madame de Pompadour, the long-term mistress of Louis XV, is said to have sought help for her frigidity from hot chocolate: she added three times as much vanilla and a pinch of ambergris so as to boost her flagging libido.

Clergymen, on the other hand, who were required to live in celibacy, were recommended coffee, considered to be an anti-erotic and sobering drink. It came into fashion in Europe following the siege of Vienna by the Turks in 1683. It was drunk in particular in Protestant regions, and in 1732 the choirmaster and organist Johann Sebastian Bach even composed a cantata in its praise. Coffee was seen as a general panacea, which supposedly strengthened the liver and gallbladder, cleansed the blood, calmed the stomach, and increased one's energy. In the Paris of the 18th century, the people downing a cup of hot coffee at the street corner in the morning were largely members of the working populace.

A few hours later, the Boucher family would drink "aristocratic" chocolate, not labour-fuelling coffee, in their comfortable boudoir. This may also be seen as an indication of the artist's ability to embrace the habits of his clients. That he was career-minded is evidenced by the addresses at which he lived. As he grew more successful, so he moved to ever "better" areas of Paris. Finally, in 1752, he moved into an apartment in the royal Louvre palace, even though it would be 1764 before he was appointed Painter to the King.

Together with the raw ingredients for the new drinks, the merchant ships arriving from distant parts also brought chinaware to go with them: coffee cups from Arabia and tea cups from China, fancy vases and pot-bellied deities, such as the ones in Boucher's boudoir. The elegant, fragile cups and saucers on his table appear to be decorated with a Chinese motif. They have no handles and are therefore hot to the touch; the ladies use spoons. Slender and graceful, such porcelain fitted well with a lifestyle in which form and elegance played an important role. Such china allowed the taking of hot drinks to become a formal social occasion, and not just something to be done alone and "by oneself".

The French upper classes were at that time searching for new and sophisticated tableware appropriate to their status. In the past, the rich had eaten from plates of silver and gold. In 1709, however, Louis XIV had made them melt down all their magnificent dinner services as a way of getting money to fund his wars. Since then the wealthy had used French faience pottery. Very few people in the years around 1739 could afford a service made of delicate porcelain. It was expensive because it had to be imported either from China or, more recently, Saxony. In 1708 the alchemist Johann Böttger and the naturalist Tschirnhausen unravelled the Chinese secret of porcelain manufacture and began producing "white gold" in Meissen.

Porcelain: Meissen was just thirty years old

Experiments were conducted in France, too. There were attempts in several cities to make porcelain, but one vital ingredient – kaolin, which gives china its hardness – was still lacking. It was eventually discovered near Limoges in 1768. Up till then, manufacturers had confined themselves to bone china, the production of which increased when Madame de Pompadour, the royal favourite, started to take an interest in it.

Madame de Pompadour turned her attention to fragile plates and cups not for economic reasons but as a means of rescuing her Louis from boredom. That was her chief occupation. She sang and danced for him on a stage in the palace, and took the opportunity to remind him that his forebear Henri IV had overseen the setting up of the Gobelin tapestry workshops. So Louis XV financed the founding of the Royal Porcelain Factory, first in Vincennes, then in Sèvres, not far from Madame de Pompadour's château de plaisance. And the favourite in turn engaged her favourite painter, Boucher. He designed patterns and motifs and thereby also helped shape the tastes of his day.

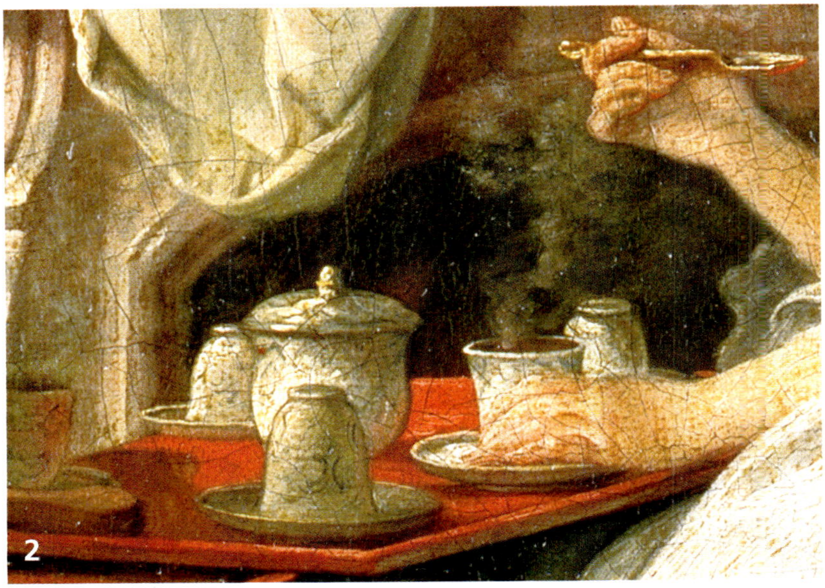

The lady sitting on the right is still in her négligé. She will get fully dressed and made up only after she has finished breakfast. She is wearing a red make-up cape. The hairdresser will arrive later to comb and powder her hair, which is still hidden beneath her lace bonnet. In the mornings, one contemporary recorded, the horde of *garçons limonadiers* in the street was joined by a swarm of hairdressers, on their way to make their wealthy clients presentable for the day.

The hairdresser comes after breakfast

Beneath her make-up cape, the lady in the painting has not yet donned her skirt and stiff corset, but is still wearing a morning gown. This gown is a status symbol: it shows that the lady does not have to work. The author Nicolas Restif de la Bretonne informs us in one of his novels that the daughter of a peasant who has become rich may be granted the form of address "Demoiselle" only if she wears such a morning gown at home.

Prosperous bourgeois wives did not lead a life purely of leisure, however. Even the daughters of the aristocracy learned how to run a household in the convents in which they were educated from the age of seven to sixteen. Later on, after all, they would have to manage their own staff. A middle-class wife had to keep a close eye on her stocks of table linen, bed linen, and clothing, a major task in itself. These stocks formed the pride of the household, represented a considerable amount of money, and – since laundry was washed at most twice a year – were extensive.

Boucher's wife did even more. She sat as a model for her husband, in this painting probably in two poses, to the right and left of the table. She also painted miniatures based on her husband's paintings and engraved them in copper; two engravings bearing her signature appear in a volume with those of her husband. Madame Boucher attained a certain independence and thereby differed from most other women of her century. Women could rise to prominence only as artists, shop-keepers, and mistresses. The most famous example in Boucher's day was Mademoiselle Poisson, in other words a young lady named Miss Fish. She became the favourite of Louis XV, who presented her with the earldom of Pompadour and thereby a finer-sounding name.

Nevertheless, a number of intelligent, rich, and socially adept women rose to positions of indirect influence via their salons. They operated through the men they manipulated. "En France, tout se fait par les femmes", it was said – everything was done by women. "They have got the upper hand over French men to such an extent … that the latter cannot think or feel except through them."

While these words may seem exaggerated, in one particular sphere France's women may indeed have influenced not only their salon guests but also broad sections of the public – namely in the validation of human emotion. Literary works testify to this shift in attitude: tears flow, even men sob. In 1731 Abbé Prévost published *Manon Lescaut*, a novel whose protagonists live only for love and passion.

This revalorization of feeling changed family life, the relationships between the spouses, and the attitude of parents towards their children. Each woman in this painting is turning towards a child. This was by no means commonplace in 1739.

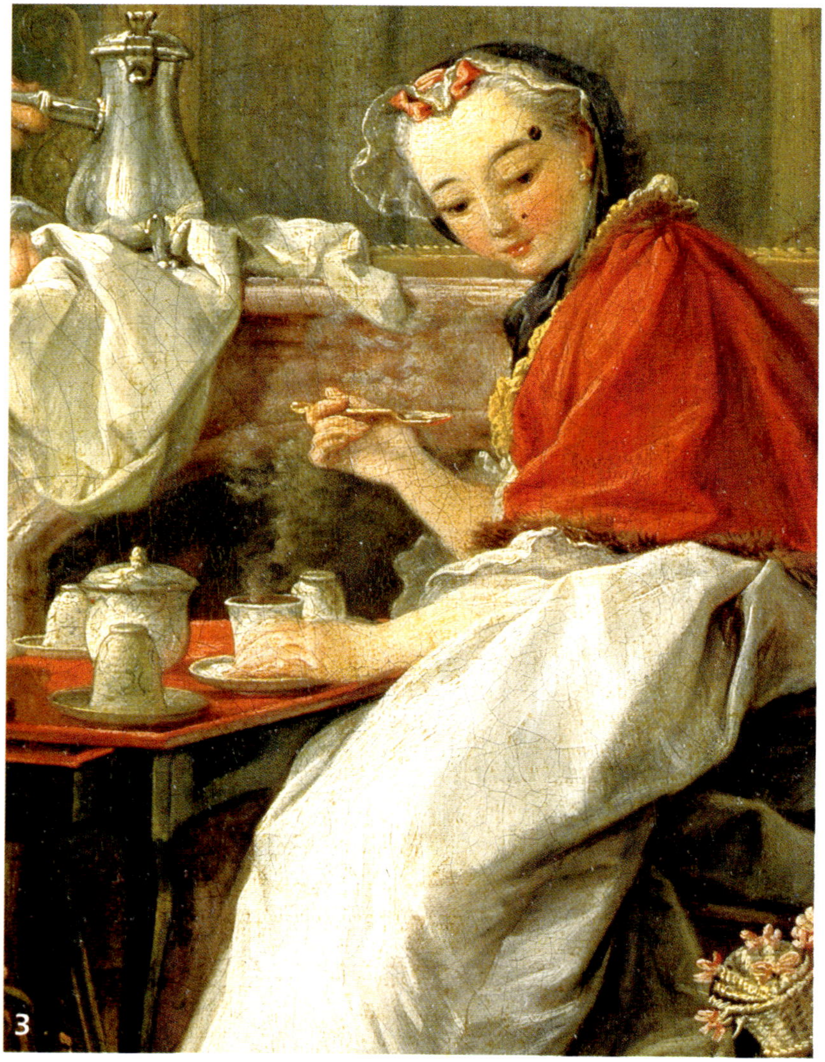

3

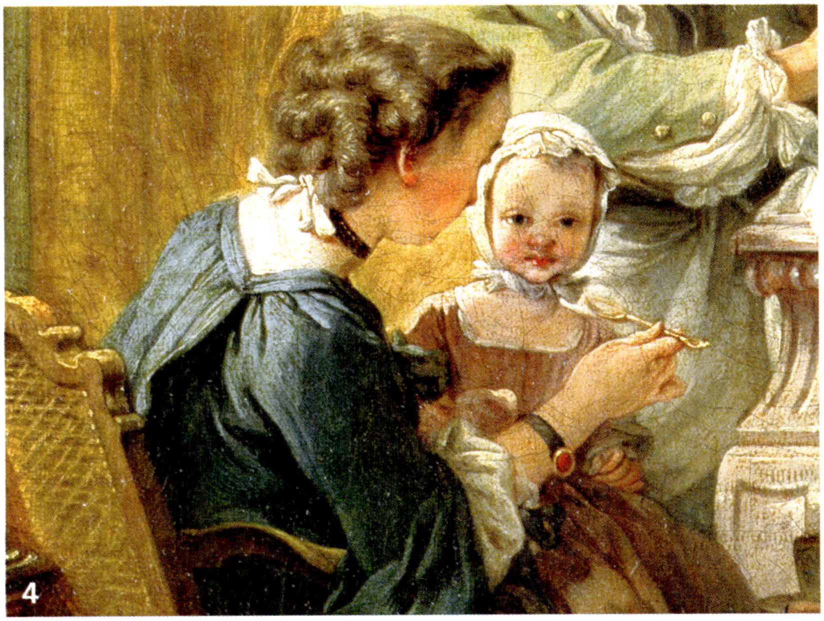

4

Children had yet to become people

It is astonishing that the children in this picture are even allowed into the boudoir with their mother. Three and four-year-olds were usually either still living with their wet-nurses in the country or were cared for in the family home by domestic servants. At the age of seven, the children of France's aristocrats and upper middle classes were sent away from home once again, the girls to convents, the boys to Jesuit boarding-schools. The loving attention being paid to the children in this painting was highly unusual for 1739.

Because small children were not thought of as people. They were considered to be closer to animals and at the mercy of the devil. Only a harsh education, it was thought, could turn them into human beings and good Christians. It was permanently feared that they would "revert back into utterly godless creatures". As soon as they started to walk, they were given reins of the kind that can be made out on the back of the right-hand child in the present picture. Such reins were not to stop children from running away, but to prevent them from "crawling around on the ground like animals". Everything animal-like was to be quickly and thoroughly eradicated.

Parents who could afford it thus kept their children at a distance. They gave them to a wet-nurse in the country. To breastfeed your own child was considered "swinish".

Only rich families with a great deal of space brought the wet-nurse into their own homes. Most parents sent their new-born infants away for several years. They placed their children through agents. For the rural population, nursing children was an important form of self-employment. A police survey of 1780 reveals how widespread the profession remained. According to the police figures, 21,000 children were born in Paris every year. Of these, some 700 were nursed by their own mothers. These were the children of the very poor. Another 700 were looked after by a wet-nurse in the parental home. These were the children of the very rich. 17,000, however, were sent away to the country by their parents. That represents 80 per cent. The remaining 2600 were abandoned at birth.

To this depressing picture can be added statistics from the city of Rouen: every third child given by its parents to a wet-nurse never returned, and of the children nursed at home, one in five died. This high rate of infant mortality may have been one of the reasons why parents rejected or avoided emotional bonding with their new-born children. A form of self-protection, of avoiding pain. It was probably a vicious circle: for ideological reasons, parents took little interest in their offspring; their neglect led to increased infant mortality; this high rate of mortality only served to encourage parental neglect as a form of self-defence.

Only a modern mother fed her child herself

The turnaround in this situation is generally dated to 1762, the year in which Jean-Jacques Rousseau published *Emile*, an essay on the education of children. Rousseau argued that mothers should breastfeed their children and that children should be allowed to develop freely in the care of their parents. He thereby gave voice to a trend that had been present beneath the surface for many years. In Boucher's painting, executed more than twenty years earlier, it is already apparent.

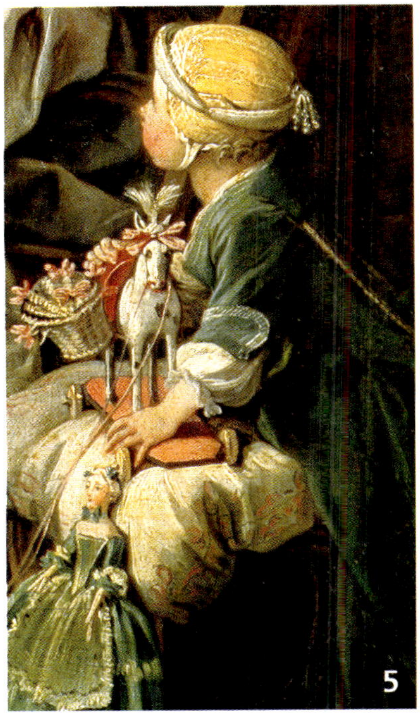

5

William Hogarth: Marriage A-la-Mode:
4. The Toilette, c. 1743

The stage is clear for the Countess and her lover

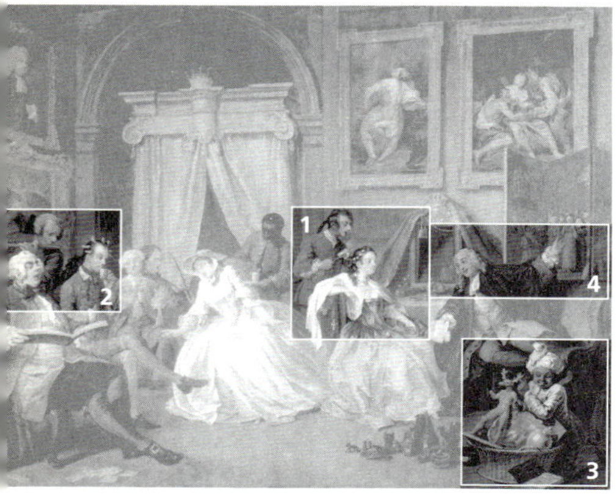

William Hogarth (1697–1764) liked to think of his pictures as a stage and his painting cycles as plays. We are here watching the fourth act of *Marriage A-la-Mode*, a tragicomedy in altogether six acts, and thus six paintings. The series opens with a marriage settlement: the impoverished Earl Squander and a wealthy middle-class businessman are forcing their children to wed. The first family thereby escapes financial ruin, while the second buys itself connections with the higher aristocracy. But the two young people don't like each other. In the second act they quarrel, in the third the husband takes a mistress, and in the fourth the wife holds court as she has her hair done. The guests drink chocolate and listen to the singer, who is accompanied by a flautist. Their sweet melodies absorb or mask the whisperings of the man on the sofa on the right. He is a lawyer by the name of Silvertongue and has already appeared in the first painting in the series, where he advises the middle-class father and comforts his daughter. The manner in which he lounges on the sofa signals his special position amongst the guests. He is showing the young Lady Squander tickets for a masked ball.

And thus fate takes its course: in the fifth act, Silvertongue the lawyer is seen escaping out of a bedroom window while the adulterous Countess kneels at her husband's feet. He has surprised them together and during the confrontation been fatally stabbed with a dagger. In the sixth and final picture, the young widow swallows poison, for her lover has been convicted of murder and hanged. A nursemaid holds out her child for a last kiss, while her embittered father strips the valuable rings from her fingers.

Hogarth's actors have no script. But the pictures tell their story and communicate their moral without words.

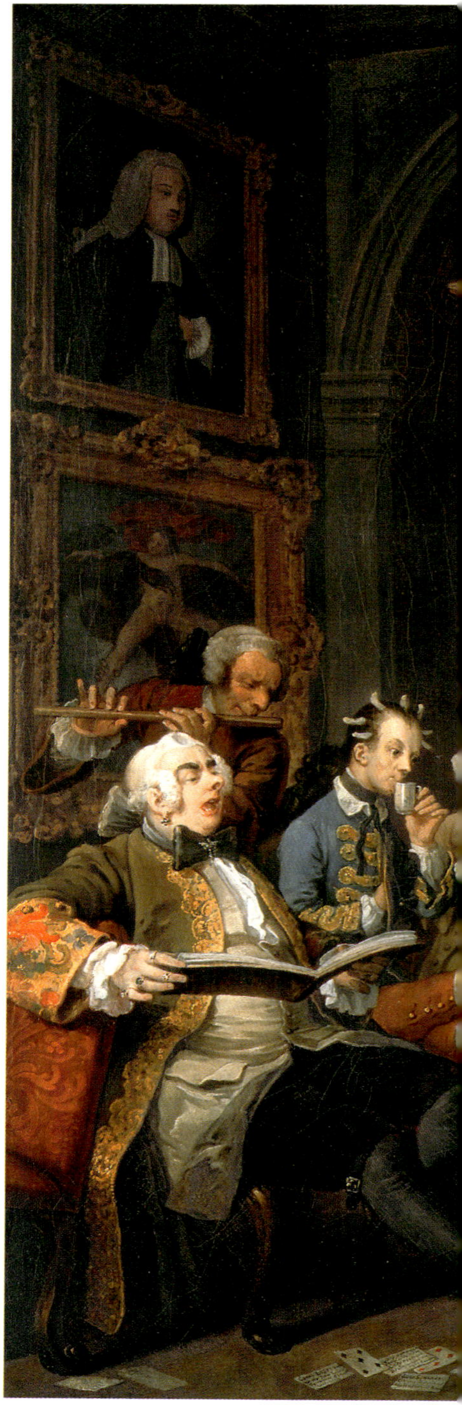

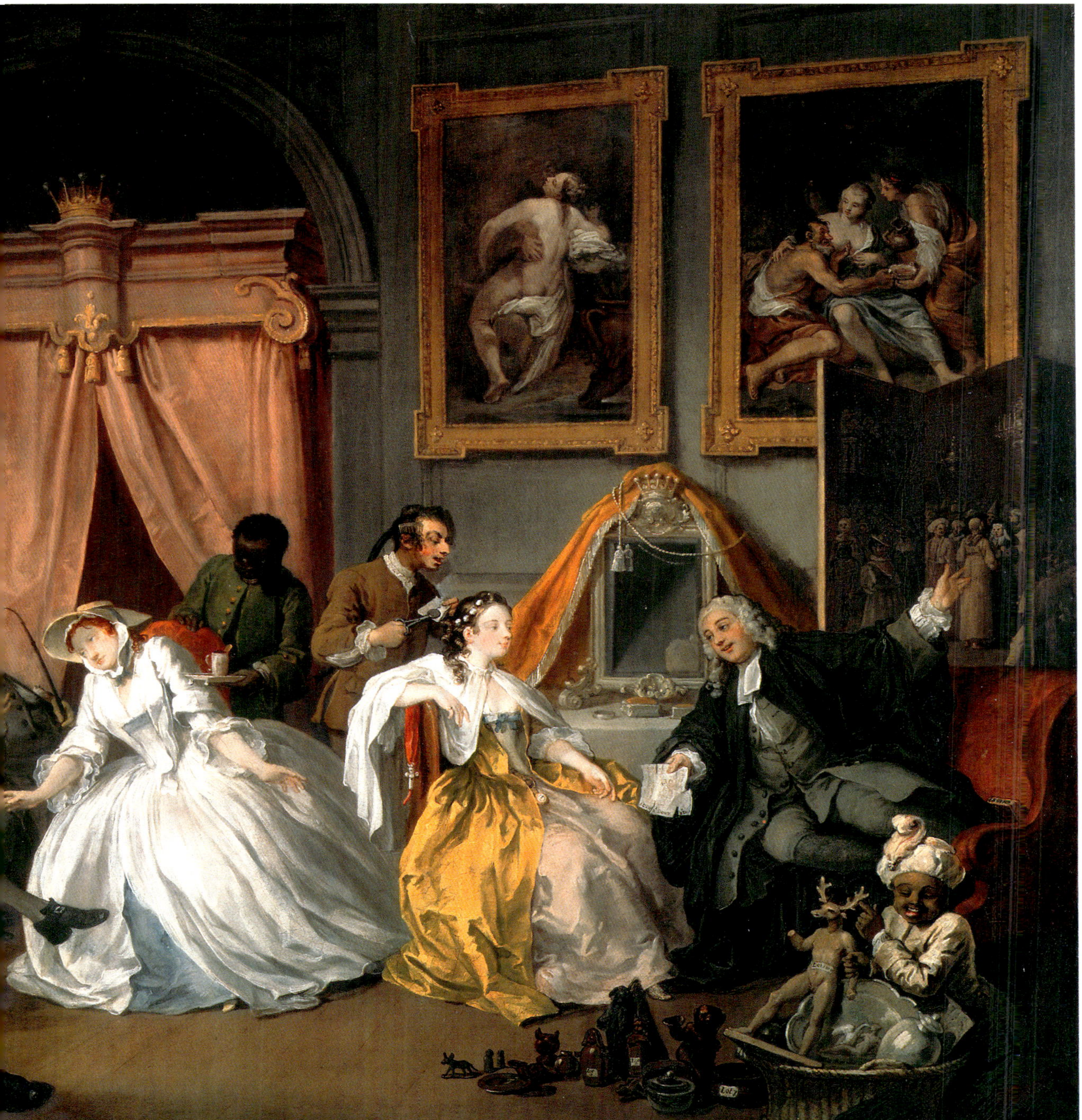

Some time has passed since the signing of the marriage settlement in the first act. The artist informs us of this by means of two details. Resplendent above the dressing table and above the alcove is in each case a coronet – the husband has become an Earl, which means his father has died. And hanging from a red ribbon on the back of the chair in which Countess Squander is sitting is a child's teething coral: she has become a mother.

The nursemaid has probably already brought the child in for its traditional morning kiss and then taken it away again. Bringing up children was not a task for parents in these circles; emotional attachment was considered inopportune. In London in the 1740s only some 25 per cent of children reached adulthood. Those that died were largely the children of the poor, but as Hogarth implies in the last painting in the series, the progeny of this arranged marriage will also not survive. The artist marks the child with a black spot as an indication of syphilis, a bequest from its father, and also gives it a crippled leg. Hogarth's unspoken moral: nothing good can come out of a bad marriage.

Forced marriages, concluded against the will of those involved, were nevertheless widespread – at least where money and property were part of the equation. Safeguarding the family fortune took first place over the wishes of the individual. Hogarth knew this from his own experience: he had to elope with his future wife, the daughter of his master, because her father would never have allowed her to wed a penniless apprentice. Hogarth's friend Henry Fielding, author of the highly successful novel *Tom Jones*, did the same. Finding a priest to conduct a secret wedding was easy.

Marriage as an institution was not highly regarded, certainly not amongst the upper classes. However strange it may sound, this was a consequence of a democratic outlook and a critical attitude towards authority. The English, long before the French, had extensively rejected the controlling role of the Church and Crown over their affairs and in the case of marriage, too, were not willing to be dictated to by a higher authority. A bill stipulating bans, a licence, witnesses, and an official ceremony conducted by an Anglican clergyman as legal requirements for marriage was opposed with the argument that it impinged on personal freedom.

The wife's role was severely restricted within marriage: legally subject to her husband, she was also seen as a lesser human being. "Women are nothing but big children", wrote the Earl of Chesterfield to his son in 1748. "A man of reason … never seeks their advice on serious matters and never confides in them." In Fielding's novel *Tom Jones*, a young girl is advised: "So far, madam, from your being concerned alone, your concern is the least, or surely the least important. It is the honour of your family which is concerned in this alliance; you are only the instrument."

The father might have addressed the same words to the young woman at her dressing table, her face turned towards her consoler, while the hairdresser tests the heat of the curling tongs on a piece of paper – the wife as the instrument by which the family can rise to the nobility. The husband, for his part, was nothing better than an instrument of financial gain; he is saving his family from ruin. Such was a "marriage a-la-mode". The suffix "a-la-mode" literally means "according to the fashion", but implied that although it might be what everyone did, it wasn't good.

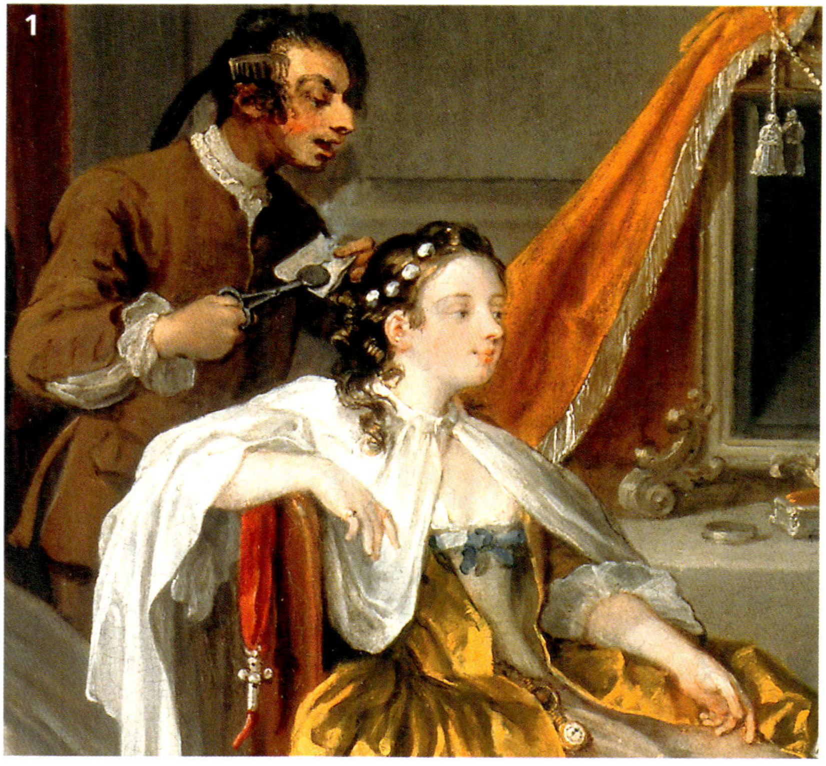

Figaro as a silent witness

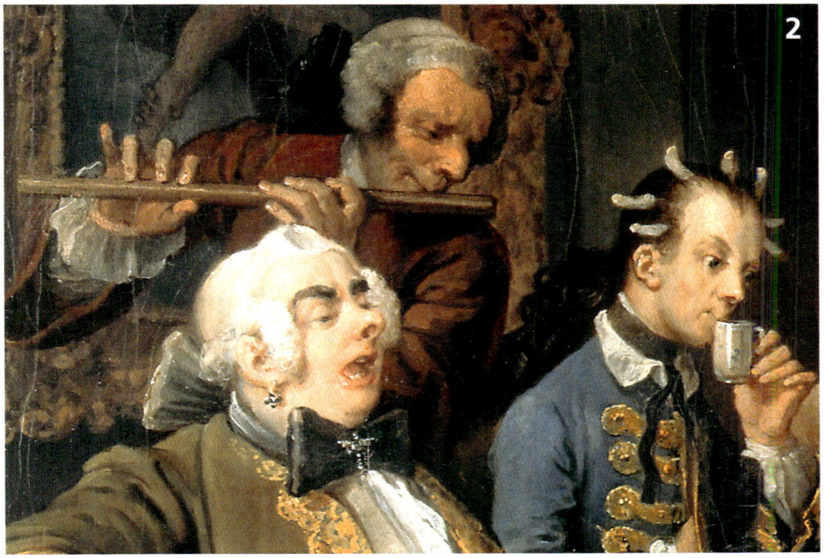

The bourgeois daughter who has risen to the aristocracy is here copying a royal ritual, the *lever du roi*, which was particularly cultivated at the French court. The royal morning toilette unfolded in two phases. The king was joined for the *petit lever* by his most senior officials, who gave him the day's news. While they talked to him, the king was given his dressing gown, was shaved and powdered, and relieved himself on his commode. This was followed by the *grand lever*, a more public morning reception, during which the king took his chocolate, was given his wig and dressed.

Countess Squander (Hogarth's names are self-explanatory) is staging a sort of *grand lever*. She has already spent money: she has been to an auction, and the bits and pieces she has purchased are standing and lying in the bottom right-hand part of the painting. She is wearing a morning gown, and the watch in her lap reads two o'clock. When the hairdresser has completed his task, she will put on a visiting gown, probably climb into her carriage and go and pay calls on her circle of acquaintances. Visiting was amongst the permitted distractions in the boring life of a lady. The numerous invitations scattered beneath the singer's chair, most of them written on the back of playing cards, serve to indicate that this was part of the daily routine. In the evening it would then be time to put on one's finery and go out to the theatre or a ball, at least during the social season. Over the summer months, the rich left their London town houses and went off to their country estates – where others earned the landed gentry their income.

The singer is probably a castrato – a man who makes up in lavish clothing for what he lacks elsewhere. He wears rings on his ear and on all his visible fingers, diamonds in his tie-pin and diamond-encrusted buckles on his knee and shoes. His silken waistcoat strains to contain his bloated body. Castrati aroused quite extraordinary passions. The woman reaching out her arms seems to want to sink at his feet. For Hogarth, however, he is but another figure of ridicule. The painter thereby took care to distance his own characters from such celebrated real-life castrati as Senesino and Farinello: "None of the Characters represented shall be personal", he announced. He had no wish to stir up trouble amongst his musician contemporaries and find himself being taken to court.

While the skinny flautist offers a comical contrast to the portly singer, the role played by the man with the curlers in his hair is unclear. It can't be the husband; we have already met him in the earlier scenes in the series and he looks quite different. Besides, he is more likely to be found with his mistress or in a tavern than at the *lever* of his own wife.

Comic strips without speech bubbles

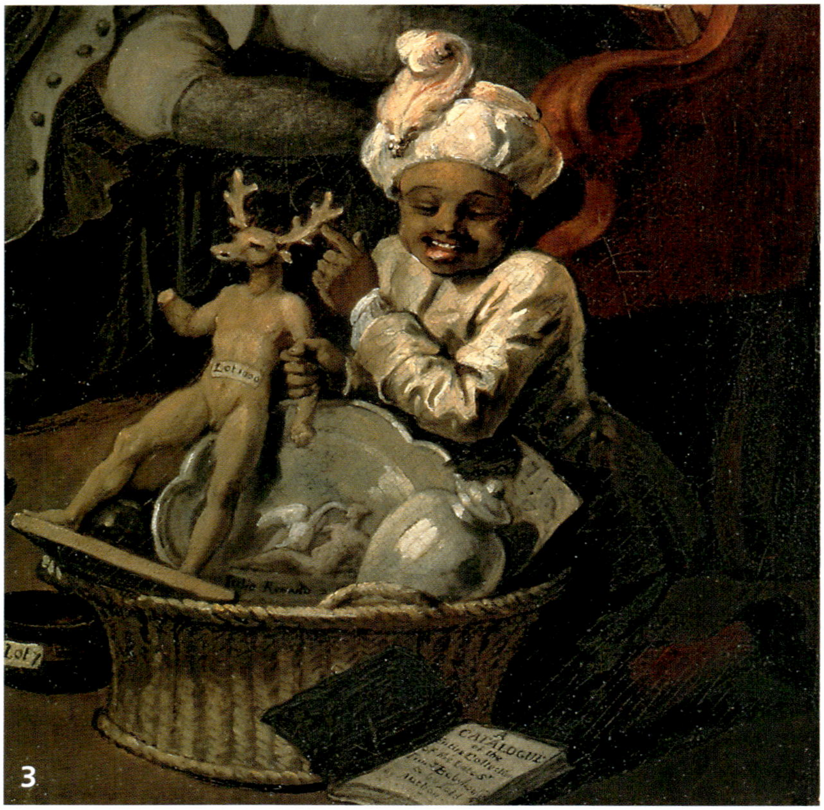

3

Hogarth's tragicomedy is set in London, at that time the largest city in Europe with a population of almost 700,000. From London, ships sailed to colonies and trading posts in Asia, Africa, and America and made the city the centre of international trade. The belief took root that England's future lay not on the European Continent, but on the seas.

Global commerce brought people of a different skin colour to England: around the middle of the 18th century, the number of black Africans in the country was estimated to be 14,000. Most of them lived in London. They were brought in as slaves and had no legal entitlement either to a salary or civil rights – unless, that is, their owner gave them their freedom. It was considered fashionable to have domesticated coloureds as servants and pages. The kneeling boy in the Indian turban evidently knows the Squander household very well. He is pointing to the figure of a man wearing antlers – a symbol of a deceived husband, but also a statue of Actaeon, the mythical hunter who surprised the goddess Diana while she was bathing naked and who was turned into a stag in punishment and torn to pieces by his own dogs. The auction number is still stuck onto the figure. The picture on the tray also recalls forbidden erotic pleasures: the married Zeus, in the shape of a swan, approaches the similarly married Queen Leda.

Hogarth's series are forerunners of the comic strip, whereby Hogarth does without speech bubbles and explanatory texts. The first important artist in the history of English painting, he had no classical training, never went to Italy, and was more interested in the society of his day than in subjects from antiquity. Relating a story unfamiliar to his public, in several pictures and without an explanation, was his invention – or at least, it was he who first raised it to the level of art. He thereby drew upon his public's general knowledge and their thought processes, preferences and prejudices. Thus even if people didn't know who Actaeon was, they were familiar with the horned image of the cuckolded husband. The heraldic coronets signalled that the father had died and the young Earl was now rich. In London society and elsewhere besides, castrati drew forth admiration and contempt like no other type of singer. The male habit of sticking one hand into one's jacket – a gesture later made famous by Napoleon – is evidently one which was laughed at: Hogarth illustrates it twice.

Although the artist does not use speech bubbles, he incorporates individual words into the painting, be it on the handwritten invitation cards or as the title of a book. One such is the French novel *Le Sopha*, which Hogarth conceals, although not too carefully, between the legs of the lawyer and the back of the oriental piece of furniture on which he is lounging – a sofa or its somewhat narrower variant. The book thus smuggled into the picture was written by Crébillon the younger. It was published in France in 1740 and in English translation in 1741 and became the favourite reading of all, male and female alike, who enjoyed indulging in erotic fantasies. Crébillon's novel is a sequel to the tales of *A Thousand and One Nights*: as an oriental narrator, he describes the wanderings of his soul, which take him to various sofas. What he sees and hears there – mostly affairs conducted out of boredom rather than passion, and often with blacks – is described in a refined prose whose elegant phrases allow the imagination to take wing. Crébillon's novel appeared at almost exactly the same time as Hogarth's painting – a French pendant to Hogarth's closer-to-home English series.

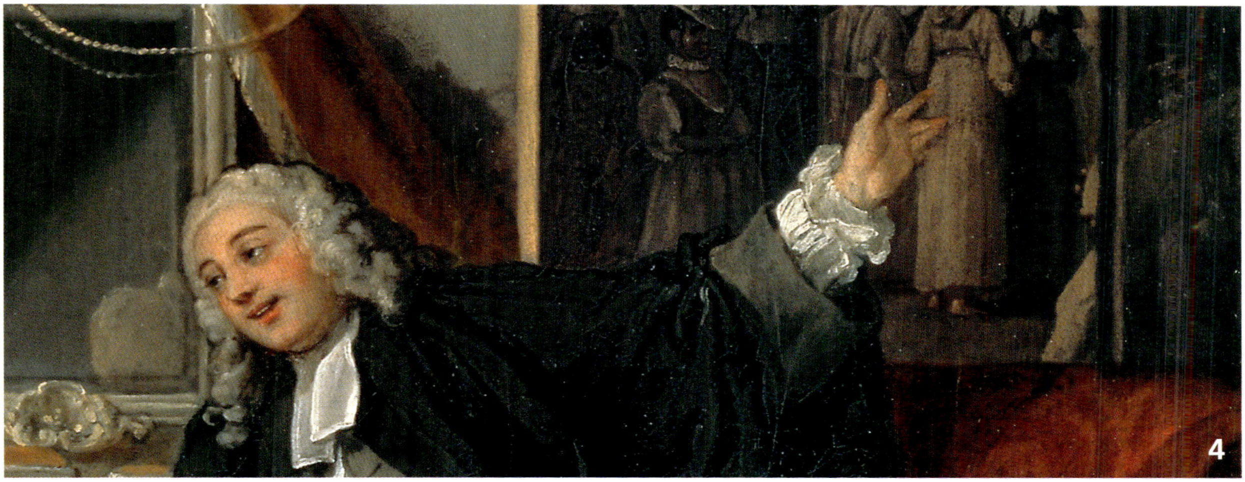

Lawyer Silvertongue is holding some tickets in his right hand and with his left hand is gesturing towards a folding screen showing a masked company – it is to such a masquerade, the viewer deduces, that he wishes to accompany Lady Squander. Costumed and masked balls permitted illicit contact, and since tickets were on general sale, anyone who paid could go. The most important of these London masquerades was held in the opera house in the Haymarket, started at nine o'clock in the evening, and often didn't end until seven o'clock the next morning. During the course of the long evening, lawyer and Lady slip away to a bagnio – a hotel of ill repute – where they are surprised by the husband, who has probably been tipped off by a spy. This can be seen in picture number five. The murder of the husband is followed, in the sixth act, by the deaths of the adulterous lovers – a moral ending in keeping with the standards of the day.

A polemic against forced marriages

Hogarth had difficulty selling his series as a complete set. Because it was not one painting but six, and because art lovers who had the money preferred to hang more conventional pictures on their walls, the sort that offered an uplifting vision of humankind and the world rather than laying society bare. *Marriage A-la-Mode* does not exist only on canvas, however. Like Hogarth's other cycles, it was also designed to be issued as engravings. These engravings brought the artist money. He sold part of the series on a subscription basis at a price of one guinea – the equivalent of two good seats at the theatre. This price rose by 50 per cent once the prints had appeared.

Since Hogarth didn't like engraving pictures, he had the plates produced by French experts. Part of the edition also went on sale in France, accompanied by an explanatory text in French that Hogarth had asked a friend to provide for the purpose. It is from this that a number of the characters' names derive, such as Silvertongue. There were about a dozen major printsellers in London at that time, and Hogarth himself had his own shop. Earning a living with socially and politically satirical prints was more easily possible in England than elsewhere – because Parliament had abolished preliminary state censorship, because a law for which Hogarth himself had lobbied for the first time protected the copyright of the author, and because ever larger numbers of English were taking an interest in social and political affairs. Newspapers were available in coffeehouses, novels described the world of the poor and disadvantaged. Not only graphic artists, but also many writers – Henry Fielding, Laurence Sterne, Jonathan Swift – combined public-friendly criticism with humour, moralizing with laughter.

The majority of graphic artists did so at the crudest level, however. Hogarth brought art into play, and also humanity. He does not portray the lawyer and the unhappily married Earl and Countess Squander as objects of ridicule, at least not as he does the singer and his audience. He gives them the familiar pale faces of cosmopolitan society, lacking in irony. For Hogarth is directing his polemic in this series not against individuals, but against forced marriages, against the treatment of bride and groom as instruments through which to improve the finances or social standing of their families. It is society he is criticizing, not its victims.

Hogarth's viewpoint also reveals itself in the design of the "set". The colourful society is gathered in a room without doors or windows. There is no exit to be seen. The enormous pink bed in the shadowy alcove lures the lovers like a trap that has been craftily laid. The actors in this comedy, it would seem, are quite unable to escape their tragic fate.

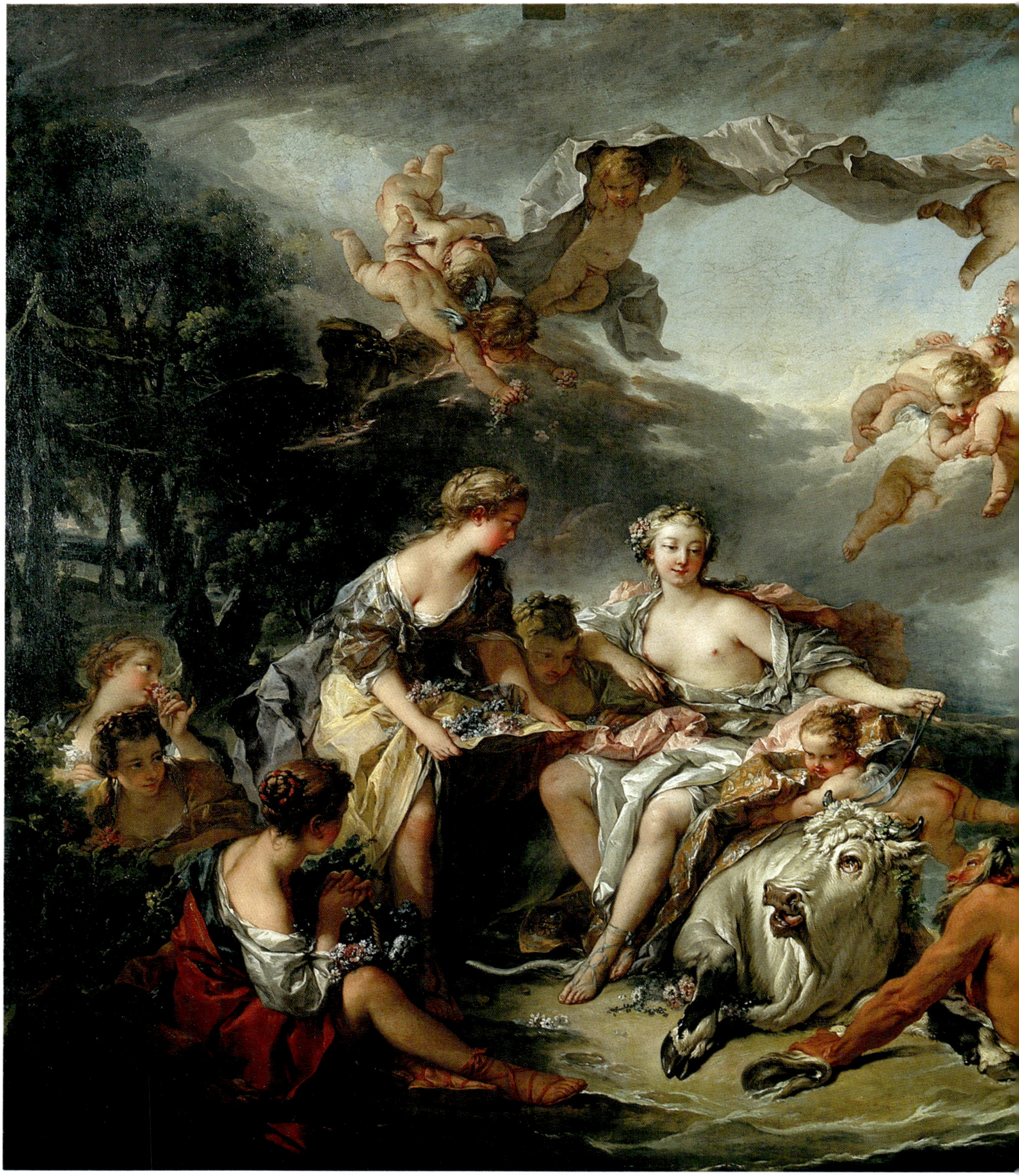

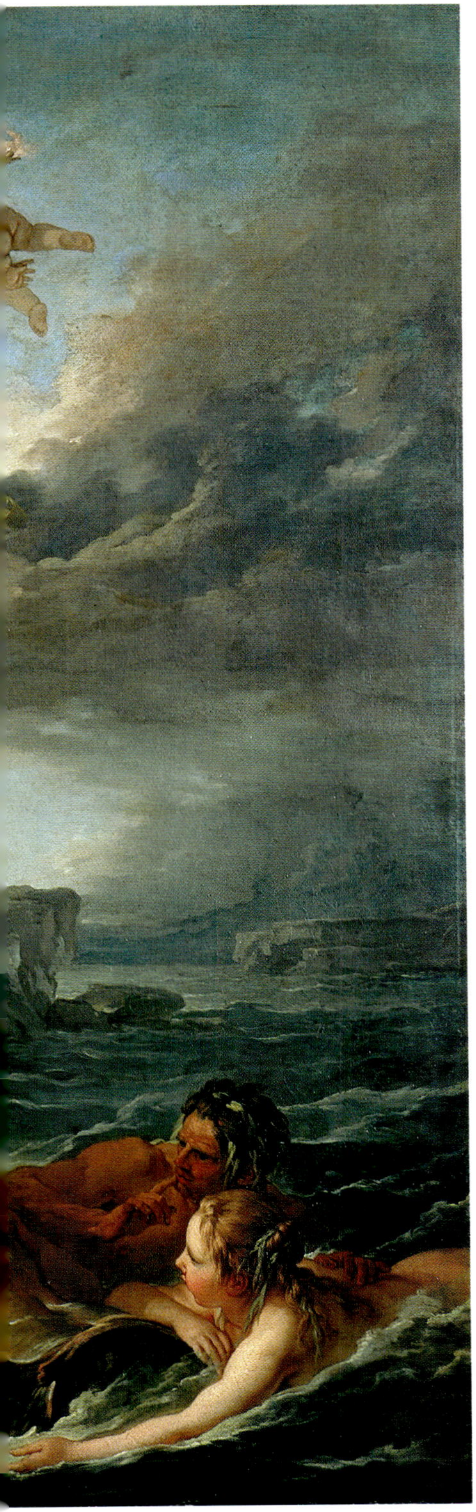

François Boucher: The Rape of Europa, 1747

A lecherous bull as sweet seducer

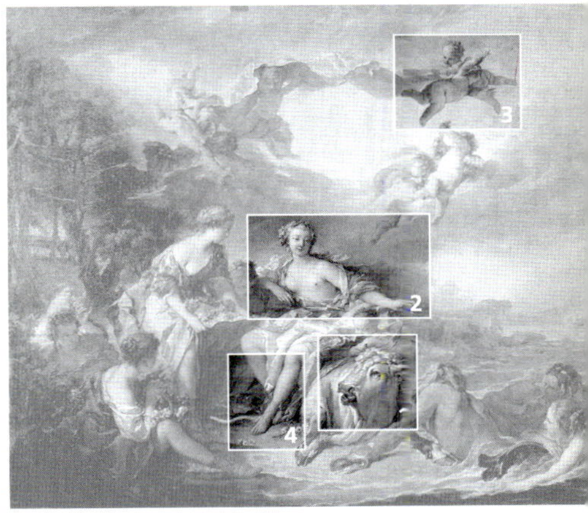

This painting was intended to hang not on a grey museum wall, but against panelling painted in white and gold and between mirrors in scalloped frames. It was destined for Versailles or for one of the châteaux de plaisance which France's King Louis XV gave to his mistress, the Marquise de Pompadour. Her taste determined the décor of the salon or boudoir in which she received her royal lover. It is known as the Pompadour style or, more familiarly, as the rococo.

The Rape of Europa is typical of this style. The picture represents Boucher's contribution to a competition held by the Director of Royal Buildings (an uncle of the Marquise de Pompadour's) amongst the most famous painters in France. All the works submitted had to employ a large-scale format and treat a "grand" subject from history or mythology, and were to be purchased by the Crown.

Boucher chose an episode from Greek myth, one of the many amorous adventures of Zeus, the father of the gods. In order to draw near to the beautiful Europa, daughter of King Agenor of Tyre, without being spotted by his jealous wife, Zeus changes himself into a bull and approaches the princess and her companions by the sea shore. His gentleness and beauty win her trust, and Europa seats herself on his back while her companions bring him flowers. The god is about to leap up and carry Europa over the sea to Crete. Fishtailed sea deities watch the scene while, in the sky overhead, naked putti hold up a billowing veil and flaming wedding torches.

The work was a great success for the 44-year-old Boucher. "There is nothing more elegant, more graceful, and more voluptuous than this composition", effused the *Nouvelles littéraires*. The artist was at the height of his fame – but, for the first time, his work was also attracting criticism. The end of the rococo was approaching.

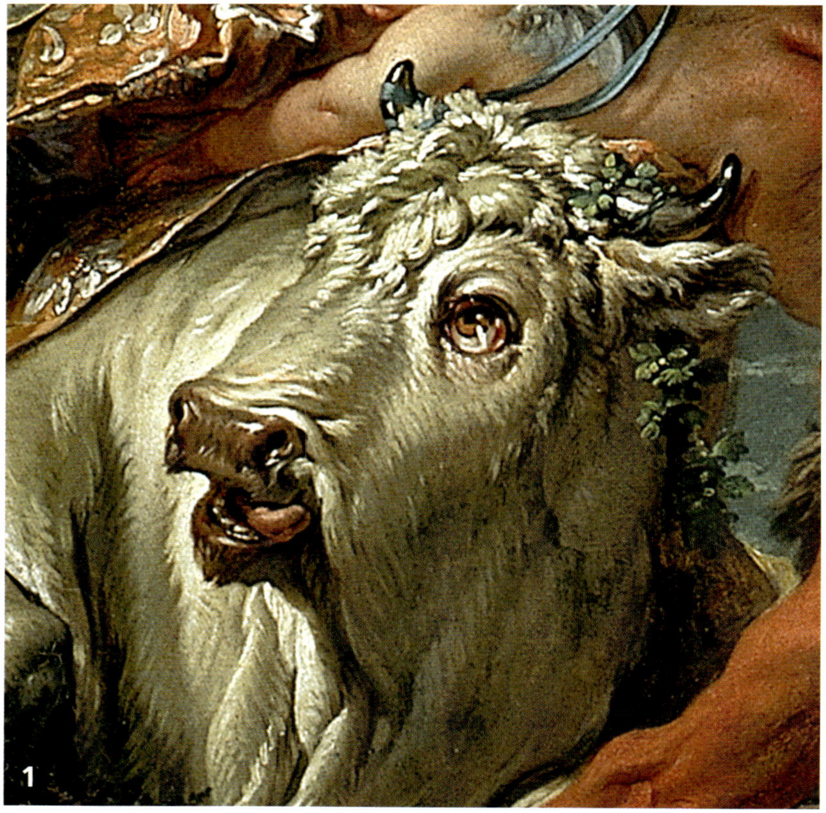

The god on a silken rein

The divine seducer presents himself as tame, on a blue silk rein, with curls, polished horns, and piously folded hooves. But he is already licking his jaws lasciviously and thereby betrays his true nature. Since time immemorial, the bull has been associated with wildness, strength, and potency: the Sumerian rulers called themselves "wild bulls" and worshipped a god in the form of a bull, whose marriage caused the rivers to rise every year and made Mesopotamia fertile.

Zeus is said to have abducted Europa from the Orient, from Tyre in Phoenicia, and carried her across the sea to Crete. Probably a memory of the sea voyages made by the Phoenicians, who with the goods they traded carried the civilization of the East to the West. The myth of the rape of Europa must have arisen in Crete, their destination, where a bull cult involving sacrifices and fertility rites also developed. It was in Crete that Zeus resumed his human form and celebrated his marriage with the king's daughter, who bore him a number of sons, including Minos, the future king and father of the dangerous bull-headed Minotaur. When the indefatigable Greek god immediately departed for new conquests, Europa was left behind to be the wife of the reigning king of Crete. Venerated as a goddess, she would eventually give her name to our continent.

In the 2nd century BC, the Greek poet Moschus of Syracuse composed a poem on the rape of Europa and thereby supplied the ingredients for later treatments of the theme: waves, dolphins, and tritons, daffodils, roses, and a handsome four-legged beast amongst maidens. The myth was subsequently handed down by Ovid, who took up the subject around the time of the birth of Christ. In his *Metamorphoses*, he recounts the various amorous transformations of Zeus/Jupiter – into a shower of golden rain, a swan, and a bull.

A French translation of Ovid appeared in 1732 and earned the myth new popularity. "Every educated person", noted Voltaire, "knows the history of the gods and heroes better than that of his own contemporaries." Studying the Latin authors was a core component of the curriculum not just in France, but right across Europe. Christianity and humanistic education at that time unified the Continent and lent an international dimension to the arts. The educated classes everywhere communicated in French, read Voltaire, and kept abreast of philosophy and fashion by following the Paris correspondence of the German Baron Grimm.

In the 18th century, France set the tone for Europe. The country was rich: having cultivated peace for almost thirty years, its economy had seen a massive upturn. With the outbreak of the Austrian Wars of Succession, however, old disputes broke out again between France and the house of Habsburg and its economic rival, England, and France was drawn into the war. Things nevertheless seemed to be going well: in 1745 Louis XV returned to Versailles from the Battle of Fontenoy as the glorious victor, celebrated as the *bien-aimé* – the well-beloved – and ready for new conquests.

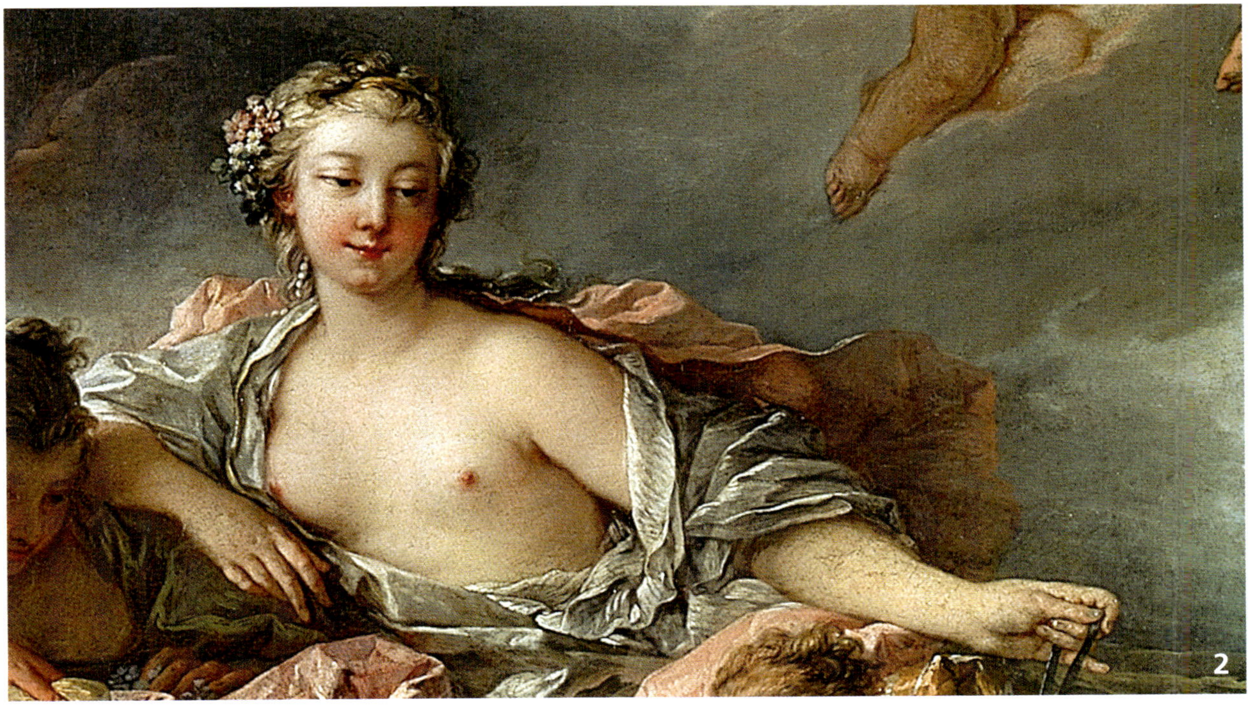

No classical beauty: Venus – Pompadour

Jupiter and Europa was the title of an opera that was performed in Versailles not long afterwards. In front of the King and a select public, in a small, mobile theatre. The star of the performance was the Marquise de Pompadour, Louis XV's official mistress since 1745, who could sing, play, and dance and who thereby relieved her lover's boredom. Surrounded by a small number of talented courtiers, she would surprise him on the stage now as a shepherdess, now as a goddess.

The myth of Europa had been popular since the 1720s. In London, for example, it had provided the material for a pantomime and a "Musical Work for the Stage". Later, in Paris, it inspired two cantatas, another opera, and a ballet. The fashion came to a close only in the 1770s, with a "Pantomime héroique" in Paris and an opera in Milan – composed by Antonio Salieri, Mozart's rival.

Boucher had already painted his first Europa in 1734 and the same theme was treated by many of his French colleagues. The subject had been popular in art since the Renaissance, and two masterpieces of the past hung in the Palais Royal in Paris: Titian's *Europa on the Bull* of 1559/62 and a copy of Paolo Veronese's *Rape of Europa* of 1568/74. Veronese's painting was commissioned by a Venetian family on the occasion of a wedding and testifies to a gradual transformation of the subject – from the representation of an abduction to that of a seduction and finally to a marriage picture, in which the bride of the god became the centre of flattering attention. Homage was paid to her and her beauty, and the princess Europa thus moved closer to Venus, the goddess of love and beauty. From Moschus onwards, the *Rape of Europa*, like the *Birth* and *Triumph of Venus*, was portrayed beside the sea, amidst nature, and offered a welcome excuse to show off a naked female body. In the 1730s the young Boucher had achieved one of his first successes with a large painting of Venus, and later executed entire series dedicated to the same goddess at the behest of Madame de Pompadour, flatteringly called "Venus-Pompadour" by the poets.

"You combine all the talents to please, you embellish/the Court, Parnassus, and Cythera". Thus Voltaire praised the King's new mistress. She met Louis XV in February 1745 at a masked ball, at which she was dressed as a goddess, but she was born a very middle-class Jeanne Antoinette Poisson within a milieu of high finance. Her father's employer and her mother's protector was the tax farmer, banker, and millionaire Charles Lenormant de Tournehem. He made sure the pretty girl was carefully educated by the best singing and dancing masters and married her at a young age to his nephew. He installed her in a small château, where her visitors included writers such as Voltaire and painters such as François Boucher, who would later capture her beauty and elegance in many portraits: no classical beauty, but entirely in line with the tastes of the 18th century, slim, with a small, high bosom, a delicate head, lively, pretty, and seductive. A description, incidentally, which equally applies to Marie-Jeanne Buseau, whom Boucher married in 1733 when she was seventeen and of whom he made so many studies that, it is said, he was able to use them for his painting for the rest of his life. For Europa, too, he is unlikely to have needed any other model.

In the many putti frolicking in Boucher's blue skies, the philosopher Denis Diderot (1713–1784) saw the ruin of all students of painting: "hardly do they know how to handle the brush and hold the palette than they torment themselves with stringing together garlands of children, with painting chubby rosy bottoms". These cousins of the pagan Cupid and the Christian angels had accompanied Europa since antiquity. Naked, they hold up wedding torches and a veil, another fixed component of all portrayals of the Europa myth since Ovid. Although childish and androgynous, the putti – like the lolling tongue of the bull – introduce the sensual note into this discreet scene of seduction. As porcelain reproductions based on Boucher's designs and manufactured by the Royal Porcelain Factory, they sold like hot cakes: they reflected the taste of a society of aristocrats and wealthy bourgeois who – like few before or after them – had the leisure time and the liking for erotic adventures.

If we are to believe the novels and memoirs of the epoch, seduction was its pastime and its life – probably as a natural reaction to the sanctimoniously strict regime imposed by Louis XIV (1638–1715). His great-grandson, also known as the "French Zeus", now maintained a "deer park" near Versailles full of pretty young women. In 1748 even the serious philosopher Diderot wrote a fairly pornographic novel, *Les bijoux indiscrets* (The indiscreet jewels), and thereby earned himself a *succès de scandale*.

Gallant mythology with putti

During the reign of Louis XIV, mythology in French art had served primarily to deify the Sun King in the allegorical figure of Apollo. Amorous stories from Mount Olympus were in those days condemned by moralists as "useless fables" and the "dirty tricks of the gods". Now, however, pictures of their erotic adventures were in demand and came into fashion as "gallant mythologies". They offered a feast for the eyes and the senses, and allowed a painter's well-off clients to contemplate, on the walls of their own salons, a reflection of the adventures they had themselves pursued or dreamed of – expressed in an exalted language, with an antique trimming and garnished with garlands of putti.

It was a genre in which Boucher excelled. Commissions were heaped upon him, especially after Madame de Pompadour became the royal mistress. As "France's First Minister of Culture" she appointed her uncle, and later her brother, Director of the Royal Buildings, and Boucher her closest colleague: he had to drop everything in order to decorate the King's palaces and above all her own châteaux de plaisance (one of which, the Elysée palace in Paris, is today the official residence of the President of France). With a cycle of nine paintings entitled *The Love Affairs of the Gods*, for example, which also provided the basis for a series of tapestries, produced by the royal factory in Beauvais.

Boucher had helped shape the tastes of the Marquise when attending her salon in the past, when she was still moving in bourgeois circles. Both came from the middle classes, were career-minded, loved glittering display, and, in art, the finely balanced overall composition as well as exquisite detail – everything was always to look graceful and pleasing. Boucher banned from his work anything that might disturb the harmonious impression of the whole. Which meant most of contemporary reality. He painted fancily dressed shepherdesses instead of toiling peasants – his customers didn't want to be reminded of to whose sweat they owed their wealth. His well-nourished putti, romping freely and happily around, had nothing in common with the infants of the 18th century, left to vegetate tightly swaddled and laced up. Those that weren't disposed of in orphanages were sent away to the country to wet-nurses, where – badly cared for and underfed – they died in their hordes. Not only the children of the very poor. Even the daughter born in 1744 of Madame de Pompadour's marriage died in 1754, after having spent the first five years of her life with a wet-nurse and the second five in a convent.

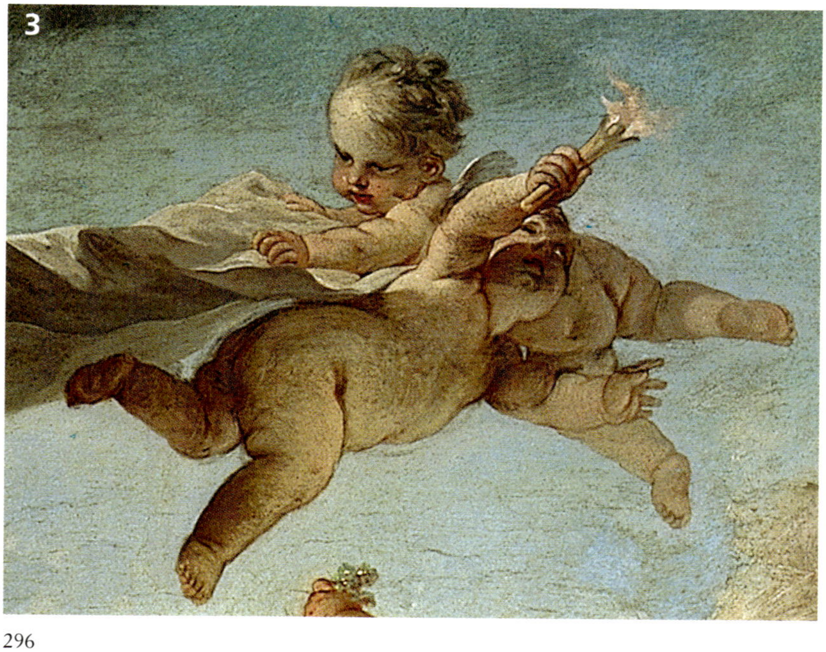

Classicism deposes the rococo

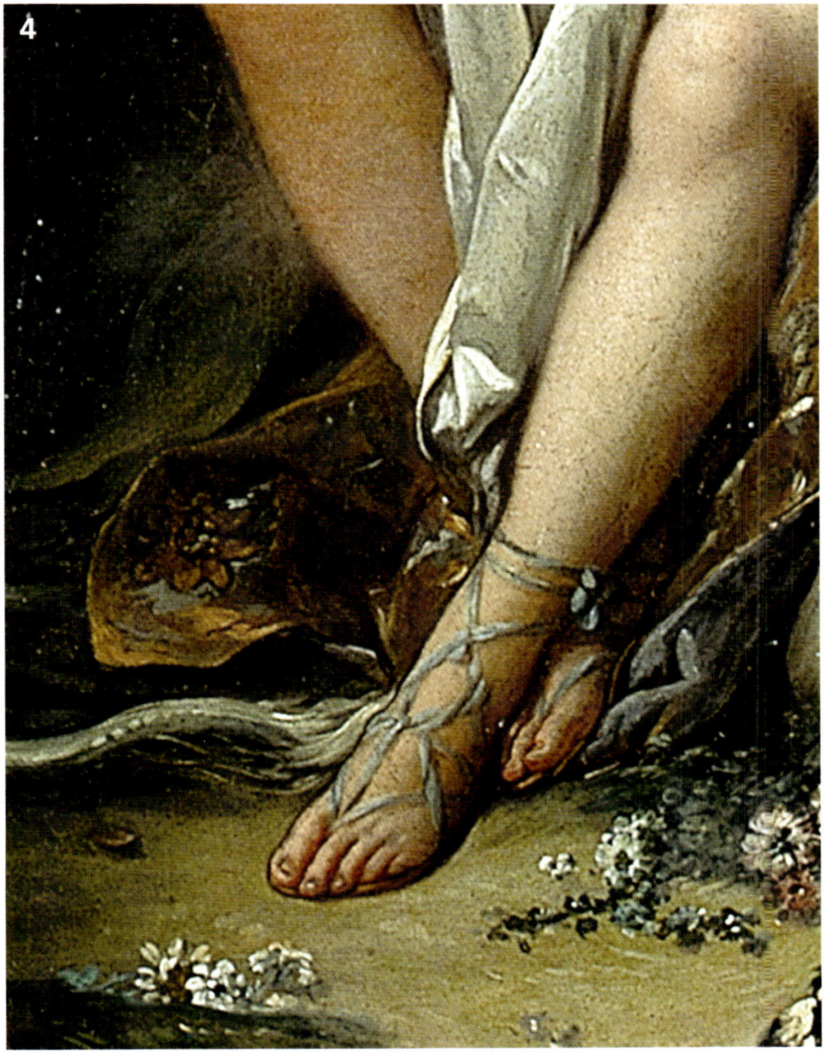

4

Boucher was rewarded with influential posts within the Academy and with pensions. His paintings fetched vast prices: 4000 to 6000 pounds for a large canvas (a labourer's wage was around a pound a day). Despite being overloaded with work – he executed some 1000 pictures over the course of his career – he remained an engaging figure and a popular guest at the salons of the day. Not so Diderot, whose dishevelled appearance was frowned upon. As a philosopher, editor, and chief author of the extensive *Encyclopédie*, the first volume of which appeared in 1751, Diderot made only a miserable living, and yet contributed, with this epoch-making work, to a change in values that would spell the end of Boucher's fame.

With the outbreak of the Seven Years' War in 1756, times had darkened. Military defeats followed on the heels of poorly judged political decisions in which Madame de Pompadour had a hand. The King had replaced the sickly mistress in his bed with younger girls, but continued to heed her advice in matters of government – with fatal consequences for France. Hated by the people and accused of being a bloodsucker, in 1764 she died. Louis XV was no longer called the Well-beloved and the first popular uprisings were reported.

Enlightenment and bad times led, in the second half of the 18th century, to a paradigm shift: frivolity was ousted by middle-class values such as morality, virtue, and truth. Diderot and his friends demanded both a "purification of morals" and a "reform of art and science". In their fight against oppression and superstition, they also devalued the ancient myths: under the heading of "Europa" in Diderot's *Encyclopédie*, we find facts about the history and geography of the continent, but nothing about a bull or an abduction.

One year after Boucher completed his *Rape*, excavations began in Pompeii. There arose a new interest in antiquity, in Roman togas and a simple, classical handling of line. The only halfway classical detail in Boucher's painting are the laced-up Greek sandals worn by his heroine. The rest – the veil, for example, and the dresses worn by Europa's companions – are derived from the wardrobe of 18th-century operas. Critics now began to find fault with the artificiality of Boucher's works, the predominance of pink in the palette, the smooth, doll-like faces. Baron Grimm was already mocking Boucher's "ornaments and pompoms" by the 1750s and denounced him as a "man of pleasures and profligacies", while Diderot aired his contempt for the artist's formal style. In his writings on art, which circulated only in manuscript form but were highly regarded, he described Boucher ten years later as "the most mortal enemy of silence that I know ... who has never known truth. People of elevated taste, of strict and antique taste", he decreed, "have no regard for him". The philosopher thereby heralded the arrival of the classicism of noble simplicity and calm magnificence with which artists such as Jacques-Louis David would make their name. Boucher outlived the rococo and was already virtually forgotten when he died in 1770. He was witness to a brief era in which, in the words of a contemporary, "the spirit glided gracefully and lightly over a thousand objects, dwelling upon none and reproducing only that which could give pleasure". For example a pretty girl, a bare bosom, or a shapely leg.

Giandomenico Tiepolo: The Minuet, c. 1754

Carnival in Venice

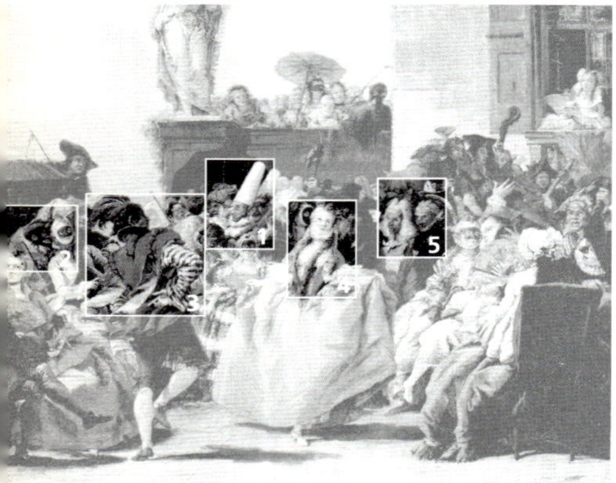

Every year, on 26 December, a representative of the Senate of the Republic of Venice, wearing a grotesque mask, emerged from the Doge's Palace onto St Mark's Square and announced to the waiting crowds that the wearing of masks was now permitted. Thus the carnival was opened. It lasted for some two months, until Ash Wednesday. And if that was not enough, there was also a pre-carnival period from 5 October until 16 December, during which people were permitted to dress up in costume in the afternoons only, and a post-carnival period for the two weeks leading up to Ascension, which coincided with Venice's large trade fair. Then there were set religious feast days and other special occasions such as the election of the doge and the election of the procurators. In total, the Venice carnival lasted not two months, but four.

During this period the theatres and casino were open. The money they raked in went primarily to the patricians, who owned the theatre buildings and were the only ones allowed to hold the bank in the casino. They could also let out their palaces to aristocratic guests. The patricians were not the only ones to make money out of the visitors – so too did the hoteliers, restauranteurs, shopkeepers, and people running the fairground booths. At times, there were as many visitors living in Venice as locals. For the city, plunged into serious economic decline, the money these visitors brought in was vital. So vital, in fact, that in 1789 the death of the doge was hushed up until Lent so as not to interrupt the celebrations.

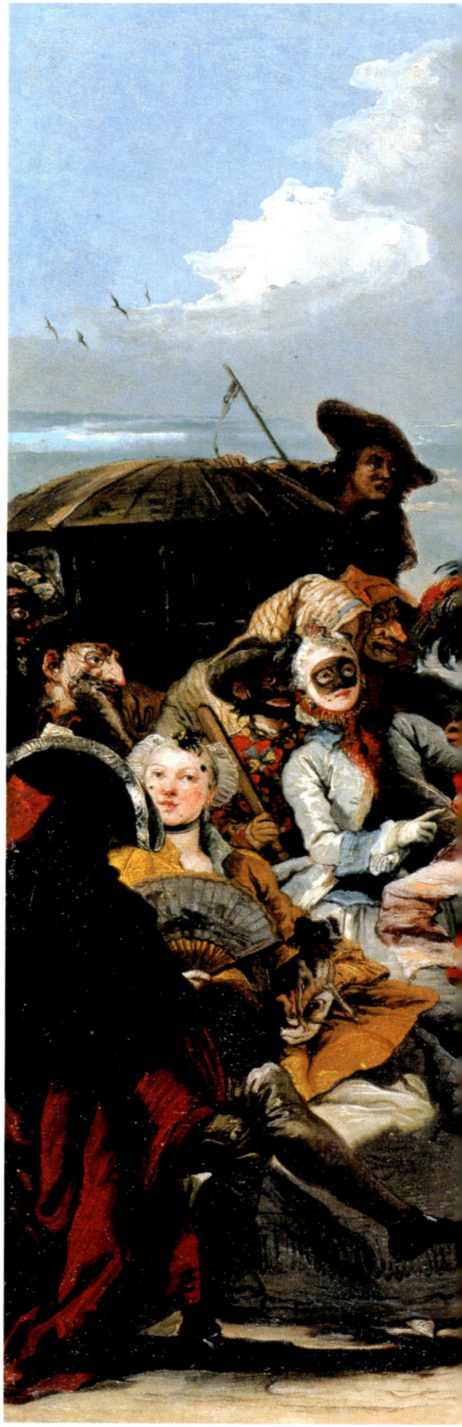

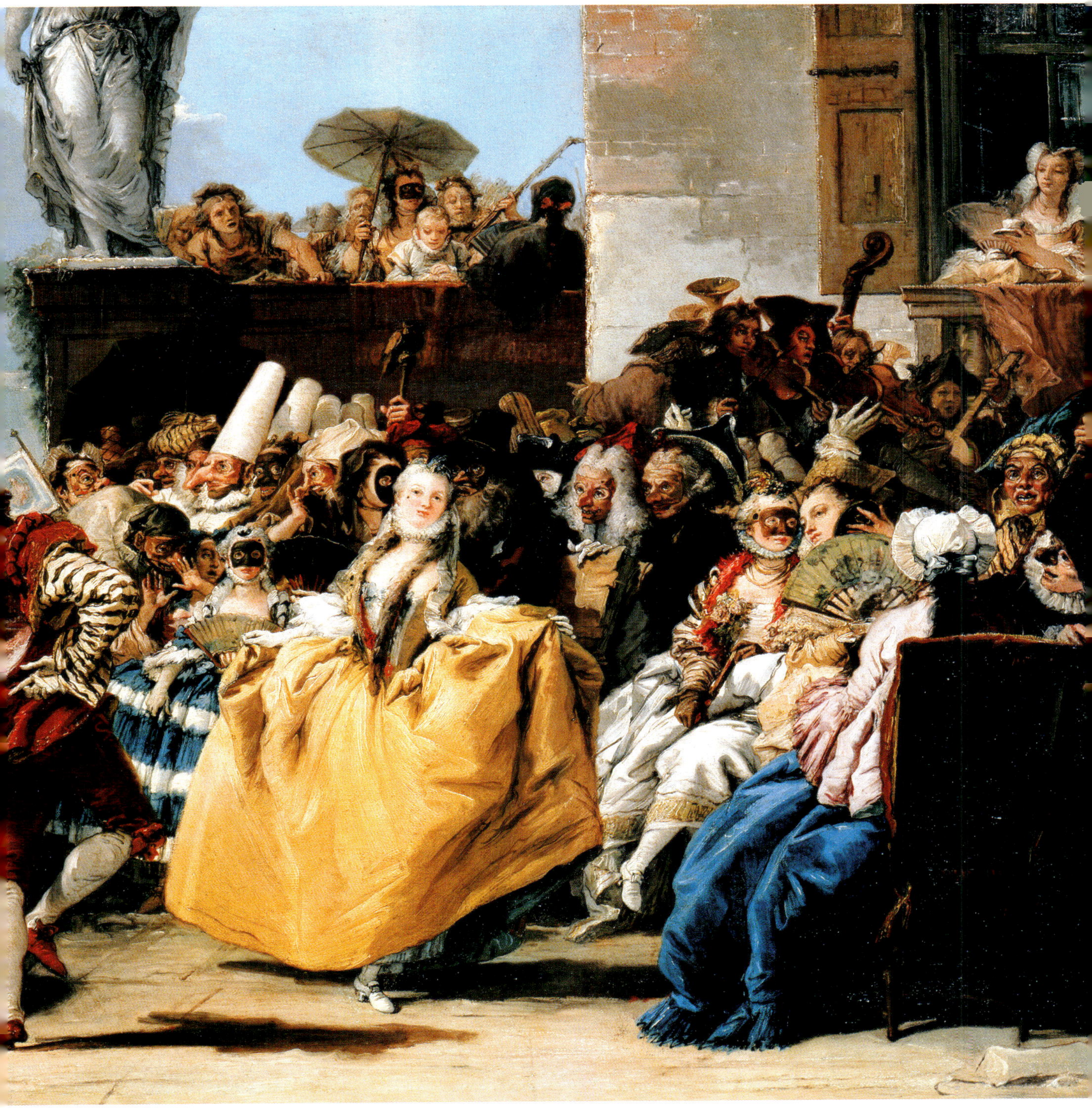

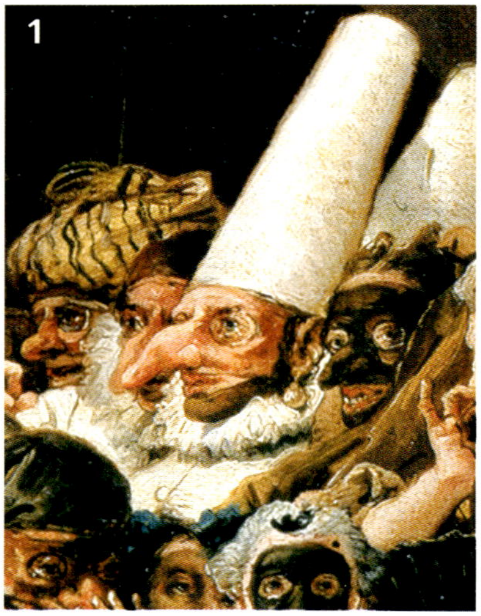

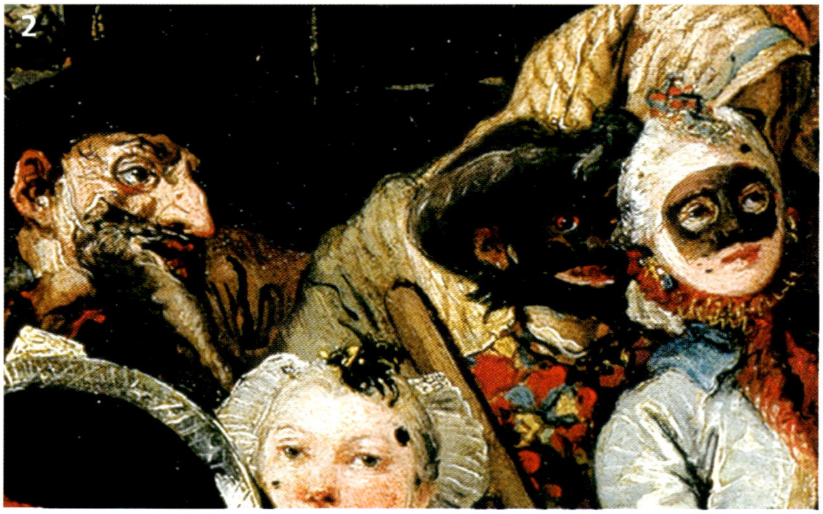

Masks, masks …

One of the reasons why Venice became the carnival capital of Europe was the Venetian love of theatre. The city boasted no less than fourteen stages; Paris, by comparison, had only three. It was also home to troupes of street players performing either opera or *commedia dell'arte* comedies. Each stock character was instantly recognizable by his or her distinctive mask and costume. The dialogue was mostly improvised, whereas the action was based on situations and exchanges typical of daily life. The connection between life on and off the Venetian stage was one that also struck Goethe, who recorded so many lively impressions during his time in Italy. "All day long in the piazzas and on the waterside", he noted, "the neighbour's wife, the lawyer, and his opponent, they all … argue and protest, shout and gesticulate, sing and play, curse and yell. And in the evenings they go the theatre and watch and listen to the life of their day, artificially constructed, more politely composed, interwoven with fairytale, distanced from reality by masks, brought close to it by its themes. They respond with childish delight, shout out again, clap, and yell."

In the carnival medley, the Venetians went a step further; they donned the masks themselves and felt as if they had stepped onto the stage. Tiepolo captures them here. On the far left, for example, the head of Pantaloon (in Italian, Pantalone) leans forward into the picture, with his pointed beard and woollen beret. On stage, Pantaloon played the part of the cuckolded husband and the old man who chases after young girls and is made a fool of by them. In the carnival throng, Pantaloon broke into conversations and offered everyone unsolicited advice.

In front of him, with a slapstick in his hand, is Arlecchino, the harlequin, clumsy but clever, greedy and as agile as an acrobat. Arlecchino is poor, comes from Bergamo, wears tattered clothes and – like Bergamo peasants – a hat topped with a hare's foot instead of feathers. On stage, he usually played the part of the servant. Beneath his black half mask, his face is sunburnt from long hours of working outside. In Venice, sun-tanned faces were considered unrefined; people cultivated a pale skin.

Next come the figures of Pulcinella, or Punch, always in groups, with their huge noses, white costumes, white hats and buckles. Just as Arlecchino came from Bergamo, Punch came from Naples. His name is derived from the Italian word for a young cockerel, hence Punch characters went about crowing. The character of Punch turned cartwheels and walked on his hands, embarked on every sort of adventure, got himself killed, and then leapt to his feet again. The Punch costume was especially popular at carnival time. Punch's lack of worry about the future, his knowledge that, however desperate the situation, life would carry on, must have resonated strongly with the Venetians in the latter years of their Republic. The end came in 1797, when the city fell to Napoleon's troops without a fight.

The adventurer

North of the Alps, minuets were usually danced in large groups. In Italy it seems to have been different. "Only those who have learned how to do it skilfully are bold enough to dance", observed Goethe. "The minuet, in particular, is quite frankly seen as a work of art and is performed, as it were, only by few couples". Should one such couple start dancing, Goethe continued, everyone else would "gather round them in a circle, watch them admiringly, and applaud them at the end."

The elegantly dressed young man who is "performing" his minuet with such obvious panache in Tiepolo's picture may be what is known in English as an adventurer – a gentleman of fortune, in other words, who owes his rank not to his parentage but to his own efforts. These men came from the lower strata of society. Their ambition was to overcome all the social obstacles in their way and attain a life of aristocratic luxury. They achieved their goal through their ability to entertain. They could dance better than other men and play cards more amusingly; they wore beautiful clothes and fascinated wealthy women. They gave the impression, if possible, of possessing esoteric knowledge, were extremely charming, and knew how to tell a gripping tale. They drew their material from their own restless lives and the travels to which they were so often compelled by creditors and the threat of imprisonment.

Adventurers, gentlemen of fortune – such impostors are to be found in every era. In the decades leading up to the French Revolution, however, they were particularly numerous. They were a product of circumstance. The ruling aristocracy by now performed few genuine functions and was becoming paralyzed; it needed entertainment. So, too, the Venetian patricians. Gone were the days of brave sea captains and bold pioneers of maritime trade, gone were the days of important diplomats. Trade with the Orient had long since collapsed, and the Republic had lost all political significance. The patricians who had made Venice great were left with nothing more fulfilling to do than run their dull Republic. They were bored. They sought distraction. In the shape of the carnival, they invented a different and

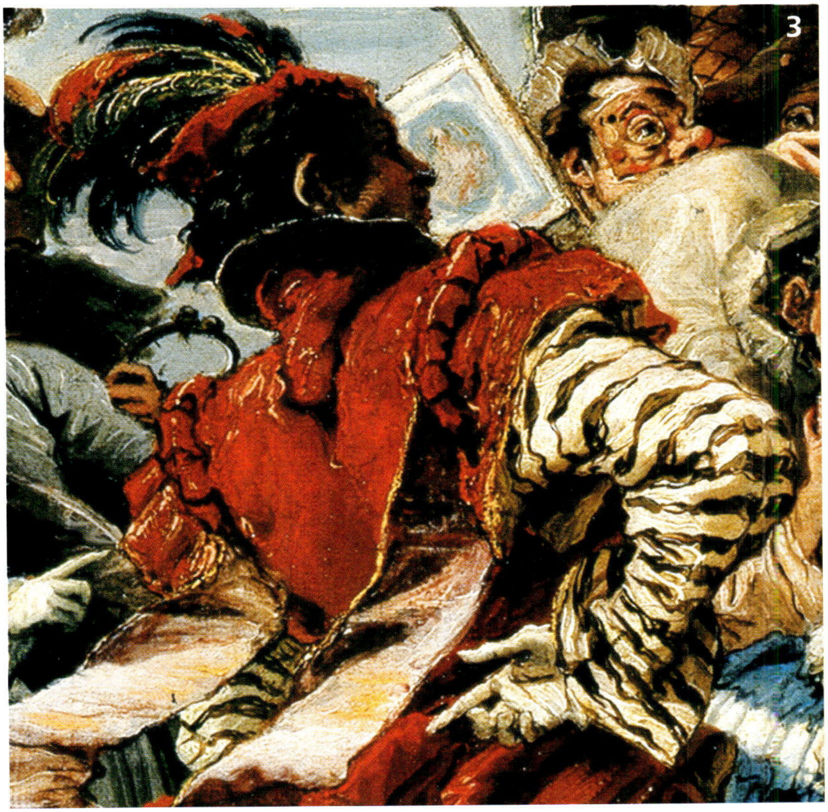
3

colourful world and thereby created a paradise for charlatans and adventurers.

It is no wonder that almost all the best-known confidence tricksters from this era should have originated from Venice or have spent much of their time there. The most famous of all was Giacomo Casanova, whose parents were both actors, and who gave himself the dubious title of Chevalier de Seingalt. By pretending to know something about medicine and the mystical significance of numbers in the cabbala, he ingratiated himself into the old patrician families. He was sometimes to be found dining at the best tables, at others imprisoned in the lead chambers, at others again entertaining his audience with tales of his daredevil escape over the rooftops of Venice.

Another was Giuseppe Balsamo of Naples, who called himself Count Cagliostro, a master of charlatanism. He promised to make old people young again and to turn stones into gold, before finding himself obliged to flee Venice at very short notice. Another again was Lorenzo da Ponte, who abandoned his real and somewhat less melodious name of Emanuele Conegliano when he converted from Judaism to Catholicism. (Conegliano sounded very similar to the Italian word for rabbit, *coniglio*.) In his memoirs, he explains that he was obliged to leave Venice on account of his political convictions. Inquisition records tell a different story: according to them, the small priest was charged with conducting an indiscreet affair with a married woman. Da Ponte's powers of invention and his talents as an entertainer are evidenced by the libretti that he wrote for three Mozart operas: *Don Giovanni*, *Cosí fan tutte* and *The Marriage of Figaro*.

All these adventurers with fancy names, these entertainment artists and darlings of society, were successful only while they were still young, as young as the man dancing the minuet in Tiepolo's painting. Life became much harder as they grew older. Cagliostro was left to rot in a papal dungeon, da Ponte scraped together a meagre living in New York by giving Italian lessons, and Casanova sat alone in a library in Dux (Duchcov) in Bohemia, laughed at by the domestics and dreaming of former times.

The female dancer has set off her pale complexion with a beauty spot; a number of other women in the painting have done the same. Beauty spots were popular in those days, and had developed into a sort of secret code: they had a different name depending on where they were applied, and signalled the wearer's current mood, her state of mind, and how she wanted to be seen. Beauty spots near the corners of the eyes, for example, meant *appassionata* – passionate. Tiepolo's dancer, with the beauty spot beneath her eye, considers herself to be *irresistibile*.

Singing, dancing, and acting allowed pretty young women to show off their particular talents to fullest advantage, and opened the door to patrician and aristocratic circles more easily than for young men. During carnival periods, Venice was full of artists of both sexes; in the 18th century the city formed one of the leading centres of music, opera, ballet, and theatre. This alone was reason enough to make Venice a firm destination along every grand tour of Europe. It seemed, moreover, that half the aristocracy of Europe had fetched its mistress from the Venetian stage.

One example was Barbarina Campanini, who was probably a cobbler's daughter. She was an outstanding dancer and a fascinating woman. Frederick the Great engaged her for his newly opened opera house in Berlin. She was in love with an English lord, however, and preferred to remain with him in Venice. Frederick commanded the Venetian Senate to send him the dancer. The Senate refused. Venice's London ambassador happened to be visiting Berlin at that time; Frederick had him imprisoned and thus put the Senate under pressure. It worked. Campanini was taken to Berlin. She danced. Frederick often visited her in her dressing room in Sanssouci. "He was a little in love with her", commented Voltaire, and added unkindly, "because she had a man's legs." She later married the son of the Prussian chancellor Cocceji, was divorced, and then elevated to the nobility, because she promised to leave her fortune to the State.

The career of Countess Campanini illustrated that it was indeed possible to rise up in society. Most girls with the same ambition, however, had less talent and less luck, and worked more or less professionally as courtesans. They lived "in sumptuous apartments along the Grand Canal" and sat "looking out of the window, beautifully dressed and made-up, in order to attract customers". The less refined dangled their legs out of the window, "dressed in red and yellow like tulips, their bosom gaping". Nor did they wait for business to come to them. On the fourth day of his stay in Venice, Goethe had the following experience: "Today, for the first time, a prostitute addressed me in broad daylight in an alleyway near the Rialto."

Like the adventurers, the masks, and the stock *commedia dell'arte* characters, so too the prostitutes were all part of the Venice carnival, that period of organized chaos when restraints were cast off, inhibitions lowered, and when all social barriers seemed to be lifted. For those who never attained the social heights or even hooked a middle-class husband, however, the future was bleak. Their old age, like that of male adventurers, was spent in the "poorhouse and on the dung heap", as Voltaire put it: the darker reality behind the glittering illusion.

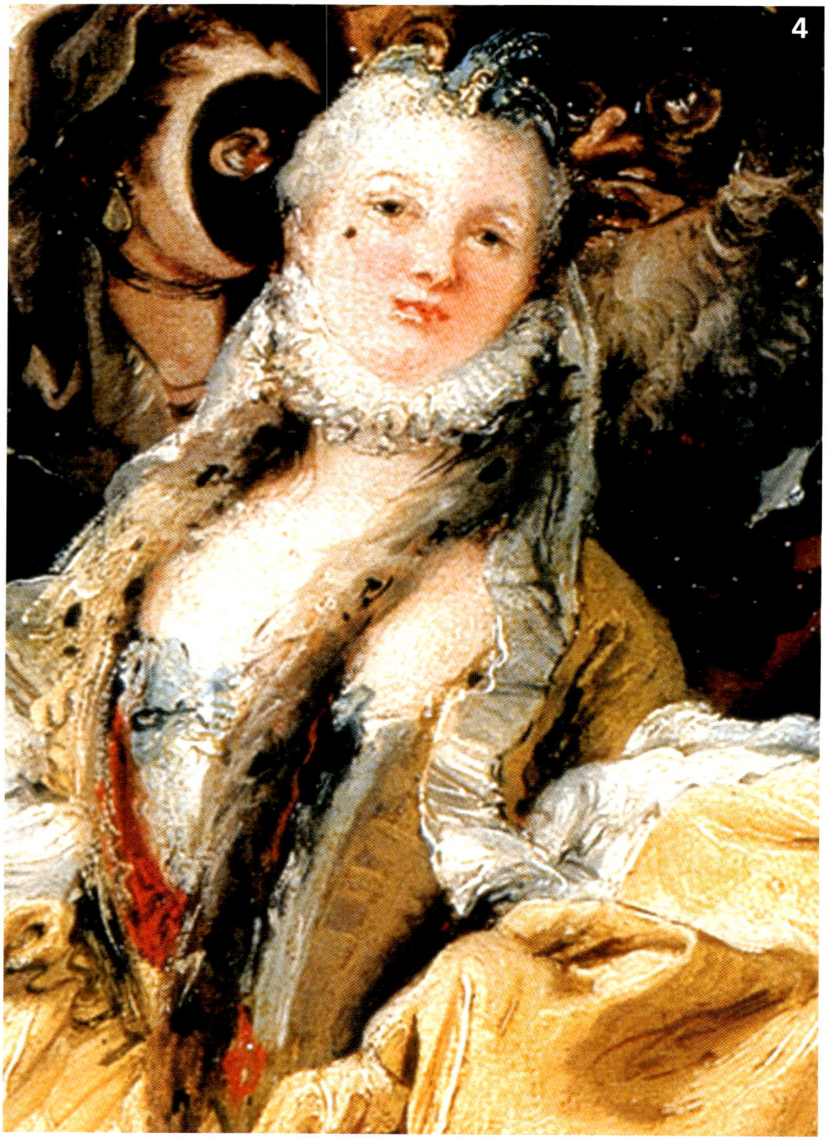

The career of a dancer

Omnipresent Inquisitors

The Venice carnival was rooted in long-standing tradition. It is mentioned in a document dating from as early as 1064. A law passed in 1268 talks about masks. Not long after this, the number of mask makers became so large that they were given their own division within the guild of painters. For reasons of state, the carnival was not merely tolerated by the rulers of Venice, but actively encouraged. They used the carnival as an opportunity to defuse social tensions. For a limited period, it was no longer possible to read from people's clothing the class to which they belonged. The barriers between the classes seemed to be lifted. For young people, especially patrician youths, it was an opportunity to indulge in sanctioned excess. The doges and their sensible advisers took the view that people who are having fun will not start a revolution. In its thousand-year history as a republic, Venice never experienced a single uprising. Foreign observers envied the city its internal stability – a stability that the carnival helped to maintain.

Only once Venice's days as a commercial power were over did its carnival also take on an economic significance. Venice in the 18th century was what Monte Carlo would be in 1900: a meeting place for the idle rich. Voltaire pokes fun at them in his *Candide*, in which he has six gentlemen taking supper together. During the course of the conversation it emerges that all six are deposed kings. Real 18th-century rulers who visited the Venice carnival more or less incognito included Frederick IV of Denmark and Norway (who stayed for three months), Karl Eugen of Württemberg (with a retinue of seventy-five), Emperor Joseph II (who came twice), the later Tsar Paul with his wife (under the pseudonym of "Conti del Nord"), and Gustavus III of Sweden, who is reported to have returned home after twelve days "tired and ill from so much entertainment, but ecstatic". Venice also offered something important to them all, namely a certain degree of security. They could feel safer in Venice than in other cities. Thanks to the Inquisition.

The Venetian Inquisition was not an ecclesiastical office but a secular institution, combining a police and a secret judiciary headed by three Inquisitors. Each had the power to order arrests; jointly they could pass the death sentence, although not on patricians. These received privileged treatment even from the Inquisition, and were either exiled or punished with fines. The Inquisitors' chief task was to protect the Church and the State. This meant that any criticism of institutions, leading figures, or the political and social circumstances was strictly forbidden. Owning a "liberal" book was as much of a crime as robbery. Goethe, too, was aware of this: "There is much, much that we'd like to talk about, including the things you're not allowed to discuss here, such as the State and its secrets ..."

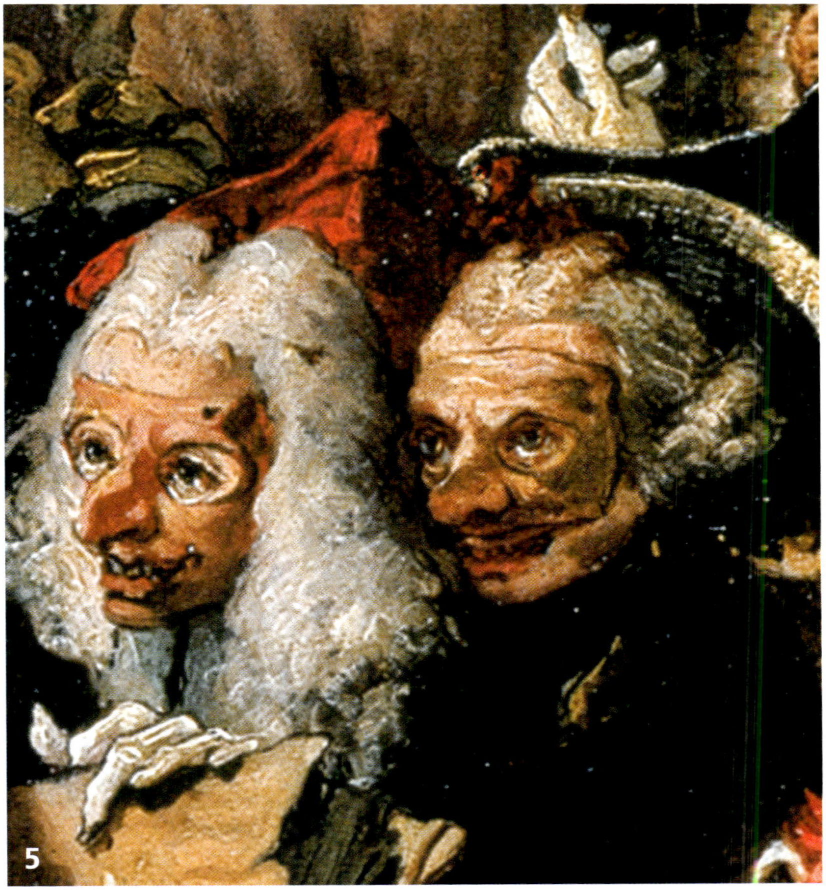

5

The secret judiciary was based on denunciation. The Inquisitors employed a wealth of spies. The worse things went for the citizens of Venice, the more of them offered their services. Casanova was just one Venetian who is supposed to have denounced others. Names could also be placed anonymously into the mouths of special stone lions. As a rule, those who were charged were not told who had denounced them. The Inquisitors justified the secrecy surrounding their trials by arguing that they had to protect their informants, whose names, in the interests of general order, they could not reveal.

The tumult and excesses of the Venice carnival were particularly easy to keep in check. A mask concealing the face made undercover surveillance simple: no one knew if the person standing next to him wasn't an agent of the Inquisition. The Inquisitors had the reputation of being all-knowing, and their envoy, the *missier grande*, needed only to show himself somewhere, and calm and order were restored.

This secret judiciary belongs firmly in the picture of the Venice carnival. On the one hand, it offered security; on the other, it made brutally sure that no marks were overstepped. Both wrong-doers and suspects simply disappeared, many of them for ever.

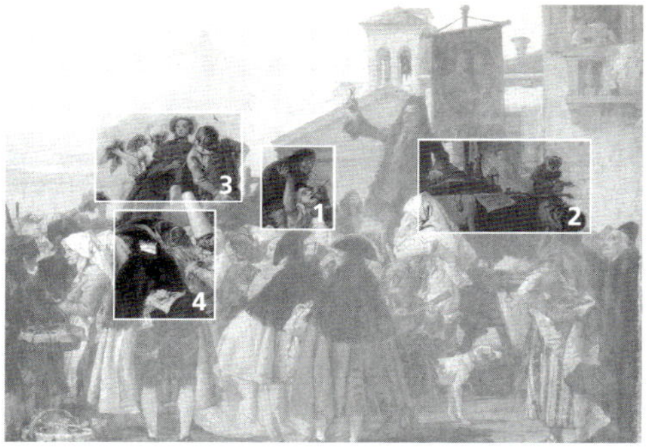
3
1
2
4

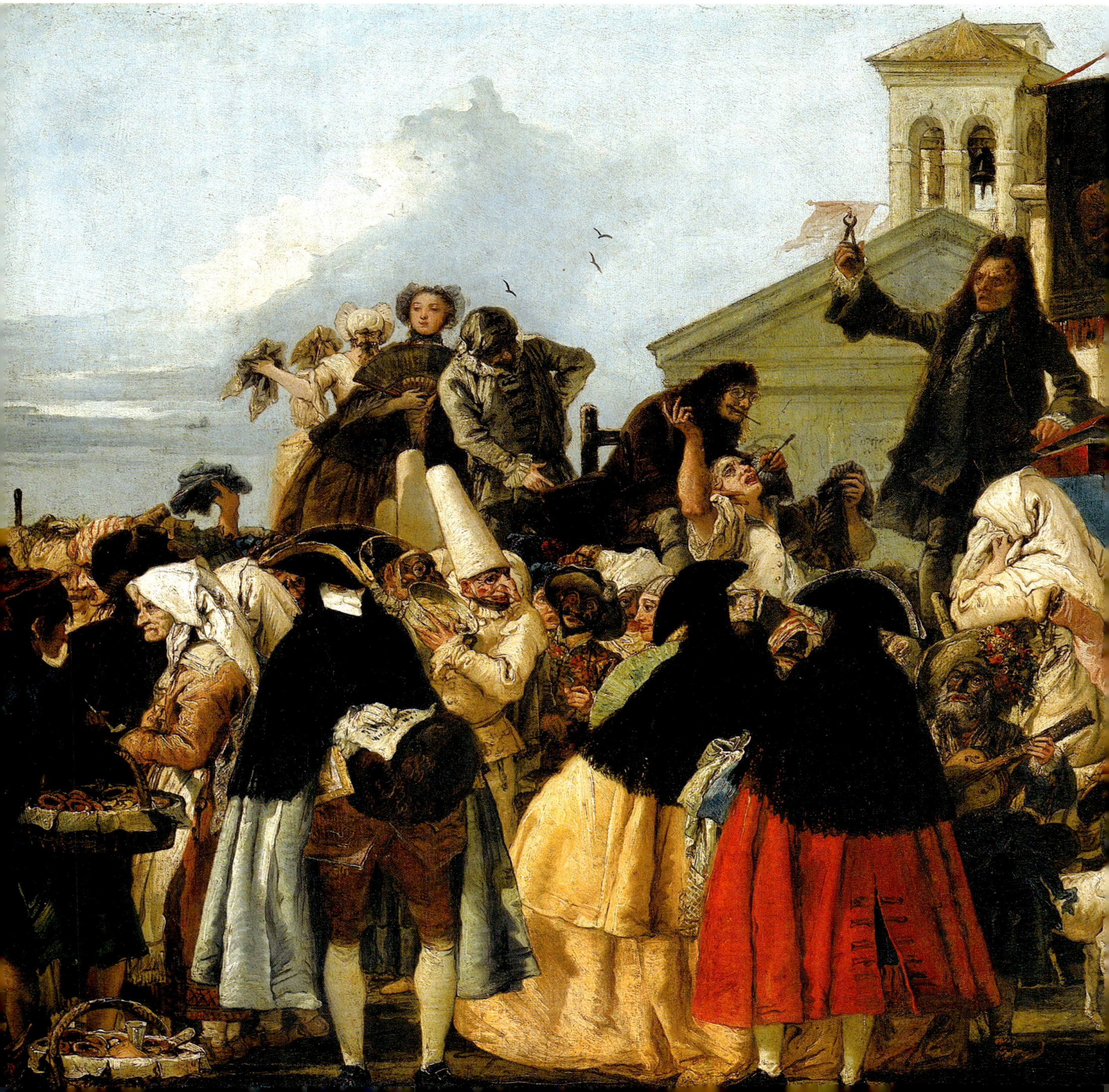

Giandomenico Tiepolo: The Tooth Drawer, c. 1754

Travelling showmen at the fair of illusions

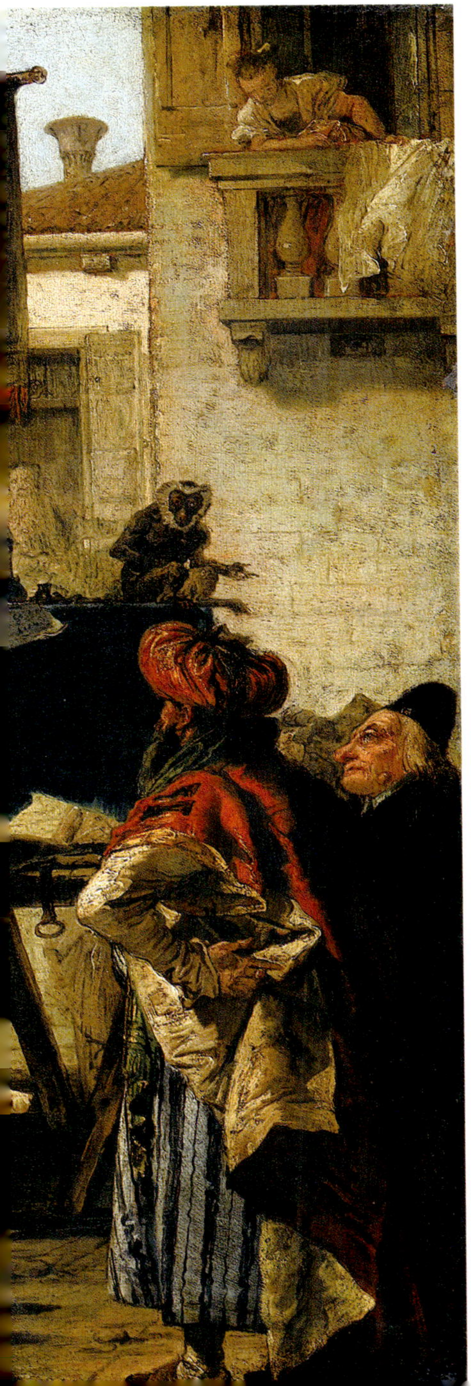

In the Venice of the 18th century, almost four months of the year were taken up with carnival celebrations. For four months the Venetians re-created an illusion of the power and splendour their Republic had long since lost. The city's population often doubled during the carnival period, swelled by the influx of actors, jugglers, musicians, street sellers, travelling doctors, and above all, of course, tourists. For the politically and economically failing Serenissima, the money they brought in was urgently needed.

Carnival time meant that the casino was open, over a dozen theatrical troupes were playing, and everyone was allowed to wear masks and fancy dress. Families and groups of people of a similar age could fetch white costumes and tall hats out of their clothes chests and transform themselves into Punch figures, for example, passing through the crowds crowing, turning cartwheels, and walking on their hands. Others disguised themselves behind grotesquely caricatured masks as old women selling pretzels, or as Turks, formerly the Venetians' deadly enemies. The domino costume, consisting of a three-cornered hat and a black cape over a wide coat, was worn by men and women alike, by people of rank as well as by those simply pretending to be so. Everyone had the opportunity to become someone else, everyone could hide behind a false identity.

Quack doctors, charlatans, and travelling faith healers blended seamlessly into the carnival scene. Giandomenico Tiepolo (1727–1804) probably painted his undated *Tooth Drawer* around 1754. It was later reproduced as an engraving, to which Tiepolo added a couplet commenting on his subject. It says something like: "With his voice and with his hand, money and teeth draws the charlatan."

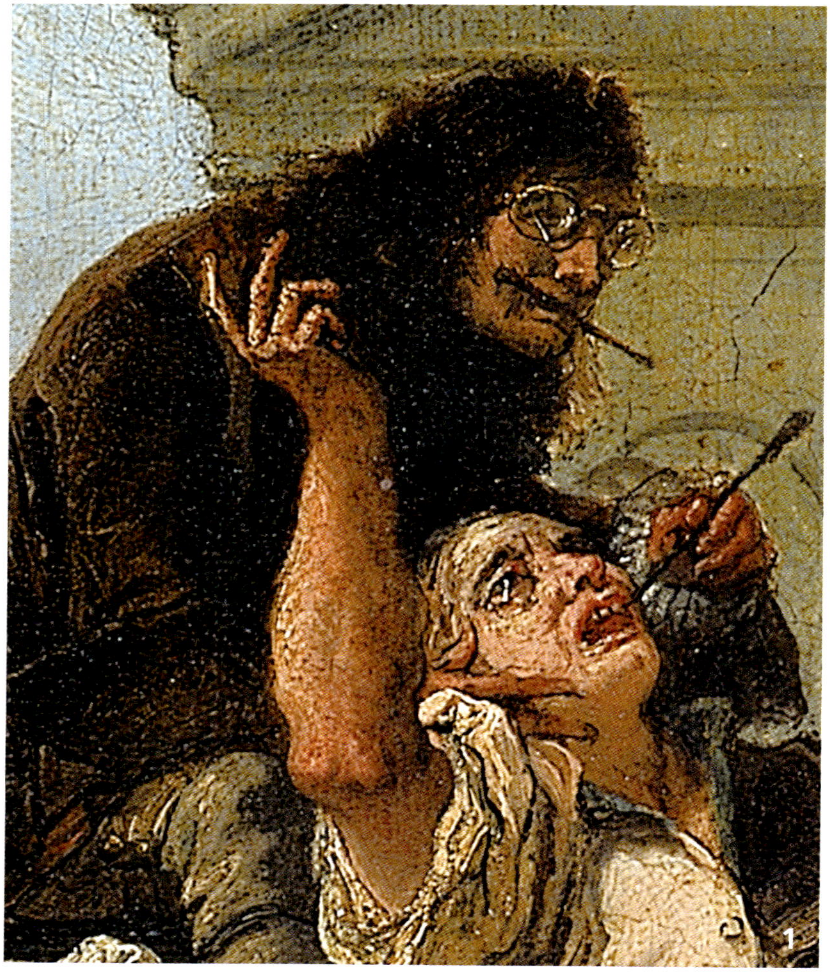

Pulling teeth was a brutal job

The artist probably knew Giuseppe Colombani, who for twenty-four years treated and extracted teeth on his stand "near the third pillar" beneath the arcades of St Mark's Square. He was considered an "onorato cavadenti", an honourable or respectable tooth drawer, in contrast to the many other travelling doctors who disappeared behind a cloud of dust before their furious customers could catch up with them.

The tooth drawer usually sat on a raised seat behind his client. Extractions were conducted without anaesthetic; Tiepolo's patient is flinging back his arm in pain. Drawing teeth was considered a lowly medical task, as were all surgical operations. Teeth pullers, surgeons, and barbers belonged to the same guild as craftsmen. Its members knew no Latin and had attended no university. They were practicians who had acted as assistant to someone else, watched how they did it, and then purchased the necessary instruments for themselves. Teeth were prodded and loosened with a "pelican" or "dental elevator", and pulled out with pincers or pliers. Afterwards the patient rinsed out his mouth with warm water, perhaps mixed with a dash of alcohol; other antiseptic measures were unknown. Infections often followed. Even if you survived an extraction, you could still die of the consequences. There are many stories of tooth drawers mistakenly extracting three good teeth instead of the bad one.

It was a bloody and brutal job, and people usually sought out a tooth drawer only when the pain was even more unbearable than the worst kind of operation. Toothache was "the most violent, most disagreeable pain, which by far exceeds all other sorts of pain in strength", wrote the Viennese surgeon Joseph Georg Pasch in 1767. The woman opposite the patient, pressing a cloth against her cheek, is probably suffering just such a toothache.

To combat this most disagreeable of all types of pain by bloodless means, tooth drawers offered a number of remedies: root extracts, powders, a *balsamus traumaticus* and "prepared crayfish eyes, mother-of-pearl or scallops, staghorn or chalk", mixed with a few drops of cinnamon or rosewood oil to improve the smell.

Most doctors held the view that holes in the teeth were made by worms, which they would proceed to try and smoke out. University doctors also recommended the treatment they recommended for every illness: bleeding and enemas. For according to traditional belief, illness resulted from an imbalance in the four fluids of the body, which could be corrected by letting blood and accelerating the digestion. Such disharmony amongst the humours was diagnosed from a urine sample, contained in a bulbous glass vessel. This urine bottle appears as a standard requisite in 18th-century pictures of doctors, and in Tiepolo's painting it can be seen beside the two figures on the standard that serves as a sort of portable shop-sign.

The 18th century brought a number of advances in dentistry. Not at the universities, however, nor amongst the fairground stalls, but in larger cities of royal residence, such as London, Paris, and Vienna. There, practitioners attempted to repair holes with fillings, developed bone dentures, and extracted healthy teeth from the poor to implant into the rich. In places where the king got toothache, dentistry moved forward.

Between the dental practitioners serving monarchs and ministers and the charlatans travelling the countryside, there were many degrees of professional competence. Giuseppe Colombani, the tooth drawer practising respectably in St Mark's Square, had seen them all. He had started out as an assistant to a Persian faith healer, who claimed to be able to make gold. He then went on to travel through Italy and Spain as a mercenary and musician, before finally settling down. In 1724 he attacked the charlatans and their tricks in a book.

One such charlatan, amongst the lowest of the low, is the hero of *The Adventurous Simplicissimus*, a novel by Hans Jakob Christoffel von Grimmelshausen, which appeared in 1669. Amidst the chaos of the Thirty Years' War, Simplicissimus must somehow find a way to feed himself, and so becomes a doctor's assistant. One day, however, he decides that he has watched the doctor enough to know how "to con a gullible peasant and earn his supper out of it". So, "with the last of his pennies", he buys the things he needs: tins, bottles, papers, and, most importantly, the ingredients

Love potions and elixirs for a long life

to make a cure-all called "theriak", which was believed to protect against poisons and the plague, and a blue water against scurvy, tooth decay, and pain in the eyes.

Both in the 17th and the 18th century, itinerant healers made most of their money out of remedies such as these. Medicines were kept in chests such as the red casket standing half-open on the blue cloth in Tiepolo's painting. Beneath the cloth is a trunk. A trunk, horse, and cart were the basic accessories of most fairground healers. In addition to medicines, they peddled beautifying and rejuvenating tinctures, elixirs for a long life, and love potions. For those who didn't want to be seen purchasing such home remedies, a carnival disguise provided the anonymity they desired.

The 18th century, the Age of Reason, was also the age of the most famous charlatans. Faith in miracle cures dominated all of Europe. The two may not have been unconnected: just as the philosophers of reason were rejecting the omnipotence of the Church, so those who were ill or lovesick no longer turned solely to the saints – the patron saint of those with toothache, for example, was St Apollonia – but increasingly to the "empiricists", popular representatives of natural science. Instead of pinning their hopes on help from on High, sufferers put their faith in the remedies in the red box.

Travelling doctors and faith healers vouched for the efficacy of their products with tales of their successes elsewhere. They frequently backed up their stories with glowing testimonials bearing impressive seals. One such letter is lying on top of Tiepolo's trunk, with its seal hanging down over the side, clearly visible. This was not all, however: upon their arrival in a town, they would arrange for circulars to be distributed in which they extolled their achievements in bragging terms. Even Simplicissimus, the young scoundrel, drew up a "French leaflet" of this kind.

More important than a circular, however, was the gift of the gab. These men had to be able to come up with an answer to any question they might be asked, just like the man resting one hand on the casket and flourishing a pair of pliers gripping a tooth in the other. Like an actor performing his role, he must persuade the crowd of his unique healing skills. The word "charlatan", as such quacks were known, derives from the Italian *ciarlare*, meaning to chatter or babble (in the sense of delivering a salesman's patter). Since chattering is a popular activity right across Italy, the word *ciarlatano* carries less derogatory overtones than in more northern parts of Europe

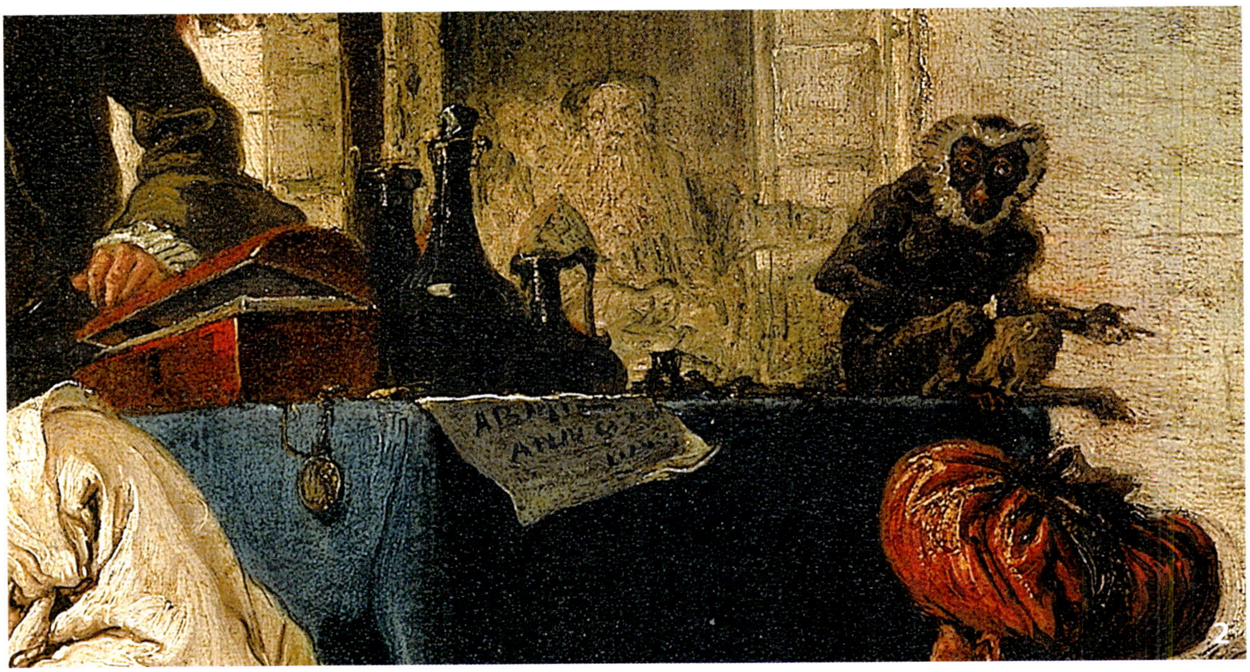

2

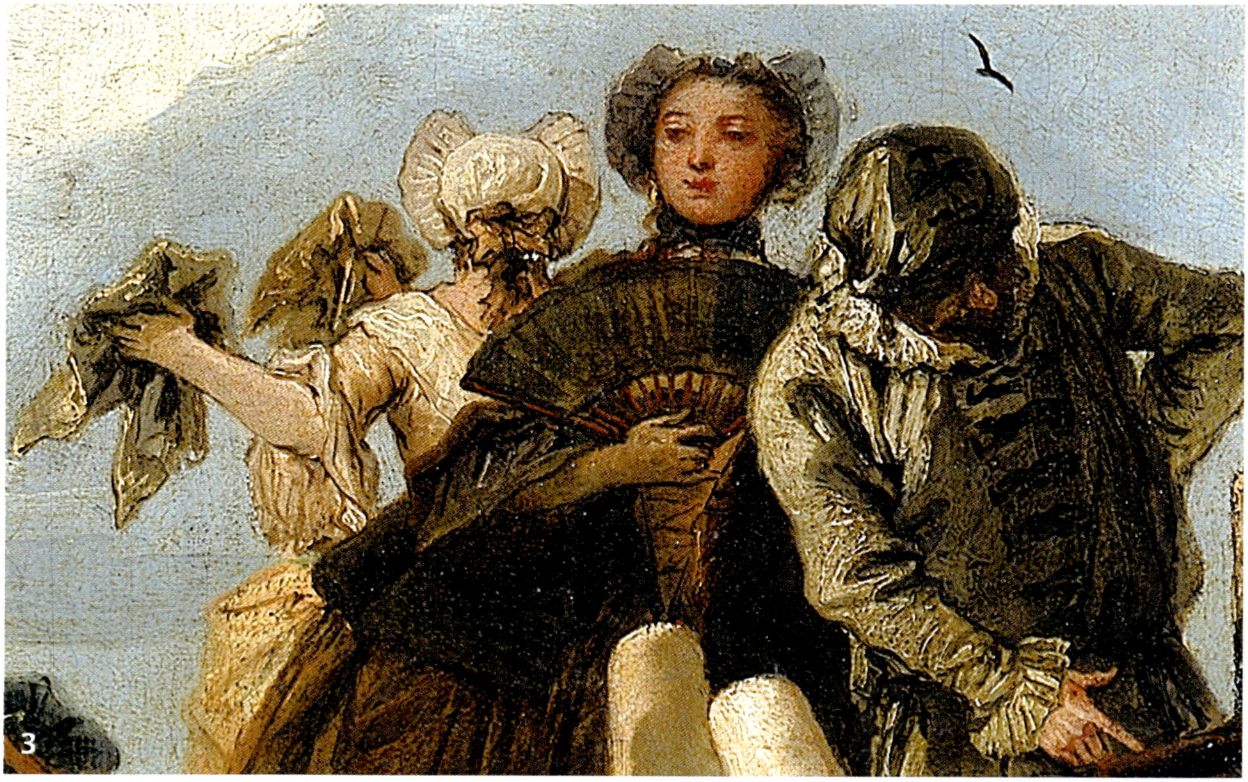

A flamboyant and noisy piece of theatre

In contrast to the many charlatans who gave themselves splendid-sounding names and titles, there was one who simply called himself "Anonymous". His real name was Buonafede Vitali. He had been a Jesuit, but had left his monastery, studied medicine, and become a professor in Palermo. The Venetian comic dramatist Carlo Goldoni (1707–1793), who knew him personally, tells us that, "because he was a better talker than writer, he gave up the respectable post he held and decided to go on the stage to harangue the public". Not rich enough to be content with simply earning applause, "he made use of his talent and sold medicines", whereby he surrounded himself with four actors as a means of entertaining the "ignorant public".

There are actors in Tiepolo's painting, too, albeit not four, but three: a harlequin – a buffoon who made the public laugh with crude jokes – in a black facemask bending down towards his audience and gesticulating; behind him, an attractive young woman silently holding her fan; and to the rear, with her back towards us, another woman with handkerchiefs in her hands. According to Goldini, the actors who worked with "Anonymous" first helped their master collect the money, "which people threw into handkerchiefs". They then "threw back these same handkerchiefs filled with little boxes", containing the miraculous remedies. The players then went on to perform a three-act comedy.

Tiepolo's painting, which measures 80 by 110 cm, is filled with accurately observed details. The actors and their handkerchiefs, the monkey and the standard – all serve to evoke the theatrical flamboyance with which every travelling charlatan had to make his appearance. For only someone with a loud voice and accompanied by the most exotic menagerie possible could draw the necessary crowd, and only someone who acted as if he was already wealthy from his successes in other parts could hope to win the confidence of his audience. Some of these faith healers travelled from town to town accompanied by a huge train of followers. One such was Johann Christian Hüber, who arrived in Memmingen on 2 July 1724 with five carriages. His retinue consisted of 50 people, including women and children, a female dwarf, two heyduck soldiers, two trumpeters, and other musicians, "who could be heard very well on their horns, as well as 18 horses and two camels". Thus the report in the town chronicle.

Giandomenico Tiepolo painted a good dozen carnival scenes, all of them treasure troves for historians of everyday 18th-century life. For the rest of us, their enduring fascination lies in the movement that infuses the canvas, the confusion that is never chaotic, the colours, and the small dramas the artist sets out before us. Above all, however, Tiepolo's carnival scenes convey the Venetian delight in illusion, the playful desire or urgent need to make the world seem different and more beautiful than it really is.

The artist thereby shows us strikingly few faces. This is true even in his portrayals of rural and urban subjects devoid of masks. Figures seen in rear view are a characteristic feature of his painting. The artist had a tendency to keep the individuality of his figures hidden.

For a long time, Giandomenico Tiepolo was himself a man without a clear identity. He was one of those many sons entirely overshadowed by their famous fathers – in his case, Giambattista Tiepolo, the celebrated artist who for many decades decorated the patrician palaces of Venice and the princely and royal residences of Europe with frescoes and paintings. It was Giambattista who conjured the four continents of the earth onto the ceiling of the archbishop's palace in Würzburg and who restored a long-faded glory to the throne room in the Spanish royal palace, with his portrayal of the famous deeds of the king's forebears. He dressed Cleopatra and the Pharaoh's daughter in splendid Venetian robes and furnished the gods and goddesses of Greek mythology with beautiful bodies. And smiling down over everything and everyone he painted was a brilliant blue sky.

Giandomenico worked for his father for over twenty years, up till the latter's death in 1770. He accompanied him to Würzburg and Madrid and executed the less important parts of the decorations covering the vast surfaces of the palace ceilings and walls – so skilfully that no one could see the difference. When painting for his father, he did not sign his work. The relationship between father and son is pointedly characterized – so it seems, at least – in the present painting. Giambattista, the father, is the man holding forth, soberly dressed and facing the public, while Giandomenico, the son, is the stooped and sullen tooth breaker. Comparisons with portraits confirm the resemblances. The same message also seems to be conveyed by the standard: instead of advertising just one person, as was usually the case, it is here publicizing two, one older and one younger.

The Tooth Drawer, perhaps executed while Tiepolo was still in Würzburg, may well offer a disguised reflection of the artist's situation: his dependence upon his father as well, perhaps, as his gratitude for what Giambattista had taught him and the financial rewards it had brought. He had already carried out a few commissions for less important churches single-handedly, albeit fully in his father's style, and even after Giambattista's death he continued to work in the same vein – without success, however. The noble, sublime world that had so uplifted viewers in his father's day no longer matched the spirit of the times. In Giandomenico's hands, it became boring.

The son's interests lay closer to real life. Instead of Zeus hurling a thunderbolt, he paints a charlatan brandishing an extracted tooth. Whereas the father had been handsomely paid to raise each of his patrons up to the heavens, the son places his hero on top of a rickety wooden platform. The beautiful woman looking down proudly onto the audience is not Aphrodite, but a cheap actress who earns her living offstage, too. But who knows, perhaps tomorrow she will be famous; upper and lower are no longer fixed social categories in the failing Serenissima, and during carnival time all such distinctions are blurred behind fans and masks.

The Tooth Drawer is the first of about a dozen carnival pictures executed by Giandomenico. He does not ennoble his figures, but repeatedly tells of their desire for a nobler, more beautiful, easier, and pain-free existence. And he paints the man who sells them such dreams – the soothsayer, faith healer, tooth drawer, charlatan, and master of eloquent speech. With ironic distance, Tiepolo portrays the tooth drawer as a colleague and his customers as Tiepolo's own comrades and fellow sufferers. The artist is painting his own society, his own world. As his father's assistant, he, too, had dealt in dreams and taken regular part in the carnival celebrations of the dying Venetian Republic.

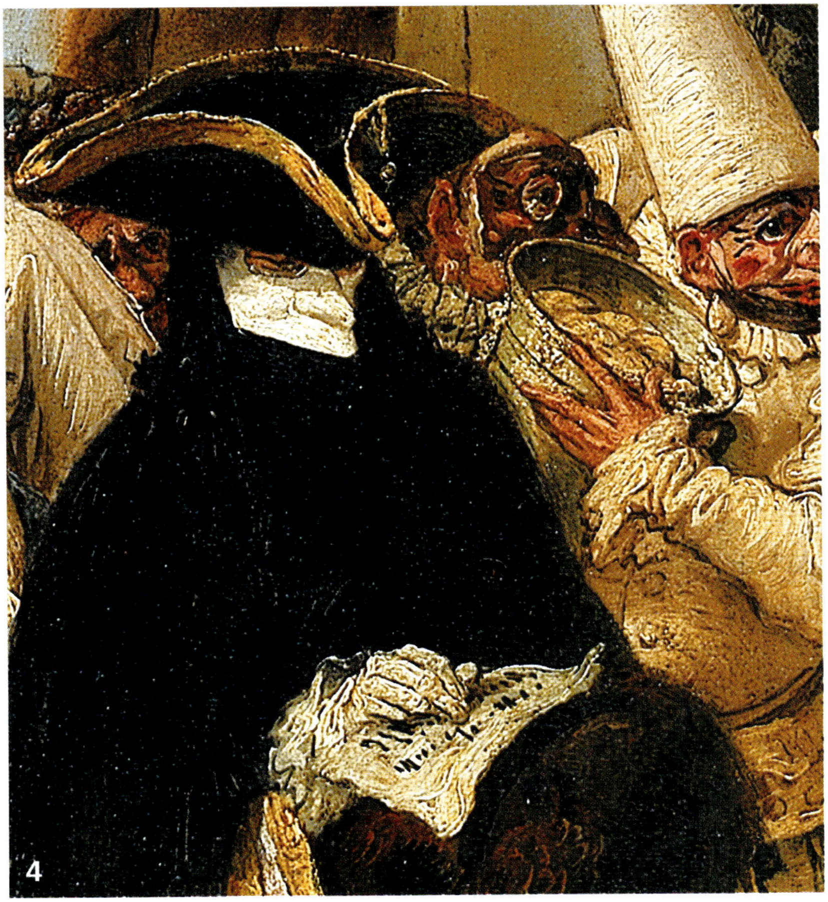

4

The artist, too, dealt in dreams

Bernardo Bellotto, called Canaletto: Dresden Old Town seen from the end of the New Town Bridge, 1765

The jewel in Saxony's crown

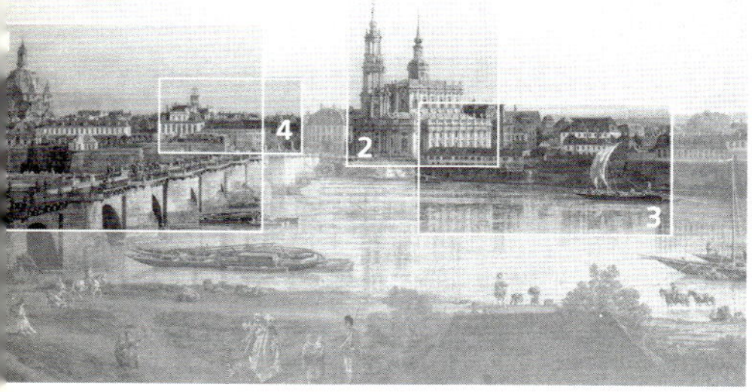

Until its destruction by aerial bombing in 1945, Dresden ranked amongst the most magnificent cities in Germany, and the present view across the river Elbe shows it from its most attractive side. Its splendid architecture arose in the 18th century. In the annals of German history, the 18th century is traditionally seen as belonging to Prussia, and in particular its king, Frederick II, who has come down to us as Frederick the Great. But if we leave aside political and military successes and think of art, culture, and architecture, it is sooner the century of Dresden than of Potsdam and Berlin.

The majority of the buildings for which the capital of Saxony would become famous were erected between 1710 and 1755, i.e. within a time span of some forty years. During this period, the old Elbe bridge was widened and given its characteristic gentle arch. On the site of the former fortifications to the left of the bridge arose a park with a summerhouse and pavilions, which became known as the Brühlsche Terrasse ("Bruhl's terrace"). Behind its leafy gardens soared the vast dome of the new Frauenkirche cathedral, consecrated in 1734. This was followed in 1755 by the Hofkirche with its open-sided spire, which was erected to the right of the bridge in front of the royal palace. Behind the building on the right-hand side of the picture we can just glimpse the Zwinger, a baroque architectural ensemble unique in Europe. It was built between 1711 and 1732.

Not visible in this view across the Elbe are the Japanisches Palais, 1715, the Coselpalais, 1746, the Dreikönigskirche and, most notably, the Stallhof behind the Frauenkirche, which housed Dresden's magnificent art collection. Agents working on behalf of the Saxon government acquired works of art from all over Europe and assembled a collection of some 4000 paintings, including virtually all the masterpieces that continue to make Dresden's Gemäldegalerie Alte Meister famous today: Raphael's *Sistine Madonna* from the monastery of San Sisto, paintings by Titian and Veronese from the collection of the bankrupt Duke of Modena, works by van Dyck, Rubens, and Tintoretto from the Imperial Gallery in Prague, and Rembrandt's *Saskia with Red Flower* from Paris, along with many others.

The buying of works of art, the commissioning of new buildings, the creation of a magnificent townscape, the lavish indulgence of a desire for beauty – all these were possible only with a great deal of money. It came – to start with, at least – from the Erzgebirge, the "Ore Mountains". Annaberg had been supplying a significant proportion of Europe's silver since the 16th century, while Freiburg had developed into a centre of ore mining. Silver and ore made the rulers of Saxony rich, and by the start of the 18th century Saxony was one of the economically most developed of the German states.

Elector of Saxony Augustus the Strong (1670–1733) used this flourishing economy as a springboard to launch him onto a wider political stage. In 1697 he had himself elected king of Poland. Saxony was approximately the size of Bavaria. Poland,

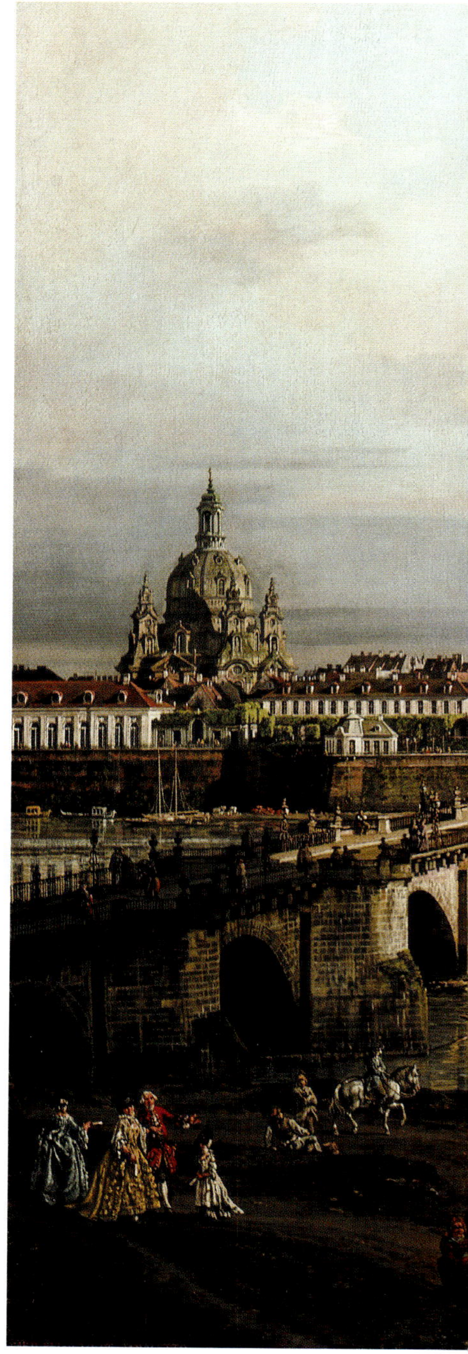

on the other hand, was larger than all the German states put together; it extended from the Baltic to the Black Sea. Augustus' son, Elector Frederick Augustus II (1696–1763), also had himself elected king of Poland. A major influencing factor in these elections was Saxony's wealth, some

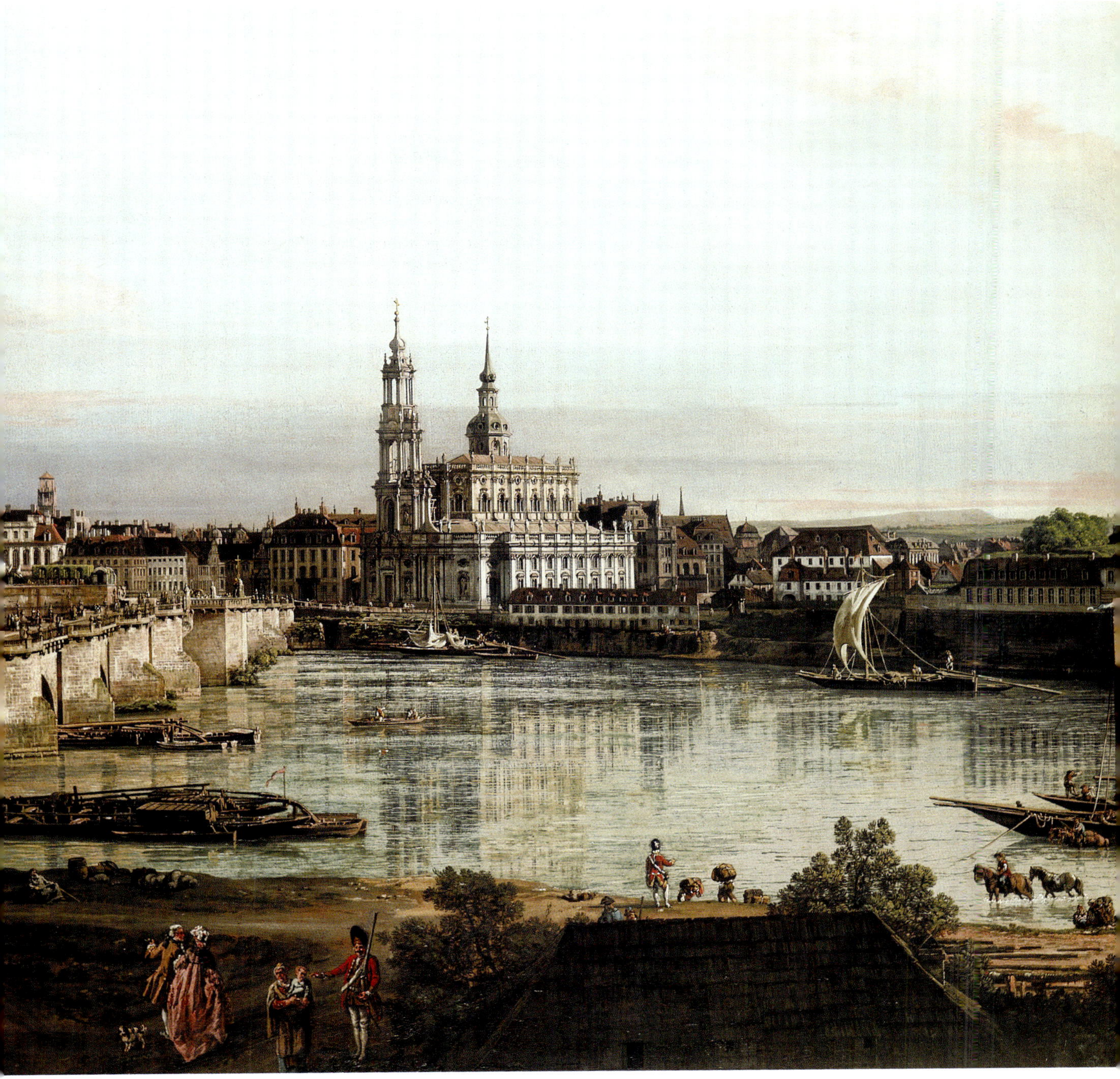

of which was used to buy the support of the Polish aristocracy. Probably no less important for the success of their campaign, however, was the glittering image that the Saxon electors sought to project, their taste for pomp and circumstance.

For the Saxon electors and many of the rulers of the day, lavish display was more than a mere luxury and indulgence. It held a meaning. In their view, the sovereign was not simply the head of his state, but actually personified it. The splendour of his person was the splendour of the State. The lavishness of life at court also drew the rural aristocracy from their regional seats. Obliged to emulate this grand lifestyle, many were forced to live beyond their means. The consequence was impoverishment and hence dependency upon the reigning sovereign. As a young man at the court of Louis XIV in Versailles, Augustus

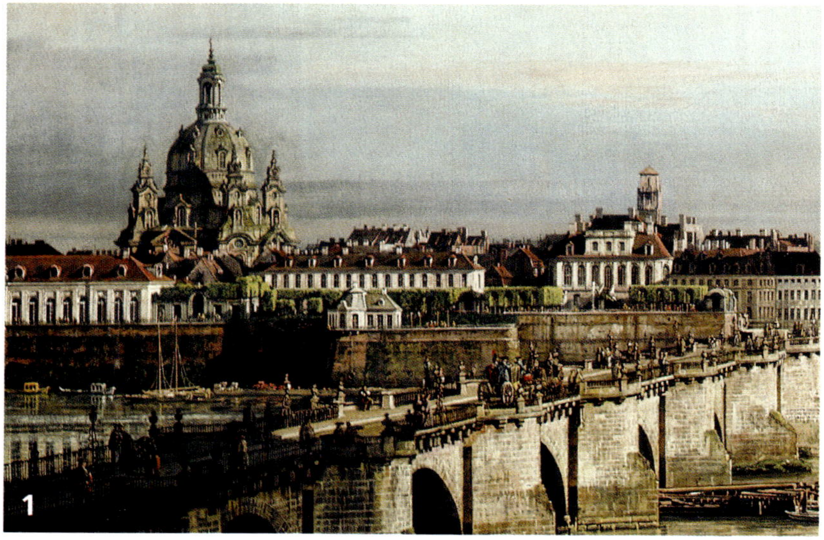

1

the Strong had been able to observe this mechanism of subjugation at work.

Augustus the Strong's appreciation of the expensive pleasures of life was, undoubtedly, at least as keen as his understanding of political necessity. He was a man of great physical strength, with an enthusiastic zest for living and an extraordinary interest in women: his love affairs and the number of children he fathered are legendary. He was not alone in his love of life, however. "The Saxon blood", wrote the Prussian Johann Michael von Loen from Dresden in 1718, "is the finest in Germany. It is fiery, affectionate, and exceedingly wanton. Their licentiousness makes the inhabitants of this land witty, pleasant, polite, and flattering, but also fickle, soft, garrulous, and gluttonous. Because nature has blessed the Saxons with such happy powers of invention, most poets and novelists are to be found amongst them ..."

In his comedy *Minna von Barnhelm*, the Saxon-born Gotthold Ephraim Lessing personifies Prussian and Saxon traits in his two protagonists. For the Prussian Major von Tellheim, honour and king are all that matter; he is a man who, denying his own desires, serves only the state. Playing opposite him is the Saxon Minna. For her, principles are less important than practice. She wants her Tellheim, not some sublime abstract. In defiance of all social convention, she follows him, and uses tricks, charm, and even intrigue in order finally to win him.

A love of beauty, a desire to follow one's feelings, an eagerness to surround oneself with the finer things in life – such characteristics were by no means exclusive to Augustus the Strong and his son Frederick Augustus II, the two electors under whom Dresden rose to become the architectural showcase of Germany. They are nevertheless qualities that might happily have exerted more influence within German history. Even if they are more appropriate to a life of state than to running the state.

The career of a favourite

Across the Elbe, next to the bridge, rise the walls of the old city fortifications. Permission to develop the site was granted to Heinrich von Brühl (1700–1763), the favourite of both the elector-kings. Brühl erected the building on the left-hand edge of the picture to house his picture gallery, and the elongated building next to it for his extensive library. To the right again, slightly set back, is the upper half of his palace. In front of this are pavilions and, on the Jungfernbastei, a small summerhouse. The pride of these gardens, however, lay outside the painting, on the left, and had by now already been destroyed. It was a belvedere offering a view over the Elbe valley, which had been demolished during the Seven Years' War.

Brühl was virtually penniless when he arrived at the Saxon court in 1719. His father was a steward in the employ of the Duke of Sachsen-Weissenfels. The duke was poor, the steward consequently also, and after his death his property had to be sold. Heinrich began his career at the age of thirteen as a page at the Weissenfels court, and at the age of nineteen joined the household of Augustus the Strong. By the age of twenty-seven he had risen to the position of chamberlain, and by thirty to treasurer. He earned his master's trust, evidently performed the tasks given to him better than others, and became the favourite. According to one contemporary: "The favour in which he is held does not seem to make him arrogant: he is gentle, honest, polite, charitable, and ... seems to have no other care but to please his master and to gather himself friends."

Under Augustus the Strong's son, Brühl was also First Minister. He governed on behalf of his master, and since the latter preferred play to work, Brühl effectively ruled single-handedly. Nobody questioned his actions, not even when he paid himself money he felt he was due. He owned extensive properties and maintained a retinue of two hundred people, comparable in size to that of the larger German rulers. Brühl's fortune was gleaned not solely from the king's coffers; he also profited from others. One minor example is Bernardo Bellotto, who arrived at the Dresden court in 1747. The elector and king had really wanted to engage Bellotto's uncle, Antonio Canal, but he was in London. So he invited the most important artist in Canal's workshop, his nephew, who like his uncle also used the name Canaletto. He was appointed court painter and was paid the highest salary ever awarded to a painter in Dresden: 1750 thalers a year. Brühl was also in charge of the king's art collection. From Bellotto's point of view, he was thus the most powerful person in Dresden. How else are we to explain the fact that Bellotto painted twenty-one views of Dresden for him, none of which Brühl ever paid for? That was only four less than the total that Bellotto, in all his eleven years in Dresden, painted for the king who paid him his annual salary. King and favourite each got identical motifs; Brühl owned the same works as his master. He used them to adorn the main room of his palace, clearly visible in the present painting with its tall windows. It was called the Canaletto Room.

In 1739, on the banks of the Elbe near the bridge and in front of the palace, the foundation stone was laid for what records describe no more specifically than as a "certain building". There were reasons for such secrecy: it was the foundation stone of the Hofkirche, the Catholic court church. Saxony, however, and the capital Dresden, were Protestant, and the elector wanted to avoid provoking unrest. For Saxony was more than just Protestant – it was the homeland of all Lutherans, and its electors had sided with the Lutheran states in opposition to the Catholic Emperor. Until 2 June 1697, that is. On that day, Augustus the Strong converted to Catholicism. Only as a Catholic could he become king of Poland, and only as the ruler of a country of that size could he become a force in European politics.

Augustus' action was that of an enlightened monarch who had modelled himself on Macchiavelli. Religion served him as a means to achieve his personal ambitions. For his fellow Saxons, however, his conversion came as a shock. They feared the Counter-Reformation would regain the upper hand; they were afraid that they would all be forced to convert, for since the Peace of Westphalia, the sovereign dictated the religion of his land. As late as 1731, 20,000 Protestants in Austria had to leave the bishopric of Salzburg because they didn't want to renounce their faith. In this respect, too, Augustus was "enlightened" in his attitude. He let it be known that his conversion was a personal affair.

It was not easy to build a Catholic church in Protestant Dresden. Augustus the Strong initially made do with a chapel inside his palace, but then converted it into an opera house. It was his son Frederick Augustus II – another convert and married to a Catholic Austrian archduchess – who finally commissioned the building of a new church. It probably carried slightly less of a risk for him than for his father, since Dresden had only just seen the completion, in 1734, of the Protestant Frauenkirche. But there were no Catholic architects in Saxony. The court had a number of plans sent from Italy and settled on Gaetano Chiaveri, who had already designed buildings in Warsaw, the second, royal seat of the Saxon electors.

Behind the Hofkirche can be seen a tower belonging to the palace; the two buildings needed to be close so that they could be linked by a covered walkway. Before the foundation stone could be laid, a number of smaller buildings had to be pulled down, the remains of the city fortifications removed, the ground level raised, and two of the bridge's arches filled in. The Hofkirche was completed in 1755. Amongst its distinctive features are the seventy-eight statues on its roof, designed by Lorenzo Mattielli. The figures on the front of the tower are those venerated by both Catholics and Protestants alike. They are succeeded towards the rear by a number of the Catholic saints whose worship Luther had so unequivocally rejected, as well as by such heroes of the Counter-Reformation as the militant Ignatius of Loyola, founder of the Jesuit Order.

The Catholic patrons had a free hand on the rooftop, but not in the Protestant streets below. According to the municipal statutes, only Protestant – and more specifically, Lutheran-churches were permitted in Dresden. Even the Calvinists had to make do with chapels. Since the Hofkirche was not recognized as a church, it was not allowed to toll any bells. Nor were the Catholics permitted to walk in procession through the streets of Dresden; instead, they staged such processions inside the church.

But the Hofkirche would not remain silent for ever. When Saxony allied itself with Napoleon, he elevated it to the status of a kingdom by way of thanks and permitted the royal court church to ring out its bells. In 1945 it was destroyed. It has since been rebuilt and is the only building in Bellotto's *veduta* that today looks exactly as it did when Bellotto painted it.

A church that wasn't allowed to be one

2

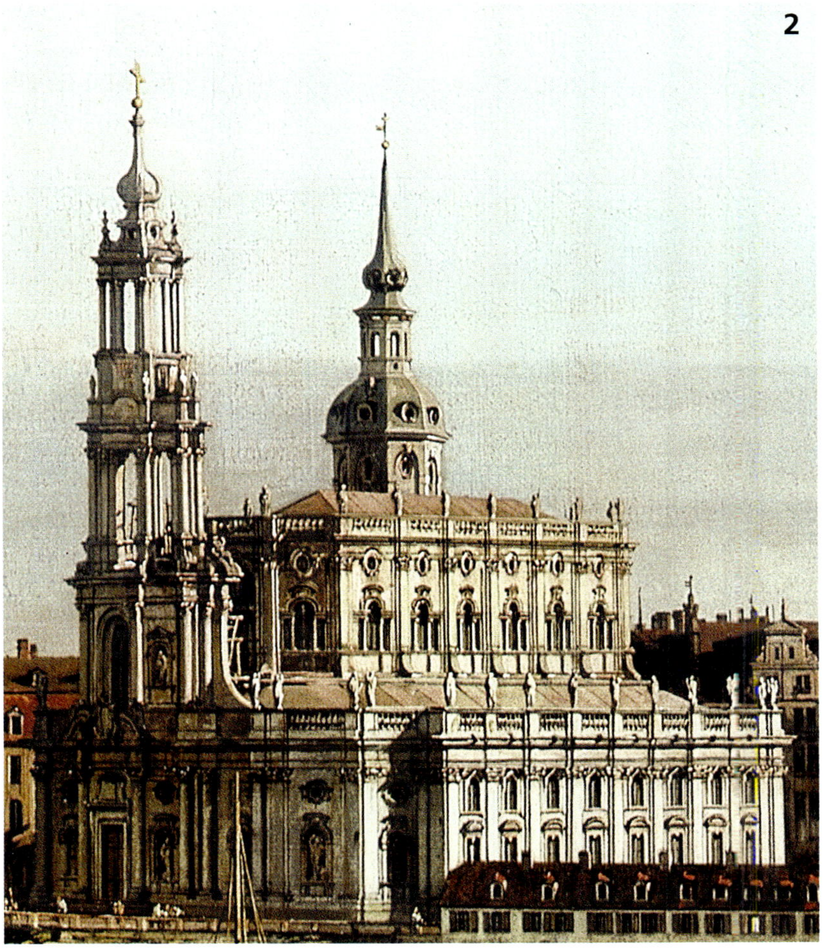

The building above the sail was the opera house; visible to the right of it is part of the French Pavilion belonging to the Zwinger complex. In the 19th century Gottfried Semper would build his new (and today restored) Opera between the old opera house and the Zwinger. Music, and in particular opera, played a dominant role in Dresden's cultural life in the 18th century, too. The pieces performed were rarely German, however. The two most important Saxon composers of the day, Bach and Handel, were working in Leipzig and London respectively. In Dresden, the Italians had the upper hand, even if a German, Johann Adolf Hasse, was engaged for a while as Kapellmeister to the Saxon court. He had studied in Venice and brought with him to Dresden his wife, Faustina Bordoni, the famous soprano.

Opera was staged at many courts; it spoke to the desire of Europe's rulers to parade the magnificence of their lifestyle. It combined music, drama, ballet, and art into a glittering tribute to an individual sovereign. Such triumphal performances did not come cheap; it cost 11,000 thalers to stage Hasse's opera *Cleofilde* in Dresden in 1731. By comparison, Brühl was supposed to pay Bellotto 200 thalers per picture. Painting was a particularly affordable art. According to reliable estimates, the 4000 pictures in the Dresden Gemäldegalerie were purchased for a total of just two million thalers. Alone the ceremonial robes that Augustus the Strong commissioned for his coronation in Poland had cost one million thalers.

The Italians living in Dresden were not all musicians. They were also stucco workers, tile layers, assistants to Chiaveri, painters, sculptors, art dealers, and cooks, for example. Thus records reveal that two court cooks by the names of Vulcani and Pereni lived in the terrace of houses in front of the Hofkirche (on the left of the detailed view shown here). The majority of these Italians lived in small houses, visible through the gap to the right of the sail, which formed part of the elector's estate and were referred to collectively as the "Italian village". A restaurant on the riverbank calls itself by this name even today.

There were some 50,000 people living in Dresden in the mid-18th century. From the First Minister and Lord Chamberlain right down to the stable lads, bakers, blacksmiths, and food suppliers, the majority were employed directly or indirectly by the court and in the running of the state. Dresden itself was not a centre of trade – that role was played by neighbouring Leipzig. As a shipping route, the Elbe was only of secondary importance: it had not been dredged or canalized and was only navigable in sections, and even then only in flat-bottomed boats with a mast that could be lowered.

Something already apparent in the present detail emerges even more clearly from city maps of Dresden from the 1700s, namely the proximity of poor and rich, of palace and humble dwellings. Despite the presence of architectural complexes such as the Zwinger, which were not open to everyone, the city had yet to evolve into distinct districts associated with different levels of income. This process would be triggered by industrialization, as cities expanded and ordinary citizens grew rich. Unable to mark themselves out with coats of arms and impressive names, these *nouveaux riches* sought to set themselves apart from their less successful fellows by establishing their own residential districts. The aristocracy of the 18th century did not yet need to do the same.

An Italian village in the Saxon capital

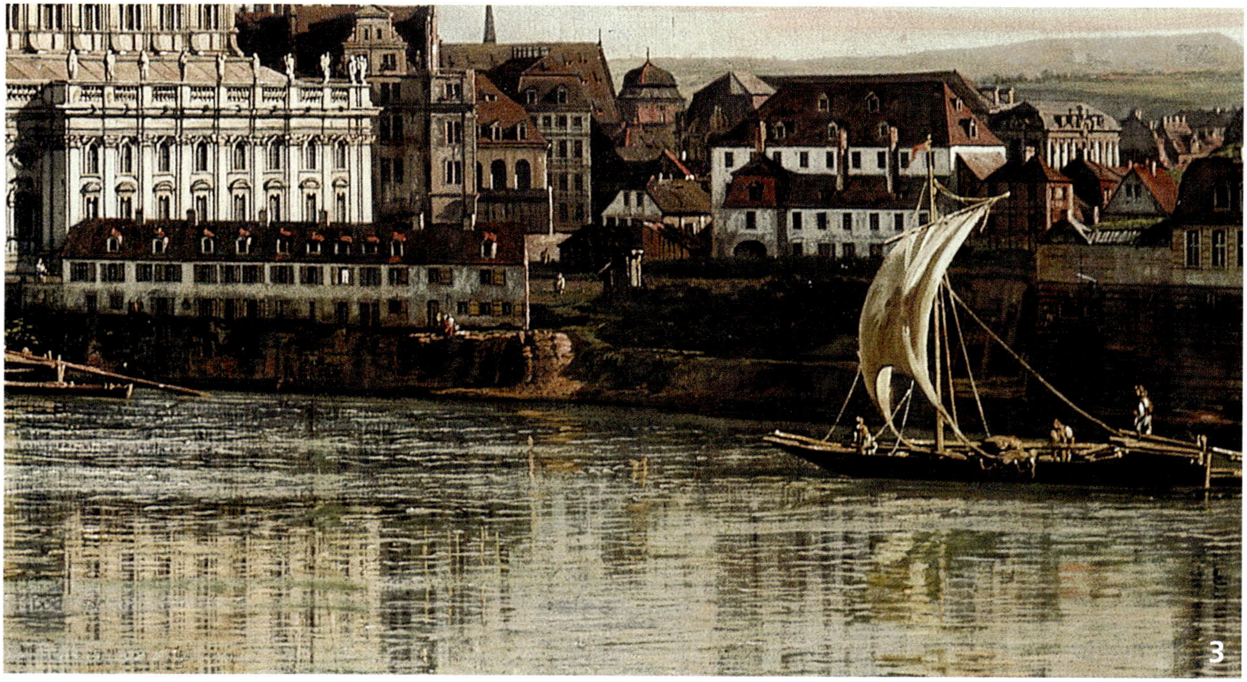

3

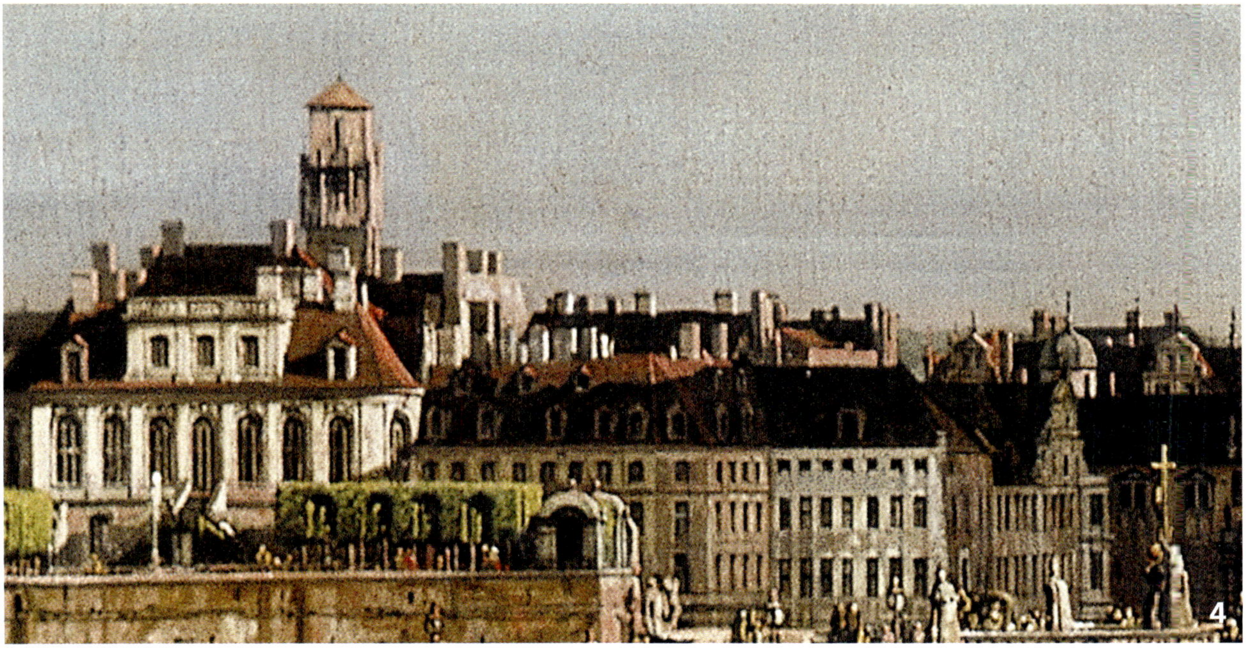

Bellotto executed his painting in 1765, probably before 22 June. He must at least have completed the drawing before then, because on this date the tower that can be seen rising behind Brühl's palace collapsed. The tower formed part of the Kreuzkirche church and had already been damaged by the Prussians in 1760.

The Seven Years' War (1756–63) had exposed Saxony's weakness. Lying helplessly between Prussia and Austria, its allegiance see-sawing between both, it became a battlefield. Dresden did not escape the consequences. In 1759 Frederick the Great occupied the city, visited the art gallery, took nothing away with him, but destroyed minister-president Brühl's pride and joy, the Belvedere. Frederick hated Brühl on account of the lack of transparency with which the favourite conducted his political affairs. In 1760 Dresden was then occupied by the Austrians. The Prussians besieged and bombarded the city for two weeks, reducing more than half its houses and many of its churches to rubble. Bellotto's beautiful view across the Elbe shows little more than a façade that has been left standing by chance.

Brühl played a major part in this disaster. He had served his master, not his country. "Amuser le Roi" was the favourite's motto, and his policy was to keep from the king anything that might upset him, while at the same time collecting in more and more money in order to finance the king's ambitions. Saxony was ruined not by the cost of palaces, churches, hunting, clothes, opera, and paintings, but by the money lavished on the Polish venture, the attempt, as an elected king, to enter the grander political arena. Saxony's millions vanished in Poland and in the Polish-Swedish war. There was nothing left to fund an army to defend the Saxon homeland. Within weeks of Frederick the Great's invasion in 1756, Saxony's generals were forced to capitulate.

If Poland had made Saxony poor, the destruction and forced contributions of the Seven Years' War ruined it. Dresden lost not just eight hundred buildings, but a quarter of its population. Many left to settle elsewhere, especially the foreigners. Art was no longer in demand. In 1759 Bellotto departed first for Vienna and then Munich, only returning to Dresden in 1761, when the end of the war was in sight. His house, too, lay in ruins.

In 1763 peace was concluded. The king and Brühl returned from Warsaw and it seemed as if the former splendour of court life would be reborn from amidst the ruins. But the king died, followed soon afterwards by his favourite. After the king's death, the court began to embrace the view that the sovereign should be there for his subjects, and not the other way round. That meant less extravagance, less money – and not just out of urgent necessity. Italian musicians and artists were dismissed, and Bellotto was given a job teaching perspective at the Academy of Art. It was for the Dresden Academy that he painted the present picture. Since private commissions were now few and far between, in 1767 he moved to Warsaw. The numerous topographical views that he proceeded to paint of Warsaw would later be consulted in the rebuilding of the city after the Second World War. He died in Warsaw in 1780.

Dresden was destroyed more than just once

In February 1945 the old Dresden was razed to the ground. By then, however, much of the cityscape recorded by Bellotto had already changed. In place of the old opera house and the Italian village lay the Theaterplatz and the Semperoper. On the site of Brühl's palace stood the parliament building. The old Elbe bridge had been pulled down and rebuilt with bigger arches to facilitate the passage of shipping. In 1814 a flight of steps was built next to the Elbe bridge, leading up to the Brühlsche Terrasse: the favourite's splendid gardens were finally to be made accessible to all citizens.

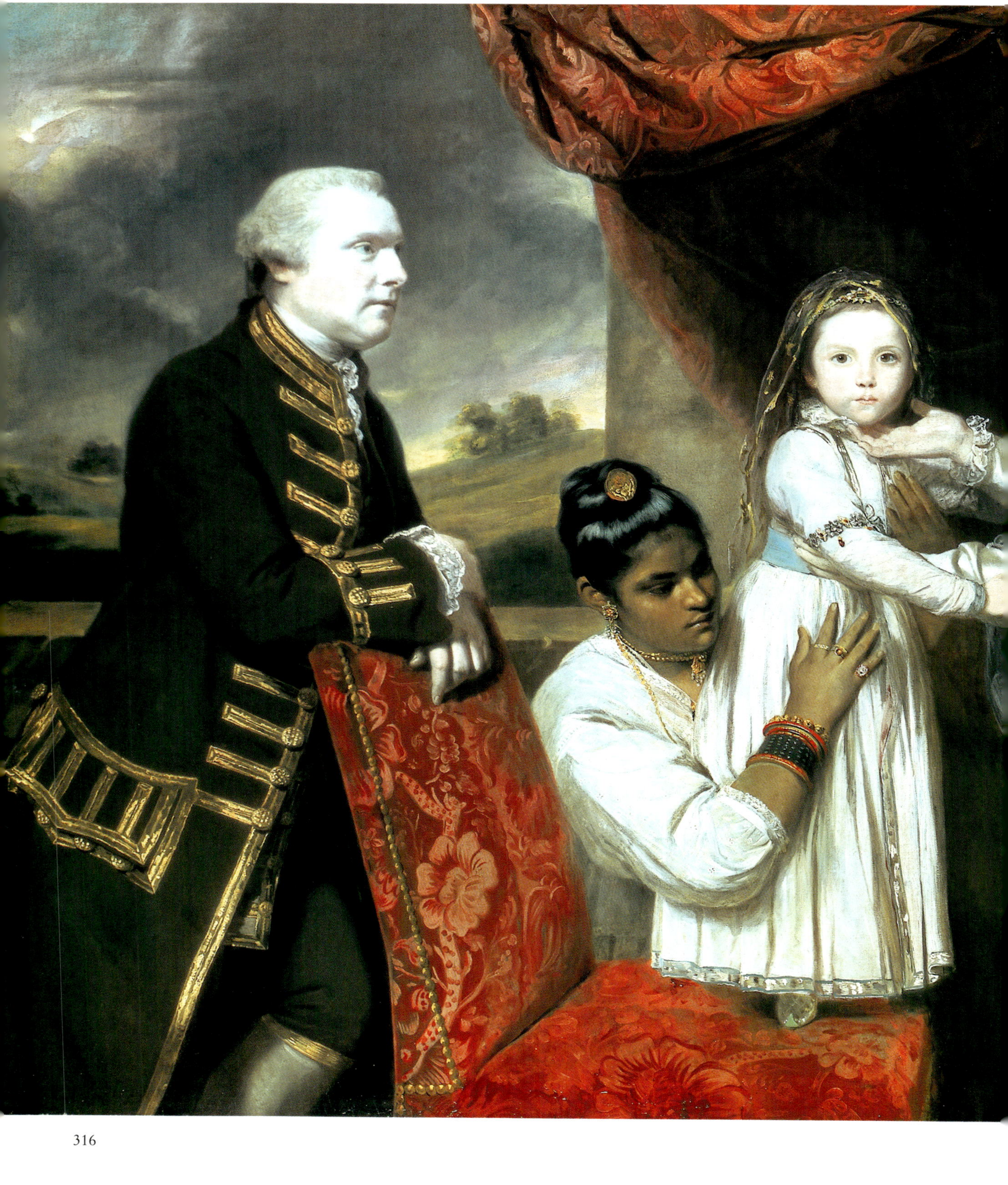

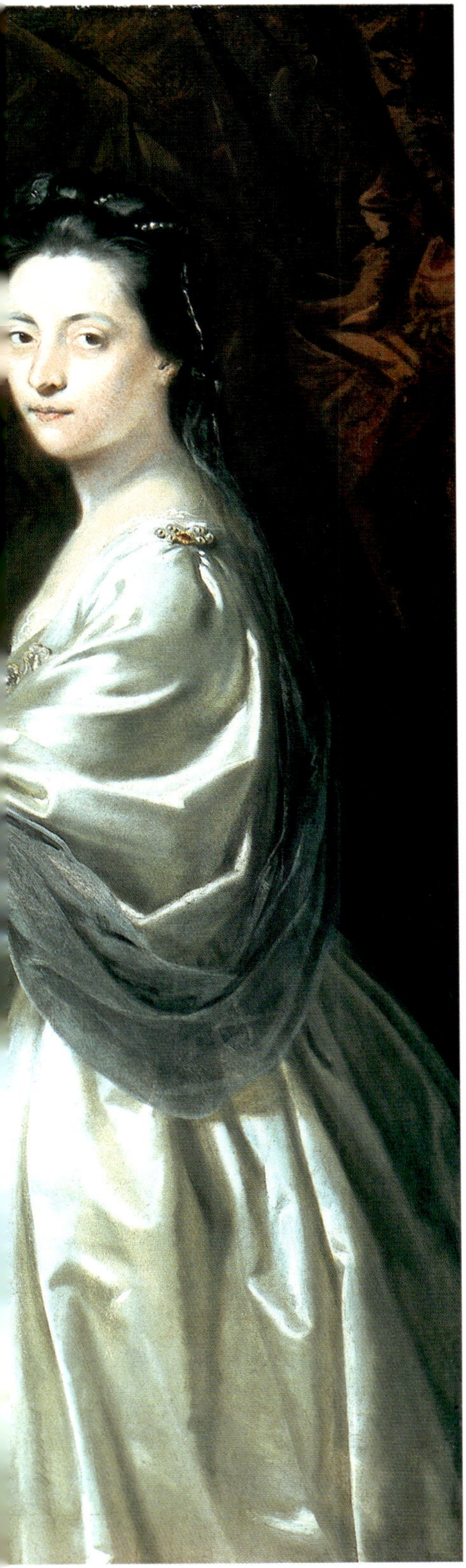

Sir Joshua Reynolds: George Clive with his Family and an Indian Maidservant, c. 1765

Those with no prospects in England go to India

Two adults, one child – and a maidservant. Sir Joshua Reynolds (1723–1792) was the portraitist of the British upper classes. With his carefully balanced compositions he created an impression of order and tradition. Heavy drapes provided a sumptuous backdrop to the individuals in front.

It was uncommon to include domestic servants in family portraits, and the nursemaid's lowly position is given visible expression in the fact that, while the parents and child are standing, she is the only one kneeling. The man is looking at his wife and child, the child and wife are looking out at the viewer; only the maidservant must lower her eyes.

Had she been a white woman, it is highly unlikely that she would have been pictured with her employers, but she is Indian. She is wearing Indian jewellery, and not only her own manner of dress, but also that of the pale little girl – silk, bangle, veil – indicate that far-off India played a role in the life of this family.

For the 1700s were not only the century of the Enlightenment, of nascent industrialization, of the French Revolution, but also the century of advancing globalization. The Europeans were establishing new trading stations and military outposts all over the world, and were fighting each other over their newly claimed territories.

England was thereby more successful than other countries. Its king, George III, was simultaneously Elector of Hanover, but his island subjects had few commercial interests on the European mainland. They saw their future on the seas, and invested in the building of merchant vessels that if necessary could also be deployed as warships.

Sea captains and merchants made their fortunes and began to change the rigid structure of English society. The old-established families of the land-owning aristocracy were now joined by those who returned from overseas as wealthy men.

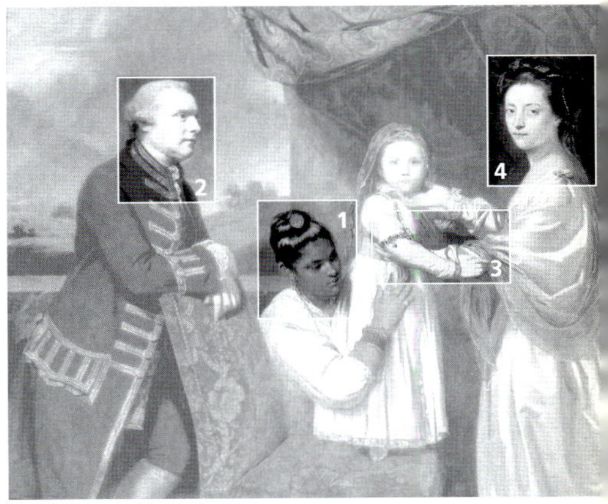

The Clives, too, were amongst the colonial profiteers who had risen in society. The Indian servant in their family portrait serves as a sort of emblem.

Not a slave, but family property

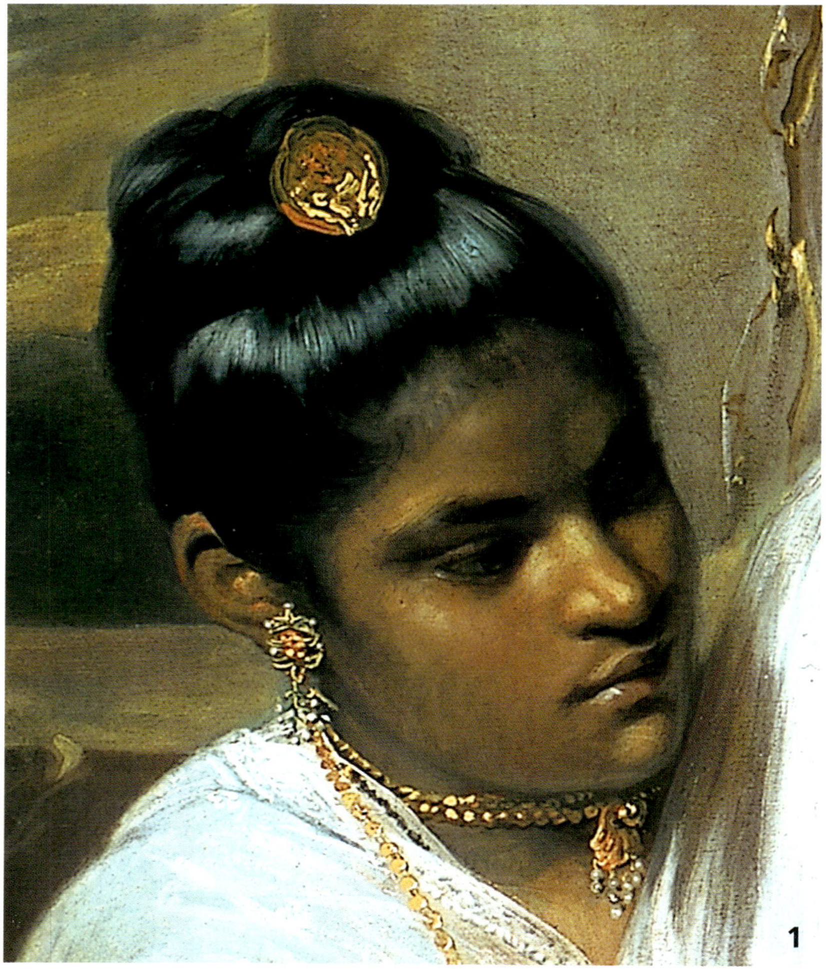

1

Overseas trade was no longer a matter of shipping gold from Mexico or spices from Asia back to Europe, as the Venetian Republic and Spain had done in the past. The 18th century saw the establishment of worldwide trading networks. The most famous example was the triangle between Europe, Africa, and the Caribbean: the British sailed out to West Africa in ships laden with arms, used the proceeds to buy slaves who they then transported to the Caribbean, where they loaded up with tobacco and sugar for England.

At the time this picture was painted, the English crown was still uninterested in India. The landowners who dominated parliament cared little about acquiring overseas territories. The vision of a global empire was still indistinct. Government involvement went only as far as regulating trade with India. In 1600, Queen Elizabeth I had granted a monopoly to the East India Company, making it the only company permitted commercial dealings with and within the distant continent.

In order to defend its foreign trading posts and friendly Indian princes, the London-based East India Company – a public corporation – maintained its own army. This army extended its protection over an ever larger area and at the same time exerted an increasing influence upon internal Asiatic trade. Not until 1773, almost a decade after the present portrait arose, would the East India Company, by now playing an almost governmental role in India, be brought under the control of the Crown.

The young, dark-skinned woman was not a slave, but belonged to that class of Indians who were treated almost like property by their own princes and by British merchants. Europeans saw India as a land of adventure and a place to make one's fortune. The journey by sea took six months, but once there the British could become vastly rich in a very short space of time. They were able to cultivate a lifestyle they could never have afforded in London: a domestic staff of one hundred was considered nothing unusual, and would include someone to carry the hookah, a hairdresser, a wig-maker, and a group of litter-bearers.

Not that any of this was possible on the fixed salaries paid by the East India Company alone. The money came from other sources. Financial bribes discreetly tendered by local princes and other traders soon added up and led the company's servants to act in their own interests rather than those of their employer. "Corruption, Licentiousness and a want of Principle seem to have possessed the Minds of all Civil Servants", wrote Robert Clive of the situation in Calcutta; "by frequent bad examples", the English had grown greedy and prodigal "beyond Conception".

The reason for the situation lay not just in the opportunities that India offered for corruption, but also in the type of ex-patriots who made it their home. Those of good standing in British society remained on their native soil; only those who saw no future for themselves in London, those unable to find a useful role, those happy to make an unscrupulous buck, set sail for Indian shores. This emerges from the diary of the Scottish author James Boswell. As a young man, he sought a commission as an officer in London. He had no luck, and became despairing. In a diary entry of 26 December 1762, he records reviewing in his head "a multitude of wild schemes" – including even the idea of "enlisting for five years as a soldier in India".

Reynolds kept a sitter-book in which he noted down all the people who sat for him for their portraits. In 1764/65 the name "Mrs. Clive" is mentioned several times. This confirms the assumption that the present painting must have been executed in the mid-1760s. When it later went under the hammer in 1817, the auctioneer no longer knew who it portrayed, and called it "Family Group with Black Maidservant".

In 1835 an art dealer claimed it portrayed the family of Robert Clive, the most famous of all English trade pioneers in India. In the 1970s the picture was purchased by the Staatliche Gemäldesammlung in Berlin and subjected to fresh scrutiny. On the basis of comparisons with other portraits and information gleaned about the family members, it is now thought to show not Robert Clive, but his nephew George Clive, who also spent time in India. But in the words of the former director of the Berlin museum, Henning Bock, "we can probably never be absolutely sure".

Both George and Robert Clive were typical of those who were obliged to seek their fortunes outside England. Robert is said to have been a difficult boy; he went from one school to the next until finally, at the age of eighteen, he was packed off to India by his father, a lawyer with a small country estate. He worked as a clerk for the East India Company in Madras, where according to the *New Encyclopædia Britannica* he "was moody and quarrelsome, attempted suicide, and once fought a duel". At the age of 25 he volunteered to go to the military assistance of an Indian prince allied with the English East India Company, who was under siege from another Indian prince allied with the rival French East India Company. With two hundred European and three hundred Indian soldiers, Clive led a diversionary attack. His tactics were successful, and he went on to pocket a fortune. Two years later he returned to England.

He arrived back in 1753. He didn't stay in London for long; by 1755 he was rounding the Cape of Good Hope on his way back to the East Indies. He had been commissioned by the English East India Company to expel the French competition once and for all. Clive won back Calcutta and was made governor of Bengal. He instated a new Indian ruler, who gratefully presented Clive with an estate that brought him in £30,000 a year, together with £234,000 in cash. When the facts of these "gifts" were later uncovered, they sparked angry attacks against him.

In 1760 Clive returned to England. Four years later, the East India Company engaged his services once again. He was sent back to Calcutta to re-establish political order and in particular to stamp out the corruption endemic among the company's servants. For this he earned himself both plaudits and enemies. After his return, he was obliged to defend himself in parliament against accusations of corruption. In 1774 he killed himself.

The *New Encyclopædia Britannica* describes him as a man of "melancholic temperament" on whose health India had by now taken its toll. "Clive's talents were outstanding", it concludes, "his character no more unscrupulous than that of many men of his day, and his work marked the real beginning of the British Empire in India."

Like Robert, George Clive also came from a middle-class family of little means. His father was a rural pastor and a headmaster. It would seem that George failed to find a career in England, for at the age of thirty he departed for India. Five years later he returned – he, too, as a wealthy man. He built himself a large house near London, procured a seat in parliament through his cousin's connections, and from there championed the latter's interests in far-away India. In 1779 he died, with little more being known about him.

A pastor's son makes good

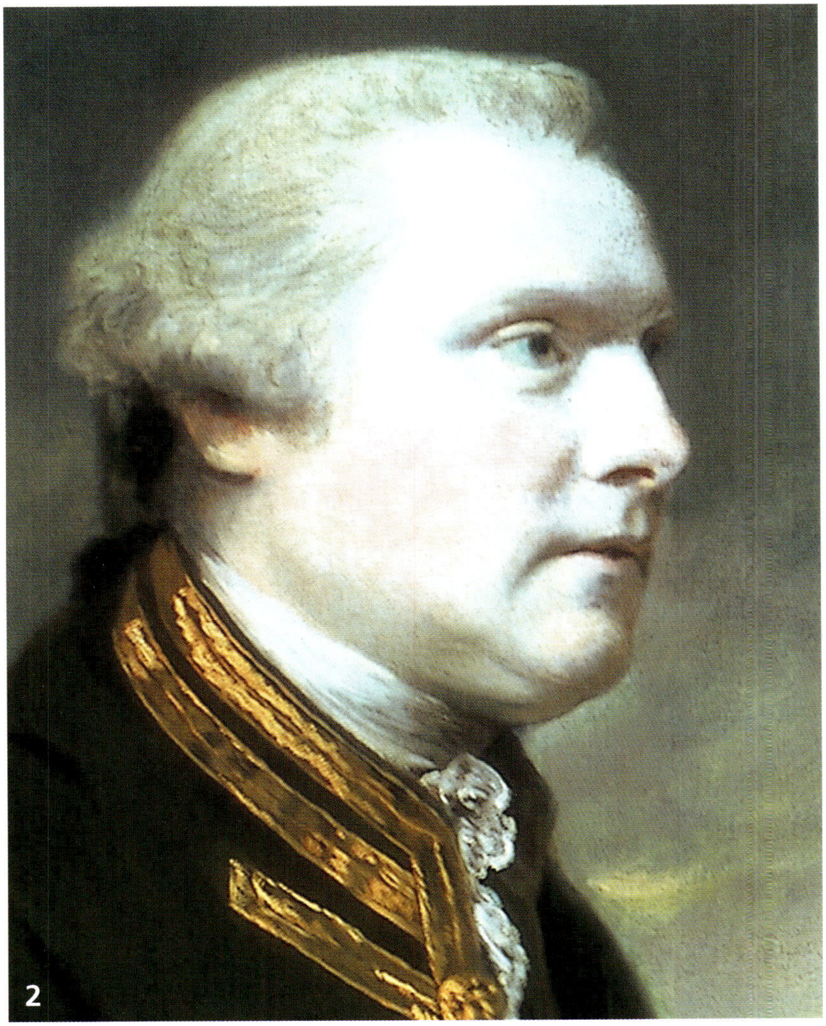

2

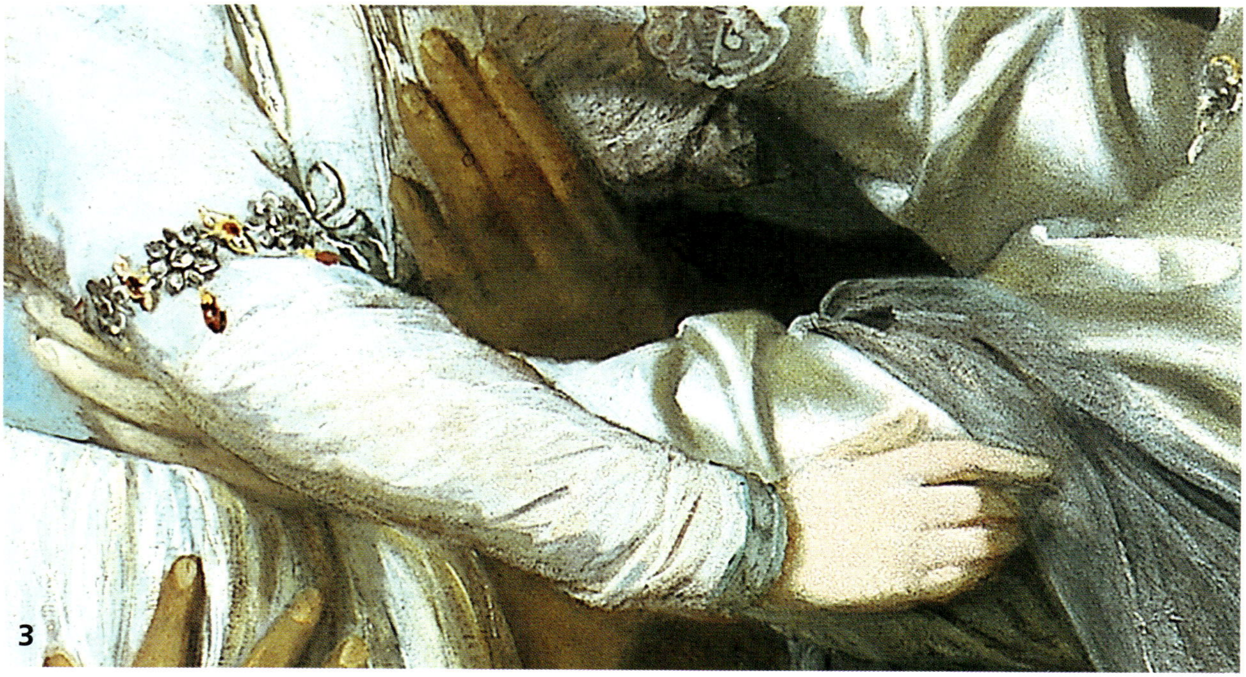

A dignified portrait in timeless dress

In 1764 George Clive's wife gave birth to a daughter. The little girl's age in this portrait can thus be reckoned in months rather than years – no wonder she has to be held up by her mother and her maid. She would not yet have possessed the well-proportioned figure that Reynolds gives her here, and she would most certainly have been incapable of such an elegant stance, in which she offers us a glimpse of a dainty foot beneath her dress. Children's hands at that age are also chubbier, and the fingers are normally curled rather than straight.

Hands were in any case never Reynolds' strong point. At times it appears as if he left them right to the end, as can be seen in the case of the maidservant. Her right hand, with its rings and bracelets, is portrayed with close attention to detail, whereas her left hand, supporting the little girl under her arm, remains ill-defined, and its fingers considerably longer than those of the hand on the front of the dress. In fact, this left hand was probably executed not by Reynolds, but by a member of his workshop. Reynolds himself usually sketched in the overall composition, painted the heads and those details he considered important, and then left the rest to his pupils or a fabrics expert.

Reynolds was considered an artist who not only captured a particularly accurate likeness of his sitters, but who also surrounded them with a discreet aura. "He ... who in his practice of portrait-painting wishes to dignify his subject", he declared in his seventh *Discourse on Art*, delivered to the Royal Academy in 1776, "will not paint her in modern dress, the familiarity of which alone is sufficient to destroy all dignity".

This is also true of Mrs Clive. Her dress, with its silk scarf fastened to the shoulder and looped over her arm, bears no relation to the fashions of the day, but is intended to capture "the general air of the antique". Such references to antiquity are even more emphatic in other paintings by Reynolds. Thus he portrayed a Mrs Hartley as a nymph, for example, and a Mrs Patrick as Juno.

Part of the artistic intention of a family portrait was to illustrate the importance of the individuals within it and their relationship to one another. In most cases, the standing husband towers above his seated wife and is thus symbolically portrayed as the head of the family. In the portrait of the Clives, this is different: husband and wife are both standing, probably for reasons of compositional symmetry. The child, on the other hand, is positioned somewhat lower, and the maidservant lowest of all, in line with her social rank.

The head of the Indian maid, however, is located at the very centre of the composition, and thus in an important place. An X-ray of the painting has revealed that it is made up of two sections of canvas sewn together. It is likely that the original plan was to paint just the mother, child, and servant, and that the decision to incorporate the husband came later. None of this can be seen on the painting's surface. The maidservant only found herself in the centre of the composition when the second canvas was added. To avoid over-emphasis upon her head, Reynolds – as the X-ray also reveals – extended the wall in the background further leftwards, painting over the bright clouds in the original background.

A striking feature of the present portrait is the close juxtaposition of the three female figures. It may have been dictated by the format of the original composition. But it also fell in line with 18th-century convention: only when the only child was a boy was he shown at his father's side, for the son would inherit the title and family estate. The bloodline was continued through the men, not the women.

Reynolds' remarkable facility for characterizing the people in his portraits is evident in the head of the young mother. Her eyes look out at the viewer from a face that is half turned towards her daughter. Reynolds thereby creates an impression of movement. Mrs Clive's expression appears reserved, perhaps timid, and her lips seem somewhat pursed. She is supporting her daughter with both hands, but – in contrast to the maidservant – at a slight distance, as if she is obliged to remember her role as wife and lady of the house as well as mother. It is a face that provokes questions and which thereby testifies to the skill of the artist.

There were some 2000 portraitists working in London in Reynolds' day, and judging their works was a social pastime. "Temple and I breakfasted with Captain Blair", noted James Boswell in his diary entry of 20 June 1763, "after which we went and saw Reynolds's portraits, which pleased us much. I then went with Erskine and had some games at billiards".

Portraiture, the only genre of art to be fashionable in England, was practised in the 18th century by a number of outstanding masters. Reynolds and Thomas Gainsborough (1727–1788) are the best known. Before them, England had strangely failed to produce any great artists. It had brought forth extraordinary talents in every other sphere – in literature, theatre, and music, for example – but not in painting and sculpture. The gap was filled by foreigners. Hans Holbein, Anthony van Dyck, and numerous Italians worked in England; agents in Venice, Florence, and Rome, acting on behalf of English collectors, bought up works, which then disappeared into castles and mansions.

This situation changed in Reynolds' lifetime, not least as a result of his own efforts. Like the two Clives, he came from modest circumstances. He was born in 1723 as the seventh of eleven children. His father was a headmaster. Like the Clives, Reynolds first had to earn his fortune. In 1760 he took a large house in Leicester Fields, a smart area of London, where he could receive clients from the ruling classes in suitable surroundings. He lived there like a prince of painters, even if – most unaristocratically – he was always working.

The king appointed him the first president of the newly founded Royal Academy of Arts, through which he was able to raise standards of training and organize public exhibitions of the work of British artists. He himself was a great buyer of paintings, and his private collection is supposed to have been the largest of its day in England. In 1792, following his death, Christie's auction house put up over 400 pictures for sale, including Rembrandt's *Susanna and the Elders*, a painting that, like the portrait of the Clive family, today hangs in the Staatliche Gemäldesammlung in Berlin.

If portraiture would awaken the urge amongst Reynolds' compatriots to establish a British school of painting, its own popularity was founded on factors unrelated to art. Portraits were a statement of social success. They had a utility value, especially for families who had amassed a rapid fortune through trade and foreign postings. Like aristocrats whose wealth accrued from the family estates, they could afford to be painted by expensive artists, in portraits that elevated them to a class into which they were not born

A face posing questions

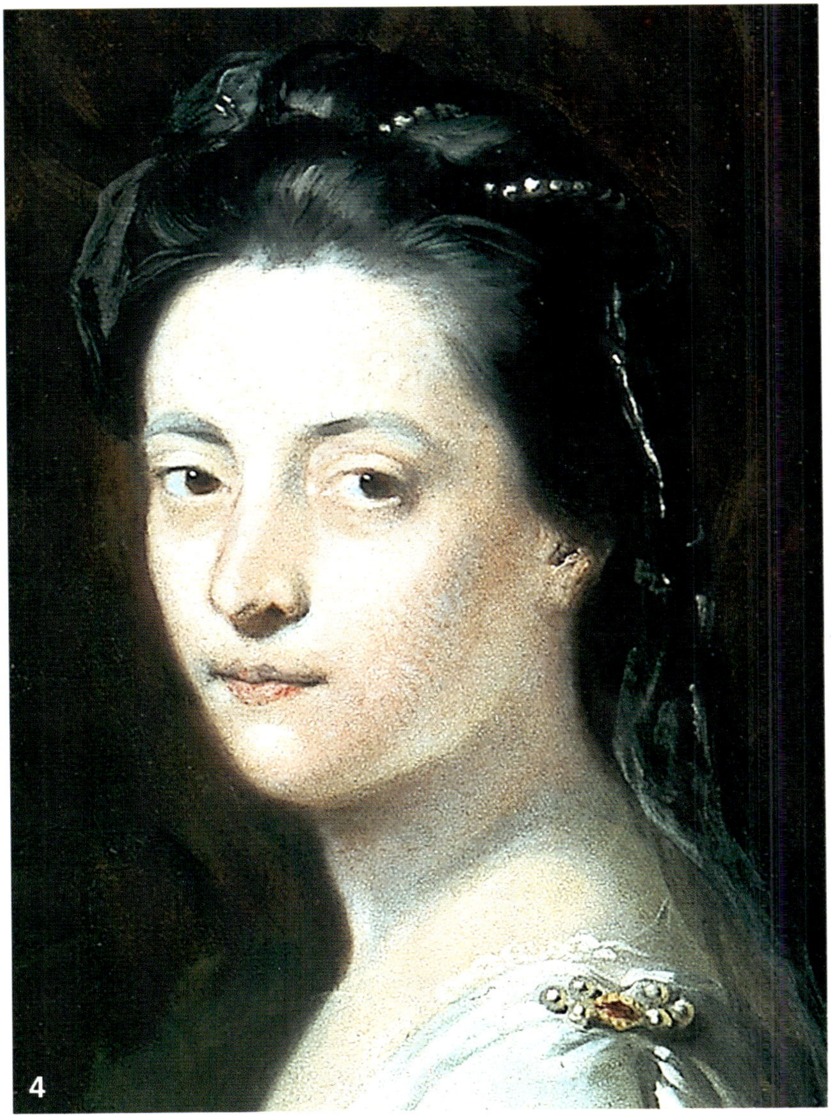

4

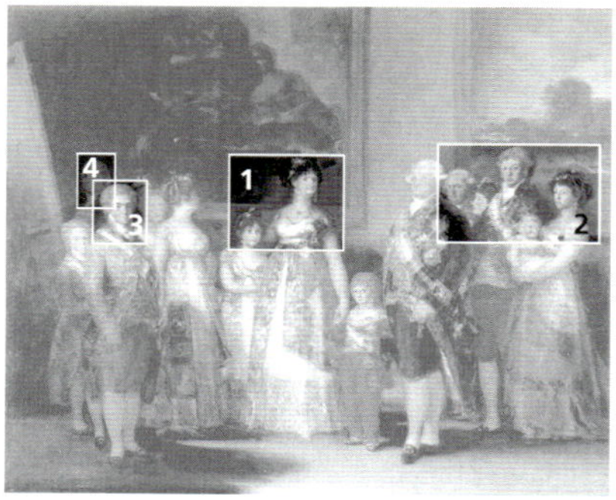
4
1
3
2

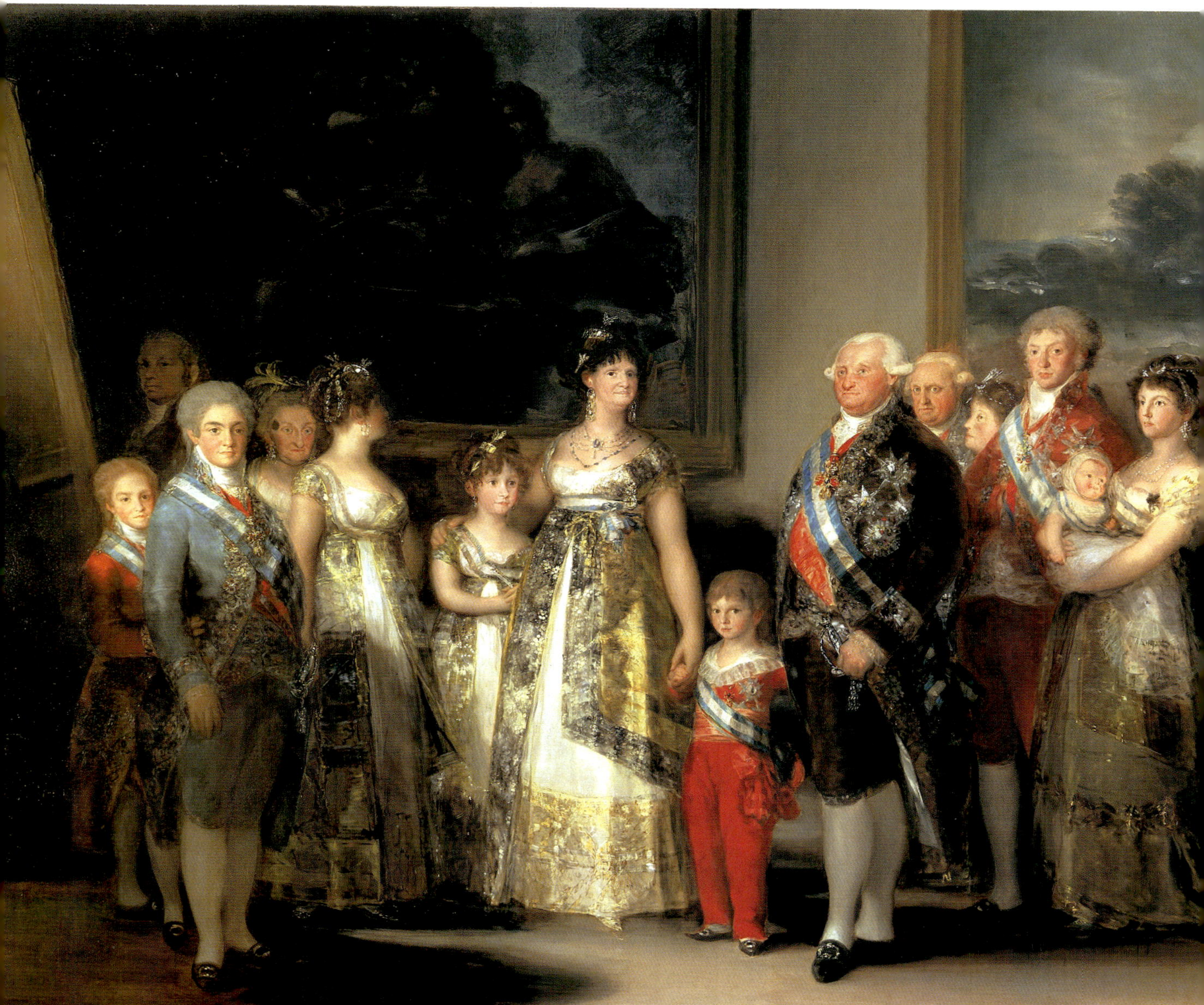

Francisco de Goya: The Family of Charles IV, 1800

Yesterday's people

On 14 July 1800 the French defeated the Austrian army at Marengo in Italy. Commander-in-chief was Napoleon Bonaparte, thirty years of age, First Consul, and leader of France for the past seven months. The *coup d'état* that had brought him to power, the forced march over the Alps to Italy, his courage and energy – all demonstrated that he was the new man.

On that same day, 14 July 1800, Queen Maria-Luisa of Spain wrote to her lover: "Goya has done my portrait, he says it's the best of them all. Now he's painting the King in the Casa del Labrador." This "farmer's house" was a small château set within the shady gardens of Aranjuez, the summer residence of the Spanish court, and was a favourite with King Charles IV. In this oasis of peace and quiet, Goya executed the preliminary studies for his painting of the royal family. It had been commissioned to commemorate the tenth anniversary of the royal couple's accession to the throne.

The celebrations at the coronation itself had been uncomfortably disturbed by the events taking place in neighbouring France. Amidst the violent upheavals of the Revolution, the Bastille had just fallen, and with it the privileged status of the nobility, to be followed just a couple of years later by the head of the king himself, Louis XVI, a close relative of Charles IV and, like him, a Bourbon.

In Spain, for the time being, nothing similar occurred, and the old order remained in place. The only uproar of the 18th century was caused in 1766, when the government tried to ban the popular wide coats and floppy hats. Two generations of Bourbon kings had striven, by means of sensible government and strategic international alliances, to straighten out their country. But it remained sparsely populated, with barely ten million inhabitants. Its army, too, was weak (60,000 men) and its economy backward. Spain remained a major power thanks only to its vast overseas possessions, but they lay far away.

As Napoleon's ambassadors reported back to Paris: "In Spain you have the common people with inferior taste, whose chief preoccupations are processions, bull fights, and love in its most brutal form. The middle classes are dissatisfied and are afflicted by the general poverty. The nobility are dying of hunger on lands that are only half cultivated. The king is a weakling, the queen a whore, the crown prince a coward, the favourite widely hated. In short, a country on its knees – it will be as easy as it is necessary to give it a new order." No wonder that Napoleon Bonaparte, in the early days still engaged in vanquishing France's enemies and reorganizing his country, saw Spain as easy game. He drew up his plans. He would thereby deploy the Spanish ruling family looking out at us in Goya's picture like pieces on the chessboard of Europe. These people belonged to the past. The future lay with Napoleon.

A phlegmatic king by the grace of God

Whether the expression reflected on the face of Charles IV is one of majestic benevolence or stupidity is a question upon which his contemporaries were not agreed. In looks, he is supposed to have born a very close resemblance to his maternal grandfather, the French king Louis XIV, who procured the Spanish throne for the Bourbons in 1700. Louis was known for his sense of duty and his passion for work, but of these characteristics the phlegmatic Charles IV inherited nothing. A quiet life was the only thing important to the Spanish king. He would allow nothing to disturb it, not even the loss of his throne and kingdom.

Just like his forebears, the fifty-two-year-old believed himself to be king by the grace of God; he was utterly impervious to "new ideas" of the sort issuing from Revolutionary France. He was the absolute, unrestricted ruler of the Spanish empire, which he viewed as his personal possession, something he could dispose of. He was accountable only to God, and certainly not to his subjects, all of whom he addressed using the familiar form of "you", be they nobles or servants. "At official receptions he liked to slap people hard on the shoulders", wrote one contemporary, "and used to laugh at this sort of joke until he cried. This demonstration of familiarity was nevertheless received with cheerfulness" by his enormous retinue. The royal household numbered some 20,000 people, who accompanied the king on his constant travels from residence to residence and who regularly consumed a tenth of the public revenue. The many courtiers reinforced Charles IV's belief in his own infallibility. This extended even into the way he made music: the king played the violin passably in a quartet. When a fellow player was so bold as to point out, respectfully, that he was playing too fast and asked him to slacken his tempo, Charles, unmoved, replied: "A prince never slows up."

With his unfortunate French relative Louis XVI he shared a love of clock-making, and like all the Bourbons he was passionate about hunting: "Every day, winter or summer, having breakfasted and heard Mass, I went out hunting until one o'clock; having eaten lunch, I carried on again until dark. In the evening, Manuel would tell me whether affairs were going well or badly, then I would go to bed. Next morning I would start all over again." Thus the king later described his day to Emperor Napoleon in person. And he would allow nothing to disturb it – not even the news that one of his children was on their deathbed. "What can I do about it?", he is supposed to have said, and then returned to shooting deer.

A popular subject of debate at court centred around the question of whether Charles IV knew about his wife's affairs or not. When his father, King Charles III, tried to illuminate him, Charles argued that a king was hardly in danger of being betrayed by his wife; she would never embark on an affair with a man of lower social standing, and those of similar rank were few and far between.

Naturally such a king was only too happy to be relieved of state business. Rather than with ministers and ambassadors, he much preferred to surround himself with carpenters, wood turners, and gunsmiths, in whose company he felt at ease.

All the while, others were running his country. When the political situation became unpleasant, when French troops marched into Spain in 1808 and there were even popular uprisings, it was easy for Napoleon to convince the king that it would be better for him to abdicate and to place Spain into Napoleon's hands. Rather like a landowner who exchanges his estate for a good pension, the king went into an exile, which at last promised him undisturbed peace of mind.

At the centre of the painting stands not the king, but his wife Maria-Luisa, something that reflects the situation at the Spanish court. The queen attached less importance to peace of mind than to power and pleasures. Goya places her against a dark painting that has recently been identified: it portrays the Old Testament story of Lot, fleeing with his daughters from the destruction of Sodom, the biblical city of depravity and sin. An appropriate background for a queen? Maria-Luisa arrived at the Spanish court at the age of fourteen, having come from Parma to be the wife of the crown prince. She, too, was a Bourbon and was related to her husband on two counts. On her father's side she was his cousin, and on her mother's side she – like he – was descended from Louis XIV. Like many ruling families, the Bourbons deliberately intermarried over the course of generations in order to preserve their power. The consequences were inescapable: the throne passed to Charles IV, for example, owing to the idiocy of his elder brother. The apathy of the king himself, which went far beyond the norm, may equally well have been the product of interbreeding, as may certain of Maria-Luisa's characteristics – one of Napoleon's chambermaids described her as the "Messalina of her age". The king, however, said of her after almost fifty years of marriage: "Look, my Louisa has given me twelve children. She is a good mother and a good wife. She has never caused me the slightest worry."

Although her husband gave her a child every year, the young crown princess was bored to death at the Spanish court. Her life, governed by rigid court protocol, ran as regularly as one of her husband's clocks. The pleasure-loving Maria-Luisa made up for the balls she was missing by occupying herself with politics and power. When, after the death of his father, Charles IV met his ministers for the first time, Maria-Luisa was with him – an unheard-of step. It became the rule. Maria-Luisa was soon at the political helm, in conjunction with her long-term lover, Manuel Godoy. She had picked out the handsome twenty-five-year-old youth from the palace guard. She made no great attempt to hide her affections, and as the French ambassador reported from Madrid: "There is not, perhaps, a single person in the whole of Spain who does not know that, to appease the Queen's unnatural sensuality ... the frequent assistance of the choicest of bodyguards" is required. The palace often rang with the queen's screams as she "regaled herself" – as the shocked French ambassador also reported – "with punches and kicks" delivered by her various playmates.

When Goya painted this portrait of the royal family in 1800, Maria-Luisa was forty-eight years old. In the words of the Russian ambassador: "Many confinements, illnesses, hereditary disease ... have wrecked her". Her complexion was "greenish" and the loss of her teeth, most of which had been replaced by false ones, had dealt her appearance a final blow. Numerous specialists worked constantly on improving her false teeth, which were made of precious stones. But they remained so inadequate that the queen was forced to take her meals alone. She suffered from such isolation, and the king often told her, however jokingly, "that she was a hideous female, that she was getting old". Only her "classically beautiful arms" survived as evidence of her former charms. Just a few years later, an ungallant Napoleon would describe Maria-Luisa as a "low-necked mummy".

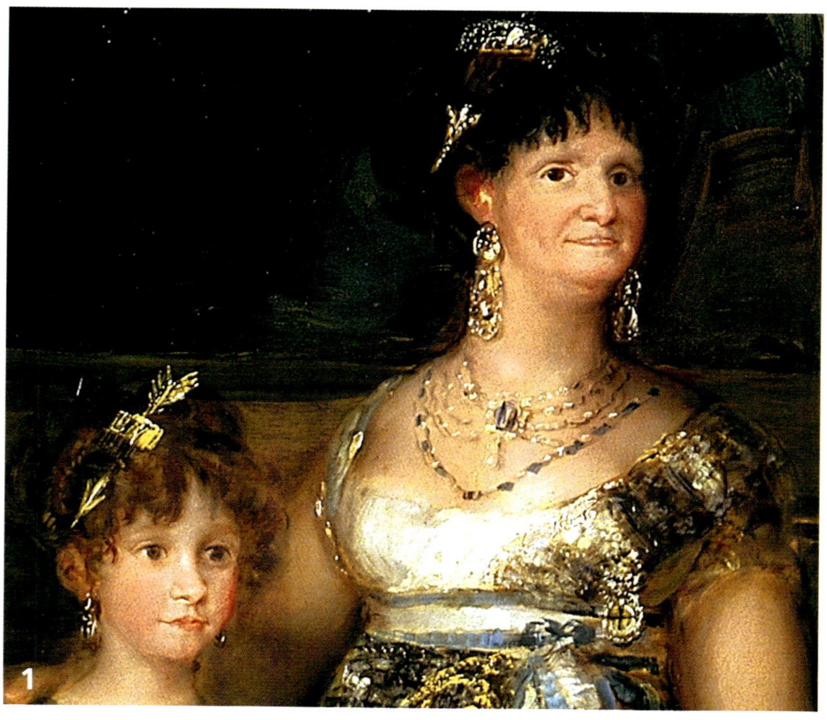

A good wife and mother

The queen found it hard to grow old; she continued to dress in young fashions. Much too young, according to her contemporaries. Maria-Luisa enthusiastically followed the latest Paris fashions, which steadily continued to be exported even during the worst years of the Revolution. Around 1800, under the influence of Napoleon's elegant wife Joséphine, Paris dictated a Grecian style of dress made of transparent, soft-draping muslins. Hairstyles, too, were curled *á la grecque*. When Napoleon, at the end of 1799, was wondering how to ingratiate himself with the Spanish queen, his ambassador recommended sending her dresses "of the kind suitable for a provocative brunette about twenty years old". They were ordered from the leading French couturier, Minette, and eagerly awaited by Maria-Luisa. But an enemy of the queen played a cruel joke on her. The Duchess of Alba, patroness and friend of the painter Goya, quickly dispatched a servant to Paris and obtained copies of the royal dresses – "only much more lavish". By the time Napoleon's dresses arrived, everywhere she went, from the theatre to the streets of Madrid, the queen could see the Duchess's ladies-in-waiting clad in the same fabrics and colours as herself. Her Catholic majesty Maria-Luisa had a reputation for being vengeful. Twice the magnificent palace of the Duchess of Alba burned down in the period that followed. In 1802 the Duchess herself died aged forty. Poisoned, they say.

Beside the queen are her two youngest children, Doña Maria Isabel and Don Francisco de Paula. There were dreams at the Spanish court of a union between the eleven-year-old girl and Napoleon Bonaparte himself, should his marriage to Joséphine continue to remain childless. But he declined. It was therefore soon decided to follow family tradition and marry Maria Isabel to a Bourbon, her cousin Franz Januarius, crown prince of Naples.

The young Don Francisco de Paula occasionally livened up the stiff court receptions by wrapping himself round the legs of the French ambassador. The courtiers laughed behind their backs: the prince had got the wrong man in uniform, but the mistake was understandable. His face bore no Bourbon features, but a resemblance instead to Maria-Luisa's lover – a resem-

The children of the earthly Trinity

blance so close, indeed, that a legislative assembly later excluded him for a while from the succession to the throne. Everyone – except the king? – knew who his father was: the two youngest members of the royal family represent in this picture the man who, in 1800, played the leading role in Spain – their father, Don Manuel Godoy.

That same summer Goya also painted a portrait of Godoy, mounted on horseback in parade uniform, a triumphant victor who has achieved all. Maria-Luisa fetched the attractive youth into her bed shortly after his arrival from the provinces, having already tried out his brother first. Manuel, unlike his brother and other members of the guard, would not be replaced. The queen kept him all her life. Other liaisons on both sides were unable to harm this relationship – even less so when it turned into a threesome.

King Charles IV namely also became fond of Manuel, be it because he took the burden of state business and his wife off his shoulders or be it out of personal inclination. King, queen, and favourite of both soon formed an unholy "earthly Trinity", as Maria-Luisa impiously termed it. The handsome Manuel was heaped with riches and offices, becoming generalissimo and prime minister. From 1792 to 1808, the real ruler of the Spanish empire was Godoy. He was the man who told the king every evening "whether affairs were going well or badly". Godoy determined Spanish policy. "He is not malicious", wrote a French ambassador, "but intoxicated by his omnipotence. He plays, so to speak, with the crown, which passion has placed in his hands." Young and politically inexperienced, Godoy was no match for Napoleon, who was pursuing his expansionist strategies with a large army. Napoleon made it impossible for Spain to remain neutral in the European conflict. In summer 1800, a treaty was negotiated between the unequal partners: Spain formed an alliance with France and ceded its naval fleet to Napoleon as a reinforcement for his planned blockade. At Trafalgar in 1805 it was sunk, precipitating the end of the Spanish overseas empire. For without a naval force, the colonies could not be held.

After the death of the royal couple in 1819, Godoy sank into poverty and oblivion. But the very two children he had fathered for the Spanish royal family would ensure the continuation of the dynasty. Maria Isabel's daughter – Godoy's granddaughter – at last provided King Ferdinand VII (1784–1833) with a female heir. She in turn married another of Godoy's grandchildren, the son of Don Francisco de Paula, who in Goya's painting is dressed in red and stands holding his mother's hand.

Some of the victims of Godoy's political weakness and Napoleon's political strength populate the right-hand side of the canvas. Relatively little affected,

Chess pieces

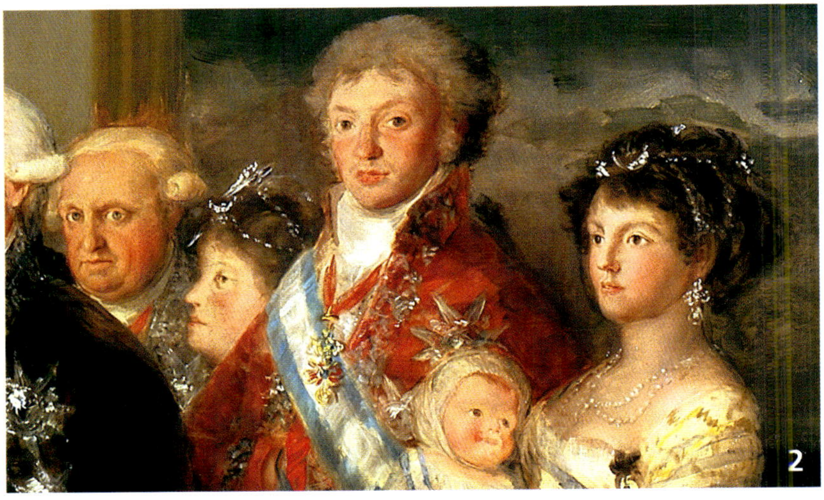

2

directly behind the king, was his somewhat younger brother Don Antonio Pascual. In 1800 he was moved out of his long-time and comfortable apartment in the royal palace to make room for Manuel Godoy's wife. Despite his rheumatism, he subsequently had to make do with a damp suite on the ground floor.

The two daughters of the royal couple had more to lose. In 1800 both were married to suitably high-ranking partners and ruled over countries of greater or lesser importance. Goya portrays Doña Carlotta Joaquina, the elder, only in profile, probably executed on the basis of sketches from an earlier date, since she had left Spain back in 1785, in order to marry the prince of Brazil, Juan, who reigned over Portugal in the name of his mad mother. Perhaps another reason why we are shown so little of her is because she was supposedly somewhat malformed.

Doña Maria Luisa Josephina, known familiarly as Louisetta, was just eighteen. Beside her is Don Luis de Bourbon, prince of Parma, her cousin and husband, and on her arm the barely one-year-old heir to the throne. He is already wearing the blue and white sash of the Maria-Luisa Order worn by all Spanish royal children and grandchildren. The royal couple greatly regretted the fact that their favourite daughter was only a princess. They asked Godoy to obtain for her the title of queen, however small the country to which the title was attached might be. Napoleon had just conquered Italy and was happy to oblige the Spanish ruling couple. The treaty signed in autumn 1800 between France and Spain granted the Duke of Parma the title of King of Etruria. In return, Godoy gave France the huge territory of Louisiana on the other side of the ocean and Spain's vital fleet.

But Louisetta would enjoy her title and her crown only for a few years. In 1807 Napoleon reorganized Italy and in so doing abolished the kingdom of Etruria. He informed Louisetta via his ambassador that she had to move out. The queen, "upset but not surprised", sold her houses, issued a few last decrees, packed her belongings into sixty carriages, including the coffin with the mortal remains of her then deceased spouse. On 4 December 1807, as French troops entered Florence, Louisetta left her kingdom and rode off across the rain-soaked country roads.

At the same time also underway, but on the high seas, was her sister Carlotta. Napoleon had finally decided to subjugate Portugal, which had long been allied with his arch enemy England and offered a hideaway for its fleet. He forced a weak Spain to allow French troops to pass through to Portugal. They marched on Lisbon. On 29 November 1807, the day before they arrived, the Portuguese royal family, together with the court, ministers, and crown jewels, boarded eight line-of-battle ships and four frigates "in a state of general agitation". Under clear skies and with a north-easterly wind, they sailed for Brazil. They, too, were fleeing from Napoleon.

The Spanish crown prince Ferdinand (1784–1833) was considered "a dreadful bore". He held the traditional title of Prince of Asturia, the Order of Charles III, and was terrified of his mother. So much so that, before a conversation with his mother, he would have his tutor write down the answers and would learn them by heart. Godoy, the idol of his parents, he detested. On 14 October 1800 Maria-Luisa wrote to her lover: "Charles and I have spoken to Ferdinand and told him that he must always love and value you ... but ah, it pains me to see that he does not share the feelings of his father and myself at all."

For this the sixteen-year-old was severely punished. He was only allowed to read books expressly approved by Godoy, and his tutor and confidantes were replaced by the favourite's cronies. It was not possible, however, to prevent the young wife wed to

Crown Prince Ferdinand, the people's choice for king

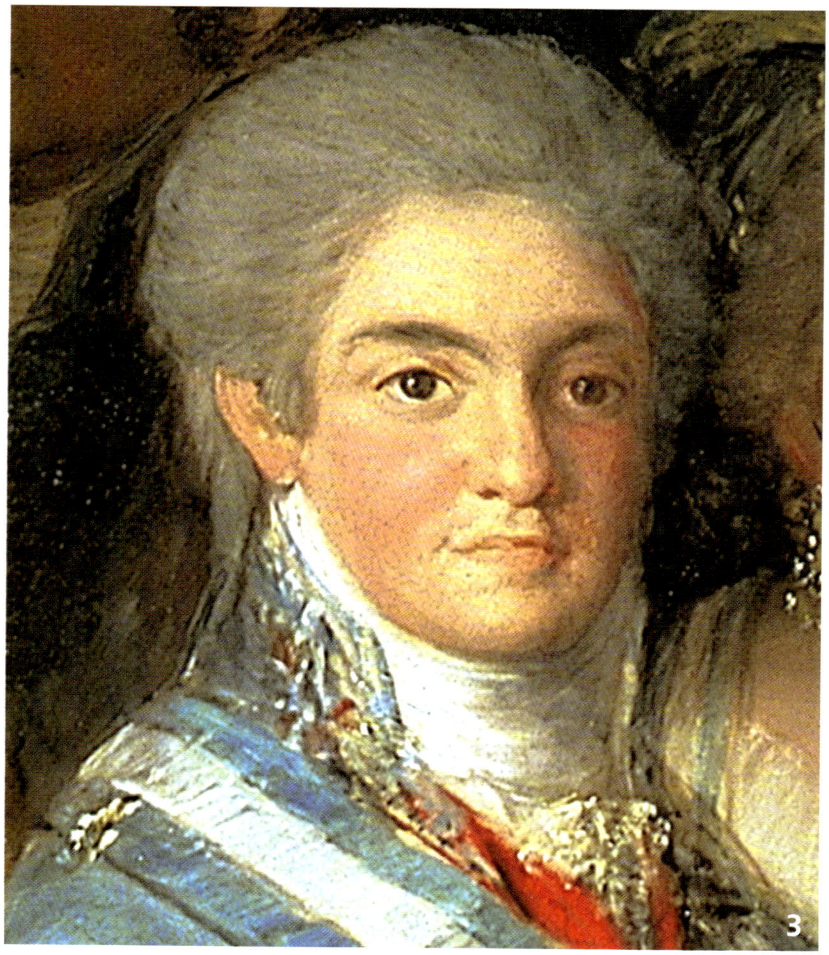

3

him in 1802, Marie Antoinette of Naples, from reinforcing his feelings of hatred. She is probably the woman beside him with her face turned away. Goya still didn't know her when he painted this picture. But Ferdinand was not a man of open resistance; he didn't fight, he kept silent, seemed to blend in, carried on hating and scheming in secret. When his intrigues came to light, he revealed that he was also a coward. Trembling and wailing he immediately revealed his accomplices.

Yet, passivity and hypocrisy did not prevent him from being elected the hero of the Spanish people. It sufficed that, as everyone knew, he shared the general hatred for the upstart Godoy, who stole the country, sold it to the French, and made the Spanish royal house into a laughing stock. Ferdinand only needed to let himself be carried along on this wave of popularity.

1808 brought a first uprising against Godoy. He was toppled, nearly torn to pieces, and owed his rescue only to French troops. When the latter then forced not only Charles IV but also Ferdinand to abdicate, and placed Napoleon's brother Joseph on the throne, the anger of the populace now turned against the French. The Spanish people rose up against their French occupiers and engaged them in a long and bitter fight. "The unfortunate Spanish war was my undoing", Napoleon later admitted on St Helena. The dull Ferdinand, *el deseado* ("the desired") of his people, waited out his time in comfortable exile in France until he was brought back to Spain in triumph in 1814 – as victor over Godoy and over Napoleon.

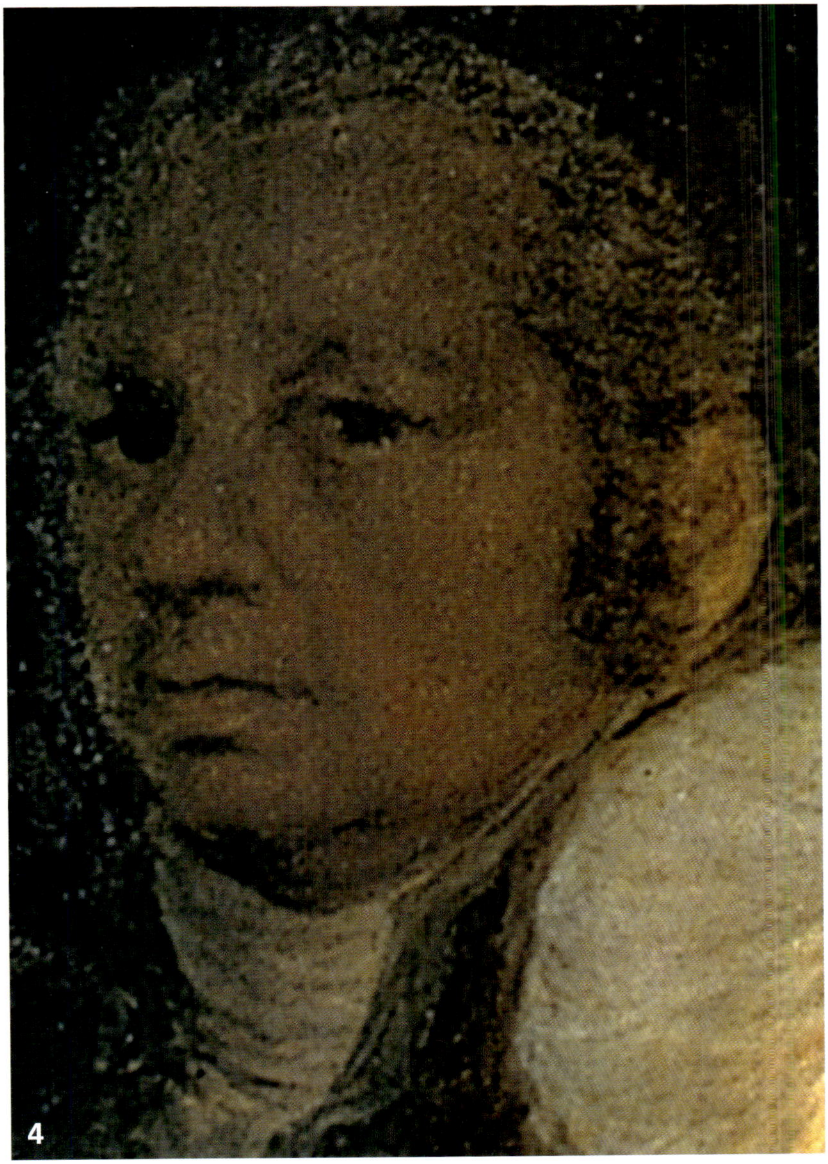

4

A self-confident artist

Goya had a high opinion of his gifts as an artist. Not only does he base the layout of *The Family of Charles IV* on that of *Las Meninas* by his famous predecessor Velázquez, but he includes himself within the composition, standing near the royal family in the left-hand background. Since autumn 1799 he had been Principal Painter to the King, earning a high salary and "a supplement of 500 ducats to maintain his own carriage". He was generally admired, his patroness was the Duchess of Alba, and Godoy, who appreciated art, took the trouble to learn sign language so that he could converse with the artist, who had been deaf for some years.

The king and queen seem to have been very satisfied with the painting they had commissioned. No contemporary took offence at the realism of the work. In June 1801 Goya was richly rewarded for the family portrait, but from this point on painted no further pictures for the royal family. Why, we do not know.

Did Goya mean this painting as a subtle criticism of the royal house? The experts are still not agreed. Probably not, because Goya always kept his political opinions separate from his work as an artist. Thus he was also able to paint the new King Joseph, by the grace of Napoleon, whom the Spanish would soon send packing. When Ferdinand returned in 1814, he dealt ruthlessly with all "collaborators". Only one man was spared his vengeance: "I ought to hang you", he said to Goya, "but you are a great artist and I'll forget everything." Goya, reinstated in his office as court painter, went on to paint portraits of this king, too.

Francisco de Goya: The Inquisition Tribunal, c. 1815

A sombre ceremony

A sombre spectacle in a sombre room. The background is crowded with people and there is a red glow in the distance – the setting sun or a blazing conflagration.

The assembly is dominated by monks in habit. The sole representative of secular authority – dressed in the powdered wig of the 18th century – is lounging, bored, in his comfortable chair. In a loggia on the left, society ladies hide behind their lace mantillas. One of the monks is reading a document by the light of a burning torch: it is the sentence passed on the figures in pale robes and conical hats. Their distinctive sanbenitos, on which the flames of Hell are flickering, brand them as heretics. Accused of offending against the Christian faith, they are here appearing before the tribunal of the Holy Inquisition – an ecclesiastical body that oversees the strict adherence to religious and moral doctrines and is about to pronounce its verdict.

In this small oil painting, which measures just 46 by 73 centimetres and today hangs in the Royal Academy of San Fernando in Madrid, Goya (1746–1828) portrays a very Spanish ritual. It was a ritual conducted countless times between the end of the 15th century and the beginning of the 19th, and one that claimed hundreds of thousands of lives. Francisco de Goya shows us an episode from an *auto de fe*, an "act of the faith".

At the climax of such an auto-da-fé, penitent heretics confessed to their heterodoxy. They professed, together with the pious crowd, their avowal of the true and sole faith and were thereupon ceremonially "reconciled" with the Church. But before they could be received back into the fold of the Church, the sinners had to do penance. The tribunal on the platform, made up of two Inquisitors, one assessor, one prosecutor, and one court attendant, announced what that should be. In most cases, the sentence consisted of flogging, lengthy imprisonment, or service on the king's galleys. Acquittals were rare.

Should a heretic prove impenitent, however, or be shown to have lapsed back into heretical ways, there was no reconciliation. He was expelled from the Church and, following the hearing by the Inquisition tribunal, handed over to the secular authorities, who were instructed to efface him "from the world through death". Far from the pomp of the act of faith, the sinner was burned alive outside the city gates and his ashes scattered in the river.

Probably the last public auto-da-fé took place in 1784, in the church of Santo Domingo el Real in Madrid. It was headed by the chief of the Madrid police, the Marqués of Cogolludo. It is possible that Goya, curious, was amongst the crowds of spectators. His undated *Inquisition Tribunal* arose over a quarter of a century later, between 1812 and 1819. Even by then, it was not altogether safe to make such a ritual the subject of a painting. The medieval institution still wielded power in Spain – as Goya had experienced at first hand.

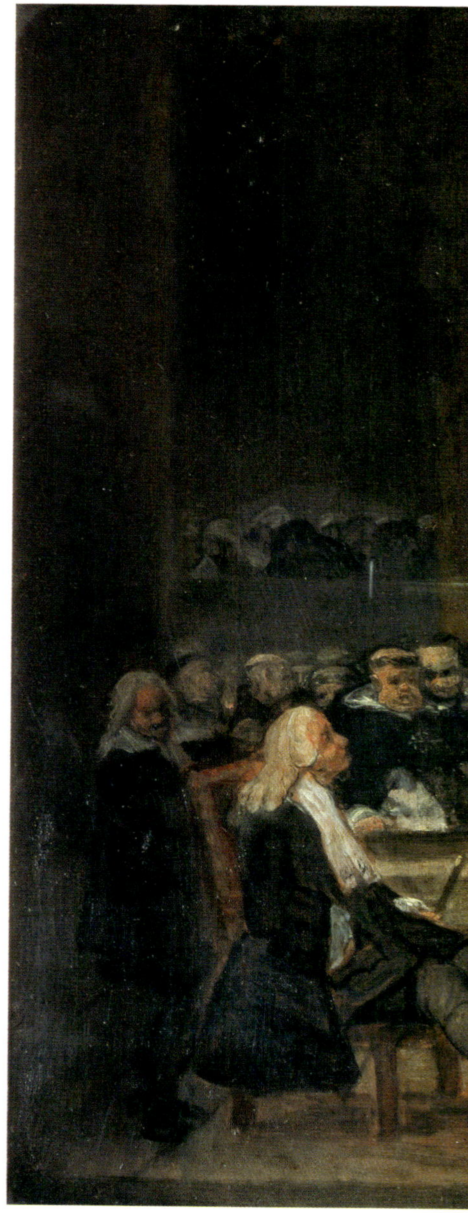

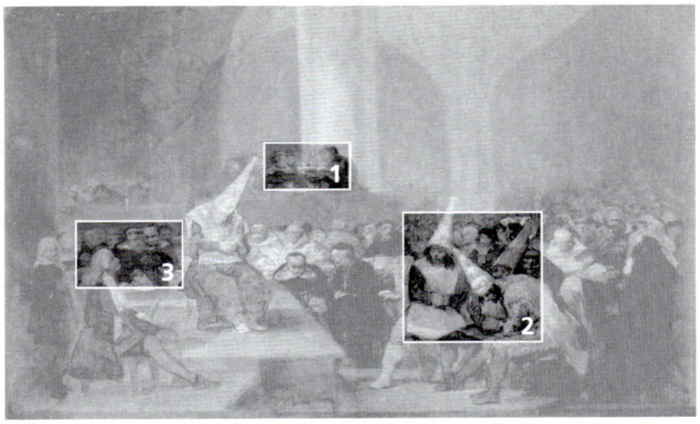
1
3
2

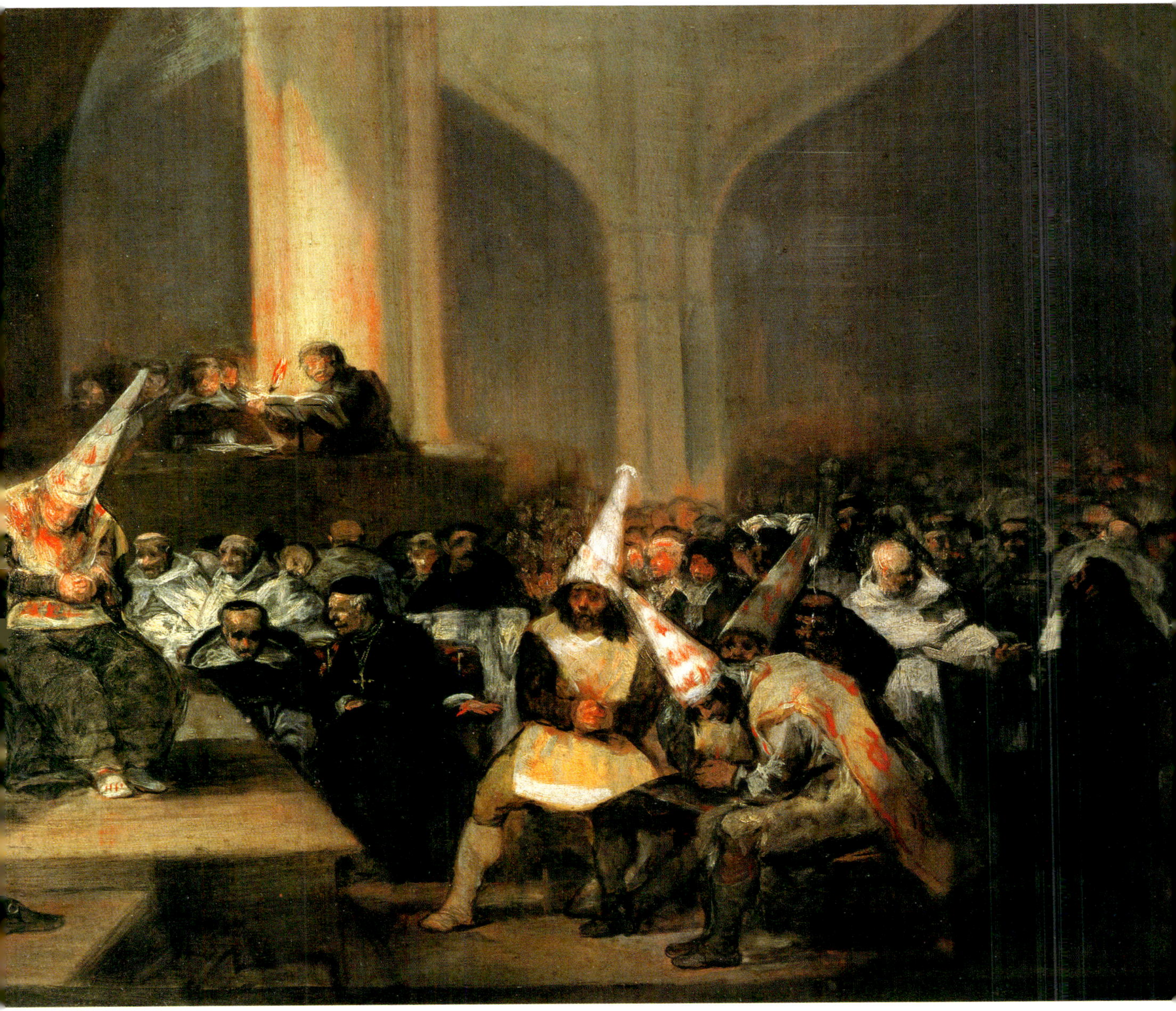

A "bulwark of the Church" was how one Spanish theologian viewed the Inquisition, a "pillar of truth, warder of the faith, and treasury of religion". God himself, it was claimed, had acted as the first Inquisitor when he asked "Adam, where are you?" after the Fall. According to canon law, "When someone who has been baptized calls himself a Christian, but obstinately denies or doubts one of the truths which must be believed according to divine and Catholic faith, then that person is a heretic." The tribunal believed it was acting on God's behalf in tracking down all those guilty of such heresy.

The Inquisition never doubted itself. Believing itself in possession of the truth, it set about saving the souls of sinners without delay. Heretics had to be ferreted out and tracked down for their own good. The Inquisition felt itself obliged to use all available means to make them see the error of their ways, to repent and do penance.

In Spain the Inquisition was introduced relatively late. In the rest of Europe it had been operating – at the Pope's behest – since the 13th century, stamping out all practices and beliefs deviating from the doctrines of Rome. Towards the end of the 15th century, the Dominican Hojeda recommended Queen Isabella of Castille to introduce the "Holy Office" of the Inquisition into her country in order to solve certain political problems. The first Grand Inquisitor was Torquemada, the queen's confessor. Under him, the religious institution became a tool in the hands of the Spanish rulers – an instrument of their expansionist, unification, and racial policies.

The large part of the Iberian peninsula had been under Islamic rule since the 8th century and was only won back extremely arduously over the following centuries in what was effectively a crusade. In 1469 the marriage of Isabella of Castille and Ferdinand of Aragon united their two realms. Granada, the last Moorish bastion, fell in 1492. The Catholic king and queen offered the Islamic population and the numerous Jews in their regained territories a stark choice between expulsion and conversion to Christianity: the new, unified Spain sought its national identity in religion. For its rulers, the "purity of the blood" was of prime importance. This, according to Isabella, was a requirement of "service to God".

Fanatics in the torch light

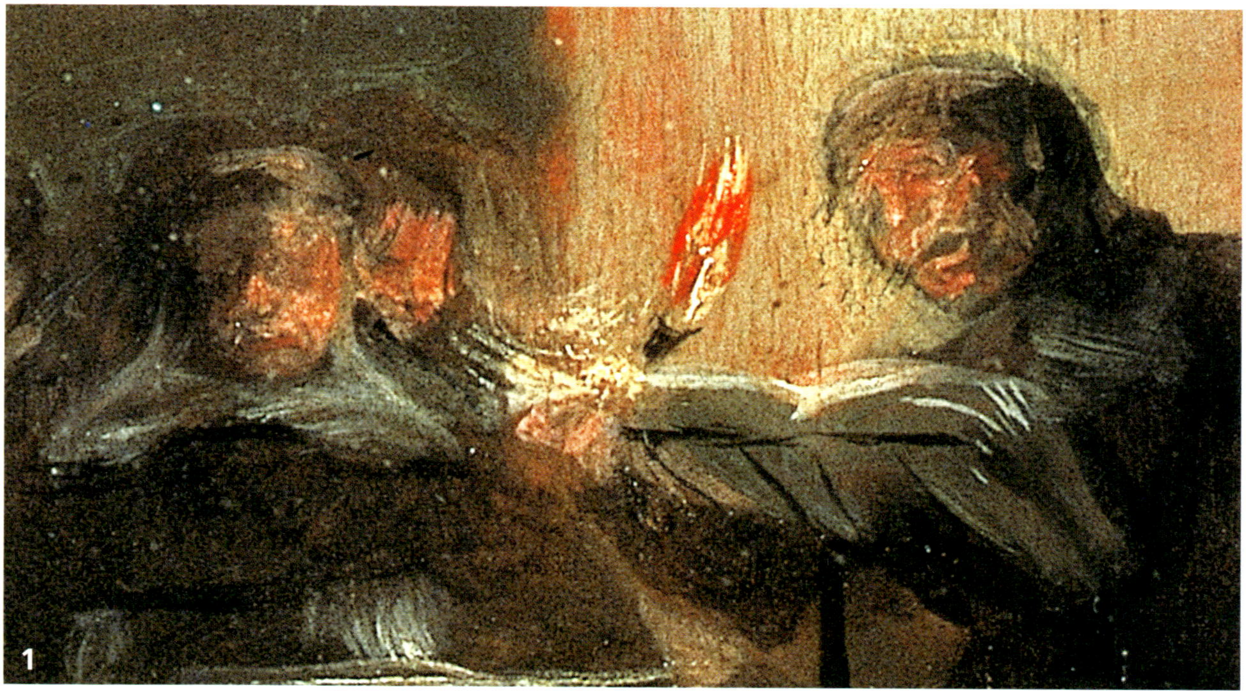

1

Many fled. Those who stayed, the Jews and Moors forced to convert to the Christian religion, were granted no peace. Still driven by the crusading spirit, the Catholic elders now turned on the "enemy within". In 1478 the Holy Office of the Inquisition was established. Its task was to keep an eye on the converts, whose Christian zeal was mistrusted. The authorities got straight to work: on 6 February 1481 six people met their deaths at the first auto-da-fé in Seville. Eating meat on a Friday or urinating against a church wall was enough to get someone denounced. By November that year, 298 had been burned at the stake in Seville and Inquisition tribunals were starting to be held all across the kingdom.

The Moors were mostly poor farm labourers. The Jews, on the other hand, having amassed large fortunes as bankers, merchants, and doctors, had long aroused envy. They were persecuted with particular zeal and merciless anti-Semitism by the Inquisitors, who financed their operations with confiscated assets. The Spanish Inquisition wiped out the converted Jews and Moors, quashed any attempt at a Reformation, and made the country a "citadel of orthodoxy".

Flames flicker menacingly on the conical "crowns" and sanbenitos, but the fact that they are light rather than black in colour indicates that these heretics will probably escape death by burning. Like the Inquisition itself, theologians traced the sanbenito (probably a distortion of *saco bendito*, holy sack) back to the Bible, namely to the animal skins with which Adam and Eve covered themselves after their expulsion from Paradise, because they were ashamed of their nakedness.

Heretics had to wear the sanbenito on the day of the auto-da-fé, and part of their penance might be to have to wear it, for years or even for the rest of their lives, every time they went out – as an instantly recognizable sign of their disgrace in a country where, at every level of society, nothing was more valuable than one's honour. The Inquisition was a master of publicity.

An auto-da-fé always took place in the largest available square in town. The evening before, the symbol of the Holy Office, the green cross, was paraded solemnly through the streets. The "act of the faith" itself began as a religious festival, with processions and Mass conducted with full ecclesiastical pomp. As the bells tolled and the faithful in every church in the town said prayers for his soul, many an "impenitent heretic" broke down.

The accused was already worn down by years of imprisonment in the dungeons of the Inquisition. There he disappeared "completely from the sight of men, as if the earth had swallowed him up", reported a witness with a shudder. The prisoner was told neither who had denounced him nor what he had been accused of. It was up to him to prove his innocence. In secret hearings he was repeatedly instructed to search his conscience. Using torture if necessary, the Holy Office eventually extracted his "voluntary" confession. He learned his sentence only at the auto-da-fé – arbitrarily passed by an institution that was simultaneously prosecutor and judge, without a public trial and without cross-examination.

Should a heretic complete his penance – and the chances of survival in prison and galleys were small – he emerged a good Catholic, but invariably also a beggar. His assets were seized, his family ruined. His descendants were prohibited from holding public office or from becoming priests, judges, notaries, lawyers, doctors, merchants, or shopkeepers.

So that his disgrace should never be forgotten and in order to be able to verify the "purity" of family trees, the sinner's sanbenito, bearing his name, form of heresy, and penance, was hung in the local church "for eternity". These relics of disgrace, regularly checked and replaced by officials of the Inquisition and the vigilant congregation, continued to adorn houses of God until well into the 19th century.

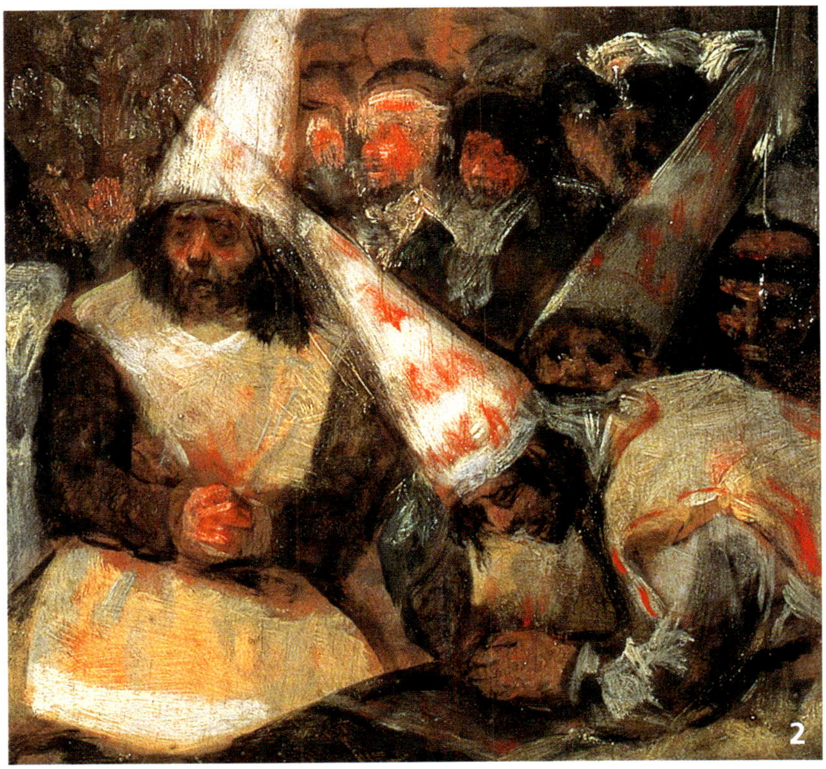

Wearing the robes of disgrace

In Spain right up to Goya's day, "not a word against the King or the Holy Office" was the maxim of the day. Not just because criticism of either institution could be dangerous, but because they had the support of every level of society. They were particularly popular with the lower classes.

When a papal delegation from Rome arrived in Spain in 1565, in order to rescue an archbishop from the clutches of the Inquisition, it had to leave again without success. It observed with astonishment that even "the most ardent champions of justice here find it better to condemn an innocent man to death than to let a blemish fall on the Inquisition".

In order to prevent heretical material entering the country, Spain sealed itself off from the rest of Europe. In 1559 everyone studying abroad was summoned to return home. Intellectual and spiritual life, churches, schools, and universities were all under the control of the Inquisition, and all publications were subjected to its strict censorship. The illegal import of foreign literature carried the death penalty. Paradoxically, the reign of the Inquisition coincided with the golden age of Spanish culture, the era during which the Spanish empire reached its greatest extent and power in the 16th and 17th centuries.

This was followed, however, by economic and political decline, and in the long term it would prove impossible to prevent new ideas from seeping into the country and challenging existing authority and tradition. In 1700 the Bourbon kings from neighbouring France acceded to the Spanish throne. They sought, through cautious and measured reforms, to lead the country out of its backwardness – with the assistance of a small, "enlightened" élite.

To reform the Inquisition, or even abolish it altogether, was something they dared not attempt. "The Spaniards want to keep it", affirmed Charles III, and the liberal politician Gaspar Melchor de Jovellanos, a friend of Goya, wrote: "The Inquisition steadfastly bans anything new, anything … that encourages intellectual … freedom". But since not all Spaniards thought the same way, "we cannot tackle this deplorable state of affairs directly".

The debate that now cautiously began nevertheless forced the Inquisition, after one last great wave of hearings around 1720, to scale down its spectacular activities. It no longer used torture, burnt only four heretics between 1759 and 1808, and contented itself for the most part with *autos particulares*, to which only a small circle of select guests were invited. The offences it chiefly pursued were fornication, witchcraft, and atheism. Senior royal officials were also amongst those accused – of "philosophizing".

In 1789 the French Revolution shocked conservative Spain and strengthened the Holy Office. In the 1790s, the "enlightened" class nevertheless rose briefly to power: in 1797 Jovellanos became Minister of Justice. But after just one year, the government was purged of liberal politicians, and Jovellanos banished and imprisoned. The Inquisition, it was whispered in Madrid, had struck again …

The secular authorities carried out the Inquisitor's sentences

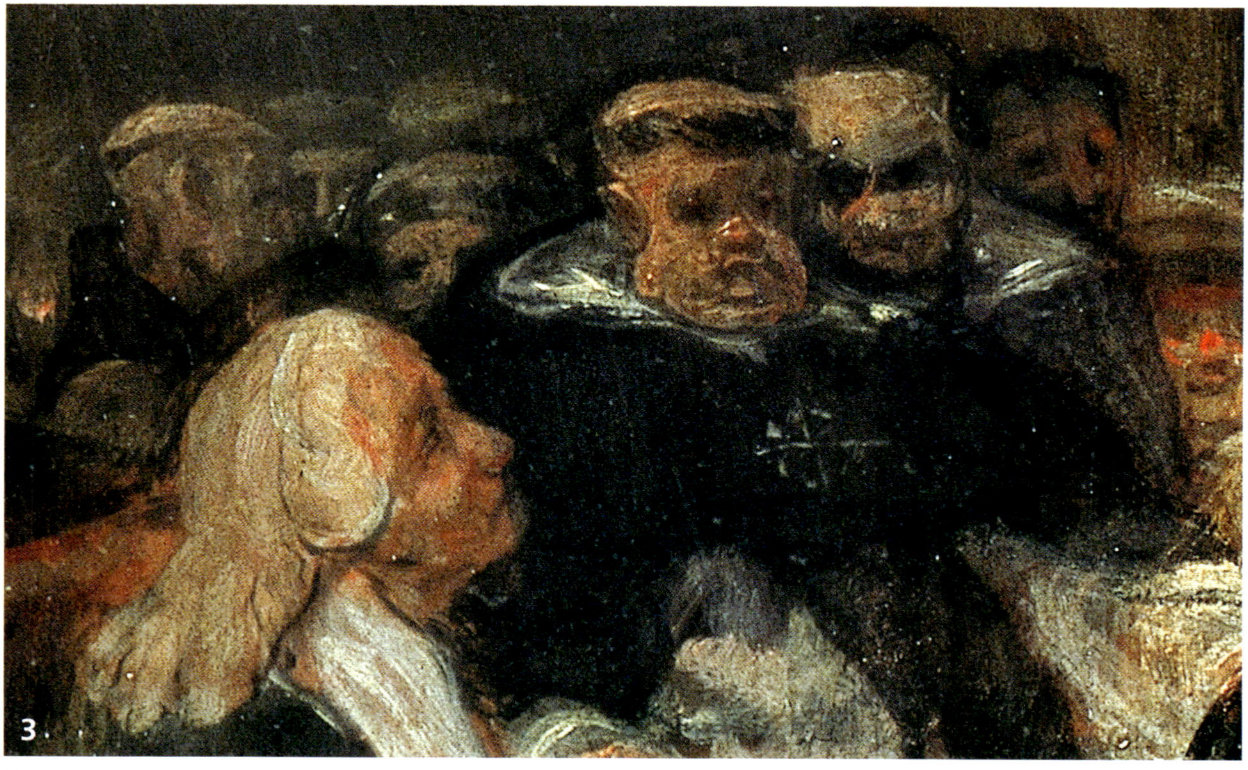

3

Goya's own encounter with the Inquisition remains – typically for this institution – shrouded in darkness. The artist himself recounted, a quarter of a century later, that he was charged by the Holy Office in 1799, following the publication of *Los Caprichos*, but how the matter ended we do not know.

Los Caprichos (Caprices) was the title of a series of eighty etchings in which Goya attacked superstition, stupidity, and repression – and naturally also the clergy and the Inquisition. No. 24 shows a scene of the kind witnessed in Valencia in as late as 1807 by the French physician Arago. There the Holy Office commanded "an alleged witch ... sitting on a donkey ... to be led through every quarter of the town ... Her upper body was bare to the waist." Goya shows her at the centre of a brutal, oppressive crowd, driven along by sheep-faced guards. "There was no remedy", he wrote resignedly underneath. There could be no doubting that the painter took the side of the victim and was attacking her tormentors.

Not until his later years did Goya turn his attention to the appalling state of the society in which he lived. Born into the lower classes, the artist devoted the first forty-five years of his life predominantly to his painting and his career. His successes brought him into contact with the élite of enlightened intellectuals, and friends such as Jovellanos opened his eyes to the backwardness of Spain. After a physical and spiritual crisis, Goya took up, in *Los Caprichos*, the fight against the "monster" born of "the sleep of reason".

After his "encounter" with the Inquisition, Goya quickly stopped selling the etchings and bequeathed the plates to a royal institute. That was probably the only way he could prevent them being destroyed. The artist became more cautious. Alongside portraits and official pictures, he continued to paint the powers of darkness, of which the Holy Office had become a symbol. But he kept such incriminating works to himself. Victims of the Inquisition from now on appeared only in his private sketchbooks or in small-format works for his friends.

The period between 1812 and 1819, during which the present painting arose, was one of uncertainty. In 1808 Spain was occupied by the French, who immediately abolished the Inquisition. It was not dead, however. After the Spanish had defeated the enemy in bitter fighting, Ferdinand VII was restored and in 1814 reintroduced the Holy Office. Monarch and Inquisition resorted to bloody repression. Thousands of "enlightened" Spaniards who had collaborated with the French were driven into exile, many of Goya's friends amongst them. In 1824, now aged seventy-eight, he, too, fled to France, where four years later he died. The "tribunal of darkness" survived the artist; it was only finally abolished in Spain in 1834.

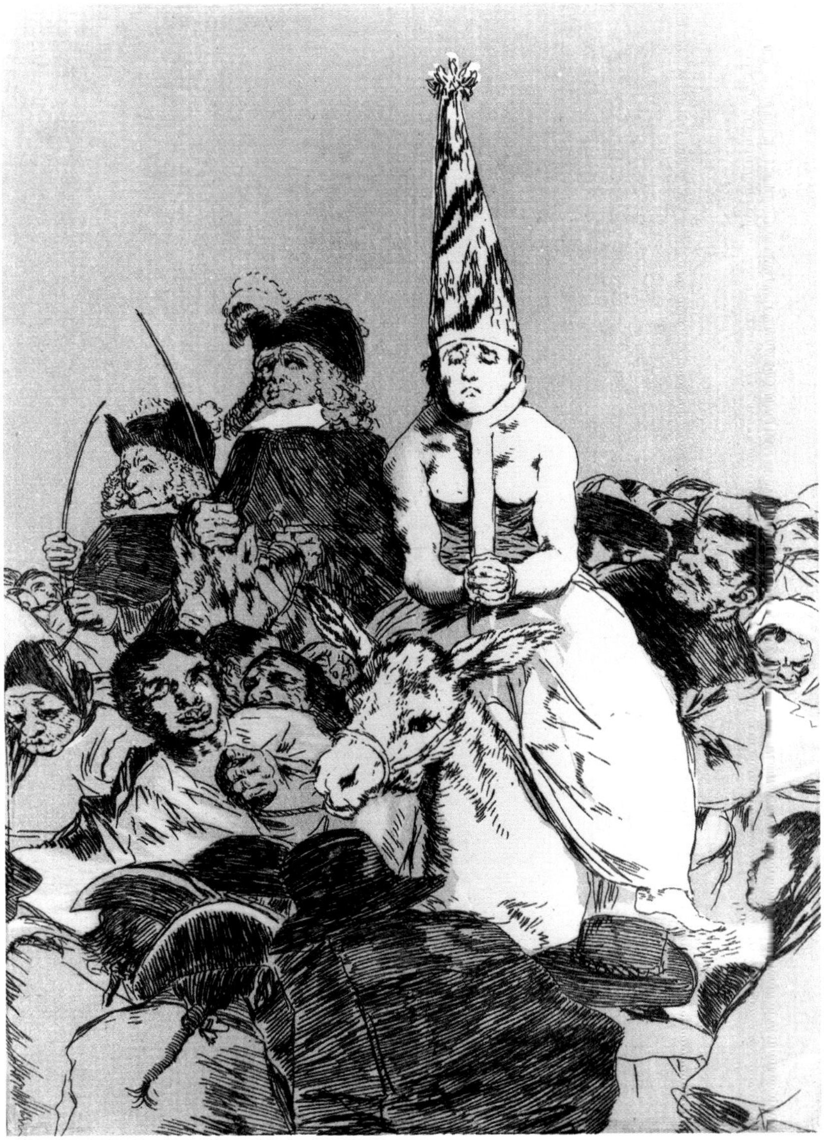

"There was no remedy", wrote Goya beneath this etching from his *Los Caprichos* series

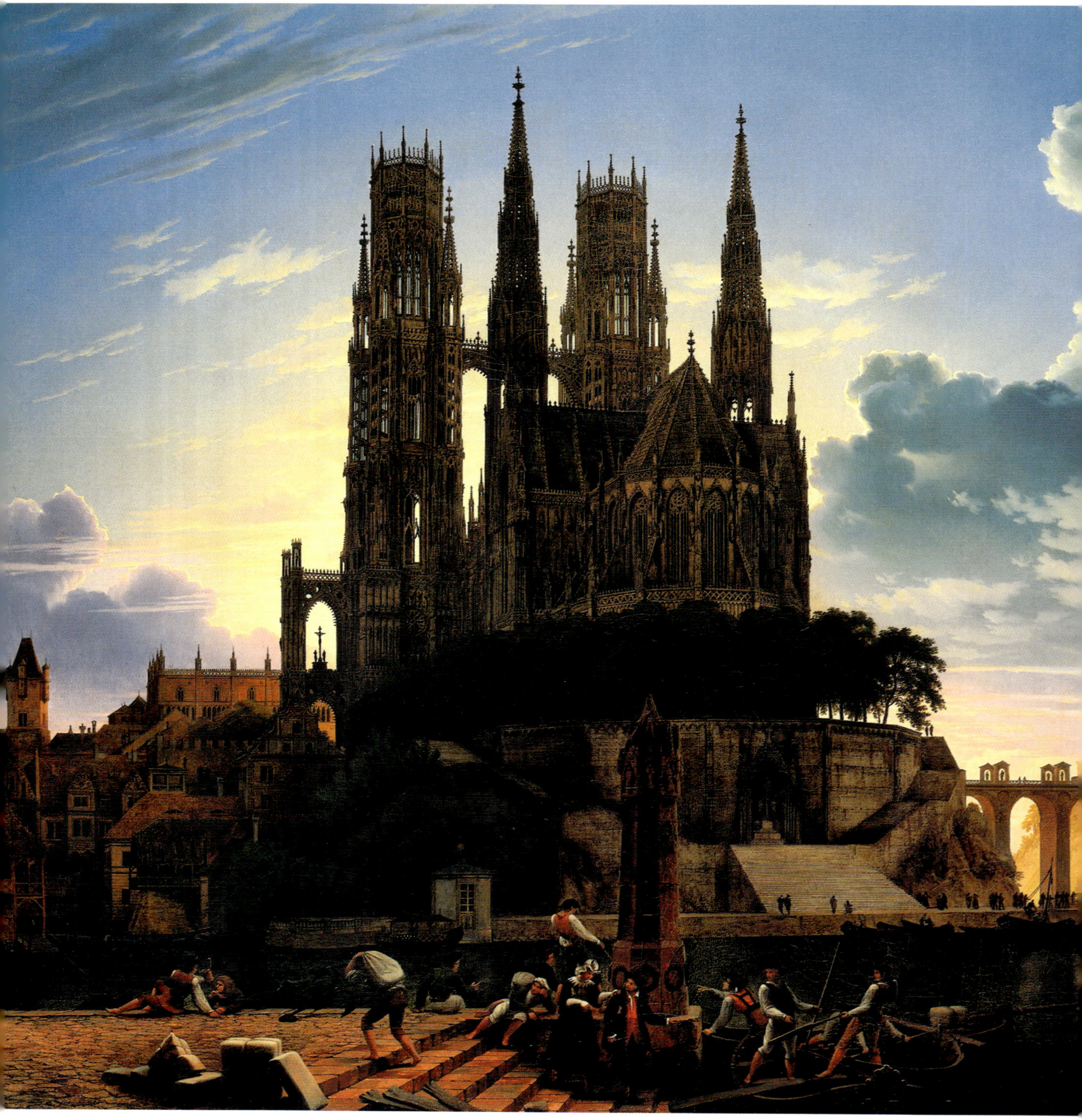

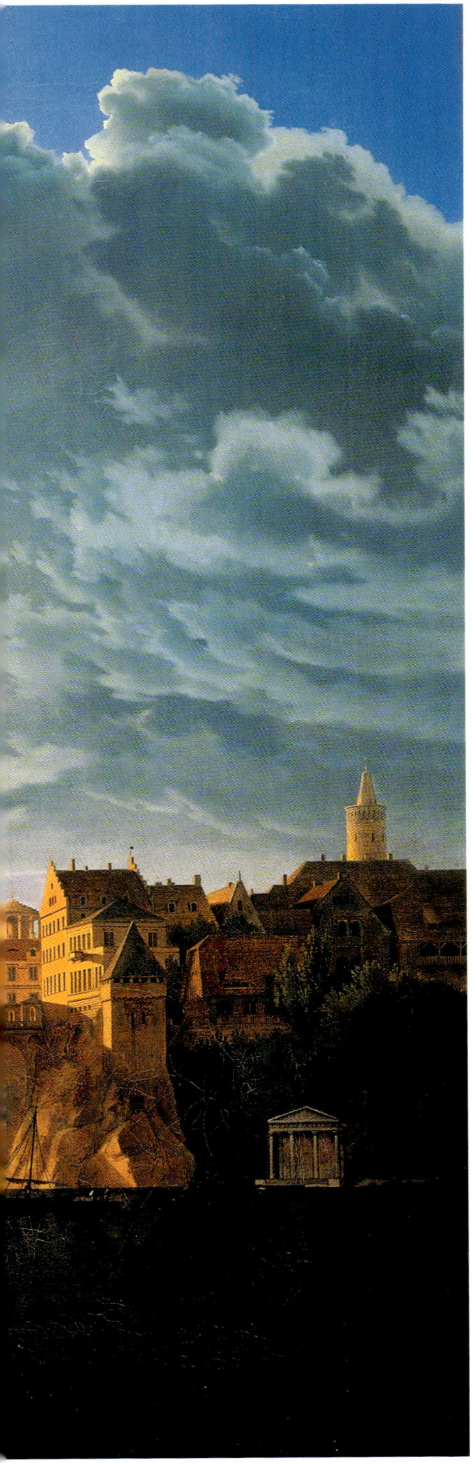

Karl Friedrich Schinkel: Cathedral Overlooking a City, 1813

Fantasy of an unemployed architect

Karl Friedrich Schinkel first showed his painting of a vast medieval cathedral rising beside the sea in 1814, at the Academy exhibition in Berlin. The work later hung in the Berlin palace of the Hohenzollern family. It then passed to the Berlin National Gallery, which loaned it to a large exhibition on the Romantics in the Munich Glaspalast. There, on 6 June 1931, it was burned to ashes, together with some 3000 other works, including nine by Caspar David Friedrich. The fire at the Munich Glaspalast was one of the greatest disasters in the history of German art exhibitions.

A second version, which Schinkel had kept for himself, fell victim to the Second World War. After Schinkel's death in 1841, it passed to the Schinkel Museum in Berlin, and later to the imperial chancellery, where it was probably destroyed in the fighting of 1945. The painting was allegedly known simply as "Schinkel 1913".

Two copies have survived. One belongs to the Nationalgalerie in Berlin, the other to the Neue Pinakothek in Munich. The Munich version shown here (94 x 126 cm) is so good that it was long thought to be another original by Schinkel. It is probably the work of Eduard Biermann, however. It is thanks to the copyists that this important composition, highly characteristic of the 19th century, can still be admired today. The original was executed in 1813, a critical juncture in European history – the year of the German wars of liberation against Napoleon and the defeat of the French emperor at the Battle of Leipzig.

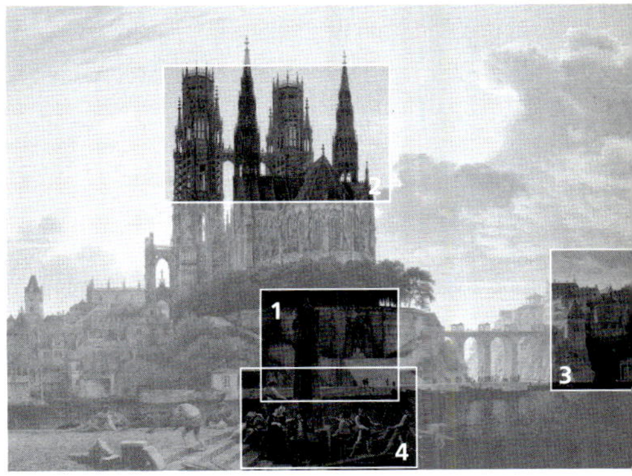

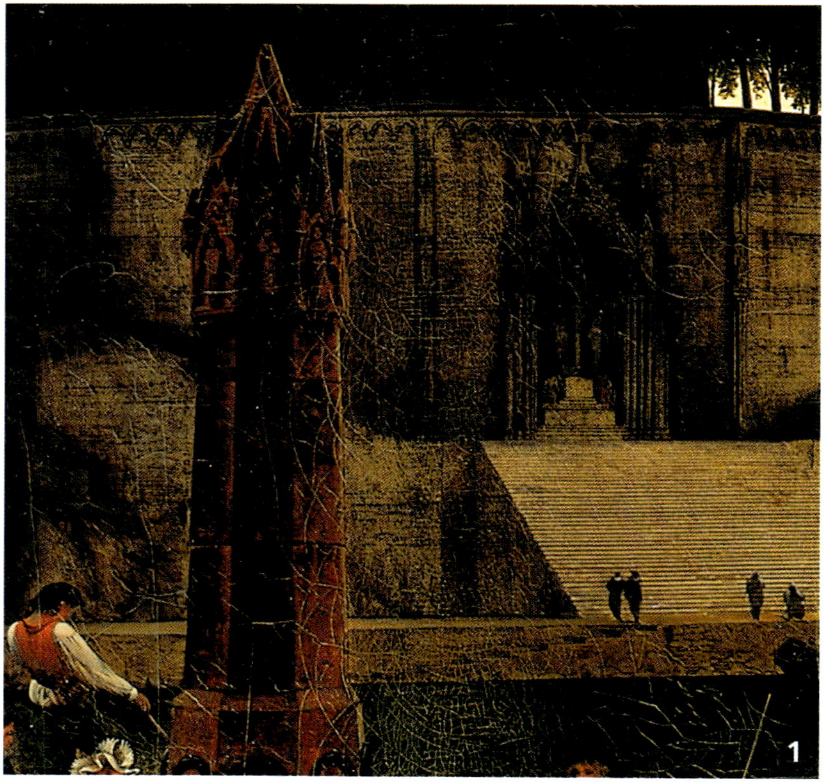

1

Schinkel paints because he can't build

Beside the flight of steps, in the shadow of the cathedral, stands a sculptural Crucifixion group and by the harbour wall in the foreground a memorial column that cannot be more specifically identified. Monuments played a major role in Schinkel's life. He designed a good number of them, even if not all went on to be built. For him, this painting too possessed the character of a memorial or monument. It was intended to symbolize a large, unified Germany.

But the reality was still quite the opposite: Germany was occupied by French troops, the nobility dependent upon Napoleon's mercy, the population divided into the friends and foes of the powerful Corsican. In 1806 the French had defeated the Prussian army at Jena and Auerstedt; the Prussian king had fled to East Prussia and Napoleon had marched into Berlin. He had ordered the goddess Victory and her quadriga to be taken down from the top of the Brandenburg Gate and shipped off to Paris – a dispiriting act of despotism.

More humiliating still were the demands for reparations that proceeded to ruin the country. The salaries of civil servants were not paid, landlords whose houses were used as quarters for the French troops lost their rents, and artisans waited in vain for commissions. In 1808 the publisher Friedrich Nicolai wrote that "in these desperately sad times since November 1806 I have lost half my fortune". During this same period, Wilhelm von Humboldt noted: "Berlin has become a village. There are hardly any carriages ... at dinners and suppers, tallow is burnt" – instead of the usual candles.

Karl Friedrich Schinkel grew up in these years of deprivation. He was born in 1781 in Neuruppin, studied architecture in Berlin, and spent the years 1803–05 in Italy. When he returned home, the prospects of getting work as an architect seemed slim. There was no money to spare for houses, churches, or palaces. Schinkel became a painter for the annual Christmas market. He produced dioramas, full-size representations that, flanked by mock columns and viewed from a distance, were dramatically lit and frequently brought to life with music and mechanical figures. He also painted a circular panorama of Palermo, which was 4.50 metres high and 27 metres long, and which could be viewed in a round wooden building. Schinkel was thereby working to entertain a large public. Illusion was in demand. The Berliners wanted to be shown an exotic location or an event from recent history. Over Christmas 1812 they were given the burning of Moscow, with which Napoleon's fall from power had begun three months earlier.

In 1813 Germany once again became a battlefield. Over 100,000 would fall at Leipzig in October alone. August had already seen a fierce skirmish at Grossbeeren, near Berlin. The Prussians were victorious, and the Berliners travelled out to the field of battle. They saw a "chaos of people, soldiers, corpses, dead horses". Many had taken food with them, and "at five o'clock everyone ate, surrounded by bodies", according to a banker by the name of Müller. The road to Berlin was full "of carts carrying nothing but wounded – a sad sight".

Schinkel's *Cathedral Overlooking a City*, in which the setting sun and low vantage-point combine to lend the cathedral a monumental grandeur, also dates to 1813. It was a year full of chaos, bloodshed, and political volatility. Only when virtually forced to by his army and subjects did Friedrich Wilhelm III, Prussia's king, openly challenge the Corsican. He also created a new military decoration, not of gold or silver, but – as appropriate to wartime and because it was intended for the troops – of iron. He made a preliminary sketch of his "Iron Cross" and instructed Schinkel, who was by now privy architectural adviser in the Department of Public Works, to produce the final design.

In March 1814 the armies allied against Napoleon marched into Paris, and Schinkel was given another commission by his king – a national cathedral that was to be erected in thanksgiving for the liberation of Prussia. The domed building with relatively low towers that he conceived in response to this request bears little resemblance to the cathedral in the present painting. What Schinkel the artist imagines soaring into the heights, Schinkel the architect kept firmly on the ground. The only Gothic features he retained were the pointed arches. Gothic, nevertheless, was what the king's commemorative cathedral was meant to be. The Gothic was considered the most quintessentially German of all architectural styles.

This misconception can be traced not least to Johann Wolfgang von Goethe. As a young man he was enraptured by Strasbourg cathedral, and in 1772 – without ever having seen the cathedrals of Milan, Reims, or Chartres – he rather ignorantly pronounced the Gothic style a "German architecture, for the Italians can boast none of their own, and even less so the French".

Goethe's enthusiasm for the Gothic style chimed in with the growing tendency to eulogize Germany's past. Young poets celebrated the bold knight Götz von Berlichingen, the Grimm brothers collected old folktales, and Dürer's Nuremberg became a symbol of peaceful civic coexistence. Everything about the old days seemed better than the present: no particularism, no despotism either at home or abroad. The Gothic was thereby chosen as the stylistic code for such retrospection; it was declared the "stirring style of medieval German architecture", which would produce the "power for the future". Thus wrote Schinkel about his cathedral project for the king. He was just one of many during this period who painted Gothic cathedrals or, like Caspar David Friedrich (1774–1840), Gothic ruins.

Schinkel would never build a national cathedral to commemorate the wars of liberation – probably because the public purse was empty. In its place, however, he erected a Gothic memorial on a hill in Berlin. It stands there still. In reference to the cross on top of the monument, the hill and the suburb that grew up around it were later renamed Kreuzberg (Cross Hill).

Gothic against Napoleon

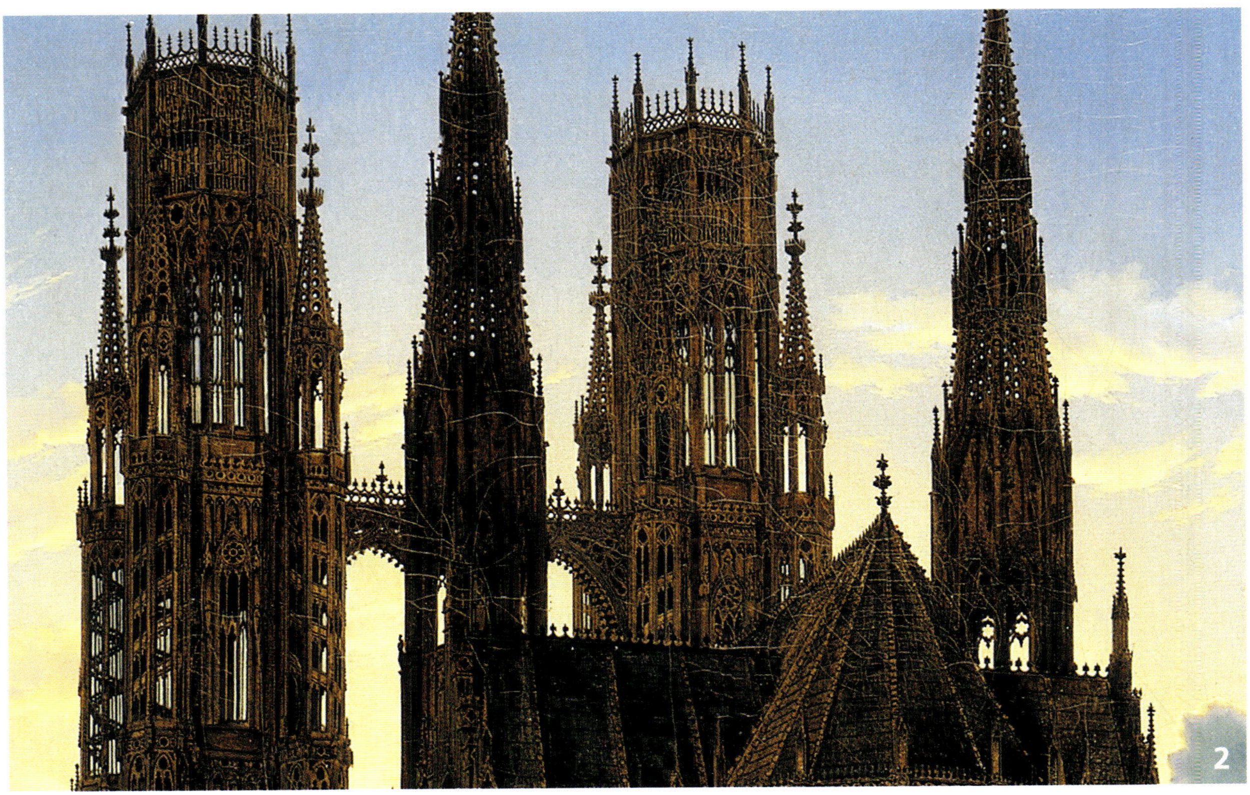
2

In 1815 Schinkel was commissioned to design a building to house the royal guard on Berlin's prestigious avenue, Unter den Linden. The resulting Neue Wache (New Guard House), which remains one of Schinkel's best-loved buildings, was furnished on its front façade with a classical portico employing ten columns and surmounted by a low-pitched triangular gable. Schinkel had employed such a gable, albeit supported on just four columns, in the very first building he ever designed, a garden temple in Potsdam. It can be seen in the present painting, too, in the small temple that appears beneath the city and which is almost identical in its proportions to the Potsdam temple.

Gothic pointed arches on the one hand, classical porticoes on the other, the curve versus the straight line – these were not just questions of artistic taste, but of political conviction. The Gothic style was associated with everything German, as well as with originality and emotion. Gothic art was considered to issue from below, from the people. The architectural language of classicism, on the other hand, spoke of order, harmony, and reason. These virtues came not from below, but from a lofty intellectual tradition, and were especially popular with rulers. For you can rule only if you can have order and control.

Love for the one did not preclude love for the other, but the older Schinkel got, the more he tended towards the classical idiom. Goethe, too, distanced himself in his later years from his youthful admiration of Strasbourg cathedral. Schinkel visited him several times in Weimar. At their last meeting, in 1826, Goethe spoke of the "character of the pointed arch in architecture as no doubt sometimes useful but lacking in beauty ...".

What Goethe called beauty, Schinkel understood as calm. For him, an impression of calm was the supreme goal of architecture. No ornamentation, just clarity and harmony. "The calmest is the building which [combines] columns and architrave ... The pointed arch, because it renders visible the conflicting forces, contains profound restlessness."

The word "calm" had a history in Prussia, albeit not in Schinkel's sense. After the Prussian defeat at Jena, announcements posted on the city walls informed the Berlin populace that "The King has lost a battle. Calm is now the first duty of all citizens." A few years later, even after Prussia and its allies had won their decisive victory over the French, the king continued to insist emphatically upon calm. Any desire for greater civil rights or national unity – causes that had also been fought for – was forcefully repressed. Like all German princes, Friedrich Wilhelm, too, was afraid of losing his power.

Whether Schinkel publicly took sides is unknown. Similarly unknown is whether a fear of revolution and chaos perhaps reinforced his personal need for calm and straight lines. Quite apart from his own artistic preferences, however, it is clear that as a Prussian civil servant he was not in a position to do anything but what his monarch and other patrons demanded, namely design buildings in the classical style.

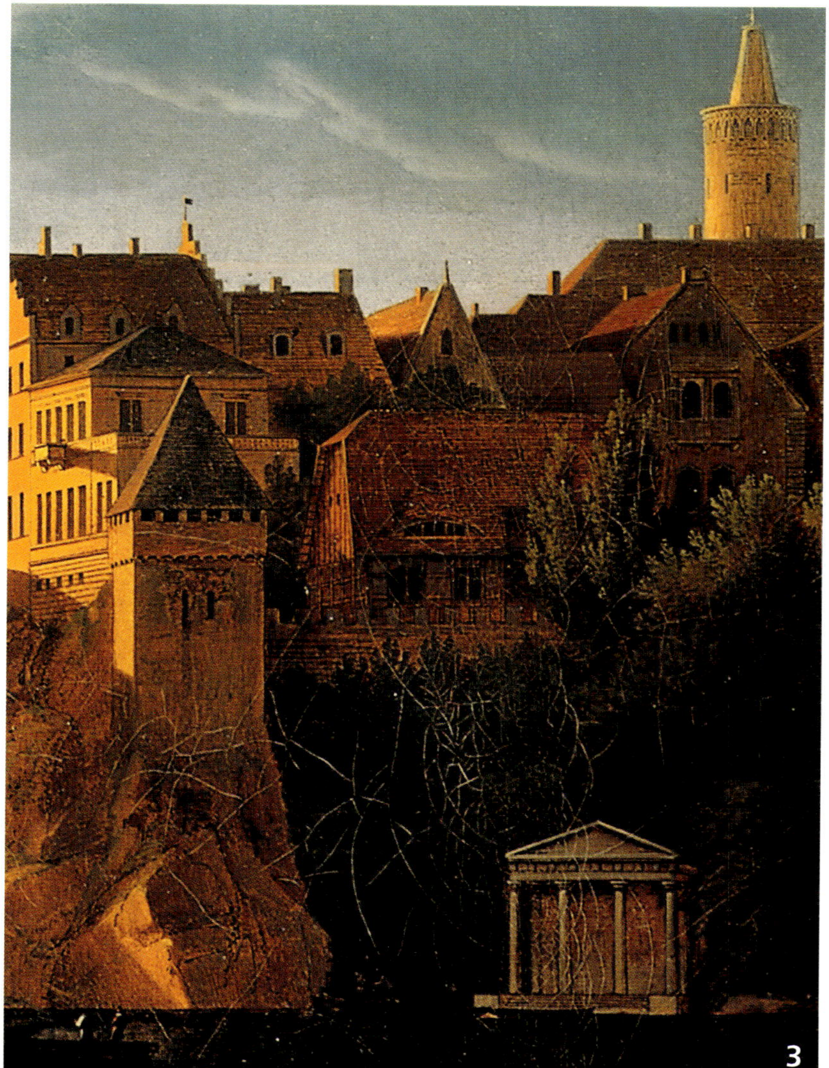

Schinkel's path to classicism

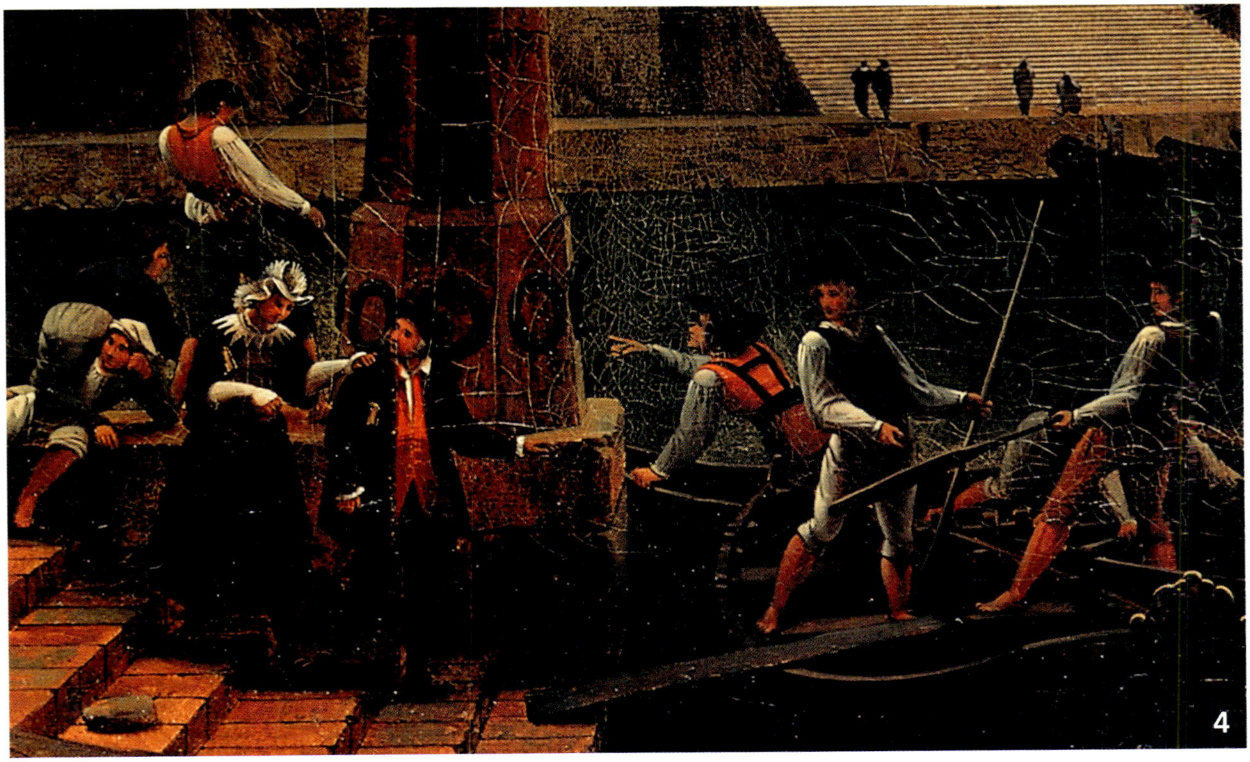

4

In paintings by Caspar David Friedrich, Schinkel's slightly older contemporary, the sea frequently appears as something mysterious, as a diffuse mass cloaked in mist or as a surface containing enormous ice floes crushing a sailing ship. Schinkel's painting is quite different. His sea is smooth. Its surface conceals nothing, and within the composition it provides a horizontal base for the soaring spires above.

The people in this painting play no more than walk-on parts. They add interest to the foreground, probably rather like the mechanical figures that stood in front of Schinkel's Christmas dioramas. Supposed to convey the impression of happy Germans in a happy epoch, they are light-footed and graceful in their poses. But their diminutive size and muted palette mean they are easily overlooked, as indeed is the intention – all eyes are drawn to the cathedral.

The cityscape that Schinkel paints here was part of a genre that had grown rapidly in popularity since the previous century. Its origins lay in the souvenir pictures painted for tourists by artists such as Francesco Guardi (1712–1793), who recorded the buildings and squares of Venice. These were followed by much grander paintings, as those executed by Bernardo Bellotto (1720–1780), for example, and intended for emperors and kings who wanted views of their magnificent capitals to hang on their walls. Both Guardi and Bellotto thereby recorded what was before their eyes. The Romantics, on the other hand, painted architecture in order to render visible something that had nothing to do with a real building. They were interested not in the pointed arch as such, but in what lay behind it. The height and the light-flooded mass of Schinkel's cathedral were understood as symbolic values.

As soon as Schinkel was able to build, in other words from 1816 onwards, he put painting aside. He had enough to do: promoted to privy councillor, inspection trips took him to all the Prussian provinces, and also to Cologne, where for more than twenty years he would be involved in the construction of the cathedral. He designed furniture, staircases, interiors, and – drawing on his experience at the Christmas market – over 100 stage sets.

The main focus of his energies remained Berlin, however. After the Neue Wache and Friedrichswerdersche church, he went

The architect of Berlin

on to build the Schauspielhaus theatre and concert hall in the Gendarmenmarkt, the Schlossbrücke, the Altes Museum in the Lustgarten and the Bauakademie school of architecture. No other architect shaped the face of the city so profoundly as Karl Friedrich Schinkel. Most of these buildings are classical in style and imbued with a sober harmony. If we compare them with the imaginary, Romantic architecture of his painted cathedrals, we can recognize something of the two faces of Prussia during these years.

Caspar David Friedrich: Hutten's Tomb, c. 1823

The tomb with no one in it

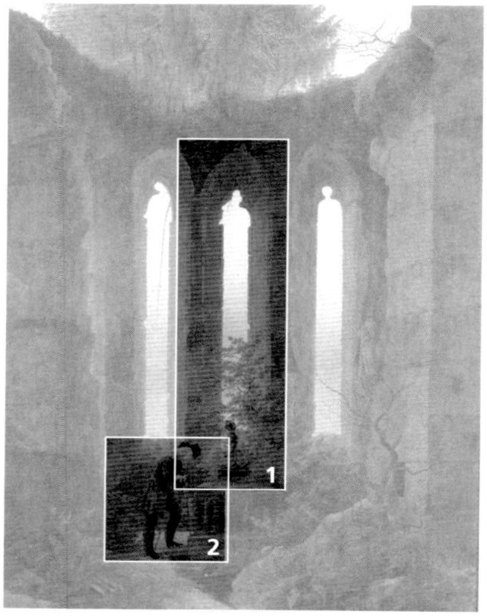

Ulrich von Hutten, born in Steckelberg castle in 1488, was a troublemaker. He was supposed to become a monk, but at the age of seventeen ran away from his monastery and travelled from one university to the next. He had to leave Vienna because he got into a dispute with the university authorities, had to leave Bologna because he took part in student uprisings, and had to flee Italy because he stabbed a soldier in a tavern.

He was thereby of weak and sickly constitution. What made him famous was his verbal, not his physical pugnacity. He called himself a "poet and orator", but was above all an agitator and pamphleteer, a hurler of insults and abuse. He was unbridled in his criticism, unrealistic in his demands. His most sustained attacks were directed at the members of the Curia in Rome, whom he called "courtesans", "tyrants", "exploiters", and "bloodsuckers": "Their practices are all directed towards taking money from the Germans."

Hutten saw himself as fighting the same battle as Luther, but his motives were different. Luther wanted religious renewal; Hutten wanted political freedom, both from Rome and from the brutal regime of some of the territorial princes. "Let us liberate our oppressed Fatherland!" he wrote to Luther, without seeing that his supposed comrade-in-arms had something else in mind.

A man who picked a fight with the Church and the ruling aristocracy was not safe in Germany. After the death of his protector Franz von Sickingen, he fled to Switzerland. Zwingli, the Swiss Protestant reformer, gave him shelter on the small island of Ufnau in Lake Zurich. There, at the age of thirty-five, he died of the consequences of syphilis. A stone tablet commemorates his name. During the summer months, ferries sail across to Ufnau, where tourists can see for themselves that the island's small Romanesque chapel bears no relation to Caspar David Friedrich's Gothic ruin. The painter never went to Ufnau.

Three hundred years later, many Germans seized upon Hutten and the example he had set. They knew little about his person or his character. They used Hutten to personify their own thoughts and feelings: their hatred for the foreign troops occupying their country, their hopes of freedom and a unified people. These were the years of Napoleonic occupation, of the German wars of liberation of 1813–15, and of reimposed princely rule.

Napoleon had Germany in his power for almost ten years. Although not everyone hated him, there were many who did, Caspar David Friedrich amongst them. "With his usual wrath against the French, Friedrich expressed his anguish at Germany's humiliation", reported a visitor. Friedrich did not take an active part in the fighting of 1813, giving money instead. He was then thirty-nine years of age and living in Dresden. After the French had been expelled from the city, he wrote a hymnic prayer: "The Lord has heard our cries and driven out our enemies ... The fugitives hasten back to their home, pursued by the sword of the North ..."

The German struggle for liberation was started less by the princes than by the people. There was a new feeling of national consciousness. Although the majority did not want to cut off the heads of their kings and princes, they demanded more rights of their own, plus a united German nation. At the Congress of Vienna of 1814/15, however, the sovereigns of Europe secured not just peace for the next few decades, but also the perpetuation of the old power structures. According to Friedrich in 1814: "It doesn't surprise me in the least that no monuments are being erected, be they in commemoration of the great cause of the people or of the courageous deeds of individual German men. As long as we remain princes' serfs, nothing noteworthy of the kind will ever happen, either. Where the people have no voice, they are not permitted to feel and honour who they are."

Friedrich painted his picture of Hutten's tomb around 1823, a year which marked a double anniversary: ten years since the start of the wars of liberation, three hundred years since Hutten's death. Friedrich may have been inspired by an edition of Hutten's works which was published in Leipzig in 1822 and 1823. The publisher spoke of the "patriotic intent" of the edition and declared: "I lead you to the tomb of the mighty figure of Ulrich von Hutten because nowhere else do I find the portrait of his times, the struggles of German patriots in the name of national glory and love of their Germanic fellows, and the endeavours of those devout reformers of the faith, given such clear and compelling expression as by the spirit which permeates his writings. Honour him! Let no one dare revile his ashes!"

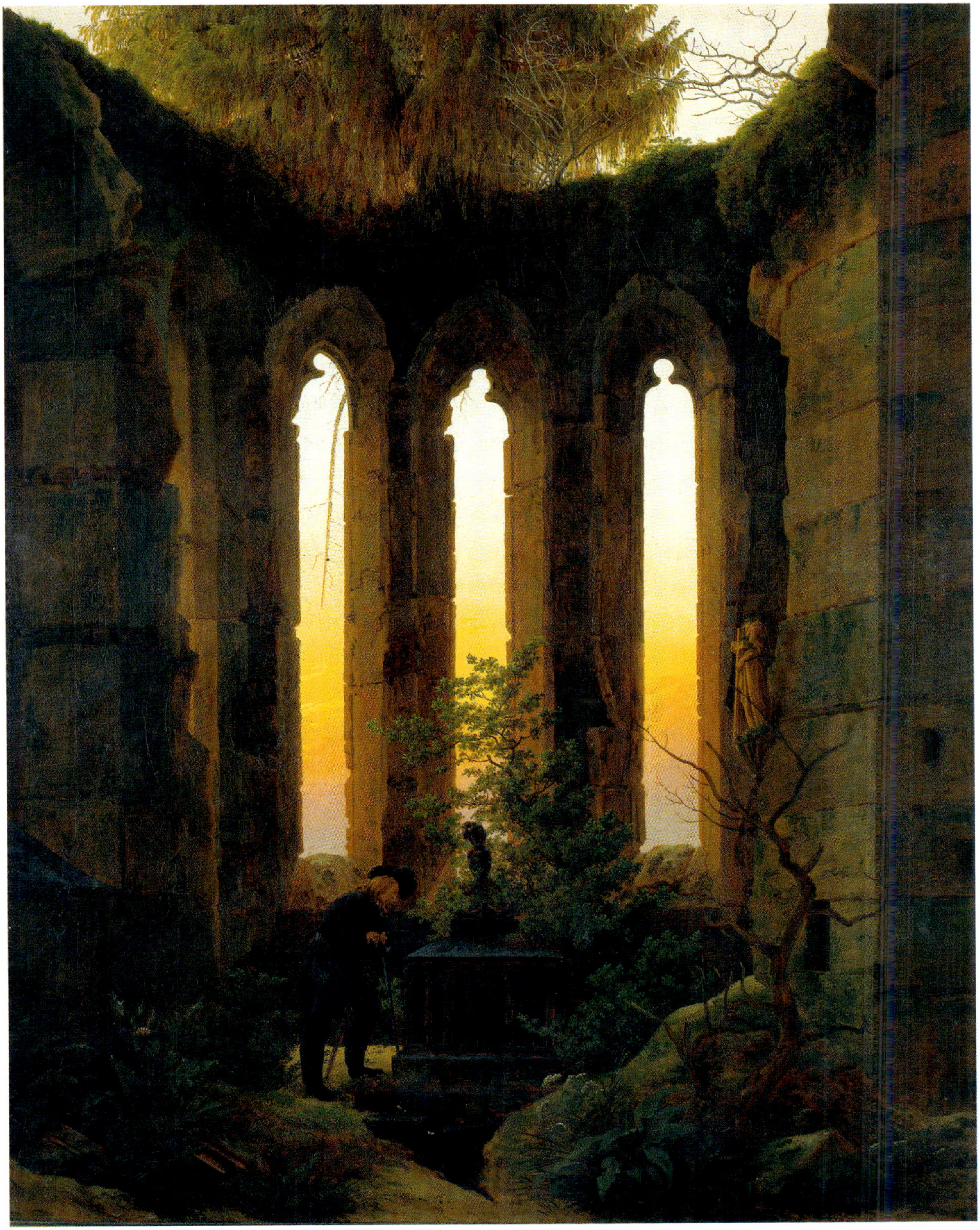

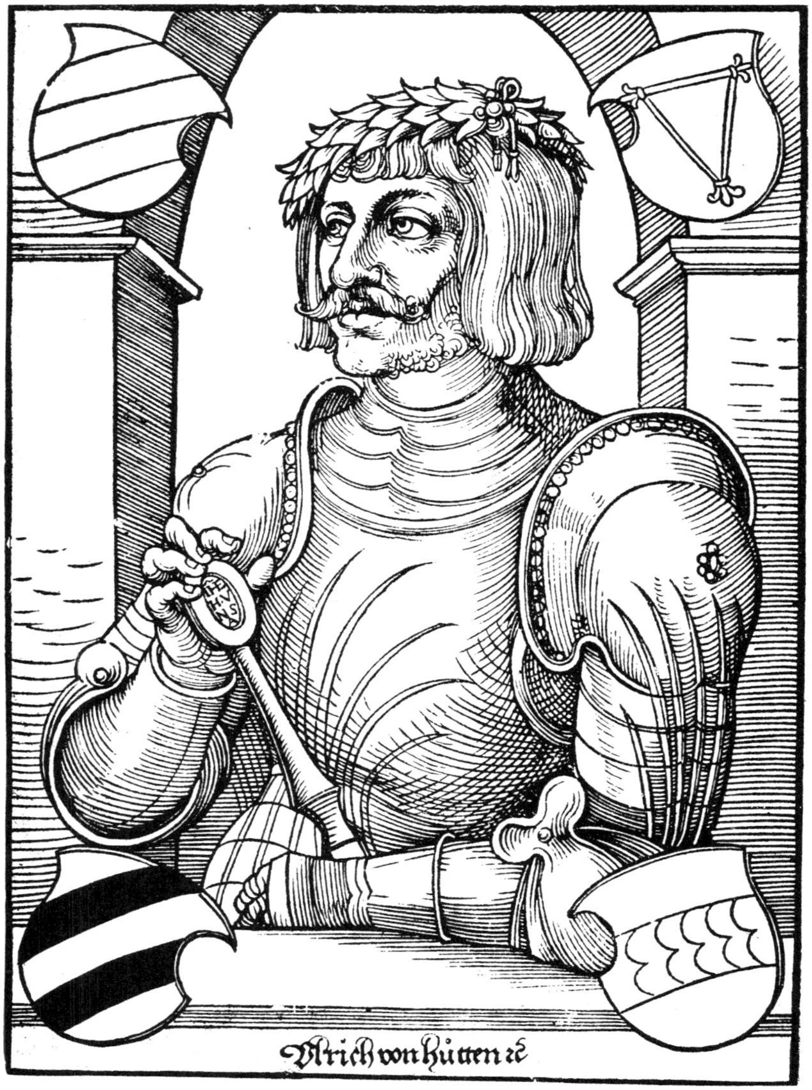

Arndt and the others

Friedrich had bemoaned princely rule and the German lack of self-confidence in a letter to the poet Ernst Moritz Arndt (1769–1860). Arndt was one of those for whom French rule was unbearable. "The Rhine, Germany's river but not Germany's border" ran one of his patriotic songs.

Friedrich has inscribed Arndt's name on the sarcophagus in writing so small as to be virtually illegible. He has listed other names, too, most of them accompanied by a date, and all linked with the attempt to shake off foreign rule, unify Germany, and give the people a voice.

Gerhard Johann David von Scharnhorst (1715–1813), Prussian military reformer: Scharnhorst recognized that, after the French Revolution, wars were no longer being waged between sovereigns but between nations, and sought to make a popular army out of the Frederician standing army. The later much-cited concept of the "citizen in uniform" goes back to his writings.

Karl Reichsfreiherr vom und zum Stein (1757–1831), Prussian administrative reformer: Baron vom und zum Stein enforced the abolition of serfdom; he sought to restrict the absolutist power of the princes by introducing self-government for cities and municipalities.

Friedrich Ludwig Jahn (1778–1852), known as the father of gymnastics: In 1811 Jahn organized the first gymnastics centre near Berlin. He propagated physical education, which he placed in the service of the national movement. He invented the German word *Volkstum* (a concept meaning the national characteristics of a people) and was one of the founders of the Lützow volunteer corps and the *Burschenschaften*, political student organizations which sprang up in the early 19th century.

Joseph von Görres (1776–1848), publisher: Görres founded the *Rheinischer Merkur*, the newspaper read by every liberal of the day, which campaigned against restoration, against the "new" system of princely rule, and against the princes' police and their snooping ways – until the paper was banned and Görres had to flee Prussia. That was in 1819, the year that Friedrich has painted after Görres' name. Görres escaped to Switzerland, like Hutten before him.

And the others? What were the others doing when Friedrich painted his picture? Scharnhorst was wounded in 1813 and died that same year. Jahn was in prison. Stein had long since been dismissed from the Prussian king's employ, had worked for the Tsar for a few years, and now lived in seclusion, far removed from politics. Ernst Moritz Arndt had lost his history professorship at Bonn University in 1820 on grounds of "demagogy".

Arndt was forbidden to teach for twenty years. After his rehabilitation, the files of his trial were published. It thereby emerged that one of the most important pieces of evidence used against him was the letter from Caspar David Friedrich in which Friedrich used the phrase "princes' serfs".

Friedrich was probably himself a victim of such "anti-demagogic" purges. From 1816 onwards, the Prussian ruling house purchased no more pictures from him. When an ordinary professorship became free at the Dresden Academy in 1824, he didn't get the job, even though it should have been awarded to a painter of his standing.

Old German dress

The man beside the tomb is wearing a half-length dark coat, long hair, and a biretta. This style of dress was deliberately adopted by men of a nationalistic and liberal frame of mind.

Ernst Moritz Arndt had already called for a "national dress" in 1814. For the man: "His usual dress is the old German frock coat, which, nowhere tailored, falls simply down so that it covers half the thigh above the knee." He had no fixed ideas as regards women's dress, however: "Let them devise their own idea of beauty."

Friedrich dressed his figures in an "old German" style as from around 1815. The men wear the frock coat and biretta, the women long dresses done up to the neck, with lace collars and puffed sleeves. This was by no means simply a whim or peculiarity of Arndt and Friedrich alone. A Russian officer observed scornfully: "Everyone was seized by the fever of Germanness and adopted the most absurd fashions in all seriousness. The women dressed in medieval German style; anything foreign was to be banned, even from the language, and replaced by German words". Many of those with patriotic feelings changed the way they spelt *deutsch* (German) to *teutsch* as Luther and Hutten had done before them. The difference of one letter made their sentiments clear.

Old German dress was worn by artists, professors, and students alike. It was particularly common amongst the political *Burschenschaft* associations. When a member of one such association murdered the dramatist August von Kotzebue, who was in Russian employ, it was a signal to the princes to take drastic action. Their Karlsbad resolutions of 1819 included the following: all newspapers to be subject to strict censorship, harsh persecution of all "demagogues", banning of *Burschenschaften*, and banning of old German dress. Friedrich continued to paint it all the same. In 1820 he was paid a visit in his studio, and showed his guests the painting *Two Men Contemplating the Moon* – in which both male figures are wearing birettas, and one of them a dark frock coat. By way of explanation, so one of the visitors later related, Friedrich said ironically: "They are plotting demagogic intrigues ..."

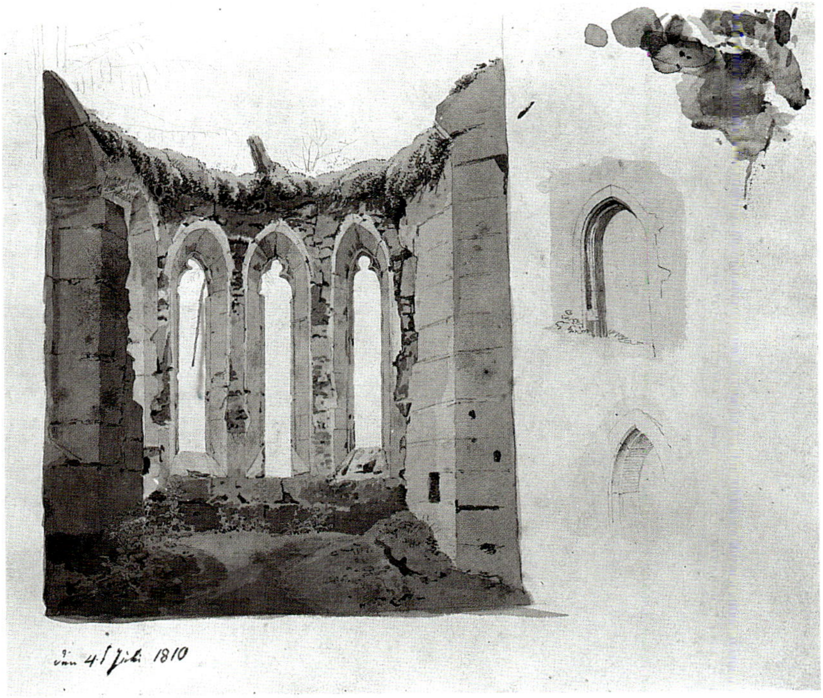

The discovery of the Gothic

In Saxony, near the small town of Zittau, lies a hill rising to some five hundred metres. Called the Oybin, it is home to the ruins of a castle and a monastery church. On his excursions from Dresden, Friedrich visited the Oybin and sketched the church ruins. A watercolour of the scene is dated 4 July 1810. Friedrich locates Hutten's "tomb" within these same ruins.

They are Gothic ruins. Gothic churches and church ruins occur repeatedly in Friedrich's paintings and held a special significance for his contemporaries, too. For them, the Gothic was not just another epoch in the history of art, like the Renaissance or the Baroque. Gothic was the code word, or rather the code symbol for a great German past. Like wearing old German dress, displaying an overt interest in the Gothic was the sign of a certain partisanship.

The veneration of the Gothic had begun with Goethe's essay on Strasbourg cathedral of 1773, in which the poet effectively rediscovered the Gothic style. Describing his previous attitude towards this style, he wrote: "Under the heading of Gothic, I lumped together all the synonymous misconceptions of something indeterminate, disorganized, unnatural, cobbled together, patched up and overladen that had ever passed through my head." But: "With what unexpected emotion the sight [of Strasburg cathedral] overtook me when first I stood before it!" The twenty-four-year-old, acquainted only with Hesse, Thuringia, Saxony, and the Alsace, pronounced the Gothic cathedral a "German architecture, for the Italians can boast noone of their own, and even less so the French."

Goethe's essay made history because it appeared at the right time. This was a period in which the Germans were liberating themselves from the cultural hegemony of France – albeit a hegemony not forced upon them by the French, but one that the Germans (and most other Europeans) had for several centuries imposed upon themselves. French was the language spoken by the aristocracy, and their tastes were also French. Hence any examples of German culture that could be held up against them inevitably came from "the people". Thus 1806 saw the publication of *Des Knaben Wunderhorn* (The Boy's Magic Horn), a collection of German folksongs, followed in 1807 by Görres' study of German folk literature, *Die teutschen Volksbücher*, and in 1812 the *Kinder- und Hausmärchen* (Fairy Tales) by the Brothers Grimm.

However strange it may seem to us today, this difference between the aristocracy and the people, between high and low, was carried over into the evaluation of the Gothic. Germany's France-oriented nobility saw its architectural ideal in classical antiquity, and its buildings were correspondingly classical, classicist, inspired by Greek temples. In his essay on Strasburg cathedral, Goethe imagines giving a piece of mock antiquity, a "container à la grecque", to a French passer-by. The cathedral's architect is simply called "Erwin". Goethe venerates the non-aristocrat; for him, as for the Romantics, the Gothic was not anti-aristocratic, but rather non-aristocratic. It was the art not of the princes, but of the people.

Of course Friedrich did not use Gothic architecture as a means of fighting the class war. His painting was never so direct, so agitatorial. And of course the Gothic was never a peculiarly German style. Only someone who was anti-French in his thinking and who was unfamiliar with English architecture could insist otherwise. But for Friedrich and many of his contemporaries, the Gothic became inextricably bound up with a vision of a great German past, in which the princes did not fight over scraps of territory, but in which sovereigns and subjects, Church and State co-existed in peaceful harmony. While this harmonious vision was intended to give strength to the liberals amongst the Germans, it more likely provided them with a refuge from the misery of the present.

The vast universe in a constricted present

Hutten's *Tomb* was exhibited for the first time in 1824 in Dresden. A sympathetic, anonymous critic structured his review around a fictitious dialogue in which a woman called Rosa says: "I wish I could stand beside the lonely traveller who is contemplating the hero's tomb so thoughtfully, particularly since I think I recognize in him the dear artist himself ..."

The man's profile bears no obvious similarity to Friedrich's own, but in a broader sense Rosa is undoubtedly right. Figures sunk in quiet contemplation stand in many of Friedrich's paintings; we know from his letters that he himself felt the need for contemplation of this kind. He was not alone: as the writings of the Romantics demonstrate, contemplation, reflection, and self-absorption were elevated almost to a cult by his contemporaries. As Novalis wrote: "But the art of quiet contemplation, of creative observation of the world, is a difficult one; it demands unceasing serious reflection and strict sobriety". And elsewhere: "The mysterious path leads inward. Within us, or nowhere, is eternity and its worlds, the past and the future."

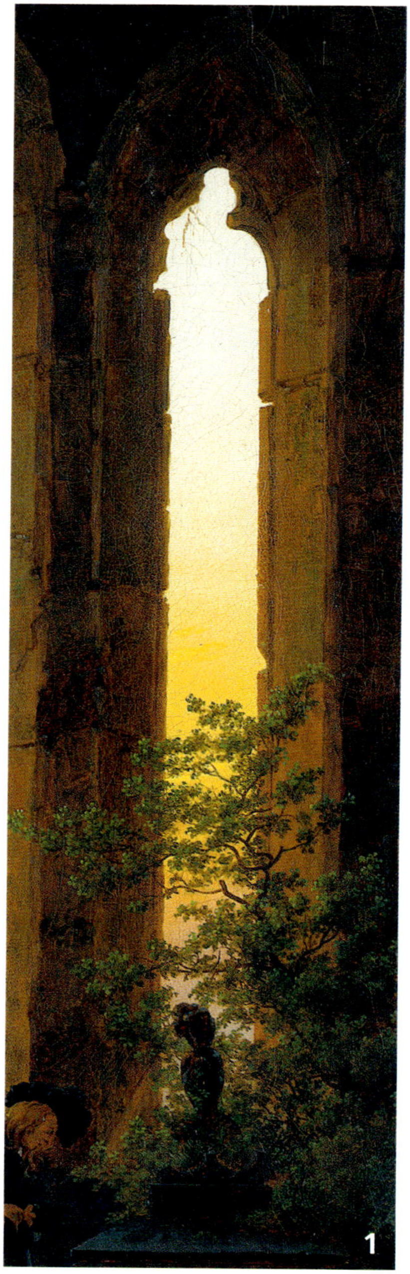
1

It is not difficult to imagine the male figure on his way "inwards", in mystical union with the universe, with nature, future, and past. Such an interpretation is easily applicable to other Friedrich pictures. But not to *Hutten's Tomb*: here we are brought firmly back to earth with names and dates. Compared with feelings of communion with the universe, they seem pedantically concrete, banally realistic, tied to the present and the political situation.

A contradiction? Certainly, but one which is resolved when one remembers the situation in which the Germans then found themselves: they wanted to become a nation and were prevented from doing so by the territorial princes; they sought to expand their personal sphere of freedom and were defeated. Apart from the few months of the wars of liberation, they were condemned to endure their fate silently. The frustration felt by Germany's citizens became one of the driving forces behind the Romantic Movement, indeed behind intellectual life as a whole, and behind the cultural flowering of these decades. One of Goethe's epigrams runs: "You hope in vain, Germans, to form yourselves into a nation; Make yourselves instead freer people."

The concept of the freer individual in outwardly unfree circumstances was one that led to the exaltation of introspection. *Hutten's Tomb* speaks not only of the freedom of the inner universe, however, but also of the social conditions that have made it necessary; not only of the harmonious vision of a medieval past, but also of the constraints of the present. There are few paintings by German artists that make an intellectual and political situation so clearly visible.

A painting is passed over in silence

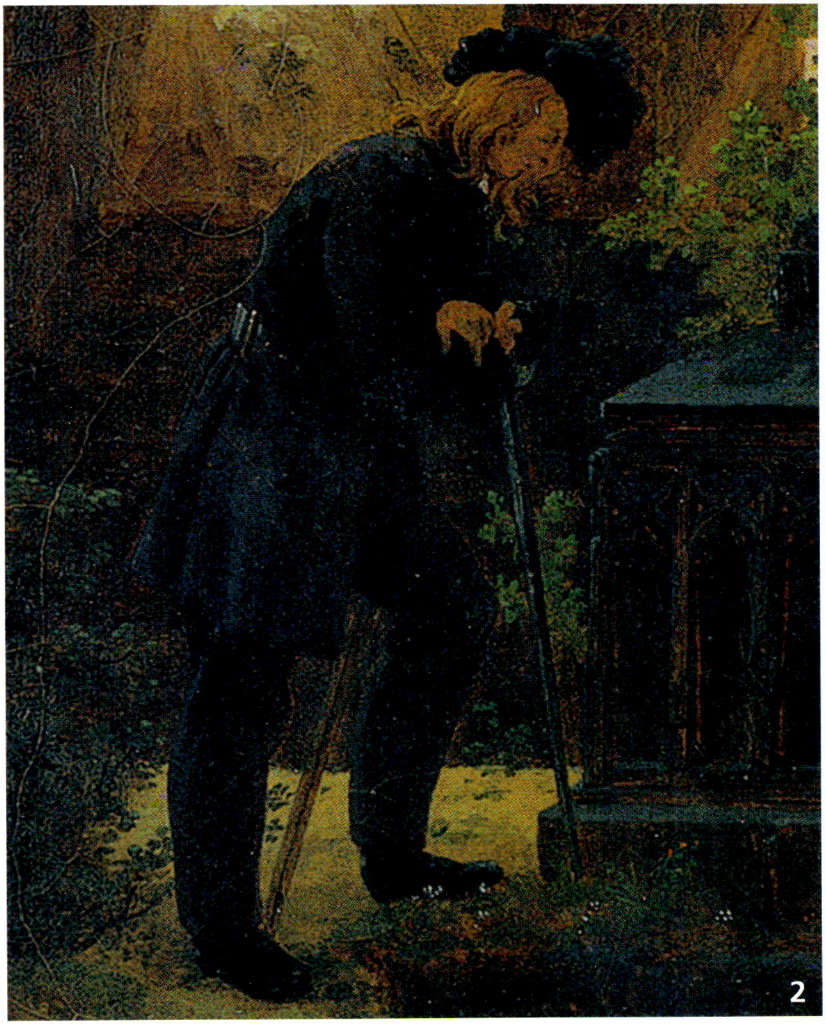

Something of the intellectual and political situation was also revealed by the reactions to the picture. The painting is undated. Art historians place it around 1823, a year that marked a double anniversary – ten years since the start of the wars of liberation, three hundred years since Hutten's death. The painting was certainly finished by 1824, when it appeared in the Dresden Art Exhibition. The exhibition catalogue lists three works by Friedrich: *A Mountainous Region*, *The Frozen Sea*, and *Ruins of an Old Chapel*. It can be concluded from the description of the anonymous reviewer and his fictitious Rosa that the scene of the ruined chapel was in fact *Hutten's Tomb*. Yet no word is breathed about Hutten, Arndt, or any of the other names included in the painting. Nor are they mentioned in the six other reviews reprinted in Helmut Börsch-Supan's 1973 catalogue raisonné of Friedrich's works! Were they written too small? Certainly, if you didn't know they were there, you could easily overlook the names and dates; but word of such a hidden message would have soon got around amongst *aficionados* of Friedrich's painting, of which the "Rosa" reviewer was undoubtedly one. He must have had other reasons for ignoring the names and dates.

In 1826 the painting appeared in Hamburg, in the first exhibition staged by the Kunstverein. Title: *View through a Ruin*. Price: 25 louis d'or. Once again, Hutten's name is missing from the catalogue, and no one would have spotted it in the painting, which was hung high up and was poorly lit. "To allow the observer to examine Friedrich's *View* properly, this picture of all pictures should have been hung near the window", wrote one reviewer. But that was precisely where the organizers chose not to place it.

That year the picture travelled to an exhibition at the Royal Academy of Arts, Berlin. The catalogue lists three landscapes by Friedrich and – at last – *Ulrich von Hutten's Memorial*. Börsch-Supan gives five reviews of the exhibition. All mention the landscapes. Two remain completely silent on the subject of the Hutten painting, two praise it without going into any depth, and one claims that it is "a picture the artist would do better in future not to submit to exhibitions". Perhaps Friedrich took this piece of advice, or perhaps he sold the picture; whatever the case, the painting is not mentioned again.

The question remains whether *Hutten's Tomb* actually hung in the Dresden and Hamburg exhibitions at all, and also whether Friedrich added the compromising names and dates at a later date. Neither possibility can be ruled out, although they are unlikely. It is more probable that writers and newspaper publishers simply didn't want to bring trouble upon themselves. They were censored – and very severely so. They did not want their newspapers to be banned, as had happened to Görres' *Rheinischer Merkur*. And the only way to ensure that was to make no mention of persons blacklisted by the authorities, to forget about the wars of liberation and the "thinking and beliefs that were once Prussia's thinking and beliefs" (Arndt).

Why, then, should Hutten's name have been mentioned in the Berlin catalogue? We are given a clue: one of the reviewers notes that Friedrich had promised to donate the sales proceeds to the "needy amongst the Greeks". This was a reference to the Greek struggle for liberation from Turkish foreign rule. It is possible that Hutten's name and this picture were considered more acceptable in the context of a foreign, far-off struggle for freedom and nationhood than as a comment on the situation in Germany: enthusiastic support for the Greek struggle for freedom as compensation for the lack of freedom at home.

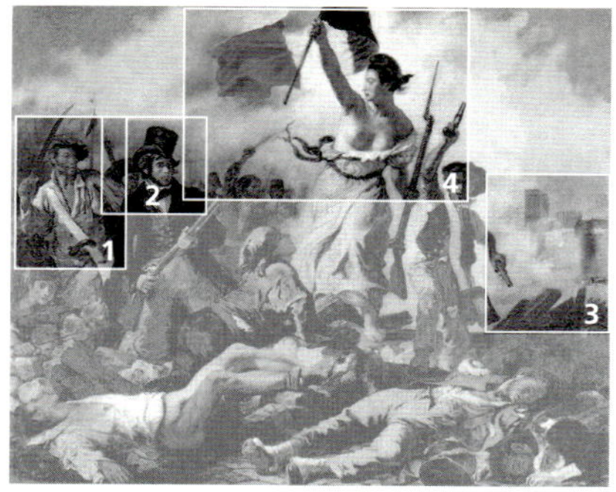
1
2
4
3

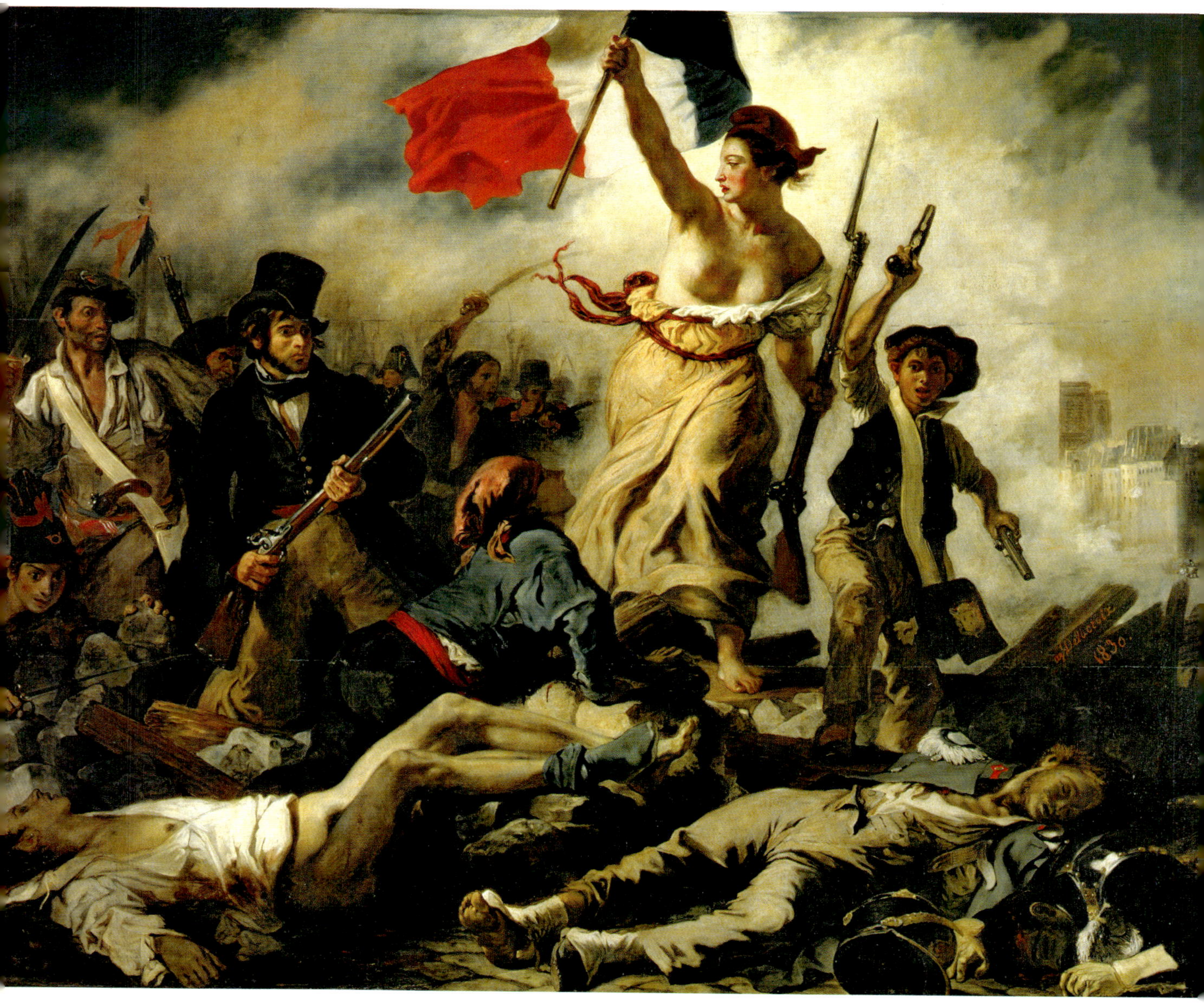

Eugène Delacroix: Liberty Leading the People, 1830

A Painter on the Barricades

The sun beats down on Paris through a haze of gun smoke. 28 July 1830 was a hot day. At the palace of St Cloud a few kilometres outside Paris, where King Charles X spent the summer months, it was already 35°C degrees in the shade before lunch, announced one of royal pages. There had been fighting in the capital since the day before. The citizens of Paris and the King's troops had formed ranks on opposite sides. Barricades had been erected. Shots had been fired. People had been killed. Early that morning, the senior commander of the royal troops informed the King: "This is no longer a riot. This is a revolution."

Fighting alongside each other on the barricades were men from widely differing backgrounds. The bourgeois, in his top hat, frock coat and neatly tied cravat, has taken up a shotgun. The worker in his cap and open-necked shirt is wielding a sabre. An adolescent street urchin is brandishing a pistol in each hand, and in the background a two-cornered hat identifies its wearer as a student of the Ecole Polytechnique. Some 7,000 to 8,000 militant Parisians fought at the barricades that day, women and children amongst them. That seems barely a handful in a city of 800,000 inhabitants. But the insurgents could count on the sympathy and active support of virtually the entire population. They were supplied all over the city with munitions and refreshments, while cobblestones and items of furniture rained down on the heads of the soldiers from the windows above.

The insurgents did not have a leader. In Delacroix'ss painting, they are headed by Liberty, personified as a Greek goddess. Over the bodies of fallen cuirassiers, she leads her followers to glory, to *gloire*. Thus the three days of 27, 28 and 29 July 1830 went down in history as *les trois glorieuses*. "Holy July days: how beautiful was the sun", wrote Heinrich Heine, the German poet who had made Paris his home, "and how great the people of Paris!"

The Parisians had gone to the barricades in revolt against the policies of a king who wanted to turn back the wheel of time. Charles X came late to power and wanted to be absolute ruler. It was an ambition that had cost his eldest brother, Louis XVI, his head. Only in 1814, after the downfall of Napoleon, had the victorious allied forces restored the Bourbons to the French throne, albeit with instructions to grant their people a parliament and a charter, a form of constitution. Because Charles X considered the newly-elected parliament of 1830 too liberal, he resolved to set aside the charter and govern by decree.

The uprising in Paris was directly sparked by three royal decrees published on 26 July. They abolished the civil rights set out in the charter and announced the introduction of censorship of the press, the dissolution of parliament and the implementation of a new electoral system that would ensure the King a compliant popular assembly. The timing seemed favourable: the new parliament had not yet met and everyone of any influence spent the summer months in the country anyway. "Whatever you do", the Prefect of Paris assured the King on 25 July, "Paris will not stir."

When the Parisians nevertheless stirred with such speed and violence, the King's generals were taken by surprise. Only some 12,000 soldiers could be mustered at short notice in the Paris area, and many of these refused to fire at civilians. Entire units deserted, and their commander, the Duke of Ragusa, was unable to quash the uprising. By the third day the revolutionaries held all the strategically important points in the city; they even stormed the Tuileries, the royal palace that Ragusa had made his headquarters. The troops were forced to withdrew from Paris and the King capitulated to the demands of his people. He could expect no assistance from any of the other European monarchs, who had guaranteed the original charter and were angered by his actions. Charles X was forced to abdicate in favour of his cousin Louis-Philippe, Duke of Orleans.

The July Revolution wrought changes in France: there was no more talk of kings "by the grace of God". The new monarch had to swear his allegiance to the constitution and called himself the "Citizen King". The events that had brought him to the throne – a violent popular uprising – made the King uneasy, however. Hence the new regime was at pains to cleanse the revolution of its threatening image and glorify it in ceremonies and with decorations.

Medals were awarded to the "courageous barricade fighters", and collections were taken for the orphans and widows of the insurgents. A column to commemorate the dead was quickly erected, unveiled with much pomp and numerous performances of the *Symphonie funèbre et triomphale* specially composed for the occasion by Hector Berlioz. (The monument can still be seen today on the Place de la Bastille.) Art, too, helped in the assimilation of the bloody events of the recent past: over 40 portrayals of the "three glorious days" filled the Paris Salon of 1831, Delacroix's canvas amongst them. It was purchased by the King for 3,000 francs and earned the artist – like the barricade fighters – an official decoration.

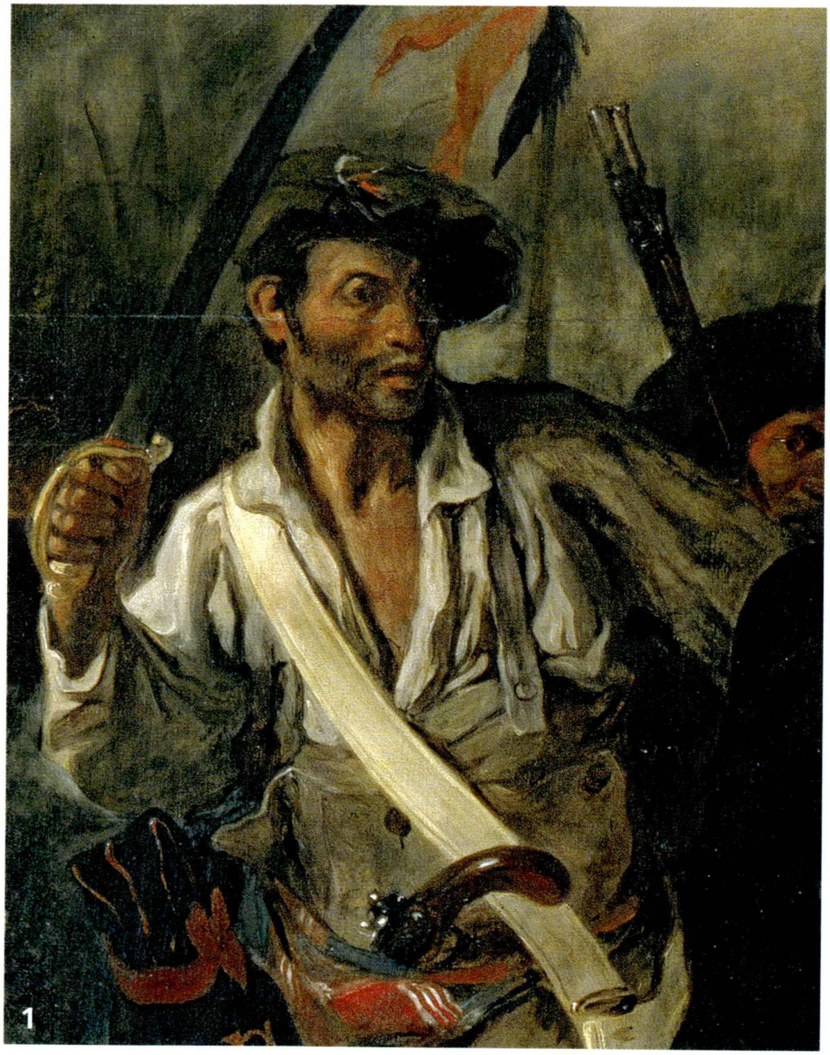

1

Wielding a sabre for the freedom of the press

His braces are not concealed beneath a jacket and waistcoat, and his pistol is thrust into the red, white and blue revolutionary's scarf around his waist. This insurgent is no bourgeois, but more likely a worker – perhaps one of the 6,000 printing workers who suddenly found themselves out on the street on the morning of 27 July because the newspapers were no longer allowed to go to press. When royal troops tried to clear the crowds thronging the centre of the city that same afternoon, it was angry printers, so it is said, who threw the first stones. The closure of the print shops was the first consequence of the royal decree curtailing the freedom of the press. Newspapers, "whatever their content", had to be submitted to the censors eight days (!) in advance of publication. They were perceived by the Ministry as "instruments of disorder and sedition"; should they appear without permission, they were impounded and their printing presses destroyed. A number of pamphlets still managed to appear that day. Inflammatory protests against the muzzling of the press were printed in secret, posted on house walls, read out in public. They whipped up emotions and created the climate in which printers armed themselves with cobblestone and soldiers, without command or warning, opened fire on the crowd.

The Parisians were driven onto the barricades first and foremost in defence of freedom of the press and their elected parliament. That workers should also join their ranks was, for many bourgeois, unexpected and unhoped-for. Why should they fight for a press that they couldn't read? For a parliament in which they had no representatives and in whose elections they were not permitted to take part, because they owned no land? Prior to 1830, no political party had concerned itself with the rights of the working classes; they were isolated, for strikes, collective agreements and gatherings of more than 20 people were all prohibited by law.

Economically, too, the workers were badly off. Of 224,000 Parisian households, 136,000 were officially classed as "needy". Unemployment was rife, wages had fallen by 22% over the past 5 years, while prices had risen by 66%. Poverty and hunger have always provided fertile ground for revolt, and when the first shots rang out, the majority of workers were quick to grasp what the uprising was really about. Old memories of 1789 were suddenly rekindled: liberty was once more at stake. "Down with the tyrants!"

The proletariat soon made up the majority of those fighting. Author and eyewitness Stendhal wrote: "On 28 July there was just one well-dressed man for every 100 men without stockings or jacket." That the workers were willing to submit to the command of the bourgeois on the barricades was something regularly commented upon. The middle classes were astonished, too, at the fact that the workers drank hardly any alcohol and were at pains to respect the property of others. There were only a few instances of looting and arson during the July Revolution.

At the end of the July Revolution, the populace dispersed back to its suburbs with just as much discipline as it had fought. The comradeship between worker and bourgeois that Delacroix portrays on the barricades quickly evaporated. The uprising brought benefits only to the land-owning bourgeoisie; apart from medals and glory, the workers gained nothing from it. The price of bread continued to soar, unemployment grew, and four years later the government of the Citizen King would open fire on striking workers.

The young Romantics loved a fight

Although Delacroix was resident in Paris during the July Revolution, according to eyewitnesses he took no active part in it. He wrote to his brother: "If I haven't lived for my country, at least I shall paint for it!" It is his eyes that stare out from beneath the fashionable silk top hat of the bourgeois on the barricades. The 32-year-old artist portrays himself as the writer Théophile Gautier (1811–1872) describes him: "his pale complexion, his abundant black hair, his eyes with their feline expression, surmounted by thick brows slightly raised ... a physiognomy of strange and exotic beauty, fierce and almost unsettling; one could have taken him for an Indian maharaja". It was often said that he looked like a prince. His real father was probably Prince Talleyrand, his mother's lover. Officially, however, he was the son of Delacroix, an official in the imperial administration, and he was brought up in a bourgeois household.

Alexandre Dumas the Elder (1802–1870) observed that the artist was not particularly enthusiastic about the uprising at first, and that his sympathies were only truly aroused by the sight of the tricolour fluttering from the towers of Notre-Dame. It was the flag for which one of Delacroix's elder brothers had died at the Battle of Friedland under Napoleon. His other elder brother had formerly served as a general. Following the restoration of the Bourbons, he had been demobilized and put on half pay: like many of Napoleon's soldiers, he mourned for the "great" times that lay in the past.

Mourning alongside the old veterans was the entire younger generation, to which Delacroix also belonged – a generation of 20 to 30-year-olds, "conceived between two wars, brought up in schools to the rolling of drums", as the poet Alfred de Musset (1810–1857) described them. They were the discontented *enfants du siècle*. They had spent their childhood hearing about and dreaming of heroic deeds and *grandeur*, and now they felt cheated: under the Bourbons, it was the cautious bankers and bourgeoisie who had the say.

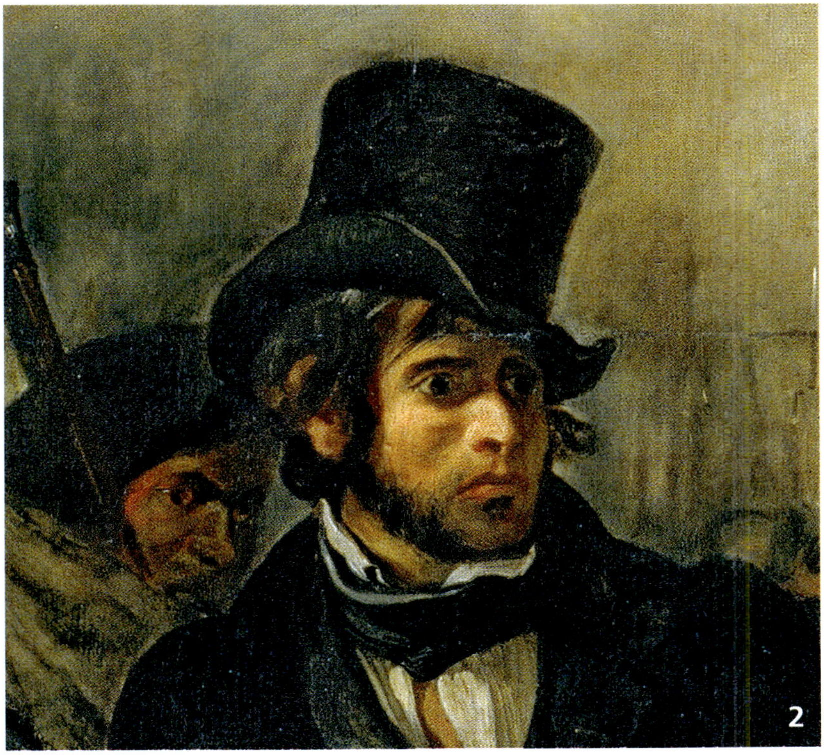

2

In the years prior to the July Revolution, this frustrated younger generation had tried to fight the battles that had otherwise escaped them by transplanting them to the intellectual and artistic arena. They sought refuge from drab reality in far-off, exotic lands or in a savage, heroic past. They thereby formed part of the Romantic movement that since the beginning of the century had been challenging the rules, authorities and traditions of art. "All power to the imagination", proclaimed the young Romantics. They mocked and provoked their "narrow-minded" enemies, and sometimes even fought them: on 25 January 1830 they staged their first great battle – in the theatre. At the première of *Hernani*, a Romantic drama by Victor Hugo (1802–1885), they set to with fists and sticks against the supporters of the Classical school. The painters, too, took part in the auditorium battle; their own preference for wild, exotic and dramatic scenes imbued with Romantic pathos had been in evidence since the Salon of 1827. Delacroix's own exhibits included *The Death of Sardanapalus* and *Greece Mourning on the Ruins of Missolonghi*.

The Romantic artists called for freedom – freedom in art, freedom in daily life and freedom, too, in politics. On 28 July 1830, however, only a few mounted the barricades themselves. The rest – for a wide variety of reasons – stayed at home. Even the liberal journalists penned their impassioned calls for resistance against the despotism of the state from the safety of their writing-desks. They were no men of action.

But their words were heard by a young generation who, filled with Romantic enthusiasm, rushed out to fight and to die. Of the 1800 insurgents who fell in the July Revolution, the majority were young men or even boys, such as the urchin brandishing the two pistols in Delacroix's painting. The Romantic author Victor Hugo (who stayed at home on 28 July because his wife was in labour) created a monument to them in his novel *Les Miserables* of 1862. Gavroche is the lad from the Paris gutter who loves humour and anarchy and who, caught on the wrong side of the barricade, faces the muskets shooting at him with a satirical song on his lips. He dies a hero's death. Perhaps Victor Hugo was inspired by Delacroix's painting, which with its stirring atmosphere and political charge has become a masterpiece of French Romanticism.

Paris invented the barricade

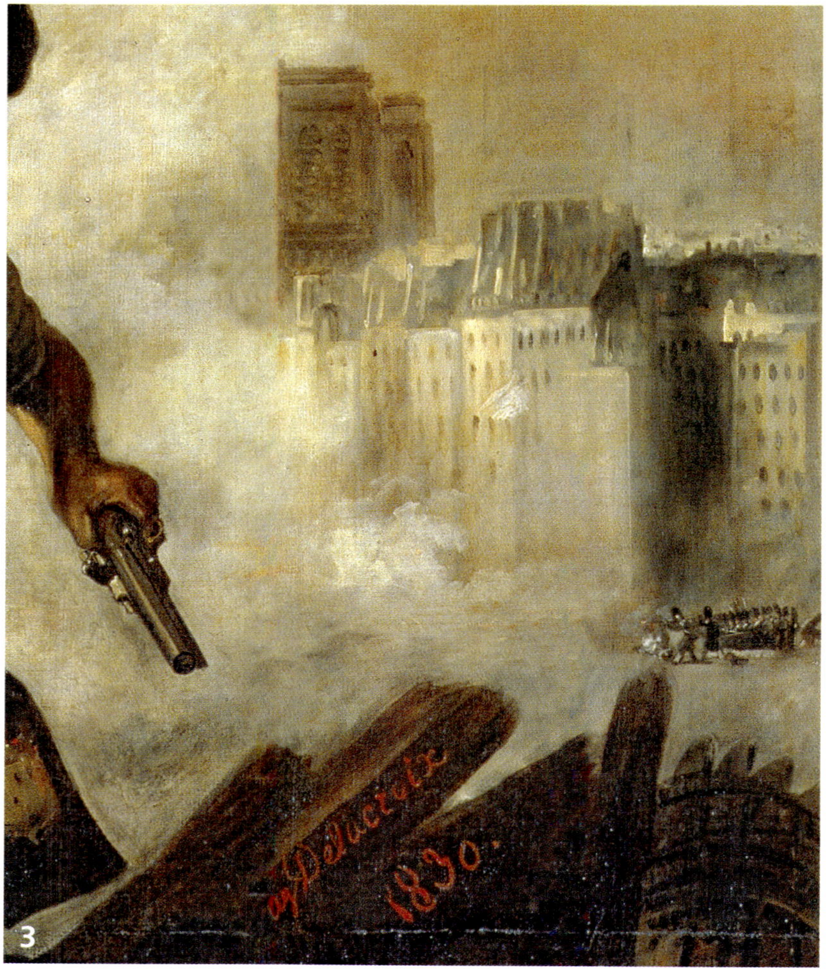

3

Weapons were in plentiful supply in Paris in 1830. Just three years earlier, after disrespectful shots had rung out during a ceremonial parade in front of the King, the government had decided to dissolve the traditional militia. Incomprehensibly, however, it failed to call in the weapons these troops held. The workers – who were excluded from the militia because they couldn't afford to equip themselves – looted the arsenals and armed themselves with shotguns, revolvers and sabres seized from the museum of historical weaponry. Anyone still left empty-handed simply waited for a comrade to fall on the barricade, and then took up their gun.

One of the dead soldiers in the foreground of Delacroix's painting has also been stripped of his shoes, stockings and trousers. The uprising brought not only workers and bourgeois out onto the streets, but also organized gangs of beggars and criminals from the Paris underworld, who appeared at the first exchange of fire.

There were some 4,000 to 6,000 barricades in Paris on 28 July 1830. The word comes from *barriques*, the barrels which, filled with earth, formed their base. Piled on top of them were felled trees, tables, cupboards from nearby houses, the occasional overturned omnibus and indeed anything else that came to hand. Sandwiched in between were mattresses, intended to absorb the bullets. The whole was nailed together with planks, and a makeshift flight of cobblestone steps was constructed on the defenders' side, so that they could storm over the top in a massed attack as the main figures in Delacroix's painting are doing.

Heinrich Heine marvelled at the speed with which the barricades were erected. "The high bulwarks which German thoroughness would need a whole day to complete", he wrote, "are here improvised in just a few minutes."

The French capital had a tradition of building barricades. Its militant citizens had already blockaded the streets in 1588 and 1648 and battled against the royal troops. On both occasions the then sovereign, first Henry III, then the young Louis XIV, had been hastily forced to leave the city. Louis never forgave the recalcitrant Parisians and later moved to Versailles.

When Heinrich Heine's compatriot Ludwig Börne arrived in Paris in September 1830, he felt the urge to take off his boots, for "one should only tread these sacred cobbles barefoot". He knew the role the hard, rounded sandstone cobbles had played in the July Revolution. They could be dug up quickly, and as well as being an important constituent of the barricades, they were also hurled out of windows onto the heads of many of the King's soldiers. Future governments would learn their lesson and rapidly replace the dangerous stones with gravel and asphalt. They would also tear down the buildings in the historical heart of the city, so as to destroy the winding alleys which offered ideal locations for barricades and which made it impossible for the royal cavalry to attack on horseback. Barricades would nevertheless continue to be built in Paris – in 1848, in 1872 and most recently in 1968 ...

Delacroix's barricade stands not in a narrow alleyway in an old part of the city, but on a spacious square, probably the former Place Saint-Antoine (today Place de la Bastille), where the royal prison once loomed and the July Column still rises. In 1830 the square was a wasteland, covered in building rubble. In the background, royal troops are marching past. The alarm bells rang out without interruption and, it is reported, the strains of the *Marseillaise*, the banned hymn of the Revolution, were regularly to be heard. The crowds cheered and wept when towards 3 o'clock in the afternoon they saw, for the first time since 1815, the old flag – the tricolour – fluttering from the distant towers of Notre-Dame.

Blue, white and red: the large flag at the centre of the picture billows over the heads of all, fighting, injured and dead. Improvised out of three scraps of cloth tied together, it also flies in the background. The three colours are repeated even in the clothes of the injured man looking up at the goddess Liberty. According to eyewitnesses, on the afternoon of 28 July they suddenly appeared all over Paris.

The tricolour had been created during the Revolution of 1789, when the Paris militia started wearing cockades in the city's two colours of red and blue. Louis XVI was obliged to accept them, but added the royal white before adopting them himself. The revolutionary troops made the tricolour the French national flag, and Napoleon retained it. In 1815 the Bourbons banned it and replaced it with their white flag. In 1830 the tricolour was accompanied by very mixed and at times contradictory emotions: for the young generation and the republicans, the old flag signified the sovereignty of the people and the victory of liberty over tyranny. For the majority of people, it evoked quite simply a patriotic nostalgia, memories of the "great" era in French history, when the tricolour under Napoleon had carried liberty, civilization and France's glory across all of Europe.

The powerfully-built woman who is waving the flag is also a relic of the Revolution. The classically-educated patriots adopted the personification of Liberty from the ancient Romans and used it to adorn their coins and letterheads. In 1789 statues of Liberty were erected everywhere. (At the end of the 19th century France would even give the United States its Statue of Liberty!)

The red cap on Liberty's head, however, would have shocked most of those who saw it. In 1792 it had served to identify the militant revolutionaries of the Jacobin club, who instituted the Reign of Terror during the 1st Paris commune. Since then the cap had symbolized both Republic and bloodthirsty Terror together. The two seemed inseparably linked: you couldn't have one without the other. This was the attitude adopted by politicians, bankers and journalists while others were battling on the barricades. To them, the safest way of ending the civil war was to keep the monarchy, but change the monarch. To the disappointment of the republicans and the young generation of insurgents, it was their solution that won the day. Instead of freedom, reforms and progress, there was order, authority and stability.

The tricolour would remain the national flag, but the canvas in which it here billows would never find its way into the throne room for which it was purchased. It disappeared instead into a gloomy palace corridor, and it was not long before Delacroix was asked to take it away. It was fetched out again briefly during the revolution of 1848, but only went on permanent display in 1855. Since 1874 it has hung in the Louvre. Prior to the introduction of the Euro, its two main figures – Liberty carrying a rifle and the pistol-touting urchin – adorned the 100-franc note of the Fifth French Republic.

The tricolour stirred every heart

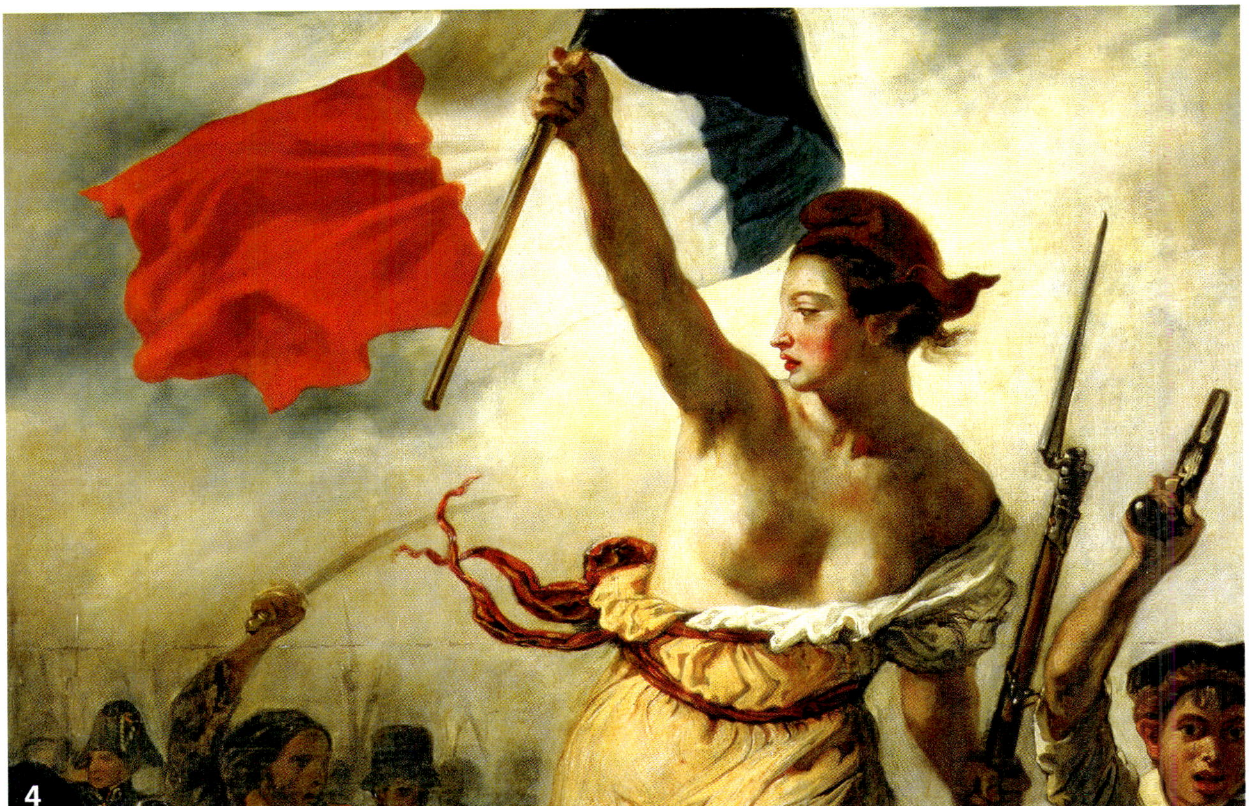
4

Ando Hiroshige: Morning Mist by Mishima, c. 1833

Japanese on their travels

Ando Hiroshige (1797–1858), master of the Japanese woodcut, liked to portray the landscape partially concealed – beneath a blanket of snow, behind a curtain of rain, or palely swathed in mist. In the present print, only the group in the foreground – two travellers, three porters, and a man leading a horse – can be clearly seen. Further back, the trees, the gateway, the roofs, and the three other figures are reduced to silhouettes and a single shade of colour. They float in the mist at a distance we cannot define. The woodcut is dominated not by the colours and forms of a specific landscape, but by what conceals them – a misty atmosphere, a diffuse light.

The red seal at the top of the picture, which measures 25 by 38 centimetres, reveals its title, *Morning Mist*. The black characters to the right state that the woodcut depicts the town of Mishima and forms part of the series *Fifty-three Stations on the Tokaido*. The Tokaido was a road some five hundred kilometres in length. It crossed mountains and rivers and linked the two most important cities in the country, Edo (present-day Tokyo) and Kyoto, the old imperial capital. The emperor's role was by then purely symbolic; real power lay with the shogun, the military dictatorship in Edo.

Hiroshige's *Tokaido* series went on sale from 1833. In those days, colour woodcuts of this kind cost between twelve and sixteen copper coins. Not a lot more than a bowl of noodle soup or a pair of straw sandals. They were particularly popular as souvenirs. In Europe, by contrast, they were accorded the status of high art. In the late 19th century, Japanese prints served as sources of inspiration for Edgar Degas, Claude Monet, Vincent van Gogh, and many other artists. Today, Japanese collectors are buying back such woodcuts for a great deal of money.

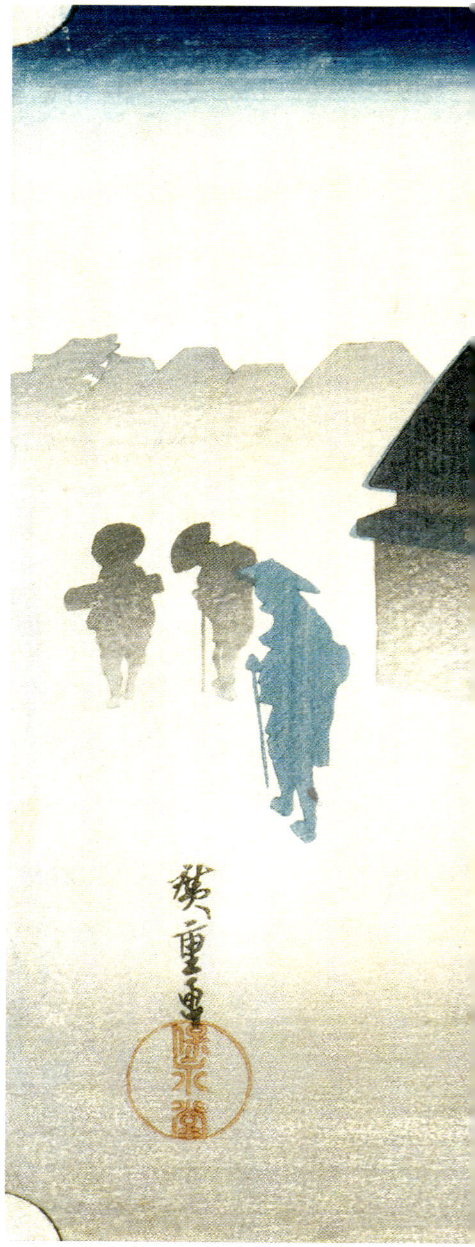

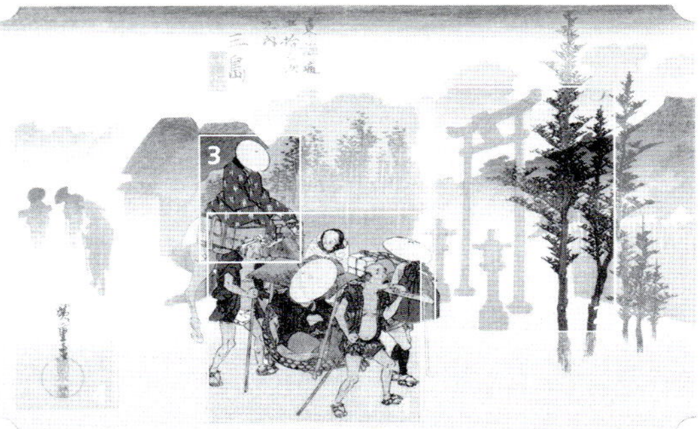

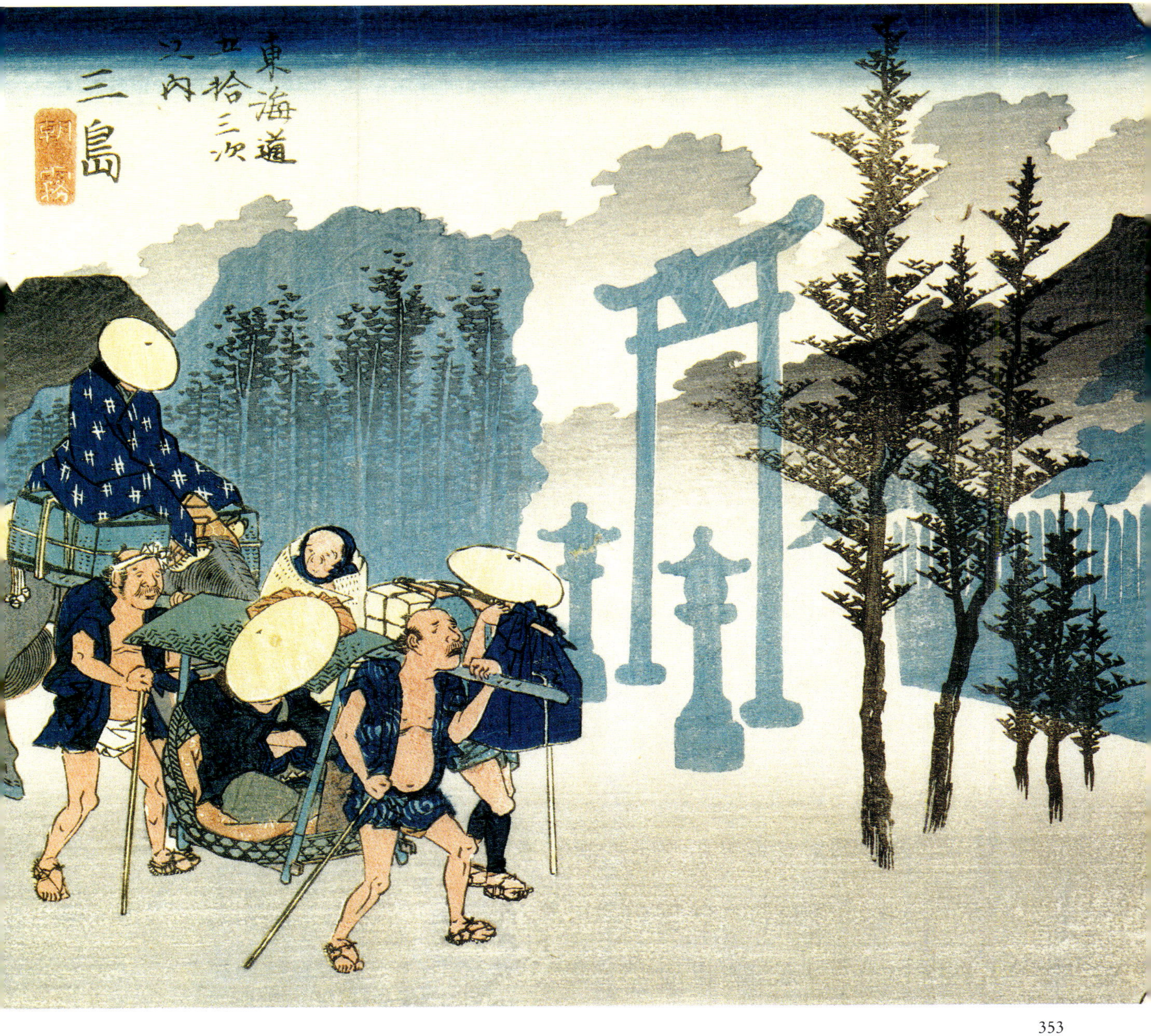
東海道
五拾三次
之内
三島
朝霧

What travelling along the Tokaido was like is described in a picaresque novel by the Japanese writer Ikku Jippensha. His heroes are called Yaji and Kita, and the two might well have bought a souvenir print to remind themselves later of the adventures, exertions, and attractions of their journey, "so that when we become old and bald we shall have something to talk about over the teacups".

The novel was published in instalments, starting in 1802, and its title might be translated as "On Shank's Pony". Journeys were usually made on foot. A fit man could walk up to forty kilometres a day, and would take between twelve and fourteen days to cover the entire distance between Edo and Kyoto. Travellers furnished themselves with a large straw hat to protect them from the sun and rain, a walking stick for slippery paths, and a protective rain covering made out of rice-straw mats, as worn in the present woodcut by the man leading the horse. Straw sandals were on sale at every station; broken sandals lay scattered along the roadside. Yaji and Kita set particular store by a good salve to massage into sore feet.

The Tokaido road was in many sections a difficult one and unsuitable for carts, but it was possible to hire a horse or litter. The type of litter that Hiroshige portrays is very simple, consisting of a woven basket into which the traveller squeezes with crossed legs and bent head. His hat lies on top of the mat designed to protect him from the rain. The litter is suspended from a pole that sways with the movements of the men carrying it; many travellers made sure they packed something for motion sickness.

All the accidents that typically occurred on such journeys naturally happened to Yaji and Kita, too. Thus the bottom of one of their baskets gave way and they "fell with a great crash onto the ground". That could have brought trouble upon the heads of the porters, for they were responsible for their customers' well-being. In the case of high-ranking individuals, they were liable for their safety with their lives.

Porters were chiefly peasants from the local vicinity. They travelled only a specific section of the road between two stations, a distance of about eight kilometres. Hiroshige portrays the men, shouldering their heavy load, with little sympathy. Perhaps because he was a town-dweller and had a low regard for impoverished samurai farmers? By contrast, he conceals the face of the person travelling – so that the viewer can identify with him more easily?

From Mishima, which lay some two hundred metres above sea level, the road rose up to the Hakone pass at an altitude of a good 1400 metres. It was a dangerous section. At the top, where no other path crossed, lay a fenced enclosure, one of the many official checkpoints. All travellers had to pass through it. Unless they were princes or samurai, the military aristocracy, they had to remove their hat, kneel down, and present themselves and their travel papers for inspection.

Japan was a surveillance state. It had been ruled for more than two hundred years by shoguns from the Tokugawa family. They were constantly on their guard against the other feudal lords, against uprisings, against secretly assembled armies.

One of their most effective means of controlling insurgent feudal lords was to compel them to spend part of the year in Edo, under the watchful eye of the shogun. If they returned to the provinces, they had to leave their families behind as hostages. There was thus much to-ing and fro-ing, especially along the Tokaido. The road was regularly blocked by princes and their large retinues, much to the annoyance of simple travellers like Yaji and Kita, and the many others who bought souvenir prints such as this one. "On some days", wrote one of the few foreigners in Japan some 140 years before this print was published, the Tokaido is "more crowded than the public streets in the biggest cities of Europe".

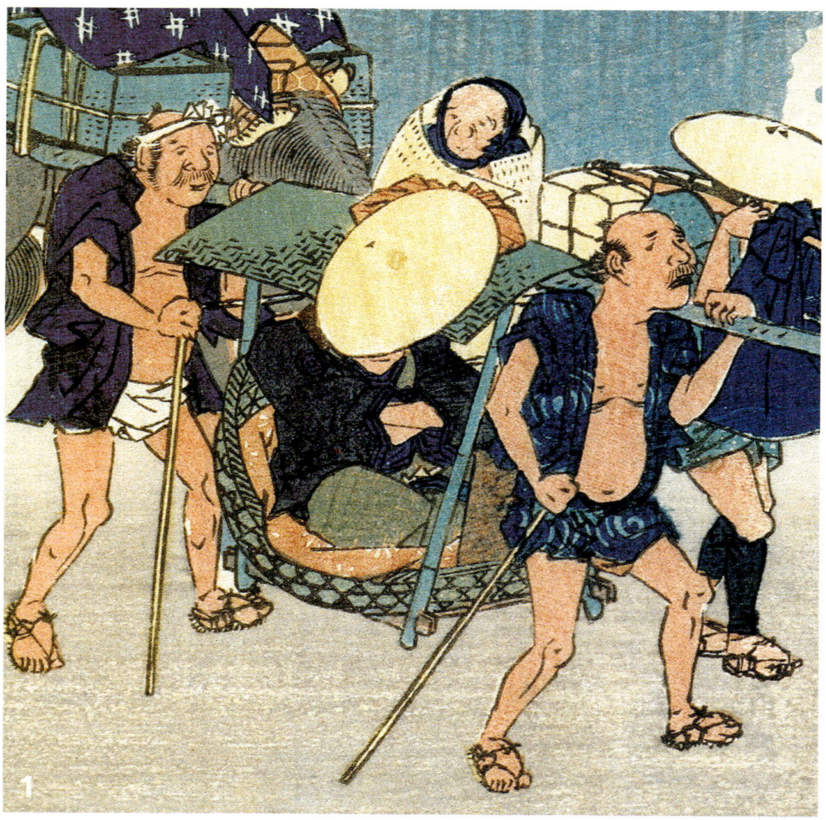
1

The road was strenuous and dangerous

Pilgrimage and holiday

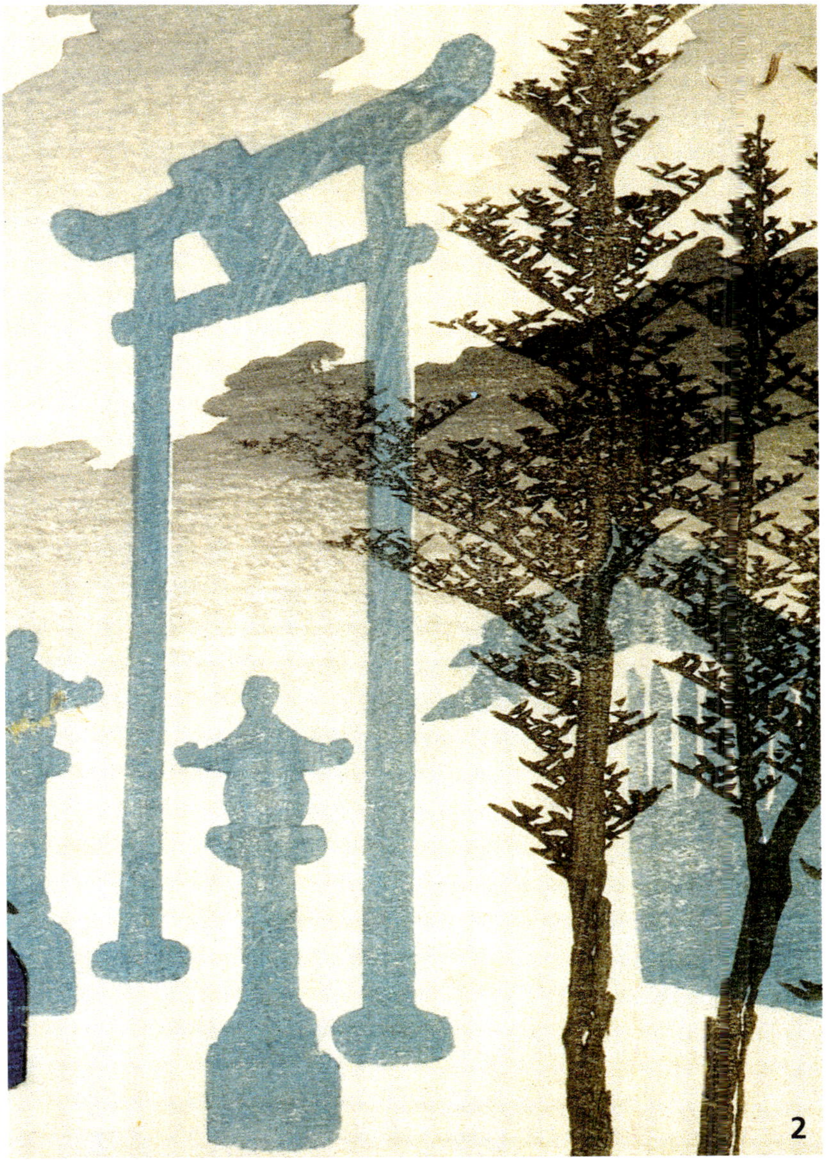

2

The Japanese believed nature was full of deities and spirits, to whom they prayed for protection and assistance in Shinto shrines. Such shrines also stood along the Tokaido. The gateway to the shrine in Mishima appears in the background of the present woodcut. Before it stand two stone lanterns. On the right-hand edge of the picture is a fence, and above it the sillhouette of the roof ridge of the main hall.

Shinto shrines and Buddhist temples were not as deserted as it would seem on this misty morning. They were besieged by pilgrims and beggars, and drew visitors by selling amulets and often, too, by holding theatre performances. Yaji and Kita remember the people selling tooth powder, who lure their customers with elaborate sword games, as well as the eating places and teahouses, and the almost overwhelming selection of culinary delights. "Ah, the sweet cakes and the fish ...!" Their novel resembles a gastronomic guide to the Tokaido.

Mishima, the town, is indicated on the left by just two houses and a few roofs. It actually comprised some fifty lodgings. The better houses offered tea, a hot bath, and a massage by a blind shampooers, and the maids were happy to join their guests in bed. That was all part of the service. In the late afternoons, they stood by their front doors in red aprons and white powdered faces, noisily drawing attention to themselves, tugging at the sleeves of arriving travellers. The visitors would certainly have to spend the night somewhere, for only the couriers of the shogun were allowed to travel at night. As we know from Yaji and Kita, your purse and your kimono could sometimes disappear next morning along with your maid.

None of the famous trade and pilgrimage routes in the Western world has ever been recorded in pictures so exhaustively as the Tokaido. Hiroshige alone made it the subject of over eight hundred woodcuts. The fact that the road was so heavily used is insufficient to explain this prodigious output. More important was the Japanese need to see somewhere different. Since 1603 Japan had been ruled by shoguns of the Tokugawa family, who had pacified the country, which had been ruined by the civil wars fought by roving armies. They had maintained peace and stability in particular by limiting mobility.

For a long time it was virtually impossible for either peasants or town dwellers to travel about. In Hiroshige's lifetime, however, this situation relaxed. The population had become more prosperous, officialdom more open to bribery, more receptive to "fees for sweets". The longing for a change of scenery, pent up for generations, the desire to embark upon an adventure, to see Japan's famous sights with their own eyes, to broaden their horizons, attracted ever more people onto the road.

This travel boom also boosted the market for souvenir prints. By publishing the woodcuts in large editions, the prices could be kept down, which in turn fuelled increased demand and the production of more and more new prints.

3

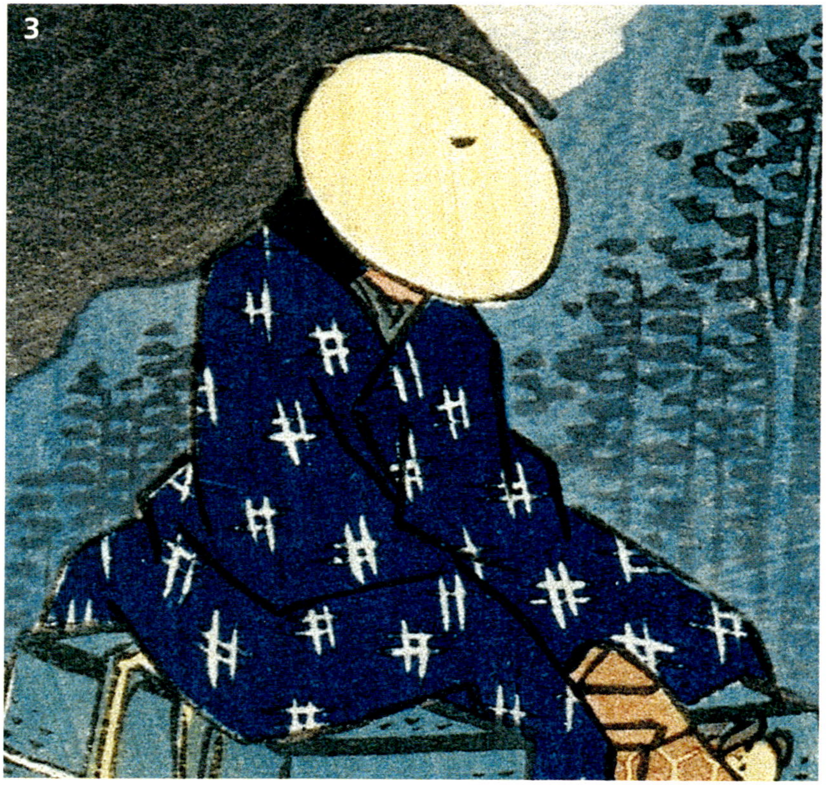

Woodcuts as souvenirs

Kimonos featuring the "water-well pattern" were worn by both sexes. Perhaps the traveller in our picture was a woman. That would only be revealed at the next checkpoint, when he or she took off his or her hat. Even then, you could never be quite sure, for women often disguised themselves as men. It was made particularly difficult for women to travel, since they were expected to stay at home with their families. "Women who go on pilgrimage and drink a lot of tea should be divorced", proclaimed a government edict of 1649.

After confining people to their own locality for more than two hundred years, however, the old rules and restrictions started to lose their hold. Pilgrimages, for example, could no longer be prevented. Officials, concerned with provisioning the population, sought only to postpone them till after the rice harvest.

In 1830, just a few years before the appearance of the *Tokaido* series, a spontaneous mass pilgrimage of women, children, and maids descended upon Ise, a Shinto shrine very near the Tokaido. It was prompted by the rumour that amulets had rained down from the sky. Over five million people are said to have set off for Ise, a fifth of the population! Another story tells of a noblewoman in northern Japan who, having said she was going on a short pilgrimage, secretly met her son and sister and spent six months travelling round the country with them, visiting all the famous sights – without any sort of travel permit.

The relaxing of travel restrictions was also bound up with the growing amount of money in circulation. The social structure was traditionally based on land ownership, and its currency was the rice ball. This was replaced by coinage. The despised merchant classes increased in prosperity and influence. The samurai, on the other hand, the military class supporting the shogun, were not allowed to engage in commercial activity. They grew poorer and poorer.

The rider between the packages tied up in woven rice matting might be a woman or alternatively a merchant. In front walks a porter. Yaji and Kita went travelling partly for financial reasons – they were running away from their debts. "On the road", so the novel says, "one has no trouble from bill collectors at the end of the month." They take repeated delight in their new freedom to move, and extol its pleasures: "The Edo man can make acquaintance with the Satsuma sweet potato and the flower-like Kyoto woman. You can go as if you were taking part in a picnic, enjoying all the delights of the road. You can sit down in the shadow of the trees and open your little tub of sake. Truly travelling means cleaning the life of care. With your straw sandals and your leggings you can wander wherever you like and enjoy the indescribable pleasures of sea and sky."

This desire to set out and explore the country gave rise to a whole new travel industry, and also a travel culture. Nowhere in Europe in the first half of the 19th century, so the experts claim, could you get a travel guide as good as the ones in Japan. Maps were painted on fans and sightseeing tours offered in the cities. When it came to buying souvenirs to take home, in first place alongside combs and white face powder were woodcuts. They were issued in editions of up to 20,000. Taking charge of their production and distribution was a publisher. It was he who engaged the artists, block cutters, and printers and financed the venture. Once the original drawing was passed by the censor, it was transferred onto wood blocks, whereby only the parts that were to be printed were left in relief; everything else was cut away. There was one block per colour. The artist checked the colours, and the printer made sure the blocks were correctly assembled.

In the case of large editions, the intensity of the colours inevitably varied. At other times, slight changes made to the woodblock meant that prints of the same scene differed. In a number of *Mishima* prints, for example, the viewer can read an advert for a well-known brand of face powder, attached to one of the stone lanterns. In another print from the series, a teahouse presents all its specialities. It was all paid advertising.

The artist, it is reported, travelled the Tokaido himself in 1832, albeit not on foot, but as a member of an official and splendidly equipped mission. Every year the shogun sent the emperor a present of valuable horses, a symbolic gift by those in power to the powerless but revered descendant of the Sun goddess.

Hiroshige, born in 1797, was a member of the military aristocracy. He spent almost his entire life in the shogun's enormous palace, serving as head of the fire brigade for twenty years. It was an important position in a city built of wood and permanently in danger of burning down. Hiroshige was thereby in charge of a great number of tattooed and – like the litter-bearers in this print – mostly scantily clad men.

Hiroshige inherited the post, and with it responsibility for his family, when he was just twelve years old, following the sudden death of his father. At thirty-three he in turn passed on both the job and the responsibility for the family to a nephew. He could earn more producing original drawings for prints.

He began with the usual portraits of actors and beautiful women. These were followed by *Famous Places in the Eastern Capital*, and in 1833 by the first and most successful *Tokaido* series, from which our print is taken. Altogether, in addition to his eight hundred views of the Tokaido, he produced some 1000 views of Edo and eight hundred of famous places in the provinces. Alongside his somewhat older contemporary Katsushika Hokusai (1760–1849), famous in particular for his *Thirty-six Views of Mount Fuji*, he was the best-known artist of his era.

Although his prints were praised as "naturalistic views with landscapes and people", by European standards the majority were not true to nature. The artist omits, condenses, suggests. On the left of the present picture, all we are shown of Mishima, a town of fifty dwellings, are vague outlines. The shrine is reduced to its roof ridge and gateway. The figures walking past in the background are merely silhouettes who take on life only through their movement. Like many Japanese artists, Hiroshige often uses symbols instead of an object itself. He empties the composition and thereby lends forcefulness to the colours and the strokes of his pen. The viewer is invited to fill in the details, both by recalling the actual scene and by using his imagination.

To achieve smooth gradations in shading, the printer used a special technique called *bokashi*. A cloth soaked in ink was dabbed onto the printing block with varying degrees of pressure, so that upon printing a correspondingly large or little amount of ink was transferred to the paper. Hiroshige also made a point of including all the various times of day and seasons of the year in his series. Thus *Morning Mist in Mishima* is followed by an evening scene, and in other prints trees in blossom

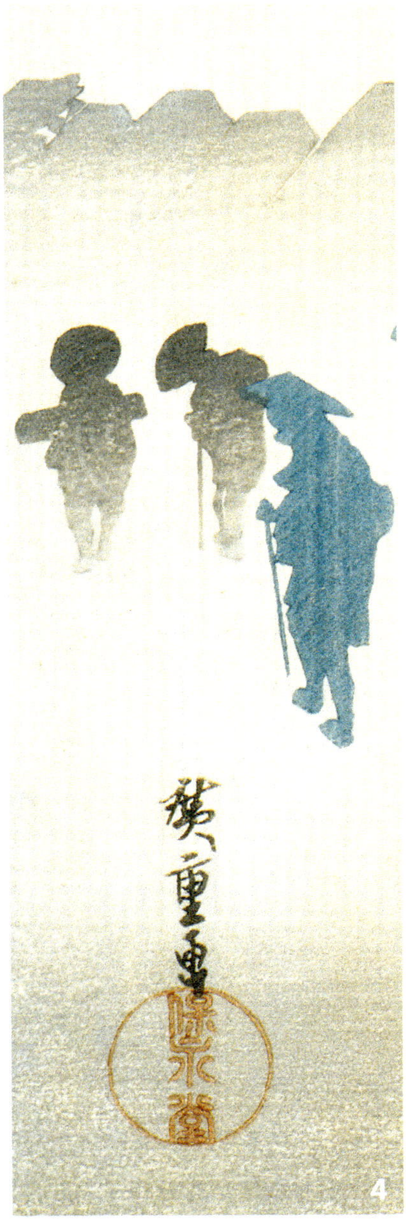

4

give way to autumn rain and snow-clad winter landscapes. Leafing through their album of woodcuts over a cup of tea, someone in their latter years would not only be reminded of specific places but invited to meditate upon distance, space, and the passage of time.

To Europeans, Hiroshige was a "wonderful Impressionist", as the painter Camille Pissarro described him in 1893. A number of Pissarro's contemporaries, including Edouard Manet, incorporated Hiroshige's prints into their own works by showing them hanging on the walls of their interiors. They were all interested in how the Japanese artist made his pictures so airy, so atmospheric, in how he suspended perspective, let three-dimensional space vanish, in how he avoided the shadows through which an artist models figures and objects, in how his figures float freely on the surface. These were all things that the Impressionists, and later the Cubists, wanted to achieve – to get away from the illusion of spatial depth, to accept a picture as a two-dimensional plane, not to let colour be dictated by reality.

The fact that Hiroshige drew so many pictures of snow, rain, and mist suggests that these subjects were his particular favourites. But they were also weather conditions that he was experiencing at first hand. Between 1830 and 1840 Japan was repeatedly struck by catastrophic rainstorms. Failed harvests led to famines that claimed tens of thousands of lives. The situation sparked civil uprisings that would contribute to the end of shogun rule. In 1868 the emperor was restored to power. The country was reformed, industrialized, and covered by a network of railways. The great age of the Tokaido was over. Hiroshige did not live to see these changes, however; he died in 1858 during a cholera epidemic.

His name appears in black characters beneath the three figures in the left-hand background, and below is the red seal of the publisher, Hoeido.

In the realm of symbols

Eugène Delacroix: Women of Algiers in their Apartments, 1834

Journey to a realm of light and colour

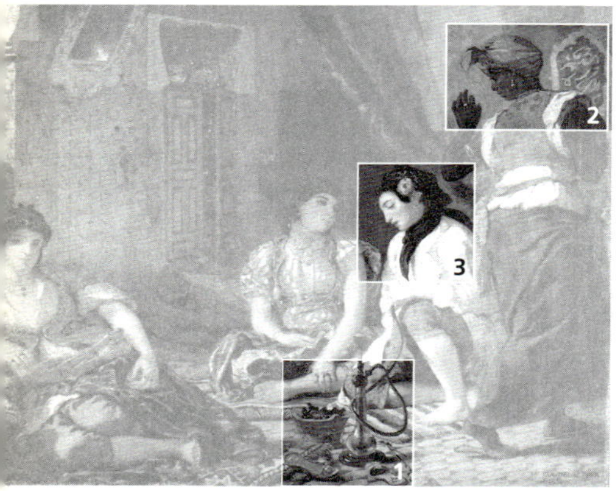

Paris, 21 November 1831: the glittering première of Giacomo Meyerbeer's opera *Robert le Diable*. Amongst the guests, the twenty-eight-year-old diplomat Charles de Mornay, who was to visit Morocco on behalf of the king. During one of the intervals, he asked his companions if they knew of an artist or draughtsman who might go with him – diplomatic missions in those days were accompanied not by reporters but in many cases by artists, whose task was to record each stage of the trip.

It was probably the diplomat's mistress, an actress, who suggested Eugène Delacroix. She described him as "a young painter, having talent and wit, a man of the world and of excellent character ... something which is not to be disdained when you have to spend four or five months together".

Delacroix (1798–1863) is known as the leader of the Romantics, and above all for his painting of the July Revolution of 1830, *Liberty Leading the People* (cf. p. 346). The hopes of the revolutionaries had been disappointed. "Everything wearies me", complained Delacroix, "the whole world, painting, and I myself."

The artist, too, was at the Meyerbeer première. De Mornay spoke to him straight away, and on 1 January 1832, after a New Year's Eve party that had lasted until three o'clock in the morning, both set off from Paris and travelled down to Toulon, where they boarded a ship headed for Barbary.

Thus a chance conversation during an interval at the opera paved the way for one of the most influential paintings in the history of European art.

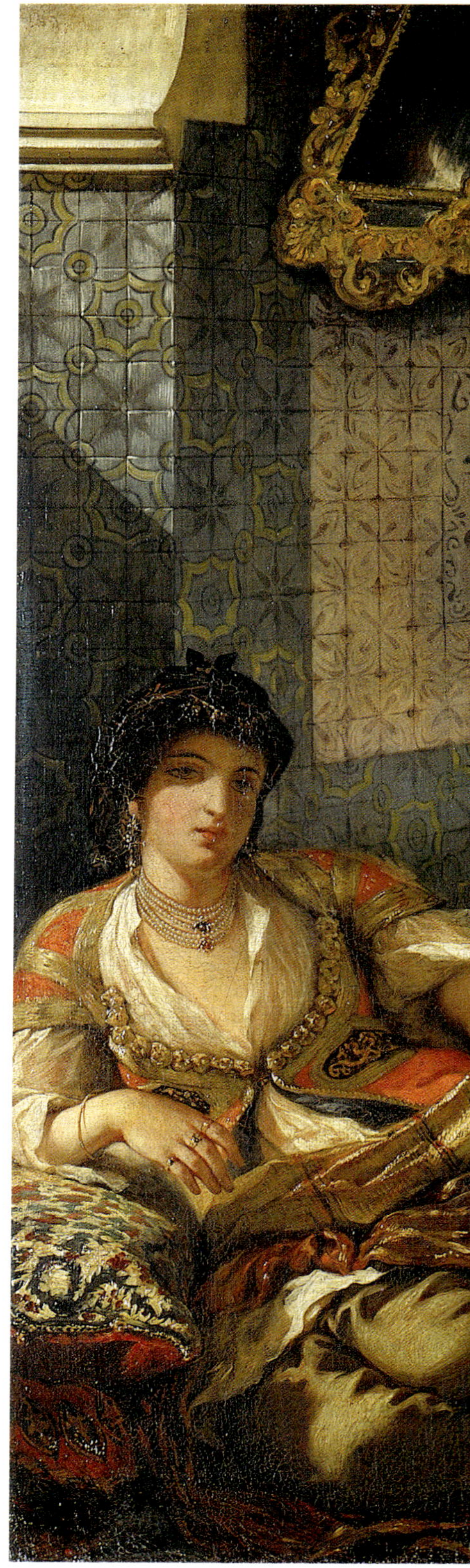

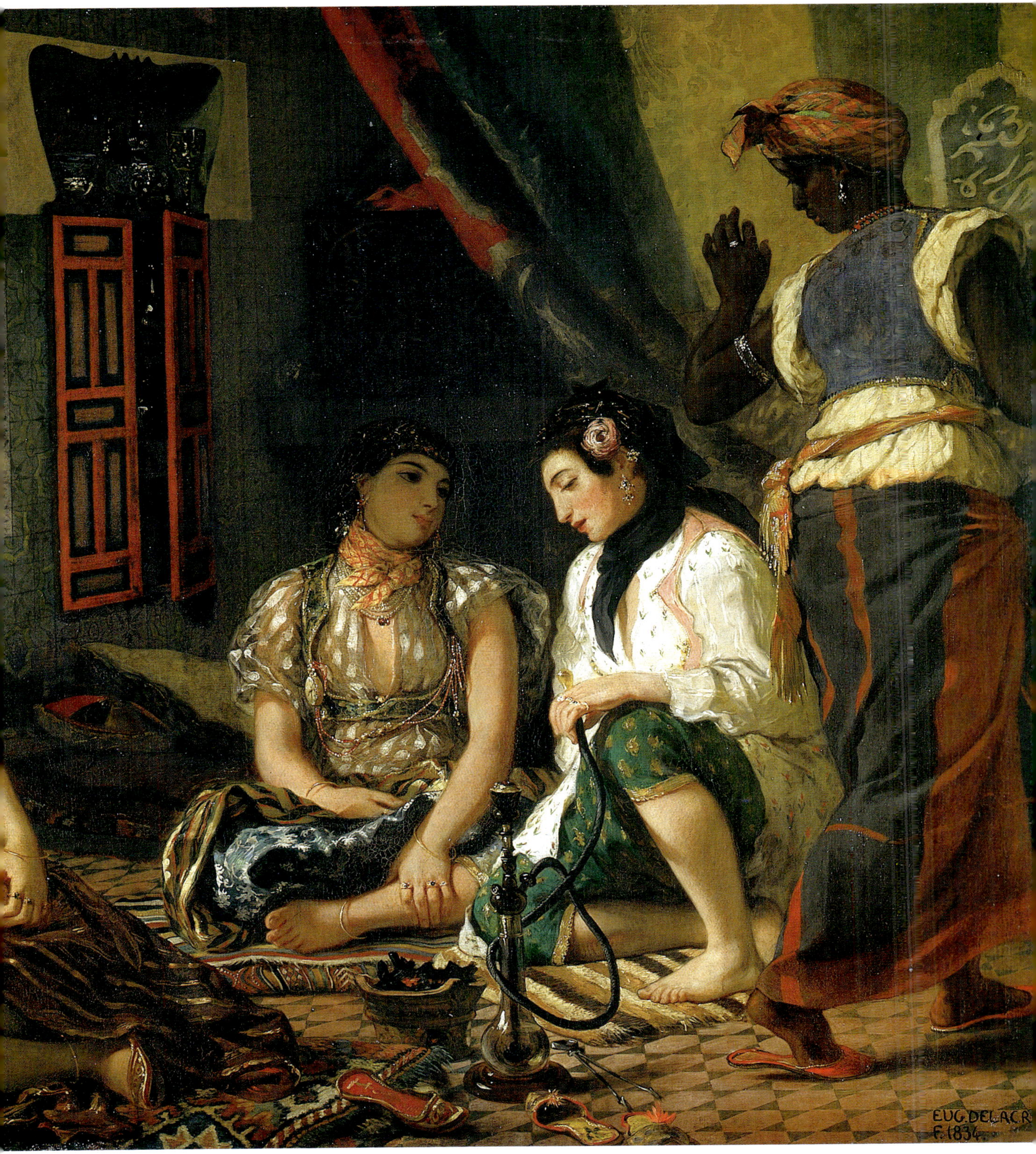
EUG. DELACR
F. 1834.

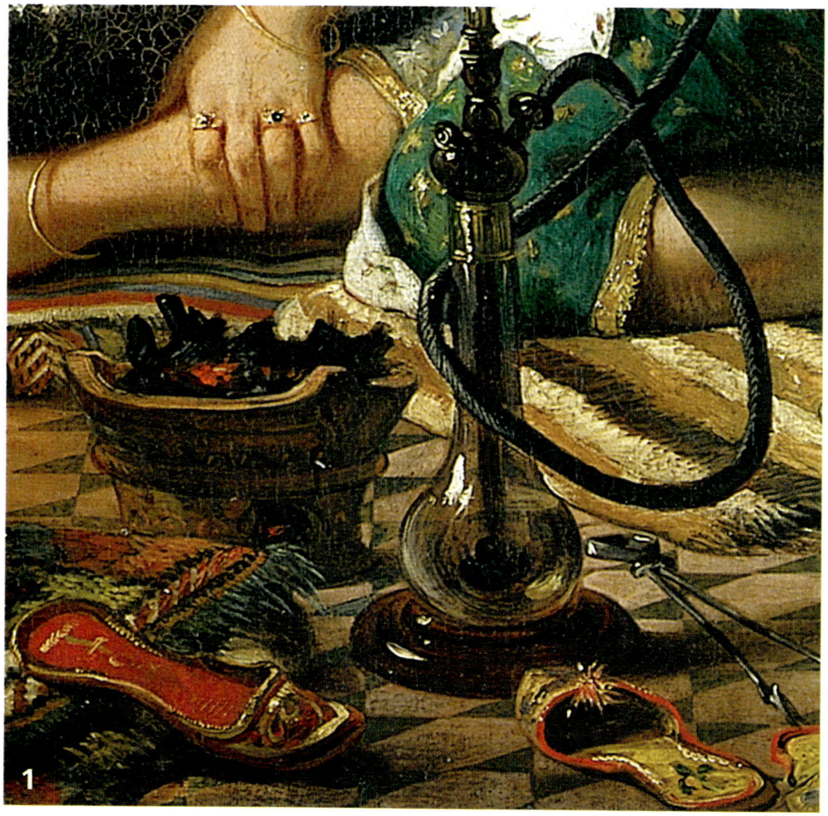

1

Wealth and atmosphere of the Orient

In 1830 a French expeditionary force occupied the city of Algiers. The French government owed money to an Algerian merchant, and the bey of Algiers had been insisting on payment. He went so far as to strike the French consul in the face with a fly-swatter during a meeting. The French used this insult as grounds to invade North Africa.

The border between Algeria and Morocco is long and difficult to patrol, and Algerian resistance fighters regularly drew on the assistance of their Moroccan neighbours. De Mornay's brief was to ask the sultan of Morocco to put a stop to this. The sultan kept the diplomat and his train of servants and translators waiting in Tangiers. He finally received him on 22 March in Meknès. The French presented him with gifts, and the sultan signed a treaty of peace and friendship.

A lavish painting that Delacroix completed in 1845 – a full thirteen years after the event – shows the sultan with his retinue, but with de Mornay absent. The apparent success of de Mornay's mission was short-lived: the Moroccans did not take the treaty seriously. Over the following years, other French diplomats had to pay several visits to the sultan to renegotiate the agreement. Only when the French took military action did the sultan fulfil their demands.

Another probable reason why Delacroix took so long to produce a large-format record of the mission is because he was overwhelmed by so many new impressions. "I am like a man in a dream," he wrote from Morocco, "seeing things he's afraid will vanish from him". He felt "indescribably happy" in Africa and was filled with curiosity for everything around him. He sought to record everything he saw: people, animals, and objects from daily life such as hookahs, slippers, a bowl containing glowing coals for a pipe, or for burning sweet-smelling herbs – objects that he combines in his *Women of Algiers in their Apartments* (180 x 220 cm) as if in a still life. "At every step there are pictures already composed which would make twenty generations of painters wealthy and famous", he wrote, albeit admitting that there was "much to be criticized with regard to human rights and equality before the law". Nevertheless, he concluded, "there is beauty in abundance".

For Count de Mornay, however, the trip was a very different experience. He was an elegant young man who was firmly rooted in Parisian high society and felt ill at ease outside the metropolis. He attached the greatest importance to the strict observation of protocol; he counted the exact number of shots fired to greet him in Tangiers, for example. The North Africans struck him as uncivilized and chaotic, and he felt only disdain for them and their "country of ignorance, barbary, and conceit".

The African mission represented a step in de Mornay's diplomatic career. For Delacroix, on the other hand, it was a point of departure into a whole new realm of light and colour. Africa transformed his palette and provided him with motifs for some eighty paintings.

Delacroix always had pencil and paper to hand, even keeping them in his saddlebag on the eleven-day ride from Tangiers to Meknès and from there back to the coast. It was a dangerous journey through wild terrain, and the diplomatic caravan survived unharmed only because it was accompanied by the sultan's horsemen.

In the watercolour study of the reclining woman, the pencil drawing can be seen beneath the paint. Delacroix usually made only rapid sketches on the spot, jotting down notes about the colours, and on this sheet writing down the name of his subject – Mounay ben Sultane. In the evenings, back in his tent, he would return to these sketches, filling out the details and adding colour. He returned to Paris with seven full sketchbooks. The extraordinary accuracy of Delacroix's observations thereby makes these sketchbooks not just a personal record of his trip, but a treasure-trove for ethnologists.

Since Islam forbids all images, drawing people was difficult. Women, furthermore, always wore veils when outside their home. When Delacroix tried, from afar, to draw some Arab women hanging out their washing on a roof terrace, they immediately fetched their husbands. Delacroix often had to work in secret, and it is not surprising that his sketchbooks contain many more portraits of men than women. Only in a Jewish household was he permitted to look around freely – an opportunity that later prompted his *Jewish Wedding*.

He sketched Mounay ben Sultane not in Morocco, but in Algiers, where he stopped for a few days on his return journey from Tangiers to Toulon. The city was at that time firmly in French hands, and Delacroix thus had another chance to do something he hadn't managed in Morocco – visit a harem.

He was invited, so the story goes, into the household of a Muslim in French service, a man who had converted to Islam from Christianity, who was less inflexible in his adherence to its precepts and who was also eager to curry favour with his colonial masters. "Having walked down some dingy corridor, you enter the part of the house which is reserved for [the women]. The eye is truly dazzled by the bright light, the fresh faces of the women and children amidst a mass of silk and gold. For a painter, it is a moment of fascination and strange happiness."

Scenes of harems in books and as paintings were popular; they were a favourite subject in the rich and colourful Oriental fantasies being spun in France at that time. This "Orientalism" reached an early climax with Napoleon's military expedition to Egypt in 1798, the year in which Delacroix was born. The French passion for all things Egyptian gave way almost seamlessly to support for the Greek war of independence from the Turks (1821/30) – a conflict which Victor Hugo celebrated in his verse work *Les Orientales*. Delacroix, too, portrayed the Greek spirit of sacrifice in two emotionally charged canvases, the *Massacre of Chios* (1824) and *Greece Mourning on the Ruins of Missolonghi* (1826).

Greece, Turkey, North Africa – for the French, and above all the Romantics amongst them, the Orient was not a specific geographical area, but rather an imaginary place of escape. Unencumbered by the realities of Parisian daily life and the political Restoration with its police dictatorship and censure, the Orient was a place where you could move freely in a society steeped in mystery and beauty.

Delacroix's pictures differ from other, effusive representations of the Orient not least in the accuracy of their details. The different patterns in the floor and wall tiles, in the cushion covers and carpets, the decorations, the doors, the various poses adopted by those lounging on the floor – all these gave his paintings an authentic air.

In 1834, two years after his return, Eugène Delacroix exhibited *Women of Algiers in their Apartments* at the Paris Salon, where it earned high praise. It was purchased by King Louis Philippe, who donated it to the Musée du Luxembourg, the museum for contemporary art. Following the artist's death, in 1874 the large painting was transferred to the Louvre.

The supposed fidelity to detail with which Delacroix offers us a glimpse into a foreign, mysterious world was undoubtedly not, however, the real reason for the painting's early success.

The artist had to sketch in secret

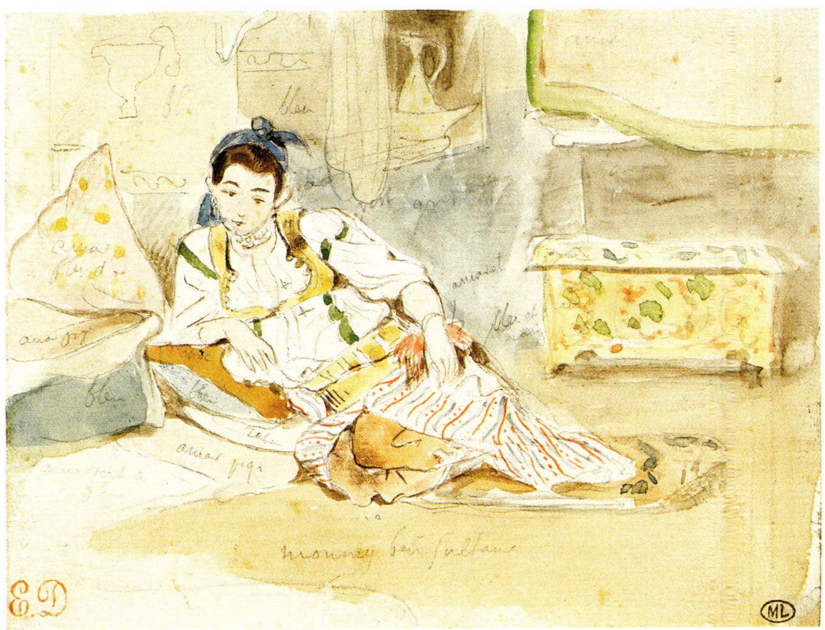

Nor is everything quite as authentic as the viewer might be led to believe. Although the pose of the woman seated on the right is taken from one of the sketchbooks, her impressive profile belongs to a Parisian model and can be found in several of Delacroix's paintings, for example as the goddess Liberty leading the people onto the barricades. Similarly, the symbols on the panel behind the negress might be assumed to be Arabic letters, but in fact they are decorative flourishes, only some of which are actually used in writing. Since the Arabic script is the script of the Koran and is therefore considered holy, for Muslims such a concoction would constitute an abuse of the language and be forbidden. Delacroix cannot have seen this panel in real life; he made it up to add a little local colour.

The profile of a Parisian model, the invention of foreign lettering – if the painter was overwhelmed by impressions while still in Africa, back in his Paris studio he adapts them to European tastes and visual conventions. The same is true of the activities of the three harem wives. Smoking was normal, but according to the notes made by the director of the museum, with whom Delacroix was acquainted, these women also took care of their children, spun, and embroidered. No sign of any such activity in this painting. The black servant-girl is the only one who seems to be busy; the women sitting on the floor are doing nothing. They remain passive, a little sleepy, with no other purpose than to wait for someone who finds pleasure in them.

"That is my idea of a woman!", the artist is supposed to have declared. All his life he avoided close relationships, because he was afraid they would get in the way of his work. In the year in which he painted the *Women of Algiers*, he took on a housekeeper who would serve him for the rest of his life as a subordinate companion.

Women as meekly waiting objects of lust, the opportunity for pleasure without commitment – Delacroix and his contemporaries (and no doubt others besides) saw this fantasy fulfilled in the Oriental harem, a forbidden, inaccessible place. In contrast to European women, the women's bodies in Delacroix's painting are not compressed inside corsets; their breasts are portrayed as bare or scantily veiled by transparent cloth. Their naked, shapely legs are casually presented to viewers who would see nothing of the sort in the streets and salons of Europe. Even to show a white-stockinged ankle was considered bold in Paris.

In the Orient of the Europeans, everything was thought to be different – instead of the civilized restraining of the instincts, a triumph of the feelings; instead of rationalism, perfumed dreams; instead of lifelong monogamy, free choice from a constantly changing harem.

The painting of Africa arose in a Paris studio

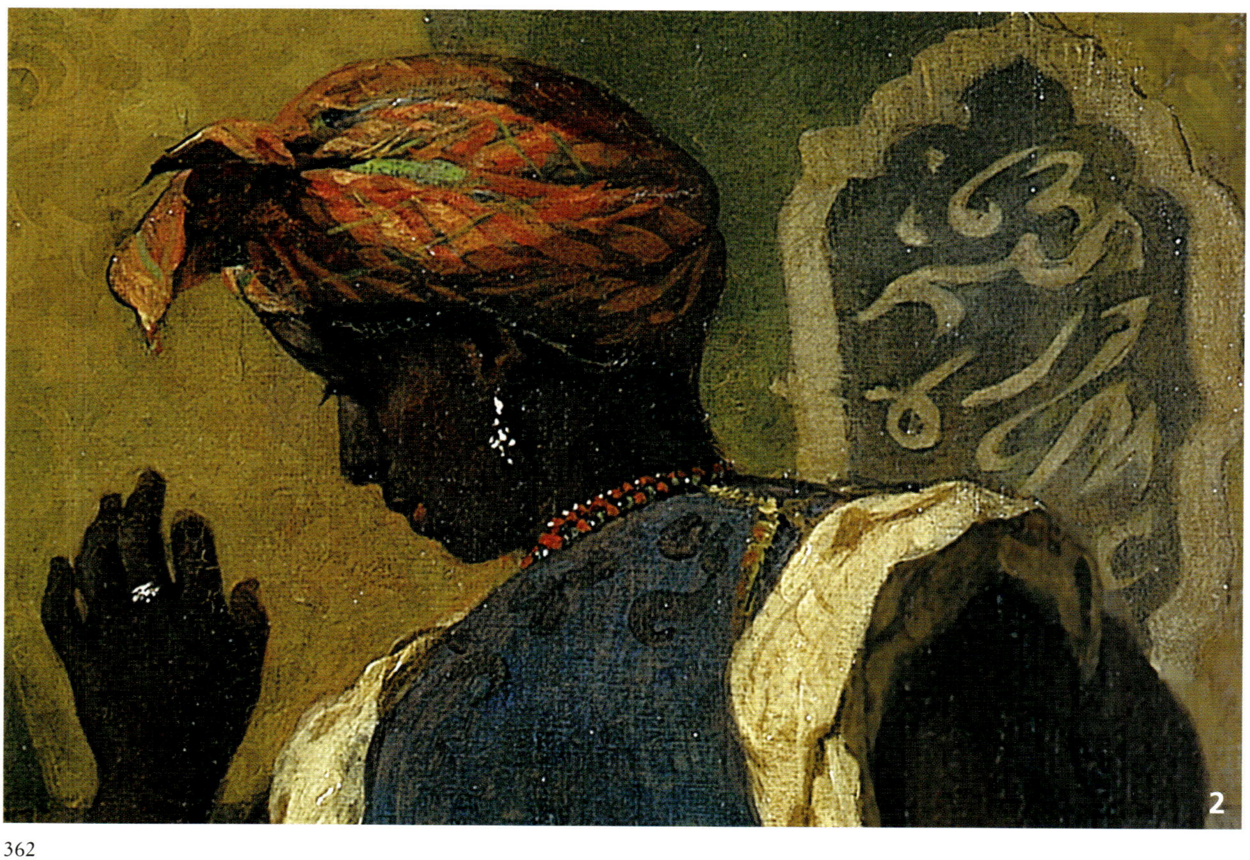
2

The woman in the harem is an old acquaintance; a Parisienne served as model

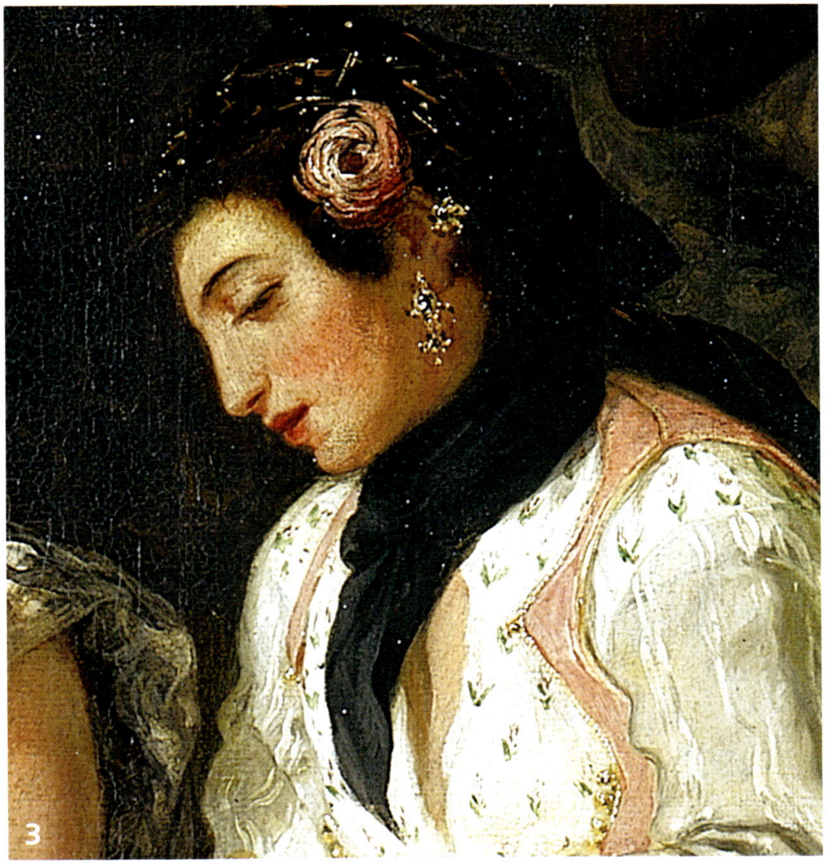

3

Even before he travelled to Morocco, Delacroix had already painted his own Oriental fantasies of pleasure and passion. Indeed, in 1828 he had caused a scandal with his *Death of Sardanapalus*, which shows the defeated Assyrian ruler resting on a mountain of cushions. The tyrant is having his horses, female slaves, and mistresses butchered, so that he can take them with him into death. The painting is a chaotic, sadistically erotic, feverish dream.

With *Women of Algiers*, Delacroix delivers a composition at the opposite end of the spectrum to his dramatically exaggerated *Sardanapalus*, one which celebrates inactivity and portrays a place of exquisite calm, far removed from the hustle and bustle of daily life. Only the black female slave is moving; she seems to be leaving the room.

The artists who painted Oriental subjects in the past are accused by Arab critics today of having behaved just like the European rulers who subjugated and exploited defenceless territories – artists as machos and colonialists.

But Delacroix ranked amongst the Romantics; he was at the forefront of those seeking happiness in far-off places. German Romantics, too, yearned for other parts; unlike the French, however, they looked back to the past. Karl Friedrich Schinkel (1781–1841) painted Gothic spires soaring above medieval cities, while Caspar David Friedrich (1774–1840) portrayed Gothic ruins in the depths of oak forests. The Gothic style and the Middle Ages thereby symbolized the united fatherland for which the Germans had fought in the wars of liberation from Napoleonic occupation. Orientalism made virtually no appearance in their art; the yearning for unity and freedom left no room for exotic dreams.

Had Delacroix attempted to view Morocco and Algiers through Arab eyes, he could never have painted this picture – the Koran forbids it. As it was, however, it became one of the most influential works of European art. It has been copied and reinterpreted many times by other artists, including Picasso, fourteen of whose paintings were inspired by the *Women of Algiers*.

The work's enduring influence derives no more from its stimulation of erotic fantasies than from its supposed authenticity. Delacroix himself wrote that he had felt dogged "by a passion for precision", a precision "which most people mistake for truth". "I began to make something tolerable of my African journey only when I had so far forgotten the trivial details as to recall in my pictures just the striking and poetic side of the subject."

He developed his poetry out of light and colour. "These pale roses, these crudely woven cushions, these slippers, this whole transparency", wrote his colleague Paul Cézanne (1839–1906), they "flow into the eye like wine down the throat and one is immediately intoxicated". And it seemed to the poet Charles Baudelaire (1821–1867) as if colour made up its own mind as to "which objects it would clothe".

Colour that liberated itself from objects, that thought for itself and assumed an autonomous life – this was something new. The painting arouses the impression that the artist, like the women staring dreamily into space, has somewhat lost track of the actual objects before him and is primarily registering their colours, as if he were seeing the world like an Oriental carpet. The contrast between the precision in the detail and the whole as a pure weave of colour is what lends the painting its fascination. It is like a first, still unconscious step towards the abstract painting of the 20th century.

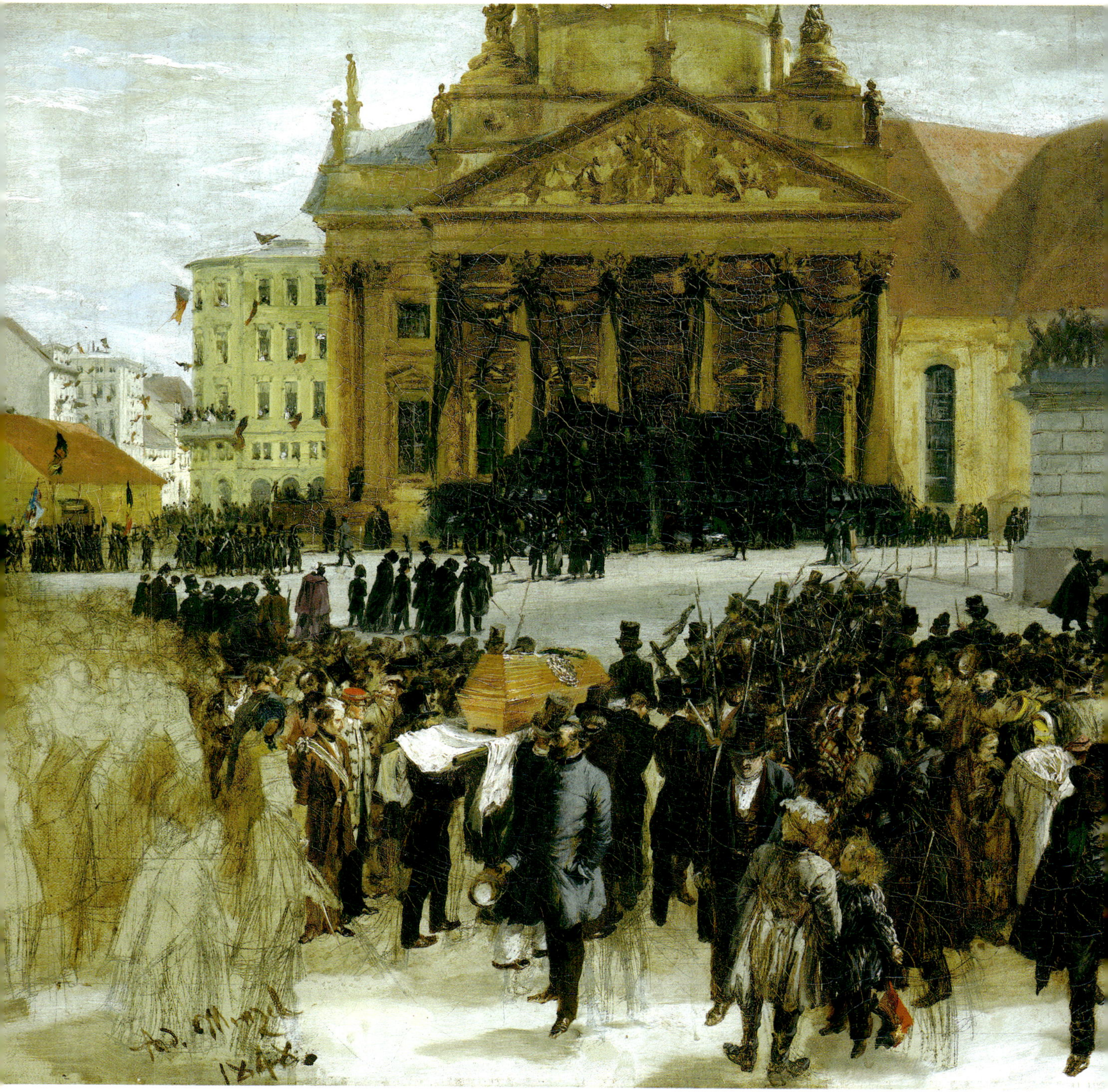

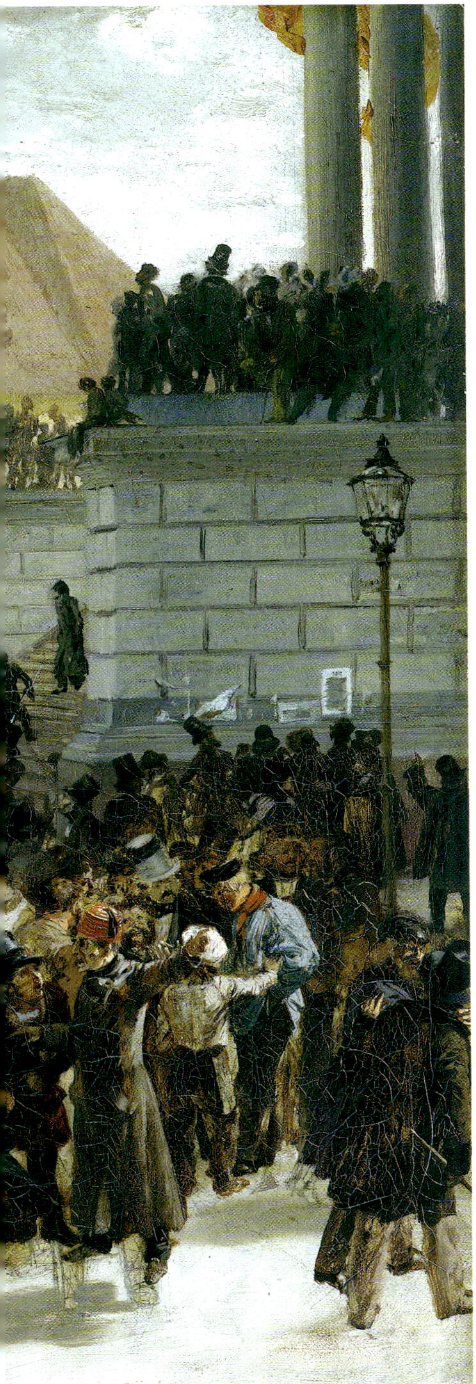

Adolph Menzel: Lying in State of the Dead in the March Revolution in Berlin, 1848

After the Uprising

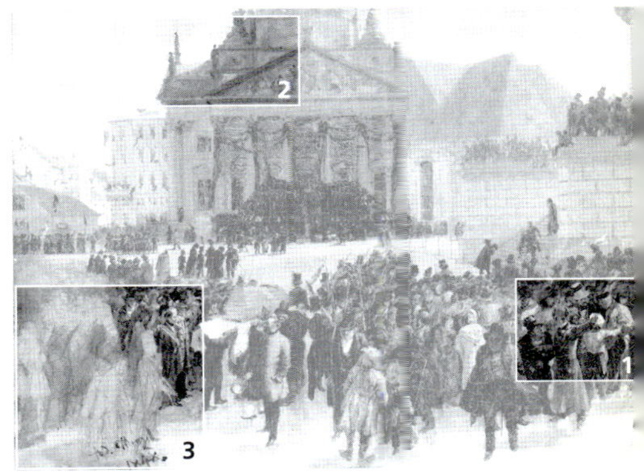

"That was a sad, solemn day", wrote Adolph Menzel, "the like of which one would never have thought to experience in Berlin". He was there, thirty-two years of age, with his sketchbook in his hand. The date: 22 March 1848. The uprising was over, the dead were being buried.

The unrest had begun a good week before. Soldiers had blocked the path of people taking part in a political meeting, leading to outbreaks of fighting and shooting. In order to see to calm and order themselves, the Berliners demanded a militia. On 18 March they gathered in front of the royal palace in order to reinforce their demands. When the king had the square cleared by force, the Berliners responded by building barricades: civil war. The monarch feared for his capital, gave in, and approved a militia.

On the morning of 22 March, the coffins of 183 dead were borne into the Gendarmenmarkt and laid out on the steps of the German Church. This is the moment captured by Menzel: no troops, no police, but civil guards with guns and bayonets mounted. What he can't show is the fact that these coffins are only those of civilians; the dead soldiers were buried separately.

From the Gendarmenmarkt, the pallbearers carried the coffins past the royal palace to Friedrichshain cemetery. Menzel wanted to watch everything, including how the humiliated king would conduct himself. "On the balcony", he noted, "stood an adjutant with a flag of mourning, opposite him a militia officer with a black, red, and yellow flag ... Every time a new procession of coffins came past, the King came out with his head bared, and remained standing until the coffins had passed. His head gleamed from afar like a patch of white. It must have been the most terrible day of his life."

Menzel was not present during the actual fighting, having been away on a trip. He had "bad luck with revolts; I'd just left Kassel when one broke out, and when I got here one had just finished". Politically, he stood firmly on the side of the liberal barricade fighters: "Berlin saved its honour in a fearful fashion!"

The majority of those who died in the uprising were artisans and workers, apprentices and journeymen in blue shirts, with red neckerchiefs and caps. Their numbers included masters, too, who wore bourgeois top hats on ceremonial occasions. Many of them were fighting less for civilian freedoms than for better living conditions: they lived in slums, had no work, and as always in spring were confronted with rising food prices. A year earlier, a "potato revolution" had broken out in the Gendarmenmarkt, during which housewives looted the market stalls, bakeries, and butcher's shops. The uprising of 1848 was also initially put down to hunger by the king and his advisers.

The people protest

It was, however, a protest against the Establishment. And the protest was international. In February, the Palais Royal in Paris had been stormed, King Louis Philippe forced to abdicate, and France declared a Republic. On 13 March there followed uprisings in Vienna; the hated Prince Metternich was obliged to flee, the Minister of War was hanged, and Milan and Venice rose up against Austrian rule. In Munich, Ludwig I abdicated in favour of his son. There was further unrest in Hesse-Darmstadt, Baden, Württemberg and Nassau.

The demands being issued by the German states were almost identical: freedom of the press, right of assembly, equality before the law, a constitution, a parliament, the end of particularism. The Berliners did not want to oust their king; they simply wanted him to guarantee civil liberties, swear to uphold and defend a constitution that guaranteed the rights of the populace, and create no obstacle to the unification of Germany.

Amongst the crowds in the lower half of the picture, Menzel includes the figures of two members of a *Burschenschaft*, a political student association. The one in front has lowered his sword in a gesture of respect. *Burschenschaft* members fought on the barricades, and a number were killed. These political organizations called repeatedly for civil rights and were spied on and banned by governments as subversive. Their colours of black, red, and gold were adopted as the flag of national democracy. Menzel has them waving from houses in the background.

For Menzel and indeed all Berliners, the men in top hats with guns and bayonets were of the utmost political significance. As members of the civil guard, they had now replaced the police and the military and represented the victory of the people. Despite the huge crowds thronging the streets, the day went off peacefully. "A people", wrote the *Vossische Zeitung*, "capable of such self-control at such a turbulent and critical time, is surely ripe for freedom."

The figures in the left-hand foreground are only sketched in with a pen, and the people making up the crowd in the lower half of the picture fall into no unified block. Some are looking at the coffin, others at the church; some are talking in small groups, and several men seem to be on the point of leaving. Are the different directions in which people are looking and moving perhaps meant to illustrate the divergent attitudes and opinions of the Berlin population? The answer is unclear. The artist himself says nothing on the subject.

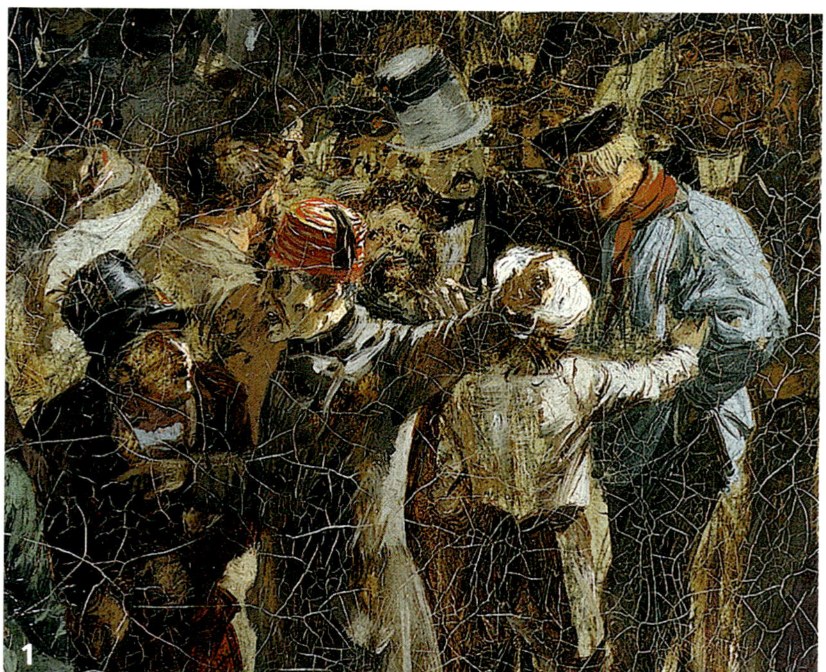
1

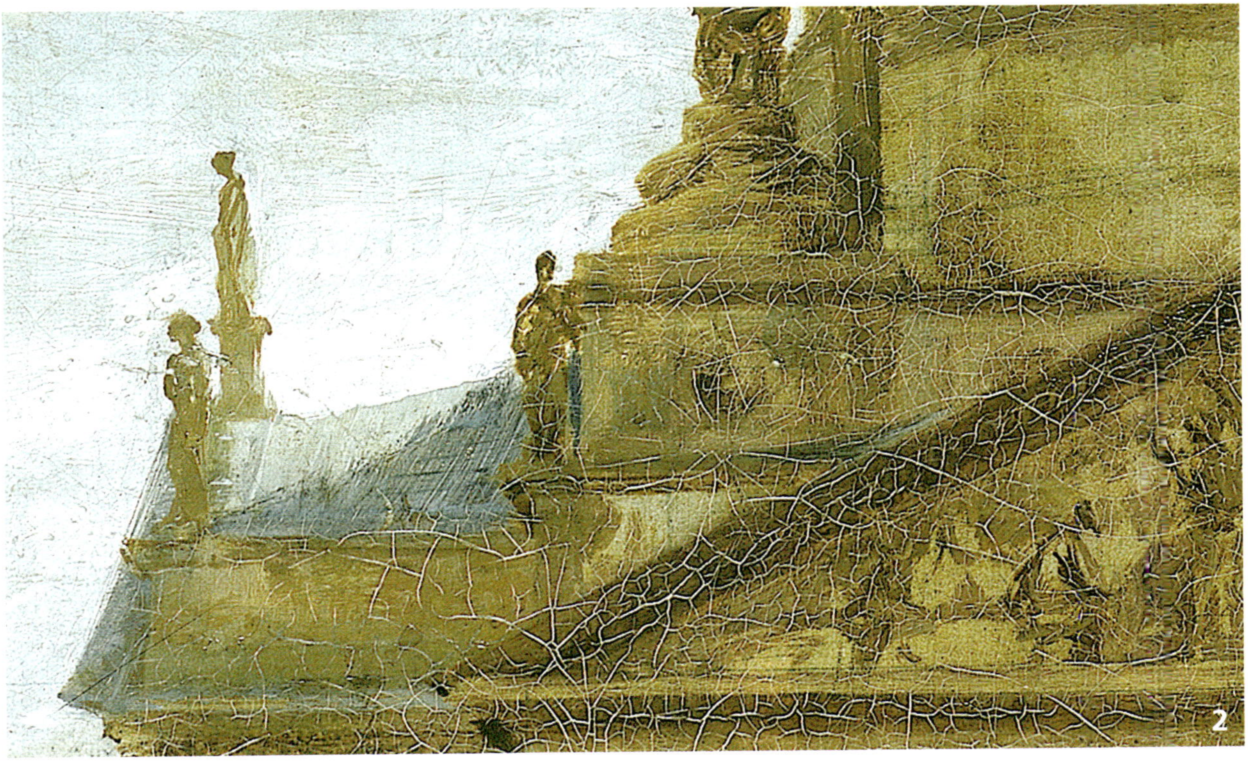

2

Menzel was passionate about real life. He always carried a sketchbook in his coat pocket. Be it his sister asleep, a corpse on the battlefield, or his own cramped bedroom, he recorded everything. He didn't paint things as they actually were, however, but how they appeared. He didn't portray what he knew something to be, but how it presented itself to his eye. He would have been thoroughly familiar, for example, with the relief in the triangular gable of the German Church which appears in the *Lying in State of the Dead*: it portrays Paul taking leave of the Ephesians, who embrace him, weeping. In his painting, however, Menzel leaves the relief indistinct. The distant statues on the church roof are not only scaled down in size in line with the laws of perspective, but also lose their outlines against the bright sky, while the flags in front of the windows dissolve into dabs of colour. The manner in which Menzel reproduced the real world made him a forerunner of Impressionism.

The classicist portico with its triangular gable was part of the base of a tower that was altogether some three times as high, rising namely to 76 metres. Menzel cuts this tower off. He was more interested in people than in imposing architecture. Frederick the Great had added the tower to the older German Church to the right of it. It is evident from the sculptural programme that he viewed it as a public rather than a religious edifice. On top of the cupola stood the triumphant figure of Virtue, and on the cornices those of her progeny whom the king considered important, such as Prudence, Fortitude, Humility, Chastity, and Charity – all virtues that a monarch might desire of his subjects. Justice is missing. That was a royal prerogative, and when the citizens demanded it, as they did in 1848, that meant revolution.

The tower was only sketchily related to the German Church and was not intended for use. For a while it housed the offices of the "Board for the Destitute". A second tower in the same architectural style was erected in front of the French Church on the opposite side of the square, where Menzel is also standing. The walls and steps on the right, on which more crowds have gathered, belong to the Schauspielhaus theatre and concert hall built by Karl Friedrich Schinkel in 1821. Menzel is himself sketching from some steps and looks

Impressionistic before Impressionism

down on the square before him and the coffins on the other side from a slight height. He leaves the ground light grey, almost white; the viewer cannot tell if it is cobbled or strewn with sand.

Menzel may have left such details for a later version. What is clearly apparent, however, is that he portrays not only the ground but also all the buildings around the tower as lighter in colour than the tower itself. He thereby lends a heaviness to the classicizing portico and conveys the impression that it weighs as profoundly on the coffins as does the feeling of grief on the people who have gathered in the square.

The March victory celebrated by a funeral procession in the Gendarmenmarkt was followed here in November by defeat. The square was occupied by troops and the Prussian National Assembly, which was drawing up a constitution in the Schauspielhaus, was forced to leave Berlin and shortly afterwards was dissolved by the king. The old balance of power was restored.

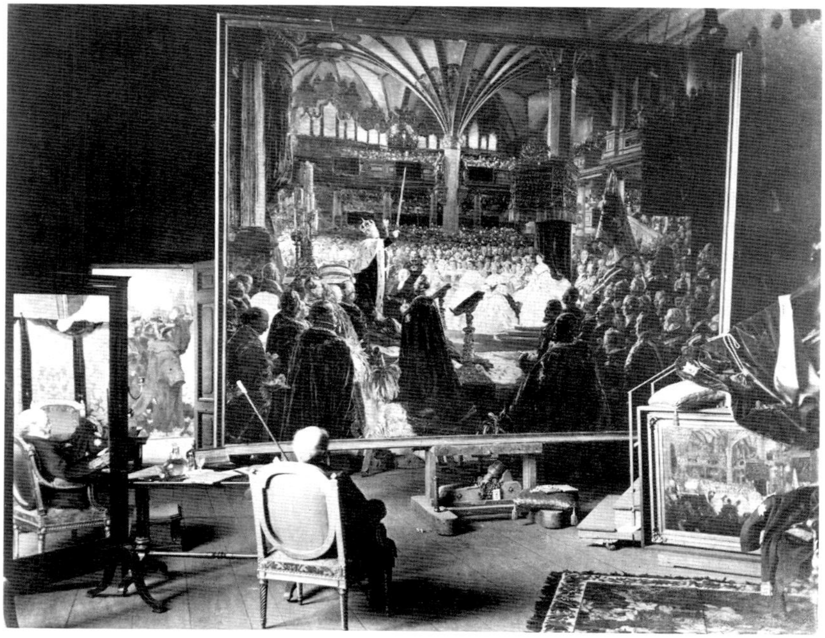

Menzel contemplates his *Coronation*

Adolph Menzel, who stood amongst the watching crowds on the steps of the French Church, was just 4' 7" tall. The military commission had officially certified him as "gnomish". "For the first time, something that made little odds to me in the past now pains me: that I haven't grown up into a big strong chap", he wrote after the March Revolution.

It is doubtful that this was the first time the thirty-two-year-old Menzel had been troubled by his height. In a society whose role models were officers, i.e. men of sound frame, restricted growth was perceived as a defect. It made Menzel an outsider. His height disadvantage was compounded by his petit-bourgeois origins and lack of education. Born in 1815, he left school at the age of just fourteen and joined his father's printing firm. When his father died two years later, the just sixteen-year-old Menzel found himself the chief provider for his family. He drew and printed vignettes for letterheads, invoices, and labels. He worked – as he would do later – deep into the night, didn't marry, and dreamed of being accepted by society.

In 1861 he achieved his ambition. Menzel was commissioned to paint the official picture of the coronation of Wilhelm I. He made sketches during the ceremony, and over the next four years made portraits of over one hundred of the most prominent figures in attendance. Every face, every detail had to be accurate. The only part he invented was the gesture of the newly crowned king raising his sword – he wanted to lend the monarch greater significance. Menzel had his photograph taken seated in front of the finished canvas.

The *Coronation* is a very different painting to the *Lying in State of the Dead in the March Revolution*. Although both record a solemn occasion, the *Coronation* appears on the canvas like the boring exercise in protocol that it probably was. No tension, no involvement. In 1848, on the other hand, Menzel was very much caught up in his subject. He commenced work with "a pounding heart and passionate enthusiasm for the ideas in whose service the victims had fallen". All the greater was his disappointment at the thwarting of the liberal movement. He was unable to continue painting; he left the unfinished canvas "with its face against the wall", reported Alfred Lichtwark, who bought the work for the Hamburg Kunsthalle in 1902. "Such was his disgust, he couldn't bring himself to lay a hand on it again."

The reason why the artist hid his *March Revolution* from himself and the public for so many years, however, may also have been because it would have formed an obstacle to his acceptance into court circles. It was a reminder, after all, of a royal defeat.

Even after Menzel became "presentable at court", it is clear from several of his paintings that his perspective was not that of the courtiers around him. In *The Departure of King Wilhelm I for the Army*, for example, he portrays the king in his carriage as a much smaller figure than the cheering Berliners lining the street (cf. p. 382), while in his *Ball Supper*, he shows tall officers trying to hold a glass, a plate and their hat all at once and appearing rather ridiculous as they do so.

Menzel kept his distance; he never painted another coronation, and occasionally encouraged the careers of artists critical of the regime, such as the young Käthe Kollwitz. As a member of a committee, he recommended her graphic series *Weavers' Rising*, shown at the Grand Berlin Exhibition of Art in 1898, for a medal. Emperor Wilhelm II rejected the idea angrily, albeit not only on political grounds. "I ask you, gentlemen, a medal for a woman – that's really going too far. It would be nothing less than a belittlement of every high distinction. Medals and honours belong on the chests of deserving men!"

On the chest of the short Herr Menzel, for example. That same year he was awarded the Order of the Black Eagle and elevated to the peerage by the emperor: 1898 – exactly fifty years after the *Lying in State of the Dead in the March Revolution*.

Menzel may have intended the present picture as a preliminary study for a larger version, a theory supported by its relatively small format of 45 by 63 centimetres. But he signed it and thereby acknowledged it as a work in its own right. In addition to his personal reasons for abandoning the composition, there may be an artistic explanation, too. It simply proved impossible to marry his dedication to documentary accuracy with his need to compose a picture that was more than a mere copy of what he was looking at. The candlelight and sunshine with whose help he was otherwise able to compose freely were here missing. The overcast sky gave only a diffuse light that cast wan shadows. And whether the people in the lower part of the composition are at a loss, upset, or resigned is almost impossible to convey in paint.

Whether unfinished or intended as a preliminary study, the picture is a rarity within German painting of the 19th century. A rarity, because it is a picture in which an important artist is obviously criticizing the existing balance of power. In France there arose a whole series of comparable paintings – by Théodore Géricault, by Edouard Manet, and above all by Eugène Delacroix, whose *Liberty Leading the People* shows a bare-breasted Liberty on the barricades, the Tricolor in her hand and armed citizens advancing at her side (cf. p. 351).

In the history of 19th-century German art, just one other painting may be said to come close to Menzel's *March Revolution*, namely *Hutten's Tomb* by Caspar David Friedrich, painted around 1823 (cf. p. 340). Friedrich portrays a grieving man beside the tomb of Ulrich von Hutten, a vociferous rebel of the 16th century. In 1823 Hutten became an inspiring example in the fight against princely rule. Friedrich hints at Hutten's relevance to the 19th-century present by inscribing on his tomb, in small lettering, the names of prominent contemporaries who had been persecuted by the Prussian authorities.

No other Romantic formulated his protest so literally and directly. In Germany, art criticizing the status quo remained only a regional phenomenon or something for rapid consumption in periodicals and broadsheets. It did not fit into the prevailing artistic trends – trends embodied by Schinkel's magnificent visions of medieval cathedrals, for example (cf. p. 334), Ludwig Richter's *Genevieve Alone in the Forest*, and Moritz von Schwind's *Water Sprites and Stag*. The Biedermeier artists celebrated the family idyll, while the Nazarenes devoted themselves to biblical scenes. The domain of art was the realm of the imagination, not political reality, except where it was required to provide an official record of events.

Alongside their criticism of the balance of power, the paintings of Friedrich and Menzel have another theme in common – mourning for the dead. Friedrich's protest is expressed as a sombre pilgrimage to a tomb in a ruined chapel; Menzel's civilian triumph takes the form of a funeral procession.

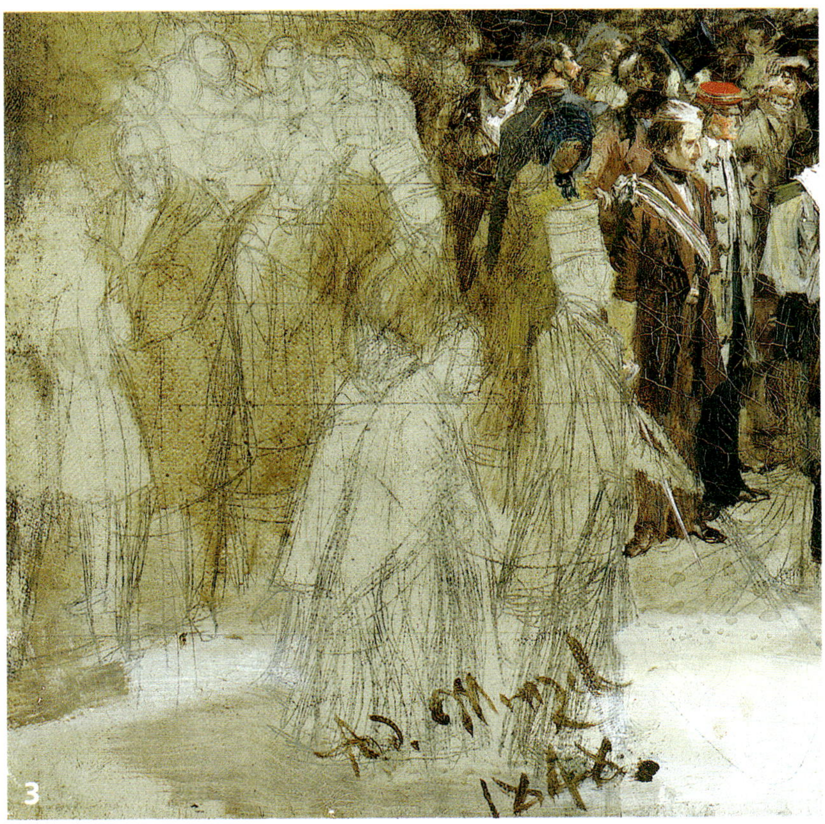

3

The picture of the Revolution remained unfinished

The programme of Modernism

Unsellable. For twenty years the painting stood in the artist's studio; no one wanted to buy it. Since 1917 it has hung in the National Gallery in London. From today's perspective, Edouard Manet's *Music in the Tuileries Gardens* marks a turning-point; it represents the earliest example of modern painting. In the spring of 1869, however, it drew heated reactions from the public. "This art is not healthy", declared one critic when the canvas went on display, and the novelist Emile Zola even recalled "an indignant amateur who went so far as to threaten to resort to violence" if the eyesore was not removed from the gallery without delay.

"Imagine, beneath the trees of the Tuileries gardens, a crowd of perhaps a hundred people moving about in the sunshine" – thus Zola described the object of the scandal. "Each person is a simple, barely determined fleck, in which the details become lines and black dots". Only, proposed Zola, when the viewer withdrew "to a respectable distance" – something that no artist had ever demanded before – did the objectionable "flecks" of colour condense into a scene from contemporary Paris: men airing their top hats and ladies showing off their new summer wardrobes, bonnets, and parasols. They converse beneath the tall trees as if in a large salon.

Summer 1862. Twice a week, a military band played fashionable tunes to an elegant audience. Edouard Manet was a regular member of the crowd. "He went to the Tuileries nearly every day from two till four o'clock, making studies in the open air, beneath the trees", recalled Manet's friend Antonin Proust. "People looked curiously at this elegantly dressed artist, who set up his canvas, armed himself with his palette, and painted." The following winter Manet completed the oil painting, measuring 76 by 118 centimetres, in his studio – it was his most ambitious work to date.

Born in 1832, the artist was full of self-confidence as he embarked on his career. Having completed his studies, he wanted to be independent. He took his own studio, left his parents' house, and moved in with the Dutch piano teacher Suzanne Leenhoff, with whom he had a son in 1852. Only later, after his father's death, did the artist dare to legalize this socially frowned-upon liaison through marriage. In private, Edouard Manet always adhered to the conventions of the wealthy upper middle classes. He maintained the well-groomed appearance of a dandy and frequented the meeting paces of the beau monde.

The year before he commenced work on the *Tuileries Gardens*, his *Spanish Singer* had been accepted by the jury into the official Salon. The painting won him an honourable mention, some early favourable reviews, and a small circle of admirers, writers and painters.

When, two years later, he exhibited fourteen new works in the Galerie Martinet on the Boulevard des Italiens, however, the success he had hoped for proved elusive. Unlike in his private life, in artistic matters Manet was not prepared to follow the conventions of his day. *Music in the Tuileries Gardens*, in particular, offended against the rules of "high" art as laid down by the Academy in both its choice of subject and its painting technique.

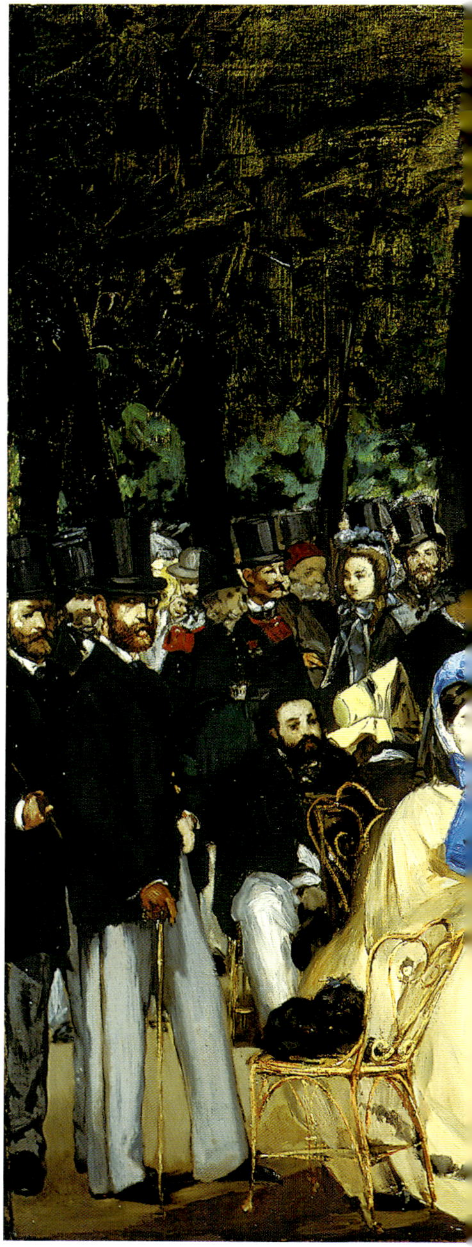

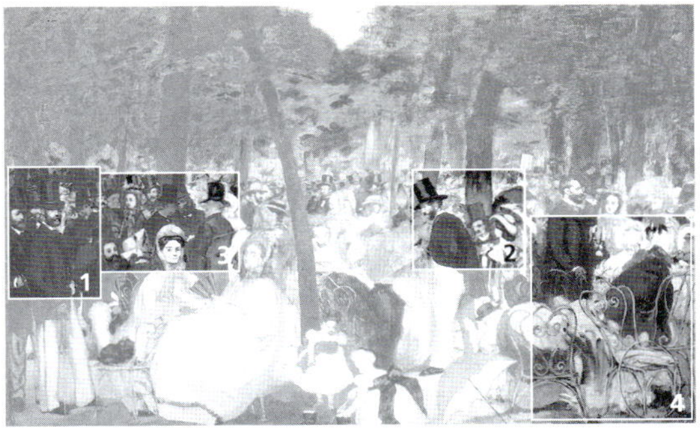
1
3
2
4

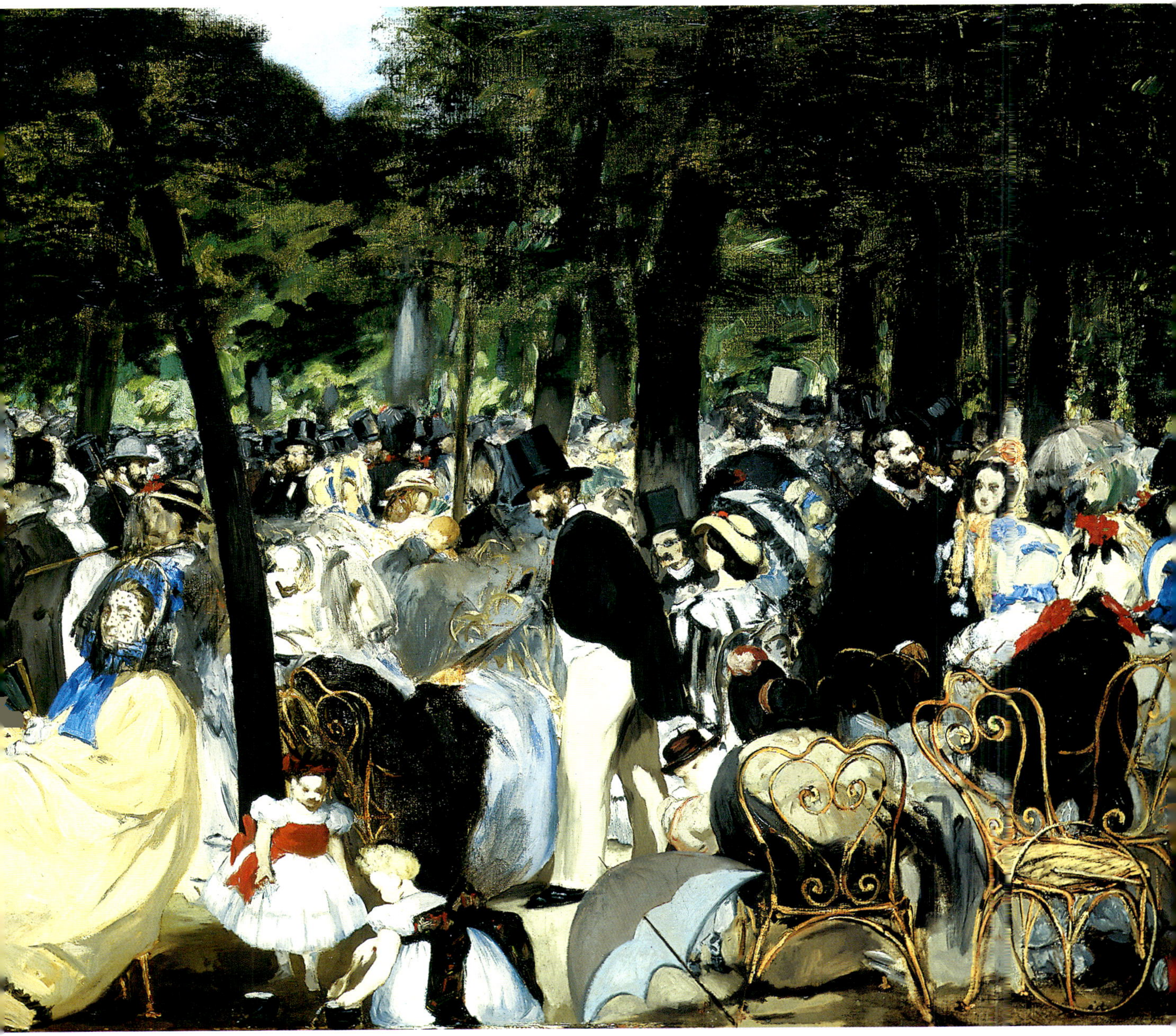

According to academic rules, objects from daily life had no place in a "proper" work of art – such things were "vulgar". The wrought-iron chairs that Manet positions so prominently in the foreground were thereby a provocative statement with a contemporary significance: only in that very summer of 1862 had the simple wooden seats in the Tuileries been replaced by the wrought-iron chairs with their decorative scrollwork, which are still found in Parisian parks today.

In the new industrial age, iron was the material of choice. Between 1852 and 1870, the Second Empire in France built its railway stations, exhibition halls, beds and chairs of iron, paradoxically – in the absence of an own style – cast in the exuberant forms of a past epoch, the 18th century. Rococo came back into fashion, as evidenced, too, by the bulky crinolines that billow over the chairs.

Emperor Napoleon III and Empress Eugénie sought to revive the pre-revolutionary glitter of the *ancien régime*. They held countless parties and balls in their Tuileries palace, where they resided with their household. The building, which at that time formed the magnificent centrepiece of the gardens, is only vaguely suggested between the trees in the background of Manet's painting. For those strolling through the park, however, it was a solid component of the gardens.

The Tuileries palace no longer exists. In 1871, after the end of Second Empire, it was looted and burned down by Communards. Rather than rebuilding it, in 1882 the Republican parliamentarians voted that the "monarchist" building should be completely destroyed. The rubble was removed, and not the slightest trace of the old building remains.

The palace was steeped in myths. There was supposed to be a curse upon it, and the dowager queen Catherine de' Medici, who had it built in the Renaissance style towards in the end of the 16th century, didn't even dare move in. Nor did the palace bring much luck to the other royal women who lived in it over the course of the years: Queen Marie-Antoinette was taken from there to prison, while the empresses Joséphine, Marie Louise and Eugénie went successively into exile.

In Manet's day, however, the proximity of the imperial palace continued to lend glamour to the Tuileries gardens – even if the empress preferred to drive up the Champs-Elysées and out to the Bois de Boulogne in the afternoons. She was followed by members of the aristocracy and moneyed classes, and all who otherwise had access to horses and a barouche. Only the emperor occasionally went for a walk in the park. The people who came to the Tuileries, mostly on foot, were primarily members of the bourgeoisie from the prosperous districts of western Paris. Dandies such as Manet and his friends also liked to stroll through its grounds.

Not that they were drawn by any strong urge to be outside in nature; the composer Daniel-François Auber, for example, declared provocatively that a few landscape engravings were the only thing he had ever seen of green leaves or indeed nature itself. The dandies were so wrapped up in themselves and their fellows that they rarely even registered the trees. These elegant idlers were happiest gathering on the new, spacious avenues that Prefect Georges-Eugène Haussmann was laying out across an ever-expanding Paris. But it was still considered chic to show oneself in the Tuileries for one or two hours in the afternoon.

Iron – the material of the industrial age

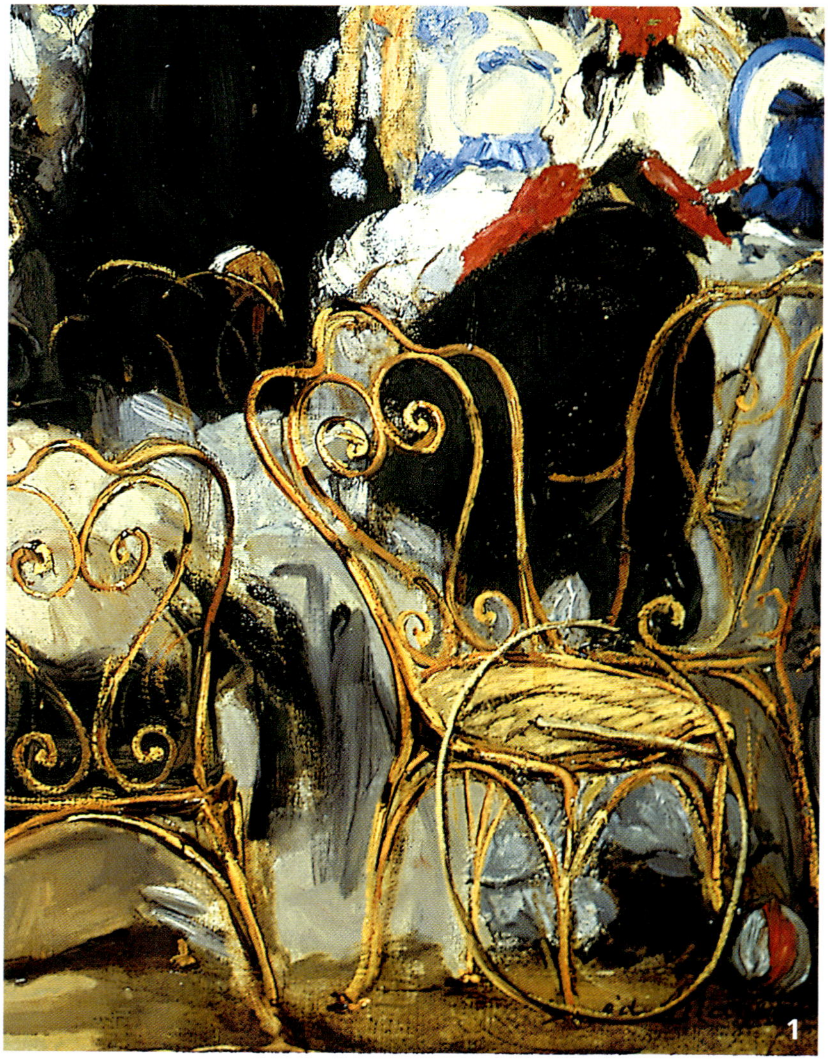
1

In place of the Greek heroes and historical individuals who traditionally peopled works of high art, viewers who stood far enough back could now make out, amidst the throng on Manet's canvas, well-known figures. The "daubs of paint" transformed themselves into individuals from contemporary society. The artist had thereby thought very hard about who he wanted to assemble beneath the trees in his painting. Friends and acquaintances, writers, critics and opinion-shapers – typical representatives of the society of the day, outstanding personalities of the Second Empire. Many can still be identified today; working from detailed preliminary studies and photographs, Manet captures their likeness with just a few skilfully placed strokes.

The bearded man with the tall top hat, for example, is probably the artist's brother, Eugène Manet; he appears in another of Manet's works, *Le Déjeuner sur l'herbe*. The man with the hooked nose, pince-nez and sideburns, sitting next to a lady by the trunk of a tree, was caricatured in the papers as a "cross between a cockerel and a grasshopper" – he is the composer Jacques Offenbach. Upbraided by the Republicans as a "corrupter of the nation", he was acclaimed by his colleague Gioacchino Rossini as the "Mozart of the Champs-Elysées". He was a typical *boulevardier*, feared nothing so much as solitude and silence, and felt happiest – even when working – in a crowd. Even as he sat here in the Tuileries gardens, the military band (not visible in the picture) was probably playing one of the catchy tunes from his operetta *Orpheus in the Underworld*, which all of Paris was humming and whistling. Offenbach provided the light, charming music that the Second Empire demanded.

In 1851 Prince Louis Napoleon, an ambitious nephew of Napoleon I, had seized power in a coup d'état. The following year he had himself elected Emperor. From then on he made sure that the nation devoted itself to non-political pursuits – a vital prerequisite for a stable dictatorship.

Industry and investment soon flourished, huge fortunes were made overnight and equally quickly spent again on luxuries and entertainment. Pleasure, fun and glamour were the order of the day, and the operetta perfectly satisfied all three.

In those days, Paris was the only city in which a Jewish artist could make a name for himself unopposed. The future composer – born Jakob Offenbach in Cologne in 1819 – was fourteen when he arrived. He began his musical career as a cellist and occasional composer. In 1855, the year of the Great Exhibition, he opened a small theatre, where he proceeded to stage one operetta after another – with phenomenal success. Not only the inhabitants of the capital itself, but also visitors from the provinces and indeed the whole of Europe proved eager to immerse themselves in the delights of *La vie parisienne*, as one of his operettas was called.

But Offenbach was hopeless with money. He repeatedly landed himself in financial difficulties and often had to hide from the bailiffs – in the Tuileries gardens, for example, which owing to its proximity to the imperial palace was considered a safe haven.

With the end of the Second Empire, however, the age of the Parisian operetta and its most popular composer were also over. Offenbach died in 1880. According to the inscription on his tomb, despite his German origins he was not just a Frenchman but "more still, a Parisian".

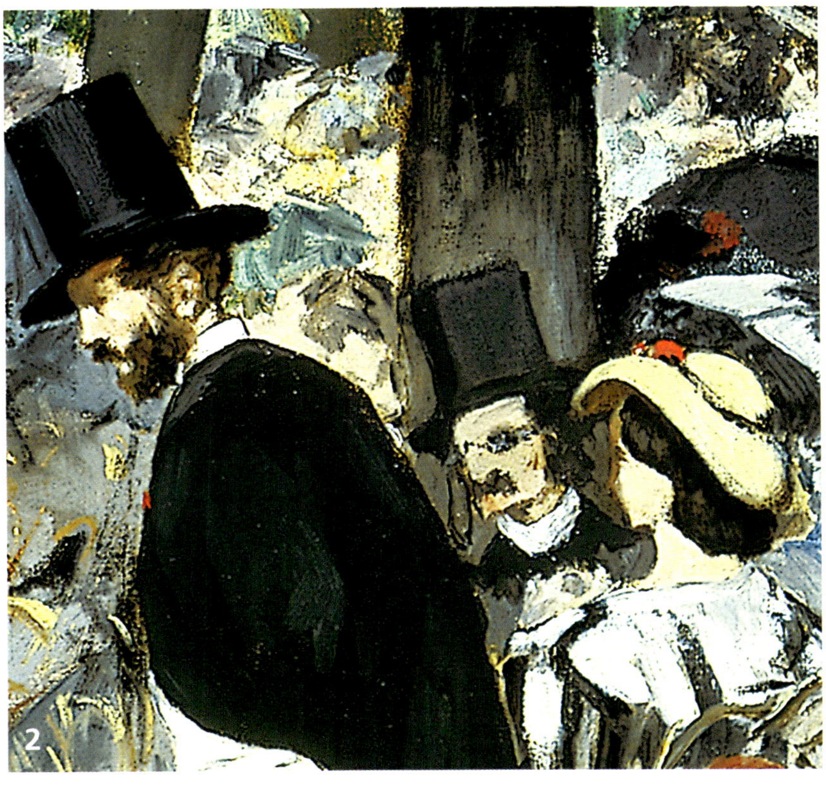

2

All of Paris was humming and whistling his tunes

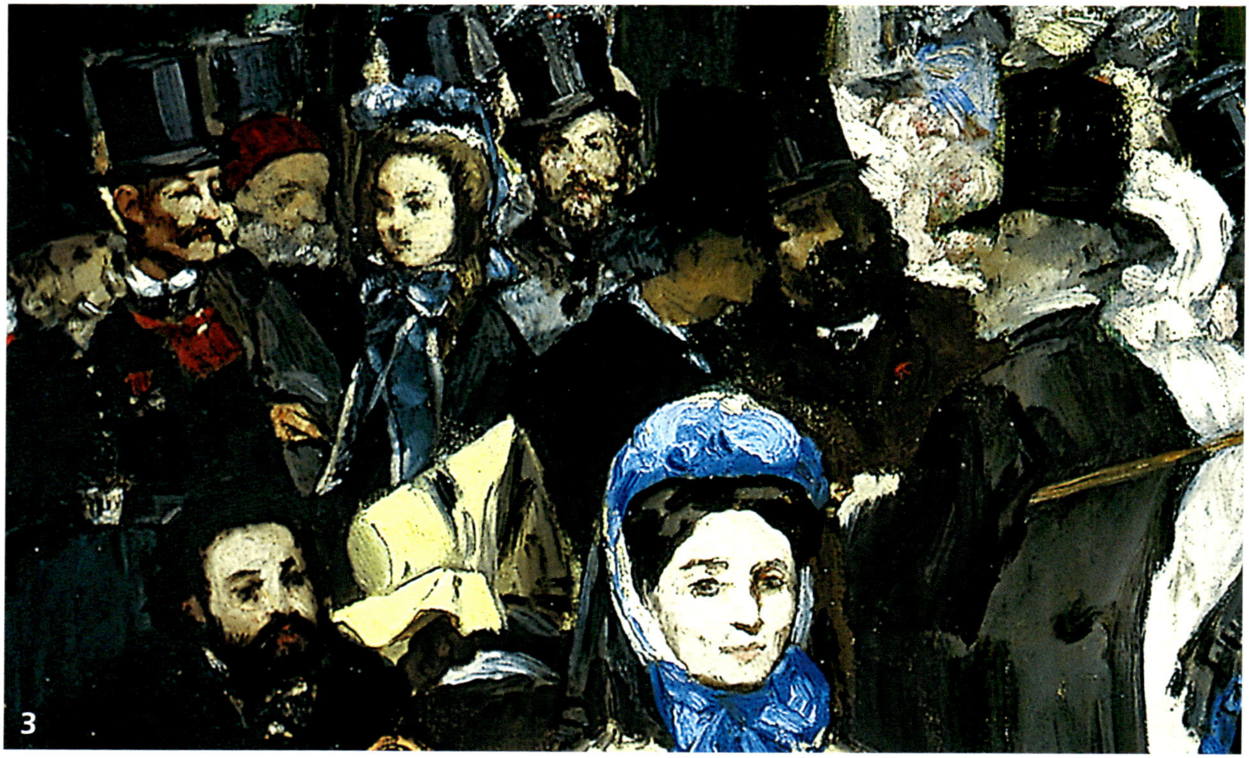

Few of the figures whom Manet assembles on his canvas are still as well known today as the composer Jacques Offenbach. Most of the ladies, for example, will have been part of the artist's circle of acquaintance; there is no sign of the famous, extravagant demi-mondaines who were as typical of the era as Offenbach's waltzes. Such women had carriages and racehorses and therefore drove out to the Bois de Boulogne for the afternoon, like the empress. Their more modest colleagues, the "lorettas", appeared in the Tuileries only after five o'clock, by which time the artist and his friends had usually already departed. For the dandies, the Tuileries gardens were an offshoot of the boulevard, a place where you showed yourself off and met your fellows. "It could be crossed in just a few paces", wrote the journalist Paul de Musset, "and yet it held the whole world!" Ludovic Halévy, the librettist of Offenbach's operettas, observed tersely: "There is no big city besides Paris. In Brussels one doesn't know anyone, doesn't see anyone", and he boasted how may acquaintances he had run into in just a single day – perhaps the painter Henri Fantin-Latour (to the left of the tree), or the men of letters Zacharie Astruc (seated) and Aurélien Scholl (behind him). Both wrote witty articles in short-lived papers that were permanently under threat of bankruptcy or a ban by the imperial censor. It was for people like them – writers, journalists, and artists – that Baron Taylor (right, with the grey beard) founded an insurance company, a sort of pension fund. Taylor, the highest official in the French museums administration, is conversing in the painting with the formerly "wild" Romantic Théophile Gauthier, who was now a contributor to the official government paper, the *Moniteur officiel*, and who in 1861 had written favourably of Manet's art.

Standing beside these two representatives of the Establishment is an outsider, the poet Charles Baudelaire. Just a "fleck" of colour, he is nevertheless the most important figure on the canvas – important for literature and art, and also for Manet. In 1862 Baudelaire was Manet's frequent companion on his walks, and his influence upon this work is clearly apparent.

With *Les Fleurs du Mal*, published in 1857 (and condemned for offending against public morality), Baudelaire wanted to "plunge into the very depths of the unconscious to find something new". In his writings on artistic theory he formulated an aesthetic programme that was radically new: "Parisian life is full of poetic and marvellous subjects", he declared in as early as 1846, and went on to demand that painters should give the immediate present precedent over historical and biblical themes. The artist, Baudelaire wrote, needed only to open his eyes to "the spectacle of fashionable life and the millions of irresolute existences that circulate in the underworld of a big city".

Manet took this advice. From the underworld he painted the *Old Musician* and the *Street Singer*; and in his *Music in the Tuileries Gardens*, painted at approximately the same time, he recorded the "spectacle of fashionable life".

The spectacle of fashionable life

Manet painted himself on the far left-hand edge of the canvas, next to the painter Albert de Balleroy with whom he had formerly shared a studio. He thereby placed himself firmly back in line with tradition. Not long previously he had copied a small oil painting in the Louvre that was attributed to the Spanish artist Diego Velázquez. It shows the famous 17th-century artist amongst his friends. Perhaps this work inspired Manet to paint his *Music in the Tuileries Gardens*. Velázquez was his idol; the fact that he adopted the older master's arrangement is an indication of Manet's self-confidence. Manet had enjoyed a solid academic training. As a student in the atelier of the celebrated history painter Thomas Couture, famous for his *Romans of the Decadence*, he had learned the traditional techniques of composition. In the *Tuileries Gardens*, too, a shaft of light divides the pictorial plane into two halves, while strongly vertical elements such as tree trunks and top hats contrast with the curving lines of armchairs and parasols, hoops and crinolines.

If the compositional structure is traditional, Manet's painting technique struck his contemporaries as revolutionary. They found that his palette "grated on the eye just as fairground music is painful to the ear". They were also shocked by his juxtaposition of realistically painted details with elements that seemed barely sketched in. The painter also spurned the conventional technique of modelling via shading, using it only in a seemingly arbitrary manner and leaving areas of pure colour to stand as such. The people in his canvas are themselves reduced to colour, to what Emile Zola described as "a simple fleck, barely determined, and in which the details become lines and black dots".

Manet is here no longer the painter of reality, but rather is inventing a new language of signs and symbols. He is risking the first, decisive step towards abstraction, towards modern art. In this, too, he was following Baudelaire: "It is an immense pleasure", effused the poet, "to lose oneself in the crowd, in the ebb and flow, in the movement, in the fleeting and the infinite ..."

The primacy of form over content was something that Baudelaire had postulated, for the first time since the Renaissance, in his review of the Salon of 1846: "The best way to tell if a painting is melodious is to view it from so far away that you cannot recognize either the subject or the lines. If it is melodious, it will already have a meaning."

As far as we know, Baudelaire the art critic made no comment on *Music in the Tuileries Gardens*. But Manet's young artist colleagues, the future Impressionists, immediately recognized the painting's significance for the development of art. Claude Monet is said to have suffered a positive shock upon viewing the exhibition in the Galerie Martinet. In 1863, after visiting the same gallery, Frédéric Bazille wrote: "You wouldn't believe how much I have learned from looking at these pictures; just one of these visits is worth a whole month of working." Even though the masterpiece would be unanimously rejected by critics and the public, Manet proceeded that same year to exhibit his *Déjeuner sur l'herbe*. Modernism in painting had begun.

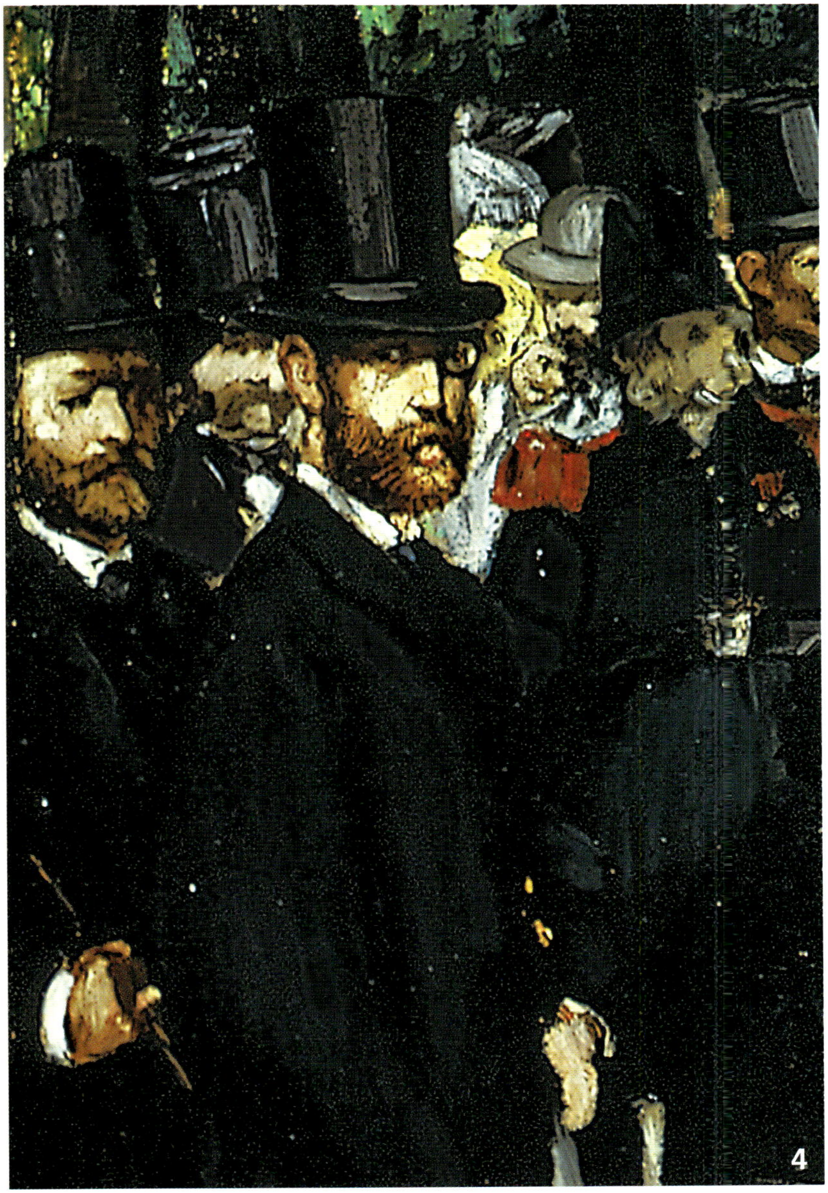

4

Manet signs his work with a self-portrait

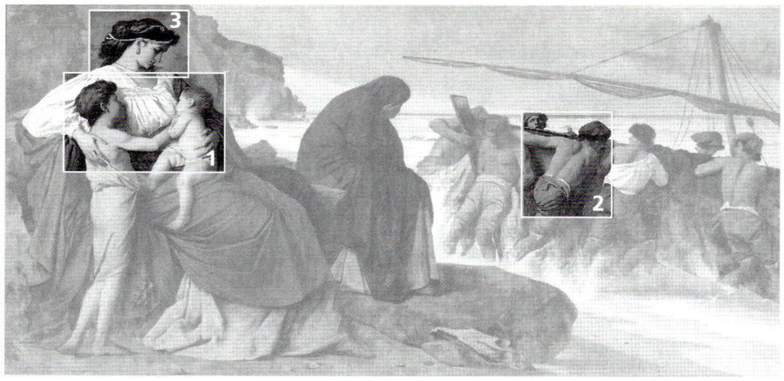
3
1
2

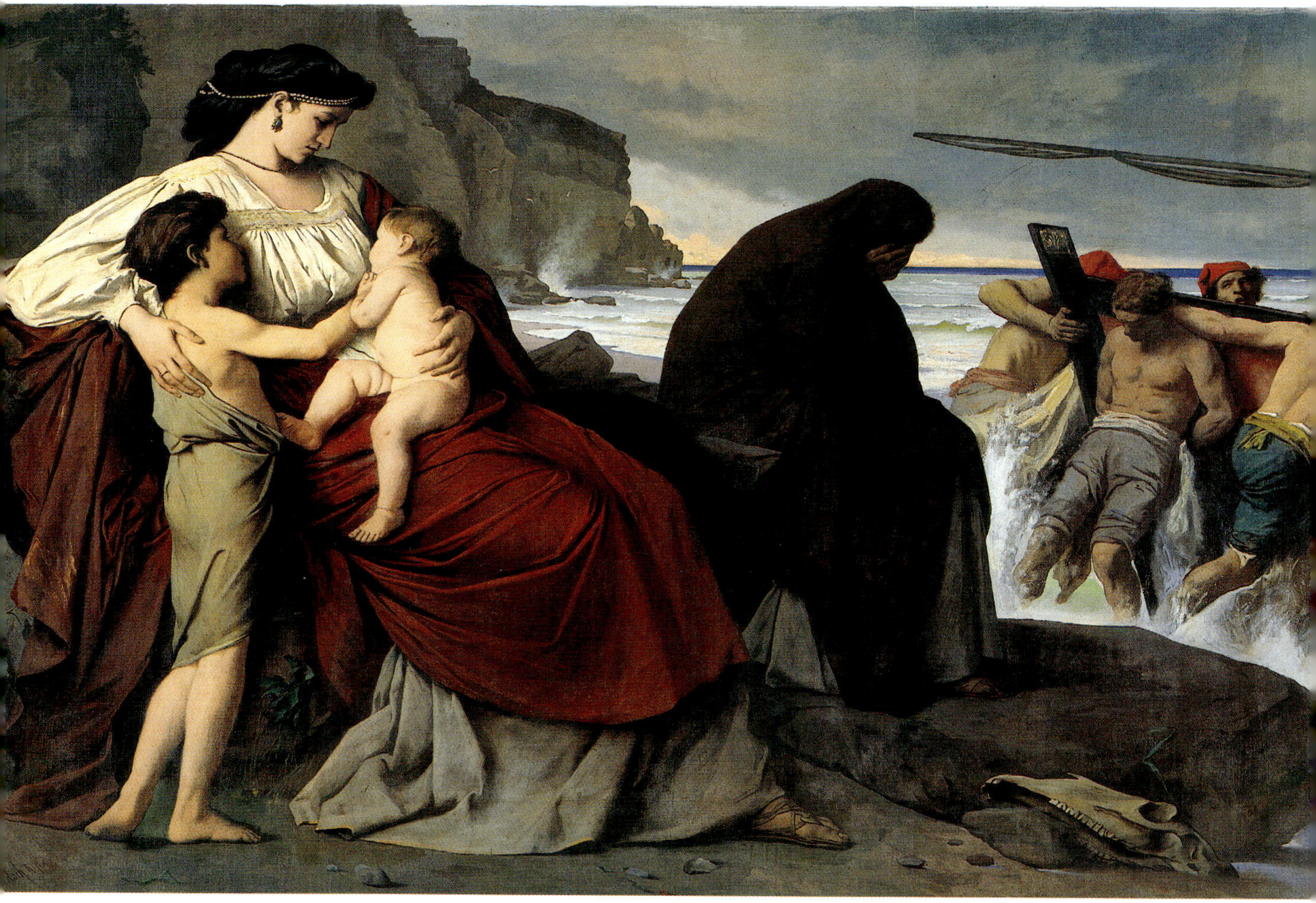

Anselm Feuerbach: Medea, 1870

The queen murders her children

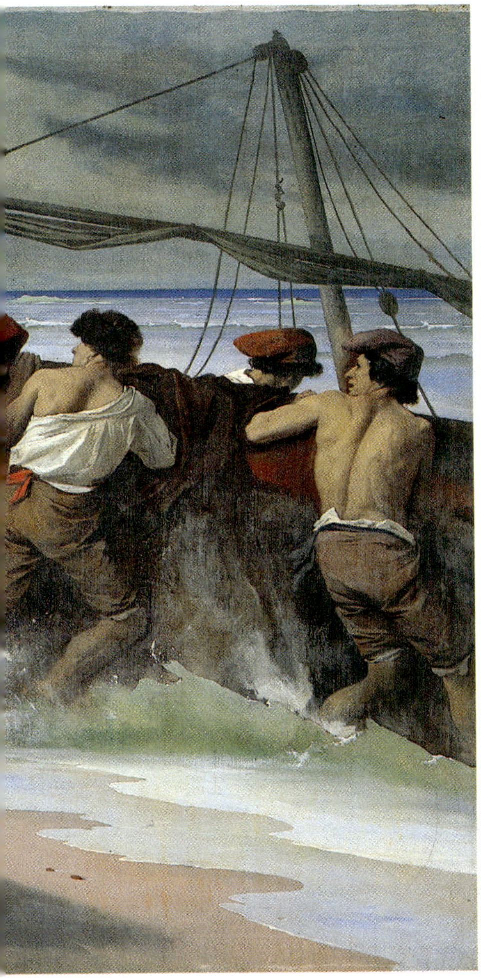

Anselm Feuerbach celebrates a woman of monumental size. Were she to stand up, she would burst out of the canvas. No one else in the composition is as large as the heroine with her children. Feuerbach makes their difference in scale plausible by locating the other figures deeper into the background

The unsettlingly large woman is seated within a precisely balanced composition. The pyramidal group of three on the left corresponds to the group of men with the boat on the right; while the mother leans to the left, the sailors are heaving the boat towards the right. The figure beneath the brown cloak provides a vertical anchor at the centre of the composition.

Feuerbach emphasizes harmony not only in the compositional structure, but also in the relationship of the mother to her children. Were the skies not overcast, nor the painting entitled *Medea* or *Medea's Farewell*, one might think that the artist was showing his public a happy family beside the sea. But the name of Medea is synonymous with murder.

Her story begins in Colchis, a kingdom in the Caucasus on the eastern shores of the Black Sea. To the Greeks, the people there were barbarians beyond the bounds of the civilized world. But the Colchians possessed a famous ram's fleece, known as the Golden Fleece, which Jason, the son of the Greek king, wanted to win. Together with his companions, later known as the Argonauts after the name of their ship, he sailed to Colchis.

The Colchian king agreed to relinquish the Fleece, but only after Jason had successfully undergone a trial of courage and strength. Jason's task was to plough a field with two fire-breathing bulls, sow it with dragon's teeth, and then defeat the armed men who would grow out the furrows. That was too much even for a Greek hero, but Medea, the king's daughter, helped him. She was a temple priestess, the granddaughter of the sun god Helios and the niece of Circe the enchantress. She knew secret charms and possessed magic powers which she used on Jason's behalf. She had fallen in love with this man from a distant country. He promised to marry her, and so she sailed away with them. She made the dragon who guarded the Golden Fleece fall asleep, killed her own brother when he came after her, and after many other adventures with the Argonauts eventually landed in Corinth, where she bore Jason two sons.

Jason later decided to abandon Medea and marry the young daughter of King Creon. Medea, insulted, enraged, unable to return to her homeland having murdered her brother, in Greece without support, Medea, the self-confident, mysterious barbarian, felt betrayed. She sought revenge, poisoned Jason's bride and stabbed her own sons to death.

The horse's skull lying at the bottom of the picture is a pointer to the impending tragedy. The figure shrouded in robes, a nurse or a servant woman, buries her face in her hands – she doesn't want to see what is coming.

In 431 BC the poet Euripides turned the legend into a play. He presented it to a society in which the position of women was closer to that of slaves than free citizens. A woman who acted in defiance of all convention and with the confidence of a man could only, as far as the Greeks were concerned, be a foreigner, a barbarian, and enchantress. At the end of the tragedy, she lays her dead sons in a chariot drawn by dragons and is carried off, rising above all human judgement. "The hand of the Most High reveals itself in many ways", Euripides writes in conclusion. "Where we do not comprehend, He knows a path."

The legend continues: Medea's dragon chariot takes her from Corinth to Athens, where she marries the king and bears him a son. But after a foiled poison attempt, she is banished and finally returns to her home of Colchis. This second part of her story did not interest Euripides, however, and was similarly ignored by virtually every artist after him. Everyone took from the material what his particular epoch wanted to hear. Thus the poet Giovanni Boccaccio (1313–1375) includes Medea in his short biographies of famous men as a cautionary example: those who follow only passion sew evil. Florentine wedding chests of the 15th century were often decorated with just the beginning of the story. Thus the Colchian princess is shown leaving her father's house and following her husband without question – just as young brides were expected to do.

Since the Renaissance, there has been no century in which the story of Medea has not been taken up and re-evaluated – right up to the present. Rolf Liebermann's opera *Freispruch für Medea* (Acquittal for Medea) was premièred in 1990, and Christa Wolf's novel *Medea: Stimmen* (Medea: Voices) was published in 1996. Both works are clearly inspired by feminist thinking. In Liebermann's opera, the Colchian becomes the representative of matriarchy, which is far superior to Jason's patriarchal society. Christa Wolf portrays Medea as an autonomous woman who, with her natural self-confidence, is intolerable to men, particularly those in power. Her murder of her children is incorporated into neither work. In the Liebermann opera, it is reduced to her decision not to carry to term a child she has conceived with Jason, while Christa Wolf turns Medea's crimes into mere rumours, spread by those wanting to drive out the strange foreigner. The bloody deed is missing – as it is in Feuerbach's canvas.

The painting was executed during the winter of 1869/70 in Rome. Feuerbach was forty years old, was unable to sell his paintings for the amount he considered they were worth, felt himself unappreciated, was almost permanently hard up, and blamed his contemporaries, especially the Germans amongst them, for his situation. He viewed society as a "complete farce" and felt he was living in a "lousy epoch". He believed the world had been a much finer place, on the other hand, when "gods still walked amongst men". He escaped into the past. "I am happy in my Hellas", the painter wrote. "One becomes a god oneself."

Every epoch views Medea differently

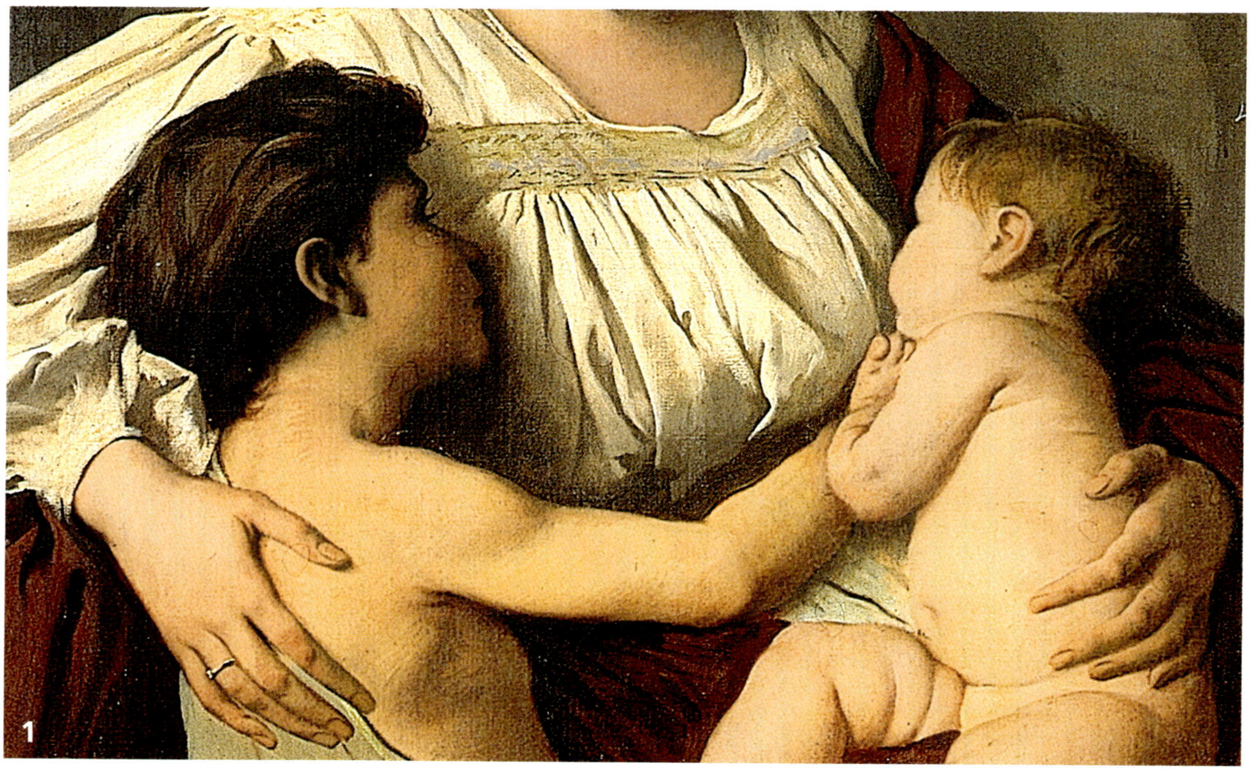
1

Eugène Delacroix portrays Medea as a wild woman

Anselm Feuerbach was born in Speyer in 1829. The son of an archaeologist, his childhood was spent moving from one town to the next. He left school without a diploma and entered the Düsseldorf Academy of Art. At the age of seventeen he executed his first large painting, *Silenus Playing the Pipes*.

After several years in Düsseldorf he went to Munich, Amsterdam and Paris. He copied Old Masters, studied under various teachers, and earned his living with portrait commissions. He was a good portraitist, but capturing the likeness of middle-class clients was not enough for him: he wanted to portray the leading characters from Greek mythology.

It was common for artists of his day to spend time in the South, in order to study the monuments of classical antiquity. At the age of twenty-five, Feuerbach, too, went to Italy. Having moved around so much in his life, he found in Rome, for the first time, something like home. He painted nymphs, bacchants, Orpheus and Eurydice, the Battle of the Amazons, the Judgement of Paris, Plato's Symposium, Iphigenia, Medea, and even Dante.

During his time in Paris, Feuerbach had probably seen – or at least heard of – Eugène Delacroix's *Médée Furieuse* (1838). In this painting, a semi-naked Medea with a wild look on her face pins her screaming children beneath her arms. In her hand she clutches the knife, and the viewer knows that she is about to strike. Deep shadows and a bright light emphasize her state of profound agitation. French Romantics such as Delacroix took the side of wild, unbridled passion. Feuerbach, the neo-classicist, wanted none of it.

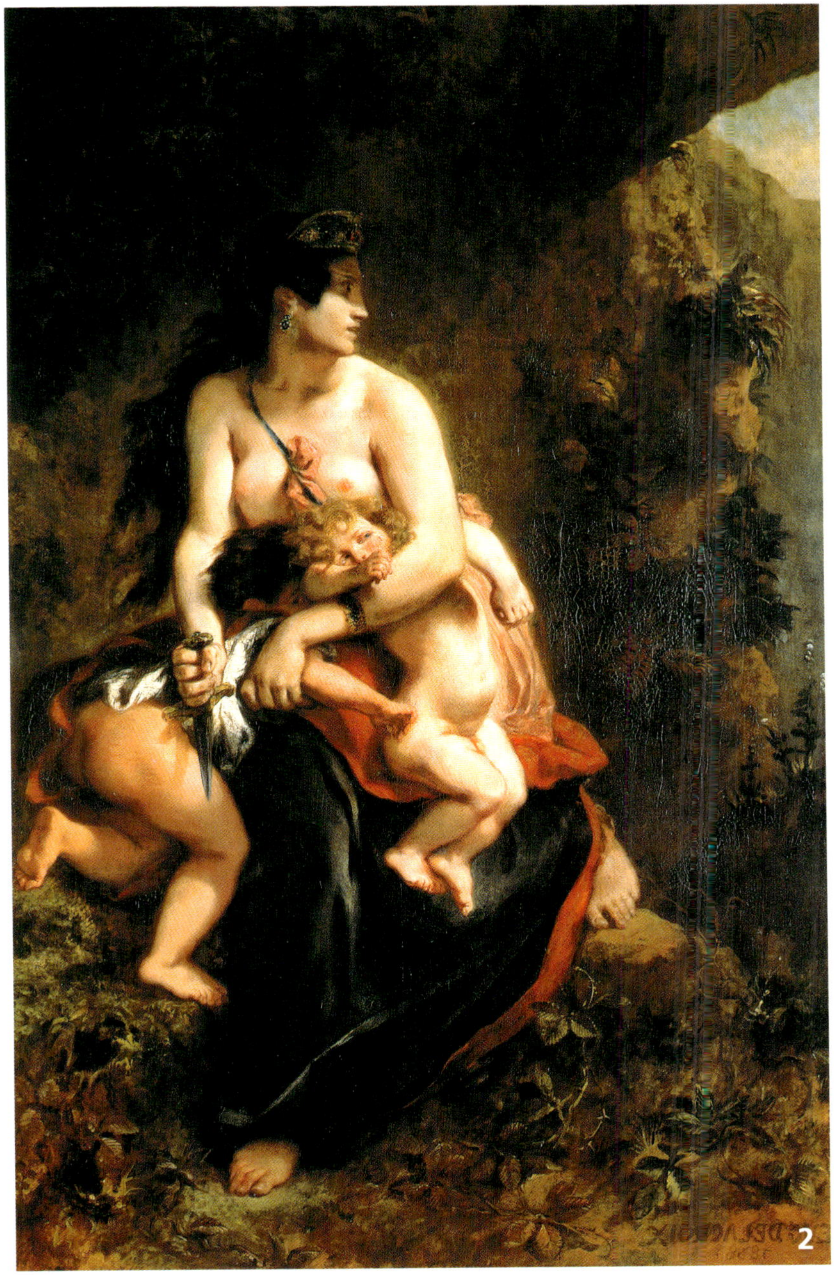

His own painting was inspired by a theatrical performance by Adélaïde Ristori, a tragic actress whose fame at that time extended right across Europe. She had a classical profile and thick black hair, which in one of the photos of her is circled by a headband or – as in Feuerbach's painting – a string of pearls.

Ristori was acting in the tragedy *Medée* written by playwright Ernest Legouvé (1807–1903). He was not a Romantic, but a writer who knew that the general public around the middle of the 19th century would not be able to accept Medea's shocking, morally offensive murder of her children without question. So (like Franz Grillparzer before him, in his *Goldenes Vlies* of 1821) he furnished it with an explanation. He portrays Medea as a darkly savage woman who keeps her children downtrodden, while Jason and his bride represent the light, bright Greek world. The sons decide to go with their father. Medea feels they have betrayed her, and this gives her a motive for murder.

The shore scene portrayed by Feuerbach only appears in Legouvé in Medea's thoughts. She is daydreaming. Medea doesn't yet know that her sons are thinking of living with their father. She wants to kill Jason's bride with a poisoned veil and then flee with her children.

Feuerbach painted Medea four times. One version – which hangs in the Mannheim Kunsthalle – shows her sitting alone, lost in thought, the knife on the ground beside her. In a painting in the Kunsthistorisches Museum in Vienna, she is similarly alone, but behind her stands an urn on which a relief decoration portrays the murder scene. A Berlin version was lost in 1945, but resembled the present painting from the Neue Pinakothek in Munich (197 x 395 cm), with its nurse, children, and sailors – and no direct mention of the bloody deed.

Why Feuerbach chose not to portray the murder is hinted at in a letter of November 1869. "Medea before the deed, Medea after the deed, Medea fleeing by the seashore at night, Medea as a loving mother, as a murderous fury" – the artist lists the possible scenarios, then concludes: "A history painting should portray a life in a situation, it should point to the future and the past and stand ... for all eternity." In other words, to show the murder scene would be to narrow the focus; by avoiding the extreme climax, the painter enables us to see Medea in the wider context of her tragic destiny.

That, at least, was his hope, and it was what he felt the works of antiquity had taught him. The art historian Johann Joachim Winckelmann (1717–1768) had described the essence of such works as "noble simplicity and quiet grandeur" – and quiet, peaceful pictures were what Feuerbach at this time also wanted. If a figure such as Medea was to be elevated above time, he first had to free her – so he believed – from all connection with real life. He took this to such an extreme that it was no longer possible to identify who the figure was meant to be – a point picked up by a number of contemporary critics.

Feuerbach celebrates his Medea as a truly monumental figure. He uses clothing to emphasize her rank: the sailors are naked from the waist up, while Medea's body is covered. The men are labouring physically, Medea does nothing. Only inside is she agitated. She wears an expression of tenderness and wistfulness. Since physical strength and the physical body are ranked lower, in Western tradition, than what we call mind and soul, the men who are trying to help Medea escape also serve to elevate her. The painter thereby raises her above the normal human scale.

Bavaria's King Ludwig II purchased Feuerbach's painting in 1876 and donated it to the Munich Neue Pinakothek. It must, therefore, have been greeted with approval in influential circles, if not by every critic. Its success was undoubtedly bound up with the general admiration for all things classical. It is also conceivable that Feuerbach's figure touched – unintentionally on the part of the artist – upon a situation widespread within contemporary society, namely the isolation experienced by women shut up at home.

Industrialization and commerce had created within society, alongside the nobility, a new, wealthy class whose women were not permitted to pursue a useful activity outside the home. The symbol of this lack of freedom of movement: the laced corset. Legally and socially, women were dependent upon men; music and maternal love were encouraged to be the chief focus of their lives. The situation of these middle-class women was discussed by Henrik Ibsen in his 1879 play *A Doll's House*, and described in 1895 by Theodor Fontane in *Effi Briest*. Many female museum visitors could have identified with Feuerbach's *Medea*; they would have seen a rocky landscape in which there was nothing for women to do, a mother absorbed in her children, and a sense of looming catastrophe.

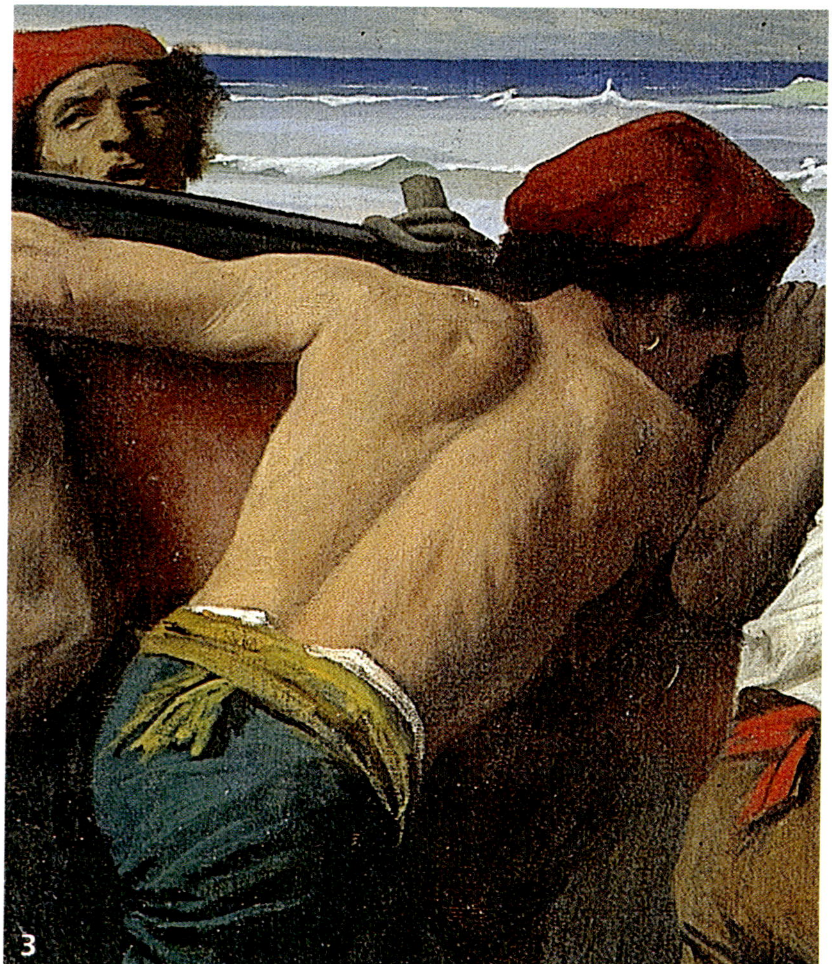

The loneliness of the middle-class wife

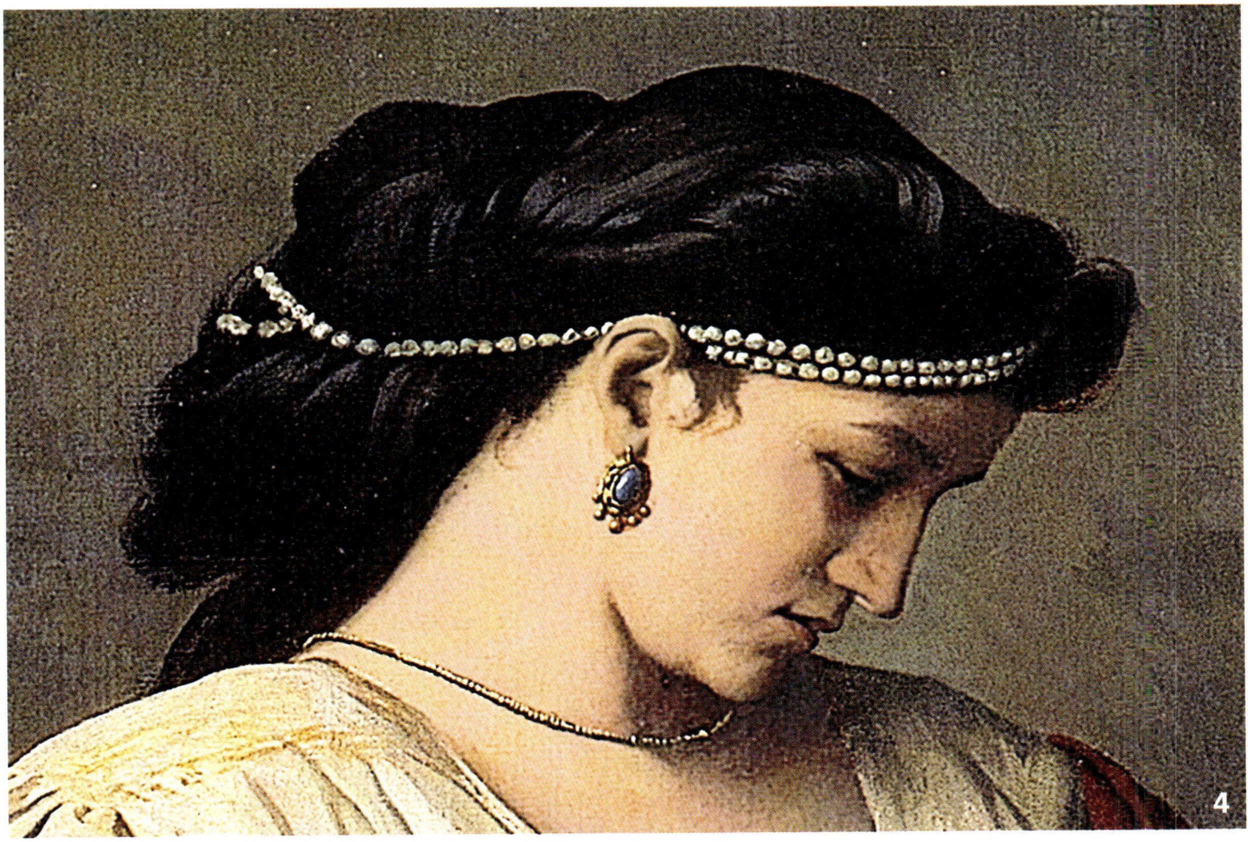

The painting exudes an air of classical distance and cool calculation, yet it is profoundly shaped by suffering and passion, and in particular by the artist's love for his father, who died while Feuerbach was still young. It was his archaeologist father who introduced the young Anselm to the world of antiquity, and his father's book on the *Vatican Apollo* would profoundly affect the direction of Feuerbach's art. He felt it was his duty to complete his father's work with artistic means. "It feels as if Father is reaching across with his dear hand and passing me the book", he wrote in 1859, and he hoped "that I may be permitted to speak his prophetic words in deeds". These deeds were his many paintings of Greece.

Although Feuerbach never married, for six years in Rome he had a mistress, the wife of a shoemaker, who appears again and again in his paintings, including in classical roles. She subsequently left him and Rome for an Englishman. A year later he met Lucia Brunnacci. She had the same thick, black hair as his former mistress, and the same classical profile. From now on, whenever he needed a female model, she was the only one he would use. Whether he loved her, or whether she simply reminded him of his unfaithful mistress, we do not know. But Lucia became his Medea.

The most important person in his life, however – and probably the reason why he never married – was his stepmother. His own mother had died shortly after his birth, and his father's new wife, Henriette, was only seventeen years older than Anselm. She loved him, he too loved her, but at times also hated, insulted, and humiliated her. Each suffered on account of the other and each physically denied the other. When Feuerbach's monumental female figures, his Medeas and Iphigenias, swathe their bodies in robes to the point that they become unrecognizable, then permeating through the Roman model is also the stepmother, beloved and unattainable.

Following the death of the artist in 1880, Henriette Feuerbach destroyed Anselm's personal correspondence and published a selection of writings which show him purely as an artist, as a genius wrestling with himself, his work and ignorant patrons. She called the book "a legacy"; it matched Feuerbach to the artist ideal of the Wilhelmine bourgeoisie and contributed to his fame over the next few decades.

The unattainable beloved

That fame has long since faded. Seen from today's perspective, the late 19th century is dominated by realism and Impressionism. In terms of mythological subjects, we think sooner of those in the ironic, playful hands of Pablo Picasso than of the monumental neo-classical figures of Anselm Feuerbach.

From time to time, nevertheless, we may venture a fresh appraisal. The fact that the human figure is returning to modern painting in pathetically exaggerated size may yet lead us to see Feuerbach's work, too, in a new light.

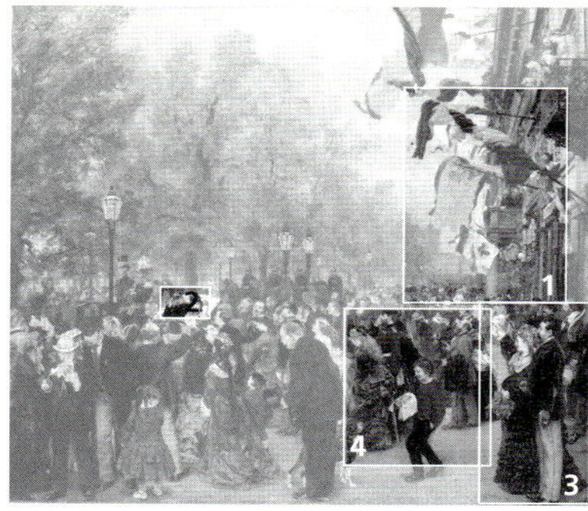
1
4
3

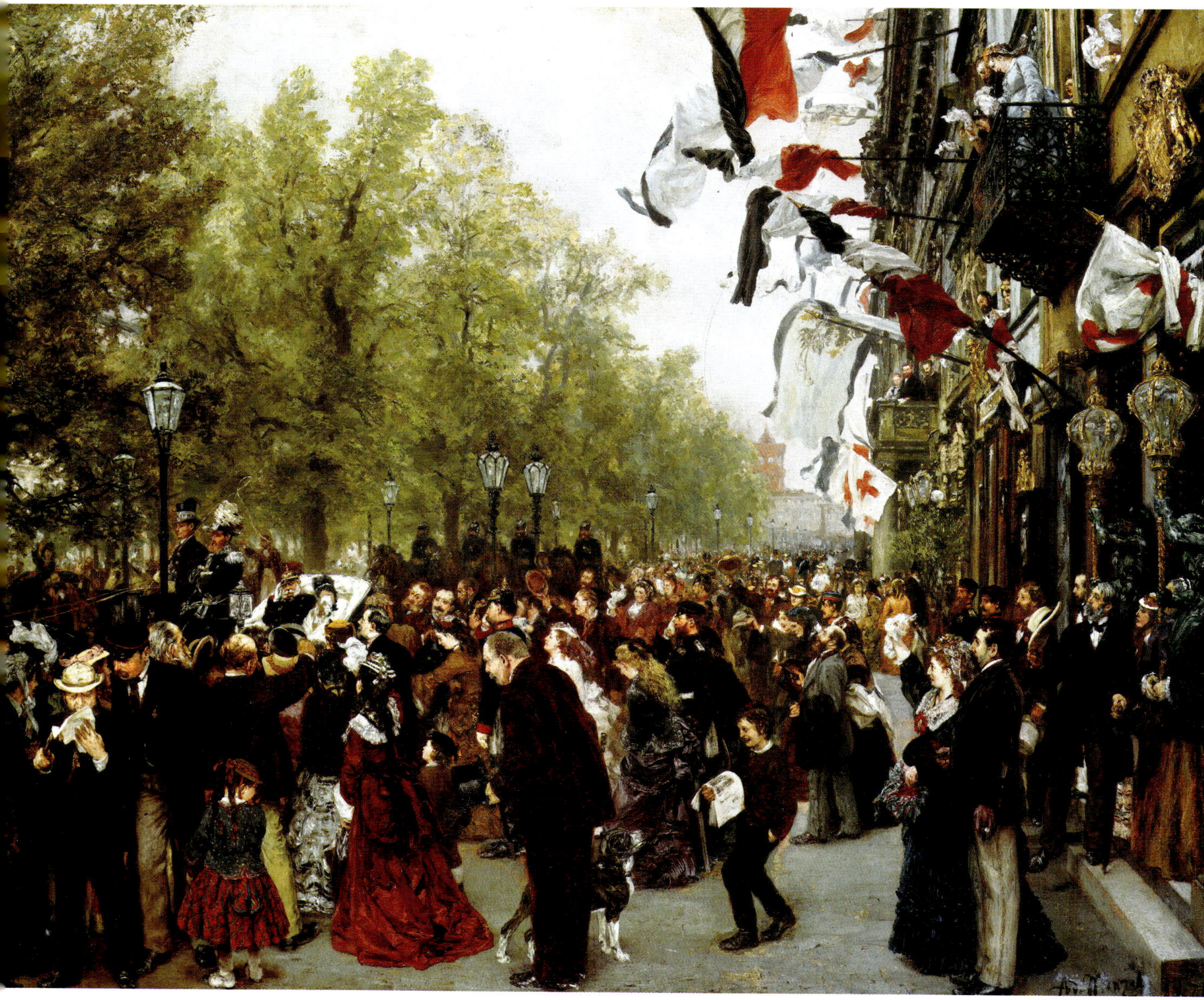

Adolph von Menzel: The Departure of King Wilhelm I for the Army on 31 July 1870, 1871

Royalty under the lime trees

31 July 1870. King Wilhelm I and Queen Augusta are passing beneath the lime trees of Unter den Linden, Berlin's most famous and splendid avenue and one that was already a good two hundred years old. It had originally been constructed at the end of the Thirty Years' War, not as a grand thoroughfare but in order to colonize the surrounding area: Brandenburg had been devastated and the Great Elector wanted to attract settlers. He therefore laid out a road in front of his palace leading into the still empty countryside. The oldest document relating to the road dates from 1647. In it, the Elector recommends that the trees to be planted "are ring-fenced so that they can't be damaged by cattle or deer and rabbits eating their bark".

The road, 1.3 kilometres long and 50 metres wide, arose under the Hohenzollerns, who would make Brandenburg Prussia a power of European importance. It would change with its rulers and with the city. It started out with just a few houses, village-like in character, with pigs snuffling between young saplings. A simple gateway with a turnpike was soon built at the end of the road, manned by a gatekeeper and a toll collector. Friedrich Wilhelm I, the Soldier King, wanted the gateway to open onto a suitably impressive square. When none of his Berlin citizens showed themselves willing to build a house so far out of town, he simply ordered them to, dictating a standard formula of three storeys, six reception rooms, four cellars and two closet rooms.

His son Friedrich II, known as Frederick the Great, built an opera house on the field beside the road. It opened in 1742. On Saturdays it staged "assemblies and masked balls", on Wednesdays French comedies and on Mondays and Fridays opera. The architect Georg Knobelsdorff described the theatre as "one of the longest and widest in the world". Frederick sought to turn the Prussian military base into a cultural metropolis. He invited Voltaire to stay, bought French paintings, crossed diplomatic swords with the Venetian Republic over a dancer whom he wanted for his opera. The walk along Unter den Linden "would be even lovelier", wrote an anonymous hand during this same period, "if you could only see through the dust occasionally."

In 1791 the "passageway through the newly erected Brandenburg Gate" was opened, and a few years later the goddess Victory with her quadriga was installed on top. In 1806 Napoleon marched through this Prussian triumphal arch and had both goddess and quadriga shipped off to Paris. After the wars of liberation, the Prussians fetched their Victory home. Heinrich Heine: "The good lady has also had her misfortunes ...".

Heine, the anti-Prussian satirist, was hugely impressed by Unter den Linden when he visited in 1822: "Truly, I know no sight more imposing ... On the right the tall, magnificent arsenal, the new guards' house, the university, and Academy. On the left the royal palace, the opera house, the library etc. Magnificent building follows magnificent building ... It is just twelve, the hour when fashionable society takes a promenade. People dressed in their best stroll up and down Unter den Linden. Can you see the elegant fellow over there wearing twelve colourful waistcoats? Do you smell the exquisite pomades and essences with which he is perfumed? And look at the beautiful ladies! What figures! Let me wax lyrical! Yes, my friend, here under the lime trees / you can delight your heart / Here you can find assembled / the most beautiful women ...".

By Heine's day the avenue had acquired all its major works of architecture, its distinctive façades, and its fashionable character as the boulevard where the upper classes promenaded. They were out walking along Unter den Linden even on Sunday, 31 July 1870 – twelve days after France had declared war on Prussia. In the diary kept by Baroness Spitzemberg, the entry for this same day reads thus: "From five o'clock Carl and I strolled around Unter den Linden, where the large numbers of people gradually formed a packed guard of honour from the palace all the way to Wilhelmstrasse. When the aged king, field cap on his head, appeared with the queen in an open carriage, enthusiastic Hurrahs rang out and many eyes filled with tears. There is something tremendously moving about seeing such an elderly gentleman setting out at the age of seventy-three to fight for his kingdom and people; God go with him!"

The biggest flag is the one bearing the black eagle of Prussia. It is flying at the centre of all the others – a position that corresponds to the political situation. Having defeated Austria at Königsgratz in 1866, Prussia was Germany's greatest power. Most of the other German states had allied themselves with Prussia to form the North German Federation. The federal colours were black, white and red.

Flags flying from private houses, from hotels, cafés, and shops, flags lining the streets in such numbers – that was a sight that wouldn't have been seen the previous century, at least not outside the city republics. They are the sign of a changed relationship between citizen and state. The state had previously been identified with the head of the royal family to the point of absolutism. The sovereign *was* the state. He *owned* his country and his subjects. Since the French Revolution, the creation of a national army by Napoleon, and the anti-Napoleonic wars of liberation, however, the mood had changed. The people no longer perceived themselves as royal subjects, but as citizens of the state. When they fought, it was no longer for their sovereign but for their country. Nationalism was born and became a factor in international politics. The sovereign's colours became the nation's colours. Everyone who was patriotic displayed them.

Beneath the Prussian and Federation flags flies a single Red Cross flag. It represents the organization that was striving to mitigate the horrors of war by increasing the numbers of medical personnel on the field and by demanding that both medical orderlies and the wounded should be respected as neutral. Its founding conference had been held in Geneva seven years previously. sixteen states attended. It was thanks to Prussia that so many came. The original initiative came from the Swiss, Henri Dunant, who approached Berlin with his proposals. They were received sympathetically and he was even given an audience with War Minister Roon. The example set by Berlin was quickly followed. Some signed up on humanitarian grounds, others for practical reasons: soldiers who know they will be looked after, should they be wounded, will fight better.

At the victory parade in Berlin after Prussia's victory over Austria, Dunant was amongst those seated in the VIP stand. Many of the guests of honour wore an armband with the Red Cross in a gesture of support. By 1870 several hundred private companies were working under the auspices of the Red Cross. They established field hospitals, dispatched nursing staff, and collected money and materials. On 31 July 1870 one of them published the following notice in the daily *Berlinische Nachrichten* newspaper: "We urgently request bandaging materials and old canvas to be delivered to the Ladies' Committee of the undersigned society, at 6a Unter den Linden. The Board of the Berlin Welfare Society for the German Armies in the Field."

Flags, flags

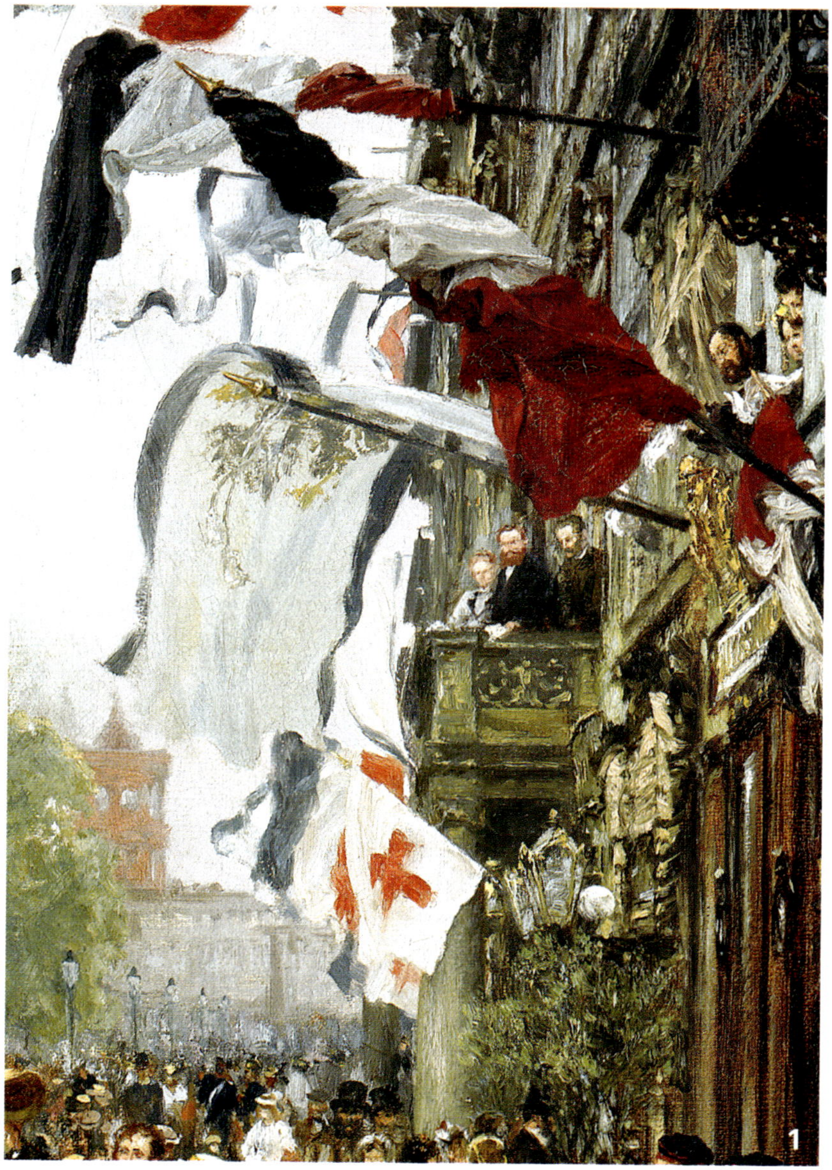
1

A king in uniform

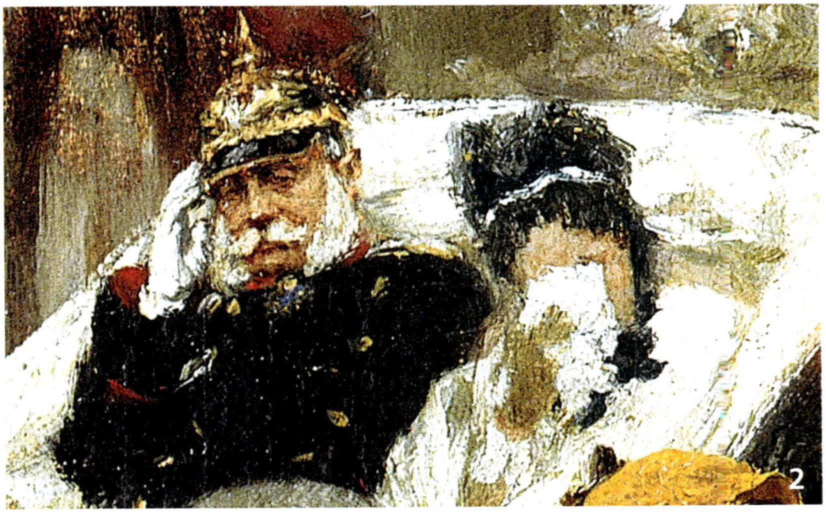

Wilhelm was departing for a war that he had never wanted. Nationalistic feelings on both sides of the Rhine had forced the conflict, and Bismarck's publication of the Ems Telegram had finally provoked the French declaration of war. Wilhelm had often had to do things he didn't want. As a ten-year-old he had fled from Napoleon with his family and for the following three years lived far from Berlin. In 1848 he fled from the Berlin revolutionaries and spent two months in London as the "case-shot king". He was not allowed to marry the woman he loved. After ascending the throne, he very quickly fell out with his parliament and had to bring in, as his partner and minister-president, a man who he didn't really like: Otto von Bismarck. When Bismarck instigated the war with Denmark, Wilhelm complained: "I am an old man and nearly seventy; how am I supposed to start thinking about war ...". Prussia's war against Austria, the "war between German brothers", Wilhelm also didn't want. No more than he wanted the imperial crown in 1871.

Menzel painted this picture of the troops departing a year after the event, and in one detail his memory has deceived him: Wilhelm wore a field cap, not a helmet. But the helmet looks more soldierly and fits better with the image of the king. He almost always wore uniform; he loved the role of commander and for him everything was "duty". Subordination to a superior or to something he accepted as a higher necessity was for him one of the most important Prussian virtues. Many admired him for precisely this readiness to comply, to submit.

On 31 July, twelve days after war had been declared, the mobilization of German troops was almost complete. The supreme commander was now departing for headquarters. Around midday Wilhelm saluted the 2nd uhlan lancers, still in Berlin. The *Berlinische Nachrichten* again: "When the commander of the regiment rode past the rostrum with the troops, the King lent forward over the railing and held out his hand to the commander [Prince Henry of Hesse]. The latter grasped it and bowed low over it, so it seemed, in order to kiss it. It was a deeply moving sight and the assembled masses erupted into cheers for the King."

In the early afternoon of 31 July a royal proclamation was issued. "To my people!", it read. "Since I am leaving today for the army, with whom to fight for Germany's honour and for the preservation of our greatest good, for the benefit of my people I wish to announce an amnesty for political crimes and offences ..."

At a quarter to six the king left his palace on Unter den Linden and travelled along the south side of the avenue towards the Brandenburg Gate. The *Berlinische Nachrichten*: "A number of court carriages, in which were seated H.M. the Queen Dowager, their royal majesties the Prince and Princess Charles, and the Duchess William of Mecklenburg, travelled at the front and were respectfully greeted by the crowd. Then followed the carriage in which the King was travelling, with the Queen beside him! Tumultuous, thunderous shouting and cheering!"

Potsdam station was adorned "with festoons, flags, garlands, and wreaths". The king's face was "serious, while the Queen could not hold back her tears." As the train drew out, the king remained standing "at the open window for the whole length of the platform ... At the middle window of the next carriage could be seen Count Bismarck ..."

A bad time for coachmen

The royal carriage on its way to Potsdam station. Up till the 19th century, long-distance travel had remained virtually unchanged for thousands of years. Then the railway arrived, financed by private companies. Each company had its own network of track. No less than five terminated in five different stations in Berlin. From Potsdam station the trains travelled west. The king's destination was Mainz.

The new railways had also changed military strategy. "The elaborate marches by Friedrich II and Napoleon are a thing of the past", wrote the *Hamburgische Correspondent* newspaper on 31 July 1870. "The armies are brought together by rail in just a few weeks and then clash with fearful force. Once the lines are facing each other, the decisive blows are struck much faster, because the troops arrive fresh from the train and do not have to overcome the exhaustion of a long march ..."

Within the cities, however, horse-drawn carriages continued to dominate the streets. The Baedeker guidebook of 1869 offers the following information for travellers arriving in Berlin by train: "At the exit of every railway terminus, an official is stationed who gives out metal tokens bearing the number of one of the hackney cabs waiting at the terminus. The metal token ... is to be given to the coachman of the cab in question, in exchange for normal travel tokens." In addition to cabs, Baedeker points out, there are the more economical omnibuses and horse-drawn trams. One horse-drawn omnibus line ran from the royal palace along Unter den Linden to the Brandenburg Gate.

In 1870 there were some 18,000 horses working in Berlin. The city had to place a certain proportion at the disposal of the troops, however. "Those with horses fit for military service who are willing to sell them for this purpose should equip them with good shoes, halter and two ropes ...", advised the *Berlinische Zeitung* of 31 July. The very same paper carried adverts such as this one: "An excellent, non-conscripted, unmarried coachman urgently seeks position owing to sale of horses. Contact Niederlagstr. 8, Thorweg bell."

Above the coachman appears a gas lamp. By the time they were installed in Berlin in 1826, they were already burning in London, Paris, and even Hanover. In terms of railways, gas lighting, and also industrial growth, Berlin was not at the forefront of Europe's metropolises.

The grandsons of Goethe and Schiller

The man with the cap reading the other man's newspaper is a student. According to Baedeker, there were 2000 of them in Berlin. Let's assume he is reading the *Berlinische Nachrichten von Staats- und gelehrten Sachen* (Berlin News of State and Learned Affairs) in the edition published by Haude and Spener on 31 July 1870. One announcement and one report might have been of immediate interest to him.

The announcement appeared on the front page. "All students of medicine in their seventh or later term entering military service" will be spared from armed combat if they sign up as medical personnel. A few pages further on, under the heading "From the Lecture Theatre", is a report from Stuttgart. During the summer semester, we learn, one Professor Vischer has been speaking on Goethe's *Iphigenie*. Following France's declaration of war, he opened his lecture thus: "While the thundering of guns begins, perhaps in the very next few days, we are to focus on verses of sublime intellectual calm ...". Professor Vischer then sought to establish a link between German classicism and war and suggested that the intellectual treasures of the nation were now also at stake. "One might say that these treasures can never be taken from us ... But they are truly our property only when the grandsons of Goethe and Schiller demonstrate through their actions that our great poets did not raise their souls high above the sombreness of life and the horror of death in vain!"

The military dictates the fashion

The man standing beside a lady on the right of the composition is wearing civilian clothes, but upon seeing the king has drawn himself as upright as a soldier, with his back straight and his hands by his sides, near the seam of his trousers. "In Berlin, the military carriage exerts the very greatest influence on the carriage of the dandies and the young bourgeoisie", noted one Frenchman, "... their stiffness, their jerky way of walking, and often, indeed more than often, their mania for clicking their heels." The man with the lady also has his heels together and his feet correctly angled.

Menzel paints the king with his hand touching his helmet. Even this military salute had entered civilian life. "If you go out early in the morning, you will see how the office workers, middle-class office workers, when they meet those they know, raise their hand to their forehead as if in a military salute and say 'Morning, morning ...'." It was what they had learned on the parade ground themselves. Virtually every man in Prussia had been in the army. Standard military service lasted three years, for men with higher academic qualifications, one year. Not so – by comparison – in France. Only a proportion of a year group was conscripted, chosen by lot, and even then it was possible to buy your way out.

The stylistically formative influence of the military, outwardly evidenced in gestures, movements, and carriage, testifies to the esteem in which it was held. Right up to the First World War, it was the most highly regarded class in society, closely linked to the monarchy: throne and eagle. Under these circumstances, under throne and eagle, it was hard for the middle classes to establish their own identity. Factory owners, doctors, academics, teachers, civil servants all conformed, fell into line. The court rewarded them for so doing with a finely graduated system of distinctions: elevation to the rank of baron, honorary titles, and an endless host of decorations.

It was no coincidence that the newspapers always carried details of titles and honours conferred by the king on their front pages. Such announcements invariably opened with the words: "His Majesty the King has most graciously deigned ..." followed by a list of awards. So it was in the issues of 31 July 1870. On that day, Working Privy Legation Councillor Abeken (he formulated the Ems Telegram, which the king sent to Bismarck) was awarded the Star to add to his Order of the Red Eagle, 2nd Class, with Oak-leaf Cluster. A major, a retired senior school teacher, and a head forester received the same decoration, 4th Class; a court surgeon and a member of the consistory in Gross-Wubiser in the Königsberg district received the General Medal of Honour.

The king also had to approve the award of foreign honours. Thus the papers of 31 July informed their readers that a Berlin counsellor of commerce was to receive a decoration from the Austrian emperor, and a stationmaster and a mason medals from the emperor of Russia.

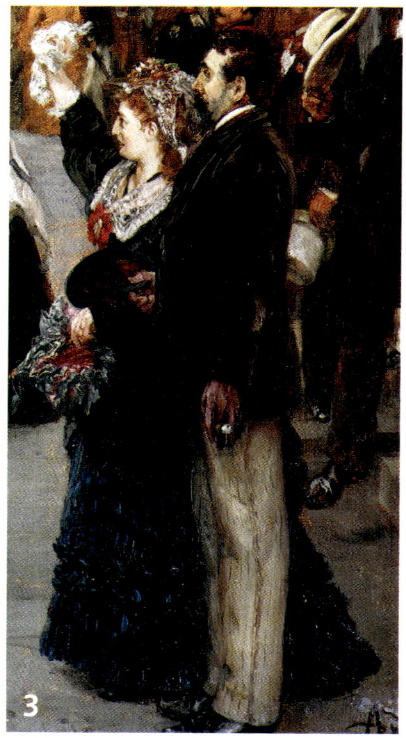

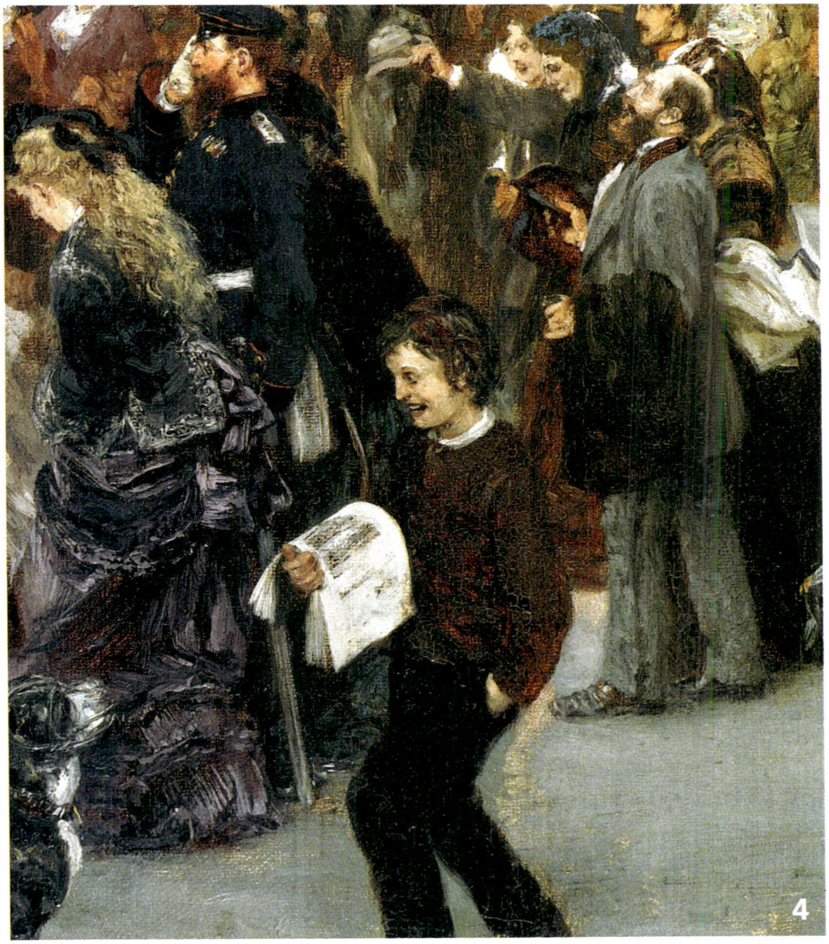

The newspaper boy

Some of those watching the royal cavalcade may have been, in the parlance of the day, "presentable at court". All, however, would have belonged to the wealthier classes. They would have been senior civil servants, officers who had inherited or married into money, land-owning nobility and factory owners, with their wives and daughters. The rest of society, making up the much larger part of the population, is absent. Its members didn't gather under the lime trees in the afternoons. Clerks, lower-grade employees, workers with their handcarts were seen there only in the mornings. With one exception: the newspaper boy. He stands apart from the crowd, interested more in the dog than the king rolling past.

Two major daily newspapers were published in Berlin, the *Berlinische Nachrichten* and the *Berlinische Zeitung*. Both also appeared on Sunday, 31 July, and both papers reflected more or less the same facet of reality that Menzel records in his painting. They start on page 1 – as their most important news – with the decorations and titles awarded by the king. Next come announcements by the court and the government, followed by reports from correspondents in the countries and courts of Europe, and finally economic affairs, financial news, and in the supplements, broadly educational articles, usually on Prussian history. In-depth features or updates on the acute housing shortages in the Berlin suburbs, for example, are absent. Housing shortages affected only the workers, people who had left the countryside and come to the city to find work. If the Berlin papers contain any hint at all of the misery of the working classes, it is only in the appeals they print from various charitable bodies. They describe not the situation itself, but what the wealthy can do to help.

Even about the latter, however, the prosperous readers of these newspapers, we learn very little. Nothing about their circumstances, nothing about their private worries. At least not in the editorial sections. Only from the classified columns can we deduce a little about their personal lives. One announcement advertises a "private maternity hospital" and emphasizes "discretion guaranteed". Another: "A respectable young lady begs someone for a loan of 5 thalers to be repaid with eternal gratitude". That there was money to be made out of war is clear from a number of advertisements: "For reconnaissance in the field I recommend my complete stock of superb military telescopes!" A supplier to the royal court "recommends for military expeditions flannel and silk campaign shirts, flannel waistbands, etc." And: "For military campaigns I recommend my instant hot chocolate, quick and easy to prepare" – just add boiling water. Under the heading of "Medical Notices" are fifteen advertisements, six of them offering a cure for syphilis. It is the disease most frequently mentioned in the "Medical" columns of 31. July 1870.

Outside the advertising section, in the editorial pages, we learn nothing about such lowly matters. The newspapers print only what is seemly; everything is selected and presented in such a way as to be acceptable to royal eyes. "Presentable at court" is how the upper and upper-middle classes wanted their newspaper to be; they were, after all, the readers who strolled down Unter den Linden on Sundays, who stood to attention in front of the king, who erupted into "tumultuous, thunderous shouting and cheering". They are captured here on Menzel's canvas. More than just a moment in history, the artist offers us a portrait of an entire society.

Claude Monet: Camille Monet on a Garden Bench (The Bench), 1873

Unease in the shade of the trees

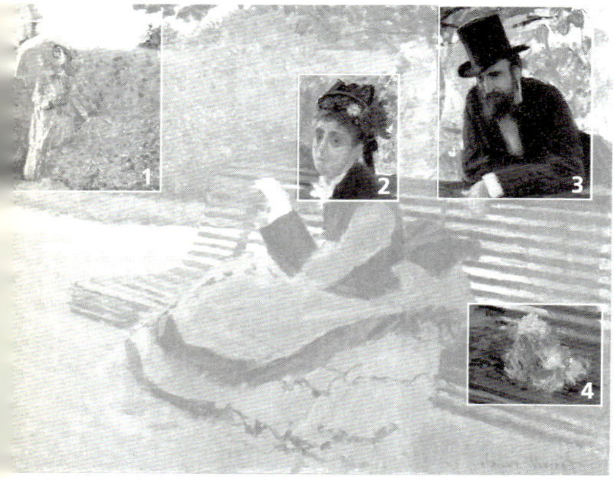

Three figures in a garden, two women, one man. The woman on the bench can be clearly identified – she is Camille, the artist's wife and his favourite model. Leaning slightly forward, she turns towards the viewer, looking out at us with large, dark eyes. Beside her lies a bouquet of flowers, perhaps brought by the gentleman leaning over the back of the bench.

A horizontal stroke of the brush indicates that Camille is holding a letter in her white-gloved hand. Art historians suspect that it may be news of a death or a letter of condolence. "A piece of bad news awaited my wife ... her father died yesterday", wrote Monet on 23 September 1873, the period during which this undated canvas must have arisen. For Claude Monet (1840–1926), these were enormously productive years; again and again he painted the banks of the Seine, meadows, fields, and the garden we see here. It lay in rural Argenteuil and belonged to the house into which Monet moved at the end of 1871 with his young wife and four-year-old son Jean. The suburb was then a popular destination amongst Parisians, who came to row and sail on the Seine. It is familiar to art lovers through the pictures of Monet, Auguste Renoir, Edouard Manet and Gustave Caillebotte, all of whom endeavoured to capture – in *plein air* painting beside the river, away from their city studios – light, air, and the reflections on the water. Argenteuil thereby became one of the chief theatres of the golden era of Impressionist painting.

Monet painted the garden, and Camille, too, over and over again. At first sight, these are harmonious, bucolic paintings that speak of elegant city-dwellers who are enjoying country life in idyllic nature. Yet there is something disquieting about a painting like *The Bench*, because the viewer is unable to fathom the relationships between the figures, because he senses a story and doesn't know what it is.

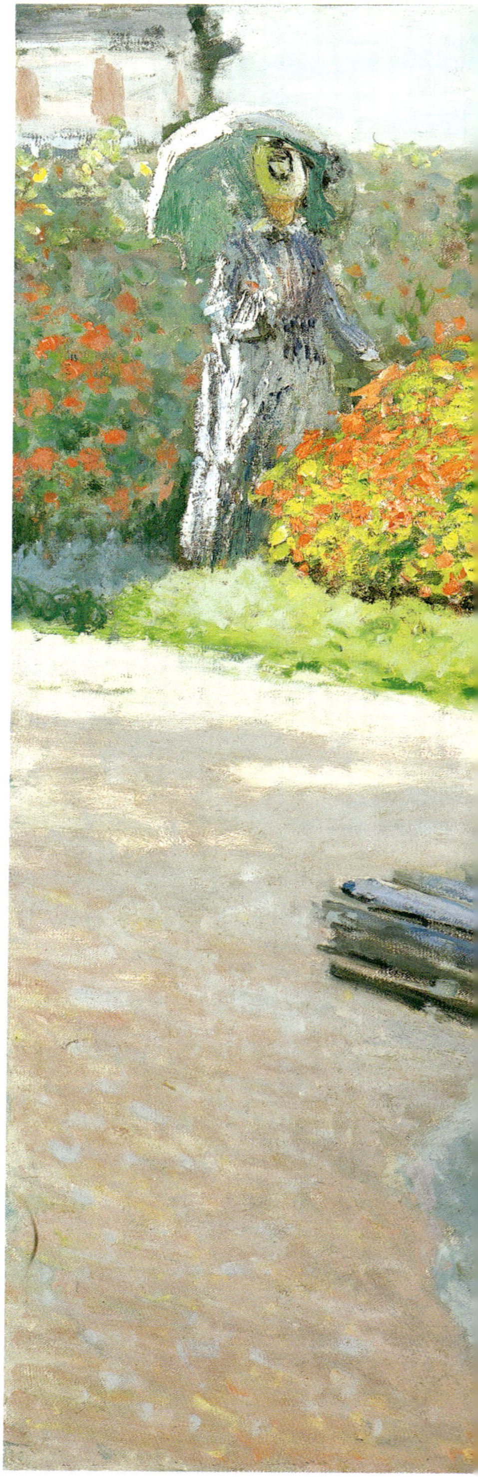

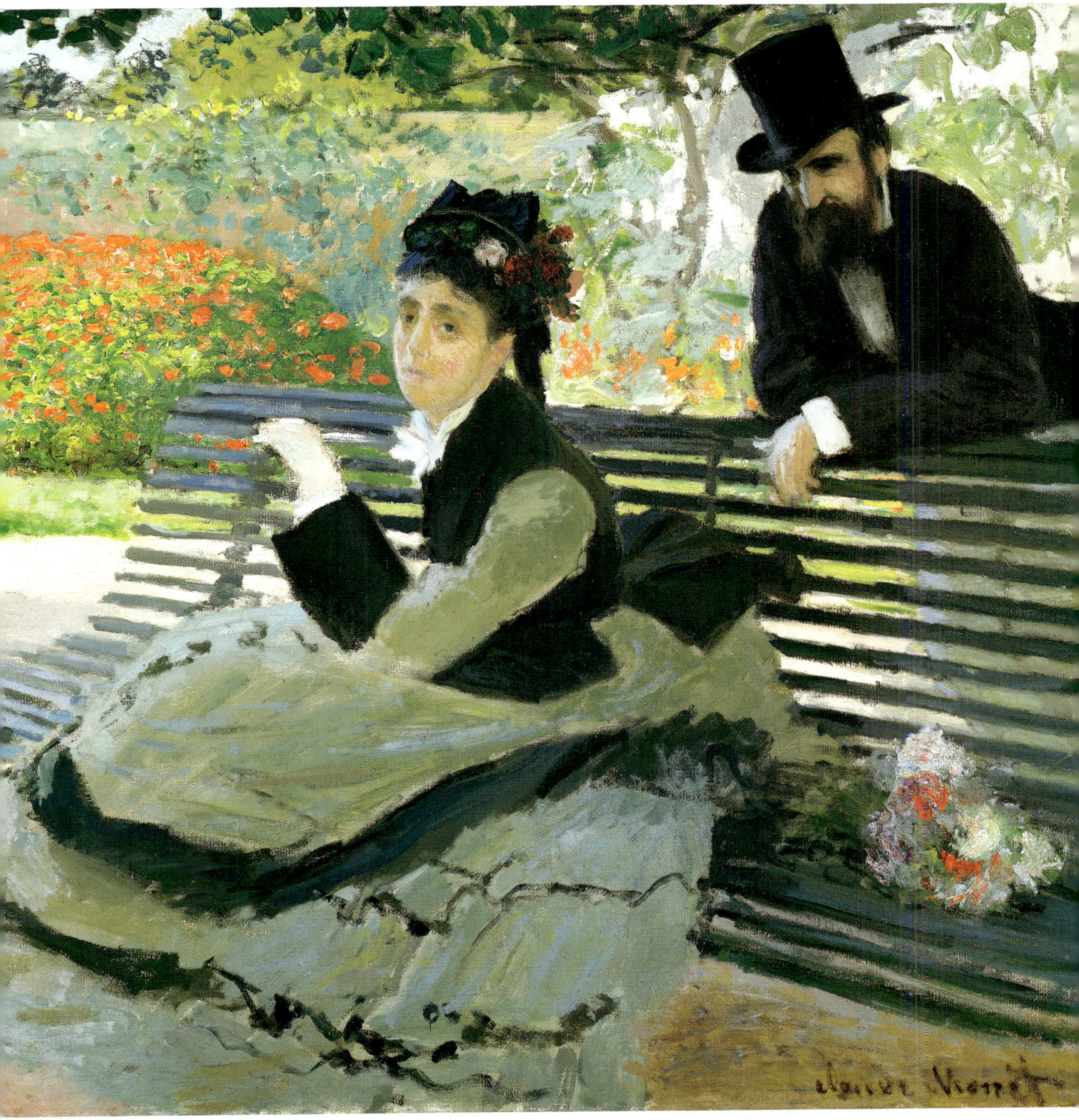

In the background, a woman beneath a parasol is studying the flourishing bed of geraniums. She is standing in such a way, however, that she can also see the other two figures. Above her parasol can be seen a corner of the house that Monet started renting in late 1871. The house and garden were situated in the better part of Argenteuil. Monet paid 1000 francs a year in rent; by way of comparison, a factory worker took home about 2,500 francs over the same period. Monet was thus now earning a decent salary, albeit only since recently.

He came from a middle-class but impoverished grocer's family from Le Havre. In 1859 he moved to Paris. He was financially supported by a wealthy aunt, Madame Lecat, who demanded in return a regular lifestyle, hard work, and professional success. If he failed her, she stopped his allowance. The young artist felt ill at ease in the established art academies, and left them in order to experiment with new motifs and techniques in the open air. Only a few of his works were accepted into the official Salons, and for years he led a life that can be romantically described as Bohemian, but which in reality bordered on absolute poverty.

Begging letters to his wealthier friends testify to his state of affairs: Monet had debts and feared the imminent arrival of the bailiffs. The painters Frédéric Bazille and Gustave Caillebotte helped the "starving" artist, and before Renoir – himself hardly rich – left his parents' house to visit Monet, he would stuff his pockets full of bread. Things with Monet, who was by now living with his model Camille, were "pitiful", reported Renoir in 1869: "they don't even eat every day".

But then Monet met the gallery-owner Paul Durand-Ruel, who became his dealer. By the age of thirty-one, the painter could afford a house and garden in Argenteuil. In 1872 he sold paintings worth a total of 12,100 francs, and in 1873 – the year in which he painted *The Bench* – he earned 24,800 francs, roughly the annual income of a Parisian doctor or lawyer. He was now able to order wine by the case from Bordeaux and hire a cook, nursemaid, and gardener. But he remained behind with the rent, didn't pay his laundry bills, and continued to ask his friends for help – old habits. Monet was a man with no head for money. A man, however, who also believed he should live as munificently as his rich aunt, upon whom he was dependent for so many years.

This is also illustrated by Monet's pictures of his garden. If we compare them both with each other and with a painting by Renoir, showing his friend Monet at his easel in the garden, it becomes clear that the garden in Argenteuil cannot have looked as park-like as it appears in *The Bench*. The flourishing bed of geraniums, if it existed at all, is a reflection less of reality than of a life Monet longed for. The same bed of geraniums is found in his painting of the gardens of his Aunt Lecat and also in a picture by Caillebotte of his family's country estate. It must thus have been something of a status symbol. The fact that Monet allocates it so much space on the canvas shows that it was important to him.

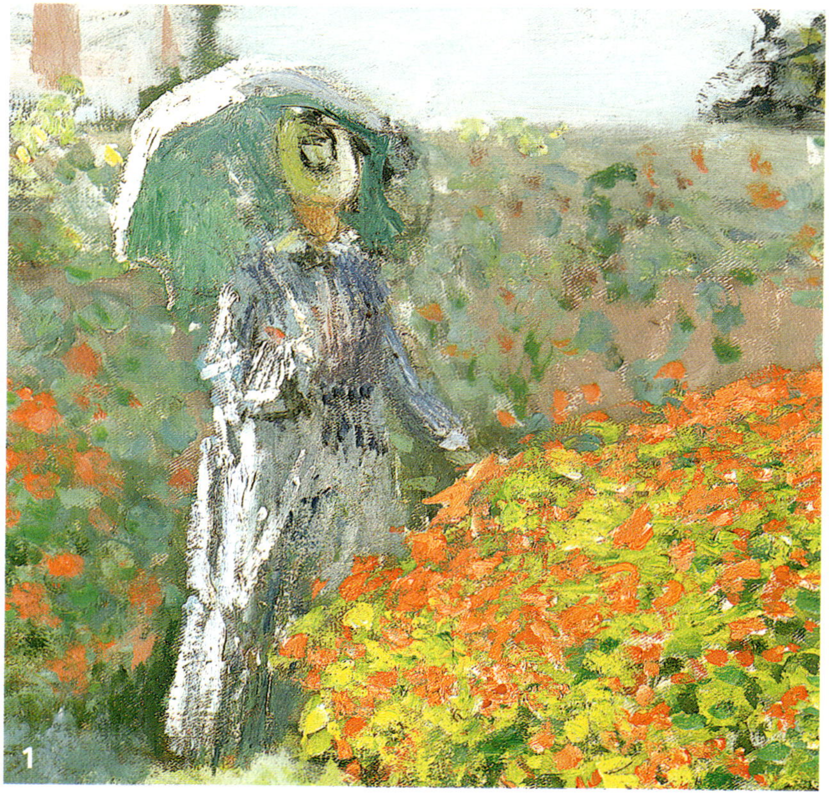

1

Out of poverty at last

For a long time she was just the artist's mistress and spurned by his family as the "unmarried mother of his bastard son". Now at last, the twenty-six-year-old Camille Léonie Doncieux could show herself in elegant surroundings as the respectable Madame Monet. Her pose seems a little strained and she is dressed more in the style of the city than the country. The dark ribbon on her hat, the black velvet of her bodice, and the black velvet trim along the hem of her dress may all be signs of mourning. All these things were expensive, elegant, and highly fashionable – as a glance through the pages of the magazine *La mode illustrée* of 1873 reveals.

Camille came from a petit-bourgeois background. In 1865 she started working as a model for Monet. A very beautiful young woman, she wore an expression of fascinating arrogance on her pale face. But "when you see Camille walking", noted a middle-class observer, "the provocative way in which she stumps along the pavement, you can immediately tell she is not a woman of the world". She was certainly not treated as one. Although, when Camille fell pregnant, Monet did not take his father's advice and immediately break off the relationship, he nevertheless departed hastily for his aunt's country estate, in order to reassure her that he had not "gone astray" and thereby safeguard his monthly cheque. He left Camille behind in Paris, heavily pregnant and penniless. He found it difficult to adjust to the new responsibilities of having a family. He acknowledged his son, but waited another three years before marrying Camille in 1870. It was the first year of the Franco-Prussian War, and as a married man Monet did not have to do military service.

In their seven years together in Argenteuil, Monet painted his wife over and over again. Apart from the fact that she remained his favourite model, however, no other evidence of his affection or love for her or his children has survived. Monet condescendingly describes Camille in a letter as a "good girl" who must be "sensible".

Monet's behaviour was not untypical. Afraid of breaching the conventions of his day and his class, Monet's elder artist colleague, Edouard Manet (1832–1883) went so far as to conceal the existence of his mistress, the piano teacher Suzanne Leenhoff, from his family and friends for thirteen whole years, maintaining her in a small apartment. He married her only after his father's death, but never recognized the son they had together. Suzanne had to refer to him all her life as her "little brother".

Camille, too, showed she could be "sensible", and even accepted the presence of another woman under her own roof. Following the ruin of his patron Ernest Hoschedé, Monet invited him, his wife, and six children to come and live with the Monet family. It was the pious and dutiful Alice Hoschedé who nursed Camille when, after the birth of a second son in 1878, she fell ill with cancer of the uterus and died the following year. In contrast to Camille, Alice was a "woman of the world". She became Monet's influential, respected companion and, after the death of her own husband, the artist's second wife.

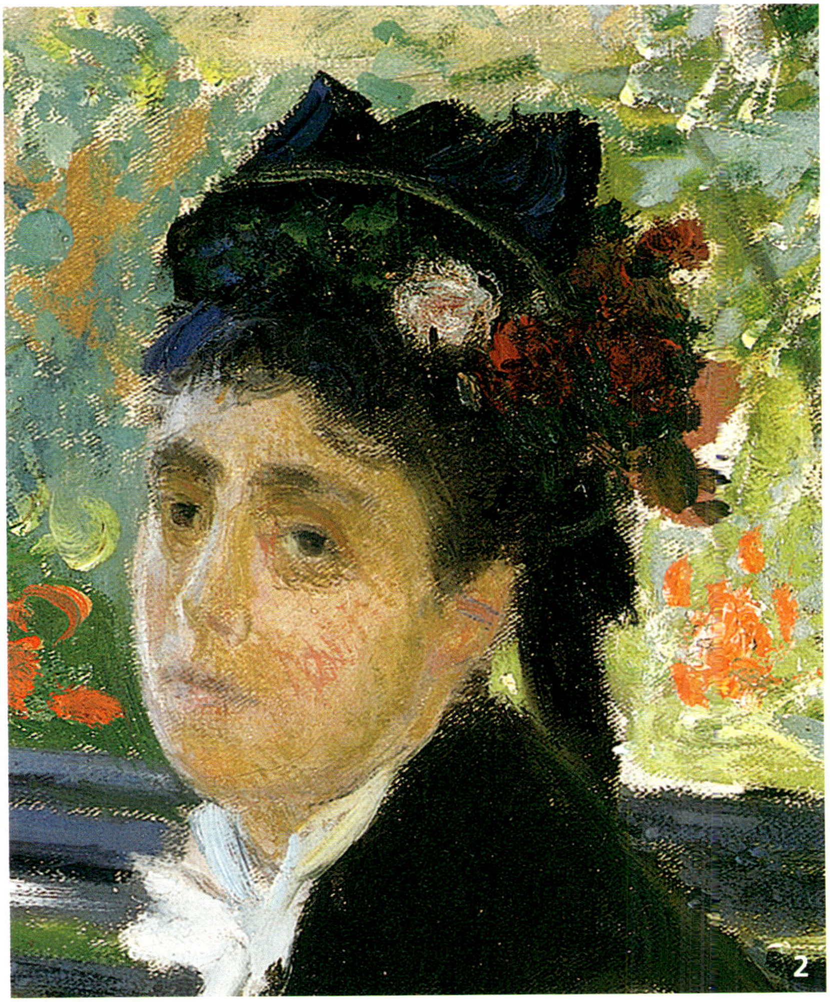
2

No woman of the world

Three figures in a summer garden, arranged in such a way that the viewer suspects there is a hidden connection between them. The black-bearded, black-coated man leaning over the back of the bench and coming very close to Camille has been interpreted by some as an admirer, by others as Death, or at least one of his messengers. Later, however, Monet remembered the man much more prosaically as a neighbour from Argenteuil.

We meet the same man again in two famous paintings by Edouard Manet. In *Le Déjeuner sur l'herbe*, the picture that caused a scandal in 1863, he is seated on the grass beside a naked female model (cf. *What Great Paintings Say*, Volume III). He is wearing a light suit, appropriate for a country picnic. In *Music in the Tuileries Gardens* of 1862, he is much more formally dressed, in a top hat, as he mingles with the elegant crowd (cf. p. 370). He thereby bears a close resemblance to the present visitor behind the bench – the same dark beard, the same sideburns, even the same slightly stooped pose.

Manet's very wealthy family had long owned a country house on the other side of the Seine from Argenteuil. Edouard became infected by Monet's enthusiasm for painting out of doors and often went to visit him, bringing his younger brother, Eugène, with him. Documentary evidence compiled by art historians indicates that this latter is the neighbour and supposed messenger of death in the present picture. When Monet painted *The Bench*, Eugène Manet was forty years old and a year later became engaged to the artist Berthe Morisot. He was very popular for his cheery disposition, and in Monet's portrait of him here, the possibility that he may be smiling behind his dark beard cannot be dismissed.

Eugène also painted, but considered himself to have little talent. His contribution to art took the form of selfless support of his artist friends. He had time to spare, was financially independent, and did not need to practice a profession. Without his ability to mediate between the egocentric personalities involved and to persuade them to reach agreement, the first exhibition of "Independent Artists", staged in 1874, might never have taken place. (It was at this exhibition that Monet would show the picture *Impression, Sunrise* that would give the Impressionists their name.) Even as he was painting *The Bench*, Monet, too, was involved in the arguments surrounding the organization of the exhibition.

Bande à Manet – Manet's gang – the group of artist friends were called. They included Renoir, who only a little while previously had stuffed his pockets full of bread for the starving Monet. They watched each other work, motivated each other. Monet recalled: "Manet, excited by the colours and the light, embarked on a picture in the open air of people beneath the trees. While he was working, Renoir came along. He in turn was captivated by the charm of the moment. He asked me for my palette, a brush, and a canvas, sat down next to Manet and started painting."

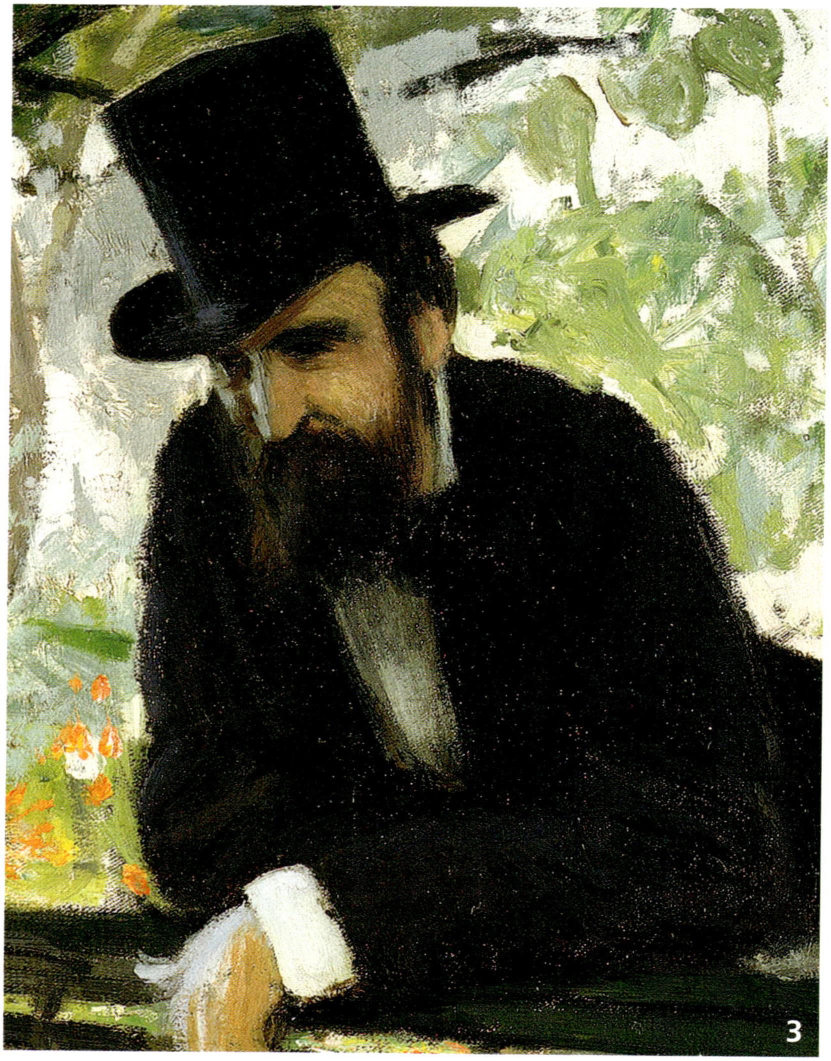

Neighbour or messenger of death?

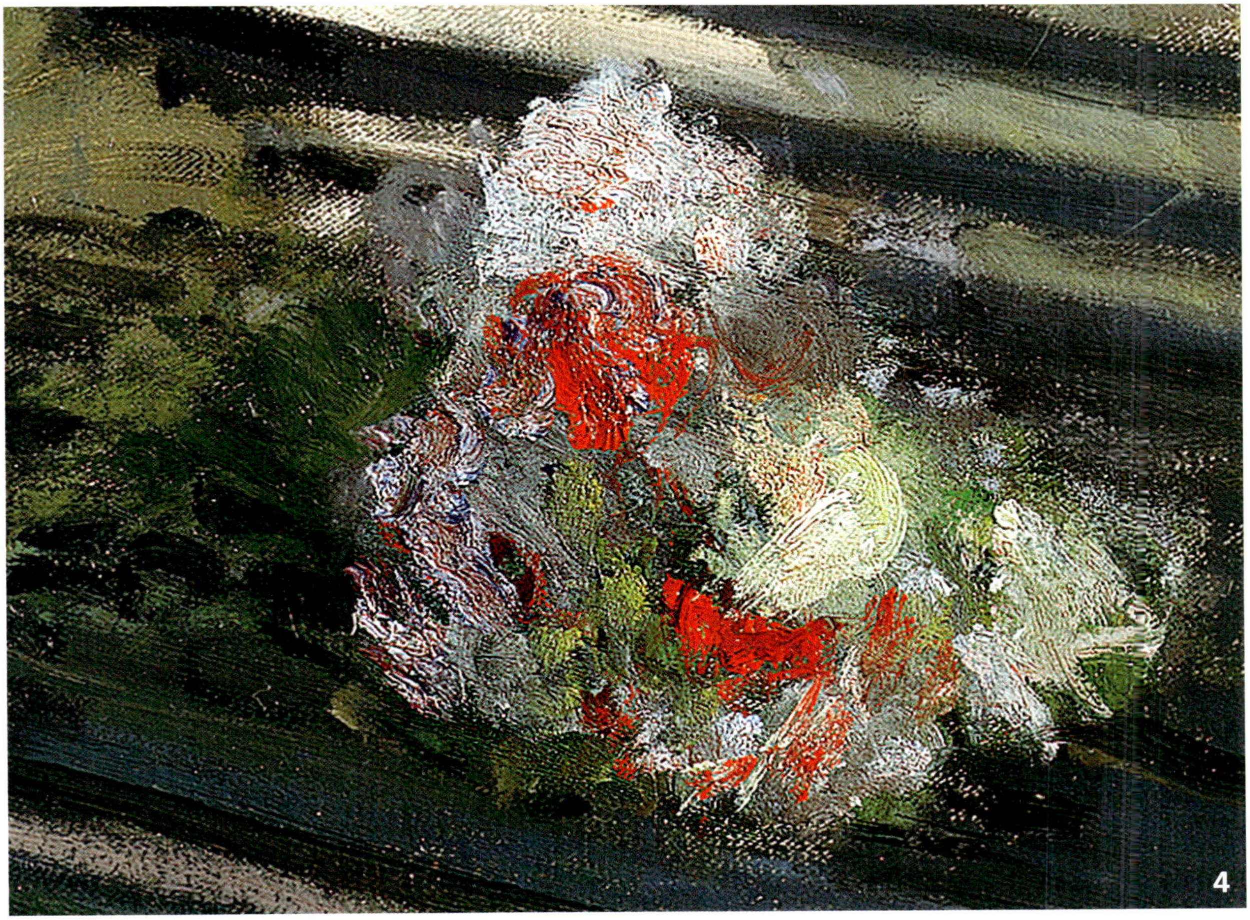

Contemporaries upbraided the Impressionists for the speed at which they worked: the bunch of flowers is tossed onto the canvas with a few passing strokes of the brush, using wet paint on wet paint and with no corrections, just an accent of colour catching the eye on the dark bench. Monet wanted to capture the mood of the moment. The bed of geraniums, the woman with the parasol, and the overgrown wall all lie in full sunlight, which brings out the vibrant red of the blooms. In the shade, by contrast, the palette is muted. Monet deploys grey-blue brushstrokes on the gravel path, bench, dress, and even bridge of the nose to characterize areas of broken light.

Capturing the changes in the light at different times of the day and year and in varying weather conditions became Monet's obsession, one which he pursued above all in series of paintings of the same subject, such as the façade of Rouen cathedral and the water lilies in his garden in Giverny.

These series show only buildings, flowers, and landscapes; people, if present at all, are reduced to brief brushstrokes. *The Bench* of 1873 marks a watershed in Monet's oeuvre; it is the last painting in which people are the main focus. That same year Monet painted another, larger-scale view of his garden from almost the same angle. Here, however, the people are relegated to the background, leaving just the bench and a table bearing the remains of a meal in the foreground. The painting is entitled *The Luncheon* – but there is no one actually eating.

Monet continued to paint single figures and portraits, but people played no further role in his cityscapes and landscapes. The three figures in his Argenteuil garden are merely – so his later pictures would seem to suggest – means to an end: they provide him with an opportunity to paint variations in light, and specifically the different effects produced by sunlight as it falls either directly or indirectly on skin, clothes, path, flowers, and bench.

People vanish

Monet was well aware that this fixation upon the visual delights of the surface was not without its dangers. "I was once standing at the bedside of one who had passed away who was and shall always remain very dear to me", he later wrote, meaning Camille. "I caught myself watching her tragic temples, almost mechanically searching for the sequence of changing shades that death was imposing upon her rigid face. Blue, yellow, grey, whatever. Such was the state I was in . . ."

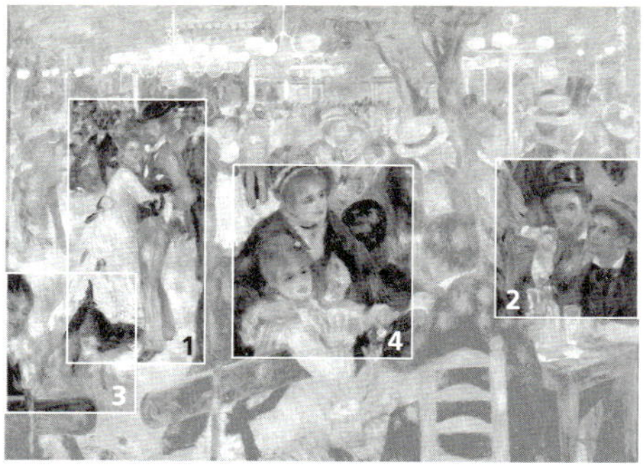
1
2
3
4

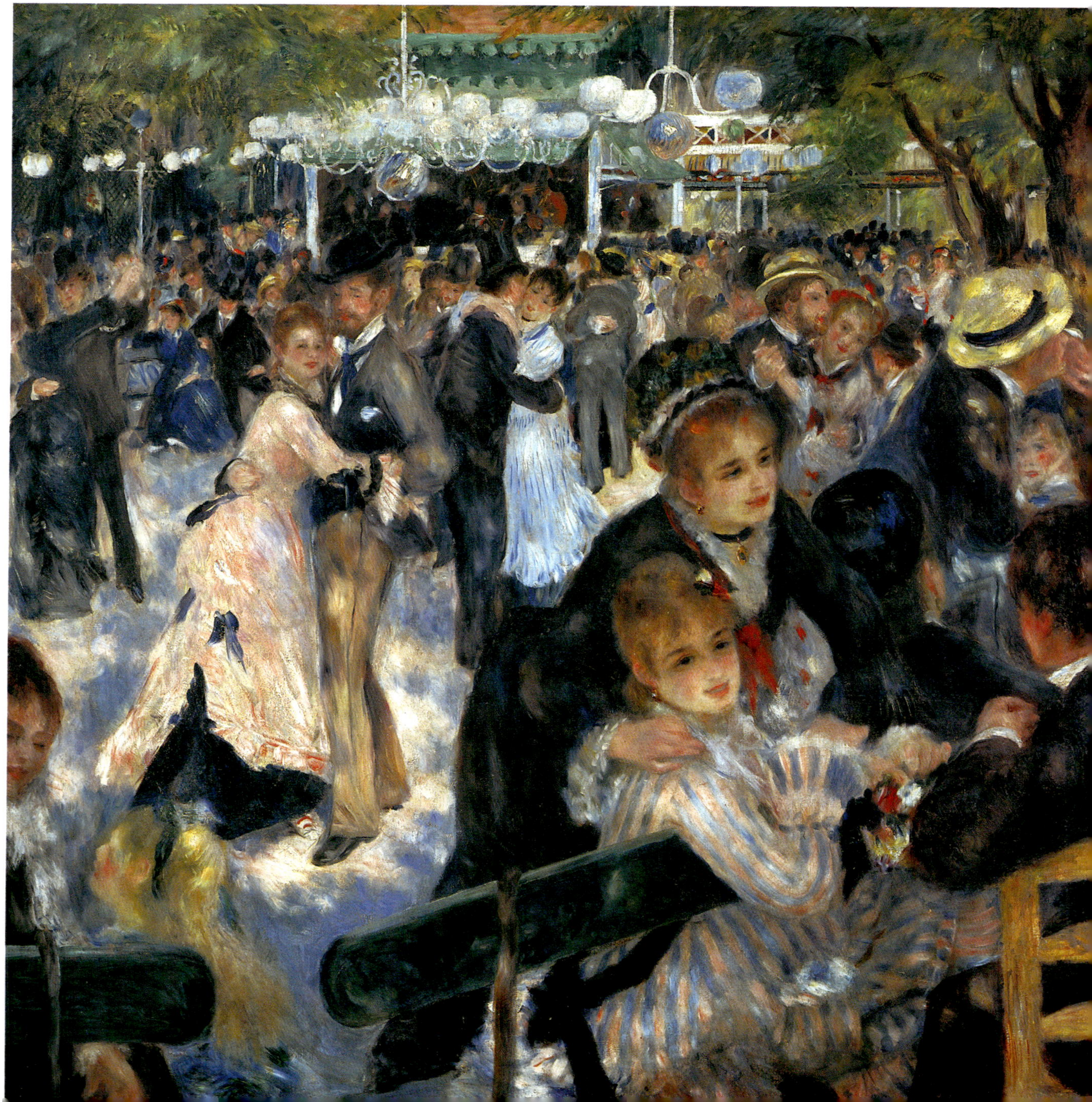

Auguste Renoir: Au Moulin de la Galette, 1876

Dancing on a Sunday on Montmartre

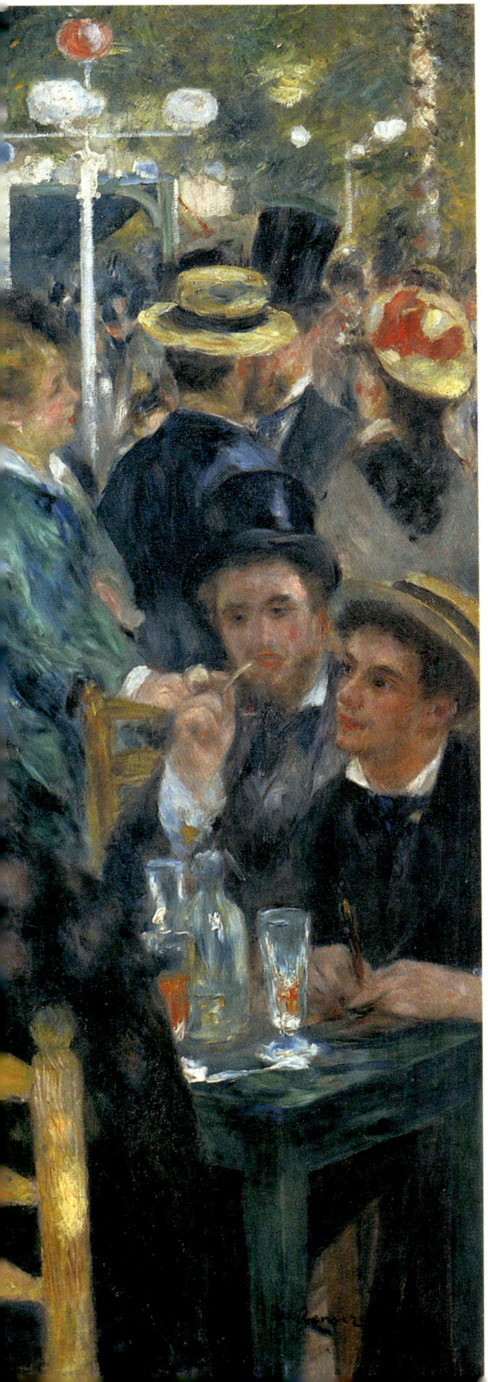

Sunday afternoon at an open-air café on top of Montmartre hill: the Moulin de la Galette was a popular dance venue, where Parisian seamstresses and workers came for a few hours of leisure. Dressed in their Sunday best, they waltzed, chatted, and enjoyed the sunshine and tranquillity.

"We rushed off into the countryside to celebrate the joy of not having to listen to any more talk about politics", wrote the author Emile Zola in 1876, the year in which Renoir painted his picture. Politics meant reflecting on France's defeat in the 1870/71 Franco-German War, on the privations suffered during the siege of Paris, on the horrors of the Commune. It was here on Montmartre that the bloody uprising had begun, and in the cemetery that lay just a few paces from the café, a mass grave contained the bodies of shot revolutionaries, victims of bourgeois repression.

"The state of siege has been lifted since yesterday morning", wrote Zola in 1876, "and Paris is now thinking only of enjoying the spring sun." Despite massive reparation payments to Germany, the economic boom of the Second Empire continued uninterrupted in the new Third Republic, and as ever after wars and catastrophes, the desire for pleasurable entertainment was particularly great. That summer, the Parisians steamed out into the countryside on the new and fashionable railway or walked up to the top of Montmartre hill, an hour by foot from the city centre and, at 130 metres, the highest point in Paris. It was famed for its good air (in the age of industrialization, something already a scarce commodity in the metropolis), its dog rose, and its lilacs. Incorporated into the city of Paris only in 1860, Montmartre still retained its village character. It offered few shops, but instead orchards, fields, cow pastures, and two windmills.

A hundred years earlier, the sails of thirty windmills could have been seen turning on the same hillside, but now there was nothing left to grind; the cornfields on the plain at the foot of Montmartre had been replaced by factory chimneys and grey tenements. Only two windmills remained on Montmartre, both of them owned by the Debray family for generations. Three Debray sons are said to have lost their lives defending their property against the Cossacks in 1814. The Russians, it was related with a shudder, had hacked the miller himself into four pieces with their sabres and hung them from the sails of his mill.

Thirsty walkers had always been able to get a glass of wine from the millers on Montmartre; the Debrays also baked their own *galette* to go with it, a flat cake that, thanks to their fine, home-produced flour, was so delicious that it eventually gave its name to the windmill. As the volume of grain to be ground grew ever smaller, Nicolas Charles Debray turned one of the windmills into a viewing tower and opened a dance hall next door: a crudely built shed decorated with plaits of straw painted green. Here and in the shady garden in front of it, a brass band played tirelessly: quadrilles, polkas, and waltzes. For 4 sous, on Sundays and public holidays you could dance there from three o'clock in the afternoon until eleven o'clock at night.

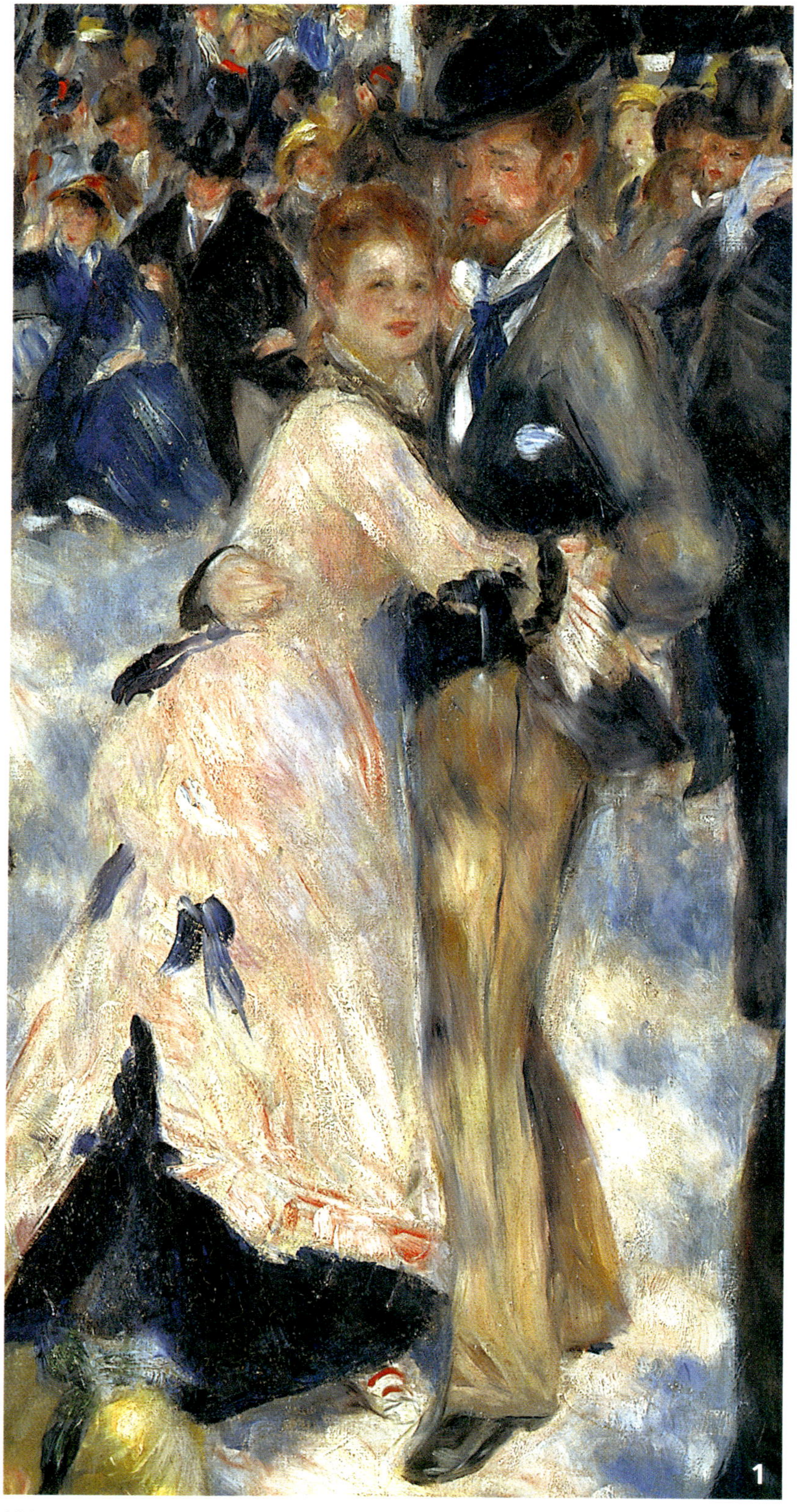

Quite different dances – the wild cancan and the lascivious *Java chaloupée* – were danced here during the week. When the many gas lamps lit up the dance floor in the evening, apaches and prostitutes with their pimps came up from the neighbouring Goutte d'Or quarter to enjoy an evening's entertainment at the Moulin de la Galette. Knifings and fights were not uncommon.

In the afternoons the public was more respectable: those who lived on the hill, mostly farmers and gardeners, junior clerks who appreciated the lower rents on Montmartre, a few artists, and above all workers from the industrial suburbs in the north of Paris. Cooped up in gloomy, cramped tenements, they sought sunshine and light at the Moulin. In the afternoons, unlike the evenings, hats were compulsory for ladies visiting the Moulin. Wearing a hat was considered – until well into the 20th century – an outward sign of middle-class respectability. If a woman went out *en cheveux*, "in her hair", it surely meant she belonged to the very lowest social classes or enjoyed a dubious reputation. Several girls are nevertheless showing their hair in Renoir's picture. Perhaps young servant-girls, who after doing the dishes are having their one Sunday afternoon off a month and have come up to the Moulin to recover from their fourteen-hour days in poorly ventilated kitchens. Or perhaps a local girl who lives on the hill and has just popped in for a quick dance, without a hat. Like Marguerite Legrand, known as Margot. She is dancing here with a painter of Spanish origin, bearing the splendid name of Don Pedro Vidal de Solares y Cardenas. He had got it into his head that he wanted to be a real Parisian, and Margot was teaching him *argot*, the language of the underworld. When the still very young Marguerite Legrand caught typhoid fever two years later, Renoir was the only person to take care of her, asking his doctor friends to treat her. When she died all the same on 25 February 1879, he paid for her funeral.

The polka on Sundays and the cancan during the week

Those with manners keep their hats on

The men, too, kept their hats on at the Moulin de la Galette – even when dancing. Either the summery straw boater or the tall black top hat. The soft felt hat with the wide brim was still considered too "oppositional" and even "revolutionary". They were worn mostly by artists, such as Don Pedro, who came to the dancehall to make sketches from life, to find models, or in search of an amorous affair. These artists were among the Bohemians who liked Montmartre because life here was cheap and uncomplicated. They lived for the day, with no thought for tomorrow.

Georges Rivière (1855–1943), on the other hand, here wearing a straw boater and seated behind a glass of *grenadine à l'eau*, grenadine syrup, had a safe middle-class job. He worked as a civil servant in the Ministry of Finance and later rose to become the Minister's head of cabinet. But he spent his youth, and the generous amount of free time that seemed to go with a post in the French administration, in the company of his artist friends. He seems here to be making notes; later he would write a book of reminiscences entitled *Renoir and his Friends*. In 1877 he published a short-lived periodical, *L'Impressioniste*, in defence of the circle around Renoir.

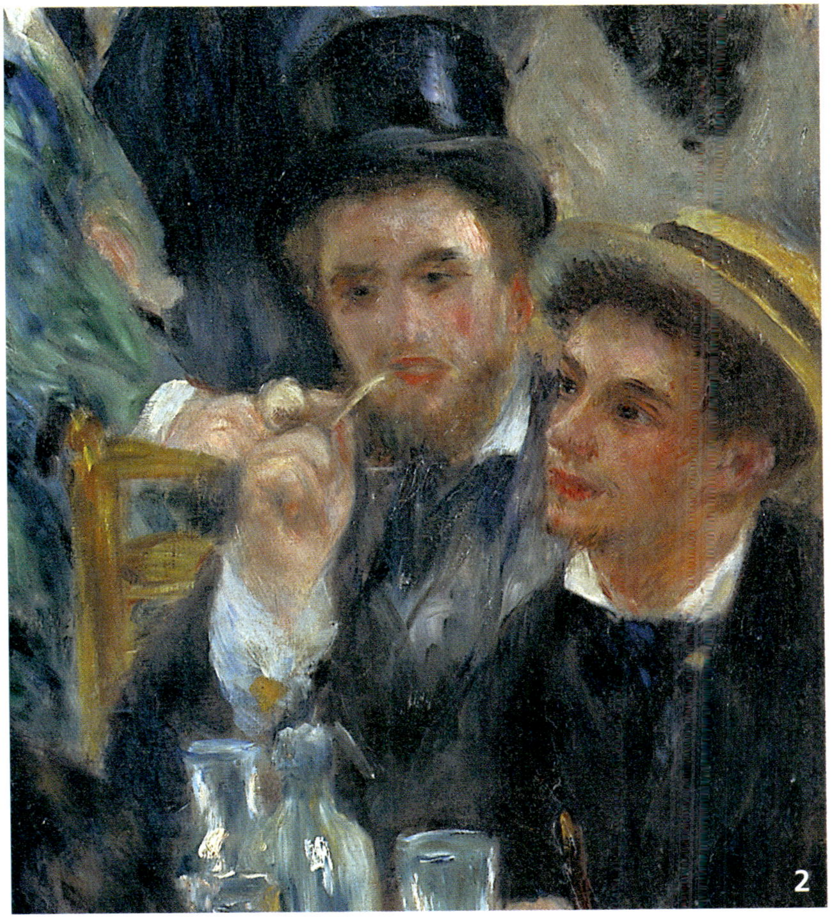
2

That circle also included the painter Norbert Goeneutte (1854–1894), seated here next to Rivière. He, too, had to learn a "proper" profession and was sent by his family to train with a notary. Only after the death of his father was he able to devote himself to his real interests.

The painters and their friends met every evening, once it had grown too dark to work, in La Nouvelle Athènes, a café at the foot of Montmartre on the Boulevard de Clichy. There Monet, Sisley, Pissarro, Bazille, Renoir, and occasionally also Cézanne would talk art. They all rejected the sort of painting that was being taught at the Academies in the second half of the 19th century and which was being exhibited in the official Salons. Instead of composing pompous history paintings in their studios, they wanted to work from nature, and they sought simple motifs in the surroundings of Paris. "Give me an apple tree in a suburban garden," said Renoir, "that's quite sufficient; I don't need a Niagara Falls." Most revolutionary of all, however, was their painting technique: they wanted, as Monet put it, "to capture light and cast it directly on the canvas".

The rebellious group of artists owed its name to a small painting by Monet. At a group exhibition of 1874, he showed a misty waterscape in the wintery sun, which he titled *Impression, Sunrise*. A critic picked up on the word "impression" in a subsequent article and ironically described the group as a whole as "Impressionists".

The critics heaped irony, rejection, and scorn on the Impressionists. "Try to explain to M. Renoir that a woman's torso is not a mass of decomposing flesh with those purplish green stains which denote a state of complete putrefaction in a corpse", ran one article in *Le Figaro*. Since the public was equally offended by such modernism, their paintings failed to sell and life for the Impressionists was a struggle. Especially for those who were without secure government jobs or who did not, like Cézanne, have a wealthy family to support them. Thus even Renoir hesitated a long time before giving up his trade as a porcelain-painter and dedicating himself solely to "art". Even when working in front of the canvas, moreover, he liked to describe himself as a craftsman.

At the beginning he reduced his material needs to a minimum and in the 1870s lived practically on beans and lentils alone, cooked on the stove in his studio. In 1875 the unexpected sale of a painting enabled him to rent two rooms at 12, rue Cortot on Montmartre hill, together with a former stable on the ground floor as a studio. When the weather was fine, he got his friends or the pretty girls in his neighbourhood to pose in the back garden. They also carried the present large canvas across to the nearby Moulin de la Galette, where our painting was executed in the summer of 1876.

Whenever a subject fired his imagination, Renoir felt the need "to immerse himself right in it", "to get to know every aspect of it". While he was painting from life in the Moulin de la Galette, therefore, Renoir plunged himself into the "village" life of Montmartre. He soon knew everybody, especially the many children who roamed the streets unsupervised while their mothers were working or "otherwise engaged". Renoir, who loved children, started to think about what he could do for them. The relatively impoverished Renoir conceived the idea of "founding an institution for them, where unemployed women would look after the infants that had to be temporarily left unattended by their mothers".

The money was to be raised through a costumed charity ball, organized by Renoir and his friends. Naturally in the Moulin de la Galette, for Monsieur Debray, the owner, was known as a kind-hearted man. "He didn't charge much for food and always had a slice of bread for the little hungry mouths." That evening the public thronged into the dancehall and the ball lasted until morning.

But when Georges Rivière counted the takings, the total was ridiculously low. "The enthusiastic crowd at the ball had consisted above all of young people of modest means, who had succeeded in talking their way past their friends selling the tickets." There was no more talk of founding a crèche for the moment. There was just enough money to pay for treatment for a poor girl who had developed phlebitis after a miscarriage.

There were many such poor girls in "merry" Montmartre. 7.5 per cent of the working-class population of the 18th arrondissement, to which the hill belonged, were classed as needy (in comparison to just 1.8 per cent in the neighbouring, middle-class 8th arrondissement). The couples who lived here were seldom legally married, but simply cohabiting. In almost every case, both partners worked, and their combined daily wages were just enough to live on.

For single women, things were much harder. In the second half of the 19th century, more and more of them found work in the textile and fashion industries, both of which were experiencing a boom following the introduction of the sewing machine. Mechanization lowered production costs, so that fashion items now become affordable for the lower classes, too. The beginnings of off-the-peg clothing brought a certain "democratization" of fashion, while the fashion designer Worth was at the same time creating the first haute couture for the moneyed aristocracy. Female employees in the fashion industry were called *midinettes*, because at midday (in French, *midi*) they flooded out of their studios. Their work laid the foundations for Paris's reputation as the international capital of fashion and became an important element in French foreign trade. But their working day lasted ten or eleven hours and they were all paid a pittance, whether they made fashion clothes, hats, or lingerie. Furthermore, there was a "quiet season" in the fashion industry of about three months a year, during which time they didn't get paid at all.

Like women teachers and shop assistants, fashion workers in the 1860s and 1870s earned only 500 francs a year. Hence many girls just ate bread and washed it down with a little milk. Anaemia and tuberculosis were amongst the consequences.

With no forms of insurance provided, illness, unemployment, or pregnancy were enough to turn this budget on its head. It was practically impossible for a woman to bring up a family on a single wage, and thus prostitution frequently became an economic necessity.

The girls whom one met in venues such as the Moulin de la Galette "belonged", according to Jean Renoir, the artist's son, "to that category of unattached girls who were typical of the Parisian morals of the day. They changed their lovers frequently, treated themselves to whatever they happened to set their heart on, and occasionally exchanged a vil-

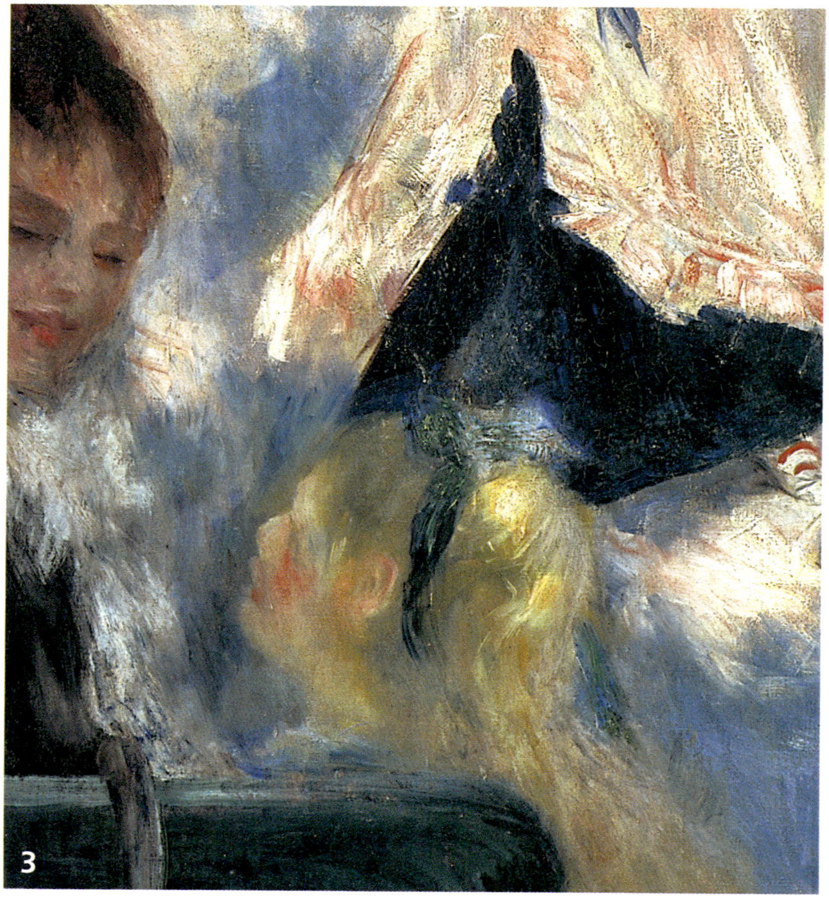

3

The *belle époque* of the lower classes

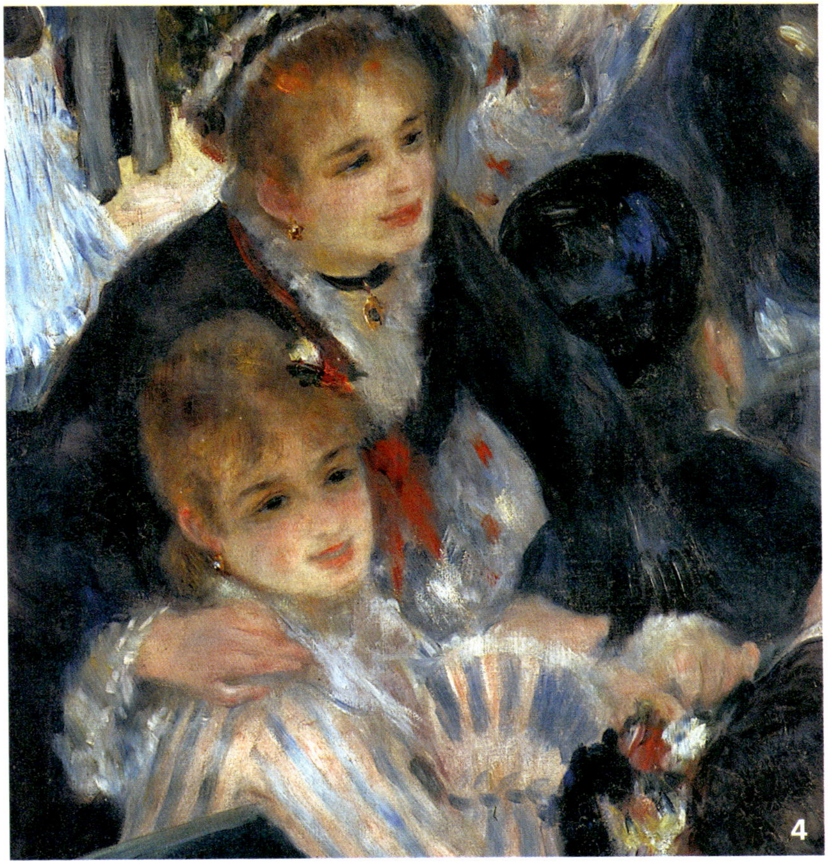

la on the Champs Elysées for an attic in the Batignolles … It is to them we owe the image of Paris during that era as radiant, witty, and full of gaiety."

Jeanne is the name of the model here bending over her younger sister. "The girl was attractive, wonderful hands, her fingertips somewhat swollen from needle pricks", Renoir much later described her to his son. If we are to believe Georges Rivière, Jeanne personified Renoir's feminine ideal, one he painted again and again throughout his life. At that time she was sixteen years old, had large black eyes, red lips, and light brown hair. Next to her sits her sister Estelle, "a small brunette with pretty ears", recalled Renoir. "I kept telling her she ought to put up her hair." Naturally, both lived on Montmartre, where the artist, who didn't like working with professional models, first approached them. Having suffered a hernia, their father, a bricklayer, preferred sitting in the pub to working; their mother was a laundress. As their fingertips betray, Jeanne and Estelle both worked as seamstresses, although neither had a permanent job. They were therefore happy to earn some extra money during the "quiet season" by modelling for Renoir, a relatively well-paid job.

We do not know what became of Jeanne and Estelle. But their lives were probably far less "radiant, witty, and full of gaiety" than Jean Renoir, looking back from his nostalgic male standpoint, remembered them. Not many girls had the chance of being married to a man such as Renoir, as happened to Aline Charigot, another young dressmaker from Montmartre hill. She, too, had started by modelling for him. From 1881 onwards they lived together and enjoyed a long and contented marriage.

Two lives typical of those led by young women from the Parisian working classes are portrayed in the novels *Nana* and *L'Assomoir* by Emile Zola, which were published in 1877 and 1879 and thus date from the same era as Renoir's painting.

Those who, like Nana and Renoir's models, had an attractive body and a delicate skin could choose a profession that, while the oldest of them all, was enjoying a particular boom in the second half of the 19th century. Such girls were "discovered" by wealthy gentlemen and kept by them in greater or lesser luxury – as prize goods, prestige objects through which, in the heyday of capitalism, the owner could put his wealth on public display. Zola's Nana soon meets a "bad end", and surely only a handful of her colleagues would have succeeded in securing themselves a dignified old age.

The other character in Zola's novel, Gervaise in *L'Assomoir*, sells not her body but her labour. All her life she toils over the washing trough and the ironing board. She is reduced to destitution, a victim of her ignorance (the large majority of the female population could neither read nor write properly), the social conditions, and men. For women were always subordinate to men; according to the Code Napoléon, they remained minors.

The first tentative attempts by a few women teachers, around the middle of the 19th century, to improve the education of women, to find decent jobs for them, and to establish childcare facilities, were smiled upon condescendingly by men. Even Marx's First International, which had been fighting since 1864 for the rights of exploited workers, did not think of doing anything for women. On the contrary, in 1866 its French section tabled a memorandum against female labour. Proudhon, the leading thinker amongst France's socialists, also endorsed the subordination of women, which he described in his writings as both unavoidable and justified. It was fine, in other words, to carry on exploiting them.

One art historian has called Renoir's painting a "testament to the carefree life of the day". But the so-called *belle époque* also had its shady side. At least for the women, it was not always Sunday at the Moulin de la Galette.

Gustave Caillebotte: Paris Street, Rainy Day, 1877

Under the umbrella, loneliness

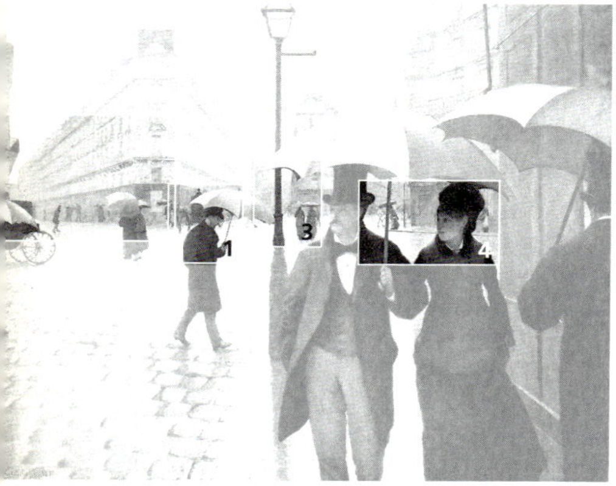

The first retrospective ever devoted to the French painter Gustave Caillebotte was mounted in 1994. By that time he had already been dead for one hundred years. The large-scale exhibition, which was subtitled "Urban Impressionist", brought together over one hundred portraits, interiors, still lifes, landscapes, and – to particularly impressive effect – large-format cityscapes. It travelled from Paris to Chicago and Los Angeles and introduced the public to an artist who had previously remained virtually unknown in both Europe and America.

Art historians were familiar with Gustave Caillebotte (1848–1894) at best as an important friend and patron of the Impressionists. He provided the impoverished artists with financial assistance and purchased their pictures at a time when virtually no one else was prepared to do so. The fact that he was himself a painter and exhibited many of his pictures alongside those of the Impressionists became lost along the way. He never sold a single one of his works, because he didn't need to. Unlike his colleagues, he was a wealthy man from a wealthy background.

Even after his death, his paintings remained in the possession of his family. Few of them entered museum collections and they were only very rarely lent out to exhibitions. Nor, in the 20th century, did they enjoy the extraordinary popularity of the other Impressionists, since they were not available as reproductions. Only in the 1950s did the Caillebotte family start to sell his paintings; art historians at last got to see them and organized the first exhibitions in the United States. In 1964 *Paris Street, Rainy Day* was purchased by The Art Institute of Chicago.

The painting, which measures 212 by 276 centimetres, portrays a complex intersection in Paris on a wintry afternoon: broad avenues, a spacious view, uniform façades. It is the Paris that can still be seen today. When Caillebotte painted it in 1877, it was new and modern.

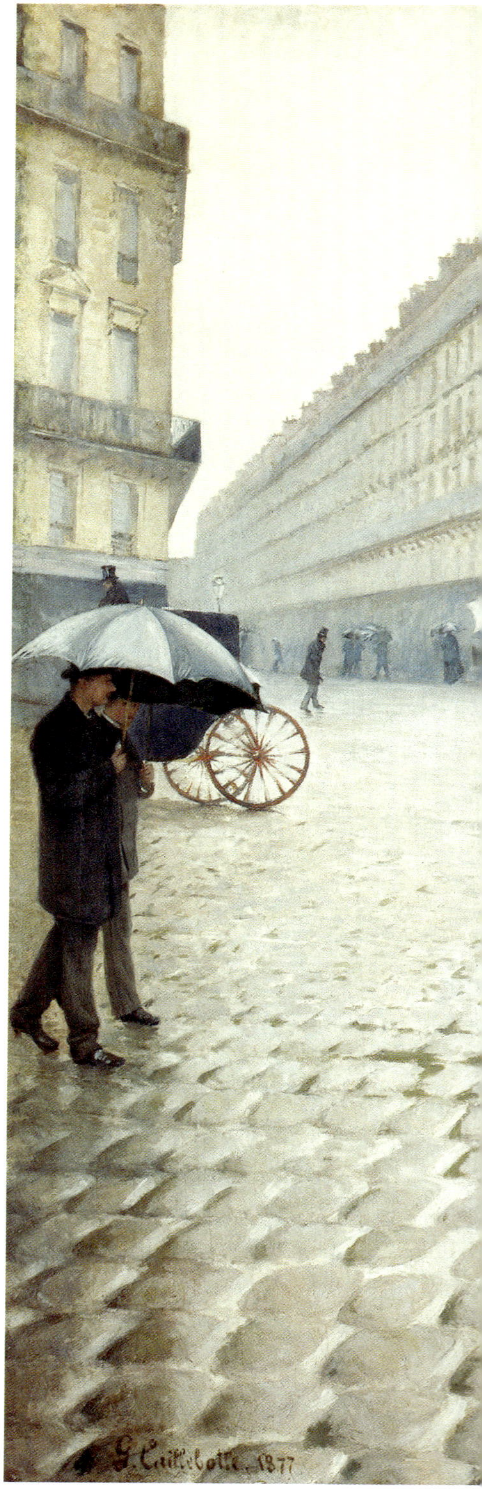

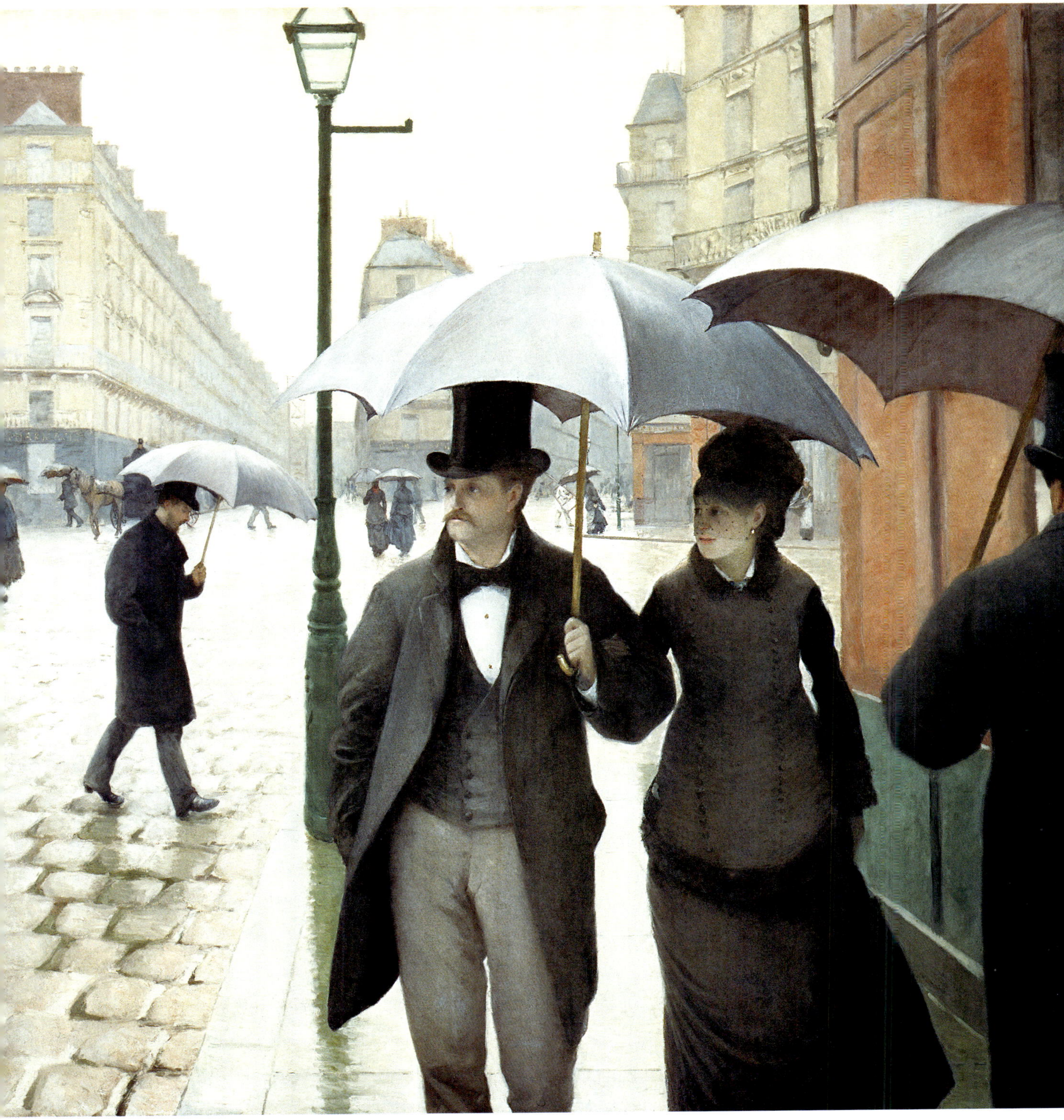

Caillebotte came from a wealthy family belonging to the *haute bourgeoisie*, a class to which a number of people in the present painting would also have belonged. His father had made his money supplying beds to the French army, and he bequeathed to his widow and four sons several apartment buildings in Paris and a country estate. At the age of twenty-six, following his father's death, Caillebotte already disposed of a considerable fortune.

He had studied law and then painting under Léon Bonnat, a highly regarded artist who remained indebted to the academic tradition. Caillebotte was unsatisfied by the mythological and historical themes of academic art, however, and joined up with a group of artists who wanted to get out of their studios and search out natural, living light and contemporary subjects. They included Auguste Renoir, Edgar Degas, Claude Monet, Camille Pissarro, and Alfred Sisley, all somewhat older than Caillebotte.

Unable or unwilling to exhibit at the official Salon, they formed a "society of painters, sculptors, and engravers" and in 1874 mounted their own exhibition. It caused a scandal. The critics were horrified; borrowing from the title of one of the works submitted by Monet, *Impression, Sunrise*, they coined the term "Impressionists" to describe the young artists. Although Caillebotte was not included in that first exhibition, he was represented by several works in the group's second show, staged in 1876. At the third show, held in 1877, he again exhibited a number of works, amongst them *Paris Street, Rainy Day*. One of the critics, Georges Rivière, noted approvingly: "An intrepid seeker, on whom we pin well-founded hopes". Three years later, the novelist Joris-Karl Huysmans predicted that "some of his canvases will one day take their place alongside the best".

Huysmans was right, but even so, for nearly a century Caillebotte was thought of simply as an impresario and patron who rented exhibition rooms for the Impressionists, got the picture frames, took care of the advertising, and put up the money. In 1878 he made Pissarro a gift of 750 francs; he paid Monet's removal costs and rent and bought a total of 18 of his paintings. He admired the colleagues who had turned their backs on tradition – perhaps because he also wanted to free himself from the bourgeois milieu from which he came.

In 1876 his younger brother died suddenly. Gustave subsequently felt prompted to draw up his own will. The terms of this will would make art history, by assuring the Impressionists belated but at long last public recognition. Caillebotte namely bequeathed his collection to the French nation, albeit with the proviso that it was exhibited "neither in an attic nor in a provincial museum" but in an appropriate setting, and only when the public would accept such painting. That, Caillebotte felt, might take "twenty years or more".

He was not mistaken. It was not until 1897, three years after his death and following heated arguments, that his bequest was officially accepted. For the first time, forty paintings by the Impressionists were now hung in a national institution, the Musée du Luxembourg.

The bequest included just one painting by Caillebotte himself, *Les Raboteurs de Parquets* (The Floor Strippers). It was added by Renoir, his executor; modesty had prevented Caillebotte from forcing his own works upon the nation along with those of his admired colleagues.

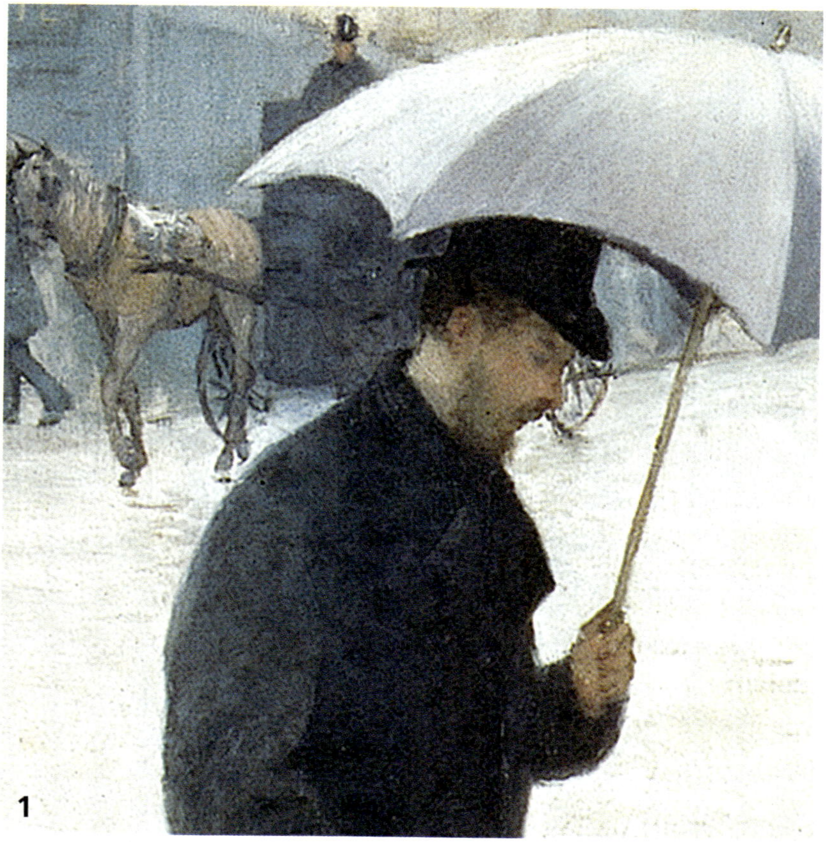

1

A selfless patron

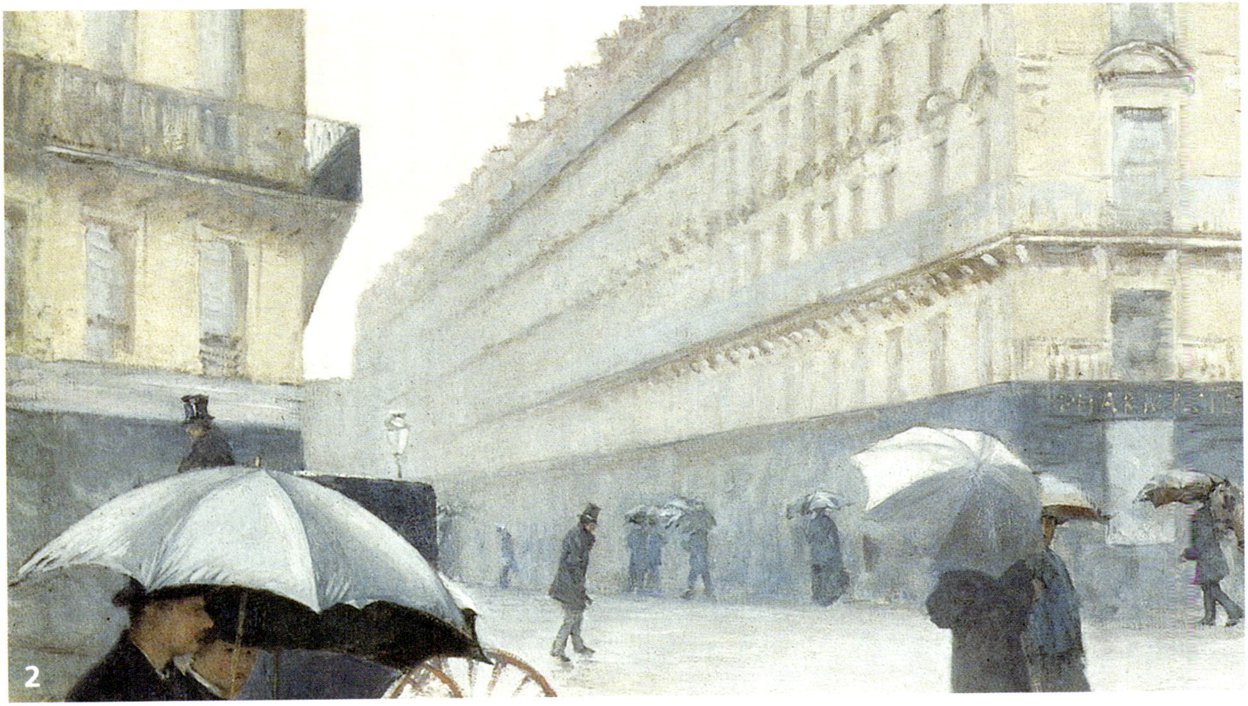

Although the title of the painting mentions just one, anonymous Paris street, there are in fact several to be seen, all of which can be identified. Running from the foreground into the background is the rue de Turin; coming in from the left and crossing the centre of the composition is the rue de Moscou; and in the background we can also see the rue Clapeyron. The intersection is today called the Place de Dublin and lies near the Gare Saint-Lazare.

These streets were laid out during Caillebotte's youth on a hill which lay beyond the old city limits and which had burgeoned into a residential district for the wealthy bourgeoisie. Not far away lay the – similarly newly designed – city centre, with its opera house and spacious boulevards lined with elegant cafés and expensive department stores.

This was all the work of Baron Georges Eugène Haussmann, Prefect of the Département of the Seine from 1853 to 1870. He had been instructed by Napoleon III to tear down the medieval city centre, with its narrow alleys and damp housing, after two cholera epidemics had claimed thousands of lives. No government had previously risked such a step, but Napoleon III wanted progress and better living conditions, and gave Haussmann his orders "to take Old Paris" with the "army" of his officials. The Baron not only took Old Paris, but also conquered new territories to the west of the city and transformed them into residential districts.

Huge loans were taken out to finance the ambitious project. The authoritarian regime gave the Prefect a free hand. Haussmann's department had sole responsibility for all new building, both public and private. From 1850, changes to the law paved the way for expropriation on a massive scale – even bypassing the legal process in the name of the public interest. Buildings were demolished and new ones were built, as property speculation fuelled increases in the price of land for development. The wheels of dispossession, wrote the novelist Emile Zola, turned like "a mighty machine which ploughed through Paris for fifteen years, producing fortunes and bankruptcies".

It was a period during which Caillebotte's father also grew rich. In 1866 he bought a plot of land with building permission "from the City of Paris, represented by Baron Haussmann," for 148,780 francs. When he died, his massive fortune lay largely apartment buildings in the splendid new districts of Paris.

Urban planner Baron Haussmann loved long lines

Although such buildings were the product of private enterprise, they were constructed under the supervision of the authorities and in line with strict regulations giving rise to the homogeneous architecture visible in Caillebotte's picture. Wide streets were to lead in a straight line from one square to another, or from one particularly important building to another, and in each case offer a spectacular view. Haussmann loved perspective and symmetry, and he liked to have streets converge upon a square like the arms of a star, as in the intersection portrayed here.

The new Paris was to consist not of detached houses, but of monumental apartment buildings housing luxury flats and employing uniform ashlar façades. The height of the eaves was stipulated for each district and usually extended to four or five storeys. The first floor and attic storey were required to have balcony railings running the entire length of the façade. Many of the city's squares and avenues continue to owe their aesthetic homogeneity and harmony to Baron Haussmann even today.

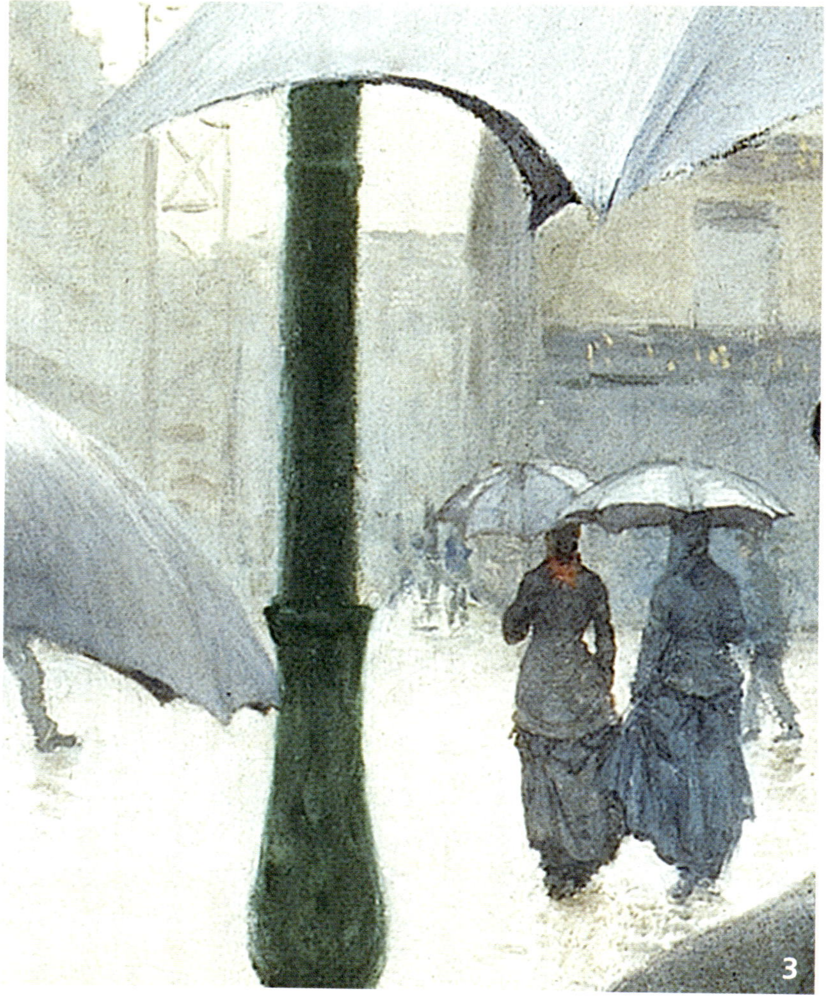

Streetlights and cobblestones recall the Commune

Caillebotte is said by his family to have executed the preparatory sketches for his canvas while seated inside a specially glazed "omnibus", a large horse-drawn carriage which protected him from the rain and cold. But "even when working from nature, one has to compose", as Degas said, and thus Caillebotte selects an angle that yields an almost geometrically structured canvas. At the centre of the composition stands a gaslight, its shadow falling towards us across the wet cobbles. Such standardized, industrially manufactured gaslights studded the streets of Haussmann's Paris at regular, rhythmical intervals, and Caillebotte, too, uses it as an ordering element, which serves to divide the composition vertically in two.

The picture is divided horizontally by the street running diagonally across it and by a line which passes through virtually every head, giving rise to a symmetrical cruciform construction that approaches Haussmann's own aesthetic preferences. This geometry is frequently and deliberately obscured, however: through the emphasis upon linear perspective, through the ever smaller figures of the passers-by, the eye is led into the background. The arching curves of the large umbrellas contrast with the verticals of the figures and façades. The man beneath the umbrella on the far right, cut off by the edge of the canvas, conveys the impression that this is merely a snapshot, a casual, momentary view, rather than a composition that has been carefully planned.

As well as *Paris Street, Rainy Day*, Caillebotte also showed his large-format *Pont de l'Europe* at the exhibition of 1877.

In the bright sunshine of a spring or summer morning, workers and members of the bourgeoisie cross a wide bridge above the tracks of Saint-Lazare station. The views of Paris exhibited by the other Impressionists in the 1877 were similarly cheerful – they celebrated the city as somewhere to stroll, to idle, and to twirl around in popular dance halls.

The mood they captured was not merely confined to art. In the war of 1870/71, France had been defeated by the Germans, and Paris besieged and bombarded. Next the revolutionary Commune had seized power in Paris, set fire to public and private buildings, and finally gone down in a bloodbath. By 1877, however, the reparations to Germany had been paid, the economy was flourishing and the Republican government was getting ready to celebrate France's recovery with the International Exhibition of 1878. In a series of articles, Renoir called upon artists to contribute to the process of democracy and to immerse the city in colour. In a third painting at the 1877 exhibition, Caillebotte portrays decorators in a grey street painting the façades of the buildings with colour.

One of them can be seen with his ladder in the background of *Paris Street*. But this is not a painting of a gay, convivial Paris that is trying to erase its memories of the past. On the contrary, most of the people in the picture seem lonely. They are not out for a stroll, but hurry through empty streets, shielding themselves with their umbrellas not just from the rain but also, so it seems, from other passers-by. And at the sight of the cobbles, which almost entirely dominate one quarter of the canvas, many viewers will have involuntarily thought of the Commune: the revolutionaries had hurled cobblestones from their barricades. They had battled for days on the Place de Clichy, which lay very close to Caillebotte's intersection. "The cobblestone", wrote Victor Hugo, "is the symbol of the people." That same uprising had also started with the streetlights being overturned.

The pearl in the woman's ear appears as a luminous dot; it is the only one in the painting, and it gleams brighter than the white shirtfront of the man beside her. Yet the person to whom the artist has thus drawn attention also wears a veil, which distances her from the viewer and signals discretion.

The two protagonists walk towards the viewer in almost life size. Their faces are highly individualized and must surely be portraits, although of whom we do not know. On one of his preparatory sketches, the artist jotted down the name of Clotilde – but who was Clotilde?

The man is wearing a frock coat and top hat, the woman a fur-trimmed outfit whose cut and colour combination struck one critic in 1877 "as modern – or should I say, the latest fashion". Even her umbrella, he thought, seemed to have been freshly purchased from one of Paris's new department stores, the Bon-Marché perhaps. It was only three years previously that umbrellas of this kind had actually been invented – by the Englishman Samuel Fox in Sheffield. Caillebotte wanted to be modern like the other Impressionists; he wanted to paint not what was past but what belonged to the present.

Characteristic of this painting and the artist is the fact that both of the main figures are looking to one side – and not at the man coming towards them, who is unable to step out of their way and whose umbrella is already dangerously close to their own. Eye contact is avoided, including with the viewer. Almost all the people in the painting are hurrying through the streets absorbed in their own thoughts, protected by their umbrellas.

Caillebotte, too, managed to shield his private life so well that few details of it have come down to us. We know that he never married. A census of 1891 records him as the head of a household with three domestic servants, four sailors, and a twenty-eight-year-old actress, registered as a "friend", who for reasons unknown called herself Charlotte Berthier but whose real name was Anne Marie Hagen. Renoir painted her.

Caillebotte was at that time living in Petit Genevilliers, a small town on the Seine near Argenteuil, where he dedicated his organizational skills, innovative thinking, and financial resources first to rowing and then to yachting. He maintained his own crew, owned his own boatyard, and designed ever faster yachts. For three years he was the best regatta sailor in France. He remained true to painting, however. When he died in 1894 at the age of just forty-five, he left some 500 pictures, even though he had long since given up exhibiting and had also withdrawn from his former circle of artist friends, no doubt fed up with their bickering. The group had by now disbanded and its individual members were no longer dependent upon his financial support. Caillebotte nevertheless continued to attend their monthly dinners at the Café Riche, and as always paid the bill for everyone.

His famous colleagues Renoir and Monet never, as far as we know, expressed an opinion about their patron's work; it is possible that a man who painted for pleasure remained an amateur in their eyes. Caillebotte's wealth was probably detrimental to his fame: his own works remained unknown long after those whom he supported had become famous. By the time they were discovered, the paintings by his Impressionist friends were already filling the pages of countless art books.

No one looks at anyone else

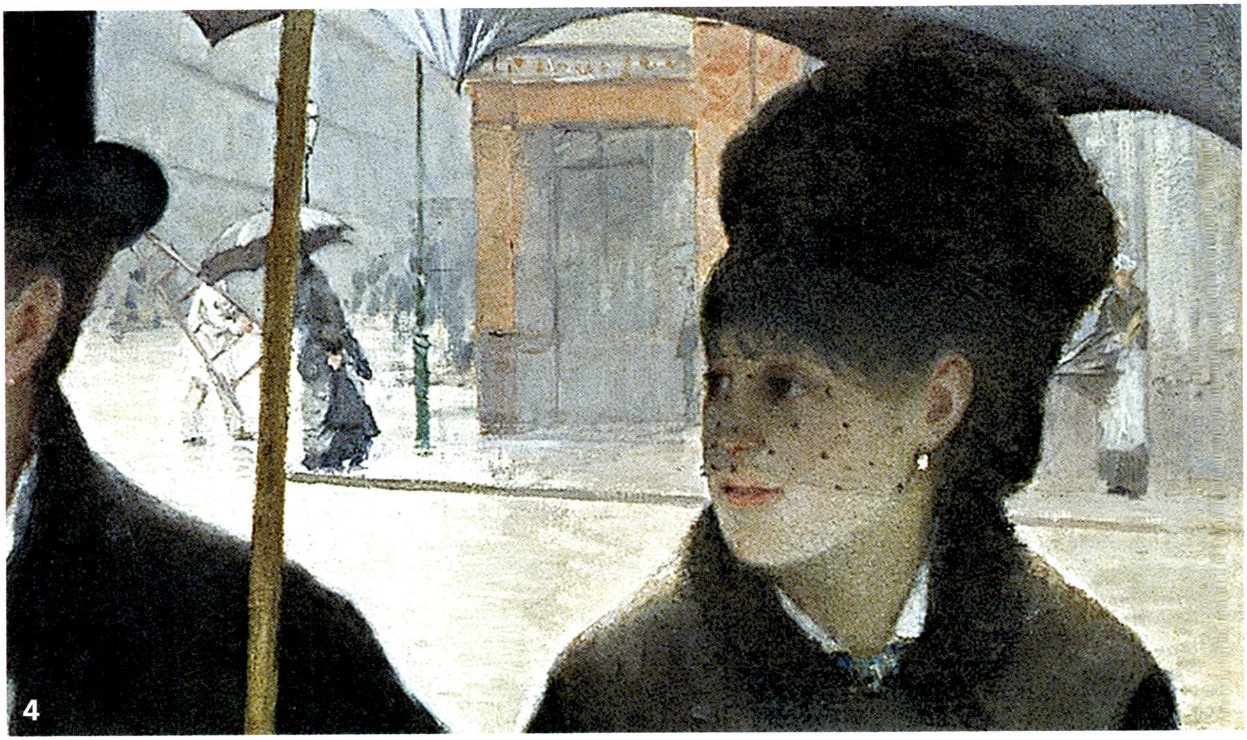
4

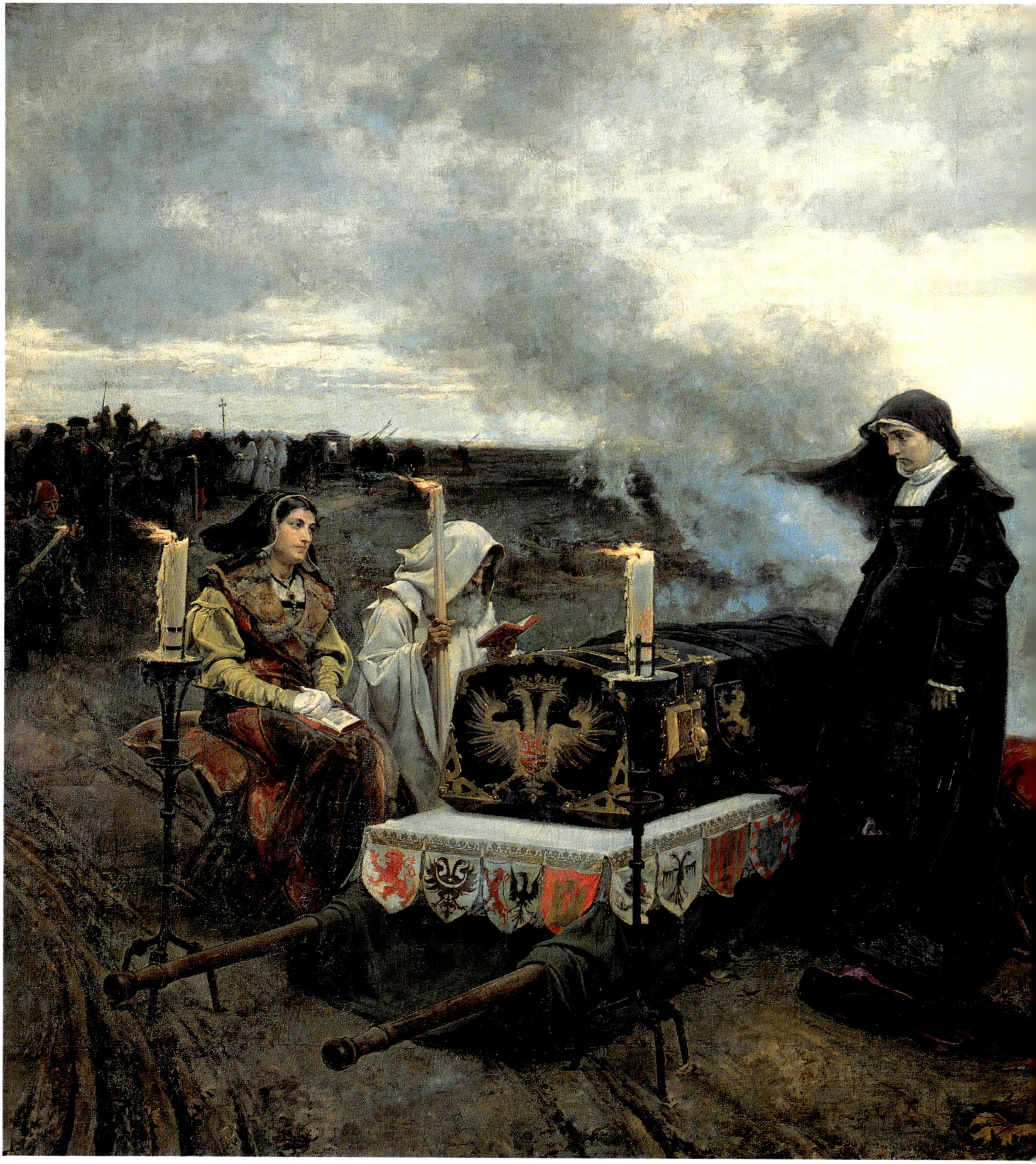

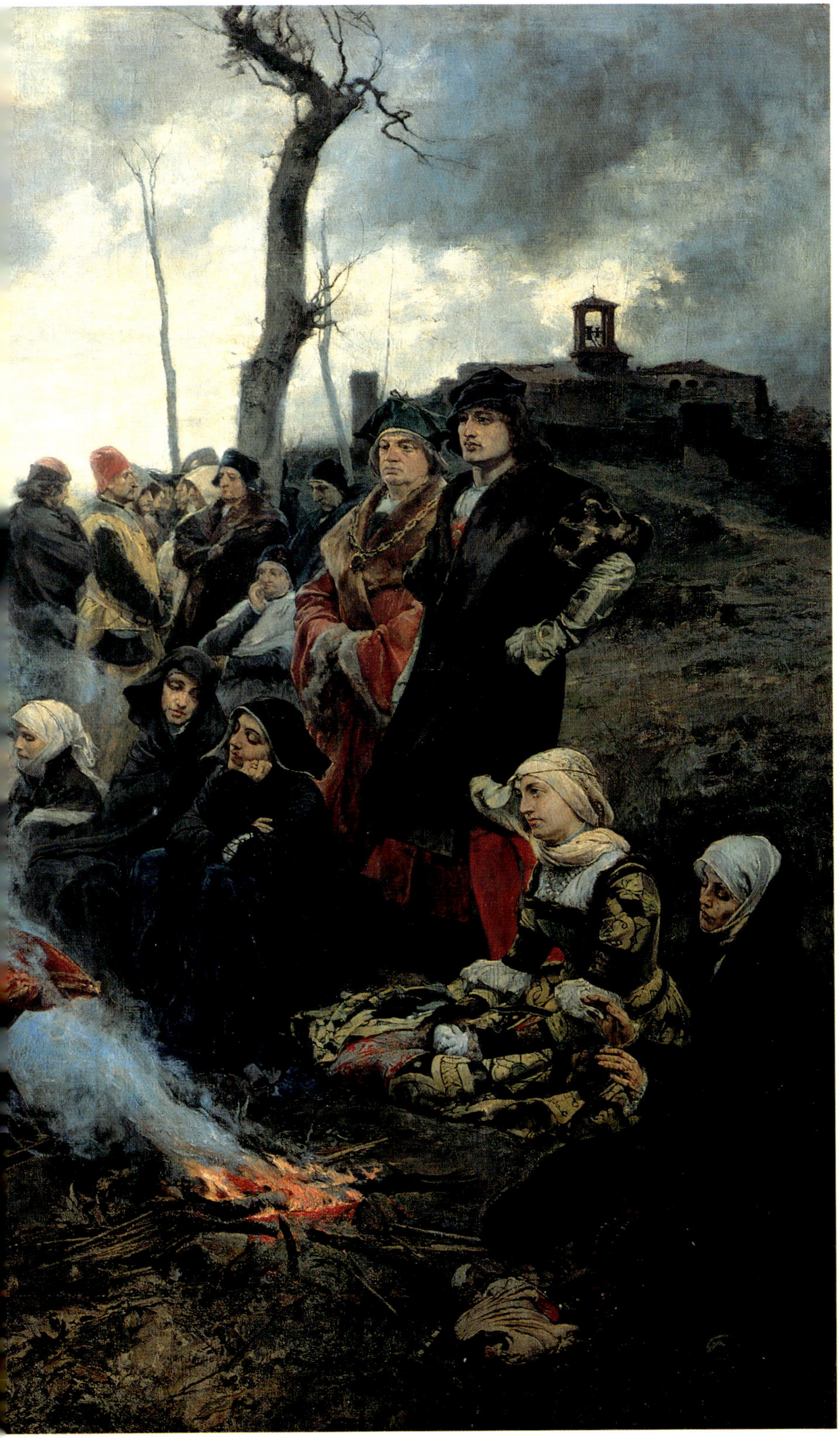

Francisco Pradilla y Ortiz: Joanna the Mad beside her Husband's Coffin, 1877

A victim along Spain's path to world power

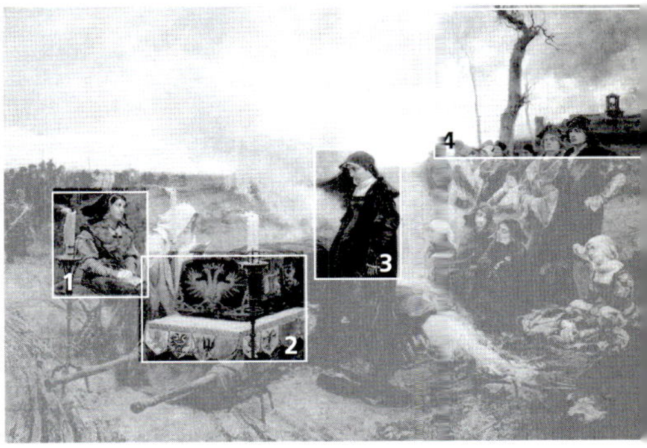

The woman dressed in black with the staring eyes and billowing veil in the centre of the picture is Queen Joanna of Castille (1479–1555). The power struggle between her father and her husband destroyed her sanity. Chroniclers relate how, after her husband's death, the heavily pregnant Joanna wandered aimlessly through Castille with her royal household in the middle of winter. Fearful that someone wanted to steal his body from her, she travelled only by night; not for a single minute would she be separated from the coffin, which was borne along on a cart. The entourage rested on the road in the wind and the cold.

Amongst the Spanish, Joanna is one of the most popular women in their country's history, thanks not least to the present painting by Francisco Pradilla. Executed in 1877, it belongs to the genre of history painting, which was at that time admired by both public and critics alike. With the birth of modern painting, however, with the rise of Impressionism, this academic "Salon art" found itself ridiculed and despised. Only since the 1970s have these works once again attracted the serious attention of art historians and become the focus of museum exhibitions.

At the Exposición Nacional de Bellas Artes of 1878, the official art exhibition in Madrid, *Joanna the Mad* won the previously unheard-of Francisco Pradilla y Ortiz (1848–1921) the highest medal of honour, never before awarded, together with the respectable sum of 20,000 pesetas. At a stroke he was famous, financially secure – and in a position to marry.

It was for lack of money that he had left school in Saragossa without a diploma, in order to earn his living, according to one of his friends, as a "door painter" and decorator. In 1866 he was to be found in Madrid in a workshop producing theatre sets, while studying painting at the San Fernando Royal Academy in his spare time. "He wasted not a minute of his free time", remembered a colleague; he would draw "in the cafés, the streets, the avenues, and on the banks of the Manzanares".

As almost everywhere in Europe, the world of art in Madrid was dominated by the state Academy, which oversaw training and organized the annual Exposición, the only opportunity for young artists to show their work.

Since Spain had virtually nothing of an educated middle class and consequently no private market for paintings, the State was effectively the only buyer of art. Most frequently, it purchased large-format history paintings to adorn government buildings. Pradilla's contemporaries considered history painting the finest of the genres because it embraced all the rest, such as portraiture and landscape painting; it thus offered the artist "the most noble sphere in which to display his talents". The Madrid Salon of 1867, for example, included eighty-three history paintings, all treating lofty subjects from biblical, Spanish, or Greco-Roman history.

If you wanted to succeed as an artist, it was imperative to take part in a competition held by the Academy. Pradilla was reticent and shy, and so one of his teachers put his name down secretly. With his *Rape of the Sabine Women*, the young painter won a three-year scholarship to Rome – an opportunity to study the art of antiquity and the Renaissance, albeit on a meagre allowance and under the strict eye of the Academy. Scholarship holders were required to send examples of the work back to Madrid every year. In the third year, it had to be a large-format history painting. Pradilla chose as his subject *Joanna the Mad.*

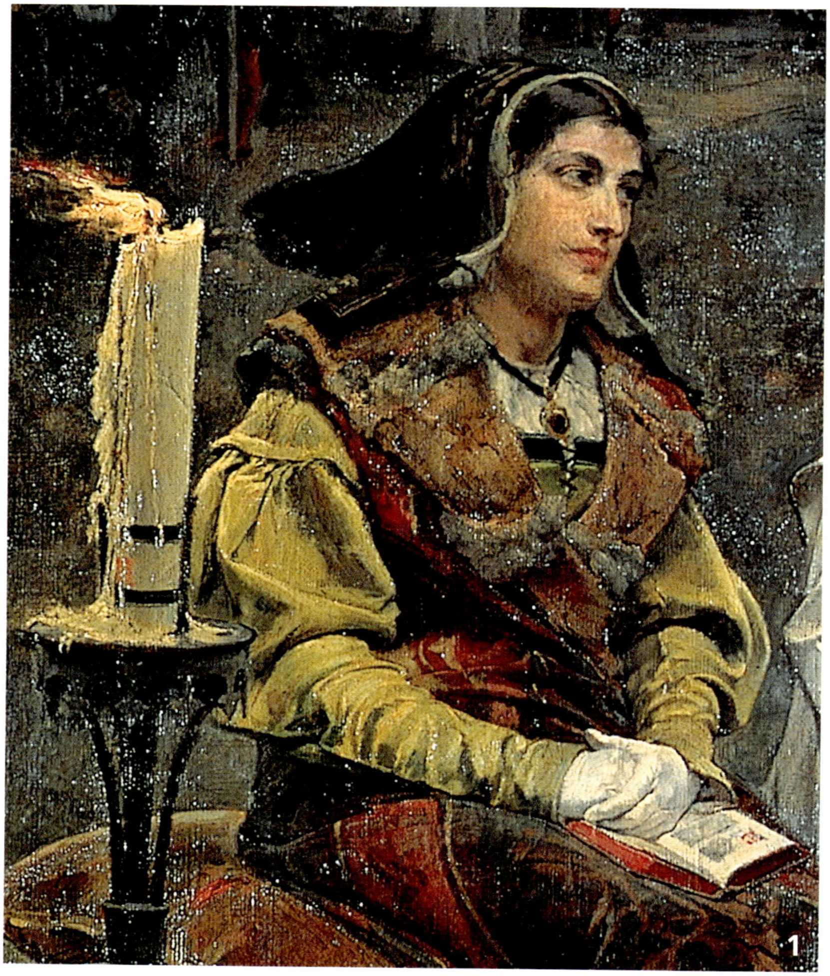
1

To paint every last inch of an enormous canvas, measuring 3.40 by 5 metres, in the smooth, minutely detailed Old Master technique prescribed by the Academy in just a year was a task worthy of Sisyphus. Pradilla's contemporaries insisted, moreover, upon historical accuracy and authenticity. Research in museums and libraries was all part of the preparatory work conducted by the artist; the fur trims, the jewellery, even the shape of the bonnet of the lady-in-waiting sitting beside the coffin – all had to be correct for the era being portrayed. Not without satisfaction did the teachers at the Academy in Madrid hear that Pradilla had often gone without lunch in order to buy a scrap of old brocade or velvet in the market so that he would have the right material to work from.

History painting was considered the noblest genre

The painting arose during a chaotic era: two civil wars, military coups, and the loss of its overseas territories had plunged Spain into a crisis of identity. This was another reason why the Academy encouraged the production of history paintings. The majority looked back nostalgically to Spain's greatest period, the final third of the 15th century, when the Catholic sovereigns Queen Isabella of Castille and King Ferdinand of Aragon had unified the country and driven the Moors out of Granada after almost eight hundred years of Muslim rule. It was during their regency that Christopher Columbus set sail on the voyages of discovery that would bring Spain a global empire.

Joanna was the daughter of Isabella and Ferdinand. She was married to Philip of Burgundy, Archduke of Austria, son of the German emperor Maximilian. Philip would one day inherit the imperial crown and the Habsburg territories and in the meantime ruled over the wealthy Netherlands. An indication of the large number of territories in Philip's possession is provided by the pall cloth covering the bier: beneath the double-headed Habsburg eagle on the end of the coffin, we can recognize the arms of Flanders, with the red lion, together with those of Brabant and Artois.

Joanna was seventeen years old when, in 1496, she went to Flanders and fell "hopelessly in love", as one eyewitness described it, with her bridegroom – something unusual in marriages arranged for political reasons and which would have tragic consequences. The vivacious Philip the Fair, as he was known, soon tired of his serious Spanish wife. News of Joanna's wild acts of jealousy (she cut off the blonde tresses of her husband's mistress) and her depressions aroused concern in Spain. For the deaths of her elder siblings meant that Joanna was now first in line to the kingdoms of Castille and Aragon.

When her mother died in 1504, both Joanna's father and her husband tried to seize the crown of Castille. They met with resistance, however, from both the populace and the aristocracy, who detested both men as foreigners and who were prepared to recognize only Joanna. It suited both men very well, therefore, to have the rightful heiress to the throne pronounced mad and unfit to rule.

The struggle for power erupted at the beginning of 1506, when Philip accompanied Joanna back to Spain. Ferdinand, her father, appeared to back down, but Philip suddenly fell ill and died, probably as a result of poisoning. The unstable Joanna suffered a breakdown; her father used her psychopathic behaviour to have her locked up, and ruled in her place.

She spent forty-five years, isolated and closely guarded, in Tordesillas castle. Her own eldest son, Emperor Charles V made no attempt to release her. If he was to rule Spain and her colonies undisturbed, Joanna had to remain in solitary confinement. She became a victim along Spain's path to world power.

The public wanted to be reminded of the glorious past

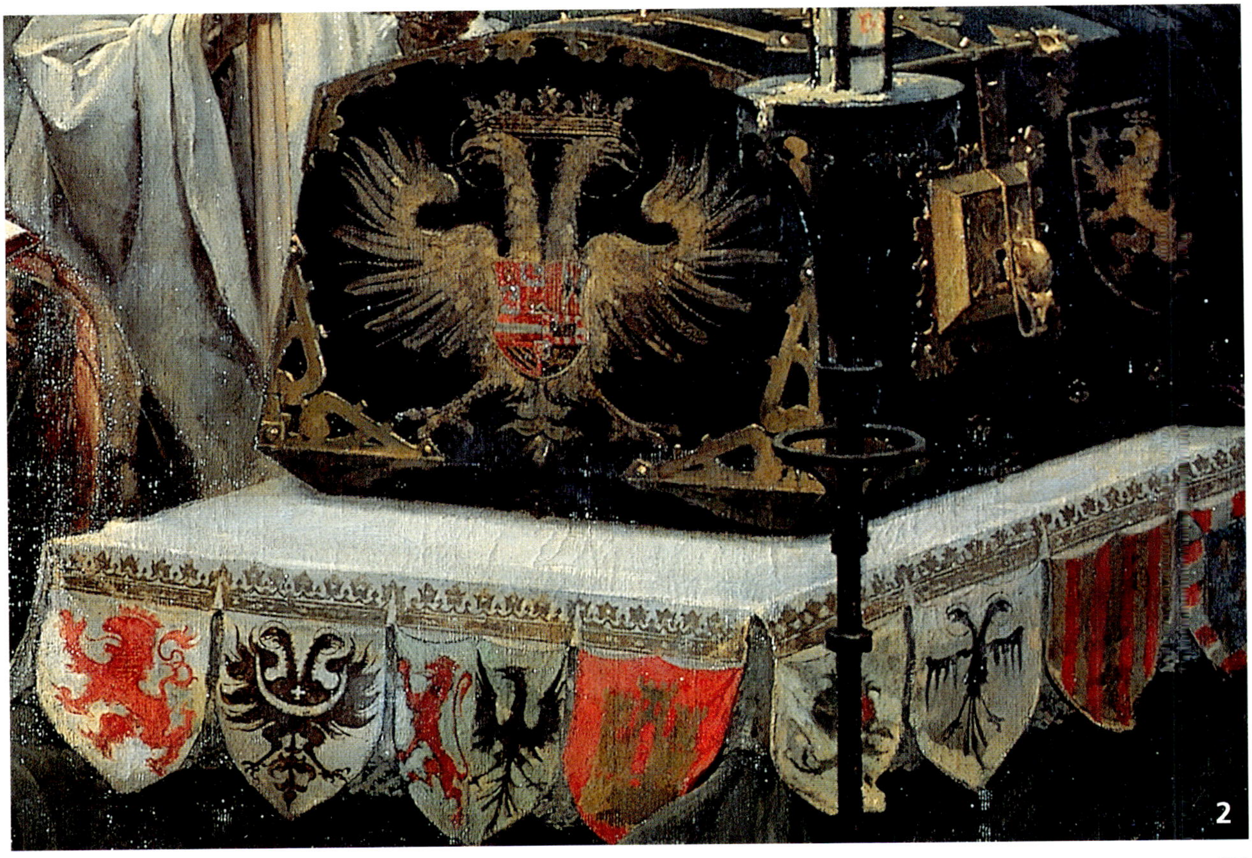

2

To what extent and from what point in time onwards Joanna was "mad" are questions difficult to answer today. One contemporary report, supplied by Pedro Mártir de Angleria, an Englishman who spent his life at the Spanish court, sheds detailed and credible light on Joanna's state of mind. Mártir accompanied the despairing widow, pregnant with her fourth child, as she travelled around the kingdom with the embalmed body of her husband for many weeks. In the delusion that people wanted to abduct her husband and take him back to the Netherlands, she watched over his lead coffin and repeatedly asked for it to be opened.

The queen's entourage, according to Mártir, "moved only at night, because a respectable woman, she said, after losing her husband who is her sun, must flee the light of day. In the villages in which we spent the day, requiems were held, but the Queen would not allow any women to enter the church ... Her jealousy, the cause of her mental confusion, tormented her even as far as the grave of the man who provoked it while alive."

Pradilla deviates from this source, which was cited in the 1878 exhibition catalogue, and portrays a number of women in the train of the misogynistic queen – probably to make his painting appeal to a wider audience.

"On one of these days", continued Mártir, "the Queen had the coffin taken into what she thought was a monastery. But as soon as she heard that it was a nunnery, she was horrified and immediately ordered the coffin to be removed and carried out to the field. There she kept her whole retinue out in the open air, suffering the severe cold of the season while the wind blew out the lamps."

In Pradilla's painting, the nunnery can be seen on a hill on the right. Other chroniclers gave gruesome accounts of the queen's obsessive devotion to her dead husband, telling how she opened his coffin again and again to kiss and caress his corpse – macabre descriptions that must have given many an exhibition visitor a shudder of pleasure. Certainly, the history painters provided their *fin de siècle* public with so many images of murder and homicide that the Paris Salon was mockingly compared to a mortuary.

History painting was also expected to provide a powerful statement of romantic emotions – and in this respect the passionate, jealous, tragic figure of Joanna was ideally suited to Spanish tastes. Furthermore, her widow's weeds and the two wedding rings on her fingers made her instantly recognizable to Spanish viewers – another important precondition of history painting.

When Pradilla, in Rome, was searching for a subject for his Academy painting, a friend recommended Joanna to him because she was "so Spanish and so dramatic".

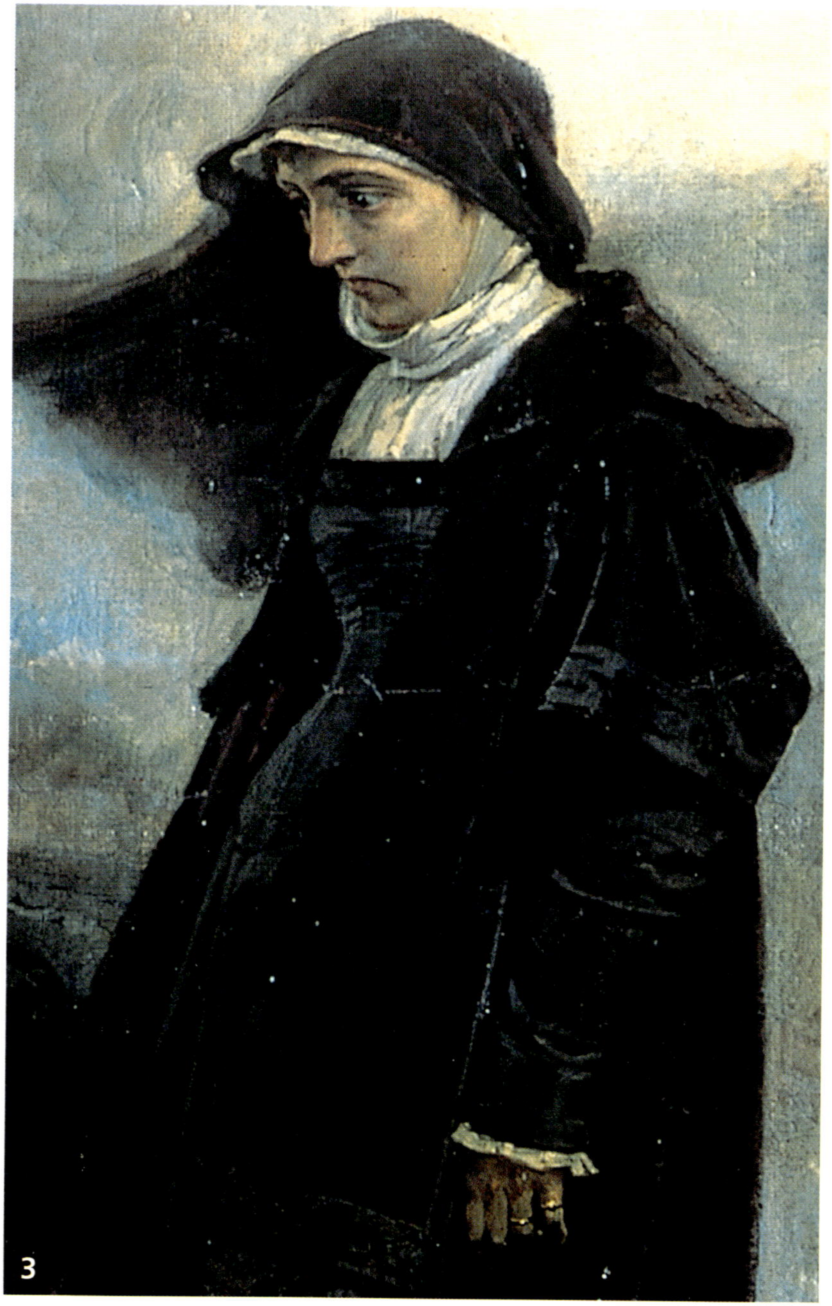

3

So Spanish and so dramatic

Other countries, too, were electrified by this Spanish woman. At the Paris International Exhibition of 1878, the painting won Pradilla a medal of honour, the Cross of the Legion of Honour and an enormous porcelain vase. He was fêted in Vienna and Munich. "Pradilla towers above all modern artists", wrote the *Rheinisch-Westfälische Zeitung*, "including Menzel and Meissonnier". Adolph von Menzel himself is said to have remarked that "the painting could be by me". The German artist, a close observer, no doubt appreciated Pradilla's solid technique and feeling for realistic detail, such as the tracks left in the frozen earth by the wheels of the cart.

Pradilla composed his works carefully and took particular pains over their background, landscape, and mood, here evoking effects of smoke and rain, the pale light of dawn and dark clouds gathering on the horizon. Force of circumstance and the dictates of the Academy had made Pradilla into a history painter, but once he had established a name for himself with such works, he was able to give them up. He now dedicated himself to genre and landscape painting and established an international clientele extending from Chile to Russia for his high-priced, small-format works. He was considered difficult: appointed director of the Spanish Academy in Rome and of the Prado Museum in Madrid, he gave up both posts after only a short time and withdrew from public life, an embittered man. His name lived on only through his history paintings, which existed in a surfeit of reproductions.

Artistic developments had overtaken him. Four years before Pradilla's *Joanna the Mad* was acclaimed by the public and the critics, the Impressionists had mounted their first exhibition in Paris. Although they were still the targets of ridicule and scorn, they would change the face of painting: the subject would become less important and objects and figures start to dissolve as new pictorial worlds were invented.

After the horrors of the First World War, history painters had nothing left to say. Their work was dismissed as *art pompier* (literally "fireman's art", meaning uninspired and conventional) and kitsch. The cumbersome canvases were taken down, banished to the storerooms, and forgotten.

In 1967 Salvador Dalí prophesied: "We will see *l'art pompier* suddenly spring up again, more alive than ever, as fresh as a rose." The Surrealist commended the flawless technique of the history painters and the attention they devoted to every last detail.

He would prove right. The public grew irritated with constantly changing styles and fashions. As one short-lived avant-garde gave way to another, the demonstrable qualities of academic Salon and history painting began to exert new attraction. The *pompiers* were rehabilitated and their works fetched out of storage, restored and exhibited – to particularly spectacular effect, since 1986, in the Musée d'Orsay in Paris.

Joanna the Mad will also be given pride of place. Once its restoration is complete, it will go on show in the Casón del Buen Retiro, part of the Prado Museum complex.

History painting was overtaken by Impressionism

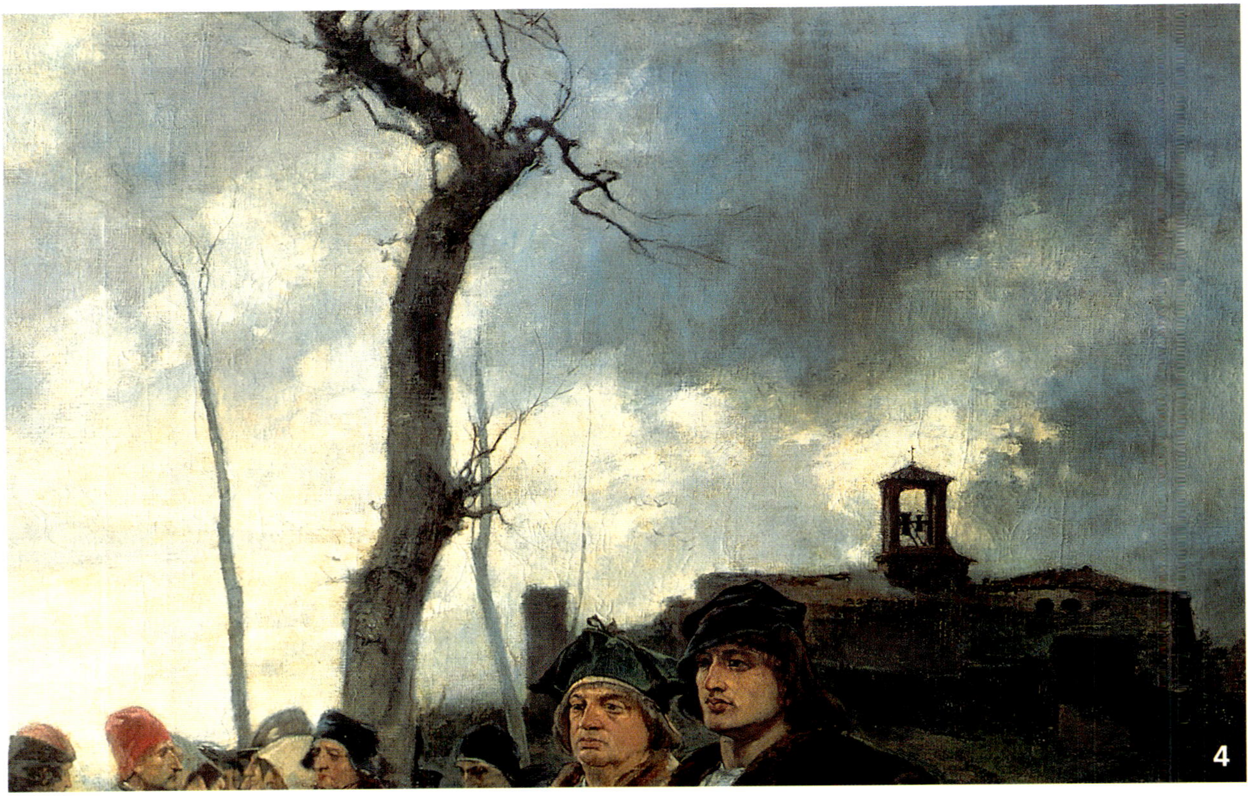

4

Arnold Böcklin: The Isle of the Dead, 1880

A dream of the South and of death

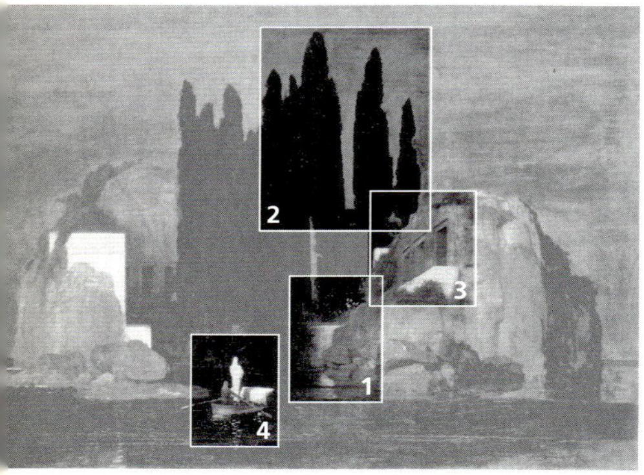

Between 1880 and 1886 Arnold Böcklin painted five versions of *The Isle of the Dead*. Four of them still exist – in Basle, Berlin, Leipzig, and New York. The Berlin picture once hung in the German Chancellery: a press photo of November 1940 shows Hitler and Molotov, the Russian foreign minister, standing in front of it. The following year, German troops would invade Russia.

Hitler had purchased "his" *Isle of the Dead* while Chancellor of the German Reich, and it had initially hung in his house in Berchtesgaden. Eleven paintings by Böcklin were also amongst the works of art purchased and requisitioned at Hitler's behest for a mammoth Nazi museum planned for Linz. For Hitler, whose tastes in art had been shaped at the start of the century, when he himself had wanted to become a painter, Böcklin ranked among the great masters. His opinion was shared by many: Arnold Böcklin was at that time one of the most popular artists in the entire German-speaking area.

Proof of this fact can be found in literature. There is scarcely an author between 1890 and 1910 who does not make some reference to Böcklin. Gottfried Keller, Paul Heyse, and Hugo von Hofmannsthal dedicated prologues and poems to him, while in his drama *Michael Kramer*, Gerhard Hauptmann even held him up as a shining example: "Always work, work, work ... Just look at a life like that, how a man like that works, someone like Böcklin. That way you make something of yourself, you accomplish something."

And what the artist accomplished again and again was *The Isle of the Dead*. Richard Dehmel left a holiday resort because "its similarity with Böcklin's *Isle of the Dead* would not have done me any good in the long term". Detlev von Liliencron and Hermann Hesse owned prints of the painting; as a young bookseller's assistant, Hesse moved to Basle "with Nietzche's works ... and a framed copy of Böcklin's *Isle of the Dead* in the trunk containing my possessions".

Just how far Böcklin's impact extended can be seen in a guide for newly married wives, entitled *In the German Home* and published by one Luise Holle in 1903. It offers pertinent advice on everything from interior furnishings and maternal duties to carnival pranks. "In the living room, the pictures should not be overly animated in either palette or subject, since when looked at every day their effect may prove unsettling", it explains on page 88. Although no specific artists are recommended by name, what it means is clear from one of its illustrations of a model room. There, in a dark frame against the dark wood panelling surrounded by a broad mount, hangs a print of *The Isle of the Dead*.

The popularization of Böcklin's works had been greatly assisted by a new printing technique, heliogravure, which permitted gradations of light and dark previously unobtainable in a print. For the first time, it was possible to create a reproduction, albeit only in black-and-white, good enough for lovers of art to hang on their wall. The Bruckmann publishing house in Munich was one of those quick to exploit this new technology. It signed exclusive contracts with artists and sold their works as prints in large-format portfolios. Menzel, Lenbach, Kaulbach, and Kalckreuth were all Bruckmann artists, as, too, was Böcklin.

When he reached his 70th birthday in 1897, he was at the pinnacle of his fame.

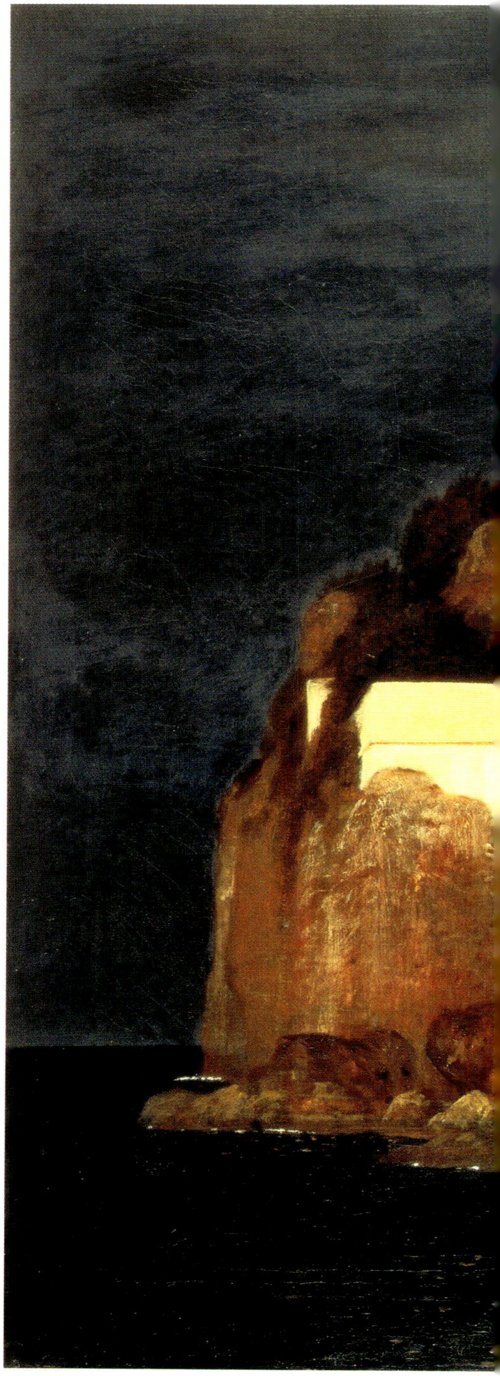

Two commemorative exhibitions were mounted in Germany, in Hamburg and Berlin: "in neither city had an exhibition ever attracted such crowds", wrote Alfred Lichtwark, at that time director of the Hamburg Kunsthalle.

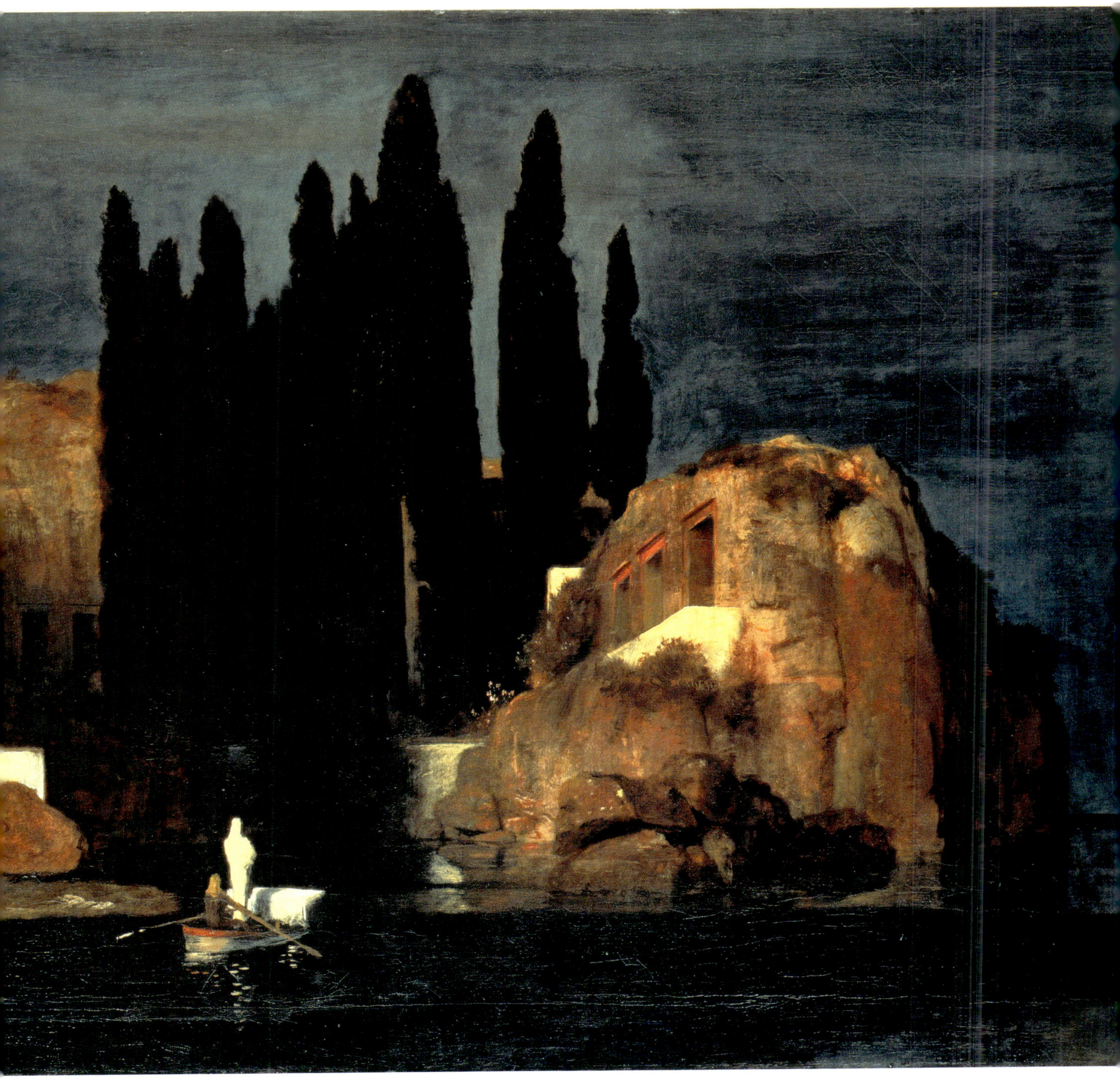

This present, first version of *The Isle of the Dead* was painted in 1880. Böcklin, who was born in Basle but who moved many times throughout his life, was at that time living in Florence. He was fifty-three years old and poor. His works were only just beginning to find acclaim. While Germany was still dominated by history painting, arriving from France were first reports of the Impressionists. Böcklin's mythological landscapes and figures, his sturdily painted fauns, centaurs, and mermaids, fell into neither of these categories, and his circle of admirers was still small. It included one Marie Berna, who was widowed young and who later married a Count Oriola in Büdesheim. She visited Böcklin in Florence and commissioned "a picture for daydreaming over".

The fact that the painting was commissioned by a woman, and that she expressly wanted something to daydream over, may simply be coincidence, but seems symptomatic of the upper middle classes of the day. Their situation is described in the novels of Theodor Fontane, the sharp-eyed observer of Wilhelmine society. His Effi Briest was no particular lover of art, but was taken to the Nationalgalerie in Berlin as a young girl to see Böcklin's *Elysian Fields*. (The work had hung there since 1878.) Effi's fate: marriage at seventeen, affair with an officer, her husband kills her lover in a duel, Effi is cast out by her husband and parents and dies. The novel appeared in 1894.

Fontane's Effi falls for the officer because she is bored as a housewife. She has nothing to do. Her house and children are looked after by domestic staff, and any latent intellectual interests she may have are never awakened. She waits for her husband to come home, plays the piano, goes for walks, and endeavours to lose herself in daydreams. Her parents know "there was nothing she loved more than gentle daydreaming, free from care".

Although Effi at times considered her daydreaming a sin, she liked doing it; what she didn't appreciate was how much she was lured into it by her middle-class society. For all but a tiny facet of the real world was closed to her. Political and social affairs were considered unpleasant. Only men were allowed to engage in such things. Nor was it considered proper for a woman of her class to work. Even after Effi has been cast out, she keeps a maidservant who continues to do everything for her. For women of the upper classes, denied the experience of reality, there remained little other than the world of the imagination, little else but to escape into dreams. Art thereby provided them with a welcome point of departure.

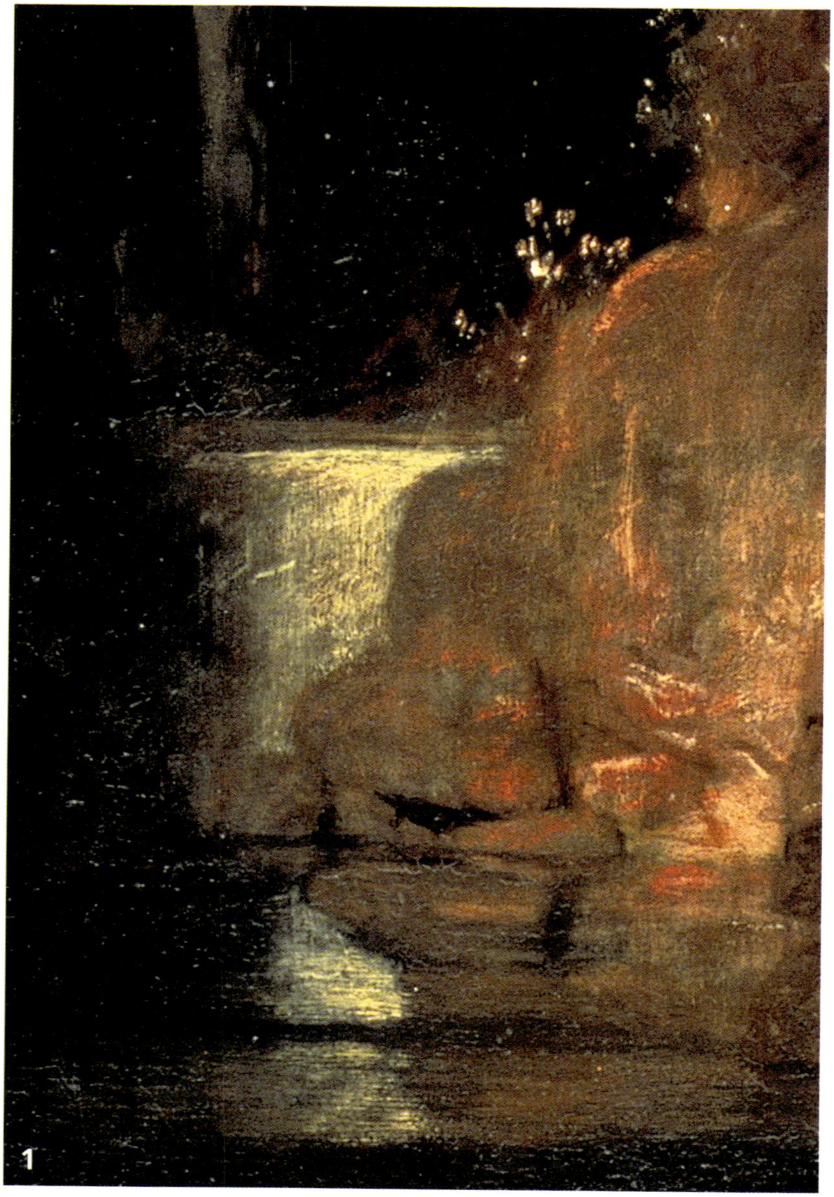
1

Lost in a daydream

Yearning for the South

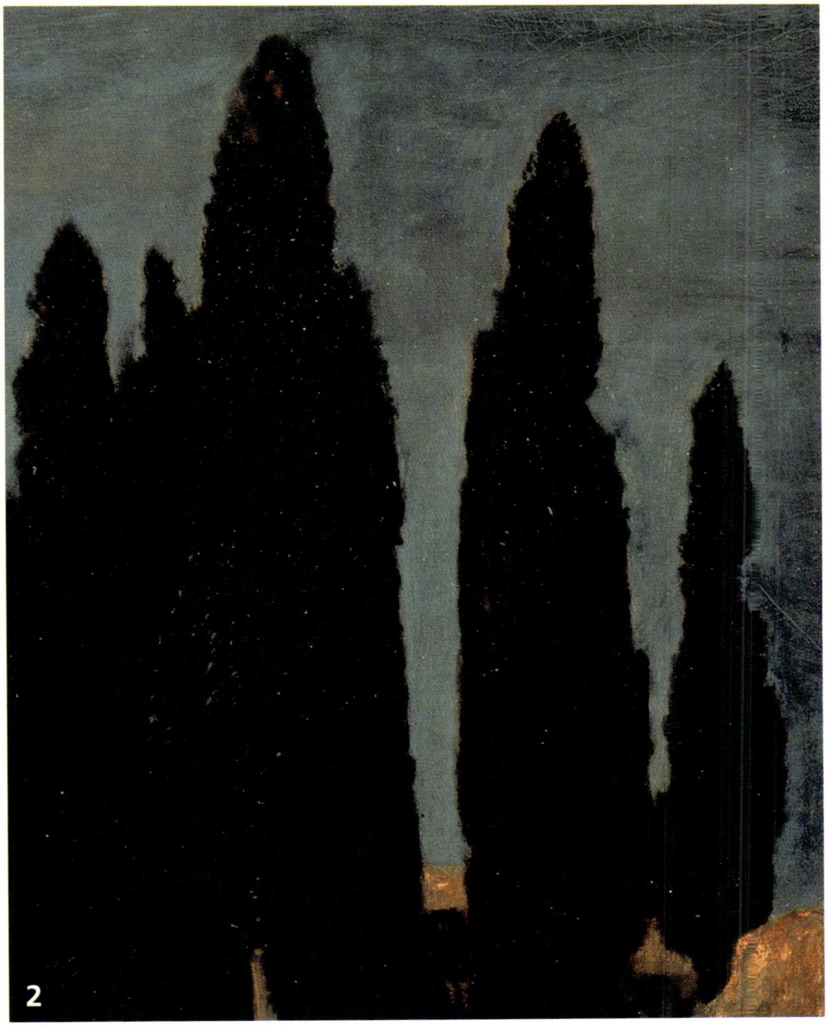

2

The centre of the composition is dominated by towering cypresses, trees that stand in almost every cemetery in southern Europe. They were planted beside temples even in antiquity. Apollo, the god of Light, is supposed to have turned a youth into a flame-shaped cypress, and gods of the underworld were also connected with the tree. Its symbolic character is ambiguous: evergreen and long-lived, it serves as a symbol both of life and of eternity after death.

The Florentines like to claim that Böcklin took his inspiration from their English cemetery with its long rows of cypresses, while in Montenegro it is said that a small island in the bay of Kotor served as Böcklin's model. The same is alleged of the fortress of Alfonso of Aragon outside Ischia, and Böcklin is certainly known to have visited Ischia in 1879, just a year before he painted the first version of *The Isle of the Dead*. Whatever the case, the motif is typical of southern Europe, and this fact undoubtedly contributed to its extraordinary popularity.

For people in Germany had always dreamed of the South, of the crucible of classical culture, and of the paradise of easier living it seemed to represent. And since the middle of the 19th century, they had been able to experience it for themselves. Up until then, those who had visited Italy were first and foremost young members of the aristocracy on their grand cultural tours of Europe, along with artists and art lovers willing to endure the hardships of travelling lengthy sections on foot and by horse and carriage. Women remained at home. The situation changed only with the advent of the railways.

In the second half of the 19th century, a network of railway track was laid down across the whole of Europe. Luxury hotels sprang up in every major town and city, travel agencies were founded, and a new strata of society started to travel to far-away places. They included Fontane's Effi Briest. Her parents had never seen the South, but on her honeymoon she travelled as far Capri and Sorrento. And when, at the end of her short life, she fell ill, the doctor declared: "We'll get [her temperature] down again, and then she must go to Switzerland or Menton." Trips to the South had become normal. As a consequence, paintings employing southern motifs began to assume a different function. For more and more people they became souvenirs, enduring mementoes in an age without photography. Pictures incorporating the most characteristic features of Mediterranean islands – cypresses, rocks, and classical-style gateways – held a particular appeal in this respect.

But it was not just this love of the South that made such paintings more popular, but also a new desire for Nature. Industrialization was causing the cities to grow, as people flocked from the countryside to find jobs in the ever increasing numbers of factories. In 1870 two thirds of Germans were still living in rural communities, with one third living in cities. By 1910 that ratio had been reversed.

Other than in earlier centuries, those living in the cities no longer owned fields and gardens outside the city walls. Not only was the population simply too big, but it was no longer the fashion. The bourgeoisie lived an emphatically urban life in dark rooms behind heavy curtains, constricted by their corsets, stiff collars, and social rules. Nature was only permitted on excursions and in flowerpots and picture frames – at least until the emergence, around the turn of the century, of the Wandervogel ("rolling stones") movement, made up of young middle-class Germans who, clad in light clothing and carrying guitars, set off out of the cities to walk in the fields and woods.

Coffin or urn – a contemporary issue

The subject of burial, however far back in time it may seem in Böcklin's painting, was in fact a current one. It was being discussed in connection with what was then a new word – crematorium. According to an issue of *Westermanns Illustrirten Deutschen Monatsheften* of 1875, "whether to be cremated or buried in the traditional way has, for the past few years, been one of the questions of the day, indeed, apart from politics and the Church, one of the most urgent questions facing a century transforming itself in every area". Three years later, Germany's first legally approved crematorium opened in Gotha. It was built by Siemens. In 1896 Böcklin's own birthplace of Basle even held a referendum on the issue, in which cremation was approved by the smallest of majorities.

There was a history to the debate surrounding cremation. For the past one hundred years or so, there had been much fear surrounding the vapours given off by decomposing bodies. They were reputed to spread epidemics. Graves became "plague pits of horror", cemeteries "birthplaces of decay". The municipal authorities responded by creating graveyards outside the city boundaries. But the cities grew and swallowed up the cemeteries, and they had to be moved even further away. The new railways made this possible: in London, a special Cemetery station was built next to Waterloo station, providing a direct rail link to Woking cemetery twenty-five miles away.

In the second half of the 19th century, however, the mood changed. In 1868 it was discussed in Paris whether to create a new cemetery thirty kilometres from the city centre. Here, too, a special "railway for the dead" was proposed. The majority was against it: "The idea that the dead should be transported by the dozen in railway trucks arouses the fury of the general public", a reader wrote to one editor; "they are obviously being treated like mere items of freight".

The Paris authorities rescued themselves from the dilemma by commissioning an investigation, designed to establish whether or not cemeteries were really harmful to the health. The conclusion: no. In the face of deep-rooted and largely irrational prejudices, however, it was hard for this latest finding to gain acceptance. Worries about "plague pits" did not disappear overnight and helped the cause of the crematorium lobby. Urns containing ashes were absolutely safe in terms of hygiene, it was argued, and could be housed in space-saving vaults within the city.

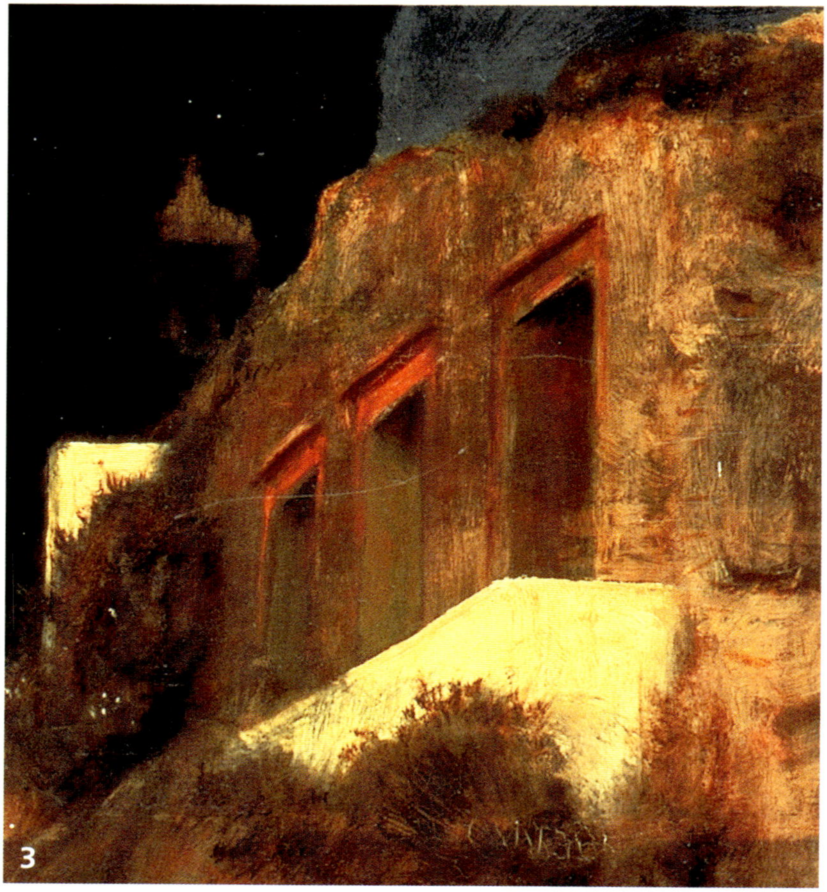
3

The spectre of industrialization appeared frequently in the burial debate. Some people rejected the prospect of corpses being carried by rail, others were against the idea of the "high-tech" crematorium. To many people, the rapid changes taking place in their cityscape and society seemed incompatible with the concepts of death and eternity. This may have been one of the reasons why those of them who often "day-dreamed" were happy to send their dead far away, to a beautiful landscape, away from the noise and dirt of the factories. For example, to an island somewhere in the South.

Böcklin not only locates his island geographically far from his German-Swiss public, but also sets it in a different time. "In the portrayal of his figures, Böcklin is supposed to have drawn upon an old Italian legend, according to which the dead person stepped into the coffin himself", wrote one earlier biographer. The standing figure might also be interpreted as an ancient priest; Böcklin leaves that open. The dark waters, which separate the realm of the living from that of the dead, evoke associations with Lethe, the river of oblivion, and the Styx, across which the dead were rowed by Charon, the ferryman. Böcklin painted him in a different picture. Names and images such as these, taken from Greek mythology, belonged to the standard repertoire of middle-class conversation.

To portray the transition from life to death as a gentle passage across water also corresponded to the tastes of the day. There is no reference to organ failure, no reference to physical decomposition. Matters relating to the body were simply not discussed in Wilhelmine – or indeed Victorian – society; everything below the waist, in particular, was taboo. This prudery and dislike of the physical body was carried over onto the dying and the dead. With the growing emphasis upon hygiene, noses had become more sensitive. Smells seemed harder to bear. Although the dying were not yet sent off to hospital, the circle of those present at their end grew smaller. Fontane, too, spares his readers Effi's death. She gives a slight cough, she runs a high temperature, and in the next chapter she already lies beneath the ground.

This revulsion at physical decomposition, at the process of putrefaction, spurred on the introduction of cremation and also gave rise to tomb statuary that would endure through the years. The memorials grew ever more elaborate, ever more emotional: marble angels raise the dead aloft, children embrace their mother, families weep for their father – in stone or metal, the body became eternal. Tomb art thereby served to suppress the aspects of death that no one wanted to think about.

In the 18th century cemeteries were viewed with horror or indifference. In the 19th century they became destinations for visitors, places of meditation. Even for Effi Briest, when she was still alive: "Here everything was in bloom, butterflies fluttered over the graves ... It was so quiet and so beautiful." She said: "I like visiting churchyards."

Like the tombstones of his day, Böcklin, too, transfigures the reality of death and decay. He also suggests the idea of life continuing after death. One of his admirers, a Professor Victor Widmann, conveyed this notion in verses written on the occasion of Böcklin's death. "A boat glides towards the Isle of Death / Its approach is watched by spirit eyes / and spirits wait to receive it." The dead are thus not dead at all; they live on as spirits, greeting the artist with singing. "Floating up to the treetop / from the calm harbour, the dark gateway, / a faint song, a majestic choir." At the end of the song there is mention of dreaming. The spirits are thereby speaking not to the viewer of the picture, however, but to Böcklin himself. They call to him: "Dream in your shade's body! / And from now on the world remains outside! / Illuminated by the radiance of your beauty."

Lethe, Styx, and a beautiful death

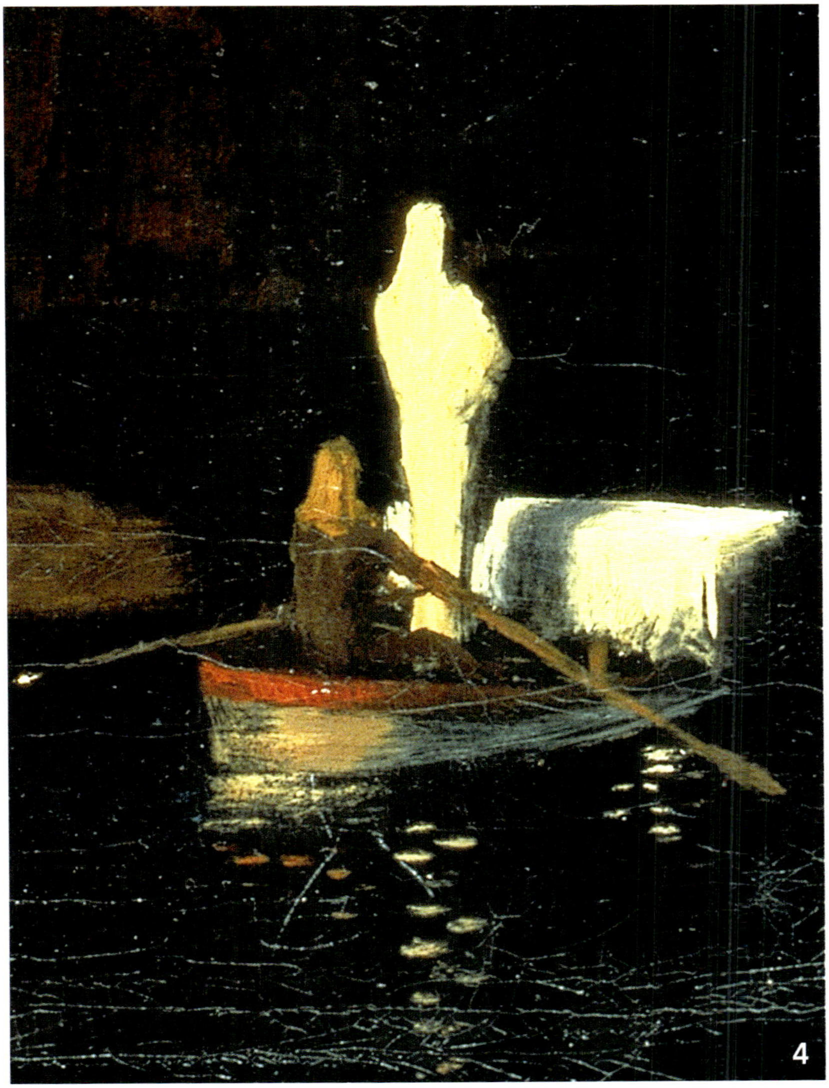

4

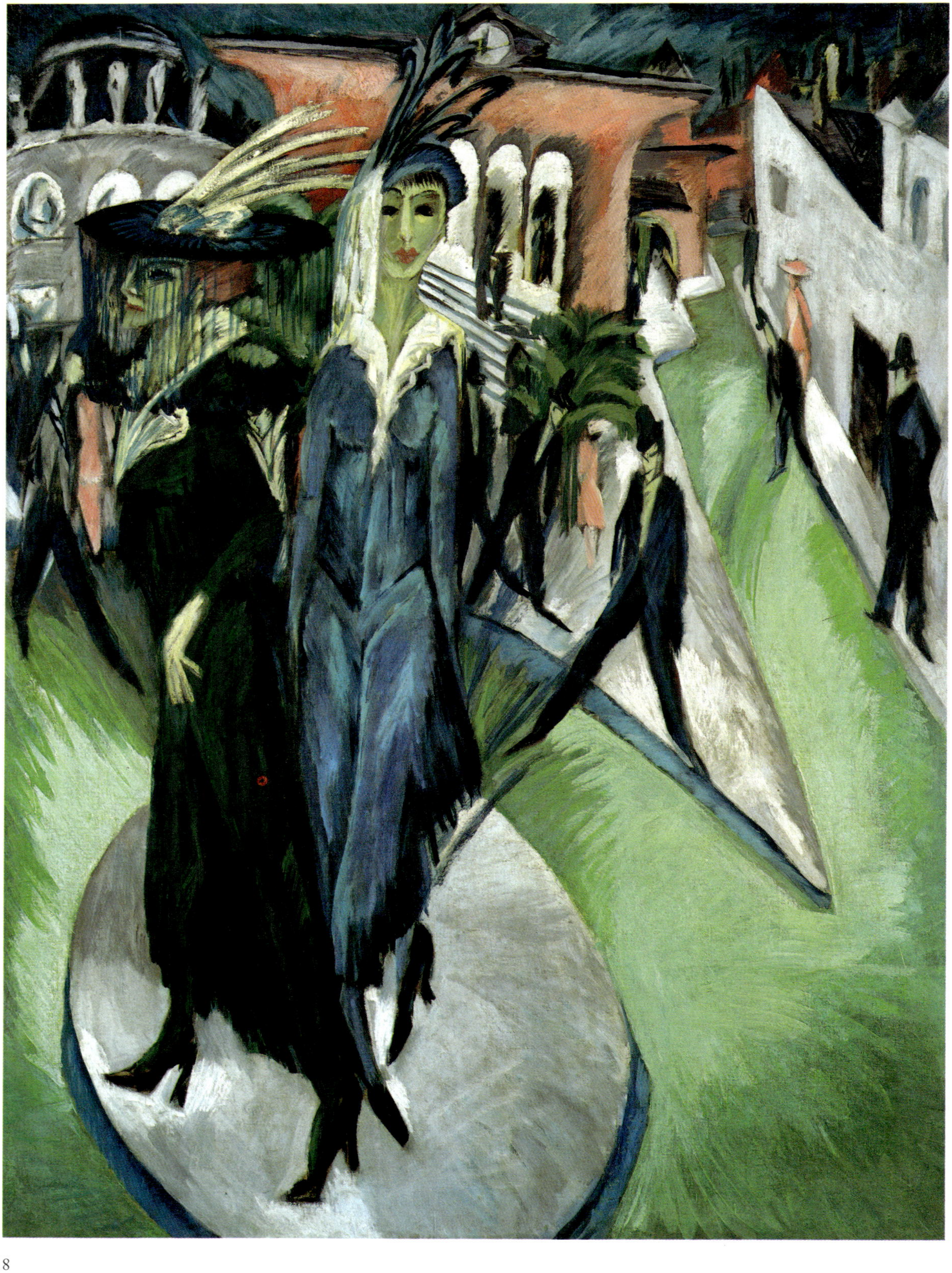

Ernst Ludwig Kirchner: Potsdamer Platz, 1914

The world is out of joint

The two women in the foreground confront the viewer in almost life size. The one in the blue dress is walking directly towards us. The other – exiting the painting to the left – cuts across her path. They almost collide. The men behind them are all darkly clad; they step out with legs apart and heads and upper bodies bent forward at more or less the same angle. In their uniformity, they resemble industrial products, robots, toys.

Although, as viewers, we face the women in this two-metre-high canvas at eye level, we see the ground on which they are standing from a much higher viewpoint. A dual perspective. As if the figures are walking across a sloping floor. The pavements and the pedestrian island are like grey slabs that have been slid over a green road surface. The red building at the top of the picture is crooked. The clock on its roof says twelve. The sky is dark – midnight. A square seems to have come out of joint.

Ernst Ludwig Kirchner painted the picture in 1914. It shows a corner of Potsdamer Platz in Berlin. He regularly sat and sketched the square from the sidewalk café lying opposite. This was not just any square, but the most heavily congested in the entire city. Five main streets and a stream of rail travellers converged upon it. A guidebook of 1910 states that it was crossed by some 5000 trams every day. Photos from the same era show horse-drawn omnibuses, hackney carriages, handcarts, and the first automobiles jostling alongside trams. "For foreigners, children, women, and the elderly", warned the guidebook, crossing Potsdamer Platz "could be hazardous to health and life".

Nowhere in Germany had such a concentration of people and vehicles ever been seen before, nor was any other city home to so many people as Berlin. In 1871 the seat of the Prussian monarchy had become the capital of the German Empire. Engineering and electrical works had made Berlin the leading centre of German industry. In 1871 it had a population of over 800,000; by 1914 this figure had swelled to well over two million. Anyone who was looking for work, who wanted to be modern, moved to Berlin – farm labourers who had lost their jobs to agricultural machinery, businessmen in search of better deals, journalists and artists who sensed that developments were unfolding faster here than in Dresden, Munich, or Hamburg. Kirchner had been living in Berlin since 1911.

As the two hands of the clock converge vertically upon twelve, we think of midnight and the witching hour, of figures from beyond the veil or the beginning of something radically new. With the benefit of hindsight, we know that 1914 and the outbreak of the first of the catastrophic wars of the 20th century did indeed mark the start of a new era. It was something no one at that time could suspect, however, including Kirchner. As his writings reveal, he took little interest in the world of politics. He was fascinated only by what lay before his eyes, with what he experienced at first hand.

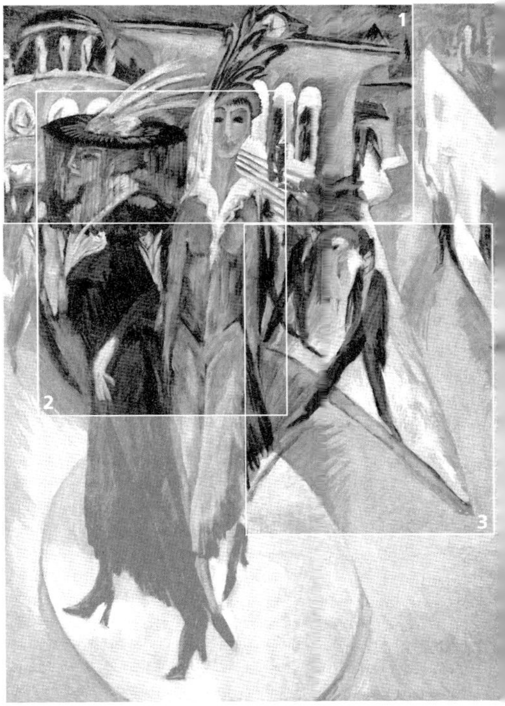

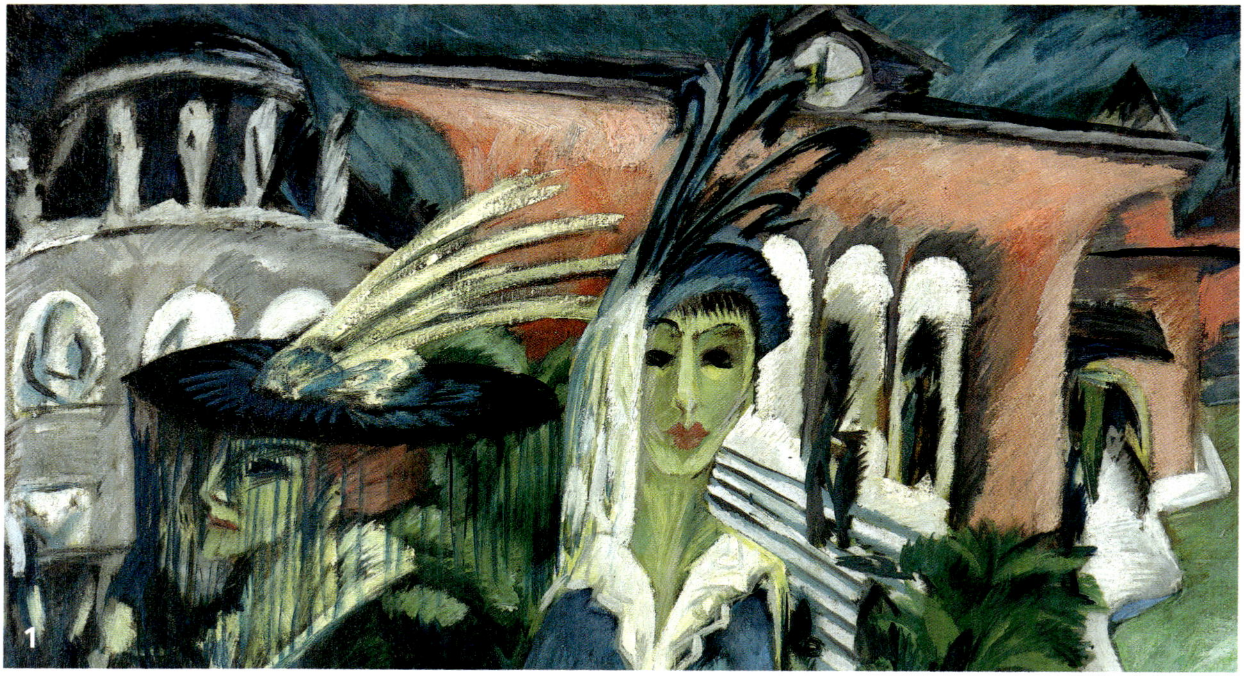

In the middle of the traffic

Railway stations in those days were hubs of activity, exerting a fascination matched at best by airports today. They were places where you could admire the latest means of high-speed transport, where guests of honour were welcomed with red carpet, a band, and an armed guard, where progressive technology was lent nobility through official pomp and circumstance. Potsdam Station was the oldest in Berlin. In 1872 it had been given a new terminal building with a façade designed to recall the Italian *palazzi* of the Renaissance. Kirchner takes away its side wings and upper loggias and allows the roof to sweep out over the walls.

To the left of the station, separated only by a street, stood a large building crowned with a cupola and statuary. It was completed in 1912, just two years before Kirchner captured it fleetingly on his canvas. A multi-purpose building, it housed a cinema, cabaret theatre, offices, and – most important of all – the Café Piccadilly, "the biggest coffee house in the world", which offered seating for 2000. Just a few steps away lay the Wertheim department store, which with its lavish interiors on several floors offered a new type of shopping experience. Everywhere new dimensions, spectacular inventions, greater numbers, fascinating for some, confusing and threatening for others.

Potsdamer Platz had evolved rather than been planned, and unlike major traffic intersections today, it was also a place where many people spent time. Flower sellers plied their trade on the pavements during the day, hotel guests looked down from their balconies, and friends met in a popular sidewalk café, where Kirchner also sat. There were restaurants, shops, a beer garden, and of course prostitutes in large numbers – all of them together making Potsdamer Platz a centre of encounters and entertainment, especially at night.

"Ach Willy, ach Willy, um sechs im Piccadilly" ("Oh Willy, oh Willy, at six in the Piccadilly") began a light-hearted song in these increasingly dark times. It was not the Piccadilly for long. In 1914, with patriotism running high following the outbreak of war, the management changed the name to Café Vaterland (Café Fatherland). Since Kirchner began his painting in the spring and finished it in the autumn, his café could call itself by both names.

The two buildings through which Kirchner identifies his location have long since disappeared. In 1945 they were bombed and burnt out; all that remained of the cupola was its steel skeleton. The rooms beneath were used for makeshift accommodation. Now finding itself on the boundary between the Allied sectors, the Vaterland acquired a dubious reputation as a hideout for black marketeers.

The ruins of the Vaterland and the station were removed in the 1950s. The border dividing East and West Berlin now ran straight across Potsdamer Platz – and when it became a wall, the formerly bustling centre of urban life and transport was transformed into a wasteland. It was patrolled on one side by East German police while, on the other, the citizens of West Berlin climbed up onto a wooden platform and stared over the wall. The fate of a very German square.

The same site today shares only its geographical location and name with the Potsdamer Platz of old. Where Kirchner paints a grey wall on the right-hand edge of the picture, the offices of the Daimler-Chrysler company now rise. Where platforms and tracks once lay behind the terminal building, a park is under construction. Today the jostling traffic is that of diggers and trucks.

Prostitutes are everywhere in male fantasies

The two women beneath their tall feathered hats are, in Kirchner's words, *Kokotten*, cocottes. Women appear in many of his street scenes, but where he describes them more specifically, it is only ever as "cocottes". He never mentions their male customers. In his portrayals of such women, he was evidently thinking less of their profession than of casual, changing relationships. "Kokotte – Zeitfrau" ("cocotte – temporary woman") is a phrase jotted down in one of his sketchbooks.

He was at that time living with Erna Schilling. She and her sister Gerda had fled the family home and were earning their living, it appears, as dancers in cheap cabarets. They modelled for the artist. Although the two cocottes in *Potsdamer Platz* bear a certain resemblance to Erna and Gerda, the artist stylizes them and refuses to be specific.

Visions of free, unbridled love were in those days a common feature of male fantasies, and the notion of the prostitute as an ideal partner was not exclusive to Kirchner. The Berlin neurologist and writer Alfred Döblin celebrated the cocotte as a "pioneer of socialism in a moral wasteland". For Döblin, sex within marriage was "as if you were only allowed to be hungry at mealtimes and in certain restaurants".

Kirchner (1880–1938) and Döblin (1878–1957) were almost the same age and knew each other well. Kirchner painted the doctor's portrait and in 1913 furnished the woodcuts for his short drama *Comtess Mizzi*. This strange play celebrates free love: in the countess's "academy", female pupils are prepared for a sort of erotic temple service; they "are our sacred daughters ... their kissing mouths closed in prayer". At the end, the institute is stormed by the police. From here to *Berlin Alexanderplatz*, Döblin's masterpiece of 1929, it was still a long way.

Erotic fantasies such as Döblin's *Comtess Mizzi* were produced in vast quantities. Another such was called *Potsdamer Platz*, like Kirchner's painting, and was written by one Curt Corrinth. It tells the story of a young man from the provinces, who sees in Berlin's prostitutes the fairy princesses of his childhood. They become "Blessed Virgins of delight" who offer men "deliverance from the flesh". Kirchner was not unfamiliar with such sublimation of whores and the sexual act: his own cocottes reveal neither bosom nor leg nor wear a seductive smile; they walk like queens, look serious, recall temple servers at the altar, resemble hetaerae sooner than whores.

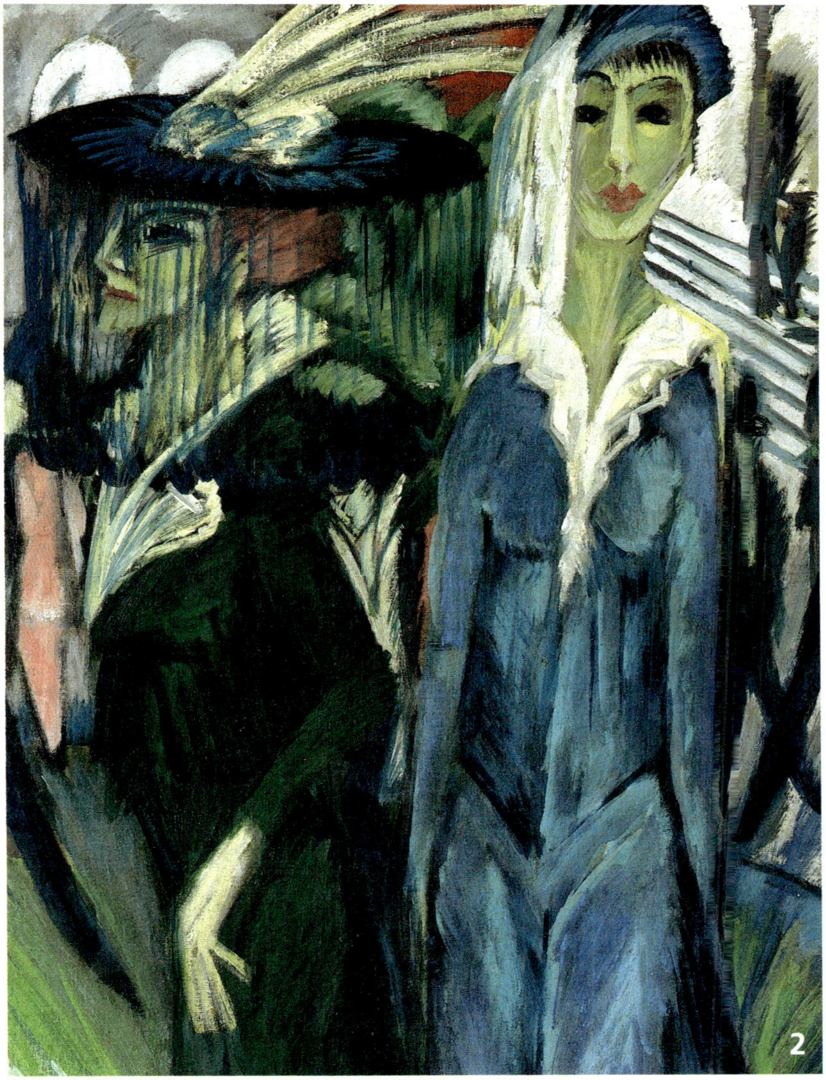

2

There were practical reasons for this display of severity, however. Prostitutes were required to be unobtrusive. According to a Berlin police regulation of 1911, it was forbidden "to stand or walk about in an indecent manner" or to proposition anyone directly. "Standing and sitting in doorways is also prohibited." Plainly clothed police officers made sure the city's prostitutes towed the line. Following the outbreak of war, it is said, many dressed themselves as widows, with a veil and black dress, in the hope that sympathy would win them extra trade.

Kirchner was called up in the spring of 1915. Military service was too much for him; he had a nervous breakdown and after a few weeks was released, "hardly able to walk". But he continued to paint. He portrayed himself as a recruit of the 75th field artillery regiment, his forehead concealed by his uniform cap, his cheeks sunken, a cigarette hanging from his lips. He would later suffer the effects of nicotine poisoning and drug abuse. He paints himself with a bloody stump for an arm, afraid of not being able to work any more, of perhaps being impotent. What does he want with the naked woman in the background? "I myself am now like the cocottes I painted. Wiped out; next time, finished."

It is a desperate, defeatist self-portrait – painted at a time when defending the fatherland was the only honourable activity for a man. Kirchner, the outsider, was born on 6 May 1880 in Aschaffenburg and was 34 years old when war broke out. He had studied architecture at his father's insistence, but had secretly attended art college at the same time. In Dresden in 1905 he and a group of friends founded Die Brücke (The Bridge), an association of impoverished artists with similar aims. They wanted to turn their backs on "the well-regarded older masters" and claim freedom in both their art and their lifestyles. That meant combating establishment art with their joint portfolios of graphic works and also developing their own, bohemian lifestyle. Kirchner lived with a succession of girlfriends in cave-like ateliers amongst furniture he had carved himself. His photographic series reveal a yearning for naked companionship.

In 1911, like many other painters and writers, he moved to Berlin, the new Babylon, the all-consuming Moloch. After his military service and nervous breakdown, friends helped him find refuge in Davos. He would stay there for the rest of his life, looked after by his Berlin girlfriend Erna Schilling, permanently under the doctors' care, pursued by panic attacks and paranoia. His former urge for freedom twisted itself into the delusion that everyone was his enemy. He felt no one understood him; his mistress lived so far beneath him that even she was unable to reach him.

Sales of his works were curtailed by external circumstances, such as the inflation which followed the end of the war, the global economic crisis of 1929 and Hitler's seizure of power in 1933. How much he nevertheless managed to sell to public collections is revealed by the number of his works impounded by the Nazis – over 600. 32 of them were included in the 1937 *Degenerate Art* exhibition in Munich, where they were held up for public derision.

The following year, he shot himself. His mistress: "The defamation in Germany, coupled with the unsuccessful November exhibition in Basle, where he again attracted nothing but criticism, led him, on the beautiful, sunny morning of 15 November, to end his life. Thank God he shot himself clean through the heart so that he died instantly."

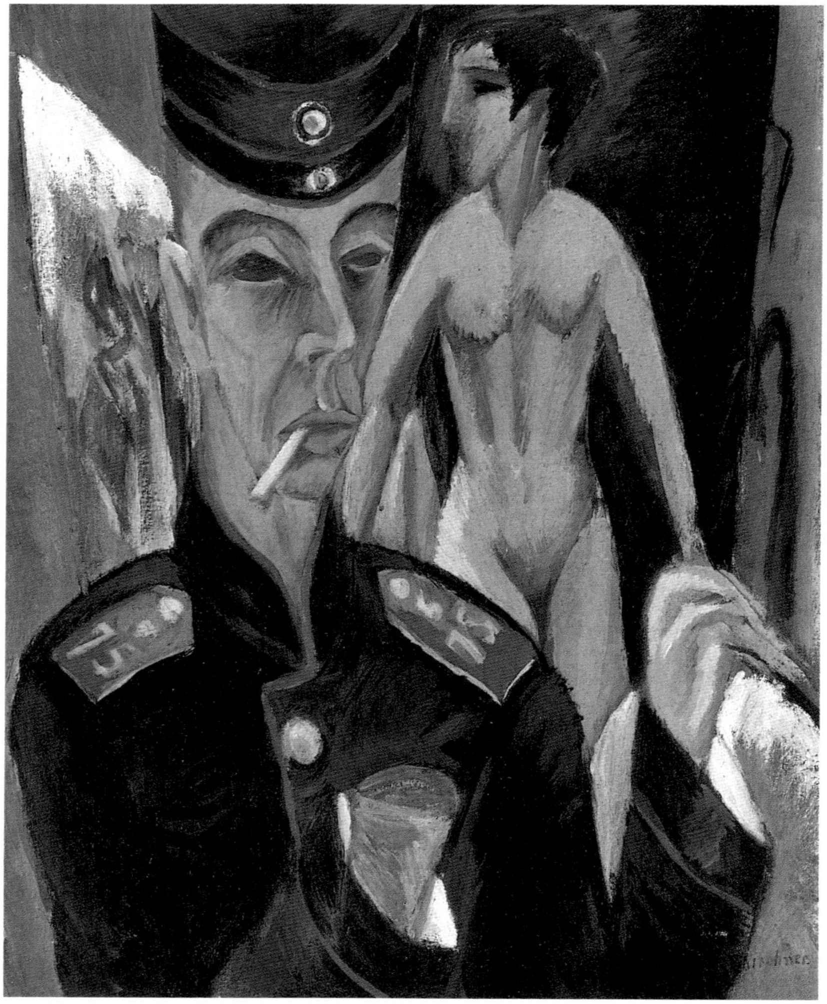

The army maims the artist

The Germans were late to discover the metropolis

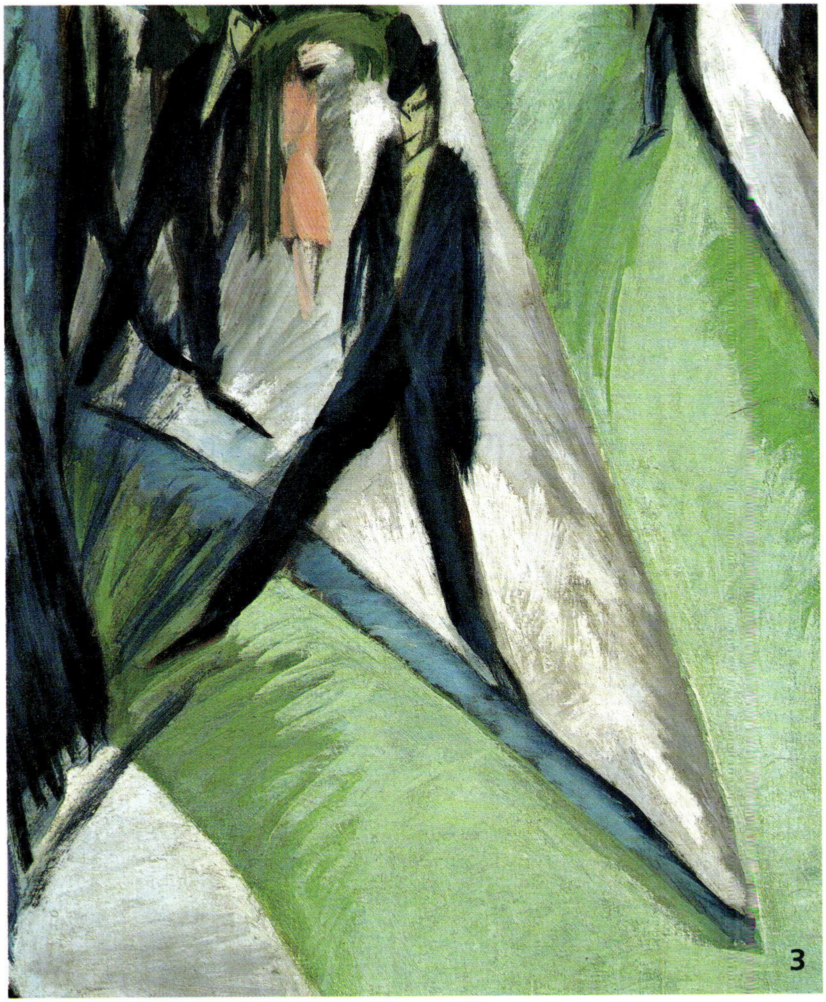

3

Kirchner lived in an era during which Europe's art disintegrated. For centuries painters had oriented themselves towards objects and how they appeared to the eye. That was now over. Figure and object were distorted, splintered, compressed into geometric forms, portrayed from several sides within a single plane. They were given strange colours, lost their three-dimensional shape or disappeared entirely into an abstract surface. Each stylistic tendency had its own name. Kirchner belonged to the Expressionists.

Over and over again he said that he didn't want to portray the world as it was, but how he experienced it. He may have had a practical reason: the demand for pictures of the real world could now be satisfied by photography, whose images could be mass-produced thanks to new printing techniques. For Kirchner, the outer world was simply a starting-point: "shapes and colours spring from the imagination of the artist."

Colours in his works rarely correspond to those of the object in real life: his kerbstones are blue, the station glows red, the road surface changes from a stronger green to a mixed yellow. This liberation of colour from its object was typical not just of Expressionist painters, but also of Expressionist writers, who spoke of "black silence", "silver coolness", and "vapours in every colour of the rainbow". The idea, suggested by some, that the green street might be intended symbolically, perhaps as a reference to the banishment of nature, does not mesh with Kirchner's aesthetic. He was concerned with expressing what life in the metropolis felt like. Judging solely by the colour combinations in *Potsdamer Platz*, there seems to be an unfriendliness, an uneasiness about the city, far removed from the feast for the eyes prepared by the Berlin Impressionists.

Dominant amongst the shapes are the circle of the pedestrian island and the pointed wedge of the pavement. Curves and acute angles are in fact repeated throughout the composition – the latter in the splayed legs of the men and the angular profile of the woman in black, the former in the arches of the building and in the face of the woman in blue. While curves suggest a pleasing, peaceful quality, acute angles are rather more aggressive, especially when pointing towards the viewer. Kirchner thereby formulates contradictory experiences.

He does the same in his figures. They are hurrying to and fro, seemingly in constant motion, but pass each other with their eyes cast down or averted to one side. Their arms appear atrophied or as if grown fast to their body, and their hands are not free to touch each other. The residents of Kirchner's Berlin neither see nor feel each other; they pass each other's lives by. Perhaps the enigmatic expression on the face of the woman advancing towards the artist and viewer offers the only option, short-term happiness: "Wiped out; next time, finished."

Industrialization and the metropolis were already being explored by French artists and novelists in the 19th century, while their neighbours to the east were still "lingering over sunrises and gooseherds", as Döblin put it. The Germans only woke up to such themes in the 20th century, following the explosion in Berlin's population. It is no coincidence, therefore, that the two outstanding works about the German metropolis, Döblin's *Alexanderplatz* and Kirchner's *Potsdamer Platz*, should bear the names of Berlin squares as their titles. The painting today hangs just a few hundred yards from the place after which it is named, in the Neue Nationalgalerie, Potsdamer Strasse, Berlin.

Appendix

Anonymous
From the Papyrus of Ani, c. 1300 BC
Sheets 3 and 4 of a papyrus roll,
38 x 2379 cm (total length)
London, British Museum

Lit.: Hornung, Erich (ed.): Das Totenbuch der Ägypter, Zurich/Munich 1979. – Suche nach Unsterblichkeit, Totenkult und Jenseitsglaube im Alten Ägypten, catalogue, Roemer und Pelizaeus Museum, Hildesheim 1990. – Kees, Hermann: Totenglaube und Jenseitsvorstellungen der Alten Ägypter, Berlin 1977.

Anonymous
The Empress Theodora with her Retinue, c. 547 BC
Ravenna, Basilica di San Vitale

Lit.: Bridge, Anthony: Theodora, Portrait in a Byzantine Landscape, London 1978. – Diehl, Charles: Théodora, Impératrice de Byzance, Paris 1904/1937. – Diehl, Charles: Byzance, Grandeur et Décadence, Paris 1919. – Ebersolt, I.: Les arts somptuaires de Byzance, Paris 1923.

Limburg Brothers (1385/1390–c. 1416)
Paul, Jean, Herman Limburg
Miniature for the month of January
from the Très Riches Heures of the
Duke of Berry,
c. 1415, 29 x 21 cm
Chantilly, Musée Condé

Lit.: Cazelles, Raymond and Longnon, Jean: The Très Riches Heures de Jean, Duke of Berry, New York 1969. – Contamine, Philippe: La vie quotidienne pendant la guerre de Cent Ans, Paris 1976. – Defourneaux, Marcelin: La vie quotidienne au temps de Jeanne d'Arc, Paris 1957. – Durrieu, Paul: Les petits chiens du Duc de Berry, in: Comptes rendus de l'Académie des Inscriptions et Belles Lettres, Paris 1909. – Lehoux, Françoise: Jean de France, Duc de Berry, 4 vols, Paris 1966/70. – Meiss, Millard: French Painting in the Time of Jean de Berry, London 1967.

Robert Campin (c. 1375–1444)
The Mérode Triptych (The Mouse-trap Annunciation), c. 1422/1430
64 x 120 cm
New York, Metropolitan Museum of Art (Cloisters)

Lit.: Châtelet, Albert: Le maître de Flémalle, la fascination du quotidien, Antwerp 1996. – Lecat, Jean-Philippe: Quand flamboyait la Toison d'or, Paris 1982. – Kemperdick, Stephan: Der Meister von Flémalle, Die Werkstatt Robert Campins und Roger van der Weyden, Turnhout 1997. – Shapiro, Meyer: Muscipula Diaboli, The Symbolism of the Mérode Altarpiece, in: The Art Bulletin, no. 27, 1945, pp. 182ff. – Thürlemann, Felix: Robert Campin, Das Mérode-Triptychon, Frankfurt a.M. 1997.

Hubert van Eyck (c. 1370–1426)
Jan van Eyck (c. 1390–1441)
The Adoration of the Lamb, 1432
134.3 x 237.5 cm
Ghent, Katedraal St Bravo

Lit.: Assmann, Erwin: Godeschalcus und Visio Godeschalci, Neumünster 1979. – Dhanens, Elisabeth: Hubert et Jan van Eyck, Anvers 1980. – Fris, Victor: Histoire de Gand, Brussels 1913. – Prevenier, Walter and Blockmans, Wim: Die burgundischen Niederlande, Weinheim 1986. – Schneider, Norbert: Jan van Eyck: Der Genter Altar, Frankfurt a. M. 1986.

Jan van Eyck (c. 1390–1441)
The Arnolfini Marriage, 1434
82 x 60 cm
London, National Gallery

Lit.: Calmette, Joseph: Les Grands Ducs de Bourgogne, Paris 1949. – Davies, Martin: The National Gallery, London, Les Primitifs Flamands, Antwerp 1954.- Dhanens, Elisabeth: Van Eyck, Anvers 1980. – Lejeune, Jean: Documents mémoires commissions: Jaen et Margarethe van Eyck et le Roman des Arnolfini, Liège 1972. -Mirot, L. and Lazzareschi, E.: Un mercante di Lucca in Fiandra, in: Bolletino Storico Lucchese XII, 1940. – Panofsky, Erwin: Early Netherlandish painting, Cambridge, Mass. 1953. – Roover, Raymond de: The rise and fall of the Medici Bank, Cambridge, Mass. 1963. – Schabacker, Peter H.: De Matrimonio ad morganaticam contracta. Jan van Eyck's Arnolfini portrait reconsidered, in: The Art Quarterly, no. 35, 1972. – Swaan, Wim: Kunst und Kultur der Spätgotik, Freiburg 1978.

Paolo Uccello (c. 1397–1475)
The Battle of San Romano, c. 1435
182 x 319 cm
London, National Gallery

Lit.: Burckhardt, Jacob: Die Kultur der Renaissance in Italien, Zurich 1956. – Defourneaux, Marcelin: La vie quotidienne au temps de Jeanne d'Arc, Paris 1957. – Griffiths, Gordon: The political significance of Uccello's Battle of San Romano, in: Journal of the Warburg and Courtauld Institutes, vol. 41, 1978. – Pope-

Henessy, John: Paolo Uccello, Paintings and Drawings, London 1969. – Trease, Geoffrey: The Soldiers of Fortune, New York 1971.

Jean Fouquet (1415/22–1446)
The Melun Diptych, c. 1456
Left wing: Etienne Chevalier mit dem heiligen Stephanus
93 x 85 cm, Berlin, Staatliche Museen
Right wing: Maria und Kind,
91.8 x 83.3 cm,
Antwerp, Museum voor Schone Kunsten.

Accompanying illustration: enamel bearing the signature "Johnes Fouquet" and a self-portrait, Paris, Musée du Louvre

Lit.: Defourneaux, Marcelin: La vie quotidienne au temps de Jeanne d'Arc, Paris 1957. – Erlanger, Philippe: Charles VII et son mystère, Paris 1945. – Huizinga, Johan: The Autumn of the Middle Ages. London (?) 1919. – Schaefer, Claude: Jean Fouquet. An der Schwelle zur Renaissance. Dresden 1994. – Vale, Malcolm G. A.: Charles VII, Berkeley/Los Angeles 1974.

Antonello da Messina (1430–1479)
St Jerome, 1460/1475
46 x 37 cm
London, National Gallery

Lit.: Howell, Jolly Penny: Jan van Eyck and St Jerome. A study of Eyckian influence on Colantonio and Antonello da Messina in Quattrocento Naples, dissertation, University of Pensylvania 1976. – Ritterbos, Bernhard: Saint and Symbol. Images of Saint Jerome in early Italian art, Groningen 1984.- Salvo, Carmen: Giurati, Feudatari, Mercadanti – L'elite urbana a Messina nell' Medioevo e Età Moderna, Rome 1995. – Scascia, Leonardo and Manedel, Gabriele: Das Gesamtwerk von Antonello da Messina (in the series "Klassiker der Kunst"), Lucerne/Stuttgart/Vienna 1987.

Hans Memling (c. 1433–1494)
The Passion, c. 1470/71,
55 x 90 cm
Turin, Galleria Sabauda

Lit.: Calmette, Joseph: Les Grands Ducs de Bourgogne, Paris 1949. – Corti, Maria and Faggin, Giorgio T.: Das Gesamtwerk von Memling, Lucerne, undated (original edition Milan 1969). – Ennen, Edith: Die europäische Stadt des Mittelalters, Göttingen 1972. -Gilliat-Smith, Ernest: The story of Bruges, London 1901, reprinted Nendeln 1971. -Roover, Raymond de: The rise and decline of the Medici Bank, Cambridge, Mass. 1963.

Antonio del Pollaiuolo (1432–1498)
Piero del Pollaiuolo (ca. 1441–ca. 1496)
The Martyrdom of St Sebastian, 1475
292 x 203 cm
London, National Gallery

Lit: Boccaccio, Giovanni: Il Decamerone, Milan 1955. – Darriulat, Jacques: Sébastien le Renaissant – Sur le martyre de saint Sébastien dans la deuxième moitié du Quattrocento, Paris 1995. – Kent, Francis William: Household and lineage in Renaissance Florence – The family life of the Capponi, Ginori and Ruccellai, Princeton 1977. – Lightbown, Ronald: Sandro Botticelli, Munich 1988. – Rocke, Michael: Forbidden friendships: Homosexuality and Male Culture in Renaissance Florence, New York 1996. – Vasari, Giorgio: Leben der augezeichneten Maler und Baumeister, Stuttgart Tübingen, 1843. – Voragine, Jacobus de: Legenda aurea, Heidelberg 1979.

Sandro Botticelli (1445–1510)
(Alessandro di Mariano Filipepi)
The Adoration of the Magi, c. 1475
111 x 134 cm
Florence, Galleria degli Uffizi

Lit.: Hatfield, Rab: Botticelli's Uffizi Adoration – A study in political content, Princeton 1976. – Lightbown, Ronald: Sandro Botticelli, Life and Work, London 1979. – Lucas-Dubreton, J.: La vie quotidienne à Florence au temps des Médicis, Paris 1958. – Roover, Raymond de: Rise and decline of the Medici Bank 1397–1494, Cambridge, Mass. 1965. – Thiébaut, Dominique: Botticelli, Cologne 1992.

Ercole de' Roberti (c. 1450–1496)
Lorenzo Costa (1460–1535)
The Ship of the Argonauts, c. 1480/1490
46 x 53 cm
Padua, Musei Civici

Lit.: Chledowsky, Casimir von: Der Hof von Ferrara, Munich 1921. – Ferino-Pagden, Sylvia: Isabella d'Este. La Prima Donna del Mondo, Vienna 1994. – Gundersheimer, Werner L.: Ferrara, The style of a Renaissance Despotism. Princeton 1973. – La Corte di Ferrara e il suo mecenatismo (The court of Ferrara and its Patronage), conference proceedings, Copenhagen 1990. – Lauts, Jan: Isabella d'Este, Hamburg 1952. – Da Bellini al Tintoretto, catalogue, Musei Civici, Padua 1992. – Schubring, Paul: Truhen und Truhenbilder der italienischen Führenaissance, Leipzig 1923.

Hieronymus Bosch (c. 1450–1516)
The Ship of Fools, 1480/1516
56 x 32 cm
Paris, Musée du Louvre

Lit.: Adhémar, Hélène: Le Musée National du Louvre, vol. 1, Les Primitifs Flamands, Brussels 1962. – Brant, Sebastian: Das Narrenschiff, ed. by Friedrich Zarncke, Darmstadt 1973. – Dörner, Klaus: Bürger und Irre, Frankfurt 1969. – Foucault, Michel: Histoire de la Folie, Paris 1961. – Kirchhoff, Theodor: Grundriß einer Geschichte der deutschen Irrenpflege, Berlin 1890. – Lefebre, Joel: Les fols et la folie, Paris 1968. -Lurker, Manfred: Der Baum in Glauben und Kunst, Baden-Baden 1962. – Tolnay, Charles de: Hieronymus Bosch, Baden-Baden 1973.

Gentile Bellini (1429–1507)
St Mark preaching at Alexandria,
1504–1507
347 x 770 cm
Milan, Pinacoteca di Brera

Brown, Patricia Fontini: Venetian narrative painting in the age of Carpaccio, New Haven 1988. – Humfrey, Peter: The Bellinesque Life of St Marc cycle for the Scuola Grande de San Marco in Venice in its original arrangement, in Zeitschrift für Kunstgeschichte, Berlin 1985. – Meyer zu Capelle, Jürgen: Gentile Bellini, Stuttgart 1988. – Müller-Wiener, Martha: Eine Stadtgeschichte Alexandrias, Berlin 1992. – Pastoureau, Michel: Bleu, Histoire d'une couleur, Paris 2000.

Giorgione (c. 1477–1510)
The Tempest, c. 1507
82 x 73 cm
Venice, Galleria dell' Accademia

Lit.: Anderson, Jaynie: Giorgione, Paris/New York 1997. – Molmenti, Pompeo: La Storia di Venezia nella Vita Privata, Bergamo 1905-8, reprinted Triest 1973, vol. 2. – Pignatti, Teresio and Pedrocco, Filippo: Giorgione, Milan 1999. – Rapp, Jürgen: Die "Favola" in Giorgiones "Gewitter", in: Bruckmanns Pantheon, Internationale Jahreszeitschrift für Kunst. International Art Journal, Revue Annuelle Internationale d'Art, LVI 1998, p. 44 ff. – Settis, Salvatore: La Tempesta interpretata, Giorgione, i committenti, il sogetto, Turin 1978

Vittore Carpaccio (c. 1460–1625/5)
St George and the Dragon, 1502/1507
141 x 360 cm
Venice, Scuola di San Giorgio degli Schiavoni

Lit.: Braunfels-Esche, Sigrid: St. Georg, Legende, Verehrung, Symbol, Munich 1976. – Brown, Patricia F.: Venetian narrative painting in the age of Carpaccio, New Haven 1988. – Catalogue: Venezia e la peste, Venice 1970. – Lauts, Jan: Carpaccio, Gemälde und Zeichnungen, Cologne 1962. – Perocco, Guido: Carpaccio nella Scuola di San Giorgio degli Schiavoni, Venice 1964. – Schöpf, Hans: Fabeltiere, Graz 1988.

Lucas Cranach the Elder (1472–1553)
The Martyrdom of St Catherine, c. 1508
112 x 85 cm
Budapest, Ráday Collection of the Reformed Church

Lit.: Blaschke, Karlheinz: Wittenberg – die Lutherstadt, Berlin 1977. – Brockhoff, Evamaria, Erichsen, Johannes and Grimm, Claus, eds.: Lucas Cranach, Ein Maler-Unternehmen aus Franken, catalogue to the exhibition in Kronach, Augsburg 1994. – Hinz, Berthold: Lucas Cranach. d. Ä., Reinbek 1983. – Pastoureau, Michel: L'étoffe du diable, une histoire des rayures et des tissus rayés, Paris 1991. – Tacke, Andreas: Der katholische Cranach, Mainz 1992.

Pinturicchio (c. 1454–1513)
(Bernardino di Betto)
Penelope and the Suitors, 1509
125 x 152 cm
London, National Gallery

Lit.: Burckhardt, Titus: Siena, Stadt der Jungfrau, Olten/Lausanne 1961. – Carli, Enzo: Il Pintoricchio (sic), Milano 1960. – Davies Martin: The National Gallery complete illustrated catalogue, London 1995. – Rovick, Patricia: The Odyssey Fresco by Pinturicchio, in: Australian Journal of Art vol VII, 1988, p. 64 ff.. – Schulz, J.: Pinturicchio and the revival of Antiquity, in: Journal of the Warburg and Courtauld Institutes, vol. 25, London 1962.

Matthias Grünewald
(1460/80–1528/1532)
The Nativity panels from the Isenheim Altar, 1512/1516
265 x 304 cm
Colmar, Musée d'Unterlinden

Lit.: Fraenger, Wilhelm: Matthias Grünewald, Munich 1983. – Lücking, Wolf: Matthis, Nachforschungen über Grünewald, Berlin 1983. – Reichenauer, Berta: Grünewald, Vienna 1992. – Seidel, Max: Mathis Gothard Nithart Grünewald, Der Isenheimer Altar, Stuttgart 1973.

Albrecht Dürer (1471–1528)
Melencholia I, 1514
24 x 19 cm
Berlin, Kupferstichkabinett der Staatlichen Sammlungen Preußischer Kulturbesitz, Hamburger Kunsthalle, Veste Coburg, etc.

Lit.: Anzelewsky, Fedja: Dürer, Werk und Wirkung, Stuttgart 1980. – Kilian, G. Werner: Eine Studie zu Dürers Melencolia, in: Wissenschaftliche Zeitschrift der Karl-Marx-Universität, Gesellschafts- und Sprachwissenschaftliche Reihe, vol. 4, Leipzig 1961. – Kirste, Hans: Albrecht Dürers Melencolia I, gesehen mit dem Auge eines Arztes, in: Die Medizinische, vol. 1, 1954, Stuttgart. – Lepenies, Wolf: Melancholie und Gesellschaft, Frankfurt a. M. 1969. – Panofsky, Erwin and Saxl, Fritz: Dürers Melencolia, Leipzig/Berlin 1923.

Niklaus Manuel Deutsch (1484–1530)
The Judgement of Paris, 1516/1528
223 x 160 cm
Basle, Kunstmuseum

Lit.: Beerli, Conrad André: Le peintre poète Nicolas Manuel Deutsch et l'evolution sociale de son temps, Geneva 1953. – El-Hiemoud-Sperlich, Inge: Das Urteil des Paris, Studien zur Bildtradition im 16.Jahrhundert, dissertation, Munich 1977. – Catalogue, Kunstmuseum Bern, Niklaus Manuel Deutsch, Maler, Dichter, Staatsmann, Bern 1979.

Netherlandish Master
Lot and his Daughters, c. 1530
58 x 34 cm
Paris, Musée du Louvre

Lit.: Kind, Joshua Benjamin: The drunken Lot and his daughters. An iconographical study of the uses of this theme in the visual arts from 1500–1650 and its bases in exegetical and literary history. Dissertation, Columbia University 1967. – Neev, David and Emery, K.O.: The destruction of Sodom, Gomorrah and Jericho; geological, climatological and archaeological background, New York/Oxford 1995. – Rank, Otto: Das Inzest-Motiv in Dichtung und Sage, Leipzig/Vienna 1926. – Rijnaarts, Josephine: Lots Töchter, Über den Vater-Tochter Inzest, Düsseldorf 1988.

Hans Holbein the Younger (1497–1543)
Portrait of the Merchant Georg Gisze, 1532
96 x 86 cm
Berlin, Gemäldegalerie der Staatlichen Museen Preußischer Kulturbesitz

Bätschmann, Oskar and Griener, Pascal: Hans Holbein, Cologne 1997. – Buck, Stephanie: Hans Holbein, Cologne 1999. – Freytag, Hermann: Das Bildnis eines Danzigers, von Holbein gemalt, in Zeitschrift des Westpreußischen Geschichtsvereins, 1932. – Klinger, D.M. and Höttler, Antje: Die Malerbrüder Ambrosius und Hans d.J. Holbein, Cheb 1998. – Werner, Theodor Gustav: Der Stalhof der deutschen Hanse in London in wirtschafts- und kunsthistorischen Bildwerken, in:Scriptae Mercature No. 2, Munich 1976.

Titian (1488/90–1576)
(Tiziano Vecelli)
Pope Paul III and his Grandsons, 1545
200 x 173 cm
Naples, Museo Nazionale di Capodimonte

Lit.: Der Glanz der Farnese, catalogue, Haus der Kunst, Munich 1995. -Reinhardt,Volker, ed.: Die großen Familien Italiens, Stuttgart 1992. – Wethey, Harold E.: The Paintings of Titian, complete edition, London 1971. – Zapperi, Roberto: Tiziano, Paolo III. e i suoi nipoti, Turin 1990. – Zapperi, Roberto: La leggenda del papa Paolo, Turin 1997.

Lucas Cranach the Elder (1472–1553)
The Fountain of Youth, 1546
121 x 184 cm
Berlin, Gemäldegalerie der Staatlichen Museen Preußischer Kulturbesitz

Lit.: Cipolla, Carlo M. and Borchardt, Knut: Die Bevölkerungsgeschichte Europas, Mittelalter bis Neuzeit, Munich 1971. – Friedländer, Max and Rosenberg, Jakob: Die Gemälde von Lucas Cranach, Basle/Boston/Stuttgart, 1979. – Hartlaub, G.F.: Lucas Cranach d.J., Der Jungbrunnen, Stuttgart 1958. – Koepplin, Dieter and Falk, Tilmann: Lucas Cranach, Gemälde, Zeichnungen, Druckgraphik, 2 vols, exhibition catalogue, Basle/Stuttgart 1974. – Martin, Alfred: Deutsches Badewesen in vergangenen Tagen, Nebst einem Beitrag zur Geschichte der deutschen Wasserheilkunde, Jena 1906. -Schade, Werner: Die Malerfamilie Cranach, Dresden 1974.

Wolf Huber (c. 1485–1553)
Crucifixion Allegory, c. 1550
154 x 131 cm
Vienna, Kunsthistorisches Museum

Lit.: Künstler, Gustav: Wolf Huber als Hofmaler des Bischofs von Passau Graf Wolfgang von Salm, in: Jahrbuch der kunsthistorischen

Sammlungen in Vienna, vol. 58, 1962. – Weinberger, Martin: Wolfgang Huber, Leipzig 1930. – Winzinger, Franz: Wolf Huber, Das Gesamtwerk, Munich/Zurich 1979.

Pieter Bruegel the Elder (1525/1530–1569)
Icarus, 1558
73.5 x 112 cm
Brussels, Musées Royaux des Beaux Arts

Lit.: Bagrow, Leo: Die Geschichte der Karthographie, Berlin 1951. – Roberts-Jones, Philippe: Bruegel, La chute d'Icare, Fribourg 1974. – Simson, Otto von and Viennaer, Matthias: Pieter Bruegel und seine Welt, Berlin 1974. – Wee, H. van der: The growth of the Antwerp market and the European economy 14th–16th century, The Hague 1963.

Pieter Bruegel the Elder (1525/1530–1569)
Dulle Griet, 1562
115 x 161 cm
Antwerp, Museum Mayer van den Bergh

Lit.: Baltrusaitis, Jurgis: Le Moyen Age Fantastique, Antiquités et Exotismes dans l'Art Gothique, Paris 1981. – Kuhn, Annette and Rüsen, Jörn (eds.): Frauen in der Geschichte, vol. 2, Düsseldorf 1982. – Jedlicka, Gotthard: Pieter Bruegel, Der Maler in seiner Zeit, Erlenbach/Leipzig 1938. – Panse, Fr. and Schmidt, H.J.: Pieter Bruegels Dulle Griet, Bildnis einer psychisch Kranken, 1907. – Wied, Alexander: Bruegel, London 1980.

Pieter Bruegel the Elder (1525/1530–1569)
The Census at Bethlehem, 1566
117 x 164.5 cm
Brussels, Musées Royaux des Beaux-Arts

Lit.: Baie Eugène: Le Siècle des Gueux, Brussels 1920. – Borst, Arno: Lebensformel im Mittelalter, Berlin 1973. – Grossmann, Fritz: Pieter Bruegel, Die Gemälde, Cologne 1966. – Guicciardini, Luigi: Beschreibung dess Niderlands ursprung, Auffnemen und Herkommens, Frankfurt 1582. – Pirenne, Henry: Geschichte Belgiens, Gotha 1907. – Simson, Otto and Winner, Matthias, eds.: Pieter Bruegel und seine Welt (colloquium held by the Kunsthistorisches Institut der Freien Universität Berlin and the Kupferstichkabinett der Staatlichen Museen Preußischer Kulturbesitz on 13th and 14th November 1975), Berlin 1979.

Pieter Bruegel the Elder (1525/1530–1659)
The Blind leading the Blind, 1568
86 x 154 cm
Naples, Museo Nazionale di Capodimonte

Accompanying illustration: Cornelys Massys, The Fall of the Blind, engraving, c. 1550, Amsterdam, Rijksmuseum, Kupferstichkabinett

Lit.: Claessens, Bob and Rousseau, Jeanne: Unser Bruegel, Antwerp 1969. – Koelbing, Huldrych M.: Renaissance der Augenheilkunde 1540–1630, Berlin/Stuttgart 1967. – Stechow, Wolfgang: Pieter Brueghel the Elder, New York 1969. – Sudhoff, Heinke: Ikonographische Untersuchungen zur "Blindenheilung" und zum "Blindensturz", Ein Beitrag zu Pieter Brueghels Neapler Gemälde von 1568, dissertation, Bonn 1981.

Annibale Carracci (1560–1609)
The Butcher's Shop, c. 1583
190 x 271 cm
Oxford, Christ Church College Picture Gallery

Lit.: Boschloo, Anton W.: Annibale Carracci in Bologna. Visible reality in art after the (2 vols), The Hague 1974. – Cooney, Patrick J.: L'opera completa di Annibale Carracci, Milan 1976. – Posner, Donald: Annibale Carracci, A study in the reform of Italian painting around 1590 (2 vols), London 1971. – The inspiration of the Carracci, catalogue, Christ Church Picture Gallery, Oxford 1991. – Mellinger, Nan: Fleisch, Ursprung und Wandel einer Lust. Eine kulturanthropologische Studie, Frankfurt 2000. – Zapperi, Roberto: Annibale Carracci, Ritratto di Artista da Giovane, Turin, 1989.

School of Fontainebleau
Gabrielle d'Estrées and one of her sisters, c. 1600
96 x 125 cm
Paris, Musée du Louvre

Lit.: Adhémar Hélène: Portraits français du 15e et 16e siècle, Musée du Louvre, Paris (undated). – Béguin Sylvie: L'Ecole de Fontainebleau, le maniérisme à la cour de France, Paris 1969. – Catalogue de l'Exposition L'Ecole de Fontainebleau, Paris 1972. – Erlanger, Philippe: La vie quotidienne sous Henri IV, Paris 1958. – Hollander, Anne: Seeing through clothes, New York 1979. – Tallemant des Réaux: Historiettes, Paris 1961. – Vaissière, Pierre de: Henri IV, Paris 1928.

Peter Paul Rubens (1577–1640)
The Dying Seneca, 1611/1615
184.5 x 155.5 cm
Munich, Alte Pinakothek

Lit.: Fuhrmann, Manfred: Seneca und Kaiser Nero, eine Biographie, Berlin 1997. – Giebel, Marion: Seneca, Reinbek 1997. – McGrath, Elisabeth: Rubens, Subjects from History, vol. II, London 1997 (Corpus Rubeanum Ludwig Burchard XIII). – Simson, Otto von: Peter Paul Rubens, Humanist, Maler und Diplomat, Mainz 1996. – Rost, Hans: Bibliographie des Selbstmords, Augsburg 1927. – White, Christopher: Peter Paul Rubens, Leben und Kunst, Stuttgart/Zurich 1988.

Georges de La Tour (1593–1652)
The Musicians' Quarrel, 1620/1630
94 x 141 cm
Los Angeles, The J. Paul Getty Museum

Accompanying illustration: Le vielleur, 162 x 105 cm,
Nantes, Musée des Beaux-Arts

Lit.: Cabourdin, Guy: La vie quotidienne en Lorraine aux 17e et 18e siècles, Paris 1984. – Foisil, Madeleine: La vie quotidienne au temps de Louis XIII, Paris 1992. – Geremek, Bronislaw: Truands et misérables dans L'Europe moderne, Paris 1980. – Georges de La Tour, catalogue, Grand Palais, Paris 1997. – Georges de La Tour and his world, catalogue, Washington/Fort Worth 1996. – Nicolson, Benedict and Wright, Christopher: Georges de La Tour, London 1974. – Ribault, Jean-Yves: Réalisme plastique et réalité sociale – A propos des aveugles musiciens de Georges de La Tour, in: Gazette des Beaux-Arts 1984, no. 104. – Rosenberg, Pierre and Macé de Lépinay, François: Georges de La Tour, Leben und Werk, Berlin 1974. – Winternitz: Musical instruments and their symbolism in western art, New Haven/New York 1967/79.

Gerard van Honthorst (1592–1656)
Jovial Company, 1622
(The Prodigal Son)
130 x 196 cm
Munich, Alte Pinakothek

Lit.: Braun, Hermann: Gerard and Willem van Honthorst. Dissertation, Göttingen 1966. – Holländische Malerei in neuem Licht: Hendrick ter Brugghen und seine Zeitgenossen, catalogue, Centraal Museum, Utrecht 1989 and Herzog-Anton-Ulrich-Museum, Braunschweig 1987. – Nicolson, Benedict: Caravaggism in Europe, Milan 1989. – Renger, Konrad: Lockere Gesellschaft, zur Ikonographie des verlorenen Sohnes und von Wirtshausszenen in der niederländischen Malerei, Berlin 1970. – Zumthor, Paul: La vie quotidienne en Hollande au temps de Rembrandt, Paris 1959.

Peter Paul Rubens (1577–1640)
Henri IV receives the portrait of Maria de' Medici, 1622/1625
394 x 295 cm
Paris, Musée du Louvre

Lit.: Avermaete, Roger: Rubens und seine Zeit, Ghent 1977. – Erlanger, Philippe: La vie quotidienne sous Henri IV, Paris 1958. – Grossmann, Karl: Der Gemäldezyklus der Galerie der Maria von Medici von Peter Paul Rubens, Strasburg 1906. – Thuillier, Jacques: Le storie di Maria de' Medici di Rubens al Lussemburgo, Milan 1967. – Vaissière, Pierre: Henri IV, Paris 1928.

Georges de La Tour (1593–1652)
The Sharper, c. 1630
106 x 146 cm
Paris, Musée du Louvre

Lit.: Ariès, Philippe: L'Enfant et la vie familiale sans l'Ancien Régime, Paris 1975. – Gizycky, Jerzy: Glück im Spiel zu allen Zeiten, Zurich 1970. – Hoffmann, Detlef: Die Welt der Spielkarte, eine Kulturgeschichte, Munich 1972. – Georges de La Tour, catalogue, Louvre, Paris 1972. – Nicolson, B. and Wright, C.: Georges de La Tour, London 1974. – Rosenberg, Pierre and Macé de Lépinay, François: Georges de La Tour, Berlin 1974.

Rembrandt 1606–1669)
(Rembrandt Harmensz. van Rijn)
(The Anatomy Lecture of Dr. Tulp, 1632
163 x 217 cm
The Hague, Mauritshuis

Lit.: Heckscher, William P.: Rembrandt's Anatomy of Dr. Nicolaas Tulp, An iconological study, New York 1958. – Zumthor, Paul: La vie quotidienne en Hollande au temps de Rembrandt, Paris 1959.

Nicolas Poussin (1594–1665)
The Rape of the Sabines, 1637/39
159 x 206 cm
Paris, Musée du Louvre

Lit.: Arikha Avigdor: Nicolas Poussin, The Rape of the Sabines, Houston 1988. – Haskell, Francis: Patrons and Painters, London/New York 1971. – Rosenberg, Pierre, ed: Nicolas Poussin, exhibition catalogue, Grand Palais, Paris, 1994/95. – Thuillier, Jacques: Nicolas Poussin, Paris, 1988.

Rembrandt (1606–1669)
(Rembrandt Harmensz. van Rijn)
The Night Watch, 1642
359 x 438 cm
Amsterdam, Rijksmuseum

Lit.: Bauch, Kurt: Rembrandt van Rijn, Die Nachtwache, Stuttgart 1957. – Gerson, Horst: Rembrandt, Gemälde, Gesamtwerk, Wiesbaden, 1968. – Haak, Bob: Rembrandt, Sein Leben, sein Werk, seine Zeit, Cologne 1969. – Heiland, Susanne and Lüdecke, Heinz: Rembrandt und die Nachwelt, Leipzig 1960. – Hijmans, Willem, Kuiper, Luitsen and Vels Heijn, Annemarie: Rembrandt's Nightwatch, The history of a painting, Alphen aan den Rijn 1978. – Walser, Paul L.: Amsterdam, Zurich 1969. – Wilson, Charles: Die Früchte der Freiheit, Holland und die europäische Kultur des 17. Jahrhunderts, Munich 1968.

Diego de Silva y Velázquez (1599–1660)
Las Meninas, 1656
318 x 276 cm
Madrid, Museo del Prado

Lit.: Defourneaux, Marcelin: La vie quotidienne en Espagne au siècle d'or, Paris 1964. – Gudiol, José: Velazquez, sa vie, son oeuvre, son évolution, Paris/Barcelona 1975. – Hume, Martin: The court of Philip IV, London 1911. – Justi, Carl: Velazquez und sein Jahrhundert, Munich, undated (reprint of the 2nd edition of 1903). – Lassaigne, Jacques: Velazquez –Les Ménines, Fribourg 1973. – Lopez-Rey, José: Velazquez, catalogue raisonné, Cologne 1996.

Jan Steen (1626–1679)
The Burgher of Delft and his daughter, 1655
82.5 x 68.6 cm
Private Collection

Lit.: Jansen, Guido M. C., ed.: Jan Steen, Maler und Erzähler, catalogue to the Steen exhibitions in Washington and Amsterdam 1996/97, German edition 1996 Stuttgart/Zurich. – Muller, Sheila D.: Jan Steen's Burgher of Delft and his Daughter, A painting and politics in seventeenth-century Holland In: Art History, vol. 12, no. 3, September 1989. – Schama, Simon: The Embarrassment of Riches, an Interpretation of Dutch Culture in the Golden Age, New York 1987. – Spicer Hinbeath: The Renaissance elbow, in: Bremmer, Jan and Roodenburg, Hermann: A cultural history of gesture, Ithaca/New York 1992.

Antoine Watteau (1684–1721)
Shop-sign for the Art Dealer Gersaint, 1720
166 x 306 cm
Berlin, Charlottenburger Schloss

Lit.: Faure, Elie: Le banqueroute de Law, 17 juillet 1720, Paris 1978. – Ferré, Jean: Watteau, Madrid 1972. – Hirschfeld, Peter: Mäzene, Die Rolle des Auftraggebers in der Kunst, 1968. – Meyer, Jean: La vie quotidienne en France au temps de la Régence, Paris 1979. – Rave, Paul Ortwin: Das Ladenschild des Kunsthändlers Gersaint, Stuttgart 1957. – Rosenberg, Pierre, ed.: Vies anciennes de Watteau, Paris 1984.

Jean Siméon Chardin (1699–1779)
The Laundress, 1733
37 x 43 cm
Stockholm, Nationalmuseet

Lit.: Chaussinand-Nogaret: La vie quotidienne des Fran(ais sous Louis XV, Paris 1979. – Fairchilds, Cissy: Domestic enemies, servants and their masters in old regime France, Baltimore/London, 1984. – Roche, Daniel: La culture des apparences, une histoire du vêtement, Paris 1989 – Rosenberg, Pierre, ed.: Chardin, exhibition catalogue, Grand Palais, Paris, Düsseldorf, London, New York 1999-2000.

François Boucher (1703–1770)
The Breakfast, 1739
81.5 x 65.5 cm
Paris, Musée du Louvre

Lit.: Ananoff, Alexandrej: François Boucher (2 vols), Lausanne 1976. – Ariès, Philippe: L'Enfant et la vie familiale sans l'Ancien Régime. Paris 1975. – Badinter, Elisabeth: L'Amour en plus, histoire de l'aman maternel du 17e au 20 e s. Paris 1980. – Chaussinand-Nogaret, Guy: La vie quotidienne des Français sous Louis XV, Paris 1979. – Schivelbusch, Wolfgang: Das Paradies, der Geschmack und die Vernunft, Munich 1980. – Shorter, Edward: Die Geburt der modernen Familie, Hamburg 1977.

William Hogarth (1697–1764)
Marriage A-la-Mode; 4. The Toilette, c. 1743
71 x 91 cm
London, National Gallery

Ball, Celia: William Hogarth's Bildsatiren als künstlerische Form der Sozialkritik, Essen

2000. – Cowley, Robert S.L.: Marriage A-la-Mode. A review of Hogarth's narrative art. Manchester 1983. – Egerton, Judy: Hogarth's Marriage a-la-mode, London 1998. – George, Dorothy: London Life in the 18th Century, London 1951. – Jarrett, Derek: England in the age of Hogarth, London/New Haven 1996.

François Boucher (1703–1770)
The Rape of Europa, 1747
161 x 194 cm
Paris, Musée du Louvre

Bluche, François: La vie quotidienne de la noblesse française au 18e siècle; Paris 1979. – Metropolitan Museum of Art, New York: Boucher. Exhibition catalogue, New York 1986. – Chaussinand-Nogaret, Guy de: La vie quotidienne des Français sous Louis XV, Paris 1979. – Kunstgewerbemuseum Berlin: Die Verführung der Europa. Exhibition catalogue, Berlin 1988. – Levron, Jacques: Madame de Pompadour. L'amour et la politique, Paris 1961/75. – Macard, Micaela von: Rokoko oder das Experiment am lebenden Herzen. Galante Ideale und Lebenskrisen. Reinbeck 1994. – Nolhac, Pierre de: Boucher, premier peintre du roi, Paris 1905/25.

Giandomenico Tiepolo (1727–1804)
The Minuet, c. 1754
79 x 110 cm
Paris, Musée du Louvre

Lit.: Goethe, Johann Wolfgang von, Italienische Reise, Munich 1963. – Jonard, Norbert: La vita a Venezia nel XVII secolo, Milan 1967. – Marius, Adriano: Giandomenico Tiepolo, Venice 1971. – Molmenti, Pompeo G.: La storia de Venezia nella vita privata, Bergamo 1905/08, reprinted Triest 1973, vol. 3.

Giandomenico Tiepolo (1727–1804)
The Tooth Drawer, c. 1754
80 x 110 cm
Paris, Musée du Louvre

Lit.: Goldoni, Carlo: Mémoires pour servir à l'histoire de sa vie et à celle de son théâtre, Paris 1787/ Milan 1943. – Francesco, Grete de: Die Macht des Charlatan, Basle 1937. – Lidforss-Stömgren, Hedvig: Die Zahnheilkunde im 18. Jahrhundert, Copenhagen 1935. – Molmenti, Pompeo: La Storia di Venezia nella vita privata. Bergamo 1905-8, reprinted Triest 1978, vol. 3. – Mariuz, Adriano: Gian Domenico Tiepolo, Venice 1971. – Geerto Snyder: Wunderglaube und Wahn, Munich 1965.

Bernardo Bellotto di Canaletto (1720–1780)
Dresden Old Town seen from the end of the New Town Bridge, 1765
99.5 x 134 cm
Karlsruhe, Staatliche Kunsthalle

Lit.: Boroviczény, Aladár von: Graf von Brühl, der Medici, Richelieu und Rothschild seiner Zeit, Zurich/Leipzig/Vienna 1930. – Kozakiewicz, Stefan: Bernardo Bellotto, genannt Canaletto, Recklinghausen 1972. – Löffler, Fritz: Das alte Dresden, Geschichte seiner Bauten, Dresden 1956. – Schlechte, Horst: Die Staatsreform in Kursachsen 1762/63, Berlin 1958. – Weinart, Benjamin Gottfried: Topographische Geschichte der Stadt Dresden und der um dieselbe herumliegenden Gegenden, Dresden 1777.

Sir Joshua Reynolds (1723–1792)
George Clive with his Family and an Indian Maidservant, c. 1765
140 x 171
Berlin, Gemäldegalerie

Lit.: Kincaid, Dennis: British social life in India 1608–1937, London/Boston 1938. – Penny, Nicolas: Reynolds, Royal Academy of Arts, exhibition catalogue, London 1986. – Prochno, Renate: Joshua Reynolds, Weinheim 1990.

Francisco de Goya (1746–1828)
The Family of Charles IV, 1800
280 x 336 cm
Madrid, Museo del Prado

Lit.: Chastenet, Jacques: Godoy, Master of Spain, London 1953. – Gassier, Pierre, Wilson, Juliet and Lachenal, François: Goya, Fribourg 1971. – Gantner, Joseph: Goya, Berlin 1974. – Gudiol, José: Goya, catalogue raisonné, Barcelona 1970. – Madol, H.R.: Godoy, Das Ende des alten Spanien, der erste Diktator unserer Zeit, Berlin 1930.

Francisco de Goya (1746–1828)
The Inquisition Tribunal, c. 1815
46 x 73 cm
Madrid, Académia Real de San Fernando

Accompanying illustration: "There was no remedy", etching no. 24 from the series Los Caprichos

Lit.: Gassier, Pierre, Wilson, Juliet and Lachenal, Fran(ois: Goya, Fribourg 1971. – Goya und das Zeitalter der Revolutionen, Kunsthalle Hamburg, catalogue, 1980. – Kamen, Henry: Die spanische Inquisition. Verfolgung und Vertreibung, Munich 1967. – Roll, Bernd: Die Inquisition und ihre Ketzer, Eichstätt 1982. – Williams, Gwyn: Goya and the Impossible Revolution. London 1976.

Karl Friedrich Schinkel (1781–1841)
Cathedral overlooking a City, 1813
94 x 126 cm
Munich, Neue Pinakothek

Lit.: Bergdoll, Barry: Karl Friedrich Schinkel, Preußens berühmtester Baumeister, Berlin 1994. – Büchel, Wolfgang: Karl Friedrich Schinkel, Reinbek 1994. – Ohff, Heinz: Karl Friedrich Schinkel oder die Schönheit in Preußen, Munich 1997. – Zadow, Mario: Karl Friedrich Schinkel, Berlin 1980.

Caspar David Friedrich (1774–1840)
Hutten's Tomb, c. 1823
93 x 73 cm
Weimar, Kunstsammlungen

Acompanying illustration:
Choir of Oybin monastic church
25.5 x 35.8 cm
Hamburg, Kunsthalle

Lit.: Arndt, Ernst Moritz: Briefe, Darmstadt 1956. – Börsch-Supan, Helmut and Jähnig, Karl Wilhelm: Caspar David Friedrich, Munich 1973. – Eimer, Gerhard: Caspar David Friedrich und die Gotik, Hamburg 1963. – Hinz, Sigrid: Caspar David Friedrich in Briefen und Bekenntnissen, Munich 1974. – Hofmann, Werner: Caspar David Friedrich, Naturwirklichkeit und Kunstwahrheit, Munich 200[illegible]. – Hutten, Ulrich von: Deutsche Schriften, Munich 1970. – Jensen, Jens Christian: Caspar David Friedrich, Leben und Werk, Cologne 1974.

Eugène Delacroix (1798–1863)
Der 28. Juli oder die Freiheit führt das Volk, 1831
260 x 325 cm
Paris, Musée du Louvre

Lit.: Adhémar, Hélène: La Liberté sur les Barricades de Delacroix, in: Gazettes des Beaux-Arts 1954. – Archaix, Guicharnaud: Juillet 1830, exhibition catalogue, Musée Carnavalet, Paris 1980. – Bory, Jean-Louis: La Révolution de Juillet, Paris 1972. – Huyghe, René: Delacroix, Munich 1967.

Ando Hiroshige (1797–1858)
Morning Mist by Mishima, c. 1833
Station no. 12 of the series "Fifty-three Stations on the Tokaido"
Woodcut, 25 x 38 cm
Rhode Island, Museum of Art

Lit.: Addiss, Stephen: Tokaido, On the Road in Old Japan, exhibition catalogue, Spencer Museum of Art, Lawrence 1980. – Forrer, Matthi: Hiroshige. Prints and drawings. Catalogue, Royal Academy of Arts, London 1997. – Ikku Jippensha: Hizakurige or Shank's Mare. Japan's Great Comic Novel of Travel and Ribaldry. Vermont/Tokyo 1960. – Vaporis, Nomiko: Breaking Barriers. Travel and the State in Early Modern Japan. Cambridge, Mass. and London 1994.

Eugène Delacroix (1798–1863)
Women of Algiers in their Appartments, 1834
180 x 229 cm
Paris, Musée du Louvre

Accompanying illustration: Mounay ben Sultane, watercolour, 10.7 x 13.8 cm, Paris, Musée du Louvre, Département des arts graphiques

Lit.: Daguerre de Hureaux, Alain: Delacroix, Das Gesamtwerk, Stuttgart 1994. – Johnson, Lee: The paintings of Eugène Delacroix, a critical catalogue, Oxford 1986. – Delacroix in Morocco, exhibition catalogue, Institut du Monde Arabe, Paris/New York 1995. – Rautmann, Peter: Eugène Delacroix, Munich 1997. – Said, Edward W.: Orientalism, New York 1978.

Adolf Menzel (1815–1905)
Lying in State of the Dead in the March Revolution in Berlin, 1848
45 x 63 cm
Hamburg, Kunsthalle

Lit.: Demps, Laurenz: Der schönste Platz Berlins, Der Gendarmenmarkt in Geschichte und Gegenwart, Berlin 1993. – Jensen, Jens Christian: Adolph Menzel, Cologne 1982. – Keisch, Claude and Riemann-Reyher, Marie Ursula, eds.: Adolph Menzel 1815–1905, Das Labyrinth der Wirklichkeit, exhibition catalogue, Cologne 1996. – Ribbe, Wolfgang, ed.: Geschichte Berlins, 2 vols, Munich 1987.

Edouard Manet (1832–1883)
Music in the Tuleries Gardens, 1862
76 x 118 cm
London, National Gallery

Lit.: Allem, Maurice: La vie quotidienne sous le Second Empire, Paris 1957. – Pierre Guiral: La vie quotidienne à l'âge d'or du capitalisme, Paris 1976. – Hillairet, Jacques: Le Palais des Tuileries, Paris 1965. – Manet 1832– 1883, exhibition catalogue, Grand Palais, Paris 1983. – Kracauer, Siegfried: Jacques Offenbach und das Paris seiner Zeit, Amsterdam 1937/ Frankfurt a.M. 1980. – Sandblad, Nils Gösta: Manet, Three studies in artistic conception, Lund 1954.

Anselm Feuerbach (1829–1880)
Medea, 1870
197 x 395 cm
Munich, Neue Pinakothek

Accompanying illustration: Eugène Delacroix, Medèe furieuse, 1838, 260 x 165 cm, Lille, Musée des Beaux-Arts

Lit.: Ecker, Jürgen: Anselm Feuerbach, Leben und Werk, Kritischer Katalog der Gemälde, Ölskizzen und Ölstudien, Munich 1991. – Kepetzis, Ekaterini: Medea in der Bildenden Kunst vom Mittelalter zur Neuzeit, Frankfurt 1997. – Kupper, Daniel: Anselm Feuerbach, Reinbek 1993. – Staatliche Kunsthalle Karlsruhe: Feuerbach, exhibition catalogue, Munich/ Berlin 1976.

Adolph Menzel (1815–1905)
The Departure of King Wilhelm I for the Army on 31 July 1870, 1871
63 x 78 cm
Berlin, Nationalgalerie

Lit.: Baedekers Reiseführer Mittel-und Norddeutschland, 14th edition, Leipzig 1869. – Herre, Franz: Anno 70/71, Cologne/Berlin 1970. – Herzfeld, Hans, ed.: Berlin und die Provinz Brandenburg im 19. und 20. Jahrhundert, Veröffentlichung der Historischen Kommission zu Berlin, vol. 25, Berlin 1968. – Höfele, Karl Heinrich: Geist und Gesellschaft der Bismarckzeit (1860– 1890). – Hofmann, Werner, ed.: Menzel, der Beobachter, exhibition catalogue, Munich 1982. – Jensen, Jens Christian: Adolph Menzel, Cologne 1982. – Laforgue, Jules: Berlin, la cour et la ville, Paris 1922. – Marcks, Friedrich: Das Rote Kreuz, Seine Entstehung und Entwicklung und seine Bethätigung in Deutschland, Gütersloh 1900. – Siebenborn, Claus: Unter den Linden, Galanter Bilderbogen um Berlins berühmte Straße 1647–1947, Berlin 1949. – Vierhaus, Rudolf, ed.: Am Hof der Hohenzollern, Aus dem Tagebuch der Baronin Spitzemberg 1865–1914, Munich 1965. – Newspapers: Berlinische Nachrichten, Königlich Privilegierte Berlinische Zeitung von Staats- und gelehrten Sachen, 1st and 2nd August 1870.

Claude Monet (1840–1926)
Camille Monet on a Garden Bench (The Bench), 1873
60.6 x 80.3 cm
New York, Metropolitan Museum

Lit.: Bailey, Colin B., Rishel, Joseph J. and Rosenthal, Mark: Masterpieces of Impressionism and Post-Impressionism. The Annenberg Collection, catalogue, Philadelphia Museum of Art 1989. – Busch, Günter: Claude Monet: Camille – Vom Realismus zum Impressionismus, Siemens Foundation lecture, Munich 1980. – Edouard Manet, exhibition catalogue, Grand Palais, Paris 1983. – Tucker, Paul Hayes: Claude Monet, Life and Art. New Haven/ London, 1995. – Wildenstein, Daniel: Monet or the Triumph of Impressionism, Cologne 1996.

Auguste Renoir (1841–1919)
Au Moulin de la Galette, 1876
131 x 175 cm
Paris, Musée d'Orsay

Lit.: Crespelle, Jean-Paul: La vie quotidienne à Montmartre au temps de Picasso, Paris 1978. – Daulte, François: Auguste Renoir, Catalogue raisonné de l'oeuvre peint, vol. 1, Lausanne 1977. – Guiral, Pierre: La vie quotidienne en France à l'âge du capitalisme, Paris 1976. – Renoir, Jean: Pierre Auguste Renoir, mon père, Paris 1985.

Gustave Caillebotte (1848–1894)
Paris Street, Rainy Day, 1877
212 x 276
Chicago, Art Institute

Lit.: Berhaut, Marie: Caillebotte, Catalogue raisonné des peintures et pastels, Paris 1994. – Gustave Caillebotte, catalogue, Paris/ Chicago/ Los Angeles 1994/95. – Jordan, David: Transforming Paris, the Life and Labours of Baron Haussmann. New York 1995. – Varnedoe, Kirk: Gustave Caillebotte, New Haven/ London 1987.

Francisco Pradilla y Ortiz (1848–1921)
Joanna the Mad beside her Husband's Coffin, 1877
340 x 500 cm
Madrid, Museo del Prado

Lit.: Diez, Jose Luis: La pintura de historia del siglo XIX en España, catalogue, Museo del Prado, Madrid 1992. – Francisco Pradilla, catalogue (in Spanish), Museo Municipal, Madrid 1987. – Hume, Martin: Queens of old Spain, London 1911. – Miller, Townsend: The Castles and the Crown. Spain 1451–1555, New York 1963. – Revero, Carlo: La pintura de historia en España, Esplendor de un genero en el siglo XIX, Madrid 1989.

Arnold Böcklin (1827–1901)
The Isle of the Dead, 1880
111 x 155 cm
Basle, Kunstmuseum

Lit.: Andrée, Rolf: Arnold Böcklin, Die Gemälde, Basle/Munich 1977. – Ariès, Philippe: L'homme devant la mort, Paris 1977. – Centre Georges Pompidou/Staatl. Kunsthalle Berlin, eds.: Die Welt der Bahnhöfe, Berlin 1980. – Holle, Luise ed.: Im deutschen Hause, Ein Ratgeber und Helfer für das gesamte häusliche Leben der deutschen Familie, Hanau, undated (1903). – Kunstmuseum Basel: Arnold Böcklin, exhibition catalogue, Basle/Stuttgart 1977. – Lichtwark, Alfred: Die Seele und das Kunstwerk, Berlin 1902. – Mendelsohn, Henry: Böcklin, Berlin 1901.

Ernst Ludwig Kirchner (1880–1938)
Potsdamer Platz, 1914
200 x 150 cm
Berlin, Neue Nationalgalerie

Accompanying illustrations: Self-portrait as a Soldier, 1915, 69 x 61 cm, Oberlin, Oberlin College, Ohio, Allen Memorial Art Museum

Lit.: Bellmann, Günther, ed.: Potsdamer Platz, Drehscheibe der Weltstadt, Berlin 1997. – Döblin, Alfred: Drama, Hörspiel, Film, Olten/Freiburg 1983. – Flexner, Abraham: Die Prostitution in Europa, Berlin 1921. – Karlheinz Gabler: E. L. Kirchner, Dokumente, exhibition catalogue, Aschaffenburg 1980. – Grisebach, Lucius and Meyer zu Eissen, Annette: Catalogue to the 1980 Kirchner exhibition in Berlin etc., Munich 1980. – Grisebach, Lothar: Ernst Ludwig Kirchners Davoser Tagebuch, Cologne 1968. – Kirchner, Ernst Ludwig and Schiefler, Gustav: Briefwechsel 1910–1935/38, Stuttgart/Zurich 1990. – März, Roland and Henkel Katharina, eds.: Catalogue to the exhibition "Der Potsdamer Platz, Ernst Ludwig Kirchner und der Untergang Preußens", Berlin 2001. – Moeller, Magdalena M.: Ernst Ludwig Kirchner, Die Straßenszenen 1913–1915, Munich 1993.

The publisher would like to thank the museums, archives and photographers for their kind co-operation and permission to reproduce photographic material. Besides the collections and institutions acknowledged in the appendix, we are grateful to:

Archiv für Kunst und Geschichte, Berlin: 22–27, 418–423.
The Art Institute of Chicago, Chicago ©: 400–405.
Artothek, Weilheim: 112–117 (Emil Bauer); 334–339, 376–378, 380–381 (Blauel); 208–209, 211–213, 220–225 (Blauel/Gnamm).
Bildarchiv Preussischer Kulturbesitz, Berlin: 268–273, 424–427, 429; 52, 54–55, 148–153, 160–165, 316–321, 368, 382–387 (Jörg P. Anders); 328–332 (Alfredo Dagli Orti); 352–357 (Jürgen Liepe); 124–128, 130–135 (Jochen Remmer).
The British Museum, London: 10–15.
Christ Church Picture Gallery, Oxford: 196–201.
The J. Paul Getty-Museum, Los Angeles ©: 214–216, 218–219.
Koninklijk Kabinet van Schilderijen, Mauritshuis, The Hague: 238–243.
Koninklijk Museum voor Schone Kunsten, Antwerp: 52–53, 56.
Kunsthistorisches Museum, Vienna: 166–171.
Kunstsammlungen zu Weimar, Photo © Louis Held: 340–341, 344–345.
The Metropolitan Museum of Art, New York ©: 28–33, 388–393.
Musée d'Unterlinden, Colmar, Photo © O. Zimmermann: 129.
Musées royaux des Beaux-Arts de Belgique, Brussels: 172–177, 184–189.
Museo del Prado, Madrid: 262–267, 322–327, 333, 406–411.
Museum Mayer van den Bergh, Antwerp: 178–183.
National Gallery Picture Library, London: 40–45, 46–51, 58–63, 70–75, 118–123, 286–291, 370–375.
National Trust Photo Library, London: 256–261.
Oberlin College, Allen Memorial Art Museum, Oberlin: 428.
Oeffentliche Kunstsammlung, Basle, Photo © Martin Bühler: 136–141, 412–417.
Réunion des Musées Nationaux, Paris: 232–237, 292–297, 304–309, 358–360, 362–363; 280–285 (Arnaudet); 217, 244–249, 379 (P. Bernard);142–147, 202–207, 298–303, 361 (G. Blot); 57, 210 (Chuzeville); 226–231 (Jean/Lewandowski); 2, 346–351, 394–399 (H. Lewandowski); 88–93 (R. G. Ojeda).
Rijksmuseum, Amsterdam: 195, 250–255.
Scala, Antella: 16–21, 64–69, 76–81, 82–87, 94–99, 100–105, 106–111, 154–159, 190–194.
St. Baafskathedraal Gent, Photo © Paul M. R. Maeyaert: 34–39.
Staatliche Kunsthalle, Hamburg: 342–343, 364–367, 369.
Staatliche Kunsthalle, Karlsruhe: 310–315.
Statens Konstmuseer, Stockholm: 274–279.